Anonymous

Cabala, Sive, Scrinia Sacra. Mysteries of State and Government

In Letters of Illustrious Persons and Great Ministers of State as well...

Anonymous

Cabala, Sive, Scrinia Sacra. Mysteries of State and Government
In Letters of Illustrious Persons and Great Ministers of State as well...

ISBN/EAN: 9783337137557

Printed in Europe, USA, Canada, Australia, Japan

Cover: Foto ©ninafisch / pixelio.de

More available books at **www.hansebooks.com**

CABALA,

Sive *SCRINIA SACRA*,

Mysteries of State
AND
GOVERNMENT:
IN
LETTERS

OF

Illustrious Persons and Great Ministers of State
As well Forreign as Domestick,

In the Reigns of King *HENRY* the Eighth,
Q: *ELIZABETH*,
K: *JAMES*, and K: *CHARLES*:

WHEREIN
Such Secrets of Empire, and Publick Affairs, as were then in Agitation,
are clearly Represented;
And many remarkable Passages faithfully Collected.

Formerly in Two Volumns.

To which is added several Choice LETTERS and
Negotiations, no where else Published.

Now Collected and Printed together in One Volumn.

With two Exact Tables, the One of the Letters, and the Other of
Things most Observable.

LONDON,
Printed for G. Bedell and T. Collins, and are to be sold at their Shop
at the Middle-Temple-Gate in Fleetstreet.
M: DC: LXIII.

THE
STATIONERS
TO THE
READER.

COURTEOUS READER,

O you this Rarity once more offereth it self; a Piece (considered in its circumstances) most remarkable, if you respect the Persons, the Language, or Sublimity of the Subject: A Collection not so much of Letters, as of Keyes to open unto you the Mysteries of Government, and the Management of Publick Transactions, in the late Reigns of the greatest Princes in *Europe*; whose principal Ministers of State, and their Negotiations, are here Presented naked; and their Consultations, Designs, and Policies, as they were Contrived, are here exposed to publick view and observation, without any the least Bias or false Gloss, and with more truth and sincerity then *Annals* usually declare to posterity: where Partiality,

The PREFACE.

Error, and Passion do oftentimes Seduce; being transported with Love or Hatred, to the Side or Person: And therefore, here is no danger of Snares, to Captivate or Inveigle any mans Judgment, nor words required to advance opinion.

Not long since, we Printed that Excellent Collection of Letters, known by the name of CABALA, with an ensuing Supplement of other Letters, of like grand Import, both which the world hath seen and approved.

Since the Publication of the two former, another Volumn of choice Letters is happily come to our hands, which will adde much Lustre and Compleatness to the other, and which you will find throughout this Volumn, Marked with *. Your kind Acceptance of the former hath encouraged us to unite them all into one Body; In the last of which you will find a little entire Volumn of Letters, from that profound, faithful, and Eminent Minister of State, Sir *William Cecil* Knight, (after Lord *Burleigh*) Secretary of State to the late Queen *Elizabeth*, to Sir *Henry Norris* Knight, her Majesties Ambassadour, Resident in *France*, during the whole time of his Negotiations in that Honourable Imployment: And therein are related (with much exactness) many memorable passages (amongst divers others) touching the Murther of the King of *Scots*, the fatal Rebellion in the North, the Sanguinary Divisions in *France*, and the *Netherlands*, reciprocal bandying of grand Agents, sowing of Factions, and such like intricate transactions, then in Agitation upon the Theatre of *Europe*: As also, several Monuments of the Incomparable Viscount St. *Alban*, richly adorned with variety of Philosophical Learning, Cabalistick mysteries

of

The PREFACE.

of State, and several passages of History, never before made publick; Likewise the fall of the Earl of *Somerset*, and the immediate Advance of the Duke of *Buckingham*, both Favourites of the first Magnitude; with many other weighty and remarkable Passages, as well Forreign as Domestick, touching the Management of Affairs, both Ecclesiastical and Political; which if compared in their Series and Dependances, you will find the frame to be very accurate, and most worthy perusal.

    The two former Parts already mentioned have been Ushered in with their several Prefaces, and, in that respect, we hope the less will be expected from us now in this Edition and Addition.

    To conclude, there has been no small care taken in the disposing of all things Alphabetically, and (as near as may be) in order of time, for the ease of the Reader; which, we doubt not, will be kindly accepted from

Your humble Servants,

Temple Gate,
June 18.
1663.

G. B.

T. C.

An Alphabetical Table of the Letters, &c. contained in this *CABALA*.

A.

	Fol.
Queen Anne of Bullen, to King Henry, from the Tower.	1
Sir Anthony Ashley, to the Duke of Buckingham.	2

Sir *Walter Aston's* Letters, &c.

Sir Walter Aston, to the Duke of Buckingham.	3
The Copy of a Memorial given to the King of Spain, translated.	ibid.
Sir Walter Aston, to the Duke.	4
Sir Walter Aston, to Secretary Conway.	5
Sir Walter Aston, to the Lord Conway.	7
Sir Walter Aston, to the Lord Conway.	8
The Abstract of a Letter from Sir Walter Aston to the Lord Conway.	10
Sir Walter Aston, to the Duke.	ibid.
Sir Walter Aston, to the Duke	11
Sir Walter Aston, to the Duke	(11)
Sir Walter Aston, to the Duke.	(12)
A Memorial to the King of Spain, by Sir Walter Aston, Embassadour in Spain.	(13)
Sir Walter Aston, to the Duke.	13
Mr. Edmond Anderson's Letter to Sir Francis Bacon.	14

B.

Sir *Francis Bacon's* Letters, &c.

Sir Francis Bacon, to the Lord Treasurer, concerning the Sollicitors place.	17
* Sir Francis Bacon, to the Lord Treasurer Burghley.	18
* Sir Francis Bacon, to the Lord Treasurer Burghley.	ibid.
A Letter framed as from Mr. Anthony Bacon to the Earl of Essex.	19
The Earl of Essex his Answer to Mr. Anthony Bacon's Letter.	21
Sir Francis Bacon, to the Earl of Salisbury, concerning the Sollicitors place.	ibid.
Sir Francis Bacon, to the Earl of Essex, when Sir Robert Cecil was in France	22
Sir Francis Bacon, to the Earl of Essex, concerning the Earl of Tyrone.	ibid.
Another to the Earl, before his going to Ireland.	23
Sir Francis Bacon, to the Earl of Essex, after his enlargement.	25
* Sir Francis Bacon, in recommendation of his service to the Earl of Northumberland, a few days before Queen Elizabeths death.	ibid.
* Sir Francis Bacon, to Mr. Robert Kempe, upon the death of Queen Elizabeth.	26
* Sir Francis Bacon, to M. David Foules, in Scotland, upon the entrance of his Majesties Reign.	ibid.
Sir Francis Bacon, to Sir Robert Cecil, after the defeat of the Spaniards in Ireland, for reducing that Kingdom to civility; with some Reasons inclosed.	ibid.
Considerations touching the Queens service in Ireland, by Sir Francis Bacon.	(49)
Sir Francis Bacon, to the Lord Treasurer, touching his Speech in Parliament.	27
Sir Francis Bacon, to the Earl of Northampton.	ibid.
* Sir Francis Bacon, to Mr. Mathew, upon sending his Book, De sapientia Veterum.	28
* Sir Francis Bacon, to the King, touching matter of Revenue and Profit.	ibid.
* Sir Francis Bacon, to the King, touching the Lord Chancellors place.	ibid.
* Sir Francis Bacon, to the King, of the Lord Chancellors amendment, and the difference begun between the Chancery and Kings Bench.	30
* Sir Francis Bacon, to Sir George Villiers, touching the difference between the Courts of Chancery and Kings Bench.	ibid.
* Sir F. Bacon, to the King, concerning the Premunire in the Kings Bench against the Chancery.	31
* Sir Francis Bacon, the Kings Attorney, to the King, touching the proceeding with Somerset.	33

An Alphabetical Table of the Letters, &c.

* Sir Francis Bacon, *the Kings Attorney, to* Sir George Villiers, *concerning the proceeding with Somerset.* 34
* Sir Francis Bacon, *the Kings Attorney, giving accompt of an Examination taken of Somerset, at the Tower.* 35
* Sir Francis Bacon, *the Kings Attorney, to* Sir George Villiers, *touching the proceeding with Somerset.* 36
* Sir Francis Bacon, *the Kings Attorney, to* Sir George Villiers, *of Account and Advice to his Majesty, touching Somerset's Arraignment.* 37
* Sir Francis Bacon, *the Kings Attorney, and some great Lords Commissioners, concerning the perswasion used to the Lord of Somerset, to a frank confession.* 38
* Sir Francis Bacon, *to the King, upon some inclination of his Majesty, signified to him, for the Chancellors place.* ibid.
* Sir Francis Bacon, *to* Sir George Villiers, *of Advice, concerning* Ireland, *from* Gorambury *to* Windsor. 39
* *The Copy of a Letter, conceived to be written to the late Duke of* Buckingham, *when he first became a Favourite to King* James; *by Sir Francis Bacon, afterwards Lord Verulam, and Viscount St. Alban: containing some Advices unto the Duke, for his better direction in that eminent place of the Favourite; drawn from him, at the intreaty of the Duke himself, by much importunity.* 40

Sir Francis Bacon, *to the Earl of* Northumberland. (51)
* *A Discourse touching Helps for the Intellectual Powers, by Sir Francis Bacon.* (52)
* Sir Francis Bacon, *to the King.* (55)
* Sir Francis Bacon, *the Kings Attorney, returned with Postils of the Kings own hand.* 53
* Sir Francis Bacon, *the Kings Attorney General, to the Master of the Horse, upon the sending of his Bill for Viscount.* 55
* Sir Francis Bacon, *to* Sir George Villiers, *upon the sending his Patent for Viscount* Villiers *to be signed.* ibid.
* Sir Francis Bacon, *to the King, about a Certificate of my Lord* Coke's. 56

Sir Francis Bacon, *to Mr.* Toby Mathew. ibid.
Sir Francis Bacon, *to the Earl of* Salisbury. 57
Lord Chancellor Bacon, *to the King.* ibid.
The Lord Chancellor Bacon, *to the King.* 58
Again *to the King.* ibid.
* Sir Francis Bacon, *to the King, upon sending unto him a beginning of a History of his Majesties time.* 59
* Sir Francis Bacon, *to the Lord Chancellor, touching the History of* Britain. ibid.

Sir Francis Bacon, *to the King, about the pardon of the Parliaments sentence.* 60
* Sir Fran. Bacon, *to the King, upon presenting his Discourse touching the Plantation of* Ireland. 61
* Sir Francis Bacon, *to the Earl of* Salisbury, *upon sending him one of his Books of Advancement of Learning.* ibid.

The Lord Chancellor Bacon, *to the Lords.* ibid.
The Lord Chancellor Bacon, *to the Duke.* 63
* Sir Francis Bacon, *to the Lord Treasurer* Buckhurst, *upon occasion of sending his Book of Advancement of Learning.* ibid.
* *A Letter of the like Argument, to the Lord Chancellor.* ibid.
* Sir Francis Bacon, *of like Argument, to the Earl of* Northampton, *with request to present the Book to his Majesty.* ibid.
* Sir Francis Bacon, *his Letter of Request, to Doctor* Plaser, *to translate the Book of Advancement of Learning into* Latine. 64
* Sir Francis Bacon, *to* Sir Thomas Bodley, *upon sending him his Book of the Advancement of Learning.* ibid.

Sir Thomas Bodley, *to* Sir Francis Bacon, *upon his new Philosophy.* 65
* Sir Francis Bacon, *to the Bishop of* Ely, *upon sending his writing, intituled,* Cogitata & visa. 68
* Sir Francis Bacon, *to* Sir Thomas Bodley, *after he had imparted to him a writing intituled,* Cogitata & visa. ibid.
* Sir Francis Bacon, *to Mr.* Mathew, *upon sending him part of* Instauratio Magna, ibid.
* Sir Francis Bacon, *to Mr.* Mathew, *touching* Instauratio Magna. 69
* Sir Francis Bacon, *to Mr.* Savil. ibid.
* Sir Francis Bacon, *to the King, touching the Sollicitors place.* 70
* Sir Francis Bacon, *to the King, his suit to succeed in the Attorneys place.* 71

An Alphabetical Table of the Letters, &c.

*Sir Francis Bacon, to Sir George Cary in France, upon sending him his Writing, In fœlicem memoriam Elizabethæ. 71
*Sir Francis Bacon, the Kings Attorney, to the King, giving some accompt touching the Commendams. 72
*Sir Fran. Bacon his Advertisement touching an holy War, to the Right Reverend Father in God, Lancelot Andrews, Lord Bishop of Winchester, and Counceller of State to his Majesty. 73
*Sir Francis Bacon, to King James, of a Digest to be made of the Laws of England. 74
*Sir Francis Bacon, to the Right Honourable his very good Lord, the Earl of Devonshire, Lord Lieutenant of Ireland. 77
Sir Francis Bacon, to the King. 86
Sir Francis Bacon, to the Lord Kinloss, upon the entrance of King James. 87
Sir Francis Bacon, to the Earl of Northumberland, concerning a Proclamation upon the Kings entry. ibid.
Sir Francis Bacon, to Sir Edward Coke, expostulatory. 88
Sir Francis Bacon, to Sir Edward Coke, after Lord Chief Justice, and in disgrace. ibid.
Sir Francis Bacon, to Sir Vincent Skinner, expostulatory. 91
Sir Francis Bacon, to the Lord Chancellor. 92
Sir Francis Bacon, to the King. ibid.

The Earl of Bristol's Letters, &c.

The Earl of Bristol, to King James. 95
The Earl of Bristol, to Secretary Cottington. 97
The Earl of Bristol, to the Lord Bishop of Lincoln. ibid.
The Earl of Bristol, to the Prince's Highness. 98
The Earl of Bristol, to the Lord Bishop of Lincoln. 99
The Earl of Bristol, to King James. 100
The Earl of Bristol, to the Duke of Buckingham. 101
The Earl of Bristol, to King James, ibid.
The Earl of Bristol, to the Lord Conway. ibid.
The Earl of Bristol, to King James. 102
The Earl of Bristol, to the Prince, touching the delivery of his Proxie to the King of Spain. 107

Several Bishops Letters, &c.

Archbishop Abbots, to Secretary Nanton. 108
The Archbishop of Canterbury, to the Bishops, concerning King James's Directions for Preachers, with the Directions. 109
The Bishops of Rochester, Oxford, and St. Davids, to the Duke, concerning Mr. Montague. 110
The Bishop of Winchester, to his Archdeacon. 112
The Bishop of Lincoln, Lord Keeper, to the Bishop of London, concerning Preaching and Catechising. ibid.
The Bishop of Exceter, to the Lower House of Parliament. 113
The Archbishop of York, to King James. ibid.
The Bishop of Lincoln, to his Majesty. 114
The Bishop of St. Davids, (Doctor Laud) to the Duke. 115
The Bishop of Landaff, to the Duke. ibid.
The Bishop of St. Davids, (Doctor Laud) to the Duke. 116
Doctor Montague, Bishop of Chichester, to the Duke. ibid.
Doctor Field, Bishop of Landaff, to the Duke. 117
Monsieur Bevayr, Chancellor of France, discharged, to the French King. 118
Monsieur Balsac, to the Cardinal de la Valette. 119
Monsieur Balsac, to King Lewis. 121
The Lord Brook, to the Duke. ibid.
Mr. George Brook, to his Wife. 123
Mr. George Brook, to a Lady in Court. ibid.
Doctor Balcanquel, to Secretary Nanton. ibid.
Sir William Beecher, to his Majesty. 125
The Duke of Buckingham, Chancellor Elect, to the University of Cambridge. 126
The University of Cambridge's Answer to the Duke. ibid.
The Lord Duke of Buckingham, to Sir Walter Aston. 127
The Duke of Buckingham, to Sir Walter Aston. 128
L. H. R. to the Duke of Buckingham. ibid.

[a] 2

An Alphabetical Table of the Letters, &c.

C.

Cecil's Letters.

Sir Robert Cecil, *after Earl of Salisbury, to the Lord* Burleigh *his Father, from* France. 133
* Certain Copies of Letters written by Sir William Cecil, Knight, Secretary of State to Queen Elizabeth, to Sir Henry Norris Knight, Ambassadour for the said Queen, Resident in France, beginning fol. 134
Sir Edward Cecil, *to Mr. Secretary* Conway. 179
Sir Edward Cecil, *to the Duke*. 180
Sir Edward Cecil, *to the Duke*. 181
Sir Edward Cecil, *to the Duke*. ibid.
Sir Edward Cecil, *to the Duke*. 182

Sir Dudley Carleton's Letters.

Sir Dudley Carleton, *to the Marquess of* Buckingham. 183
Sir Dudley Carleton, *to the Duke of* Buckingham. 186
Sir Dudley Carleton, *to the Duke*. 187
Sir Dudley Carleton, *to the Duke*. 189
Sir Dudley Carleton, *to the Duke*. 190
Sir Dudley Carleton, *to the Duke*. 192
Sir Dudley Carleton, *to the Duke*. 193
Sir Dudley Carleton, *to the Duke*. 195
Sir Dudley Carleton, *to the Duke*. ibid.
Sir Dudley Carleton, *to the Duke*. 196
Sir Dudley Carleton, *to the Duke*. 197
Sir Dudley Carleton, *to the Duke*. 198
Sir Charles Cornwallis, *Lieger in* Spain, *to the* Spanish *King*. ibid.
Sir Charles Cornwallis, *to the Spanish King*. 199
Sir Charles Cornwallis, *to the Spanish King*. 200
Sir Charles Cornwallis, *to the Spanish King*. 201
King Charles, *to the Earl of* Bristol. 203
King Charles, *to the University of* Cambridge, *in approbation of the Election*. ibid.
The University of Cambridge's *Answer to King* Charles. 257
King Charles *his Instructions to the Vice-Chancellor, and Heads of* Cambridge, *for Government, &c.* 204
King Charles, *to the Lords Spiritual and Temporal*. ibid.
King Charles, *to the University of* Cambridge, *for a new Election*. 205
A Commission to divers Lords, for the delivery of Flushing, Brill, &c. 206
A Commission to Viscount Lisle *Governour, to deliver up* Flushing, &c. 207
The Council of Ireland *to King* Charles, *in defence of the Lord Deputy* Faulkland. 208
A Council Table Order, against hearing Mass in Embassadours houses. 210
The Collection of the Passages and Discourses, between the Embassadours of the King of Spain *and Sir* Arthur Chichester. 211
Sir Arthur Chichester, *to the Duke*. 212
The Earl of Carlisle, *to his Majesty*. 213
The Earl of Carlisle, *to the Duke*. 214
The Earl of Carlisle, *to the Duke*. 215
Mr. Edward Clark, *to the Duke*. ibid.
Mr. Edward Clark, *to the Duke*. 216
* *The Lord* Coke, *to King* James, *touching trial of Duels out of* England. ibid
Sir Francis Cottington, *to the Duke*. 217
Sir George Cary, *to the Marquess of* Buckingham. 218
Don Carlos, *to the Lord* Conway. 219
Doctor Corbet, *to the Duke*. 220
Carr, *Earl of* Somerset, *to King* James 221
Vide *the rest concerning* Somerset, *in Sir* Francis Bacons *Letters*.
Lord Conway, *to the Earl of* Bristol. 414
Lord Cromwel, *to the Duke*. 413

D.

The Earl of Desmond, *to the Earl of* Ormond. 223
Sir Kenhelm Digby, *to Sir* Edward Stradling. ibid.

An Alphabetical Table of the Letters, &c.

Doctor Donne, to the Marquess of Buckingham.	228
Doctor Donne, to the Duke.	ibid.
A Defiance sent by the Grand Seignior, to Maximilian the Second.	229

E.

Queen Elizabeth's Letter to the Lady Norris, upon the death of her Son.	ibid.
Sir John Elliot, to the Duke.	412
The Earl of Essex, to King James, concerning Secretary Davison.	229
The Earl of Essex, to Secretary Davison.	230
The Earl of Essex, to Mr. Secretary Davison.	ibid.
The Earl of Essex, to Mr. Secretary Davison.	231
The Earl of Essex, to Secretary Davison.	ibid.
The Earl of Essex, to Secretary Davison.	ibid.
The Earl of Essex, to Mr Secretary Davison, upon the death of Mr. Secretary Walsingham.	232
The Earl of Essex, to the Queen.	ibid.
The Earl of Essex, to the Queen.	233
Sir Thomas Egerton, Lord Chancellor, to the Earl of Essex.	ibid.
The Earl of Essex his Answer to the Lord Chancellor.	234
Sir Thomas Egerton, Chancellor, after Lord Ellesmere, to the Earl of Essex.	235
Lord Chancellor Ellesmere, to King James.	ibid.
Lord Chancellor Ellesmere, to King James.	236

F.

Ferdinand the Emperour, to Don Balthasar de Zuniga.	237
The Lord Faulkland's Petition to the King.	238
A Declaration of Ferdinand Infanta of Spain.	239

G.

Mr. Gargrave, to the Lord Davers.	240
Ab ignoto, to the Conde Gondomar, concerning the death of Philip the 3d.	ibid.
To Count Gondomar.	242
The Conde de Gondomar, to the Duke.	244

H.

King Henry the Eighth, to the Clergy of the Province of York, Anno 1533. touching his Title of Supreme Head of the Church of England.	ibid.
Sir John Hipsley, to the Duke.	248
The Lord Herbert, to his Majesty.	249
The Earl of Holland, to his Majesty.	250
The Earl of Holland, to the Duke.	251
The Earl of Holland, to the Duke.	152
The Earl of Holland, to the Duke.	253
The Earl of Holland, to the Universitie of Cambridge.	254
The Lady Elizabeth Howard, to the King.	
* The History of the Reign of King Henry the Eighth, K. Edward the Sixth, Queen Mary, and part of the Reign of Queen Elizabeth.	ibid.

I.

King James, to the Major and Aldermen of London, after he was proclaimed.	257
King James, to the Universitie of Cambridge.	ibid.
* A Copy of a Letter from his Majesty, to the Lords, read at the Board, Nov 21. 1617. touching the abatement of his Majesties Houshold charge.	258
* A Copy of his Majesties second Letter.	ibid.
King James, to the Earl of Bristol, Embassadour in Spain.	259
King James, to Ferdinand the Emperour, concerning the Palatinate.	260
His Imperial Majesty, to King James.	261
King James, to Pope Gregory the 15th.	412
The Earl of Worcester, Arundel and Surrey, Montgomery, to the King.	262
King James, to the Earl of Bristol.	ibid.
The Earl of Bristol, in Answer to King James.	263
King James his Instructions to the Arch-bishop of Canterbury, concerning Orders to be observed by Bishops in their Dioceses, 1622.	265
King James, to the Palsgrave.	266
The Palsgraves Answer to King James.	267
* King James, to the Lord Bacon, by occasion of a Book, it was the Organon.	270

* King

An Alphabetical Table of the Letters, &c.

King James his Letter to his Trusty and welbeloved Tho. Coventry, our Attorney General. 270
To King James, ab ignoto, from Madrid. ibid.
Ab ignoto, of the Affairs of Spain, France, and Italy. 271
Ab ignoto, concerning the Estate of Rochel after the surrender. 272
To King James, ab ignoto. 273
To King James, ab ignoto. 274
To the King, ab ignoto. 276
To his sacred Majesty, ab ignoto. 277
To King James, ab ignoto. 414
The Copy of a Letter, written by his Majesty King James, to the Lord Keeper, the Bishops of London, Winton, Rochester, St. Davids, and Exceter, Sir Henry Hubbert, Mr. Justice Dodderidge, Sir Henry Martin, and Doctor Steward, or any six of them, whereof the Lord Keeper, the Bishops of London, Winton, and St. Davids, to be four. 279
The Justices of Peace in the County of Devon, to the Lords of the Councel. ibid.
Instructions for the Ministers and Church-wardens of London. 280

K.

The Lord Keeper *Williams*, his Letters.

Lord Keeper, to the Duke, about the Liberties of Westminster. 283
The Lord Keeper to the Duke. ibid.
The Lord Keeper, to the Duke. 284
The Lord Keeper, to the Duke, concerning the Earl of Southampton. 285
The Lord Keeper, to the Duke, concerning the Earl Marshals place. ibid.
The Lord Keeper, to the Duke. 286
The Lord Keeper, to the Duke, concerning the Lord of St. Albans. 287
The Lord Keeper, to the Duke. 288
The Lord Keeper, to the Duke, about Mr. Thomas Murrey's dispensation, &c. 289
Passages between the Lord Keeper, and Don Francisco. 290
The Lord Keeper, to the Duke, concerning Sir Iohn Michel. 291
The Lord Keeper, to the Duke. ibid.
The Lord Keeper, to the Duke, about the Lord Treasurer. 292
The fair and familiar Conferences which the Lord Treasurer had with the Lord Keeper, after some expostulations of his own, and the issue joyned thereupon, at White-hall, Septemb. 7. 1622. ibid.
The Lord Keeper, to the Lord Viscount Anan. 293
The Lord Keeper, to the Duke. 295
The Lord Keeper to the Duke. 296
The Lord Keeper, to the Duke. 297
The Lord Keeper, to the Duke. 298
The Lord Keeper, to the Duke. ibid.
A Relation sent by the Lord Keeper to the Duke, containing the Heads of that discourse which fell from Don Francisco. April. 7. 1624. at 11 of the Clock at night. 300
The Lord Keeper, to the Duke, concerning Sir Richard Weston. 301
The Lord Keeper, to the Duke. 302
The Lord Keeper, to the Duke. ibid.
The Lord Keeper, to the Duke. 303
The Lord Keeper, to the Duke, concerning the Countess of Southampton. 304
The Lord Keeper, to the Duke. ibid.
The Lord Keeper, to the Duke, concerning Doctor Scot. 305
The Lord Keeper, to the Duke. ibid.
The Lord Keeper, to the Duke, about Sir Robert Howard. 306
The Lord Keeper, to the Duke. 307
The Lord Keeper, to the Duke. 308
The Lord Keeper, to the Duke. ibid.
The Lord Keeper, to the Duke. 309
The Bishop of Lincoln, (sometimes Lord Keeper) to the Duke. 310

The Lord of *Kensingtons* Letters.

The Lord of Kensington, to the Duke. 311
The Lord of Kensington, to the Prince. 312
The Lord of Kensington, to the Prince. 313

An Alphabetical Table of the Letters, &c.

The Lord of Kensington to the Duke. 314
The Lord of Kensington, to the Duke. 315
The Lord of Kensington, to the Lord Conway. 316
The Lord of Kensington, to the Duke. 318
The Lord Kensington to the Duke. 320

L

Mr. Lorkin, to the Duke. 320
Mr. Lorkin, to the Duke. 321
The Lords of the Councel in England, to the Lords of the Councel in Ireland. Jan. 31. 1629. 322

M

Sir Robert Mansel, to the Duke. 323
Sir Robert Mansel, to the Duke. 325
Padre Maestre, at Rome, to the Spanish Embassadour in England. 326
Magdibeg, to his Majesty. ibid.
The Earl of Middlesex, to his Majesty. 327
The Earl of Middlesex, to the Duke. ibid.
Sir Toby Mathew, to the Duchess of Buckingham. 328
Sir Toby Mathew, to the King of Spain. 329
The Lord Mountjoy, to the Earl of Essex. 330
The Duke of Modena, to the Duke of Savoy. ibid.

N

Thomas Duke of Norfolk, to Queen Elizabeth. 331
Sir Francis Norris, to King James. ibid.
The Countess of Nottingham, to the Danish Embassadour. 332
The Lord Nithisdale, to the Duke. ibid.
The Lady Elizabeth Norris, to the Duke. 333

O

Sir Iohn Ogle, to the Duke. ibid.
The Earl of Oxford, to the Duke. 334
An Order made at White-hall, betwixt the University and Town of Cambridge, 4. Decemb. 1629, 335

P

SIR Iohn Perrots Commission for Lord Deputy of Ireland. ibid.
The whole contents of the Commission. 336
The Queens Warrant to the Lords &c, of Ireland, for ministring the Oath, and delivery of the Sword to him, Jan. 31. 1583. ibid.
Another for his entertainment there. ibid.
The Queens Instructions to Sir Iohn Perrot. 337.
Sir Iohn Perrot, to the Lords of the Council. ibid.
The Petition of Francis Philips, to King James, for the release of Sir Robert Philips, Prisoner in the Tower. 338
Sir Robert Philips, to the Duke of Buckingham. 340
K. Philip the Third of Spain, to the Conde Olivarez. 341
Conde Olivarez, his Answer to the King. 342
The Protestants of France, to Charles King of Great-Britain. 343
The Pope, to the Duke of Buckingham. Gregory P. P. XV. 345
The Lady Purbeck, to the Duke 346
Mr. Iohn Packer, to the Lord Keeper. ibid.
Passages between the Lord Nithisdale, and the Spanish Embassadours. 347
Captain Iohn Pennington, to the Duke. 348
Captain Pennington, to the Duke. 351
A Patent for the Admiralty of Ireland. ibid.

R

Sir Thomas Roe, to the Marquess of Buckingham, Lord Admiral. 352
Cardinal Richlieu, to the Roman Catholiques of Great-Britain. 353
The Duke of Roban, to his Majesty of Great-Britain. ibid.
Sir Walter Raleigh, to the Duke. 354
Sir Walter Raleigh, to King James, before his Tryal. 355
Sir Walter Raleigh, to Sir Robert Carr, after Earl of Somerset. ibid.
Monsieur Richer, forced, recants his Opinions against the Papal Supremacy over Kings. 356

The

An Alphabetical Table of the Letters, &c.

The Lord Viscount Rochford, *to the Duke of* Buckingham. 356
Mr. Ruthen, *to the Earl of* Northumberland. 357

S.

THe Copy of a Letter sent from Spain, concerning the Princes arrival there, &c. ..... ibid.
A Privy Seal, for transporting of Horse. 359
The Earl of Suffolk, *to his Majesty.* ..... ibid.
The Earl of Southampton's *Letter to the Bishop of* Lincoln. ..... ibid.
The Lord Keepers Answer to the Earl of Southampton's *Letter.* 360
Oliver St. Iohn, *to the Major of* Malborough, *against the Benevolence.* 361
The Earl of Suffolk, *to the Duke* 362
The Earl of Suffolk, *to his Majesty.* ..... ibid.
* Sir Philip Sidney, *unto Queen* Elizabeth, *touching her Marriage with Monsieur.* 363
* *The Lord* Sanquir's *Case.* 368
* *The: Lady* Shrewsbury's *Case.* 369
Doctor Sharp, *to King* James. 370
Doctor Sharp, *to the Duke of* Buckingham. 372
The King of Spain, *to Pope* Urban. 415

T.

SIr Nicholas Throckmorton, *then Embassadour in* France, *to Queen* Elizabeth, *touching a free Passage for the Queen of* Scots, *through* England *into* Scotland. 374
Monsieur Toyrax, *to the Duke of* Buckingham. 380
Mr. Trumbal, *to the Secretary.* ..... ibid.
Mr. Trumbal, *to the Secretary.* 382
Mr. Ch. Th. *to the Duke of* Buckingham. 383

U.

POpe Urban, *to* Lewis *the Thirteenth, of* France. 386
The University of Cambridge, *to the Duke.* 387
The Dukes Answer. ..... ibid.
The Vice-chancellor of Cambridge, *to the King, upon the Dukes death.* 388
The University of Cambridge, *to the King.* ..... ibid.
The University of Cambridge, *to the Archbishop of* York. 389
The University of Cambridge *to the Earl of* Manchester. ..... ibid.
The University of Cambridge, *to Sir* Humphrey May. 390
The University of Cambridge, *to the Lord Chief Justice* Richardson. ..... ibid.

W.

SIr Henry Wallop, *to the Queen.* 391
Sir Isaac Wake, *to the Secretary.* ..... ibid.
Sir Isaac Wake, *to Mr. Secretary.* 393
Sir Isaac Wake, *to the Duke.* 395
Sir Isaac Wake's *Proposition for the King of* Denmark. 396
Sir Henry Wotton, *to the Duke.* 397
Sir Henry Wotton, *to the Duke.* 398
Sir Henry Wotton, *to the Duke.* 399
Sir Henry Wotton, *to the Duke.* 400
Sir Henry Wotton, *to the Duke.* ..... ibid.
Sir Henry Wotton, *to the Earl of* Portland, *Lord Treasurer.* ..... ibid.
Sir Richard Weston, *to the Duke.* 401
Sir Richard Weston, *to the Duke.* 402
Sir Richard Weston, *to the Duke.* 403
Sir Richard Weston, *to the Duke.* ..... ibid.
Sir Richard Weston, *to the Duke.* 404
Sir Richard Weston, *to the Duke.* ..... ibid.
The Lord Wimbledon, *to the Duke.* ..... ibid.
The Lord Wimbledon, *to the Duke.* 406
Sir Francis Walsingham, *Secretary, to Monsieur* Critoy, *Secretary of* France. ..... ibid.
Doctor Williams, *to the Duke.* 408

Y.

The Marquess Ynoyosa, *to the Lord* Conway. 409
Sir Henry Yelverton, *to the Duke.* ..... ibid.
Sir Henry Yelverton's *submission in* Star-chamber. 410

CABALA:
SIVE,
Scrinia Sacra.

IN
LETTERS of Illustrious Persons, and Great Ministers
of *STATE*, &c.

Queen Anne *of* Bullen *to King* Henry, *from the Tower*, May 6. 1536.

SIR,

Our Graces displeasure, and my imprisonment, are things so strange unto me, as what to write, or what to excuse, I am altogether ignorant. Whereas you send unto me (willing me to confess a truth, and so to obtain your favour) by such a one whom you know to be my ancient professed enemy, I no sooner received this message, then I rightly conceived your meaning: And if, as you say, confessing a truth indeed may procure my safety, I shall with all willingness and duty perform your command; but let not your Grace ever imagine that your poor wife will ever be brought to acknowledge a fault, where not so much as a thought ever proceeded: And, to speak a truth, never Prince had wife more loyal in all duty, and in all true affection, then you have ever found in *Anne Bullen*; with which name and place I could willingly have contented my self, if God, and your Graces pleasure, had so been pleased. Neither did I at any time forget my self in my exaltation, or received Queenship, but that I always look'd for such an alteration as now I find, the ground of my preferment being on no surer foundation then your Graces fancie, the least alteration whereof, I knew, was fit and sufficient to draw that fancie to some other subject.

You have chosen me from a low estate to be your Queen and Companion, far beyond my desert, or desire: If then you find me worthy of such honour, Good your Grace, let not any light fancie, or bad counsel of my Enemies, withdraw your Princely favour from me; neither let that stain, that unworthy stain of a disloyal heart towards your good Grace, ever cast so foul a blot on your most dutiful wife, and the Infant-Princess your daughter. Try me, good King, but let me have a lawfull trial, and let not my sworn enemies sit as my Accusers and Judges: Yea, let me receive an open Trial, for my truthes shall fear no open shames; then shall you see, either my innocency cleared, your suspition and conscience satisfied, the ignominy and slander of the world stopped, or my guilt openly declared: So that whatsoever God or you may determine of me, your Grace may be freed from an open censure; and my offence being so lawfully proved, your Grace is at liberty, both before God and man, not onely to execute worthy punishment on me as an unfaithfull wife, but to follow your affection, already setled on that party for whose sake I am now as I am, whose name I could some while since have pointed to, your Grace not being ignorant of my suspicion therein. But if you have already determined of me, and that not onely my death, but an infamous slander must bring you the enjoying of a desired happiness, then I desire of God, that he will pardon your great sin herein, and likewise my enemies the instruments thereof; and that he will not call you to a strict accompt for your unprincely and cruel usage of me, at his general Judgment-seat, where both you and my self must both shortly appear, and in whose just Judgment, I doubt not, whatsoever the world may think of me, my innocency shall be openly known, and sufficiently cleared.

My last and onely request shall be, That my self may bear the burthen of your Graces displeasure, and that it may not touch the innocent souls of those poor Gentlemen, who, as I understand, are in streight imprisonment for my sake. If ever I have found favour in your sight, if ever the name of *Anne Bullen* hath been pleasing in your ears, let me obtain this last request, and I will so leave to trouble your Grace any further, with my earnest prayers to the Trinity, to have your Grace in his good keeping, and to direct you in all your actions.

From my dolefull prison in the Tower,
this sixth of May, 1536.

Your most loyal and faithfull Wife,
ANNE BULLEN.

Sir Anthony Ashley *to the Duke of* Buckingham.

May it please your good Lordship,

IF any thing had happened worth your knowledge, I had either come or sent to *Theobalds* in your absence, being ascertained, that your Lordship had been already particularly informed of what passed in the Higher House betwixt the Earl of *A.* and the *L.S.* which is the onely thing of note, and is thought will beget some novelty.

Your Lordship may be most assured, that your Adversaries continue their meetings and conferences here in *Holborn*, how to give his Majestie some soul distaste of you, as making you the onely author of all grievances and oppressions whatsoever, for your private ends. And I hope to be able, within few days, (if promise be kept) to give you good overture of a mutual oath taken to this purpose amongst them.

The rumour lately spread, touching his Majesties untimely pardon of the late Lord Chancellors Fine and Imprisonment, with some other favours intended towards him, (said to be procured by your Lordships onely intimation) hath exceedingly exasperated the rancour of the ill-affected; which, albeit it be false, and unlikely, because very unseasonable, it doth yet serve the present turn, for the increase of malice against you. I can but inform your Lordship of what I understand, you may please to make use thereof as your self thinketh best.

I most humbly intreat your good Lordship, to keep Letters of this nature, either in your own Cabinet, or to make Hereticks of them; for I am very well acquainted with the disposition of some Pen-men in Court. Upon message even now received of my poor Daughters sudden dangerous sickness, I am constrained unmannerly to post unto her, being the onely comfort I have in this world; and do purpose, God willing, a speedy return. In the mean time, and even with my hearty prayer, I commend your good Lordship to Gods mercifull and safe keeping. This 12th. of *May*, 1621.

Your honourable good Lordships faithfully devoted,
A. A.

Sir WALTER ASTON'S
Letters, &c.

Sir Walter Aston *to the* Duke *of* Buckingham.

May it please y'ur Grace,

Y Lord of *Bristol* intended to have dispatched away a Post unto his Majesty this night, with the advice of the arrival of the Dispensation, which came to Town the 12th. of this moneth, hoping that he should have been likewise able to have given to his Majesty and his Highness a clear account of all things concerning it. But the delivery of the Queen this morning (who is brought to bed of a Daughter) hath stopped all negotiation; and I believe it will be these two days before he can be ready to send him away. There is no novelty (as I yet understand) that is come with the Dispensation; there will be something desired for better explanation of his Majesties and his Highness intentions; and some omissions there are, which, as they understand, was his Highness intention should have been in the Capitulation, they being promised by his Highness. But I do not find that these will be any stop to the business; For they do press my Lord of *Bristol* very much to proceed presently to the *Desposorios*. Your Grace shall understand all things more particularly by the next Post. I do now make the more haste, forbearing to trouble you with other occurrences, lest my Letters come short of the departure of the Post, as they did of his who was last dispatched from hence.

I do most humbly desire your Grace to continue the doing me those offices that may continue me in his Majesties and his Highness good opinion; and I doubt not but I shall be ever able to let your Grace see, that you have not a more faithfull servant, then he which your Grace hath most bound to be so, and that shall ever remain

Novemb. 15. 1623.

Yours, &c.
W. A.

The Copy of a Memorial given to the King of Spain. Translated.

SIR,

SIR *Walter Aston*, Embassador of the King of Great *Britain*, saith, That the King his Master hath commanded him to represent unto your Majesty, that having received so many promises from hence to procure the intire restitution of the *Palatinate*, and Electoral Dignity to the Prince his Son in Law, He commanded his Embassador to press your Majesty with all diligence, that the said promises might take effect, not as a condition of the Marriage, but desiring infinitely to see setled, together with the marriage, the peace and quiet of his Son in Law, his Daughter, and Grandchildren; and having understood that this his desire hath received an interpretation far differing from his intention, hath commanded him anew, for the greater demonstration of the desire which he hath to preserve the good Correspondence with your Majesty, to declare unto you, that he hath not propounded the said restitutions as a condition of the marriage, but according to that which he understood was most conformable with the intention of your Majesty, declared by the *Conde de Olivarez*, for the surest, and most effectual means, to make the amity which is betwixt your Majesties firm and indissoluble: And that there might not remain any doubt or matter hereafter, that should cause dispute, he hath required that every thing might he settled under your Majesties hand; desiring it likewise for the greater comfort of his onely Daughter, and for to make the coming of that most excellent Princess of more esteem unto his Subjects, bringing with her (besides the glory of her own virtue and worth) the security of a perpetual peace and amity, and an everlasting pawn to his Kingdomes of the constancy and real performance of your Majesties promises, with such satisfaction to his hopes grounded on the said promises, not as a Condition, but as the fruit and blessing of the alliance. Moreover he saith, That the King his Master hath commanded him to make this Declaration unto your Majesty, that you may know the truth and the sound intentions of his proceedings, with the good end to which it aims, having renewed the powers, and deferred the delivery of them, onely to give time for the accomplishing and setling that which hath been promised for the satisfying his expectation, and assuring the amity betwixt your Majesties Persons and Crowns; the King his Master hoping that your Majesty will likewise lay hold of this occasion, which you now have in your hand, to give him full satisfaction in that which with so much reason he desires, and therewithal a reciprocal and everlasting blessing to both your Majesties Crowns.

Jan. 19. 1623.
Stil. Vet.

Sir Walter Aston *to the Duke*.

May it please your Grace,

HOwsoever upon the arrival of Mr. *Greisley*, I took the occasion of the ordinary, the day following, to acknowledge unto your Grace the Comfort which I had received by your Letters; understanding by them the favour which you have done me, in diverting from me his Majesties and his Highness displeasure, I shall notwithstanding intreat here leave, by the same means by which I received so much happiness, to renew my humble and most thankfull acknowledgment unto your Grace. I most earnestly intreat your Grace to look upon me here as a servant that loves you in his heart, and that shall faithfully in all things comply with what you can expect from such an one; and that therefore you will be pleased to preserve me still in the way, how I may serve his Majesty and his Highness to their Content, and perform towards your Grace those offices of a servant, which may be most to your satisfaction. For I am now here in a dangerous time, in the greatest businesses that have been treated of many years, and the bitterest storms threatning betwixt these Crowns, that have been these many ages. I have therefore no hope to save my self, without I be guided by his Highness and your Graces trust and care of me.

The Marquess of *Ynoisa* hath lately advertised hither, That he hath several times desired to have private audience with his Majesty, and hath not been able to procure any, but what your Grace assists at. It is likewise advertised unto this King and his Ministers, that your Grace hath many meetings with the Sea-Captains, and that your Counsels are how the War is to be made against *Spain*. For the avoiding of unnecessary repetitions, I do here inclosed send your Grace a Copy of my Letter to Mr. Secretary *Conway*, wherein you will find a relation of all things that are come to my hands at this present, that may any way have reflection unto his Majesties service. And this is the course which I intend, and conceive most convenient to hold hereafter with your Grace, without you command me the contrary. In the said Copy your Grace will find a discourse of what hath lately passed betwixt my Lord of *Bristol*, and the *Conde* of *Olivarez*, in the *Pardo*. Now that I may more fully discharge my duty, I have thought fit here to acquaint your Grace, that since the putting off of the *Deposories*, at a meeting that my Lord and my self had with the *Conde*, he did make a solemn protestation, that if the Treaty of the Match did ever come on again with effect, it should onely be by his Lordships hand, and no other. I then understood it, and still do, but for a frothy protestation, yet have held it my duty to advertize, it having passed in my hearing; the truth is, that my Lords answer was in Conformity to his last in the *Pardo*, every way rejecting it, saying, That he had rather be confined to any Town in *Africk*, then

Sir Walter Aston *to Secretary* Conway.

then that his person should be any hinderance to the Match. Thus forbearing to trouble your Grace any farther, with my hearty prayers unto God for the continuance of his blessings unto you. I rest

Your Graces &c.

January. 22. 1623. Stil. Vet. W. A.

Sir Walter Aston *to Secretary* Conway.

Right Honourable,

BY the return of this Bearer Mr. *Greisley,* you will understand of the safe coming to my hands of your dispatch of the 30th of the last moneth, with his Majesties Letters therein inclosed. I do now herewithall send an account unto his Majestie of my proceedings upon his Commands, which I do intreat your Honour to be pleased to present unto him, as also farther to acquaint his Majesty, that I have already spoken with divers of these Ministers, and given them such a declaration of his Majesties good intentions in the pressing at this season for the restitutions of the *Palatinate,* and Electoral dignity, unto the Prince his Son in Law, as I have order to do by the said Letter, but do find they are here so possessed with the ill relations they receive out of *England,* that I with much difficultie can scarce give them any kind of satisfaction. I have acquainted the *Conde Olivarez* with the answer, which your Honour, and Mr. Secretarie *Calvert* had received from their Embassadours touching their audiences, the *Conde* himself having formerly acquainted me with their Complaint. His answer now was, That he understood they had acknowledged unto your Honours to have received from his Majesty in that point all kind of satisfaction, but that after you were gone to the Marquess of *Ynoisa* wrote a Letter to Secretarie *Calvert,* telling him, that he did not well remember himself of what had passed at his being there, but had since called to mind, that he had procured some audiences with the Prince with much difficultie. To which I answered the *Conde,* That it seemed the Marquesse was very light of his advertisements, to give such informations as might breed ill understandings betwixt Princes, and esteem them of no more Consequence, then to forget what he had advertised with so much ease. Concerning that malicious report here raised of the Prince's treating a marriage in *France,* I desire your Honour to let his Majesty know, that it is advertised hither out of *England* as a thing so certain, that there is not a Minister of State (excepting the *Conde* of *Gondomar*) that hath not given some credit unto it. I have therefore, according to his Majesties directions, given such declarations touching the author and believers of it, as your Honour in his Majesties name hath commanded me. I have likewise received by Mr. *Greisley* your Letter of the 31. of the last: In answer of which, all that I shall need to say here unto your Honour is, that my Lord of *Bristol* hath received your former Letter, acquainting him with his Majesties pleasure concerning the same business, from whom his Majestie will receive an account thereof. This is all that I have to say to your Honour, at this present, touching those particulars mentioned in your Letter; I shall now here further acquaint you with such advertisements as I conceive may any waies have reference unto his Majesties service. My Lord of *Bristol,* and my self, repairing some few daies since unto the *Pardo,* having conference with the *Conde* of *Olivarez,* his Lordship acquainted the *Conde* with the Letters of revocation, which he had received from his Majesty, and withal desired that he would procure him licence to take his leave of the King. The *Conde* answered his Lordship, That he had much to say unto him by order from his Majesty, the substance of his speech was; That they had received large advertisements out of *England,* by which they understood the hard measure that he was there likely to suffer by the power of his enemies, and that the onely crime which they could impute unto him, was for labouring to effect the marriage, which his Master could not but take much to heart, and held himself obliged to publish to the world the good service that my Lord had done unto the King of Great *Britain*; and therefore, for the better encouragement likewise of his own, and all other Ministers that should truly serve their Masters, he was to offer him a blank paper signed by the King, wherein his Lordship might set down his own Conditions, and demands; which he said he did not propound to corrupt any servant of his Majesties, but for a publique declaration of what was due unto his Lordships proceedings. He said further, that in that offer, he laid before him the Lands and Dignities that were in his Masters power to dispose of; out of which he left it at his pleasure to choose what estate, or honour, he should think good, adding thereunto some other extravagant and disproportionable offers. My Lords answer was, That he was very sorry to hear this language used unto him, telling the

Conde

Sir Walter Aston *to Secretary* Conway.

Conde, that his Catholique Majesty did owe him nothing, but that what he had done was upon the King his Masters Commands, and without any intention to serve *Spain*. And that howsoever he might have reason to fear the power of his enemies, yet he trusted much upon the innocency of his own Cause, and the Justice of the King, and that he could not understand himself in any danger: but were he sure to lose his head at his arrival there, he would go to throw down himself at his Majesties feet and mercy, and rather there die upon a Scaffold then be Duke of *Infantada* in *Spain*. On the 16th of this moneth, there was declared here in Councel a resolution of this King, to make a journey to his frontier Towns in *Andaluzia*, with an intention to begin his journey upon the 29: of this moneth, *Stil. Vet*. And, as I am informed, his Majesty will there entertain himself the greatest part of these three moneths following; so that his return hither will not be until the beginning of *May*. My Lord of *Bristol* hath sent divers to the *Conde* for leave to dispeed himself of the King; but in respect of his Majesties being at the *Pardo*, he hath been hitherto delayed, and hath yet no certain day appointed for it: But I conceive it will be sometime this week. The Cause of the delaying of his Lordships admittance to the King, as I understand, is, that the same day that his Lordship shall declare his revocation to the King, they will here in Councel declare the revocation of the Marquess of *Ynoisa*. Howsoever in respect of the Kings departure, (at which time they use here to embarge all the mules, and means of carriage in this Town) I beleeve his Lordship will not begin his journey so soon as he intended.

All the relations which are lately come out of *England* do wish them to entertain themselves here with no farther hopes, that there is any intention to proceed to the Match; and this advice comes accompanied with such a report of the state of all things there, that hath much irritated all these Ministers, and let loose the tongues of the people against the proceedings of his Majesty, and Highness. I labour as much as I can, and as far as my directions will give me latitude, to give them better understandings of the real intentions of his Majesty and Highness: but divers of them cleerly tell me, That I profess one thing, and the actions of his Majesty and Highness (upon the which they must ground their belief) are differing from it. I shall therefore here, in discharge of my duty, advertize your Honour, that they do here expect nothing but a War, about which they have already held divers Councels, and go seriously to work, preparing themselves for what may happen. Which I desire your Honour to advertize his Majesty, being high time, as far as I am able to judge, that am here upon the place, that his Majesty do either resolve upon some course for the allaying of these storms; or that he goe in hand with equal preparations. Having observed, in former times, the strange rumours that have run in *England* upon small foundations, I have thought it fit to prevent the credit which may be given to idle relations, by advertizing your Honour that I cannot conceive how any great attempt can be made from hence this year, howsoever businesses should go. The Squadron of the Kings Fleet (under the Command of *Don Fadrique de Toledo*) is come into *Cadiz*, and joyned with that which *Don Juan Taxardo* is Captain of. And as I am credibly informed, this King will have by the end of *April* between fifty and sixty Gallions at Sea. It is true, that other years the number commonly falls short of what is expected, and their setting forth to Sea some moneths later then the time appointed; but there is extraordinary care taken this year, that there be no default in neither; the chief end (that I can understand) of this Kings journey being to see the Fleet of Plate come in, to take view of his Armado, and see them put to Sea. That which I understand is onely left alive of the Marriage here is, that the Jewels which the Prince left with this King for the Infanta and her Ladies, are not yet returned; but it is intimated unto me, that if the Letters which they shall receive out of *England*, upon the answer they have given to his Majesty about the business of the *Palatinate* be no better then such as they have lately received, they will return the Jewels, and declare the business of the Match for broken. I shall therefore intreat your Honour to know his Majesties pleasure how I shall carry my self, if they be offered unto me, being resolved in the mean time, until I shall know his Majesties pleasure, if any such thing happen, absolutely to refuse them. The Princess some few daies since fell sick of a *Calentura*, of which she remaineth still in her bed, though it be said she is now somewhat better. I will conclude, with many thanks for your friendly advertizements concerning my own particular, which (God willing) as far as I can, I will observe; and do earnestly intreat you, that you will please to continue the like favours unto me, which I shall highly esteem of. And so with a grateful acknowledgement of my obligations, I rest

Your Honours, &c.

January, 22. 1623.

W. Aston.

Sir Walter Aston to the Lord Conway.

Right Honourable;

I Have advertised by former dispatches, that the Parliament here had granted unto his King 60 millions of Ducates to be paid in 12 years, which with 12 millions which remain yet unpaid of what was given the King at the last session, this King was to receive 72 millions in the 12 years next following. I shall now acquaint your Honour that there are only 19. Cities that have voice in this Parliament, and that each of them do send hither two *Procuradores*, (as they call them here) but these have no power finally to conclude any thing, but what is agreed on by them is to be approved of by the said Cities, or the greatest number of them, before it have the force of an Act of Parliament, and that therefore there hath been all possible art used to procure the Cities to confirm what hath been granted by their *Procuradores* touching the 60 millions; and it is here thought that one of the motives of this Kings journey was, hoping by the authority of his presence to procure the consent unto the said gift of the 4. Cities which he is to pass by in this journey, namely *Cordova, Sivil, Joen*, and *Granado*, it being here doubted, that the said Cities might make great opposition to the said grant, notwithstanding his Majesty hath not had such success as was expected. But *Cordova* which was the first City with which his Majesty began, hath absolutely refused to give their Consent, letting his Majesty understand, though in as fair and respectful terms as they could express themselves, That it was a demand impossible for them to Comply withall. What the success of this may be is doubtful, *Cordova* having given but an ill example to the other Cities; and yet it is rather believed here, that the greatest number of them being under the Command of such as are either this Kings servants, or absolutely under his dispose, that his Majesty will be able to overcome the business; and they are now busie how to settle the manner of the leavie of the said sum by yearly and equal portions.

They having found here divers inconveniences in their new Government of *Portugal* by way of Governours, are resolved to place Vice-Kings again there. And for to gratifie the Emperour, have elected for that charge his third Brother *Don Carlos*, who is presently to make his repair thither. On the 27th. of the last moneth, my Lord of *Bristol* took his leave of the Queen and the Infanta, and on the Sunday following, being the 29. of the said moneth, his Lordship delivered unto me the Powers which his Highness left with him, and those which have been since sent hither. His Lordship is preparing for his journey, and saith that he is already in such a forwardness, as upon the arrival here of Mr. *Greisly*, or any other from *England*, whereby he shall receive means for the taking up of moneys here, he will presently put himself upon the way. The Queen here some few daies since fell suddenly ill, and swooned two or three times; but her indisposition lasted not above two or three daies; Her Majestie is now (thanks be to God) very well again. The King having received advice thereof intended (as it is said) to come presently post hither; but upon better news, His Majesty proceeds in his journey; and for any thing that I can understand, it will be *May* before his return to this Town.

There are lately thrown abroad in this Town divers Copies of a Proclamation pretended to be published in *Ireland*, bearing date the 27 of *January* last. It hath made a great noise here, and divers of their Ministers have spoken with me about it, they conceiving it to be contrary to what hath been lately Capitulated. For my part, I have been able to give them no answer, not having yet understood from your Honour, nor any of his Majesties Ministers, of any such Proclamation. I have seen the Proclamation as it came Printed from thence, and do here inclosed send your Honour a Copy thereof, desiring you that you will acquaint his Majesty therewithal, that he may be pleased to Command therein what to his wisdom shall seem fit. To those that have spoken with me about this Proclamation (having first disclaimed the having had knowledg of any such thing) I have used discourses of mine own touching the abuses of those which are called titulary Archbishops, Bishops, &c. letting them understand here, that if those kind of people have ben busie there to plant secretly their Government, they have far exceeded the favour which was promised them, and given his Majesty just cause to give order for the reformation.

My last to your Honour was of the 7th of *February* last by *Albert Rivas*, whom I dispatched with all diligence to you, since when I have received nothing from your Honour. I shall therefore, &c.

Your Honours, &c. W. Aston.

Sir Walter Aston *to the Lord* Conway.

Right Honourable,

IN a former Dispatch which I lately made unto your Honour, I sent unto you the Copy of a Letter, which I then had newly received from the Secretary *Den Andreas de Prada*, by which he advertised me, That the King his Master (according to what I had requested by Memorial) had commanded, that all English Commodities and Manufactures which I have long since advertised, were prohibited by *Pramatica's* published here for the reformation of abuses) should enter into these Kingdoms. I have long since performed divers diligences my self, both with the Secretary, and President of *Castile*, for the procuring a Declaration of the said Order, being careful to prevent such inconveniences as the King our Masters Subjects might fall into, for want thereof: But having been tossed up and down between the Secretary and the President with several delays, the one remitting me to the other; I repaired to the *Conde of Olivarez* (suspecting some novelty in the business) and acquainted him, that upon the receipt of a Letter sent me from the Secretary *Den Andreas de Prada*, concerning the free entrance of English Commodities, I had given notice, by a Copy of the said Letter, unto the King my Master of what was therein Commanded, and had likewise advertised the Merchants that reside in these Kingdoms, of the said Order: I also gave him account of the several diligences which I had performed with the President, and the Secretary, for the procuring a Declaration thereof, and desired, that he would presently command, that there might be such course taken, that there should be no further delayes used therein, since I should be loath to see the King my Masters Subjects, encouraged by the said Order, to repair hither with their Merchandizes, and fall into inconveniences for want of notice given thereof unto their Ministers in the Ports. The *Conde* fell into discourses far from my expectation, asking me, whether it were not free for any King, in his own Kingdom, to Command his own Subjects to wear what he pleased? saying further, That the English were not prohibited to bring in their Commodities, but that the King his Master might command his Subjects to spend the Byes, and other Commodities of his own Kingdoms, and not to make use of those that came from forreign parts, as to his wisdome, for the good of his Kingdoms, should seem best: That there should be a suspension of the execution of the said *Pramatica's* until St *James-tide*, and no longer. To which I answered, That I made no doubt of the power that every King had over his own Subjects; notwithstanding, where it was articled betwixt two Kings, that there should be a free admittance of each others Commodities unto their several Kingdomes, and after, a Command should be given, prohibiting, either of them unto their Subjects, the making use thereof, it could not but be understood a defrauding and deluding of the Articles, and the true intention of them: but I told him, I came not to dispute this now, for the Secretaries Letter had desired me to take notice of another resolution; therefore I desired, that there might be a speedy and publick Declaration made of what was therein signified unto me: or if there were any new resolution, that I might understand it. To which he answered (pretending that he spake it as a freedom which he used with me, but came out with it in such a manner, as I saw he was full of it) That the truth was, that they would proceed here, as they were proceeded withal in *England*: That the King my Master had lately given leave to the *Hollanders* to transport Artillery out of *England*, and had denied the like to their Embassadors, having required it; which was (as he said) directly against the Articles of Peace, wherein it was Capitulated, That neither should assist, with any kind of Arms, the enemy of the other. He said further, That the *English* had taken *Ormuz*, and there was no satisfaction given concerning that business, nor appearance of any intention to do it; and concluded, That when the Articles of Peace should be observed to them, they would do the like. I told the *Conde*, I had not understood any thing of those particulars which he mentioned, and therefore could say nothing unto him; neither thought I fit to give him any further answer, being loath, in a business of this importance, where the Articles of Peace between these Kingdoms are in question, to do any thing at guess, but to advertise it to the King my Master, and to proceed according to such order as he shall please to give me. I do therefore intreat your Honour, that you will be pleased to acquaint his Majesty with what hath passed, wherein I doubt not but his Majesty will observe the distraction, and inconstancy of their proceedings here at present, in Commanding what his Majesty will have found by this Secretaries Letter, and taking presently after new resolutions. After this language which the *Conde* hath used unto me, I cannot expect any reason or Justice here; and the Merchants have many suits depending, wherein

Sir Walter Aston *to the Lord* Conway.

in they have received great injuries, whereof I have not hitherto complained, because I was in continual hope of procuring redress; and their suits proceeded on, I cannot say as I would have wished, but according to the stile here, and in such manner as they have done in former times. I doubt not but his Majesty will therefore likewise please to consider what a stop there is likely to be here of all businesses concerning the Commerce, and either proceed as occasion shall there be offered, in the like manner, or take such a Course for setling things in better order, as to his wisdom shall seem best. I have since had some overtures made unto me, that the said declaration shall presently come out; in the mean time, I would not with that the Merchants should adventure any thing trusting to their courtesie here. By my last unto your Honour which was of the 20th of *May*, I advertised the advice which was given hither, That the Galeons that bring the Plate were upon the way for these parts; Since when there is news of their arrival at S. *Lucar*, excepting two of them, which perished in their journey hitherward; the one sprung a leak in a calm day, and sunk so fast, that there were only saved 52 men; the rest, which were about 200 persons, were all drowned, neither was any of her fraight saved. The other was their *Admirante*, which corresponds with our Vice-Admiral, which likewise sprung a leak, but all the men aboard were saved, and a good part of her silver. There is lost, upon Register, in these two Ships three millions; and it is thought that there perished in them above a million, in silver, and goods unregistred.

Upon order that was lately sent unto the *Assistente* of *Sevil*, for the perfecting the Grant of the Millions to the King by the said City, there being doubt made whether it was a lawful Concession, or no; The *Assistente* called together those that had voices in the said Grant of the said Millions, and made a speech unto them, wishing a general Conformity to what his Majesty had desired of them; but the proposition was very distastful unto the greater number, who little expected to have heard that business revived again. And the people having gotten notice, upon the breaking up of that meeting, of what had been there propounded, in a tumultuous manner ran after the *Assistente*, who was returning to his house; and hearing such a clamour behind him, thought that the people had been disquieted by some accident, and stayed to have appeased them; but by the curses which he heard, and the blows he received by the stones which were thrown at him, he quickly found against whom the fury of the people was bent, and so made all the haste he could to his own house; which at length he recovered sore wounded, and with much hazard of his life.

The *Irish* Priests, and others of that Kingdom which reside in this Court, begin to grow very busie here, and do promise great matters unto this King in the assistance which his Majesty shall find in *Ireland*, whensoever he shall please to attempt any thing against that Kingdom; but for any thing I can learn, there hath been as yet so little ear given unto them, that they have not descended to make any particular offer. But they are treated here with much Courtesie, *Tyr-Connel* being made a Page to the Queen, and the rest receiving good satisfaction. I will be as vigilant as I can to trace out their steps, and I hope I shall be able to give seasonable advertisement of their proceedings. Howsoever, since secret Councels may be held, and resolutions taken, which I may miss of; I doubt not but the King our Master, considering the present jealousies and distasts betwixt these Crowns, will be vigilant to secure that Kingdom, that there may be nothing neglected upon which they may here take any sudden advantage. By the English Merchants that reside at *Malaga* I have received advice, that 3 *Scotish* Masters of Ships have lately had a sentence pronounced against them by the D. of *Medina Sidona*, wherein their Ships and all their goods are confiscated, for having brought *Holland* Commodities to that Port, and their persons condemned to the Galleys; which, notwithstanding their appellation unto the Councel of War here, (which ought to have been admitted them) was presently put into execution. The same day that I received the advice, I gave in a Memorial to the Councel of State, representing the rigorous and unjust proceeding against the said *Scotish* Masters, and desired that they would send their order, that the Appellation might be admitted, and that their persons might be presently returned off of the Gallies. I likewise repaired to the *Conde* of *Olivarez*, acquainting him with the proceedings of the Duke, and was able to give him some examples of divers *Hollanders* that had been treated, in the like occasion, with far less rigour. Whereupon there is Command given, according to what I have desired; and whatsoever shall become of their goods, I have a promise from the *Conde* of *Olivarez*, that their persons shall be treated with all Courtesie. It is published by the Ladies of the Palace, that the Queen is with Child, which hath filled this Court with much joy, and her Majesty hath so much better health now upon her being new with Child, then she hath had of the rest, that they are already here full of hopes that she will bring them a Prince, &c.

June 5. 1624. *Your Honours*, &c. W. Aston.

Sir Walter Aston to the Duke.

The Abstract of a Letter from Sir Walter Aston *to the Lord* Conway.

HE acknowledgeth the receipt of his Majesties Letters of the 27 of *June* by Mr. *Wych*, and is busie in preparing to put those Directions in execution; and that being done, will give a speedy and full account. The Marquess *Iniosa* dispatched away a Post to *Spain* from *Calice*, and by him give as malicious an account of his usage at his departure from *England*; and also of all other late passages there, as malice it self could have dictated. He omits no libels or infamous songs, nor spares his own inventions where they may serve to incense. The Credit they are like to give to their Embassadour, the height of discontent they are now in, the assurance given them of the weak and mean estate of all things in *England*, may tempt them to offer the giving us a blow, where we are weakest. And therefore no necessary preparations for defence to be neglected on our part. None of their Armado stirres yet, but only four Gallions appointed to accompany for some dayes the *Nova Espagna* Fleet that put to Sea the fourth of this present.

Sir *Walter Aston* doubts, that the light he hath received of the present state of things in *England*, and the Arguments to answer their Objections, will hardly be applyed to give any satisfaction, (things being in so much distemper there.) And where the best answers on both sides are recriminations, he conceives little is to be expected but a direct falling out. The cause of their retarding *Mendoza*'s coming for *England* hath been their desire to see the issue of the proceedings with their Embassadour. All the Grandees, and principal persons of *Spain*, are summoned to give their attendance with their armes, which is done by three Letters. 1. *Admonitoria*. 2. *Mandatoria*. 3. *Executoria*. The two first are already set forth. And there is order likewise given for the *Battalon* to be in a readiness, which is the same as the Trained Bands in *England*. This is an ancient practice there, upon suspition of forreign invasion, or domestick Commotion. There are leavies new making according to custome, for supplying of Garrisons; and though these Leavies are greater then usually, yet not much worthy of note. An Embassadour arrived there from *Denmark*; his coming being given out to be to negotiate the businefs of the *Palatinate*, and to make overtures for a Peace with *Holland*: but if nothing be heard of this in *England*, it is not like to be true. A Request presented unto the King by a *Consulta* from the Inquisitor general, &c. to procure a *Jubile* from *Rome* for expiation of the late great Contempt done by a *Frenchman* to the Sacrament. The King promiseth to do it, and he, the Queen, and the whole houshold will endeavour to deserve it by fasting, and other duties. In his answer to the *Consulta* there is a passage, that intimates his intention of looking abroad with his armes. The *Frenchman* was condemned, burnt publiquely, and dyed a Roman Catholique. There have been divers processions in expression of the general grief for that action. The King, Queen, his Brothers and Sister, with the Grandees, and the Councel, went in procession about the two square Courts of the Palace, where there were four Altars built, one by the Kings care, the rest by the Queen, the Infanta, Cardinal, *Don Carlos*, and *Dona Maria*, who joyned in the care of one of them. The greatest riches of Diamonds and Pearls that were in the Churches thereabouts, and in the Kings store, were presented on those Altars, and were at ten millions. They intend to dispatch one *Jaques Brones*, Secretary of the Council of *Flanders*, by Post into *England*, to bring *Don Carlos* warrant to come away, and to stay Agent in *England* until the arrival of another Embassadour, which will not be long. They stay the giving out of the order for the free admittance of English Merchandizes, until they see what will be done with their Ships in the Downs, &c.

July 17. 1624.

Sir Walter Aston to the Duke.

May it please your Grace,

I Assure my self that your Grace is very confident, that I have not onely pursued the Complaint which I here made against the Marquess of *Tniosa* with the duty of a Minister in obedience to the King my Masters Command, but as passionately interested against his person, who maliciously attempted to stain (if it had been possible) the honour of the Prince, his Highness, and your Graces, my noblest friend. And certainly, my Lord, I should be infinitely afflicted in not having brought this businefs to that issue which I thirsted after, could I accuse my self of omitting any thing that might have sharpned them here against him:

Sir Walter Aston *to the Duke*.

But the *Conde* of *Olivarez* with a strong and violent hand hath delivered the Marquess from any exemplary punishment, which would certainly have been inflicted upon him, had he been left to the Councel of State; and without care either of the King his Masters honour or engagement, hath saved the Marquess, and left the envy of it upon his Majesty, if the King our Master will so please to understand it.

In my last unto your Grace, which was of the 24th of the last moneth, I humbly intreated you to procure me his Majesties leave to return into *England* for some few moneths; which suit I do here again renew unto your Grace. Howsoever in respect of this novelty in the Marquess his business, I will forbear putting my self upon the way until I hear of the receipt of this dispatch: since if his Majesty shall please to give any demonstrations here of his sence of their unworthy proceedings, I would be loath that those Commands should find me out of the way: with the remembrance of my duty, I rest

Your Graces, &c.

20. of *Octob.* 1624.   W. Aston.

Sir Walter Aston *to the Duke*.

May it please your Grace,

THE Arch-Duke *Don Carlos*, brother to the Emperour, made his entrie into this Town on the 15th of the last moneth, *Stil. Vet.* He was met by the Almirante of *Castile* two days journey from this place, who went from hence well accompanied, and attended by many Liveries richly set forth. Some 400 paces without a Gate of this Town, called *Alcala*, the Arch-Duke was received by the two Infants *Don Carlos* and the Cardinal, and about 200 paces without the said Gate by the King himself, who came attended with the greatest part of this Court, and in his Coach accompanied with the Duke of *Newbergh*, and the *Conde* of *Olivarez*: The King lighted out of his Coach to receive the Arch-Duke, and some complements being past between them, returned into his Coach, and set the Arch-Duke by him on his left hand; in the other end of the Coach sate the two Infants; in one boot the Duke of *Newbergh*, and the *Conde* of *Olivarez*; and in the other the Emperours Embassadour, and the Almirante; the Almirante taking place of the Embassadour. Being come to the Palace, the King accompanied the Arch-Duke to the Queens Quarter, where his Majesty left him to be conveyed from thence to his own Quarter (which is the same was given to the Prince his Highness at his being in this Court,) by the Infants his Brothers, as he was, having finished his complements with the Queen, and the Infanta *Dona Maria*. There were preparations here making for the honouring his reception with several feasts, and entertainments after their manner here; but these have been stopped by the Arch-Dukes sickness, who felt himself indisposed the day after his arrival, and applying some Physical remedies by the advice of a Physitian which he brought along with him, his distemper increased, and (as it is pretended by these Physitians) by a wrong course held with him. What hath been the true cause of his infirmity, I leave to be disputed by them; He hath been held divers days with a terrible Calenture, which proved at last a *Tabardillo*, whereupon there was little hope conceived of his life; but he hath since received some ease, and is now in a good way of amendment. In respect of the Emperours unworthy proceedings with the King our Master, I have not dared to visit him, until I shall have notice of his Majesties pleasure therein, which I shall be glad to understand from your Grace.

Since the expiring of the Truce betwixt this Crown and the *Hollanders*, this King hath given License to divers Port Towns on the Coasts of *Biscay* to arm out what ships they shall think good, and to make prize to their own particular benefit of what they shall light upon belonging to the enemies of this Crown: by which means it is here hoped, That these Coasts will be much the better secured from the daily pillages of the Holland men of War, and the Turkish Pyrates. For the advancing whereof, upon request made of those of *Sevil*, there is License given unto them to arm what men of War they can find means. The Duke of *Maqueda* likewise with leave hath lately set forth six ships which are abroad in Pyracy.

There is advice given hither, that the Duke of *Brandenbergh* hath given his consent to the conferring of the Electoral dignity upon the Duke of *Bavaria*, which I can hardly believe, though I find it assured from very good hands.

The Duke of *Newbergh* remains still in this Court, and presses to carry a cleer resolution

Sir Walter Aston *to the Duke.*

in his businesses from hence; but for any thing I can yet learn, his negotiation remains in the same estate as I advertised in my last to Mr. Secretary *Conway.*

The Armado prepared in *Portugal* for the recovering of *Brasil* is gone to Sea; and whereas, they were to have stayed at the *Cape* St. *Vincent* for the Armado of *Castile*, upon advice that is given hither, that the Hollanders in *Brasil* are not able to make any resistance of consideration, they have order to proceed in their journey. Twenty ships of war, and 4000 land Souldiers (which is the force of that Fleet) being here held sufficient for that enterprize. The Armado in *Cadiz* is not yet departed, but hath her men aboard, and there is daily expectation of news that it is gone to Sea. The Duke of *Saxonie* having received letters from the King our Master, and the King of *Denmark*, sent presently copies of them unto the Emperour, with his answers unto their Majesties, and accompanied them with a letter of his own unto the Emperour. All which the Emperour sent unto the King. The carriage of the Duke is much esteemed here, for having given (as I am informed) by his Letters unto the King our Master, and the King of *Denmark* such an answer as they are here much satisfied withal. Notwithstanding in this Letter to the Emperour, with many reasons, and much instance, he adviseth him to apply himself to the setting of the peace in *Germany*; and expressing much affection to the composing of the affairs of the Prince Palatine, doth earnestly intreat his Majesty not to destroy that ancient house. In the mean time the Duke of *Bavaria* uses all diligence to combine himself with this Crown, and now doth offer to cast off all other thoughts of leagues, and to depend wholly upon *Spain*, so that this King will protect him in his Electoral dignity, and what he hath lately possessed himself of in those parts. This offer of the Dukes hath been several days debated in Councel, where the Marquess *Yniosa* hath been busie in the behalf of the Duke: but the wiser part of this Councel seeing how prejudicial the increase of the Dukes greatness may prove to the Empire, do no way favour his pretensions. They likewise hold fit to continue the state of things in possibility of an accommodation without our Master.

The Arch-Duke *Don Carlos* hath brought power from the Emperour to proceed to the consummation of a marriage between the Emperours son and the Infanta *Donna Maria*, wherein, he says, he hath nothing to Capitulate, but brings them a blank paper, and hath power and order to confirm what conditions they shall here set down. The Emperours Embassadour doth much press to proceed to the Capitulations, but there is yet nothing done. The Infanta of *Brussels* hath lately written hither, importing this King to admit of a Treaty of marriage betwixt the Prince of *Polonia*, and the Infanta his Sister, extolling with many expressions the worth and parts of that Prince.

There hath been some moneths a general stop of their proceedings here in all suits of English Merchants depending in this Court; but I have at last procured a *Junto* to be assigned for the hearing of all English Causes, wherein I am promised there shall be a speedy Resolution taken of whatsoever is at present in Question.

The Duke of *Feria* hath lately advertised hither from *Millain*, that the French King, and the Duke of *Savoy* do minister much occasion of jealousie, that they intend to attempt some novelty in those parts, and doth therefore desire, that his Troops may be augmented; whereupon (above the ordinary charge) there was instantly remitted unto him 2000 Ducates.

The great annual *Assiento* which this King makes with the *Genoeses* is newly concluded; it is for 7 millions, whereof 4 are remitted for *Flanders*, to be paid by monethly portions.

In a late meeting of the Councel of State, upon a discourse that passed amongst them, taking into consideration this Kings wants, and the present distemper of his affairs, the Inquisidor General expressing how necessary a time it was for his Majesties Subjects to assist his present occasions, made offer of 100 Ducates for his part, which the *Conde* of *Olivarez* followed with a tender of 300; the *Conde* of *Monterrey* of 100; all the rest of the Councel of State following their example, gave according to their quality. Notice being taken of this abroad, the Condestable wrote a Letter unto this King, wherein he made tender of 200 Ducates, the Marquess of *Castel Rodrigo* of 100; the Marquess of *Carpio* of the like sum. Divers others have likewise declared themselves in this donative; and it is hoped that it will go over the whole Kingdom, and bring in an extraordinary Treasure into the Kings purse. Thus, with the remembrance of my duty, I rest

December, 10.   *Your Graces*, &c.
1624.   W. A.

Sir Walter Aston, to the Duke.

May it please your Grace,

I Have received so much comfort by the care which I see in your Grace to take all occasions to honour, and favour me, that I should be glad (if it were possible in my affection to your person, and in my desire to serve you, that your Grace might see something in me above what you could find in any other servant. What an honest thankfulness can be, I am, and what an honest servant can yield you, shall be ever vigilant in me to serve you. Since the departure of the last Post (by whom I wrote lately unto your Grace) my Lord of *Bristol* hath had audience with this King (taking me along with him) to whom his Lordship represented the King our Masters desire concerning the Palatinate in conformity to what his Majesty hath commanded by his late letters; we are now solliciting to hasten this Kings answer, which we hope we shall shortly send unto his Majesty; and there is no diligence omitted by my Lord of *Bristol*, nor my self (that we can think on) to negotiate such an answer as may be to his Majesties good liking. The dispatches from *Rome* are not yet come; but by Letters which they have lately received from the Duke of *Pastrana*, it is advertised, that all things are concluded, and that he would send them away within a few daies. By my Lord of *Bristols* Letter to his Majesty, your Grace will understand the resolution which his Lordship hath taken concerning his proceedings upon the arrival of the dispatches from *Rome*; his Lordship hath communicated with me his Majesties Letter, and desired my opinion concerning the resolution which he had taken, wherein I have concurred with his Lordship, not understanding it any way to be differing in substance from his Majesties directions; the altering of the day mentioned in his Majesties letters being only the changing it from a time when the powers are of no force, to a time when they may be of use: the putting of any thing in execution in the one time, or in the other, depending upon his Majesties, and his Highnesses further directions. I have hitherto understood, that his Majesty and his Highness have really affected this match, and have laboured faithfully to second their desires with my utmost endeavyurs. There is none, I am sure, a better witness then my self of the affection which your Grace hath born unto it, which I have seen remain constant through many tryals, And therefore until I understand the contrary from your self, I must believe that your desires are the same which I have seen them. I must ever speak my heart freely unto your Grace, and confess that upon the letter which I received from his Highness, and upon the sight of his Majesties to my Lord of *Bristol*, I have been jealous of his Majesties heart and his Highness, that they are not that to the match which they have been; but these are but distrusts of my own, and not foundation sufficient to slacken or cool those diligences which I daily perform, in conformity to his Majesties, and his Highness Commands, and to what remains apparent of their desires. I shall therefore humbly desire your Lordship to open mine eyes, and, if I am out of the way, to set me straight; for I have no affections of mine own, but what agrees with my Masters, and will ever submit, with all humility, my self, and my judgment unto his Majesties wisdom, and faithfully labour to serve him accordingly to what I shall understand to be his will and pleasure. But until I know by your Graces favour by what Compass to guide my Course, I can only follow his Majesties revealed will; and will once take the boldness to represent unto your Grace, in discharge of what I owe you, these Considerations, which my desire to serve you forceth from me. I do look upon your Grace as a person infinitely provoked to be an enemy to this match, and believe, that you have had represented unto you many reasons, shewing how much it concerns you to seek to break it, with all the force you have: But I can neither believe, that the errour of one man can make you an enemy to that which brings along with it so much happiness and content unto his Majesty, and his Highness: nor that your Graces judgment can be led by those arguments, that under the colour of safety, would bring you into a dangerous labyrinth. Your Grace hath given noble testimony, how little you have valued your own safety in respect of his Majesties service; and therefore I assure my self you would contemn all Considerations concerning your self, that might hinder the advancement of his Majesties ends. In the proceeding to this match, there is the same conveniency to his Majesty that ever hath been, there is the same Lady, the same portion, the same friendship desired, they professing here an exact complying with what is capitulated, and a resolution to give his Majesty satisfaction in whatsoever is in their power. From your Grace none can take away the honour of having been the Principal means by which this great business hath been brought to a conclusion. And whatsoever others may suggest against your Grace, the *Infanta* truly informed cannot but understand you the person to whom she owes most in this business.

Sir Walter Aston, to the Duke.

busines. Your Grace, and the Cond. Olivarez have fallen upon different waies, that which concerns the honour of the King our Master, being different to that which he understood concerned most his Master; your ends were both one for concerning of the match, and with the Conclusion of it, he cannot but better understand you. Would your Grace would commit it to my charge to inform the *Infanta* what you have merited, and accommodate all other mistakes here concerning the proceeding. If your Grace would reconcile your heart, I would not doubt, but, with the Conclusion of the Match, to compose all things to your good satisfaction, and to bring them to a truer understanding of you, and of their obligation unto you. In what a Sea of Confusions the breaking of this alliance would engage his Majesty, I will leave to your Lordships wisdom to consider of, it being too large a discourse for a Letter.

I will therefore onely desire your Lordship to consider, that even the most prosperous War hath misfortune enough in it to make the Authour of it unhappy: of which how innocent soever your Lordship is, the occasions that have been given you, will ever make you lyable to the aspersion of it. This I write not unto your Grace, as thinking to divert you from what you are falling into; for I am confident your heart runs a more peaceable way: but I am willing that you should see, that howsoever others should be inclined to carry you into this tempest, it concerns you, in your care of their happines, and your own, to divert them from it. I humbly desire your Grace to pardon this errour of mine (if it be one) which I can excuse with the affection, and infinite desire which I have to see you ever happy and flourish.

Concerning my self, your Grace knows my wants, and I doubt not but your Care is what I could wish. I should be glad when you have done with *Peter Wych*, to see him dispatched away with some supplies unto me, which I shall be in extream want of by Christmass, my debts besides in *England* being clamorous upon me for some satisfaction. I leave all to your Graces care and favour, Everresting.

Your Graces humblest, and most bounden servant,
Walter Aston.

Postscript.
The *Condessa* of *Olivarez* bids me tell you, that she kisses your Graces hands, and doth every day recommend you particularly by name in her prayers to God.

Sir Walter Aston, to the Duke.

May it please your Grace,

I Have committed to the trust and secrecie of this bearer Mr. *Clark* (whom I find your Graces faithful servant) certain advertisements to be delivered by him unto you; which as one that shall (God willing) in all things shew himself your passionate servant, I could no way conceal from you. And howsoever your Grace may have many advertisements from hence (the relations that come from *England* giving occasion to many discourses censuring the Prince, and your Grace) yet I hope to be so vigilant, that there shall hardly be any resolution taken by these Ministers which may have any reflexion on your Person, that I shall not one way or other get notice of, and advertize unto you.

I have in all things with so much affection desired to serve your Grace every way to your satisfaction, that it hath infinitely afflicted me, that I should have done any thing, whereby I might lessen your favourable opinions towards me; but I hope your Grace hath by this time set me straight both with his Majesty, and his Highness, and restored me to the same place in your affection which I have formerly had. Which I am the rather confident of since I cannot accuse any action, or thought of mine, that hath not born towards your Grace all possible respect and love. I found by experience here, that the favour which by your Graces means I received from his Highness, and that which you were pleased likewise to honour me withall, had raised me many enemies; And I have reason to fear, upon this occasion, there may be some that will be busie to do me ill offices with you; but I trust so much upon my own sincerity, that as I never made any second means unto your Grace, but to have ever singly depended upon the constancy of your goodness to me, finding my self the same that I have been, I make no means to resist such injuries as others may offer to do me, but continue depending wholly upon that goodness, and justness, which I know in your Grace, and which I assure my self will never fail me. I have not been so carelefs a Servant of your Graces, as not to have debated over and over with my self, how far the proceedings or breaking of the present treaty here might concern your Grace,

which

which I have discoursed largely to Mr. *Clark*, thinking them of too large a body to be contained in a Letter; but I shall, in all things, submit my self to your better wisdom: And when you shall please to impart unto me, wherein his Majesty and his Highness shall be best served, your Grace shall find, in all my actions, that my affections, with all obedience, shall run the same way; and that my proceedings shall have those respects in them towards your Grace, as you may expect from your faithfull servant. And so, &c.

Decemb. 22. 1623.

Your G. &c.
W. A.

A Memorial to the King of Spain, by Sir Walter Aston, Ambassadour in SPAIN.

SIr *Walter Aston*, Embassadour to the King of *Great Britain*, saith, That the King, his Master, hath commanded him to represent to your Majesty, That having declared to your Majesty the Reasons why he could receive no satisfaction by your Majesties Answer of the first of *January*; and that thereby, according to the unanimous consent of his Parliament he came to dissolve both the Treaties of the Match and *Palatinate*, he received another Answer from your Majesty, wherein he finds less ground to build upon: and having understood, that either by the *Padre de Maestro*, or your Majesties Ambassadours which have assisted these days past in this Court, there was something to be propounded and declared touching the business of the *Palatinate*, whereby he might have received satisfaction; the said Embassadours, until now, have not said any thing at all to purpose: Which comparing with other circumstances of their ill carriage, he gathers and doubts, that according to the ill-affection, and depraved intentions, wherewith they have proceeded in all things, but especially, in particular, they have laboured to hinder the good correspondency, and so necessary and desired intelligence which should be conserved with your Majesty. Furthermore, he saith, That the King his Master hath commanded him to give account to your Majesty, that in an Audience which he gave to the Marquess *de Tnoyosa* and *Don Carlo Colomma*, they under cloak and pretext of zeal and particular care of his person, pretended to discover unto him a very great conjuration against his Person and Royal Dignity; and it was,

That at the beginning of the Parliament, the Duke of *Buckingham* had consulted with certain Lords, of the arguments and means which were to be taken touching the breaking and dissolving of the Treaties of the *Palatinate* and Match; and the consultations passed thus far, That if his Majesty would not accommodate himself to their counsels, they would give him a house of pleasure, whither he might retire himself to his sports, in regard that the Prince had now years sufficient to, and parts answerable for, the Government of the Kingdom.

The Information was of that quality, that it was sufficient to put impression in him of perpetual jealousies, in regard, that through the ribs of the Duke he gave wounds to the Prince his Son, and the Nobility; and it is not probable, that they could bring to effect such designs, without departing totally from the Obligation of Faith and Loyalty which they owed, to his Person and Crown, because the Lords made themselves culpable as concealers: And it is not likely that the Duke would hurl himself into such an enterprize, without communicating it first with the Prince, and knowing his pleasure.

And because this information might be made more clear, he did make many instances unto the said Embassadors, that they would give him the Authors of the said Conjuration, this being the sole means whereby their own honour might be preserved, &c. whereby their great zeal and care they had pretended to have of his person might appear. But instead of confirming the great zeal they had pretended to bear him, all the answer they made him consisted of Arguments against the discovery of the Conspirators: So that, for the confirmation of the said report, there remained no other means then the examination of some of his Council of State, and principal Subjects; which he put in execution, and made them take Oath every one particularly in his own presence, and commanded, that such interrogatories and questions should be propounded unto them that were most pertinent to the accusation; so that neither part, particle, or circumstance, remained, which was not exactly examined and winnowed; and he found in the Duke, and the rest that were accused, a sincere innocency touching the accusations and importation wherewith they were charged.

This being so, he turned to make new instances unto the said Embassadours, that they should not prefer the discovery of the names of the Conspirators to the security of his Royal person, and truth and honour of themselves, and the hazard of an opinion, to be held and judged the Traytors of a plot of such malice, sedition, and danger: But the Embassadours remaining in a knotty kind of obstinacy resolved to conceal the Authors. Nevertheless, afterwads he gave them an Audience, wherein the Marquess of *Ynojosa* took his leave.

Few days after, they demanded new Audience, pretending, that they had something to say that concerned the publick good, and conduced to the entire restitution of the *Palatinate*, with desire to lose no opportunity that might conduce thereunto, and therewith the confirmation and conservation of the friendship with your Majesty, His Majesty having suspended some few days to give them Audience, thinking, that being thereby better advised they would resolve upon a wiser course, and declare the Authors of so pernicious an action: And having since made many instances, and attended the success of so long patience, he sent his Secretary, and Sir *Francis Cottington*, Secretary to the Prince, commanding them, that they should signifie unto the Embassadours, that he desired nothing more then the continuance of the friendship 'twixt both the Crowns; and if so be they had any thing to say, they would communicate it to the said Secretaries, as persons of so great trust, which he sent to that end: And if they made difficulty of this, that they would choose, amongst his Councel of State, those which they liked best, and he would command that they should presently repair unto them: And if this did not likewise seem best unto them, that they would send what they had to say, in a Letter sealed up, by whom should seem best unto them, and he would receive it with his own hands. But the Embassadours mis-behaving themselves in all that was propounded, the said Secretaries, according to the Order which they brought, told them, That they, being the Authors of anInformation so dangerous and seditious, had made themselves uncapable to treat further with the King their Master; and were it not for the respect to the King, his dear and beloved Brother, and their Master, and in contemplation of their condition as Embassadours of such a Majesty, he would, and could, by the Law of Nations, and the right of his own Royal Justice, proceed against them with such severity as their offence deserved; but, for the reasons aforesaid, he would leave the reparation hereof to the justice of their King, of whom he would demand and require it.

In conformity whereof, the said Embassadour of the King of *Great Britain* saith, That the King his Master hath commanded him to demand reparation and satisfaction of your Majesty against the said Marquess *de Ynojosa*, and *Don Carlos Colomma*, making your Majesty Judge of the great scandal and enormous offence which they have committed against them and the publick right, and expect Justice from your Majesty, in the demonstrations and chastisements which your Majesty shall inflict upon them; which, for his proceeding sake with your Majesty, and out of your Majesties own uprightness and goodness, ought to be expected.

Furthermore, he saith, That the King his Master hath commanded him to assure your Majesty, that till now he hath not mingled the correspondence and friendship he held with your Majesty,with the faults and offences of your Ministers, but leaves and restrains them to their own persons; and that he remains with your Majesty in the true and ancient friendship and brotherhood as heretofore; and that he is ready to give hearing to any thing that shall be Reason,and to answer thereunto: and when your Majesty is pleased to send your Embassadors thither, he will make them all good treaty, and receive them with that good love that is due.

For conclusion, the said Embassadour humbly beseecheth your Majesty will be pleased to observe and weigh the care and tenderness wherewith the King, his Master, proceeded with your Majesties Embassadours, not obliging to precipitate resolutions, but giving them much time to prove and give light of that which they had spoken; and besides, opening unto them many ways that they might comply with their orders, if they had any such. Which course if they had taken, they might well have given satisfaction to the King his Master, and moderated the so grounded opinion of their ill proceedings against the peace, and so good intelligence and correspondence betwixt both the Crowns.

Madrid, Aug. 5. 1624.

Sir

Sir Walter Aston *to the Duke.*

May it please your Grace,

THE Portugal Armado put to Sea on the 12th of the last moneth, *Stil. Vet,* It consists of 22 Ships of War, 4 Victuallers, and two small Pinnaces of Advice: There goeth in it neer upon 4000 Land Souldiers. From Cadiz I have now fresh advice, That *Don Frederique* is still in the Port, with the Fleet which he Commands, but himselfand his men all embarqued. That Armado consisteth of some 35 Ships of War, and about 8000 Souldiers, and both the Fleets are victualled for 8 moneths. That of Portugal had first order to expect *Don Frederique* at the *Cape* St. *Vincent,* but hath since received command to proceed on the journey. It being now 27 days since the Fleet departed, and this remaining still in Harbour, doth give me much cause of jealousie: especially understanding, that they have here advice, (which they give credit to) that the Troops lately delivered to Count *Mansfelt* are sent to succour *Breda,* fearing (if it be so) that they laying hold of it as a breach of the Peace (which interpretation I meet with in every discourse) should presently fall with this Armado upon some part of *Ireland.* I have no farther ground for this distrust, then what I have here represented, which your Grace weighing with the importancy of their enterprise in hand for the recovering the *Baya,* and the occasions that will be given them from *England,* do best know what rigid judgement to make. Sithence I wrote my other Letter unto your Grace, (which accompanies this) I understand the *French* Embassadour, by order from the King his Master, hath given account unto this King of the Conclusion of the Match betwixt the Prince his Highness, and Madam *Christiene* his Masters Sister. Whereupon this King, and the whole Court, put on *Galas:* I conceive (howsoever I have not heard any thing thereof by any Letter unto me) that this is ground enough to Congratulate with your Grace this good beginning which I shall affectionately wish may in the success, in all times prove a happiness to his Highness, and a particular blessing to your Grace. The *Conde* of *Gondemar* hath newly received a Command from the King his Master (signified unto him by the Secretary *Don Andreas de Prada*) to put himself presently upon the way for *England,* which, he hath answered, he will obey; howsoever I believe he will keep his *Christmass* here. Mr. *Butler,* whom your Grace left here placed with this King, meets often with such discourses in the Palace, that, as a faithful servant to your Grace, he hath no patience to bear; which he hath reason to believe, will in a short time throw him out of this Court, which he would be glad to prevent, if he might have your Graces command to return, being infinitely desirous that your Grace would dispose otherwise of him. I will conclude with the same suit for my self, there being none that hath more need of comfort from your Grace. I best know, that I have no way deserved any change or decay in your Graces favour towards me, having not been slow in upbraiding this Nation with their obligations to your Grace, and their shameful ungratefulness, nor without a constant and passionate desire to serve your Grace every way to your content, if your Graces Commands would but direct me what to do; I do therefore rest confident of your care and goodness, towards me. And so, with my prayers to God to continue his blessings upon you, I rest

The 10th of *Decemb.*
1625.

Your Graces, &c.

W. Aston.

Mr.

Mr. Edmond Andersons *Letter to Sir* Francis Bacon.

Noble Sir,

THere is ever a certain presumption to be had of the favour of great men, so as there be a reason added to accompany their justice; mine, that gives boldness to call upon your succour, is, that I am fallen more under the malignity of rumor, then severity of laws, though that hath ever set mine offence at the blackest mark: to force this latter cloud away, none can but the breath of a King; th'other which threatneth and oppresseth more, every good Spirit may help to disperse. In this name, honourable Sir, I beseech your goodness to spend some few words to the putting of false fame to flight, which hath so often endangered even the innocent: And if the saving of a poor penitent man may come to be part of your care, let it ever be reckoned to your vertue, that you have not only assisted to preserve, but create a person so corrected by necessity, as the example of his repentance was not worthy to be lost; who will live and die thankfully yours,

Edmond Anderson.

SIR

Sir Francis Bacon's
LETTERS,
&c.

Sir FRANCIS BACON'S Letters, &c.

Sir Francis Bacon to the Lord Treasurer, concerning the Sollicitors Place.

Fter the remembrance of my humble duty, though I know by late experience how mindfull your Lordship vouchsafeth to be of me and my poor fortune; and since it pleased your Lordship, during your indisposition, when her Majesty came to visit your Lordship, to make mention of me for my imployment and preferment: yet being now in the Countrey, I do presume that your Lordship, who of your self had an honourable care of the matter, will not think it a trouble to be sollicited therein. My hope is this, that whereas your Lordship told me, her Majesty was somewhat gravelled upon the offence she took at my Speech in Parliament, your Lordships favourable endeavour, who hath assured me that for your own part you construe that I spake to the best, will be as a good tide to remove her from that shelve; and it is not unknown unto your good Lordship, that I was the first of the ordinary sort of the Lower House that spake for the Subsidy; and that which I after spake in difference, was but in circumstance of time; which methinks was no great matter, since there is variety allowed in Councel, as a Discord in Musick, to make it more perfect.

But I may justly doubt her Majesties impression upon this particular, as her conceipt otherwise of my insufficiency and unworthiness; which though I acknowledge to be great, yet it will be the less, because I purpose not to divide my self between her Majesty, and the causes of other men, as others have done, but to attend her business onely; hoping that a whole man, meanly able, may do as well as half a man better able: And if her Majesty thinketh that she shall make an adventure in using one that is rather a man of study then of practice and experience, surely I may remember to have heard, that my Father (an example, I confess, rather ready then like) was made Sollicitor of the Augmentation (a Court of much business) when he had never practised, and was but 27 years old: And Mr. *Brograve* was now, in my time, called Attorney of the Dutchy, when he had practised little or nothing, and yet hath discharged his place with great sufficiency. But those, and the like things, are as her Majesty shall be made capable of them: wherein knowing what authority your Lordships commendations have with her Majesty, I conclude with my self, that the substance of strength which I may receive, will be from your Lordship. It is true, my life hath been so private, as I have had no means to do your Lordship service; but yet, as your Lordship knoweth, I have made offer of such as I could yield. For, as God hath given me a mind to love the publick, so incidently I have ever had your Lordship in singular admiration, whose happy ability her Majesty hath so long used to her great honour and yours. Besides, that amendment of state, or countenance, which I have received, hath been from your Lordship: And therefore, if your Lordship shall stand a good friend to your poor Allie, you shall but *tueri opus* which you have begun; and your Lordship shall bestow your benefit upon one that hath more sense of obligation, then of self-love.

Thus humbly desiring pardon of so long a Letter, I wish your Lordship all happiness.

Your Lordships in all humbleness to be commanded,

June 6. 1595.   FR. BACON.

Sir Francis Bacon *to the Lord Treasurer* Burghley.

My Lord,

With as much confidence as mine own honest and faithfull devotion unto your service, and your honourable correspondence unto me and my poor estate, can breed in a man, do I commend my self unto your Lordship. I wax now somewhat ancient; one and thirty years is a great deal of sand in the hour-glass: My health, I thank God, I find confirmed, and I do not fear that action shall impair it, because I account my ordinary course of study and meditation to be more painfull then most parts of action are. I ever bare a mind (in some middle place, that I could discharge) to serve her Majesty; not as a man born under *Sol*, that loveth Honour; nor under *Jupiter*, that loveth business, (for the contemplative Planet carrieth me away wholly;) but as a man born under an excellent Sovereign, that deserveth the dedication of all mens abilities. Besides, I do not find in my self so much self-love, but that the greater parts of my thoughts are to deserve well (if I were able) of my friends, and, namely, of your Lordship, who being the *Atlas* of this Common-wealth, the Honour of my house, and the second founder of my poor estate, I am tied by all duties, both of a good Patriot, and of an unworthy Kinsman, and of an obliged servant, to imploy whatsoever I am, to do you service. Again, the meanness of my estate doth somewhat move me: for, though I cannot accuse my self, that I am either prodigal, or slothfull; yet my health is not to spend, nor my course to get. Lastly, I confess, that I have as vast contemplative ends, as I have moderate civil ends; for I have taken all knowledge to be my providence; and if I could purge it of two sorts of Rovers, whereof the one with frivolous disputations, confutations, and verbosities; the other with blind experiments, and auricular traditions and impostures, hath committed so many spoils; I hope I should bring in industrious Observations, grounded Conclusions, and profitable Inventions and Discoveries, the best state of that providence. This, whether it be curiosity, or vain-glory, or nature, or (if one take it favourably) *Philanthropia*, is so fixed in my mind, as it cannot be removed: And I do easily see, that place of any reasonable countenannce doth bring commandement of more wits then of a mans own, which is the thing I greatly affect. And for your Lordship, perhaps you shall not find more strength, and less encounter, in any other. And if your Lordship shall find now, or at any time, that I do seek or affect any place, whereunto any that is neerer unto your Lordship shall be concurrent, say then, that I am a most dishonest man. And if your Lordship will not carry me on, I willnot do as *Anaxagoras* did, who reduced himself, with contemplation, unto voluntary poverty: But this I will do, I will sell the inheritance that I have, and purchase some lease of quick revenue, or some Office of gain that shall be executed by Deputy, and so give over all care of service, and become some sorry Book-maker, or a true Pioneer in that Mine of Truth, which (he said) lay so deep. This which I have writ unto your Lordship, is rather thoughts then words, being set down without all Art, disguising, or reservation. Wherein I have done honour, both to your Lordships wisdom, in judging that that will be best believed of your Lordship, which is truest; and to your Lordships good nature, in retaining nothing from you. And even so I wish your Lordship all happiness, and to my self, means and occasion to be added to my faithfull desire to do you service.

From my Lodging, at Grays-Inn.

Sir Francis Bacon *to the Lord Treasurer* Burghley.

My singular good Lord,

Your Lordships comfortable Relation of her Majesties gracious opinion and meaning towards me, though, at that time, your leisure gave me not leave, to shew how I was affected therewith; yet upon every representation thereof, it entreth, and striketh more deeply into me, as both my Nature and Duty presseth me, to return some speech of thankfulness. It must be an exceeding comfort and encouragement to me, setting forth, and putting my self in way towards her Majesties service, to encounter with an example, so private and domestical, of her Majesties gracious goodness and benignity, being made good and verified in my father, so far forth, as it extendeth to his Posterity.

Accepting them as commended by his service, during the Nonage (as I may term it) of their own deserts, I, for my part, am very well content, that I take least part, either of his abilities of Mind, or of his worldly Advancement; both which he held, and received, the one of the gift of God immediately, the other of her Majesties Gift: Yet in the loyal and earnest Affection which

he

he bare to her Majesties service, I trust, my portion shall not be with the least, nor in proportion with the youngest Birth. For, me thinks, his president should be a silent charge, upon his blessing, unto us all, in our degrees, to follow him afar off, and to dedicate unto her Majesties service, both the use and spending of our lives. True it is, that I must needs acknowledge my self prepared and furnished thereunto with nothing, but with a multitude of lacks and imperfections; but calling to mind, how diversly, and in what particular providence, God hath declared himself to tender the state of her Majesties Affairs, I conceive and gather hope, that those whom he hath, in a manner, prest for her Majesties service, by working and imprinting in them a single and zealous mind to bestow their duties therein, he will see them accordingly appointed of sufficiency convenient for the Rank and standing where they shall be imployed; so as under this her Majesties blessing, I trust, to receive a larger allowance of Gods Graces. And as I may hope for this, so I can assure and promise for my Endeavour, that it shall not be in fault; but what diligence can intitle me unto, that, I doubt not, to recover. And now, seeing it hath pleased her Majesty to take knowledge of this my mind, and to vouchsafe to appropriate me unto her service, preventing any desert of mine with her Princely liberality; first, I humbly do beseech your Lordship, to present to her Majesty my more then humble thanks for the same: And withal, having regard to mine own unworthiness to receive such favour, and to the small possibility in me to satisfie and answer what her Majesty conceiveth; I am moved to become a most humble suitor to her Majesty, that this benefit also may be affixed unto the other, which is, That if there appear in me no such towardness of service as, it may be, her Majesty doth benignly value and assess me at, by reason of my sundry wants, and the disadvantage of my nature, being unapt to lay forth the simple store of those inferiour gifts which God hath allotted unto me, most to view; yet that it would please her Excellent Majesty, not to accompt my thankfulness the less, for that my disability is great to shew it; but to sustain me in her Majesties gracious opinion, whereupon I onely rest, and not upon any expectation of desert, to proceed from my self, towards the contentment thereof. But if it shall please God to send forth an occasion whereby my faithful affection may be tried, I trust, it shall save me labour for ever making more protestation of it hereafter. In the mean time, howsoever it be not made known to her Majesty, yet God knoweth it, through the daily sollicitations wherewith I address my self unto him in unfeigned Prayer for the multiplying of her Majesties prosperities: to your Lordship also, whose recommendation, I know right well, hath been material to advance her Majesties good opinion of me, I can be but a bounden servant. So much may I safely promise, and purpose to be, seeing publick and private bonds vary not, but that my service to her Majesty and your Lordship draw in a line, I wish therefore to shew it with as good proof, as I can say it in good faith. &c.

Your Lordships, &c.

Two Letters framed, one as from Mr. Anthony Bacon *to the Earl of* Essex, *the other, as the Earls answer.*

My singular good Lord,

THis standing at a stay doth make me, in my love towards your Lordship, jealous lest you do somewhat, or omit somewhat, that amounteth to a new errour: For I suppose, that of all former matters there is a full expiation; wherein, for any thing which your Lordship doth, I, for my part, (who am remote) cannot cast or devise wherein my errour should be, except in one point, which I dare not censure, nor dissuade; which is, that as the Prophet saith, in this affliction you look up *ad manum percutientem,* and so make your peace with God. And yet I have heard it noted, that my Lord of *Leicester,* who could never get to be taken for a Saint, yet in the Queens disfavour waxed seeming religious. Which may be thought by some, and used by others, as a case resembling yours, if men do not see, or will not see the difference between your two dispositions. But, to be plain with your Lordship, my fear rather is, because I hear how some of your good and wise friends, not unpractised in the Court, and supposing themselves not to be unseen in that deep and unscrutable Centre of the Court, which is her Majesties mind, do not onely toll the bell, but even ring out peals, as if your fortune were dead and buried, and as if there were no possibility of recovering her Majesties favour; and as if the best of your condition were, to live a private and retired life, out of want, out of peril, and out of manifest disgrace. And so, in this perswasion to your Lordship-wards, to frame and accommodate your actions and mind to that end; I fear (I say) that this untimely despair may in time bring forth a just despair, by causing your Lordship to slacken and break off your wise, wife, loyal, and seasonable endeavour and industry for reintegration to her Majesties favour, in comparison whereof, all other circumstances are but as *Atomi*, or rather is a *Vacuum*, without any substance at all.

Against this opinion, it may please your Lordship to consider of these reasons, which I have collected; and to make judgment of them, neither out of the melancholy of your present fortune, nor out of the infusion of that which cometh to you by others relation, which is subject to much tincture, but *ex rebus ipsis*, out of the nature of the persons and actions themselves, as the truest, and less deceiving, ground of opinion. For, though I am so unfortunate as to be a stranger to her Majesties eye, much more to her nature and manners, yet by that which is extant I do manifestly discern, that she hath that character of the Divine nature and goodness, as *quos amavit, amavit usque ad finem*; and where she hath a creature, she doth not deface nor defeat it: insomuch as, if I observe rightly, in those persons whom heretofore she hath honoured with her special favour, she hath covered and remitted, not onely defections and ingratitudes in affection, but errors in State and service.

2. If I can, Scholar-like, spell and put together the parts of her Majesties proceedings now towards your Lordship, I cannot but make this construction; That her Majesty, in her Royal intention, never purposed to call your doings into publick question, but onely to have used a cloud without a shower, and censuring them by some restraint of liberty, and debarring from her presence. For both the handling the cause in the Star-Chamber was inforced by the violence of libelling and rumours, wherein the Queen thought to have satisfied the world, and yet spared your appearance: And then after, when that means, which was intended for the quenching of malicious bruits, turned to kindle them, because it was said your Lordship was condemned unheard, and your Lordships Sister wrote that private Letter, then her Majesty saw plainly, that these winds of rumours could not be commanded down, without a handling of the Cause, by making you party, and admitting your defence. And to this purpose, I do assure your Lordship, that my Brother *Francis Bacon*, who is too wise to be abused, though he be both reserved in all particulars more then is needfull, yet in generality he hath ever constantly, and with asseveration, affirmed to me, That both those dayes, that of the Star-Chamber, and that at my Lord Keepers, were won of the Queen, meerly upon necessity and point of Honour, against her own inclination.

3. In the last proceeding, I note three points, which are directly significant, that her Majesty did expresly forbear any point which was irrecuperable, or might make your Lordship in any degree uncapable of the return of her favour, or might fix any character indeleble of disgrace upon you: For she spared the publick places, which spared ignominy; she limited the Charge precisely, not to touch disloyalty, and no Record remaineth to memory of the Charge or Sentence.

4. The very distinction which was made in the sentence of Sequestration, from the places of service in State, and leaving to your Lordship the place of Master of the Horse, doth, in my understanding, point at this, that her Majesty meant to use your Lordships attendance in Court, while she exercises of other places stood suspended.

5. I have heard, and your Lordship knoweth better, that now since you were in your own custody, her Majesty, *in verbo Regio*, and by his mouth to whom she committeth her Royal Grants and Decrees, hath assured your Lordship, she will forbid, and not suffer your ruine.

6. As I have heard her Majesty to be a Prince of that magnanimity, that she will spare the service of the ablest Subject or Peer, where she shall be thought not to stand in need of it; so she is of that policy, as she will not blaze the service of a meaner then your Lordship, where it shall depend meerly upon her choice and will.

7. I held it for a principle, That those diseases are hardest to cure, whereof the cause is obscure; and those easiest, whereof the cause is manifest. Whereupon I conclude, that since it hath been your errours in your lowness towards her Majesty which have prejudiced you, that your reforming and conformity will restore you, so as you may be *Faber fortunæ propriæ*.

Lastly, Considering your Lordship is removed from dealing in Causes of State, and left onely to a place of Attendance, methinks the Ambition of any which can endure no Partners in State-matters may be so quenched, as they should not laboriously oppose themselves to your being in Court. So as upon the whole matter, I cannot find, neither in her Majesties Person, nor in your own person, nor in any third person, neither in former presidents, nor in your own case, any cause of peremptory despair. Neither do I speak this, but that if her Majesty out of her resolution should design you to a private life, you should be as willing, upon the appointment, to go into the Wilderness, as into the Land of Promise;

onely

The Earl of Essex to Mr. Anthony Bacon.

only I wish that your Lordship will not despair, but put trust (next to God) in her Majesties grace, and not be wanting to your self. I know your Lordship may justly interpret, that this which I perswade may have some reference to my particular, because I may truly say, *te stante non virebo*, for I am withered in my self; but *manebo*, or *renebo*, I should in some sort be, or hold out. But though your Lordships years and health may expect return of grace and fortune, yet your Eclipse for a time is an *ultimum vale* to my fortune: And were it not that I desired and hope to see my Brother established by her Majesties favour, as I think him well worthy for that he hath done and suffered, it were time I did take that course from which I disswade your Lordship. Now in the mean time, I cannot choose but perform those honest duties unto you, to whom I have been so deeply bound, &c.

The Earl of Essex his Answer to Mr. Anthony Bacons Letter.

Mr. Bacon,

I Thank you for your kind and careful letter; it perswadeth that which I wish for strongly, and hope for weakly, that is, possibility of restitution to her Majesties favour: Your arguments that would cherish hope, turn into despair: You say the Queen never meant to call me to publick censure, which sheweth her goodness; but you see I passed it, which sheweth others power. I believe most stedfastly, her Majesty never intended to bring my cause to a publick censure; and I believe as verily, that since the sentence she meant to restore me to tend upon her person: but those which could use occasions (which it was not in me to let) and amplifie and practise occasions to represent to her Majesty a necessity to bring me to the one, can and will do the like to stop me from the other. You say, my errors were my prejudice, and therefore I can mend my self. It is true; but they that know that I can mend my self, and that if I ever recover the Queen, that I will never lose her again, will never suffer me to obtain Interest in her favour: and you say, the Queen never forsook utterly where she hath inwardly favoured; but know not whether the hour-glass of time hath altered her, but sure I am, the false glass of others informations must alter her, when I want access to plead mine own cause. I know I ought doubly, infinitely to be her Majesties, both *jure creationis*, for I am her creature; and *jure redemptionis*, for I know she hath saved me from overthrow. But for her first love, and for her last protection, and all her great benefits, I can but pray for her Majesty; and my endeavour is now to make my prayers for her and my self better heard. For thanks be to God, that they which can make her Majesty believe I counterfeit with her, cannot make God believe that I counterfeit with him; and they that can let me from coming near to her, cannot let me from drawing nearer to him, as I hope I do daily. For your brother, I hold him an honest Gentleman, and wish him all good, much rather for your sake; your self, I know, hath suffered more for me, and with me, then any friend that I have: But I can but lament freely, as you see I do, and advise you not to do that I do, which is, to despair. You know Letters what hurt they have done me, and therefore make sure of this: and yet I could not, as having no other pledge of my love, but communicate openly with you for the ease of my heart and yours;

Your loving friend,
R. ESSEX.

Sir Francis Bacon to the Earl of Salisbury, concerning the Sollicitors place.

It may please your Lordship,

I Am not privy to my self of any such ill deserving towards your Lordship, as that I should think it an impudent thing to be a suitor for your favour in a reasonable matter, your Lordship being to me as (with your good favour) you cannot cease to be: but rather it were a simple and arrogant part in me to forbear it.

It is thought Mr. *Attorney* shall be chief Justice of the Common-Place; in case Mr. *Sollicitor* rise. I would be glad now at last to be Sollicitor: chiefly because I think it will increase my practice, wherein, God blessing me a few years, I may mend my state, and so after fall to my studies and ease; whereof one is requisite for my body, and the other serveth for my mind; wherein if I shall find your Lordships favour, I shall be more happy then I have been, which may make me also more wise. I have small store of means about the King, and to sue my self is not fit; and therefore I shall leave it to God, his Majesty, and your Lordship: for

I must still be next the door. I thank God, in these transitory things I am well resolved. So beseeching your Lordship not to think this Letter the less humble, because it is plain, I rest, &c.

FR. BACON.

Sir Francis Bacon *to the Earl of* Essex, *when Sir* Robert Cecil *was in* France.

My singular good Lord,

I Do write, because I have not yet had time fully to express my conceit, nor now to attend you, touching *Irish* matters, considering them as they may concern the State; that it is one of the aptest particulars that hath come, or can come upon the stage, for your Lordship to purchase honour upon. I am moved to think for three reasons: because it is ingenerate in your house in respect of my Lord your Fathers noble attempts; because of all the accidents of State at this time, the labour resteth upon most that; and because the world will make a kind of comparison between those that set it out of frame, and those that shall bring it into frame: which kind of honour giveth the quickest kind of reflection. The transferring this honour upon your self consisteth in two points: The one, if the principal persons imployed come in by you, and depend upon you; the other, if your Lordship declare your self to undertake a care of that matter. For the persons, it falleth out well, that your Lordship hath had no interest in the persons of imputation: For neither Sir *William Fitz-Williams*, nor Sir *John Norris* was yours: Sir *William Russel* was conceived yours, but was curbed: Sir *Conier's Clifford*, as I conceive it, dependeth upon you, who is said to do well; and if my Lord of *Ormond* in this interim do accomodate well, I take it he hath always had good understanding with your Lordship. So as all things are not only whole and entire, but of favourable aspect towards your Lordship, if you now chuse well: wherein, in your wisdom, you will remember there is a great difference in choice of the persons, as you shall think the affairs to incline to composition, or to war. For your care-taking, popular conceit hath been, that *Irish* causes have been much neglected, whereby the very reputation of better care will be a strength: And I am sure, her Majesty and my Lords of the Council do not think their care dissolved, when they have chosen whom to imploy; but that they will proceed in a spirit of State, and not leave the main point to discretion. Then if a resolution be taken, a Consultation must proceed; and the Consultation must be governed upon information to be had from such as know the place, and matters in fact: And in taking of information I have always noted there is a skill and a wisdom. For I cannot tell what accompt or inquiry hath been taken of Sir *William Russel*, of Sir *Ralph Bingham*, of the Earl of *Tomond*, of Mr. *Wilbraham*: but I am of opinion, much more would be had of them, if your Lordship shall be pleased severally to confer, not *obiter*, but expresly, upon some *Caveat* given them to think of it before; for, *bene docet qui prudenter interrogat*. For the points of opposing them, I am too much a stranger to the business, to deduce them: but in a——Topick methinks the pertinent interrogations must be either of the possibility and means of Accord, or of the nature of the War, or of the reformation of the particular abuses, or of the joyning of practice with force in the disunion of the Rebels. If your Lordship doubt to put your sickle in other mens harvests, yet consider you have these advantages. First, Time being fit to you in Mr. Secretaries absence: Next, *Vis unita fortior*: Thirdly, the business being mixt with matters of war, it is fittest for you: Lastly, I know your Lordship will carry it with that modesty and respect towards aged Dignity, and that good correspondencie towards my dear Ally, and your good friend, now abroad, as no inconveniencie may grow that way. Thus have I plaid the ignorant Statesman, which I do to no body but your Lordship, except I do it to the Queen sometimes, when she trains me on. But your Lordship will accept my duty and good meaning, and secure me touching the privateness of that *I* write;

Your Lordships, to be commanded,
FR. BACON.

Sir Francis Bacon *to the Earl of* Essex, *concerning the Earl of* Tyrone.

THose advertisements which your Lordship imparted to me, and the like, *I* hold to be no more certain to make judgement upon, then a Patients water to a Physitian: Therefore for me upon one water to make a judgement, were indeed like a foolish bold Mountebank,

Sir Francis Bacon *to the Earl of* Essex.

or Doctor *Birket*; Yet for willing duties sake, *I* will set down to your Lordship what opinion sprung in my mind upon that *I* read. The Letter from the Councel there leaning to distrust, *I* do not much rely upon, for three causes. First, because it is always both the grace, and the safety from blame of such a Councel, to erre in caution: whereunto add, that it may be, they or some of them are not without envy towards the person who is used in treating the Accord. Next, because the time of this Treaty hath no shew of dissimulation, for that *Tyrone* is now in no streights; but like a Gamester that will give over because he is a winner, not because he hath no more money in his purse.

Lastly, I do not see but those Articles whereupon they ground their suspicion, may as well proceed out of fear as out of falshood, for the reteining of the dependance of the protracting the admission of a Sheriffe, the refusing to give his son for hostage, the holding from present repair to *Dublin*, the refusing to go presently to accord, without including *O. Donell* and others his associates, may very well come of a guilty reservation, in case he should receive hard measure, and not out of treachery; so as if the great person be faithful, and that you have not here some present intelligence of present succours from *Spain*, for the expectation whereof *Tyrone* would win time, I see no deep cause of distrusting the cause if it be good. And for the question, her Majesty seemeth to me a winner three ways, First, her purse shall have rest: Next, it will divert the forreign designes upon that place. Thirdly, though her *Majesty* is like for a time to govern *Precario* in the North, and be not in true command in better state there then before, yet besides the two respects of ease of charge, and advantage of opinion abroad, before mentioned, she shall have a time to use her Princely policy in two points: In the one, to weaken by division and disunion of the heads; the other, by recovering and winning the people by justice, which of all other causes is the best. Now for the *Athenian* question, you discourse well, *Quid igitur agendum est?* I will shoot my fools bolt, since you will have it so. The Earle of *Ormond* to be encouraged and comforted above all things, the Garrisons to be instantly provided for; For opportunity makes a thief: and if he should mean never so well now, yet such an advantage as the breaking of her Majesties Garrisons, might tempt a true man. And because he may as well waver upon his own inconstancy as upon occasion, and wont of variableness is never restrained but with fear, I hold it necessary he be menaced with a strong war; not by words, but by Musters and preparations of forces here, in case the accord proceed not; but none to be sent over lest it disturb the Treaty, and make him look to be over-run as soon as he hath laid down Arms. And, but that your Lordship is too easie to pass, in such cases, from dissimulation to verity, I think, if your Lordship lent your reputation in this case, it is to pretend, that it not a defensive war, as in times past, but a full reconquest of those parts of the Countrey be resolved on, you would accept the charge, I think it would help to settle him, and win you a great deal of honour gratis. And that which most properly concerneth this action, if it prove a peace, I think her Majesty shall do well to cure the root of the disease, and to profess by a commission of peaceable men chiefly of respect and countenance, the reformation of abuses, extortions, and injustices there, and to plant a stronger and surer government then heretofore, for the ease and protection of the subject; for the removing of the sword, or government in Arms, from the Earle of *Ormond*, or the sending of a Deputy, which will ecclipse it, if peace follow, I think unseasonable. Lastly, I hold still my opinion, both for your better information, and your fuller declaration of your care, and evermore meriting service, that your Lordship have a set conference with the persons I named in my former writing. I rest,

At your Lordships service

FR. BACON.

Another to the Earl, before his going to Ireland.

MY singular good Lord, your note of my silence in your occasions hath made me set down these few wandring lines, as one that would say somewhat, and can say nothing touching your Lordships intended charge for *Ireland*; which my endeavour I know your Lordship will accept graciously and well; whether your Lordship take it by the handle of the occasion ministred from your self, or of the affection from which it proceedeth, your Lordship is designed to a service of great merit and great peril; and as the greatness of the perill must needs include no small consequence of peril if it be not temperately governed: for all immoderate success extinguisheth merit, and stirreth up distaste and envy, the

assured

assured fore-runner of whole changes of peril. But I am at the last point first, some good spirit leading my pen to presage to your Lordships success: wherein it is true, I am not, without my Oracle and Divinations, none of them superstitious, and yet not all natural: For first, looking into the course of Gods providence in things now depending, and calling into consideration how great things God hath done by her Majesty, and for her collect he hath disposed of this great dissection in *Ireland*, whereby to give an urgent occasion to the reduction of that whole kingdom, as upon the rebellion of *Desmond* there ensued the reduction of that Province. Next, your Lordship goeth against three of the unluckiest vices of all other, Disloyalty, Ingratitude, and Insolence; which three offences in all examples have seldome their doom adjourned to the world to come. Lastly, he that shall have had the honour to know your Lordship inwardly, as I have had, shall find *bona exta*, whereby he may better ground a divination of good, then upon the dissection of a Sacrifice. But that part I leave; for it is fit for others to be confident upon you, and you to be confident upon the cause; the goodness and justice whereof is such, as can hardly be matched in any example, it being no ambitious war of Forreigners, but a recovery of subjects, and that after lenity of conditions often tried; and a recovery of them not onely to obedience, but to humanity and policy, from more then *Indian Barbarism*. There is yet another kind of divination familiar in matters of State, being that which *Demosthenes* so often relieth upon in his time, where he saith, That which for the time past is worst of all, is for the time to come the best, which is, that things go ill, not by accident, but by error; wherein though your Lordship hath been a waking Censor, yet you must look for no other now, but, *Medice, cura te ipsum*: and although your Lordship shall not be the blessed Physician that cometh to the declination of the disease, yet you imbrace that condition which many Noble Spirits have accepted for advantage, which is, that you go upon the greater peril of your fortune, and the less of your reputation; and so the honour countervaileth the adventure: of which honour your Lordship is in no small possession, when that her Majesty, known to be one of the most judicious Princes in discerning of spirits, that ever governed, hath made choyce of you meerly out of her Royal judgement (her affection inclining rather to continue your attendance) into whose hands and trust to put the commandement and conduct of so great forces, the gathering in the fruit of so great charge, the execution of so many Counsels, the redeeming of the defaults of so many former Governors, and the clearing of the glory of so many happy years reign onely in this part excepted. Nay further, how far forth the peril of that State is interlaced with the peril of *England*; and therefore how great the honour is to keep and defend the approaches of this Kingdom, I hear many discourse; and indeed there is a great difference, whether the *Tortoise* gather her self into her shell hurt or unhurt: And if any man be of opinion, that the nature of an enemy doth extenuate the honour of a service, being but a Rebell and a Savage, I differ from him; for I see the justest Triumphs that the *Romans* in their greatest greatness did obtain, and that whereof the Emperours in their stiles took additions and denominations, were of such an enemy, that is, people barbarous and not reduced to civility, magnifying a kind of lawless liberty, prodigal of life, hardened in body, fortified in woods and bogs, placing both justice and felicity in the sharpness of their swords. Such were the *Germans* and ancient *Britains*, and divers others. Upon which kind of people whether the victory be a Conquest, or a Reconquest upon a Rebellion or revolt, it made no difference, that ever I could find, in honour. And therefore it is not the inriching predatory war that hath the preheminence in honour; else should it be more honour to bring in a Carrack of rich burthen, then one of the twelve Spanish Apostles. But then this nature of people doth yield a higher point of honour (considering in truth and substance) then any war can yield which should be atchieved against a civil enemy, if the end may be——*Paciq; imponere morem*, To replant and refound the policie of that Nation, to which nothing is wanting but a just and civil Government. Which design, as it doth descend to you from your noble Father, (who lost his life in that action, though he paid tribute to nature, and not to fortune) so I hope your Lordship shall be as fatal a Captain to this war, as *Africanus* was to the war of *Carthage*, after that both his Uncle and his Father had lost their lives in *Spain* in the same war.

Now although it be true, that these things which I have writ (being but representations unto your Lordship of the honour and appearance of success of the enterprize) be not much to the purpose of my direction, yet it is that which is best to me being no man of war, and ignorant in the particulars of State: for a man may by the eye set up the white right in midst of the But, though he be no Archer. Therefore I will only add this wish, according to the English phrase, which termeth a wel-wishing advice a wish, that your Lordship in this whole action, looking forward, set down this Position; That merit is worthier then fame;

and

and looking back hither would remember this text, That obedience is better then sacrifice. For designing to fame and glory may make your Lordship, in the adventure of your person, to be valiant as a private Souldier, rather then as a General; it may make you in your commandments rather to be gracious then disciplinary; it may make you press action, in the respect of the great expectation conceived, rather hastily then seasonably and safely; it may make you seek rather to atchieve the war by force, then by intermixture of practice; it may make you (if God shall send you prosperous beginnings) rather seek the fruition of that honour, then the perfection of the work in hand. And for your proceeding like a good protestant (upon warrant, and not upon good intention) your Lordship knoweth, in your wisdom, that as it is most fit for you to desire convenient liberty of instruction, so it is no less fit for you to observe the due limits of them, remembring that the exceeding of them may not onely procure (in case of adverse accident) a dangerous disavow, but also (in case of prosperous success) be subject to interpretation, as if all were not referred to the right end.

Thus I have presumed to write these few lines to your Lordship *in methodo ignorantiæ*, which is, when a man speaketh of any subject not according to the parts of the matter, but according to the model of his own knowledge: And most humbly desire your Lordship, that the weakness thereof may be supplied in your Lordship, by a benign acceptation, as it is in me by my best wishing.

FR. BACON.

Sir Francis Bacon *to the Earl of* Essex *after his Enlargement.*

My Lord,

NO man can expound my doings better then your Lordship, which makes me need to say the less; only I humbly pray you to believe that I aspire to the conscience and commendation of *Bonus Civis* and *Bonus Vir*; and that though I love some things better, I confess, then I love your Lordship; yet I love few persons better, both for gratitudes sake, and for vertues, which cannot hurt but by accident. Of which my good affection it may please your Lordship to assure your self, of all the true effects and offices that I can yield: for as I was ever sorry your Lordship should flie with waxen wings, doubting *Icarus*'s fortune; so for the growing up of your own feathers, be they Ostriches or other kinde, no man shall be more glad; and this is the Axel-tree, whereupon I have turned, and shall turn. Which having already signified unto you by some neer means, having so fit a Messenger for mine own Letter, I thought good to redouble also by writing. And so I commend you to Gods protection. From *Grays Inne*, &c.

July 19. 1600.   FR. BACON.

Sir Francis Bacon *in recommendation of his service,* to the Earl of Northumberland, *a few days before* Queen Elizabeths *death.*

It may please your good Lordship,

* AS the time of sowing of seed is known, but the time of coming up and disclosing is casual, or according to the season; So I am a witness to my self, that there hath been covered in my mind a long time a seed of affection and zeal towards your Lordship, sown by the estimation of your vertues, and your particular honours and favours to my brother deceased, and to my self, which seed still springing, now bursteth forth into this profession. And to be plain with your Lordship, it is very true, and no winds or noyses of civil matters can blow this out of my head or heart, that your great capacity and love towards studies and contemplations, of an higher and worthier nature then popular, a Nature rare in the world, and in a person of your Lordships quality almost singular, is to me a great and chief motive to draw my affection and admiration towards you: and therefore, good my Lord, if I may be of any use to your Lordship by my Head, Tongue, Pen, Means, or Friends, I humbly pray you to hold me your own: and herewithal, not to do so much disadvantage to my good mind, nor partly, to your own worth, as to conceive, that this commendation of my humble service proceedeth out of any streights of my occasions, but meerly out of an election, and indeed, the fulness of my heart. And so wishing your Lordship all prosperity, I continue.

Sir Francis Bacon *to Mr.* Robert Kempe, *upon the death of Queen* Elizabeth.

* Mr. *Kempe*, This alteration is so great, as you might justly conceive some coldness of my affection towards you, if you should hear nothing from me, I living in this place. It is in vain to tell you, with what a wonderfull still and calme this wheel is turned round, which whether it be a remnant of her felicity that is gone, or a fruit of his reputation that is coming, I will not determine; for I cannot but divide my self, between her memory and his name. Yet we account it but as a fair morn before Sun rising, before his Majesties presence; though, for my part, I see not whence any weather should arise. The Papists are conteined with fear enough, and hope too much. The French is thought to turn his practice upon procuring some disturbance in *Scotland*, where Crowns may do wonders. But this day is so welcome to the Nation, and the time so short, as I do not fear the effect. My Lord of *Southampton* expecteth release by the next dispatch, and is already much visited, and much well wished. There is continual Posting, by men of good quality, towards the King, the rather, I think, because this Spring time it is but a kinde of sport. It is hoped, that as the State here hath performed the part of good Attorneys, to deliver the King quiet possession of his Kingdom; so the King will re-deliver them quiet possession of their places, rather filling places void, then removing men placed. So, &c.

Sir Francis Bacon *to Mr.* David Foules *in* Scotland, *upon the entrance of His Majesties Reign.*

* SIR, The occasion awaketh in me the remembrance of the constant and mutual good offices which passed between my good brother and your self; whereunto, as you know, I was not altogether a stranger, though the time and design (as between brethren) made me more reserved. But well do I bear in minde the great opinion which my brother (whose Judgement I much reverence) would often express to me of the extraordinary sufficiency, Dexterity, and temper, which he had found in you, in the business and service of the King our Sovereign Lord. This latter bred in me an election, as the former gave an inducement, for me to address my self to you, and to make this signification of my desire, towards a mutual entertainment of good affection, and correspondence between us; hoping that some good effect my result of it, towards the Kings service; and that, for our particulars, though occasion give you the precedence, of furthering my being known by good note unto the King; so no long time will intercede, before I, on my part, shall have some means given to requite your favours, and to verifie your commendation. And so with my loving commendations (good Mr *Foules*) I leave you to Gods goodness.

From *Graies Inne*, this 25th of *March*.

Sir Francis Bacon *to Sir* Robert Cecil, *after defeat of the* Spaniards *in* Ireland, *for reducing that Kingdom to civility, with some Reasons inclosed.*

It may please your Honour,

AS one that wisheth you all increase of honour, and as one that cannot leave to love the State, what interest soever I have, or may come to have in it, and as one that now this dead Vacation time have some leisure *ad aliud agendum*, I will presume to propound unto you that which though you cannot but see, yet I know not whether you apprehend and esteem it in so high a degree, that is, for the best action of importation to your self, of sound honour and merit to her Majesty, & this Crown, without ventosity or popularity, that the riches of any occasion, or the tide of any opportunity can possibly minister or offer. And that is, the Causes of *Ireland*, if they be taken by the right handle: For if the wound be not ripped up again, and come to a festered sense, by new forreign succours, I think that no Physitian will go on much with letting blood *in declinatione morbi*, but will intend to purge and corroborate. To which purpose, I send you mine opinion, without labour of words in the inclosed; and sure I am, that if you

Sir Francis Bacon *to the Lord Treasurer,* &c.

you shall enter into the matter according to the vivacity of your own spirit, nothing can make unto you a more gainful return: for you shall make the Queens felicity compleat, which now (as it is) is incomparable: and for your self, you shall make your self as good a Patriot, as you are thought a Politick; and to have no less generous ends, then dexterous delivery of your self towards your ends; and as well to have true arts and grounds of government, as the facility and felicity of practice and negotiation; and to be as well seen in the periods and tides of estates, as in your own circle and way: then the which I suppose nothing can be a better addition and accumulation of honour unto you.

This I hope I may in privateness write, either as a Kinsman, that may be bold; or as a Scholar, that hath liberty of discourse, without committing of any absurdity. If not, I pray your honour to believe, I ever loved her Majesty and the State, and now love your self; and there is never any vehement love without some absurdity, as the Spaniard well saith; *Desuario con la calentura.* So desiring your honours pardon, I ever continue, &c.

FR. BACON.

Sir Francis Bacon *to the Lord Treasurer, touching his Speech in Parliament.*

It may please your good Lordship,

I Was sorry to find by your Lordships speech yesterday, that my last Speech in Parliament; delivered in discharge of my conscience, my duty to God, her Majesty, and my Countrey, was offensive: if it were misreported, I would be glad to attend your Lordship, to disavow any thing I said not; if it were misconstrued, I would be glad to expound my words, to exclude any sence I meant not; if my heart be mis-judged by imputation of popularity, or opposition, I have great wrong, and the greater, because the manner of my Speech did most evidently shew, that I spake most simply, and onely to satisfie my conscience, and not with any advantage or policy to sway the cause; and my terms carried all signification of duty, and zeal towards her Majesty and her service. It is very true, that from the beginning, whatsoever was a double Subsidy, I did wish might for presidents sake appear to be extraordinary, and for discontents sake might not have been levied upon the poorer sort, though otherwise I wished it as rising as I think this will prove, or more. This was my mind, I confess it: and therefore I most humbly pray your good Lordship, first, to continue me in your own good opinion, and then, to perform the part of an honourable good friend, towards your poor servant, and ally, in drawing her Majesty to accept of the sincerity and simplicity of my zeal, and to hold me in her Majesties favour, which is to me dearer then my life. And so, &c.

Your Lordships most humble in all duty,

FR. BACON.

Sir Francis Bacon *to the Earl of* Northampton.

May it please your good Lordship,

AS the time of sowing of a seed is known, but the time of coming up and disclosing is casual, or according to the season; so I am witness to my self, that there hath been covered in my mind a long time a seed of affection and zeal towards your Lordship, sown by the estimation of your vertues, and your particular honours and favours to my brother deceased, and to my self; which seed still springing, now bursteth forth into this profession. And to be plain with your Lordship, it is very true, and no winds or noyses of evil matters can blow this out of my head or heart, that your great capacities and love towards studies and contemplations, of an higher and worthier nature then popular, a matter rare in the world, and in a person of your Lordships quality almost singular, is to me a great and chief motive to draw my affection and admiration towards you: and therefore, good my Lord, if I may be of any use to your Lordship, I humbly pray your Lordship, to hold me your own: and therefore withal, not to do so much disadvantage to my good mind, as to conceive, that this commendation of my humble service proceedeth out of any streights of my occasions; but meerly out of an election, and indeed, the fulness of my heart. And so wishing your Lordship all prosperity, I continue yours, &c.

FR. BACON.

A Letter to Mr. Matthew, upon sending his Book De Sapientia Veterum.

Mr. *Matthew*, I do very heartily thank you for your Letter of the 24th of *Aug.* from *Salamanca*; and in recompence thereof, I send you a little work of mine, that hath begun to pass the world. They tell me my Lattin is turn'd into Silver, and become currant. Had you been here you had been my Inquisitor, before it came forth. But I think the greatest Inquisitor in *Spain* will allow it. But one thing you must pardon me, if I make no haste to believe, that the world should be grown to such an extasie, as to reject truth in Philosophy, because the Author dissenteth in Religion; no more then they do by *Aristotle*, or *Averrois*. My great work goeth forward, and after my manner, I alter ever when I adde. So that nothing is finished till all be finished. This I have written in the midst of a Term and Parliament, thinking no time so precious, but that I should talk of these matters with so good and dear a friend. And so, with my wonted wishes, I leave you to Gods goodness.

From *Graies Inne*, *Febr.* 17. 1610.

A Letter to the King, touching matter of Revenue and Profit.

It may please your Majesty,

I May remember what *Tacitus* saith, by occasion that *Tyberius* was often and long absent from *Rome*, *In Urbe*, *& parva & magna negotia Imperatorem simul premunt*. But saith he, *in recessu, dimissis rebus minoris momenti, summæ rerum magnarum magis agitantur*. This maketh me think, it shall be no incivility to trouble your Majesty with business, during your aboad from *London*, knowing your Majesties Meditations are the principal wheel of your estate, and being warranted by a former commandment, which I received from you.

I do now onely send your Majesty these papers inclosed, because I greatly desire so far forth to preserve my Credit with you, as thus: That whereas lately (perhaps out of too much desire which induceth too much belief) I was bold to say, that I thought it as easie for your Majesty to come out of want, as to go forth of your Gallery, your Majesty would not take me for a dreamer, or a projector. I send your Majesty therefore some grounds of my hopes. And for that paper which I have gathered of increasements *sperare*; I beseech you to give me leave to think, that if any of the particulars do fail, it will be rather for want of workmanship in those that shall deal in them, then want of materials in the things themselves. The other paper hath many discarding cards; and I send it chiefly, that your Majesty may be the less surprised by projectors, who pretend sometimes great discoveries and inventions, in things that have been propounded, and perhaps after a better fashion, long since. God Almighty preserve your Majesty.

April 25. 1610.

Your Majesties most humble and devoted Servant and Subject.

A Letter to the King, touching the Lord Chancellors place.

It may please your most Excellent Majesty,

YOur worthy Chancellor, I fear, goeth his last day. God hath hitherto used to weed out such Servants as grew not fit for your Majesty, but now he hath gathered to himself a true sage, or *salvia*, out of your Garden; But your Majesties service must not be mortal.

Upon this heavy accident, I pray your Majesty, in all humbleness and sincerity, to give me leave to use a few words. I must never forget, when I moved your Majesty for the Attorneys place, it was your own sole act; more then that *Somerset*, when he knew your Majesty had resolved it, thrust himself into the business, for a Fee. And therefore I have no reason to pray to Saints.

I shall now again make oblation to your Majesty, first of my heart, then of my service, thirdly, of my place of Attorney (which I think is honestly worth 6000*l.* *per annum*) and fourthly, of my place of the Starchamber, which is worth 1600*l. per annum*, and with the favour and countenance of a Chancellor, much more.

I hope I may be acquitted of presumption, if I think of it, both because my Father had the place, which is some civil inducements to my desire: And I pray God your Majesty may have twenty no worse years in your Greatness, then Queen *Elizabeth* had in her Model, (after my Fathers placing) and chiefly, because, if the Chancellors place went to the law, it was ever conferred upon some of the Learned Councel, and never upon a Judge. For *Audley* was raised from K. Serjeant, my Father from Attorney of the Wards, *Bromley* from Sollicitor, *Puckering* from Serjeant, *Egerton* from Master of the Rolls, having newly left the Attorneys place. Now I beseech your Majesty, let me put you the present case, truly. If you take my Lord *Coke*, this will follow; first, your Majesty shall put an over-ruling nature into an over-ruling place, which may breed an extream: Next, you shall blunt his industries in matter of finances, which seemeth to aime at another place. And lastly, popular men are no sure Mounters for your Majesties Saddle. If you take my Lord *Hubbard*, you shall have a Judge at the upper end of your Councel-board, and another at the lower end: Whereby your Majesty will finde your Prerogative pent. For though there should be emulation between them, yet as Legists they will agree, in magnifying that wherein they are best, He is no States-man, but an *Oeconomist*, wholly for himself. So as your Majesty (more then an outward form) will find little help in him, for the business. If you take my Lord of *Canterbury*, I will say no more, but the Chancellors place requires a whole man. And to have both Jurisdictions, Spiritual and Temporal, in that height, is fit but for a King.

For my self, I can onely present your Majesty with *Gloria in obsequio*: yet I dare promise, that if I sit in that place, your business shall not make such short turns upon you, as it doth; but when a direction is once given, it shall be pursued and performed; and your Majesty shall onely be troubled with the true care of a King, which is to think what you would have done in chief, and not how, for the passages.

I do presume also, in respect of my Fathers memory, and that I have been always gratious in the Lower House, I have interest in the Gentlemen of *England*, and shall be able to do some good effect, in rectifying that Body of Parliament men, which is *Cardo rerum*. For let me tell your Majesty, that that part of the Chancellors place which is to Judge in equity, between party and party, that same *Regnum judiciale* (which since my Fathers time is but too much enlarged) concerneth your Majesty least, more then the acquitting your Conscience for Justice. But it is the other parts of a Moderator, amongst your Councel, of an Overseer over your Judges, of a planter of fit Justices, and Governors in the Country, that importeth your affairs and these times most.

I will adde also, that I hope by my care, the inventive part of your Councel will be strengthened, who now commonly, do exercise rather their Judgements, then their inventions: And the inventive part cometh from projectors, and private men, which cannot be so well; In which kinde, my Lord of *Salisbury* had a good method, if his ends had been upright.

To conclude, if I were the man I would be, I should hope, that as your Majesty hath of late wonne hearts by depressing; you should in this leese no hearts by advancing. For I see your people can better skill of *Concretum* then *Abstractum*, and that the waves of their affections flow rather after, persons then things. So that acts of this nature (if this were one) do more good then twenty Bills of Grace.

If God call my Lord, the Warrants and Commissions which are requisite for the taking the Seal, and for the working with it, and for the reviving of Warrants under his hand, which dye with him, and the like, shall be in readiness. And in this time presseth more, because it is the end of a Term, and almost the beginning of the Circuits: So that the Seal cannot stand still. But this may be done, as heretofore, by Commission, till your Majesty hath resolved of an Officer. God ever preserve your Majesty.

Febr. 12.
1615.

Your Majesties most humble Subject,
and bounden Servant.

Sir Francis Bacon *to the* King.

A Letter to the King, *of my Lord* Chancellors *amendment, and the difference begun between the* Chancery *and* Kings Bench.

It may please your most excellent Majesty,

✻ I Do finde (God be thanked) a sensible amendment in my Lord Chancellor, I was with him yesterday in private conference, about half an hour, and this day again, at such time as he did seal, which he endured well almost the space of an hour, though the vapour of the wax be offensive to him. He is free from a fever, perfect in his powers of memory and speech, and not hollow in his voice nor looks. He hath no panting, or labouring respiration, neither are his coughs dry or weak. But whosoever thinketh his disease to be but Melancholy, maketh no true judgement of it; for it is plainly a formed and deep cough, with a pectorall surcharge, so that, at times, he doth almost *animam agere*. I forbear to advertise your Majesty of the care I took to have Commissioners in readiness, because Master Secretary *Lake* hath let me understand he signified as much to your Majesty. But I hope there shall be no use of them for this time.

And as I am glad to advertise your Majesty of the amendment of your Chancellors person, so I am sorry to accompany it with an advertisement of the sickness of your Chancery Court; though (by the grace of God) that cure will be much easier then the other. It is true, I did lately write to your Majesty, that for the matter of *Habeas corpora* (which was the third matter in Law you had given me in charge) I did think the Communion of service between my Lord Chancellor, and my Lord Chief Justice, in the great business of examination, would so joyn them, as they would not square at this time. But pardon me (I humbly pray your Majesty) if I have too reasonable thoughts. And yet that which happened the last day of the Term concerning certain indictments; in the nature of Præmunire, preferred into the Kings Bench, but not found, is not so much as is noysed abroad, (though I must say, it was *Omni tempore nimium, & hoc tempore alienum*.) And therefore I beseech your Majesty not to give any believing eare to reports, but to receive the truth from me that am your Atturney Generall, and ought to stand indifferent for jurisdictions of all Courts; which account I cannot give your Majesty now, because I was then absent, and some are now absent, which are properly and authentically to informe me, touching that which passed. Neither let this any way dis-joynt your other business; for there is a time for all things, and this very accident may be turned to good; not that I am of opinion, that that same cunning Maxime of *Separa & Impera*, which sometimes holdeth in persons, can well take place in jurisdictions; but because some good occasion by this excess may be taken, to settle that which would have been more dangerous, if it had gone on, by little and little. God preserve your Majesty.

Febr. 15th   *Your Majesties most humble subject,*
1615.   *and most bounden servant.*

A Letter to Sir Geo: Villiers, *touching the difference between the Courts of* Chancery *and* Kings Bench.

Sir,

✻ I Received this morning from you two Letters by the same bearer, the one written before the other, both after his Majesty had received my last. In this difference between the two Courts of Chancery and Kings Bench (for so I had rather take it at this time, then between the persons of my Lord Chancellor, and my Lord Chief Justice) I marvaile not, if rumour get any way of true relation; for I know Fame hath swift wings, specially that which hath black feathers; but within these two dayes (for sooner I cannot be ready) I will write to his Majesty both the Narrative truly, and my opinion sincerely, taking much comfort, that I serve such a King, as hath Gods property, in discerning truly of mens hearts. I purpose to speak with my Lord Chancellor this day, and so to exhibit that Cordial of his Majesties grace, as I hope this other accident will rather rowse and raise his spirits, then deject him, or incline him to a relapse; Mean while, I commend the wit of a mean man that said this other day; Well (saith he) next Term you shall have an old man come with a besom of Worm-wood in his hand, that will sweep away all this. For it is my Lord Chan-

Chancellor his fashion, especially towards the Summer, to carry a posie of Worm-wood. I writ this Letter in haste, to return the Messenger with it. God keep you, and long and happily may you serve his Majesty.

Feb. 19. 1615. *Your true and affectionate servant.*

POST-SCRIPT.

Sir, I humbly thank you for your inward Letter: I have burned it as you commanded, but the flame it hath kindled in me will never be extinguished.

Sir Francis Bacon *to the* King, *concerning the* Præmunire *in the* Kings Bench *against the* Chancery.

It may please your most Excellent Majesty,

I Was yesterday in the afternoon with my Lord Chancellor, according to your commandment, which I received by the Mr. of the Horse, and finde the old man well comforted, both towards God and towards the world. And that same middle comfort, which is a divine and humane proceeding from your Majesty being Gods Lievtenant on earth, I am perswaded hath been a great cause, that such a sicknefs hath been portable to such an age. I did not faile in my conjecture, that this businefs of the Chancery hath stirred him. He sheweth to despise it, but yet he is full of it, and almost like a young Duellist that findeth himself behind hand.

I will now (as your Majesty requireth) give you a true relation of that which passed; neither will I decline your royall commandment, for delivering my opinion also, though it be a tender subject to write on. But I that accout my being but an accident to my service, will neglect no duty upon self-safety. First, it is necessary I let your Majesty know the ground of the difference between the two Courts, that your Majesty may the better understand the Narrative.

There was a Statute made 27. *Ed:* 3. *Cap:* 1. which (no doubt) in the principal intention 27 E. 3. thereof, was ordained against those that sued to *Rome*, wherein there are words somewhat *Cap.* 1. generall, against any that questioneth or impeacheth any judgement given in the Kings Courts, in any other Courts. Upon these doubtfull words (other Courts) the Controversie groweth; For the founder interpretation taketh them to be meant of those Courts which though locally they were not held at *Rome*, or where the Popes Chair was, but here within the Realme, yet in their jurisdiction had their dependency upon the Court of *Rome*; as were the Court of the Legat here, and the Courts of the Arch-bishops and Bishops, which were then but subordinate judgement seats, to that high Tribunal of *Rome*.

And for this Construction, the opposition of the words, (if they be well observed) between the Kings Courts and other Courts, maketh very much; For it importeth as if those other Courts were not the Kings Courts. Also the main scope of the Statute fortifieth the same; and lastly, the practice of many ages. The other interpretation (which cleaveth to the letter, expoundeth the Kings Courts to be the Courts of Law only, and other Courts to be Courts of Equity, as the Chancery, Exchequer-Chamber, Dutchy, &c. though this also flyeth indeed from the letter; for that all these are the Kings Courts.

There is also another Statute, which is but a simple Prohibition, and not with a penal- 4 H. 4. ty of Præmunire as the other is, That after judgements given in the Kings Courts, the par- *Cap.* 23. ties shall be in peace, except the judgments be undone, by Error, or Attaint, which is a legall forme of reversall. And of this also, I hold the founder interpretation to be, to settle possessions against disturbances, and not to take away remedy in equity, where those judgements are obtained *ex rigore juris*, and against good Conscience.

But upon these two Statutes, there hath been a late conceipt in some, that if a judgement passe at the Common Law against any, he may not after sue for reliefe in Chancery; and if he doe, both he and his Councel, and his Sollicitor, yea and the Judge in, equity, himself, are within the danger of those Statutes. There your Majesty hath the true state of the question, which I was necessarily to shew you first, because your Majesty calleth for this relation, not as newes, but as businefs. Now to the Historicall part; It is the Course of the Kings Bench, that they give in Charge to the Grand Jury offences of all natures to be presented within *Middlesex*, where the said Court is; and the manner is to enumerate them, as it were in Articles. This was done by Justice *Crooke*, the wednesday before the Term ended; and that Article, *if any man after a judgement given had*
drawn

drawn the said judgement to a new examination in any other Court, was by him especially given in Charge, which had not used to be given in charge before. It is true, it was not solemnly dwelt upon, but as it were, thrown in amongst the rest.

The last day of the Terme (and that which all men condemn) the supposed last day of my Lord Chancellors life) there were two Indictments preferred of Præmunire, for suing in Chancery after judgement at Common Law; The one by *Richard Glanvile*, the other by *William Allen*; the former against *Courtney* the party in Chancery, *Gibb* the Councellor, and *Deurst* the Clerk. The latter against Alderman *Bowles*, and *Humfrey Smith*, parties in Chancery, Serjeant *Moore* the Councellor, *Elias Wood* Sollicitor in the Cause, and Sir *John Tyndall* Master of the Chancery, and an Assesser to my Lord Chancellor. For the cases themselves, it were too long to trouble your Majesty with them; but this I will say, if they were set on that preferred them, they were the worst work-men that ever were that set them on; for there could not have been chosen two such causes, to the honour and advantage of the Chancery, for the justness of the Decrees, and the fowlness and scandall, both of fact, and person, in those that impeach the Decrees.

The Grand Jury, consisting (as it seemeth) of very substantiall and intelligent persons, would not finde the Bills, notwithstanding that they were much clamoured by the parties, and twice sent back by the Court; and in conclusion, resolutely 17 of 19 found an *Ignoramus*; wherein, for that time, I think *Ignoramus* was wiser then those that knew too much.

Your Majesty will pardon me, if I be sparing in delivering to you some other circumstances of aggravation, and concurrences of some like matters the same day, as if it had been some fatall constellation. They be not things so sufficiently tryed, as I dare put them into your eare.

For my opinion, I cannot but begin with this Preface, that I am infinitely sorry that your Majesty is thus put to salve and cure, not only accidents of time, but errours of servants. For I account this a kinde of sickness of my Lord *Coke's*, that comes almost, in as ill a time, as the sickness of my Lord Chancellor. And as I think it was one of the wisest parts that ever he plaid, when he went down to your Majesty to *Royston*, and desired to have my Lord Chancellor joyned with him. So this was one of the weakest parts that ever he plaid, to make all the world perceive that my Lord Chancellor is severed from him at this time.

But for that which may concern your service, which is my end (leaving other men to their own wayes.) First, my opinion is plainly, that my Lord *Coke*, at this time, is not to be disgraced, both because he is so well habituate for that which remaineth of these capitall causes, and also for that which I finde is in his breast touching your finances, and matters of repaire of your estate. And (if I might speak it) as I think it were good his hopes were at an end in some kinde, so I could wish they were raised in some other. On the other side, this great and publique affront, not only to the reverend and well deserving person of your Chancellor (and at a time when he was thought to lye a dying, which was barbarous) but to your high Court of Chancery (which is the Court of your absolute power) may not (in my opinion) passe lightly, nor end only in some formall atonement; but use is to be made thereof, for the setling of your authoritie, and strengthening of your Prerogative, according to the true rules of Monarchy. Now to accommodate and reconcile these advices, which seeme almost opposite.

First, Your Majesty may not see it (though I confesse it be suspitious) that my Lord *Cooke* was any way aforehand privie to that which was done, or that he did set it, or animate it, but only took the matter as it came before him, and that his Error was only that at such a time he did not divert it in some good manner.

Secondly, If it be true (as is reported) that any of the puisne Judges did stirre this business, or that they did openly revile and menace the Jury for doing their Conscience (as they did honestly and truly) I think that Judge is worthy to lose his place. And to be plain with your Majesty, I do not think there is any thing, a greater *Polycreston, ad multa utile*, to your affaires, then upon a just and fit occasion, to make some example against the presumption of a Judge, in causes that concern your Majesty; whereby the whole body of those Magistrates may be contained in better awe; and, it may be, this will light upon no unfit subject, of a person that is rude, and that no man cares for.

Thirdly, If there be no one so much in fault (which I cannot yet affirme, either way, and there must be a just ground, God forbid else) yet I should think, that the very presumption of going so far in so high a cause deserveth to have that done, which was done

in

Sir Francis Bacon *to the* King.

in this very cafe, upon the Indictment of Serjeant *Heale*, in Queen *Elizabeth's* time, that the Judges fhould anfwer it upon their knees before your Majefty, or your Councel, and receive a fharp admonition; at which time alfo, my Lord *Wrey*, being then Chief Juftice, flipt the Collar, and was forborn.

Fourthly, for the perfons themfelves, *Glanvile* and *Allen*, which are bafe fellows, and turbulent, I think there will be difcovered and proved againft them (befides the preferring of the Bill) fuch combination, and contemptuous fpeeches and behaviour, as there will be good ground to call them, and perhaps fome of their petty Councellors at Law, into the Star-Chamber.

In all this which I have faid, your Majefty may be pleafed to obferve, that I do not engage you much in the main point of the Jurifdiction, for which I have a great deal of reafon, which I now forbear. But two things I wifh to be done: the one, That your Majefty take this occafion to redouble unto all your Judges your ancient and true Charge and Rule; That you will endure no innovating in the point of jurifdictions; but will have every Court impaled within their own prefidents, and not affume to themfelves new Powers, upon conceipts and inventions of Law: The other, That in thefe high Caufes, that touch upon State and Monarchy, your Majefty give them ftreight charge, That upon any occafions intervenient, hereafter, they do not make the vulgar party to their conteftations, by publick handling them, before they have confulted with your Majefty, to whom the reglement of thofe things appertaineth. To conclude, I am not without hope, that your Majefties managing this bufinefs, according to your great wifdom, unto which I acknowledge my felf not worthy to be Card-holder, or Candle-holder, will make profit of this accident, as a thing of Gods fending.

Laftly, I may not forget to reprefent to your Majefty, that there is no thinking of Arraignments, until thefe things be fomewhat accommodated, and fome outward and fuperficial reconciliation, at leaft, made between my Lord Chancellor and my Lord Chief Juftice; for this accident is a banquet to all *Somerfets* friends. But this is a thing that falleth out naturally of it felf, in refpect of the Judges going Circuit, and my Lord Chancellors infirmity, with hope of recovery. And although this protraction of time may breed fome doubt of mutability, yet I have lately learned, out of an excellent Letter of a certain King, That the Sun fheweth fometimes watry to our eyes, but when the cloud is gone, the Sun is as before. God preferve your Majefty.

Febr, 21. 1615.

*Your Majefties moft humble fubject,
and moft bounden fervant.*

Your Majefties commandment fpeaketh for pardon of fo long a Letter; which yet I wifh may have a fhort continuance, and be punifhed with fire.

Sir Francis Bacon, *the* Kings Attorney, *to the* King, *touching the proceeding with* Somerfet.

It may pleafe your moft excellent Majefty,

AT my laft accefs to your Majefty, it was fit for me to confider the time, and your journey, which maketh me now trouble your Majefty with a remnant of that I thought then to have faid, befides your old Warrant, and Commiffion to me, to advertife your Majefty; when you are *aux champs*, of any thing that concern'd your fervice, and my place. I know your Majefty is *Nunquam minus folus quam cum folus*; and, I confefs, in regard of your great judgment (unto which nothing ought to be prefented, but well weighed) I could almoft wifh, that the manner of *Tiberius* were in ufe again, of whom *Tacitus* faith, *Mos erat quamvis præfentem fcripto adire*; much more, in abfence.

I faid to your Majefty, that which I do now repeat, that the Evidence, upon which my Lord of *Somerfet* ftandeth indicted, is of a good ftrong thred, confidering, impoyfoning is the darkeft of offences; but, that the thred muft be well fpun, and woven together. For, your Majefty knoweth, it is one thing to deal with a Jury of *Middlefex* and *Londoners*, and another to deal with the Peers, whofe objects, perhaps, will not be fo much what is before them in the prefent cafe (which, I think, is as odious to them as to the vulgar) but what may be hereafter. Befides, there be two difadvantages, we that fhall give in evidence fhall meet with, fomewhat confiderable: the one, that the fame things, often open'd, lofe their frefhnefs,

except

except there be an aspersion of somewhat that is new; the other is, the expectation raised, which makes things seem less then they are, because they are less then opinion. Therefore I were not your Attorney, nor my self, if I should not be very carefull, that in this last part, which is the pinnacle of your former Justice, all things may pass *sine offendiculo, sine scrupulo*. Hereupon I did move two things, which (having now more fully explained my self) I do in all humbleness renew. First, That your Majesty will be carefull to chuse a Steward of Judgment, that may be able to moderate the Evidence, and cut off Digressions; for I may interrupt, but I cannot silence: The other, That there may be special care taken, for the ordering of the Evidence, not onely for the knitting, but for the lift, and (to use your Majesties own word) the confining of it. This to do, if your Majesty vouchsafe to direct it your self, that is the best; if not, I humbly pray you, to require my Lord Chancellor, that he, together with my Lord Chief Justice, will conferr with my self, and my fellows, that shall be used for the marshalling and bounding of the Evidence; that we may have the help of his opinion, as well as that of my Lord Chief Justice, whose great travels as I much commend; yet that same *Plerophoria*, or over-confidence, doth alwayes subject things to a great deal of chance.

There is another business proper for me to crave of your Majesty at this time, (as one that have in my eye a great deal of service to be done) concerning your casual Revenue; but considering times and persons, I desire to be strengthened by some such form of Commandment, under your royal Hand, as I send you here inclosed. I most humbly pray your Majesty, to think, that I understand my self right well in this which I desire, and that it tendeth greatly to the good of your service. The Warrant I mean not to impart, but upon just occasion. Thus, thirsty to hear of your Majesties good health, I rest.

Jan. 22. 1615.

Sir Francis Bacon, *the Kings Attorney, to Sir* George Villiers, *concerning the proceeding with* Somerset.

SIR,

I Thought it convenient to give his Majesty an accompt of that which his Majesty gave me in charge in general, reserving the particulars for his coming. And I find it necessary to know his pleasure in some things, ere I could further proceed.

My Lord Chancellor, and my self, spent Thursday and Yesterday, the whole forenoons of both days, in the examination of Sir *Robert Cotton*, whom we find, hitherto, but empty, save onely in the great point of the Treaty with *Spain*.

This examination was taken before his Majesties Warrant came to Mr. Vice-Chamberlain, for communicating unto us the secrets of the Pensions; which Warrant I received yesterday morning, being Friday, and a meeting was appointed at my Lord Chancellors, in the evening, after Councel: Upon which conference, we find matter of further examination for Sir *Robert Cotton*, of some new Articles, whereupon to examine *Somerset*, and of entring into examination of Sir *William Mounson*.

Wherefore, first, for *Somerset*, being now ready to proceed to examine him, we stay onely upon the Duke of *Lenox*, who, it seemeth, is fallen sick, and keepeth in; without whom, we neither think it warranted by his Majesties direction, nor agreeable to his intention, that we should proceed; for, that will want, which should sweeten the cup of Medicine, he being his Countrey-man and friend. Herein then we humbly crave his Majesties direction, with all convenient speed, whether we shall expect the Dukes recovery, or proceed by our selves; or that his Majesty will think of some other person (qualified according to his Majesties just intention) to be joyned with us. I remember we had speech with his Majesty of my Lord *Hay*, and I, for my part, can think of no other, except it should be my Lord Chancellor of *Scotland*, for my Lord *Binning* may be thought too neer allied.

I am further to know his Majesties pleasure concerning the day: For my Lord Chancellor, and I, conceived his Majesty to have designed the Munday and Tuesday after S*t*. *Georges* Feast; and, neverthelefs, we conceived also, that his Majesty understood, that the examinations of *Somerset*, about this, and otherwise, touching the *Spanish* practices, should first be put to a point; which will not be possible, as time cometh on, by reason of this accident of the Dukes sickness, and the cause we find of Sir *William Mounsons* examination; and that divers of the Peers are to be sent for, from remote places.

It may please his Majesty therefore, to take into consideration, whether the days may not well be put off till Wednesday and Thursday after the Term, which endeth on the Munday, being the Wednesday and Thursday before *Whitsontide*; or, if that please not his Majesty, (in respect it may be his Majesty will be then in Town, whereas these Arraignments have been still in his Majesties absence from Town) then to take Munday and Tuesday after Trinity-Sunday, being the Munday and Tuesday before Trinity Term.

Now for Sir *William Mounson*, if it be his Majesties pleasure that my Lord Chancellor and I shall proceed to the examination of him (for that of the Duke of *Lenox* differs, in that there is not the like cause as in that of *Somerset*) then his Majesty may be pleased to direct his Commandment and Warrant to my Lord Chief Justice, to deliver unto me the examinations he took of Sir *William Mounson*, that those, joyned to the information which we have received from Mr. Vice-Chamberlain, may be full instructions unto us for his examination. Further, I pray, let his Majesty know, that on Thursday in the evening my Lord Chief Justice and my self attended my Lord Chancellor at his house, for the setling of that scruple which his Majesty most justly conceived in the examination of the Lady *Somerset*; at which time, resting on his Majesties opinion, that that Evidence, as it standeth now unclear'd, must *secundum leges sanæ conscientiæ* be laid aside; the question was, Whether we should leave it out? or try what a re-examination of my Lady *Somerset* would produce? Whereupon, we agreed upon a re-examination of my Lady *Somerset*, which my Lord Chief Justice and I have appointed for Munday morning. I was bold, at that meeting, to put my Lord Chief Justice a posing question, which was, Whether that opinion which his Brethren had given upon the whole Evidence, and he had reported to his Majesty, *viz.* (That it was good Evidence, in their opinions, to convince my Lord of *Somerset*) was not grounded upon this part of the Evidence now to be omitted, as well as upon the rest. Who answered confidently, That, no: and they never saw the exposition of the Letter, but onely the Letter.

The same Thursday evening, before we entred into this last matter, and in the presence of Mr. Secretary *Winwood* (who left us when we went to the former business) we had conference concerning the frauds and abusive Grants passed to the prejudice of his Majesties state of Revenue; where my Lord Chief Justice made some relation of his collections which he had made of that kind; of which I will say onely this, that I heard nothing that was new to me, and I found my Lord Chancellor, in divers particulars, more ready then I found him. We grew to a distribution both of times and of matters: For we agreed what to begin with presently, and what should follow; and also we had consideration what was to be holpen by Law, what by Equity, and what by Parliament; Wherein, I must confess, that in the last of these (of which my Lord Chief Justice made most accompt) I make most doubt. But the conclusion was, That upon this entrance, I should advise and conferr at large with my Lord Chief Justice, and set things in work. The particulars I referr till his Majesties coming.

The Learned Councel have attended me now twice at my Chamber, to conferr upon that which his Majesty gave us in commandment, for our opinions upon the Case set down by my Lord Chancellor, whether the Statutes extend to it, or no. Wherein, we are more and more edified and confirm'd, that they do not; and shall shortly send our Report to his Majesty.

Sir, I hope you will bear me witness, I have not been idle; but all is nothing to the duty I ow his Majesty, for his singular favours past and present; supplying all with love and prayers, I rest

April 13. 1616.   *Your true friend, and devoted servant.*

Sir Francis Bacon, *the Kings Attorney, giving accompt of an Examination taken of* Somerset *at the Tower.*

SIR.

* I Received from you a Letter of very brief and clear directions, and I think it a great blessing of God upon me and my labours, that my directions come by so clear a Conduit, as they receive no tincture in the passage.

Yesterday, my Lord Chancellor, the Duke of *Lenox*, and my self, spent the whole Afternoon at the Tower, in the examination of *Somerset*, upon the Articles sent from his Majesty, and some other additionals, which were in effect contained in the former, but extended to more particularity, by occasion of somewhat discovered by *Cottons* examination, and Mr. Vice-Chamberlains information.

He is full of protestations, and would fain keep that quarter toward *Spain* clear, using but

but this for Argument; That he had such fortunes from his Majesty, as he could not think of bettering his conditions from *Spain*, because (as he said) he was no military man. He cometh nothing so far on (for that which concerneth the Treaty) as *Cotton*, which doth much aggravate suspicion against him. The further particulars I reserve to his Majesties coming.

In the end, *tanquam obiter*, but very effectually, my Lord Chancellor put him in mind of the state he stood in for the imprisonment; but he was little moved with it, and pretended carelesness of life, since ignominy had made him unfit for his Majesties service. I am of opinion, that the fair usage of him, as it was fit for the *Spanish* examinations, and for the questions touching the Papers and Dispatches, and all that; so it was no good preparative, to make him descend into himself touching his present danger: and therefore my Lord Chancellor, and my self, thought not good to insist upon it at this time.

I have received from my Lord Chief Justice the examinations of Sir *William Mounson*: with whom we mean to proceed to further examination with all speed.

My Lord Chief Justice is altered touching the re-examination of the Lady, and desired me that we might stay till he spake with his Majesty, saying, it could be no casting back to the business; which I did approve.

My self, with the rest of my fellows, upon due and mature advice, perfected our Report touching the Chancery; for the receiving whereof, I pray you, put his Majesty in mind, at his coming, to appoint some time for us to wait upon him all together, for the delivery in of the same, as we did in our former Certificate.

For the Revenue matters, I reserve them to his Majesties coming; and in the mean time, I doubt not but Mr. Secretary *Winwood* will make some kind of Report thereof to his Majesty.

For the conclusion of your Letter, concerning my own comfort, I can say but the Psalm of *Quid retribuam?* God, that giveth me favour in his Majesties eyes, will strengthen me in his Majesties service. I ever rest,

April 18. 1616. *Your true and devoted servant.*

To requite your Post-script of excuse for scribling, I pray you excuse that the Paper is not gilt, I writing from *Westminster Hall*, where we are not so fine.

Sir Francis Bacon, the Kings Attorney, to Sir George Villiers, touching the proceeding with Somerset.

SIR,

* I Have received my Letter from his Majesty, with his marginal Notes, which shall be my directions, being glad to perceive I understand his Majesty so well. That same little Charm, which may be secretly infused into *Somersets* ear some few hours before his Tryal, was excellently well thought of by his Majesty, and I do approve it, both for matter, and time; onely, if it seem good to his Majesty, I would wish it a little enlarged: For, if it be no more but to spare his bloud, he hath a kind of proud humour, which may over-work the Medicine. Therefore I could wish it were made a little stronger, by giving him some hope that his Majesty will be good to his Lady and Child; and that time (when Justice, and his Majesties Honour, is once saved and satisfied) may produce further fruit of his Majesties compassion; which was to be seen in the example of *Southampton*, whom his Majesty, after attainder, restored; and *Cobham* and *Gray*, to whom his Majesty (notwithstanding they were offendors against his own person) yet spared their lives; and for *Gray*, his Majesty gave him back some part of his estate, and was upon point to deliver him much more; he, having been so highly in his Majesties favour, may hope well, if he hurt not himself by his publick misdemeanor.

For the Person that should deliver this message, I am not so well seen in the Region of his friends, as to be able to make choice of a particular; my Lord Treasurer, the Lord *Knolles*, or any of his neerest friends, should not be trusted with it; for they may go too far, and perhaps, work contrary to his Majesties ends. Those which occurr to me, are my Lord *Hay*, my Lord *Burghley* (of *England*, I mean) and Sir *Robert Carr*.

My Lady of *Somerset* hath been re-examined, and his Majesty is found, both a true Prophet, and a most just King, in that scruple he made: For now she expoundeth the word *He*, that should send the Tarts to *Helwiss*'s wife, to be of *Overbury*, and not of *Somerset*; But for the person that should bid her, she saith, it was *Northampton* or *Weston*, not pitching upon certainty, which giveth some advantage to the Evidence. Yester-

Sir Francis Bacon *to* Sir George Villiers.

Yesterday being Wednesday, I spent 4 or 5 houres with the Judges whom his Majesty designed to take consideration with the four Judges of the Kings Bench, of the Evidence against *Somerset*. They all concurre in opinion, that the questioning him, and drawing him on to tryal is most honourable and just, and that the Evidence is fair and good.

His Majesties Letter to the Judges concerning the *Commendams* was full of magnanimity and wisdome. I perceive his Majesty is never less alone, then when he is alone; for I am sure there was no body by him to informe him, which made me admire it the more.

The Judges have given day over, till the second Saturday of the next terme; so as that matter may indure further consideration for his Majesty, not onely not to lose ground, but to win ground.

To morrow is appointed for the examination of *Somerset*, which by some infirmitie of the Duke of *Lenox*, was put off from this day. When this is done, I will write more fully, ever resting,

May 2. 1616.   *Your true and devoted servant*,

Sir Francis Bacon, *the Kings Attorney, to Sir* George Villers, *of account and advice to his Majesty touching* Somersets *Arraignment.*

SIR,

* I am far enough from opinion, that the *Ridentegration* or *Resuscitation* of *Somersets* fortune can ever stand with his Majesties honor and safety; and therein I think I express my self fully to his Majesty in one of my former letters: and I know well any expectation or thought abroad will do much hurt. But yet the glimmering of that which the King hath done to others, by way of talke to him, cannot hurt, as I conceive; but I would not have that part of the Message as from the King, but added by the messenger, as from himself. This I remitt to his Majesties Princely judgment.

For the person, though he trust the Lieutenant well, yet it must be some new man; for in these cases, that which is ordinary worketh not so great impressions, as that which is new and extraordinary.

The time I wish to be the Tuesday, being the even of his Ladies Arraignment. For as his Majesty first conceived, I would not have it stay in his stomack too long, lest it sowre in the digestion; and to be too neer the time, may be thought but to tune him for that day.

I send herewithal the substance of that which I purpose to say nakedly, and onely in that part which is of tenderness; for how I conceive was his Majesties meaning.

It will be necessary, because I have distributed parts to the two Serjeants (as that paper doth express) and they understand nothing of his Majesties pleasure, of the manner of carrying the Evidence, more then they may guess by observation of my example, (which they may ascribe as much to my nature, as to direction) therefore that his Majesty would be pleased to write some few words to us all, signed with his own hand, that the matter it self being Tragical enough, bitterness and insulting be forborne; and that we remember our part, to be to make him Delinquent to the Peers, and not odious to the People. That part of the Evidence of the Ladies exposition of the Pronoune (He) which was first caught hold of by me, and after by his Majesties singular wisdome and Conscience, excepted to, and now is by her re-examination retracted, I have given order to Serjeant *Mountague* (within whose part it falleth) to leave it out of the Evidence.

I do yet crave pardon, if I do not certifie touching the point of Law for respiting the Judgement, for I have not fully advised with my Lord Chancellor concerning it: but I will advertise it in time.

I send his Majestie the Lord Stewards Commission in two several instruments; the one to remain with my Lord Chancellor, which is that which is written in Secretary hand for his Warrant, and is to pass the Signet; the other, that, whereunto the Great Seal is to be affixed, which is in Chancery hand. His Majesty is to Sign them both, and to transmit the former to the Signet, if the Secretaries either of them be there; and both of them are to be returned to me with all speed. I ever rest,

May 5. 1616.   *Your true and devoted servant*

Sir,

Sir Francis Bacon *the Kings Attorney, and some great Lords Commissioners, concerning the perswasion used to the Lord of* Somerset *to a frank Confession.*

It may please your Majesty.

WE have done our best endeavours, to perform your Majesties Commission both in matter and manner, for the examination of my Lord of *Somerset,* wherein that which passed (for the general) was to this effect; that he was to know his own case, for that his day of Tryal could not be farre off; but that this dayes work was that which would conduce to your Majesties Justice little or nothing, but to your Mercy much, if he did lay hold upon it, and therefore, might do him good, but could do him no hurt; For as for your Justice, there had been taken great and grave opinion, not onely of such judges as he may think violent, but of the most saddest and most temperate of the Kingdome, who ought to understand the state of the proofs, that the Evidence was full to convict him, so as there needed neither Confession, nor supply of examination. But for your Majesties mercy (although he were not to expect, we should make any promise) we did assure him, that your Majesty was compassionate of him, if he gave you some ground whereon to work; that as long as he stood upon his Innocency, and Tryal, your Majesty was tied in honour to proceed according to Justice, and that he little understood (being a close prisoner) how much the expectation of the world, besides your love to Justice it self, ingaged your Majesty, whatsoever your inclination were: but nevertheless, that a frank and cleer Confession might open the gate of mercy, and help to satisfie the point of honour.

That his Lady (as he knew, and that after many Oathes, and Imprecations to the contrary) had nevertheless in the end, been touched with remorse, confessed, that she that led him to offend might leade him likewise to repent of his offence. That the confession of one of them could not fitly doe either of them much good; but the confession of both of them might work some further effect towards both. And therefore, in conclusion, we wished him not to shut the gate of your Majesties mercy against himself, by being obdurate any longer. This was the effect of that which was spoken, part by one of us, part by another, as it fell out: adding further that he might well discern who spake in us, in the course we held: for that Commissioners for examination might not presume so farre of themselves.

Not to trouble your Majesty with Circumstances of his answers, the sequel was no other, but that we found him still, not to come any degree further on to confess; onely his behaviour was very sober, and modest, and milde (differing apparantly from other times) but yet, as it seem'd, resolv'd to expect his Tryal.

Then did we proceed to examine him upon divers questions, touching the Impoysonment, which indeed were very material, and supplemental to the former Evidence: wherein either his affirmatives gave some light, or his negatives do greatly falsifye him, in that which is apparantly proved.

We made this further observation, that when we asked him some question that did touch the Prince, or some Forreign practice (which we did very sparingly at this time) yet he grew a little stirred; but in the questions of the Impoisonment very cold and modest. Thus not thinking it necessary to trouble your Majesty with any further particulars, we end with prayer to God ever to preserve your Majesty;

Your Majesties most Loyal and faithful servant, &c.

If it seem good unto your Majesty, we think it not amiss some Preacher (well chosen) had access to my Lord of *Somerset,* for his preparing and comfort, although it be before his Tryal.

Sir Francis Bacon *to the King, upon some inclination of his Majesty, signified to him for the Chancellors place.*

It may please your most Excellent Majesty,

THe last day when it pleased your Majesty to express your self towards me in favour, far above that I can deserve, or could expect, I was surprised by the Princes coming in; I most humbly pray your Majesty, therefore, to accept these few lines of acknowledgement.

I never had great thoughts for my self, further then to maintain those great thoughts which,

Sir Francis Bacon *to* Sir George Villiers.

which I confess I have for your service. I know what honour is, and I know what the times are; but I thank God with me my service is the principal, and it is far from me, under honourable pretences, to cover base desires, which I account them to be, when men refer too much to themselves, especially serving such a King. I am afraid of nothing, but that the Master of the Horse, your excellent servant, and my self, shall fall out about this, who shall hold your Stirrup best: but were your Majesty mounted, and seated without difficulties and distastes in your business, as I desire and hope to see you, I should *ex animo* desire to spend the decline of my years in my studies, wherein also I should not forget to do him honour, who besides his active and politique vertues, is the best pen of Kings, and much more the best subject of a pen. God ever preserve your Majesty.

April 1. 1616.

Your Majesties most humble Subject,
and more and more obliged Servant,

Sir Francis Bacon *to Sir* George Villiers, *of advice concerning* Ireland, *from* Gorambury *to* Windsor.

S I R,

Because I am uncertain whether his Majesty will put to a point some resolutions touching *Ireland*, now at *Windsor*; I thought it my duty to attend his Majesty by my Letter, and thereby to supply my absence, for the renewing of some former Commissions for *Ireland*, and the framing of a new Commission for the Wards, and the alienations, which appertain properly to me, as His Majesties Attorney, and have been accordingly referred by the Lords, I will undertake that they are prepared with a greater care, and better application to his Majesties service, in that Kingdome, then heretofore they have been; and therefore of that I say no more. And for the Instructions of the new Deputy, they have been set down by the two Secretaries, and read to the board, and being things of an ordinary nature, I doe not see but they may pass. But there have been three propositions and Councels, which have been stirred, which seem to me of very great importance, wherein I think my self bound to deliver to his Majesty my advice, and opinion, if they should now come in question. The first is touching the Recusant Magistrates of the Towns of *Ireland*, and the Commonalties themselves, and their Electors what shall be done; which consultation, ariseth from the late advertisements from the two Lord Justices, upon the instance of the two Towns *Linrick* and *Kilkenny*; in which advertisements, they represent the danger onely without giving any light for the remedy, rather warely for themselves, then agreeable to their duties and places. In this point, I humbly pray his Majesty to remember, that the refusal is not of the Oath of Allegiance, (which is not enacted in *Ireland*) but of the Oath of Supremacy, which cutteth deeper into matter of Conscience.

Also that his Majesty, will out of the depth of his Excellent Wisdome and providence, think, and as it were Calculate with himself, whether time will make more for the Cause of Religion in *Ireland*, and be still more and more propitious; or whether differing remedies will not make the case more difficult. For if time give his Majesty the advantage, what needeth precipitation of extream remedies; but if the time will make the case more desperate, then his Majesty cannot begin too soon. Now, in my opinion, time will open and facilitate things for reformation of Religion there, and not shut up or lock out the same. For first, the plantations going on, and being principally of Protestants, cannot but mate the other party in time. Also His Majesties care in placing good Bishops, and good Divines; in amplifying the Colledge there, and looking to the education of Wards, and such like; as they are the most natural means, so are they like to be the most effectual and happy, for the weeding out of Popery, without using the temporal sword; so that I think I may truly conclude, that the ripeness of time is not yet come.

Therefore my advice is, in all humbleness, that this hazardous course of proceeding to tender the Oath to the Magistrates of Towns, proceed not, but die by degrees. And yet, to preserve the authority and reputation of the former Councel, I would have somewhat done, which is, that there be a proceeding to seisure of liberties, but not by any act of power, but by *quo Warranto*, or *Scire Facias*, which is a legal course, and will be the work of three or four Termes; by which time the matter will be somewhat coole.

But I would not (in no case) that the proceeding should be with both the Towns which stand now in contempt, but with one of them onely, choosing that which shall be most fit.

For

For, if his Majesty proceed with both, then all the Towns that are in the like case will think it a common Cause, and that it is but their case to day, and their own to morrow. But if his Majesty proceed but with one, the apprehension and terror will not be so strong; for, they may think, it may be their case to be spared, as well as prosecuted. And this is the best advice that I can give to his Majesty, in this streight; and of this opinion seemed my Lord Chancellor to be.

The second Proposition is this; It may be, his Majesty will be moved to reduce the number of his Councel of *Ireland* (which is now almost Fifty) to Twenty, or the like number, in respect that the greatness of the number doth both imbase the Authority of the Councel, and divulge the business. Nevertheless, I hold this Proposition to be rather specious, and solemn, then needfull at this time; for certainly, it will fill the State full of discontentment, which, in a growing and unsetled State, ought not to be. This I could wish, that his Majesty would appoint a select number of Councellors there, which might deal in the improvement of his Revenue (being a thing not to pass through too many hands) and the said selected number should have dayes of sitting by themselves, at which the rest of the Councel should not be present; which being once setled, then other principal business of State may be handled at these sittings; and so the rest begin to be dis-used, and yet retain their countenance, without murmur, or disgrace.

The third Proposition, as it is moved, seemeth to be pretty, if it can keep promise; for it is this, That a means may be found to re-enforce his Majesties Army by Five hundred, or a Thousand men, and that without any penny increase of charge. And the means should be, That there should be a Commandment of a local removing, and transferring some companies from one Province to another, whereupon it is supposed, that many that are planted in House and Lands, will rather lose their entertainment, then remove; and thereby new men may have their pay, yet the old be mingled in the Countrey, for the strength thereof. In this Proposition two things may be feared; the one, discontent of those that shall be put off; the other, that the Companies shall be stuffed with Novices, (*Tirones*) in stead of *Veterani*. I wish therefore, that this Proposition be well debated, before it be admitted. Thus having performed that which Duty binds me to, I commend you to Gods best preservation.

July 5. 1616. *Your most devoted and bounden servant.*

The Copy of a Letter, conceived to be written to the late Duke of Buckingham, *when he first became a Favorite to King* James, *by Sir* Francis Bacon, *afterwards Lord* Verulam, *and Viscount S.* Alban: *Containing some Advices unto the Duke, for his better direction in that eminent place of the Favourite; Drawn from him at the intreaty of the Duke himself, by much importunity.*

Noble Sir,

✻ WHat you requested of me by word, when I last waited on you, you have since renewed by your Letters. Your requests are commands unto me; and yet the matter is of that nature, that I find my self very unable to serve you therein, as you desire. It hath pleased the King to cast an extraordinary eye of favour upon you, and you express your self very desirous to win upon the Judgment of your Master, and not upon his Affections onely. I do very much commend your noble ambition herein; for, Favour so bottomed, is like to be lasting; whereas, if it be built but upon the sandy foundation of personal respects onely, it cannot be long-lived.

Yet in this you have erred, in applying your self to me, the most unworthy of your servants, to give assistance upon so weighty a subject.

You know, I am no Courtier, nor vers'd in State-affairs; my life, hitherto, hath rather been contemplative, then active; I have rather studied Books, then Men; I can but guess, at the most, at these things, in which you desire to be advised: Nevertheless, to shew my obedience, though with the hazard of my discretion, I shall yield unto you.

Sir,

Sir Francis Bacon, *to the Duke of* Buckingham. 4.

Sir, In the first place, I shall be bold to put you in minde of the present condition you are in; you are not only a Courtier, but a Bed-chamber man, and so are in the eye and eare of your Master; but you are also a favourite; The Favourite of the time, and so are in his bosome also; The world hath so voted you, and doth so esteem of you, (for Kings and great Princes, even the wisest of them, have had their friends, their favourites, their Privadoes, in all ages; for they have their affections, as well as other men) of these they make severall uses: sometimes to communicate and debate their thoughts with them, and to ripen their judgements thereby; sometimes to ease their cares by imparting them; and sometimes to interpose them, between themselves and the envie or malice of their people (for Kings cannot erre, that must be discharged upon the shoulders of their Ministers; and they who are neerest unto them must be content to bear the greatest load;) Truly Sir, I do not believe or suspect that you are chosen to this eminency, out of the last of these considerations; for you serve such a Master, who by his wisdome and goodness, is as free from the malice or envie of his Subjects, as, I think I may say truly, ever any King was, who hath sat upon his throne before him: But I am confident, his Majesty hath cast his eyes upon you, as finding you to be such as you should be, or hoping to make you to be such as he would have you to be; for this I may say, without flattery, your out-side promiseth as much as can be expected from a Gentleman: But be it in the one respect, or other, it belongeth to you to take care of your self, and to know well what the name of a Favourite signifies; If you be chosen upon the former respects, you have reason to take care of your actions and deportment, out of your gratitude, for the Kings sake; but if out of the latter, you ought to take the greater care, for your own sake.

You are as a new-risen starre, and the eyes of all men are upon you; let not your own negligence make you fall like a Meteor.

The contemplation then of your present condition must necessarily prepare you for action; what time can be well spar'd from your attendance on your Master will be taken up by suitors, whom you cannot avoid, nor decline, without reproach; for if you do not already, you will soon finde the throng of suitors attend you; for no man, almost, who hath to do with the King will think himself safe, unless you be his good Angel, and guide him, or, at least, that you be not a *Malus Genius* against him; so that, in respect of the King your Master, you must be very wary, that you give him true information; and if the matter concern him in his Government, that you do not flatter him; if you do, you are as great a Traytor to him, in the Court of Heaven, as he that draws his sword against him; and in respect of the suitors which shall attend you, there is nothing will bring you more honour and more ease, then to do them what right in justice you may, and with as much speed as you may; for believe it, Sir, next to the obtaining of the suite, a speedy and a gentle deniall (when the case will not bear it) is the most acceptable to suitors; they will gaine by their dispatch; whereas else they shall spend their time and money in attending; and you will gaine in the ease you will finde in being rid of their importunity. But if they obtaine what they reasonably desired, they will be doubly bound to you for your favour; *Bis dat qui cito dat*, it multiplies the courtesie, to do it with good words, and speedily.

That you may be able to do this with the best advantage, my humble advice is this; when suitors come unto you, set apart a certain hour in a day to give them audience: If the business be light and easie, it may by word only be delivered, and in a word be answered; but if it be either of weight, or of difficulty, direct the suitor to commit it to writing, (if it be not so already) and then direct him to attend for his answer at a set time to be appointed, which would constantly be observed, unless some matter of great moment do interrupt it; when you have received the Petitions (and it will please the Petitioners well, to have access unto you to deliver them into your own hand) let your Secretary first reade them, and draw lines under the material parts thereof (for the matter, for the most part, lies in a narrow room) The Petitions being thus prepared, do you constantly set apart an hour in a day to peruse those Petitions; and after you have ranked them into severall files, according to the subject matter, make choice of two or three friends, whose judgements and fidelities you believe you may trust in a business of that nature, and recommend it to one or more of them, to informe you of their opinions, and of their reasons for or against the granting of it; and if the matter be of great weight indeed, then it would not be amiss to send severall Copies of the same Petition to severall of your friends, the one not knowing what the other doth, and desire them to return their answers to you by a certain time, to be prefixed in writing; so shall you receive an impartiall answer, and by comparing the

G one

one with the other, you shall both discern the abilities and faithfulness of your friends, and be able to give a judgement thereupon, as an Oracle. But by no means trust not to your own judgement alone, for no man is omniscient; nor trust only to your servants, who may mislead you, or mis-informe you; by which they may perhaps gain a few crowns, but the reproach will lie upon your self, if it be not rightly carried.

For the facilitating of your dispatches, my advice is further, that you divide all the Petitions, and the matters therein contained, under severall heads, which, I conceive, may be fitly ranked into these eight sorts.

1. Matters that concern Religion, and the Church and Church-men.
2. Matters concerning Justice, and the Laws, and the professors thereof.
3. Councellors, and the Councell table, and the great offices and officers of the Kingdome.
4. Forreign Negotiations and Embassies.
5. Peace and warr, both forreign and civill, and in that the Navie and Forts, and what belongs to them.
6. Trade at home and abroad.
7. Colonies, or forreign Plantations.
8. The Court, and Curiality.

And whatsoever will not fall naturally under one of these heads, believe me, Sir, will not be worthy of your thoughts, in this capacity we now speak of. And of these sorts, I warrant you, you will finde enough to keep you in businefs.

I begin with the first, which concerns Religion.

1. In the first place, be you your self rightly perswaded and setled in the true Protestant Religion, professed by the Church of *England*; which doubtless is as sound and orthodox in the doctrine thereof, as any Christian Church in the world.

2. In this you need not be a Monitor to your gracious Master the King; the chiefest of his imperiall titles, is, to be *The Defender of the Faith*; and his learning is eminent, not only above other Princes, but above other men; be but his scholar, and you are safe in that.

3. For the Discipline of the Church of *England*, by Bishops, &c. I will not positively say, as some do, that its *Jure Divino*; but this I say, and think, *ex animo*, that it is the neerest to Apostolicall truth; and confidently I shall say, it is fittest for Monarchy, of all others: I will use no other authority to you, then that excellent Proclamation set out by the King himself in the first year of his Reign, and annexed before the Book of Common Prayer, which I desire you to reade; and if at any time there shall be the least motion made for innovation, to put the King in minde to reade it himself: It is most dangerous in a State to give ear to the least alterations in Government.

4. Take heed, I beseech you, that you be not an instrument to countenance the *Romish Catholicks*; I cannot flatter, the world believes that some neer in blood to you are too much of that perswasion; you must use them with fit respects, according to the bonds of nature; but you are of kin, and so a friend to their persons, not to their errours.

5. The Arch-bishops and Bishops, next under the King, have the government of the Church and Ecclesiasticall affaires; be not you the mean to preferre any to those places, for any by-respects; but only for their learning, gravity and worth; their lives and Doctrine ought to be exemplary.

6. For Deanes, and Canons or Prebends of Cathedrall Churches: In their first institution they were of great use in the Church; they were not only to be of Councell with the Bishop for his revenue, but chiefly for his Government in causes Ecclesiasticall; use your best means to preferre such to those places who are fit for that purpose, men eminent for their learning, piety, and discretion, and put the King often in minde thereof; and let them be reduced again to their first institution.

7. You will be often sollicited, and perhaps importuned to preferre Scholars to Church-livings; you may further your friends in that way, *caeteris paribus*; otherwise, remember, I pray, that these are not places meerly of favour, the charge of souls lies upon them; the greatest account whereof will be required at their own hands; but they will share deeply in their faults who are the instruments of their preferment.

8. Besides the Romish Catholicks, there is a generation of Sectaries, the Anabaptists, Brownists, and others, of their kindes, they have been severall times very busie in this Kingdome, under the colour of zeale for reformation of Religion: The King your Master knows their disposition very well; a small touch will put him in mind of them; he had experience of them in *Scotland*, I hope he will beware of them in *England*; a little countenance or connivency sets them on fire.

9. Order

9. Order and decent ceremonies in the Church, are not only comely but commendable; but there must be great care, not to introduce innovations, they will quickly prove scandalous; men are naturally over-prone to suspition; the true Protestant Religion is seated in the golden mean; the enemies unto her, are the extreams on either hand.

10. The persons of Churchmen are to be had in due respect, for their works sake, and protected from scorn; but if a Clergie man be loose and scandalous, he must not be patronized nor wink't at, the example of a few such, corrupt many.

11. Great care must be taken, that the patrimony of the Church be not sacrilegiously diverted to lay uses: his Majesty in his time hath religiously stopped a leak that did much harm, and would else have done more. Be sure, as much as in you lies, stop the like upon all occasions.

12. Colledges and Schools of learning are to be cherished and encouraged, there to breed up a new stock to furnish the Church and Common-wealth, when the old store are transplanted. This kingdome hath in latter ages been famous for good literature; and if preferment shall attend the deservers, there will not want supplies.

Next to Religion, let your care be to promote Justice. By Justice and mercy is the Kings throne established.

1. Let the rule of Justice be the Laws of the Land, an impartiall arbiter between the King and his people, and between one Subject and another: I shall not speak superlatively of them, lest I be suspected of partiality, in regard of my own profession; but this I may truly say, they are second to none in the Christian world.

2. And, as far as it may lie in you, let no Arbitrary power be intruded; the people of this Kingdome love the Laws thereof, and nothing will oblige them more, then a confidence of the free enjoying of them; What the Nobles, upon an occasion, once said in Parliament, *Nolumus leges Angliæ mutari*, is imprinted in the hearts of all the people.

3. But because the life of the Lawes lies in the due execution and administration of them, let your eye be, in the first place, upon the choice of good Judges; These properties had they need to be furnished with; To be learned in their profession, patient in hearing, prudent in governing, powerfull in their elocution to perswade and satisfi eboth the parties and hearers, just in their judgement: and, to sum up all, they must have these three Attributes; They must be men of courage, fearing God, and hating covetousness; An ignorant man cannot, a Coward dares not, be a good Judge.

4. By no means be you perswaded to interpose your self, either by word or letter, in any cause depending, or like to be depending in any Court of justice, nor suffer any other great man to do it where you can hinder it, and by all means disswade the King himself from it, upon the importunity of any for themselves or their friends; If it should prevail, it perverts justice; but if the judge be so just, and of such courage (as he ought to be) as not to be inclined thereby, yet it alwayes leaves a taint of suspition behinde it; Judges must be as chaste as *Cæsars* wife, neither to be, nor to be suspected to be, unjust; and Sir, the honour of the Judges in their judicature, is the Kings honour, whose person they represent.

5. There is great use of the service of the judges in their circuits, which are twice in the year held throughout the Kingdome; the triall of a few causes between party and party, or delivering of the gaols in the severall Counties, are of great use for the expedition of justice; yet they are of much more use for the government of the Counties through which they passe, if that were well thought upon.

6. For if they had instructions to that purpose, they might be the best intelligencers to the King of the true state of his whole Kingdome, of the disposition of the people, of their inclinations, of their intentions and motions, which are necessary to be truly understood.

7. To this end, I could wish, that against every circuit all the judges should, sometimes by the King himself, and sometimes by the Lord Chancellor or Lord Keeper, in the Kings name, receive a charge of those things which the present times did much require; and at their returne should deliver a faithfull account thereof, and how they found and left the Counties through which they passed, and in which they kept their Assises.

8. And that they might the better perform this work, which might be of great importance, it will not be amiss that sometimes this charge be publick, as it useth to be in the Star-Chamber at the end of the Terms next before the circuit begins, where the Kings care of justice, and the good of his people, may be published: and that sometimes also it may be private, to communicate to the judges some things not so fit to be publickly delivered.

9. I could wish also that the judges were directed to make a little longer stay in a place then usually they do; a day more in a County would be a very good addition, (although their

wages for their circuits were increased in proportion) it would stand better with the gravity of their imployment; where-'s now they are sometimes enforced to rise over-early, and to sit over-late, for the dispatch of their business, to the extraordinary trouble of themselves and of the people; their times indeed not being *horæ juridicæ*; And, which is the maine, they would have the more leisure to informe themselves (*quasi aliud agentes*) of the true estate of the Country.

10. The attendance of the Sheriffs of the Counties, accompanied with the principall Gentlemen, in a comely, not a costly equipage, upon the Judges of Assize at their coming to the place of their sitting, and at their going out, is not only a civilitie, but of use also: It raiseth a reverence to the persons and places of the Judges, who coming from the King himself on so great an errand, should not be neglected.

11. If any sue to be made a Judge, for my own part, I should suspect him; but if either directly or indirectly he should bargaine for a place of judicature, let him be rejected with shame; *vendere jure potest, emerat ille prius*.

12. When the place of a chief Judge of a Court becomes vacant, a puisne Judge of that Court, or of another Court who hath approved himself fit and deserving, would be sometimes preferred, it would be a good encouragement for him, and for others, by his example.

13. Next to the Judge, there would be care used in the choice of such as are called to the degree of Serjeants at Law (for such they must be first, before they be made Judges) none should be made Serjeants but such as probably might be held fit to be Judges afterwards, when the experience at the barr hath fitted them for the bench: Therefore by all means cry down that unworthy course of late times used, that they should pay moneys for it: It may satisfie some Courtiers, but it is no honour to the person so preferred, nor to the King, who thus preferres them.

14. For the Kings Councel at the Law, especially his Atturney and Sollicitor generall, I need say nothing; their continuall use for the Kings service, not only for his revenue, but for all the parts of his Government, will put the King, and those who love his service, in mind to make choice of men every way fit and able for that employment; they had need to be learned in their profession, and not ignorant in other things; and to be dexterous in those affairs whereof the dispatch is committed to them.

15. The Kings Atturney of the Court of Wards is in the true quality of the Judges; therefore what hath been observed already of Judges, which are intended principally of the 3 great Courts of Law at *Westminster*, may be applied to the choice of the Atturney of this Court.

16. The like for the Atturney of the Dutchy of *Lancaster*, who partakes of both qualities, partly of a Judge in that Court, and partly of an Atturney generall; for so much as concerns the proper revenue of the Dutchy.

17. I must not forget the Judges of the 4 circuits in the 12 Shires of *Wales*, who although they are not of the first magnitude, nor need be of the degree of the coyse (only the chief Justice of *Chester*, who is one of their number, is so) yet are they considerable in the choice of them, by the same rules as the other Judges are; and they sometimes are, and fitly may be, transplanted into the higher Courts.

18. There are many Courts (as you see) some superior, some provinciall, and some of a lower orb; It were to be wished, and is fit to be so ordered, that every of them keep themselves within their proper spheres. The harmony of Justice is then the sweetest, when there is no jarring about the jurisdiction of the Courts; which me-thinks wisdome cannot much differ upon, their true bounds being for the most part so clearly known.

19. Having said thus much of the Judges, somewhat will be fit to put you in mind concerning the principall Ministers of Justice: and in the first, of the high Sheriffs of the Counties, which have been very ancient in this Kingdome, I am sure before the Conquest: The choice of them I commend to your care, and that at fit times you put the King in minde thereof, That as neer as may be they be such as are fit for those places; for they are of great trust and power; The *posse Comitatus*, the power of the whole County, being legally committed unto him.

20. Therefore it is agreeable with the intention of the Law, that the choice of them should be by the commendation of the great Officers of the Kingdome, and by the advice of the Judges, who are presumed to be well read in the condition of the Gentry of the whole Kingdome: And although the King may do it of himself, yet the old way is the good way.

21. But I utterly condemn the practice of the latter times, which hath lately crept into the Court (at the back staires) That some who are prick'd for Sheriffs, and were fit, should get out of the bill, and others who were neither thought upon, nor worthy to be, should be nominated, and both for money.

22. I

22. I must not omit to put you in mind of the Lords Lieutenants, and deputy Lieutenants, of the Counties: their proper use is for ordering the military affairs, in order to an invasion from abroad, or a rebellion or sedition at home; good choice should be made of them, and prudent instructions given to them, and as little of the Arbitrary power as may be left unto them; and that the Muster-Masters, and other Officers under them, incroach not upon the Subject; that will detract much from the Kings service.

23. The Justices of peace are of great use; Antiently there were Conservators of the peace; these are the same, saving that several Acts of Parliament have altered their denomination, and enlarged their jurisdiction in many particulars: The fitter they are for the peace of the Kingdom, the more heed ought to be taken in the choice of them.

24. But negatively, this I shall be bold to say, that none should be put into either of those Commissions with an eye of favour to their persons, to give them countenance or reputation in the places where they live, but for the Kings service sake; nor any put out for the disfavour of any great man: It hath been too often used, and hath been no good service to the King.

25. A word more, if you please to give me leave, for the true rules of the moderation of Justice on the Kings part. The execution of Justice is committed to his Judges, which seemeth to be the severer part; but the milder part, which is mercy, is wholly left in the Kings immediate hand: And Justice and Mercy are the true supporters of his Royal Throne.

26. If the King shall be wholly intent upon Justice, it may appear with an over-rigid aspect; but if he shall be over remiss and easie, it draweth upon him contempt. Examples of Justice must be made sometimes for terrour to some; Examples of mercy, sometimes, for comfort to others: the one procures fear, and the other love. A King must be both feared and loved, else he is lost.

27. The ordinary Courts of Justice I have spoken of, and of their Judges and judicature; I shall put you in mind of some things, touching the High Court of Parliament in *England*, which is superlative; and therefore it will behove me to speak the more warily thereof.

28. For the Institution of it, it is very antient in this Kingdom: It consisteth of the two Houses, of Peers and Commons, as the Members, and of the Kings Majesty, as the head of that great body; By the Kings authority alone, and by his Writs, they are Assembled, and by him alone are they Prorogued and Dissolved, but each House may Adjourn it self.

29. They being thus Assembled, are more properly a Councel to the King, the great Councel of the Kingdom, to advise his Majesty in those things of weight and difficulty, which concern both the King and People, then a Court.

30. No new Laws can be made, nor old Laws abrogated or altered, but by common consent in Parliament, where Bills are prepared and presented to the two Houses, and then delivered, but nothing is concluded but by the Kings Royal assent; They are but Embryos, 'tis he giveth life unto them.

31. Yet the House of Peers hath a power of Judicature in some cases; properly, to examine, and then to affirm; or if there be cause, to reverse, the judgements which have been given in the Court of Kings Bench, (which is the Court of highest jurisdiction in the Kingdom; for ordinary Judicature) but in these cases it must be done by Writ of Error *in Parliamento*: And thus the rule of their proceedings is not *absoluta potestas*, as in making new Laws (in that conjuncture as before) but *limitata potestas*, according to the known Laws of the land.

32. But the House of Commons have onely power to censure the members of their own House, in point of election or misdemeanors, in or towards that House; and have not, nor ever had power, so much as to administer an oath to prepare a judgement.

33. The true use of Parliaments in this Kingdom is very excellent, and they would be often called, as the affairs of the Kingdom shall require; and continued as long as is necessary, and no longer; for then they be but burthens to the people, by reason of the priviledges justly due to the members of the two Houses and their attendants; which their just rights and priviledges are religiously to be observed and maintained; but if they should be unjustly enlarged beyond their true bounds, they might lessen the just power of the Crown, it borders so neer upon popularity.

34. All this while I have spoken concerning the Common Laws of *England*, generally, and properly so called, because it is most general and common to almost all cases and causes, both civil and criminal: But there is also another Law, which is called the Civil or Ecclesiastical Law, which is confined to some few heads; and that is not to be neglected: and although I am a professor of the Common Law, yet am I so much a lover of truth and of

Learning,

Learning, and of my native Country, that I do heartily perswade that the professors of that Law, called Civilians (being that which now is their guide) should not be discountenanced nor discouraged; else whensoever we shall have ought to do with any forreign King or State, we shall be at a miserable loss, for want of Learned men in that profession.

III. I come now to the consideration of those things which concern Councellors of State, The Council Table, and the great Offices and Officers of the Kingdom, which are those who for the most part furnish out that honourable Board.

1. Of Councellors, here are two sorts: The first, *Consiliarii nati*, (as I may term them) such are the Prince of *Wales*, and others of the Kings Sons (when he hath more,) of these I speak not, for they are naturally born to be Councellors to the King, to learn the art of Governing betimes.

2. But the ordinary sort of Councellors are such as the King, out of a due consideration of their worth and abilities, and withal, of their fidelities to his person and to his Crown, calleth to be of Councel with him, in his ordinary Government. And the Council Table is so called from the place where they ordinarily assemble and sit together; and their oath is the onely ceremony used, to make them such, which is solemnly given unto them, at their first admission: These honourable persons are from thenceforth of that Board and Body: They cannot come until they be thus called, and the King at his pleasure may spare their attendance; and he may dispense with their presence there, which at their own pleasure they may not do.

3. This being the quality of their service, you will easily judge what care the King should use, in his choice of them; It behoveth that they be persons of great trust and fidelity, and also of wisdom and judgment, who shall thus assist in bearing up the Kings Throne; and of known experience in publick affairs.

4. Yet it may not be unfit to call some of young years, to train them up in that trade, and so fit them for those weighty affairs, against the time of greater maturity; and some also for the honour of their persons; But these two sorts not to be tyed to so strict attendance, as the others from whom the present dispatch of business is expected.

5. I could wish that their number might not be so over great, the persons of the Councellors would be the more venerable. And I know that Queen *Elizabeth*, in whose time I had the happiness to be born, and to live many years, was not so much observed, for having a numerous, as a wise, Councel.

6. The duty of a Privy Councellor to a King, I conceive, is, not onely to attend the Councel Board, at the times appointed, and there to consult of what shall be propounded; But also to study those things which may advance the Kings honour and safety, and the good of the Kingdom, and to communicate the same to the King, or to his fellow Councellors, as there shall be occasion. And this, sir, will concern you more then others, by how much you have a larger share in his affections.

7. And one thing I shall be bold to desire you to recommend to his Majesty: That when any new thing shall be propounded to be taken into consideration, that no Councellor should suddenly deliver any positive opinion thereof; it is not so easie with all men to retract their opinions, although there shall be cause for it: But onely to hear it, and at the most but to break it, at first, that it may be the better understood against the next meeting.

8. When any matter of weight hath been debated, and seemeth to be ready for a resolution; I wish it may not be at that sitting concluded (unless the necessity of the time press it) lest upon second cogitations there should be cause to alter, which is not for the gravity and honour of that Board.

9. I wish also that the King would be pleased sometimes to be present at that Board, it addes a Majesty to it: And yet not to be too frequently there, that would render it less esteemed when it is become common; Besides, it may sometimes make the Councellors not to be so free in their debates, in his presence, as they would be in his absence.

10. Besides the giving of Counsel, the Councellors are bound by their duties *ex vi termini*, as well as by their oaths, to keep Councel, therefore are they called *de Privato Consilio Regis, & a secretioribus consiliis Regis*.

11. One thing I adde, in the negative, which is not fit for that Board, the entertaining of private causes, of *meum & tuum*, those should be left to the ordinary course and Courts of Justice.

12. As there is great care to be used, for the Councellors themselves to be chosen, so there is of the Clerks of the Councel also, for the secretting of their Consultations, and me thinks, it were fit that his Majesty be speedily moved, to give a strict charge, and to bind it

Sir Francis Bacon, *to the Duke of* Buckingham. 47

it with a solemn order (if it be not already so done) that no copies of the orders of that Table be delivered out by the Clerks of the Councel, but by the order of the Board; nor any not being a Councellor, or a Clerk of the Councel, or his Clerk, to have access to the Councel Books: and to that purpose, that the servants attending the Clerks of the Councel be bound to secrecy, as well as their Masters.

13. For the great Offices and Officers of the Kingdom, I shall say little; for the most of them are such, as cannot well be severed from the Councellorship; and therefore the same rule is to be observed for both, in the choice of them; In the general, onely, I advise this, let them be set in those places for which they are probably the most fit.

14. But in the quality of the persons, I conceive it will be most convenient, to have some of every sort, (as in the time of Queen *Elizabeth* it was) one Bishop at the least, in respect of questions touching Religion, or Church Government; one or more skilled in the Laws; some for Martial affairs; and some for Forreign affairs: By this mixture, one will help another, in all things that shall there happen to be moved; But if that should fail, it will be a safe way, to consult with some other able persons well versed in that point which is the subject of their Consultation, which yet may be done so warily, as may not discover the main end therein.

IV. In the next place, I shall put you in mind of Forreign Negotiations and Embassies, to or with Forrein Princes or States, wherein I shall be little able to serve you.

1. Onely, I will tell you what was the course in the happy days of Queen *Elizabeth*, whom it will be no dis-reputation to follow: she did vary, according to the nature of the employment, the quality of the persons she employed; which is a good rule to go by.

2. If it were an Embassy of Gratulation or Ceremony (which must not be neglected) choice was made of some noble person, eminent in place, and able in purse, and he would take it as a mark of favour, and discharge it without any great burthen to the Queens Coffers, for his own honours sake.

3. But if it were an Embassy of weight, concerning affairs of State, choice was made of some sad person of known judgement, wisdom and experience, and not of a young man, nor wayed in State matters: nor of a meer formal man, whatsoever his title or outside were.

4. Yet in company of such, some young towardly Noblemen or Gentlemen were usually sent also, as assistants or attendants, according to the quality of the persons; who might be thereby prepared and fitted for the like imployment, by this means, at another turn.

5. In their company were always sent some grave and sad men, skilful in the Civil Laws; and some in the Languages, and some who had been formerly conversant in the Courts of those Princes, and knew their ways; these were assistants in private, but not trusted to manage the affairs in publick; that would detract from the honour of the Principal Embassadour.

6. If the Negotiation were about Merchants affairs, then were the persons employed for the most part Doctors of the Civil Law, assisted with some other discreet men; and in such the charge was ordinarily defrayed, by the Company or Society of Merchants, whom the Negotiation concerned.

7. If Legier Embassadors or Agents were sent to remain in or neer the Courts of those Princes or States (as it was ever held fit, to observe the motions, and to hold correspondency with them, upon all occasions) such were made choice of, as were presumed to be vigilant, industrious, and discreet men, and had the Language of the place whither they were sent; & with these were sent such as were hopeful to be worthy of the like imployment at another time.

8. Their care was, to give true and timely Intelligence of all Occurrences, either to the Queen her self, or the Secretaries of State, unto whom they had their immediate relation.

9. Their charge was alwaies born by the Queen, duely paid out of the Exchequer, in such proportion, as, according to their qualities and places, might give them an honourable subsistence there: But for the reward of their service, they were to expect it upon their return, by some such preferment as might be worthy of them, and yet be little burthen to the Queens Coffers or Revenues.

10. At their going forth, they had their general Instructions in writing, which might be communicated to the Ministers of that State, whither they were sent; and they had also private instructions, upon particular occasions; and at their return, they did always render an account of some things to the Queen her self, of some things to the body of the Councel, and of some others to the Secretaries of State; who made use of them, or communicated them, as there was cause.

11. In those days there was a constant course held, that by the advice of the Secretaries, or some principal Councellors, there were always sent forth, into several parts beyond the

Seas

Seas some young men, of whom good hopes were conceived of their towardliness, to be trained up, and made fit for such publick imployments, and to learn the Languages. This was at the charge of the Queen, which was not much, for they travelled but as private Gentlemen; and as by their industry their deserts did appear, so were they farther imployed or rewarded. This course I shall recommend unto you, to breed up a nursery of such publick Plants.

V. For peace and war, and those things which appertain to either; I in my own disposition and profession am wholly for peace, if please God to bless this Kingdom therewith, as for many years past he hath done: and,

1. I presume I shall not need to perswade you to the advancing of it; nor shall you need to perswade the King your Master therein, for that he hath hitherto been another *Solomon*, in this our *Israel*; and the Motto which he hath chosen (*Beati Pacifici*) shews his own judgement: But he must use the means to preserve it; else such a jewel may be lost.

2. God is the God of peace (it is one of his Attributes) therefore by him alone we must pray, and hope to continue it: there is the foundation.

3. And the King must not neglect the just ways for it; Justice is the best Protector of it at home, and providence for war is the best prevention of it from abroad.

4. Wars are either Forreign or Civil; for the Forreign war by the King upon some Neighbour Nation, I hope we are secure; the King, in his pious and just disposition, is not inclinable thereunto, his Empire is long enough; bounded with the Ocean, as if the very Scituation thereof had taught the King and People to set up their rests, and say, *Ne plus ultra*.

5. And for a war of invasion from abroad; only we must not be over-secure, thats the way to invite it.

6. But if we be alwaies prepared to receive an enemy, if the ambition or malice of any should incite him, we may be very confident we shall long live in peace and quietness, without any attempts upon us.

7. To make the preparations hereunto the more assured: In the first place, I will recommend unto you the care of our out-work, the Navy Royal and Shipping of our Kingdom, which are the walls thereof: and every great Ship is as an impregnable fort; & our many safe & commodious Ports and Havens, in every of these Kingdoms, are as the redoubts to secure them.

8. For the body of the Ships, no nation of the world doth equal *England*, for the Oaken Timber wherewith to build them; and we need not borrow of any other, Iron for Spikes, or Nailes to fasten them together; but there must be a great deal of providence used, that our Ship-Timber be not unnecessarily wasted.

9. But for Tackling, as Sails and Cordage, we are bebolden to our neighbours for them, and do buy them for our money; that must be foreseen and layed up in store against a time of need, and not sought for when we are to use them: But we are much to blame, that we make them not at home, only Pitch and Tar we have not of our own.

10. For the true Art of building of Ships, for burthen and service both, no nation in the world exceeds us: Ship-wrights and all other Artisans belonging to that Trade must be cherished and encouraged.

11. Powder & Ammunition of all sorts we can have at home, and in exchange for other home commodities we may be plentifully supplied from our neighbors, which must not be neglected.

12. With Mariners and Seamen this kingdom is plentifully furnished, the constant Trade of Merchandizing will furnish us, at a need; and navigable rivers will repair the store, both to the Navy Royal, and to the Merchants, if they be set on work, and well payed for their labour.

13. Sea Captains and Commanders and other Officers must be encouraged, and rise by degrees, as their fidelity and industry deserve it.

14. Our strict League of amity and alliance with our neer neighbors the Hollanders is a mutual strength to both; the shipping of both, in conjuncture, being so powerful, by Gods blessing, as no Forreiners will venture upon; This League and friendship must inviolably be observed.

15. From *Scotland* we have had in former times some Alarms, and Inrodes, into the Northern parts of this Kingdom; but that happy union of both Kingdoms under one Soveraign, our gracious King, I hope, hath taken away all occasions of breach between the two nations; let not the cause arise from *England*, and I hope the *Scots* will not adventure it; or if they do, I hope they will find, that although to our King they were his first-born Subjects; yet to *England* belongs the birthright: But this should not be any cause to offer any injury to them, nor to suffer any from them.

16. There remains then no danger, by the blessing of God, but a Civil War, from which God of his mercy defend us, as that which is most desperate of all others. The Kings wisdom and Justice must prevent it, if it may be; or if it should happen, *quod absit*, he must quench that wild-fire, with all the diligence that possibly can be.

17. Com-

17. Competition to the Crown, there is none, nor can be, therefore it must be a fire within the bowels, or nothing, the cures whereof are these, *Remedium præveniens*, which is the best physick, either to a natural body, or to a State, by just and equal Government to take away the occasion; and *Remedium puniens*, if the other prevail not: The service and vigilancy of the Deputy Lieutenants in every County, and of the High Sheriff, will contribute much herein to our security.

18. But if that should not prevail, by a wise and timous Inquisition, the peccant humors and humorists must be discovered, and purged, or cut off; mercy, in such a case, in a King, is true cruelty.

19. Yet if the Heads of the Tribes can be taken off, and the mis-led multitude will see their errour, and return to their obedience, such an extent of mercy is both honourable and profitable.

20. A King, against a storm, must fore-see, to have a convenient stock of treasure; and neither be without money, which is the sinews of war, nor to depend upon the courtesie of others, which may fail at a pinch.

21. He must also have a Magazine of all sorts, which must be had from forreign parts, or provided at home, and to commit them to several places, under the custody of trusty and faithfull Ministers and Officers, if it be possible.

22. He must make choice of expert and able Commanders to conduct and manage the War, either against a forreign invasion, or a home rebellion; which must not be young and giddy, which dare, not onely to fight, but to swear, and drink, and curse, neither fit to govern others, nor able to govern themselves.

23. Let not such be discouraged, if they deserve well, by mis-information, or for the satisfying the humors or ambition of others, perhaps, out of envy, perhaps, out of treachery, or other sinister ends: A steddy hand, in governing of Military affairs, is more requisite then in times of peace, because an error committed in war, may, perhaps, prove irremediable.

24. If God shall bless these endeavours, and the King return to his own house in peace, when a Civil-war shall be at an end, those who have been found faithfull in the Land must be regarded, yea, and rewarded also; the traiterous, or treacherous, who have mis-led others, severely punish'd; and the neutrals, and false-hearted friends & followers, who have started aside like a broken bowe, be noted, *Carbone nigro*; and so I shall leave them, and this part of the work.

VI. I come to the sixth part, which is Trade; and that is either at home, or abroad. And I begin with that which is at home, which enableth the Subjects of the Kingdom to live, and layeth a foundation to a forreign trade by traffique with others, which enableth them to live plentifully and happily.

1. For the home-trade, I first commend unto your consideration the encouragement of tillage, which will enable the Kingdom for corn for the Natives, and to spare for exportation: And I my self have known, more then once, when, in times of dearth, in Queen *Elizabeths* days, it drained much coin of the Kingdom, to furnish us with corn from forreign parts.

2. Good husbands will find the means, by good husbandry, to improve their lands, by Lyme, Chalk, Marl, or Sea-sand, where it can be had: But it will not be amiss, that they be put in mind thereof, and encouraged in their industries.

3. Planting of Orchards, in a soil and air fit for them, is very profitable, as well as pleasureable; Sider and Perry are notable Beverage in Sea-voyages.

4. Gardens are also very profitable, if planted with Artichokes, roots, and such other things as are fit for food; whence they be called Kitchin-gardens, and that very properly.

5. The planting of Hop-yards, sowing of Woad, and Rape-seed, are found very profitable for the Planters, in places apt for them, and consequently profitable for the Kingdom, which for divers years was furnished with them from beyond the seas.

6. The planting and preserving of Woods, especially of Timber, is not onely profitable, but commendable, therewith to furnish posterity, both for building, and shipping.

7. The Kingdom would be much improved, by draining of drowned lands, and gaining that in from the over-flowing of salt waters and the sea, and from fresh waters also.

8. And many of those grounds would be exceeding fit for Dairies, which, being well hous-wived, are exceeding commodious.

9. Much good land might be gained from Forests and Chases, more remote from the Kings access, and from other commonable places, so as always there be a due care taken, that the poor Commoners have no injury by such improvement.

10. The making of navigable Rivers would be very profitable; they would be as so many in-draughts of wealth, by conveying of commodities with ease from place to place.

11. The planting of Hemp and Flax would be an unknown advantage to the Kingdom, many places therein being as apt for it, as any forreign parts.

12. But add hereunto, that it be converted into Linen-cloth, or Cordage, the commodity thereof will be multiplied.

13. So it is of the Wools and Leather of the Kingdom, if they be converted into manufactures.

14. Our *English* Dames are much given to the wearing of costly Laces; and, if they be brought from *Italy*, or *France*, or *Flanders*, they are in great esteem; whereas, if the like Laces were made by the *English*, so much thred as would make a yard of Lace, being put into that manufacture, would be five times, or perhaps, ten, or twenty times the value.

15. The breeding of cattel is of much profit, especially the breed of Horses, in many places, not onely for travel, but for the great saddle; the *English* horse, for strength, and courage, and swiftness together, not being inferiour to the horses of any other Kingdome.

16. The Minerals of the Kingdom, of Lead, Iron, Copper, and Tynn, especially, are of great value, and set many able-bodied subjects on work; it were great pity they should not be industriously followed.

17. But of all Minerals, there is none like to that of Fishing, upon the coasts of these Kingdoms, and the seas belonging to them: our neighbours, within half a dayes sail of us, with a good wind, can shew us the use and value thereof; and, doubtless, there is sea-room enough for both Nations, without offending one another; and it would exceedingly support the Navie.

18. This Realm is much enriched, of late years, by the trade of Merchandize which the *English* drive in foreign parts; and, if it be wisely managed, it must of necessity very much increase the wealth thereof; care being taken, that the exportation exceed in value the importation, for then the ballance of trade must of necessity be returned in Coin, or Bullion

19. This would easily be effected, if the Merchants were perswaded, or compelled, to make their returns in solid commodities, and not too much thereof in vanity, tending to excess.

20. But especially care must be taken, that Monopolies, which are the Cankers of all trading, be not admitted, under specious colours of publick good.

21. To put all these into a regulation, if a constant Commission, to men of honesty and understanding, were granted, and well pursued, to give order for the managing of these things, both at home and abroad, to the best advantage; and that this Commission were subordinate to the Councel-board; it is conceived, it would produce notable effects.

VII. The next thing is that of Colonies and forreign Plantations, which are very necessary, as out-lets, to a populous Nation, and may be profitable also, if they be managed in a discreet way.

1. First, in the choice of the place, which requireth many circumstances; as, the scituation, neer the sea, for the commodiousness of an intercourse with *England*; the temper of the air and climate, as may best agree with the bodies of the *English*, rather inclining to cold, then heat; that it be stored with Woods, Mines, and Fruits, which are naturally in the place; that the soil be such as will probably be fruitful for Corn, and other conveniencies, and for breeding of cattel; that it hath Rivers, both for passage between place and place, and for fishing also, if it may be; that the Natives be not so many, but that there may be elbow-room enough for them, and for the Adventures also: All which are likely to be found in the *West-Indies*.

2. It would be also such as is not already planted by the Subjects of any Christian Prince, or State, nor over-neerly neighbouring to their Plantation. And it would be more convenient, to be chosen by some of those Gentlemen or Merchants which move first in the work, then to be designed unto them from the King; for it must proceed from the option of the people, else it founds like an exile; so the Colonies must be raised by the leave of the King, and not by his Command.

3. After the place is made choice of, the first step must be, to make choice of a fit Governor, who, although he have not the name, yet he must have the power of a *Vice-Roy*; and if the person who principally moved in the work be not fit for that trust, yet he must not be excluded from command; but then his defect in the Governing part must be supplied by such Assistants as shall be joyned with him, or as he shall very well approve of.

4. As at their setting out they must have their Commission, or Letters Patents from the King, that so they may acknowledge their dependency upon the Crown of *England*, and under his protection; so they must receive some general instructions, how to dispose of themselves, when they come there; which must be in nature of Laws unto them.

5. But the general Law, by which they must be guided and governed, must be the Common Law of *England*; and to that end, it will be fit, that some man, reasonably studied in the Law, and otherwise qualified for such a purpose, be perswaded (if not thereunto inclined of himself, which were the best) to go thither as a Chancellor amongst them, at first; and when the Plantation were more setled, then to have Courts of Justice there, as in *England*.

6. At the first planting, or as soon after as they can, they must make themselves defensible both against the Natives, and against strangers; and to that purpose, they must have the assistance

sistance of some able military man, and convenient Arms and Ammunition for their defence.

7. For the Discipline of the Church in those parts, it will be necessary, that it agree with that which is setled in *England*; else it will make a schism, and a rent, in Christs coat, which must be seamless; and, to that purpose, it will be fit, that by the Kings supreme power in Causes Ecclesiastical, within all his Dominions, they be subordinate under some Bishop and Bishoprick of this Realm.

8. For the better defence against a common Enemy, I think it would be best, that forreign Plantations should be placed in one Continent, and neer together; whereas, if they be too remote the one from the other, they will be dis-united, and so the weaker.

9. They must provide themselves of houses, such as, for the present, they can, and, at more leisure, such as may be better; and they first must plant for corn and cattel, &c. for food, and necessary sustenance; and after, they may enlarge themselves for those things which may be for profit and pleasure, and to traffique withall also.

10. Woods for shipping, in the first place, may doubtless be there had, and minerals there found, perhaps, of the richest; howsoever, the mines out of the fruits of the earth, and seas, and waters adjoyning, may be found in abundance.

11. In a short time they may build Vessels and Ships also, for traffique with the parts neer adjoyning, and with *England* also, from whence they may be furnished with such things as they may want, and, in exchange or barter, send from thence other things, with which quickly, either by Nature, or Art, they may abound.

12. But these things would, by all means, be prevented; That no known Bankrupt, for shelter; nor known murderer, or other wicked person, to avoid the Law; nor known Heretick, or Schismatick, be suffered to go into those Countreys; or, if they do creep in there, not to be harboured, or continued: else, the place would receive them naught, and return them into *England*, upon all occasions, worse.

13. That no Merchant, under colour of driving a trade thither, or from thence, be suffered to work upon their necessities.

14. And that to regulate all these inconveniences, which will insensibly grow upon them, that the King be pleased to erect a subordinate Councel in *England*, whose care and charge shall be, to advise, and put in execution, all things which shall be found fit for the good of those new Plantations; who, upon all occasions, shall give an account of their proceedings to the King, or to the Councel-board, and from them receive such directions as may best agree with the Government of that place.

15. That the Kings reasonable profit be not neglected, partly, upon reservation of moderate rents and services; and, partly, upon Customes; and, partly, upon importation and exportation of Merchandize: which, for a convenient time after the Plantation begin, would be very easie, to encourage the work; but, after it is well setled, may be raised to a considerable proportion, worthy the acceptation.

VIII. I come to the last of those things which I propounded, which is, the Court, and Curiality.

The other did properly concern the King, in his Royal capacity, as *Pater patriæ*; this more properly, as *Pater familias*: And herein,

1. I shall, in a word, and but in a word onely, put you in mind, That the King in his own person, both in respect of his Houshold, or Court, and in respect of his whole Kingdom, (for a little Kingdom is but as a great Houshold, and a great Houshold, as a little Kingdom) must be exemplary, *Regis ad exemplum, &c.* But for this, God be praised, our charge is easie; for your gracious Master, for his Learning and Piety, Justice and Bounty, may be, and is, not onely a president to his own subjects, but to forreign Princes also; yet he is still but a man, and seasonable *Memento's* may be useful; and, being discreetly used, cannot but take well with him.

2. But your greatest care must be, that the great men of his Court (for you must give me leave to be plain with you, for so is your injunction laid upon me) your self in the first place, who is first in the eye of all men, give no just cause of scandal, either by light, or vain, or by oppressive carriage.

3. The great Officers of the Kings Houshold had need be both discreet and provident persons, both for his Honour, and for his Thrift; they must look both ways, else they are but half-sighted: Yet in the choice of them, there is more latitude left to affection, then in the choice of Councellors, and of the great Officers of State, before touched, which must always be made choice of meerly out of judgment, for in them the publick hath a great interest.

4. For the other ministerial Officers in Court (as, for distinction sake, they may be termed) there must be also an eye unto them, and upon them; they have usually risen in the Houshold

by degrees, and it is a noble way, to encourage faithfull service: But the King must not bind himself to a necessity herein, for then it will be held *ex debito*; neither must he alter it, without an apparent cause for it: but to displace any who are in, upon displeasure, which for the most part happeneth upon the information of some great man, is, by all means, to be avoided, unless there be a manifest cause for it.

5. In these things you may sometimes interpose, to do just and good offices; but for the general, I should rather advise, meddle little, but leave the ordering of those Houshold affairs to the White-staffs, which are those honourable persons, to whom it properly belongeth, to be answerable to the King for it; and to those other Officers of the Green-cloth, who are subordinate to them, as a kind of Council, and a Court of Justice also.

6. Yet for the Green-cloth Law, (take it in the largest sence) I have no opinion of it, further then it is regulated by the just Rules of the Common-Laws of *England*.

7. Towards the support of his Majesties own Table, and of the Princes, and of his necessary Officers, his Majesty hath a good help by purveyance, which justly is due unto him; and, if justly used, is no great burthen to the subject; but by the Purveyors, and other under Officers, is many times abused. In many parts of the Kingdome, I think, it is already reduced to a certainty in money; and if it be indifferently and discreetly managed, it would be no hard matter to settle it so throughout the whole Kingdom; yet to be renewed from time to time, for that will be the best, and safest, both for the King, and People.

8. The King must be put in mind, to preserve the Revenues of his Crown, both certain, and casual, without diminution, and to lay up treasure in store against a time of extremity; empty coffers give an ill sound, and make the people many times forget their Duty, thinking that the King must be beholden to them for his supplies.

9. I shall by no means think it fit, that he reward any of his servants with the benefit of forfeitures, either by Fines in the Court of Star-Chamber, or High Commission Courts, or other Courts of Justice, or that they should be farmed out, or bestowed upon any, so much as by promise, before judgment given; it would neither be profitable, nor honourable.

10. Besides matters of serious consideration, in the Courts of Princes, there must be times for pastimes and disports: When there is a Queen, and Ladies of Honour attending her, there must sometimes be Masques, and Revels, and Enterludes; and when there is no Queen, or Princess, as now, yet at Festivals, and for entertainment of Strangers, or upon such occasions, they may be fit also: Yet care would be taken, that, in such cases, they be set off more with wit and activity, then with costly and wastefull expences.

11. But for the King and Prince, and the Lords and Chivalry of the Court, I rather commend, in their turns and seasons, the riding of the great Horse, the Tilts, the Barriers, Tennis, and Hunting, which are more for the health and strength of those who exercise them, then in an effeminate way to please themselves and others.

And now the Prince groweth up fast to be a man, and is of a sweet and excellent disposition; it would be an irreparable stain and dishonour upon you, having that access unto him, if you should mis-lead him, or suffer him to be mis led by any loose or flattering Parasites: The whole Kingdom hath a deep interest in his virtuous education; and if you, keeping that distance which is fit, do humbly interpose your self, in such a case, he will one day give you thanks for it.

12. Yet Dice and Cards may sometimes be used for recreation, when field-sports cannot be had; but not to use it as a mean to spend the time, much less to mis-spend the thrift of the Gamesters.

SIR, I shall trouble you no longer; I have run over these things as I first propounded them; please you to make use of them, or any of them, as you shall see occasion; or to lay them by, as you think best, and to add to them, as you daily may, out of your experience.

I must be bold, again, to put you in mind of your present condition; you are in the quality of a Sentinel; if you sleep, or neglect your charge, you are an undone man, and you may fall much faster then you have risen.

I have but one thing more to mind you of, which neerly concerns your self; you serve a great and gracious Master, and there is a most hopefull young Prince, whom you must not desert; it behoves you to carry your self wisely and evenly between them both: adore not so the rising Son, that you forget the Father, who raised you to this height; nor be you so obsequious to the Father, that you give just cause to the Son, to suspect that you neglect him: But carry your self with that judgment, as, if it be possible, may please and content them both, which, truly, I believe, will be no hard matter for you to do; so may you live long beloved of both, which is the hearty prayer of

Your most obliged and devoted servant.

Sir

Sir Francis Bacon's *Considerations*, touching the *Queens service* in Ireland.

The Reduction of the Countrey as well to Civility and Justice, as to Obedience and Peace, which things as the affairs now stand I hold to be inseparable, consisteth in four points.
1. The extinguishing of the Reliques of War.
2. The Recovery of the hearts of the People.
3. The removing of the root and occasions of new troubles.
4. Plantation and buildings.

For the first, concerning the places, times and particularities of further prosecution in fact, I leave it to the opinion of men of War, onely the difficulty is to distinguish and discern the propositions which shall be according to the ends of the State here, that is, fin I and summary towards the extirpation of the troubles from those, which though they pretend the publick ends, yet may referr indeed to the more private and compendious ends of the Councel there, or other particular Governours or Captains. But still, as I touched in my letter, I do think much letting blood, in *declinatione morbi*, is against method of cure, and that it will but exasperate necessity and despair, and perchance discover the hollowness of that which is done already, which none blazeth to the best shew: For *Tailles* and proscription of two or three of the principal Rebels, they are, no doubt *jure Gentium* lawful, in *Italy* usually practised upon the *Banditti*, best in season when a side goeth down, and may do good in two kinds; the one, if it take effect, the other, in the distrust which followeth amongst the Rebels themselves. But of all other points (to my understanding) the most effectual is, the well expressing or impressing of the design of this State upon that miserable and desolate kingdom, containing the same between these two lists or bound ries. The one, that the Queen seeketh not an extirpation of the people, but a reduction; and now that she hath chastised them by Royal power and Arms, according to the necessity of the occasion, her Majesty taketh no pleasure in effusion of blood, or displanting of ancient generations; the other, that her Majesties Princely care is principally and intention lly bent upon that action of *Ireland*; and that she seeketh not so much the ease of charge, as the Royal performance of her office of Protection, and reclaim of those her Subjects: And in a word, that the case is allowed as far as may stand with the honour of the time past, which it is easie to reconcile, as in my last note I shewed. And again I do repeat, that if her Majesties design be, *ex professo*, to reduce wild and barbarous people to civility and Justice, as well as to reduce Rebels to obedience, it maketh weakness true Christianity, and conditions turn graces, and so hath a fineness in turning utility upon point of honor of these times. And besids, if her Majesty shall suddenly abate the lists of her Forces, and shall do nothing to countervail it in the point of reputation of a publick proceeding, I doubt things may too soon fall back in o the state they were in. Next to this, adding reputation to the cause, by imprinting an opinion of her Majesties care and intention upon this action, is the taking away the reputation from the contrary side, by cutting off the opinion and expectation of forreign succours: to which purpose, this enterprize of *Algiers*, if it hold according to the advertisement, and if it be not wrapped up in the period of this Summer, seemeth to be an opportunity *Cœlitus demissa*. And to the same purpose, nothing can be more fit then a Treaty, or a shadow of a Treaty of a Peace with *Spain*; which, methinks, should be in our power to fasten, at least *rumore tenus*, to the deluding of as wise a people as the *Irish*. Lastly, for this point, that the Ancients called *potestas facta redeundi ad sanitatem*, and which is but a mockery, when the Enemy is strong or proud, but effectual in his declination; that is, a liberal Proclamation of grace and pardon to such as shall submit and come in within a time prefixed, and of some further reward to such as shall bring others in, that ones sword may be sharpned against anothers, as a matter of good experience, and now, I think, will come in time. And perchance, though I wish the exclusions of such a Pardon exceeding few, yet it will not be safe to continue some of them in their strength, but to transfer te them and their generation into *England*, and give them recompence and satisfaction here, for their possessions there, as the King of *Spain* did by divers families of *Portugal*. The effecting of all the which fall within the points aforesaid, and likewise those which fall within the divisions following: Nothing can be, in priority, either of time, or matter, precedent to the sending of some Commission of the continuance *ad res inspiciendas & componendas*. For it must be a very significant demonstration of her Majesties care of that Kingdom, a credence to any that shall come in and submit, a bridle to any that have their fortunes there, and shall apply their Propositions to private ends, and

Considerations touching the Queens service in Ireland.

an evidence of her Majesties politick courses without neglect or respiration, and it hath been the wisdom of the best examples of Government. Towards the recovery of the hearts of the people, there be but three things *in natura rerum*.

1. Religion. 2. Justice and Protection. 3. Obligation and reward. For Religion, to speak first of piety, and then of Policie. All Divines do agree, that if Consciences be to be inforced at all wherein they differ, yet two things must precede their inforcement; th'one, means of information; th'other, time of operation: Neither of which they have yet had. Besides, till they be more like reasonable men then they yet are, their society were rather scandalous to true Religion then otherwise, as pearl cast before swine: For till they be cleansed from their blood, incontinency, and theft, and which are now not the lapses of particular persons, but the very laws of the Nation, they are incompatible with Religion formed with Policie. There is no doubt but to wrestle with them now is directly opposite to their reclaim, and cannot but continue their alienation of mind from this government. Besides, one of the principal pretences whereby the heads of the Rebellion have prevailed both with the people and the Forreigner, hath been the defence of the Catholick Religion; and it is that likewise hath made the Forreigner reciprocally more plausible with the Rebel. Therefore a Toleration of Religion for a time not definite, except it be in some principal Towns and Precincts, after the manner of some French Edicts, seemeth to me to be a matter warrantable by Religion, and in Policie of absolute necessity; and the hesitation of this, I think, hath been a great casting back of the affairs there. Neither if any English Papist or Recusant shall for liberty of his conscience transfer his person, family and fortunes thither, do I hold it a matter of danger, but expedient to draw on undertaking, and to further population. Neither if *Rome* will cozen it self by conceiving it may be some degree to the like Toleration in *England*, do I hold it a matter of any moment, but rather a good mean to take off the fierceness and eagerness of the humour of *Rome*, and to stay further Excommunications and Interjections of *Ireland*. But there would go hand in hand with this some course of advantage. Religion indeed, where the people is capable of it, is the sending over of some good Preachers, especially of that sort which are vehement and zealous perswaders, and not Scholastical, to be resident in the principal Towns, endowing them with some stipend out of her Majesties revenues, as her Majesty hath most religiously and graciously done in *Lancashire*; and the recontinuing and replenishing the Colledge begun at *Dublin*, the placing of good men Bishops in the See there; the taking care of the versions of Bibles, Catechisms, and other books of Instruction, into the Irish language, and the like religious courses, both for the honour of God, and for the avoiding of scandal and insatisfaction here, by a toleration of Religion there. For instance, the Barbarism and desolation of the Country considered, it is not possible they should find any sweetness at all of it, (which hath been the error of times past) formal and fetched far off from the State, because it will require running up and down for process of polling and exactions by fees, and many other delays and charges: And therefore there must be an interim in which the Justice must be only summary, the rather because it is fit and safe for a time the Country do participate of Martial government. And therefore I do wish in every principal Town or place of habitation there were a Captain or a Governour, and a Judge, such as Recorders and learned Stewards are here in Corporations, who may have a Prerogative-Commission to hear and determine *secundum sanam discretionem*, and as near as may be to the Laws and Customs of *England*, and that by Bill or Plaint without Original Writ, reserving from their sentence matter of Freehold and Inheritance to be determined before a superior Judge itinerant, to be reversed if cause be, before the Councel of the Province to be established with fit Informations.

For obligation and reward, it is true, no doubt, which was anciently said, That a State is contained in two words, *Præmium & Pœna*: And I am perswaded, if a penny in the pound which hath been spent *in pœna*, a chastisement of Rebels, without other fruit or emolument of this State, had been spent *in præmio*, that in rewarding, things had never grown to this extremity. But to speak forwards: The keeping of the principal Irish persons in terms of contentment, and without particular complaint, as generally the carrying of an eaven course between the English and the Irish, whether it be in competition, or whether it be in controversie, as if they were one Nation, without the same partial course which hath been held by the Governours and Councellours, that some have favoured the Irish, and some contrary, is one of the best medicines for that State. And as for other points of governing their Nobility as well in this Court as there, of Knighthood, of Education of their Children, and the like points of comfort and allurement, they are things which fall into every mans consideration.

For

Sir Francis Bacon, to the Earl of Northumberland.

For the extirpating of the seeds of troubles, I suppose the main roots are but three : The first, the ambition and absoluteness of the chief of the Families and Setts; the second, the licentious idleness of their Kerns and Souldiers that lie upon their Countrey by seffes and such oppressions; the third, the barbarous customs in habits of apparel, in these Poets or Heralds that enchant them in savage manners, and sundry other such dreggs of Barbarism and Rebellion, which by a number of politique Statutes of *Ireland*, meet to be put in execution, are already forbidden, unto which such additions may be made as the present time requireth. But the reducing of this branch requireth a more particular notice of the State and manners there then falls within my compass.

For Plantations and buildings, I do find it strange, that in the last plot for the population of *Munster*, there were limitations how much in Demesnes, and how much in Farm and Tennantry, how many buildings should be erected, how many *Irish* in mixture should be admitted; but there was no restraint that they might not build *sparsim* at their pleasure, much less any condition that they should make places fortified and defensible, the which was too much secureness, to my understanding. So as for this last point of plantations and buildings, there be two considerations which I hold most material; the one of quickning, the other for assuring: The first is, that choyce be made of such persons for the government of Towns and places, and such undertakers be procured as be men gracious and wel-beloved, and are like to be well followed; wherein for *Munster* it may be, because it is not *Res integra*, but that the former undertakers stand interessed there, will be some difficulty; but surely (in mine opinion) either with agreeing with them, or by over-ruling them by a Parliament in *Ireland* (which in this course of a politique proceeding, infinite occasions will require speedily to be held) it will be fit to supply fit qualified persons for undertakers. The other, that it be not left, as heretofore, to the pleasure of the undertakers and adventurers, where and how to build and plant, but that they do it according to a prescript or formality. For first, the places both Maritime and Inland, which are fittest for Colonies or Garrison, as well for doubt of Forreigners, as for keeping the Countrey in bridle, would be found surveighed and resolved upon; and then that the Patentees be tyed to build those places only, and to fortifie as shall be thought convenient. And lastly, it followeth of course in Countreys of new populations, to invite and provoke inhabitants by ample liberties and Charters.

FR. BACON.

The Reader is to take notice, That these Considerations referr to the Letter written by Sir Francis Bacon *to Sir* Robert Cecil, *after the defeat of the* Spaniards *in* Ireland, *in fol.26.of this Cabala.*

Sir Francis Bacon, to the Earl of Northumberland.

It may please your Lordship,

I Would not have lost this journey, and yet I have not that I went for: For I have had no private conference to purpose with the King, no more hath almost any other *English*; for the speech his Majesty admitteth with some Noblemen, is rather matter of grace then matter of business: with the Attorney he spake, urged by the Treasurer of *Scotland*, but no more then needs must. After I had received his Majesties first welcome, and was promised private access, yet not knowing what matter of service your Lordships Letter carried, for I saw it not, and knowing that primeness in advertifement is much, I chose rather to deliver it to Sir *Thomas Hoskins*, then to let it cool in my hands, upon expectation of access: Your Lordship shall find a Prince the furthest from vain-glory that may be, and rather like a Prince of the ancient form then of the latter time; his speeches swift and cursory, and in the full Dialect of his Nation, and in speech of business short, in speech of discourse large: he affecteth popularity by gracing them that are popular, and not by any fashons of his own; he is thought somewhat general in his favours; and his vertue of access is rather because he is much abroad, and in press, then that he giveth easie audience: he hasteneth to a mixture of both Kingdoms and Nations, faster perhaps then policy will well bear. I told your Lordship once before my opinion, that methought his Majesty rather asked councel of the time past, then of the time to come. But it is yet early to ground any setled opinion. For other particularities I refer to conference, having in these generals gone further in these tender arguments then I would have done, were not the bearer hereof so assured. So I continue your, &c,

FR. BACON.

A Discourse touching Helps for the Intellectual Powers, by Sir Francis Bacon.

I Did ever hold it for an insolent and unluckie saying, *Faber quisque fortunas suas*, except it be uttered onely as an hortative, or spur, to correct sloth: For otherwise, if it be believed as it soundeth, and that a man entreth into an high imagination that he can compass and fathom all Accidents, and ascribeth all successes to his drifts and reaches, and the contrary to his errours and sleepings; it is commonly seen, that the evening fortune of that man is not so prosperous, as of him that, without slacking of his industry, attributeth much to felicity and Providence above him, But if the sentence were turned to this, *Faber quisque ingenii sui*, it were somewhat more true, and much more profitable: Because it would teach men to bend themselves to reform those imperfections in themselves which now they seek but to cover, and to attain those vertues and good parts which now they seek but to have onely in shew and demonstration. Yet, notwithstanding, every man attempteth to be of the first Trade of Carpenters, and few bind themselves to the second; whereas, nevertheless, the rising in fortune seldom amendeth the mind; but, on the other side, the removing of the stones and impediments of the mind, doth often clear the passage and current to a mans fortune. But certain it is, whether it be believed or no, that as the most excellent of metals, Gold, is of all others the most pliant, and most enduring to be wrought; so of all living and breathing substances, the perfectest, Man, is the most susceptible of help, improvement, impression, and alteration; and not onely in his Body, but in his Mind and Spirit; and there again, not onely in his Appetite and Affection, but in his powers of Wit and Reason.

For, as to the Body of Man, we find many and strange experiences, how Nature is overwrought by custom, even in actions that seem of most difficulty, and least possible. As first, in voluntary motion, which, though it be termed voluntary, yet the highest degrees of it are not voluntary; for it is in my power and will to run, but to run faster then according to my lightness, or disposition of body, is not in my power nor will. We see the industry and practice of Tumblers and *Funambulo's*, what effects of great wonder it bringeth the Body of man unto. So for suffering of pain, and dolour, which is thought so contrary to the nature of man, there is much example of Penances, in strict Orders of Superstition, what they do endure; such as may well verifie the report of the *Spartan* Boys, which were wont to be scourged upon the Altar so bitterly, as sometimes they died of it, and yet were never heard to complain. And to pass to those faculties which are reckoned more involuntary, as long fasting and abstinency, and the contrary extreme, voracity; the leaving and forbearing the use of drink for altogether, the enduring vehement cold, and the like; there have not wanted, neither do want, divers examples of strange victories over the body, in every of these. Nay, in respiration, the proof hath been of some, who by continual use of diving and working under the water, have brought themselves to be able to hold their Breath an incredible time; and others, that have been able, without suffocation, to endure the stifling breath of an Oven or Furnace, so heated, as though it did not scald nor burn, yet it was many degrees too hot for any man, not made to it, to breathe or take in: And some Impostors and Counterfeits, likewise, have been able to wreathe and cast their bodies into strange forms and motions; yea, and others to bring themselves into Trances and Astonishments. All which Examples do demonstrate, how variously, and to how high points and degrees the Body of Man may be (as it were) molded and wrought. And if any man conceive, that it is some secret propriety of nature that hath been in those persons which have attained to those points, and that it is not open for every man to do the like, though he had been put to it; for which cause such things come but very rarely to pass: It is true, no doubt, that some persons are apter then others; but so, as the more aptness causeth perfection, but the less aptness doth not disable: So that, for example, the more apt child that is taken to be made a *Funambulo* will prove more excellent in his feats; but the less apt will be *Gregarius Funambulo* also. And there is small question, but that these abilities would have been more common; and others of like sort, not attempted, would likewise have been brought upon the Stage, but for two Reasons: The one, because of mens diffidence, in prejudging them as impossibilities; for it holdeth, in these things, which the Poet saith, *Possunt, quia posse videntur*; for no man shall know how much may be done, except he believe much may be done: The other Reason is, Because they be but practices base and inglorious, and of no

great

great use, and therefore sequestred from reward of value; and, on the other side, painfull, so as the recompence balanceth not with the travel and suffering.

And as to the Will of man, it is that which is most manageable and obedient, as that which admitteth most Medicines to cure and alter it. The most sovereign of all is Religion, which is able to change and transform it in the deepest and most inward inclinations and motions. And next to this, Opinion and Apprehension, whether it be infused by Tradition and Institution, or wrought in by Disputation and Perswasion. And the third is Example, which transforms the Will of man into the similitude of that which is most obversant and familiar towards it. And the fourth is, when one affection is healed and corrected by another: As when Cowardise is remedied by shame and dishonour; or sluggishness and backwardness by indignation and emulation; and so of the like. And lastly, when all these means, or any of them, have new framed or formed humane Will, then doth Custom and Habit corroborate and confirm all the rest, Therefore it is no marvel, though this faculty of the mind, (of Will and Election) which inclineth Affection and Appetite, being but the inceptions and rudiments of Will, may be so well governed and managed, Because it admitteth access to so divers Remedies to be applied to it, and to work upon it. The effects whereof are so many, and so known, as require no enumeration: But, generally, they do issue, as Medicines do, into kinds of cures; whereof the one is a just or true Cure, and the other is called Palliation: For either the labour and intention is, to reform the Affections really and truly, restraining them, if they be too violent, and raising them, if they be too soft and weak; or else it is to cover them, or, if occasion be, to pretend them, and represent them. Of the former sort whereof, the Examples are plentifull in the Schools of Philosophers, and in all other Institutions of Moral Vertue: And of the other sort, the Examples are more plentifull in the Courts of Princes, and in all Politick Traffick; where it is ordinary to find, not onely profound dissimulations, and suffocating the Affections, that no note or mark appear of them outwardly, but also lively simulations, and affectations, carrying the tokens of Passions which are not; as *Risus jussus*, and *Lachrymæ coactæ*, and the like.

Of Helps of the Intellectual Powers.

The Intellectual Powers have fewer means to work upon them, then the Will, or Body of Man: But the one that prevaileth, that is exercise, worketh more forcibly in them then in the rest.

The ancient habit of the Philosophers; *Si quis quærat, in utramque partem, de omni Scibili.*   *These that follow, are but indigested Notes.*
  The Exercise of Scholars, making Verses *ex tempore*;
     Stans pede in uno.
  The Exercise of Lawyers, in Memory Narrative.
  The Exercise of Sophists, and *Jo. ad oppositum*, with manifest effect.
  Artificial Memory greatly holpen by Exercise.
  The Exercise of Buffons, to draw all things to conceits ridiculous.
  The Means that help the Understanding, and Faculties thereof, are not Example, (as in the Will, by Conversation; and here, the conceit of Imitation, already digested; with the confutation, *Obiter, si videbitur*, of *Tullies* Opinion, advising a man to take some one to imitate. Similitude of faces analalysed.)
  Arts, Logick, Rhetorick; The Ancients, *Aristotle, Plato, Thastetus, Gorgias, Livigiosus, vel Sophista, Protagoras, Aristotle, Schola sua.* Topicks, *Elenchs.* Rhetoricks, *Organon, Cicero, Hermogenes.*
  The Neotericks, *Ramus, Agricola. Nil sacri Lullius.* His *Typocosmia.*, Studying *Coopers* Dictionary; *Matthews* Collections of proper Words for Metaphors; *Agrippa, de vanitate, &c.*
  Quær. if not here, of Imitation.
  Collections preparative. *Aristotles* similitude of a Shoo-makers shop, full of shooes of all sorts: *Demosthenes Exordia Concionum: Tullies* Precept of Theses of all sorts preparative.
  The relying upon Exercise, with the difference of using and tempering the Instrument: And the similitude of prescribing against the Laws of Nature, and of Estate.

Five

Five Points.

I. That Exercises are to be framed to the life; that is to say, to work Ability in that kind, whereof a man, in the course of Action, shall have most use.

II. The indirect and oblique Exercises which do, *per partes,* and *per consequentiam,* enable these Faculties, which, perhaps, direct Exercise, at first, would but distort: And these have chiefly place where the Faculty is weak, not *per se,* but *per accidens.* As if want of Memory grow through Lightness of Wit, and want of stayed Attention; then the Mathematicks, or the Law, helpeth, Because they are things, wherein if the mind once roam, it cannot recover.

III. Of the advantages of Exercise; as, to dance with heavy shooes, to march with heavy Armour and carriage; and the contrary advantage, (in natures very dull, and unapt) of working alacrity, by framing an Exercise with some delight or affection;

——— *Veluti pueris dant crustula blandi*
Doctores, elementa velint ut discere prima.

IV. Of the Cautions of Exercise; as, to beware, lest by evil doing (as all beginners do weakly) a man grow not, and be inveterate, in an ill Habit, and so take not the advantage of custom in perfection, but in confirming ill.   Slubbering on the Lute.

V. The marshalling and sequel of Sciences and Practices: Logick, and Rhetorick, should be used to be read after Poesie, History, and Philosophy: First, exercise to do things well and clean; after, promptly and readily.

The Exercises in the Universities and Schools, are of Memory and Invention; either to speak by heart that which is set down *verbatim,* or to speak *ex tempore*; whereas there is little use, in Action, of either of both. But most things which we utter, are neither verbally premeditate, nor meerly extemporal; therefore exercise would be framed to take a little breathing, and to consider of Heads, and then to fit and form the Speech *ex tempore.* This would be done in two manners; both with writing in tables, and without: For in most actions, it is permitted, and passable, to use the Note; whereunto if a man be not accustomed, it will put him out.

There is no use of a Narrative Memory in Academies, *viz.* with circumstances of Times, Persons, and Places, and with Names; and it is one Art, to discourse, and another, to relate and describe; and herein, use and action is most conversant.

Also, to sum up, and contract, is a thing in action of very general use.

Sir

Sir Francis Bacon *to the King.*

May it please your most excellent Majesty,

IN the midst of my misery, which is rather asswaged by remembrance, then by hope, my chiefest worldly comfort is, to think, that since the time I had the first vote of the lower House of Parliament for Commissioner of the Union; untill the time that I was this Parliament chosen by both Houses, for their Messenger to your Majesty in the Petition of Religion, (which two, were my first and last services) I was evermore so happy, as to have my poor services graciously accepted by your Majesty, and likewise, not to have had any of them miscarry in my hands. Neither of which points I can any wayes take to my self, but ascribe the former to your Majesties goodness, and the latter to your prudent directions, which I was ever carefull to have, and keep. For, as I have often said to your Majesty, I was towards you but as a Bucket, and a Cistern to draw forth, and conserve, and your self was the fountain. Unto this comfort of nineteen years prosperitie there succeeded a comfort even in my greatest adversitie, somewhat of the same Nature, which is, That in those offences wherewith I was Charged, there was not any one that had special relation to your Majesty, or any your particular Commandments. For as towards Almighty God, there are offences against the First and Second Table, and yet all against God; so with the servants of Kings, there are offences more immediate against the Sovereign, although all offences against Law are also against the King. Unto which comfort there is added this circumstance, that as my faults were not against your Majesty, otherwise then as all faults are; so my fall is not your Majesties act, otherwise then as all acts of Justice are yours. This I write, not to insinuate with your Majesty, but as a most humble appeal to your Majesties gracious remembrance, how honest and direct you have ever found me in your service, whereby I have an assured belief, that there is in your Majesties Princely thoughts a great deal of serenitie and clearness to me, your Majesties now prostrate, and cast-down servant.

Neither (my most gracious Sovereign,) do I by this mentioning of my services, lay claim to your Princely grace and bounty, though the priviledge of calamity do bear that form of Petition. I know well, had they been much more, they had been but my bounden duty; Nay, I must also confess, that they were, from time to time, far above my merit super-rewarded by your Majesties benefits, which you heaped upon me. Your Majesty was, and is, that Man to me, that raised and advanced me nine times, thrice in dignitie, and six times in office. The places indeed were the painfullest of all your service, but then they had both honour and profit, and the then profits might have maintained my now honour, if I had been wise. Neither was your Majesties immediate liberalitie wanting towards me, in some gifts, if I may hold them. All this I do most thankfully acknowledge, and do herewith conclude, that for any thing arising from my self, to move your eye of pitie towards me, there is much more in my present misery then in my past services; save that the same your Majesties goodness, that may give relief to the one, may give value to the other.

And indeed, if it may please your Majesty, This Theme of my misery is so plentifull, as it need not be coupled with any thing else. I have been some body, by your Majesties singular and undeserved favour, even the prime Officer of your Kingdom. Your Majesties arm hath been often over mine in Councell, when you presided at the Table, so neer I was. I have born your Majesties Image in metall, much more in heart. I was never, in nineteen years service, chidden by your Majesty, but contrariwise, often over-joyed, when your Majesty wou'd sometimes say; *I was a good husband for you, though none for my self*; Sometimes, *That I had a way to deal in business*, suavibus modis, *which was the way which was most according to your own heart*; and other most gracious speeches of affection and trust, which I feed on, till this day. But why should I speak of these things, which are now vanished, but onely the better to express my down-fall.

For now it is thus with me; I am a year and a half old in misery, though (I must ever acknowledge) not without some mixture of your Majesties grace and mercy. For I do not think it possible, that any you once loved should be totally miserable. My own means, through mine own improvidence, are poor and weak, little better then my Father left me. The poor things which I have had from your Majesty, are either in question, or at courtesie. My dignities remain marks of your past favour, but yet burdens withall of my present fortune. The poor remnants which I had of my former fortunes, in Plate or Jewells, I have spread upon poor men, unto whom I owed, scarce leaving my self bread. So as, to conclude, I must pour out my misery before your Majesty, sofar, as to say; *Si deseris tu, perimus.*

But

Sir Francis Bacon, to the King.

But as I can offer to your Majesties compassion little arising from my self to move you, except it be my extreme misery, which I have truly laid open; so looking up to your Majesty your self, I should think I committed *Cains* fault, if I should despair. Your Majesty is a King, whose heart is as unscrutable, for secret motions of goodness, as for depth of wisdom. You are, Creator-like, factive, and not destructive; you are a Prince, in whom I have ever noted an aversion against any thing that savoured of a hard heart; as, on the other side, your Princely eye was wont to meet with any motion that was made on the relieving part. Therefore, as one that hath had the happiness to know your Majesty neer hand, I have (most gracious Sovereign) faith enough for a Miracle, much more for a Grace, That your Majesty will not suffer your poor creature to be utterly defaced, nor blot that Name quite out of your Book, upon which your sacred Hand hath been so oft for new Ornaments and Additions. Unto this degree of compassion, I hope, God above (of whose mercy towards me, both in my prosperity, and adversity, I have had great testimonies and pledges, though mine own manifold and wretched unthankfulness might have averted them) will dispose your Princely heart, already prepared to all Piety. And why should I not think, but that thrice Noble Prince, who would have pulled me out of the Fire of a Sentence, will help to pull me (if I may use that homely phrase) out of the Mire of an abject and sordid condition, in my last days? And that excellent Favourite of yours (the goodness of whose Nature contendeth with the greatness of his Fortune, and who counteth it a Prize, a second Prize, to be a good Friend, after that Prize which he carrieth to be a good Servant) will kiss your hands with joy, for any work of Piety you shall do for me? And as all commiserating persons (specially such as find their hearts void of malice) are apt to think, that all men pity them, I assure my self, that the Lords of the Council (who out of their Wisdom and Nobleness cannot but be sensible of humane events) will, in this way which I go for the relief of my estate, further and advance your Majesties goodness towards me. For there is a kind of Fraternity between great men that are, and those that have been, being but the several Tenses of one Verb: Nay, I do further presume, that both Houses of Parliament will love their Justice the better, if it end not in my ruine. For I have been often told by many of my Lords (as it were, in excusing the severity of the Sentence) that they knew they left me in good hands. And your Majesty knoweth well, I have been, all my life long, acceptable to those Assemblies, not by flattery, but by moderation, and by honest expressing of a desire to have all things go fairly and well.

But (if it may please your Majesty) for Saints, I shall give them reverence, but no adoration. My address is to your Majesty, the Fountain of Goodness: Your Majesty shall, by the grace of God, not feel that in gift, which I shall extremely feel in help; for my desires are moderate, and my courses measured to a life orderly and reserved; hoping still to do your Majesty honour in my way. Onely I most humbly beseech your Majesty, to give me leave to conclude with those words which necessity speaketh; Help me, dear Sovereign Lord and Master, and pity me so far, as I, that have born a bag, be not now, in my age, forced, in effect, to bear a wallet; nor I, that desire to live to study, may not be driven to study to live. I most humbly crave pardon of a long Letter, after a long silence. God of Heaven ever bless, preserve, and prosper your Majesty.

Your Majesties poor ancient Servant and Beadsman,

Fr. St. Alban.

Sir Francis Bacon to the King, &c.

Sir Francis Bacon, *the Kings Attorney, returned with Postils, of the Kings own hand.*

It may please your most excellent Majesty.

YOur Majesty hath put upon me a work of providence in this great Cause, which is to break and distinguish future events into present Cases, and so to present them to your Royal judgement, that in this action which hath been carried with so great Prudence, Justice, and Clemency, there may be (for that which remaineth) as little surprize as is possible, but that things duly foreseen may have their remedies and directions in readiness; wherein I cannot forget what the *Poet Martial* saith; *O ! quantum est subitis casibus ingenium !* signifying, that accident is many times more subtil then foresight; and overeacheth expectation; and besides, I know very well the meaness of my own judgement, in comprehending or forecasting what may follow.

It was your Majesties pleasure, also, that I should couple the suppositions with my opinion in every of them, which is a harder taske; but yet your Majesties commandment requireth my obedience, and your trust giveth me assurance.

I will put the case which I wish; That *Somerset* should make a cleer Confession of his offences, before he be produced to Tryal.	In this case, it seemeth your Majesty will have a new consult. The points whereof will be. (1) whether your Majesty will stay the Tryal, and so save them both from the Stage, and that publique Ignominy. Or (2) whether you will (or may fitly by law) have the Tryal proceed, and stay or reprieve the Judgement; which saveth the Lands from forfeiture, and the blood from corruption. Or (3) whether, you will have both Tryal and judgment proceed, and save the blood onely, not from corrupting, but from spilling.
REX. *I say with* Apollo, Media tutius itur, *if it may stand with Law; and if it cannot, When I shall hear that he confesseth, I am then to make choice of the first, or the last.*	

These be the depths of your Majesties mercy which I may not enter into; but for honour and reputation, they have these grounds.

> That the blood of *Overbury* is already revenged by divers Executions.
>
> That Confession and Penitency are the foot-stools of Mercy, adding this circumstance likewise, that the former offenders did none of them make a cleer confession.
>
> That the great downfall of so great persons carrieth, in it self, a heavy punishment, and a kinde of civil death, although their lives should not be taken.

All which may satisfie honour, for sparing their lives.

But if your Majesties mercy should extend to the first degree, which is the highest, of sparing the Stage and the Tryal; Then three things are to be considered.

REX. *This Article cannot be mended in point thereof.*	First that they make such a submission or deprecation, as they prostrate themselves, and all that they have, at your Majesties feet, imploring your mercy. Secondly, that your Majestie, in your own wisdome, do advise what course you will take, for the utter extinguishing of all hope of resuscitating of their fortunes and favour; whereof if there should be the least conceit, it will leave in men a great deal of envy, and discontent. And lastly, whether your Majesty will not suffer it

it to be thought abroad, that there is cause of further examination of *Somerset*, concerning matters of Estate, after he shall begin once to be a Confessant, and so make as well a politique ground, as a ground of Clemency, for further stay.

And for the second degree of proceeding to Tryal, and staying Judgement, I must better inform my self, by presidents, and advise with my Lord Chancellor.

The second Case is, if that fall out which is likest (as things stand, and which we expect) which is, that the Lady Confess: and that *Somerset* himself plead not guilty, and be found guilty.

REX. *If stay of Judgement can stand with the Law, I would even wish it in this Case; In all the rest this Article cannot be mended.*

In this Case, first, I suppose your Majesty will not think of any stay of judgement, but that the publique process of Justice pass on.

Secondly, for your Mercy to be extended to both, for pardon of their execution, I have partly touched, in the considerations applyed to the former Case; whereunto may be added, that as there is ground of mercy for her, upon her Penitency and free Confession, and will be much more upon his finding guilty, because the malice on his part will be thought the deeper source of the offence; So there will be ground for Mercy, on his part, upon the nature of the proof, because it rests chiefly upon Presumptions. For certainly, there may be an Evidence so ballanced, as it may have sufficient matter for the Conscience of the Peers to convict him, and yet leave sufficient matter in the Conscience of a King, upon the same Evidence, to pardon his life; because the Peers are astringed by necessity, either to acquit or condemn; but Grace is free. And for my part, I think the Evidence in this present Case will be of such a nature.

Thirdly, It shall be my care so to moderate the manner of charging him, as it might make him not odious beyond the extent of Mercy.

REX. *That danger is well to be foreseen, lest he upon the one part commit impardenable Errors, and I on the other part seem to punish him in the spirit of revenge.*

Lastly, all these points of Mercy and favour are to be understood with this limitation, if he do not, by his contemptuous and insolent carriage at the Bar, make himself uncapable and unworthy of them.

The third Case is, if he should stand mute, and will not plead, whereof your Majesty knoweth there hath been some secret question.

In this case, I should think fit, that, as in publique, both my self, and chiefly my Lord Chancellor (sitting then as Lord Steward of *England*) should dehort and deter him from that desperation; so nevertheless, that as much should be done for him, as was done for *Weston*, which was to adjourne the Court for some dayes, upon a Christian ground, that he may have time to turn from that mind of destroying himself; during which time your Majesties further pleasure may be known.

REX. *This Article cannot be mended.*

The fourth Case is that, which I should be very sorry should happen; but it is a future contingent, that is, if the Peers should acquit him, and finde him not guilty.

REX. *This is so also.*

In this Case, the Lord Steward must be provided what to doe. For as it hath been never seen, (as I conceive it) that there should be any rejecting of the Verdict, or any respiting of the judgement of the acquittal, so on the other side, this Case requireth, that because there be many high and heynous offences (though not Capital) for which he may be questioned in the Star-Chamber, or otherwise, that there be some touch of that in general, at the conclusion, by my Lord Steward of *England*. And that therefore he be reminded to the *Tower*, as Close-Prisoner.

Sir Francis Bacon, *to the Master of the Horse.*

For matter of examination, or other proceedings, my Lord Chancellor, with my advice, hath set down,

To morrow, being Monday, for the Re-examination of the Lady.

Wednesday next, for the meeting of the Judges, concerning the Evidence.

Thursday, for the Examination of *Somerset* himself, according to your Majesties Instructions.

Which three parts, when they shall be performed, I will give your Majesty advertisement with speed, and in the mean time be glad to receive from your Majesty (whom it is my part to inform truly) such directions, or significations of your pleasure, as this advertisement may induce, and that with speed, because the time cometh on. Well remembering who is the person, whom your Majesty admitted to this secret; I have sent this Letter open unto him, that he may take your Majesties times to report it, or shew it unto you, assuring my self that nothing is more firme then his Trust, tyed to your Majesties commandments;

April 28. 1616.
Your Majesties most humble, and most bounden Subject and Servant.

Sir Francis Bacon, *the Kings Attorney General, to the Master of the Horse, upon the sending of his Bill for Viscount, &c.*

SIR,

I send you the Bill for his Majesties Signature, reformed according to his Majesties amendments, both in the two places (which, I assure you, were altered with great judgement) and in the third place, which his Majesty termed a question onely. But he is an idle body, that thinketh his Majesty asketh an idle question; and therefore his Majesties questions are to be answered, by taking away the cause of the question, and not by replying.

For the name, his Majesties will is a Law in those things; and to speak the truth, it is a well-sounding, and noble name, both here and abroad; and being your proper name, I will take it for a good signe, that you shall give honour to your dignity, and not your dignity to you. Therefore I have made it Viscount *Villiers*; and for your Barony, I will keep it for an Earldome. For though the other had been more orderly, yet that is as usual; and both alike good in Law.

For *Ropers* place, I would have it by all means dispatched; and therefore I marvaile it lingreth. It were no good manners, to take the business out of my Lord Treasurers hands; and therefore I purpose to write to his Lordship, if I hear not from him first, by Mr. *Deckome*; but if I hear of any delay, you will give me leave (especially since the King named me) to deal with Sir *Joseph Roper* my self; for neither I, nor my Lord Treasurer, can deserve any great thanks in this business of yours, considering the King hath spoken to Sir *Jo. Roper*, and he hath promised; and besides, the thing it self is so reasonable, as it ought to be as soon done, as said. I am now gotten into the Countrey to my house, where I have some little liberty, to think of that I would think of, and not of that which other men hourly break their head withall, as it was at *London*. Upon this you may conclude, that most of my thoughts are to His Majesty, and then you cannot be farre off. God ever keep you, and prosper you. I rest alwaies,

The 5 of *August*, one of the happiest days.
Your true and most dutiful servant,

Sir Francis Bacon, *to Sir* George Villiers, *upon the sending his Patent for Viscount Villiers to be signed.*

SIR,

I have sent you now your Patent, of Creation of Lord *Bletchly* of *Bletchly*, and of Viscount *Villiers*. *Bletchly* is your own, and I liked the sound of the name better then *Whaddon*; but the name will be hid, for you will be called Viscount *Villiers*. I have put them in a Patent, after the manner of the Patent for Earls, where Baronies are joyned; but the chief reason was, because I would avoid double prefaces, which had not been fit; nevertheless the Ceremony of Robing, and otherwise, must be double.

And now, because I am in the Countrey, I will send you some of my Countrey fruits, which with me are good Meditations, which, when I am in the City, are choked with business.

After

After that the King shall have watered your new Dignities, with the bounty of the Lands which he intends you, and that some other things concerning your means, which are now likewise in intention, shall be setled upon you; I do not see, but you may think your private fortunes established; and therefore it is now time, that you should referr your actions to the good of your Sovereign, and your Countrey. It is the life of an Oxe, or beast, alwayes to eat, and never exercise; but men are born (and specially Christian men) not to cramb in their Fortunes. but to exercise their Vertues; and yet the other hath been the unworthy, and (thanks be to God) sometimes, the unlucky, humour of great persons, in our times: Neither will your future Fortune be the further off; for, assure your self, that Fortune is of a Womans nature, and will sooner follow by sleighting, then by too much wooing. And in this dedication of your self to the Publick, I recommend unto you, principally, that which, I think, was never done since I was born, and which, because it is not done, hath bred almost a wildernesse and solitude in the Kings service; which is, That you countenance, and encourage, and advance able men, in all kinds, degrees, and professions. For in the time of the *Cecils*, the Father and the Son, able men were, by design, and of purpose, suppressed: and though of late, choice goeth better, both in Church and Common-wealth, yet money, and turn-serving, and cunning canvasses, and importunity, prevaileth too much. And, in places of moment, rather make able and honest men yours, then advance those that are otherwise, because they are yours. As for cunning and corrupt men, you must (I know) sometimes use them, but keep them at a distance; and let it appear rather, that you make use of them, then that they lead you. Above all, depend wholly (next unto God) upon the King, and be ruled (as hitherto you have been) by his Instructions, for that is best for your self. For the Kings care and thoughts for you are according to the thoughts of a great King; whereas your thoughts concerning your self, are, and ought to be, according to the thoughts of a modest man. But let me not weary you; the sum is, that you think Goodness the best part of Greatness; and that you remember whence your rising comes, and make return accordingly. God keep you.

Aug. 12. 1616.

Sir Francis Bacon *to the King, about a Certificate of my Lord* Coke's.

It may please your Excellent Majesty,

* I Send your Majesty, inclosed, my Lord *Coke's* answers, I will not call them rescripts, much less Oracles. They are of his own hand, and offered to me (as they are) in writing, not required by me to have them set down in writing, though I am glad of it, for my own discharge. I thought it my duty, as soon as I received them, instantly to send them to your Majesty, and forbear, for the present, to speak further of them. I, for my part, (though this *Muscovia*-weather be a little too hard for my constitution) was ready to have waited upon your Majesty this day, all respects set aside; but my Lord Treasurer, in respect of the season, and much other business, was willing to save me. I will onely conclude, touching these Papers, with a Text divided; I cannot say, *Oportuit haec fieri*, but I may say, *Finis autem nondum*. God preserve your Majesty.

Feb. 14. at 12. a Clock.

Your Majesties most humble, and devoted subject and servant.

I humbly pray your Majesty, to keep the Papers safe.

Sir Francis Bacon, to Mr. Toby Matthews.

Mr. *Matthews*,

DO not think me forgetfull, or altered towards you: But if I should say, I could do you any good, I should make my power more then it is. I do fear that which I am right sorry for, that you grow more impatient and busie then at first; which makes me exceedingly fear the issue of that which seemeth not to stand at a stay. I my self am out of doubt, that you have been miserably abused, when you were first seduced; and that which I take in compassion, others may take in severity. I pray God, that understands us all better then we understand one another, continue you, as I hope he will, at least, within the

bounds

bounds of loyalty to his Majesty, and natural piety to your Countrey. And I intreat you much, to meditate sometimes upon the effect of Superstition in this last *Powder-treason*, fit to be tabled and pictured in the chambers of *Meditation*, as another Hell above the ground; and well justifying the censure of the Heathen, that *Superstition is far worse then Atheism*, by how much it is less evil to have no good opinion of God at all, then such as are impious towards his Divine Majesty and goodness. Good Mr. *Matthews*, receive your self back from these courses of perdition. Willing to have written a great deal more, I continue

Your, &c.
FR. BACON.

Sir Francis Bacon, *to the Earl of* Salisbury.

It may please your good Lordship,

I Am not ignorant how mean a thing I stand for, in desiring to come into the Sollicitors place: For I know well, it is not the thing it hath been, time having wrought an alteration, both in the profession, and in that special place. Yet because I think it will increase my practice, and that it may satisfie my friends, and because I have been voiced to it, I would be glad it were done. Wherein I may say to your Lordship, in the confidence of your poor Kinsman, and a man by you advanced, *In idem fer opem qui spem dedisti*: For I am sure, it was not possible for a man living to have received from another more significant and comfortable words of hope: your Lordship being pleased to tell me, during the course of my last service, That you would raise me; and, that when you were resolved to raise a man, you were more carefull of him, then himself; and, that what you had done for me in my marriage, was a benefit for me, but of no use to your Lordship; and therefore I might assure my self you would not leave me there, with many like speeches; which I know too well my duty to take any other hold of, then the hold of a thankfull remembrance: And I know, and all the world knoweth, that your Lordship is no dealer of Holy-water, but noble and real; and on my part, on sure ground, that I have committed nothing that may deserve any alteration; and if I cannot observe you as I would, your Lordship will impute it to my want of experience, which I shall gather better, when I am once setled.

And therefore my hope is, your Lordship will finish a good work, and consider, that time groweth precious, and that I am now *vergentibus annis*; and although I know your fortune is not to want an hundred such as I am, yet I shall be ever ready to give you my best and first fruits, and to supply, as much as in me lieth, a worthiness by thankfulness.

FR. BACON.

Lord Chancellor Bacon, *to the King.*

I Dare not presume any more to reply upon your Majesty, but reserve my Defence till I attend your Majesty at your happy return, when I hope verily to approve my self not onely a true servant to your Majesty, but a true friend to my Lord of *Buckingham*; and for the times also, I hope to give your Majesty a good account, though distance of place may obscure them. But there is one part of your Majesties Letter, that I could be sorry to take time to answer; which is, that your Majesty conceives, that whereas I wrote, That the heighth of my Lords Fortune might make him secure, I mean, that he was turned proud, or unknowing of himself. Surely, the opinion I have ever had of my Lord (whereof your Majesty is best witness) is far from that. But my meaning was plain and simple; That his Lordship might, through his great Fortune, be the less apt to cast and fore-see the unfaithfulness of friends, and the malignity of enemies, and accidents of times. Which is a judgment (your Majesty knoweth better then I) that the best Authors make of the best, and best tempered spirits, *ut sunt res humanae*; insomuch as *Guicciardini* maketh the same judgment (not of a particular person, but) of the wisest State of *Europe*, the Senate of *Venice*, when he saith, Their prosperity had made them secure, and under-weighers of perils. Therefore I beseech your Majesty, to deliver me, in this, from any the least imputation to my dear and Noble Lord and Friend. And so expecting, that that Sun, which when it went from us, left us cold weather, and now it is returned towards us hath brought with it a blessed harvest, will, when it cometh to us, dispel and disperse all mists, and mistakings.

July 31. 1617.   *I am, &c.*

The Lord Chancellor Bacon, to the King.

It may please your most Excellent Majesty,

I Do many times, with gladness, and for a remedy of my other labours, revolve in my mind the great happiness which God (of his singular goodness) hath accumulated upon your Majesty every way, and how compleat the same would be, if the state of your means were once rectified, and well ordered; your people military, and obedient, fit for war, used to peace; your Church illightened with good Preachers, as an heaven of Stars; your Judges learned, and learning from you, just, and just by your example; your Nobility in a right distance between Crown and People, no oppressors of the People, no over-shadowers of the Crown; your Councel full of tributes of care, faith, and freedom; your Gentlemen, and Justices of Peace, willing to apply your Royal Mandates to the nature of their several Counties, but ready to obey; your Servants in awe of your wisdom, in hope of your goodness; the Fields growing every day, by the improvement and recovery of grounds, from the desert, to the garden; the City grown from wood to brick; your Sea-walls, or *Pomerium* of your Island, surveyed, and in edifying; your Merchants embracing the whole compass of the World, East, West, North, and South; the times give you Peace, and yet offer you opportunities of action abroad; and lastly, your excellent Royal Issue entaileth these blessings and favours of God to descend to all posterity. It resteth therefore, that, God having done so great things for your Majesty, and you for others, you would do so much for your self, as to go through (according to your good beginnings) with the rectifying and setling of your estate and means, which onely is wanting. *Hoc rebus defuit unum.* I therefore, whom onely love and duty to your Majesty, and your Royal Line, hath made a *Financier,* do intend to present unto your Majesty a perfect book of your estate, like a perspective-glass, to draw your estate neerer to your sight; beseeching your Majesty to conceive, that if I have not attained to do that that I would do, in this, which is not proper for me, nor in my element, I shall make your Majesty amends in some other thing, in which I am better bred.

Jan. 2. 1618.   *God ever preserve, &c.*

The Lord Chancellor Bacon, to the King.

It may please your most Excellent Majesty,

Time hath been, when I have brought unto you *Gemitum Columbæ* from others, now I bring it from my self. I flie unto your Majesty with the wings of a Dove, which, once within these seven dayes, I thought would have carried me a higher flight. When I enter into my self, I find not the materials of such a tempest as is come upon me. I have been, (as your Majesty knoweth best) never author of any immoderate Counsel, but alwayes desired to have things carried *suavibus modis.* I have been no avaricious oppressor of the people. I have been no haughty, or intolerable, or hatefull man, in my conversation, or carriage: I have inherited no hatred from my Father, but am a good Patriot born. Whence should this be? for these are the things that use to raise dislikes abroad.

For the House of Commons, I began my Credit there, and now it must be the place of the Sepulture thereof. And yet this Parliament, upon the message touching Religion, the old love revived, and they said, I was the same man still, onely Honesty was turned into Honour.

For the Upper House, even within these dayes, before these troubles, they seemed as to take me into their arms, finding in me ingenuity, which they took to be the true streight line of nobleness, without crooks or angles.

And for the briberies and gifts wherewith I am charged; when the books of hearts shall be opened, I hope, I shall not be found to have the troubled fountain of a corrupt heart, in a depraved habit of taking rewards to pervert Justice, howsoever I may be frail, and partake of the abuses of the Times.

And therefore I am resolved, when I come to my answer, not to trick my innocency (as I writ to the Lords) by cavillations, or voidances; but to speak to them the language that my heart speaketh to me, in excusing, extenuating, or ingenuous confessing; praying God, to give me the grace to see to the bottom of my faults, and that no hardness of heart do steal upon me, under shew of more neatness of Conscience, then is Cause.

But

But not to trouble your Majesty any longer, craving pardon for this long mourning Letter; that which I thirst after, as the Hart after the streams, is, that I may know, by my matchless friend that presenteth to you this Letter, your Majesties heart (which is an *abyssus* of goodness, as I am an *abyssus* of misery) towards me. I have been ever your man, and counted my self but an usu-fructuary of my self, the property being yours. And now making my self an oblation, to do with me as may best conduce to the honour of your Justice, the honour of your Mercy, and the use of your Service, resting as

Mar. 25. 1620.   *Clay in your Majesties gracious hands,*
                                             Fr. S*t*. Alban. Canc.

Sir Francis Bacon, *to the King, upon the sending unto him a beginning of a History of his Majesties time.*

It may please your Majesty,

* Hearing that you are at leisure to peruse Story, a desire took me to make an experiment what I could do in your Majesties times; which, being but a leaf, or two, I pray your pardon, if I send it for your recreation, considering, that love must creep, where it cannot go. But to this I add these petitions: First, that if your Majesty do dislike any thing, you would conceive I can amend it upon your least beck. Next, that if I have not spoken of your Majesty encomiastically, your Majesty will be pleased onely to ascribe it to the Law of an History, which doth not clutter together praises, upon the first mention of a name, but rather disperseth them, and weaveth them throughout the whole Narration: And as for the proper place of commemoration (which is in the period of life) I pray God I may never live to write it. Thirdly, that the reason why I presumed to think of this oblation, was, because whatsoever my disability be, yet I shall have that advantage which almost no writer of History hath had, in that I shall write the times, not onely since I could remember, but since I could observe. And lastly, that it is onely for your Majesties reading.

Sir Francis Bacon, *to the Lord Chancellor, touching the History of* Britain.

It may please your good Lordship,

* Some late act of his Majesty, referred to some former speech which I have heard from your Lordship, bred in me a great desire, and by strength of desire a boldness, to make an humble Proposition to your Lordship, such as, in me, can be no better then a wish; but if your Lordship should apprehend it, it may take some good and worthy effect. The Act I speak of, is the order given by his Majesty for the erection of a Tomb or Monument for our late Sovereign Queen *Elizabeth*: wherein I may note much, but this at this time, That as her Majesty did always right to his Majesties hopes, so his Highness doth, in all things, right to her memory; a very just and Princely retribution. But from this occasion, by a very easie ascent, I passed further, being put in mind, by this representative of her person, of the more true and more perfect representative, which is, of her Life and Government. For, as Statues and Pictures are dumb Histories, so Histories are speaking Pictures; wherein (if my affection be not too great, or my reading too small) I am of this opinion, that if *Plutarch* were alive to write Lives by Parallels, it would trouble him, for Vertue and Fortune both, to find for her a parallel amongst Women. And though she was of the Passive Sex, yet her Government was so active, as, in my simple opinion, it made more impression upon the several States of *Europe*, then it received from thence. But, I confess unto your Lordship, I could not stay here, but went a little further into the consideration of the times which have passed since King *Henry* the Eighth; wherein I find the strangest variety, that, in so little number of Successions of any hereditary Monarchy, hath ever been known; the Reign of a Child; the offer of an Usurpation, though it were but as a diary Ague; the Reign of a Lady married to a Forreigner, and the Reign of a Lady solitary and unmarried: So that, as it cometh to pass, in massive bodies, that they have certain trepidations, and waverings, before they fix and settle; so it seemeth, that, by the providence of God, this Monarchy (before it was to settle in his Majesty and his generations, in which I hope it is now established for ever) hath had these preclusive changes in these barren Princes. Neither could I contain my self here, (as it is easier for a man to multiply, then to stay a wish) but calling to remembrance the unworthiness of the History of *England*, in the main continuance thereof, and the partiality

lity and obliquity of that of *Scotland*, in the latest and largest Author that I have seen; I conceived, it would be honour for his Majesty, and a work very memorable, if this Island of great *Britain*, as it is now joyned in Monarchy for the Ages to come, so it were joyned in History for the times past; and that one just and compleat History were compiled of both Nations. And if any man think, it may refresh the memory of former discord, he may satisfie himself with the Verse, *Olim hæc meminisse juvabit*. For, the case being now altered, it is matter of comfort and gratulation, to remember former troubles. Thus much, if it may please your Lordship, was in the Optative mood, and it was time that I should look a little into the Potential; wherein the hope that I received was grounded upon three Observations: The first, of these times, which flourish in Learning, both of Art, and Language; which giveth hope, not onely that it may be done, but that it may be well done. Secondly, I do see, that which all the world sees, in his Majesty, a wonderfull judgment in Learning, and a singular affection towards Learning, and Works which are of the mind, and not of the hand. For, there cannot be the like honour sought in building of Galleries, and planting of Elms along high-ways, and the outward ornaments wherein *France* now is busie, (things rather of magnificence then of magnanimity) as there is in the uniting of States, pacifying of Controversies, nourishing and augmenting of Learning and Arts, and the particular action appertaining unto these; of which kind *Cicero* judged truly, when he said to *Cæsar*, *Quantum operibus tuis detrahet vetustas, tantum addet laudibus*. And lastly, I called to mind, that your Lordship, at some times, hath been pleased to express unto me a great desire, that something of this matter should be done, answerable, indeed, to your other noble and worthy courses and actions; joyning, and adding unto the great services towards his Majesty, (which have, in small compass of time, been performed by your Lordship) other great deservings, both of the Church, and Common-wealth, and particulars: So as the opinion of so great and wise a man doth seem to me a good warrant, both of the possibility, and worth of the matter. But all this while, I assure my self, I cannot be mistaken by your Lordship, as if I sought an Office or imployment for my self; for no man knows better then your Lordship, that if there were in me any faculty thereunto, yet neither my course of life, nor profession, would permit it, But because there be so many good Painters, both for hand and colours, it needeth but encouragement and instructions to give life unto it. So, in all humbleness, I conclude my presenting unto your Lordship this wish, which if it perish, it is but a loss of that which is not. And so craving pardon, that I have taken so much time from your Lordship, I remain, &c.

Sir Francis Bacon, *to the King, about the Pardon of the Parliaments sentence.*

Most gracious and dread Soveraign,

* Before I make my Petition to your Majesty, I make my Prayers to God above, *pectore ab imo*, That if I have held any thing so dear as your Majesties service, (nay) your hearts ease, and your honour, I may be repulsed with a denial. But if that hath been the principal with me, That God, who knoweth my heart, would move your Majesties royal heart to take compassion of me, and to grant my desire.

I prostrate my self at your Majesties feet; I, your ancient servant, now sixty four years old in age, and three years and five moneths old in misery. I desire not from your Majesty, means, nor place, nor imployment; but onely, after so long a time of expiation, a compleat and total remission of the sentence of the Upper House, to the end that blot of ignominy may be removed from me, and from my memory with posterity, that I die not a condemned man, but may be to your Majesty, as I am to God, *Nova creatura*. Your Majesty hath pardoned the like to Sir *John Bennet*, between whose case and mine, (not being partial to my self, but speaking out of the general opinion) there was as much difference, I will not say, as between black and white, but as between black and gray, or ash-coloured. Look therefore down (dear Sovereign) upon me also in pity. I know, your Majesties heart is inscrutable for goodness; and my Lord of *Buckingham* was wont to tell me, you were the best natured man in the world; and it is Gods property, that those he hath loved he loveth to the end. Let your Majesties grace, in this my desire, stream down upon me, and let it be out of the fountain and spring-head, and *ex mero motu*, that living or dying, the print of the goodness of King *James* may be in my heart, and his praises in my mouth. This my most humble request granted may make me live a year or two happily; and denied, will kill me quickly. But yet the last thing that will die in me, will be the heart and affection of

Your Majesties most humble and true devoted servant,

July 30. 1624.

Fr. St. Alban.

Sir Francis Bacon, to the Earl of Salisbury.

Sir Francis Bacon, *to the King, upon presenting his discourse, touching the Plantation of* Ireland.

It may please your excellent Majesty.

I know no better way how to express my good wishes of a New-year to your Majesty, then by this little book, which in all humbleness I send you. The stile is a stile of business, rather then curious or elaborate; And herein I was encouraged by my experience of your Majesties former Grace, in accepting of the like poore field-fruits, touching the union. And certainly I reckon this action as a second brother to the Union. For I assure my self, that *England, Scotland,* and *Ireland,* well united, is such a Trifoil, as no Prince except your self (who are the worthiest) weareth in his Crown, *Si Potentia reducatur in actum.* I know well, that for me to beat my brains about these things, they be *Majora quam pro fortuna,* but yet they be *Minora quam pro studio & voluntate.* For as I do yet bear an extream zeal to the memory of my old Mistris Queen *Elizabeth,* to whom I was rather bound for her trust, then for her favour; so I must acknowledge my self more bound to your Majesty, both for trust and favour: whereof I will never deceive the one, as I can never deserve the other. And so in all humbleness kissing your Majesties Sacred hands, I remain;

Sir Francis Bacon, *to the Earl of* Salisbury, *upon sending him one of his books of advancement of Learning.*

It may please your Good Lordship,

I present your Lordship with a work of my vacant time, which if it had been more, the work had been better. It appertaineth to your Lordship (besides my particular respects) in some proprietie, in regard you are a great Governor in a Province of Learning; and (that which is more) you have added to your place affection towards Learning, and to your affection judgement, of which, the last I could be content were (for the time) less, that you might the less exquisitely censure that which I offer to you. But sure I am, the Argument is good, if it had lighted upon a good Author; but I shall content my self to awake better spirits, like a Bell-ringer which is first up, to call others to Church. So, with my humble desire of your Lordships good acceptation, I remain,

---

The Lord Chancellor Bacon, *to the Lords.*

It may please your Lordships,

I shall humbly crave at your Lordships hands a benigne interpretation of that which I shall now write; for words that come from wasted spirits, and an oppressed mind, are more safe in being deposited in a noble Construction, then in being Circled with any reserved caution. Having made this as a protection to all which I shall say, I will go on, but with a very strange entrance (as may seem to your Lordships, at the first,) for in the midst of a state of as great affliction as I think a mortal man can endure, (honour being above life) I shall begin, with the professing gladness in some things:

The first is, that hereafter the greatness of a Judge or Magistrate shall be no Sanctuary, or protection to him against guiltiness; which, in few words, is the beginning of a golden world.

The next, that after this example, it is like that Judges will flie from any thing in the likeness of Corruption (though it were at a great distance) as from a Serpent; which tendeth to the purging of the Courts of Justice, and reducing them to their true honour and splendour. And in these two points, God is my witness (though it be my fortune to be the anvile, upon which these good effects are beaten and wrought) I take no small comfort. But to pass from the motions of my heart, whereof God is onely Judge, to the merits of my Cause, whereof your Lordships are onely Judges, under God, and his Lieutenant, I do understand, there hath been expected from me, heretofore, some justification; and thereof I have chosen one onely justification instead of all others, out of the justification of *Job*; for after the clear submission and Confession which I shall now make unto your Lordships, I hope I may say, and justifie with *Job*, in these words; *I have not hid my sin as did Adam, nor concealed my faults in my bosome.* This is the only justification I will use. It resteth therefore, that, without fig-leaves, I do ingenuously confess and acknowledge, that having understood the

the particulars of the charge, not formally from the house, but enough to inform my Conscience and memory, I find matter both sufficient and full, to move me to desert the defence, and to move your Lordships to condemn and censure me. Neither will I trouble your Lordships by singling out particulars, which I think may fall off. *Quid te exempta juvat spinis de millibus una?* Neither will I prompt your Lordships to observe upon the proofes, where they come not home, or the scruples touching the credit of the Witnesses: Neither will I present unto your Lordships, how far a defence might in divers things extenuate the offence, in respect of the time, or manner of the gift, or the like circumstances; but onely leave these things to spring out of your own noble thoughts, and observations of the evidence, and examinations themselves, and charitably to wind about the particulars of the charge here and there, as God shall put in your minds, and so, submit my self wholly to your piety and grace.

And now that I have spoken to your Lordships, as Judges, I shall say a few words unto you as Peers, and Prelates, humbly commending my cause to your noble minds, and magnanimous affections.

Your Lordships are not onely Judges, but Parliamentary Judges, you have a farther extent of arbitrary power, then other Courts: and if you be not tyed to the ordinary course of Courts, or presidents, in point of strictness and severity, much more in points of mercy and mitigation. And yet if any thing I should move might be contrary to your honourable and worthy ends to introduce a reformation, I should not seek it. But herein I beseech your Lordships to give me leave to tell you a story. *Titus Manlius* took his sons life for giving battail against the prohibition of his General. Not many years after, the like severity was pursued by *Papirius Cursor* the Dictator, against *Quintus Maximus*, who being upon the point to be sentenced, was by the intercession of some principal persons of the Senate spared; whereupon *Livie* maketh this grave and gracious observation, *Neque minus firmata est disciplina militaris periculo Quinti Maximi, quam miserabili supplicio Titi Manlii*, The discipline of War was no less established by the questioning onely of *Quintus Maximus*, then by the punishment of *Titus Manlius*. And the same reason is of the reformation of Justice; for the questioning of men of eminent place hath the same terror, though not the same rigor with the punishment. But my Case stayeth not there; for my humble desire is, that his Majesty would take the Seal into his hands, which is a great downfall, and may serve, I hope, in it self, for an expiation of my faults.

Therefore, if mercy and mitigation be in your Lordships power, and do no waies cross your ends, why should I not hope of your favours and Commiserations? Your Lordships may be pleased to behold your chief pattern, the King our Sovereign, a King of incomparable Clemency, and whose heart is inscrutable for wisdom and goodness. You well remember, that there sate not these hundred years before in your House a Prince (and never such a Prince) whose presence deserveth to be made memorable by records, and acts, mixt of mercy and justice, Yourselves are either Nobles (and Compassion ever beateth in the veins of noble bloud,) or Reverend Prelates, who are the servants of him that would *not break the bruised Reed, nor quench smoaking flaxe.*

You all sit upon a high Stage, and therefore cannot but be more sensible of the changes of humane Condition, and of the fall of any from high places. Neither will your Lordships forget that there are *vitia temporis*, as well as *vitia hominis*, and that the beginning of reformation hath a contrary power to the pool of *Bethesda*; for that had strength onely to cure him that was first cast in, and this hath strength to hurt him onely that is first Cast in; and for my part, I wish it may stay there, and go no further.

Lastly, I assure my self, your Lordships have a noble feeling of me, as a member of your own body; and one, that in this very Session had some taste of your loving affections, which I hope was not a lightning before the death of them, but rather a spark of that grace which now in the Conclusion will more appear. And therefore, my humble suit to your Lordships is, that my voluntary Confession be my sentence, and the loss of the Seal my punishment; and that your Lordships will spare any farther sentence, but recommend me to his Majesties grace and pardon for all that is past. And so, &c.

Your Lordships, &c.
Francis St. Alban Can.

Sir Francis Bacon, to the Lord Buckhurst.

The Lord Chancellor Bacon, to the Duke.

My very good Lord,

MY Lord of *Suffolk's* cause is this day sentenced. My Lord, and his Lady, fined at 30000 l. with imprisonment in the Tower at their own charges. *Bingley* at 2000 l. and committed to the Fleeet. Sir *Edward Cook* did his part, I have not heard him do better; and began with a fine of an 10000 l. But the Judges first, and most of the rest, reduced it as before. I do not dislike that things pass moderately, and all things considered it is not amiss, and might easily have been worse. There was much speaking of interceding for the Kings mercie, which (in my opinion) was not so proper for a sentence: I said, in conclusion, that mercy was to come *ex mero motu*, and so left it. I took some other occasion pertinent to do the King honour, by shewing how happy he was in all other parts of his Government, save only in the manage of his treasure by these Officers.

I have sent the King a new Bill for *Suffex*: for my Lord of *Nottingham's* Certificate was true, and I told the Judges of it before, but they neglected it. I conceive the first man (which is newly set down) is the fittest. God ever preserve and keep you, &c.

Sir Francis Bacon, to the Lord Treasurer Buckhurst, upon the same occasion, of sending his book of Advancement of Learning.

May it please your good Lordship,

* I have finished a work touching the advancement or setting forward of learning, which I have dedicated to his Majesty, the most learned of a Sovereign, or temporal Prince, that time hath known. And upon reason not unlike, I humbly present one of the books to your Lordship, not onely as a Chancellor of an University, but as one that was excellently bred in all learning; which I have ever noted to shine in all your speeches and behaviours. And therefore your Lordship will yield a gracious aspect to your first love, and take pleasure in the adorning of that wherewith your self are so much adorned. And so humbly desiring your favourable acceptation thereof, with signification of my humble duty, I remain,

---

A Letter of the like Argument, to the Lord Chancellor.

May it please your good Lordship,

* I humbly present your Lordship with a work, wherein as you have much commandment over the Author, so your Lordship hath also great interest in the argument. For to speak without flattery, few have like use of Learning, or like judgement in learning, as I have observed in your Lordship. And again, your Lordship hath been a great Planter of Learning, not onely in those places in the Church which have been in your own gift, but also in your commendatory Vote, no man hath more constantly held, *detur digniori*; and therefore both your Lordship is beholden to Learning, and learning beholden to you. Which maketh me presume, with good assurance, that your Lordship will accept well of these my labours, the rather because your Lordship in private speech hath often begun to me, in expressing your admiration of his Majesties Learning, to whom I have dedicated this work; and whose vertue and perfection in that kind did chiefly move me to a work of this nature. And so, with signification of my most humble duty and affection towards your Lordship, I remain, &c.

Sir Francis Bacon, of like argument, to the Earl of Northampton, with request to present the book to his Majesty.

It may please your good Lordship,

* HAving finished a work touching the Advancement of Learning, and dedicated the same to his sacred Majesty, whom I dare avouch (if the records of time erre not) to be the learnedst King that hath reigned; I was desirous, in a kind of congruity, to present it by the learnedst Councellor in this Kingdome, to the end, that so good an argument, lighting upon so bad an Author, might receive some reparation, by the hands into which, and by which, it should be delivered. And therefore I make it my humble suit to your Lordship to present this mean, but well meant writing to his Majesty, and with it my humble and zealous duty; and also my like humble request of pardon, if I have too often taken his name in vain, not onely in the dedication, but in the voucher of the authority of his speeches, and writings. And so I remain, &c.

Sir

Sir Francis Bacon, *his Letter of request to* Doctor Plaſer, *to tranſlate the book of* Advancement of Learning *into Latine.*

Mr. Doctor Plaſer,

* A great deſire will take a ſmall occaſion to hope, and put in Tryal that which is deſired. It pleaſed you a good while ſince, to expreſs unto me, the good liking which you conceive of my book, of the advancement of Learning, and that, more ſignificantly (as it ſeemed to me) then out of curteſie, or civil reſpect. My ſelf, as I then took contentment in your approbation thereof, ſo I ſhould eſteem and acknowledge, not onely my contentment increaſed, but my labours advanced, if I might obtain your help in that nature which I deſire. Wherein before I ſet down in plain terms my requeſt unto you, I will open my ſelf, what it was which I chiefly ſought, and propounded to my ſelf, in that work, that you may perceive that which I now deſire to be purſuant thereupon. If I doe not erre, (For any judgement that a man maketh of his own doings had need be ſpoken with a *Si nunquam fallit Imago,*) I have this opinion, that if I had ſought my own commendation, it had been a much fitter courſe for me, to have done as Gardners uſe to doe, by taking their Seeds and Slips, and rearing them firſt into plants, and ſo uttering them in pots, when they are in flower, and in their beſt ſtate. But for as much as my end was, merit of the ſtate of Learning, to my power, and not glorie; and becauſe my purpoſe was rather to excite other mens wits, then to magnifie my own, I was deſirous to prevent the incertaineſs of my own life and times, by uttering rather ſeeds then plants; nay and further, as the Proverb is, by ſowing with the Basket, then with the hand. Wherefore, ſince I have onely taken upon me to ring a Bell, to call other wits together; (which is the meaneſt office) it cannot but be conſonant to my deſire, to have that Bell heard, as farre as can be. And ſince that they are but ſparks, which can work but upon matter prepared; I have the more reaſon to wiſh, that thoſe ſparks may flye abroad; that they may the better find, and light upon thoſe minds, and ſpirits, which are apt to be kindled. And therefore the privateneſs of the language conſidered, wherein it it is written, excluding ſo many readers, (as on the other ſide, the obſcurity of the argument, in many parts of it, excludeth many others) I muſt account it a ſecond birth of that work, if it might be tranſlated into Latine, without manifeſt loſs of the ſence and matter. For this purpoſe, I could not repreſent to my ſelf any man, into whoſe hands I do more earneſtly deſire that work ſhould fall, then your ſelf; for by that I have heard and read, I know no man a greater Maſter in commanding words to ſerve matter. Nevertheleſs, I am not ignorant of the worth of your labours, whether ſuch as your place and profeſſion impoſeth on you, or ſuch as your own vertue may, upon your voluntary election, take in hand. But I can lay before you no other perſwaſions, then either the work it ſelf may affect you with, or the honour of his Majeſty, to whom it is dedicated, or your particular inclination to my ſelf; who, as I never took ſo much comfort in any labours of my own, ſo I ſhall never acknowledge my ſelf more obliged in any thing to the labour of another, then in that which ſhall aſſiſt this. Which your labour if I can, by my place, profeſſion, means, friends, travel, word, deed, requite unto you; I ſhall eſteem my ſelf ſo ſtraitly bound thereunto, as I ſhall be ever moſt ready, both to take and ſeek occaſions of thankfulneſs. And ſo leaving it, nevertheleſs, *Salva amicitia* (as reaſon is) to your own good liking, I remain, &c.

Sir Francis Bacon, *to Sir* Thomas Bodley, *upon ſending him his book of the advancement of Learning.*

SIR,

* I Think no man may more truly ſay with the Pſalm, *multum incola fuit anima mea.* For I do confeſs, ſince I was of any underſtanding, my mind hath, in effect, been abſent from that I have done, and in abſence, errours are committed, which I do willingly acknowledge; and amongſt the reſt, this great one that led the reſt; that knowing my ſelf by inward calling to be fitter to hold a book, then to play a part, I have led my life in civil Cauſes; for which I was not very fit by nature, and more unfit by the pre-occupation of my mind. Therefore, calling my ſelf home I have now for a time enjoyed my ſelf; where likewiſe I deſire to make the world partaker, My labours (if ſo I may term that which was the comfort of my other labours) I have dedicated to the King; deſirous, if there be any good in them, it may be as fat of a Sacrifice, incenſed to his honour; and the ſecond

second Copy have sent unto you, not only in good affection, but in a kinde of congruity, in regard of your great and rare desert of Learning: For Books are the Shrines where the Saint is, or is believed to be. And you having built an Ark, to save Learning from deluge, deserve, in propriety, any new instrument or engine, whereby Learning should be improved or advanced. So, &c.

Sir Thomas Bodley, *to Sir* Francis Bacon, *upon his new Philosophy.*

Sir,

AS soon as the Term was ended, supposing your leisure was more then before, I was coming to thank you two or three times, rather chusing to do it by word then letter; but I was still disappointed of my purpose, as I am at this present upon an urgent occasion, which doth tie me fast to *Fulham*, and hath now made me determine to impart my mind in writing. I think you know I have read your *Cogitata & visa*; which, I protest, I have done with great desire, reputing it a token of your singular love, that you joyned me with those your friends, to whom you would commend the first perusal of your draught: for which I pray give me leave to say but this unto you; First, that if the depth of my affection to your person and spirit, to your works and your words, and to all your ability, were as highly to be valued as your affection is to me, it might walk with yours arm in arm, and claim your love by just desert; but there can be no comparison, where our states are so uneven, and our means to demonstrate our affections, so different; insomuch as for mine own, I must leave it to be prized in the nature that it is; and you shall evermore find it most addicted to your worth. As touching the subject of your Book, you have set afoot so many noble speculations, as I cannot chuse but wonder, and I shall wonder at it ever, that your expence of time considered in your publick profession, which hath in a manner no acquaintance with Scholarship or Learning, you should have culled forth the quintessence, and sucked up the sap of the chiefest kind of Learning. For howsoever, in some points, you do vary altogether from that which is and hath been ever the received doctrine of our Schools, and was always by the wisest (as still they have been deemed) of all Nations and Ages, adjudged the truest; yet it is apparent, in those very points, in all your proposals and plots in that Book, you shew your self a Master workman. For my self, I must confess, and I speak it *Ingenue*, that for the matter of Learning, I am not worthy to be reckoned in the number of smatterers; and yet, because it may seem that being willing to communicate your Treatise with your friends, you are likewise willing to listen to whatsoever I or others can except against it; I must deliver unto you, for my private opinion, that I am one of the crew, that say there is, and we profess a greater holdfast of certainty in your Sciences, then you by your discourse will seem to acknowledge: For where, at first, you do object the ill success and errors of practitioners of Physick, you know, as wel they do proceed of the Patients unruliness: for not one of an hundred doth obey his Physitian in their own indisposition; for few are able in that kind to explicate themselves; or by reason their diseases are by nature incurable, which is incident, you know, to many sorts of maladies; or for some other hidden cause, which cannot be discovered by course of conjecture, Howbeit, I am full of this belief, that as Physick is ministred now adays by Physicians, it is much to be ascribed to their negligence or ignorance, or other touch of imperfection, that they speed no better in their practice: for few are found, of that profession, so well instructed in their Art, as they might by the precepts which their Art doth afford; which though it be defective in regard of such perfection, yet for certain it doth flourish with admirable remedies, such as tract of time hath taught by experimental effects, and are the open high-way to that knowledge that you recommend. As for Alchimie, and Magick, some conclusions they have that are worthy the preserving: but all their skill is so accompanied with subtilties and guiles, as both the Crafts and the Crafts-masters are not only despised, but named with derision. Whereupon, to make good your principal assertion, me-thinks you should have drawn the most of your examples from that which is taught in the liberal Sciences, not by picking out cases that happen very seldom, and may by all confession be subject to reproof, but by controlling the generals, and grounds, and eminent Positions and Aphorisms, which the greatest Artists and Philosophers have from time to time defended: for it goeth for currant among all men of learning, that those kind of Arts which Clerks in times past did term *Quadrivials*, confirm their propositions by infallible demonstrations. And likewise in *Trivials*, such lessons and directions are delivered unto us, as will effect very neer, or as much altogether, as every faculty doth promise.

Now in case we should concur to do as you advise, which is, to renounce our common notions, and cancel all our Theorems, Axioms, Rules and Tenents, and so to come babes *ad regnum naturæ*, as we are willed by Scriptures to come *ad regnum cœlorum*. There is nothing more certain, in my understanding, then that it would instantly bring us to Barbarism, and after many thousand years, leave us more unprovided of Theorical furniture, then we are at this present: For that were indeed to become *Tabula rasa*, when we shall leave no impression of any former principles, but be driven to begin the world again, to travel by trials of actions and sense, (which are your proofs by particulars) what to place in *intellectu* for our general conceptions, it being a Maxim of all mens approving, *In intellectu nihil esse quod non prius fuit in sensu*. And so in appearance it would befal us, that till *Plato*'s year be come about, our insight in learning would be of less reckoning then now it is accounted. As for that which you inculcate, of a knowledge more excellent then now is among us, which experience might produce, if we would but Essay to extract it out of Nature by particular probations, it is no more, upon the matter, but to incite us unto that which, without instigation, by a natural instinct men will practise of themselves: for it cannot in reason be otherwise thought, but that there are infinite, in all parts of the world, (for we may not in this case confine our Cogitations within the bounds of *Europe*) which embrace the course which you purpose, with all diligence and care, that any ability can perform. For every man is born with an appetite of knowledge, wherewith he cannot be glutted, but still, as in a dropsie, thirst after more. But yet, why men should so hearken to any such perswasions, as wholly to abolish those setled opinions, and general Theorems to which they have attained by their own and their Ancestors experience, I see nothing alledged to induce me to think it. Moreover, I may speak, as I suppose, with good probability, that if we should make a mental survey, what is like to be effected all the world over; those five or six inventions which you have selected, and imagined to be but of modern standing, would make but a slender shew among so many hundreds of all kinds of natures, which are daily brought to light by the enforcement of wit or casual events, and may be compared, or partly preferred, above those that you have named. But were it so here, that all were admitted that you can require, for the augmentation of our knowledge, and that all our Theorems and general Positions were utterly extinguished with a new substitution of others in their places, what hope may we have of any benefit of learning by this alteration? Assuredly, as soon as the new are brought *ad ἀκμήν* by the Inventors and their followers, by an interchangeable course of natural things, they will fall by degrees in oblivion to be buried, and so in continuance to perish outright; and that perchance upon the like to your present pretences, by proposal of some means to advance all our knowledge to a higher pitch of perfectness; for still the same defects that antiquity found, will reside in mankind, and therefore other issues of their actions, devices and studies, are not to be expected then is apparent by Records were in former times observed. I remember here a note which *Paterculus* made of the incomparable wits of the *Grecians* and *Romans*, in their flourishing state; that there might be this reason of their notable downfal, in their issue that came after, because by nature, *Quod summo studio petitum est ascendit in summum, difficilisque in perfecto mora est:* insomuch that men perceiving that they could not go further, being come to the stop, they turned back again of their own accord, forsaking those studies that are most in request, and betaking themselves to new endeavours, as if the thing they sought had been by prevention fore-prized by others. So it fared in particular with the eloquence of that age, that when their successors found that hardly they could equal, by no means excel, their predecessors, they began to neglect the study thereof, and speak, for many hundred year, in a rustical manner, till this later resolution brought the wheel about again, by inflaming gallant spirits to give the onset a-fresh, with straining and striving to climb unto the top and height of perfection, not in that gift alone, but in every other skill in any part of learning. For I do not hold it any erroneous conceit to think of every science, that, as now they are professed, so they have been before in all precedent ages, though not alike in all places, nor at all times alike in one and the same; but according to the changes and turning of times with a more exact and plain, or with a more rude and obscure kind of teaching.

And if the question should be asked, what proof I have of it; I have the doctrine of *Aristotle*, and of the deepest learned Clerks, of whom we have any means to take any notice: That as there is of other things, so there is of Sciences, *ortus & interitus:* which is also the meaning (if I should expound it) of *nihil novum sub sole*, and is as well to be applied *ad facta* as *addicta; ut nihil neque dictum neque factum, quod non est dictum aut factum prius*. I have further, for my warrant, that famous complaint of *Solomon* to his son, against the infinite making of Books in his time, of which, in all congruity, great part were of observations and

instructions

Sir Thomas Bodley, to Sir Francis Bacon.

instructions in all kind of literature, and of those there is not now so much as one Pamphlet (only some parcels of the Bible excepted) remaining to posterity. As then there was not in like manner to be found any footing of millions of Authors that were long before *Solomon*; and yet we must give credit to that which he affirmed; that whatsoever was then or before, it could never be truly pronounced of it, *Behold, this is new*. Whereupon I must for my final conclusion infer, Seeing all the endeavours, study and knowledge, of mankind, in whatsoever Art or Science, have ever been the same as they are at this present, though full of mutabilities, according to the changes and accidental occasions of Ages, and Country's, and Clerks dispositions; which can never but be subject to intention and remission, both in their devices and practices of their knowledge. If now we should accord in opinion with you; First, to condemn our present knowledge of doubt and incertitude (which you confer but by averment) without other force of argument, and then to disclaim all our Axioms and Maxims, and general assertions that are left by tradition from our Elders to us; which (for so it is to be pretended) have passed all probations of the sharpest wits that ever were *Abecedarii*, by the frequent spelling of particulars, to come to the notice of new generals, and so afresh to create new principles of Sciences, the end of all would be, that when we should be dispossessed of the learning which we have, all our consequent travel will but help us in a circle, to conduct us to the place from whence we set forwards, and bring us to the happiness to be restored *in integrum*, which will require as many ages as have marched before us, to be perfectly atchieved. And this I write, with no dislike of increasing our knowledge with new-found devices (which is undoubtedly a practice of high commendation) in regard of the benefit they will yield for the present, that the world hath ever been, and will for ever continue, very full of such Devisers; whose industry that way hath been very obstinate and eminent, and hath produced strange effects, above the reach and the hope of mens common capacities; and yet our Notions and Theorems have always kept in grace both with them, and with the rarest that ever were named among the learned.

By this you see to what boldness I am brought by your kindness; That (if I seem to be too saucy in this contradiction) it is the opinion that I hold of your noble disposition, and of the freedom in these cases, that you will afford your special friend, that hath induced me to it. And although I my self, like a Carriers horse, cannot bawk the beaten way, in which I have been trained; yet since it is my censure of your *Cogitata* that I must tell you, to be plain, you have very much wronged your self and the world, to smother such a treasure so long in your coffer: For though I stand well assured (for the tenor and subject of your main discourse) you are not able to impanel a Jury in any University that will give up a verdict to acquit you of Error; yet it cannot be gainsaid, that all your Treatise over doth abound with choice conceipt of the present state of learning, and with so worthy contemplations of the means to procure it, as may perswade with any Student to look more narrowly to his business, not only by aspiring to the greatest perfection, of that which is now adays divulged in the Sciences, but by diving yet deeper, as it were, into the bowels and secrets of nature, and by inforcing of the powers of his judgment and wit to learn of St. *Paul*, *Consectari meliora dona:* which course, would to God (to whisper so much into your ear) you had followed at the first, when you fell to the study of such a study as was not worthy such a Student. Nevertheless, being so as it is, that you are therein setled, and your Country soundly served; I cannot but wish with all my heart, as I do very often, that you may gain a fit reward, to the full of your deserts. Which I hope will come with heaps of happiness and honour.

From Fulham, Febr. 19.
1607.

Yours to be used, and commanded,
THO. BODLEY.

Sir, one kind of boldness doth draw on another; insomuch as me-thinks I should often to signifie, that before the transcript of your Book be fitted for the Press, it will be requisite for you to cast a Censors eye upon the Stile and the Elocution; which, in the framing of some periods, and in divers words and phrases, will hardly go for current, if the Copy brought to me be just the same that you would publish.

THO. BODLEY.

Sir Francis Bacon, *to the Bishop of* Ely, *upon sending his writing intituled,* Cogitata & visa.

My very good Lord,

NOW your Lordship hath been so long in the Church and the Palace, disputing between Kings and Popes, me-thinks you should take pleasure to look into the field and refresh your mind with some matter of Philosophy; though that science be now, through age, waxed a child again, and left to boyes and young men. And because you are wont to make me believe you took liking to my writings, I send you some of this Vacation fruits, and thus much more of my mind and purpose. *I hasten not to publish, perishing I would prevent.* And I am forced to respect as well my times, as the matter; for with me it is thus, and I think with all men, in my case: If I bind my self to an argument, it loadeth my mind; but if I rid my mind of the present Cogitation, it is rather a recreation: This hath put me into these Miscellanies, which I purpose to suppress, if God give me leave to write a just and perfect Volumne of Philosophy, which I go on with, though slowly. I send not your Lordship too much, lest it may glut you. Now, let me tell you what my desire is. If your Lordship be so good now, as when you were the good Dean of *Westminster*, my request to you is, that not by Pricks, but by Notes, you would mark unto me whatsoever shall seem unto you, either not currant in the stile, or harsh to credit and opinion, or inconvenient for the person of the writer. For no man can be Judge and party; and when our minds judge by reflexion on our selves, they are more subject to error. And though, for the matter it self, my judgment be in some things fixed, and not accessible by any mans judgment that goeth not my way, yet even in those things the admonition of a friend may make me express my self diversly. I would have come to your Lordship, but that I am hastning to my house in the Country. And so I commend your Lordship to Gods goodness.

Sir Francis Bacon, *to Sir* Thomas Bodley, *after he had imparted to him a writing intituled,* Cogitata & visa.

SIR, in respect of my going down to my house, in the Country, I shall have miss of my Papers, which I pray you therefore return unto me. You are, I bear you witness, sloathful, and you help me nothing; so as I am half in conceipt, that you affect not the argument; For my self, I know well you love and affect. I can say no more to you, but, *non canimus surdis, respondent omnia silvæ.* If you be not of the Lodgings chaulked up (whereof I speak in my Preface) I am but to pass by your door. But if I had you but a fortnight at *Gorambury*, I would make you tell me another tale, or else I would adde a Cogitation against Libraries, and be revenged on you that way: I pray you send me some good news of Sir *Thomas Smith*, and commend me very kindly to him. So I rest.

Sir Francis Bacon, *to Mr.* Matthew, *upon sending him part of* Instauratio Magna.

Mr. *Matthew*, I plainly perceive by your affectionate writing touching my work, that one and the same thing affecteth us both, which is the good end to which it is dedicated: For as for any ability of mine, it cannot merit that degree of approbation: For your Caution for Church-men, and Church-matters; (as for any impediment it might be to the applause and celebrity of my work) it moveth me not; but as it may hinder the fruit and good which may come of a quiet and calme passage to the good Port to which it is bound, I hold it a just respect, so as to fetch a fair wind, I go not too far about: But troth is, I shall have no occasion to meet them in my way, exceptit be, as they will needs confederate themselves with *Aristotle*; who, you know is intemperately magnified with the Scholemen, and is also allyed (as I take it) to the Jesuits by *Faber*, who was a companion of *Loyola*, and a great *Aristotelian*. I send you at this time, the only part which hath any harshness, and yet I framed to my self an opinion, that whosoever allowed well of that Preface, which you so much commend, will not dislike, or at least ought not dislike, this other speech of Preparation; For it is written out of the same spirit, and out of the same necessitie. Nay, it doth more fully lay open, that the question between me and the Ancients is not of the vertue of the race, but of the rightness of the way. And to speak truth, it is to the other but as *Palma* to *Pugnus*, part of the same thing, more large. You conceive aright, that in this, and the other, you have Commission to impart, and communicate them to others, according to your discretion: other matters I write not of: My self am like the Miller of *Huntington*, that was wont to pray for peace amongst the willowes; for while the windes blew the wind-mills wrought, and the watermill was less customed. So I see that Controversies of Religion must hinder the advancement of Sciences. Let me conclude with my perpetuall wish towards your self, that the approbation of your self by your own discreet and temperate carriage may restore you to your Country, and your friends to your society. And so I commend you to Gods goodness.

 Graies Inne, this 10th
  of *October*. 1609.

Sir Francis Banon, *to* Mr Matthew, *touching* Instauratio Magna.

* **M**r *Matthew*, I heartily thank you for your Letter of the 10th of *Feb:* and am glad to receive from you matter both of encouragement and advertisment, touching my writings. For my part, I do wish that since there is almost no *lumen siccum* in the world, but all, *Madidum*, *Maceratum*, infused in affections, and bloods, or humours, that these things of mine had those separations that might make them more acceptable; so that they claim not so much acquaintance of the present times, as they be thereby the less like to last. And to shew you that I have some purpose to new mould them, I send you a leaf or two of the Preface, carrying some figure of the whole work. Wherein I purpose to take that which is reall and effectuall of both writings; and chiefly, to add pledge, if not payment, to my promise. I send you also a Memoriall of Queen *Elizabeth*, to requite your Elogie of the late D. of *Florences* felicitie. Of this, when you were here, I shewed you some Model, though at that time, me-thought you were as willing to hear *Julius Cæsar*, as Q: *Elizabeth* commended. But this which I send is more full, and hath more of the Narrative; and further, hath one part that I think will not be disagreeable, either to you, or that place, being the true tracts of her proceeding towards the Catholicks, which are infinitely mistaken. And though I do not imagine they will pass allowance there, yet they will gain upon excuse. I find Mr *Lezure* to use you well (I mean his tongue, of you) which shews you either honest or wise. But this I speak meerly; for in good faith, I conceive hope, that you will so govern your self, as we may take you as assuredly for a good Subject, and Patriot, as you take your self for a good Christian; and so we may again enjoy your company, and you your Conscience, if it may no otherwise be. For my part, assure your self, that (as we say in the Law) *Mutatis mutandis*, my love and good wishes to you are not diminished. And so I remain.

Sir Francis Bacon, *to* Mr Savill.

* **M**r. *Savill*, Coming back from your Invitation at *Eaton*, where I had refreshed my self with company which I loved, I fell into a consideration of that part of Policie whereof Philosophy speaketh too much, and Laws too little; And that is, of education of youth; whereupon fixing my minde a while, I found straitwayes, and noted, even in the discourses of Philosophers, (which are so large in this argument,) a strange silence concerning one principall part of that subject. For as touching the framing and seasoning of youth to moral vertues, tolerance of labour, continency from pleasures, obedience, honour, and the like, they handle it: but touching the improvement and helping of the intellectuall powers, as of conceipt, memory, and judgement, they say nothing; whether it were that they thought it to be a matter wherein Nature only prevailed; or that they intended it, as referred to the severall and proper Arts which teach the use of Reason, and speech. But for the former of these two reasons, howsoever it pleaseth them to distinguish of habits, and powers, the experience is manifest enough, that the motions and faculties of the will and memory may be not only governed and guided, but also confirmed and enlarged, by customë and exercise duly applyed; as, if a man exercise shooting, he shall not only shoot

                   neerer

neerer the mark, but also draw a stronger bow. And as for the latter, of comprehending these precepts within the Arts of Logick and Rhetorick, if it be rightly considered, their office is distinct altogether from this point; for it is no part of the doctrine of the use, or handling of an instrument, to teach how to whet or grinde the instrument, to give it a sharper edge, or how to quench it, or otherwise, whereby to give it a stronger temper. Wherefore finding this part of knowledge not broken, I have but *tanquam aliud agens*, entred into it, and salute you with it, dedicating it after the ancient manner; first, as to a dear friend, and then as to an apt person; forasmuch as you have both place to practise it, and judgement, and leisure, to look deeper into it, then I have done, Herein you must call to minde, *αεις ν ωξ ϋδως*. Though the argument be not of great height and dignitie, neverthelesse, it is of great and universall use. And yet I do not see, why (to consider it rightly) that should not be a learning of heighth, which teacheth to raise the highest and worthiest part of the minde. But howsoever that be, if the world take any light and use by this writing, I will, that the Gratulation be to the good friendship and acquaintance between us two. And so I commend you to Gods divine protection.

Sir Francis Bacon, *to the King*, *touching the Sollicitors place*.

✱ HOw honestly ready I have been (most gracious Sovereign) to do your Majesty humble service to the best of my power, and in a manner beyond my power, (as I now stand) I am not so unfortunate, but your Majesty knoweth. For both in the Commission of Union (the labour whereof, for men of my profession, rested most upon my hand,) and this last Parliament in the bill of the Subsidie, (both body, and preamble;) in the bill of Attainders of *Tresham*, and the rest; in the matter of Purveyance, in the Ecclesiasticall Petitions, in the grievances, and the like; as I was ever carefull, (and not without good successe) sometimes to put forward that which was good, sometimes to keep back that which was not so good; so your Majesty was pleased to accept kindly of my services, and to say to me, such conflicts were the warrs of peace, and such victories, the victories of peace; And therefore such servants that obtained them were by Kings, that reign in peace, no lesse to be esteemed then services of Commanders in the warrs. In all which, neverthelesse, I can challenge to my self no sufficiency, but that I was diligent and reasonably happy to execute those directions which I received either immediately from your royal mouth, or from my Lord of *Salisbury*; At which time it pleased your Majesty to promise, and assure me, that upon the remove of the then Atturney, I should not be forgotten, but brought into ordinary place. And this was, after, confirmed to me by many of my Lords, and towards the end of the last Term, the manner also in particular was spoken of, that is, that Mr. Sollicitor should be made your Majesties Serjeant, and I Sollicitor; for so it was thought best, to sort with both our gifts and faculties, for the good of your service. And of this resolution both Court and Country took knowledge. Neither was this any Invention or Project of mine own, but moved from my Lords; and I think, first, from my Lord Chancellor. Whereupon resting, your Majesty well knoweth, I never opened my mouth for the greater place, though I am sure I had two Circumstances, that Mr. Atturney that now is, could not alledge. The one, nine years service of the Crown; The other, being Cosen German to the Lord of *Salisbury*, whom your Majesty esteemeth and trusteth so much. But for the lesse place, I conceived it was meant me. But after that M. Atturney *Hubbert* was placed, I heard no more of my Preferment, but it seemed to be at a stop, to my great disgrace and discouragement. For (gracious Sovereign) if still when the waters are stirred, another shall be put before me, your Majesty had need work a Miracle, or else I shall be still a lame man to do your Majesty service. And therefore my most humble suite to your Majesty is, that this which seem'd to me was intended, may speedily be perform'd. And I hope my former service shall be but beginnings to better, when I am better strengthned. For sure I am, no mans heart is fuller (I say not but many have greater hearts, but I say, not fuller) of love and duty towards your Majesty, and your Children, as I hope time will manifest against envie and detraction, if any be. To conclude, I most humbly crave pardon for my boldnesse, and rest.

Sir Francis Bacon, *to the King, his suite to succeed in the Atturneys place.*

It may please your Majesty,

Your great and Princely favours towards me in advancing me to place, and that which is to me of no less comfort, your Majesties benigne and gracious acceptation from time to time of my poor services, much above the merit and value of them, hath almost brought me to an opinion, that I may sooner perchance be wanting to my self in not asking, then finde your Majesties goodness wanting to me, in any my reasonable and modest desires. And therefore, perceiving how at this time preferments of Law fly about mine ears, to some above me, and to some below me, I did conceive your Majesty may think it rather a kinde of dulness, or want of Faith, then Modestie, if I should not come with my Pitcher to *Jacobs* well, as others do. Wherein I shall propound to your Majesty, that which tendeth not so much to the raising of my Fortune, as to the setling of my minde, being sometimes assayled with this Cogitation, that by reason of my slowness to sue and apprehend sudden occasions, keeping on one plain course of painfull service, I may (*in fine dierum*) be in danger to be neglected and forgotten. And if that should be, then were it much better for me now while I stand in your Majesties good opinion (though unworthy) and have some reputation in the world, to give over the Course I am in, and to make Proof to do you some honour by my Pen; either by writing some faithfull Narrative of your happy (though not untraduced) times, or by recompiling your Laws, which, I perceive, your Majesty laboureth with, and hath in your head, (as *Jupiter* had *Pallas*,) or some other the like work (for without some endeavour to do you honour I would not live) then to spend my wits and time in this laborious place, wherein now I serve, if it shall be deprived of those outward ornaments, and inward comforts, which it was wont to have in respect of an assured succession to some place of more dignitie and rest, which seemeth now to be a hope altogether casual, if not wholly intercepted. Wherefore (not to hold your Majesty long) my suit (then the which I think I cannot well go lower) is, that I may obtain your royal promise to succeed (if I live) into the Atturneys place, whensoever it shall be voyd, it being but the natural, and immediate step and rise, which the place I now hold hath ever (in sort) made claim to, and almost never fayled in. In this suite I make no friends to your Majesty, but relie upon no other motive then your Grace, nor any other assurance but your word, whereof I had good experience when I came to the Sollicitors place, that they were like to the two great Lights, which in their motions are never Retrograde. So, with my best prayer for your Majesties happiness, I rest.

Sir Francis Bacon, *to Sir* George Cary *in* France, *upon sending him his writing,* In fœlicem memoriam Elizabethæ.

My very good Lord,

Being asked the question by this bearer, an old servant of my brother *Anthony Bacon*, whether I would command him any service into *France*, and being at better leisure then I would, in regard of sickness, I began to remember, that neither your business nor mine, (though great and continuall) can be, upon an exact account, any just occasion why so much good will as hath passed between us should be so much discontinued as it hath been. And therefore, because one must begin, I thought to provoke your remembrance of me, by my Letter. And thinking how to fit it with somewhat besides salutations, it came to my minde, that this last Summer by occasion of a factious Book that endeavoured to verifie *Misera fœmina* (the addition of the Popes Bull) upon Queen *Elizabeth*; I did write a few lines in her memorial, which I thought you would be well pleased to reade, both for the argument, and because you were wont to bear affection to my pen. *Verum, ut aliud ex alio,* if it came handsomly to pass, I would be glad the President *de Thou* (who hath written a History, as you know, of that same and diligence) saw it; chiefly because I know not, whether it may not serve him for some use in his Story; wherein I would be glad he did right to the truth, and to the memory of that Lady, as I perceive by that he hath already written, he is well inclined to do; I would be glad also, it were some occasion (such as absence may permit) of some acquaintance or mutual notice between us. For though he
hath

hath many ways the precedence (chiefly in worth) yet this is common to us both, that we serve our Sovereigns in places of Law eminent, and not our selves only, but that our Fathers did so before us; and lastly, that both of us love Learning, and Liberal Sciences, which was ever a bond of Friendship, in the greatest distances of places. But of this I make no farther request, then your own occasions and respects (to me unknown) may further or limit; my principal purpose being to salute you, and to send you this token. whereunto I will adde my very kind commendations to my Lady. And so commit you both to Gods holy protection.

Sir Francis Bacon, *the Kings Attorney, to the King, giving some accompt touching the* Commendams.

It may please your most excellent Majesty,

* I Am not swift to deliver any thing to your Majesty, before it be well weighed. But now that I have informed my self of as much as is necessary, touching this proceeding of the Judges, to the Argument of the *Commendams*, (notwithstanding your Majesties pleasure signified by me upon your Majesties Commandment, in presence of my Lord Chancellor and the Bishop of *Winchester*, to the contrary) I do think it fit to advertise your Majesty what hath passed; the rather, because I suppose the Judges, since they performed not your Commandment, have at least given your Majesty their reasons of their failing therein; I being to answer for the doing of your Majesties Commandment, and they for the not doing.

I did conceive, that in a cause that concern'd your Majesty and your Royal power, the Judges having heard your Attorney General argue the *Saterday* before, would of themselves have taken further time to be advised.

And (if I fail not in memory) my Lord *Coke* received from your Majesties self, as I take it, a precedent Commandment, in *Hillary* Term; That both in the *Rege inconsulto*, and in the *Commendams*, your Attorney should be heard to speak, and then stay to be made of further proceeding, till my Lord had spoken with your Majesty.

Nevertheless, hearing that the day appointed for the Judges Argument held, contrary to my expectation, I sent on *Thursday* in the evening, (having received your Majesties Commandment but the day before, in the afternoon) a Letter to my Lord *Coke*, whereby I let him know, that upon some Report of my Lord of *Winchester* (who by your Commandment was present at my Argument) of that which passed, it was your Majesties express pleasure, that no further proceeding should be, untill your Majesty had confer'd with your Judges; which your Majesty thought to have done at your being now last in Town; but by reason of your many and weighty occasions, your Princely times would not serve; and that it was your pleasure he should signifie so much, to the rest of the Judges, whereof his Lordship might not fail. His answer, by word, to my man was; That it were good the rest of the Judges understood so much from my self. Whereupon I (that cannot skill in scruples, in matter of service) did write, on *Friday*, three several Letters of like content, to the Judges of the Common Pleas, and the Barons of the Exchequer, and the other three Judges of the Kings Bench, mentioning, in that last, my particular Letter to my Lord Chief Justice.

This was all I did, and thought all had been sure, insomuch as the same day being appointed in Chancery, for your Majesties great Cause (followed by my Lord *Hunsdon*) I writ two other Letters, to both the Chief Justices, to put them in mind of assisting my Lord Chancellor at the hearing. And when my Lord Chancellor himself took some notice upon that occasion, openly in the Chancery, that the *Commendams* could not hold, presently after, I heard the Judges were gone about the *Commendams*; which I thought, at first, had been only to adjourn the Court. But I heard after, that they proceeded to Argument.

In this their doing, I conceive they must either except to the Nature of the Commandment, or to the credence thereof; both which, I assure my self, your Majesty will maintain.

For if they should stand upon the general ground, *Nulli negabimus, nulli differemus Justitiam*, it receiveth two answers. The one, that reasonable and mature advice may not be confounded with delay; and that they can well alledge, when it pleaseth them. The other, that there is a great difference between a Case meerly between Subject and Subject, and where the Kings interest is in question directly, or by consequence. As for the Attorneys Place, and Commission, it is as proper for him to signifie the Kings pleasure to the Judges, as for the Secretary to signifie the same to the Privy Councel, and so hath it ever been.

These

These things were a little strange, if there came not so many of them together, as the one maketh the other seem less strange: But your Majesty hath fair occasions to remedy all, with small aid. I say no more for the present.

I was a little plain with my Lord *Coke* in these matters; and when his answer was, that he knew all these things, I said, he could never profit too much, in knowing himself, and his duty.

Sir Francis Bacon *his Advertisement touching an Holy War, to the Right Reverend Father in God,* Lancelot Andrews, *Lord Bishop of* Winchester, *and Counsellor of Estate to his Majesty.*

My Lord,

* AMongst consolations, it is not the least, to represent to a mans self like examples of calamity in others. For Example gives a quicker impression then Arguments; and besides, they certifie us of that which the Scripture also tendereth for satisfaction, *That no new thing is happened unto us.* This they do the better, by how much the Examples are liker, in circumstances, to our own case; and more especially, if they fall upon persons that are greater and worthier then our selves. For as it savoureth of vanity, to match our selves highly, in our own conceit; so, on the other side, it is a good sound conclusion, That if our betters have sustained the like events, we have the less cause to be grieved.

In this kind of consolation, I have not been wanting to my self, though, as a Christian, I have tasted (through Gods great goodness) of higher remedies. Having therefore, through the variety of my reading, set before me many examples, both of ancient, and latter times, my thoughts, I confess, have chiefly stayed upon three particulars, as the most eminent, and the most resembling; all three, persons, that had held chief place of Authority in their Countreys; all three ruined, not by war, or by any other disaster, but by Justice and Sentence, as Delinquents, and Criminals; all three famous Writers: Insomuch, as the remembrance of their calamity is, now, as to posterity, but as a little Picture of Night-work, remaining amongst the fair and excellent Tables of their Acts and Works: and all three, (if that were any thing to the matter) fit examples to quench any mans ambition of rising again, for that they were, every one of them, restored with great glory, but to their further ruine and destruction, ending in a violent death. The men were, *Demosthenes, Cicero,* and *Seneca,* persons that I durst not claim affinity with, except the similitude of our fortunes had contracted it. When I had cast mine eyes upon these examples, I was carried on further to observe, how they did bear their fortunes, and, principally, how they did employ their times, being banished, and disabled for publick business; to the end, that I might learn by them, and that they might be as well my Counsellors, as my Comforters. Whereupon I happened to note, how diversly their fortunes wrought upon them, especially, in that point at which I did most aim, which was, the employing of their times and pens. In *Cicero*, I saw, that during his banishment (which was almost two years) he was so softened and dejected, as he wrote nothing but a few womanish Epistles: And yet, in mine opinion, he had least reason of the three to be discouraged; for that although it was judged, and judged by the highest kind of judgment, in form of a Statute, or Law, That he should be banished, and his whole estate confiscated and seized, and his houses pulled down, and that it should be highly penal for any man to propound his repeal; yet his case, even then, had no great blot of ignominy, but it was thought but a tempest of Popularity which overthrew him. *Demosthenes*, contrary-wise, though his case was foul, being condemned for bribery, and not simple bribery, but bribery in the nature of Treason and disloyalty; yet, nevertheless, he took so little knowledge of his fortune, as, during his banishment, he did much busie himself, and intermeddle with matters of State, and took upon him to counsel the State, as if he had been still at the Helm, by Letters, as appears by some Epistles of his which are extant. *Seneca*, indeed, who was condemned for many corruptions, and crimes, and banished into a solitary Island, kept a mean: for, though his Pen did not freeze, yet he abstained from intruding into matters of business; but spent his time in writing Books of excellent Argument, and use for all Ages, though he might have made better choice, sometimes, of his Dedications.

These examples confirmed me much in a resolution (whereunto I was otherwise inclined) to spend my time wholly in writing, and to put forth that poor Talent, or half Talent, or what it is, that God hath given me, not, as heretofore, to particular exchanges, but to tanks or Mounts of Perpetuity, which will not break.

L   Therefore

Therefore having, not long since, set forth a part of my *Instauration*, which is the work that, in mine own judgment (*Si nunquam fallit Imago*) I may most esteem, I think to proceed in some few parts thereof. And although I have received, from many parts beyond the Seas, testimonies touching that work, such, as beyond which I could not expect at the first, in so abstruse an Argument; yet, nevertheless, I have just cause to doubt, that it flies too much over mens heads: I have a purpose, therefore, (though I break the order of time) to draw it down to the sense, by some patterns of a Natural Story, and Inquisition. And again, for that my Book of *Advancement of Learning* may be some preparative, or Key, for the better opening of the *Instauration*, because it exhibits a mixture of new conceipts, and old; whereas the *Instauration* gives the new unmixed, (otherwise then with some little aspersion of the old, for tastes sake;) I have thought to procure a Translation of that Book into the general Language, not without great and ample additions, and enrichment thereof, especially in the second Book, which handleth the partition of Sciences; in such sort, as I hold it, may serve in lieu of the first part of the *Instauration*, and acquit my promise in that part. Again, because I cannot altogether desert the civil person that I have borne, (which, if I should forget, enough would remember) I have also entred into a work touching Laws, propounding a Character of Justice in the middle Term, between the speculative and reverend discourses of Philosophers, and the writings of Lawyers, which are tied, and obnoxious to their particular Laws. And although it be true, that I had a purpose to make a particular Digest, or re-compilement, of the Laws of mine own Nation; yet because it is a Work of assistance, and that that I cannot master, by my own forces and pen I have laid it aside. Now having, in the work of my *Instauration*, had in contemplation the general good of men, in their very being, and dowries of Nature; and in my work of *Laws*, the general good of men in Society, and the dowries of Government, I thought in duty I owed somewhat unto mine own Countrey, which I ever loved; insomuch as although my place hath been far above my deserts, yet my thoughts and cares concerning the good thereof were beyond, and over, and above my place. So now, being, as I am, no more able to do my Countrey service, it remained unto me to do it honour, which I have endeavoured to do, in my Work of the Reign of King *Henry* the Seventh. As for my Essays, and some other particulars of that Nature, I count them but as the Recreations of my other Studies; and in that sort I purpose to continue them, though I am not ignorant, that those kind of Writings would, with less pains and embracement, perhaps, yield more lustre and reputation to my Name, then those other which I have in hand. But I accompt the use that a man should seek, of the publishing of his own Writings before his death, to be but an untimely anticipation of that which is proper to follow a man, and not to go along with him.

But revolving with my self my Writings, as well those I have published, as those which I had in hand, methought they went all into the City, and none into the Temple; where, because I have found so great consolation, I desire likewise to make some poor oblation. Therefore I have chosen an Argument, mixt of Religious and Civil Considerations; and likewise mixt between Contemplative and Active: For, who can tell, whether there may not be an *Exeriere aliquis?* Great matters (especially, if they be Religious) have (many times) small beginnings, and the Plat-form may draw on the Building. This Work, because I was ever an enemy to flattering Dedications, I have dedicated to your Lordship, in respect of our ancient and private acquaintance, and because, amongst the men of our times, I hold you in especial reverence.

Sir Francis Bacon, *to King* James, *of a Digest to be made of the Laws of* England.

Most Excellent Sovereign,

Amongst the Degrees and Acts of Sovereign, or rather Heroical Honor, the first, or second, is the person and merit of a Law-giver. Princes that govern well are Fathers of the People: But if a Father breed his Son well, and allow him well, while he liveth, but leave him nothing at his death, whereby both he, and his Children, and his Childrens Children, may be the better, it is not in him compleat. So Kings, if they make a portion of an Age happy by their good Government; yet if they do not make Testaments (as God Almighty doth) whereby a perpetuity of good may descend to their Countrey, they are but mortal, and transitory benefactors. *Domitian*, a few dayes before he died, dreamed, that a Golden Head did rise upon the Nape of his Neck; which was truly performed, in the Golden Age that followed his times, for five Successions. But Kings, by giving their Subjects good Laws, may, if they will, in their own time, joyn and graff this Golden Head

upon

upon their own necks, after their death: Nay, they make *Nabuchodonosors* Image of Monarchy, golden from head to foot. And if any of the meaner sort of Politicks, that are sighted onely to see the worst of things, think, That Laws are but Cobwebs, and that good Princes will do well without them, and bad will not stand much upon them; the discourse is neither good, nor wise. For, certain it is, that good Laws are good bridles to bad Princes, and as a very Wall about Government. And if Tyrants sometimes make a breach into them, yet they mollifie even Tyranny it self, as *Solons* Laws did the Tyranny of *Pisistratus*; and then commonly they get up again, upon the first advantage of better times. Other means to perpetuate the memory and merits of Sovereign Princes, are inferiour to this. Buildings of Temples, Tombs, Palaces, Theatres, and the like, are honourable things, and look big upon posterity: But *Constantine* the Great gave the name well to those works, when he used to call *Trajan,* who was a great builder, *Parietarius,* because his name was upon so many walls. So that, if that be the matter, that the King would turn Wall-flower, or Pelitory of the wall, with cost he may. *Adrians* vein was better, for his mind was to wrastle a fall with Time; and being a great progressor over all the *Roman* Empire, when ever he found any decays of Bridges, or High-ways, or cuts of Rivers, and Sewers, or Walls, or Banks, or the like, he gave substantial order for their repair. He gave also multitudes of Charters, and Liberties, for the comfort of Corporations, and Companies in decay, so that his bounty did strive with the ruines of time. But yet this, though it were an excellent disposition, went but, in effect, to the Cases and Shells of a Common-wealth; it was nothing to Virtue, or Vice. A bad man might indifferently take the benefit and ease of his Ways and Bridges, as well as a good; and bad people might purchase good Charters. Surely, the better works of perpetuity, in Princes, are they that wash the in-side of the Cup; such as are foundations of Colledges and Lectures, for learning, and education for youth; likewise foundations and institutions of Orders and Fraternities, for Nobleness, Enterprize, and Obedience, and the like: But yet these also are but like plantations of Orchards and Gardens in plats and spots of ground, here and there; they do not till over the whole Kingdom, and make it fruitfull, as doth the establishing of good Laws and Ordinances, which make a whole Nation to be as a well ordered Colledge or Foundation.

This kind of work, in the memory of times, is rare enough to shew it excellent; and yet not so rare, as to make it suspected for impossible, inconvenient, and unsafe. *Moses,* that gave Laws to the *Hebrews,* because he was the Scribe of God himself, is fitter to be named for Honours sake to other Law-givers, then to be numbred and ranked amongst them. *Minos, Lycurgus,* and *Solon,* are examples for Themes of Grammar-Scholars. For ancient Personages, and Characters, now a days, use to wax Children again. Though that Parable of *Pindarus* be true, *The best thing is water;* for common and trivial things are many times the best, and rather despised upon pride, because they are vulgar, then upon cause or use. Certain it is, that the Laws of those three Law-givers had great prerogatives; the first, of fame, because they were the pattern among the *Grecians;* the second, of lasting, for they continued longest without alteration; the third, a spirit of reviver, to be often expressed, and often restored.

Amongst the seven Kings of *Rome,* there were four Law-givers: For it is most true that a Discourse of *Italy* saith, *There was never State so well swadled in the infancy, as the* Roman *was, by the vertue of their first Kings;* which was a principal cause of the wonderfull growth of that State in after-times.

The *Decemvirs* Laws were Laws upon Laws, not the Original; for they graffed Laws of *Græcia* upon the *Roman* stock of Laws and Customs: But such was their success, as the twelve Tables which they compiled were the main Body of the Laws which framed and welded the great Body of that State. These lasted a long time, with some supplementals; and the *Prætorian* Edicts in *Albo,* which were, in respect of Laws, as Writing-tables in respect of Brass; the one to be put in and out, as the other is permanent. *Lucius Cornelius Sylla* reformed the Laws of *Rome:* For that man had three singularities, which never Tyrant had but he; That he was a Law-giver; that he took part with Nobility; and that he turned private man, not upon fear, but upon confidence.

Cæsar, long after, desired to imitate him onely in the first; for otherwise, he relied upon new men; and for resigning his power, *Seneca* describeth him right, *Cæsar gladium cito condidit, nunquam posuit:* And himself took it upon him, saying, in scorn, of *Sylla's* resignation, *Sylla nescivit literas, dictare non potuit.* But, for the part of a Law-giver, *Cicero* giveth him the Attribute; *Cæsar, si ab eo quæreretur quid egisset in Toga, leges se, respondisset, multas & præclaras tulisse.* His Nephew *Augustus* did tread the same steps, but with deeper print, because of his long Reign in peace; whereof one of the Poets of his time saith,

Pace data terris, animum ad Civilia vertit,
Jura suum legesque tulit justissimus Author.

From that time, there was such a race of Wit and Authority, between the Commentaries and Decisions of the Lawyers, and the Edicts of the Emperours, as both Laws and Lawyers were out of breath: whereupon *Justinian*, in the end, re-compiled both, and made a Body of Laws, such as might be wielded, which himself calleth glorious, and yet not above truth; the edifice or structure of a sacred Temple of Justice, built indeed out of the former ruines of Books, as materials, and some novel constitutions of his own.

In *Athens* they had *sex viri*, as *Æschines* observeth, which were standing Commissioners, who did watch to discern what Laws were unproper for the times, and what new Law did, in any branch, cross a former Law, and so, *ex officio*, propounded their Repeal.

King *Edgar* collected the Laws of this Kingdom, and gave them a strength of a faggot bound, which formerly were dispersed; which was more glory to him, then his sailing about this Island with a great Fleet: for that was, as the Scripture saith, *Via navis in mari*, it vanished; but this lasteth.

Alphonso the Wise, the Ninth of that name, King of *Castile*, compiled the Digest of the Laws of *Spain*, intituled, The *six Partidas*; an excellent work, which he finished in seven years: And, as *Tacitus* noteth well, that the Capitol, though built in the beginnings of *Rome*, yet was fit for the great Monarchy that came after; so that building of Laws sufficeth the greatness of the Empire of *Spain*, which since hath ensued.

Lewis the Eleventh had in his mind, though he performed it not, to have made one constant Law of *France*, extracted out of the Civil *Roman* Law, and the Customs of Provinces, which are various, and the Kings Edicts, which with the *French* are Statutes. Surely he might have done well, if, like as he brought the Crown (as he said himself) *hors de Page*, so he had brought his People from *Lacquay*, not to run up and down for their Laws, to the Civil Law, and the Ordinances of Courts, and Discourses of Philosophers, as they use to do.

King *Henry* the Eighth, in the 27. year of his Reign, was authorized by Parliament to nominate 32. Commissioners, part Ecclesiastical, part Temporal, to purge the Common-Law, and to make it agreeable to the Law of God, and the Law of the Land; but it took not effect: For the Acts of that King were, commonly, rather proffers and fames, then either well grounded, or well pursued. But I doubt I err, in producing so many examples: for, as *Cicero* said to *Cæsar*, so may I say to your Majesty, *Nil vulgare, te dignum videri possit*; though, indeed, this, well understood, is far from vulgar; for that the Laws of both Kingdoms and States have been, like buildings, of many pieces, and patched up, from time to time, according to occasions, without frame or model.

Now for the Laws of *England*, if I shall speak my opinion of them, without partiality, either to my Profession, or Countrey; for the matter and nature of them, I hold them wise, just, and moderate Laws; they give to God, they give to *Cæsar*, they give to the Subject, what appertaineth. It is true, they are as mixt as our Language, compounded of *British, Roman, Saxon, Danish, Norman* customs; and surely, as our Language is thereby so much the richer; so our Laws are likewise, by that mixture, the more compleat. Neither doth this attribute the less to them, then those that would have them to stand out the same, in all mutations. For no tree is so good first set, as by transplanting and graffing. I remember what happened to *Calisthenes*, that followed *Alexanders* Court, and was grown into some displeasure with him, because he could not well brook the *Persian* adoration: At a Supper (which with the *Grecians* was a great part) he was desired, the King being present, because he was an Eloquent man, to speak of some Theme; which he did, and chose for his Theme, the praise of the *Macedonian* Nation. Which though it were but a filling thing, to praise men to their faces; yet he performed it with such advantage of truth, and avoidance of flattery, and with such life, as was applauded by the hearers. The King was the less pleased with it, not loving the man, and, by way of discountenance, said, It was easie to be a good Orator in a pleasing Theme: But, saith he to him, turn your stile, and tell us now of our faults, that we may have the profit, and not the praise onely. Which he presently did, with such quickness, that *Alexander* said, That Malice made him Eloquent then, as the Theme had done before. I shall not fall into either of these extremes, in this subject, of the Laws of England. I have commended them before for the matter; but, surely, they ask much amendment for the form; which to reduce and perfect, I hold to be one of the greatest Dowries that can be conferred upon this Kingdome; which work, for the excellency, as it is worthy your Majesties Acts and Times, so it hath some circumstance of propriety agreeable to your Person. God hath blessed your Majesty

with

with posterity and I am not of opinion, that Kings that are barren are fittest to supply perpetuitie of generations by perpetuitie of noble acts; but contrariwise, that they that leave posterity, are the more interessed in the care of future times, that as well their Progeny as their people may participate of their merit. Your Majesty is a great Master in Justice, and Judicature, and it were pity, the fruit of that your vertue should not be transmitted to the ages to come. Your Majesty also reigneth in learned times, the more, no doubt, in regard of your own perfection in learning, and your Patronage thereof, and it hath been the mishap of works, that the less learned time hath sometimes wrought upon the more Learned, which now will not be so. As for my self, the Law was my profession, to which I am a debtor; some little help I have of other Arts, which may give forme to matter; and I have now by Gods merciful chastisement, and by his special providence, time and leasure to put my Talent, or half Talent, or what it is, to such exchanges, as may perhaps exceed the interest of an active life. Therefore as in the beginning of my troubles, I made offer to your Majesty to take pains in the story of *England*, and in compiling a method, and digest of your Laws; so have I performed the first (which rested but upon my self) in some part. And I do in all humbleness renew the offer of this Letter, (which will require help and assistance) to your Majesty, if it shall stand with your good pleasure to imploy my service therein.

Sir Francis Bacon, *To the Right Honourable his very good Lord, the Earl of Devonshire, Lord Lieuteuant of* Ireland.

IT may please your good Lordship, I cannot be ignorant, and ought to be sensible of the wrong which I sustain, Common speech, as if I had been false or unthankful, to that noble, but unfortunate Earl, the Earl of *Essex*: and for satisfying the vulgar sort, I do not so much regard it; though I love a good name; but yet as an hand-maid and attendant of honesty and vertue. For I am of his opinion, that said pleasantly, *that it was a shame to him that was a Suitor to the Mistress, to make Love to the Waiting-Woman*. And therefore, to Wooe or Court common fame, otherwise then it followeth upon honest courses, I, for my part, find not my self fit nor disposed. But on the other side, there is no worldly thing that concerneth my self, which I hold more dear, then the good opinion of certain persons, amongst which there is none I would more willingly give satisfaction unto, then to your Lordship. First, because you loved my Lord of *Essex*, and therefore will not be partial towards me, which is part of that I desire; next, because it hath ever pleased you, to shew your self to me an honourable friend, and so no baseness in me to seek to satisfy you. And lastly, because I know your Lordship is excellently grounded in the true rules and habits of duties and moralities, which must be they which shall decide this matter: wherein (my Lord) my defence needeth to be but simple and brief; namely, that whatsoever I did concerning that action and proceeding, was done in my duty and service to the Queen, and her State; in which I would not shew my self falshearted nor faint-hearted, for any mans sake living. For every honest man, that hath his heart well planted, will forsake his King, rather then forsake God; and forsake his Friends, rather then forsake his King; and yet will forsake any earthly Commodity, yea and his own life, in some cases, rather then forsake his Friend. I hope the world hath not forgotten his degrees, else the Heathen saying, *amicus usque ad aras*, shall judge them: and if any man shall say, that I did officiously intrude my self into that business, because I had no ordinary place; the like may be said of all the business, in effect, that passed the hands of the learned Councel either of State or Revenue, these many years, wherein I was continually used; for, as your Lordship may remember, the Queen knew her strength so well, as she looked her word should be a warrant; and after the manner of the choicest Princes before her, did not alwaies tye her trust to place, but did sometimes divide private favour from office. And I, for my part, though I was not unseen in the world, but I knew the condition was subject to envie and peril; yet because I knew, again, she was constant in her favours, and made an end where she began; and especially, because she upheld me with extraordinary access; and other demonstrations, confidence and Grace, I resolved to endure it in expectation of better. But my scope and desire is, that your Lordship would be pleased to have the honourable patience to know the truth, in some particularity of all that passed in this cause, wherein I had any part; that you may perceive how honest a heart I ever bare to my Sovereign, and to my Countrey, and to that Nobleman who had so well deserved of me, and so well accepted of my deservings; whose fortune I cannot remember without much grief. But for any action of mine, towards him, there is nothing that passed me in my life-time that cometh to my remembrance with

more

more clearness, and less check of Conscience: For, it will appear to your Lordship, that I was not onely not opposite to my Lord of *Essex*, but that I did occupy the utmost of my wits, and adventured my fortune with the Queen, to have redintegrated his; and so continued faithfully and industriously, till his last fatal impatience (for so I will call it;) after which day, there was not time to work for him, though the same my affection, when it could not work upon the subject proper, went to the next, with no ill effect towards some others, who (I think) do rather not know it, then not acknowledge it. And this I will assure your Lordship, I will leave nothing untold that is truth, for any enemy, that I have to add; and on the other side, I must reserve much which makes for me, upon many respects of Duty, which I esteem above my Credit: And what I have here set down to your Lordship, I protest, as I hope to have any part in Gods favour, is true.

It is well known, how I did, many years since, dedicate my travels and studies to the use, and (as I may term it) service of my Lord of *Essex*; which, I protest before God, I did not, making election of him as the likeliest mean of mine own advancement; but out of the humour of a man that ever from the time I had any use of Reason (whether it were reading upon good Books, or upon the example of a good Father, or by nature) I loved my Countrey more then was answerable to my fortune; and I held, at that time, my Lord to be the fittest instrument to do good to the State: and therefore I applied my self wholly to him, in a manner, which I think happeneth rarely amongst men. For I did not onely labour carefully and industriously in that he set me about, whether it were matter of advice, or otherwise; but neglecting the Queens service, mine own fortune, and, in a sort, my vocation, I did nothing but devise and ruminate with my self, to the best of my understanding, Propositions and Memorials of any thing that might concern his Lordships honour, fortune, or service. And when, not long after I entred into this course, my Brother, Mr. *Anthony Bacon*, came from beyond the seas, being a Gentleman whose abilities the world taketh knowledge of, for matter of State, specially, Forreign, I did likewise knit his service to be at my Lords disposing. And, on the other side, I must, and will, ever acknowledge my Lords love, trust, and favour, towards me; and last of all, his liberality, having enfeoffed me of land which I sold for 1800. *li.* to Mr. *Reynold Nicholas*, and I think was more worth, and that at such a time, and with so kind and noble circumstances, as the manner was as much as the matter: Which, though it be but an idle digression, yet because I will not be short in commemoration of his benefits, I will presume to trouble your Lordship with the relating to you the manner of it.

After the Queen had denied me the Sollicitors place, for the which his Lordship had been a long and earnest suitor on my behalf, it pleased him to come to me from *Richmond* to *Twiknam*-Park, and brake with me, and said; Mr. *Bacon*, the Queen hath denied me the place for you, and hath placed another: I know you are the least part of your own matter; but you fare ill, because you have chosen me for your mean and dependance; you have spent your time and thoughts in my matters: I die (these were the very words) if I do not somewhat towards your fortune; you shall not deny to accept a piece of land which I will bestow upon you. My answer, I remember, was; That for my fortune, it was no great matter; but that his Lordships offer made me call to mind what was wont to be said, when I was in *France*, of the Duke of *Guise*, That he was the greatest Usurer in *France*, because he had turned all his estate into obligations; meaning, that he had left himself nothing, but onely had bound numbers of persons to him: Now, my Lord, (said I) I would not have you imitate this course, nor turn your state thus by greatest gifts into obligations, for you will find many bad Debtors. He bad me take no care for that, and pressed it; whereupon I said, I see, my Lord, that I must be your Homager, and hold land of your gift; but do you know the manner of doing homage in Law? always it is with a saving of his faith to the King, and his other Lords; and therefore, my Lord, (said I) I can be no more yours then I was, and it must be with the ancient savings; and, if I grow to be a rich man, you will give me leave to give it back again to some of your un-rewarded followers.

But to return: Sure I am, (though I can arrogate nothing to my self, but that I was a faithfull Remembrancer to your Lordship) that while I had most credit with him, his fortune went on best; and yet in too many points we always directly, and contradictorily differed; which I will mention to your Lordship, because it giveth light to all that followed. The one was, I always set this down, That the onely course to be held with the Queen, was, by obsequiousness and observance: and I remember, I would usually gage confidently, that if he would take that course constantly, and with choice of good particulars to express it, the

Queen would be brought in time to *Ahasuerus* question to aske, what should done to the man that the King would honour: meaning that her goodness was without limit where there was a true concurrence, which I knew in her nature to be true: My Lord, on the other side, had a setled opinion that the Queen should be brought to nothing but by a kind of necessity and authority; and I well remember when by violent Courses at any time he had got his will, he would aske me; now sir, whose principles be true? and I would again say to him, my Lord, these courses be like to hot waters, they will help at a pang, but if you use them you shall spoil the stomach, and you shall be fain still to make them stronger and stronger, and yet in the end they will lose their operation; with much other variety wherewith I used to touch that string. Another point was, that I alwaies vehemently perswaded him from seeking greatnefs by a military dependence, or by a popular dependence, as that which would breed in the Queen jealousie, in himself presumption, and in the State perturbation; and I did usually compare them to *Icarus* two wings, which were joyned on with wax, and would make him venter to soare too high, and then fail him at the height. And I would further say unto him, my Lord stand upon two feet, and flye not upon two wings. The two feet are the two kinds of *Justice*, commutative and distributive; use your greatnefs, for advancing of merit and vertue, and relieving wrongs and burthens, you shall need no other art of finenefs: but he would tell me that opinion came not from my minde, but from my robe. But it is very true, that I that never meant to enthrall my self to my Lord of *Essex*, nor any other man, more then stood with the publique good, did (though I could little prevail) divert him by all means possible from courses of the wars and popularity: for I saw plainly, the Queen must either live or dye; if she lived, then the times would be, as in the declination of an old Prince; if she died, the times would be, as in the beginning of an new; and that if his Lordship did rise too fast in these courses, the times might be dangerous for him, and he for them. Nay, I remember, I was thus plain with him, upon his voyage to the *Islands*, when I saw every spring put forth such actions of charge and provocation, that I said to him, my Lord, when I came first to you, I took you for a Physitian, that desired to cure the diseases of the State; but now I doubt you will be like to those Physitians which can be content to keep their Patients long, because they would alwaies be in request: which plainenefs he neverthelefs took very well; as he had an excellent care, and was *patientissimus veri*, and assured me the case of the Realm required it; and I think, this speech of mine, and the like renewed afterwards, pricked him to write that Apology which is in many mens hands.

But this difference in two points, so main and material, bred, in procefs of time, a discontinuance of privatenefs (as it is the manner of men seldom to Communicate where they think their courses not approved) between his Lordship and my self, so as I was not called, nor advised with, for some year and a half before his Lordships going into *Ireland*, as in former time; yet neverthelefs touching his going into *Ireland*, it pleased him expresly, and in a set manner, to desire mine opinion, and Counsel; at which time I did not only diffwade, but protest against his going, telling him, with as much vehemency and affeveration as I could, that absence in that kind would exulcerate the Queens minde, whereby it would not be possible for him to carry himself so, as to give her sufficient contentment, nor for her to carry her self so, as to give him sufficient countenance, which would be ill for her, ill for him, and ill for the State. And because I would omit no argument, I remember, I stood also upon the difficulty of the action, setting before him, out of histories, that the Irish was such an enemie, as the ancient *Gaules*, or *Britains*, or *Germans* were, and that we faw how the Romans who had such discipline, to govern their souldiers, and such Donatives to encourage them, and the whole world in a manner to leavie them; yet when they came to deal with enemies which placed their felicities only in liberty, and the sharpnefs of their sword, and had the natural and elemental advantages of woods and boggs, and hardnefs of bodies, they ever found they had their hands full of them, and therefore concluded, that going over with such expectation as he did, and through the churlishnefs of the enterprise, not like to answer it, would mightily diminish his reputation and name; other reasons I used, so as I am sure, I never in any thing, in my life-time, dealt with him in like earnestnefs by speech, by writing, and by all the means I could devise. For, I did as plainly see his overthrow, chained as it were by destiny to that Journey, as it is possible for any man to ground a Judgement upon future contingents. But, my Lord, howsoever his ear was open, yet his heart and resolution was shut against that advice, whereby his ruine might have been prevented.

After

After my Lords going I saw how true a Prophet I was, in regard of the evident alteration which naturally succeeded in the Queens minde, and thereupon I was still in watch to find the best occasion, that, in the weakness of my power, I could either take, or minister, to pull him out of the fire, if it had been possible, and not long after, me thought I saw some overture thereof, which I apprehended readily; a particularity which I think to be known to very few, and the which I do the rather relate to your Lordship, because I hear it should be talked, that while my Lord was in *Ireland*, I revealed some matter against him, or I cannot tell what; which if it were not a meer slander, as the rest is, but had any, though never so little colour, was surely upon this occasion. The Queen one day being at *Non-such*, a little, (as I remember) before *Cuffers* coming over where I attended her, shewed a passionate distaste of my Lords proceedings in *Ireland*, as if they were unfortunate, without Judgement, Contemptuous, and not without some private end of his own, and all that might be, and was pleased, as she spake of it to many that she trusted less, so to fall into the like speech with me; whereupon I that was still awake, and true to my grounds which I thought surest for my Lords good, said to this effect: Madam, I know not the particulars of Estate, and I know this, that Princes occasions must have no abrupt periods or conclusions; but otherwise, I would think that if you had my Lord of *Essex* here with a white staff in his hand, as my Lord of *Leicester* had, and continued him still about you, for society to your self, and for an honour and ornament to your attendance and Court, in the eyes of your people, and in the eyes of Forreign Ambassadors, then were he in his right Element : for to discontent him as you do, and yet to put armes and power into his hands, may be a kind of temptation to make him prove combersome and unruly. And therefore, if you would *imponere bonam clausulam*, and send for him, and satisfie him with honour here neer you, if your affairs (which as I have said) I am not acquainted with, will permit it, I think were the best way, which course; your Lordship knoweth, if it had been taken, then all had been well; and no contempt in my Lords coming over, nor continuance of these jealousies which that imployment of *Ireland* bred, and my Lord here in his former greatness: well, the next news that I heard was, that my Lord was come over, and that he was committed to his Chamber, for leaving *Ireland* without the Queens Licence : this was at *Non-such* where (as my duty was) I came to his Lordship and talked with him privately, about a quarter of an houre, and he asked my opinion of the course that was taken with him; I told him, my Lord, *Nubecula est, cito transibit*, it is but a mist : but shall I tell your Lordship it is as mists are, if it go upwards it may haply cause a showre; if downward, it will cleer up; and therefore, good my Lord, carry it so, as you take away by all means all umbrages and distastes from the Queen, and especially, if I were worthy to admonish you (as I have been by your Lordship, thought, and now your question imports the continuance of that opinion) observe three points. First, make not this cessation or peace which is concluded with *Tyrone* as a service wherein you glory, but as a shuffling up of a prosecution which was not very fortunate; next, represent not to the Queen any necessity of State, whereby, as by a coercion or wrench, she should think her self enforced to send you back into *Ireland* ; but leave it to her. Thirdly, seek access *importune, opportune*, seriously, sportingly, every way. I remember, my Lord was willing to hear me, but spake very few words, and shaked his head sometimes, as if he thought he was in the wrong; but sure I am, he did just contrary in every one of these three points. After this, during the while my Lord was committed to my Lord Keepers, I came divers times to the Queen, as I had used to do, about cause of her Revenue and Law business, as is well known: by reason of which accesses, according to the ordinary charities of Court, it was given out that I was one of them that incensed the Queen against my Lord of *Essex*. These speeches I cannot tell, nor I will not think that they grew any waies from her own speeches, whose memory I will ever honour : if they did, she is with God, and *miserum est ab illis Lædi, de quibus non possis queri*. But, I must give this testimony to my Lord *Cecill*, that one time, in his house; at the *Savoy*, he dealt with me directly, and said to me, Cousin, I hear it, but I believe it not, that you should do some ill office to my Lord of *Essex*; for my part, I am meerly passive, and not active, in this action, and I follow the Queen, and that heavily, and I leadher not; my Lord of *Essex* is one that in nature I could consent with, as with any one living; the queen indeed is my Sovereign, and I am her creature; I may not lose her, and the same course I would wish you to take; whereupon I satisfied him how farre I was from any such mind. And, as sometimes it comes to pass, that mens inclinations are opened more in a toy then in a serious matter ; A little before that time, being about the middle

of

of *Michaelmass* Term, her Majesty had a purpose to dine at my lodging at *Twittnam* Park, at which time I had (though I profess not to be a Poet) prepared a Sonnet, directly tending to draw on her Majesties reconcilement to my Lord, which I remember also I shewed to a great person, and one of my Lords neerest friends who commended it: this though it be (as I said) but a toy, yet it shewed plainly in what spirit I proceeded, and that I was ready not only to do my Lord good offices, but to publish and declare my self for him; and never was I so ambitious of any thing in my life time, as I was to have carried some token or favour from her Majesty to my Lord, using all the art I had, both to procure her Majesty to send, and my self to be the Messenger; for as to the former, I feared not to alledge to her, that this proceeding towards my Lord was a thing towards the people very implausible; and therefore wished her Majesty, howsoever she did, yet to discharge her self, and to lay it upon others; and thereso that she should intermix her proceedings with some immediate graces from her self, that the world might take knowledge of her Princely nature and goodness, lest it should alienate the hearts of her people from her; which I did stand upon, knowing very well that if she once relented, to send or visit, those demonstrations would prove matter of substance for my Lords good: And to draw that imployment upon my self, I advised her Majesty, that whensoever God should move her to turn the light of her favour towards my Lord, to make signification to him thereof; that her Majesty, if she did it not in person, would at the least use some such mean as might not intitle themselves to any part of the thanks, as persons that were thought mighty with her, to work her, or to bring her about; but to use some such as could not be thought but a meer Conduct of her own goodness; but I could never prevaile with her, though I am perswaded she saw plainly whereat I levelled; but she had me in jealousie that I was not hers entirely, but still had inward and deep respects towards my Lord, more then stood at that time with her will and pleasure.

About the same time, I remember an answer of mine in a matter which had some affinity with my Lords Cause; which though it grew from me, went after about in others names; for her Majesty being mightily incensed with that Book which was dedicated to my Lord of *Essex*, being a story of the first year of King *Henry* the 4th. thinking it a seditious prelude to put into the peoples heads boldness and faction, said, she had an opinion there was treason in it, and asked me if I could not finde any places in it that might be drawn within Case of Treason: Whereto I answered; for treason, sure I found none; but for felony, very many. And when her Majesty hastily asked me, wherein: I told her, the Author had committed very apparent theft; for he had taken most of the sentences of *Cornelius Tacitus*, and translated them into *English*, and put them into his text. And another time, when the Queen could not be perswaded that it was his writing whose name was to it, but that it had some more mischievous Author, and said with great indignation, that she would have him racked to produce his Author, I replied; Nay, Madam, he is a Doctor, never rack his person, but rack his stile, let him have pen, Ink, and paper, and help of books, and be enjoyned to continue the story where it breaketh off, and I will undertake, by collating the stiles, to judge whether he were the Author, or no. But for the main matter, sure I am, when the Queen at any time asked my opinion of my Lords Case, I ever, in one tenour, said unto her, that they were faults which the Law might term Contempts, because they were the transgression of her particular directions and Instructions: but then, what defence might be made of them in regard of the great Interest the person had in her Majesties favour, in regard of the greatness of his place, and the ampleness of his Commission, in regard of the nature of the business, being action of war, which in common cases cannot be tyed to strictness of Instructions, in regard of the distance of the place; having also a Sea between his demands and her Commands, must be subject to winde and weather, in regard of a Councel of State of *Ireland*, which he had at his back to avow his actions upon; and lastly, in regard of a good Intention that he might alledge for himself, which, I told her, in some religions, was held to be a sufficient dispensation for Gods Commandments, much more for Princes: in all these regards I besought her Majesty to be advised again and again, how she brought the Cause into any publick question: Nay, I went further, for I told her my Lord was an eloquent and well spoken man: and besides his eloquence of nature or art, he had an eloquence of accident; which passed them both, which was, the pitie and benevolence of his hearers; and therefore when he should come to answer for himself, I doubted his words would have so unequall passage above theirs that should charge him, as would not be for her Majesties honour;

and therefore wished the Conclusion might be, that they might wrap it up privately between themselves, and that she would restore my Lord to his former attendance, with some addition of honour, to take away discontent: But this I will never deny, that I did shew no approbation generally of his being sent back again into *Ireland*, both because it would have carried a repugnancy with my former discourse, and because I was in mine own heart fully perswaded, that it was not good, neither for the Queen, nor for the State, nor for himself; and yet I did not disswade it neither, but left it ever as *locus lubricus*. For this particularitie I do well remember, that after your Lordship was named for the place in *Ireland*, and not long before your going, it pleased her Majesty, at *Whitehall*, to speak to me of that nomination: at which time I said to her; surely, Madam, if you mean not to imploy my Lord of *Essex* thither again, your Majesty cannot make a better choice; and was going on to shew some reason, and her Majesty interrupted me with great passion; *Essex* (said she) whensoever I send *Essex* back again into *Ireland*, I will marry you, claim it of me: Whereunto I said, well Madam, I will release that Contract, if his going be for the good of the State. Immediately after the Queen had thought of a Course (which was also executed) to have somewhat published in the *Star-Chamber*, for the satisfaction of the world, touching my Lord of *Essex* his restraint, and my Lord not to be called to it, but occasion to be taken by reason of some libells then dispersed, which when her Majesty propounded unto me, I was utterly against it, and told her plainly, that the people would say that my Lord was wounded upon his back, and that Justice had her balance taken from her, which ever consisted of an accusation, and defence, with many other quick and significant terms to that purpose; insomuch, that I remember, I said that my Lord, *in foro famæ*, was too hard for her; and therefore wished her, as I had done before, to wrap it up privately. And certainly, I offended her at that time, which was rare with me; for I call to minde, that both the *Christmas*, *Lent*, and *Easter* term following, though I came divers times to her upon Law-businesses, yet me-thought her face and manner was not so cleare and open to me as it was at the first: And she did directly charge me that I was absent that day at the *Star-Chamber*, which was very true; but I alledged some indisposition of body to excuse it; and during all the time aforesaid, there was *altum silentium*, from her to me, touching my Lord of *Essex* causes. But towards the end of Easter term her Majesty brake with me, and told me that she had found my words true; for that the proceeding in the *Star-Chamber* had done no good, but rather kindled factious bruits (as she termed them) then quenched them, and therefore that she was determined now, for the satisfaction of the world, to proceed against my Lord in the *Star-Chamber* by an Information *ore tenus*, and to have my Lord brought to his Answer: howbeit, she said she would assure me, that whatsoever she did should be towards my Lord, *ad castigationem, & non ad destructionem*, as indeed she had often repeated the same phrase before: Whereunto I said (to the end utterly to divert her,) Madam, if you will have me to speak to you in this Argument, I must speak to you as frier *Bacon*'s head spake, that said; first, *Time is*, and then *Time Was*, and *Time would never be*; for certainly (said I) it is now farr too late, the matter is cold, and hath taken too much winde; whereat she seemed again offended, and rose from me, and that resolution for a while continued; and after in the beginning of *Midsomer* term, I attending her, and finding her setled in that resolution, (which I heard of also otherwise) she falling upon the like speech, it is true, that seeing no other remedy, I said to her sleightly, Why, Madam, if you will needs have a proceeding, you were best have it in some such sort as *Ovid* spake of his Mistress; *Est aliquid luce patente minus*; to make a Councel-table matter of it, and end; which speech again she seemed to take in ill part, but yet I think it did good for that time, and help to divert that Cause of proceeding by Information in the *Star-Chamber*: Neverthelesse, afterwards it pleased her to make a more solemn matter of the proceeding; and some few dayes after, when order was given that the matter should be heard at *York-House*, before an Assembly of Councellors, Peers, and Judges, and some audience of men of qualitie to be admitted; then did some principal Councellors send for us of the learned Councel, and notifie her Majesties pleasure unto us; save that it was said to me openly, by some one of them, that her Majesty was not yet resolved whether she would have me forborn in the businesse or no. And hereupon might arise that other sinister and untrue speech that I heare is raised of me, how I was a suitor to be used against my Lord of *Essex* at that time; for it is very true, that I that knew well what had passed between the Queen and me, and what occasion I had given her both of distaste and distrust in crossing her disposition by

standing

Sir Francis Bacon, to the Earl of Devonshire. 83

standing stedfast for my Lord of *Essex*; and suspecting it also to be a stratagem arising from some particular emulation, I writ to her two or three words of Complement, signifying to her Majesty, that if she would be pleased to spare me in my Lord of *Essex*'s cause, out of the Consideration she took of my obligation towards him, I should reckon it for one of her highest favours; but otherwise desiring her Majesty to think that I knew the degrees of duties, and that no particular obligation whatsoever to any Subject could supplant or weaken that entireness of dutie that I did owe and bear to her and her service; and this was the goodly suite I made, being a respect no man that had his wits could have omitted, but nevertheless, I had a further reach in it; for I judged that dayes work would be a full period of any bitterness or harshness between the Queen and my Lord; and therefore if I declared my self fully according to her minde at that time, which could not do my Lord any manner of prejudice, I should keep my credit with her ever after, whereby to do my Lord service.

Hereupon, the next news that I heard was, that we were all sent for again, and that her Majesties pleasure was we should all have parts in the business; and the Lords falling into distribution of our parts, it was allotted to me that I should set forth some undutifull carriage of my Lord, in giving occasion and Countenance to a seditious Pamphlet, as it was termed, which was dedicated unto him, which was the book before mentioned, of King *H:* 4. Whereupon I replied to that allotment, and said to their Lordships, that it was an old matter, and had no manner of Coherence with the rest of the Charge, being matters of *Ireland*, and therefore that I having been wronged by bruits before, this would expose me to them more: and it would be said, I gave in evidence mine own tales. It was answered again, with good shew, that because it was Considered how I stood tied to my Lord of *Essex*, therefore that part was thought fittest for me which did him least hurt; for that whereas all the rest was matter of Charge and accusation, this only was but matter of Caveat and admonition; wherewith though I was in mine own Conscience little satisfied; because I knew well a man were better to be Charged with some faults, then admonished of some others: yet the Conclusion binding upon the Queens pleasure directly, *volens nolens* I could not avoid that part that was layed upon me; which part if in the delivery I did handle not tenderly (though no man before me did in so clear terms free my Lord from all disloyaltie as I did) that your Lordship knoweth must be ascribed to the superior duty I did owe to the Queens fame and honour in a publick proceeding; and partly, to the intention I had to uphold my self in credit and strength with the Queen, the better to be able to do my Lord good offices afterwards; for assoon as this day was past, I lost no time, but the very next day following (as I remember) I attended her Majesty, fully resolved to try and put in use my utmost endeavour, so far as I in my weakness could give furtherance, to bring my Lord speedily again into Court, and into favour; and knowing (as I supposed at least) how the Queen was to be used, I thought that to make her Conceive that the matter went well then, was the way to make her leave off there: and I remember well, I said to her, You have now, Madam, obtained victory over two things, which the greatest Princes in the world cannot at their wills subdue: the one is, over fame; the other is, over a great minde; for surely the world is now, I hope, reasonable well satisfied; and for my Lord, he did shew that humiliation towards your Majesty, as I am perswaded he was never in his life time more fit for your Majesties favour then he is now: therefore if your Majesty will not marr it by lingring, but give over at the best (and now you have made so good a full point, receive him again with tenderness;) I shall then think that all that is past is for the best. Whereat, I remember, she took exceeding great Contentment, and did often iterate and put me in minde, that she had ever said, that her proceeding should be *ad reparationem*, and not *ad ruinam*, as who saith, that now is the time I should plainly perceive that that saying of hers should prove true. And further, she willed me to set down in writing all that passed that day; I obeyed her commandment, and within some few dayes after brought her again the Narration, which I did reade unto her in two several after-noons: and when I came to that part that set forth my Lords own answer (which was my principall care,) I do well bear in minde that she was extraordinarily moved with it, with kindness and relenting towards my Lord, and told me afterwards (speaking how well I had expressed my Lords part) that she perceived old love would not be forgotten: Whereto I answered suddenly, that I hoped she meant that by her self. But in Conclusion, I did advise her, that now she had taken a representation of the matter to her self, that she would let it go no further: (for Madam, said I) the fire blazeth well already,

M 2 what

what should you tumble it? And besides, it may please you keep a conveniencie with your self in this Case; for since your express direction was there should be no Register nor Clerk to take this sentence, nor no record or memoriall made up of the proceeding; why should you now do that popularly which you would not admit to be done judicially? Whereupon she did agree that that writing should be suppressed; and I think there were not five persons that ever saw it. But from this time forth, during the whole latter end of that Summer, while the Court was at *Non-such* & *Oatland*, I made it my task and scope to take and give occasions for my Lords redintegration in his fortunes. Which my intention I did also signifie to my Lord, assoon as ever he was at libertie; whereby I might without perill of the Queens indignation write to him, and having received from his Lordship a courteous and loving acceptation of my good will and endeavours, I did apply it in all my accesses to the Queen, which were very many at that time, and purposely sought and wrought upon other variable pretences, but only and chiefly for that purpose. And on the other side, I did not forbear to give my Lord from time to time faithfull advertisement, what I found, and what I wished. And I drew for him, by his appointment, some Letters to her Majesty, which though I knew well his Lordships gift and stile was far better then mine own, yet because he required it, alledging that by his long restraint he was grown almost a stranger to the Queens present conceipts, I was ready to perform it; and sure I am, that for the space of six weeks, or two moneths, it prospered so well, as I expected continually his restoring to his attendance. And I was never better welcome to the Queen, nor more made of, then when I spake fullest and boldest for him: in which kinde the particulars were exceeding many, whereof, for an example, I will remember to your Lordship one or two; as, at one time, I call to minde, her Majesty was speaking of a fellow that undertook to cure, or at least to ease my brother of his gout, and asked me how it went forwards; and I told her Majesty, that at the first he received good by it, but after, in the course of his Cure, he found himself at a stay or rather worse: the Queen said again, I will tell you, *Bacon*, the errour of it: the manner of these Physicians, and especially these Empiricks, is, to continue one kinde of medicine, which at the first is proper, being to draw out the ill humour; but after they have not the discretion to change their medicine, but apply still drawing medicines, when they should rather intend to cure and corroborate the part. Good Lord Madam (said I) how wisely and aptly can you speak and discern of Physick ministred to the body, and consider not that there is the like reason of Physick ministred to the minde: as now, in the Case of my Lord of *Essex*, your Princely word ever was, that you intended ever to reforme his minde, and not ruine his fortune: I know well, you cannot but think you have drawn the humour sufficiently; and therefore it were more then time, and it were but for doubt of mortifying or exulcerating, that you did apply and minister strength and comfort unto him: for these same gradations of yours are fitter to corrupt then to correct any minde of greatness. And another time, I remember, she told me for newes, that my Lord had written unto her some very dutifull Letters, and that she had been moved by them; and when she took it to be the abundance of his heart, she found it to be but a preparative to a suite for the renewing of his farme of sweet wines: Whereto I replied, Alas Madam, how doth your Majesty construe of these things, as if these two could not stand well together; which indeed Nature hath planted in all Creatures; For there are but two sympathies, the one, towards *Perfection*, the other, towards *Preservation*; That to *Perfection*, as the Iron tendeth to the Loadstone; that to *Preservation*, as the Vine will creep unto a stake or prop that stands by it, not for any love to the stake, but to uphold it self. And therefore, Madam, you must distinguish, my Lords desire to do you service, is as to his perfection, that which he thinks himself to be bound for; whereas, his desire to obtain this thing of you, is but for a sustentation; and not to trouble your Lordship with many other particulars like unto this, it was at the same time that I did draw, by my Lords privitie, and by his appointment, two Letters, the one written as from my brother, the other, as an answer returned from my Lord; both to be by me in secret manner shewed to the Queen; which it pleased my Lord very strangely to mention at the barr: the scope of which were, but to represent and picture forth unto her Majesty my Lords minde to be such as I know her Majesty would fainest have had it; which Letters whosoever shall see (for they cannot now be retracted or altered, being by reason of my brothers, or his Lordships servants delivery, long since come into divers hands) let him judge, specially if he knew the Queen, and do remember those times, whether they were not the labours of one that sought to bring the Queen about for my Lord of *Essex* his good. The truth is, that the issue of all this dealing grew to this, that the Queen by some slackness of my Lord, as I imagine, liked him worse and worse, and grew more incensed towards him;

Then

Sir Francis Bacon, *to the* Earl *of* Devonshire. 85

Then, she remembring belike the continual and incessant, and confident, speeches and courses that I had held on my Lords side, became utterly alienated from me, and for the space of at least three moneths, (which was between *Michaelmas* & *New-years-tide* following) would not so much as look on me, but turned away from me with expres, & purpose-like discountenance wheresoever she saw me; and at such time as I desired to speak with her about Law business, ever sent me forth very sleight refusals; insomuch as it is most true, that immediately after *New-years-tide* I desired to speak with her, and being admitted to her, I dealt with her plainly, and said: Madam, I see you withdraw your favour from me; and now I have lost many friends for your sake, I must lose you too; you have put me like one of those that the French men call *Infans perdus*, that serve on foot before horsemen, so have you put me into matters of envy without place or without strength; and I know, at Chess a pawn before the King is ever much plaid upon: a great many love me not, because they think I have been against my Lord of *Essex*; and you love me not, because you know I have been for him: yet will I never repent me that I have dealt in simplicity of heart towards you both, without respect of Cautions to my self, and therefore *vivus vidensque pereo*: If I do break my neck, I shall do it as *Derrington* did, which walked on the Battlements of the Church many days, and took a view and survey where he should fall; and so, Madam (said I) I am not so simple, but that I take a prospect of mine own overthrow; only I thought I would tell you so much, that you may know, it was faith and not folly that brought me into it; and so I will pray for you: upon which speeches of mine, uttered with some passion, it is true, her Majesty was exceedingly moved, and accumulated a number of kind and gracious words upon me, and willed me to rest upon this, *Gratia mea sufficit*, and a number of other sensible and tender words and demonstrations, such as more could not be; but as touching my Lord of *Essex*. *ne verbum quidem*. Whereupon I departed, resting then determined to meddle no more in the matter, as that that I saw would overthrow me, and not be able to do him any good. And thus I made mine own peace, with mine own Confidence, at that time; and this was the last time I saw her Majesty, before the 8th of *February*, which was the day of my Lord of *Essex* his misfortune: After which time, for that I performed at the Bar in my publick service, your Lordship knoweth, by the rules of duty, I was to do it honestly, without prevarication: but for any putting my self in it, I protest before God, I never moved the Queen, nor any person living, concerning my being used in the service, either of evidence or of examination; but it was meerly laid upon me with the rest of my fellows. And for the time that passed between the arraignment and my Lords suffering, I well remember I was but once with the Queen, at what time, though I durst not deal directly for my Lord, as things then stood; yet generally I did both commend her Majesties mercy, terming it to her as an excellent balme, that did continually distil from her Sovereign hands, and made an excellent odour in the scents of her people; and not only so, but I took hardiness to extenuate, not the fact (for that I durst not) but the danger, telling her, that if some base or cruel minded persons had entred into such an action, it might have caused much bloud and combustion; but it appeared well, they were such as knew not how to play the Malefactors, and some other words, which I now omit. And as for the rest of the carriage of my self in that service, I have many honourable witnesses that can tell; that the next day after my Lords arraignment, by my diligence and information, touching the quality and nature of the offendours, six of nine were stayed, which otherwise had been attainted; I bringing their Lordships Letter for their stay, after the Jury was sworn to pass upon them; so neer it went: and how careful I was, and made it my part, that whosoever was in trouble abont that matter, assoon as ever his case was sufficiently known and defined of, might not continue in restraint, but be set at liberty; and many other parts, which, I am well assured of, stood with the duty of an honest man. But indeed, I will not deny, for the case of Sir *Thomas Smith* of *London*, the Queen demanding my opinion of it, I told her I thought it was as hard as many of the rest; but what was the reason? because, at that time I had seen only his accusation, and had never been present at any examination of his; and the matter so standing, I had been very untrue to my service, if I had not delivered that opinion. But afterwards, upon a re-examination of some that charged him, who weakned their own testimony; and especially hearing himself *viva voce*, I went instantly to the Queen, out of the soundness of my Conscience, not regarding what opinion I had formerly delivered, and told her Majesty, I was satisfied and resolved in my Conscience, that for the reputation of the action, the plot was to countenance the action, farther by him in respect of his place, then they had indeed any interest or intelligence with him; it is very true also, about that time her Majesty taking a liking of my pen, upon that which I

formerly

formerly had done concerning the proceeding at *York* house, and likewise upon some former Declarations, which in former times by her appointment I put in writing, commanded me to pen that Book which was published for the better satisfaction of the world; which I did, but so as never Secretary had more particular and express directions and instructions in every point, how to guide my hand in it; and not only so, but after that I had made a first draught thereof, and propounded it to certain principal Councellors, by her Majesties appointment, it was perused, weighed, censured, altered, and made almost a new writing, according to their Lordships better consideration, wherein their Lordships and my self both were as religious, and curious of truth, as desirous of satisfaction: and my self, indeed, gave only words and form of stile, in pursuing their directions: And after it had passed their allowance, it was again exactly perused by the Queen her self, and some alterations made again by her appointment; nay, and after it was set to Print, the Queen, who, as your Lordship knoweth, as she was excellent in great matters, so she was exquisite in small: and noted, that I could not forget my ancient respect to my Lord of *Essex*, in terming him ever my Lord of *Essex*, in almost every page of the Book, which she thought not fit, but would have it made *Essex*, or the late Earl of *Essex*: whereupon, of force it was Printed *de novo*, and the first Copies suppressed, by her peremptory commandment. And this, my Lord, to my furthest remembrance, is all that passed, wherein I had part, which I have set down as near as I could in the very words and speeches that were used, not because they are worth the repetition, I mean those of mine, but to the end your Lordship may lively and plainly discern between the face of truth, and a smooth tale. And the rather also, because in things that passed a good while since, the very words and phrases did sometimes bring to my remembrance the matters, wherein I refer me to your honourable Judgment, whether you do not see the traces of an honest man; and had I been as well believed, either by the Queen or my Lord, as I was well heard by them both; both my Lord had been fortunate, and so had my self in his fortune.

To conclude, therefore, I humbly pray your Lordship to pardon me, for troubling you with this long Narration, and that you will vouchsafe to hold me in your good opinion, till you know I have deserved, or find that I shall deserve the contrary; and even so I continue,

At your Lordships honourable Commandments,
very humble, F. B.

Sir Francis Bacon, to the King.

MAY it please your most excellent Majesty: It is observed, upon a place in the *Canticles* by some, *Ego sum Flos Campi, & Lilium Convallium*; that it is not said, *Ego sum flos horti, & lilium montium*: because the Majesty of that Person is not inclosed for a few, nor appropriate to the great. And yet, notwithstanding, this Royal vertue of access, which nature and judgment hath placed in your Majesties mind, as the portal of all the rest, could not of it self (my imperfections considered) have animated me to have made oblation of my self immediately to your Majesty, had it not been joyned to a habit, of like liberty which I enjoyed with my late dear Sovereign Mistress, a Princess happy in all things, but most happy in such a Successor. And yet further, and more neerly, I was not a little encouraged, not only upon a supposal, that unto your Majesties sacred ears (open to the aire of all vertues) there might have come some small breath of the good memory of my Father, so long a principal Councellor in your Kingdom, but also, by the particular knowledge of the infinite devotion, and incessant endeavours, beyond the strength of his body, and the nature of the times, which appeared in my good Brother towards your Majesties service, and were on your Majesties part, through your singular benignities, by many most gracious and lively significations and favours accepted and acknowledged, beyond the thought of any thing he could effect: All which endeavours and duties, for the most part, were common to my self with him, though by design between brethren dissembled. And therefore, most high and mighty King, my most dear and dread Sovereign Lord, since now the corner-stone is laid of the mightiest Monarchy in *Europe*, and that God above, who is noted to have a mighty hand in bridling the floods and fluctuations of the seas, and of peoples hearts, hath by the miraculous and universal consent, (the more strange, because it proceedeth from such diversity of causes) in your coming in, given a sign and token, what he intendeth in the continuance; I think there is no Subject of your Majesty, who loveth this Island, and is not hollow and unworthy,

unworthy, whose heart is not on fire, not only to bring you Peace-offerings to make you propitious; but to sacrifice himself as a Burnt-offering to your Majesties service: Amongst which number, no mans fire shall be more pure and fervent; but how far forth it shall blaze out, that resteth in your Majesties imployment. For since your fortune, in the greatness thereof, hath for a time debarred your Majesty of the fruitful vertue which one calleth the principal, *(Principis est virtus maxima nosse suos)* because your Majesty hath many of yours, which are unknown unto you, I must leave all to the trial of further time; and thirsting after the happiness of kissing your Royal hand, continue ever

Your, &c.
FR. BACON.

Sir Francis Bacon, *to the Lord* Kinloss, *upon the entrance of* K. James.

My Lord,

THE present occasion awakeneth in me a remembrance of the constant amity and mutual good offices which passed between my Brother deceased and your Lordship, whereunto I was less strange, then in respect of the time I had reason to pretend; and withal I call to mind the great opinion my Brother (who seldom failed in judgment of a person) would often express to me of your Lordships great wisdom and soundness, both in head and heart, towards the service and affairs of our Sovereign Lord the King. The one of those hath bred in me an election, and the other a confidence, to address my good will and sincere affection to your good Lordship, not doubting, in regard my course of life hath wrought me not to be altogether unseen in the matters of the Kingdom, that I may be in some use both in points of service to the King, and your Lordships particular: And on the other side, I will not omit to desire humbly your Lordships favour, in furthering a good conceit and impression of my most humble duty, and true zeal towards the King, to whose Majesty words cannot make me known, neither mine own nor others, but time will, to no disadvantage of any that shall fore-run his Majesties experience, by their humanity and commendations. And so I commend your Lordship to Gods protection.

Your, &c.
From *Graies Inne,* &c.
FR. BACON.

Sir Francis Bacon, *to the Earl of* Northumberland, *concerning a Proclamation upon the Kings entry.*

It may please your Lordship,

I Do hold it a thing formal and necessary, for the King to fore-run his coming, be it never so speedy, with some gracious Declaration for the cherishing, entertaining, and preparing of mens affections. For which purpose I have conceived a draught, it being a thing to me familiar, in my Mistress her times, to have my pen used in politick writings of satisfaction. The use of this may be in two sorts: First properly, if your Lordship think convenient to shew the King any such draught, because the veins and pulses of this State cannot but be known here; which if your Lordship should, then I would desire your Lordship to withdraw my name, and onely signifie that you gave some heads of direction of such a matter to one of whose stile and pen you had some opinion. The other collateral, that though your Lordship make no other use of it, yet it is a kind of pourtraicture of that which I think worthy to be advised by your Lordship to the King, to express himself according to those points which are therein conceived, and perhaps more compendious and significant then if I had set them down in Articles. I would have attended your Lordship, but for some little Physick I took. To morrow morning I will wait on you. So I ever continue, *&c.*

FR. BACON.

Sir Francis Bacon, to Sir Edward Coke, expostulatory.

Mr. Attorney,

I Thought best, once for all, to let you know, in plainness, what I find of you, and what you shall find of me; you take to your self a liberty to disgrace and disable my Law, experience and discretion, what it pleases you; I pray think of me. I am one that know both mine own wants & other mens; and it may be, perchance, that mine may mend when others stand at a stay: And surely, I may not in publick place endure to be wronged, without repelling the same to my best advantage, to right my self. You are great, and therefore have the more enviers, which would be glad to have you paid at anothers cost. Since the time I missed the Sollicitors place, the rather I think by your means, I cannot expect that you and I shall ever serve as Attorney and Sollicitor together; but either, to serve with another, upon your remove, or to step into some other course. So as I am more free then ever I was from any occasion of unworthy conforming my self to you, more then general good manners, or your particular good usage shall provoke: And if you had not been short-sighted in your own fortune (as I think) you might have had more use of me; but that tide is past. I write not this to shew any friends what a brave Letter I have writ to Mr. Attorney, I have none of those humours: but that I have written is to a good end, that is, to the more decent carriage of my Masters service, and to our particular better understanding one another. This Letter, if it shall be answered by you in deed, and not in word, I suppose it will not be the worse for us both; else, it is but a few lines lost, which for a much smaller matter I would adventure. So this being to you self, I for my part rest,

Yours, &c.
FR. BACON.

Sir Francis Bacon, to Sir Edward Coke, after Lord Chief Justice, and in disgrace.

My very good Lord,

THough it be true, that who considereth the wind and the rain shall neither sow nor reap, *Eccles. 9. 15.* yet there is a season for every action: And so there is a time to speak, and a time to keep silence; there is a time when the words of a poor simple man may profit: and that poor man, in the *Preacher,* which delivered the City by his wisdom, found, that without this opportunity, the power both of wisdom and eloquence lose but their labour, and cannot charm the deaf Adder. God therefore, before his Son that bringeth mercy, sent his servant the Trumpeter of repentance to level a very high hill, to prepare the way before him, making it smooth and straight. And as it is in spiritual things, where Christ never comes before his Way-maker hath laid even the heart with sorrow and repentance (since self-conceited and proud persons think themselves too good and too wise to learn of their inferior, and therefore need not the Physician) so in the rules of earthly wisdom, it is not possible for nature to attain any mediocrity of perfection, before she be humbled by knowing her self and her own ignorance. Not only knowledge, but also every other gift (which we call the gifts of fortune) have power to pull up earthly——Afflictions only level these Mole-hils of pride, plough the heart, and make it fit for Wisdom to sow her seed, and for Grace to bring forth her increase. Happy is that man therefore, both in regard of heavenly and earthly wisdom, that is thus wounded, to be cured; thus broken, to be made straight; thus made acquainted with his own imperfections, that he may be perfected.

Supposing this to be the time of your affliction, that which I have propounded to my self is, by taking this seasonable advantage, like a true friend (though far unworthy to be counted so) to shew you your true shape in a glass, and that not in a false one, to flatter you, nor yet in one that should make you seem worse then you are, and so offend you; but in one made by the reflexion of your own words and actions, from whose light proceeds the voice of the people, which is often not unfitly called the voice of God: but therein (since I purposed a truth) I must intreat liberty to be plain, a liberty that at this time I know not whether or no I may use safely, I am sure at other times I could not: yet of this resolve your self, it proceedeth from love, and a true desire to do you good, that you knowing the general opinion may not altogether neglect or contemn it, but mend what you find amiss in your self, and retain what your judgement shall approve; for to this end shall truth be delivered as naked as if your self were to be anatomized by the hand of opinion. All men

can

Sir Francis Bacon, *to* Sir Edward Coke.

can see their own profit, that part of the wallet hangs before. A true friend (whose worthy office I would perform, since, I fear, both your self, and all great men, want such, being themselves true friends to few or none) is first to shew the other, and which is from your eyes.

First, therefore, behold your errours: In discourse, you delight to speak too much, not to hear other men; this, some say, becomes a Pleader, not a Judge: for by this sometimes your affections are entangled with a love of your own Arguments, though they be the weaker, and rejecting of those, which, when your affections were setled, your own judgment would allow for strongest. Thus while you speak in your own Element, the Law, no man ordinarily equals you; but when you wander, (as you often delight to do) you then wander indeed, and give never such satisfaction as the curious time requires. This is not caused by any natural defect, but first for want of election, when you, having a large and fruitfull mind, should not so much labour what to speak, as to find what to leave unspoken: Rich soils are often to be weeded.

Secondly, you cloy your Auditory; when you would be observed, speech must either be sweet, or short.

Thirdly, you converse with Books, not Men, and Books specially humane, and have no excellent choice with men, who are the best books: For a man of action and imployment you seldom converse with, and then but with your underlings; not freely, but as a Schoolmaster with his Scholars, ever to teach, never to learn. But if sometimes you would, in your familiar discourse, hear others, and make election of such as know what they speak, you should know many of these tales you tell to be but ordinary, and many other things, which you delight to repeat, and serve in for novelties, to be but stale. As, in your pleadings, you were wont to insult over misery, and to inveigh bitterly at the persons (which bred you many enemies, whose poyson yet swelleth, and the effects now appear) so are you still wont to be a little careless in this point, to praise, or disgrace, upon sleight grounds, and that sometimes untruly; so that your reproofs, or commendations, are, for the most part, neglected and contemned; when the censure of a Judge (coming slow, but sure). should be a brand to the guilty, and a crown to the vertuous. You will jest at any man in publick, without respect of the persons dignity, or your own: This disgraceth your gravity, more then it can advance the opinion of your wit; and so do all actions which, we see, you do directly with a touch of vain-glory, having no respect to the true end. You make the Law to lean too much to your opinion, whereby you shew your self to be a legal Tyrant, striking with that weapon where you please, since you are able to turn the edge any way. For thus the wise Master of the Law gives warning to young Students, that they should be wary, lest while they hope to be instructed by your integrity and knowledge, they should be deceived with your skill armed with authority. Your too much love of the world is too much seen, when having the living of 10000*l.* you relieve few or none, The hand that hath taken so much, can it give so little? Herein you shew no bowels of compassion, as if you thought all too little for your self; or that God had given you all that you have (if you think wealth to be his gift, I mean, that you get well, for I know sure, the rest is not) onely to that end you should still gather more, and never be satisfied, but try how much you could gather, to accompt for all at the great and general Audit-day. We desire you to amend this, and let your poor Tenants in *Norfolk* find some comfort, where nothing of your estate is spent towards their relief, but all brought up hither, to the impoverishing of your Countrey.

In your last, which might have been your best, piece of service to the State, affectioned to follow that old Rule, which giveth Justice leaden heels, and iron hands, you used too many delays, till the Delinquents hands were loosed, and yours bound: In that work you seemed another *Fabius*; here the humour of *Marcellus* would have done better: What needed you have sought more evidences then enough? While you pretended the finding out of more, (missing your aim) you discredited what you had found. This best judgments think, though you never used such speeches as are fathered upon you, yet you might well have done it, and but rightly: For this crime was second to none, but the Powder-plot: That would have blown up all at one blow, a mercifull cruelty; this would have done the same by degrees, a lingring, but a sure way; one might by one be called out, till all opposers had been removed: Besides, that other Plot was scandalous to *Rome*, making Popery odious in the sight of the whole world; this hath been scandalous to the truth of the whole Gospel; and since the first nullity to this instant, when Justice hath her hands bound, the Devil could not have invented a more mischievous practice, to our State and Church, then this hath been; is, and is like to be. God avert the evil.

But herein you committed another fault, that you were too open in your proceedings, and so taught them whereby to defend themselves; so you gave them time to undermine Justice, and to work upon all advantages, both of affections, and honor, and opportunity, and breach of friendship; which they have so well followed, sparing neither pains nor cost, that it almost seemeth an higher offence in you to have done so much indeed, then that you have done no more: you stop the confessions and accusations of some, who perhaps, had they been suffered, would have spoken enough to have removed some stumbling-blocks out of your way; and that you did not this in the favour of any one, but of I know not what present unadvised humors, supposing enough behind to discover all, which fell not out so. Howsoever, as the Apostle saith in another case, you went not rightly to the truth; and therefore, though you were to be commended for what you did, yet you were to be reprehended for many circumstances in the doing; and doubtless God hath an eye, in this cross, to your negligence; and the briars are left to be pricks in your sides, and thorns in your eyes. But that which we commend you for, are those excellent parts of Nature, and knowledge in the Law, which you are indued withall; but these are only good in their good use: wherefore we thank you heartily for standing stoutly in the Commonwealths behalf, hoping it proceedeth not from a disposition to oppose Greatness (as your enemies say) but to do justice, and deliver truth indifferently without respect of persons; and in this we pray for your prosperity, and are sorry that your good actions should not alwaies succeed happily. But in the carriage of this you were faulty; for you took it in hand in an evil time, both in respect of the present business which it interrupted, and in regard of his present sickness whom it concerned, whereby you disunited your strength, and made a gap for the enemies to pass out at, and to return and assault you.

But now, since the case so standeth, we desire you to give way to power, and so to fight that you be not utterly broken, but reserved entirely to serve the Commonwealth again, and do what good you can, since you cannot do all the good you would; and since you are fallen upon this rock, cast out the goods to save the bottom, stop the leaks and make towards land; learn of the Steward, to make friends of the unrighteous Mammon. Those *Spaniards* in *Mexico* who were chased of the *Indians*, tell us what to do with our goods in our extremities; they being to pass over a River in their flight, as many as cast away their gold swam over safe; but some more covetous, keeping their gold, were either drowned with it, or overtaken and slain by the Savages; you have received, now learn to give. The *Beaver* learns us this lesson, who being hunted for his stones bites them off: You cannot but have much of your estate (pardon my plainness) ill got; think how much of that you never spake for; how much by speaking injustly or in unjust causes. Account it then a blessing of God, if thus it may be laid out for your good, and not left for your heir, to hasten the wasting of much of the rest, perhaps of all; for so we see God oftentimes proceeds in judgment with many hasty gatherers; you have enough to spare, being well laid, to turn the Tide, and fetch all things again. But if you escape (I suppose it worthy of an *if*) since you know the old use, that none called in question must go away uncensured; yet consider that accusations make wounds, and leave scarres; and though you see your tale behind your back, your self free, and the Covert before, yet remember there are stands; trust not a reconciled enemie, but think the peace is but to secure you for further advantage, expect a second and a third encounter; the main battel, the wings are yet unbroken, they may charge you at an instant, or death before them: walk therefore circumspectly; and if at length, by means of our good endeavors and yours, you recover the favour that you have lost, give God the glory in action, not in words onely, and remember us with sense of your past misfortune, whose estate hath, doth, and may hereafter lye in the power of your breath. There is a great mercy in dispatch, delays are tortures wherewith we are by degrees rent out of our estates: do not you (if you be restored) as some others do, fly from the service of vertue to serve the time, as if they repented their goodness, or meant not to make a second hazard in Gods House; but rather let this cross make you zealous in Gods cause, sensible in ours, and more sensible in all, which express thus. You have been a great enemy to Papists, if you love God, be so still, but more indeed then heretofore: for much of your zeal was heretofore wasted in words: call to remembrance that they were the persons that prophesied of that cross of yours long before it hapned; they saw the storm coming, being the principal contrivers and furtherers of the plot, the men that blew the coals, heat the Iron, and made all things ready, they owe you a good turn, and will, if they can, pay it you; you see their hearts by their deeds, prove then your faith so too. The best good work you can do, is to do the best you can against them, that is, to see the Law severely, justly, and diligently executed. And now we beseech you, my Lord, be sensible both of the stroak, and hand that striketh: learn of

David

David, to leave *Shimei*, and call upon God; he hath some great work to do, and he prepareth you for it; he would neither have you faint, nor yet bear this cross with a Stoical resolution. There is a Christian mediocrity, worthy of your greatness. I must be plain, perhaps, rash. H. d some notes which you have taken at Sermons been written in your heart to practise, this work had been done long ago, without the envy of your enemies: But when we will not mind our selves, God (if we belong to him) takes us in hand; and because he seeth that we have unbridled stomacks, therefore he sends outward crosses; which, while they cause us to mourn, do comfort us, being assured testimonies of his love that sends them. To humble our selves therefore before God, is the part of a Christian: but, for the world, and our enemies, the counsel of the Poet is apt, *Tune cede malis, sed contra audentior ito.*

The last part of this counsel you forget; yet none need be asham'd to make use of it, that so being armed against casualties, you may stand firm against the assaults on the right hand, and on the left. For this is certain, the mind that is most prone to be puft up with prosperity, is most weak, and apt to be dejected with the least puff of adversity. Indeed she is strong enough to make an able man stagger, striking terrible blows; but true Christian wisdom gives us armour of proof against all assaults, and teacheth us in all estates to be content: for, though she cause our truest friends to declare themselves our enemies, though she give heart then to the most cowardly to strike us, though an hours continuance countervail an age of prosperity, though she cast in our dish all that ever we have done, yet hath she no power to hurt the humble and wise, but onely to break such as too much prosperity hath made stiff in their own thoughts, but weak indeed, and fitted for renewing; when the wise rather gather from thence profit and wisdom, by the example of *David*, who said, *Before I was chastised, I went wrong.* Now then, he that knoweth the right way, will look better to his footing. *Cardan* saith, That weeping, fasting, and sighing, are the chief purgers of griefs. Indeed, naturally they help to asswage sorrow; but God, in this case, is the onely and best Physician: the means he hath ordained, are, the advice of friends, the amendment of our selves; for amendment is both Physician and Cure. For friends, although your Lordship be scant, yet, I hope, you are not altogether destitute; if you be, do but look on good books, they are true friends, that will neither flatter, nor dissemble; be you but true to your self, applying what they teach unto the party grieved, and you shall need no other comfort, nor counsel. To them, and to Gods holy Spirit, directing you in the reading of them; I commend your Lordship, beseeching him to send you a good issue out of these troubles; and from henceforth to work a reformation in all that is amiss, and a resolute perseverance, proceeding, and growth in all that is good, and that for his glory, the bettering of your self, this Church and Common-wealth; whose faithfull servant whilest you remain, I remain a faithfull servant to you.

Sir Francis Bacon, to Sir Vincent Skinner, *expostulatory.*

Sir *Vincent Skinner,*

I See that by your needless delays this matter is grown to a new question: wherein, for the matter it self, if it had been stayed at the beginning, by my Lord Treasurer, and my Lord Chancellor, I should not so much have stood upon it: For, the great and daily travels which I take in his Majesties service, either are rewarded in themselves, in that they are but my duty, or else may deserve a much greater matter. Neither can I think amiss of any man, that, in furtherance of the Kings benefit, moved the doubt, that I knew not what warrant you had: But my wrong is, that you, having had my Lord Treasurers, and Mr. Chancellors warrant for payment, above a moneth since, you (I say) making your payments, belike, upon such differences as are better known to your self, then agreeable to due respect of his Majesties service, have delayed all this time, otherwise then I might have expected either from our ancient acquaintance, or, from that regard, that one in your place may owe to one in mine. By occasion whereof, there ensueth to me a greater inconvenience, that now my name, in sort, must be in question amongst you, as if I were a man likely to demand that that were unreasonable, or to be denied that that is reasonable: and this must be, because you can pleasure men at pleasure. But this I leave, with this, that it is the first matter wherein I had occasion to discern of your friendship; which I see to fall to this, That whereas Mr. Chancellor, the last time, in my mans hearing, very honourably said, that he would not discontent any man in my place, it seems you have no such caution. But my writing to you now, is, to know of you, where now the stay is, without being any more beholden to you, to whom indeed no man ought to be beholden in those cases in a right course. And so I bid you farewell.

FR. BACON.

Sir Francis Bacon, *to the Lord Chancellor.*

It may please your Lordship,

AS I conceived it to be a resolution, both with his Majesty, and among your Lordships of his Councel, that I should be placed Sollicitor, and the Sollicitor to be removed to be the Kings Serjeant; so I most humbly thank your Lordships furtherance and forwardness therein, your Lordship being the man that first devised the mean: Wherefore my humble request unto your Lordship is, That you would set in with some strength to finish this your work; which (I assure your Lordship) I desire the rather, because being placed, I hope, for your many favours, to be able to do you some better service: for, as I am, your Lordship cannot use me, nor scarcely indeed know me; not that I vainly think I shall be able to do any great matters; but certainly, it will frame me to use a more industrious observance and application to such as I honour so much as I do your Lordship, and not, I hope, without some good offices, which may deserve your thanks. And herewithal, good my Lord, I humbly pray your Lordship to consider, that time groweth precious with me, and that a married man is seven years older, in his thoughts, the first day: And therefore, what a discomfortable thing it is for me to be unsetled still. For surely, were it not that I think my self born for to do my Sovereign service, and therefore in that station will I live and die; otherwise, for mine own private comfort, it were better for me, that the King should blot me out of his book, or that I should turn my course to endeavour to serve him in some other kind, then for me to stand thus at a stop, and to have that little reputation which by my industry I gather to be scattered and taken away by continual disgraces, every new man coming in before me; and sure I am, I shall never have fairer promises and hope from all your Lordships, and I would believe you in a far greater matter: And if it were nothing else, I hope the modesty of my suit deserveth somewhat, for I know well, the Sollicitors place is not as your Lordship left it, time working alteration, somewhat in the profession, much more in that special place. And were it not to satisfie my wife's friends, and to get my self out of being a common gaze, and a speech, (I protest before God) I would never speak word for it. But to conclude, as my honourable Lady was some mean to make me to change the name of another: so, if it please you to help me, as you said, to change mine own name, I cannot be but more and more bounden to you; And I am much deceived, if your Lordship find not the King well inclined: as for my Lord of *Salisbury*, he is forward, and affectionate.

Yours, &c.
FR. BACON.

Sir Francis Bacon, *to the King.*

It may please your Excellent Majesty,

HOw honestly ready I have been, most gracious Sovereign, to do your Majesty humble service to the best of my power, and, in a manner, beyond my power, as I now stand, I am not so unfortunate but your Majesty knows; both in the Commission of Union, the labour whereof, for men of my profession, rested most upon my hands: and this last Parliament, for the Bill of Subsidy, both Body, and preamble: In the Bill of Attainders, of *Tresham*, and the rest; in the matter of Purveyance, in the Ecclesiastical Petitions, in the Grievances, and the like; as I was ever carefull, not without good success, sometime to put forward that which was good, sometime to keep back that which was worse; so your Majesty was pleased, kindly to accept of my services, and to say to me, Such conflicts were the wars of peace, and such victories the victories of peace; and therefore, such servants as obtained them, were, by Kings that reign in peace, no less to be esteemed then Conquerors in the wars. In all which, nevertheless, I can challenge to my self no sufficiency, that I was diligent

gent, and reasonably happy, to execute those directions which I received, either immediately from your Royal mouth, or from my Lord of *Salisbury*. At that time, it pleased your Majesty also to assure me, that upon the remove of the then Attorney, I should not be forgotten, but be brought into ordinary place: and this was after confirmed unto me by many of my Lords. And towards the end of the last Term, the manner also in particular spoken of, that is, that Mr. Sollicitor should be made your Majesties Serjeant, and I Sollicitor; for so it was thought best to sort with both our gifts and faculties for the good of our service, And of this resolution both Court and Countrey took notice. Neither was this any invention or project of mine own, but moved from my Lords, I think, first from my Lord Chancellor: whereupon resting, your Majesty well knoweth, I never opened my mouth for the greater place, although, I am sure, I had two circumstances that Mr. Attorney that now is could not alledge; the one, nine years service of the Crown; the other, the being Cousin-german to my Lord of *Salisbury*; for of my Fathers service I will not speak. But for the less place, I conceive, it was never meant me: But after that Mr. Attorney *Hubbard* was placed, I heard no more of any preferment, but it seemed to be at a stop, to my great disgrace and discontentment. For, gracious Sovereign, if still, when the waters be stirred, another shall be put in before me, your Majesty had need work a miracle, or else I shall be a lame man to do your services. And therefore, my most humble suit unto your Majesty is, That this, which seemed to me intended, may speedily be performed; and I hope, my former services shall be but as beginnings to better, when I am better strengthened: For, sure I am, no mans heart is fuller; I say not, but many may have greater hearts, but I say, not fuller of love and duty towards your Majesty and your Children, as I hope time will manifest against envy and detraction, if any be. To conclude, I humbly crave pardon for my boldness, &c.

Yours, &c.

FR. BACON.

The

The EARL of BRISTOL'S
Letters, &c.

The Earl of Bristol, *to King* James.

May it please your most Excellent Majesty,

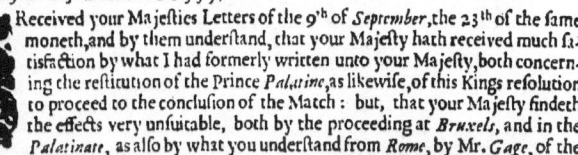

Received your Majesties Letters of the 9th of *September*, the 23th of the same moneth, and by them understand, that your Majesty hath received much satisfaction by what I had formerly written unto your Majesty, both concerning the restitution of the Prince *Palatine*, as likewise, of this Kings resolution to proceed to the conclusion of the Match: but, that your Majesty findeth the effects very unsuitable, both by the proceeding at *Bruxels*, and in the *Palatinate*, as also by what you understand from *Rome*, by Mr. *Gage*, of the Popes demands. I hope, by the arrival of Mr. *Cottington*, your Majesty will have received satisfaction, in some measure; at least, that there hath been no diligence or time omitted, either for the redressing of any thing that hath been amiss, or for the advancing of your Majesties affairs.

The very day I received your Letters I sent a Gentleman post unto the King, who was gone into the *Escurial*, to demand audience; which he presently granted me, and I repaired thither unto him upon the third of *October*, the Conde *de Gondomar* being likewise commanded to wait upon the King: I was there well received; and presently upon my arrival, the Conde *de Olivarez* came to me, to the lodgings which were appointed for me to rest in. To him I delivered fully, in the presence of Sir *Walter Aston*, and the Conde *de Gondomar*, what I had to negotiate with the King, both in the business of the Match, and of the Palatinate. In the Match, I represented how much it imported your Majesty, that a speedy resolution might be taken therein, both in regard of the Prince, being your Majesties onely son, now arrived to the age of 22. years, and for the setling of your affairs in *England*. I repeated unto him all the passages in this Treaty, how many years had been already spent in it; that after so long an expectation, the diligences used in *Rome* for the obtaining of the Dispensation had wrought but small effect, since the Pope had lately made such demands as were altogether impossible for your Majesty to condescend unto; and therefore your Majesty, seeing the business still delayed, held it fit, that some such course might be taken, that both your Majesties might speedily know what you were to trust unto; and therefore had commanded me, to signifie unto this King your uttermost resolution, how far you would condescend, in point of Religion, towards what the Pope had demanded: and if herewith this King could be satisfied, your Majesty desired, that we might proceed to a final and speedy conclusion; otherwise, that this King would likewise cleerly declare himself, that your Majesty might lose no more time in the disposing of the Prince your Son. Hereunto the Conde *de Olivarez* answered with some length, the substance I shall onely presume to set down, briefly, to your Majesty. He proposed a sincere intention and resolution in the King to make the Match, and that there should not be one day lost; for the speedy dispatch thereof imported them as much as your Majesty: and to the end that no time may be lost, this King had, the next day after, for Don *Balthazar de Zuniga*, appointed Don *Ferdinando de Giron* in his place in the Commission: That for the going of Mr. *Gage* from *Rome*, and the Popes demands, they were absolutely ignorant of them; That the King had done all that I my self desired, for the redress of this errour; That I might assure your Majesty, that you shall find all sincerity and cleer proceeding, without an hours delay, more then of necessity the nature of the business requires. As

The Earl of Bristol, to the King.

As for the business of the *Palatinate*, I presented at large the merits of your Majesties proceeding, the many promises made from hence; yet notwithstanding the while your Majesty was treating at *Bruxels*, *Heidelberg* one of the three places which were onely left, and where your Majesty had Garrisons, was besieged by the Archduke *Leopold* and Monsieur *Tilly*; that this King had withdrawn his Forces, and so exposed the *Palatinate* absolutely to the Emperour, and the Duke of *Bavaria*. The Conde *de Olivarez* answered me, by acknowledging how much your Majesties proceedings had deserved at the Emperour and this Kings hands: That whatsoever your Majesty could expect, or had been at any time promised, should by this King be really performed: That the Prince Palatines own courses hitherto had been the only hinderance of the effecting of it: That he referred it unto your Majesties own just judgement, whether the calling of this Kings forces out of the *Palatinate* were with any ill intention, or meerly for the defence of *Flanders*, which otherwise had been put in great hazard by Count *Mansfield*, as your Majesty saw by what had really passed: That the siege of *Heidelbergh* was no way by the consent or knowledge of this King or any of his Ministers, but was generally disapproved by them all.

I told them, I conceived that was not enough; for that your Majesty had engaged your self to this King, that in case your Son-in-law would not conform himself, you would not only forsake him, but would declare your self against him, and give the Emperour assistance for the reducing of him to reason, and that your Majesty could not but expect a like reciprocal proceeding from the King. He answered, your Majesty should see the Kings sincerity by the effects; and that if *Heidelbergh* should be taken, and the Emperour refuse to restore it, or to condescend to such accommodation as should be held reasonable, this King would infallibly assist your Majesty with his Forces. And this he spake with great assurance, and wished me to desire your Majesty to be confident you would find nothing but real and sincere proceedings from hence.

I was then presently called for to the King, to whom I spake first in the business of the Match, and delivered him the contents thereof in writing, which I have sent to Mr Secretary. I received from him the same answer, in effect, as from the Conde *de Olivarez*, That he desired the Match no less then your Majesty; That on his part there should be no time lost for the bringing of it to a speedy conclusion. In the business of the *Palatinate*, I spake unto the King with some length, repeating many particulars of your Majesties proceedings, and how much your honour was like to suffer, that now, whilst you are treating, *Heidelbergh* defended by your Garrisons was like to be taken. The King answered me, He would effectually labour that your Majesty should have entire satisfaction; and rather then your Majesty should fail thereof, he would imploy his Arms to effect it for you. My Lord Ambassador Sir *Walter Aston*, accompanied me at my audience, and was a witness of all that passed, as well with the King, as with the Conde *de Olivarez*.

Within few dayes after the news of the taking of *Heidelbergh* came hither: whereupon I dispatched again to the King in such sort as I have at large advertised Mr. Secretary *Calvert*. The effect of my Negotiation was, that they on the 13 of *October* dispatched Letters away of the Emperors and Duke of *Bavarias* proceedings. But pressing them further, in regard their former Letters have wrought so little effect, they have given me at present a second dispatch, which I have sent to the *Infanta*, and whereof Mr. Secretary will give your Majesty an account, which I conceive will procure your Majesties better satisfaction then hitherto you have received from the Emperor and his party.

For the business of the match, I have written to Mr. Secretary what is to be said at present; and will only add, that as I should not willingly give your Majesty hope upon uncertain grounds, so I will not conceal what they profess, which is, That they will give your Majesty real and speedy satisfaction therein. And if they intended it not, they are falser then all the Devils in hell; for deeper oaths and protestations of sincerity cannot be made.

It will only remain, that I humbly cast my self at your Majesties feet, for that addition of Title wherewith it hath pleased you to honour me, and my posterity. My gratitude and thankfulness wanteth expression, and shall only say unto your Majesty, That as all I have, either of fortunes or honour, I hold it meerly of your bounty and goodness; so shall I ever cheerfully lay them down, with my life into the bargain, for the service of your Majesty and yours.

So with my humble prayers, for the health and prosperity of your Majesty, I humbly commend your Majesty to Gods holy protection, and rest,

Madrid, Octob. 21.
1622.

Your Majesties most humble servant and subject,
BRISTOL.

The Earl of Bristol, to Secretary Cottington.

Good Mr. Secretary Cottington,

THere is no man living knoweth better then your self, how zealous I have been unto the Princes service; and whilest I thought he desired the Match, I was for it against all the World. Now the Treaty is ended, the world shall see I never had, nor will have any affections of my own, but will wholly follow my Masters, as I have written unto you in my former Letters, and have not these four moneths spoken a word in the marriage. If his Majesty and the Prince will have a war, I will spend my life and fortunes in it, without so much as replying, in what quarrel soever it be. And of thus much I intreat you let his Highness be informed by you. And I intreat you let me know his directions, what he will have me do, and how to behave my self; for I absolutely cast my self at his feet, which I desire to do the first thing after my landing, to the end that understanding his pleasure I may commit no errour. I beseech you to dispatch this bearer back unto me with all possible speed, though it be with not one word more but what the Prince will have me do, wherewith I shall come *muy Consolado*. I understand that I have been much bound to the Prince for the procuring the 4000*l*. to be payed, and for my Pension.

I pray present unto him my most humble thanks: and I confess, I have been much more comforted with that demonstration of his favour, then I can be with the money. I doubt not but at this time I shall have the effects of a real friendship from you in this particular. And so desiring to have my service remembred to my Lady *Cottington*, I rest,

Poitiers. April 15. 1623.   *Yours*, &c.
                                BRISTOL.

POST-SCRIPT.

I Pray move the Prince, that one of the Kings Ships may be presently appointed to waft me over; For I have a great charge of the Princes with me.

W. Greisly met me within 10 posts of *Burdeaux*, and is passed on to *Madrid*: I think he shall find the *Blandones* for his Highness in a readiness; for Mr. *Stone* taketh care of them, and hath the money in his hand.

The Earl of Bristol, to the Lord Bishop of Lincoln.

My very worthy Lord,

I Give you many thanks for your Letter of the 23d of *July*, by which I understand your great care of me, by seconding a former motion it pleased your Lordship to make, of having me reconciled to my Lord Dukes favour, (A thing which I have infinitely desired) and have esteemed the good offices you have been pleased to do therein, as a very high obligation your Lordship puts upon me. But I conceive your Lordship will find that any motion you have made in that kind unto his Grace hath been despised, rather then received with any thankfulness, or that he hath returned you any answer of his inclination thereunto. For the truth is, my Lord doth look down upon my poor Condition with that scorn and contempt, that I conjecture the very moving of any such thing, especially under the term of reconciliation, hath not been pleasing unto his Lordship. But thereof your Lorship can make the best judgment, by the answer you received from him. I do but guess thereat, by what I have heard he hath been pleased to say, and the manner wherewith he hath used me. Which hath been such, that the *Spaniards* themselves (which most afflicted me) have out of compassion pitied me. Yet I may with much truth assure your Lordship, that I have not omitted towards him either any respect of service, that was fit for me to perform; either towards his person, or the high place he holdeth in my Masters favour, or unto his present imployment; (well knowing, how undecent and scandalous a thing it is, for the Ministers of a Prince to run different ways in a strange Court) but have attended him in all his publick audience, and used in all kinds that respect and observance towards him, that I think malice her self cannot charge me with an omission. And my Lord, this is the truth, whatsoever may be said or written to the contrary: It is true, that some four moneths since, in a business that no lesse concerned his Majestie and the Prince's service, then abruptly to have broken off all our Treaty, I was far differing from my Lords opinion; And thereupon happened

betwixt

betwixt us some dispute in debate of the business, but without any thing that was personal; and there was no creature living at it but the Prince, to whose Censure I shall willingly refer my self. In me, I protest it unto your Lordship, it made no alteration, but within half an hour I came to him with the same reverence and respect that I was wont to do, the which I have continued ever since; so that I have much wondered how it cometh to be so much spoken of in *England*, that my Lord Duke and my self should live here at too much distance. And I cannot find any other reason for it, but that every body hath taken so much notice of my ill and contemptible usage, that they think it impossible for any Gentleman, but to be sensible of it. But if any one dis-respect, or omission from me, towards my Lord Duke, can be truly instanced in by any man, I will be contented to incur his Majesties high displeasure, and your Lordships censure.

For the present news here, it is, that the ninth of this Moneth, the Prince intendeth (God willing) to begin his journey for *England*. And the day before, I conceive the Contract will be. The *Infanta* is to follow in the Spring, and the Prince hath commanded my stay here. I know not how things may be reconciled here before my Lord Dukes departure; but at present, they are in all extremity ill, betwixt this King and his Ministers, and the Duke; and they stick not to profess, that they will rather put the *Infanta* headlong into a Well, then into his hands. I write unto your Lordship, you see, with much freeness, and I intreat you let it remain with you. And so, in much haste, I onely intreat your Lordship to believe, that you have not living an honester, nor a true-hearteder friend, and servant, then

August 20. 1623.

Your Lordships ever to be commanded,
BRISTOL.

The Earl of Bristol, to the Prince his Highness.

WHen your Highness shall remember, that your Highness being here in person, it was not possible in less then a moneth to get that dispatch'd which you were promised Mr. Secretary *Cottington* should have carried with him, if your Highness would have but stayed him 24 hours; I hope you will pardon your servants, although they sometimes mistake in the time which they limit for the procuring of the dispatch of business, especially if they depend upon the dispatches that are to be procured from them. I have these 10 daies had *Grisly* in a readiness to depart, having every day expected a resolution from the *Junto*. First, in point of the portion, and since in the daies of payment; and at last, I have received their answer in them both, in such sort as your Highness will see in the paper inclosed, which is an extract of the heads of the temporal Articles that we have agreed, although I have onely consented unto them *de bene esse*, until I shall receive his Majesties approbation and yours: In the point of the portion, I have had a tough and a knotty piece of work, by reason that not onely the *Conde de Olivarez*, but all the *Junto* were absolutely ignorant of what had passed in the late Kings time, which I foresaw; and that was the cause that I moved so earnestly, at the *Escurial*, to have the *Conde de Gondomar* remain here. They made many presidents to be searched, and found that the *two millions* demanded was four times as much as ever was given with any daughter of *Spain* in money. They alleadged, that it would be said, that the King of *Spain* was fain to purchase the friendship and alliance of *England*; that this would be such a president, as that *Spain* hereafter must marry no more daughters. I only insisted, that it was a thing by the last King setled, and agreed with me; that this King had, by several answers in writing to me, undertaken to pursue the business as it was left by his father, and to make good whatsoever he had promised. And thereupon desired that the original Papers, and *Consultos* of the last King, might be seen, which very honestly by the *Secretary Cirica* were produced, and appeared to be such, that I dare say, there was not a man that saw them that doubteth of the last Kings real intention of making the Match. And questionless, this had been the usefullest occasion to have disavowed former proceedings, and I was resolved to put them to it. But both the King and his Councel, upon the sight of what had been promised by his father, presently took resolution to make good the two millions, onely to remonstrate unto his Majesty the vastness of the Portion, and to desire him to consider how far the King had stretched himself in this particular for his satisfaction. And therefore, that he would have Consideration of it in such things, for the future, as might be treated of betwixt them and their Kingdoms. As for the days of payment, I insisted to have had half a Million upon the *Deposorio's*, half a Million

The Earl of Bristol, to the Lord Bishop of Lincoln.

Million to be carried along with the *Infanta*, and the other Million at their Fleets, the two next years after by equal portions. But I have now received the Kings answer in this particular, which your Highness will see in the enclosed paper; as likewise what I have done therein by the Copy of the dispatch, which I now write about it to Mr. Secretary. So not having any thing more to adde concerning this particular, I recommend your highness to Gods holy protection, &c.

Madrid. Septemb. 24. 1623.

The Earl of Bristol, to the Lord Bishop of Lincoln.

My singular Lord,

I Have dispatched this Bearer, my servant *Greislie*, with the draught of the temporal Articles, which I hope will be to the King and Prince his satisfaction, and he will let your Lordship have a sight of them.

Since the departure of the Prince, there have every day passed Letters of extraordinary affection between the King, and the Prince; and the love that is here generally born unto the Prince, is such, as cannot be well believed by those that daily hear nor what passeth both from the King and his chief Ministers. And to say the truth, his Highness hath well deserved it; for in the whole time of his being here, he hath carried himself with the greatest affability, patience and constancy, and at his departure, with the greatest bounty and liberality, that I think hath been known in any Prince in our times. And I protest unto your Lordship, as a Christian, that I never heard in all the time of his being here, nor since, any one exception taken against him, unless it were for being supposed to be too much guided by my Lord Duke of *Buckingham*, who is indeed very little beholden to the *Spaniards*, for their good opinion of him, and departed from hence with so little satisfaction, that the *Spaniards* are in doubt, that he will endeavour all that shall be possible to cross the Marriage: Wherein certainly they are very much mistaken; For my Lord cannot but be obliged, as a servant, for any particular distastes of his own, not to cross the advancement of his Majesty, and the Prince's service, especially in a business of so high consequence as this.

It may be your Lordship will hear many complaints, and that the Match never was, nor yet is intended; I beseech your Lordship to give little belief in that kind, and the effects will now speedily declare the truth, if the fault be not on our side. It is true that the *Spaniards* have committed many errours in their proceedings with the Prince; but the business is now by the Prince overcome, if we our selves draw not back: For which, I confess, I should be heartily sorry, and so I conceive would most honest men; for if this Match, and the alliance with *Spain*, hath been so long desired by his Majesty, and that for it he hath been pleased to do so much, and the Prince to take so hazardous a voyage, if all the same reasons are yet on foot, which have ever moved the King and Prince to wish the Match; if to this may be added, that his majesty hath overcome all the difficulties on his part, and that both he and the Prince do stand engaged for the performance of it, as far as Princes can be, God forbid, that any particular distastes, or misunderstandings (which God knoweth have little relation to the business) should be of power to disturb it, especially now, when the Match is past all danger of miscarrying, the Portion and all temporal Articles setled, and I hope to the Kings Content, and all other good effects that could be expected by this alliance in a very fair way. I hope there will be no cause of doubt in this kind; if there should be, I am sure that your Lordship would put to a helping hand, to keep the business from being overthrown, since you have done so much for the overcoming of former difficulties, and the bringing it to the pass 'tis now in. If there be no cause of writing this, I beseech your Lordship to impute it to my zeal to the business, and my freeness with your Lordship, upon whose true love and friendship I so much rely, as I shall not forbear to tell you any of my fears. I hope within 3 days Sir *Francis Cottington* will be able to begin his journey towards your Lordship. He will tell you many truths, being, on my knowledge, as hearty a servant and friend as 'tis possible for your Lordship to have. He hath told me how much I am bound to your Lordship for your love and favour, and truly I will deserve it the best I can, and that I think wil be only by loving you; for otherwise I conceive I am like to have little means of meriting at any bodies hands, yet at your Lordships it may be I may, by being a man of honesty and honour; And such an one I will labour to be, and your affectionate friend and servant. And so I kiss your Lordships hands.

Madrid, &c. 24th of *Septemb.* 1623.

The Earl of Bristol, to King James.

May it please your most excellent Majesty,

I Find that upon the news that is now come from the Duke of *Pastrava*, that the Pope hath cleerly passed the Dispensation, which is now hourly expected here. There is an intention to call presently upon me, for the Princes powers for the marriage left in my hands, the which I know not upon what ground or reason to detain, the Prince having engaged (in the said powers) the faith and word of a Prince, no way to revoke and retract from them, but that they should remain in full force till *Christmas*, and delivered unto me a politick declaration of his pleasure, that upon the coming of the Dispensation I should deliver them unto this King, that they might be put in execution, and hereof, likewise, was there by Secretary *Serita*, as a publick Notary, an Instrument drawn, and attested by all the witnesses present. If I shall alleadge your Majesties pleasure of having the marriage deferred until one of the Holidays, although they should condescend thereunto, that is impossible, for the powers will be then expired. If I shall insist upon the restitution of the Palatinate, this King hath therein delared his answer; and it would be much wondred why that should be now added for a condition of the marriage, having ever hitherto been treated of as a businefs apart, and was in being at the granting of the said powers, and hath been often under debate, but never specified, nor the powers delivered upon any condition, of having any such point first cleered; and I must confess unto your Majesty, I understand not how, with honour, and that exact dealing which hath ever been observed in all your Majesties actions, the powers can be detained; unless there should appear some new and emergent cause since the granting of them, whereof as yet I hear none specified: Therefore being loath to be the instrument by whose hands any thing should pass that might have the least reflection upon your Majesties or the Princes honour, (which I shall ever value more then my life or safety) and judging it likewise to conduce more to your service, and assuring my self that your Majesties late direction, to have the marriage upon one of the Holy-days in *Christmas*, was for want of due information that the powers will be then expired, I have thought it fit (with the advice of Sir *Walter Aston*) to raise no scruple in the delivery of the said powers, but do intend, when they shall be required, to pass on to the nominating of a prefixed day, for the Deposorio's: but I shall endeavour to defer the time, untill I may be advertised of your Majesties pleasure, if it may be within the space of 24 daies, and will labour to find some handsom and fair occasion for the deferring of them, without alleadging any directions, in that kind, from your Majesty or the Prince.

The reasons why I have thought it fit to take this resolution, are; First, I find by your Majesties letters, and the Princes; that your intent is to proceed in the marriage, and to that purpose your Majesty and the Prince have set me free to deliver the powers according to the first intentions, by removing that scruple of the Infanta's entring into Religion, whereupon they were only suspended.

Secondly, your Majesties Letter only intimateth a desire, not a direction, of having the marriage upon one of the Holy-days of *Christmas*: which I conceive is to be understood, if it may well and fittingly be so, not, if there shall be impossibility therein, by reason of the expiring of the powers before, and that the intention of having it then should be overthrown thereby, when I am confident that what your Majesty writeth is for want of due information of the clause of expiration of the powers.

Thirdly, if your Majesty, upon these reasons, and such as I have formerly alleaged unto your Majesty, should (as I no way doubt but your Majesty will) give me order for the present proceeding to the marriage, yet by my refusing of the powers, and alleadging your Majesties or the Princes directions, although afterwards all things should be cleered, yet would it cast some kinde of aspersion and jealousie upon the sincerity of your Majesties and the Princes proceedings. On the contrary side, if your Majesties intention be not to proceed in the match, whereof I see no ground, the intimation of that may be as well a moneth hence as now: And I judge it duty in a servant, especially in a businefs of so high a consequence, and wherein your Majesty hath spent so much time, to give his master leisure to repair to his second cogitations, before he do any act that may disorder or overthrow.

This I offer, with all humility, unto your Majesties wise and just consideration, and beseech you to make interpretation of my proceedings herein, according to my dutiful and zealous care of your honour and service. I have of purpose dispatch'd this Post with this Letter, to

the

The Earl of Bristol to the Duke of Buckingham.

the end I may receive your Majesties directions, in this particular, with all possible speed; which, I hope, shall be to proceed directly to the marriage according to the Capitulations, and so to order all things for the Princess her journey in the Spring. And for the *Palatinate*, your Majesty may be confident, there shall be diligence used in procuring a speedy and good resolution. So, &c.
Novemb. 1. 1623.

The Earl of Bristol, to the Duke of Buckingham.

May it please your Grace,

THe present estate of the Kings affairs requireth the concurrency of all his servants, and the Co-operation of all his Ministers; which maketh me desirous to make unto your Grace this tender of my service; that if there have happened any errours, or mis-understandings, your Grace would for that regard pass them over: and for any thing that may personally concern my particular, I shall labour to give you that satisfaction as may deserve your friendship. And if that shall not serve the turn, I shall not be found unarmed with patience against any thing that can happen unto me. And so wishing, that this humble offer of my service may find that acceptation as I humbly desire, I rest,

Madrid. Decemb. 6. 1623.
      Your Graces most humble servant,
         Bristol.

The Earl of Bristol, to King James.

May it please your most excellent Majesty,

I Hope your Majesty will not be displeased that I continue unto you that most humble and just suit, which I have often made unto your Majesty, and your Majesty hath been often graciously pleased to promise, which was, that I should be no wayes lessened, or diminished in your Majesties favour, and good opinion, until you should be first pleased graciously to hear me, and my Cause. And although your Majesty, for just respects, hath not been pleased hitherto to admit me into your presence, which I esteem an infinite mis-fortune to me: Yet, I hope, that time will no way confirm those impressions of displeasure, which I do no way doubt, but will be fully cleered, whensoever I shall be so happy as by your Majesty to be heard. For I take God to record, that I have faithfully and honestly served you, and exactly pursued your ends to the best of my understanding, and abilities. And I do no way doubt, but your Majesty will in the end protect so faithful a servant as I have been, and shall appear to be to your Majesty. And in the interim, my most humble suit unto your Majesty is, that since I am neither admitted my self, nor any man else will speak any word in my defence, or justification, your Majesty, according to your Justice, will let nothing that may be said of me redound to my prejudice in your gracious opinion: For it shall be found, that I will in all things wholly conform my self unto your Majesties will and pleasure. So wishing unto your Majesty a happy journey, and a safe return, with the increase of all happiness, I humbly, &c.

London. July 27. 1624.
      Your Majesties, &c.
         Bristol.

The Earl of Bristol, to the Lord Conway.

My Lord,

I Received your Letter of the 25 of *February*, and therein a Commandment from his Majesty, and in his Majesties name, to make a cleer and plain answer, Whether I desire or rest in the security I am now in, and to acknowledge the gracious favour of his late Majesty, and of his which now is, who have been pleased not to question my actions, &c.
                     Here-

The Earl of Bristol, to the King.

Hereunto I have laboured exactly to obey, but finde that a plain and clear answer cannot possibly be made, untill there be a cleer understanding of the thing propounded; so that I may crave pardon, if my answer be not so cleer as I could wish it: for I must freely acknowledge, that I no way understand what is meant by the security I am now in, whether it be by the present estate I am now in, or not: If it be so, I conceive a man cannot be under a harder Condition; for your Lordship knoweth, that by order my person is restrained, and you were pleased lately to send me word, that you would not advise me to make use of the liberty which his late Majesty had given me of coming to *London*, although that were only to follow my private affairs, and for the recovery of my decayed health. I stand likewise prohibited to come to the Court, or to the Kings presence, (I pass by my being removed from all my places, and offices, and wholly depending upon his Majesties royal pleasure.) But being a Peer of this Realm, I have not only by Commandment been formerly stayed from the Parliament, but of late, my writ hath been detained, as though my honour were forfeited. And this is truly the Condition I am now in, but I cannot imagine that this is the security intended I should rest in; but am in hope, that the security intended is, that *I may for the future enjoy the liberty of a free Subject, and the priviledges of a Peer of the Kingdom*. Which being so, I shall with all humility acknowledge his Majesties grace and favour, and be ready to serve him with all fidelity, even to the laying down of my life, not thinking it to stand with the duty of a Subject to press his being questioned, since such being the pleasure of his Sovereign, it were not in the power of any Subject to avoid it. But in case his Majesty shall be pleased to bring me to any legal trial, I shall most willingly and dutifully submit my self thereunto, and doubt not but my innocency in the end will be my best Mediatour for his Majesties future favour. And in that Case I am a suitor that my Writ of Parliament as a Peer of this Realm may be sent unto me, and that my present repair to *London* may not displease his Majesty; As for the pardon of the 21. *Reg. Jacobi*, which you mention, I should renounce, but that I know that the justest and most cautious man living may through ignorance or omission offend the Lawes; so that as a Subject I shall not disclaim any benefit which cometh in the general, as it doth usually to all other Subjects in the Kingdom: But as for any Crime in particular, that may trench upon my imployments in point of Loyalty, fidelity, or want of affection to the King or State, I know my innocency to be such, that I am confident, I shall not need that pardon. I shall conclude, with a most humble suit unto your Lordship, that out of your nobleness, and that friendship that hath been betwixt us, you will use your best endeavours, both with his Majesty and the Duke, that this unfortunate business may be past over, by the renewing whereof I can see little use that can be made, but the adding to a mans mis-fortunes already sufficiently humbled; For I am ready to do all that a man of honour and honesty may do; but rather then to do any thing that may be prejudicial to me in that kind, to suffer whatsoever it shall please God to send. And so with the remembrance of my humble service unto your Lordship, I recommend you unto Gods holy protection, And rest,

March 4. 1625.
Sherborn Lodge, &c.

Your Lordships humble servant,

Bristol.

The Earl of Bristol, to King James.

Most gracious Sovereign,

IT may please your Majesty to remember, that at my coming out of *Spain* I signified unto your Majesty, how far the Duke of *Lerma* had upon severall occasions intimated unto me an extraordinary desire of this King and State, not only to maintain peace and amity with your Majesty, but to lay hold of all things that may be offered for the neerer uniting of your Majesty and your Crowns; and that from this generality he had descended often to have discourse with me of a match for the Prince's Highness with the second daughter of *Spain*, assuring me, that in this King and his Ministers, there was a forward disposition thereunto. But from me he received no other answer, but to this effect, That I in the treaty of the former match for the late Prince, had received so strange and unexpected answer from them, and that their demands seemed so improper and unworthy, that I conceived that your Majesty had little reason to be induced again to give eare to any such overture, or that I should

again

again enter into any such treaty, much less to be the motioner thereof: Although I would confess, that if I were fully perswaded of the sincerity of their intentions, and of a possibility of having the said match effected, I know not any thing wherein I would more willingly imploy my endeavours, but as the case now stood, I was certain, that if I should but make any such motion in *England*, I should but draw imputation of much weakness upon me there, and no whit advance the cause; for that your Majesty and your Ministers would make no other construction of the motion, but as construed to divert the Match of *France*; which was treated of, for that your Majesty who but the year before had received so unpleasing and unequal an answer, should now be perswaded that there was here so great a change, as that a match was really desired, there would now need more then ordinary assurance. But the Duke of *Lerma* continuing severall times the same profession, and telling me besides that the greatest Cases might be altered by circumstances, and that the Age of this Prince was much more proper then that of his brother; I freely let the Duke know, that in case I might see that it was really desired here, and that I might be able to propound unto my Master conditions of so much advantage and certainty as might put him and his ministers out of doubt that this overture was not again revived from hence, either for diversion, or winning of time, I would then willingly intimate unto your Majesty the inclination and desire I found here of having a proposition for this match once again set on foot. The Duke told me, he would have a further conference with me; and that he then no wayes doubted to give such satisfaction as might well assure your Majesty and your Ministers, that they sincerely desired the match, in general, & would omit nothing on their side for the accommodating of particulars that might give furtherance unto it. But the very night before the Duke had appointed a meeting with me, there came a Post dispatcht out of *England* from the *Spanish* Embassador, upon the arrivall of Sir *Thomas Edmonds* into *England*, who brought word that the match with *France* was absolutely concluded, and that within few days it was to be published: Whereupon the Duke, at our meeting the next morning, told me that it would be needless now to descend to any particulars in the business whereof we are to treat, since that they had newly received advertisement that the match with *France* was fully concluded. And thus, for the present, the matter rested untill some five or six weeks after, about which time my self was to go into *England*; and so taking leave of the Duke, he asked me whether I had not received advertisement that the match with *France* was published. I told him, no, but I had certainly heard that it was not as yet fully concluded: Whereupon he intreated me, that in case I found not the *French* match in such forwardness as it could not be stayed, I would let him know of it; and that if I should see any kinde of possibility that the business we had spoken of might be set on foot, I would advertise him; and that thereupon he would proceed to those particulars which he formerly intended for my satisfaction.

Herewith I acquainted your Majesty, and finding the *Spanish* Embassador in *England* had notice from the Duke of our former proceedings, and order to further them by all possible means he could, especially if he should understand that your Majesty were not fully resolved of the *French* match, I thought it fit by this means to let the Duke understand in what estate I found those businesses in *England*; and thereupon, with your Majesties permission, I wrote a Letter unto him, to this effect.

That although it were true that the Match with *France* had been treated of with much earnestness on both sides, and with great likelihood of being concluded; yet there daily arose so many difficulties, and new cases of delay, that I judged it far from any perfect conclusion; neither did I see cause absolutely to despair of the businesses which our selves pretended, unless the difficulty of the Conditions should make it desperate. But if those things should be expected by *Spain* which in the Treaty for the late Princess were demanded, it were better by much not to renew the business, then by impossible or unfitting propositions on either side to give distaste, or lessen the friendship which now was betwixt your Majesties. And therefore, except that, in *Spain*, they would be contented with such conditions as your Majesty most fittingly and conveniently might yield unto, and all other Catholique Princes were willing to content themselves with, I neither saw cause to hope for good success, or reason to set the treaty on foot. But in case I might know that the conditions, in point of Religion, might be such as I should see a possibility of your Majesties condescending unto them, I should be far from desparing of some good effect; for that I knew that divers, not of the meanest nor least power with your Majesty, were hereunto well inclined, and would give their helping hands.

Hereupon the *Spanish* Embassador dispatch'd his Secretary into *Spain*, and received answer from the Duke, that he should give me all assurance that there was a great desire and inclinaclination to the making of the Match, and that at my return into *Spain* they no way doubted but that I should receive such satisfaction, as should make it appear, on their part, there should be nothing wanting for the effecting of it.

It now remaineth, what hath passed herein since my last coming to this Court. I arrived here in *Madrid* only a day or two before *Christmass*; and having some six dayes after my audience appointed by the King, whilst I was in a with-drawing Chamber expecting the Kings coming forth, the Duke of *Lerma* came thither to bear me company; and after many respectful demands of your Majesty, and the Queens; and the Princes health, and some few complements unto my self concerning my welcome again unto this Court, he fell to speak of the false Alarm we had in *England* concerning a Spanish Armado; seeming much to be displeased that any credit should be given to any thing to his Majesties dishonour and want of fidelity, (as he termed it,) But your Majesty (he said) did never believe it: And it seems he heard of some pleasant answer your Majesty should make to some one of your Ministers, that in great haste came unto your Majesty when you were a hunting, and told you that the Spanish Fleet was in the Channel. From this he entred into great protestations of the sincerity of this Kings affection and intention towards your Majesty, telling me that I should now see how much they desired to work a greater neerness and uniting between your Majesties: And that of the principal business of which we had in former time spoken, meaning the Marriage, he desired to speak with me, but it must be at more leisure. I answered, that I would not fail shortly to wait upon him, and that he should find me answerable to the profession I had made, which was, that being induced thereunto by such sufficient and good grounds as might satisfie my Master both for the conveniency and fittingness of having such a Treaty set on foot, and likewise might take away all objections of their intents of entertaining and diverting your Majesty hereby, I would be as ready to do all good offices, and give furtherance to the business, as any Minister the King of *Spain* had. And this was all that at our first meeting passed in this business.

About some eight days after, I having not in all this time stirred out of my house, under colour of being ill disposed, though the truth was, indeed, to inform my self of some particulars which concerned your Majesties service, before I would speak with the Duke: He being (as I have since understood) something troubled that in all this time I made no means to come unto him, one morning, by nine of the clock, very privately came to my house, without advertising of his coming (as the custom is here) untill the Coach stayed at my gate; and then he sent in a Gentleman to me, telling me that the Duke was there to speak with me. When I had conducted the Duke into a room where we were private, he fell into the aforesaid matter, and in the manner as I shall here set down unto your Majesty, without making any other pretence or intent of his coming, or without using, in the space of an hour, any speech touching any other business.

After some few questions of your Majesty and the Queen, he began to ask many things of the Prince; as of his age, his stature, his health, his inclination, to what sports he was chiefly given? And then suddenly, as it were with a passionate expression of affection, he desired God to bless him, and to make him the means by which your Majesties might be conjoyned in a neerer alliance, and your Kingdoms in a perpetual amity: saying unto me, that he was out of doubt of my good inclination to this business, both by what had formerly passed between our selves, as likewise by my proceedings in *England*, whereof he had been fully informed by the Spanish Embassadour. And therefore he would, in few words, deal with me with much cleerness and freeness, assuring himself he should receive the like measure from me; and thereupon entred into a solemn protestation, how much this King desired the Match; and for himself, he solemnly swore, there was no one thing in the world he more desired to see before he dyed, then the effecting thereof. But my Lord Embassador (said he) you must deal as justly with me, to let me understand whether you conceive the like desire to be in the King of *England*, and his Ministers, and then I shall proceed to speak further unto you.

I answered the Duke, That I ever esteemed more the reputation of a man of truth and integrity, then of skill and subtilty: which I did hope he did well perceive by what I was to say, for that I was much more desirous fairly to go off from this business, then easily to go into it. And therefore, if he would have me speak my conscience, I neither conceived that either in your Majesty, or any of your Ministers, there was any kind of inclination thereunto; for that they having formerly given so resolute and distastefull an answer, your Majesty had just cause never again to cast so much as your thoughts this way: And though it might be alledged, that the fitness of the Prince his years, and other civil regards, might cause new reso-

resolutions, yet the differences of Religion were still the same, and the same were the truths and opinions of Divines in matter of Conscience; and therefore it would not but be a thing of great difficulty, to perswade your Majestie, and your Ministers, that a Match should be hearkened unto, much less desired, from hence, but upon the same terms, the very thought and remembrance whereof is yet unpleasing in *England*. So that, to deal plainly with him, I neither found in your Majestie, or in the Councel, any kind of thought or imagination of any possibility of having any such motion again revived. But this I found not to grow from any particular dislike or want of affection in your Majestie to *Spain*, or that many of the greatest, or the principallest persons in *England*, judged not the neernefs and alliance of *Spain* equally valuable with any other of Christendom; but that, out of a distastfulnefs of the former answer given from hence, all expectation of any businefs of this nature was absolutely extinguished; and therefore again to revive it, there would need more then ordinary endeavours, or ordinary assurances : But in case that they might be given, I know that this Match would neither want well-willers, nor assistants. And, for my own part, I would freely make profession, that no man more desired it then my self, nor would more willingly imploy his endeavours for the furthering thereof, when by the descending to particulars I should see, both in regard of the conditions, and the assurances of sincere proceedings, the motion worthy and fit by a discreet and good servant to be offered to his Master; neither then should I be wholly out of hope of good success, though I would not but esteem it a businefs of infinite difficulty.

The Duke replied, That any discourse that I thought fit herein should be condescended unto, for that all time was lost that was spent in generalities : and therefore, if I so liked, he would move this King, that one or two, besides himself, might be appointed to have conference with me; for that, if he should onely retain it in his hands, by reason of his many occupations, it would have a flower progrefs then he wished : but if I would, by way of conference, digest the difficulties into heads and particulars, he would, as often as he might, be present at our meeting: but for his own part, he said, he apprehended few, but what would arise out of the difference of Religion.

I told the Duke, that I very well approved of the descending into particulars, neither should I refuse conference with any herein whom the King would appoint to speak with me : But if his meaning were, that these persons should be nominated or joyned by way of Commission, I thought fit to let him understand, that I neither had any time, nor did at present speak of this businefs, either by order, or direction, no nor so much as by your Majesties privity, but as a Minister that desired to lay hold of all occasions for the increasing of further love and neernefs betwixt his Master and the Prince to whom he is imployed, I should be glad, to the uttermost of my power, to advance and further this cause, as that which I apprehended to be the greatest which the world now affordeth, for the firm uniting of your Majesties and your estates.

The Duke told me, that the King would make no scruple to declare his good inclination and desire to have this Match proceeded in; and that for the accommodating of the difficulties, he had already used divers diligences with the Pope, as likewise with the greatest Divines of this Kingdom, whereof he named some unto me, whom he said he found very well inclined to the Match : He told me also, he would be glad they might speak with me, to the end I might truly understand of them all kind of scruples that could be alledged. I answered, I desired nothing more; and that I could not but approve of those courses he prescribed, as the most probable to produce a good effect; and that I hoped God would give a happy success unto the businefs : But I should be bold in one thing to deliver my opinion, which was, No ways to interefs our Masters herein, unlefs, by the understanding and cleering the difficulties on both sides, there should be great appearances and probabilities that the businefs would take effect; for if their names should be herein used, and after their Treaty should not be successfull, it would but exasperate and breed a greater distafte betwixt your Majesties. The Duke told me, he himself milliked not my opinion; though he said, that howsoever that businefs succeeded, yet your Majesty should have reason to accept kindly this Kings good intention; for that, if it miscarried, it should appear, not to be their default, but that they had stretched as far as honour and conscience would give them leave. And thus much, he said, I might write unto your Majesty, if I thought fit, or to my confident friends in *England*, upon his word and assurance : and so telling me, that he would presently appoint those that should conferr with me in this businefs, we then parted.

Within two dayes after, I went to the Duke; and after that I had spoken with him about the businefs of *Cleves*, according to my instruction, whereof I gave an account unto Mr. Secretary in a difpatch directed unto him, we fell again into the fpeech of the Match.

The Duke told me; he had well confidered of that which I had faid unto him, and much approved it, not to intereft our Mafters in the bufinefs, until we fhould fee fome likelihood of good fuccefs.

And for that he fuppofed the difference of Religion like to prove the onely difficulty of confideration, he thought it fit, that it fhould be firft cleared; and therefore he would break the matter with the Cardinal of *Toledo* and the Kings Confeffor, and with them he joyned another learned man; one Father *Frederick*, who, fince I underftand, is a Jefuite, but, truly, hath the report of a moderate man. Thefe, the Duke faid, fhould have order to conferr with me as far as might be, referving fafe the grounds and fincerity of their Religion. I anfwered the Duke, that I was well fatisfied herewith; and that if their demands were fuch as might content any other Catholick Prince, I fhould have hope of good fuccefs; if otherwife, I fhould judge it a happinefs to be put out of doubt and fufpence: and fo we paffed from this fubject.

I prefume to fet down to your Majeftie all the paffages of this bufinefs, with fo much length and fulnefs, for that I no way dare adventure to offer unto your Majeftie any opinion or belief of my own, either for the fitnefs of the Match, or the fincerity of their intention, or the poffibility of accommodating differences of Religion. But your Majeftie feeing, undifguifed, all that hath hitherto paffed, with every circumftance, may be pleafed, out of the confideration and knowledge of thofe particulars, to frame unto your felf both fuch a belief of their direct meaning, and fuch a refolution of the further proceeding herein, as fhall be moft fuitable to your Majefties wifdom: Onely I think it fit, to fet down further unto your Majeftie, the particular ends which may be conceived they aim at, by fetting this bufinefs afoot at this prefent, in cafe they fhould not intend really to perform it: The firft may be, to ftagger and divert your Majefties Treaty with *France*: The fecond, for entertaining your Majeftie with fair hopes and promifes, thereby to keep you from declaring your felf oppofite unto them, in the prefent bufinefs of *Juliers* and *Cleves*, which remaineth ftill uncompounded. But this being fo, your Majeftie may be pleafed to underftand, that they ferve themfelves with this occafion; not that there could be any fuch thing primarily in their intention, for that the expreffion of their defire to the Match was the laft year, long before thefe differences happened.

Further, the Duke of *Lerma* fhould be the moft falfe and difhonourable man living, without Chriftianity or Soul, if he fhould voluntarily damn himfelf with Oaths and Proteftations of a thing that he fincerely meant not; and, truly, he fhould deal contrarily to the wifdom of his other proceedings, wherein he layeth all occafions of diftafte or difcourtefie upon other inferiour Minifters, labouring ftill to clear himfelf of the imputation of them, if in this he fhould make himfelf the author and inftrument of fo unjuft and indirect proceeding between Princes. But the courfe of moft fecurity and caution, is, that your Majeftie fuffer none of your other refolutions to be interrupted by this overture; onely, if your Majeftie be pleafed for a while to entertain and fufpend the conclufion of the Match with *France*, I conceive it can be little to your Majefties difadvantage.

It, laftly, now remaineth, that I become an humble fuitor unto your Majeftie, for your clear and full directions in this bufinefs, defiring, if your Majeftie will have it further entertained, that I may have ample inftructions from your Majeftie, both that I may intimate what may be expected in point of Dowrie, and in all other things to be required by your Majeftie, as likewife how far I may proceed in fatisfying in point of Religion. For it is not to be fuppofed, that they will proceed with that freenefs and directnefs which is to be wifhed, unlefs in a fitting meafure they fhall fee me likewife able and willing to declare my felf in fuch points wherein they may expect fatisfaction. I intend not hereby to move for a formal Commiffion to treat, but onely a private inftruction, for my direction and warrant, how to behave my felf as may be moft advantagious to the caufe, and your Majefties ends. So humbly defiring your Majeftie to command this Bearer to be difpatched back with all convenient fpeed, I commend your Majeftie to the holy protection of God.

Your Majefties faithfull fubject and fervant,

DIGBY.

The Earl of Briſtol, *to the Prince, touching the delivery of his Proxie to the King of* Spain.

May it pleaſe your Highneſs,

IN this Letter, I ſhall onely ſpeak unto your Highneſs concerning that particular whereof you were pleaſed to write unto me, after your departure from St. *Lorenzo*, and have preſumed to ſet down exactly the caſe as it ſtands; in what ſort, a woman betrothed, and *poſt Matrimonium ratum*, may, before the Conſummation of Marriage, betake her ſelf unto a Religious life: I have likewiſe ſet down unto your Highneſs all ſorts of ſecurity, that may be taken before the betrothing, for the preventing of any ſuch courſe in the parties that are to be betrothed. To this, your Highneſs may add any other you can think of; for that the King, and his Siſter, and all the Miniſters, profeſs ſo really the punctual and preſent performance of all that is capitulated with your Highneſs; That they will refuſe no kind of ſecurity, that, in reaſon, can be demanded in this behalf; ſo that your Highneſs may ſet down whatſoever you think this King and his Siſter may do, with decency, and honour, and they will be ready to perform it.

I muſt now crave leave to ſpeak unto your Highneſs like a faithfull plain ſervant, which is, If your Highneſs pleaſure be, to have uſe made of the Powers you have left in my hands, I no way doubt, but in this particular ſuch ſatisfaction will be given, as will appear reaſonable to all the world: But if your Highneſs deſire, that theſe Powers ſhould not be uſed, they may be detained upon other juſt reaſons, which will ariſe in the treaty of the temporal articles. And I doubt not but the *Depoſorio's* may be deferred for ſome few dayes, upon other fair pretexts. But theſe inconveniencies, I conceive, will follow. Firſt, it will be of great diſcomfort to the *Infanta*, who until the *Depoſorio's* are paſt, is not her own woman, but muſt be governed by the pleaſure of the *Junto*, which I think ſhe is very weary of; neither till then may ſhe declare her ſelf to be yours, nor comply with your Highneſs, in anſwering of your Letters, and Meſſages, and giving you thoſe reſpects, and comforts, which I know ſhe would be glad to do. But if ſhe ſhould any way judge, that the delay of the *Depoſorio's* ſhould ariſe from your Highneſs part, I conceive ſhe would take it moſt heavily. Secondly, it will certainly raiſe great jealouſies in this King, and his Miniſters, and retard the reſolutions that are fit to be taken with ſpeed, for the putting in execution that which is capitulated. I therefore offer it unto your Highneſs wiſdom, Whether, upon the ſatisfaction which they will give in this particular, which will be whatſoever you can deſire, and upon the agreement of the temporal articles, your Highneſs would, upon the coming of the Popes approbation, make any further ſcruple in the delivering of your Highneſs powers? If I ſhall, I am confident they will not preſs it, as not decent for the womans part to urge the haſting of the Marriage: But, I conceive, it will caſt ſuch a cloud of Jealouſie and diſtruſt upon the buſineſs, that, beſides the diſcontent and affliction which I know it will give the Infanta (which moſt worketh upon me) it will ſo diſorder the buſineſs, that it will make a ſtand in your whole proceedings, and preparations, wherein they now go on chearfully and confidently, and, I conceive, will punctually perform all that they have capitulated with your Highneſs. I dare not ſo much as give my ſelf leave once to queſtion your Highneſs intentions of proceeding to the real effecting of the Match, which makes me deſirous that all things may be executed, that may any way retard or diſturb it: Onely I ſhall, like a faithfull poor ſervant, preſume to ſay thus much to your Highneſs; That, for divers years paſt, I know the King your Father, and your ſelf, have held this the fitteſt Match in the world; and by a deſire of effecting it, your Highneſs was induced to undertake that hazardous journey of coming to this Court in perſon. In the time of your being here, admitting that their proceedings have been in many things unworthy of you, and that divers diſtaſtes have grown by intervenient accidents; now things are reduced to thoſe terms, that the Match it ſelf is ſure, the portion, and the temporal Articles ſetled (I hope, to the Kings liking, and yours) all other good effects that could be hoped for by this alliance, are in a fair way. If to theſe reaſons may be added, That on his Majeſty and your Highneſs part, you have already paſſed by, and overcome the main difficulties; and your Highneſs by your journey hath ſatisfied your ſelf of the perſon of the *Infanta*; God forbid, that either any perſonal diſtaſtes of Miniſters, or any indiſcreet or paſſionate carriage of buſineſſes, ſhould hazard that which his Majeſty and your Highneſs have done ſo much to obtain, and whereby, doubtleſs, ſo much good and peace is to accrew to Chriſtendom, by the effecting of it;

and, contrariwise, so much trouble and mischief by the miscarrying of it; besides the individual happiness of your Highness in such a Wife, which the world supposeth you infinitely esteem for her Person; and for her Birth, and Portion, is no where to be matched; and questionless, for her Vertue, and setled Affection to your Highness, deserveth you better then any Woman in the World. I humbly crave pardon for writing unto your Highness in this manner, which, I hope, your Highness well enough knows, neither the benefits I have received from Spain, nor their gratefull usage of me upon occasions, (nor, I protest unto your Highness, any other earthly respect) moveth me unto it, but the zeal and love I bear to your service, for which I shall ever under-value any thing that may concern my self. And therefore I shall conclude, by intreating your Highness, that if you would have things go well, that a Post may instantly be dispatched back unto me, authorizing me to deliver the said Powers, upon the arrival of the Dispensation, and having taken fitting securitie in this particular point. And this I earnestly beseech your Highness may be done with all possible speed and secrecie, and that the *Spanish* Embassadors may not know, that ever there was any suspension made of the delivery of the Powers. In the *interim*, I will find means, if the Dispensation come, for 20, or 24. dayes, to alledge some other fair pretexts for the deferring of the *Deposorios*: but herein I desire I may know your Highness resolution with all possible speed, *&c.* And so with, *&c.*

Madrid.   BRISTOL.

Archbishop Abbots, *to Secretary* Nanton.

Good Mr. Secretary,

I Have never more desired to be present at any Consultation, then that which is this day to be handled; for my heart, and all my heart, goeth with it: But my foot is worse then it was on Friday, so that, by advice of my Physician, I have sweat this whole night past, and am directed to keep my bed this day.

But for the matter, my humble advice is, That there is no going back, but a countenancing of it against all the world; yea, so far, as with ringing of Bells, and making of Bon-fires in *London*, so soon as it shall be certainly understood that the Coronation is past. I am satisfied in my Conscience, that the Cause is just, wherefore they have rejected that proud and bloudy man; and so much the rather, because he hath taken a course to make that Kingdom not elective, but to take it from the donation of another man. And when God hath set up the Prince, that is chosen to be a mark of honour through all Christendom, to propagate his Gospel, and to protect the oppressed; I dare not, for my part, give advice, but to follow where God leads.

It is a great honour to the King our Master, that he hath such a Son, whose Virtues have made him thought fit to be made a King. And methinks, I do, in this, and that of *Hungary*, foresee the work of God, that by piece and piece, the Kings of the earth, that gave their power unto the beast, (all the Word of God must be fulfilled) shall now tear the Whore, and make her desolate, as St. *John* in his Revelation hath fore-told. I pray you, therefore, with all the spirits you have, to put life into this business; and let a return be made into *Germany* with speed, and with comfort, and let it really be prosecuted, that it may appear to the world, that we are awake when God in this sort calleth us.

If I had time to express it, I could be very angry at the shuffling which was used toward my Lord of *Doncaster*, and the sleighting of his Embassage so, which cannot but touch upon our Great Master who did send him: and therefore, I would never have a Noble Son forsaken, for respect of them who truly aim at nothing but their own purposes.

Our striking in will comfort the *Bohemians*, will honour the *Palsgrave*, will strengthen the Union, will bring on the States of the Low-Countreys, will stir up the King of *Denmark*, and will move his two Uncles, the Prince of *Orange*, and the Duke of *Bovillon*, together with *Tremoville* (a rich Prince in *France*) to cast in their shares; and *Hungary*, as I hope, (being in that same Cause) will run the same fortune. For the means to support the war, I hope *Providebit Deus*: The Parliament is the old, and honourable way, but how assured at this time, I know not; yet I will hope the best: certainly, if countenance be given to the action, many brave spirits will voluntarily go. Our great Master, in sufficient

want

want of money, gave some ayd to the Duke of *Savoy*, and furnished out a prettie army in the cause of *Cleve*. We must trie once again what can be done in this businesse of a higher nature, and all the money that may be spared is to be turned that way. And perhaps God provided the Jewels that were laid up in the Tower to be gathered by the Mother for the preservation of her Daughter; who like a noble Princesse hath professed to her Husband, not to leave her self one Jewel, rather then not to maintain so religious, and righteous a cause. You see that lying on my bed I have gone too far; but if I were with you, this should be my language; which I pray you humbly and heartily to represent to the King my Master, telling him, that when I can stand, I hope to do his Majestie some service herein. So commending me unto you, I remain,

Your very loving friend,
Geo. Cant.

The Archbishop of Canterbury, *to the Bishops, concerning King* James *his Directions for Preachers, with the Directions.*

Right Reverend Father in God, and my very good Lord and Brother, I have received from the Kings most excellent Majesty a Letter, the tenor whereof here ensueth.

Most Reverend Father in God, right trusty, and right entirely beloved Councellor, we greet you well. Forasmuch as the abuses and extravagancies of Preachers in the Pulpit have been in all times repressed in this Realm, by some Act of Councel or State, with the advice or resolution of grave and learned Prelates, insomuch as the very licencing of Preachers had beginning by an Order of *Star-Chamber*, the 8. day of *July*, in the 19. year of King *Henry* 8. our Noble Predecessor: and whereas at this present divers young Students by reading of late Writers, and ungrounded Divines, do broach many times unprofitable, unsound, seditious and dangerous Doctrine, to the scandal of the Church, and disquieting of the State and present Government; We upon humble representation to us of these inconveniences by your self and sundry other grave and reverend Prelates of this Church, as also of our Princely care and zeal for the extirpation of schisme and dissention growing from these seeds, and for the setling of a religious and peaceable government both of the Church and State, do by these our special Letters streightly charge and commandyou, to use all possible care and diligence that these limitations and cautions herewith sent unto you concerning Preachers, be duly and streightly henceforth observed, and put in practice by the several Bishops in their several Diocesses within your jurisdictions. And to this end, our pleasure is, that you send them forthwith several Copies of these Directions, to be by them speedily sent and communicated to every Parson, Vicar and Curate, Lecturer and Minister, in every Cathedral and Parish Church within their several Diocesses; and that you earnestly require them to imploy their uttermost endeavor in the performance of this so important a businesse, letting them know that we have a special eye to their proceedings, and expect a strict account thereof both of you and them, and every of them. And these our Letters shall be your sufficient Warrant and Discharge in that behalf. Given under our Signet, at our Castle of *Windsor*, the fourteenth day of *August*, in the twentieth year of our reign of *England*, *France*, and *Ireland*, and of *Scotland* the fifty sixt.

Directions concerning Preachers.

1. That no Preacher, under the degree of a Bishop, or a Dean of a Cathedral or Collegiat Church, and that upon the Kings days, and set Festivals, do take occasion by the expounding of any Text of Scripture whatsoever, to fall to any set Discourse or Commonplace, otherwise then by opening the coherence and division of his Text, which be not comprehended and warranted in essence, substance, effect, or natural inference, within some one of the Articles of Religion, set forth by authority in the Church of *England*, and the two books of Homilies set forth by the same authority, in the year 1562. or in some of the Homilies set forth by authority of the Church of *England*, not onely for the help of non-preaching, but withall for a Pattern or a Boundary, as it were, for the preaching Ministers; and for their further instruction for the performance hereof, that they forthwith read over and peruse diligently the said Book of Articles, and the two Books of Homilies.

2. That no Parson, Vicar, Curate, or Lecturer, shall preach any Sermon, or Collation, hereafter, upon Sundays or Holy-days in the afternoon, in any Cathedral or Parish-Church throughout the Kingdome, but upon some part of the Catechisme, or some Text taken out of the Creed, the ten Commandments, or the Lords prayer, (Funeral sermons only excepted) And

And that those Preachers be most encouraged and approved of who spend their afternoons exercises in the examination of children in their Catechism, which is the most ancient and laudable custom of teaching in the Church of *England*.

3. That no Preacher, of what title or denomination soever, under the degree of a Bishop, or Dean at the least, do from henceforth presume to preach in any popular Auditory the deep points of Predestination, Election, Reprobation, or the universality, efficacy, resistibility or irresistibility of Gods grace; but leave these Theams to be handled by learned men, and that moderately and modestly by way of use and application, rather then by way of positive doctrine, as being fitter for Schools and Universities, then for simple Auditories.

4. That no Preacher, of what title or denomination soever, shall presume from henceforth in any Auditory within this Kingdome to declare, limit, or bound out by way of positive doctrine, in any Sermon or Lecture, the power, prerogative, jurisdiction, authority, right or duty of soveraign Princes; or otherwise meddle with these matters of State, and the differences betwixt Princes and people, then as they are instructed and presidented in the Homilies of Obedience, and in the rest of the Homilies and Articles of Religion;set forth, as before is mentioned, by publick Authority; but rather confine themselves wholly to these two heads, Faith, and good life, which are all the subject of ancient Homilies and Sermons.

5. That no Preacher, of what title or denomination soever, shall causelesly, or without invitation of the Text, fall into bitter invectives, or undecent railing speeches against the persons of either Papists or Puritans; but modestly, and gravely, when they are occasioned thereunto by the text of Scripture, cleer both the doctrine and discipline of the Church of *England* from the aspersions of either adversary, especially when the Auditory is suspected with the one or the other infection.

6. Lastly, That the Archbishops and Bishops of this Kingdom (whom his Majesty hath good cause to blame for their former remisness) be more wary and choice in the licensing of Preachers, and revoke all grants made to any Chancellor, Official or Commissary, to pass Licences in this kind. And that all the Lecturers throughout the Kingdom, a new body, and severed from the ancient Clergie of *England*, as being neither Parsons, Vicars, nor Curates, be licensed henceforward in the Court of Faculties, only upon recommendations of the party from the Bishop of the Diocess under his hand and seal, with a *Fiat* from the Archbishop of *Canterbury*, and a confirmation under the great seal of *England*; and that such as transgress any of these Directions be suspended by the Lord Bishop of that Diocess, or, in his default, by the Lord Archbishop of that Province *(ab officio & beneficio)* for a year and a day, until his Majesty, by the advice of the next Convocation, shall prescribe some further punishment.

By this you see his Majesties Princely care, that men should preach Christ crucified, obedience to the higher powers, and honest and Christian conversation of life, but in a regular form; and not that every young man should take unto himself an exorbitant liberty to teach what he listeth, to the offence of his Majesty, and to the disturbance and disquiet of the Church and Commonwealth. I can give unto your Lordship no better directions for the performance hereof, then are prescribed to you in his Majesties Letter, and the Schedule hereunto annexed. Wherefore I pray you be very careful, since it is the Princely pleasure of his Majesty to require an exact account both of you and of me for the same. Thus not doubting, but by your Register, or otherwise, you will cause these instructions to be communicated to your Clergy, I leave you to the Almighty, and remain your Lordships loving brother,

Croydon. Aug. 15. 1622.   George Cant.

The Bishops of Rochester, Oxford, *and* St. Davids, *to the Duke, concerning Mr.* Montague.

May it please your Grace,

WE are bold to be suitors to you, in the behalf of the Church of *England*, and a poor member of it, Mr. *Montague*, at this time not a little distressed. We are not strangers to his person, but it is the Cause which we are bound to be tender of.

The Cause, we conceive, (under correction of better judgment) concerns the Church of *England* meerly; for that Church when it was reformed from the superstitious opinions broached, or maintained by the Church of *Rome*, refused the apparent and dangerous errours, and would not be too busie with every particular School-point. The cause why she held this moderation, was, because she could not be able to preserve any unity amongst Christians, if men were forced to subscribe to curious particulars, disputed in Schools.

Now

The Bishops, of Rochester, &c. to the Duke.

Now may it please your Grace, the opinions which at this time trouble many men in the late book of Mr. *Montague*, are some of them such as are expresly the resolved doctrine of the Church of *England*, and those he is bound to maintain. Some of them such as are fit onely for Schools, and to be left at more liberty for learned men to abound in their own sence, so they keep themselves peaceable, and distract not the Church. And therefore, to make any man subscribe to School-opinions, may justly seem hard in the Church of Christ, and was one great fault of the Councel of *Trent*. And to affright them from those opinions in which they have (as they are bound) subscribed to the Church, as it is worse in it self, so it may be the Mother of greater danger.

May it please your Grace further to consider, that when the Clergy submitted themselves, in the time of *Henry* the 8th. the submission was so, that if any difference, doctrinal, or other, fell in the Church, the King and the Bishops were to be Judges of it in a National Synod, or Convocation, the King first giving leave under his broad Seal, to handle the points in difference.

But the Church never submitted to any other Judge, neither indeed can she, though she would. And we humbly desire your Grace to consider, and then to move his most Gracious Majesty (if you shall think fit) what dangerous Consequences may follow upon it. For first, if any other Judge be allowed in matter of Doctrine, we shall depart from the ordinance of Christ, and the continual course and practice of the Church.

2. Secondly, if the Church be once brought down beneath her self, we cannot but fear what may be next strook at.

3. Thirdly, it will some way touch the honour of his Majesties dear Father, and our most dread Sovereign of Glorious and ever blessed memory, King *James*, who saw and approved all the opinions in this book; and he in his rare wisdom and judgement would never have allowed them, if they had Crossed with truth and the Church of *England*.

4. Fourthly, we must be bold to say, that we cannot conceive what use there can be of Civil Government in the Common-Wealth, or of preaching, and external ministrie in the Church, if such fatal opinions as some which are opposite, and contrary to these delivered by Mr. *Montague*, are, and shall be publiquely taught and maintained.

5. Fifthly, we are certain, that all or most of the contrary opinions were treated of at *Lambeth*, and ready to be published, but then Queen *Elizabeth* of famous memory, upon notice given, how little they agreed with the Practice of piety, and obedience to all Government, caused them to be suppressed, and so they have continued ever since, till of late some of them have received countenance at the Synod of *Dort*. Now this was a Synod of that nation, and can be of no authority in any other National Church, till it be received there by publique authority. And our hope is, that the Church of *England* will be well advised, and more then once over, before she admit a forreign Synod, especially of such a Church as condemneth her discipline and manner of Government, to say no more.

And further, we are bold to commend to your Graces wisdom this one particular. His Majesty (as we have been informed) hath already taken this businesse into his own care, and most worthily referred it in a right course to Church-consideration. And we well hoped, that without further trouble to the state, or breach of unity in the Church, it might so have been well, and orderly composed, as we still pray it may. These things considered, we have little to say for Mr. *Montagues* person : onely thus much we know ; He is a very good Scholar, and a right honest man. A man every way able to do God, his Majesty, and the Church of *England* great service. We fear he may receive great discouragement, and, which is far worse, we have some cause to doubt this may breed a great backwardnesse in able men to write in the defence of the Church of *England*, against either home, or forreign adversaries, if they shall see him sink in fortunes reputation, or health, upon his book-occasion.

And this we most humbly submit to your Graces judgment, and care of the Churches peace, and welfare. So recommending your Grace to the protection of Almighty God,

We shall ever rest, at your Graces service

2. August 1625.

Jo. Roffens.
Jo. Oxon.
Guil. Meneven.

The Bishop of Lincoln, *to the Bishop of* London.

The Bishop of Winchester, *to his Arch-deacon.*

Salutem in Christo. I have received Letters from the most Reverend Father in God, the Lord Arch-bishop of *Canterbury*, the tenor whereof followeth.

Right Reverend Father in God, my very good Lord and brother, I have received from the Kings most excellent Majesty a Letter, the tenor whereof here ensueth.

Most Reverend Father in God, right trusty, and right entirely beloved Councellor, we greet you well. Forasmuch as the abuses and extravagancies of Preachers in the Pulpit have been, &c.

According to the tenor of these Letters, you are to see that these limitations and cautions herewith sent unto you be duly and strictly from henceforth observed and put in practice, and that several Copies of those Directions be speedily communicated to every one of those whom they shall concern, and that you may imploy your uttermost endeavours in the performance of so important a business, considering that his Majesty will have a special eye over you and me, and expect a strict account at both our hands; whereof praying you to have all possible care, I commend your endeavours therein to the blessing of God.

Your very loving friend,

From Farnham, Aug. 15, 1622.   Lan. Winton.

The Bishop of Lincoln, *Lord Keeper, to the Bishop of* London, *concerning Preaching and Catechizing.*

My very good Lord,

I Doubt not, before this time you have received from me the directions of his most excellent Majesty concerning Preaching and Preachers, which are so graciously set down, that no godly or discreet man can otherwise then acknowledg that they do much tend to edification, if he take them not up upon report, but do punctually consider the tenor of the words as they lie, and doth not give an ill construction to that which may receive a fair interpretation. Notwithstanding, because some few Church-men and many of the people have sinisterly conceived, as we here find, that those Instructions do tend to the restraint of the exercise of Preaching, and do in some sort abate the number of Sermons, and so consequently by degrees do make a breach to ignorance and superstition, his Majesty in his Princely wisdome hath thought fit that I should advertise your Lordship of the grave and weighty reasons which induced his Highness to prescribe that which was done.

You are therefore to know, that his Majesty being much troubled and grieved, at the heart, to hear every day of so many defections from our Religion both to Popery and Anabaptism, or other points of Separation, in some parts of this Kingdom; and considering, with much admiration, what might be the cause thereof, especially in the reign of such a King who doth so constantly profess himself an open adversary to the superstition of the one, and madness of the other, his Princely wisdome could fall upon no one greater probability, then the lightness, affectedness, and unprofitableness of that kind of Preaching which hath been of late years too much taken up in Court, University, City and Countrey.

The usual scope of very many Preachers is noted to be, soaring up in points of Divinity, too deep for the capacity of the people, or mustering up of so much reading, or displaying of their own wit, or an ignorant medling with Civil matters, as well in the private several Parishes and Corporations, as in the publique, of the Kingdom, or a venting of their own distastes, or a smoothing up those idle fancies (which when the Text shall occasion the same, is not onely approved, but much commended by his Royal Majesty) both against the persons of Papists and Puritans.

Now the people bred up with this kind of teaching, and never instructed in the Catechism and fundamental grounds of Religion, are, for all this airy nourishment, no better then a Brass Tabret, new Table-books to be filled up either with Manuals and Catechismes of the Popish Priests, or the papers and pamphlets of Anabaptists, Brownists, and Puritans.

His Majesty therefore calling to mind the saying *Tertullian, Id verum quod primum*; and remembring with what doctrine the Church of *England* in her first and most happy Reformation did drive out the one, and keep out the other from poysoning and infecting the people of this Kingdom, doth find that the whole scope of this doctrine is contained in the Articles of Religion, the two books of Homilies, the lesser and the greater Catechism, chifm, which his Majeſtie doth therefore recommend again in theſe Directions, as the Themes and proper ſubjects of all ſound and edifying Preaching.

And ſo far are theſe directions from abridging, that his Majeſty doth expect at our hands, that it ſhould increaſe the number of Sermons, by renewing, every Sunday in the afternoon, in all Pariſh-Churches throughout the Kingdom, that primitive and moſt profitable Expoſition of the Catechiſm, wherewith the people, yea, very children, may be timely ſeaſoned and inſtructed in all the heads of Chriſtian Religion. The which kind of Expoſition (to our amendment be it ſpoken) is more diligently obſerved in all the Reformed Churches of *Europe*, then of late it hath been here in *England*. I find his Majeſtie much moved with this neglect, and reſolved (if we, that are Biſhops, do not ſee a reformation thereof, which I truſt we ſhall) to recommend to the care of the Civil Magiſtrate: ſo far is his Highneſs from giving the leaſt diſcouragement to ſolid Preaching, or diſcreet and religious Preachers.

To all theſe I am to add, That it is his Majeſties Princely pleaſure, that both the former Directions, and thoſe Reaſons of the ſame, be fairly written in every Regiſters Office, to the end, that every Preacher, of what denomination ſoever, may, if he be ſo pleaſed, take out Copies of either of them with his own hand *gratis*, paying nothing in the name of fee, or expedition: But if he do uſe the pains of the Regiſter, or the Clerk, then to pay ſome moderate Fee, to be pronounced, in open Court, by the Chancellor and Commiſſaries of the place, taking the direction and approbation of my Lords the Biſhops.

Laſtly, That from henceforward a courſe may be taken, that every Parſon, Vicar, Curate, or Lecturer, do make, and exhibit an account, for the performance of theſe his Majeſties Directions, and the Reaſons for the ſame, at the enſuing Viſitation of the Biſhops and Archdeacons, paying to the Regiſter 6 d. for the exhibiting. And ſo wiſhing, but withall, in his Majeſties name, requiring your Lordſhip to have a ſpecial and extraordinary care of the premiſes, I leave you to the Almighty.

Septemb. 3. 1622.

Your very loving friend,
J. Lincoln, C. S.

The Biſhop of Exceter, to the Lower Houſe of Parliament.

Gentlemen,

FOR Gods ſake, be wiſe in your well meant zeal: Why do we argue away precious time, that can never be revoked, or repaired? Wo is me, whileſt we diſpute, our friends periſh, and we muſt follow them. Where are we, if we break? and (I tremble to think it) we cannot but break, if we hold too ſtiff. Our Liberties and Properties are ſufficiently declared to be ſure, and legal; our remedies are clear and irrefragible; what do we fear? Every Subject now ſees the way chalked out before him for future Juſtice, and who dares henceforth tread beſides it? Certainly, whileſt Parliaments live, we need not miſdoubt the like violation of our freedoms and rights; may we be but where the Loans found us, we ſhall ſufficiently enjoy our ſelves, and ours: it is now no ſeaſon to reach for more. O let us not, whileſt we over-rigidly plead for a higher ſtrain of ſafety, put our ſelves into a neceſſity of ruine, and utter deſpair of redreſs; let us not, in a ſuſpicion of evil that may be, caſt our ſelves into a preſent confuſion: if you love your ſelves, and your Countrey, remit ſomething of your own Terms; and ſince the ſubſtance is yielded by your noble Compatriots, ſtand not too curiouſly upon points of circumſtance. Fear not to truſt a good King, who, after the ſtricteſt Law made, muſt be truſted with the execution: Think, that your Countrey, yea, Chriſtendom lieth in the mercy of your preſent reſolution: Relent, or farewell. Farewell from him, whoſe faithfull heart bleeds in a vowed ſacrifice for his King and Countrey.

The Archbiſhop of York, to King James.

May it pleaſe your Majeſty,

I Have been too long ſilent, and am afraid, that by ſilence I have neglected the dutie of the place it hath pleaſed God to call me unto, and your Majeſtie to place me in: But now I humbly beſeech, that I may diſcharge my Conſcience towards God, and my Dutie towards your Majeſtie. And therefore, I beſeech you, Sir, to give me leave freely to de-

Q liver

liver my self, and then let it please your Majesty to do with me as you please.

Your Majesty hath propounded a Toleration of Religion: I beseech you, to take into your Consideration, what your Act is, and what the Consequence may be. By your Act, you labour to set up that most damnable and heretical Doctrine of the Church of *Rome*, the Whore of *Babylon*. How hatefull will it be to God, and grievous to your Subjects (the true professors of the Gospel) that your Majesty, who hath often defended, and learnedly written against those wicked Heresies, should now shew your self a Patron of those Doctrines which your Pen hath told the world, and your Conscience tells your self, are superstitious, idolatrous, and detestable. Also, what you have done, in sending the Prince without consent of your Councel, and the privity and approbation of your People: For although, Sir, you have a large interest in the Prince, as the Son of your flesh, yet have your People a greater, as the Son of the Kingdom, upon whom (next after your Majesty) are their eyes fixed, and their Welfare depends. And so llenderly is his going apprehended, that, believe it Sir, however his return may be safe, yet the drawers of him unto that action, so dangerous to himself, so desperate to the Kingdom, will not pass away unquestioned, and unpunished.

Besides, this Toleration you endeavour to set up by your Proclamation, it cannot be done without a Parliament, unless your Majesty will let your Subjects see, that you now take unto your self a liberty to throw down the Laws of the Land at your pleasure. What dreadfull Consequence these things may draw after, I beseech your Majesty to consider.

And above all, lest by this Toleration, and discountenance of the true profession of the Gospel (wherewith God hath blessed us, and under which this Kingdom hath flourished these many years) your Majesty doth draw upon the Kingdom, in generall, and your self in particular, Gods heavie wrath and indignation.

Thus, in discharge of my duty to your Majestie, and the place of my Calling, I have taken the humble boldness to deliver my Conscience. And now, Sir, Do with me what you please.

The Bishop of Lincoln, *to his Majesty.*

Most Mighty, and dread Sovereign,

I Have now these four moneths, by the strength of those gracious speeches your Majestie used, (when I took my leave of your Majestie at *Salisbury,*) and the conscience of mine own innocencie from having ever wilfully or maliciously offended your Majestie, comforted my self in these great afflictions, to be thus enjoyned from your Majesties presence, (the onely Heaven wherein my soul delighted,) having submitted my self (I hope, dutifully, and patiently) to the discharge from that great Office, (for the execution whereof I was altogether unworthy;) my required absence from the Councel-Table; my sequestration from attending your Majesties Coronation; and your Majesties favourable pleasure (for so I do esteem that) to spare my presence at this next Parliament: And, I trust in God, I shall most readily obey any other Command that bears the image and superscription of your Majestie, without any desire of searching after the hand that helps to press and engrave it. Yet because I suffer in some more particulars, then, peradventure, is explicitely known to your Majestie; and that I have no friend left about your Majestie, that dares, for fear of displeasure, relate unto your Majesty my griefs, and necessities; I humbly crave your gracious pardon, to make some two representations, and some few Petitions unto your most Excellent Majestie.

First, I humbly shew unto your Majestie, that, besides my former calamities, I am not paid that part of my Pension which should pay the Creditors who lent me money to buy the same; notwithstanding your Majestie hath been graciously pleased to order otherwise.

Secondly, I have not yet received my Writ of Summons unto the Parliament (denied to no Prisoners, or condemned Peers, in the late Reign of your blessed Father,) that I might accordingly make my Proxie; the which I cannot do, the Writ not received: nor can I my self go into the Countrey, as I had done long ere this, had not the expectation of this Writ, together with the special service of my Lord Duke, and no other occasion whatsoever, detained me.

These two particulars I present, with all submission, unto your Majestie, and shall rest satisfied with what royal resolution your Majestie shall make therein.

These Petitions that follow, I must earnestly beg at your Majesties hands, and for Gods sake,

The Bishop of St. David's, to the Duke.

sake, and your blessed Fathers sake, whose Creature, and most painfull servant, I was.

First, that your Majesty would be pleased to mitigate and allay the causeless displeasure of my Lord Duke against me; who is so little satisfied with any thing I can do, or suffer, that I have no means left to appease his anger, but my prayers to God, and your Sacred Majesty.

Secondly, I beseech your Majesty, for Christ Jesus sake, not to believe news, or accusations against me, concerning my carriage past, present, or to come, whilest I stand thus enjoyned from your Royal presence, before you shall have heard my answer and defence unto the particulars. Those that inform your Majesty may (God he knoweth) be oftentimes mis-informed.

My last supplication unto your Majestie is, That in my absence, this Parliament, no use may be made of your sacred Name to wound the reputation of a poor Bishop, who, besides his Religion, and Dutie to that Divine Character you now bear, hath ever affectionately honoured your very Person above all the objects in this world, as he desires the salvation of the world to come. But I crave no protection against any other accuser, or accusation whatsoever. So shall I never cease to pray to the Almighty God, to make your Majestie the Happiest and Greatest King that ever was Crowned and Anointed; which shall be the continual Orisons of

Your Majesties most dutifull and most humble Vassal,
JO. LINCOLN.

The Bishop of St. Davids, (Dr. Laud) to the Duke.

My most gracious Lord,

I May not be absent, and not write: And since your Grace is pleased with the trouble, I must profess my self much content with the performance of the dutie. I am not unmindfull of the last business your Grace committed to me; but I have as yet done the less in it, because I fell into a relapse of my infirmity: but, I thank God, I am once more free, if I can look better to my self, as I hope I shall.

My Lord, I must become an humble suitor to your Grace. I hear, by good hand, that my Lord of *Canterbury* intends shortly to renew the High Commission: Now I am to acquaint your Grace, that there is never a Bishop that lives about *London* left out of the Commission but my self, and many that live quite absent are in, and many inferiours to Bishops. The Commission is a place of great experience, for any man that is a Governour in the Church; and since, by his Majesties gracious goodness, and your Grace's sole procurement, I am made a Governour, I would be loath to be excluded from that which might give me experience, and so enable me to perform my duty. I am sure, my Lord of *Canterbury* will leave me out, as hitherto he hath done, if his Majestie be not pleased to Command that I shall be in. This I submit to your Grace; but humbly desire, even against my own ease and quiet, that I may not be deprived of that experience which is necessary for my place. I most humbly beseech your Grace to pardon this boldness, and to know, that in my daily prayers for your Grace's happiness, I shall ever rest

Novemb. 18. 1624.

Your Grace's most devoted and affectionate servant,
Guil. Menevensis.

The Bishop of Landaffe, to the Duke.

My most honourable good Lord,

IT is meet, before I beg anew, that I should first acknowledge those benefits, and more especially, give thanks for the last noble favour your Lordship did me, in standing up the last day of Parliament, and pleading my cause. Never was poor man more bound to a gracious Lord for protecting his innocency; and it came seasonable, like a showr of rain in the time of drought: My very heart was parched with grief till it came, and it had ere this been broken, had not your Lordships Speech then dropt comfort, in strength whereof it yet lives. For an abortive thought, which never came into act, some two or three years ago conceived, and that tending to a work of mercy, and charity, a deed of justice, and due thankfulness, how far, how foully have I been traduced! your Honour cannot imagine how

deeply

deeply I have been wounded in my good name, as if I had deserved deprivation, degradation, yea, to be hanged, drawn, and quartered. This can none cure, but God, or the King, *Deus in monte*, God hath done his part in providing an occasion: Besides *London* (which is too high for me to look after) and the removes which may be thereby, *Hereford*, the next Seat to mine, (whither my Predecessors have oft been removed) is said to be now void. Now, good my Lord, speak once more seasonably: it is a doubled, and redoubled, an infinitely multiplied benefit, which is so given. Never had I more need of the Cordial his Majesty gave me at my going into *Wales*, which was, That I should not stay long there. It would be a restorative too, not onely of my Credit, so cruelly crackt with the sharp teeth of the wide mouth of vulgar lying Fame, but of my estate also, always poor, but lately much more impoverished, and made crazie, by occasions of the Church, which drew me to *London* (a place of great expences, as the busie times were) to little purpose: And the Parliament overtaking me, which have held me long, and longer yet are like to hold me here, even to the undoing of my self, my wife, and six children, from whom I have now lived six or seven moneths. And what shall I carry home with me, but disgrace and infamy? Yet, my good Lord, at least procure me of my Lord the King a *Nunc dimittis*, leave to depart. I shall be further out of the reach of pursuing malice, there in the Countrey; do his Majesty better service, in gathering up his Subsidies, praying, and teaching my Children (whilest I read a Lecture to them, my self was never yet able to get by heart, of parcimony, which must be to them in stead of a patrimony,) to pray for his Majesties long life, health and happiness. In which prayer shall your Lordship ever be duly remembred by

Your Lordships daily devout Readsman.
Theophilus Landavensis

The Bishop of St. Davids, (Doctor Laud) to the Duke.

My most gracious Lord,

I Am heartily glad to hear your Lordship is so well returned, and so happily as to meet so great joy. God hath, among many others his great blessings (and I know your Grace so esteems them) sent you now this extraordinary one, a Son to inherit his Fathers honours, and the rest of Gods blessings upon both. So soon as I came to an end of my journey, I met the happy news of Gods blessing upon your Grace, and it seasoned all the hard journey I have had out of *Wales* through the snow. When I had rested my self a little at my friend's house in the Forest (Mr. *Windebank*, a servant of your Grace's, whom I made bold to make known to your Honour) I came to *Windsor*, in hope to have been so happy as to meet your Grace at the great solemnity: but when I came, I found that which I suspected, that your Grace's greater joy would carry you further. Which journey, and the cause, and the end of it, I heartily wish, and pray, may be full of joy, and all contentment to your Grace. I made bold to trouble your Grace with a Letter, or two, out of *Wales*, which I hope Mr. *Windebank* took the best care he could to see delivered. I have no means to do your Grace any service, but by my prayers; and they do daily attend, and shall ever, while I breathe to utter them. I hope, though I have missed this opportunity, yet I shall be so happy as to see and wait upon your Grace at *London*. In the mean time, and ever, I leave your Grace, and all your home-blessings, to the protection of the Almighty, and shall ever be found

Windsor, Decemb. 13.   *Your Grace's most devoted and affectionate servant,*
1625.   Guil. Menevēn.

Doctor Montague, Bishop of Chichester, to the Duke.

May it please your Grace,

YOur Highness vouchsafed, at *Windsor*, to let me understand, that his Majesty, my gracious Master and Sovereign, had taken me off from that trouble and vexation which by some mens procurement I was put unto in the House of Commons. They, as I understand, think not so, but intend to proceed against me so far as they can, as having returned his Majesty no other answer, but that I was freed from imprisonment. It is true, that besides 20*l.* which the Serjeant had of me by exaction of fees, they bound me unto him in a Bond of 2000*l.*

The Bishop of Landaffe, to the Duke.

to appear before them, the first day of the next Sessions. I beseech your Grace, that as you have been pleased to tie me unto your excellent, not onely self, but also most honourable Sister, in that bond of obligation, as never was poor Scholar to such Worthies: so you would be pleased to let his Majesty understand the case, that, by your means, I may be absolutely discharged, with the re-delivery of my Bond from them whom I never offended, who (under correction) have nothing to do with me; and, as his Majesties servant, be left unto himself, especially, for that which was authorized by himself, and commanded by his Father, my late Master, of ever blessed memory. If his Majesty will be pleased to call for their accusations against me, if I do not really and throughly answer whatsoever is, or can be, imputed to me out of my Books, I will no further desire favour and protection of his Majesty, and your Gracious self, but be willingly left unto my enemies. I must crave pardon for presuming thus to trouble your Grace, the rather, because, through a grievous affliction of the Collick and Stone, I am not able personally to attend your Grace, whom, according unto my most bounden duty, I daily recommend unto the Almighty, being more obliged unto your noble self, then ever to any one. So remaining

Petworth, July 29.   *Most humbly at your Graces service ever*,
Ri. Montague.

1. IF any, or all the Papists living, can prove, That the *Roman* Church, as it now stands in opposition to the Church of *England*, is either the Catholick Church of Christ, or a sound member of the Catholick Church,
                       I will subscribe.

2. If any, or all the Papists living, can prove unto me, That the Church of *England*, as it standeth at this day, is not a true member of the Catholick Church,
                       I will subscribe.

3. If any, or all the Papists living, can prove unto me, That any one Point at this day maintained by the Church of *Rome* against the Church of *England* was the received Doctrine of the Catholick Church, or concluded by any General Councel, or particular approved Councel, or resolved of by any one Father, of Credit, to be such, for Five hundred years, at least, after Christ,
                       I will subscribe,
Ri. *Montague*.

Doctor Field, *Bishop of* Landaffe, *to the Duke*.

My gracious good Lord,

IN the great Library of men, that I have studied these many years, your Grace is the best Book, and most Classick Author, that I have read, in whom I find so much goodness, sweetness, and nobleness of nature, such an Heroick spirit, for boundless bounty, as I never did in any. I could instance in many, some of whom you have made Deans, some Bishops, some Lords, and Privy Councellors; none, that ever looked toward your Grace, did ever go empty away. I need go no further then my self (a gum of the earth) whom some eight years ago you raised out of the dust, for raising but a thought so high as to serve your Highness. Since that, I have not played the Truant, but more diligently studied you then ever before: and yet (Dunce that I am) I stand at a stay, and am a *Non-proficient*, the Book being the same that ever it was, as may appear by the great proficiency of others. This wonderfully poseth me, and sure there is some guile, some wile in some of my fellow Students, who hide my Book from me, or some part of it. All the fault is not in mine own blockishness, that I thrive no better: I once feared this before, that some did me ill offices. Your Grace was pleased to protest, no man had; and to assure me, no man could. My heart tells me, it hath been always upright, and is still most faithfull unto you. I have examined my actions, my words, and my very thoughts, and found all of them, ever since, most sound unto your Grace. Give me leave, after so long patience (for which vertue you were once pleased to commend me to my old Master, King *James*, and I have not yet lost it) now that for these twelve Moneths almost, I have been, not onely upon the Stage, but upon the rack of expectations, even distracted between hope and fear, to comfort my self with recordation of your Loving kindnesses of old, when on that great Feast-day of your being inaugured our Chancellor, my look was your book, wherein you read sadness, to which I was bold to answer, I trusted your Grace would give me no cause. You replyed with (loss of blood rather) that was your noble expression. But God forbid so precious an effusion. (I would empty all my veins rather then you should bleed one drop) whenas one blast of your breath is able to bring me to the haven where I would be. My Lord, I am grown an old man, and am like old Housholdstuffe, apt to be broke upon often removing. I desire it therefore but once for all, be it *Eli*, or *Bathe* and *Wells*; and I will spend the remainder of my dayes in writing an History of your good deeds to me and others, whereby I may vindicate you from the envie, and obloquy of this present wicked age wherein we live, and whilest I live, in praying for your Grace,

Whose I am totally and finally
Theophilus Landaven.

Monsieur Bevayr, *Chancellor of* France *discharged*, *to the* French *King.*

LO, Sir, I willingly resign into your hands the charge with which you were pleased to honour me, and with the same Countenance that I received it, without seeeking for it, I leave it without grieving for it ; the Law had sufficiently taught me to obey your Majesty, so that I needed not to have been sent for by a Captain of the Guard, and twenty Archers; violence should only be used against those that resist, and not against me that know how to obey, and that have ever esteemed this honour a heavy burthen, rather then a dignity, which yet I had accepted for the good of your service, because every able man owes his cares and his years to the publick good; and because it had been a shame for me to refuse to die with the stern in my hand, being able to hinder, or at the least delay, the shipwrack that threatens us. God grant, Sir, that I be the greatest loser in this disfavour, and that you and your State be the least touched in it. This accident hath not taken me on the suddain, having ever well foreseen, that as I followed as much as I could the integrity and vertues of *Monsieur de Villeroy*, and the President *Janin*; so I ought to expect the like fortune to theirs: your commandment in this agrees with the choice my self had made, if I had been at full liberty; for I love a great deal better to be companion in their disgraces, (if I ought so to stile the being disburthened of affairs) then to be imployed in the managing the State with them that there remain; since I might in time have taken an ill day by the Company of such people, to whom I no whit envy the increase of authority, which is given them at my cost; for I have not used to give account of my actions every morning by stealth, neither will I be prescribed what I ought to do, if the States good, and reason do not counsell me unto it. This is much more honourable for me, then to have betrayed your Majesty, in sealing a discharge to an accountant of 80000 pound, in the great poverty of the Treasury, and that to further the good of a man that blushes not (besides this) to demand the Dutchy of *Alanson* by way of mortgage, which is the portion of the Kings Sons, and to pretend to the office of Constable, which the late Kings will expresly was, should be suppressed after the death of the late Lord *Monmorency*. Think not, Sir, that in not giving my consent to this, I desired to oppose my self against your Authority; I know well that that hath no bounds but those of your will; but yet are you bound to rule your self according to reason, and to follow the Counsel of those which have entred into the managing of the State, by the choice which the late King had made of them, as being more able to give it you, then certain new comers drawn out of the dregs of business and of the people. This exchange which is made of us for them, is the trick of the Wolves to the Sheep, when they took their doggs from them; doth not your Majesty perceive it, or dare you not redress it for fear of disobedience ? Sir, you owe obedience by nature to those that preach it to you, but they themselves owe it you both by divine and humane right; and though you should yield them less, they have given you but too many examples so to do. Remember, if it please you, that you are past fifteen years old, and Kings are of age at fourteen. *Isaac* followed *Abraham* his Father to be sacrificed, because he was not old enough to fear any thing: I believe if he had been a man grown, and had foreseen the danger, he would not himself have carried the sticks upon his shoulders; he was but the appearance of a sacrifice, I pray God in these occasions keep you from the effect: for when I see that men move the Authority of the Court when they will, that men set to sile and dispose of the Officers of the Crown, without being

once

once hindred by any; the Princes of the blood having been some imprisoned, and other Princes having retired themselves for the security of their persons; when I see that among the great ones, they that are made see some shadow of better fortunes are fain to lend their hands to bring themselves into bondage; that they which have attained some setlednesse in this alteration, maintain it onely for fear of returning to the former misery of their former condition———. Besides, it seems also that the people, and the Provinces partake of this change, after the example of the great ones, seeing the help of the law is unprofitable; every thing being out of order, by canvasing, by violences, and by corruptions; the Louvre it self hath put on a new face, as well as the affairs of the Kingdome; there remains nothing of the old Court but the walls, and even of them the use hath been changed; for they were wont to serve for the safeguard of Princes, and now they serve for their prison, and for yours it may be, (if it be lawful to say so:) for it is not without some end, that when you goe abroad, you have a company of light horse to attend you, chosen by a suspected hand; this is your Guard after the fashion of the Bastile, this distrust counsels you enough what you ought to do, and you need no other advice. I am hist at, I am scoft at, and my discourse; so was *Cassandra* used, when she foretold the destruction of *Troy*. Sir, I have nothing left but my tongue to serve you with; If I were so happy to draw you out of the error in which you are fed, I would bless a thousand times my disgrace, for having emboldened me to speak freely in a time wherein even words are punished. The falsenesse of the *Alcharon* is onely authorised, by that it is forbidden under pain of death to speak of it. The incroachment which is made upon your Authority takes footing onely by the danger that is in telling it you freely; consider, (if it please you) that those which usurp power over you are of a Country where every body would reign; thence it is that there is not a City on the other side the Alpes, that hath not her republick or her petty King; and if your Majesty had but a little tasted the History of your own Kingdom, you would have found that the most learned Tragedies that were ever seen in *France* have come from that side: the last ——— upon occasion of a little book which I published, touching *Constancy and Comfort in publick calamities*, I fear much that (contrary to my designe) this is a Work for your Reigne, if the goodness of God take not pity on us. Think not, Sir, that the grief to see my self removed from the State Affairs breeds so bold a discourse; If I had felt any grief for that, 'tis but as new married Wives weep to leave the subjection of their Fathers, to enter into the equality of Marriage: Yet it is true, that owing you my service, I should with more contentment have imployed it in your Councels of State, then in your Parliaments, where the matters are of lesse importance. For I, suppose, that if the Carpenter which made the frame of the Admiral, wherein *Don John de Austria* commanded at the Battel of *Lepanto*, had known that she should have served in so important an occasion, wherein depended the safety of the rest of Europe, he would have taken more pleasure in the making her, then if he had made a Vessel destined onely for Traffick. Notwithstanding, since your Majesty commands me to retire my self, in a good hour be it, the lesser Stars bear a part in a perfection of the Universe, though they contribute less to it then the Sun or Moon. In what condition soever I live, I will ever bring all I shall be able to the good of your service: and if there be any of those which are neer you, that lament mine absence, for my own sake, I would willingly say to them, Weep for your selves children of *Jerusalem*, that for want of courage suffer your Majesty to be betrayed; and not for me, that have no other fault, then that I am an honest man. I take leave therefore of you, Sir, praying God to take pity of your *Estate*, and care of your Breeding.

Monsieur Balsac, *to the Cardinal* de la Valette.

My Lord,

I am retired here into *Cicero's* house, where I take the fresh aire, and the shade of every houre of the day, and laugh at those that broil themselves at *Rome*. But although I be come hither as well to untire my spirit, as to recreate my body, notwithstanding it is impossible that the first can rest, but must do businesse where it finds none; it crosses the Sea, and passes over the Alpes without my consent; and because there is nothing to do at *France*, it goes to seek some at *Constantinople*, at *Madrid*, at *London*, and at *Montauban*. Now, to the end you may not think me a lyar, and that under an honest pretext I would palliate a reproveable idlenesse; I am going to write you the adventures of my yesterday daies walk, and speak to you in the same stile, and the same sort as I rave. While the King is busied to make warre, the King of *Spain* passeth his time with Ladies, and into places that may not honestly be named; I will give no judgement upon the different inclination of these two Princes, but I very well know, that so long as they live in that fashion, the King of *Spain* shall take no Townes, nor the King of *France* the Pox. You have surely heard it reported, that the *Polanders* have defeated the *Turks* Army, which was composed of two hundred thousand Combatants, the halfe whereof lay dead upon the place. It must necessarily be granted, that but he only, after such a loss, could make such a second, and that he hath a source of men that cannot be drawn dry, either by warrs, by plagues, or by any other ill disposition of the aire, seeing that in the abundance of all things, that his Empire produces, there is nothing at so low a price, as the lives of Souldiers. When I dream that the Duke of *Bouillon* is shut up in *Sedan*, from whence he cannot come forth to goe and make his party, I imagine to my self, a poore mother standing upon the brink of a River, seeing her sonne slain on the other side, neither being able to help him or bid him farewell: never was man so assaulted with such diversity of thoughts, nor opprest with unprofitable cares; one while it vexes him that sufficient resistance was not made at St. *Jehan de Angeli*; and again, I find that they made not use of the advantage which they might have taken. At one and the same time I would have been at *Montauban* to defend, and in *England* to get succour for it. But why dwels so great a spirit in a body that hath no more heat in it then a fever gives it, and which is never removed but by *Amber-Greece* and Physick? its known that the better part of it dwels in the history of troubles, and that in this world it holds but the place of another. In the mean time, the affairs of the Rebels grow to ruine; and if they make any small attempts, it is not that their hopes increase, nor their courage strengthens; but it is Gods will that they shall not have either victory or peace.

The Duke of *Bouillon* sees all this, not being able to remedy, and if sometimes to divert his spirit from so vexing an object, he thinks to seek some comfort out of the Kingdome, and amongst strangers affairs, of one side he discovers a puissant Army under the conduct of *Spinola*, which threatens all *Germany*; and on the other side he sees his Nephew, who from having been *Count Palatine*, and King of *Bohemia*, is become pensioner to the *Hollanders*, and a Gentleman of the Prince of *Orange* his train; as the beasts, in time past, were wont to be crowned, which ought to be sacrificed; so fortune presented a Kingdome to this poore man, to the end he should lose his life, but not to lie, he hath shewed himself craftier then she, and fled so he could never be overtaken. Notwithstanding, to speak home, the gain which he got by not dying at the battail of *Prague*, is not so great as the reproach which shall be cast upon him for living by his own fault, and for having witnessed to all the people of the world, that the end of his desires was only to attain to be old; and without doubt, as it is a great advantage to be the Grand-child of an usurper, so there is not a more miserable condition, then to have been a King, and now to be no more but the subject, or tragedy, to playes. Let men then, as much as they please, praise the designes of this man, and his good intention. I, for my part, find nothing so easy as to fly, and lose; and posterity shall put him rather in the number of Thieves that have been punished, then of conquerours which have triumphed on the earth. Since it is true, that the persecution ceases in *England*, and that the King wearieth himself with giving us Martyrs, it may be, that within a short time, he will altogether set souls at liberty, that still makes one step to his mother Church. As for my part, I despair not of this great conversion, that all honest men will, with salt tears, desire this from Heaven, knowing to the contrary, that he hath a reasonable spirit, and may be perswaded upon a thing that he determined on. I assure my self that he studies every day the truth of the instructions the great Cardinal *Peron* left him, and that will be the strongest in his Kingdomes, assoon as his Conscience ————authority better re-stablished then his. His predecessors knew not how to reign in regard of him, no not she that plaid with so many heads, and who was more happy then needful for the Christian Common-wealth. It is certain, that heretofore *England* believed in God, but this day it only believes in its Prince, and Religion makes but a part of the obedience yielded unto him; insomuch, that if he would but set in the place of all the points of Faith all the fables of Poesie, he should find in his subjects complying enough to bring them to his will, and perswade himself, that he may make all things just that he does, and all things culpable that he condemns; his Authority came not so far at the first stroak; and there must be time to make men lose Reason, but at this time when all

spirits

spirits are vanquished, and that the great belief that he hath given of his judgement takes away the liberty of theirs; they can imagine nothing above the wisdome of the King, and without medling with any thing that passes between God and him; they believe that if he command them to tread under-foot all the Holy things, and to violate all the Lawes, all that were but for the safety of their Consciences. But it is to be believed, that this Divine providence, which conducts things to their ends, by means which in appearance are contrary, will use the bloodiness of this people to procure their salvation, and cause them to come again into the Church, by the same door they went out of it. And since the hearts of Kings are in the hands of God, there wants nothing but a good motion sent unto him, to build again the Altars which he hath beaten down, and at one clap to turn to the true Religion the souls of three Kingdomes. A while ago he sent a Gentleman expresly to this Court, that it might not be contrary with the Marriage which he treated with *Spain*, and to endeavour to make the *Romans* think well of it; and that one of these dayes, it may be, he will call his Holiness, and the sacred Colledge of Cardinals; but hitherto these are termes of a tongue unknown to him. Furthermore, in this Country we imagine, that there will be no lack of warrs till *Rochel* be reduced to extremity: It is very true, that the forces which the King hath left before it, are not great; but for how many men, think you, they count the Captain into whose hands he hath put them! It is not permitted to judge of that which he will do by the ordinary course of the things of this world; his actions cannot be drawn into example; and though he be infinitely wise, notwithstanding it is certain, that in what he undertakes, it alwayes appears somewhat greater then mans wisdome; Yet truly, my Lord, after having considered the motion of the Stars, which are so just; the order of the seasons, which are so governed; the beauties of Nature, which are so divers; I find in the end, that there is nothing in the world, wherein God sheweth himself so admirable, as in the guiding of the life of my Lord your Father. But to the purpose, behold this that I added yesterday to the great discourse, which I made by your Commandment, and which you much praised the first time.

Monsieur Balsac, *to King* Lewis.

SIR,

THe late King your Father hath not done more, and neverthelesss, not to speak of the Actions of his life; your Majesty knows that his last thoughts made all the Kings of the earth to tremble, and his memory untill this day is reverenced to the uttermost ends of the world. Notwithstanding, Sir, be it that you are come in a better time then he, be it that God hath destinated your Majesty for higher things, the glory which you have gotten at the going out of your infancy is not less, then that which that great Prince deserved when he was grown old in Armes: and in affaires as he, so you make your self redoubted without tyranny, as he, so you govern your people. But I am constrained to avow that your Majesty must needs yield to him in one thing, which is, that you have not yet begot a Son that resembles you. But certainly, Sir, we cannot any longer time have this advantage over you. All *Europe* requires Princes and Princesses of you; and it is certain, that the world ought not to end, but when your race shall fail: if you will then that the beauty of the things we see pass to another age; If you will that the publick tranquillity have an assured foundation, and that your victories may be eternal, you must talk no more of working powerfully, nor of doing great Acts of State, but with the Queen.

The Lord Brook, *to the Duke*.

May it please your Grace,

OUt of *Spain* we hear, the world comes so fast after you, (since your departure,) as we assure our selves, this great work is at a good end, with contentment to our blessed Prince, and like a Princely treaty, with addition of honour to the Monarchy he intends to match with.

But, Sir, we hear of a new treaty sprung up between the *Palsgraves* Eldest Son, and the Emperours youngest Daughter. A Labyrinth, into which what hope soever leads us, I fear no one thread will be able to guide us well out. Because in the passages between these far distant Princes, education of children seems like to be demanded; Balancing of

R   Counsels

Counsels to the jealousie of friends, I Question whether the *Palatinate* shall be delivered in the Nonage before marriage, or after; Then whether sequestred into a Catholick, or Protestant hands. If into a Catholick, a probable argument that both it and the *Valtoline* are equally reserved free to fall with associated forces upon our ancient Bulwark the *Netherlands*, at pleasure. Lastly, whether the Miter, and these Scepters thus united, with their advantage in number of swords, and Desks abroad, their new springing party at home, strengths by sea and land, Constant ambition of adding Crown to Crown, and perfect Audit of their neighbours powers, and humors (even while the second Heir-male of this Kingdom shall live in the hands of enemies, and strangers) I say whether these will no t prove fearful inequalities, casual to the lives of our King and Prince, dangerous to the Crown, by changing successive rights into tenures of Courtesie, and charging of the peoples consciences with visions of confusion or bondage.

Again (Sir) admit this new project should vanish into smoak, as undigested vapours use to do, yet give me leave to question, whether to your Grace you have overtly protested against the intricate Courses of the *Spaniard*, even the specious issue of the *Palatinates* delivery, before consummation of marriage, but not like to prove Mother of many Colourable and unavoydible delays. Because, suppose the proposition should be granted, yet who sees not that the effecting of it will prove an act of so many parts. *Viz.* the Pope, Emperour, King of *Spain*, Duke of *Bavaria*, &c. and of so great consequence joyntly, and severally, to them all, and must of necessity require divers assemblies, commissions, perchance Diets, &c. And then what time the execution of the Minutes under these Heads will demand, he that knows the divers natures of Nations in treating may easily conceive.

To begin with the least; what money or other conditions can be offered like to satisfie the honour, humour, and huge expence of the *Bavarian*, for quitting his Conquest to so unreconcileable a neighbour: and if there be possibility, yet out of whose estate or treasury are these conditions, or large proportions of Dowry, probably to be expected? touching the Emperour; Is there any forreign alliance able to perswade this Prince, who having by an untimely war changed all tenures of Election into succession, and thereby shaken the ancient freedom of our *Germany* Princes, what, I say, can in likelihood win him to restore these dead forces to his Enemies, to the prejudice of all he injoyes, or aspires to. Besides, what shall move this Emperour to take away the Bann from the *Palsegraves* person, who hath so desperately hazarded, not only his own private Kingdoms, and Provinces, but by his undertaking, waved the main ambition of the *Austrian* familie. For the Spanish King, if he be prest, his answer will be ready, and fair, that he hath no right in him (but mediation) as appeares by the divisions already made. Notwithstanding, how little right soever he pretends, yet his Councel, his instruments, his charge, by diversion, *Overt Ayde*, insensible succours (the world sees) have been used in all these wars; so as this together with his right by strong hand gotten (and kept by arts of depositing) upon the *Valtoline*, may lead us to discern clearly, that he finds the passage of his forces through them equal, and so resolves both, to over-run the Low Countries when he please. Against which little State (whether out of revenge, or ambition of greater conquests by them) he will constantly carry a watchfull and griping enemies hand.

Concerning the Pope, who knows not, that his universal affected supremacy (howsoever dissembled) yet hath, doth, and ever will urge his Holiness to stir up colourable Warres of Religion. Since Warres, Contentions, and tumults among Princes, have been his old way of adding more wealth, and power to his sanctified Sea. How, I say, this new fashion'd Monarch shall be won to suffer *Heidelberg* (the most dangerous nest of Hereticks, after *Geneva*) to return to her former strength, is a poynt beyond my Capacity.

By these short, hasty, and imperfect images, your Grace may yet judge, that except the restitution of the *Palatinate* be instantly pressed (and like a work of Faeries either furnished, or broken off at once) we may easily be over-shot in our own bowes, by having the strengths and free Councels of *England*, *Scotland*, and *Ireland*, during this treaty kept under a kind of Covert-baron, and so long made a forge for other Princes ends, as my Blessed Sovereigns trust may perchance find it self compelled to play an After-Game, amongst discouraged friends, and combination of powerful enemies; such as under characters of *Alliance* will think they have won one great Step towards their inveterate Ambition of a Western Monarchy.

Noble Duke, If you find me lifted above my earth, in handling a subject to which I am utterly a stranger, yet bear with a Monks humour, in a man that is prisoner to old age. Hide my folly from the eyes of Criticks. And pardon my freedom that hath wearied you, with a mind ever to remain,

Novemb. 11. 1623.   Your Graces loving Grand-child, and humble servant,
    Tho. Brook.

To his Wife.

Let me intreat you to reade my Letter once again, and if you can find no cause of quarrell, do but then think what you have done all this time to send me such a Cartell; you cannot be more void of fault, then I of suspirion, and what you speak I cannot understand. But doth my imprisonment abridge me that I cannot give you counsel? Or have you resolved to follow the counsel of the Lady you know? Know then, as my ill fortune cannot deject me, so ought it much less to make you brave and insolent. You have your choyce of two courses, let me know which you will take, that I trust not to a broken Reed. And yet what need I care, seeing that you who were my chief care, do now begin to sever your self: I will not yet condemn you; you may see how unapt I am to entertain ill thoughts. I will yet both hold and write my self,

Your loving Husband,

G. BROOK.

Mr. George Brook, to a Lady in Court.

Madam,

The message which you sent me, of her Majesties gracious purpose altered towards me, hath put me into that extasie, that I know not whereupon to rest my self, not having power to believe that which I am bound to know. Is it possible that you should be so weak in grace with her Majesty, as not to prevail in so small a matter for any man but of an intire reputation? or shall I believe that her Majesty, who suffers not the merit of her servants to be buried with them, should not hold me equivalent with any new *Melchisedech* without father or mother. I protest (Madam) I could not presage any ill success to my self, but only out of the means of my ambition, and have held it therefore superfluous to claim any favour in vertue of supererogation, esteeming it too great a derogation from my self, for so poor a thing as a Spittle-house, to raise the dead to speak for me, or challenge any thing more then my own. But it is neither the strangeness of the matter, nor the hardness of my belief, that can alter the decree of a Prince. But I must take it in good payment that is no less then for as great a disgrace as can outwardly befall me; yet must I ever hold my self beholden to this suit; for though I lose the Hospital, yet have I lost many errors; withall I have weighed my friends in a balance, and taken a just measure of my fortune. I must not despair, it is not impossible for a man well taught to make a retreat into himself; neither will I yet despair of my suit, only for this reason, that this change cannot proceed of her Majesties proper motion, but must be procured by some blind practice that dares not see the light, though it may be my fortune to bring it forth blushing; howsoever it be, it shall never distemper my dutifull affection towards her Majesty, though that be for ever barred from her knowledge: for they who are able to prevent her goodness will be ever likely to prevent my service. That the place is already meant to a Divine cannot be true, nor my impediment: For there is no kind of her Majesties servants and subjects so provided for, there being such store of places that fall daily both better then this in value, and more proper for their function. Your Ladiship hath been hitherto an honorable and faithfull intercessor for me; Good Madam, be not weary to continue so still, as I shall do ever to acknowledge it; and if I be able, in part to deserve it,

G. B.

Dr. Balcanquel, to Secretary Nanton.

Right Honourable,

The reason why I have not of late written to your Honour, is, the discontinuance of our Sessions of the Synod this great while; but since my last unto your Honour, we have thus spent our time. The publick Reading of all the Collegiate judgements upon the 5. Articles was made an end of. In which (God be thanked for it) there was a greater harmony and consent then could almost be hoped for, in such variety of learned men, who did not know one of anothers judgement: The only difference was in the second Article. After that the President (never asking advice from the Synod) took upon him to conceive, and dictate the Canons himself to us; but we who were sent by his Majesty, conceiving that

that course to be altogether against the dignity of the Synod, consulted with some of the Delegates, who approved our Counsel, and thought it fit, that there should be some deputed by the Synod, and joyned to the President for conceiving of the Canons, that so whatsoever was done might be done by publick authority. This motion did trouble the President not a little, who hath all the Provincials at his beck, and some of the forreign Divines too, but especially the *Palatines*. Yet there was a publick Synod called for this purpose, where the President of the Delegates did make a speech, desiring the Synod to depute some who joyning with the President and the Assessours might take pains for moulding of the Canons. In the delivering of the voices most testified their dislike of this course, and their singular respect to the Presidents credit; but *Scultetus* did by many reasons approve the course which the President had begun, and disprove this new course, which was suggested, yet he taxed no man personally. But *Sibrandus* (when he came to deliver his voice) like a mad-man did inveigh against those who were the suggesters of this change, and said, That strangers should not take upon them to prescribe what was good for the estate of their Church, and that some others who had joyned in that were worthy to be noted *Censura Ecclesiastica*: therein he aymed at the South *Holland*, who did likewise much dislike the Presidents his Course. *Sibrandus* spake so furiously, that both the *Præses Politicus*, and the *Præses Ecclesiasticus*, desired him either to hold his peace, or else speak that which might not disturb the peace of the Synod. Yet since it was the Delegates pleasure, the whole Synod added to the President and the Assessours three forreign Divines, viz. my Lord of *Landaff*, *Scultetus*, and *Deodatus*; three Provincials, viz. *Polyander*, *Valleus*, and *Triglandius*; who should mould and conceive the Canons upon every Article, and then send a Copie of what they have done to every Colledge, that they may adde power, and change what they will, the Colledges observations being considered by them, and the Canons according to them amended, they are to be returned to the Colledges, and the Colledges to return them again, & so to keep the course ever till there be no exceptions against them. When they are thus agreed upon by all the several Colledges, they shall publickly be concluded, and approved by the Synod.

We are now hard at polishing the Canons which these Deputies send us. All our trouble is in the second Article: The most part oft the Synod would cry us down with voices for the restriction of the general propositions in Scripture, & the Confessions of the Reformed Churches concerning Christs death, *ad Solos Electos*. We stand for leaving them unexpounded, and unrestricted, as we found them, and rejoyce exceedingly, that the Directions which my Lord Embassadour sent us from his Majesty concerning this point, agreeth so fully with our judgement subscribed with our hands, given in to the Synod, upon the second Article. By this doing we, first, leave a sound and sufficient ground for preaching of the Gospel to all men. Next, we shun a great deal of offence, which otherwise we must needs have given to the *Lutheran* Churches. Thirdly, we retain the same phrases, and forms of speaking, which those Fathers did, who wrestled with the *Pelagians* in the same point. If this Article be well looked into, I hope there shall moderation enough be observed in all the rest. If it were not for the moderation of the forreign Divines, we should have such Canons as I think have not been heard of: for there is never a Provincial Minister here, who hath delivered any rigid Proposition, and hath been taxed by the Remonstrants for it, but he would have that Proposition thrust into one Canon or another, that so he may have something to shew for that which he hath said. As soon as the Canons are agreed upon, I shall, by Gods grace, with all expedition send them unto your Honour. Our next work will be *Vorstius*, whose book they would censure, without citation of himself. The President wrote to our Colledge, in the Delegates name, to know, whether we thought it fit to have him personally cited; but especially to know what we thought would be most agreeing to his Majesties mind.

To the latter, concerning his Majesties mind, we answered, That we thought my Lord Embassadour could give them the best resolution for that point.

For the former, we thought it would be evil taken, If any man should be condemned, not being first heard. But because they doubted that *Vorstius* would keep them as long as the Remonstrants had done; We told them, That we desired they would not suffer him to make any defences, or explications, of his blasphemous propositions, but simply to answer *per ita vel non*, whether he would plainly abjure them, or not; And so accordingly proceed against him, and so we should make no great loss of time; so I think he shall be personally cited.

This is all; for we have had no Synodical meeting these twelve dayes. I can see no end of
the

Sir William Beecher, to the King.

the Synod before *Whitsontide.* With my best prayers for your Honour, and the remembrance of all my faithful respects, I take my leave; And am

March 26.

Your Honours
In all true observance and service,
Walter Balcanquel.

Sir William Beecher, to his Majesty.

Most Gracious Soveraign,

BEsides the relation of the appearance, of change in the affairs of the Court, wherewith my dispatch to Mr. Secretary *Lake* will acquaint your Majesty; I thought it my duty to give you particular account, that being yesterday with the Prince of *Jainville*, after some earnest protestations made to me of his desire to do your Majesty service, falling into discourse of those occurrences, he grew into these terms. That the complaints of the Queen Mother were founded upon good reason; that if she had offended the King, or the State, why did they not make her process? if she had not offended, why should she not see the King, and her children? that when the Queen fell upon these complaints, they thought to fright her, by pretending to bring forth the Prince of *Conde*; but that the Queen had astonished them, by telling them; That she was so far from opposing, as she desired the liberty of the Prince. That the Queens friends would be glad of his liberty, for that it could not be prejudicial, but rather advantagious, at the least, it would be honourable for them, if his liberty were wrought, if not by their intercession, at least by their occasion; further he told me, That he was confident, that the Queen would not be gained by their fair words, but would persist in her resolution. Which discourse of his, with some other advertisements, doth perswade me, that this matter hath a farther root, and is likely to bring forth some great alteration here, in no long time. And I doubt not but that *Monsieur de Luine* will find; with repentance, how much better it had been for him, to have furthered your Majesties advice for the delivery of the Prince, whereby he might have acquired to the King a reputation of Justice, and to himself, an obligation of a powerful friend in the Prince, rather then to leave him to the adventure of the changes that time may produce. But if your Counsel did prove fruitless to them by their misconceit of it, yet it doth, and will every day; prove more honourable to your Majesty, who by your wisdom have foreseen, and by your goodness have premonished all your neighbours of the mischiefs that threatned them.

Peradventure they may overcome this *effort* of the Queens by fair words to her Person, and threats signified afar off, and continue the state of affairs in the same condition that now it is, which is, in few words, extreamly Romish, Jesuitish, and, by consequence, *Spanish*.

Monsieur *de Luine* seemeth to me a man in himself capable of Reason, and by the death of the Marshall *d' Anchre*, eternally bound to be a good Patriot, but that he applies himself wholly to the Kings person, and that distrusting his own judgment relies upon the judgment of the Ministers of the State, and principally *Du Augen*, the Chancellor, and the Gardeseaux.

Du A gen.

They utterly neglect all the Alliances of our Religion abroad, and care not how inconsiderately they oppress it at home. Onely they seem desirous to entertain themselves well with the King of *Spain*, by the intervention of the *Nuncio*, and do think that no advantage which they can give the *Spaniard* by this proceeding in other parts, can equal that which they pretend to receive at home, by suppressing the State, and doctrine of those of the Religion.

If they proceed long in this train, it will undoubtedly breed mischievous designs, which there is no so ready way to prevent, as to let them generally perceive, that they are discovered; whereby the proceedings of the Ministers of State will grow so detestable to all those here, that have any sense of the love of their Countrey, that it will produce either a change of their persons, or of their Counsels.

But I do humbly submit the censure hereof to your Majesties most exquisite judgment; whom I do beseech the Almighty long to preserve in health and all perfect happiness.

February 4.

Your Majesties
Most humble Subject, and Loyal Servant,
Will. Beecher.

The Duke of Buckingham, *Chancellor elect, to the University of* Cambridge.

MR. Vice-Chancellor, and Gentlemen of the University of *Cambridge*, there is no one thing that concerneth me more near, then the good opinion of good and learned honest men; amongst which number as you have ever held the first rank in the estimation of the Common-wealth, and fame of the Christian world; so in conferring of this Honour of Chancellorship upon me, I must confess, you have satisfied a great ambition of mine owne, which I hope will never forsake me, and that is, To be thought well of by men that deserve well, and men of your profession. Yet I cannot attribute this Honour to any desert in me, but to the respect you bear to the Sacred memory of my Master deceased, the King of Scholars, who loved you, and honoured you often with his presence; and to my gracious Master now living, who inherits, with his blessed Fathers vertues, the affection he bore your University. I beseech you, as you have now made your choice with so many kinde and noble circumstances, as the manner is to me as acceptable and grateful as the matter; so to assure your selves, that you have cast your votes upon your servant, who is as apprehensive of the time you have shewed your affection in, as of the Honour you have given him. And I earnestly request you all, that you would be pleased not to judge me comparatively, by the success and happiness you have had in your former choice of Chancellors, who as they knew better, perhaps by advantage of education in your University, how to value the deserts of men of your qualities and degrees; so could they not be more willing to cherish you then my self, who will make amends for want of Scholarship, in my love to the professors of it, and unto the Source from whence it cometh: having now most just cause more chiefly to employ my uttermost endeavours, with what favour I enjoy from a Royal Master, to the maintaining of the Charters, Priviledges, and Immunities of your University in general, and to the advancing of the particular merits of the Students therein. And since I am so far engaged unto you, I will presume upon a further courtesie, which is, That you will be pleased to supply me with your advice, and suggest a way unto me (as my self likewise shall not fail to think on some means) how we may make Posterity remember you have a thankful Chancellor, and one that both really loved you, and your University. Which is a resolution writ in an honest heart, by him that wanteth much to express his affection to you; who will ever be

York house, *Junii* 5. *Your faithful friend, and humble servant*,
1626. Geor. Buckingham.

The University of Cambridge's *Answer to the Duke.*

Illustrissime Princeps, atq; auspicatissime Cancellarie,

NEptunum perhibent gratum cum Minerva iniisse certamen, utrum re magis mortalibus conferret donum: ille potens maris Deus illico effudit equum; Illa pacis & musarum numen, suppeditavit oleam; utrumque certe Deo dignum munus. Adeo nostrum non est tantam litem dirimere, quin sacessat potius litis importuna vox, ubi non alia quam Amoris propinantur pignora. Perinde tecum se res habet, excellentissime Dux, quem jam olim potentissimus Oceani Britannici Neptunus, non solum suprema Maris Præfectura cohonestavit, sed & Prætorio donavit Equo: adeo ut illius munere & propria virtute, unus audiat, Terræ Marique summus Dictator, ut sic dicamus Classis, & Magister Equitum. Post tanta honorum vestigia, ecce, nostra Minerva, tua jam Cantabrigia, supplex suas obtendit oleas, tanquam inter victrices lauros lambentes hederas; oleas quidem quibus & tuis rebus, & rebus tum publicis tum Literariis precatur simul & auspicatur pacem. Nec ad usque sumus gens togata impotenter superbi, ut hoc Cancellariatu arbitremur. Nos tantillos tibi in id Meritorum & Gratiæ culmen evecto, quicquam vel testimonii ad æstimationem, vel tituli ad gloriam contulisse. Quod autem ipse aliter opinaris, vestra illa pietas est, haud ambitio, major tua tum virtus tum decus est, quam ut eis aut nostra quidpiam suffragia adderes, aut aliorum possit Invidia detrahere: stellæ in primo orbe, quas fixas vocant, altiores sunt, quam ut ad eas valeat terrarum umbra pertingere, quamquam fælicissimæ memoriæ Jacobo, pientissimæque Carolo, non est, quod hoc quicquid est nominis te debere dicas, citra est, misellum munus Academicum, citra est quam ut tantos auctores mereatur, quin vestram potius celsitudinem, vestrum tutelare numen, Nos illis

Principibus

Principibus imputabimus, qui inde ex illius petitissimum voto te elegimus, unde non nisi immortalia accipere beneficia solebamus. Quod si nostrum hoc in vestram Excellentiam studium tibi ipsa, uti scribis, commendat tempestivitas, nos illud saltem debituri sumus temporibus, cæterum non nimis fœlicibus, quod tibi vel inde gratiores sumus; quanquam suspicamur, ut hæc totum quod de opportunitate insinuas meram sit, nec magnis ingeniis insolens bene de suis cultoribus merendi artificium, quæ eo consilio singula suorum officia maxima tempestive adiument, quo uberius sibi remunerandi argumentum aucupentur: nam faciles credimus honorificis quibus nos dignaris promissis. Jamdiu est, ex quo te animo atque opera Cancellarium sensimus, nihilque tibi hoc tempore nostra poterit suffragia, quam nomen adjicere. Nobis tamen, ut cum illustrissimis heroibus præcessoribus tuis, te committamus, in quo sunt tua prædicanda modestia illorum honori & memoriæ consuluit, ne tanti fulgoris claritudine effuscentur; ut enim nulla re magis se jactat Cantabrigia quam præteritorum gloria ac splendore Patronorum; hodie tamen, nescio quid solito augustius spirat, & tuis superba auspiciis, quasi Buckinghamiensis, arcta tutelis, magnaque spe gravida intumescit. Ad extremum, nos ad concilium vocas, qua petitissimum ratione, quo digno monumento tuo, in nos amoris memoriam posteritati censeres; verum enim vero (Illustrissime Dux, indulgentissimeque Cancellarie) major est ea provincia, quam ut nos eam subeundo simus, quod tuo amori par sit monumentum, tuum potest solummodo excogitare ingenium. Nos interea alia manebit cura, quibus nimirum apud Deum precibus, quibus studiorum vigiliis, officiorum obsequiis, tantæ Clientelæ fœlicitatem nobis propriam & perpetuam despondeamus.

Datæ, frequentissimo Senatu nostro,   *Vestræ Excellentiæ humillimi*
     sexto Idus Junii, 1626.   *devotissimiqne Clientes Servique,*

                               Procancellarius, & reliquus
                               Senatus Cantabrigiensis.

The Lord Duke of Buckingham, *to Sir* Walter Aston.

IN your Letter of the 5th of *December,* you desire me to give you my opinion; my ancient acquaintance, long custome of loving you, with constancy of friendship invites me to do you this office of good will, and to serve you according to your request. And for your more intire satisfaction, I will deliver the things in the past and present. You, in all the beginning of the Treaty, wonne to your self a good estimation, while you were only at large in the Treaty, and had communication of the passages from the Lord of *Bristol,* as by courtesie: and in his absence handled no farther in the Treaty of marriage, then by direction from him. When the Prince was there, your carriage gave his Highness and my self all satisfaction. Now you must give me leave to put you in mind of the freedom used with you, whilest we were at *Madrid,* and of the explanation the Prince made of himself to you, by his Letters from St. *Andreas.* From which you might observe the resentment the Prince had of their proceedings with him. And by his Highness Declaration to you from thence you might see, both his care and resolution, not to ingage himself into the marriage without good conditions for the Palatinate, and Conservation of his honour every way. My care and my intentions were to move increase of honour to you, and to recompence, by a good understanding, to be layed in his Majesty towards you, which I pursued so soon as I came to the Kings presence. And the Princes confidence was so great in you, as he joyned you in the Commission; besides, he declared himself to you by his Letters, not leaving you thereby to guess at his Majesties directions to the Earl of *Bristol,* which he was to communicate to you. Now you may think how strange it was to the Prince, and how much I was troubled (not being able to make your excuse) when your joynt Letters made known, how you had concurred with the Earl of *Bristol,* to engage his Highness, by prefixing a day for the *Desposories,* without making certain the restitution of the Palatinate and Electoral dignity, the portion, and temporal Articles. Which proceeding of yours with the Earl of *Bristol* was so understood by the Lords of the Committee, as they took resolution once, to advise his majesty to revoke both the Lord of *Bristol,* and you, upon those grounds, which you will understand by his Majesties own Letters, and Secretary *Conways* Letters, written to you with this dispatch. I was not able at first, by any endeavour, to oppose the resolution of your revocation, so far had you cast your self into misconstruction, and given stop to the progress of your own advancement. But with constant industry and time, I have won this point, of qualifying all ill opinion of you, and
                                                                  sufferance

sufferance of your continuing there. So as it wil be now in your power (by your Carriage) to come off without reproof. And I shall hope to overcome the rest with time, to bring you again to the condition of honour and recompence. Being confident that since you see your own errour, and acknowledge it, you will be careful, by a stiff and judicious carriage, to warrant all your present and succeeding actions. If you think, at first sight, I press you a little hard upon this point, you may be pleased to interpret it to be a faithful way of satisfying your request, and expression of my affection, to have you to do all things suitable to your wisdom, virtue, and honour, and according to the wishes of

Yours, &c.
G. Buckingham.

The Duke of Buckingham, to Sir Walter Aston.

I Had not leisure in my former dispatch, being hastie to write the reason why I wondered at the errour you committed in the last dispatch of my Lord of *Bristols* and yours; for the matter is, that his Majesty having plainly written unto you, both in his former dispatch, that he desired to be assured of the restitution of the Palatinate, before the *Depsorium* was made, seeing he would be sorry to welcome home one Daughter with a smiling cheer, and leave his own onely Daughter, at the same time, weeping and disconsolate. And the Prince having also written unto you, that he never meant to match there, and be frustrated of the restitution of the Palatinate so often promised, that notwithstanding this clear Language, you should have joyned with my Lord of *Bristol* in a resolution of so hastie a delivery of the Prince's *Proxie*, before you had his Majesties answer to your former dispatch, wherein my Lord of *Bristol* urged of his Majesty a harsh answer and direction; and his Majesty cannot but take it for a kind of scorn, that within 4 daies after he had urged his Majesties answer, ye should, in the mean time, take resolutions of your own heads. You may do well, because there is no leisure in this hastie dispatch, for his Majesty to answer my Lord of *Bristols* last Letter (which will be done, by the next duplicate of this same dispatch) to acquaint him in the mean time with this Letter, which his Majesty himself hath dictated unto me. And so in haste I bid you farewel.

Yours, &c.
G. B.

L. H. R. to the Duke of Buckingham.

My dear Lord,

I Have since my departure from you used all diligence in the Princes service, and punctually observed all his Commands. Onely, with the King I have dealt so freely in my relation of the Prince his carriage, and your extraordinary care of working his content in all points, that I did move him to shed tears in expressing his happiness for such a Son; and likewise his good fortune in having a Favourite, who is framed according to his own heart in all points. Neither have I pressed any thing to injure, any farther then my duty bound me, and my faithful love to your service, which shall alwaies have a prime place in my heart.

My Lord, there are contrary opinions in Court and City, by the one you are much admired for your noble expressions of true honour, and love to your King, Prince, and Country, with many observations of your special care and zeal to Religion, and your immovable resolution to contest with all oppositions to the contrary. By the other, you are maligned, and they give it out, That you have with your wilfulness occasioned these delaies, by diverting and changing their waies, wherein they had begun to treat: but the falseness hereof hath been shewn; and it appears malice without ground, the which though heretofore I have told you, not out of any other end then to do you service, yet have you so sleightly regarded me for it, and so much respected those ill-deserving Great ones, (as if you had intended to receive your enemies into your bosome, and to cast off your faithfullest friends;) yet shall not any usage discourage me from discharging the office of a most loving and zealous affected friend, and servant; yea insomuch, that I will rather displease you, in doing you that faithful service that both my honour and love obligeth me to, then be silent, and they let you run into apparent danger.

My

L. H. R. to the *Duke* of Buckingham.

My Lord, amongst the Protestants you are divulged (as much as ill disposed ones dare) a Papist. Among the Papists, it is avowed you are the greatest enemy they have. For which reports, I am not troubled, for they have made you the much more pitied, and as highly esteemed, and honoured amongst the most judicious, and best deserving subjects, as any thing could do. And I dare assure you, that since your being at *Madrid*, you are much better beloved of all people (who have not ends) then you were before. Noble Lord, I find the King both resolute, and couragious, but wise, and secret, to my own hearts joy, and not to be won upon by the subtil and false policie of any: I made it my humble suit upon my knees, that he would consent to no proposition of this Spanish Embassadour, concerning peace or war, till the Princes return. Which suit he took well at my hands, and granted. I have told him freely what I have observed in *Spain*, both of their manners, usage, and honestie, and left it to his wisdom, to make what use he pleased. His Majestie longs to see the Prince and you, and so do all the subjects, and will not be satisfied with any thing, but your speedy return. Except you have jealousies put into the Spaniards heads, and prevent the danger, which will be by hasting the marriage with all possible speed ; for there are some whose buttons break with venom, that you have got so much honour, and so well deserved of the King and Prince. But you believe me not, but think I speak of Spleen, when God knows I never bore any to any man, but for your sake. Your most vertuous Lady mourns for your absence, and will not be comforted. Your fair Daughter deserves your staying withal; and your faithful friends, and the good of the Kingdom, want you most of all.

And for your greater comfort, the King is so reserved in the Princes affairs, as that he neither imparts the business of *Spain*, nor his intents therein, to any of his privie Councel. Since your patent, the Earl *Marshal* is become a great stranger at the Court. But all men finde you so fast riveted into the Kings heart, that they see it is an impossibility to work you any way displeasure in your absence, and therefore forbear to express what willingly they would effect, but find it in vain to go about it. But let not the Kings love to you, or their small ability to do you harm, make you too careless or too credulous of those your enemies, lest it give too great encouragement to them, and too great disheartning to your faithful friends. I am sorrie, at my being with you at *Madrid*, that you durst not impart those secrets wherein I am sure my faithfulness and love unto you would have done you all service (as the thing I most desire) but I see the zeal of my heart to you is not rightly considered ; yet am I confident that time will make me best known, and better esteemed by you, as one whose true heart is alwaies watchful, of taking all opportunities to do you service. My Lord, you shall find me not onely a word-friend, but an active, who never am better pleased, then when I find most opposition. And for conclusion, I am so far from shunning dangers, to do you service, as that I would willingly wade in blood at any time to manifest my self yours. And therefore, I should receive great content, if you knew, how truly I were yours, because, then I am sure, in the Nobleness of your nature, it would be impossible for any to be able to do me wrong in your honourable thoughts. My dear Lord, pray suffer no longer delaies in *Spain*, but either dispatch what you went for quickly, or else return speedily ; for assure your self, their desire to have you continue there is for no love to you, but to further thereby their own designs elsewhere. Nay, I dare justifie it out of my own weak judgement, that the longer you stay, the farther off you shall be from obtaining what you desire. And if you resolutely purpose your return with speed, you will force them out of their dull pace, and put them upon the rock from which they cannot escape, except they fulfil your desires. Besides, your presence is most necessary here for home-affairs, for your absence hath caused too great insolencie in the Court, by such as bear themselves very loftily, and insult very much over yours, especially your poor servant *Mewtis* is much threatned as being yours, and must suffer till you come back. Some other things likewise are otherwise carried in your absence, then would be in your presence ; therefore for Gods sake return, but with the Prince, and count delaies denials. And the longer you stay there, the stronger you make them, and your selves the weaker. My Lord of *Bristol* hath a great and more powerful party in Court then you imagine ; in so much, that I am confident, were the King a neuter, he would prevail ; and I do not much marvail at it, for you trust upon the honour, and justification of your actions, desirous to make no friends, because you need none ; but he deals with a great deal of cautelous wisedom : and as he hath wrought into the Kings opinion, by reason of some pleasing services, so hath he into all those who are about the King, or powerful, that they may better his good services, and smother his bad. Besides, the man who is suspitious (as he must needs be) hath far greater care of after-reckonings, how to make fair glosses, then he who doth all things with the avowment of all honour, and the onely intent of service to his King, and Country. It grieves me, I am not thought worthy to hear from you any word by these last messengers, especially being promised the imployment from which I was put. Farewel (dear Lord) and the Almighties protection be upon our unmatchable Prince, upon whose worth, and brave atchievements, all eyes are fixed; and the same protection light upon you, his right hand, and give you the good fortune, to make as brave a return, as you did voyage thither, to the eternal praise of your future memories. And upon these hopes, I rest happie to think my self

Yours

H. R.

CECIL'S

CECILS
LETTERS,
&c.

133

CECIL'S
Letters, &c.

Sir Robert Cecil, *after Earl of* Salisbury, *to the Lord* Burleigh, *his Father, from* France.

Y duty humbly remembred to your Lordship: Having lately made dispatches from *Deip*, and having made little way in *France*, by reason of Sir *Thomas Wilks* indisposition, your Lordship can expect little from me; especially having joyned with my associates in a letter to your Lordship: Neverthelesse, because love and duty will find easily occasion to expresse themselves, I am bold to yield your Lordship some more trouble by my private Letter. I have met here with the primier President of *Roan*, a man of great credit and reputation, one that untill meer necessity did force him, kept much hold here for this King: he afterward retired, and kept the Parliament at *Caen*; he is learned, grave, of good person, good discourse, and well affectionate to *England*, his name is *Claude Grollart*; he is now next the Duke *Monpensier*, the stay of all those quarters, insomuch that when the King will be merry with him, he calls him one of the petty Dukes in *Normandy*: he did visit me with great respect, and fell into familiar discourse with me of your Lordship, whom he had known in *England* many years since, and hath had correspondency with your Lordship by letters in Mr. Secretary *Walsinghams* time: And being talking thereof, he desired me to tell your Lordship by occasion, that when these troubles were like to grow by the League, you writ him a letter of advice to stick fast to the King, and not to be doubtful, though he saw difficulties; for you did hold it for a true Oracle, That the Kings on earth are like the Sun, and that such as do seek to usurp, are like falling Stars: For the Sun, although it be eclipsed and obfuscated with mists and clouds, at length they are dispersed; where the other are but figures of stars in the eyes view, and prove no more but exhalations, which suddenly dissolve and fall to the earth; where they are consumed. Because I have little else to fill my paper, I presume to trouble your Lordship thus far, to whom I think it cannot be offensive to hear that for your sake I am by many the better used, and that by your own wisdom, you are by men of place and gravity both honored and remembred. The marriage of the Duke of *Tremoville* to the Count *Maurice* his sister hath drawn the Duke of *Bovillion* towards *Britany*, where, I am informed by this President, that he meaneth to stay, and to attend the King, to whom he will clear himself if he take any knowledge of any jealousie; and the rather because he is there well fortified in a Countrey full of those that are of the Religion. It shall behove me being there to carry my self tenderly towards him. The Kings prosperity in *Britany* hath already made his Catholicks begin to quarrel with the Accord which hath been made at the Assembly: For the persons that were appointed to frame the Articles into an Edict have varied upon some principal points, onely to trifle out the time, thereby to discover whether the King may need

their

Sir William Cecil, to Sir Henry Norris.

their resistance, or no. But the Duke of *Bovillon* hearing inckling of it, made more haste, and hath been with the King, and doth return forthwith to him, as soon as he hath been at the marriage of the Lady *Tremeville*. Your Lordship knows the circumstances of my journey are not such as can afford me any means to judge; but this your Lordship may assure, that by that time I have spoken to the King, things will break out one way or other, so far as it will appear whether it be worth the tarrying to treat, or no; after once the King has been dealt with, to which I will address my self with all speed, and not tarry for the States, who may be come to *Paris* by that time I do return: for I believe they will be content to treat any where. I should have a miss of Sir *Thomas Wilks*, were it not we were well instructed; and surely, he was grown very heavy of late, and dull: If I should stay here to attend his recovery, it would consume me to no purpose. I have written a Letter to the Queen of some such gathering as I have gotten, and of the speeches between me and the President, because her Majesty may not be offended that I write not particularly to her self of something. Although the *Spaniards* from *Callis* have spoiled *Base-Bologne*, yet it is not holden here that the Cardinal will sit down before any Town speedily, for he will not be able. Nevertheless, the Constable is come into *Picardy*, to give stay to the Province; if that be the fruit of the Treaty, we shall have less need to disswade the King.

I much fear Sir *Tho.Wilks* to be in a Lethargy. Since your Lordships Letter of *Feb.*15. which found me at *Dover* a little before my imbarking, the wind hath not served to bring me any Letter out of *England*. The Lord of heaven send me tidings of your Lordships health, for whom I will daily pray. I received also a Letter from the Earl of *Essex*, of the 16. and did imbark the 17. I humbly take my leave, and rest

Feb. 26. 1597.

Your Lordships humble and obedient Son,
Ro. Cecil.

Certain Copies of Letters written by Sir William Cecil *Knight, Secretary of Estate to Queen* Elizabeth, *to Sir* Hen. Norris *Knight, Ambassador for the said Queen, Resident in* France.

SIR,

✻ I Am constrained to use the hand of my servant in writing unto you, because I find it somewhat grievous to use mine own at this present: The Queens Majesty hath received your letters with very good contentation, and alloweth your manner of beginning and proceeding, aswell, I dare assure you, as your self could devise; which I do not in words onely speak, but wish you to take them for as good a truth as I can inform.

Entertainment above ordinary.

The rare manner of your entertainment hath moved the Queens Majesty to Muze upon what course it should be, being more then hath been used in like cases to her Ambassadors; and such as besides your own report hath been by others very largely advertised; and for that in such things guesses be but doubtful, I pray you by your next advertise me what your self doth think of it; and in the mean time, I know you, are not untaught to judge of the difference of fair words from good deeds, as the saying is, *Fortuna cum adblanditur captum advenit*:

To know the cause thereof.

The Queens Majesty meaneth to require this Ambassador expresly to write unto the King there, in how good part she taketh this manner of gratefull acceptation of you her servant there, giving him to understand how good report you have made thereof, and how much comforted you are, by this manner, to proceed in her service there.

I would have had her Majesty to have written her own letters to the King hereof; But her Majesty made choice rather to speak with the Ambassador, which she will do to morrow, who cometh hither, and *La Croq* which cometh out of *Scotland*, and departeth shortly from hence thither into *France*, having been a good time in manner as an Ambassador with the *Scotish* Queen.

Monsieur *Moret* is, I think, on the way coming hither out of *Scotland*; my Lord of *Bedford*, who came long ago out of *Scotland*, arrived here but of late, and hath brought us good report from the *Scotish* Queen, of her good disposition to keep peace and amity with the Queens Majesty.

Of late *Shane Oneal* hath made means to the Lord Deputy of *Ireland*, to be received into Grace, pretending that he hath not meant any manner of unlawfulness unto the Queen; by which is gathered, that he groweth weary of his lewdness; and yet I think he is not otherwise to be reformed, then by sharp prosecution, which is intended to be followed no whit the less for any his fair writings, as reason is.

Of

Sir William Cecil, to Sir Henry Norris.

Of the troubles of the Low Countries, I think you be as well advertised there as we can be here; and of the likelihood of the Kings not coming into the Low Countries.

I cannot tell whether you are yet acquainted with Captain *Cockburne*, whose humor when you know, as I think *Barnaby* can shew you, I doubt not but you shall have of his hand no lack of intelligence, which you must credit as you shall see cause by proof of the event; he writeth almost weekly to me, and looketh for as many answers, which I cannot have leisure to make him; but I pray let him understand that I accept his writing in very good part.

The manner of the dealing with them there for the particular causes contained in your instructions is very well to be liked; and I wish the success of the answers to prove as good as the beginning hath appearance, and especially for the relief of the poor Prisoners in the Gallies, whose stay, I fear, will grow indirectly by Monsieur *de Foix*, to get thereby the acquital of *Lestrille*, whom surely he is bound in honor to see restored.

Since I had written thus much by my servants hand, and meant yester-night to have ended the letter; I thought good to stay untill this present, that I knew by the *French* Ambassador, what *De la Crocq* should do here; and amongst other things, the Queens Majesty hath very earnestly expressed to the Ambassador her good liking and estimation of your Honorable entertainment, whereof you did advertise her Majesty; and contrary to her former determination, did tell *La Crocq*, that he should carry her Majesties letters to the *French* King, of special thanks for the same; besides words of visitation, nothing passed this day otherwise; and therefore meaning not to keep your servant any longer, I end, with my very hearty commendations to your self, and my Lady, and wish as well to you and all yours, as to my self:

Feb. 10. 1566.
                                                      Yours assuredly,
                                                      W. Cecil.

To the Right Honorable, Sir Hen. Norris *Knight, the Queens Majesties Ambassador in* France.

SIR,

* THe Queens Majesty continueth her good liking of your manner of negotiation; and your advertisements to her Majesty, which she wisheth you to continue. She also alloweth your discretion, in writing apart to me, in matters containing trouble and business, and to her of Advice; of all other things, she most marvelleth at the answer sent you by Monsieur *De Foix*, who seemeth not disposed to perform his promise made to the Queens Majesty, by a cavillation, alledging it to have been for his Master; wherefore you shall do well to say to him, That upon his answer reported hither, the Queens Majesty seemeth to make doubt that you have not rightly conceived it; and therefore she hath re-charged you to speak with himself, and to require his answer; for you may say, her Majesty advertised you that she can not be well perswaded that you will forget your promise firmly made to her self, for the safe delivery of *Lestrille*; and when he was escaped of your advertisement, that he was taken; and that he should be returned into *England*, and if such a promise be no otherwise kept, being made unto other, you may say her Majesty shall finde it strange how to credit an Ambassador; and so her Majesty would that you should charge him in fair words, and good manners, the best you can, to obtain *Lestrille*. You may do well to learn how many prisoners do remain in the Gallies.

The strange news of the death of the King of *Scots* will be come thither before these letters; but by your son you shall know as much as I have.

The Queens Majesty would fain have a Taylor that had skill to make her Apparel, both after the *French* and *Italian* manner; and she thinketh that you in sight use some mean to obtain some one such there as serveth that Queen, without mentioning any manner of request in the Queen Majesties name. First, to cause my Lady, your wife, to use some such means to get one, as thereof knowledge might not come to the Queen Mothers ears, of whom the Queens Majesty thinketh thus, That if she did understand that it were a matter wherein her Majesty might be pleasured, she would offer to send one to the Queens Majesty: Nevertheless, if it cannot be so obtained by this indirect means, then her Majesty would have you devise some other good means to obtain one that were skillful.

I have staid your Son from going hence now these two days, upon the Queens Majesties Commandment, for that she would have him to have as much of the truth of the circumstances of the murther of the King of *Scots* as might be; and hitherto the same is hard to come by, otherwise then in a generality, that he was strangled, and his lodging razed with Gunpowder; his Father was first said to have been slain; but it is not true, for he was at *Glasco* at that time. It is constantly affirmed that there were thirty at the killing of him.

We

We look hourely for *Robert Melvin* from the Queen of *Scots*, by whom we must have that which he hath order to report.

The Queens Majesty sent yesterday my Lady *Howard*, and my wife, to the Lady *Lenox* to the Tower, to open this matter unto her, who could not be by any means kept from such passions of minde, as the horriblness of the fact did require. And this last night were with the the said Lady, the Dean of *Westminster*, and Doctor *Huick*; and I hope her Majesty will shew some favourable compassion of the said Lady, whom any humane nature must needs pity. After I had written thus far, Master *Melvin* came hither from *Scotland*, by whom we looked that we should have heard many of the circumstances of this murther; but he cannot, or may not, tell us any more then we heard before; the most suspition that I can hear, is, of the Earl *Bothwell*; but yet I would not be the Author of any such report, but onely do mean to inform you, as I hear, and as I mean, when I shall have more.

The Queens Majesty caused the *French* Ambassador to be informed of the answer made to you by Monsieur *de Foix* concerning *Lestrille*, who saith, when he hath spoken with the Queens Majesty here, he will advertise the King then thereof. He seemed to understand, first, how some bargain might be made for *Lestrille*. Secondly, whether the Queens Majesty could not be pleased to have him delivered to you; but the messenger answered him, that he knew no other, but to have him returned hither according to the promise; and so you may do well therein to persist.

Now seeing I am come to no more knowledge from *Scotland*, I will stay your Son no longer, wishing him well to come to you, and long to enjoy both you and my Lady;

From *Westminster*,   *Yours assuredly,*
20. Feb. 1566.   W. Cecill.

Postscript.
I thank you for your offer, to send me the Book *de translation' de Religion'*, which I have, but if there be any particular Charts new printed, I pray you send me a Callender thereof, and of any new Books, whereupon I may chance crave of you some.

To the Right honorable, Sir Henry Norris Knight, the Queens Majesties Ambassador, Resident in France.

⁂ AFter my very hearty commendations, I send you herewith a Letter from the Queens Majesty, by which you shall understand what her pleasure is for you to deal with the *French* King; whereunto you may add, as you see occasion, That you are informed, very credibly, that *Monluets* Company, now at their return, are suffered to make Port sale of all that they have brought home from the Isles of *Medera*. And therefore, if it might please his Majesty to give direct order and charge, for due restitution of that which was spoiled from the Queens Subjects; It is likely the parties shall be able enough to make recompence, my meaning herein is, that the *French* King and his Council may perceive that it is well known, how these Pirates are suffered to do what they will, notwithstanding contrary Proclamations; and yet you shall so utter this matter, as not that you finde fault with this manner of sufferance, for that ought properly to be to the *Spanish* or *Portugal* Ambassador, with whom you may sometime deal, to understand how they do know what is done, and how they do interpret it.

You shall shortly hear of some special person, that shall be sent thither in Ambassage, to joyn with you for the demanding of *Callis*, which is due, by the Treaty of *Cambray*, to be restored to the Queens Majesty the second day of *April* next; but who it is that shall come, as yet I cannot advertise.

The manner of the death of the King of *Scots* is not yet discovered to us, for the knowledge of the Author thereof; but there hath been Proclamation made, that whosoever would reveal the offendors shall have two thousand pound *Scotish*; and if he were a party, should have his pardon and five hundred pounds; the day after a Bill was set up in *Edenburgh*, in this sort, *I, according to the Proclamation, have made inquisition for the slaughter of the King, and do finde the* Earle Bothwell, *Mr.* James Beafour, *Parson of* Flisk, *Mr.* David Chamber, *and Black Mr.* John Spence, *the principal devisers thereof; and if this be not true, spir at* Gilbert Basour. There were also words added, which I am loth to report, that touched the Queen of *Scots*, which I hold best to be supprest: Further, such persons anointed are not to be thought ill of without manifest proof.

The next day following, a second Proclamation was made, repeating the former Bill, willing

Sir William Cecil, to Sir Henry Norris. 137

the party to subscribe his name, and he should be pardoned, and have the money according to the first Proclamation. The next day, being the nineteenth of *February*, a second Bill was set up in the former place, offering to compear and avow the matter; so as the money might be put into indifferent hands; and that Sir *Francis Bastine*, *Joseph* and *Moses Misse* be taken; and then he the exhibitor of the Bill would avow the whole;matter, and declare every mans act. Thus far things passed till that day, and since that, I hear that much unquietness is like to grow about that matter; and the common speech toucheth the Earles, *Bothwell* and *Huntly*, who remain with the Queen; but how true the accusations are, I will not take upon me to affirm the one or the other; neither would I have you to utter any of these things, to make condemnation of any of them, but as reports, not doubting but shortly God will cause the truth to be revealed. There do adhere together with the Earl of *Lenox*, the Earles of *Argile*, *Morton*, *Athell*, *Murrey*, *Catness*, and *Glencarne*, who mean to be at *Edenburgh* very shortly, as they pretend, to search out the malefactors.

Of late you wrote unto me of one *King* an *Englishman*, who doth misuse himself very much; of whom if you would write unto me somewhat more particularly, for the proof of his Traiterous speeches, whereby there might be some good ground made; how to have him demanded, you shall hear more thereof, and so shall (percase) by the next, though I do not hear from you; and so fare you heartily well.

Westm. 5. *March*, 1566.

Yours assuredly
W. Cecil.

Postscript.

Because I have not presently leisure to write to Mr. *Man*, Ambassador in *Spain*, I pray you to let him understand of such advertisments as I send you, and such other things as you shall think meet; And to convey the letters by the *Spanish* Ambassadors means, Resident there in that Court.

To the Right honorable, Sir Henry Norris Knight, the
Queens Majesties Ambassador, Resident in France.

SIR,

I wrote of late to you, that Sir *Thomas Smith* should come shortly thither, but I think he shall not be there now so speedily as was meant; for he shall first secretly pass over to *Callis*, to be there the 3. *April*, to demand the Town; not that we think the Governour will deliver it, But to avoid all Cavillation which they might invent (for by Law it must be demanded at the very place, and being not delivered, the sum of five hundred thousand pounds is forfeited;) Master *Winter* shall pass secretly with him to take possession thereof, if they shall deceive our expectation; but not past three of the Council know of *Winters* going.

The common fame in *Scotland* continueth upon the Earl *Bothwell*, to be the principal Murtherer of the King, and the Queens name is not well spoken of; God amend all that is amiss: We heard before your writing, of the *French* attempt for the Prince.

We have no news, but all well here; the matters of *Flanders* go very hard for the Protestants; and if God do not provide for their safety, I look for their ruine. I heard, this day, that *Danvile* should be slain: fare you well.

Westm. 21. *March* 1566.

Yours assuredly,
W. Cecil.

To the Right Honorable, Sir Henry Norris Knight, the
Queens Majesties Ambassador, Resident in France.

SIR,

BY the Queens Majesties letters, and by this bearer, you shall understand how earnestly her Majesty is inclined to help the Count *Recandelle*; and since the writing of her Majesties letters, she hath commanded me that you should make it a principal part of your request to the King, and the Queen mother; that considering the Count is a stranger born, and is of the Order of *France*, that his cause might be heard and ordered by the King, and the others of the same order; and to that end you shall prosecute your request, that the whole cause may be removed from the Court of Parliament at *Paris*; wherein her Majesty would have you by all good means to persist, as in a request that of it self is honorable, and sometimes, as she thinketh, usual. At the least such as if any the like person being a stranger in her Realm, and being honored with the Order of the Garter, if he would require to have his causes, (wherein his

T   life

Sir William Cecil, *to* Sir Henry Norris.

life or honor were touched) to be heard by her Majesty, and her Knights of her Order; he should not be denyed, nor should be by any other Judges molested.

Thus I report to you her Majesties good pleasure; and thereto do add my poor private request, to beseech you not to be weary in the prosecution of this suit.

Westm, 9. *March,* 1567.

Yours assuredly,
W. Cecil.

To the Right Honorable, Sir Henry Norris *Knight, Her Majesties Ambassador, Resident in* France.

SIR,

* Yesterday Mr. *Smiths* Son arrived with some Letters from you and him, containing your troublesome negotiation, whereof we here thought very long. He saith he was constrained to tarry six days at *Hull,* and that his Father would be here this night; you shall hereafter hear of some ill news out of *Ireland;* and though it be not of great moment, thanks be to God, yet by report of ill friends, they wil be amplified. Indeed the 21. of *April,* a Fire happened in a little Fort upon the Sea side, at a place called the *Dirrye,* which Mr. *Randolphe* first took, in such sort as the houses being all covered with Straw, the soldiers were forced to abandon it, being two hundred, and with their Captain Mr. *Sentlo,* came by Sea to *Kneckvergus,* a Castle of the Queens; but for all this it is meant to take again the place, or a better, and to prosecute the Rebel, who is in declination.

The Queen of *Scots,* I think, will be wooed to marry the Earl *Bothwell*; the principal of the Nobility are against it, and are at *Sterling* with the Prince. Fare ye well; and as I wrot by Mr. *Shute,* so assure your self of me, as you mean your self to me:

May 12. 1567.

Yours assuredly,
W. Cecil.

To the Right Honorable, Sir Henry Norris *Knight, her Majesties Ambassador, Resident in* France.

SIR,

* By your last Letter of   I understand of the intelligence was given unto you, of preparation of eight Ships, to be set out to the Seas, which seemeth very strange; and therefore the Ambassador here, who could not get Audience of the Queens Majesty, although he often demanded it, since Mr. *Smiths* return, was sent for to come to the Council, and was roundly charged with certain depredations committed upon *English* Merchants in the West; and also with this new preparation, and therewith warned to advertise his Master, that we could not long suffer such attempts unrevenged; and being somewhat amazed with the charge, he denyed the things very flatly, and promised to write very earnestly therein to the King his Master. And for conclusion, he said, that we would write unto you, to move the King to make restitution, and to prohibit the going to the Seas of any other but of those that were good Merchants in this time of peace, according to the Treaty; of which our negotiation you shall hear more shortly by Letters from the Council, although I thought it good, by this my private Letter, somewhat to touch it unto you.

This speech with the Ambassador was on Saturday, the fourth of this present; and upon importunity of the Ambassador, he had Audience of the Queens Majesty this day, to whom he shewed a Letter from the King, that *Percivall* coming over with Letters of late thither, was stayed at *Deip*; and the King hearing that he had Letters from the Queens Majesty; ordered to dismiss him, and willed the Ambassador to pray the Queen to think no offence in it, for the said *Percivall* was to be Arrested in *France* for great debts which he ow'd there; besides that, as the Ambassador saith, he is to be charged there with a murther. After he had shewed this Letter to her Majesty, she called the Lord Chamberlain and me to her in his presence, there being no more of her Council then; and in very round speeches told the Ambassador, that she did not take the *French* Kings answer, for the matter of *Callis,* in good part; and so much the worse, because the Queen Mother, by her Letters sent by Mr. *Smith,* wrote that her Son had given very benign Audience, and so reasonable an answer, as ought well to content her Majesty. In which manner of speech, she saith, she is not well used, considering the answer was altogether unjust and unreasonable, and if hereof the Ambassador shall make any sinister report, you may, as you see cause, well maintain the Queens answer to be very reasonable, as having cause to mislike the manner of writing of the Queen thereon; which, neverthelefs, you may impute to the unadvisedness of the Secretaries, for so the Queens Majesty here did impute it.

Upon

Sir William Cecil, to Sir Henry Norris.

Upon Sunday last I received Letters from *Barnaby*, your Secretary, who therein did very well advertise me of the staying of *Percival* at *Deip*, and indeed I do find that the cause hath grown from the Ambassador here, either of displeasure, or of suspition that he hath against the State *Ro. Condulphe*, for whom he knew *Percival* was specially sent; and finding this day the Ambassador very earnest in private speech with my Lord of *Leicester* and my self, that *Percivall* would be Arrested in *France*, after that he had delivered the Queens Letters; I advised him to write to the contrary, for otherwise he might provoke us to do the like with his Messengers; and surely, if I may be suffered, so will I use them.

I have no more to write unto you; But I can assure you that the Queen of *Scots* was married the 15. of this *May*, and the Nobility therewith so offended, as they remain with the Prince, and keep apart from her; what will follow, I know not. My Lady your Wife is safely arrived, and was long with the Queen on Sunday: I thank you for the little *French* Book which she brought me, the like whereof I had before.

May 27. 1567.
To the right honorable, Sir Henry Norris *Knight*, the
Queens Majesties Ambassador, Resident in France.

         Yours assuredly,
         W. Cecil.

SIR,

* The matters of *Scotland* grow so great, as they draw us to be very careful thereof; I think not but you do hear of them by the reports; but briefly these they be: The best part of the Nobility hath confederated themselves, to follow, by way of Justice, the condemnation of *Bothwell* and his Complices, for the murther of the King; *Bothwell* defends himself by the Queens maintenance and the *Hambletons*, so as he hath some party, though it be not great. The 15. of this moneth he brought the Queen into the field, with her power, which was so small, as he escaped himself without fighting, and left the Queen in the field; and she yielding her self to the Lords, flatly denyed to grant Justice against *Bothwell*; so as they have restrained her in *Lothleven*, untill they may come unto the end of their pursuit against *Bothwell*.

The *French* Ambassador, and *Villeroy*, who is there, pretend to favour the Lords with very great offers, and, it may be, they do as much on the other side.

At this time I send unto you certain Packets of Letters, left here by Mr. *Melvin*, who lately came hither from the Queen of *Scots*; the sending of those to my Lord of *Murray* requireth great haste, whereof you may not make the *Scotish* Ambassador privy; but I think you may make *Robert Steward* privy, with whom you may confer, for the speedy sending away of the same letters.

His return into *Scotland* is much desired of them; and for the Weal both of *England* and *Scotland*, I wish he were here; and for his manner of returning, touching his safety, I pray require Mr. *Steward* to have good care.

Our Wars in *Ireland* are come to a good pass; for the Arch-Traytor *Shane-Oneale* is slain by certain *Scots* in *Ireland*, of whom he sought aid (one murtherer killed by many murtherers) hereby the whole Realm, I trust, will become quiet; I pray you, of those things that our Ambassador in *Spain*, by your letters, may be advertised, whereof I cannot at this time make any special letter unto him, for lack of leisure; and so, I pray, advertise him from me: I am pitifully overwhelmed with business.

Sir *Nicholas Throckmorton* is shortly to pass into *Scotland*, to negotiate there for the pacification of those troubles.

Richmond, 26. June 1567.
To the right honorable, Sir Henry Norris *Knight*, the
Queens Majesties Ambassador, Resident in France.

         Yours assuredly,
         W. Cecil.

SIR,

* This your Lackquey brought me letters from you, and also from your servant Mr. —— whom he left at *Rye*; for such business as by his letter he hath certified me, whereof I have informed the Queens Majesty, wherein she also well alloweth of your circumspection; and I wish all to succeed as you advise, for otherwise the peril were great. Sir *Nicholas Throckmorton* hath been somewhat long in going into *Scotland*, and entred by *Berrick* on Munday last; I think the two Factions of the *Hambletons* and the *Lenox's* shall better accord then your neighbors where you now live would; if *Bothwell* might be apprehended, I think the Queen, there, shall be at good liberty, for the Nobility.

Sir William Cecil, to Sir Henry Norris.

My Lord of *Pembrocke* perceiving likelihood of troubles there in that Country, would gladly have his Son Mr. *Edward Herbert* to return home; and so, I pray, with my hearty commendations to him, declare my Lord his Fathers minde; and if my Lord of *Murray* should lack credit for money, my Lord Steward would have his Son give him such credit as he hath, for my Lord alloweth well of his friendship. I am sorry that at present I am unfurnished to help you with a Secretary; my servant *Windebanke* is sick, Mr. *Sommers* will not be induced to leave his place. So as, neverthelefs, if I can procure you any other meet person, by the next Meffenger, you shall hear.

I thank you for the Chart of *Paris*, and for a written Book to the Queens Majestie, whereof her Majesty would gladly know the Author; And so I end.

Richmond, 14. *July*, 1567.

Yours affuredly,
W. Cecil.

To the right honorable, Sir Henry Norris *Knight, the Queens Majesties Ambaffador, Resident in* France.

SIR,

AT my last writing by Master *Jenny*, I did not make any mention of answer to your request for the provision of a Secretary, Because I heard that you meant to place one *Melennx*, if he might be recommended by me; and truly if he be meet for the place, I do well allow thereof; for howfoever he did in times past misufe me, I have remitted it, and wish him well.

My Lord Keeper prayeth you to use some good means, to inquire by the way of *Orleans*, of Sir *Ralph Pawlet*, what is become of him, and where he is, and how he doth.

It is certain, on the 29. of *July*, the Prince of *Scotland* was Crowned King at *Sterling*, with all the Ceremonies thereto due, and with a general applaufe of all sorts; the Queen yet remaineth where she was.

Windsor, 5. *Aug.* 1567.

Yours affuredly,
W. Cecil.

To the right honorable, Sir Henry Norris *Knight, the Queens Majesties Ambaffador, Resident in* France.

SIR,

YOu shall perceive by the Queens Majesties Letter to you, at this present, how earnestly she is bent in the favor of the Queen of *Scots*; and truely, since the beginning, she hath been greatly offended with the Lords; and howfoever her Majesty might make her profit by bearing with the Lords in this Action, yet no councel can stay her Majestie from manifesting of her misliking of them; So as, indeed, I think thereby the *French* may and will easily catch them, and make their present profit of them, to the damage of *England*; and in this behalf her Majesty had no small misliking of that Book which you sent me, written in *French*, whose name yet I know not; but howfoever I think him of great Wit, and acquaintance in the affairs of the world: It is not in my power to procure any reward, and therefore you must so use the matter, as he neither be discouraged, nor think unkindnefs in me.

When all is done, I think my Lord of *Murray* will take the Office of Regency; and will so band himself with the rest, as he will be out of peril at home. And as for External power to offend them, I think they are so skillful of other Princes causes and needs, as I think they will remain without fear.

We are occupied with no news greater then this of *Scotland*; We begin to doubt of the King of *Spains* coming out of *Spain*, finding it more likely for his Son to come.

In *Ireland* all things proceed smoothly, to make the whole Realm obedient; the Deputie hath leave to come over to confer with the Queens Majesty upon the affairs.

My Lord of *Suffex* wrote from *Augusta*, the 24. of *July*, that he meant to be at *Vienna* the last of *July*, and also that the Emperor meant to be there at the same time.

I must heartily pray you to bear with my advice, that in your expences you have consideration not to expend so much as by your Bills brought to me by your servant *Cartwright* it seemeth you do; for truely I have no Warrant to allow such several Fees as be therein contained, neither did I know any of the like allowed to any of your predecessors; and in the paying for your intelligences, if you be not well ware, you shall, for the most part, have counterfeited ware for good money.

In matters of importance, or when you are precifely commanded to profecute matters of weight, it is reason your extraordinary charges be born; but as to the common Advifees of the

Sir William Cecil, to Sir Henry Norris.

Occurrents abroad, they are to be commonly had for small value, and many times as news for news, for at this day the common Advisees from *Venice*, *Rome*, *Spain*, *Constantinople*, *Vienna*, *Geneva*, *Naples*, yea and from *Paris*, are made so currant, as every Merchant hath them with their letters from their Factors. If I did not know your good Nature, I would not thus plainly write; and yet if I should not hereof warn you, your expences might increase, and I know not how to procure your payment; and yet hereby I mean to do my best, at all times to help you to allowance for all necessary expences; and so I take my leave.

From the Mannor of
  Guilford, 19. *Aug.* 1567.
To the right honorable, Sir Henry Norris Knight, the
  Queens Majesties Ambassador, Resident in France.

Yours assuredly,
W. Cecil.

SIR,

* I Have had no good Messenger of good time to write unto you; the Queens Majesty hath been abroad from *Windsor* these twenty dayes, and returned on Saturday very well.

Lignerolls is come out of *Scotland* with very small satisfaction, as I think; he could not speak with the Queen, no more then Sir *Nicholas Throckmorton*, who also is returning.

The *Hambletons* hold out, the Earl of *Murray* is now Regent; the Queens Majesty our Sovereign remaineth still offended with the Lords, for the Queen, the example moveth her.

In *Ireland* all things prosper and be quiet; Sir *Henry Sydney* shall come onely to confer, and shall return to keep a Parliament in *Ireland*.

My Lord of *Sussex* was honorably received the fifth of *August*, lodged and defrayed by the Emperor, had his first Audience on the eight; the Arch-Duke *Charles* was looked for within five days; and now we daily look for Sir *Henry Cobham* to come in Post; at the least, within these ten days.

All things are quiet within this Realm, thanked be Almighty God.

I have presently a paper sent me from *Antwerp* in *French*, very strange, containing an Edict, to compell all Judges, Governors, all Officers and Councellors, to give Attestation of the Catholick Faith; if it should be true, it should be a hazard to make a plain civil war.

My Lady your Wife came this night hither to *Windsor*, whom I have warned to write to you by this bearer.

Septem. 3. 1567.
To the Right honorable, Sir Henry Norris Knight, the
  Queens Majesties Ambassador, Resident in France.

Yours assuredly,
W. Cecil.

SIR,

* YOu may perceive by the Queens letter, how this noble man is partly of his own minde, partly by perswasion stayed; and surely, if either the *French* King or the Queen should appear to make any force against them of *Scotland*, for the Queens cause, we finde it credibly, that it were the next way to make an end of her; and for that cause her Majesty is loth to take that way, for avoiding of slanders that might grow thereby.

I had provided a young man for you, which could have served very well for writing and speaking of *French* and *English*; but I durst not allow him to serve you in your negotiations, although I know no thing in him to the contrary; but hearing that you have men that can both speak and write *French*, and perceiving by the superscription of your letters, that you have one who writeth a good Secretary hand, I have thought fit to forbear to deal further with the said party.

I thank you for your offer to send me any Charts that I should name; and if you would send me a note of the names of the Charts that are thought thought newest, and of the Author of their setting forth, and the places where they be printed, I may chance to trouble you with craving of some.

I would be glad to have from you a note of the names of the chiefest Nobility of *France*, and with whom they be married; adding thereto any other thing that may belong to the knowledge of their Lineage and Degrees, as you shall think meet. And so for this time I end.

Windsor, 27. *Sept.* 1567.
To the right honorable, Sir Henry Norris Knight, the
  Queens Majesties Ambassador, Resident in France.

Yours assuredly,
W. Cecil.

Sir William Cecil, to Sir Henry Norris.

SIR,

After my very hearty Commendations, with my like thanks for all your courteous letters to me, and specially for the friendly trust which I see you put in me, to the due answering whereof you shall never finde me wanting.

My Lady, your good Wife, can sufficiently report to you all things from hence, so as I need write nothing presently, but my hearty commendations.

And where it seemeth you think some hardness, in not allowance of your expences, expressed in sundry your Bills; surely it is not lack of my good will that stayeth me, but power; for truly I never subscribed so many extraordinary Bills for any, as I have done for you; and, as I understand by your servant *Cartwright*, I have subscribed more in some of them then will be as yet paid. Generally, I will subscribe all charges reasonable for carriage of Letters; but concerning entertainment of men to continue at the Court, or for rewards, given extraordinarily, I never did, nor could allow them; and yet I wish them paid, being laid out in the service of her Majesty. And, in this manner, I heartily pray you to interpret my good will to the best; for surely if you were either my Brother or Son, I have no more power to shew you and yours good will, then I do.

The Duke of *Chastilherant* is at *Deip*, and meaneth within these ten days to be here, as his servants report; I think he shall not be able to annoy the *Lowth*, as he and his, I see, do desire. *Bothwell* is not yet taken, to our knowledge, though it be said he should be taken on the Seas, by a Ship of *Bremes*: And so I end, as I began.

Windsor, 2. Octob. 1567.   *Yours, as your own,*
To the right honorable, Sir Henry Norris *Knight, the*   W. Cecil.
Queens Majesties Ambassador, Resident in France.

SIR,

* Your servant *Jenny* arrived here yesterday, with your letters of the first day of *September*, by which the Queen was greatly satisfied, for that we had received divers brutes of the troubles of *France*, whereunto we know not what credit to give; and now considering the Ice is thus broken, you must think we shall daily be molested with uncertain reports.

The Queens Majesty advertised the *French* Ambassador, and Monsieur *de Pasquiers*, of as much as she heard from you, who were not a little troubled before, by reason of strangers news spread abroad, and more dangerous to the King; for otherwise they had heard no manner of thing of credit out of *France*, although of late time they had sent three several Messengers; so as I do guess that the passages be stopped to them, and I wish they be not also to you too.

I finde her Majesty disposed, upon the next hearing from thence, to send some special Gentlemen thither; before which time, her Majesty being moved by me according to your desire, yet will not agree to send to you any Currier.

My Lady, your Wife, was ready to depart towards you upon Wednesday last, and would not be stayed from her journey by any perswasion; what she will do now upon your servants coming, I know not; but, in my opinion, she shall do well to forbear the venture.

This Letter which I do write, I do send by your Footman, wherein I dare, as the time is, write nothing but that which may be seen of all sorts.

That which you wrote of late to me touching *Jenny* your servant, I assure you ought not to be imputed to him, but to such in *Scotland*, to whom being uttered for their good, they could not use it as was meet.

We have nothing in *Scotland*, but all things therein be quiet since the last of *September*, at which time the Castle of *Dunbar* was rendred to the Earl of *Murray*; and one named the Lord *Wamghton*, follower of the Earl *Bothwell*, which kept the Castle as long as he could, was adjudged to pay for the charges of them which besieged it; and the charge of the Carriage of the Ordinance back to *Edenburgh*, a new kind of punishment, sufficient enough for such a beggar. And so wishing that we may hear often from you; I end with this also, that it shall behove you to take good heed, whose reports you credit in this variety.

9. Oct. 1567.   *Yours assuredly,*
To the right honorable, Sir Henry Norris *Knight, the*   W. Cecil.
Queens Majesties Ambassador, Resident in France.

SIR,

* I Heartily thank you for your gentle letters sent to me by your two last Messengers, *William Wade* and *Crips*; both which persons come to me, being at *London*, because it was Term time,

Sir William Cecil, to Sir Henry Norris.

time, where I am for the more part, saving Sundays and Holidays; by which occasion, I have at both times sent your letters to the Queens Majesty, so as I have not had the commodity to see your advertisements; nevertheless, you shall do well to continue your accustomed manner of advertising her Majestie as fully as you can, for in these troublesome times, the accidents being so diversly reported as they are, it is meet that her Majesty should be largely advertised; and because it may be that your letters may come in this Term time whiles I am at *London*, I pray let me have some repetition of your advises in such letters as you shall write to me. This bearer your servant *Crips* can make full report to you of all matters here.

My Lady your Wife also hath been very careful to have him return to you; and would have some other of more weight; but the Queens Majestie forbeareth to send any, because of the uncertainty of the time. H+ *Dover* A 1 m̃ in misliking o 1t € and of F wherein all is done that can be by B, and to cover the same, as I think the principal is for that A is 42 91 11 ♀ ᴅ, and doubtful of giving Ω·ωɒɔ5 5∖ subjects; nevertheless, you shall do well as occasion shall serve 5∖ ♃ G n⅗ ♀ 5: :♓ For this we here well perceive that ↗7 ♃ is it ᴍᴍ115 we look daily to hear a certainty of the m̃ W⁺ R, howsoever perceive they there mean to let it.

In *Scotland* all is quiet, the Queen continueth in *Lough Levin*, in very good health; and the Earle of *Murray* ruleth quietly as Regent; and so I end.

Hampton Court, 3. *Nov.* 1567.   *Yours assuredly as your own,*
To the Right Honorable, Sir Hen. Norris *Knight, the*   W. Cecil.
Queens Majesties Ambassador, Resident in France.

(Marginal notes: Her Majestie much misliketh of the Pr̃ince of Conde and Thadmar Lords of France. The Lords of the Council do all they can to cover the same. Her Majesty holdeth is doubtful to give comfort to subjects. Our Ambassador to comfort them, nevertheless, as occasion serves. Expectation of the Queens wars trying with the Archduke Charles. In Scotland all quiet, the Scotish Queen still in Lough Levin and in health. Murray ruleth quietly as Regent.)

SIR,

BEfore Mr. *Bridges* came, who arrived here on Saturday last, with your letters dated the 16. We were much troubled with variety of reports, of the encounter betwixt the Constable and the Prince; and by him we are well satisfied to hear that we think to be truth, although otherwise men report on the other side.

Your servant *Crips* was sent hence, and as I hear, was stayed for lack of winde to pass, six or seven days at *Rye*; but seeing Mr. *Bridges* met him so neer *Paris*, I think he came in safety to you. And now, for your further satisfaction, I send this Bearer Mr. *Jenny*, whom truly I think honest and careful, and in the matter imputed unto him, I take him to be clear.

Mr. *Bridges* shews himself towards you very friendly, and, in his reports, very wise and discreet; surely I do like him well.

The oftner you can send, the better it is, in this busie time.

The *French* Ambassador perswadeth us, that all our Merchants at *Rohan* are by his means at good liberty to use their Trade; which if they be, I know the thanks belong to you.

I wish to have a Callender of them which are with the Prince, and also to see the Edicts that have lately passed from the King against them.

Yours assured, to continue,
To the right honorable, Sir Henry Norris *Knight, the*   W. Cecil.
Queens Majesties Ambassador, Resident in France.

AFter my very hearty commendation, my Lady, your Bedfellow, having not heard from you this good while, hath thought good to send over one of hers purposely to see you, and to bring her word again from you; by whom I would not fail to write these few words unto you; not having any thing to write at this time, but of the prosperous state of all things on this side. The last letters from you hither were by your servant *Henry Crips*, who was dispatched home again towards you the fourth of this moneth, the want whereof is not imputed to be in you for lack of diligence and good will to write, but partly to the dangerous time, and hard means to send when you would, and partly, for lack of knowledge of the doings of the contrary part, which in such a time are not easily known; but, as you may, you shall do well to advertise how things pass there, at the full.

The *French* Ambassador was with the Queens Majesty on Wednesday the 12. of this present, who had no great news to impart to her Majesty, but came onely, as he said, to see her Majesty. His last letters out of *France*, he said, were of the 27. of *October*; In talk with me he told me, that by his letters he understood, that the King had sent for you at the time of the sending away of his dispatch, whereby he judged that you might have occasion to write hither shortly; and that your Messenger was, in likelihood, on the way hitherwards; so as if he be not hindred by the way, your letters are looked for very shortly, or for lack of his com-

Sir William Cecil, to Sir Henry Norris.

coming, it will be, indeed, thought that he is stayed; your next advertisement will shew it, which is daily looked for: And thus I wish you, in this dangerous time, all safety and health.

From the Court at Hampton-
Court, 15. Nov. 1567.
                 Your very assured loving friend,
                          W. Cecil.

To the right honorable, Sir Henry Norris Knight, the Queens Majesties Ambassador, Resident in France.

SIR,

* You must think, that seeing all the parts of Christendom are intentive to hear of the maters of *France*; we cannot be careless, to whom the same belongeth next of all, whatsoever the end thereof shall be.

Your last letters brought hither came with good speed, being dated the 28. of *December*, they came the fourth of this *January*. Of the news therein contained, mentioning the encounter betwixt *Mountgomery* and the Kings Vantguard, about the 23. of *December*, I had letters dated in *Paris* the 20. which did express the same more particularly, but I dare not credit them.

Your good advise given to her Majesty in the said letter, is well to be commended. Of the state of our things here, there is no new thing to write; all things, thanked be God, are quiet.

In *Scotland* they have ended their Parliament; wherein, as I hear, they have Enacted the Coronation of the King, the Authority of the Regent to be good, and have noted the Queen to be privy to the murther of her husband.

My Lady, your wife, hath been a little sick, but now well recovered, and hath instantly required me to send away this bearer, because she had writings to send you; otherwise I would have had him stayed two days to have heard some more news from thence.

I thank you for the Articles which you last sent me; but lacking the Articles of the other side, I could not well understand those which you sent me: And so I end,

Westm. 8. Jan. 1567.
                 Yours assuredly to use or command,
                          W. Cecil.

To the right honorable, Sir Henry Norris Knight, the Queens Majesties Ambassador Resident in France.

SIR,

* It is to us here thought very long since we heard from you, your last being of the fourth of this moneth, sent by young *Cornwallis*, specially because we are troubled with such diversity of reports, that what may be taken for truth, is uncertain. Beside this, I cannot but let you understand, that the Lords of the Council are desirous to hear more largely and particularly how things do pass; wherein they seem to require such a dilligence, as Sir *Tho. Smith* was wont to use, who sought to understand, and so continually did write what was done, almost every other day, making as it were, a Journal or a *Diarium*. But, in my opinion, I have shewed them that it is not so easie for you to do it in this time, considering the Armies and their accidents are far from *Paris*, and as I think, very great heed given, that no advertisements should be given you, but such as you should not think worthy of writing: Nevertheless, for their contentations, I wish you would write of as many things as you can, whereby they shall both be content, and what they hear from other places of the same things, they shall better discern what to think true.

[13] § 19 79'7052 λ ⨯ 5. m. 3. to the disadvantage of R. All things here are in quietness, I think Master Vice-Chamberlain shall be Deputy of *Ireland*, for that Sir *H. Sydney* is sore vexed with the Stone in the Bladder; and so I take my leave, thanking you for the offer you have made me to provide for me certain Charts, of the which I am bold to name nine, as I have noted them in the paper included.

26. January, 1567.
                  Yours assured,
                          W. Cecil.

To the right honorable, Sir Henry Norris Knight, the Queens Majesties Ambassador, Resident in France.

SIR,

* After my hearty commendations, the Queens Majesty, and my Lords of her Council, have been reasonably well satisfied of late by your two dispatches, wherein you have largely written, the last being of the 29. sent hither by the means of *Glover* of *Rohane*, the other of the 23. brought hither by this bearer your servant; before the coming whereof, we had plenty of uncertain news brought hither by the means of the passages, sometimes from *Diep*, sometime

from

Sir William Cecil, to Sir Henry Norris.

from *Bulloigne*; but comparing them with yours, we make them as refuse, and yours as clean metal. And truely I finde that to be true which you write, that you see good cause to forbear writing of every thing there, finding by experience that the greater part of reports brought thither prove not the truest. I am glad there is no occasion here to require you with any news, for God blesseth us with continuance in our accustomed quietness; for the which, I wish, we might but yield half the thanks. The Queens Majesty is in good health, and was purposed of late to have gone abroad for her Pastime, as she did this time twelve moneths, but the foulness of the weather hath letted it. There were certain *Scots*, which newly returned into *Ireland*, about *November* last, but they found themselves disappointed of such aide as they looked for, and so are gone, and feared, whereby the Realm remaineth quiet. The Earl of *Desmond*, and his brother Sir *John*, be here in the Tower, chargeable rather with disorders for private quarrels then for any untruth; whereupon some think, that whilst they remain here, good order may be better stablished there. In *Scotland* things are quietly Governed by the Regent, who doth acquit himself very honorably, to the advancement of Religion and Justice, without respect of persons. My Lord of *Sussex*, by his last letters of the 27. of *January*, looked for his resolute answer in such sort at that time, as he hoped to be at *Antwerp*, before the end of this moneth. What his answer is like to be, I assure you, on my Faith, neither do I know, nor can likely conjecture. I perceive by some of your letters of late, that you were somewhat troubled with light reports of news from hence, and therein you thought it strange that you could not hear thereof from me. You may be sure, that in such a case I would have given you some knowledge, if any thing had hapned.

More as yet I have not at this present, but heartily to thank you for the young horse you have bestowed upon me; wherein you see my overmuch boldness of your friendship, as in many other things; and so I heartily take my leave: I wish to have a Bill of the names of the principal persons, with the place.

Westm. 12. *Feb.* 1567.
To the right honorable, Sir Henry Norris *Knight, the Queens Majesties Ambassador, Resident in* France.

Yours assured,
W. Cecil.

SIR,

Your last letters be dated the 10. of *February*, by which (as I perceive) you did, two days before, make earnest suit on the behalf of the poor men at *Marseiles*, wherein surely you did very charitably; besides that, it toucheth the Queens Majesty, in honor, to have them delivered; and so her Majesty alloweth your doings therein; and therefore you may do well to continue it. I doubt the former answer will be renewed, that is, to have the interest of *D'Estrill* fully remitted, which belongeth properly to some of the Queens Subjects, who have spent a great deal of money in the pursuit thereof, by attendance onely for that purpose upon this Court, more then two or three years, which of my own knowledge I understand to be true; insomuch as they have been forced to be relieved out of prison, for very debt grown by this their suite. Of late they of *Rye* took certain Fishers of *Diepe*, which had come upon our shoar in the night, and Fished with sundry Nets of unlawful size, such as are both by the Ordinances of *France* and *England*, on both sides, condemned; and being kept in Ward by them of *Rye*, the Ambassador made earnest suite for them; but after the Nets were brought up, and some of the parties also, and plainly proved before them, that they were far unlawful; It was agreed by my Lord Steward and the Officers of the houshold, here, in the favor of them, That they should be released, and have their Nets, with faithful promise, never to use the same again upon our Coast: Hereof it may be you shall hear, but I assure you, considering the unreasonableness of their Nets, I think they had too much favor, in that the Nets were not burned. The Queens Majesty, this morning, willed me to write unto you, that you should obtain licence of the *French* King, to send for, by safe conduct, your Nephew *Champernoune*, which is with the Count *Mountgomery*, whom his father thought to have remained in *Normandy* with the Countess; but now since dinner, I perceive by Sir *Arthur Champernoune*, he would be loth to seem to send for him, and therefore you may do herein as Sir *Arthur Champernoune* shall, by his letter sent unto you at this time, move you; for indeed I think the Count *Mountgomery* would be very loth to part with him, for opinion sake. The Lord of *Arbreth* came lately out of *Scotland* this way, and spake with the Queens Majesty, pretending to go into *France* to sollicite aide for the delivery of the Queen of *Scots*; he came out of *Scotland* without licence or knowledge of the Regent there ⚻— ♃ 30–05♈ 2♉ 157 ♂ ♌ ♎ this way of late, but I trust shortly to hear from ♄ ♆ ♃ of such things as he carryed with him. Your admonition of O was well allowed of, but about that matter we are otherwise occupied, if things may fall out as are meant, whereof I cannot write any more, bec use as yet the Iron is not in the Forge. I thank you for the Edicts published and printed in *Paris*, which you sent me, praying you that you will hereafter continue, in the same manner, to send me any thing that is there published.

Having not heard of any thing from you since the 9. of this moneth, (this being the 26) I am in some perplexity what to think of matters there; for howsoever rumors and news be brought from the Sea coast; neither do I believe any for the truth, but such as are confirmed by you; And hereby you may perceive that the oftner you write, the more pleasure you do me.

West. 26. Feb. 1567.   *Yours assuredly,*
                        Postscript.   W. Cecil.

I hear that *Glover* of *Rohan* is very ill used. I wish you could help him, as you shall understand his grief.

To the right honorable, Sir Henry Norris *Knight, the*
   Queens Majesties Ambassador, Resident in France.

SIR,

* Your last letters that have come to my hands, were of the 12. of *Feb.* brought hither by one *Bogg*, of the *French* Kings Guard, who having tarryed, as he said, fourteen days at *Diep* for lack of passage; by that means came very slowly hither; and therefore you must think we be here much troubled for lack of certain advertisements from you, whilst we hear from other parts reports so diversly: Nevertheless, I do think and affirm, that there be some letters dispatched from you since the date aforesaid. Those which you wrote last to the Queens Highness, were well and amply written; and so I wish you should do with the rest hereafter.

You may perceive by the Queens Majesties letter, which I send at this time, her sincere meaning, which if it be well taken, it is well bestowed; and yet I think she should not finde the like courtesie and good meaning, if she had need of the like, from the which I pray God long keep her. Her Majesty is well disposed to send some thither, if she thought she might do good towards the peace, against which I think, plainly, all Ambassadors but your self are vehemently disposed; and so it appeareth by the fruits of their Councils; and if you told the Queen mother, so as of your own head, as a thing you hear spread abroad in the world, I think you might do well and speak truely; for as for the Popes Ministers, their profession is to prefer the State of their corrupted Church before the Weal of any Kingdom in the earth; and whatsoever come of any thing, they look onely to the continuance of their own ambitious ruling; and as for other Ministers of Princes, or for men of War; it is a truth infallible, the more they do impoverish that Monarchy of *France*, the better they think their own estates; and if the Queen-mother and other good Councellors of the King, do not understand this, you may say, if you can in good terms, *Oculos Habent & non vident*. Our matters here in *England* remain as hitherto they have long done, by the goodness of God, in great quietness.

This day I had letters from my Lord of *Sussex*, of the first of thismoneth, from *Antwerp*, who, I perceive, meaneth to pass over the Seas hitherwards this night; so as, I think, he will be here by Munday; what he bringeth, I know not at all. *Bredrood* is dead at *Collen*; the Count of *Berry*, eldest son to the Prince of *Orange*, is in *Zealand*, ready to be carryed into *Spain*; it is doubted that the Counts of *Egmond* and *Horne* shall follow.

March, 6. 1567.   *Yours assuredly,*
To the right honorable, Sir Henry Norris *Knight, the*   W. Cecil.
   Queens Majesties Ambassador, Resident in France.

SIR,

* You have done very well, in this doubtful time, to write so often hither as you have done, for that the Queens Majesty hath been in great expectation, what to judge to be the truth in the middest of so many divers advertisements; for howsoever we be from other places advertised, we measure the same even by yours. The last letters which you sent were dated the 30. of *March*, which came hither yesterday, being the 7. And considering the last accident hapned the 29. by a treachery to have supplanted the good meaning of the peace, I am in opinion that the Prince and his should have a reasonable occasion offered unto them to mend their bargain, in certain points tending to their own surety; which surely if they do not better foresee, me thinks, their danger wil not be far off, I pray you to continue your vigilancy in exploring of ♄ ♃ ♆ ⚹ ☍ 2V. wherein you may do very well to procure that the K may be induced to withstand that enterprize, as being a matter very prejudicial to the whole

* ∗ 73 A o London 2 ⊓ o–o o– ♃ ♅ ☿ ♄ ♒ Paris, &c.   Here

Sir William Cecil, to Sir Henry Norris.

Here hath been, of good long time, one *Emmanuel Tremelius*, who heretofore, in King *Edwards* time, read the *Hebrew* Lecture in *Cambridge*; and hath now been sent hither by the Count *Palatine* the Elector, to inform the Queens Majesty of the proceedings of the said Elector, in sending his Son into *France*, without intention to offend the King and the Realm, or to assist the Prince of *Conde* in any thing; but onely in the defence of the common cause of Religion, who now upon the ending of these causes in *France* will depart hence; and truely, in my opinion, the said Elector hath shewed himself to be a Prince of great honor in this Action.

The Prince of *Orange*, hath also sent hither a special Gentleman, to declare unto her Majesty his innocency in such causes as are objected against him, touching any part of his duty towards the King of *Spain*: And further, also, to shew good cause why he doth not return into the Low Countries, to appear before the Duke of *Alva*, whom he noteth to be a Judge not competent, because he hath already notoriously broken the Laws and ancient priviledges of the same Countries. Out of *Scotland*, I hear, that the *Hambletons* continue in that Faction against the Regent; and I believe they be nourished out of *France*, by means of the Abbot of *Arbroth*, who lately came thorough this way. Of my Lady, your wifes, dangerous sickness (out of the which she was newly escaping, when your Son arrived here) I doubt not but you are well advertised; so as I need not to write any other thing, but onely to rejoyce, with you, that she is so well amended. You see, by my writing, that this Country, thanked be God, is as barren of news, as that of *France* is plenteous.

Sir *Ambrose Cave* is departed this life, and as yet it is not known who shall succeed him; some name Mr Vice-Chamberlaine, some Sir *Henry Sydney*, some Sir *Ralph Sadler*, some Sir *Nic. Throckmorton*; her Majesty can make no ill choice of any of these: And so trusting ere this letter can come to your hands, I shall receive some of yours, containing the resolution of this long lingring peace.

April, 8. 1568.

Yours assuredly,
W. Cecil.

SIR,

This evening, *Harcourte* arrived here with your letters, which were long looked for, and be now welcome; for your satisfaction, by this bearer, you shall understand of the recovery of my Lady, your Wife. The Gentleman that lately came hither, named Monsieur *de Beamont*, one of the late disorder of *France*, passeth into *Scotland*, which is not much to be liked.

The book which you sent, of the peace, hath not printed in it certain Articles, by way of request, made to the King by the Commissaries on the Princes part; what answers Marginal of the King, I fear much the surety of the Prince and his Colleagues.

I hear by him that came last, now, of strange news at *Diep*, of the King and Prince of *Spain*; I pray you, if there be any of moment, send us word.

Here is an Ambassador arrived from *Portugal*, for to brawle about Merchants and Maritime matters: For haste, I can write no more.

April, 14. 1568.

Yours assuredly,
W. Cecil.

Postscript.

I send you the beginning of the Parliament of *Scotland*; when I have more, you shall have more sent you.

To the right honorable, Sir Henry Norris Knight, the Queens Majesties Ambassador, Resident in France.

SIR,

Your last letters brought hither, are of the 18. of *April*, which came hither the 29. of the same moneth, by which I looked to have heard where the Prince and the Admiral was, and what they did; and how they intended to prosecute the enjoying of the peace, for here we are troubled with very many fond tales; and I never make good resolution of doubts without your advertisment; and therefore, I pray, write from time to time, what is done on both parts: You shall do well to give good respect to the σ pretending to ☾ ♈ ♓ ♌ † ♅ ♈ ⊢ wherein surely may be seen the very intent of the practicers.

I heartily thank you, Sir, for your plentiful present of so many Countries, as you lately sent by *Harcourte*, who indeed did in former times serve me, and with my good favor departed from me; but if he may serve you, I am glad, for I never knew but good honesty by him :t 2 i: [♍ ♃. o V ♎ ♎ is not a little afraid of these ♃ ♉ ♌ ⊢ ♒ ⊥ ♐. ♁ ♈ ♌ ♉, ♁ G and H.

Sir William Cecil, to Sir Henry Norris.

We hear newly of great attempts towards *Flanders*, and so having nothing more to write, I am by business forced to end, being assured, that both by your Son, and otherwise, you are advertised of all our seen matters here. From *Greenwich* the first of *May*, which is become a very cold day, 1568.

Yours assured at all times,
W. Cecil.

To the right honorable, Sir Henry Norris Knight, the Queens Majesties Ambassador, Resident in France.

SIR,

BY the Queens Majesties letter you may perceive what is her pleasure at this time; *Beaton* is passing thither, so as I think he will be at the Court before the coming of this bearer: In your speaking with the King, you may not, by your speech, seem to utter that you know of *Beatons* coming for aid there, upon advertisement given from hence; for he being advised not to seek aid there, and promised aid here, for his Mistris, hath in words allowed thereof; and saith, that he will forbear to require aide from thence, and will onely but notifie the Queens liberty. But yet, surely I am not bound to believe him; but he hath required us here to say nothing of that which he, at his first coming, told us, That the Queen his Mistris sent him to *France*, to require aide of one thousand Harquebusiers, and a sum of money, with some Ordnance. Wherefore, except you shall learn there that he demandeth aid, you shall not speak thereof; but if he do, then shall ye do well to make mention thereof to the King.

I hear daily of the evil observation of the last peace towards the Protestants.

In *Flanders* and the Low Countries, I see things will prosper too well in hurt of the Religion; and onely for lack that the Prince of *Orange* his party hath of money.

Greenwich, 16. of *May*, 1568.

Yours assuredly,
W. Cecil.

Postscript.

And I think Mr. Vice-Chamberlaine shall be Controller, Mr. *Sydney* Treasurer, Mr. *Throckmorton* Vice-Chamberlain, and Sir *Ralph Sadler* Chancellor of the Duchy.

To the right honorable, Sir Henry Norris Knight, the Queens Majesties Ambassador, Resident in France.

After our very hearty commendations, we being made privy to such Letters and Message as you lately sent by this bearer your Secretary, to me Sir *William Cecil*, have well considered the same, and do well allow of the good ⟨cipher⟩ because ⟨cipher⟩ the ⟨cipher⟩ And do not mislike the overture, made to you by *Paris* ⟨cipher⟩ 40 ⟨cipher⟩ n. o. ⟨cipher⟩ for the diverting of the ⟨cipher⟩ Low ⟨cipher⟩ good ⟨cipher⟩ o Q *Callis* and *Dover*; and although there is no likelyhood of the sequel of this overture for sundry respects; yet we do allow so well thereof, as we wish you would make such answer to the said party, as ⟨cipher⟩ xx: And to that end we are content that you may, if need so require, 3 ⟨cipher⟩ 170 :tt 442 5. 193 the ⟨cipher⟩ 70 ⟨cipher⟩ 70 ⟨cipher⟩ 72 ⟨cipher⟩ giving him to understand, that we will gladly if the matter shall ⟨cipher⟩ the ⟨cipher⟩ to us, use our credit towards xx the A ⟨cipher⟩, who we hope surely neither can nor will but accept the good will of ⟨cipher⟩ in every good part; and so we require you to further that matter with all ttt xx ⟨cipher⟩ that you can; and on our part you may assure the party that it shall be also xx ⟨cipher⟩ low ⟨cipher⟩ 4. 5. the 13 ⟨cipher⟩ ⟨cipher⟩ ⟨cipher⟩. And so fare ye well heartily.

From the Court at Greenwich,
28. of June, 1568.

Your assured loving friends,
Pembroke, R. Leicester, W. Cecil.

To the right honorable, Sir Henry Norris Knight, her Majesties Ambassador Resident in France.

SIR,

YEsterday being the 12. of this month, Mr. *Bridges* came to the Court as we were going from *London* towards *Havering*, in such sort, as the Queens Majesty her self seeing him, and knowing that you would not have sent him but with matter of some importance, commanded me forthwith to decipher your letter, which I did, and shewed her Majesty; whereupon she comfortably and constantly seemed not to fear any such Devillish practice

Sir William Cecil, to Sir Henry Norris. 149

ctice; but yet she is earnest in the further discovery of the matter, and liketh well of your advertisement: But she marvelleth that you did not advise more particularly of more special means, to know the XX ❡ ♌ ♈ ♉ ♃ ♒ E, for as he is described to be of chiefest might un with the ③ T 2 ♃ ♍ ♈ ☌ as also with ④ we cannot truly hit of no man; for as there be 4. or 5. that do sometime accompany the ③ so are there men of that Nation, but they do resort to the ⑭ wherefore it is necessary that you speak again with the party that gave you this intelligence; and if the matter be of truth, and not a disguising to some other purpose, he can as well obtain you the knowledge of the party in certainty; s this to give a guess at him; for as he hath his intelligence of the matter which he uttered to you (if it be true) so may he attain to a more perfect knowledge; and if the matter be true, and shall be discovered by his means, you may promise him reward of the Queens Majesty, as of a Prince of honor, and so indeed shall he have it; on the other side, if the matter be not true, but a device, surely he and they that do participate with him are much to blame; wherefore, Sir, I earnestly require you to use all the speed you can herein, and advertise as plentifully as you can, to the satisfaction of her Majesty; For though her Highness words have comfort, yet it cannot be but she shall rest perplexed untill more certainty be had.

Likewise her Majesty would have you cause diligent inquisition to be made of the other matter concerning the vi g prepared by :t 4L 4 5 u ♈ ♍ L u σ J ♐ T 2 i n where and when, and to what end the prepation shall be.

We marvail that you write nothing at this time of the Prince of *Conde*, &c. For the *French* Ambassador reporteth that he shall come to the King to *Galliau*, the Cardinal *Burbons* house; and that the Cardinal of *Lorrein* shall depart from the Court, which to me is unlikely for truth.

The *Scotish* Queen is ordered to remove from *Carlile*, to a Castle of the Lord *Scroops* in the edge of *Terk-shire* next *Cumberland*, called *Bolton*; for where she was appointed to come to *Tutbury*, the Queens Majesty, finding her great misliking therein, hath forborn the same.

Her desires are these, in sundry degrees: First, to come to the Queens Majesties person, and to have present aid to be restored: Secondly, if that cannot be, to have licence to pass into *France*; and to these it hath been answered, untill her cause may appear more probable for her innocency, the Queens Majesty cannot with honor receive her personally; but if the Queen will by any manner of means, honorable, let her cause appear to be void of the horrible crime imputed to her for the murthering of her husband, she shall be aided, and used with all honor; whereunto she will give no resolute answer, other then that, if she may come personally to the Queens Majesty, then she will let it appear how she standeth in the cause: Hereupon we stand at a brawl; she much offended that she hath not her requests, and we much troubled with the difficulties, finding neither her continuance here good, nor her departing hence quiet for us. We here speak of one *La Mote* that should come hither.

From Havering, the 13. of
July, *in haste*.   *Postscript*.   *Yours assured*,
                                     W. Cecil.

And for ♁ and *x*, I pray you put them in comfort, that if extremity should happen, they must not be left; for it is so universal a cause as none of the Religion can separate themselves one from another; we must all pray together, and stand fast together; and further, &c.

To the right honorable, Sir Henry Norris *Knight, the*
Queens Majesties Ambassador, Resident in France.

AFter my hearty commendations, though here be no great cause of present dispatch to you; yet for the return of this bearer your servant *Darrington*, having been long here; and also to let you understand of the Queens Majesty proceedings with the Queen of *Scots* since her being in this Realm, and since my last letters to you, I have taken this occasion to return him to you. The Queen of *Scots* having long laboured the Queens Majesty, both by Messages and Letters, to have aid of her Majesty against the Lords of *Scotland*, and by force to restore her to her Realm; her Majesty could not finde it meet in honor so to do, but rather to seek all other good means to compass it with quiet and honor; wherein much travailing hath been spent. Finally, the Queen of *Scots* hath agreed that her matter shall be heard in this Realm, before some good personages, to be deputed by the Queens Majesty, to meet with some of the Lords of *Scotland*, about *New-Castle*, or *Durham*, or neer this way, as shall be found fit; and so to be reported to her Majesty. This way being now resolved upon, and accepted of all parts, the Earl of *Murray* hath offered to come himself in person (if her Majesty finde it good) accompanyed with others of meet condition, to any place, and at any time that her Majesty will appoint; and because the Lord *Herrejs*, having long

Sir William Cecil, to Sir Henry Norris.

been here for the Queen of Scots, and lately gone to her, hath on his Mistrisses behalf required that speed might be used in this matter; the Queens Majesty hath by her special letters required the Earle of Murray, that all expedition may be made, either for his own, or else that some others may come chosen, to be persons of wisdom and dexterity, and void of all particular passion in such a cause as this is, and upon his answer of the persons that shall be thus appointed there, the Queens Queens Majesty will, with all speed, send like fit personages from hence to meet with them; and in the mean time, where they the Lords of Scotland had summoned a Parliament of their three Estates, to assemble in this next August; her Majesty hath required them to suspend the holding of the Parliament, untill the issue of this matter to be heard by her Majesty, may come to some end. In this meeting the Queens Majesty doth not mean to charge the Queen of Scots, but will hear what the Lords can alleadge for themselves, to defend all their doings and proceedings, for imprisoning and deposing their Queen, and other matters published by them; and thereof to cause report to be made to her to be answered; and likewise to carry such matters as are to come from her, against them; and upon hearing of all parts, as matters shall in truth fall out, so doth her Majesty mean to deal further therein, as honor will lead and move her to do.

Whilst these things have been in doing, the Queens Majesty hath been advertised, though not from the Queen of Scots, that she hath deputed the whole Government of her Realm of Scotland to the Duke of Chastilherault, thereby both to make a party (as may be supposed) betwixt him and the Earl of Murray; and also to be the earnester to procure Forreign aid for his maintenance, whereof her Majesty is informed there is great appearance, having obtained of the French King good numbers of Harquebuziers and others, ready to embarque for Scotland; which being true, her Majesty hath good cause to let the said King understand, that it is against his promise, as your self knoweth best. And so hath also the said Queen assured her Majesty, that she will not procure any Strangers to come into Scotland for her use, untill it may appear what will ensue of this meeting; But if the contrary fall out, either by her own means, or by the procuring of the said Duke of Chastilherault in France; the Queens Majesty will not onely forbear to deal any further for the benefit of the Queen of Scots, as hitherto her Highness hath done with all honor and sincerity, having had as great care of her cause, as she her self could have; but shall be justly moved to do otherwise then the said Queen or her friends abroad would wish. Thus much I thought good to impart unto you of these matters, to the end that if you (being there) finde indeed, that the said Duke doth obtain any such aide there to be sent into Scotland, you may take occasion to deal therein with the King, or with such as you know fittest for the stay thereof.

The Queen is now removed lately from Carlile to Bolton Castle, a house of the Lord Scroops, about 30. miles within the land, fitter in all respects for her to lye at then Carlile, being a Town for Frontier and War; the Queens Majesty doth cause her to be very well and honorably used and accompanied. And thus having no other present matter to write unto you, I thought good herewith to return your servant to you, wishing you right heartily well to do. From the Court at Endfield, the 25. of July, 1568.

After the end of this letter, your servant Wall arrived here with your letters to the Lord Steward, the Earl of Leicester, and to me, for answer to the letter which we wrote to you; which letter, after I had caused to be deciphered, I sent to the Court, to them, my self being at my house near Waltham, not well at ease, nor in case to go to Court.

I long much to hear answer of letters sent by your Lackque, touching the matter of an Italian, whereof I doubt the Queens Majesty is more careful to hear then she doth here express; at this time, I have received a letter from an Italian there with you, who subscribed his name, who seemeth very importune to have answer, becuse he may be entertained; and if he be the party of whom you writ about a moneth past, surely, as I did advertise you, the Queens Majesty will in no wise hear of any such offers, which she thinketh are but chargeable, without fruit, although I had earnestly moved her Majesty to have adventured some small piece of money upon such a man; therefore I see no remedy but to pay him as well as may be with good words. And thus I wish you better to fare, then I did at the writing hereof.

Your assured loving friend,
W. Cecil.

To the right honorable, Sir Henry Norris Knight, the Queens Majesties Ambassador, Resident in France.

SIR,

BY yours of the 23. of the last moneth, for answer of mine of the 13. of the same, I unde... you have very diligently and circumspectly travailed in the great dangerous

Sir William Cecil, to Sir Henry Norris.

rous matter, to satisfie the Queens Majesty, whereof you gave before that intelligence; and though I perceive that you can come to no more understanding therein, for further satisfaction of her Majesty, yet she is very well satisfied with your diligence and care; and so hath specially willed me to give you knowledge of her allowance of your doings therein. Methinketh the parties which tell you such pieces of tales, if the whole were true, might as well tell you the whole as such obscure parts; which if they do not, you might well alleadge them to be but devices to breed unquietness and suspition; and as I wrote before unto you, they might be tempted with offer of rewards, that the troth of the matter might be disclosed.

The Queens Majesty, as I am informed (for presently I am not at the Court, by reason of my sickness) meaneth to have the matter between the Queen of *Scots* and her subjects heard in this Realm, and compounded (as I think) with a certain manner of restitution of the Queen; and that limited with certain conditions, which how they shall be afterwards performed; wise men may doubt; the Queen of *Scots* her self, at length, seemeth content to commit the order of this cause to her Majesty; wherein if her Majesty's own interest should not be provided for, the world might think great want in her self, which I trust, she will regard.

I am willed by her Majesty to require you to continue your diligence in inquisition, what preparations are meant or intended in that Country to sent into *Scotland*; and as you shall finde any, to give speedy knowledge thereof, as I know you would do if you were not thus advertised.

There is coming out of *Spain* a new person to be Resident Ambassador here, who is a Commendatory of an Order; in whom I wish no worse conditions, then I have found in this man, for maintenance of amity.

Our whole expectation (as yours there is) resteth upon the event and success of these matters in the Low Countries, which as they shall fall out so, are like to produce consequences to the greater part of Christendom; and therefore, I beseech God, it may please him to direct them to his honor, and quietness (if it may be) of his universal Church here in earth; and so I end, being occasioned to use the hand of another my self, being very unable to write, and fully wearied with inditing thus much: Fare you heartily well, from my house in *Cheston*, the 3. of *August*, 1568.

Sir, this bearer, Mr. *Hudleston*, acknowledgeth himself so much beholden to you, as he is desirous to return thither to spend his time, where he may shew himself thankful to you, and to that end hath requested me to write to you by him; he hath required to be accepted into my service; but I think him worthy of some better Master, and my self am overburthened with numbers, or else I would gladly have accepted him.

Yours assure',
W. Cecil.

SIR,

* MY late sickness, hath been cause of my rare writing, and I am sorry to hear of your lack of health; which I trust you have ere this time recovered.

Your letters sent by the *Frenchman* of *Southwark* came one day onely before *Cockhorne*, who came also safely with your letters on Saturday last. I have made the Queens Majesty privy to both your letters; and as to the unhappy news of *Flanders*, we had the same worse reported by the *Spanish* Ambassador here, then yours did there, who hath made triumphant story thereof, as far uncredible as any in *Amadis de Gaule*; for in the fighting continually one whole day, there was on *Lodowicks* part slain and devoured 8000. and on the other part but eight, so every one of them killed ten hundred.

I understand, that within these three days we shall have the report more reasonable; for I also hear that the greater number of the men slain, were of the Dukes part, which I wish to be true ⇾ £3℞ is in words content to commit H† *Dover* ϡ ≀ 2 ⊹ ✢ 7 ⨍ s ∧ A but yet x doth not omit to stir new troubles in v.

Touching the ≠ λ ш 3 ✚ 𝛿 2 149 whereof you have often writ, order is taken to deal with ⊤ 2 ⁃, m ‡ ʃ ʌ s: λ *Paris*; and surely methinks still since the informers will not be known of the particulars in more certainty, that these things are intended to bring us into their play; but yet no diligence is to be omitted. I think the Duke of *Norfolk*, my Lord of *Sussex*, and Sir *Walter Mildmay*, shall be Commissioners to treat in the North betwixt the Queen of *Scots*, and her subjects. And so I end.

Dunstable, 10. *August*. 1568.

Yours assuredly,
W. Cecil,
SIR,

To the Right Honorable, Sir Henry Norris Knight, her
Majesties Ambassador, Resident in France.

Sir William Cecil, to Sir Henry Norris.

SIR,

*THe sufficiency of the bringer hereof is such, as I need not to write any thing to you by him of importance, to whom any thing may be well committed; He can best tell you upon what occasion the Queens Majesty sendeth this Message to the *French* King at this time, which because it is long and of great importance, the Queens Majesty would have you first transl te it into *French*; and well digest it with your self; so as you may very perfectly and readily express it in such sort as it is conceived; And I think, if you would in the translating thereof distribute it into sundry members, by way of Articles, you should the better carry it in your minde, making thereby an account with your self of the better delivery thereof; and you shall do well, to let some such as favor the intention of the Queens Message, to see the Copy of the letter, whereby they may, per-case, being called to give advice to the King, further the cause, to the benefit of them of the Religion.

This day I received your letters, of the date of the 20. of this moneth by *Glover*, who of late time dwelt in *Roan*, whom I take to be a good honest person; but of the matter of the Jewels, whereof you wrote, upon his report, I my self know no certainty.

As for the occurrents of *Scotland*, you shall understand that where the Queens Majesty hath determined with the Queen of *Scots*, to hear the whole matter, and (as it seemeth) to the advantage of the Queen, she took such comfort thereof, as she made the Earl of *Arguile* Lieutenant in one part, and the Earl of *Huntly* in another; and the Duke of *Chastilherault* over all; so as they forthwith leavyed Forces, and by Proclamation threatned the Regent, and all his, with fire and sword, who upon the Queens request had forborn hostility, until the matter might be heard; and upon the 16. day of this moneth, the said Regent beginning a Parliament, which was appointed six weeks before quietly, and holding the same without any Armes; about the 19. word came to him that the Earl of *Arguile* was come to *Glasco* with 2000. and the Earl of *Huntley* coming out of the North with a great power to joyn with *Arguile*, and so to come to *Sterling* to surprise both the place, and the King; upon which occasion, the Earl of *Murray* brake up the Parliament, and sent all the power that he had to stay their joyning together; and (as I heard) the Earl of *Huntley* is put to the worse, and so fled home-ward; hereof the Queen of *Scots* maketh great complaint to the Queens Majesty; you may do well when you have done your great Message, as you see cause, you may charge the Queen Mother with the breach of promise, if the Duke of *Chastilherault* be gone forwards towards *Scotland* with power.

Bissiter, 27. Aug. 1568.

Yours assuredly,
W. Cecil.

Postscript.

I have boldly received from you sundry books; and I am bold to pray you to provide for me a book concerning Architecture, intituled according to a paper here included, which I saw at Sir *Tho. Smith's*; or if you think there is any better of a late making, of that argument.

To the Right Honorable, Sir Henry Norris *Knight*,
Her Majesties Ambassador, Resident in France.

SIR,

*YOur Lackquey arrived here on Friday in the afternoon; and because the Bishop of *Reynes* hath not yet his audience, I stay your servant *Wall*, to bring the knowledge of that shall pass.

The Ambassador sent his Nephew *Willcob* to require Audience, and that it might be Ordered to have her Majesties Council present at the Bishops Missado; Her Majesty answered that they forgot themselves, in coming from a King that was but young, to think her not able to corceive an answer without her Council; and though she could use the advice of her Council as was meet; yet she saw no cause why they should thus deal with her being of full years, and governing her Realm in better sort then *France* was; so the audience being demanded on Saturday, was put off untill Tuesday, wherewith I think they are not contented. The Cardinal *Castillon* lyeth at *Shene* ⵜⵜ ⱵⲘ⳽ⵡ 370Пo—73 : ⵁⵏ⏀9 A *Paris*, the rather to displease ⱵⵜⲦ ∘∘4⟂4⊦ Ᵽ8o⧫ for *Callis*. I think xx⎞ ⲞΔ⸴ Ω^23T-0⧫³·⸲⸲ 5. 0-0⸵ Ⅹⳋⴣu⸵: E[3:7 −∘∓ ℞ⵎⵦⲟ⟩ⴥ⸌⸍ for E *London* 4 3 8 o T 2 J demanded.

The Duke of *Norfolke, &c.* are gone to *Yorke*, where the Dyet shall begin the last of this moneth.

It is ⵡ ⟩⸝⸝⸝ⵔⵒ ⱖⵎ⸴: ⸳ⵙ *Callice* c 3 : c ⧫∘-{t 4 ⵔ⸴⸲ ⵔuⵏⵎ⸲{⸳-⸦ 9 0 :t o⸲⸴ ⸴ⵉ⸲⸳⸞⸴. *London* 2Ᵽ ∏ 8 o N 3 c o⸲⸴ⵔ⸴⸲⸴ ⴑⴑⵝ⸲70⸲: ⸲ ⸵.c ⸲ ⸲⸲ ⵔ⸲uⵏⵎ⸵T

Sir William Cecil, *to Sir* Henry Norris.

9: ≈1⁷⊤ ≢ to the contrary ⲭ♏♄⸺⸴ shal be there any ℰ§ℰ☾⅄⏉L ⨯○♑ ♄⅏ ♃♌ ♃‧9:
7 ‥5 5 9 0-0 *Dover*, &c. The succefs of the matters for good ○ ‥ ♃ ⊥ ⴹ ⊦ ⨅ ⤵ ⤴⨅
3: [E u.

Sir, I pray advertife me what you may reafonably think of 3 9 ≈ ♃ ∧⁵ Π ♃ 5   3 5 ⊦⊎
⁓ ♃ L practices what D or any like to him. I thank you for the book you fent me of Architecture; but the Book which I moft defired is made by the fame Author, and yet intituled, *Novels inftitutions per bien baftir, per Philemont de L'orn.* I thank you for your Placarts, and inftruments that you fent me by your Lackquey,

Yours affuredly, as
your brother,

Septem. 27. 1568.   *Poftfcript.*   W. Cecil.

And is well ufed by *A* the rather to difpleafe all Papifts, I think he hath or shall shortly have fuch comfort for *E* as *Steward* demanded. It is not meant if *x* shall be proved guilty of the Murther, to reftore her to V. howfoever her friends may brag to the contrary; nor yet shall there be any hafte made of her delivery, untill the fuccefs of the matter of F and F be feen: I pray you, Sir, advertife me what you may reafonably think of Sir *Robert Staffords* practices with D or any like him.

To the right honorable, Sir Henry Norris *Knight, the*
Queens Majefties Ambaffador, Refident in France.

SIR,

*A*Fter the letters of the Queens Majefty were clofed up at *Biffiter*, her Majefty ftayed your Son, that he might carry with him a letter for the Marshall *Mentmorancis* wife, for thanks for favor to my Lord Chamberlains daughter; and for a token which her Majefty now fendeth by your Son, being a Ring with a pointed Diamond. I befeech you caufe the letter to her to be endorfed as you shall think meet: for I know not whether she be intituled Madam, Lady, Duchefs of *Calsho*, or *Montmorancy*, or otherwife. I write this upon the 29. being Sunday in the afternoon, in *Rycot*, where the Queens Majefty is well lodged, to her great contentation, as she hath commanded me to write to you; lacking onely the prefence of your felf, whom she wisheth here untill Thurfday, that she shall depart from hence; of which Meffage I pray you take knowledge, and give her Majefty thanks, for she bad me to write thus very earneftly; and fo fare you well from your own houfe, where alfo I am better lodged then I was in all this Progrefs, We are truly certified by our own Ambaffador from *Spain*, who is on the way thorough *France* to return, that the Prince is fuddainly dead; but by what occafion it is doubtful.

Yours affuredly,

29. Aug. 1568.   W. Cecil.

To the right honorable, Sir Henry Norris *Knight, the*
Queens Majefties Ambaffador, Refident in France.

SIR,

I Have, as I lately fignified unto you, ftayed this bearer, *John Wall*, your fervant, to the time that this Bifhop of *Rhemes* should have his Audience and be anfwered; he was heard on Tuefday, and at his departure was required, briefly to put in writing the fum of his fpeech, which he did, as shall appear by the Copy herewith fent unto you; and yet in his fpeech he touched an offence in the latter end of your Meffage, noting noting the Doctrine of *Rome* to be contrary to Chrifts, wherein he amplified before the Queens Majefty, that feeing his Mafter holdeth the Doctrine of *Rome*, therefore your Majefty should repute him no Chriftian, which fpeech, he faid, was hardly born by the king in an open Audience; whereunto fome anfwer hath been made, as you may fee, to falve the matter, by turning the fence, that the Doctrine of *Rome* was contrary to Chrifts, in derogating, *&c.* Onely in this was fome difference made, although, indeed, your writing was warranted by the Queens Majefties letter; and therefore no fault in any wife found in your doings. I do fend you, herewith, the copy of the Bifhops writing exhibited, and the anfwer of her Majefty thereto, which being put in *French* was yefterday, before the Ambaffadors, were admitted to her Majefties prefence, read unto them by one of the Clerks of the Council, in the prefence of the Council; and afterward they were brought unto her Majefty, who did confirm her former anfwer, and fo they departed without further debate thereof. It was thought they would have ufed fome fpeeches concerning the Cardinal *Chaftillon*, whom they finde very well and courteoufly ufed here by the Queens Majefties order; but they have not hitherto fpoken a word of him. At their firft being here, on Tuefday, they told the Queens Majefty, that they had newly received letters out of *France*, by which they were given to underftand, that *Martignes* purfued *Dandelet*

X
and

Sir William Cecil, to Sir Henry Norris.

and overthrew all his force, and made him to flye; which news was onely heard and not credited; insomuch, as the next day following, we heard credibly that *Martignes* had indeed pursued certain followers of *Dandelot*, at the passage of *Leyer*, which *Dandelot* had before safely passed with all his Forces, Footmen and Horsemen; and perceiving that *Martignes* had used some cruelty upon a small number of simple people that followed *Dandelot*, he returned over the water with his Horsemen, and avenged the former injury upon *Martignes*, and from thence went to *Rhemes*; where finding certain of the Presidents or Judges, which had given order to destroy all that could be found of the Religion, he executed their own Law upon some of them, and hanged some of the Judges; which news being brought unto us the day after he had given us the other for a farewell, he was this day welcomed with these; the rather because they touched his own Town of *Reynes*; and I wish them to be true, to cool their heating of lying. The Cardinal *Castillons* wife is come over, whom I think the Queen means to use very well. The Duke of *Chastilherault* comes hither to morrow to the Queens Majesty, but I think he shall not be permitted to go to the Queen of *Scots* very hastily.

If by the next letters it shall not appear, that you can have *Rowland* delivered, and your letters restored, I perceive the Queens Majesty will be well content that some one of theirs shall be stayed in the like manner: And so I end,   *Yours assuredly,*

Windsor, 1. Oct. 1568.   W. Cecil.

Postscript.

I pray you send me word whether you thought ⚹⚹ ♀♃ diot × 3 9⅞ 2 ʌ ⊓ 2 5. ⊟⟃⟅ 3 5. ⎯ 30 ʌ 2♀ ⌐ to be suspected of the matter concerning the 4 ʌ 9 3 ʌ ⊔⊔ 9:3 ⟶ 0 ⋀ or no. ⟃ ℰ By the next, which shall be by my Lady your wife, I will change my Cipher.

To the right honorable, Sir Henry Norris *Knight, the*
Queens Majesties Ambassador, Resident in France.

SIR,

⁎ THis present, being the 18. your servant came with your letters of the 12. which I longed much for, not having of a great time heard from you. The Prince of *Orange* passing the   and his proceeding cannot be unknown to you; and therefore I leave to write thereof.

The *French* Ambassador promised once to write favorably in this poor mans behalf; but this morning he sent his Nephew to me, declaring that considering he perceived much favor shewed by us to the King his Masters Rebels, he could not, without some misliking, write in favor of our Countrymen; I required of him, whom, in particular, he could name as Rebels, that had favor of us; he would name none; I told him, we accepted the Cardinal *Chastillon* as a Nobleman, and a good faithful subject and Councellor to the King; for that upon pride and inveterate malice done to him by the Cardinal of *Lorrein*, he was by him and his so persecuted, as he could not live in *France* without danger of his life; and I told him we had the more cause to favor him, and all such, because the said Cardinal *Lorrein* was well known to be an open enemy to the Queens Majesty, our Sovereign. So he departed, with no small misliking, and I well contented to utter some round speeches. The Queens Majesty is resolved to set out certain of our Ships to *Britain* and *Guyen*, to preserve our *Burdeaux* Fleets from depredations; whereupon I think there will be some misliking uttered thereto you, But considering the frequent Piracies already committed; and the menacing of the Pyrats to our *Burdeaux* Fleet, we can do no other, and so you may answer. I think this Ambassador will advertise many devices of suspitions, of our aiding of the Prince with Money, Shot, and Powder; but the King shall never finde her Majesty to do any thing therein to be reprehended, If in case of Merchandize for Salt or Wine, the Princes Ministers can borrow things of our Merchants; I know not how to remedy secret bargains, where Merchandize is in use. The Treaty of *Yerk* shall cease for a while, for that some of the Commissioners on either side are sent for hither, to confer with her Majesty. The Queen of *Scots* case appeareth not defensible by her own   In so much as they intend another course, to make the Duke of *Chastilherault* their head, and provide for themselves. And so having no more at this present, I end with my hearty thanks for your kind accepting of my friendly good will that I bear you.

Westm. 28. Oct. 1568.   *Yours assuredly,*
                                                                                         W. Cecil.

To the right honorable, Sir Henry Norris *Knight, the*
Queens Majesties Ambassador, Resident in France.

SIR,

⁎ IT seemeth long since I heard from you, trusting that my Lady and your Son came safely to you, although their passage was very hard at *Rye*. We hear many divers news of the

mat-

matters in *France*; But I give no credit, *untill you shall play the Bishop and confirm them*. Our Commissioners at *York* have heard the Queen of *Scots* complaint, and the answer of the other part; wherein they have forborn to charge the Queen with the murther, upon some reasonable respects, not knowing what end they will make if they should charge and prove her guilty; hereupon the Queens Majesty hath sent for some on either part. Sir *Ra. Sadler* came hither yesterday, and the Bishop of *Ross*, and the Lord *Herreys* for the *Scotish* Queen came this day, and so shall *Liddington* and *Mackgill* for the Prince. It is mentioned to have a composition, whereto the *Scotish* Queen, as they say is very willing, ⊞ *Dever* ⚡ But *A* and *B*, for the more part, are earnestly disposed 5∧ ⊃ ⊢ 7 ‖ x a / and if 3 ⊃ ⊓ ⟆ ⊣ 9 ∪ ⅋ [↓ 7 8 o ɪ 9 ✝ ∧ ⊎ / ⊔ ⊃ ⊎ ⊓ / as it is thought very probable, then so to be ⎫ 7: ⨏ ⊼ ⊏ ⌊ for otherwise quietness will never long continue. The Queens Majesty finding her subjects continually spoiled by the *French* upon the Seas, is forced to send Mr. *Winter* to the Seas with four Ships of her Majesties, and two Barks; I know how many tales will be spred of his going; but truly you may avow that his going is wholly to preserve our Fleet at *Burdeaux* from Piracy, and therefore he is appointed to go towards *Burdeaux* x ✚✚ xx ⊃ [3 T 4 0 ⊓ ⊓. c4 EF: ∫ ω :t 9 ⊓ 1 ; [E ⊓ ⨏ ⊏ with ⊃ 7 ⫙ 6 ⩲ 9: ⩎ ⊓ *A* hath agreed ☉ —09 to ⚬⚬ ⊏ ⫙ ⊐ E ⫟ and for the son to have 3 ⊥ 0–0 5. I hear say, that some of our Merchants in *London* have bargained with certain Merchants of *Rochell*, and thereabout, to buy a quantity of Salt, wherewith it is likely that the King there, when he shall hear thereof, will be very suspicious; but in such cases Merchants must be permitted to make their bargains, and so you shall have reason to maintain their doings. The Cardinal *Chastillon* sheweth himself so quiet a person; and in all his languages so faithful a servant to the King his Master, as he meriteth great commendations; he medleth in nothing here, but wholly occupyed in exercise of his Religion; he continually lamenteth, that grave Councellors perswading peace are not of more power and credit in the Court. Whatsoever this *French* Ambassador shall report of him, he cannot truly report any evil of him: I hear that *La Mot* is on his way, at *Callis*, to come hither. I think surely some of yours are on the way. I pray send me a Register or List of the Chieftains on the Kings part, and also on the contrary. Sir, I do send you herewith a new Cipher.

To the right honorable, Sir Henry Norris *Knight, the*   *Yours assuredly,*
   Queens Majesties Ambassador, Resident in France.   W. Cecil.

SIR,

Your last letters that came to my hands were of the 29. of the last moneth; by which you signified to me the advertisements which you then had of the taking of *Angulesme*; since which time sundry reports are brought hither of Battels that should be betwixt the parties, whereof lacking advertisements from your self, I do give credit unto none, by reason of the diversities of the reports. On Sunday last *La Mot* was presented by Mounsieur *de la Forest*, the former Ambassador, whom the Queens Majesty hath admitted as Ambassador for the *French* King, and seemeth to like well of his wisdom; whereof hitherto, for mine own part, I have not had any proof. The cause of the Queen of *Scots* is now to be heard here; for which purpose the Duke of *Norfolk*, and the Earl of *Sussex*, are sent for from *York*, and are to be here within these two days; and presently the Earl of *Murray*, the Earl *Morten*, with certain other Noble men of his part, are already come; and on the Queens part the Bishop of *Ross*, and the Lord *Herryes* be at *London*, and do daily look for some other Commissioners to joyn with them; because her Majesty meaneth to have the whole matter advisedly heard, she hath appointed an Assembly, not onely of her whole Council, but of all the Earls of the Realm, to be here the 18. of this moneth; at which time her Majesty meaneth to have this cause of the Queen of *Scots* fully heard, and therein to take such resolution and end as she shall be advised unto by her said Council and Estates. The last letters which you sent unto the Queen, wherein, as her Majesty saith, you made declaration of your Message done to that King, concerning the Cardinal *Chastillons* being here, was by her Majesty casually let fall in the fire, and so burnt; whereupon her Majesty being sorry for that she had not advisedly perused it, willed me to write unto you for the copy of the same letter again, which I pray you to send me by the next. I would be glad to hear a brief, or, as they call it, a list of the names of the principal persons that have a charge now in these wars in *France* on both parts, with the contents, as near as you can, of their numbers.

After the writing hereof this present evening, as the bearer hereof can tell, Mr. *Edmonds* came hither with your letters to the Queens Majesty, by which I am satisfied for those reports that were made of the great fights at *Angulesme*; and of that which hath been here reported by the *French* Ambassador, of the overthrow of *Mouvaus*, which I am glad is not true

as he reported; and so finding nothing else to be answered, I have thought good to dispatch this bearer with this my letter, to the intent we might the sooner hear of your news, whereupon dependeth the whole expectation of the Christian world. *Yours assuredly,*
Hampton-Court 16. Nov. 1568. W. Cecil.

Postscript.
Before Mr. *Edmonds* came you may see what I wrote of the ☉♄♃♅♆♇.
To the Right honorable, Sir Henry Norris Knight, the
Queens Majesties Ambassador, Resident in France.

SIR,

* BY your last letter sent to me by this bearer your servant, I perceived how good hap it was, for our satisfaction here, that your letters came not away with the report of the victory, whereof the King there advertised you by a special Messenger, untill you had also knowledge of the truth thereof, by *Villeroys* coming from the Camp after the first message; for like as the former part of your letters made mention of a great Victory for the King, and an overthrow of the Princes whole Infantry; So have many letters been written hither from *Paris* and other places, according to the partial affections of the Writers, in affirmance thereof, adding, for their confirmation, certain solemnities by Processions, and such like, used at *Paris* for the same; nevertheless, I account the truth to be as in the latter part of your letter you write, that there was no such manner of battel, but certain skirmishes, wherein there was no great inequality; and yet because I hear it also credibly reported that the Prince of *Conde* lodged and kept the field, where the skirmishes were, I think his losses were less then the others; whereof I think, within a while, to know the truth more particularly.

This matter of the Queen of *Scots* began to be heard and treated on at *Westminster* the 25. of the last moneth, since which time there hath been sittings five or six several days; and yesterday the Queen of *Scots* Commissioners, having matter to answer, whereby the Queen their Mistriss was charged with the murther of her husband; they alleadged that they would go no further, being so commanded by letters from her, received since the beginning of this Commission; and have required to speak with the Queens Majesty, of whom they pretend they will desire to have the Queen their Mistriss to come to the presence of her Majesty, and answer these causes her self; whereunto how they shall be answered, I cannot tell; but for that purpose, and others, her Majesty, hath presently sent for her Council, who be here at present; and so shall the Queen of *Scots* Commissioners be to morrow; and hereafterward, as matters shall fall out, I will advertise you further, and so take my leave.

Hampton-Court, 2. Decemb. 1568. *Yours assuredly,*
To the Right honorable, Sir Henry Norris Knight, her W. Cecil.
Majesties Ambassador, Resident in France.

SIR,

* SInce my last writing by your servant *Buffin*, I have forborn to write, because I thought both to hear somewhat more from you; and to have also somewhat here to write unto you. Since which time, I have received no letters from you, but such as the poor Merchants of *Ireland* brought me, being dated the 25. of the last moneth, which came hither on Saturday last, being the 11. of this moneth; and considering the multitude of tales reported here to us, of the conflict about the 18. I was nothing satisfied with the said last letters; because touching that matter they did refer me to your former, against which the *French* Ambassador here hath precisely given unto us news, in the name of the King his Master, wholly to the disadvantage of the Prince; and therefore, I wish you had written thereof now at the latter time somewhat more particularly. I did of late write to you for the copy of the letter which you wrote unto the Queens Majesty, touching the speech that was uttered unto you by the King there, concerning the Cardinal *Chastillon*, for that, as I wrote unto you, the same letter by casualty was burned before it was thoroughly read and perused, and hitherto I have not heard your answer to the same. We have been here of late much occupied, in the conference with the Commissioners of *Scotland*, wherein there hath been eight or nine several Sessions; the sum of the matter is this, the Queens party began at *York* to accuse the Regent and his party, whereunto they made their answer and defence; after which the Queens party, by replication, maintained their accusation, and then the conference there stayed; whereupon the Regent being here with the Queens Majesty, vehemently charged, was driven, for his defence, to disclose a full Fardel of the naughty matter, tending to convince the Queen as deviser of the murther; and the Earl of *Bothwell* her Executer; and now t' e Queens party finding the burthen

so

Sir William Cecil, to Sir Henry Norris.

so great, refuse to make any answer, and press that their Mistris may come in person to answer the matter her self, before the Queens Majesty, which is thought not fit to be granted, untill the great Blots of the marriage with her husband the murtherer, and the evident charges by letters of her own, to be the deviser of the murther, be somewhat razed out or recovered; for that as the matters are exhibited against her, it is far unseemly for any Prince, or chaste ears, to be annoyed with the filthy noise thereof; and yet, as being a Commissioner, I must and will forbear to pronounce any thing herein certainly; although as a private person, I cannot but with horror and trembling think thereof. In your letters of the 25. you recommended unto me a cause of your own between you and one *Brabrook*, wherein you write, that one *Tetterfall* your Atturney should have informed me, but herein I have not a good while now dealt withall, but whensoever any shall, I shall be glad to shew you any friendship to my power, *& sic de ceteris.* I am sorry to understand of the sickness of your Son, Mr. *William Norris*, and therefore I would be glad to hear from you of his recovery, for indeed I do heartily like him and his condition. I have also dealt with my Lord of *Norfolks* grace in your matter, for your right to the Lord *Dacres* Lands, wherein his Grace, at the Council table, openly promised his favor.

I pray you, Sir, commend me to my good Lady your wife; if there be any good Charte of *France*, made since Mr. *Oliver Trunkets* impression having no date; I would be glad to have one, to behold therein the particular voyages and passages of these contrary powers: And so I end.   *Yours assuredly as your own,*

Hampton-Court, 14. Decemb. 1568.
To the right honorable, Sir Henry Norris Knight, the   W. Cecil.
  Queens Majesties Ambassador, resident in France.

SIR,

THis bearer your servant came hither the last of *December*, with your letters of the 25. and 26. of the same, wherein he used good diligence; and for the contents thereof, her Majesty is very well satisfied with the diligence of your advertising, being before by reason of contrarious reports in great suspence what to think; for this *French* Ambassador now being here, useth an ordinary manner to write unto her Majesty, in a certain general sort of the news of that Country, as favorably as he may on the Kings behalf, as reason is he should; but yet not without danger of discrediting himself by reporting untruths. As I conjecture by your advertisements, it is likely that God hath already permitted some great effect to be wrought about this *Christmas* time, by some Battail stricken betwixt the two Armies; and howsoever it is, I do not doubt but you will advertise; and therein the will of God is to be obeyed with thinks, or with patience, as it pleaseth him to give his grace, or to chastise.

By your letters also, it appeared that the Prince of *Orange*, at the writing thereof, was still in the *French* Kings Dominions; and yet the common report at the same time was that he was departed towards *Germany*, whereof the Duke of *Alva's* friends, in the *Low Countries*, begin to make some triumph. The matter of the Queen of *Scots* remains in these termes; upon the accusation produced by her Commissioners, against the Earl of *Murray*, they have for their defence shewed so much matter to charge her with the procuring of the murther of her husband, as thereupon motion is made, on her behalf, for covering of her honor, to have some appointment betwixt her and her subjects, which is communed of secretly by two or three manner of wayes; that is to say, That she should affirm her resignation of her Crown to her Son, as it hath been made, and live here in *England*. Or else her self and her Son to joyn in Title, and the Earl of *Murray* to remain Regent: Or, thirdly, her self to remain in Title Queen, and to live here in *England* secluded, and the Earl of *Murray* to continue Regent; which matters have so many pikes, as the venture is great to take hold of any one of them, nevertheless, in the mean time outwardly she offereth to prove her self innocent, so she may be permitted to come to the Queens presence and answer for her self; which is thought to be the more earnestly required, because it is also thought assured it will be denyed; and now what is like to grow to be the end thereof, surely I cannot well guess; for as for my self, I finde my insufficiency to wade so deep, and the violence of the stream so great, as without good company assisting in Council, I dare not venture to make any passage. Here is a stay made of certain treasure that came out of *Spain* to pass into *Flanders*, which we take to be Merchants, and not the Kings, as is alleadged; if it shall prove Merchants, we may be bolder to take the use of it, upon good Bonds, for an interest; and so wishing you and my Lady, and yours, a fortunate good year. I end,   *Yours assuredly,*

Jan. 3. 1568.   W. Cecil.
   SIR,

Sir William Cecil, to Sir Henry Norris.

SIR,

Heartily thank you for your last letters of the first of this month, wherein you did well deliver us from some perplexity, being by the *French* Ambassador here otherwise advertised, to the advantage of the Cardinalists; his letters are dated the 30 of *December* from the King; and I marvel to perceive by your letters that the skirmish should be the 23. and the advise should not come to you before the 28. for thereby it seemeth the Camp should be so far off, as in four or five days tidings could not come; but this I think may be said, that evil news are brought to that Court slowly, at the least they are uttered slowly. Of this accident of Arrest, you shall be by her Majesties letters fully advertised; at the signing whereof, her Majesty said that she would have sent a Gentleman expresly to the King; but she considered that being sent by Sea, the journey in this Winter time will be very dangerous and uncertain; and to send him thorow *France*, where the troubles are such as she could not (either without mistrust of the *French* King, because the party should pass thorow *Gascoigne*, and the Queen of *Navarrs* Country, or without certain danger by souldiers;) and thereupon you shall so advertise that Ambassador of *Spain*, and require him to make advertisement acordingly; whereunto you may add, that her Majesty hath thought of three or four meet persons to be sent thither, for one of them to be an Ambassador Resident; but none will be gotten, that with good will will serve, in respect of Mr. *Mans* strange and hard handling; which things her Majesty would have you set out more plainly to him, that the King may finde that onely to be the cause why there is no Resident Ambassador there. And thus I end, having willed *Harcourte* to take some of the Proclamations, if they be ready printed in *French*. Yours assuredly,

Jan. 8. 1568. W. Cecil.

Postscript.

I finde, in a Bill of Petitions, beginning from the 28. of *August* to *December*, sundry sums of money pressed by you for carriage of Packets, to whom I have not answered; and therefore, hereafter, I pray you write expresly, of what you do there, for avoiding of double charge.

To the right honorable, Sir Henry Norris *Knight*,
her Majesties Ambassador, Resident in France.

SIR,

Since the writing the other letter, dated the 8. of *January*, my Lady caused her servant to stay for a Passport for two Geldings; and sithence my other letter, we have here news from *Flanders* ⱻ ʌ 𝔰. V. 𝛑 ⅔ ℒ touching R and therefore we are in a continual expectation what were the very news of a matter that was reported to have hapned the 23. of *December*. The more particulars you write hither, and the oftner, the more thankful is your service; and surely I see nothing so meet for us to understand, as to be often advertised from you, which considering, you may write in your Cipher, the oftner you hazard your letters, the less is the peril. We have no news from *Scotland*, but that their Parliament is ended; and amongst other things they have all assented, by Act, to decline the Queen of *Scots* obtaining to be lawful, because she was privy to the murther of her husband. There were none of the Nobility absent, but such as were of the *Hambletons*. And thus I end my suddain letter, being in a great longing to hear from you.

January 10. 1568. Yours assuredly,
W. Cecil.

To the Right Honorable, Sir Henry Norris *Knight*,
Her Majesties Ambassador, Resident in France.

SIR,

After, I had written my other letters sent in this Packet unto you, which I was to have sent away by one of your Footmen; your servant this bearer, *Henry Crispe*, came hither upon Thursday last with your letters, dated the 22. of this moneth; and perceiving him earnestly disposed to return unto you, I thought best to stay the sending away of your Footman; and to send, as I do, this dispatch by this bearer, which is partly because my former letters shall seem to bear so old a date. And herewith I send unto you, which was not ready before, a memorial, in the *Spanish* tongue, of the matters passed concerning this late Arrest; which memorial her Majesty would have you procure with her letters to the King of *Spain*; and therefore after you have perused it, I wish you should retain a Copy thereof, either in *Spanish* or in *French*, for your better instruction; and that done, to use all the expedition you may for the conveyance of her Majesties letters and the said Memorial to the King of *Spain*.

Since the finishing of the said memorial, you shall understand that *D' Assenleville* hath been here a good time, being not as yet accepted as an Ambassador; for that he hath no
special

Sir William Cecil, to Sir Henry Norris.

special letters nor Commission from the King, but from the Duke of *Alva*; And all that he can say for himself, is, That he cometh in the Kings name, as one of his Privy Council, and whatsoever he shall do shall be confirmed by the King, before he will depart out of the Realm. He would also privately confer with the *Spanish* Ambassador, which hath been hitherto denyed, for that it is meant that the mis-behaviors of the said Ambassadors should be openly disclosed to *D' Assonleville*, thereby to let it appear how unmeet a man he is to be a Minister for Amity here, which yesterday was declared to *D' Assonleville* at my Lord Keepers house, where he came to these of the Council following, my Lord Keeper, the Duke of *Norfolk*, the Earl of *Leicester*, the Lord Admiral, my self, Mr. *Sadler*, and Mr. *Mildmay*; and that done, he seemed sorry for things past, and yet pressed still to speak with the Ambassador, which was not then granted by us, for that we did intend that resolution should grow from her Majesty, which, though it be not yet known, I think he shall not be denyed. In these matters we have cause to be somewhat slow to satisfie them, lest they should, according to their accustomed manner, grow too audacious; what will be the end thereof, I cannot judge, but I trust it will appear that they have begun upon a wrong ground; and, as it falleth out, I think they shall be found to be behinde hand with us. Yesterday, word came to *London*, that all the *English* Fleet, which are feared should have been Arrested in *Spain*, came home safe; and this day I have heard for certainty that *Hawkins* is arrived at *Mounts Bay*, with the Queens Ship the *Minion*, having in her the Treasure, which he hath gotten by his Trade in the *Indies*, and by rigor of the *Spaniards* near *Mexico* was forced to leave the *Jesus* of *Lubeck* upon a Leek; which also he destroyed, that they took no profit thereof; hereafter I will write unto you, as I shall learn the further truth of this matter, with what cruelty he was used, under pretence of friendship, and of a compact made betwixt him and the Vice-Roy of the *Indies*, and Pledges delivered on both sides for the performance thereof. The Queens of *Scots* was removed from *Bolton*, by my Lord *Scrope*, and Mr. Vice-chamberlain, on Wednesday last; so as I think on Monday or Tuesday, she shall be at *Tetbury*, where the Earl of *Shrewsbury* is already, and there shall take the charge of her; and with him shall Mr. *Hen. Knollis*, brother to Mr. Vice-Chamberlain, remain to assist him. Of late the Queens Majesty understanding out of *Scotland*, that the Queen of *Scots* faction there had published sundry things, being very false and slanderous (meaning thereby to withdraw the Earl of *Murrays* friends from him, and to bring the Queens Majesty doings into some question, whereof we also be credibly informed) the Queen of *Scots*, by her letters, was the very cause; thereupon her Majesty ordered to have the contrary notified upon her Frontiers, for maintenance of the truth, as by the same you shall understand, which I send you herewith in Print. The advertisements which you gave both to my Lord of *Leicester*, and me, of the secret cause of the Kings going to *Metz*, seemeth to be of such importance, as it is requisite for us to provide with speed some remedy, and so we here, for our part, will do our best as A ☌ 🜚 ♁ ♏ serve, which you may consider ☉ ☐ ⁂ ☌ ♃ ♃ ♃ considering the +4 3 : 0 : o-o *Je* 228; and therefore I pray you attempt all the means you can to advise all parts that shall take the harm. I have no more to write to you, meaning to expect, within three or four days, somewhat from you; and then I will write by one of your Footmen, and so I take my leave.

The *French* Ambassador hath been informed of the stay of our Ships at *Rhoan*, and on Thursday last my Lords of the Council sent Mr. *Hampton* to him to move him, that they might be released within 15. days, or else we must do the like; his answer was, that he would do his best, and he trusted they should be, imputing the cause to our sufferance of the Prince of *Conde* his party on the Sea to make Port-sale in our Havens, which surely is not by us permitted; and therefore for his satisfaction, we did yesterday write letters to all Officers of Ports, to prohibit utterly the vent of any Commodities brought in by such men; and besides this, the Ambassador hath required that you would be earnest with the King for the release of our Ships, which we told him was not neglected by you; and so, I doubt not, but you do your best therein.

This day the Ambassador sent unto me his Secretary to complain, that the Currier of *Callis* carrying his Packet from hence should be searched, and certain Packets of letters taken from him, which I told him was true; and the cause thereof such, as we had more reason to complain thereof then he; For true it is, that the said Currier having but one small Packet of the *French* Ambassadors, under pretence thereof, had carryed with him two great Fardels of letters of the Merchants of the *Low Countries*, who were here Arrested with their goods, a matter also whereof the said Ambassador was forewarned; and so is the matter to be proved by the letters of the said strangers, which I at present have in my custody; and so the Post was permitted freely to depart with all manner of letters, which he had of the

said

Sir William Cecil, *to* Sir Henry Norris.

said Ambassador. And so I pray you to make answer therein, as you shall see cause, for so is the truth, and no otherwise.   *Yours assuredly,*
Hampton-Court, Jan. 30. 1568.   W. Cecil.
To the Right honorable, Sir Henry Norris *Knight, the Queens Majesties Ambassador, Resident in* France.

SIR,

OF late I have received three several letters from you, the first of the 11. the second of the 13. and the last of the 15. of *February*, although that of the 13 of *February* was written to be in *January*, but I am sure to be mistaken. By the first it appeared, that you could not obtain of Mounsieur *Morviller* the names of any Ships or Merchants of that party which were stayed here; although they pretended the stay of ours at *Rhoane* to be for that cause: In the same letter you make mention of two dis-courtesies, or as I may rather say, injuries done unto you; the one by taking *Rogers* your servant, the other by imprisoning the Physician to my Lady your wife; of which two matters, you may see by the answer made to the *French* Ambassador, I have made mention. The second letter, of the 13. which was brought to me by this bearer, containeth matter of burthening you by the Queen Mother for soliciting the Queens Majesty, to take some enterprize for *Callis* or *Rochel*, wherein I think your wisdom sufficient to satisfie your self what to think; for if you had so done, as I know not what you have, it were not unlike, but they there would invent and set abroach, for their advantage, the like matter if the circumstances were theirs, as they be ours. And where you are charged with conveyance of the Rebels letters (as they call them) in your Packets; I think the same and the former part are fed with one humor, which is, that though you do not in this sort, yet they surely would so do in the like; wherefore I wish you to be no ways troubled herewith; but as the end of the verse is, *Contra audentior ito*; and yet to hold this rule, to be a Minister of good amity betwixt the Princes, *usque ad aras*, that is, as far forth as it be not against the honor of God, and the safety of the Queen our Soveraign.

By your letter of the 15. which was written after you had closed up the Packet brought by this bearer, you advertised me of the news which you had of Monsieur *Gengez*; and of the joyning together of the Prince of *Orange* and the Duke *Pipantine*, whereof, saving your advertisements, otherwise we hear nothing, but rather the contrary, being spred so by the *French* Ambassador here, with affirmations of great credit. In the latter end of your letter of the 13. it appeareth you had not then sent away the Queens Majesties letters to the King of *Spain*, whereof I am very sorry, for her majesty maketh an assured account, that they had been in *Spaine* by this time, which I see you did not, because the *Spanish* Ambassador was not at Court but at *Paris*; for remedy whereof, all speed possible would be used to send them by a special man to the Ambassador at *Paris*, with some excuse to him of sending the same so late. You shall understand that Monsieur *D' Assonleville*, who came onely from the Duke of *Alva*, hath been here of long time, hovering to have had access to the Queen as an Ambassador, which her Majesty would not allow of, nor would so much prejudice her self in respect of the unkinde usage of the Duke of *Alva*; and yet nevertheless allowed unto him as much conference as he would with her Council; to whom although he did open, as we think, the sum of his negotiation, yet he pretended to have somewhat more to her Majesty, if he might have audience of her, which, otherwise, he said he could open to no body.

As to that which he opened to the Council, which was a request to have the money released, and the Arrest set at liberty; It was answered, That the money belonged to Merchants, and that he could not deny, but added that it was meant to have been lent unto the Duke of *Alva* in the *Low Countries*, and so as they termed it, destined to the Kings use; as to the restitution of the money, and putting the Arrest at liberty, she would neither deny nor grant the same to him, considering he lacked authority to make sufficient contract thereupon; but when the King himself should send one sufficiently authorized, both to understand, and to redress the injuries done by the Duke of *Alva* to her Majesties subjects; it should well appear that the King should be reasonably satisfied on her Majesties behalf, and amity and peace should be conserved according to the Treaties. And besides this, it was added, that seeing the Duke of *Alva* began the Arrest first, it was reason they should also begin the release; and so in the end *D' Assonleville* appearing to be much miscontented, was licensed to depart, and so is gone, having used all good gentle speech that could be, during his being here; notwithstanding the report made of his great bravery made at *Callis* before his coming, which either was not true, or else purged his choler upon the Seas coming hither. Thus having, as time could serve me, enlarged my letter, I end, with my hearty thanks to you for the Charts of

France

Sir William Cecil, to Sir Henry Norris.

France, which I perceive are of the like as I had some before, so as I think there is no newer Printed. *Yours assuredly, as your own,*
Westm. March, 7. 1568. *Postscript.* W. Cecil.

I would gladly know, whether the paper you sent me, containing the Emperors answer to the *French* Kings demand, be to be allowed as true.

To the right honorable, Sir Henry Norris *Knight*, &c.

SIR,

BY the Queens Majesties letters you shall perceive in what sort the *French* Ambassador hath sought to frame a tale of a slander against you, her Majesty hath answered for you, and as long as no other thing can be produced to touch you, it is reason that her Majesty should answer for you, as she doth. Your servant *Madder* came safely hither four days past, and I have heard from my Lady, of *Harts* taking, and the Queens Majesties letters from him. Whereof, as I know, upon her advertisement to you, you will use some roundness of speech by way of complaint there; so have we here not forborn to charge the Ambassador with these dis-courteous dealings, who promises earnestly to write to the King thereof. The *French* Ambassador giveth out store of News of the overthrow of *Montgomery*, the taking of his brother, of *Gonliss* death, of the Duke of *Biponts* sickness; of his want of money to go to the Field, but we heard of many contraries to these; and so I wish you your hearts desire.

Westm. 14. March. 1568. *Yours assuredly,*
To the Right Honorable, Sir Henry Norris *Knight, her Majesties Ambassador, Resident in* France. W. Cecil.

SIR,

YOur servant *Crips* came hither yesternight, as I perceive, constrained to follow and accompany Monsieur *de Montasser*, who this day was brought to the Queens Majesties presence to report the Victory which God had given to the *French* King by a Battail, as he termed it, wherein was slain the Prince of *Conde*; whereunto, as I could conceive, her Majesty answered, that of any good Fortune hapning to the King, she was glad; but she thought it also to be condoled with the King, that it should be counted a Victory to have a Prince of his blood slain; and so with such like speech, not fully to their contentation. Before the coming of your letters, we could not firmly believe the reports of the Prince of *Conde's* death; but now the will of God is to be interpreted in this and all things to the best.

I am sorry to see you so troubled, whereof her Majesty is so informed, as she told the *French* Ambassador, that if he will not procure the King his Master to cause you and yours to be otherwise entreated, she will revoke you; In the mean season I pray you keep your former courage, *& contra audentior ito*. I have been, and yet am, not in sure health, as your Son can inform you, whereby I am not able to write any long letter; when *Madder* was here, I gave him a Memorial of sundry things, of which I trust he hath by this time informed you at length. We have heard nothing from *Rochel* since this re-encounter at *Cognac*; but from *Paris* we hear, that saving the loss of the Princes person, the other part hath the greater loss in numbers; and that the Admiral did defeat fourty Ensigns of Mounsieurs Army that offered to besiege him in *Cognac*, hereof shortly the truth will be known. I note that this 13. of *March* last past had two sundry great effects; for upon that day, when the Regent of *Scotland* should have fought with the Duke of *Chastilherault*, they did notably accord the same day in this sort, that the Duke acknowledged the young King, and went with the Regent to *Sterling*; and with him, besides other Noblemen, the Lord *Herryes*, who had been here a vehement Commissioner for the Queen of *Scots*. Besides, it is accorded, that for redress of all private quarrels, there were four Noblemen named of either part to end all, who should come to *Edenburgh* the tenth of *April*, to treat thereupon; and this was unwilling to the Queen of *Scots*, who must needs be greatly perplexed therewith; what will follow, I know not, but the Regent is now well obeyed; the same day we see what was done in *Poytiers*; wherein Gods judgements are not to be over much searched.

I send you within the Queens Majesties letter, a paper in a new Cipher to ⊡ ⊤ ⊽ *Je* ♄ 29: 3 ♃ 9. ⑲ ∇ *le* 0 ◠ 91 ☉ ⊙ U8 7: ◠ 95 which he desireth forasmuch as all power legal to be ℮ to 't O U A 8 Z♄♄ which I pray you do.

And thus I finde my self not able to indure any longer writing, and therefore end;
Westm. 6. April, 1568. *Yours assuredly,*
W. Cecil.

Sir William Cecil, to Sir Henry Norris.

SIR,

* After I had closed up this other Packet, I had occasion to stay the bearer, partly by indisposition of my health, and also, within a day after, by reason of the coming of your Son, *John Norris*, with your letters of the 15. of this moneth, who gave us here to understand of certain discomfortable news which were told him at *Abeville*; and as it appeareth, were in great haste sent before him by the Marshal *de Cosse* to the *French* Ambassador, containing an absolute Victory by the Kings brother, in a battail besides *Cognac*; in which it was written, that the Prince of *Conde*, and the rest of the Nobility with him, saving the Admiral and *Dandelot* (who were fled) were all slain; and this news being here dispersed abroad, I thought good to stay the sending away of this bearer, untill we might better understand what to think truth herein; which being now four days, and therein no confirmation of the aforesaid news, but a doubtful maintenance of them; whereby it is thought that either no part was true, or not in such sort as was reported; and therefore knowing the necessity of your mans service, I do return him unto you. We understand certainly out of *Scotland*, that there hath been an accord by certain Articles made betwixt the Regent and the Duke of *Chastilherault* and his party, wherein the obedience to the King is acknowledged, and a Surcease untill the tenth of *April*; at which time the Duke, and eight more, chosen on both parts, shall meet at *Edenburgh*, to confer of the estate of the Queen of *Scots*, how she shall be reputed; and likewise of recompences for the losses on both parts sustained in these civil wars; and for performance of this Treaty, the Duke, the Earle of *Cassels*, and the Lord *Herryes*, remain with the Regent, untill they put in their Sons for Hostages; and the Regent in the mean time intendeth to use his force to subdue the Out-laws upon our Frontiers.

I received letters even now out of *Ireland*, by which it is written of the defeat of four hundred *Irish* and *Scots*, onely by sixscore *Englishmen*; I shall continually hearken for your letters, to declare to us the truth of this great tale of the Battail of *Cognac*. We hear that the Count *Meighen* is newly departed and fled into *Germany* upon fear. Yours assuredly,

27. *March*, 1568. W. Cecil.

Postscript.

The time serveth me not to write to you of your self, for your motion of leaving that place.

To the right honorable, Sir Henry Norris *Knight, &c.*

SIR,

* Since the coming hither of *Harcourt*, who came hither on St. *George* his day, as it seemeth, with good haste, we here have been much unsatisfied, for that we could not imagine what to conceive to be the cause that in so long space we heard not from you; having in the mean time so many divers tales, as we were more troubled with the uncertainty, then glad of the news; and to add more grief, we could not hear from *Rochel* since the Re-encounter, untill now by a Merchant that came hither within these two dayes past, by whom we are more ascertained then before; by him we understand, that the loss of the Prince is more in reputation then in deed, for that now the whole Army is reduced to better Order then it was before. The Vidame of *Charles* is come to *Plimouth*, and his wife, as it is thought, not being well liked of amongst the Nobility, because he married so meanly; indeed it must needs be some reproof to him to come away when service is requisite. Since the accord made in *Scotland* the 13. of *March*, at *Easter* last, the Duke of *Chastilherault* and his part, hearing, as it is thought, of the death of the Prince of *Conde*, and by brute, that the Admiral and all that party were utterly subverted, did go back from their agreement, which was, to acknowledge the young King and the Regent; whereupon, as we hear, the Duke himself, the Archbishop of St. *Andrew*, the Lord *Herryes*, and the Lord *Rosbim*, are committed to the Castle of *Edenburgh*, what will follow I know not; God stay these troubles that increase so near us; I think you do hear from Mr. *Killigrew*, who is sent to the *Palsgrave* of the *Rheine*, and so I end.

April, 27. 1569. Yours assuredly,

W. Cecil.

Postscript.

Sir, to avoid some length of my own writing, I do send you herewith the sum of the Negotiation lately with the *French* Ambassador, and thereto have adjoyned the Copy of the Proclamation, that is meant to be made by the Queens Majesty, which is mentioned in the other writing; and a Copy also of a clause contained in the *French* Kings Proclamation; by all means you may, well understand that which hath passed in this matter, and shape your own speech there accordingly.

W. Cecil.

To the right honorable, Sir Henry Norris
Knight, Ambassador in France.

SIR,

Sir William Cecil, to Sir Henry Norris.

SIR,

You have much satisfied us here with your letters sent by Mr. *Madder*, who is able to explicate the affairs very sensibly; and now I have thought good to address to you *Hart-curte* knowing that he is very serviceable unto you. And as for any news to make recompence to you, I have not; and glad I am that our Country doth not yield any such as *France*; and yet in the way of Christian charity, I do lament the misfortune of *France*, marvailing that a Country that hath had so many wise men, able to offend other Countries, hath none to devise help for themselves. I wish that you would learn of the *Spanish* Ambassador there, whether he sent the letters which you delivered to him from the Queens Majesty. There is some secret means made hither, to come to accord with the *Low Countries*; and therein I see the most doubt will be in devising assurance how to continue the accords. Our Navy hath been ready these fourteen days at *Harwich*, to go with the Merchants Fleet of Wooll and Cloth to *Hamburgh*; and our Fleet that was appointed to *Rochel* is, as we think, there, by means of the Easterly winds that have hindred and stayed the other Fleet. God send them both a good return, for they are no small offence to our neighbors; that to *Hamburgh*, to the Duke of *Alva*; and the other, to the *French*. The *French* Ambassador continueth a suitor, that no Ambassador be sent to *Rochell*; and that our Merchants cannot forbear, specially for Salt, which cannot be had in other places, although even now great likelihood is of sufficiency to be had, within these 12 moneths, in *England*.

The Earl of *Murray* proceedeth still in uniting to him the Lords that were divorced from him; and specially, of late, the Earl of *Arguile* is reconciled to him; and the like is looked for of the Earl of *Huntley*. I have no more, but to end with my commendations.

Greenwich, 15. *May*, 1569.
          Yours assured at command,
                W. Cecil.

SIR,

Your last letters, that came hither to my hands, were written the 27. by which, amongst other things, you wrote of the brute, of the impoisoning *Dandelot* by the means of an *Italian*, of which matter we were here advertised almost ten days before; the report was in part before he was sick, such assurance have these Artizans of their works; the will of God be fulfilled, to the confusion and shame of such as work them, and such great iniquities. We have certain news from *Rochell*, that *Dandelot*, being opened, the very poison was manifestly found in him. The Queens Majesty, of late, was very credibly advertised by sight of original letters, of persons of no small reputation in that Kings Court, which have entreated of the matter, whereof heretofore your self hath also advertised concerning the ⊙ V ♂ D and ☉ Π ☍ ☌ ♃ ♄ for the transferring ♓ 4 ; V ∧ ♌ 8 ♃ ♌ 3. And now her Majesty would have you use all good means that you can possible, to learn some more truth hereof, and thereof with speed to advertise her Majesty; for it is so precisely denyed on the other part here, as nothing can be more. The *French* Ambassador continueth complaining of lack of restitution in general; yet I assure you he never is refused restitution upon any particular demand; where, contrarywise, our Merchants are daily evil used at *Rhoan*, and specially *Callis*; and, as it seemeth, the Governor of *Callis* regardeth not the Ambassadors speeches or promises here; or else it is Covenanted betwixt them to Boulster out their doings.

Original letters intercepted by persons of credit in the French Court, of Advertisement concerning the Q. of Scots and Duke of Anjou. That the said Scottish Queen should transfer her Title on the said Duke. To learn note with hereof, and advertise with speed. This precisely denyed by the other side.

Mr. *Winter* departed from *Harwich* the 19. of *May*, and came to *Hamburgh* the 23. remained there untill the 28. and returned safe to *Harwich* the first of *June*, all in good safety, with the Queens Ships, leaving two there to return with our Merchants. It is found that all the Ships in the Country dare not deal with six of the Queens, being armed as they are; motion is made of accord betwixt us and the *Low Countries*. The Earl of *Murray* hath no resistance in *Scotland*.

Greenwich, 4. *June*, 1569.
          Yours assuredly,
               W. Cecil.

Postscript.

SIR; It is now accorded, that three of the Merchants shall pass over to *Rohan*, to prove what restitution the *French* will make there, and the like shall be here. Because I doubt your slack servants, I do presently send away this bearer; otherwise I would have staid him to have seen what manner of news this Ambassador hath to declare upon Tuesday next, at which time he hath required to be heard. I am ready, as I told your Son, Mr. *William Norris*, to do any thing in my power to pleasure you in your particular causes or suites here; as the last Term, I did deal for you in such as I was required;

          Yours assuredly,
               W. Cecil.

To the right honorable, Sir Henry Norris Knight, the Queens Majesties Ambassador, Resident in France.

Sir William Cecil, to Sir Henry Norris.

SIR,

* Your last letters are of the 8, of *June*, brought by a Merchant residing at *Rehan*; and now our daily expectation is to hear, either of the joyning of the Duke *Bipont* with the Admiral, or else that they have been kept asunder by fight; we have no news here, being contented with continuance of quietness, which we think to possess, except the motions of the contrary shall come from thence, whereof we have great cause to fear, and the like to prevent. Upon a Reprizal made by Mr. *Winter* here of certain *Portugals* goods, We hear, for certainty, that the King of *Portugal* hath Arrested the goods of our Merchants there, whereof will follow some jarr, which we think our foes will increase. The Queen of *Scots* hath sent one *Borthick*, by whom, at his request, I wrot yesterday, and her Secretary *Rowlye* into *France*, to procure from the King and his brother *D' Anjou*, some satisfaction to the Queens Majesty, for avoiding of the opinion conceived of her transaction with Monsieur *D' Anjou*; how they shall well satisfie her Majesty, I cannot tell, but, as of late I wrote to you, her Majesty would have you explore, by all means that you can, what hath been in truth done heretofore in that case, besides the advertisement; for her Majesty hath seen letters passed betwixt no mean persons of Authority there, being adversaries to the Religion; by which it manifestly appeareth, that such matters have been secretly concluded; and yet the more tryals are made hereof, the better it is. We have, at length, accorded with the *French* Ambassador here, as you shall see by a Copy of writing herewith sent you; and so I take my leave of you. I wish that you would always when you send any with your letters, write what you impress to them for their charges, for I make full allowance to them all: And so with my hearty commendations to you and my Lady, I end. Our Progress is like to be to *Southampton*.

Greenwich, 18 *June* 1569.

Your assured friend at command,
W. Cecil.

To the right honorable, Sir Henry Norris *Knight*, the *Queens Majesties Ambassador, Resident in* France.

SIR,

* This bearer Mr *Borthick*, servant to the Queen of *Scots*, hath required me to have my letters unto you, to signifie the cause of his coming; wherein I can certifie, of my knowledge, no other than thus; the Queen of *Scots*, of late time, amongst other things, to move the Queens Majesty to be favourable unto her in her causes, offered to do any thing reasonable to satisfie her Majesty, concerning her surety in the right of this Crown, as she now possesseth it to her self and her issue; whereupon answer was given, that though there was no need, for the Queens Majesties assurance, to have any Act pass from her, yet as things were understood, the Queen of *Scots* was not now a person able or meet to contract therein; for it was understood that she had made a Concession of all her Title to this Crown, to the Duke of *Anjou*; with which answer we finde the Queen of *Scots* much moved as a thing devised by her enemies in *France*; and thereupon she advertiseth the cause to be of the sending of her servants into *France* to the King his Brother, Uncles, &c. to make perfect testimony in what sort this surmise is untrue; and so, as I am informed, this is the occasion of the coming of Mr. *Borthick* this Bearer, who, truly, I have found always a good servant to the Queen his Mistriss, and a tractable Gentleman at all times; and so I pray you accept him upon my commendations.

Yours assuredly,

Westm. 16. *June*, 1569.
W. Cecil.

To the right honorable, Sir Henry Norris *Knight*, the *Queens Majesties Ambassador, Resident in* France.

SIR,

* Your advertisement of the Duke of *Bipont* came hither so speedily, as untill seven days after the *French* Ambassador could not understand thereof; but when he did, he used no sparing to divulge it abroad; where the Count *Ernest* of *Mansfelt* is we cannot as yet understand; but from *Rochell* we hear that he is well allowed of the Army, and not inferior in knowledge to the Duke. The will of God must be patiently received and obeyed; and what shall ensue hereof to his glory, we must, if it be good, affirm it to be beyond our deserts; if otherwise, not so evil as we have deserved. Of late, about the 15. of *June*, a Rebellion began in the West part of *Ireland* about *Cork*; wherein we care not for the force of the inhabitants, so they be not aided with some *Spaniards* or *Portugals*, whereof we are not void of suspicion; and therefore we do presently send certain Captains with a Force by Sea from *Bristoll* to *Cork*, meaning to provide for the worst, as reason is.

Our

Sir William Cecil, to Sir Henry Norris.

Our *Rochell* Fleet is safely returned with Salt; and I think the Merchants have not as yet brought their whole accomplement. Upon your last advertisement of the delays used in giving you Passports, I did peremptorily admonish the *French* Ambassador, That if he did not procure you some better expedition at the Kings hands there, he should have the like measure there; and therefore I think you shall hear somewhat, whereof I pray you advertise me: And so I take my leave. *Yours assuredly,*

Greenwich, 3. *July,* 1569. — W. Cecil.

Postscript.

An unfortunate Accident is befaln to my Lord of *Shrewsbury*, being first stricken with a Palsey, and now stricken lamentably with a Phrensie, God comfort him; It is likely the Queen of *Scots* shall remove to *Belvoir*, in the charge of my Lord of *Bedford*.

To the right honorable, Sir Henry Norris *Knight, the Queens Majesties Ambassador, Resident in* France.

SIR,

AS my leisure is small to write much, so have I not much matter to write unto you at this time; but onely to send away this bearer your servant unto you, because I think in this time you have cause to use them all. Your Son, Mr. *John Norris*, I think shall be the next by whom you shall understand all our matters here better then I can express in my letters; and therefore I do forbear to write divers things at this present unto you; which by him you shall more certainly understand; onely at this time I wish that you could finde the means to send some trusty person to ⟨cipher⟩ there to understand the certainty of the matter, whereof you did last adverse her Majesty concerning the ⟨cipher⟩. For herein it is necessary to be better ascertained, then by reports, lest some may inform you of things to move us here, to enter further then will be allowable. Your constancy in opinion for the maintenance of Gods cause is, here, of good Councellors much liked, and in that respect I assure you, I do earnestly commend you. *Yours assuredly,*

Greenwich, 11. July, 1569. W. Cecil.

To send a trusty person to Marseilles.

Postscript:

I pray that I may be commended to my good Lay, whom I see void of fear of Wars, for love of your company.

To the right honorable, Sir Henry Norris *Knight, the Queens Majesties Ambassador, Resident in* France.

SIR,

YOur last letters brought unto me by the *French* Ambassadors Secretary were of the 9. of this moneth, the advertisement wherein being in Ciphers contented me so much, as I wish you could by the next make me good assurance of the truth thereof; and if the same be true, methinketh the contrary party should not forbear to take advantage of the time. This day the *French* Ambassador had to dinner with him, the Duke of *Norfolk*, the Earl of *Arundel*, the Earl of *Leicester*, my Lord Chamberlain, and my self; having invited us four or five days past; where my Lord of *Leicester* and I had privately reported the misusage of you by them of your house by the Parisians, who seemed to be ignorant thereof; imputing the same to their insolency, reporting, for example, their late boldness in executing of the two Merchants which the King had pardoned, whereof your self also of late wrote unto the Queens Majesty. Afterward he entred more privately with me in discoursing of the causes why you were misliked there, to be onely for the intelligence which you had with his Masters Rebels; a matter, as he said, if he should attempt the like here, he knew that I would so mislike, as he could not be suffered to remain here as an Ambassador. I told him that for any thing to me known therein, he did as much here to his power; but we had no such cause of suspicion as they had, and therefore he heard nothing of us. I confess that I thought you as well-willing to the cause of Religion as any Minister the Queen had, and I liked you the better; neither would I ever consent that any other manner of person should be sent to be our Ambassador there. In the end, he required me to write earnestly unto you, by way of advice, that you would forbear your manner of dealing with the Kings Rebels; and I told him that so I would, and durst assure him that you would deal with none whom you could account as Rebells; percase, you would wish well to the Kings good servants, that were afflicted for their consciences; and so after such like advisings, we went to dinne. When I consider by whom I send this letter, I mean your Son, I finde my self ensured of writing, being also, as he knoweth, oppressed at present with business; I am bold to end, with my heartiest tieft commendations to you, and my Lady; I thank you for your good entertainment of Mr. *Borthick*, for he hath written thereof very well.

20. July, 1569. W. Cecil.

To the right honorable, Sir Henry Norris *Knight, the Queens Majesties Ambassador, Resident in* France.

SIR,

Since the time that we first sent the Merchants to *Rohan*, to confer with the Marshall *de Crosse*, for restitution to be made on either side, we never heard from them but once, at which time they advertised us, that the Merchants pretended ignorance of those things which the Ambassador here had alleaged, both in the Kings name, and in his; nevertheless he entreated them well, and caused them to stay untill he might send and have answer from the King, which they did; and since that time we have not heard of them; but making report thereof to the Ambassador, he would not seem to believe our Merchants, pretending the mistaking of the Marshals words; and so in the end, by his frequent sollicitation, the Queens Majesty hath accorded, by advice of her Council, in such manner as you perceive, by a Copy hereof in writing sent herewith; the like whereof is sent at this present unto the said Merchants remaining at *Rohan*. In which accord, you shall see a division of the matters in question according to their natures; That is, for things plainly and openly Arrested and staid, to be restored within a time, without suit in Law; the rest of the things to be restored, by order of Law, with favorable expedition; whereas the Ambassador would have had the accord made, that all things, of what nature soever they were, being proved to have been taken by any of the Queens subjects; or any other that should be proved to have brought the same into any Port or Creek of this Realm, that immediate restitution or recompence should be made for the same, whereby you can guess what matters he meant to have drawn to their advantage, by such large words. Thus much of this matter I have thought good to write unto you for your information; and for the enlargement thereof, I have at present written to the Merchants, to advertise you of their proceedings. We have report come to us from *Callis*, that the King there is come to *Paris*, and that his brother, with his Army, is at *Orleance*, with many other things, to the advantage of the Prince of *Navarr*; but hereof I make no certainty nor account, untill I may hear from you. You shall, perchance, hear of some troubles in *Ireland*, which also may be by our ill-willers increased; and therefore I have thought good to impart unto you briefly the state of those matters, *Fitz Morris* of *Desmond*, one that pretendeth title to the Earldom of *Desmond*, hath traiterously conspired with divers Rebels in the South-West part, with one *Mac Cartemore*, late time made Earl of *Clancarty*, to withstand the Authority of the Queens Majesty; and pretendeth to make a change of Religion, being provoked thereto by certain Friars, that have offered to get him aid out of *Spain* and *Portugall*; and upon comfort hereof, hath with a Rebellious number over-run divers parts in the West; and especially made great spoil upon certain Lands belonging to Sir *Warham* St. *Leger*, neer *Corke*. And besides this, have procured the Earl of *Ormonds* younger brethren to commit like riotous acts, pretending, on their part, that they do the same, not of any disobedience to the Queen, but to maintain their private Titles and Lands against Sir *Peter Carew*, whom indeed the Lord Deputy there findeth very serviceable against them; and in that respect, it seemeth, they would cover their disorders, But thanked be God, the brothers powers are dispersed, and they driven into desert places; and the Deputy was the 27. of the last moneth in a Castle of Sir *Edward Butlers*, which was taken by force, and from thence marched with his Army against the other Rebells, who also fled from him. And so, although indeed it be a matter to be pitied, to have any such disorder to be begun, yet with Gods goodness there is great likelihood of due avenge to be had of them all; and no small profit to grow to the Queens Majestie, by the forfeitures and escheats of their Lands, wherewith the better subjects may be rewarded. The *French* Ambassador hath been here this day, and shewed the Queens Majesty, that the King is come to *Paris* to levy mony for increase of his Army, and that there are coming six thousand more *Switzers* to his service.

The 25. of the last, the Earl of *Murray* began a convention at St. *Johns* Town, and meaneth to send, as I think, the Lord *Lydlington* hither with his minde concerning the Queen of *Scots*; and so I end with my hearty commendations, both to your self, and my Lady.

Otlands, 3. Aug. 1569. Yours assuredly,
 W. Cecil.

Postscript.

[cipher] here is very desirous that [cipher] might be [cipher] hither.

To the right honorable, Sir Henry Norris *Knight, the Queens Majesties Ambassador, Resident in* France.

SIR,

Sir William Cecil, to Sir Henry Norris.

SIR,

Your last letters brought hither to my hands, came by Mr. *Huddleston*, whom surely I think you shall finde an honest servitor; I have no matter presently to write of, but to take occasion to send away this bearer your servant, and I wish to hear from you of some good success at *Poictiers*; I do lye in wait for the *Italian*, of whom you lately made mention in your letters, that is sent hither to attempt his devillish conclusions. Out of *Ireland*, since my last, I have heard nothing of any moment, but I trust all shall be in quiet there; and so is the state of this Realm also, howsoever any other shall report, having a disposition of malicious prophesying. In *Suffolk*, a lewd Varlet, not disposed to get his living by labor, motioned a number of light persons to have made a rout in manner of Rebellion, to have spoiled the richer sort; but the matter was discovered, and the offenders taken before they did attempt any thing more then had passed by words, so as thereby they are punishable, but as conspirers by words, and not as actual Rebels. The convention of St. *Johns*-Town in *Scotland* was dissolved about the second of this moneth; and one Wednesday last came hither one *Alexander Hume* from the Regent, with letters, declaring that he had an universal obedience in *Scotland*, and that the States there would not consent to any thing concerning the Queen of *Scots* restitution by any manner of Degree; wherewith her Majesty is not well pleased, because she hath a disposition to have her out of the Realm, with some tollerable conditions to avoid perill, which is a matter very hard, at the least to me, to compass; I think you shall hear someways of an intention of ⊤ ⊙ a ♏ D ⊖ ♈ and ⊙ ♐ ♓ ♄ ♃ ♀ ♉. Certainly, if the Queens Majesty may or shall be thereto perswaded, I think it likely to succeed, it hath so many weighty circumstances in it, as I wish my self as free from the consideration thereof, as I have been from the intelligence of the devising thereof, I thought not good to have you ignorant; I know ♃ hath not allowed of it.

Sir, I thank you for the *French* story which you lately sent me by *Huddleston*; the next that shall come to you, I think, will be Mr. *William Norris*.   *Yours assuredly,*

Fernham, 13. *August*, 1569.   W. Cecil.

Postscript.

Immediately after your last servant departed with letters to you, making mention of our accord with the *French* Ambassador, came the two Merchants, *Patrick* and *Offly*, to *London*, with an accord propounded by the Marshall *de Cross*, but not accepted, for that thereby was required a general restitution of all things, which on our part indeed cannot be; and now the *French* Ambassador will not be here on Wednesday, to enter into a new communication. I send you a late Proclamation, which you may impart there as you list.

SIR,

Although the bearer hereof, Mr. *Norris*, your Son, is well able to satisfie you of all our Occurrents here, both because of his continual attendance about the Court, and for his understanding; yet in one onely thing I am most fit to inform you; That his stay here of long time hath been principally by my occasion, whom I have at all times, of late, when he hath desired to come over unto you, moved to stay, upon expectation to have some matter of more weight to be by him imparted unto you; but finding the same not so to fall out, and perceiving him the more importune to resort unto you, since the repair of *Harcourte*, by whom he understood of your sickness, I have thought it good no longer to defer him; and therefore without any other great matter, but to send him where he would be, he now cometh; and if I should enter into writing of any particular things here past; he is as well able to express the same of his own knowledge, as I am by writing; and therefore you shall justly hold me excused, if I forbear my writing, having so sufficient a person to make report of all things, as well such as are meet for letters, as also not meet for some respects. Of the matters of *Ireland*, he shall make you full report. Of *Scotland* he can do the like; of our Trade to *Hamburgh*, he is not ignorant; of the matters betwixt us and *France* for Arrests of Merchandizes, I have made him Privy; and for the matters in this Court, he hath seen and understands as much thereof as I doubt not but shall satisfie; so as he shall serve you at this time in stead of many long letters: And so I end, with a good hope that he shall finde you well amended; whereof I shall also be glad to hear, wishing that the same might be joyned with the winning of *Poictiers*, of which we here live, on all sides, in no small expectation, though with sundry meanings.   *Your assured friend at command,*

Southampton, 9. *Sept.* 1569.   W. Cecil.

To the right honorable, Sir Henry Norris Knight, the
Queens Majesties Ambassador, Resident in France.

SIR,

Sir William Cecil, to Sir Henry Norris.

SIR,

Since your Sons departing from *Southampton*, I have deferred to write untill this time, perceiving some likelihood of some greater matters to ensue, and yet the event thereof draws out at some length, which hath moved me to defer the same untill now, and doubting that otherwise rumors may be brought unto you, I have thought good to send away this bearer. You shall understand, that according as your Son was able to inform you, the Duke of *Norfolk* departed towards *London* about the 16. of this moneth, promising to return to the Court within 8. days; the Queens Majesty having shewed her self towards him offended with his dealing in the marriage, was newly offended with his departure; but being by me assured (as I earnestly thought) that he would return, her Majesty was quieted; contrary hereunto, notwithstanding that he wrote on Thursday the 23. that he would be at the Court before Munday, yet he went away secretly from *London* to *Reninghale* that same night, whereof we had no knowledge untill Sunday in the morning, that his own letters written on Friday at night at *Reninghale* came hither, by which he signified the cause of his departure to be a vehement fear, that he conceived by reports made to him, that he should be committed to the Tower; and therefore he did withdraw himself, to have means to seek the Queens Majesties favor, which he offered to do as a quiet humble subject. Hereupon, the same Sunday Mr. *Edmund Garret* was sent to him, who found him at *Reninghale* on Munday at night, in a fervent Ague; so as the Duke required respite, untill Friday, with which answer Mr. *Garret* returned, and therewith the Queens Majesty was offended, and began, by reason also of other lewd tales brought to her Majesty, to enter into no small jealousie, and therefore sent again Mr. *Garret*, with a peremptory commandment, that he should come notwithstanding his Ague; and so even now, whilst I am writing, I have word, that Mr. *Garret* coming on Thursday at night, found him ready to come of his own disposition, and surely is now on the way, whereof I am glad; First, for the respect of the State, and next for the Duke himself, whom of all subjects I honored and loved above the rest, and surely found in him always matter so deserving. Whilst this matter hath been in passing, you must not think but the Queen of *Scots* was nearer looked to then before; and though evil willers to our State would have gladly seen some troublesome issue of this matter; yet God be thanked, I trust they shall be deceived. The Queens Majesty hath willed my Lord of *Arundel*, and my Lord of *Pembroke*, to keep their lodgings here, for that they were privy of this marriage intended, and did not reveal it to her Majesty, for I think none of them so did with any evil meaning; and of my Lord of *Pembrokes* intent herein, I can witness that he meant nothing but well to the Queens Majesty; my Lord *Lumly* also is restrained; the Queens Majesty hath also been grievously offended with my Lord *Leicester*, but considering he hath revealed all that, he saith, he knoweth of himself, her Majesty spareth her displeasure the more towards him; some disquiets must arise, but I trust not hurtful, for that her Majesty faith, she will know the truth, so as every one shall see his own fault, and so stay. Thus have I briefly run over a troublesome passage full of fears and jealousies; God send her Majesty the quietness that she of her goodness desireth. My Lord of *Huntington* is joyned with the Earl of *Shrewsbury*, in charge for the *Scotish* Queens safety. This 3. of *October*, the Duke is come to Mr. *Paul Wentworths* house, where Sir *Henry Nevill* hath charge to attend upon him; I hope, as I know no offence of untruth in him, so the event of things will be moderate; and so, for my part, I will endeavor all my power, even for the Queens Majesties service.

I know there will be in that Court large discourses hereupon, but I trust they shall lack their hope. The Plague continueth in *London*, the Term is prorogued untill *All-hallentide*.

All the former part of this letter hath been written these three days, and stayed untill the Dukes coming. *Yours assuredly*,

3. *Octob*. 1569.   W. Cecil.

To the right honorable, Sir Henry Norris Knight, the Queens Majesties Ambassador, Resident in France.

SIR,

Even when this bearer was departing, I heard that *Crips*, your servant, was come from you as far as *Amiens* or *Abberville*, and there was faln sick, but whether he hath any letters of yours, or no, I cannot tell; I do mean to send one thither to see his estate, and to bring your letters, which will come very late; and therefore I think we shall also have some later from you as soon as they shall come to my hands. This bearer seemeth to be in Religion good enough, but yet you know how he politickly serveth the *French* King. Howsoever any evil bouts shall come thither, at this present all the Realm is, as yet, as at any time it hath been, and no doubt of the contrary, and yet the Duke of *Norfolk* is in custody, and so are the

Earl

Sir William Cecil, to Sir Henry Norris.

Earl of *Arundel*, and Lord *Lumley*, but the Lord Steward onely keepeth his Chamber in the Court, and I trust shall shortly do well; And so I end.

Windsor-Castle, 10. Oct. 1569.
To the right honorable, Sir Henry Norris Knight, the
Queens Majesties Ambassador, Resident in France.

Your assured friend,
W. Cecil.

SIR,

* AS you have with grief written your advises, so have they with grief been received of us, and yet in all these accidents of the world, we must accept, with humbleness, the Ordinances of Almighty God, and expect his further favor with patience, and with prayer, and intercession to move the Majesty of God to draw his heavy hand over us, which is provoked by our sins. Of our late matters here, by the Queens Majesties letter you shall further understand, which being as you see, long, I know you will well consider and advise how to express the same to the *French* King in the *French* tongue; wherein we have this disadvantage, that their Ministers speak in their own tongue, and we in theirs. Whatsoever you shall hear by lewd reports from hence, assure your self that I know no cause to doubt, but that all things are and will continue quiet. The Queen of *Scots*, I trust, is and shall be so regarded, as no trouble will arise thereof; the Duke of *Norfolk* doth humbly accept the Queens Majesties dealings with him; and I know of none that are thought to have favored his part, but either they plainly alter their opinions, and follow the Queens; or if they do not so inwardly, yet outwardly they yield to serve and follow her Majesty order. Before you sent us your letters which you received from *Spain* concerning *Ireland*, we had knowledge of the same from the same place, and much more, and have made provision to our power. These your sinister accidents in *France* will cause some that were in a slumber here to awake; and so beseeching you to pardon me, if my letter be hasty and very short,

Windsor-Castle, 26. Oct. 1566.
To the Right honorable, Sir Henry Norris Knight, the
Queens Majesties Ambassador, Resident in France.

Yours assuredly,
W. Cecil.

SIR,

* THis bearer, your Footman, having brought your letters hither a good while since is desirous to return, though I think both the season of the year and the weather will not suffer him to make much haste, yet I have thought good to let you partly to understand of the state of things here. About the midst of the last moneth, the Earls of *Northumberland* and *Westmerland*, assembling themselves with some Companies (after refusall to come in to the Lord President) came to *Duresme*, where they have made Proclamations, in their own names, for reformations of the disorders of the Realm (as they termed it) and for restitution of the ancient Customes and liberties of the Church, and so directed the same generally to all of the old and Catholike Religion. In their Companies they have Priests of their Faction, who, to please the people thereabouts, give them Masses, and some such trash of the spoils and wastes where they have been; and upon the sudden having levyed of all sorts (as it is thought) of Footmen about four thousand, simply appointed for the wars, and of Horsemen about a thousand, wherein indeed all their strength is; and with these numbers (before the Earl of *Sussex* could gather numbers meet to resist them) they came down to *Todcaster*, *Ferry-brigs* and *Doncaster*, being twelve miles, or thereabouts, wide from *Yorke*, and were not indeed resisted, untill at *Doncaster* the Lord *Darcy* of the *North*, with certain numbers, which he was leading to *Yorke*, did very valiantly repulse a number of them; hereupon they are retired to *Richmondshire*, and know not what to enterprise by their stragling in this sort. The Earl of *Sussex* is at *Yorke*, where Sir *Ralph Sadler* is, and hath levyed the power of *Yorkshire* against them; the Lord *Hunsden* is sent to *Berwick*, and to the Borders, to levy the like there; Sir *John Forster* to do the like in his marches, the Lord *Screope* also in his Wardenry, the Earl of *Cumberland* and the Lord *Wharton*, to joyn with their Forces in *Westmerland*, and that side; and besides, the Lord Admiral with the Forces of *Lincoln-shire*, and the Earl of *Warwick*, with other numbers of *Nottinghamshire*, *Darbyshire*, *Warwick-shire*, and other parts of the South, are appointed Lieutenants of the Army, who are to joyn with my Lord of *Sussex*; and to do further as shall be found meet. And by this means you shall hear shortly, I doubt not, of the confusion of this Rebellious enterprise, who, as you may perceive, by the Queens Majesties Proclamation, are proclaimed thorough the Realm, as they have behaved themselves. The Queens Majesty hath, besides, ready upon all occasions an Army of fifteen thousand near to her own person. The Queen of *Scots* is removed from

Sir William Cecil, to Sir Henry Norris.

Tutbery to *Coventry*, where attends on her the Earls of *Shrewsbury*, and *Huntington*. Under the Conduct of the Army of the Southern parts is the Viscount *Hereford*, with the power of *Staffordshire*, very well appointed; and divers Gentlemen of credit and service of the Court, and other places, of themselves, are gone thither to serve under the said Lieutenants.

In company with those said Rebels are not many Gentlemen of name, but *Norton* an old man, who carryeth the Cross, *Markinfield*, *Swynbourne*, and an Uncle of the Earl of *Westmerland*, named *Christopher Nevill*; all the Realm, and all the Nobility, besides these only two Rebels, are as obedient as ever they were, and surely so like to be, whatsoever our ill-willers may report.

2 *Novemb.* 1569.

Yours assured,
W. Cecil.

To the right honorable, Sir Henry Norris *Knight*, the Queens Majesties Ambassador, Resident in France.

SIR,

✱ I Have forborn these two or three days to write unto you, because I could not by occasion of some sickness use my own hand, and also because I would not detain here any longer this bearer Mr. *Rogers*, who is both serviceable for you, and desirous to be returned thither. I have thought good to dispatch him towards you, who can inform you of such news as we have here; and that he may the better do it, I have imparted to him such things as I think meet for you to know; and for that I am not well able at present to write any more, I trust you will be for this time satisfied with such declaration as this bearer shall make unto you. Thus fare you heartily well, From *Windsor* the 10. *Nov.* 1569.

I think long to hear from you, because I have not received any letters from you since the tenth of the last month, which *D'amons* brought; but I doubt not but some of yours be on the way, whereby we may understand how things pass there. Since the writing hereof, came yesterday your Lackquey with letters of the   of   wherein you make mention that *Lodowick* the Count *Nassau* should be slain, which I trust is not so, because of other letters which I have seen, that came hither by the way of *Rochell*, that testifie nothing of his death, but great praise of his service, the day of the battle. At this present I am unable to write by reason of some sickness, as this bearer can report. Herewith I send you a copy in writing of such things as after long debate betwixt the *French* Ambassador and us hath been here accorded; which I wish may be as well performed on their part as they have promised. I pray you, Sir, commend me to my good Lady, and your Sons.

Yours assuredly,
W. Cecil.

12. *Novemb.* at night.

To the right honorable, Sir Henry Norris *Knight*, the Queens Majesties Ambassador, Resident in France.

SIR,

✱ Though I think this bringer will deliver you my letter, yet I know not with what readiness he will impart to you our state here; and therefore have thought good to advertise you thus much, that, thanked be God, our Northern Rebellion is fallen flat to the ground and scattered away. The Earls are fled into *Northumberland*, seeking all ways to escape, but they are roundly pursued; Sir *John Forster* and Sir *Henry Percy* in one company, my Lord of *Sussex* in another. The 16. hereof they broke up their sorry Army, and the 18. they entred into *Northumberland*, the 19. into the Mountains, they scattered all their Footmen, willing them to shift for themselves; and of a thousand Horsemen there fled but five hundred. By this time they be fewer, and I trust either taken or fled into *Scotland*, where the Earl of *Murray* is in good readiness, to chase them to their ruine; yesternight came Mr. *Madder*; and upon the next letters from my Lord of *Sussex*, I will send away *Crips* or some other. The Queens Majesty hath had a notable Tryal of her whole Realm, and subjects, in this time, wherein she hath had service readily of all sorts, without respect of Religion.

Yours assuredly,
W. Cecil.

Windsor, 24. *Decemb.*

To the right honorable, Sir Henry Norris *Knight*, the Queens Majesties Ambassador, Resident in France.

SIR,

✱ I Have long time determined to send away this bearer, your servant, *Henry Crips*, but my delay hath grown of a desire that I had to see some good issue of this Rebellion, which as it hath had a time of declination, and is now suppressed; so could I not well before this

time

Sir William Cecil, to Sir Henry Norris.

time send this bearer away, who now bringeth her Majesties letters unto you, by which you shall understand how her pleasure is, that you should impart the events thereof in that Court; and indeed hitherto we have no certain and manifest proofs that it should have any other ground, but as it is expressed in her Majesties letters; nevertheless, we have discovered some tokens, and we hear of some words uttered by the Earl of *Northumberland*, that maketh us to think this Rebellion had more Branches, both of our own and strangers, then did appear; and I trust the same will be found out, though, perchance, when all are known in secret manner, all may not be notified. Of all other Occurrents, I know your Son, Mr. *William*, and other your servants here doth advertise you; and therefore I pray you to bear with my shortness, for I am almost smothered with business. We look to hear of the apprehension of more of the Rebels; I send you extracts of our letters out of the North, as of late time they have come.

Windsor-Castle, 7. Jan. 1569.
To the right honorable, Sir Henry Norris Knight, the Queens, &c.
                                      Yours assuredly,
                                            W. Cecil.

Advertisements from Lyexham, 22. Decemb. 1569.

* THe two Rebellious Rebels went into *Liddesdale* in *Scotland* yesternight, where *Martin Elwood*, and others, that have given pledges to the Regent of *Scotland*, did raise their forces against them; being conducted by black *Ormeston*, an Out-law of *Scotland*, that was a principal murtherer of the King of *Scots*, where the fight was offered, and both parties alighted from their horses; and in the end, *Elwood* said to *Ormeston*, he would be sorry to enter deadly feud with him by bloodshed; but he would charge him and the rest before the Regent, for keeping of the Rebels; and if he did not put them out of the Country, the next day he would do his worst against them; whereupon the two Earls were driven to leave *Liddesdale*, and to flye to one of the *Armestronges* a Scot upon the batable on the borders between *Liddesdale* and *England*; the same day the *Liddesdale* men stole the horses of the Countess of *Northumberland*, and her two women, and ten others of their Company; so as the Earls being gone, the Lady of *Northumberland* was left there on foot at *John* of the Sides house in a Cottage, not to be compared to many a Dog-kennel in *England*, at their departing from her, they went not above fifty horse, and the Earl of *Westmerland*, to be the more unknown, changed his Coat of Plate and sword with *John* of the Sides, and departed like a *Scotish* Borderer. The rest of the Rebels are partly taken in the West Borders of *England*, and partly spoiled by the *English* and *Scotish* Borderers.

By letters of the 24.

The Rebels be driven to change their names, their Horses and apparel, and to ride like *Liddesdale* men. The Regent of *Scotland* will be this night upon the Borders of *Liddesdale*. The Earl of *Cumberland*, the Lord *Scroop*, and Mr. *Leonard Dacre* have shewed themselves very Honorable and diligent in their service at the Rebels entring into the West Marches; and upon the scaling of the Rebels, there be great numbers of them taken there.

There be in every of the Marches against *Scotland* sundry Bands of Horsemen, and shot laid, it they shall enter into the Realm again.

By letters of the last of December.

The Regent of *Scotland* is gone from *Jedworth* to *Edenburgh*, and hath taken the Earl of *Northumberland*, and six of his men with him. Before his departure from *Jedworth* he sent for the Gentlemen of *Tividale*, to come before him, where all came saving the Lord of *Fernehurst*, and the Lord of *Bucklugh*, whereupon the Regent rode towards them, but they hearing thereof suddainly rode away. *Robert Collingwood*, *Ralph Swynton*, with others of their company, were taken in East *Tividale*, and delivered to the Regent, who re-delivered them to their takers, and charged them for their safe keeping, *Egremont Ratcliff* with certain with him remain about *Liddesdale*. And it is thought the Countess of *Northumberland*, the Earl of *Westmerland*, *Norten*, *Markenfield*, *Swynborne*, and *Tempest*, are removed out *Liddesdale* to the Lords of *Fernhurst* and *Bucklugh*.

SIR,

* I Doubt not but the report of the cruel murther of the Regent in *Scotland* will be diversly reported in those parts; and diversly also received, by some with gladness, and by some with grief, as I am sure it shall be of you; the manner of it was thus (as I have been advertised) the 22. of the last moneth, the Regent coming thorough the Town of *Lithgo*, which is in the midway between *Sterling* and *Edenburgh*, having in his company about a hundred persons, was stricken with a Courrier about the Navell, with the Pellet coming out about his Hucklebone, which also slew a horse behinde him; and of this wound he dyed the next day afterward within night; the murtherer was one *Hambleton* of *Bothwell-Hall*, who lay secretly in a house to attempt this mischief, having shut the doors towards the street in such sort, as no man could enter on the foreside to take him; and so he escaped on the backside, where he had a horse to serve his turn, although he was pursued; which is like to follow miserably to that Land, I dare not judge; but do fear that the death of so good a man will prove *Initium malorum*. At the writing hereof, I know not what is done or intended; but some write from thence, That the Earls of *Marr* and *Morton*, and other friends to the young King, are come to *Edinburgh*, and do in the Kings name preserve the State, and do purpose to have the Land ruled by four Regents; and one to be a Lieutenant for the wars to execute their directions; a matter more probable in talk than in effect; as I shall hereafter understand more, so will I write, It hapned that at this time, Sir *Henry Gates*, and the Marshal of *Berwick* were at *Edinburgh*, having been at *Sterling* with the Regent, the Fryday before, for the demanding in the Queens Majesties name, of the Earl of *Northumberland*, and other the Rebels, and by direction of the Regent they attended at *Edinburgh* for answer to be given the day of his death, which now is; as our Lawyers call it, *fine die*. Mr. *Randolph* went from hence towards *Scotland*, the 29. upon knowledge of the hurt, and doubt of his life. The same day also came *Montluct* to her Majesties presence with the *French* Ambassador, bringing his letters dated the 27. of *December*, at which time I think they understood not of the stay of our Rebellion. The sum of *Montluets* message consisted upon these two heads, request for restitution, and liberty of the Queen of *Scots*, and a declaration of the Kings inclination to peace with his subjects, and their disguising with him by treating and suing for peace, and yet amassing of new Forces in *Almaine*, and seeking also to surprise the Kings Towns, as *Burdeaux*, and other like, whereupon the King requireth the Queens Majesty not to favor his Rebels if they should seek any further succours from hence, as they have done, as persons unworthy of any favor. They have made great instance to be answered for the first matter, but the Queens Majesty hath hitherto deferred them; but I think upon Munday next they shall have audience. I forgat to shew you, that in the request for the Queen of *Scots*, he desired liberty to go to her, and from thence to pass into *Scotland*, which thing would not be granted unto him. Upon the death of the Regent, the Earl of *Sussex* and Mr. *Sadler* were admonished to stay there, for that it was thought good that Mr. *Sadler* should have gone from thence into *Scotland*; but they both being come upon former licence near the City on the way, upon desire to see her Majesty, came hither yesterday unlooked for; and although in the beginning of this Northern Rebellion her Majesty sometimes uttered some misliking of the Earl, yet this day she meaning to deal very Princely with him, in presence of her Council, charged him with such things as she had heard, to cause her misliking, without any note of mistrust towards him for his fidelity; whereupon, he did with such humbleness, wisdom, plainness, and dexterity, answer her Majesty, as both she and all the rest were fully satisfied, and he adjudged by good proofs to have served in all this time faithfully, stoutly, and so circumspectly, as it manifestly appeareth, that if he had not so used himself in the beginning, the whole North part had entred into the Rebellion.

Usque ad 3. *Febr*.

We have now letters out of *Scotland*, that the Nobility which favoreth the young King have assembled themselves, and made a reconciliation of divers persons that had particular quarrels one against another; and as they pretend, they will all joyn firmly in the revenge of the Murther, and defence of their King; the Lord *Grange*, who keepeth the Castle of *Edenburgh*, is reconciled to the Earl *Morton*, and become one of this Bonde, and so doth *Liddington* also offer to be another. The Duke of *Chastilherault* is streighter kept then he was before; and it is commonly reported, that the *Hambletons* were the workers of this murther; thus much being known of certain, that the murtherer was a neer kinsman of the Dukes; and that the Peece wherewith he murthered the Regent, and the spare horses whereupon he escaped, did all belong to the Abbot of *Arbroth*, the Dukes second Son, and the murtherer was received into *Hambleton* the Dukes house; all which, I trust, God will see revenged. The Rebellion moved in the West parts of *Ireland* this last Summer, being also cherished with comfort out of *Spaine*, is fully suppressed; and the Country reduced to such quietness and obedience, as the like hath not been in those parts these many yeers, the heads being all taken and reduced to obedience, saving one only, named *James Fitz Maurice*, who wandreth in the deserts without any succor, making means to be received to mercy, but he is of so little value, as it is refused unto him. For your own revocation from thence, I am not unmindful, but have attempted the same; and so mean to continue it, as I hope you shall shortly receive comfort.

Usque

Sir William Cecil, to Sir Henry Norris.

Usque ad 5. Febr.

This day, the 6 of *Febr.* the *French* Ambaſſador came with *Montlovet* to her Majeſty, to require anſwer to their demands, which were three; Firſt, to have the Queen of *Scots* delivered and reſtored; Secondly, that *Montlovet* might repair to the Queen of *Scots*; Thirdly, that he might repair into *Scotland*: To all theſe her Majeſty, having her whole Council in her preſence, That, for the firſt, ſhe ſaid, ſhe had uſed the Queen of *Scots* with more honor and favor, then any Prince, having like cauſe, would have done; and though ſhe was not bound to make account to any Prince of her doings, yet ſhe would impart to the King, her good brother, ſome reaſonable conſideration of her doings; and ſo ſhe ended her anſwer to that. The other two requeſts depended ſo upon the firſt, as ſhe ſaid ſhe could not accord the eunto; and ſo though ſhe uſed good loving ſpeech to ſatisfie him, yet in brief they departed without obtaining their requeſts, as ſhortly you ſhall underſtand more at length by the next Meſſenger, and letters, which in this behalf ſhall be ſent unto you. We hear that two Ships of war of St. *Malloes*, under the conduct of the Lord *Flemings* brother, arrived in *Don Brittons Frith* the tenth of *January*, and have, as I think, victualled the Caſtle of *Don Britton*, whereof will follow ſome further annoyance to *Scotland*. And thus I am forced to end for the preſent, by reaſon of multitude of other affairs. *Yours aſſuredly,*

Hampton-Court, Feb. 7. 1569.   W. Cecil.

To the right honorable, Sir Henry Norris Knight, the Queens Majeſties Ambaſſador, Reſident with the French King.

SIR,

* AFter all the other letters in this Packet were ſealed up, your honeſt ſervant, Mr. *Rogers*, arrived here with your letters; of the contents whereof, concerning the crazed ſhaken Treaty of peace betwixt the King and his ſubjects, I had plainly heard four or five days paſt from *Rochel*. Your intelligences accord with the like, as I have received lately from *Rochel*; and as you do expreſs to us the dangerous practiſes of our Adverſaries here, ſo I aſſure you the ſame are not by Councellors here neglected, although I can give no aſſurance how they ſhall be avoided; and yet I would not doubt, but with Gods goodneſs, their whole deſigns ſhould prove fruſtrate if our Councels might take place. I have named to the Queens Majeſty two to be your ſucceſſors, both to be well liked, if their livelihoods were anſwerable to their other qualities; the one is Mr. *Francis Walſingham*, the other is Mr. *Hen. Killigrew*, who is indeed in livelihood much inferior. If I can procure that either of them, or ſome other, might relieve you, I aſſure you there ſhall not lack any good will in me.

Hampton-Court, 7. Febr. 1569.   *Yours aſſuredly,*
  W. Cecil.

To the right honourable, Sir Henry Norris Knight, the Queens Majeſties Ambaſſador, Reſident in France.

SIR,

* YOur laſt letters are thus come to my hands; *Crips* came with thoſe of yours the 9. then *Neal* with thoſe of the 25. of the laſt month, and yeſterday came the *French* Ambaſſadors Secretary with thoſe of the firſt of *March*; by all which is manifeſt the inward natural care that you take for the Queens Majeſty, and therein her Highneſs accepteth your zeal and duty moſt thankfully. And yet, I know not by what means, her Majeſty is not much troubled with the opinion of danger; neverthelesſ, I and others cannot be but greatly fearful for her, and do, and will do, that in us may lye to underſtand, thorough Gods aſſiſtance, the attempts; as for ⌧ ☉ D many here, and the moſt of this Council think the peril no leſs, but rather greater, if ♀ ♃ D foraſmuch ſhould ⊢ ☉ 7: ♉ 9: ♎ li ⌧. Since the death of the Regent, the Borderers have maintained our Rebels, and invaded *England*; wherefore for which purpoſe my Lord of *Suſſex* is now ordered with an Army to invade them and make revenge; whereof the *Scots* hearing do make all means they can to be reconciled, but they muſt feel the ſword and the fire-brand; and becauſe I will end my letter, I will deliver to this bearer a ſhort memorial of words to ſerve him for informing of you of the things of our State; and ſo with my moſt hearty commendations, I end, being ſorry that as yet I cannot perfect my intent for your return.   *Your aſſured friend,*
  W. Cecil.

Hampton-Court, 22. March, 1569.
To the right honorable, Sir Henry Norris Knight, the Queens Majeſties Ambaſſador, Reſident in France.

Sir William Cecil, to Sir Henry Norris.

SI',
*BY the Queens Majesties long letter you shall perceive her Majesties meaning in such sort, as I need not to repeat or enlarge the same; and the sooner that her Majesty may have answer hereof, the better she will be content, especially if the answer shall be good.

I send to you the Copies of the advertisements of my Lord of Sussex journey into Scotland the 17. of April, and returning the 22. his Lordship entred the 27. to besiege (as I think) Hume Castle; for the same hath been the receptacle of all the Rebels; but at the writing hereof, I am not ascertained what his Lordship hath done. Of late the Bishop of Ross caused one of his servants secretly to procure the printing of a Book in English, whereof before eight leaves could be finished, intelligence was had; which Book tendeth to set forth to the world, that the Queen of Scots was not guilty of her husbands death, a parable in many mens opinion; next, that she is a lawful heir to the Crown, and herewith such reasons inserted as make unsound conclusions for the Queens Majesties present state. Besides this, a notable lye is there uttered, That all the noblemen that heard her cause did judge her innocent; and therefore made suite to her Majesty, that she might marry with my Lord of Norfolk. With these and such like enterprises, her Majesty hath been grieved with the said Bishop, whereupon she hath the longer kept him from her presence; but I think he will be spoken withall to morrow, and so within two or three days, it is likely, he shall have access to her Majesty. The Secretary in Scotland hath so discovered himself for the Queen of Scots, as he is the instrument to increase her party, having such credit with Grange, who keepeth Edenburgh Castle, as the Duke of Chastilherault, the Lord Herries, &c. are now at liberty, and thereby the party for the King is diminished, you can judge what is ment to be done; and I wish her Majesty to take such a way herein, as may preserve her estate, the device and execution whereof is found, upon consultation, very difficult; and yet in all evils the least is to be chosen. My Lord of Worcester and my Lord of Huntington are chosen Knights of the Order. I cannot procure any resolution for your revocation, untill it may be seen what will fall out there of the war betwixt the King and his subjects, whereof daily there is expectation of some issue; and the French Ambassador doth constantly affirm that the peace shall follow: And so I end.

Hampton-Court, 4. May, 1570.   Yours assuredly,
To the right honorable, Sir Henry Norris Knight, the   W. Cecil.
Queens Majesties Ambassador, Resident with the French King.

A Note of a Journey into Tividale *by the Earl* Sussex, *her Majesties Lieutenant in the North, begun the* 17. *of* April, 1570. *and ending the* 22. *of the same.*

*THe 17. of April, 1570. the Earl of Sussex, and the Lord Hunsdon, Governor of Berwick, with all the Garrisons and power of the East Marches, came to Warke, and entered into Tividale in Scotland the 18. at the break of the day, and burnt all Castles and Towns as they went, untill they came to the Castle of Moss, standing in a strong Marsh, and belonging to the Lord of Fernhurst, which they burnt and razed, and so burnt the Country untill they came to Craling. The same day, Sir John Foster, with all the Garrisons and force of the middle marches, entred into Tividale and Expesgate head 16. miles from Warke, and so burnt all the Country, untill they came to a strong Castle, called   in the possession of the mother of the Lord of Fernhurst, which he burnt and razed, and so burnt all other Castles and Towns, untill he came to Craling, where both Companies met, and so went up the River of Tivit, and burnt and threw down all the Castles and Towns upon that River, untill they came to Jedworth, where they lodged.

This day the Lord of Chesford, Warden of the middle marches, with the principal men of his kinde, who had never in person received the Rebels, nor invaded England, and yet had evil men that had done both, came in to the Lord Lieutenant, and submitted himself, and offered to abide order for his mens offences, whereupon he was received as a friend, and he and all his were free from any hurt.

The 19. the Army was divided into two parts, whereof the one did pass the River of Tivit, and burnt and razed the Castle of Fernhurst, and all other Castles and Towns of the Lord of Fernhurst, Huuthill, and Bederoll, and so passed on to Minte; and the other part of the Army burnt in like sort on the other side of the River Tivit, untill he came to Hawick, where it was intended to have lodged that night, for that the Bailiffs had the same morning offered to
receive

Sir William Cecil, to Sir Henry Norris.

receive the Army, and had therefore their Town assured; but at the coming thither of the Army, they had unthetched their houses, and burnt the Thetch in the streets, and were all fled, so as no person could well enter for smoak, which caused lack of victuals, lodging, and horsemeats; and therefore the fire began by themselves in the Straw burnt the whole Town, after saving *Donn Lamorecks* Castle, which for his sake was spared, and all the goods of the Town in it. The 20. the Army went to *Branshaw*, the Lord of *Buckleughs* house, which was wholly overthrown with Powder, and there divided and burnt, on the North the River of *Tivies*, more into the inland, all the Castles and Towns in that Country, which belonged wholly to the Lord of *Bucklough* and his kinsmen, and returned that night to *Jedworth*. The 21. the Army divided, and one part went to the River of *Bowbeat*, and burnt all on both sides of that River; and the other part went to the River of *Caile*, and burnt all on both sides of the River, and met neer to *Kelsam*, where the Lord Lieutenant lodged that night of purpose to beset *Hume* Castle in the night, and the Lord *Hunsdon* and the other part went to *Warke*, to bring the Ordnance thence in the morning, which was disappointed by the negligence of such as were left in charge, who suffered the carriage horses to return after the Ordnance was brought thither; so as for lack of horses to draw the Ordnance, the Army was forced to return to *Bernwick* the 22. All which time there was never any shew of resistance. And the same time the Lord *Scroope* entred *Scotland*, from the West Marches, the 18, &c. During which time the Marches in all places were so guarded, as the *Scots* that did not shew themselves to offer fight in the field, durst not offer to enter into *England*; so as in the absence of the Army there was not one house burnt, nor own Cow taken in *England*; and it is conceived by such as know the enemies part of *Tividale*, that there is razed, overthrown, and burnt in this journey, above fifty strong Castles and Piles, and above 300 Villages; so as there be few in that Country that have received the Rebels, or invaded *England*, that have either Castle for themselves, or houses for their Tenants, besides the loss and spoils of their other goods, wherein nothing is reckoned of that was done in the other parts by the Lord *Scroope*, for that it was not done within the County of *Tividale*, &c.

The Rode of the Lord Scroope, *Warden of the West marches of* England, *into* Scotland.

- Who the 17. of *April* at ten of the clock at night, with three thousand Horse and Foot, came to *Ellesingham* on the Wednesday at night, and burned that Town in the morning, being from *Carlile* twenty miles.

On Thursday he burned; besides *Hoddom* the *Maymes*, the Town and all the houses, which is the Lord *Herryes*, and from *Carlile* sixteen miles.

That day they burned *Trayle-trow*, which is the Lord *Maxwells*, from *Carlile* 16. miles.

They burned the Town of *Reywell*, which is the Lord *Coplands*, and the Lord *Homeyns*, from *Carlile* eighteen miles.

They burned the house of *Copewell*, and the Demesne of the Lord *Coplands*, from *Carlile* nineteen miles.

They burned the Town of *Blackshieve*, which is the Lord *Maxwells*, from *Carlile* 20. miles.

Item, The Town of *Sherrington*, of the same, twenty miles.

Item, The blank end of the same Lords, twenty miles.

Item, The Town of *Lowzwood* of the same Lords, twenty miles.

Goods taken the same Rode, one thousand Neat, and one thousand Sheep and Goats.

Of the *Scots*, are taken one hundred Horsmen, within a mile of *Dunnscrest*. Some say that *Swynborne* is taken.

SIR,

* BY letters from my Lords of *Sussex* and *Hunsdon* of the 29. of *April*, it is advertised that the Castle of *Hume* being besieged by them, and the Battery laid the 27. of *April*, the day following the Captain sent out a Trumpet to desire a Parlie, which was granted; the Castle desired licence to send a Messenger to the Lord *Hume* to know his pleasure what they should do, whereupon it was agreed a Messenger should pass; and one was sent with him to see that delay should be used; the Messenger at his return brought Commission from the Lord *Hume* to deliver the Castle, simply, without condition, trusting to their Honors for a favourable dealing with his men; whereupon the Castle was received, and all the Armor and Weapons, and the people licenced to depart without Bag or Baggage; and now the same remaineth newly fortified to the Queens Majesties charge, more stronger then it was before, to the intent the Rebels may not have their refuge thither as they had before. By other letters of the first of *May* from my Lord of *Sussex*, it is advertised, that the most part of the March of East *Tividale*, *Esdale*, *Ewesdale*, *Wawcopdale*, and other parts upon the Borders from the East to the

West

Sir William Cecil, to Sir Henry Norris.

West Seas, whom their continuance of obedience to their King, desire the Amity betwixt both Realms, offer to spend their lives in the resisting of any Forreign power that shall offer the disturbance of either; refuse dependence upon the *French*; offer to depend upon the Queens Majestie; and in their actions have refused to receive the Rebels, or to assist the invaders of *England*, the like whereof all others do offer that acknowledge that authority. The contrary part openly receive the Rebels, maintain the invaders of *England*, share in their actions and ill meaning to *England*, and seek dependence and maintenance of the *French*. The Earls of *Morton*, *Murray*, and *Glincarne*, with others of the Kings Council, prepared to be at *Edinburgh* the 29. of the last, whereupon the Duke of *Chastilheranlt* and *Huntley* went to *Lithgo* the 28. to stop their meeting; and the 26. *Morton* went out of *Edenburgh* with a thousand men to meet the other Earls a By-way, and so came together that night to *Edinburgh* with all their Forces, or to fight for it; in which time the Lords of *Hume* and *Liddington* be entred the Castle with *Grange*; so as it is likely they will try shortly by the sword which side shall have the Authority.
                                                             W. Cecil,

* IT may please you to be advertised, according to my Lord Lieutenants direction, I entered into *Scotland* on Tuesday at night last, the 18. of this *April*, and on Wednesday at night encamped at *Heclesenghham*, within *Hoddom*, distant from *Carlile* 18. miles, and within *Scotland* 12. miles; and on Thursday in the morning I sent forth *Simon Musgrave*, appointed by me as General of the Horsemen, to burn and spoile the Country, and to meet me at a place called *Cambretreys*, and the said *Simon* burnt the Towns of *Hoddome* and the *Maynes*, *Treltrow*, *Revel* and *Calpoole*, the Town of *Blackshaw Sherrington*, the Banck end, within three miles of *Drumfriese*, *Lowgher*, and *Lowgherwood*, and *Hecklsengham*, which Towns were of the Lands of the Lord *Herryes* and *Maxwell*, the Lord of *Cockpoole*, and the Lord of *Helmends*; and as the said *Simon* and his company came to old *Cockpool*, there was the Lord *Maxwell* with his Forces, and the Inhabitants of *Drumfriese* assembled, and skirmished with the Couriers, and compelled them to return unto the said *Simon*; and then the said *Simon* marched unto the Town of *Blackshaw* with his Company, where the Lord *Maxwell* was in order, and his Forces; and the said *Simon* and *Fargus Graime*, with the number of a hundred Horsemen, did give the charge upon the said Lord *Maxwell*, and made him flee, and his Company also; In which fight there were a hundred prisoners taken, whereof the principal was the Alderman of *Drumfriese*, and 16. of the Burgesses thereof, the rest were Footmen; the chase was followed within one mile of *Drumfriese*; after which conflict, the said *Simon* returned to *Blackshaw* aforesaid, and burnt it, and seised a great number of Cattle, and delivered the same unto certain Gentlemen and others to convey unto me; and he, the said *Simon*, Rode with a hundred Horsemen to burn the Banck end *Lowgher* and *Lowgherwood*; and as the said Gentlmen, with their Company, came to a streight place neer unto Old-*Cockpool*, the said Lord *Maxwell*, the Lord *Carlile*, the Lords of *Holme-ends*, *Closburne Lorge*, *Hempsfeild Cowhill*, and *Tenoll*, with the number of four hundred horsemen, and six hundred footmen, charged them very sore, and forced them to alight and draw their company to a strong place, to abide the charge of their enemies; and so they remained untill the said *Simon* came unto them, and alighted, and put his Company in Order, and set his Horses between his Company and the Sea, and so stood in order to receive the enemy; and in this sort continued charging, and receiving their charges, the space of three hours, I being at *Cambretreys*, aforesaid, a place before appointed between me and the said *Simon* for his relief (being distant from him three miles) understanding of some distress sent my Band of Horsmen, with my brother *Edward Scroope*, and a hundred and fifty shot with Mr. *Awdley*, and Mr. *Herbert*, to their relief; and the said *Simon*, upon the coming of the said Band of horsemen and Shot, gave the enemies the charge with all his Forces, whereupon they fled; in which flight there was taken a hundred prisoners, whereof some were of the petty Lords of the Country; but the Lord *Maxwell*, the Lord *Carlile*, the Lord *Johnson*, and the rest before named, escaped by the strength of the Lord of *Cockpools* house, and a great Wood, and a Mauress that was neer there adjoyning; and so the said *Simon* repaired to me with his Company, and so we returned home. And thus, for this time, I commit you to the Almighty.   *Yours assured to command*,
   Carlile, 21. April, 1570.   *Postscript.*   H. Scroop.

Drumlangricks servants and Tenants, whom I had given charge that they should not be dealt withall, for that he favored the Kings faction, and the Queens Majesties, were as cruel against us as any others. Sir, I have written to my Lord Lieutenant for 500. men, but for fourteen dayes; and with them, I will undertake to march to *Drumfriese*, and lye in that Town, and burn and spoil it, if the Queen Majesties think it good; for the open receipt of her Majesties Rebels is there manifest.   SIR,

SIR.

* MY leisure serveth me, as I was wont to have it; all my time at command of others, and none for my self, and little for my private friends. By the Queens Majesties Letters you may perceive the state of things here: God send her Majesty a good issue of this *Scotish* matter, whereinto the entry is easie, but the passage within doubtfull, and I fear the end will be monstrous.

By your Letters of late time, it hath seemed, that your opinion was, for the Queens Majesty to be delivered of the *Scotish* Queen: But, surely, few here amongst us conceive it feasible, with surety.

My Lord of *Sussex* useth his charge very honourably, and circumspectly, upon the Frontiers; where indeed he hath made revenge, and that onely almost upon the guilty.

I do send you, herewith, a printed thing, or two, sent me from *Scotland*; and so take my leave, wishing, for your own sake, that peace might be seen there, so as you might bring it; for which purpose, I trust, surely, her Majesty will send one for you.

May 23. 1570.
Yours most assured,
W. Cecill.

To the Right Honourable, Sir Henry Norris Knight, the Queens Majesties Embassador, Resident in France.

SIR,

* THis Bearer came hither with good speed. I do send you, herewith, a Note of my Lord of *Sussex* his last Letters from *Berwick*: I do also send you, in writing, the Copy of that which the *French* Embassadour lately sent thither, containing the sum of that which lately passed here betwixt the Queens Majesty and him, wherein, truly, he hath not much differed from that which was accorded.

The Bishop of *Rosse* departed, on Friday last, to the *Scotish* Queen, to deal with her, that some of her part might come hither out of *Scotland*, to treat of her causes, and that Arms might cease on both sides.

Since his going thither, the Queens Majesty understandeth of a practice that he had, two days before his departure, with a Noble-man of this Realm, being a professed Papist, contrary to his manner of dealing with the Queens Majesty: whereupon, her Majesty is not a little moved against him; and therefore, I think, she will not deal with him at his return.

We look daily that peace will there be made, though we see not how it shall continue; But, I trust, thereby you shall be revoked, and, I think, Mr. *Walsingham* shall come in your place. I have no more at this present.

I received yesterday a Letter from *Paris*, of the 19th of *May*; but I did, before that, receive another of the 24th.

Hampton-Court, June 8. 1570.
Yours assuredly,
W. Cecill.

To the Right Honourable, Sir Henry Norris, Knight, the Queens Majesties Embassador, Resident in France.

By Letters from Berwick, *June* 3.

THe Marshal of *Berwick*, being at *Edenburgh* with certain Forces, dealt with the Earls of *Grange* and *Liddington*, to procure a surcease of Arms; which taking no effect, he went, with the Noble-men of *Scotland* that joyned with him, to *Glasco*, from whence the Duke, and his associates, fled, upon their setting forth. From thence the Marshal sent to the Bishop of *S. Andrews*, and the Lords who were in *Dumbarton* Castle, to parley with them, to procure an abstinence of Arms; who appointed to meet them the next day, at a Village half way betwixt *Glasco* and *Dumbarton*: where missing them at the time appointed, went neerer to *Dumbarton*, whereof he sent them word; and thereupon they returned his messengers, and appointed to meet and speak with him out of the Castle, so as he would bring but one or two with him, and to put away his Companie: And assoon as he had so done, and that he was within their shott, they sent him word, to look to himself, and that they would not come to him; and as he turned his Horse, divers Harquebusiers

A 2   laid

Sir William Cecill, to Sir Henry Norris.

laid for the purpose, shot at him, and they discharged a Falcon at him out of the Castle, but he escaped without hurt. Hereupon, the Noble-men which were with him burnt the Countrey thereabouts that belonged to the *Hamiltons*, burnt the Town of *Hamilton*, and rized the Castle of *Hamilton*, and two other principal Houses of the said Duke's, one in *Lithgo*, and another called *Kennel*; they have also thrown down the Abbot of *Kilwrenings* House, and, in effect, all the principal Houses of the *Hamiltons*, and have dealt with no other persons, but with an *Hamilton*; and so our Marshal is returned to *Berwick*, &c.

SIR,

Yesterday did *Crips* arrive, with your Letters from *Argenton*; and two days before, came *Rogers*.

The Queens Majestie takes the Kings answer doubtfull, for his sending of Forces into *Scotland*; and therefore hath caused the *French* Embassadour to understand, and to advertise the King, That if the King will send Forces thither, she will take her self free from her promise of delivering the Queen of *Scots*: of which matter, I think, he will advertise the King; and as you have occasion, you may take knowledge thereof. For already her Majestie hath revoked her Forces out of *Scotland*, leaving onely in *Hume*, and *Fast-Castle*, a small Garrison, where our Rebels were most maintained, when they invaded *England*, until her Majestie may have some amends for her Subjects losses.

My Lord of *Sussex* hath fully avenged their wrongs; but yet our people have not recompence.

Mr. *Drury*, the Marshal, with a thousand Foot, and four hundred Horse, hath so plagued the *Hamiltons*, as they never had such losses in all the wars betwixt *England* and *Scotland* these forty years.

The Queens Majestie hath hurt her foot, that she is constrained to keep her Bed-chamber; and therefore the *French* Embassador could not yesterday have Audience when he required, but is willed to write that he hath to say. I am sorry that your servants, when they come, tarry so long here as they do; for it is not my fault. And so I end,

Oatlands, June 22.   Yours assuredly,
1570.   W. Cecill.

Post-script.

The Earl of *Southampton* lately being known to have met, in *Lambeth*-Marsh, with the Bishop of *Ross*, is, for his foolish audacity, committed to the Sheriff of *London*, closely to be there kept. The fond Lord *Morley*, without any cause offered him, is gone, like a Noddy, to *Lorrein*.

SIR,

I Stayed this Bearer two days longer then first I intended, because the *French* Embassador required Audience, affirming, That he had Answer from the *French* King, wherewith the Queens Majesty would be satisfied. And yesterday he was here, and shewed her Majesty the *French* Kings Letters to him; and thereof gave her Majesty a Copy, which I have; and do send to you herewith an extract of a clause tending to the matter, the Letter being of it self long, and full of good words, purporting his desire to have the *Scotish* Queen restored, and Concord established betwixt the two Queens. The Letter is dated the 10 of *June*; and I note, that your Letter is dated the 15th. And by his foresaid Letter, the King writeth, That he will, within two days, speak with you at *Alanson*.

Now how the Kings promise will be kept, a short time will declare; or how, if he break it, there shall be some cavillations found, wherein, I doubt, that they will seek illusions, for that we do yet keep *Hume*-Castle, and *Fast*-Castle, which are kept with not past fourscore men; and being the Houses of the Lord *Hume*, the Warden, who aided our Rebels with his Forces to invade, burn, and spoil *England*, and therefore is, by the Laws of the Borders, answerable to the Subjects of *England*: it is reason they be kept, until he will return, or authorize some for him, to make answer, or to take order with the Complainants; which being done, the Queens Majesty will readily restore them. Thus much I have thought meet to impart.

Oatlands, June 25. 1570.   Yours assuredly,
    W. Cecill.

To the Right Honourable, Sir Henry Norris Knight, the
    Queens Majesties Embassador, Resident in France.

SIR,

*I Am thrown into a Maze at this time, that I know not how to walk from dangers. Sir *Walter Mildmay*, and I, are sent to the *Scotish* Queen, as by the Queens Majesties Letters you may see : God be our guide ; for neither of us like the Message.

I trust, at my return, when Mr. *Walsingham* shall be returned, to help you home. Your sufficient is sufficient to impart unto you all our occurrents : And so I end, from

Reading, Septemb. 26. 1570.

Your assured Friend,
W. Cecill.

To the Right Honourable, Sir Henry Norris, *Knight, the Queens Majesties Embassador, Resident in* France.

Sir Edward Cecill, to Mr. Secretary Conway.

My very good Lord,

IT hath pleased your Lordship to write me three Letters lately : the one, a particular List of Officers, that should be sent from hence ; the second, for Mr. *Hopton* ; the third, an acknowledgment onely of the receipt of my Letter to your Lordship. The first I have put in execution, and have written to your son, Sir *Edward Conway*, to give them all notice of your Lordships care of them ; and to let them know, how welcome any one shall be to me, that you think fit to be imployed. For one of them, called Ensign *Rainsford*, I had set him down, because I received your Lordships direction from himself. For Mr. *Hopton*, I have written unto him, according to your desire, with your Letter inclosed. Concerning the last, I give your Lordship many humble thanks, for having expressed the acceptance by your answer. Touching your business here, the State hath been as contrary to us, as the wind : For, though they see a great action likely to be performed to their own good, with little cost to themselves ; yet they desire to be so wise, as to make benefit both ways, and not to balk any advantage, which makes them stand so stiff upon the denying of us Officers and Souldiers by election, and will yield to send none but whole companies, onely to abate so much upon the repartitions. But Sir *William St. Leiger*, and I, have utterly refused their offer, as a Proposition against his Majesties service : for, by this ignorant Winter-war our Companies are grown half new men, having lost most of our old ; and of those new men; the half are sick besides ; so that his Majestie should be beholden to them, rather for names, then men : And again, for the Officers, and Souldiers, it is like they should be most of them the worst in the Regiment from whence they are to come : Whereas, if we might have had those Officers we made choice of, which were but ten Captains, and other inferiour Officers, to the number of thirty, they might have been fit for imployment upon a double enemie. And I could wish, that whensoever his Majestie shall be once furnished with good Officers, it would please him to make account of them, as these men do, who have had long experience, and known their value.

It pleased my Lord the Duke, to write to me a Letter, and to let me know he had chosen me his Officer, to attend, and obey him, in this journey : an honour too great for me, because I did never expect it ; but nothing shall excuse my faults, saving my life. And, among many other Directions, he commanded me to provide for the Army such necessary things as cannot be had in *England* : whereof I have thought of many, which, I fear, I shall not have the time to get. In my care belonging to these provisions, I have considered the use of our small pieces of Ordnance here, which they call Drakes, that shoot 70. Musquet-bullets : They will be of great use in this service, both in regard of the quick landing, and of the passing of such mountainous places as, perhaps, we may meet withall ; and likewise in respect of the little hope we have to get any good Musquetiers, or, at least, any great store of them : But they are in such favour here, as we can obtain none from hence, and so are forced, by a general consent, to buy ten of them here that were provided for the King of *France* ; and the reputation they carry is such, as they are ready money every where. They cost not much more then 400 *l.* sterling, and, I hope, they will prove the profitab'est pieces that were ever used in the quarrel of his Majesties Friends. We have likewise

A a 2 considered

Sir Edward Cecill, to the Duke.

considered, of what service a Company of Fire-locks would be to the action; but the time is so short, we cannot raise them. Howsoever, we are promised of the States to have leave for a Company of Harquebusiers, which are of such use, upon all occasions, that we cannot miss them; and we have chosen a brave and worthy Gentleman, his Majesties servant and subject, who is willing to leave any service for this, being the service of the King. If they should have been raised in *England*, his Majestie must have paid for the Horses, Arms, Saddles, and Pistols, and yet not find any able to have served in that kind.

The wind (as yet) holds contrary, which hath made me send this by Sir *Henry Vane*, who goes a way that I dare not pass. But (I hope) if the wind serve, not to be many days behind him, to receive your Lordships command more particularly, which I will obey, as

Hague, June 2. 1625.   *Your Lordships most humble servant,*
                                                                Ed. Cecill.

Post-script.

MY Lord, now, in this time of necessity for the getting of good Musquetiers, there are many hundred to be found in *England*, that have served in this Land, which, by Proclamation and promise of money in hand, or more pay, will easily discover themselves; whom some of the new men (to be released) will be glad to satisfie, without charge to his Majestie.

Sir Edward Cecill, to the Duke.

My most excellent Lord,

THere are some Letters of mine that had come to your Lordships hands a good many days since, had not the wind been contrary, and withstood their passage: The substance whereof was onely to shew you, how thankfull I hold my self to your Excellencie, for so great and infinite a favour as it hath pleased your Excellencie to think me worthy of: But, as it is a favour that will set me on work all the days of my life, so is it greater then I can ever deserve; howsoever, my resolution is, to do my best. And I humbly beseech your Excellencie to believe, that with my diligence, and the best understanding I have, I will seek nothing but to please you, and to honour you; and if God say Amen, to make the world speak of your design, as much (I hope) as ever our Nation hath given cause. And for the faults of my self, and those I shall bring with me, they shall not be excused, but with our lives, and bloods; for, I hope, I shall bring none, but such as know what to do, and, when they come to it, will bite sooner then bark. I do promise my self, your Excellencie will have no cause to doubt, or repent you of your favours; for I know what men have done, and what they can do, in my conclusion: But God is God, and men are but men.

All my discouragement is, that the States answer not his Majesties expectation, being fearfull (especially, since the loss of *Breda*) to part with any of their old Officers, or old Souldiers; but my hope is now better, for we have put them to another resolution, by answering all their objections. By this disposition of the States to the keeping all their old Souldiers, I wish your Excellencie will be pleased to be as carefull in your choice, as you are desirous of great designs; for otherwise, the honour, and the charge, will both be cast away, as your Excellencie may perceive in some of our latter expeditions; seeing that although there are many called Souldiers in the world, yet but a few there be that are so: For, so long a man must live in the profession, to enable him sufficiently, that many grow unable to perform what they know, before they have attained to the knowledge of what to perform; the knowledge of War being the highest of humane things that God suffereth mans understanding to reach unto.

I have, according to your Excellencies command, made as many provisions as I can, for the shortness of the time, of such things as cannot be gotten in *England*: And I could have wished, I had known of this imployment but some moneths sooner; for then I could have saved his Majesty somewhat, and have added many things that would very much have advanced the service. For, in our profession, the preparing of things belonging to the war doth more shew a mans experience and judgment, then any thing else, by reason the first errours are the begetting of many more, that afterwards cannot be avoided. Your Excellencie may be pleased to inform your self of all the exploits and undertakings of our Nation, that none of them hath suffered (for the most part) more, then through the negligence of provisions, as in Victual, Munition, Boats for Landing, and for the receiving of sick men, to keep the rest from infection. In this point of provision, it is not good to trust upon a particular man, for gain is a corrupter where the care is not publique. And in so great an expedition, one must do with living men, as they do with the dead; there must be overseers and executors to have a true intent well performed.

I have presumed to write thus much, to shew my thankfulness to your Excellency, and my great affection to his Majesties service, whereof I am infinitely possessed. I hear your Excellency is in *France*, but my Prayers to God are to send you safe and happy home, for the World holds you the soul of advancing his Majesties affairs, wherein his Honour is ingaged as it is, especially in this action, being the first, and a Great One.

And as for my self, who am now a creature you have made, I know not what I shall do when I come to *England*, being your Excellencies shadow only.

I have here attended the wind, and since I cannot force it, I am glad of the opportunity to send the Letters by Sir *Henry Vane*, who goes over Land, a passage I am not capable of, having been so long their enemie. But I hope God will send me soon after, leaving Sir *William* St. *Lieger* here for the dispatch of that which remains. I have written more particularly to my Lord *Conway*, which I dare not set down here, for fear of being tedious, and knowing his Lordship will give your Excellency an account of it. And so, in all humbleness and duty, I pray God send your Excellency honour, and length of life for his Majesties affairs, and for the happiness of

                                 Your Lordships most humble, faithful, and obedient servant,
Hague, June 3. 1625.   Ed. Cecill.

Sir Edward Cecill, to the Duke.

My most excellent Lord,

THe occasion of my boldness in presenting your Excellency with these lines, is, for that contrary to my expectation, I hear that there is a Commission a drawing to make Sir *Horace Vere* a Baron of *England*. It is strange to me at this time to hear it, for that I know not what worth there is more in him, then in those that are equal in profession, and before him in birth. If your Excellency have made choice of me to be your second in this journey of so much charge, and expectation, and to make me less then I was, what courage shall I have to do you service? or what honour will redound to your Excellency? But although I write it, yet I cannot believe it, for that I know you of that judgement and nobleness, that you will rather adde to your faithful servants, although they beg it not, then to disgrace them, and make them less. Therefore I will continue my belief, and rest,

                                 Your Excellencies most humble, and devoted servant,
July, 19 1625.   Ed. Cecill.

Sir Edward Cecill, to the Duke.

My very good Lord,

HOw much my affection and ambition hath been to serve your Lordship before other men, I hope I shall not need now to express, considering it hath been clear and manifest to your own tryal, whereof I do bear still the Testimony, and the continuance in mine own heart. But in your nobleness it will not appear impertinent to your Lordship, that I put you in mind, how much I suffered in the disgrace my enemies cast upon me, about the imployment for the Palatinate, when I was under your protection; whether I suffered for mine own sake, or for your Lordship, I know not: howsoever of this I am assured, the greatest cause I gave them, that had least reason, was because I sought not them, but your Lordship only. And for the success, you may see by the miracles the imployment hath brought forth, that it was carried another way, rather for private malice, then for any great zeal to the advancement of the publique Cause.

Now my Lord, for your own honour, and for the upholding of your servant, make me so happy, if there be any imployment for men of my profession (as there is in opinion) that I may be the man by your Lordships means, wherein you shall make me your obliged, as I am now your affectionate servant. For which you shall be assured of as thankful a heart, as any

breathes

Sir Edward Cecil, to the Duke.

breathes in the whole world. In the enjoyning of which kind of service, though you are accounted the most happy among great men, yet you cannot have too much of it. I could remember your Lordship of his Majesties gracious promise, for my imployment before any other, in the presence of the Prince and your Lordship, and that I am the first General his Majesty ever made, and that I had no ill success in the perfecting of that service; yet for all this, I will only trust in your Nobleness, if you resolve to make me your Creature.

And if it shall please his Majesty to hold me worthy of this honour, I will undertake to save his Coffers (as I have heretofore done) the sixth part of the imployments charge and cost that any other man shall require, who makes not a computation for the managing of it, by a sufficient expence of his own.

I will not write more at this time, but to wish your Lordship as much happiness as your heart can desire, and that you will give me an occasion to shew how much I am, and will be,

From our Army, Novemb. 20.

Your Lordships most faithful and affectionate servant,
Ed. Cecill.

Sir Edward Cecil, to the Duke.

May it please your Excellency,

THis Gentleman, Sir *George Blundel,* hath now cleerly quitted the service of the States, for this especial reason (as he assures me) to be the more absolutely imployed in your Excellencies service. This I know, his friends here that love him (which are many) are very sorrie to part with him, for there is no melancholly where he goes. And therefore, considering the condition of this place, we shall be great losers, being upon a melancholly place, and service, ill payed, sick (of all diseases in the world, in a place that is next neighbour to hell, if the book printed say true, which saith, that the Low-Countreymen are next neighbours to the devil. And I am sure, we are now seated lower then any part of these Countries; for the waters are above us, and about us, and we live in more fear of them, then of the enemy:; for we may be drowned at an hours warning. if we do not continually work against it; and yet, if it shall please your Excellency, this is a Seat for a Winter War. Many more inconveniencies we are daily sensible of, of which I have endured so much, as I dare say, without vanity, that few of my rank and fortune have suffered more, or longer then I have done, in these Countries; having served these 27 years together without intermission; and all this for no other end (for I am 900 l. a year the worse for the Wars) then to make me able to serve my Prince and Countrey, when occasion should be offered.

But since the time is come, that opinion doth so govern, as strangers get the Command, and new Souldiers are imployed, which was never heard of before amongst men of our occupation, It is high time for me to retire, and wish I had been of any other profession then this. For if long service can get no honour, nor reward, nor imployment, but the contrary; it would touch a mans discretion to be more and more unfortunate: All my comfort is, that I shall have the honour and good fortune, in my retreat, to draw neerer to your Excellencies service, if not in my profession, (which I desire above all) yet in something whereof your Excellency may make use of me. For I am ambitious of nothing more, then to prove my self by action, and not by recommendation,

From our Army at Wallike,
Decemb. 4.

Your Excellencies most faithfull, devoted, and humble servant,
Ed. Cecill.

Sir DUDLEY CARLETON'S
Letters, &c.

Sir Dudley Carleton, *to the Marquess of* Buckingham.

Right Honourable,

BY the dispatch of the fourteenth of this present (which I sent by *Johnson* the Post) I advertised your Honour at large in the two several Letters of the occurrents of these parts, and therewith sent a copie of my second proposition which I made the day before in the Assembly of the States General, touching the businesse of *Cleves*, and *Juliers*, in conformity to your Honours Letters of the 30.th of the last.

The answer thereunto was deferred until yesterday, and then brought me only by word of mouth from the States by *Mounsieur Magnus* of *Zealand*, and *Monsieur Zulestein* of *Utrecht*, and was to this effect, That the States having sent my former proposition of the third of *December* to their several provinces, from which this later did not differ in substance, save onely in respect of the time for the restitution of the Towns, which was prolonged for the space of a moneth, all they could do, according to the constitution of their government, was, to send this my second proposition likewise unto their provinces, which they had done the day after I made the same; and until they receive more expresse order from their principals, they were to rest upon their former answer. Wherein they declared their good intentions to accommodate this businesse, so it might be with safety to themselves, and satisfaction of their neighbours. And herein they were to expect the resolution of the Elector of *Brandenbergh*, from whom the time did not yet serve to know his mind. Mean while they humbly beseech his Majesty to make a gracious construction of their proceedings.

I was the day before with Monsieur *Barnevelt*, (who is President this week) to sollicite their answer, who excused himself upon the smallnesse of their number, many of the States being absent, and of two Provinces all the Deputies: So as to give a determinate resolution according as was required, they could not: and to make answer in general terms, since his Majesty rested not satisfied with the former, he doubted another of the same kind would not please him. So, as it seems, this Message in place of an answer in writing, proceeded of his Counsel.

By discourse both with him, and those which came unto me, upon this subject, I find their diffidence of the purpose of the *Spaniard* rather increased then otherwise, upon the news of Leavies intended on the Arch-Dukes side, to the number of 9000 foot, and 1000, or 1200 horse; and their delay in taking a determinate resolution, no way disswaded, but rather counselled by all other Princes, who have interest in this businesse. Their Embassadour at *Paris* having advertised them by reiterated Letters, That *Don Pedro di Sarmientos* his offer to his Majesty, touching the execution of the Treaty of *Zanten*, is absolutely disavowed by both the Kings of *France* and *Spain*. And this *French* Embassador *Mounsieur de Maurier*, having made it appear unto them, that at *Brussels* they have the same conceit of it, as a thing done without authority. Besides, the Princes of the Union have written lately expresse Letters to the States, wherein they perswade them to extraordinary vigilance upon the

Spaniards,

Sir D. Carleton, to the Marq. of Buckingham.

Spaniards, and particularly in this business of *Cleves*, and *Juliers*, the translated Copies of which Letters I send your Honour herewith. And the Prince of *Brandenbergh* being young himself, and having his Councel divided in opinion, doth nothing absolutely without reference to this State; and when I put them in mind, how they themselves were the authors and framers of the Treaty of *Zanten*, they stick not to say plainly, *Tempora mutantur, & nos:* So as I am daily more and more confirmed in my former opinion, That there is no way left to accommodate this business, but by a private agreement between the Princes Pretendents. But *Strickius*, the Agent of *Brandenbergh*, being absent at *Cleves*, I do not hear how this Negotiation proceeds.

Amongst the particularities which passed in discourse between *Monsieur Magnus* and my self, I insisting upon restitution of the Townes, as the means to prevent an imminent war upon the quarrel, he asked to whom they should restore them, unless the Princes were agreed, and that they might know which of the Princes should receive him, and whom they should have for their neighbour. Whereby it appears, this course will on this side remove all difficulties.

It is advertised hither, by *Monsieur Langrack*, the States Embassadour at *Paris*, that the apprehension they had in the Court, to have this business ended without the French Kings intervention, caused *Monsieur de Refuges* to be summoned to make another journey expresly hither, in regard he had formerly the managing thereof, Notwithstanding that *Monsieur de la Nove* was already named for this extraordinary Embassage: But *Refuges* excusing himself upon his indisposition, sent all his memorial of what passed when he was here in the Treaty of *Zanten*, with his private opinion upon the whole matter, to serve as an instruction to *la Nove*.

By the other Letters, of the 28 of this present, *Stilo Nov. Monsieur Langrack* hath given this State many important advertisements; as first, that he hath obtained of the *French* King a continuance of the succours of the 3 Regiments of Foot, and 2. Troops of Horse of that Nation for one year longer, notwithstanding the opposition of the *Spanish*, and Arch-Dukes Emb. ssadours, who advised the recalling of them upon occasion of the present troubles in *France*. That there is order given and assignation for 120000 Crowns towards the arrearages of their pay. That a resolution is taken in that Court, by the advice of the new Councellours, contrary to the opinion of the old, to prosecute the Princes by war, and maintain the Kings authority henceforward by force. That, to this effect, the King desires the State should perform their promises of sending towards the river of *Burdeaux* 5. Men of War. That he likewise requires of them in conformity of the last treaties betwixt the Crown and this State, an assistance of men to the number of the *French*, which are here in service, under some good Commander; But the *French* themselves the King will not have, for fear when they shall come into *France*, of their revolting to the Princes. That he demands free passage through these Countries, down the *Mause*, and the *Rheine*, of 3000. Souldiers, with their armes, which are leavied by the Count *John Giacomo Belioysa* in *Luke-Land*, and thereabouts, and shipping to transport them into *France*.

All these particulars were moved unto him (as he writes) by the Marshal *de Ancre*; to which he adds, that the King is so much incensed against the Duke of *Bouillon*, for seeking to this State for protection; whereof by Letters I advertised your Honour, in my last, that there is a resolution taken to declare him *Criminel de lese Majestate*.

These *Grauntes* are so scantie (the continuance of the *French* Troops in the service of the State being but for a year only, and the payment of them arriving only to the tenth part of what is already due) that they here interpret them to proceed from the *Marshal de Ancre Pourtenir* (as they say) *le bee en Leau*, and the demands are so large and extravagant, that they are thought *iniquum petere, ut aquum ferant*; whereby, on the one side to keep this State in devotion to the *French* King, and on the other, to prevent the like requests of the Princes: for there is small appearance, they will give passage to so many men through their Countries armed, and commanded by an *Italian*, who hath born armes against them, and is married into the Arch-Dukes Countrey. And when it comes to question, of sending forces of their own thither, it is like they will find as good excuses for that point, as they have hitherto done for the sending of the ships now three moneths since promised, and still sollicited: for howsoever the chief Persons here have been long particularly interested and ingaged (as your Honour knows) by neer dependence on this Crown, I find them of late very much alienated, in consideration that it is so much governed by Spain, which in the end, they apprehended, will turn to the ruine of this State.

In

Sir Dudley Carleton, to the Duke. 185

In *France* they are jealous of this coldness, and have of late expostulated the matter with *Monsieur Langrack*, as if they here did incline to the Princes, there being a bruite raised in *Paris*, that Count *Maurice* would go in Person to their assistance; whereof the Queen Regent was very sensible; but I do not find here, that there was any ground for that report.

Here hath been lately a fame spread and nourished by such as desire to weaken the correspondence between his Majesty and this State, that his Majesty is in neer terms of matching our Prince with *Spain*. Which report is now the more credited, by an adviso out of *Spain*, from a secret Minister this State entertains, under colour of solliciting Merchants causes. That this match hath been there, by order of the King of *Spain*, debated in the inquisition, and judged necessary, in regard it would serve for introduction of Popery into *England*.

This I find to be the *Remora* of my chief affairs with this State, my pressing the restitution of the Towns in *Cleves* and *Juliers* being thought by many of these jealous people to hang on this thread, as a thing very acceptable, and agreeable, at this time, to the King of *Spain*, and much advantagious in this present conjuncture to his affairs; and my insisting upon sending of Commissioners to his Majesty, in the business of our Merchants, they apply the same way, as if the opinion which would be conceived of this Embassage, (howsoever Merchants affairs were pretended, the chief intent was to play *Davus in Comœdia*) should according to the use of *Nitimur in Vetitum*, rather kindle, then quench the desire of the Spaniard, and draw the match to a more speedy conclusion.

At my last being with *Monsieur Barnevelt*, I did expostulate the States delay of sending Commissioners to his Majesty upon this occasion, as neither answereth to Sir *Noel Caron's* word and promise to his Majesty, nor to that which, from his mouth, I did advertise your Lordship of the States inclination in general, and the resolution, in particular, of those of *Holland*. To which he answered me, That with much difficulty and opposition he had obtained the assent of *Holland*, and that now the matter rested with *Zealand*; but he doubted, that his Majesty restoring the old Company of Merchants, would make a stay of any farther proceeding, as now less requisite, howsoever, that Sir *Noel Carone* had advertised, that notwithstanding this change, he thought the sending of Commissioners very necessary.

The Questions here, about Religion, rest in the same state as I advertised your Lordship in my last, the Assembly of *Holland* being separated until the end of *February*, stil. no. when they are to meet again. Mean while a provisional order is taken, that the *Contra-Remonstrants* shall continue their preaching in our English Church, which they have accommodated with Scaffolds, to make it more capable of their number.

There was much question, in this Assembly, whether his Excellency should be present, or no: but in the end, he was called by the major part of voices, contrary to *Monsieur Barnevelt's* opinion, and his authority over-swayed the matter in favour of the *Contra-Remonstrants*, for the continuance of their preaching, which it was proposed to hinder by some violent Courses.

By example of this place, there is the like provisional order taken for preaching at the *Brill*, and *Rotterdam*; and certain of the Burghers are established in *Tergow*, who were put from their Trade and Commerce, for their expostulating with the Magistrate upon this quarrel.

I have been spoken unto by divers particular persons well affected in this cause, to procure a Letter from his Majesty to his Excellency, whereby to comfort and encourage him in his Zeal for the maintenance of the true doctrine, and the professors thereof, against these Novelists and their opinions, Which I most humbly refer to his Majesties wisdom, (in case he judge this office necessary) whether it be fit to be done by Letter or Message; the former of which will be of greater vertue, but the latter less subject to cross construction of the Arminian faction, which your Honour knows how potent it is here amongst those who have chief rule in this State. Thus I humbly take leave, ever resting

Hague, Febr. 24.
1616. Stil. Vet.

Your Lordships
Most faithfully to be commanded;

Dudley Carleton.

B b

Sir Dudley Carleton, to the Duke of Buckingham.

My most honourable Lord,

Immediately upon receipt of your Lordships Letter concerning Sir *John Ogle*, I moved the Prince of *Orange* not onely for his leave for Sir *John* to go into *England*, but likewise for his Letters of recommendation, whereby to give your Lordship subject, upon some such testimonies of his Excellencies good satisfaction, to set him upright in his Majesties favour, both which he granted unto me: though against the first, he alleadged the absence of all the *English* Colonels, and touching the latter, he called to mind old matters; which notwithstanding (upon what I undertook for Sir *John's* future intentions) he was content to forget. I did once again upon Sir *John's* instance, put his Excellency in mind of his dispatch, wherein I found no difficulty. Since I find Sir *John* hath changed his purpose of going, and his excuse will be made at his intreaty by his Excellency, who hath since let me know, Though he would not deny me his leave, yet he is better content, in regard he is so slenderly accompanied with Colonels, in a time when the State hath need of their service, with his stay. So as Sir *John* hath the obligation to your Lordship of a favourable recommendation; and for his not prevailing himself of his leave when it was granted, he must leave to himself to render a reason. For my part, having accomplished what I find by your Lordships Letter, to be agreeable both to his Majesties pleasure, and your Lordships, I thought it my duty to advertise, That there is an ancient difference between Sir *Horatio Vere*, and Sir *Edward Cecil*, about the extent of their Commands; whereupon followeth a great inconveniency, to the dishonour of our Nation, which (as it appears, when they were last in the field before *Reez*) are divided hereby, and march, and lodge in several bodies, and quarters. Much endeavour hath been formerly used in these parts to reconcile them, but all in vain, by reason of some ill Instruments, who wrought upon both their discontents, to set them farther asunder. Now, they are both in *England*, and are both written for, to come over; It were a work worthy of your Lordship to make them understand one another better; and what they will not yield to of themselves, to over-rule by his Majesties authority. I may not conceal from your Lordship, that I am intreated by the Prince of *Orange* himself to do this office, both with his Majesty, and your Lordship, wherein he would not be seen himself, because having dealt between them fruitlesly heretofore, he doubteth of the like success now. But when their agreement shall be made, he will acknowledge his obligation to your Lordship; and for the better proceeding therein, I sent your Lordship a Copy of an order formerly set down betwixt them, with the translate of Sir *Horatio Vere's* Commission, (both which I had of his Excellency) and likewise the beginning, and proceeding of their difference, as I have collected the same in brief out of other mens reports.

The projects I sent your Lordship with my last, of a *West-Indian* Company having been proposed to the States of *Guelderland* for their ratification, (who have the leading voice in the Assembly of the States general, and were ever least forward in that business) hath thus far their allowance, that they will concur therein with the rest of the Provinces. But withal I do understand, they have given their Deputies secret charge not to give way thereunto, in case they find it prejudicial to the Truce. Which makes the matter evident, that the project of the Company (though it be never so advanced) will stand or fall, according to the proceeding of the Truce. The expiration whereof approaching so neer, and here being advertisements from *Paris*, that a French Gentleman, one *Belleavium* (who was lately employed hither to the Prince of *Orange* about the difference betwixt him and the Prince of *Conde*) had secret instructions to sound the States, how they stood affected to the renewing thereof. I have used all diligence to know how far he went; and am well informed, he hath done nothing therein of consideration: only this past between him and his Excellency.

He telling his Excellency from *Monsieur Desdiguieres*, and some of the French Kings Councel, how acceptable the extraordinary Embassage intended from hence will be in that Court, thereupon perswaded a speedy embracing the opportunity.

From whence (said his Excellency, after his round manner) cometh this alteration?

To speak plainly (said he) they fear in *France*, you will renew the Truce without them, and therefore, by your Embassadours, they would interpose themselves.

Here are good advertisements both from *Bruxels* and *Paris*, that the Spaniards intent is not to renew the Truce, but to have a Peace proposed with these plausible conditions;

That

Sir Dudley Carleton, to the Duke.

That the King of *Spain* will pretend nothing in the Regiment of these United Provinces, nor require any thing of them in the point of Religion, but leave all in terms as it now stands, with recognition onely of some titular Sovereignty, which he cannot in honour relinquish.

This is already proposed to *France*, as a glorious work, to establish a setled Peace in these parts of the world, but with this condition; That if it be not imbraced here, then *France* shall refuse to give this State any further support, or countenance, of which it is here believed, that *Spain* hath already obtained a firm promise in that Court. And that either the like overture is already made, or will be within few daies, to his Majesty.

Under which doth lie hidden many mysteries much to the advantage of the *Spaniard*, and prejudice of this State: for the very proposition of a new Treaty will distract them here very much, in regard of their unsettlednefs, and aptness upon any dispute to relapse into faction, besides many Considerations of importance, belonging properly to the Constitution of their Government; but the acceptation of the old, by renewing of the Truce upon the former terms, for so many years, more or less, as shall be thought fitting, will in my poor opinion (which notwithstanding is not slenderly grounded) take place, without much difficulty. The importance of this business hath made me give your Lordship this trouble, and your Lordship may be pleased to let his Majesty understand as well that little as is done by *Monsieur Belleavium*, as what they here conceive to be further intended by the *Spaniard*. So I most humbly take leave, ever resting

Hague this 10th of
June, 1620.

Your Lordships
Most faithful servant,

Dudley Carleton.

Sir Dudley Carleton, to the Duke.

Most honourable,

I Observe in such Letters from the Prince Electour to her Highness, with the sight of which she is pleased sometimes to favour me, a mis-understanding betwixt him and his Uncle the Duke of *Bovillon*, who groweth weary of his Guest, doubting lest in his Consideration some danger may be drawn upon his Town of *Sedan*; And the jealousie the Prince conceiveth, what may be done with him in case of a Siege, (against which that is no place to make long resistance) besides the discomforts of living in another mans house, and being ill looked on, makes him wish himself any where else; but chiefly here, where he is as much desired, as missed by her Highness, his children and Family: And where the Prince of *Orange*, and the States (apprehending very well his present danger, and incommodity) will give him very willingly his wonted welcome. Your Lordship may be pleased to make thus much known to his Majesty: And if your Lordship can so dispose of the matter, that with his Majesties good liking he may return hither again, I know nothing your Lordship can do more agreeable to her Highness, though she doth wholly submit her affections and desires to his Majesties pleasure.

The wars were never warmer then they are already, and now likely more and more to kindle in these parts: The Siege of *Ostend*, by those which were present there, and are now in *Berghen*, being esteemed sport in comparison of the fury is used in disputing the outworks of that Town. Where on Monday last in the night an assault was given, and maintained six hours, by the *Spaniards*, upon a half Moon kept by the Dutch on the North side; out of which they were three several times repulsed, with the loss of betwixt 3 and 400 men of their best, and on this side under 40. All that they gained being (after the same manner as their former attempt on the other side, wherein Colonel *Hynderson* was slain) to lodge in the foot of the work. Two of our old Captains, Sir *Michael Everard*, and *Lovelace* (hurt in that, and the like assault, given on that side within few daies after) are both dead of their wounds within these two daies. One at *Dort*, the other at *Rotterdam*, whither they were retired to be cured: which is imputed by the Chirurgeons to some malignity is used to the Bullets: but that is not to be believed amongst Christians; yet I have seen some brought hither shot by the Enemy, sufficient to break all quarter.

We shall have now, questionless, many and sharp encounters in the field: Count *Mansfelt* being on his way hitherwards with his Army, much weakned during his abode in the Frontiers of *France*; but of strength sufficient to march through the open Countries of *Henault*, and *Brabant*. Which course he takes directly with intention to come to *Breda*. And where by computation, he should be by *Munday*, or *Tuesday* next at the furthest, unless he be overtaken by *Don Gonzales de Cordova*, or met with by the Count *Henrie Vandenbergh*, or the Marquess *Spinola*, in any of which there is small appearance. *Cordova* going forward at leisure with 16 pieces of Cannon, and the 18th of this present, when *Mansfelt* passed a bridge at *Marpin* over the *Sambre* in *Henault* (which was the onely passage of difficulty, and that as our advertisements here say, he crossed without resistance) being some hours March behind him, who having three field pieces onely, and small store of baggage, and in effect his whole Armie on horseback, may make great expedition

If *Vandenbergh* stir, he will be followed by the Prince of *Orange*. And the Marquess *Spinola* cannot go strong enough to encounter him, without raising his Siege at *Berghen*, which though he should do, the *Campaigne* is large enough, and *Mansfelt* lightly laden, to take and leave at pleasure, it being in his power, (if his way to *Breda* be stopped) to fall down towards such places the States hold in *Flanders*.

The States furnish him with 6000 *Florins* for the time of three moneths they entertain him and his Armie. In which space, the service they hope to draw from him, is, the raising the Siege of *Berghen*, by cutting off the Convoyes betwixt *Antwerp* and the Spanish Leaguer, which can no longer continue in the place it now remains, then it can keep the way of *Antwerp* open, by which only their Victuals and Munition is conducted.

This time of three moneths expired, there is small appearance of longer entertainment of *Mansfelt* by this State, who doth then purpose to retire to the Duke *Christien* of *Brunswick's* old Quarter at *Lipstadt*: Where they intend to winter their Army, and augment the same against the next Spring, to return again into *Germany*, if the Peace of those parts be not concluded, or some mischance do not happen in the mean time. Which resolution of theirs, for such it is (as I am very well informed) deserves the more to be cherished, by how much the more disrespect is shewed his Majesties Embassadour in the *Palatinate*, by burning and spoyling her Highness Joynture even in his view, (as *Don Gonzales* did whilest he remained in those parts) and since besieging his Majesties Garrison *Heidelbergh*; before which place, we understand here by Letters of the 14^h, from *Frankford*, that Baron *Tillie* began his approaches the 12th of this present.

I have not heard what is the issue of Captain *Brett's* business, but hope the best. Colonel *Hynderson's* Regiment was given, upon the first news of his death, to Sir *Francis Hynderson* by the Prince of *Orange*, with which the States are much displeased, as contrarying their Act. And I have lamented my self to them, as a wrong done my Lord of *Buckleugh*, and his Majestie, in his behalf: which they promise me to repair, as they possibly may be able. And I press them to it, by those means which your Lordship will find contained in an abstract of a Letter I wrote lately to his Excellencie, chiefly to this purpose.

Her Highness having received a fair Present from the Prince her Brother, doth render his Highness thanks, by the inclosed. I know not so great a Lady in the world, nor ever did, (though I have seen many Courts) of such natural affections: An obedient Daughter; A loving Sister; And a tender Wife, whose care of her Husband doth augment with his misfortunes.

Your Lordship cannot therefore shew your care of her more, then by bringing them again together with the soonest. Of which I beseech your Lordship, that with the soonest I may know what hope there is, and that (if your Lordship please) by Mr *Ashburnham*, whose return with a favourable dispatch is daily expected. Thus I most humbly take leave,

Hague, August 23. 1622.

Your Lordships
Most humble, and most devoted Servant,

Dudley Carleton.

Sir Dudley Carleton, to the *Duke*.

Most Honourable,

NOT to give your Lordship the trouble of often Letters, I render an account of his Majesties Commandments, by the same hand I usually receive them. One I had lately by an express Letter from his Majestie, accompanied with another from your Lordship, touching my Lord of *Buckleugh*, to demand full satisfaction of the States, for all his Lordships pretensions, and to that effect to procure Instructions and Commission to be sent to Sir *Noel Carone*, to end this businesse.

To which effect I have moved both his Excellencie and the States, and whilest they were treating thereof, Colonel *Bregue* arrived here out of *Scotland*: with whom they are now handling to put him to Pension, and to give my Lord the Command of his Regiment in lieu of his Pretensions. Which when they come to calculate, my Lord will find a short reckoning of them; and to send accounts out of their accountants hands, and refer them to others, they will never be moved.

Wherefore if the course they now take can be gone thorough with (which Colonel *Bregue* doth most unwillingly hear of) it will be then in my Lords choice, whether he will remain satisfied or not. And within few daies I hope to return my Lords Secretary with advertisement of what is done. Mean time I assure your Lordship, nothing is omitted in my endeavours to procure him that which may be most to his contentment.

In the present condition of publick affairs, your Lordship knoweth well, how at this instant we have all *buone Parolle* out of *Spain*, and *Cattivi-fatti* of all the rest of the house of *Austria*. In so much as these Low-Country Troops under the Governance of the Infanta assist in the blocking up of a poor town, all which remains of his Majesties onely Daughters Jointure in the *Palatinate*. And the Emperour not content with having chased her Husband out of the Empire, in the Proposition of the *Diet* of *Ratusbone*, makes this one Article, to make war upon these Provinces, because (amongst other quarrels) they give refuge to the Prince *Palatine*. Where will this persecution cease? And what place in the world, to which they are driven from hence (and is easily guessed in all their extremitie, whither they will be forced to flie) is not subject to the same quarrel ? within this week that I now write (betwixt Sunday and Sunday) we were here in that state, if God had not prevented it, this Country had been too hot for them to remain in; and it had been a happinesse for them, if they could have got a poor scheveling Boat to have transported them else-where. This Bearer, my Nephew, will inform your Lordship more particularly thereof.

Now, *de agendis*, there rests no more, then question of maintaining the Army of *Mansfelt*, and *Branswick*, which is lodged at the present in a place out of which it can hardly march, and more hardly be removed. If it have pay, and countenance, it may do good service in *Germany*; if not, I will tell your Lordship what I conceive may be the consequence. It will be hedged into *East-frizeland* by *Tillie*, (whose Troops already draw that way) *Cordova* and *Anhalt*, against which, keeping it self within that Country, it wil be able to make resistance, as the poor Peasants thereof did heretofore against the Spanish Army, by reason of the difficulty of accesse. From this State it will have all assistance; and though it be kept in by land, it will have the Sea open betwixt *Griett* and *Norden*, (both which places are in *Mansfelts* possession) a Haven fit for a Fleet of *Gallions*. If by that means they, with correspondencie with this State, may support themselves, it will be very ill for many important consequences. If they and this State, (which will be forced to run a fortune together) be overcome, much worse; for what can keep the rest of *Europe* from subjection to the *Austriaci*? We see how in *Terra firma* the *Walloons* joyned to *Spaniards*, both make and maintain their Conquests. Joyn the *Hollanders* to them by Sea, they will reap the like service by them. The fruit we have reaped heretofore of the shiping of these Provinces, both for defence in the year 88, and offence in the *Cadiz* journey, sheweth what a strong addition this is to a greater power.

My most honourable Lord, I am so full of such like speculations, that these have broken out *ex Plentitudine Cordis*, surcharged with grief to see, *in Plenitudine temporis*, that to come to effect in the publick affairs which was discovered long since, by the Emperours intercepted Letters, sent by the *Capuchine* into *Spain*, and to hear the judgement made every where, that the publick opposition of the Spanish Embassadour (*D'Ognates* words) to the Emperours proceeding *de facto*, is but a patelinage, with secret understanding to abuse his
Majesties

Majesties goodness. Of which it lyeth yet in his Majesties power to vindicate himself; but there is no time to spare. I humbly crave pardon for this liberty of discourse I use with your Lordship, who am,

Hague, 31. Jan.
1622.

Your Lordships, most humble, and most faithful servant,

Dudley Carleton.

Sir Dudley Carleton, *to the Duke*.

May it please your Grace,

THe general knowledge the Queen of *Bohemia* received from your Grace, by my Nephew, of the disposition of our affairs at home, since his Highness, and your Graces return out of *Spain*, upon the true understanding you have bred in his Majesty of the Spanish proceedings, being more particularly both for the state of the matter, and the manner, fit to be held here in disposing these men to such overtures as are necessary, expressed unto me by Sir *George Goring*, with special caution of secrecie and celeritie:

I have thought fit to set down at large (whilest it is fresh in my memory) an opportunitie as properly given unto me this day by the Prince of *Orange*, (who is the only person of power and confidence we have here to treat withal) as I hope your Grace will judge it seasonably taken.

And that was an occasion of business concerning a mutiny at *Breda*, which drew the Councel of State (where I have my Seance) to the States general, with whom we found the Prince. That business ending in good time gave him a long hours leisure with me afterwards in his Garden, which he himself desired of me, because somewhat was farther to be digested between us concerning the English Troops, which shewed themselves most in this Mutiny: And hereupon the consideration of the necessitie of this State, and impossibility of giving their Troops full contentment, gave us subject of further discourse, both of the means of better payment they have here at home, and the helps they might conceive from abroad, which making appear unto me to be coldest from *England*, as long as our Match with *Spain* is still in treaty, he asked me bluntly (after his manner,) *Qui a't'il de vostre Mariage?* I told him, it was now at a stay upon this point, That the restitution of the *Palatinate* must be first concluded. And that the Queen of *Bohemia* was not only well comforted with this assurance, but pleased her self with a further conceit, that the opportunity was never fairer for this State to regain the King her Fathers favour, and return to the ancient support of his Crowns, which by the way of gratitude for her good usage, since she had her refuge into these parts, she could not but admonish his Excellencyof, and advise him not to let it slip. This he did not so suddenly lay hold of, as not first to cast many misdoubts, as if the alienation were too great, and his Majesty too much wedded in affection, if not in Alliance to new friends, to be so soon reconjoyned to his old, as their necessities did require.

Here I took occasion to play my own Part, and to remember unto him how things had passed within the compass of my experience, from the beginning; letting him know what friendship his Majesty had shewed this State, in the making their *Truce*; what sincerity, in rendring their Cautionary Towns according to contract, when they were demanded; what affection, in supporting their affaires during their late domestick disputes; what care, in setling our *East-Indian* differences; finally, what Patience in conniving at all the misdemeanours, and insolencies of their Sea-men, without seeking revenge.

And hereupon concluded, that I found them here in the same errour as men are which put first from Land to Sea, and believe the Land passes from them, not they from the Land, in that the Alienation, which hath long been nourished betwixt his Majesty and this State sprang originally from them.

First, by *Barnevelt*, and his faction of Arminians, carrying the State to new Alliances, with the Hans-Towns, and otherwise by themselves, refusing somuch as the knowledge of them to my Predecessour in this place, Sir *Ralph Winwood*, with much scorn and contempt.

Next, by a harsh and peremptory stile, used in all we had then to do with them, savouring rather of pride and presumption, then any due respect or desire of friendship.

Lastly, by a precipitate course taken at Sea by their Ships of war, and Merchants, against
his

Sir Dudley Carleton, *to the* Duke.

his Majesties Subjects, making prize of some, shouldering others out of their places of trade, and entring in the *East-Indies* into open hostilitie, avowed by a publick Act of the States General. This ill course begun and pursued for some years continuance, breeding a deserved distaste in his Majesty on this side; and on the Spanish part fair overtures of friendship, being continually made, and confirmed by the tender of a Match of a potent Prince. None can marvel that his Majesty did embrace the same, unless it should be expected of him, that for love of this State, how ill soever deserving, he should lend a deaf eare to all other friendships that did not concurre with the interest of this State. And the remembrance of these things not being so old as to be worn out, they might here very well conceive, that the suspition of Alienation and dis-affection, is as strong on our side for their giving the cause of our leaning another way, as on theirs, for the effect which hath since followed. And now the cause is removed, the effect may possibly cease in like manner, if we may have good assurance, that breaking with our new friends upon the occasions now presented, we might fasten, after the wonted manner, with an old; and the King be satisfied in such doubts, he may upon good reason cast, and know certainly what to trust to. To this conclusion he answered (confessing first their many obligations to his Majesty, both for his favour, and sufferance,) that nothing could be more certain, then the affection of this State to a Prince embracing their cause of opposition to *Spain*. And if his Majesty could take that resolution, he might dispose of them, their lives and their fortunes. I told him, that more (in a case of this importance, when there was question of alteration of the whole course of a great Princes affaires) would be required then bare professions and protestations; and the rather, because he knew I was not ignorant, how many Billets, and Papers have been heretofore brought hither by * Madam *Sercluus*, and others, tending to *Truce*, or peace, and how much such a matter was thirsted after by their Frontier Provinces, which being free for them to take, or leave, after their own humours, it was not likely his Majesty would discharge them of their burthen, to pull it upon his own Shoulders; But to enter into the common cause of defence, and add a powerful hand in supporting them, might be seisable in the present conjuncture, upon good assurance he should never be left single in the quarrel. Whereunto he answered, that true it was, the woman I named, and divers others, had been tampering heretofore about such Treaties, and that he had continually put their Papers into his Pocket, and so suppressed them (with consent of some of the States, of whom he was most confident) lest such propositions, being brought into their publick Assemblies, might have driven them into distraction, and dispute one with another, according to their several affections, either to Peace, or War, and thereby slacken their Contributions, wherewith they pay their Army, and by consequence expose them to the mercy of the enemy.

And that this course of his being finally discovered by the Marquess *Spinola*, and *Peckius*, their purpose now was (as he is privately advertised from *Bruxels*) to steal over some person hither by the usual means of Pass-ports for Merchants and Travailers, to make some such like Proposition at the several Assemblies of the States of these united Provinces: which it should be his study to prevent, because of the mischief may be bred thereby amongst them; And this he assured me for conclusion, That as their affections and affaires now stand, nothing but despair can bring these Provinces to Peace, or Truce, with Spain.

To this I yielded, but said, That was not enough, because of such changes to which the world was daily subject. Neither did Queen *Elizabeth* undertake their protection upon such bare presumptions, wherefore some further assurance must be thought on; which he consented unto, as a thing requisite on both sides, and joyned issue with me in this point; That when the King would be to this State, as Queen *Elizabeth* was; this State would be to him, as it was to Queen *Elizabeth*.

This being *opus unius diei*, not unlike the first day of the Creation of the world, in distinguishing light and darkness, I will give your Grace this further light, of what belongs to negotiation with this State.

The present opportunitie of the Prince of *Orange's* good affection, and strength of these Provinces both by Sea and Land, as it yet stands, (but not possible so long to continue) being seasonably laid hold of, his Majesty may have with this State a firm and fruitful alliance.

But if the Prince of *Orange* should die, (as he is much broken, and the last year at this time, we did not think he could live till *May*) or the enemy break into the borders of this State, (as this last Summer, if the *Imperialists* had joyned with the *Spaniards*, they had undoubtedly done; and unless some Change or Alteration happen, as is feared, will do this next year) the best link we have for a bond of friendship would fail, and as much difference

An old Popish Gentlewoman of this towne, who's passport on both sides trusts so she is known by the title of la Maquerelle de la Tresue.

Sir Dudley Carleton, to the Duke.

be betwixt this State, as it now is, and what it is like to be upon any such ill accident, (as was now feared, and still hangs over them) as betwixt a strong Staffe, and a broken Reed. So I cease to give your Grace any further trouble.

Your Graces

Hague, 9. Decemb.
1623.

Most humble, and most faithful servant,

Dudley Carleton

Sir Dudley Carleton, to the Duke.

May it please your Grace,

WHat Comfort and Contentment the Queen of *Bohemia* receives in your Graces Message and Letter by my Nephew, I leave to her own expression, which never fails her, when her heart goeth with her hand, as I can assure your Grace, it doth in this subject. And this I will say more, who can say nothing but truth, I never knew your Grace ill with this good and gracious Princesse; but now you are so well setled in her good opinion and favour, that I know none hath more interest therein.

And this use your Grace may make thereof to his Majesties service, that now this King and Queen are both of them no less confident of your affection, then they are of your sinceritie; what you advise them in their affairs will be of much weight to sway them in the balance of their judgement.

Whereas now a Proposition is made unto them, on which their whole estate doth depend as well for themselves, as their posteritie, full of doubtful circumstances on both sides, (the choice not being, as they conceive, betwixt one thing certain, and another uncertain; but betwixt two unequal uncertainties) it is hard to say which way they incline: but if they be left to themselves, I perceive they will rather stand to the hazard of the latter, with preservation of their honour and lawfull pretensions, then submit themselves to the former with shame and disgrace, and no assurance of better dealing then was used to the deported House of *Saxony*, by a better Emperour then this, accounted, of which we have the Heir (one of the worthiest Princes in *Germany*) here in hard Conditions amongst us. And he serves as a spectacle to these Princes of their fortunes, by the same way as his Predecessors took, of submission. Yet other things being before agreed of, and setled in that sort as his Majesty hath alwayes assured these Princes to be his full intention of restitution to their Patrimonial Honours and Estate; This King, I finde, will conform himself to what his Majesty shall think fit, touching a due submission.

But this being a matter of ceremony, the other of substance, he judgeth, that if this precede, (that is, the Submission) the other of restitution will never follow. Neither can it be well seen, how in possibility it may be effected, considering that (whilest things have been held sometimes in terms, alwayes in talk of accommodation) the Electoral is given to *Bavaria* by the Emperour, and avowed by a Congratulatory Embassage from *Bruxels*: the upper *Palatinate* setled in his possession, with some portion to *Newburgh* for his Contentation, and engagement. A principal part of the lower *Palatinate* (the *Bergstrate*) given to the Elector of *Mentz*, with the consent of those of *Bruxels*, (where he was lately in person to obtain it) though they grossely dissemble it, and promises of parts of the rest made to other Princes.

So as what is now pretended (I must deal plainly with your Grace) is no otherwayes interpreted, then as experience doth teach of these three former years proceedings: Ever new Overtures in Winter, and new Ruptures in the Summer. And as of two former Treaties with this Prince, which passed my hands, (one a Consent to a Submission sent to *Vienna*, the other a Ratification of a Suspension oftentimes sent to *Bruxels*) no other use was made, but with the first to accelerate *Bethlem Gabor* in his Treatie of Peace with the Emperour as then on foot, and with the second to intimidate both the Electours *Saxony*, and *Brandenburgh*, with the Princes of the *Nethes, Saxony*, and *Creyts*, from entring into Armes, to which they were well disposed, upon the discontentment they received of the preposterous courses that were taken in the Diet at *Ratisbone*; (and to this effect Copies of the very projects of the said Treaties were dispersed by the *Imperialists*, before the Instruments themselves

were

Sir Dudley Carleton, to the Duke.

were perfected,) so it is here believed, that now *Gabor* is again in Arms, and other Princes ready to imbrace any good occasion of redress of affairs, time is onely sought to be gained by this new Overture, and the King of *Bohemia's* Credit with his Friends and well-wishers in *Germany* to be weakned, if not lost; for, if once he submit himself, allowing the translation of the Electoral, he shall thereby avow the Emperours undue proceedings in that cause, (which have been protested against by *Saxony*, and *Brandenburgh*, and all the other *German* Princes, excepting those onely of the Catholick League) and by whom afterwards, upon any ill dealing, can he expect to be befriended, who forsakes himself, and his own Cause? This is the discourse of these Princes, upon this occasion: But when they are asked, What then can you trust unto? their recourse is to his Majesty, who, they hope, knoweth the means to effect, in their behalf, what he hath so long, and so constantly, undertaken for them. And though, for these three or four years past, affairs on this side have gone in a continual decadence, and now threaten a final ruine, unless it be withstood by some Princely resolution, (not of petty, but of great Princes,) yet here is no such discouragement, but that it is thought, there is yet strength and vigour enough left in the good Party, not onely to subsist, but to rise and flourish again as well as ever. And in this cogitation the King and Queen remain, not prescribing any thing to his Majesty, nor willing to submit themselves anew to the same rod with which they have been so often scourged.

Your Grace was lately invited, with my Lord of *Richmond*, to Christen their young Son; which being excused by my Lord of *Richmond*, in both your names, and the King of *France* undertaking that office, it was performed by that King, and the King of *Swedes*, yesterday was sevennight (represented by the *French* Embassadour here resident, and the Prince of *Orange*) in the same manner, and the same Church, as the Princess *Louise*, bearing the same name, was christned the last year: when the Duke *Christien* of *Brunswick* being invited to be Godfather, though absent, and, for some respects of precedence, could not have a Deputy, was understood notwithstanding to be one of the *Parrins*; and so do the King and Queen hold both your Grace, and my Lord of *Richmond*.

I must now render your Grace my humble thanks, for your manifestation of your favour to my self, which you are pleased to do in such ample manner, as to tell me further, for my comfort, who are my friends; and a further effect of friendship I could not expect of them, then to procure me the assurance I now receive from your Grace, who have won the reputation by your constancy to those you take into your care, that your word is taken for your deed. And though that which I thought fittest for my self fails me, if your Grace can think me fit for any thing else, towards the amendment of my poor fortune, I shall attend the same with much patience of mind, though great extremity, otherwise, by reason of a small estate charged with great debts, (which are no small burthen to an honest mind,) And ever remain

Hague, Decemb. 13. 1623.

Your Grace's most faithfull devoted servant,
Dudley Carleton.

Sir Dudley Carleton, *to the Duke*.

May it please your Grace,

THe Queen of *Bohemia*, desirous to draw the Prince of *Orange* to more then general professions of service to his Majesty, hath sometimes, in my presence, when I waited on her Highness, given occasion of discourse her self, and at other times I have spoken in her name with his Excellency to the like effect, as in my former Letter to your Grace: which caused his Excellency to take three of the States, such of whom he is most confident, (one of *Guelderland*, another of *Holland*, the third of *Zealand*) unto him, to strengthen himself by their concurrence in that which is his own inclination, of carrying this State to a strict alliance with his Majesty; in which he told them, That first their minds must be known, and next, such assurance thought of, as not onely must give his Majesty present contentment, but likewise free him from all misdoubt for the future, that either upon offers from *Spain* to these Provinces, or any sinister accidents of War, they should be induced to make Peace or Truce, without his Majesties consent.

Whereunto they answered him, (as I have it from himself this day,) That nothing could be more agreeable to their affections, and interests, in all respects, then to be under his Majesties protection: And for assurance of their remaining constant to that course, they
doubted

doubted not, but when the matter should be treated of, the Provinces would willingly condescend to what should be necessary to that purpose.

His Excellency, in relation hereof unto me, went so much further, as to instance in their new resolution here, now finally put in practice, of making Voyages into the *West-Indies*, after the same forms as they have done into the *East*; both which joyned together, make them irreconcileable with *Spain*. Yet if his Majesty will have a further tie on them, they will not refuse it: But he saith, the States will expect, that such obligation be mutual, and that they, in like manner, may rest assured, when they put themselves wholly under his Majesties wings, his Majesty will not flie from them, and make his peace without them.

I told him, the case was not equal betwixt his Majesty and them, they being actually in War, his Majesty in Peace; so as, to come to a conjunction, his Majesty must change condition, not they; and therefore hath the more reason to look, before he leap out of Peace into War: And so did Queen *Elizabeth*, who had reigned twenty seven years, before she openly took upon her the protection of these Countreys; but after, continued her War in their Cause to her dying day. This he confessed; but remembred withall, That there was a Treaty of *Burburck*, with which the States were much startled; and he thought, that when this business should be more particularly scanned amongst them, as they would willingly give, so they would expect to receive good assurance.

In this point of declaration of their affection, and willingness to warrant his Majesty sufficiently, I asked him, How far I might go, not to be disavowed, so as, if his Majesty should take any sudden resolution, according as affairs require, he might confidently build upon the concurrence of this State? He answered me, that a resolution in this kind would require a further proceeding then was fit, until his Majesty would be content to make his mind known, by such private means as might seem best to his own wisdom; and then, according to his own liking, they would enlarge this matter here, to more mens knowledge, then the small circle in which it hitherto walked, and guide it in that manner as may be fit for the form of it, to his Majesties honour, and, for the substance, to his full contentment: Which he offered to do now, if I would press him to it; but withall, told me his opinion, that it would raise nothing but bruit and noise, without effect, when we had here no better ground to work upon; and therefore wished the business might expect a return from his Majesty, if he could be content it should be proceeded in. In these terms remains this business, not free from many cautions, and nice circumstances; and yet, on this side, (I can assure your Grace) full of good affection: but these are the true reasons of their coming on no faster. They hold it for a Maxime, That *Spain* will never match with his Majesty for love, but either for hope, or fear; if *Spain* can entertain hope of reducing these Provinces to obedience by the Match; or fear, that unless the Match proceed, his Majesty will joyn with these Provinces in opposition to *Spain*: they hold, in either of these cases, the Match as made. And therefore, lest some use should be made of their presentations of themselves, to their own prejudice, they are thus shie and circumspect. Besides, as they have had some help of money out of *France* this last year, so they are entertained with hopes of more against the next; which, they fear, would be excused, upon any offer they should make of themselves towards his Majesty; and therefore, are loth to adventure the exchange of a substance for that which appears unto them, hitherto, no better then a shadow: And they are indeed very umbragious; for they suspect, that Tentatives of this kind, of which some have been made heretofore amongst them, tend to no other end, then to endear our Merchandize with *Spain*, and let the Ministers of that Crown know, that we refuse their contemplation. But when his Majesty shall resolve in his own heart, and be pleased to make himself so understood, it will be no hard matter, by his Excellencies means (who is a Prince full of good intentions, and real affections to his Majesty, and his Royal Family) to make these men lay by their jealousies, and be as true to his Majesty, and the support of his Crowns, as his own Kingdoms: Which is no more then they ow, for the protection which these that are now in Government had of his Majesty, when they were, lately, sinking under the burthen of a contrary faction; and no more then, upon a good knowledge of their interests and affections, I can undertake for them, they will really and readily pay, if the matter be well managed. In which, the confidence and freedom I have used with this Noble Gentleman, Sir *George Goring*, may give your Grace some further light, as any doubts shall arise concerning the business. So I most humbly take leave,

Hague, Decemb. 18. 1623.

Your Graces most humble, and most faithfull servant,
Dudley Carleton.

Sir Dudley Carleton, *to the Duke.*

May it please your Grace,

IT were a sin against the publick service, in which your Grace doth employ your self so much to the common good, and your own honour, to molest you with Letters, in this busie time; which must serve me for excuse of silence, since the beginning of the Parliament. What I write now, is by commandment of the Queen of *Bohemia*, concerning this Bearer, Captain *Gifford*, an old Sea-man of our Nation; who, having a private suit to the States, hath made a journy over hither, with recommendation to me from our two Secretaries, for advancement thereof; but with a further purpose to be employed by the Queen against the *Spaniard*, in a matter of no less moment then taking of a Galeon, which usually bringeth the treasure over the Gulph of *Mexico*, from *Nova Spagna* to the *Havana*: which he designs after this manner; To go out, with two Ships, and a Pinnace, onely fitted for fight, without more in number, because if the Alarm would be taken at a greater Fleet, and to lie under covert of a small Island in the entry of the Gulph of *Mexico*; where the Galeon, coming usually alone, unless it be accompanied with some Merchants Ships, which he sets light by, and which, encumbred with goods and passengers, he thinks may be mastered, and taken, building upon the security in which that Galeon, with the rest of that *Nova Spagna* Fleet, do sail scattering in the Gulph, till they meet with the Fleet of *Terra Firma* at the *Havana*; where he having been heretofore a prisoner made this observation, and doth now offer himself to put the design in execution; with a demand of between 10000. and 11000 *l.* for the whole equipage.

The Queen, in recompence of his good will, returns him with this address to your Grace, as a man fit for employment, for so he is generally reputed: But for the particularity of the Exploit, she doth not entertain any thought thereof, but referrs it wholly to your Grace's consideration, and to the opportunity, according as affairs shall succeed betwixt his Majesty and *Spain*.

Here are come Letters from some of the King and Queens servants on that side, and one to my self from a private friend, advertising, That there is a readiness in divers of his Majesties Subjects, of good abilities, to put to Sea with Letters of Mart, in the name of this King and Queen, against the *Spaniard*; and of a likelihood, that if such Commissions were given by these Princes, they would not be ill understood by his Majesty.

Monsieur *Aertsens* hath likewise written hither, in a private Letter to the Prince of *Orange*, that he hath been spoken with to move the States to increase the number he and his Colleague have mentioned of ten or twelve Ships, to joyn, in any good occasion, with his Majesties Fleet, to twenty: And that the purpose is to set out fifty sail on that side, and that both shall go under the name of the King and Queen of *Bohemia*. Wherein, though the motion be not directly made, yet the Prince of *Orange* hath discoursed enough, that when it shall come to issue, they will stretch themselves to furnish, to the full, what is required on this side. In both these businesses, as well the granting Letters of Mart by these Princes, as their lending their names to any greater action, they intend to govern themselves onely as they shall understand to concur with his Majesties pleasure; and therefore hope they shall receive advice from his Highness, and your Grace, what is fit for them to contribute to such occasions as they see much to their comforts, you advance with so great care and vigilance. Thus I most humbly take leave,

Your Grace's most humble, and most devoted servant,

Hague, April 16. 1624.
Dudley Carleton.

Sir Dudley Carleton, *to the Duke.*

May it please your Grace,

SUch commandments as I received from your Grace, by double Dispatches of the 4th of the last, by way of provision, whilest Sir *William Saint Leiger* lay sick, were prevented by his own presence, he bringing the first of those Packets with him, and thereby bad commodity to assist at the breaking of the business to the States, by virtue of his Majesties Credence given him and my Lord General *Cecill*; which, since, he hath sollicited both at the Camp, and in this place, with all possible care and industry; and I have not failed of my utmost endeavours.

Sir Dudley Carleton, to the Duke.

But the unfetlednefs of this Government, which ftill continueth, fince the late change of Governours, hath bred delay to fome, and direct impediments to other points we had in charge; which we have endeavoured to fupply by other means. And now, in what ftate he leaves the whole bufinefs, he will relate to your Grace. Such Patents as your Grace required from the King and Queen of *Bohemia*, I have committed to his delivery, in divers forms, with a Blank, figned and fealed, wherein to frame fuch an one as may be better to your minds: but if your Grace make no ufe of it, you may pleafe to return it to me again; to the end I may reftore it.

What concerns my felf, I abfolutely remit, and fubmit to your Grace: onely I will renew the requeft I made to your Grace by my Nephew; That your Grace will not prefer any before me in your formerly intended favour, out of belief, that any can be more, then I refolve to reft, whileft I live, *a toutes Efpreves*,

Humbly and faithfully devoted to your Grace's perfon and fervice,

Hague, June 20.
1625.

Dudley Carleton.

Sir Dudley Carleton, to the Duke.

May it pleafe your Grace,

AFter long attendance, the wind is come good for *Plymouth*, which, I hope, will carry thither, fpeedily and fafely, the States whole Fleet, though in three parts; twelve Ships with the Admiral *de Naffau*, who hath long waited in the *Texel*; four but newly ready, provided by thofe of *Zealand* at *Amfterdam*; and four, which have layen fome time before the *Brill*, whereof one is to land the Marfhal *Chatillion* in paffing by *Calice*, the other three to convoy the *Englifh*-men: And Arms I fend in ten other Ships I have hired at *Rotterdam*; before which place they have layen twenty days a Ship-board, by reafon of contrary winds, with fome impatiency, but no diforder; which what courfe I took to prevent, as likewife what may happen in their voyage, my Lord *Conway* (to whom I give a particular account of all) will inform your Grace.

I have obtained leave for Sir *John Proud* to go the voyage, according to his Majefties Letter, though it was fomewhat ftood upon by the States, and he hath taken his paffage by *Zealand*.

When I call to mind, what Patents I procured of the King of *Bohemia*, and fent your Grace by Sir *William Saint Leiger*, (amongft which was one of fubmiffion to any accommodation his Majeftie fhall at any time like well of, for the King of *Bohemia*) I think it neceffary to advertife your Grace, That knowledge being come hither of the *Infanta*'s fending the Count *Shemburgh* to the King of *Denmark*, with a fair Meffage, and the Count *Gondomar*'s overtures to Mr. *Trumbal*, tending to reconcilement, and reftitution of the *Palatinate*, it is fo willingly hearkened unto by the King of *Bohemia*, that there is no doubt of his confent: But withall he well confiders, that if Treaty alone be trufted unto, and thereupon Arms now levied by his Majefty and his Friends be laid afide, all will prove as fruitlefs as formerly. For howfoever the King of *Spain* (for more free profecution of other quarrels, or defigns) may be induced to quit what he poffeffeth in the *Palatinate*; the fhares which the Emperour, the Duke of *Bavaria*, and the two Electors of *Mentz* and *Triers*, with a great rabble of Popifh Priefts and Jefuites, have therein, will require more then bare negotiation, to wring it out of their hands; and nothing but Victory, or, at leaft, a well-armed Treaty, can ferve that turn.

The time feems long both to the King and Queen, and grows very irkfome, every day more then other, of their abode here in this place; which indeed doth prove, in all refpects, very uncomfortable; and that your Grace will gather out of Mr. Secretary *Morton*'s report, and my Letters to my Lord *Conway*. In this very confideration, I befeech your Grace, be the more mindfull of,

Your Grace's moft humble, and moft devoted fervant,

Hague, Auguft 20.
1625.

Dudley Carleton.

Sir Dudley Carleton, *to the Duke.*

May it please your Grace,

THe business of strict conjunction betwixt his Majesty and this State (touching which the Queen of *Bohemia* hath received his Highness, and your Graces Letters, and I your Graces of the 9th. of this present) goeth on the right foot (according as your Grace will see more particularly by my Letters to Mr. Secretary *Conway*,) and as the matter is here embraced with much affection, so, for the manner, I doubt not but it will be well ordered in that sort, as will be for his Majesties honour, and contentment. But in regard of jealousies towards us, and emulations amongst these men, in matters of imployment, (to which all men are subject, especially in good and advantagious businesses, some time will be required, to set all in the right way, yet no unlimited time; for I hope, within a week all will be resolved of, and within a few dayes more put in execution fully to expectation. Sir *Noel Carone* writes, a league offensive and defensive will be embraced by his Majesty, if it be proposed from hence, with offer of assurance; And I assure my self, both the overture and offer will be made and really effected, if it be answered on our side with good correspondence. That which busieth my cogitations is, that *tempus agendi* may be lost *Consultando*; and therefore seeing how both his Majesty, and this State stand affected, I will take the liberty to give your Grace two advertisements in matters of action, which will be of exceeding fruit, if they be thought of in tin time, and for which there is no time to spare.

One is, that your Grace doth inquire after in your Letter to the Queen of *Bohemia* (who excuseth writing either to his Highness, or your Grace, till the States have resolved of their sending) that is, the States preparation for the *West-Indies*, which way, the Company for those parts newly erected in these, hath set out one Fleet of 32 Sayl now already at Sea, with some Land-men amongst them, to put on ground, and fortifie as they shall find occasion; for which they have men for the purpose, and all materials ready embarqued with them.

A second Fleet they are now preparing against April next, about which all their Admiralties and some of the Deputies of this new *West-Indian* Company, are here at this present. And the design is, for the Admiralties to set out at the charge of the generality twelve good ships of war, besides what they have already on the coast of *Spain*, and in the narrow Seas; which they will still continue.

To these 12. ships they require the *West-Indian* Company to joyn 12. more, which will make a good Fleet; and this they intend shall be ready (as I said) in April next, to attend the coming of the *Spanish West-Indian* Fleet, which here they understand is put into the *Havana*, with intention there to winter, as it did the last year.

Now if his Majesty will give leave to his Subjects, to erect a Company for the *West-Indies*, and joyn with these men in those parts, as they do in the East, (and upon moree quall conditions, since the business is now but in the beginning) it will be here gladly embraced. And if he will frame a Fleet betwixt his own ships and his Merchants, to joyn with the States Fleet prepared for April next, to intercept the *Spanish West-Indian* Fleet, nothing more will be desired by these men, and there is nothing of which for the present they promise themselves greater fruit: for either they hope to take, or to stop the silver of those parts (both which are good services, considering the need of money the *Spaniards* have in these,) or else they resolve with the ships which belong to the company to pursue their voyage to the *West-Indies*.

The second is a Truce with the Pyrates of *Algier*; such an one as this State hath made in conformity to their peace with the Grand Seigniour, which will be no more observed for unmolesting all and every one of our Merchants ships as they are straglingly lighted on, then it is with these men, who suffer many losses in particular; but those are recompensed in the general. For the *Spaniards* are much amazed with this correspondence; And the men of War of this State, or such Merchants as can make any reasonable defence, are most medled withall. Besides, in any matter of offence they concurr together; And even now a proposition is made from *Algier* to the Prince of *Orange*, (which I have from his own mouth to acquaint your Grace therewith) that in case this State against the beginning of next summer will set out twenty Sayl of ships upon any good service against the *Spaniards*, they will joyn unto them 60. Sayl to pursue the design, whatsoever it shall be, of this State. The acceptation of which offer, being now in deliberation, it will be suspended till it be seen how this unexpected business with his Majesty may proceed; and then they will here do nothing but that as

they

may concurr with our common Interests. But becaue the negotiation of this matter with those of *Algier* (that is, a truce betwixt his Majesties subjects and those men) will require time, your Grace may provisionally move his Majesty (if the matter be well liked) to use such endeavours as may conduce thereunto. Here they use to write, and send through *France*, by *Marseilles*, to the Consul they have continually at *Algier*, by whose means (if no better present it self) any thing may be proposed his Majesty shall find fitting.

Other things I will within few daies remonstrate to your Grace, for his Majesties service, in this change of affairs, which require all possible industries, and diligences, to be used both far and neer; And those not neglected, I doubt not, but they who have so grossly abused his Majesties friendship will soon repent themselves, and by their harms see their own errours. Thus I most humbly take leave,

Your Graces most humble, and most faithful servant,

Hague, January 24, 1625.
Dudley Carleton.

Sir Dudley Carleton, *to the Duke.*

May it please your Grace,

ACcording as I advertised your Grace, the 24 of the last, of the disposition of the Prince of *Orange*, and such of the States as he called unto him to Councel, they procured the rest soon after to resolve of an Embassage to his Majesty, and now they have dispatched the same with as much expedition as could possibly be used. The persons are *Aertsens* of *Holland*, and *Joachim* of *Zealand*, both able, and well affected persons, and both sufficiently known to his Majesty by former employments. They go amply authorized for what they shall treat: but that as yet is an Embrion onely, which must receive form and life from his Majesty, in whose hands it lyeth to preserve this State, and dispose for ever of the whole strength thereof for his own service, and his Royal Families: Which after more debates and distastes then have passed with all the world besides, I am glad I can say upon good warrantize: whereof this is one proof, that when his Majesty is constrained by the necessity of affairs to send, and seek to his other friends, he is sent, and sought, and sued to from hence. I doubt not but it will be objected (as hath been formerly) that it is for their own Interest, and that they would gladly engage his Majesty in their quarrel, which it were a folly to deny: but there is alwaies the friendship strongest when the Interests are most conjoyned. And if that which is principally for one mans benefit turn likewise to another mans advantage, *Hoc non facere* (saith an old School-book) *summa est imprudentiæ*.

The affairs of these parts for matter of Action (which have more then ordinarily succeeded in this cold season, but have been more coldly pursued then was feared) I refer to this Bearer, my Nephew, his report; who having the honour to be his Majesties servant, I imploy him the more willingly, as able to give account of such particularities, either of this Negotiation, or otherwise, of which his Majesty and your Grace may require knowledge. And I humbly beseech your Grace to give him encouragement by your accustomed noble favour, So rests

Your Graces most humble, and most devoted servant,

Hague, February 16. 1625.
Dudley Carleton.

Sir Charles Cornwallis, *Lieger in* Spain, *to the* Spanish *King.*

YOur Majesty hath shewed the sincerity of your Royal heart in applying remedy to many inconveniences and injustice offered by your Ministers to the King my Masters subjects in their goods and bodies, and therein have performed not only what belongeth to your Kingly dignity, but also what might be expected from a Prince so zealous of justice, and of so good intention. It resteth, that now I beseech you to cast your Royal eyes upon another extream injustice offered not only to their bodies and goods, but to their very souls; who being by your Majesties agreement, confirmed with your oath, to live within these your Kingdoms free from molestation for matter of opinion and conscience, except in matters of scandal to others, are here laid hold on and imprisoned by your Majesties Officers of Inquisition, continually, upon every light occasion of private information of some particular persons of their own Countrey, who being fugitives out of their own houses, and having according to the nature of our people removed not only their bodies, but their hearts, from the soil that

bred

Sir Dudley Carleton, to the Duke.

bred them, and from their Brethren that were nourished with them, do here seek to grace themselves, by professing and teaching the observations of the *Romish* Church; and that, not out of any zeal, but, as plainly appeareth by many of their actions, out of malice and envy. By the Commissioners, authorized by both your Majesties for the agreeing of the Peace, it was clearly discerned, that if, upon private or particular informations, his Majesties vassals here should be questioned for matter of Religion, It was not possible that they should exercise any commerce in these Kingdoms, where they should be no one moment assured either of their goods or liberties. It was therefore provided, that they should, in no sort, be impeached, but in case of scandal, and that scandal, with your Majesties favour, must be understood to grow out of some publick action, not out of private opinion, or single conscience; for if otherwise, very vain and inutil had been that provision. How the word *scandal* is, in the most usual and common sence, to be understood, is in no Books more evident then in the Divine Scriptures themselves. Our Saviour, in regard of his publick teaching of the Gospel, and the abolishing of the Law-Ceremonial, was said to be, to both houses of *Israel, a stone of scandal*. The sin of *David*, if it had layen covered in his own heart, or been committed in private, should not have been, either published, or punished, as a scandal to the enemies of God. St. *Paul* himself declareth, that his own eating of flesh offered to Idols could not be an offence, but onely his eating before others of weak conscience, whereby to give the scandal. Besides, I humbly beseech your Majesty, consider, how fitly that of the Apostle, *Quis es qui judicas alienum servum*, may be applied to those Officers of the Inquisition, attempting to lay hands on the Subjects of another Prince, your Majesties confederate, offering none offence to the Laws, or publick prejudice to their profession: yea, in divers parts of your Majesties dominions, the Subjects of my Master have suffered this restraint. The Inquisitor-General, lately deceased, who in all his actions shewed himself a considerate Minister, and carefull, in regard of your Majesties honour, of the observing of what you have capitulated, upon my complaint, never failed to give the remedy that in justice I required. He being now with God, and one of my Sovereigns subjects having been long, without cause, detained by the Inquisitors in *Lisbon*; and another of good account, a man moderate and temperate in all his actions, lately apprehended by that Office in *Ayemonte*, and restrained in their prison at *Sevil*: I am commanded from his Majesty, and importuned by my Countrey-men, who all, with one voice, complain, and protest, that they dare not longer continue their commerce, without present order for remedy of so extream and perillous an injustice, to beseech your Majesty, that you will be pleased, not onely to give present order for the release of those that without scandal are known, for the present, in your prisons; but also, that in time to come the true intention of that Article be observed, which is, That, without known offence and scandal, the King my Masters subjects be not molested. The accomplishment of this (considering how much it imports your Majesty in honour, your Majesty and the Arch-Duke having in that Article, in no other sort then in all the rest, covenanted by especial words, that your selves would provide, that in no case, but onely in giving scandal to others, the subjects of my Sovereign should be troubled for their consciences) I cannot but expect from so just and sincere a Prince: and therefore will not trouble your Majesty with more words; but offering my self, in all things within my power, to your Majesties service, I remain, with a desire to be reckoned in the number of your Majesties humble and affectionate servants,

July 23. *stilo novo*, 1608.   C. C.

Sir Charles Cornwallis, to the Spanish King.

THe largeness and liberality of your Majesties Royal hand being such, that it hath made your Greatness and Munificence of much so note through most parts of this world; I assure my self, it is far removed from the thoughts of your Princely heart, to streighten in matter of Justice, that so naturally and necessarily belongeth to your Kingly Office. Your Majesty hath been pleased to refer to the Constable, the Duke of *Infantasque*, and two of the Regents of your Councel of *Arragon*, the understanding and determining of the extreme and barbarous usage, outrage and spoil, committed by ships set out in course under the Commission, and at the charge of your Majesties Vice-Roy of *Sardinia*, and his Son-in-law *Don Lewis de Calatana*, and others by their procurement: Those Lords, and others, there authorized by that Commission, very nobly and justly desiring, that of the spoil committed there might be made entire satisfaction, gave order divers moneths since; but your Majesties

Viceroy adding to his former offence contempt of your Majesties authority, hath not only disobeyed in his own person, but contradicted and withstood in others the accomplishment of your commandements; it seemeth that God is pleased, for the good of your Majesties Estate and Government, to dis-vizard that man, and make apparent to the world how unfit he is to be trusted with your command of so great importance, whose covetous and ungodly condition is come to such height, as hath drawn him not only to spoil unlawfully, and so barbarously to use the subjects of so great a King, your confederate, and thereby to hazard a breach of the amity between your Majesties so necessary for both your Estates, and so utile to the whole Commonwealth of Christendom, but also to neglect and contemn the authority of your Majesty his own Sovereign, to whom, besides the obligation of his natural allegiance, he is so inhnitely bound for preferring and trusting him with a matter of so great consequence and dignity. By this paper inclosed your Majesty shall understand the manner of proceeding of the King my Master against such of his subjects as commit the like crimes and outrage against any of yours, and thereby conceive what my said Sovereign expecteth of your Majesty in this and the like, and what I am commanded, in conformity thereof, to require; which is, that there be no proceeding in so clear and plain a case, by way of protest or suit in Law, which in this Kingdom (as by experience is known,) are immortal; but that according to the sixth Article of the Peace, and the most Christian and just example shewed by my Sovereign, who so punctually and conscionably in all things observeth with your Majesty, you will be pleased that there be not only an entire and emmediate satisfaction to the parties, but that as well your said Viceroy, and *Don Lewis* his Son-in-Law, as all others their aiders, partners, and receivers in that crime, may be criminally proceeded against, and suffer such punishment, as so enorm and unlawful actions have justly deserved: The performance of this (considering with what patience the King my Master, out of his love to your Majesty, notwithstanding the daily complaints and importunities of the parties, and the general exclamation of other his subjects, who hold it rather agreeable with his honor and Kingly Office, not so long to permit unsatisfied or unpunished so intollerable an outrage, hath more then three whole years attended it) I cannot but expect from so just and pious a Prince, without further delay or protraction of time.

Jan. 16. *novo stilo*. 1608.

Sir Charles Cornwallis, *to the Spanish King.*

WEll knoweth your Majesty, in your Royal wisdome, how necessary to Kings is the conservation of authority and respect to their Kingly dignities; as also that the greatest and most absolute precept of Justice, is, to do to others what we would be done unto our selves: How religiously and punctually the King my master hath observed these unto your Majesty, hath appeared by many demonstrations, (and not the least) in the denial he made to *Antonio de Perez* to abide in his Kingdome, or to have access to his person; only out of a conceit he had, that he came with a mind determined to dis-authorize your Majesty in his speeches, or to make offer of some practice against your Estates in his overcures. Your Majesties own Royal and gratefull inclination I know to be such, as you are not without desire to pay my Sovereign with the like equivalent retribution: but with your Majesties pardon and favour, duty inforceth me plainly to tell you, that the Ministers of these your Kingdoms shew not the like affection; where not one, but many, of my Sovereigns worst affected subjects are daily received, cherished, and honoured with entertainments in your service. Were that sort of people contented only to abuse your Majesties Kingly munificence and Christian charity, and to deceive your Ministers with their falsified genealogies, and with putting the *Don* upon many whose fathers and Ancestors were so base and beggerly as they never arrived to be owners of so much as convenient apparrel to cover their nakedness, it were much more tolerable: but when having here tasted the warmth of your Majesties liberal and pious hand, they become furnished in such ample and abundant manner, as their poor and miserable Ancestors durst never so much as dream of, like *Æsops* Serpent', they turn their venemous slings towards the bosoms that gave them heat and life, and endeavour with all the force and Art they have, to give cause of distaste, and by consequence of division, between your Majesty and your faithfullest and most powerfull Confederate, in uneven payment for your Majesties so great and gracious a favour. With generalities for the present I will not deal, as he whose cares and desires have ever been to soften, and not to sharpen.

Two

Sir Charles Cornwallis, to the Spanish King.

Two *Irish* in your Court, the one a son, as by his own Country-men is generally reported, either to a vagabond Rimer, a generation of people in that Country of the worst account; or to give him his best title, of a poor Mechanical Surgeon. The other descended rather of more base and beggarly parents; neglecting what by the Laws of God they ow to their own Sovereign, and as little regarding their obligation to your Majesty, who from the dust of the earth and miserable estate hath made them what they are, notwithstanding that they cannot be ignorant of the strict charge and commandments your Majesty hath given, that all due respect be had to the King my Master, and his Ministers and subjects; the first, in irreverent and irrespective behaviour towards my self and some of mine; the other, in obstinate defending his companions unmannerliness, delivering, by way of direct asseveration, that I am an heretick, and such an one as to whom it is not lawful, under the pain of deadly sin, to use any courtesie or reverence whatsoever, have of late miscarried themselves, as I hold it not agreeable either with what I ow to the King I serve, or the honour I have to represent his person, to pass over with silence, but to present it instantly to your Majesty. The names of the parties are, *Magg Ogg*, a Sollicitor (as here is said) for the fugitive Earl of *Tyrone*, condemned by the verdict of his own Countrymen, besides his delict of Treason, of thirteen several murders. The other names himself *Cordio Mauricio*, and is here (as I am informed) allowed for —— for his vagabonding Countrymen, hath put on the habit of a Priest, and hath of your Majesty thirty crowns a moneth in Pension. The parties and the offences I have made known unto your Secretary of State, and I cannot doubt, but your Majesty, in conformity of what the King my Master hath by so many arguments demonstrated towards your Majesty and your Ministers, will command such exemplary punishment to be made of them, as a behaviour so undecent, a slander and reproach so intolerable, and an opinion so desperate and dangerous, and so contrary to what your Majesty and all those of your Councel, Nobility and Clergy, do practise, do worthily merit, &c. *Feb.* 1608.

Sir Charles Cornwallis, to the Spanish King.

Your Majesty to whom God hath given so large an Empire, and so much exceeding that of other Princes, and whom he hath blessed with so great an inclination to piety, clemency, and other vertues becoming your Royall dignity and Person, will, I know, hold it evil beseeming so rare a greatness to come behind any King, how pious and vertuous soever, either in the observance of the laws of mutual charity and friendship, or in love or zeal to justice, which to all Kingdoms and Governments gives the assuredst foundation; and in defect whereof, by the Spirit of God himself Kingdoms are said to be translated from one Nation to another. The first King that God gave unto his people, he elected of higher stature then the rest, by the shoulders upwards, signifying thereby how much Kings are to strive to exceed and excell in the height and measure of vertue and justice; also how fit it is for them to overlook with their authorities & providences the highest head of their Ministers, and to observe how they guide themselves.

By the contents of this paper inclosed, your Majesty shall perceive the Christian and Kingly care the King my Master hath had, not only of the observances of the Articles of Peace, since the same between your Majesties were concluded; but of the punctual accomplishment of the true Laws of amity and friendship, which are more surely and expressively imprinted in Royall and Noble hearts, then possibly they can be written or charactered by any pen in paper. In your Majesties Kingdoms (pardon I humbly beseech you, if I speak plainly) much contrary to that example, the King my Masters subjects suffer all manner of spoils, oppressions and miseries, and are (as well I may term them) made a very prey to the hungry and greedy; your Viceroyes and others enter their ships under cover and colour of Peace and Justice; finding them rich, they lay crimes to their charge, whereof there appears neither proof nor probability; yet serve their pretences to possess them of their goods, and to put the poor Merchants to a demand in Law: wherein were truth alone the balance they should be weighed by, (though that form of redress were far short of the immediate remedy provided by the King my Sovereign for your Majesties subjects) yet were it much more allowable and to be endured; but having here complained two whole years without any course at all taken for redress, as in the cause with the Duke of *Feria* three intire years, as in that with the Viceroy of *Sardinia* one year and more, as in that of his Majesties servant *Adrian Thibaut*, taken and spoiled by your Majesties Generall *Don Luis*; as in that of *Estry* and *Bispich*, imprisoned and bereaved of their goods by *Juan de Vendoza Alcalde* of *Madrid*, we are after so long a time spent in misery and charge countervailing a great part of the value of the goods taken from us, inforced still to all punctualities and extremities of forms of law, and to abide the uttermost perill of all adventages that by the inventions, wits and tongues of Lawyers, can be devised, to obscure and hide the light and right of truth. The false colour given by every of these, and the barbarous cruelty used to the parties, would require too long and tedious a declaration. It satisfieth that none of their pretences are proved; nay, which is more, they are so false and fabulous, as to no indifferent understanding they appear so much as probable.

My humble desire is, your Majesty would be pleased to pass your own Royal eyes upon this paper; and therefore to affect all possible brevity, I will pass unto your Majesties other inferior Ministers of your Ports, of which few there are (those in *Biscay*, and some in *Portugal* only excepted) where we have not divers oppressions, imprisonments, and unjust imbargements, in *Sevil* especially; whereof forty several suits, and as many false sentences given, raised and pursued by a man now dead, and therefore in charity left unnamed. We have hitherto in your Majesties Councel of war (where before those noble Lords all passed by the equal line of Justice) not failed, in my remembrance, in the overthrowing of any, save one mistaken that passed in a wrong name, and another, concerning merchandise that had their manufacture in *Embden*, (whereof I suppose those Lords were not rightly informed) only excepted. In that Court, I must acknowledge, we have had redress, but yet with your Majesties favour a miserable one; our gain being whether we shall be owners of our own or not, our expences and charges certain, and the time without measure large, whereby many have been undone, some dead in prison in *England*, for want of what was unjustly detained from them here. Yet neither the false Judges in *Sevil*, nor Promoters, ever chastised, or for any thing that I yet have understood, so much as ever reprehended or found fault with.

I haste to a conclusion, fearing lest I should dwell too long on a matter so unsavoury and unpleasing to your Majesties pitiful ears and Christian heart, so much of it self disposed to all clemency and piety. I will, for the next, resort to the ships, cordage, corn, and other victuals and provisions taken from the King my Sovereigns subjects for your Majesties own services, and the relief of the extreme necessity in your Gallies, and Garrisons of the Navy, of whom some have been enforced for want of payment of their moneys to send their ships home unfreighted; a loss extreme to poor Merchants that live by trade and time, to repair to this Court, and here remain, some of them fourteen moneths, and others two years and more, till their very charges had eaten out a great part of what was due unto them, and in the end recover only their own, without any relief or recompence, either for their expences, times lost, or dammages. I will only instance two, because their causes are most strange and pitiful, and yet unsatisfied; the one named *Thomas Harrison*, and the other *Richard Morris*: The first served your Majesty with his ship, till the same, with one of his sons and all his men, were swallowed with the Seas, and hath been here more then four years suing for his recompence and salary, recommended by the King my Sovereign, by Letters from your Majesties Embassadors in *England*, and by my self all that long time furthered with my earnest sollicitation; which hath begot infinite promises, but to this day no manner of payment or performance: The other, who sometimes hath been a man of wealth and reputation, and falling into great poverty, served your Majesty with all that in the world he was worth, and all that in value above 6000 Ryals. I blush, I protest, to think of it, and my heart is grieved to mention it to so great a King, of whose liberality and magnificence the world taketh so much notice. His right and his necessity being well known unto your Officers, he hath been more then three years and a half fed with hopes, and put off with schedules, and sending from one Port to another for the receipt of his money, till he hath indebted himself the most part of the sum, and at present wanteth wherewith both to feed and cover him. Now, at last, he is promised payment here out of your Royal chests, but after so many ceremonies and circumstances to be performed with your Officers in other parts, as God knows hunger may end the poor man before they begin to satisfie him. By all this will plainly appear to your Majesty, that your Majesties subjects are by the favour and Christian Justice of the King my Master entred into the new Testament and law of Grace, having restitution and remedy without the delays of ceremony and formality; and we still remain under the old, and tyed in all things to the hand-writing of the Law, to the burthenous circumstances and intolerable dilatory formalities of proceeding in this your Kingdom, and what else your unpitiful Ministers will out of uncharitable and unsensible minds of other mens harms, charge and impose upon us.

Well doth your Majesty conceive, that would the King my Master wink at the like courses to be taken by his subjects and ministers with such of yours as they might meet upon the Seas, the English are not of so little invention, but they could devise as good colours

and

and pretences; nor their Lawyers of so small skill, and so much conscience, but they could form and protract suits; nor the Ships of *England* so weakened and lessened, but they could equal and surmount their losses. I have out of mine own humble affection to your Majesty, out of my generall and ever continuing desire to hold firm the ancient amity so necessary for your own estates, and utile for the whole Common-weal of Christendom, out of the force of duty I owe to my King and Country, thus far adventured to unburthen my soul and thoughts, not doubting but your Majesties magnanimous and Christian heart will be moved as well in desire to equal the pious and immutable example of the King my Master, as in a just compassion of a Nation now confederate with you, and that so gladly would entertain any cause to love and serve you, to give present remedy to those woful and intolerable oppressions; and that since you have confirmed, and consented by your Articles of Peace of new orders (which being confirmed by your oath stand now in force of Laws) you would be pleased, in like manner, to give them a new form of indilatory execution, conformable to that of the King my Sovereign, &c.

King Charles, *to the Earl of* Bristol.

WE have read your Letter addressed to us by *Buckingham*; and We cannot but wonder that you should through forgetfulness make such a request to us of favour, as if you stood eavenly capable of it; when you know what your behaviour in *Spain* deserved of Us, which you are to examine by the observations We made, and know you well remember, how at our first coming into *Spain*, taking upon you to be so wise as to foresee our intentions to change our Religion, you were so far from dissuading us, that you offered your service, and secrecy, to concur in it, and in many other open Conferences, pressing to shew how convenient it was for us to be a *Roman Catholick*, it being impossible, in your opinion, to do any great action otherwise; how much wrong, disadvantage, and disservice you did to the Treaty, and to the right and interest of our dear Brother, and Sister, and their Children; what disadvantage, inconvenience, and hazard you intangled us in by your artifices, putting off, and delaying our return home. The great estimation you made of that State, and the vile price you set this Kingdome at, still maintaining, that we, under colour of friendship to *Spain*, did what was in our power against them, which (you said) they knew very well. And last of all, your approving of those Conditions, that our Nephew should be brought up in the Emperours Court; to which Sir *Walter Aston* then said, he durst not give his Consent, for fear of his head; you replying to him, that without some such great action, neither marriage nor peace could be had, &c.

Jan. 21. 1625.

King Charles *to the University of* Cambridge, *in approbation of the Election.*

TRusty and Welbeloved, We greet you well. Whereas upon Our Pleasure intimated unto you by the Bishop of *Durham* for the choice of your Chancellor, you have with such duty as We expected highly satisfied Us in your election, We cannot in Our Princely nature (who are much possessed with this testimony of your ready and loyal affections) but for ever to let you know, how much you are therein made partakers of Our Royal approbation: and as We shall ever conceive, that an Honour done to a person We favour, is out of a loyal respect had unto Our Self; and as we shall ever justifie *Buckingham* worthy of this your Election, so shall you finde the fruits of it: for We have found him a faithful servant to our dear Father of blessed memory; and Our Self cannot but undertake that he will prove such a one unto you; and will assist him with a gracious willingness, in any thing that may concern the good of the University in general, or the particular merits of any Students there.

Given under Our Signet, at Our Palace of Westminster, *the sixth of* June, *in the second year of Our Reign.*

June 6. 1626.

King Charles *his Instructions, to the Vice-Chancellor, and Heads of* Cambridge, *for Government,* &c.

CHARLES REX.

First, that all those directions and orders of our Father of blessed memory, which at any time were sent to our said University, be duly observed and put in execution.

2. Whereas we have been informed, that of late years many Students of that our University, not regarding their own birth, degree, and quality, have made divers contracts of marriage with women of mean estate, and of no good fame, in that Town, to their great disparagement, the discontent of their parents and friends, and the dishonour of the Government of that our University; we will, and command you, that at all times hereafter, if any Taverner, Inholder, or Victualer, or any other inhabitant of the Town, or within the Jurisdiction of the University, shall keep any daughter, or other woman in his house, to whom there shall resort any Scholars of that University, of what condition so ever, to misspend their time, or otherwise to mis-behave themselves in marriage, without the consent of those that have the Gardiance and tuition of them, that upon notice thereof, you do presently convent the said Scholars or Scholar, and the said woman or women thus suspected, before you, and upon due examination, if you find cause therefore, that you command the said woman or women, according to the form of your Charter against women, *de malo suspectis*, to remove out of the University, and foure miles of the same : And if any refuse presently to obey your commands, and to be ordered by you herein, that you then bind them over with sureties to appear before the Lords of our Privy Counsel, to answer their contempt, and such matters as shall be objected against them. And if any refuse presently to obey, to imprison them till they either remove, or put in such bonds with sureties.

3. That you be careful that all the Statutes of our University be duly executed, especially those *de vestitu Scholarium, & de modestia, & morum urbanitate.* And whereas we are informed, that Batchelors of Law, Physick, and Masters of Arts, and others of higher degree, pretend they are not subject to your censure, if they resort to such houses and places as are mentioned in the said Statutes, to eat, drink, play, or take Tobacco, to the misspending of their time, and corrupting of others by their ill example, and to the scandalizing of the government of our said University : Our will and pleasure is, by these presents, that you do also command them, and every of them, to forbear coming to any such houses, otherwise, or at other times, then by the said Statute others of inferiour order and degree, are allowed to do, any Statute or Concession whatsoever to the contrary notwithstanding. And if any refuse to obey you herein, that you proceed against them as contumacious; and if there be cause, that you also signifie their names to us, or the Lords of our privy Counsel.

4. That you do severely punish all such of your body, of what degree or condition soever, as shall contemn their superiors, or mis-behave themselves, either in word or deed, towards the Vice-Chancellor or Proctors, or any other Officers of our University, especially in the executing of their office.

5. Lastly, we will and command, that a Copy of these our directions be delivered to the Master of every Colledge, and that he cause the same to be published to those of his Colledge, and then to be Registred in the Registers of their Colledges, and duly observed and kept by all persons whom they concern.

Examinatur, & concordat cum Originali. Ita attester, Jacobus Fabor *Registrarius,* *March* 4. 1629.

King Charles, *to the Lords Spiritual and Temporal.*

WE being desirous of nothing more then the advancing of the good peace and prosperity of our people, have given leave to free debates of highest point of our prerogative royal, which in the times of our Predecessors, Kings and Queens of this Realm, were ever restrained as matter they would not have disputed; and in other things we have been willing so far to descend to the desires of our good Subjects, as might fully satisfie all moderate minds, and free them from all just feares and jealousies, which those messages we have sent unto the Commons House will well demonstrate to the world; and yet we find it still insisted on, That in no case whatsoever, should it never so neerly concern matters

ters of State and Government, we or our Privy Councel have power to commit any man without the cause be shewed. The service it self would be thereby destroyed and defeated; and the cause it self must be such as may be determined by our Judges of our causes at *Westminster*, in a legal and ordinary way of Justice; whereas the cause may be such, as these Judges have not capacity of Judicature, nor rules of Law to direct and guide their Judgements in cases of transcedent nature, which happening so often, the very intermitting of the constant rules of Government, for so many ages within this Kingdom practised, would soon dissolve the very frame and foundation of our Monarchy; wherefore, as to our Commons, we made fair propositions, which might equally preserve the just liberties of the subject: So my Lords, we have thought good to let you know, that without the overthrow of our Sovereignty, we cannot suffer this power to be impeached; yet notwithstanding, to clear our conscience and intentions, this we publish, that it is not in our heart or will, ever to extend our Royal power (lent unto us from God) beyond the just rule of moderation, in any thing which shall be contrary to our Laws and Customes, wherein the safety of our people shall be our only aim. And we do hereby declare our Royal pleasure to be, which (God willing) we will ever constantly continue and maintain, that neither we nor our Privy Councel shall, or will, at any time hereafter, commit or command to prison, or otherwise restrain, the person of any for not lending money unto us, or for any other cause which in our conscience doth concern the publick good, and safety of us and our people; we will not be drawn to pretend any cause which in our conscience is not, or is not expressed, which base thought, we hope no man can imagine, can fall into our Royal breast: and that in all causes of this nature which shall hereafter happen, we shall upon the humble Petition of the patty, or address of our Judges unto us, readily and really express the true cause of their commitment or restraint, so soon as with conveniency or safety the same is fit to be disclosed and expressed; and that in all causes Criminal, of ordinary Jurisdiction, our Judges shall proceed to the deliverance and bailment of the Prisoner, according to the known and ordinary rules of the Laws of this Land; and according to the Statute of *Magna Charta*, and those other six Statutes insisted on, which we do take knowledge stand in full force; and which we intend not to weaken, or abrogate, against the true intent thereof.

This we have thought fit to signifie unto you, the rather for the shortning of any long debate upon this question, the season of the year being so far advanced; and our great occasions of State not lending us many days of long continuance of this Session of Parliament.

Given under our Signet, at our Palace at Westminster, *the Twelfth day of* May, *in the Fourth Year of our Reign.*

CAROLUS REX.

King Charles, *to the* University *of* Cambridge; *for a new Election.*

Right Trusty and Welbeloved, We greet you well. As We took in gracious part your due respect, in Electing heretofore for your Chancellor a man who for his parts and faithful service was most dear unto Us: so now We are well pleased to understand, that you are sensible of your own and the common loss, by the bloody assassinate of so eminent a person, and that you desire and expect, for your comfort, an intimation from Us of a capable Subject to succeed in his room. This expression on your part hath begotten in Us a Royal affection towards you, and more care for your good; out of which, We commend unto free Election, of you the Vice-chancellor and Heads, and of the Masters Regents, and Non-Regents, (according to Our ancient Custom) Our Right Trusty and Right Welbeloved Cousin and Counsellor, *Henry* Earl of *Holland*, lately a member of your own Body; and well known unto you all: whose hearty affection to advance Religion and Learning generally in Our own Kingdoms, and especially in the Fountains, cannot be doubted of. Not that We shall cease to be your Chancellor in effect according to Our promise; but the rather for your advantage, We advise you to the choice, that you may have a person acceptable unto Us, and daily attending on Our person, to be Our Remembrancer and Sollicitor for you upon all occasions. And your general concurring herein shall be to Us a pledge of Our affections; which We are willing to cherish.

Given at our Court, the 28 *h of* August, *in the Fourth year of Our Reign.*

CAROLUS REX.

A Commiſsion to divers Lords, &c. for the delivery of
Fluſhing, Brill, &c.

JAMES by the Grace of God King of England, &c. To the Right Reverend Father in God, our Right Truſty and Welbeloved Councellor George Lord Archbiſhop of Canterbury, and to our Right Truſty and Welbeloved Councellor Tho. Ellſmere, Lord Chancellor of England; and to our Truſty and Welbeloved Couſins and Councellors, Tho. Earl of Suffolk, Lord Treaſurer of England; Edward Earl of Worceſter, Lord Keeper of our Privy-Seal; Lodowick Duke of Lenox, Lord Steward of our houſhold; Charles Earl of Nottingham, Lord Admiral of England; William Earl of Pembroke, Lord Chamberlain of our houſhold; Tho. Earl of Exeter, John Earl of Mar, and Alexander Earl of Dumfermlin; and to our Right Truſty and Welbeloved Councellors, Tho. Viſcount Fenton, Tho. Biſhop of Winton, Edward Lord Zouch, Lord Warden of our Cinque-Ports; William Lord Knowls, Treaſurer of our houſhold; John Lord Stanhop, and Tho. Lord Banning; and to our Right Truſty and Welbeloved Councellors, Sir John Digby Knight, our Vice-Chamberlain; Sir John Herbert Knight, one of our Principal Secretaries of State; Sir Fulk Grevil Knight, Chancellor and Under-Treaſurer of our Exchequer; Sir Tho Parry Knight, Chancellor of our Dutchy of Lancaſter; Sir Edward Coke Knight, Chief Juſtice of our Bench; and Sir Julius Ceſar Knight, Maſter of the Rolls; Greeting.
 Whereas the States-General of the United Provinces of the Low-Countries have divers times ſollicited us by their reſident Embaſſadour, Sir Noel Carone Knight; that we would be pleaſed to render into their hands the Town of Fluſhing in Zealand, with the Caſtle of Ramakins; and of Brill in Holland, with the Forts and Sconces thereunto belonging, which we hold by way of Caution, until ſuch ſums of money as they owe unto us be re-imburſed, upon ſuch reaſonable conditions as ſhould be agreed on between us and them, for the re-imburſing and repayments of the ſaid monies: And whereas we have recommended the conſideration of this ſo weighty and important an affair, to the judgment and diſcretion of you the Lords of our Privy Councel, and have received from you after long and mature deliberation and examination of the circumſtances and advice; That as the preſent condition of our State now ſtandeth, and as the nature of thoſe Towns is meerly cautionary, wherein we can challenge no intereſt of propriety; it would be much better for our ſervice, upon fair and advantagious conditions to render them, then longer to hold them at ſo heavy a charge. Now for as much as, in our Princely wiſdom, we have reſolved to yield up our ſaid Towns, with the ſaid Caſtle and Sconces belonging unto them, upon ſuch conditions as ſhall be moſt for our advantage, as well in point of honour as of profit, Know ye therefore, that we have aſſigned and appointed you the ſaid Archbiſhop, Lord Treaſurer, Lord Privy-Seal, Lord Steward, Lord Admiral, Lord Chamberlain, Earl of Exeter, Earl of Mar, Earl of Dumfermlin, Viſcount Fenton, Lord Biſhop of Winton, Lord Zouch, Lord Knowls, Lord Stanhop, Lord Banning, Sir John Digby, Sir John Herbert, Sir Ralph Winwood, Sir Tho. Lake, Sir Fulk Grevil. Sir Tho. Parry, Sir Edw. Coke, Sir Julius Ceſar, our Commiſſioners, and do by theſe preſents give full power and authority unto you, or the more part of you, for us and in our name, to treat and conclude with the ſaid Sir Noel Carone Knight, Embaſſadour from the States of the United Provinces, being likewiſe for that purpoſe ſufficiently authorized from the ſaid States his ſuperiors, touching the rendition and yielding up of the ſaid Town of Fluſhing, with the Caſtle of Ramakins in Zeland, and of the Town of Brill in Holland, with the Forts and Sconces thereto belonging, and of the Artillery and Munition formerly delivered by the States, with the ſame which are now remaining in them, or any of them, and have not been ſpent and conſumed; And for the delivery of them into the hands of the ſaid States on ſuch terms as by you ſhall be thought fit for our moſt honour and profit; and for the manner thereof to give inſtructions to our ſaid ſeveral Governours of the ſaid Garriſons, according to ſuch your concluſion. And this our Commiſſion or the enrollment or exemplification thereof ſhall be unto you, and every of you, a ſufficient warrant and diſcharge in that behalf. In witneſs &c.
 Witneſs our ſelf at Weſtminſter, the 31 day of May, in the 14th year of our Reign, &c. and of Scotland the 49th.

A

A Commission to Viscount Lisle, Governour, to deliver up Flushing, &c.

JAMES by the Grace of God, &c. To our Right Trusty and Welbeloved Cousin, *Robert* Lord Viscount *Lisle*, Lord Chamberlain to our dear Consort the Queen, and our Governour of our Town of *Flushing*, and of the Castle of *Ramakins*, Greeting. Whereas, we by our Letters Patents Sealed with our great Seal of *England*, bearing date at *Westminster* the 22 day of *April*, in the fifth year of our Reign of *England*, *France*, and *Ireland*, of *Scotland* 36, for the consideration therein expressed, did make, ordain, and constitute you the said Viscount *Lisle*, by the name of Sir *Robert Sydney* Knight, for Us to be the Governour and Captain of the said Town of *Flushing*, and of the Castle of *Ramakins* in the *Low Countries*, and of all the Garrisons and Souldiers that then were, or hereafter should be there placed for our service and guard of the said Town and Castle, to have, hold, exercise and occupy the Office of the said Governour and Captain of the said Town and Castle by your self, or your sufficient Deputy or Deputies, to be allowed by Us during Our pleasure; giving unto you full power and authority, by your said Letters Patents, to take the Oath and Oaths of all Captains and Souldiers then serving, or that hereafter should serve in the same Town and Castle, as in like causes was requisite, with divers other powers therein mentioned, as by Our said Letters Patents at large appeareth. And whereas the States General of the United Provinces of the *Low Countries* have divers and sundry times for many years together sollicited Us by their Resident Embassadour Sir *Noel Carone* Knight, that We would be pleased to render into their hands the said Town of *Flushing* in *Zealand*, with the said Castle of *Ramakins*, and the Town of *Brill* in *Holland*, with the Forts and Sconces thereunto belonging, which We hold by way of Caution, until such sums of money as they owe unto Us be re-imbursed upon such reasonable conditions as should be agreed upon between Us & them, for the re-imbursing and repaiment of the said monies. And whereas thereupon We recommended the consideration of this so weighty and important an affair to the judgment and discretion of the Lords of the Privy Councel, and have received from them (after long and mature deliberation and examination of Circumstances) an advice, that as the present condition of Our State now standeth, and as the nature of those Towns is lying only Cautionary, wherein we can challenge no interest of propriety, it should be much better for our service, upon fair and advantagious conditions to render them, then longer to hold them at so heavy a charge. Now forasmuch as in Our Princely Wisdom We have resolved to yield up our said Towns, with the said Castle and Sconces belonging unto them, upon such conditions as shall be most fit for our advantage, as well in point of honour as of profit: And to that end, by our Commission under our great Seal of *England*, have assigned and appointed the Lords and others of our Privy Councel our Commissioners, and thereby give full power and authority unto them, or the more part of them, for Us, and in our name, to treat and conclude with the said Sir *Noel Carone* Knight, Embassadour from the States of the United Provinces, being likewise for that purpose sufficiently authorized from the said States his superiors, touching the rendition and yielding up of the said Town of *Flushing*, with the Castle of *Ramakins* in *Zealand*, and of the said Town of *Brill* in *Holland*, with the Forts and Sconces thereunto belonging, and of the Artillery or Munition formerly delivered by the said States, with the same Towns, and Castles, and Forts, and which are now remaining in them, or any of them, and have not been spent or consumed. And for the delivery of the said Towns, Castle, Forts, Artillery, and Munition, into the hands of the said States, upon such terms as by the said Lords, and other of our Privy Councel, or the more part of them, shall be thought fit for our most honour and profit, and for the manner thereof to give instructions to our several Governours of our said Garrisons according to such their conclusion, which conclusion, according to our said Commission, is already made and perfected.

We do therefore hereby give power and authority unto, and do charge and command you the said Lord *Lisle*, for us and in our name, to render and yield up into the hands of the said States of the United Provinces, or to such persons as shall be lawfully deputed by them, the aforesaid Town of *Flushing*, and Castle of *Ramakins*, whereof now you have charge by vertue of our Letters Patents aforesaid, together with the Artillery and Munition now remaining in them or any of them, heretofore delivered by the said States with the said Town and Castle, and as yet not spent or consumed; observing and performing in all points such instructions as you shall receive under the hands of the said Lords and others of our

Privy

Privy-Councel, or the more part of them, concerning the rendring up and delivery of the said Town. And we do further give you full power and authority, and by these presents do charge and command you, for us and in our name, to discharge and set free all the subordinate Officers, Captains and Souldiers under your charge, of that oath and trust which heretofore they have taken, for the keeping and preserving of that Town and Castle to our use and service; and for that purpose to make such Declaration, Proclamation, and other signification of our Royal pleasure, commandment and ordinance in that behalf, as in your wisdom you shall think fit; and these our Letters-Patents, or the inrolment or exemplification thereof shall be your sufficient warrant and discharge in that behalf. In witness, &c.

Witness our self at Westminster, *the* 22 *day of* May, *in the* 14th *year of our reign of* England, France, and Ireland, *and of* Scotland *the* 49th.
May 22. *Jac.* 14.

The Councel of Ireland, to King Charles, in defence of the Lord Deputy Faulkland.

May it please your most excellent Majesty,

WE stand so bounden to your Royal Self, and your most blessed Father, our late deceased Sovereign Lord and Master, as we are urged in duty to prostrate this act of our faith at your Majesties feet, as an assay to cleer some things, wherein misinformation may seem to have approached your high wisdom. We understand that it is collected out of some late dispatches from hence, that there are such disorders in the Government here, as by the present Governors are remediless; all which is ascribed to the differences between persons of chief place; We do, in all humility, testifie and declare that we have not seen or known any inconvenience to the publick service, between your Majesties Deputy and Chancellor, neither have of late seen or heard any act or speech of contention between them. Other difference between persons of any eminent Action we understand none; neither are any disorders here yet so overgrown as to surpass the redress of the present Governour; especially, so long as he hath such a standing English Army as your Majesty now alloweth; if only we may receive some supply of Arms and Munition, which we have often written for, and do daily expect, and which shall be no loss to your Majesty. It is true, most gracious Sovereign, that in some late dispatches we mentioned three grievances in this Government, which in extent may threaten much, if we be not timely directed from thence concerning them, *viz.* the insolence and excrescence of the Popish pretended Clergy, the disorder and offence of the Irish Regiment, and the late outragious presumption of the unsetled Irish, in some parts; towards all which (being parties perhaps otherwise conceived of there, then understood here) your Deputy and Councel have of late used particular abstinence, holding themselves somewhat limited concerning them, by late Instructions, Letters and directions from thence. And therefore, lest countenance of that course might turn to greater dammage, we make choice seasonably to crave expression of the good pleasure of your Highness, and the most Honourable Lords of your Councel, lest our actions and zeal therein might vary from the purposes on that side, and so wanting of unanimity in both States, break the progress of the Reformation; Not that we any way make doubt to give your Majesty a good accompt of our selves therein, and of the full eviction of those evils in due time, so we might be assured of your Majesties and their Lordships good allowance of our endeavours, being confident, in all humility, to declare and affirm to your Sacred Majesty, that the rest of this great body (as to the civil part thereof) is in far better order at this time, then ever it was in the memory of man; as well in the current and general execution of Justice according to the Laws, in the freedom of mens persons and estates, (the present charge of the Army excepted) and in the Universal outward subjection of all sorts of setled inhabitants to the Crown and Laws of *England*, and also in the advancement of the Crown Revenues; and lastly, in the competent number of Bishops, and other able and Learned Ministers of the Church of *England* of all sorts, which we especially attribute to the blessedness of your time, and to the Industries, Zeal, Judgment and moderation of your Deputy, as well in your Majesties service, as towards this people, having now well learned this great office; and to the good beginnings of the two last precedent Deputies, under direction of your most Renowned Father.

Secondly, we understand that your Deputy and Councel are blamed, for the present surcharge of your Revenues here, far beyond the support thereof.

Herein

Herein your Royal Majesty may be pleased to cause a review of our dispatch from hence, in *August*, 1627. wherein it will appear, that their part in that offence hath been onely obedience to extraordinary Warrants from thence; and that if those Warrants had not been fully performed out of your Revenues, you had had about 40000 *l. Irish*, to pay Pensioners, in your Coffers, and answer other necessities which have since increased.

So as we humbly crave pardon freely to affirm, that the fault hath not been here; and further also to say, for your Majesties honour, and our comfort, That during 200. years last past, *England* hath never been so free of the charge of *Ireland*, as now it is.

Thirdly, we understand, that your Deputy is accused for miscarriage in the legal prosecution of *Phelim Mac Frogh*, and others adhering to him in certain treasonable Acts and Practices. Herein, we most humbly beseech your Majesty, that a review may be of a Declaration sent from hence about the beginning of your Deputies Government, signed by him, and all the Councel then here; whereby will appear, how the parts of *Lemster*, at least, have been, from age to age, infested by him and his predecessors, and the inhabitants of the territory of *Ranelagh*, wherein he took upon him a Chiefery; and therein will also appear, that it was the special affection and endeavour of several worthy Deputies here, to have cleered that offensive plot, which no wise State could suffer so neer the seat thereof, and that they also severally attempted it by force, the said *Phelim*'s Father being slain in actual Rebellion by Sir *William Russel*'s prosecution; but the general Rebellion of the Kingdom always interrupted the settlement thereof. This being, at that time, the Declaration of the State, moved your Deputy, being a stranger, to have a wary aspect upon the people, for the common peace, which he hath carefully performed. Afterwards, at the time when the general voice was amongst the *Irish*, that the *Spaniards* would be here, your Deputy had cause to examine several persons and causes concerning that Rumour, whereby fell out to be discovered to him, among others, that this *Phelim* had confederated for raising a Commotion in *Lemster*, and murthering a *Scotish* Minister, and Justice of Peace (a ready instrument in Crown Causes) inhabiting about the border of the said Territory : Before which time we never heard of any displeasure or hard measure borne by your said Deputy to him, or offence taken by him, at any particular done to him, unless he were offended, that your Deputy refused his money offered to blanch your Majesties title to the Lands in *Ranelagh*, now granted to undertakers; discovered and prosecuted, at first, by his Brother *Redmond*, and his Councel *Peter de la Hoyd* : We do also herein, in all humility, testifie and declare, that he acquainted several Privie Councellors here, and others of judgment, with the same; and also, in every act and passage thereof, used the labour and presence, either of your Majesties Privie Councellors, Judges, or learned Councel; always professing, publickly and privately (which we also in our Consciences do believe) that he had no particular envie or displeasure to *Phelim*'s person, or any of his, neither had any end in what might fall out upon that discovery or pains, or any act done concerning that Countrey, other then the reducement thereof to the conformity of other Civil parts, the common peace of your Majesties good Subjects adjacent, and the legal and plenary effecting of that which by so many good Governours, in times of disturbance, could not be done, there being no power in him to make any particular benefit of the Escheat, either in Lands, or Goods : and before any thing was to be done for the Trial of him and the rest for their lives, he made a speedy and immediate address to your Majesty, dated 27 *August*, 1628. upon the Indictment found, to inform you of the then present estate of that business, which we have seen, not doing it before (as he affirms) for that he had formerly received gracious approbations of his proceedings in the like discoveries.

We also, in all humbleness and duty, do declare and protest, That if, upon their evil demerits, and the due proceedings of Law, those now questioned may be taken away, and the Territory setled in Legal Government, and *English* Order, (towards which a strong Fort is already almost built in the midst of it, by your Majesties Undertakers lately planted there : It will be a service of the greatest importment to bridle the *Irish*, assure the inhabitants of other parts, and strengthen the general peace of the Kingdom (next to the great Plantation of *Ulster*) that hath been done in this age. If otherwise they shall by fair Trial acquit the course of your Majesties free and indifferent Justice, it will make them wary in point of Duty and Loyalty hereafter. And we do further, in all submission, declare, That in these discoveries, (the Persons and Causes considered) it was of necessity, that the personal pains of your Highness Deputy should be bestowed; the rather, for that the Evidences being to be given, for the most part, by persons involved in the same confederacies, and who were to become actors, they would not be drawn to confess truths to any inferiour Ministers, being of stubborn and malign spirits; besides the dissivations of Priests, and of the Dependents, and manifold Allies of the said *Phelim*, if they had not been warily look'd after.

Lastly, We, in all humbleness of heart, and freedom of faithfull servants, do beseech your most sacred Majesty to consider, how much the sufferings of your zealous servants may prove to your dis-service, especially in this place, where discouragement of your most dextrous service is most aimed at, by multitudes of several qualities, and cannot but soon perplex the present happy state of your affairs. We beseech the eternal God to guide and prosper your Majesties advices and designs.

April 28. 1629.

Your most humble and obedient Subjects and Servants,

Signed by
L. *Primate.*
V. *Valentia.*
V. *Kilmalleck.*
V. *Ranelagh.*
L. *Dillon.*

L. *Cauffeild.*
L. *Aungier.*
L. *Pr. of Munster.*
L. *Chief Justice.*

Sir *Adam Loftus.*
Mr. of the *Wards.*
L. *Chief Baron.*
Sir *Charles Coote.*

A Councel-Table Order, against hearing Mass at Embassadours houses.

At *White-Hall*, the tenth of *March*, 1629.

PRESENT

Lord *Keeper.*
Lord *Treasurer.*
Lord *President.*
Lord *Privy Seal.*
Lord *Steward,*
Lord *Chamberlain.*
Earl *of* Suffolk.
Earl *of* Dorset.
Earl *of* Salisbury.

Lord *Wimbleton.*
Lord *Viscount* Dorchester.
Lord *Viscount* Wentworth.
Lord *Viscount* Grandison.
Lord *Viscount* Faulkland.
Lord *Savile.*
Lord *Newbergh.*
Mr. *Vice-Chamberlain.*
Mr. *Secretary* Cooke.

AT this Sitting, the Lord Viscount *Dorchester* declared, That his Majesty being informed of the bold and open repair made to several places, and specially to the houses of Forreign Embassadours, for the hearing of Mass, which the Laws and Statutes of this Kingdom do expresly forbid his Subjects to frequent: and considering, in his Princely wisdom, both the publick Scandals, and dangerous consequence thereof, is resolved to take present order for the stopping of this evil before it spread it self any further; and for this purpose had commanded him to acquaint the Board with his pleasure in that behalf, and what course he thinketh fit to be held therein; and withall, to demand the opinion and advice of their Lordships concerning the same, his Majesty being desirous to use the best and most effectual expedient that can be found. Hereupon, his Lordship, proceeding, did further declare, that his Majesty (to shew the cleerness and earnestness of his intention herein) hath begun at his own house, *viz.* Wheresoever the Queens Majesty hath any Chappel being intended for the onely service of her, and for those *French* who attend her; for which the Earl of *Dorset*, Lord Chamberlain to her Majesty, hath been commanded to take special care, according to such directions as he hath received from his Majesty. That for so much as concerneth the repair to the houses of Forreign Embassadours, at the time of Mass, his Majesty thinks fit, that some Messengers of the Chamber, or other Officers or Persons fit for that service, shall be appointed to watch all the several passages to their houses, and, without entring into the said houses, or infringing the freedoms and priviledges belonging unto them, observe such persons as go thither; but at their coming from thence, they are to apprehend them, and bring them to the Board: and such as they cannot apprehend, to bring their names. But to the end that the said Forreign Embassadours may have no cause to complain of this proceeding, as if there were any intention to wrong or dis-respect them, his Majesty doth likewise think fit, that

for

for the preventing of any such mistaking, and sinister interpretation, the said Embassadors shall be acquainted with the truth of this business; and likewise assured, in his Majesties name, that he is, and will be, as carefull to conserve all priviledges and rights belonging to the quality of their places, as any of his Progenitors have been, and in the same manner as himself expecteth that their Princes shall use towards his Embassadours.

Lastly, That it is his Majesties express pleasure, that the like diligence be used for the apprehending of all such as repair to Mass in prisons, or other places.

The Board having heard this Declaration, did unanimously conclude, That there could not be taken a more effectuall course for the preventing of these evils, then this which his Majesty in his wisdom hath set down; and therefore the same be immediately put in strict and carefull execution. And it was likewise thought fit, that the Lord Viscount Dorchester, and Mr. Secretary Cooke, should be sent to the forreign Embassadors severally, to acquaint them with his Majesties intention, as is before mentioned; and that the Messengers of the Chamber to be employed in the service before specified, shall be appointed, and receive their charge from the Lord Archbishop of Canterbury, the Lord Bishop of London, and the Secretaries, who are to take a speciall care to see this put in execution.

March 10. 1629.

The Collections of the Passages and Discourses between the Embassadours of the King of Spain, and Sir Arthur Chichester.

These Passages were sent to the Duke, inclosed in the following Letter.

ON Sunday, the 18. of this present *January*, the two Embassadours of *Spain* came to visit me at my house in *Drury-Lane*. At their first entrance, they took occasion to speak of the profession of Souldiers, and of the *Spanish* Nation, affirming them to be the bravest Friends, and the bravest Enemies. I approved it in the Souldier, and contradicted it not in the Nation.

When they were come into an inner Room, looking upon the Company, as if they desired to be private, I caused them to withdraw; but noting that they had brought an Interpreter with them, I prayed Sir *James Blount*, and *Nathaniel Tomkins*, Clerk of the Princes Councel, (who doth well understand the *Spanish* tongue) to abide with me.

Being private, they said they came to visit me, because of the good intention and well-wishing they understood I had to the accommodation of businesses, and because I stood named by his Majesty for the employment into *Germany*.

I acknowledged their coming to visit me, as a particular favour, professing my self to be one of those who was able to do least, but that I must and would in all things conform my self to the will and good pleasure of the King my Master.

They were pleased to remember, and to take for argument of his Majesties good opinion of me, to make me one of the *Junto* (as they called it) of the selected Councellors, and his employment given me the last year, as his Extraordinary Embassadour into *Germany*.

I told them, I had been bred a Souldier, as their Excellencies had been, but that I wanted the capacity and abilities which they had; and that for want of Language (not affecting to speak by an Interpreter) I had forborn to wait on their Excellencies, as otherwise I would have done.

To that, they returned the like Complement, and then said, Their Master had sent a good answer touching the *Palatinate*; and they assured me, that he would perform what he had promised, with advantage.

I said, If it were so, I then hoped all things would sort to a good end.

They then asked me, How his Majesty and the Lords were affected? and whether therewith they were satisfied, or no?

I answered, That I conceived, their Excellencies knew his Majesties mind as well as the Lords, for that they had so lately Audience of him.

They said, It was true, they had so, but not a private Audience; nor could they obtain any, though they had much desired the same, but that others were still present.

I said, merrily, That they were two, and I believed that the King their Master had sent as able and experienced Ministers as he had any; and therefore his Majesty might, peradventure, think fit not to hear them alone.

They

They said, His Majesty might alone hear a thousand Ministers of any Kings, but if he should be otherwise pleased, they well liked of the Princes being present: But they said, there were also other great Ministers of the Kings, who wished not well to their Masters affairs.

I said, There might therein be a mistaking, or mis-understanding on their part: for if the King their Master mean so really as they said, I conceived, that no body would be willing to remove his Majesty from those purposes, and that good affection which he bore unto his dear Brother, the King of *Spain*.

The Marquess said, in *English*, The King was a good King, and the Prince a good Prince; but some of their Ministers, they doubted, were ill-willers to them.

I asked, if greater demonstrations of reality could be devised, then had been given on the part of the King and Prince? instancing in the Prince his going in Person into *Spain*.

They confessed it; but as the times now were, they said, ill offices were done them.

I assured them, That I neither knew, nor understood of any; neither did I ever hear them spoken of, but with due respect had unto them, as to the Ministers of a great King, and his Majesties dear Brother.

They said, Their meaning was not, that the ill offices were done to their Persons, but to the great Businesses, which a certain Person had shewed a willingness to disturb; but they hoped, that the intended amity between our Masters would hold, and proceed nevertheless.

I professed, that I knew nothing to the contrary, neither understood I the particular at which they aimed.

The Marquess swore, As he was a Christian, he knew that the King his Master did so truly and really esteem his dear Brother the King of *England*, and the Prince of *Wales*, that if they needed part of his blood, they should have it for their good: But he complained, that they could not have their Messages delivered, nor returned from the King, of late, but qualified according to the pleasures of others.

I said, they mis-conceived it; for I thought they had no cause to complain, seeing they now had, or might have (as I supposed) the Kings Ear, when they craved it in due and befitting times.

They seemed to deny it, alledging, That they could not get their Messages and Papers answered, as aforetime.

I said, When the Prince was in *Spain*, they had free access to his Majesty, whensoever they desired it.

Yea, said the Marquess in Latine, *Tunc*; but now, he said, the case was altered.

I said, The King had given many testimonies to the world, of his willingness to comply with their Master, and them: And if either his Majesty, or the Prince, seemed now more reserved and deliberate in their actions then heretofore, it might be, that his Highness had learned that wary and circumspect proceeding in *Spain*, where they are said to use it in matters of far less moment.

They smiled hereat, and prayed me to continue my good intentions and respects towards them, and to the joynt affairs of both our Masters.

I said, I would always serve the King my Master with a true and faithfull heart; and so far as should be agreeable to his desires, and good liking, I would, to my small power, be ready to serve them.

In conclusion, they said, They came but to visit me; but being come, they could not choose but say something, and touch upon business.

January 18. 1623.   *Arthur Chichester.*

Sir Arthur Chichester, *to the* Duke.

May it please your Grace,

WHen you went last from *White-Hall*, I waited on the Prince and you into the Gallery, where your Lordship spake something unto me which I understood not, to wit, *Are you turned too?* As I knew not the ground of the Demand, I could make no present answer; nor now, but by conjecture. When I turn from the Prince, (whom I know to be the worthiest of Princes,) or from you, (who by your favours have so bound me to serve you,) or from the truth, (as I conceive it,) God, I know, will turn from me: until then, I humbly pray your Lordship to believe, that I am your honest servant.

The Sunday after your Lordships departure, the Embassadours of the King of *Spain* came unto

The Earl of Carlisle, to the King.

unto me under the pretext of a visit. I have herewith sent your Grace a brief of what passed between us. I judge some man hath done me an ill office, by insinuating me into their good opinions of me; sure I am, I never spake of them, nor of the affairs they have to manage, but what I have said, when the selected Councel were assembled. I cannot be so dull, but to know that they meant your Grace to be the Interposer of their desires, and the Man whom they wished to be absent when they have their private audience. They are exceeding Cautelous, and I conceive the late Dispatch from *Spain* is like a gilded bait, to allure and deceive; your Lordship, perceiving their Malice, will be wary to avoyd their Venom. I am

25 Jan. 1623.

Your Graces humble, and faithfull servant,
Arthur Chichester.

The Earl of Carlisle, to his Majesty.

May it please your most Excellent Majesty,

THough my present indisposition deprives me of the honour to attend your Majesty, with the rest of the Commissioners, with whom your Majesty was pleased to associate me; yet I most humbly beseech your Majesty to give me leave, in all humility, to represent unto your Majesty what my heart conceiveth to be most for your Majesties service, in the present conjuncture of your affairs. During this time of my distemper I have been visited by divers Gentlemen of quality, who are Parliament-men, none of those popular and plausible Oratours, but solid, and judicious good patriots, who fear God, and honour the King. Out of their discourses I collect, That there are three things, which do chiefly trouble your people.

The first, that for the subsidies granted, the two last Parliaments, they have received no retribution by any bills of Grace.

The second, that some of their Burgesses were proceeded against after the Parliament were dissolved.

And the third, that they misdoubt, that when they shall have satisfied your Majesties demands and desires, you will nevertheless proceed to the conclusion of the *Spanish* match. It would be too much importunity to trouble your Majesty with the several answers which I made to their objections, and would be too great presumption in me to advise your Majesties incomparable wisdom what should be fittest to be done for your Majesties honour, and the contentment of the people; yet if it would please my Lord the King to give his humblest Creature leave to give vent to the loyal fervour of his heart, restless, and indefatigable in continual meditation of his Gracious Masters honour and service, I would thus with all humble submission, explain my self: That there is nothing which either the enemies of this State, or the perverse industry of false-hearted servants, could invent more mischievous, then the misunderstandings which have grown between your Majesty and your people: nothing that will more dishearten the envious Maligners of your Majesties felicity, and encourage your true-hearted friends, and servants, then the removing of those false fears, and jealousies, which are meer imaginary Phantasms, and bodies of ayr easily dissipated, whensoever it shall please the sun of your Majesty to shew it self clearly in its native brightness, lustre, and goodness.

God and the World do know the scope and the end of all your Majesties pious affections, and endeavours, to have been no other, then the setling of an universal peace in Christendom; (a felicity only proper for your Majesties time, and only possible to be procured by your incomparable goodness, and wisdom) but since the malice of the Devil, and deceitfull men, have crossed those fair waies wherein your Majesty was proceeding, abusing your trust and goodness, (as Innocencie and goodness are alwaies more easily betrayed, then wiliness and malice) you must now cast about again, and sail by another point of the compass; and I am confident your Majesty will more securely and easily attain your noble and pious end, though the way be different.

The means are, briefly, these three.

First, let your Majesties enemies see, that the Lion hath teeth, and claws.

2. Next, embrace and invite a strict and sincere friendship and association with those whom neighbourhood and alliance, and common interest of state, and religion, have joyned unto you.

3. And

3. And last of all, cast off, and remove jealousies, which are between you Majesty and your people.

Your Majesty must begin with the last, for upon that foundation you may afterwards set what frame of building you please. And when should you begin (Sir) but at this overture of your Parliament, by a gracious, clear, and confident discovery of your intentions to your People. Fear them not (Sir) never was there a better King, that had better subjects, if your Majesty would trust them. Let them but see that you love them, and constantly rely upon their humble advice, and ready assistance, and your Majesty will see, how they will tear open their breasts, to give you their hearts; and having them, your Majesty is sure of their hands and purses. Cast but away some Crums of your Crown amongst them, and your Majesty will see those crums will make a miracle, they will satisfie many thousands. Give them assurance that your heart was always at home, though your eyes were abroad; invite them to look forward, and not backward, and constantly maintain, that with confidence you undertake, and your Majesty will find admirable effects of this harmonious concord. Your Majesty as the head directing, and your people as the hands and feet, obeying and co-operating for the honour, safety, and welfare of the body of the State. This will revive, and reunite your friends abroad, and dismay, and disappoint the hopes of your enemies, secure your Majesties person, assure your Estate, and make your memorie glorious to posterity.

Pardon, I most humbly beseech your Majesty, this licentious freedom, which the zeal of your safety and service hath extorted from a tongue-tyed man, who putteth his heart into his Majesties hand, and humbly prostrateth himself at your Royal feet, as being

Feb.14.1623.
Your Majesties most humble, most obedient obliged Creature, Subject, and Servant,
Carlile.

The Earl of Carlile, to the Duke.

My most Noble dear Lord,

SInce my last to your Lordship by Mr. *Endimion Porter*, there hath not happened any matter of great moment, or alteration, here, saving the resolution (which his Majesty hath taken by the advice of his Councel) for the disarming of all the Popish Lords. In the execution whereof there fell out a brabble at the Lord *Vaux* his house in *North-hamptonshire*, wherein there were some blows exchanged between the said Lord, and Mr. *Knightly*, a Justice of the Peace, who assisted the Deputy Lieutenant in that action. Whereof complaint being made, his Majesty was pleased himself in Councel to have the hearing of the businefs; and upon examination to refer the judgement thereof to the Star-Chamber the next Term. But at the issuing out of the Councel-Chamber, the Lord *Vaux* taking occasion to speak to Sir *William Spencer*, (who with the rest had given information in favour of Mr. *Knightly*,) told him, that though he neglected his reputation before the Lords, yet he doubted not, but he would have more care of his oath when the businefs should come to Examination in the Star-Chamber. Herewith Sir *William Spencer* finding his reputation challenged, presently complained, and thereupon, the words being acknowledged, the Lord *Vaux* was committed prisoner to the Fleet.

In the disarming of the Lords-Recusants, there was as much respect had of some, who have relation to your Lordship, as you your self would desire.

The Papists in general here do give some cause of jealousie by their Combinations and Murmurings, wherein it is suspected, that they are as fondly, as busily encouraged by the pragmatical *Monsieurs*. But his Majesties temper and wisdom will be sufficient to prevent all inconveniencie, which their folly or passion may contrive. There is one Sir *Thomas Gerrard* a Recusant brought up hither out of *Lancashire*, being accused of some treacherous design against his Majesties Person. *Rochel* is so streightly blocked up by Sea and Land, as no Intelligence can be sent into the Town. We have not as yet any clear Categorical answers touching the restitution of our ships. As soon as any thing more worthy of your Lordships knowledg shall occur, you shall not fail to be advertised from him that is eternally vowed,

Novemb. 20. 1625.
Your Graces most faithfull friend, and most humble servant,
Carlile.

The Earl of Carlile, to the Duke.

My most Noble dear Lord,

I Must ever acknowledge my self infinitely obliged to your Lordship for many Noble favours; but for none more, then the freedom, and true cordial friendship expressed in your last Letter, touching my son; And I shall humbly beseech your Lordship, in all occasions, to continue that free and friendly manner of proceeding, which I shall ever justly esteem as the most real testimony of your favour towards me. Your Lordship will now be pleased to give me leave with the same freedom and sincerity to give your Lordship an account, that it is now 4. moneths since the Count of *Mansfelt* made the proposition to me, to nominate my son to be one of his Colonels, as he did likewise to my Lord of *Holland*, for his Brother Sir *Charles Rich*; which at the first (I must deal plainly with your Lordship) I took for a piece of art, as if he knowing, that next to the benefit and assistance he received from your Lordships favour and protection, we were the most active instruments imployed in this business, and therefore he sought to ingage us so much the farther by this interest. But afterwards I found, that under the shadow of this Complement put upon me, he had a desire to gratifie Sir *James Ramsey*, whom he designed to be my sons Lieutenant, having regard to his former deserts, and the courage and sufficiency he hath found in him. I profess unto your Lordship sincerely, that he received no other encouragement or acceptance from me, then a bare negative; Insomuch as he afterwards sent a Gentleman to tell me, That he perceived whatsoever he should expect from me in the furtherance of his business, must be only for the respect I bear to my Masters service, and nothing for love of his person, since I accepted not the profer of his service. My Lord of *Holland* can justifie the truth of this assertion, who alone was acquainted with that which passed: for I protest, upon my salvation, that I neither spake of it to any creature living, not so much as to my Son, neither have I written one word thereof to the Count *Mansfelt*, neither knew I any thing of his proceedings, till by the last Currier Mr. Secretary was pleased to acquaint me with the nomination of my son. If I had seriously intended any such thing, I want not so much judgment and discretion, as not first to discover my desire to my gracious Master, humbly craving his leave and allowance: And I should not have failed to have recourse to your Lordships favourable assistance therein. And thus (my Noble Lord) have I given you an account what entertainment I gave to the Count *Mansfelts* Complement. And I will be bold also to give your Lordship this further assurance, that no particular interest, or consideration of mine own, shall have power to alter my constant course of serving my gracious Master faithfully, and industriously. And so humbly submitting all to his Majesties good pleasure, and your Lordships wisdom, I remain eternally,

Your Graces most faithful friend, and humble servant,
Carlile.

Postscript.

I most humbly beseech your Lordship that this unfortunate Complement put upon my son may be no prejudice to the deserts of Sir *James Ramsey*.

Mr. Edward Clark, to the Duke.

May it please your Grace,

I Have been hitherto very unfit (by reason of my sickness) to give your Lordship any account of my time at *Madrid*. So that without your Lordships favourable construction, I may be thought forgetfull of the trust committed to my charge; and the rather, in that as yet your Lordship hath only heard what I have done, but not why. I presume I have faithfully followed the Princes direction, and on such probable inducements, as will, I hope, both in his Highnesses and your Lordships opinion, plead my excuse at least. The very day the Prince arrived at St. *Andera*, my Lord of *Bristol*, seeing me very weak, told me he was very sorry I was not able to perform my journey for *England*, for that now there was an extraordinary occasion of a dispatch, not only in respect of the ratification come the night before; but because also they were almost come to a final conclusion of all articles, which were to be engrossed, and signed the next day. Hereupon I was inquisitive to know what assurance he had the Ratification was come. He answered, that, that very day, he had been summoned to attend the *Junto*, and that there they had earnestly pressed

him;

him, that the Articles might be speedily drawn up, and signed, since they had now received full warrant to authorize them to proceed; And that the next day was appointed accordingly. Thereupon unwilling to omit the present opportunity, conceiving withall the purpose of the Princes Letter to be, either to express his Highness further pleasure before the meeting of the *Junto*, or to prevent the concluding of some other particular Article they might otherwise fall upon: I delivered his Letter to his Lordship (pretending it came to my hands amongst other Letters that same day) I found them exceedingly troubled in reading it, nor did he forbear to tell me, it must for a time be concealed; for he feared, if they should come to the knowledge of it they would give order to stay the Prince. Upon these motives, and in this manner, I parted with it; wherein I humbly submitting my self to his Highness Construction, I remain

Madrid, Octob. 1. 1623.

Your Graces humblest servant to command,
Ed. Clark.

Mr. Edward Clark, *to the Duke.*

My Lord,

THe Infanta's preparation for the *Deposorios* was great, but greater sorrow (good Ladie) to see it deferred. It hath bred in them all some distraction. The multitude know not what to conjecture, what to say, but cry *Piden el Palatinato.* They confess the demand just, but unseasonable, and do publish, that (the *Deposorios* past) the Infanta on her knees should have been a suitor to the King to restore it, making it thereby her act, and drawing the obligation wholly to her. I must confess, I want faith to believe it, and the rather, because I see it reflect secretly, and maliciously upon your Lordship, who are made the author of all the impediments that happen, not by your enemies onely, but by those that should suppress it. Which troubles me so much, that I hasten all I can my return; since I know no other then to be,

Madrid, 6. September. 1623.

Your Graces faithfull servant,
Edw. Clark.

The Lord Coke *to King* James, *touching tryal of Duels out of* England.

May it please your most Excellent Majesty,

* I Have received a commandment by Mr. Sollicitor, from your Majesty, consisting upon two parts; First, to answer whether I informed not your Majesty, that if two of your subjects should goe over beyond Sea to fight in a forreign Kingdome, and there in fight the one killeth the other, that in this case, the same might be punished by appeal before the Constable and Marshal of *England*; Secondly, if I made any such information, what authority and reason I had to maintain it.

To the first, the truth is, that I did informe your Majesty so; and I well remember I said then that it was *Dowries* case, your Majesty then speaking of Duels.

To the second, this is by authority of an Act of Parliament, made in the first year of King *Henry* the fourth, in the 14th. Chapter, in these words.

For many inconveniencies and mischiefs that have oftentimes happened by many appeals made within the Realm before this time; It is Ordained and Established from henceforth, that all appeals to be made of things done within the Realm shall be tryed and determined by the good Laws of this Realm, made and used in the time of the Kings noble Progenitors; And that all appeals to be made of things done out of the Relam, shall be tryed before the Constable and Marshal of *England* for the time being; and that no appeals be from henceforth made, or in any wise pursued in Parliament, in any time to come.

Note that for this Statute criminal Causes were handled, judged in Parliament.

In the late Queens time a Case fell out upon this Statute; Sir *Francis Drake* having put *Dowrie* to death beyond Sea, the Brother and Heir of *Dowrie* sued by Petition to the Queen, that she would be pleased to appoint a Constable *hac vice*, to the end he might have an appeal against Sir *Francis Drake* for the death of his Brother. This Petition the Queen referred to Sir *Thomas Bromley*, and the two Chief Justices, and others; and it was resolved by them (which I being of Councel with *Dowrie*, set down briefly for my learning)

ing) that if two English men go beyond the Sea, and in combat the one killeth the other, this offence may be determined before the Constable and Marshal of *England*, and so was the Satute of 1 *Hen*. 4. to be intended.

But after upon the true circumstance of the case, the Queen would not constitute a Constable of *England*, without whom no proceeding could be.

And I take this resolution to be well warranted by the Satute ; and no small inconvenience should follow, and a great defect should be in the Law, if such bloody offences should not be punished, and your Majesty should lose a flower of your Crown, in losing this power to punish these growing and dangerous offences. I shewed to Mr. Sollicitor my report and memorial of *Dowties* Case, and I shall ever remain.

Febr. 19. 1616.
To the Kings most excellent Majesty.

Your Majesties Loyal and faithful Subject,
Edw. Coke.

Sir Francis Cottington, *to the Duke.*

May it please your Honour,

MY last unto you was of the 23 of *September* by Mr. *Berrie*, who that day departed from hence towards *England*, with intention to take passage by Sea from St. *Sebastins*: and although I conceive, that this conveyance will be much speedier (it being by an extraordinary dispatched for *Flanders*) yet for that I hold the other to be sure; I will not forbear to trouble your Honour with any repetition of that dispatch.

The strength and boldness of the Pyrats (or rather of the Turks) is now grown to that height, both in the Ocean, and *Mediterranean* Seas, as I have never known any thing to have wrought a greater sadness and distraction in the Court, then the daily advice thereof. Their whole Fleet consists of 40 Sail of tall Ships, of between 200 and 400, Tuns apiece ; Their Admiral of 500 Tuns. They are divided into 2 Squadrons, the one of 18 Sail, remaining before *Malaga*, (in sight of the City) the other about the *Cape* St. *Marie*, which is between *Lisbone* and *Sevil*. That Squadron within the *Streights* entred the road of *Mostil* (a Town by *Malaga*) where with their Ordnance they beat down a part of the Castle, and had doubtless taken the Town, but that from *Granado* there came Souldiers to succour it; yet they took there divers Ships, and amongst them 3 or 4 of the West part of *England* Two bigg English Ships they drave on shoar, not past four Leagues from *Malaga*; and after they went on shoar also, and burnt them, and to this day they remain before *Malaga*, intercepting all Ships that pass that way, and absolutely prohibiting all Trade into those parts of *Spain*. The other Squadron, at the *Cape* St. *Marie*, doth there the like, intercepting all shipping whatsoever. They lately met with seven Sail of English Ships, (all of *London*, as I take it) but loaden only with pipe-staves, which they had taken on the Coast of *Ireland* by the way. Five of these, viz. the *Marie Anne*, the *Marie* and *John*, the *Rebecca*, and *Gibbs* of *Sandwich*, and one *John Cheyney* of *London*, they took, and the other two escaped. They roob'd them only of their victuals, their Ordnance, and some Sails, and so let them go ; but in their company was also taken a great Ship of *Lubeck*, said to be very rich, which they still keep with all the men. They have few or no Christians aboard them. But all either *Turks* or *Moores*, and the most part are of those which of late years were turned out of *Spain* for *Moriscos*. They attend (as it seems) and as themselves report to them that have been aboard them, the coming of the *West Indian* Fleet, which is now very near. But from hence they have commanded the *Armado* (which was divided into three Squadrons) to be joyned together, and advice is brought that it is so, and now consists of 20 strong Ships ; *Den John Faxardo* (the General) hath also express order to fight with the Pyrats, not admitting any excuse whatsoever ; but the Common opinion is here, that we will be able to do them little harm, because his Ships are of great burthen, and they will be able to go from him at their pleasure. And the other Squadron within the *Streights* will always be able to secure their retreat thither. I doubt not but, in my next dispatch, I shall be able to tell your honour what *Don John Faxardo* either hath or will do to them. If this year they safely return to *Argier* (especially if they should take any of the Fleet) it is much to be feared that the King of *Spains* forces by Sea will not be sufficient to restrain them hereafter, so much sweetness they find by making prize of all Christians whatsoever. The Secretary of the Councel of war hath hereupon discoursed much unto me, & by him I perceive, that here is an intention, to move his Majesty (the King our Master) that he will be pleased to joyn some of his Sea-forces (upon good terms) with this King, for the suppressing

suppressing of these Pyrats, if they should hereafter grow, and increase as hitherto they have done. Seeing they now profess themselves the common enemies of Christendom. Many reasons he gave me, that he thought might move his Majesty thereunto; but that whereon, I for my part, most reflect, is, that these courses of the Pyrats do but exercise the forces of the King of *Spain* by Sea, and put an obligation on him by all means to strengthen, and increase his Armada, and keep in practice his Sea-souldiers, without doing him any great harm. for that the greatest damage will always fall upon the Merchants that Trade into those parts (of which the English will ever be the greatest number, and the greatest losers) And as for the taking of his Fleet, it is not to be imagined, for that besides, they come very strong (consisting of 50 great Ships, of which eight are Gallions of war) they shall always be met, and guarded by the *Armado*. Your Honour may be pleased to acquaint his Majesty with what I here write; for I perceive it is expected, that I should advertise what the Secretary hath discoursed to me, which I would have done more at large; but I am streightned with want of time. Yet I may not forbear to advertise your Honour, that the said Secretary told me withall, that the last year the States desired leave of this King, that certain Ships of war (which they armed against Pyrats) might have safe recourse into these parts, which was accordingly granted them; but that instead of offending the Pyrats, the same Ships sold in *Argeir* as much Powder, and other warlike provision, (especially Powder) unto the *Turks*, as furnished the foresaid Fleet which they have now at Sea, a thing which is here very ill taken. I doubt not but, from *Piedmont* your Honour hath better advertisement (at the least more speedier) then I can give you from hence; yet have I thought it fit to advertise you, that in a late ambush, which the Duke of *Savoy* had laied, at *Don Pedro de Tolledo's* entrance into *Piedmont*, the *Maestro de Campo* of the Spanish Army was slain; the Son of the Prince of *Astuli* was hurt : so was the Prince of *Morveles* (who serves this King there) and many other Captains, and Gentlemen of note, slain and hurt. They here say, that the number of men *Don Pedro* lost were but few; but their custom is to dissemble their losses; howsoever, it is to be conceived, that when so many principal men were touched, the common Souldiers could not well escape.

At *Lisbone* there are arrived two Caracks, and a Gallion, from the *East Indies*, the Caracks very rich, and much richer then in former years; but (as in a former Letter I advertised you) two others as rich as they, and that should have come in company with these, were cast away coming home.

Don Roderigo Calderon (now the Marquess *de Las Siete Iglesias*) is suddenly commanded from this Court, and confined to a small Village, and Judges are appointed to examine by what means he is so suddenly grown to so great an estate (which in my time is risen from nothing to above 60000 Duckets a year rent, besides an infinite treasure in moveables) and doubtless some heavy sentence will fall upon him, for he hath many enemies and I understand that the Duke of *Lerma* hath much withdrawn his favour.

New supplies of Souldiers are here raised for the Governour of *Millian*, and 30 Companies are ready to be embarqued at *Valencia*, where the Gallies attend them.

Here is lately come hither one who calls himself Sir *James Mackonel* a Scotchman, and saies he is Cousin German to the Earl of *Arguile* : I have not seen him, but I hear he discourses of his breaking out of the Castle of *Edenborough*, of the unjustness of his imprisonment there, of his integrity in the Popes Religion, and so desires to be entertained into this Kings service; which doubtless he shall obtain, if he can make it here be believed, that he hath a true fugitives heart.

My Lord *Ross* is now much hearkned after, and they think he staies very long. By the ordinary (God willing) I shall write again to your Honour. And so, for this time, I humbly take my leave :

Madrid, the first of
Octob. 1616. *Stil. Vet.*

Your Lordships
to be Commanded.
Fran. Cottington.

Sir George Cary, to the Marquess of Buckingham.

Your Lordship

WIll be satisfied, before this of mine will have the happiness to kiss your Noble hands, that the great Mystery of iniquity, in the Star-chamber, is now revealed, and as many as could be discerned to have the mark of the beast upon them have undergone
their

their censure. Some, I must confess, and great fishes too, have broken out of the net. But that escape must be objected to the errours of some of the pursuers, whose courses in some things were not enough direct to warrant what otherwise might have been done And your Lordship, who are a good Woodman, well knows, unless the Wind-lace be well carried, the Bowes which stand up can never shoot.

Notwithstanding all the defaults of the meaner Agents, the Court maintaining the honour of their own uprightness and integrity, hath, with moderation too, (yet such as leaves subject to his Majesties mercy to work upon some particulars) raised in Fine some 130000*l.* or thereabouts. If no errours had been committed, (whereupon those Defendants, which escaped, took advantage to be safe) by this which is done, you may imagine what it would have amounted to. For my part, I rejoyce to conceive, how with the shortest of the daies, we are at the worst of our estate, hoping by this means, with the return of the Sun, to see some such return of the money, (the riches of his Majesties Treasury, and blood of the Common-wealth, as that the Exchequer may flow, and the Veins of the State may fill again, and both, with the Spring, renew their strength, lustre, and complexion. I have now stayed here so long attending this business, that I hold it too late to wait upon you at *Newmarket*. That gives me cause to crave your pardon for this presuming imperfect Accompt of this daies action, and withla to desire the assurance, that I live in your estimation, the same I will ever be

Decemb. 8. 1619.

Your Lordships
Most sincerely honest and humble servant,
G. Cary.

Don Carlos, *to the Lord* Conway.

Sir,

I Have understood by Mr. *Strada*, with particular contentment, the news of your good health, which God continue for many years. I see by yours, received by *Strada*, what his Majesty hath been pleased to order concerning the ships of the *Indies*, which is as much in effect as could be hoped for from so great a King, so zealous of Justice and Equity.

In the Conduct of this business, we will observe the order given by his Majesty, in confidence that the Subjects of the King my Master shall obtain their ends, and his Catholick Majesty receive the contentment to know, that the excesses of those that shall be convinced have been punished.

By the last Currier of *Flanders*, we received neither from the Infanta nor any other person, any other news then what Mr. *Trumbal* sent by his Letters.

I confess freely, that the Marquess and my self have been much troubled, both of us being exceedingly desirous, that his Majesty should receive in every thing (even in words, and formalities) the same satisfaction which we hope he shall receive in the effects. Nevertheless, in discharge of her Highness, I will say that which is fit for me as I am her servant, and which I pray you from me to deliver unto his Majesty; but thus understood, that it is onely my own particular discourse.

By the displeasure his Majesty hath been pleased to testifie unto me, upon many occasions, of the Prince *Palatines* refusal to sign, and ratifie the Treaty of suspension of Arms; He may be also pleased to judge, how it may have been taken by the King my Master in *Spain*, and the Infanta in *Flanders*; and the rather because of the continual reports that at the same time went up and down and increased (as ordinarily it falls out) of the descent of *Allerstat* with a mighty Army of 20000 foot, and 6000 horse, not any more to make war in *Germany*, but to joyn with the Prince of *Orange*, and fall upon those Provinces in obedience to his Catholick Majesty, which was no other, but directly to aim at the vital parts of the Spanish Monarchy.

If for these just fears (which cannot certainly be held vain being considered with those of the year past, proceeding from one and the same Cause, both of which have been scattered by the Almighty hand of God, in his secret Judgments) it hath not onely been lawful, but also necessary, to conserve the ancient alliances, & procure new, I leave it to the judgment of every man of understanding, not doubting but for this respect you will be of the same opinion with me: And much more his Majesty, whom God hath endowed with so great knowledge, and royal qualities, as are known to all the world.

Moreover,

Moreover, let us see if in the Law of gratitude, the Infanta could do less then acknowledge towards the Duke of *Bavaria* the valour wherewith his Army had resisted the pernicious designs of *Alberstat*, having hazarded his own estate, to hinder the imminent danger of the King my Master.

Again, let us consider if the Infanta sending to visit, and give him thanks, could excuse her self from giving him all those titles which the Duke of *Bavaria* gives himself, and desires should be given him. And if he might not, if she had done otherwise, have thought the ingratitude greater then the acknowledgment. And therefore, things being in this state, the Infanta could not excuse her self from sending to visit him, seeing he had succoured her in a time of need, and in visiting him to give him that which he desired should be given him. And the like is to be said for the King my Master, in case he had done; the like, as Mr. *Trumbel* writes the Infanta should tell him, and with a great deal more reason, because the Countries are his own. And therefore, since his Majesty of Great *Britain* is so great a King, and hath so great a reputation of the exact performing of his Royal obligations, I doubt not but he will judge, that in this formality, the King my Master, and the Infanta his Aunt, have but acquitted themselves of their obligations. For the rest, if at the conference of *Cullen*, which his said Majesty and her Highness have desired, and do yet desire, his Majesty of great *Britain* shall see, that they are wanting on their part to proceed with that sincerity and truth which they have so often offered, and which the Marquess of *Yuciosa* doth still offer, on the behalf of the King my Master, so that only the Prince *Palatine* make the submissions due to the Emperour as his natural Lord, and resolve to follow the Paternal counsels of his Majesty of great *Britain*, his Majesty shall then have reason to complain. And in the mean time the Prince *Palatine* should do but well, not to entertain those Amities he endeavours to conserve, nor to sollicit those Leagues which he labours to procure, not only with the declared rebels of the King my Master, and of the House of *Austria*, but also with the enemies of all Christendom. I will engage my head, if following this way, his Majesty and his son in law find themselves deceived.

You know sir, that I treat in truth and freedom, and do therefore hope you will impute my excuses to that, and will not call this liberty of my discourse, rashness, but an immortal desire in me, in all things to procure the service of our Kings, laying aside all occasions of misunderstanding, now we treat of nothing else, but uniting our selves more by the strict bonds of love, over and above those of our Alliance.

I do humbly beseech you to say thus much to his Majesty, and to assure him from me, that when he shall be pleased to employ me in this matter, as in all other, he shall ever find me faithful and real, as I have offered my self, and always continue; being well assured, that even in that I shall serve my Master. And I pray you to believe, in your particular, that I am, and will be eternally

Septemb. 3.

Yours, &c.

Dr. Corbet, *to the Duke.*

May it please your Grace,

TO consider my two great losses this week; one in respect of his Majesty, to whom I was to preach; the other in respect of my Patron, whom I was to visit. If this be not the way to repair the latter of my losses, I fear I am in danger to be utterly undone. To press too neer a great man, is a means to be put by; and to stand too far off, is the way to be forgotten: so *Ecclesiasticus*. In which mediocrity, could I hit it, would I live and die. My Lord, I would neither press neer, nor stand far off, choosing rather the name of an ill Courtier, then a saucy Scholar,

From Your Graces most humble servant,
Rich. Corbet.

Post-script.

Here is news, my noble Lord, about us, that in the point of Allegiance now in hand, all the Papists are exceeding Orthodox, the onely Recusants are the Puritanes.

The Earl of Somerset, to King James.

BY this Gentleman, your Majesties Lieutenant, I understand of some halt you made, and the cause of it, at such time as he offered to your Majesty my Letters. But soon after, your Majesty could resolve your self, and behold me nothing so diffident of you, but in humble language petitioning your favour; for I am in hope, that my condition is not capable of so much more misery, as that I need to make my self a passage to you by such way of intercession. This which follows after I offer your Majesty, though not as to your self, for upon less motive you can find favour for me: Now I need onely move, not plead, before your Majesty, as my Case doth stand for what I seek to have done follows upon what you have already done, as a Consequence and succeeding growth of your own act. But to the effect, that your Majesty may see that there is enough to answer those (if any such there be) as do go about to pervert the exercise of your power, and to turn it from its own clear excellency, for to minister unto their passions: I have presumed, to this end, to awake your Majesties own conceipt upon this subject, which can gather to it self better and more able defences in your behalf upon this view; for though the acts of your mercy, which are not communicable, nor the causes of them with others, as derived from those secret motives which are only sensible and privy to your own heart, and admit of no search or discovery to any general satisfaction, and that under this protection I might guard my particular sufficiently; yet my Case needs not hide it self, but attend the dispute with any that would put upon it a monstrous and heavy shape. For though that I must acknowledge, that both life and estate are forfeit to you by Law, yet so forfeited, as the same Law gives you the same power to preserve, as it doth to punish, whereby your Majesties higher prerogative doth not wrestle with it; nor do you infringe those grounds by which you have ever governed; so as the resistance is not great that your Majesty hath, for to give life, and which is less in the gift of estate; for that the Law casts wholly upon your self, and yields it as fit matter for the exercise of your goodness. Once it was your Majesties gift to me, so it may be better not taken then a second time given; for it is common to all men for to avoid to take that which hath been once their own. And I may say farther, that Law hath not been so severe upon the ruine of innocent posterity, nor yet cancelled, nor cut off the merits of Ancestors, before the politick hand of State had contrived it into those several forms, as fitted to their ends and government. To this I may adde, that that whereupon I was judged, even the Crime it self, might have been none, if your Majesties hand had not once touched upon it, by which all access unto your favour was quite taken from me. Yet as it did at length appear, I fell, rather for want of well defending, then by the violence or force of any proofs: for I so far forsook my self, and my Cause, as that it may be a question, whether I was more condemned for that, or for the matter it self which was the subject of that days Controversie. Then, thus far nothing hath appeared, wherein your Majesty hath extended for me your power beyond the reasonable bound; neither doth any thing stand so in the way of your future proceedings, but rather make easie the access of your Majesties favour to my relief.

What may then be the cause, that Malice can pitch upon, wherefore your Majesty should not proceed for to accomplish your own work? Aspersions are taken away by your Majesties letting me become subject to the utmost power of Law, with the lives of so many of the offendours, which yieldeth the world subject of sorrow rather then appetite to more blood; but truth and innocency protect themselves in poor men, much more in Kings. Neither ever was there such aspersion (God knows) in any possibility towards your Majesty, but amongst those who would create those pretences to mislead your Majesty, and thereby make me miserable. If not this (whereof the virtue and use was in the former time, and now determined) there is not any but your pleasure. It is true, I am forfeited to your Majesty, but not against you, by any treasonable or unfaithful act. Besides, there is to be yielded a distinction of men, as in faults; in which I am of, both under the neerest degrees of exception; yet your Majesty hath pardoned life and estate to Traytors, and to strangers, sometimes the one, sometimes the other; Nay to some concerned in this business wherein I suffer you have pardoned more then I desire; who (as it is reported) if they had come to the test, had proved Copper, and should have drunk of the bitter Cup as well as others. But I do not by this envy your favours to any person, nor seek I to draw them in the yoke with my self, but applaud your Majesties goodness, being in that respect in a

neerer

The Earl of Somerset, to the King.

In. Si W. Elvish.

neerer possibility to come at me. Besides this, to *Elvish* your Majesty hath given estate, which is a greater gift then life, because it extends to posterity, who was the worst deserver in this business; an un-offended instrument might have prevented all after-mischief, who for his own ends suffered it, and by the like arts afterwards bewrayed it. To this I

Sr Lewis Tresham.

may adde *Tresham*, in the Powder Treason, upon whose successours I do not cast any of his infamy, yet he preserved himself to posterity; so as what he, or others such as he, have defrauded by the arts of Law, and whom their own unfaithfulness made safe, I have much ado to hold by ingenuity, and Confidence. How may it be, that because I distrusted not your Majesty, or because it returned into your power from whom I had it, it is in danger to be broken or dismembred. Let me hope that there is nothing which by favour may be excused, or by industry might have been avoided, that will fail me, where your Majesty is to determine. It is not I who thus put your Majesty in mind importunely: It is he that was your Creature, it is *Somerset*, with all your honours, and envious greatness, that is now in question. Kings themselves are protected from the breach of Law by being Favorites and Gods anointed, which gives your Majesty the like priviledge over yours; As I took

Dr. Donne.

from Dr. *Donne* in his Sermon, that the goodness of God is not so much acknowledged by us in being our Creator, as in being our Redeemer; nor in that he hath chosen us, as that nothing can take us out of his hands; which in your Majesties remembrance let me challenge, and hope for: For the first accesses of favour, they may be ascribed to ones own pleasing themselves; but that appears to be for our sakes, and for our good, when the same forsakes not our civil deserts. This redemption I crave, not as to my own person, but with your benefits once given; nor do I assume them very deep, for I have voluntarily departed from the hopes of pension, place, office; I only cleave to that which is so little, as that it will suffer no paring, or diminution.

And as in my former Letters, so by this, I humbly crave of your Majesty not to let the practices of Court work upon your Son the Prince, not fearing your sufferance of my loss in that particular so much, (for I cannot lose it, but willingly all with it) as for to take off the Stage that which in the attempt may prove inconvenient. And consider, I pray your Majesty, that my hope in desiring to pass these bad times, was to be restored to my fortunes; others are made unhappy by me, if otherwise, and then I lose my end. I speak of empairing, of changing, or supplying, as of any other way, all such alterations, and ruine, are alike, without I be worthy of your gift, and that I can be worthy of all that Law can permit you to give, or cast upon your Majesty by a more neerer title, as it doth by this; I shall account them equal evils, that leave nothing, or a patched and proportioned one, changed or translated from one thing to another.

But if your Majesty have any respects to move you to suspend your good intention towards me, let that which is mine rest in your own hands, till that you find all opposite humours conformed to your purpose. I have done wrong to my self, thus to entertain such a doubt of your Majesty; but of the unrelenting of adversaries, which when you will have them, will sooner alter; and that all this while I have received nothing of present notice for direction, or to comfort me, from your Majesty, hath made me to expostulate with my self thus hardly. For God is my Judge, Sir, I can never be worthy to be, if I have these marks put upon me, of a Traytor; as that tumbling and disordering of that estate would declare the divorce from your presence, lays too much upon me, and this would upon both.

I will say no farther, neither in that which your Majesty doubted my aptness to fall into, for my Cause, nor my Confidence is not in that distress as for to use that mean of intercession, nor of any thing besides, but to remember your Majesty, that I am the Workmanship of your hands, and bear your stamp deeply imprinted in all the characters of favour; that I was the first plant ingrafted by your Majesties hand in this place, therefore not to be unrooted by the same hand, lest it should taint all the same kind with the touch of that fatalness; And that I was even the Son of a Father, whose services are registred in the first honours and impressions I took of your Majesties favour, and laid there as a foundation-stone of that building; These, and your Majesties goodness for to receive them, is that I rely upon; So praying for your Majesties prosperity, I am, in all humbleness,

Your Majesties loyal servant,
and Creature,

R. Somerset.

Earl

Sir Kenhelm Digby, to Sir Edward Stradling.

Earl of Desmond, to the Earl of Ormond.

My Lord,

GReat is my grief when I think how heavily her Majesty is bent to dis-favour me; and howbeit I carry the name of an undutifull Subject, yet God knoweth that my heart and mind are alwayes most lowly inclined to serve my most loving Prince, so it may please her Highness to remove her heavy displeasure from me. As I may not condemn my self of disloyalty to her Majesty, so cannot I excuse my faults, but must confess that I have incurred her Majesties indignation; yet when the cause and means which were found and devised to make me commit folly, shall be known to her Highness, I rest in an assured hope that her most gracious Majesty will both think of me as my heart deserveth; and also of those that wrung me into undutifulness, as their cunning device meriteth. From my heart I am sorry, that folly, bad counsels, sleights, or any other thing hath made me to forget my duty: And therefore I am most desirous to get conference with your Lordship, to the end I may open and declare to you how tyrannously I was used, humbly craving that you will vouchsafe to appoint some time and place where and when I may attend your Honour, and then I doubt not to make it appear how dutifull a mind I carry, how faithfully I have at mine own charge served her Majesty before I was proclaimed, how sorrowfull I am for my offences, and how faithfully I am affected ever hereafter to serve her Majesty. And so I commit your Lordship to God, the 5. of *June*, 1583. Subscribed   *GIRALD DESMOND*

Sir Kenhelm Digby, to Sir Edward Stradling.

To my Honourable Friend, Sir Edward Esterling, alias Stradling, aboard his ship.

MY much honoured friend, I am too well acquainted with the weakness of my abilities (that are farre unfit to undergo such a task as I have in hand) to flatter my self with the hope that I may either informe your understanding, or do my self honour by what I am to write. But I am so desirous that you should be possessed with the true knowledge of what a bent will I have, upon all occasions, to do you service, that obedience to your Command weigheth much more with me then the lawfulness of my excuse can, to preserve me from giving you in writing such a testimony of my ignorance and erring fantasie, as I fear this will prove. Therefore, without any more circumstances, I will as near as I can, deliver to you, in this paper, what the other day I discoursed to you upon the 22ᵈ Staffe of the ninth Canto, in the second book of that matchless Poem, *The Fairy Queen*, written by our *English Virgil*, whose words are these.

> *The frame thereof seem'd partly Circular,*
> *And part Triangular : O work Divine!*
> *These two the first and last proportions are,*
> *Th'one imperfect, mortal, faeminine;*
> *Th'other immortal, perfect, masculine:*
> *And twixt them both a quadrat was the base,*
> *Proportion'd equally, by seven, and nine;*
> *Nine was the Circle set in heavens place,*
> *All which compacted made a goodly Diapase.*

In this Staff, the Author seemeth to me to proceed in a differing manner from what he doth elsewhere, generally, through his whole book; for in other places, although the beginning of this Allegory or mystical sence may be obscure, yet in the process of it he doth himself declare his own conceptions in such sort, that they are obvious to any ordinary capacity: But in this, he seemeth only to glance at the profoundest notions that any science can deliver to us; and then of a suddain, as it were recalling himself out of an Enthusiasme, he returneth to the gentle relation of the Allegorical history that he had begun, leaving his readers to wander up and down in much obscurity, and to rove with much danger of erring at his intention in these lines; which I conceive to be dictated

by

by such a learned spirit, and so generally a knowing soul, that were there nothing else extant of *Spencers* writings, yet these few words would make me esteem him no whit inferiour to the most famous men that ever have been in any age, as giving an evident testimony herein, that he was throughly versed in the Mathematicall sciences, in Philosophy and Divinity; unto all which this might serve for an ample Theame to make large Commentaries upon ; In my praises upon this subject I am confident, that the worth of the Author will preserve me from this censure, that my ignorance only begetteth this admiration, since he hath written nothing that is not admirable. But that it may appear I am guided somewhat by my own Judgement, (although it be a very mean one) and not by implicit faith, and that I may in the best manner I can comply with what you may expect from me, I will not longer hold you in suspence, but begin immediately (though abruptly) with the declaration of what I conceive to be the true sence of this place; which I shall not go about to adorn with any plausible discourses, or with authorities and examples drawn from others writings; (since my want both of conveniency and learning would make me fall very short herein) but it shall be enough for me to intimate my conceptions, and to offer them up unto you in their own simple and naked forme, leaving to your better Judgement the examination of the weight of them; and after perusal of them, beseeching you to reduce me, if you perceive me to erre. It is evident, that the Authors intention in this Canto, is, to describe the body of man informed with a rational soul ; and in prosecution of that design, he setteth down particularly the several parts of the one, and the faculties of the other. But in this *Stanza* he comprehendeth the general description of them both, as (being joyned together to frame a compleat man) they make one perfect compound; which will appear better by taking a survey of every several Clause thereof by it self.

> *The frame thereof seem'd partly circular,*
> *And part triangular.* ———

By these figures, I conceive, that he meaneth the Mind and the Body of man; the first being by him compared to a Circle, and the latter to a Triangle; for as the Circle of all figures is the most perfect, and includeth the greatest space, and is every way full, and without angles, made by the continuation of one only line ; so mans soul is the noblest and most beautiful creature that God hath created, and by it we are capable of the greatest gifts which God can bestow, which are Grace, Glory, and Hypostatical union of the humane Nature to the divine : and she enjoyeth perfect freedom and liberty in all other actions, and is made without composition, (which no figures are that have angles ; for they are caused by the coincidence of several lines) but of one pure substance , which was by God breathed into a body made of such compounded earth, as in the preceding Stanza the Author describeth ; and this is the exact image of him that breathed it, representing him as fully as it is possible for any creature which is infinitely distant from the Creator. For as God hath neither beginning nor ending, so neither of these can be found in a Circle ; although that being made of the successive motion of a line, it must be supposed to have a beginning some where. God is compared to a circle whose centre is every where, but whose Circumference no where; but mans soul is a circle whose circumference is limited by the true centre of it, which is only God. For as a circumference doth in all parts alike respect that indivisible point, and as all lines drawn from the inner side of it do make right angles with it when they meet therein ; so all the interior actions of mans soul ought to have no other respective point to direct themselves unto but God : and as long as they make right angles, which is, that they keep the exact middle of vertue, and decline not to either of the sides, where the contrary vices dwell, they cannot fail but meet in their Centre.

By the Triangular figure he very aptly designeth the Body : For as the Circle is of all other figures the most perfect, and most capacious ; so the Triangle is the most imperfect, and includeth the least space: It is the first and lowest of all figures ; for fewer then three right lines cannot comprehend and inclose a superficies ; having but three angles, they are all acutes (if it be equilateral) and but equall to two right ones ; in which respect all other regular figures, consisting of more then three lines, do exceed it : May not these be resembled to the three great and compounded Elements in mans body, to wit, Salt, Sulphur, and Mercury ? which mingled together do make the natural heat, and radicall moisture, the two qualities whereby man liveth: for the more lines that do go to comprehend a figure, the more and greater the angles are, and the neerer it cometh to the perfection of a Circle.

A Triangle is composed of several lines, and they of points, which yet do not make a
quantity

quantity by being contiguous one to another, but rather the motion of them doth describe the lines. In like manner, the Body of man is compounded of the four Elements, which are made by the four primary qualities, not compounded of them, (for they are but accidents,) but by their operation upon the first matter.

And as a Triangle hath three lines, so a solid body hath three dimensions, to wit, Longitude, Latitude, and Profundity: but of all bodies mans is of the lowest rank (as the Triangle is among figures) being composed of the Elements, which make it liable to alteration and corruption. In which consideration of the dignity of bodies, I divide them, by a general division, into sublunary, which are the elementated ones; and into the æthereal (which are supposed to be, of their own nature, incorruptible:) and peradventure there are some other species of corporeal substances, which is not in this place to dispute.

———*O work Divine!*

Certainly, of all Gods works, the noblest and the perfectest is man, and for whom, indeed, all others were done: for, if we consider his soul, it is the very Image of God; if his body, it is adorned with the greatest beauty and excellent symmetry of parts, of any created thing; whereby it witnesseth the perfection of the Architect, that of so drossie mold is able to make so excellent a Fabrick; if his operations, they are free; if his end, it is eternal glory; and if you take him all together, man is a little world, an exact type of the great world, and of God himself.

But in all this, me thinketh, that the admirable work, is, the joyning together of the two different, and indeed opposite, substances in man, to make one perfect compound, the Soul and the Body, which are of so contrary a nature, that their uniting seemeth to be a miracle: for how can one inform and work in the other, since there is no mean of operation, that we know) between a spiritual substance and a corporeal? yet we see that it doth. As hard it is to find the true proportion between a Circle and a Triangle; yet that there is a just proportion, and that they may be equal, *Archimedes* hath left us an ingenious demonstration: but, in reducing it to a Probleme, it faileth in this, That because the proportion between a crooked line and a straight one is not known, one must make use of a mechanical way of measuring the Peripherie of the one, to convert it into the side of the other.

These two the first and last proportions are.

What I have already said concerning a Circle and a Triangle doth sufficiently unfold what is meant in this Verse; yet it will not be amiss to speak one word more hereof in this place. All things that have existence may be divided into three Classes; which are, either what is pure and simple in it self, or what hath a nature compounded of what is simple, or what hath a nature compounded of what is compounded. In continued quantity, this may be exemplified by a Point, a Line, and a Superficies, or Body; and in numbers, by an Unity, a Denary, and a Centenary. The first, which is onely pure and single, like an indivisible Point, or an Unity, hath relation onely to the Divine Nature; that point then moving in a spherical manner (which serveth to express the perfections of Gods actions) describeth the circle of our souls, and of Angels, and of intellectual substances, which are of a pure and simple nature; but receiveth that from what is so in a perfecter manner, and that hath his from none else; like lines that are made from the flowing of points, or denaries that are composed of unites, beyond both which there is nothing.

In the last place, Bodies are to be ranked, which are composed of the Elements, and they likewise suffer composition, and may very well be compared to the lowest of figures, which are composed of lines, that ow their being to points, (and such are Triangles;) or to Centenaries, that are composed of Denaries, and they of Unites. But if we will compare these together by proportion, God must be left out, since there is an infinite distance between the simplicity and perfection of his nature, and the composition and imperfection of all created substances, as there is between an indivisible point, and a continuate quantity; or between a simple unite, and compounded number: so that onely the other two kinds of substances do enter into this consideration; and of them I have already proved, that mans soul is one of the noblest, being dignified by Hypostatical Union above all other intellectual substances, and his elementated body of the other, the most low and corruptible: whereby it is evident, that these two are the first and last proportions, both in respect of their own figures, and of what they express.

The one imperfect, mortal, feminine;
Th' other immortal, perfect, masculine.

Mans body hath all the properties of imperfect matter; it is but the patient, of it self alone

alone it can do nothing, it is liable to corruption and diſſolution, if it once be deprived of the form, which actuateth it ſelf, and is incorruptible and immortal.

And as the Feminine Sex is imperfect, and receiveth perfection from the Maſculine; ſo doth the Body from the Soul, which to it is in lieu of a Male: And as in corporal generations the Female doth afford but groſs and paſſive matter, unto which the Male giveth active heat, and prolifical vertue; ſo in ſpiritual generations, (which are the operations of the Mind) the Body adminiſtreth only the Organs, which, if they were not employed by the Soul, would of themſelves ſerve to nothing. And as there is a mutual appetence between the Male and the Female, between matter and form; ſo there is between the Body and Soul of a man: but what Ligament they have, that our Author defineth not; (and, peradventure, Reaſon is not able to attain unto it) yet he telleth us, what is the Foundation that this Machine reſteth upon, and what keepeth the Parts together, in theſe words:

And 'twixt them both a Quadrat was the Baſe.

By which Quadrat, I conceive that he meaneth the four principal Humours in mans body, to wit, Choler, Blood, Phlegm, and Melancholy; which, if they be diſtempered, and unfitly mingled, the diſſolution of the whole doth enſue: like to a Building, which falleth to ruine, if the Foundation or Baſe of it be unſound or diſordered. And in ſome of theſe the vital ſpirits are contained and preſerved, which the other do keep in a convenient temper; and as long as they do ſo, the Soul and the Body dwell together like good friends: So that theſe four are the Baſe of the conjunction of the other two; both which, he ſaith, are

Proportion'd equally by Seven and Nine.

In which words, I underſtand, that he meaneth the influences of the ſuperiour ſubſtances, which govern the inferiour, into theſe two differing parts of man, to wit, of the Stars (the moſt powerfull of which are the ſeven Planets) into his Body, and of the Angels (which are divided into nine Hierarchies or Orders) into the Soul, which, in his Aſtrophel, he ſaith, is

By Sovereign choice from th' Heavenly Quires ſelect,
And lineally deriv'd from Angels race.

And as much as the one do govern the Body, ſo much the other do the Mind: wherein it is to be conſidered, that ſome are of opinion, how at the inſtant of the conception of a child, or rather, more effectually, at the inſtant of his birth, the conceived Sperm, or the tender body, doth receive ſuch influence of the Heavens as then reigneth over that place where the conception or birth is made; and all the Stars, and virtual places of the Celeſtial Orbs, participating of the qualities of the ſeven Planets; according to the which they are diſtributed into ſo many Claſſes, or the compounds of them, it cometh to paſs, that according to the variety of the ſeveral aſpects of the one and of the other, there are various inclinations and qualities in mens bodies, but all reduced to ſeven general heads, and the compounds of them, which being to be varied innumerable ways, cauſeth as many different effects, yet the influence of ſome one Planet continually predominating: but when the matter in the womans womb is capable of a Soul to inform it, then God ſendeth one from Heaven into it.

——— *Eternal God*
In Paradiſe did whilome plant this flower,
Whence he it fetch'd out of her native place,
And did in ſtock of earthly fleſh enrace.

And this opinion the Author expreſſeth himſelf more plainly to be of, in another Work, where he ſaith,

There She beholds, with high aſpiring thought,
The Cradle of her own Creation,
Amongſt the ſeats of Angels, heavenly wrought.

Which whether it hath been created ever ſince the beginning of the world, and reſerved in ſome fit place until due time, or be created upon the emergent occaſion, no man can tell: but certain it is, that it is immortal, according to that I ſaid when I ſpake of the Circle, which hath no ending, and an uncertain beginning.

The meſſengers to convey which ſoul into the body are the Intelligences that move the Orbs of Heaven; who, according to their ſeveral natures, do communicate unto it ſeveral proprieties, and they who are governours of thoſe Stars that have at that inſtant the ſuperiority in the Planetary aſpects; whereby it cometh to paſs, that in all inclinations there is much affinity between the Soul and the Body, being that the like is between the Intelligences

gences and the Stars; both which communicate their vertues to each of them. And these Angels being, as I said before, of nine several Hierarchies, there are so many principal differences in humane souls, which do participate most of their properties with whom, in their descent, they make longest stay, and that had most active power to work upon them, and accompanied them with a peculiar *Genius*; which is, according to their several governments, like the same kind of water that running through various conduits, wherein several aromatical and odoriferous things are laid, doth acquire several kinds of taste and smells; for it is supposed, that in their first Creation all souls are alike, and that their differing proprieties arrive unto them afterwards, when they pass through the spheres of the governing Intelligences: so that by such their influence it may truly be said,

Nine was the Circle set in Heavens place.

Which Verse, by assigning his office to the nine, and the proper place of the Circle, doth give much light to what is said before.

And for further confirmation that this is the Authors opinion, read attentively the sixth Canto of the third Book, where most learnedly he delivereth the Tenets of this Philosophy; and of that, I recommend to you to take particular notice of the second, and thirty second Stanza's, and also of the last Staff of his *Epithalamium*; and surveying his works, you shall find him to be a constant Disciple of *Plato*'s School.

All which compacted made a goodly Diapase.

In nature, there is not to be found a more compleat and more excellent concordance of all parts, then that which is between the compaction and uniting together of the body and soul of man; both which, although they consist of many and most differing faculties and parts, yet when they keep due time with one another, do all together make the most perfect harmony that can be imagined. And as the nature of sounds (that consist of friendly consonants and accords) is, to mingle with one another, and to slide into the ear with much sweetness, where by their unity they last a long time, and delight it; whereas, on the contrary side, discords do continually jar, and fight together, and will not mingle with one another; but all of them striving to have the victory, their reluctation and disorder giveth a soon end to their sounds, which strike the ear in a harsh and offensive manner, and they die in the very beginning of their conflict. In like sort, when a mans actions are regular; and that being directed towards God they become like the lines of a Circle which all meet in the Centre; then his musick is excellent and compleat, and all together are the Authors of that blessed harmony which maketh him happy in the glorious vision of Gods perfections, wherein the mind is filled with high knowledges, and most pleasing contemplations, and the senses are, as it were, drowned with eternal delight; and nothing can interrupt this joy, this happiness, which is an everlasting Diapase: Whereas, on the contrary part, if a mans actions be disorderly, and consisting of discord, which is, when the sensitive part rebelleth, and wrastleth with the rational, and striveth to oppress it, then this Musick is spoiled; and instead of eternal life, pleasure, and joy, it causeth perpetual death, horrour, pain, and misery; which unfortunate estate the Poet describeth elsewhere, as in the conclusion of this Staff he intimateth. The other happy one, which is the never-failing reward of such an obedient Body, and Æthereal and Vertuous Mind, as he maketh to be the seat of the bright Virgin *Alma*, mans worthiest inhabitant, Reason. Her I feel to speak within me, and to chide me for my bold attempt, warning me to stray no further: For what I have said, (considering how weakly it is said) your Commandment is all that I can pretend in excuse; but since my desire to obey may as well be seen in a few lines, as in a large discourse, it were indiscretion in me to trouble you with more words, and to discover unto you more of my ignorance. I will onely beg pardon of you for this blotted and interlined paper, whose contents are so mean, that it cannot deserve the pains of a transcription; which if you make difficulty to grant unto it for my sake, let it obtain it for having been yours, and now returning again to you, as also doth the Book that containeth my Text which yesterday you sent me, to fit this part of it with a Comment: which, peradventure, I might have performed better, if either I had afforded my self more time, or had had the convenience of some other Books, apt to quicken my invention, to whom I might have been beholden for enlarging my understanding in some things that are treated here, although the application should still have been my own: with these two helps, peradventure, I might have dived farther into the Authors intention, the depth of which cannot be founded by any that is less learned then he was. But I perswade my self very strongly, that in what I have said there is nothing contradictory to it; and that an intelligent and well-read man, proceeding upon my grounds, might compose a worthy and true Commentary upon this Theme; upon which I wonder how I stumbled, considering how many learned men have failed in the interpreting of it, and have all approved my opinion, at the first hearing it: but it was fortune that made me to light upon it, when first this Stanza was re-d unto me for an undissoluble riddle: And the same discourse that I made upon it, the first half quarter of an hour that I saw it, I send it you here, without having reduced it to any better form, or added any thing at all unto it; which I beseech you receive benignly, as coming from

Your most affectionate friend, and humble servant,
Kenhelm Digby.

Dr Donne, to the Marquess of Buckingham.

My most honoured Lord,

I Most humbly beseech your Lordship, to afford this rag of Paper a room amongst your Evidences. It is your evidence, not for a Mannor, but for a man. As I am a Priest, it is my sacrifice of Prayer to God for your Lordship; and as I am a Priest made able to subsist, and appear in Gods service, by your Lordship; it is a sacrifice of my self to you. I deliver this Paper as my Image; and I assist the power of any Conjurer with this imprecation upon my self, that as he shall tear this paper, this picture of mine, so I may be torn in my fortune, and in my fame, if ever I have any corner in my heart dispossessed of a zeal to your Lordships service. His Majesty hath given me a royal Key into your Chamber, leave to stand in your presence; and your Lordship hath already such a fortune, as that you shall not need to be afraid of a suitor, when I appear there. So that, I protest to your Lordship, I know not what I want, since I cannot suspect, nor fear my self, for ever doing, or leaving undone, any thing by which I might forfeit that title, of being always

Septemb. 13. 1621.

Your Lordships, &c,
J. D.

Dr. Donne, to the Duke.

My honoured Lord,

ONce I adventured to say to the Prince his Highness, That I was sure he would receive a Book from me the more graciously, because it was dedicated to your Grace: I proceed justly, upon the same confidence, that your Grace will accept this, because it is his by the same title. If I had not overcome that reluctation which I had in my self, of representing devotions, and mortifications, to a young and active Prince, I should not have put them into your presence, who have done so much, and have so much to do in this world, as that it might seem enough to think seriously of that. No man, in the Body of Story, is a full President to you, nor may any future man promise himself an adequation to his president, if he make you his. Kings have discerned the seeds of high vertues in many men, and upon that Gold they have put their stamp, their favours upon those persons: But then those persons have laboured under the jealousie of the future Heir; and some few have had the love of Prince and King, but not of the Kingdom; and some, of that too, and not of the Church; God hath united your Grace so to them all, that as you have received obligations from the King and Prince, so you have laid obligations upon the Church and State: They above, love you out of their judgment, because they have loved you; and we below, love you out of our thankfulness, because you have loved us. Gods Privie-Seal is the Testimony of a good Conscience, and his Broad-Seal is the outward Blessings of this Life: But since his Pillar of Fire was seconded with a Pillar of Cloud, and that all his temporal Blessings have some partial Eclipses, and the purest Consciences some remorses; so though he have made your way to Glory Glory, and brought you, in the arms and bosom of his Vicegerent, into his own arms and bosom, yet there must come a minute of twi-light in a natural death. And as the reading of the actions of great men may assist you for great actions, so for this one necessary descent of dying, (which, I hope, shall be the onely step of lowness that ever you shall pass by, and by that, late) you may receive some Remembrances, from the Meditations and Devotions of

Your Grace's devoutest servant,
J. Donne.

Queen Elizabeth, to the Lady Norris.

A Defiance sent by the Grand Seigniour to Maximilian *the second.*

BY the sufferance of the great God, We *Solyman*, God in earth, great and high Emperor of all the word, Patron and Distributer of all Christians, We send and declare unto thee *Maximilian*, all wrath and ill fortune and infidelity, and to all thy Princes, subjects and helpers: We give it known unto thee, That We, by the sufferance of the great God, named The Perpetual and Universal God in Earth, most mighty Emperour, *Selden* in *Babylon*, Lord of *Armenia*, the most mightiest in *Persepolis* and *Numidia*, the great helper of God, Prince for the Rode of *Barbary* unto the mountains of *Achaia*, King of Kings from the *Meridian* to the *Septentrion* of the earth, from the rising place of the Sun to the setting of it, the first and chiefest, placed in the Paradise of *Mahomet*, the destroyer of all Christendom, and of all Christians, and that do profess Christianity, the keeper and defender of the Sepulchre of thy God crucified, the onely victorious and triumphant Lord of all the world, and of all Circuits and Provinces thereof: Thou *Maximilian*, which writest thy self King of our Kingdom of *Hungary*, which is under our Crown and obeysance, we will visit thee for that cause, and also perswade thee that with our strength and force of thirteen Kingdoms, with might and strength, to the number of one hundred thousand as well Horsemen as Footmen prepared for war, with all the power and strength of Turkish munition, and with such power as thou nor none of thy servants have seen, heard, or had knowledge of, even before thy chief City *Vienna*, and the Country thereabouts: We *Selyman*, God on earth, against thee, with all thy assisters and helpers, with our warlike strength, do pronounce and protest your utter destruction and depopulation, as we can by all means possible devise it. And this we will signifie unto thee, to the which thou and thy miserable people may prepare your selves. With us it is determined, with our men appointed, thee and all thy *German* Kingdoms and Provinces altogether to spoil: This misery we have consented unto against thee and thy Princes, and have thou no doubt but we will come. Dated in the City of *Constantinople*, out of which we did expulse your Predecessors, their wives, children and friends, and made them most miserable slaves and Captives, the year of our Reign fourty seven.

Queen Elizabeths *Letter to the Lady* Norris, *upon the death of her Son.*

ALthough we have deferred long to represent unto you our grieved thoughts, because we liked full well to yield you the first reflections of our misfortunes, whom we have alwaies sought to cherish and comfort; yet knowing now that necessity must bring it to your ears, and nature consequently must move many passionate affections in your heart, we have resolved no longer to smother either our care for your sorrow, or the sympathy of our grief for his death; wherein if society in sorrowing work diminution, we do assure you by this true messenger of our mind, that nature can have stirred no more dolorous affections in you as a mother, for a dear son, then the gratefulness and memory of his services past had wrought in us his Sovereign apprehension of the miss of so worthy a servant. But now that natures common work is done, and he that was born to die hath paid his tribute, let that Christian discretion stay the flux of your immoderate grieving, which hath instructed you both by example and knowledge, that nothing of this kind hath happened but by Gods providence; and that these lines from your loving and gracious Sovereign, serve to assure you, that there shall ever appear the lively characters of you and yours that are left, in our valuing rightly all their faithfull and honest endeavours. More we will not write of this subject, but have dispatched this Gentleman to visit both your Lord, and condole with you in the true sense of your love, and to pray you, that the world may see, that what time cureth in weak minds, that discretion and moderation may help in you in this accident, where there is so opportune occasion to demonstrate true patience and true moderation.

The Earle of Essex, *to King* James, *concerning Secretary* Davison.

MOst excellent King, for him that is already bound for many favours, a stile of thankfulness is much fitter then the humour of suing; but so it falls out, that he which to own advantage would have sought nothing in your favour, but your favour it self, doth no
so.

The Earl of Essex, to Mr. Secretary Davison.

for another become an humble petitioner to your Majesty: your Majesty cannot be such a stranger to the affairs of this Countrey, but as you know what actions are done in this place, so you understand the minds of the men by whom they are done. Therefore I doubt not, but the man for whom I speak is somewhat known to your Majesty, and being known, I presume of greater favour, (Mr. Secretary Davison being fallen into her Majesties displeasure and disgrace) beloved of the best and most religious of this land, doth stand as barred from any preferment or restoring in his place; except out of the honour and noblenesse of your own Royal heart, your Majesty will undertake his cause. To leave the nature of his fault to your Majesties best judgment, and report of your own servant, and to speak of the man, I must say truly, that his sufficiency in Councel, and matters of State, is such, as the Queen her self confesseth, in her Kingdom she hath not such another; his vertue, religion, and worth in all degrees, is of the world taken to be so great, as no man in his good fortune hath had more general love, then this Gentleman in his disgrace: And if to a man so worthy in himself, and so esteemed of all men, my words might avail any thing, I would assure your Majesty, you would get great honour, and great love, not onely here amongst us, but in all places of Christendom where this Gentleman is any thing known, if you should now be the author of his restoring to his place, which in effect he now is, but that as a man not acceptable to her Majesty, he doth forbear to attend. I do in all humblenesse commend this cause to your Majesty, having the warrant of a good conscience, that I know to be both honourable and honest; and your Majesty to the blessed protection of that mighty God, to whom will pray for your Majesties happy and prosperous estate, He that will do your Majesty all humble service,

Greenwich, April 18. 1589.   R. ESSEX.

The Earle of Essex, to Secretary Davison.

SIR,

As at my departure, so upon my return, I must needs salute you, as one whom then, and now, and ever, I must love very much. I would gladly see you, but I am tied here a while; when I may have occasion to shew my love to you, I will do more then I now promise. In the mean time, wishing you that happinesse which men in this world ought to seek, I take my leave,

Your assured Friend,

At the Court, July 11. 1589.   R. ESSEX.

The Earl of Essex, to Mr. Secretary Davison.

SIR,

I Have as I could, taken my opportunity since I saw you, to perform as much as I promised you; and though in all I have been able to effect nothing, yet even now I have had better leisure to sollicite the Queen, then in this stormy time I did hope for. My beginning was, as being amongst others intreated to move her in your behalf: my course was to lay open your sufferings and your patience; in them you had felt poverty, restraint and disgrace, and yet you shewed nothing but faith and humility; faith, as being never wearied nor discouraged to do her service; humblenesse, as content to forget all the burthens that had been laid upon you, and to serve her Majesty with as frank and willing a heart as they that have received greatest grace from her. To this I received no answer, but in general terms, that her honour was much touched, your presumption had been intollerable, and that she could not let it slip out of her mind. When I urged your accesse, she denied it, but so as I had no cause to be afraid to speak again. When I offered in them both to reply, she fell into other discourse, and so we parted. So all that I have done you know; what I shall do ye shall prescribe. If your any mans else ——— I pray you let me know, for so I shall perceive whether she will open heart more to me then them, which being known I may deal accordingly. And so I com out to God:

Your most assured friend,

Windsor, Octob. 2.   R. ESSEX.

The Earl of Essex, to Mr. Secretary Davison.

IF this Letter do not deliver you my very affectionate wishes, and assure you that I am both carefull to deserve well, and covetous to hear well of you, it doth not discharge the trust that I have committed unto it. My love to your worthy father, my expectation that you will truly inherit his vertues, and the proof that I have seen of, your well spending your time abroad, are three strong bands to tie my affection unto you; to which when I see added your kindness to my self, my Reason tells my heart, I cannot value you, or affect you too much: you have laid so good a foundation of framing your self, as if now you do not perfect the work, the expectation you have raised will be your greatest adversary: slack not your industry, in thinking you have taken great pains already, *Nusquam enim nec sine emolumento, nec emolumentum sine impensa opera est: Labor voluptasque dissimilia natura, societate quadam naturali inter se conjuncta sunt.* Nor think your self at any time so rich in knowledge or reputation, as you may spend on the stock: For as the way to vertue is steep and craggy, so the descent from it is headlong. It is said of our bodies, that they do *lente augescere, & cito extinguuntur;* it may be as properly said of our minds. Let your vertuous Father, who in the midst of his troubles and discomforts hath brought you, by his care and charge, to what you are now in, you receive perfect comfort and contentment; Learn *virtutem ab illo, fortunam ab aliis.* I write not this, as suspecting you need be admonished, or as finding my self able to direct; but as he that when he was writing took the plainest and naturallest stile of a friend truly affected to you: Receive it, therefore, I pray you, as a pledge of more love then I can now shew you. And so desiring nothing more then to hear often from you, I wish you all happiness, and rest,

White-hall, Jan. 8.

Your affectionate and assured friend,
R. ESSEX.

The Earl of Essex, to Secretary Davison.

SIR,

AS I have ever loved you, so now taking leave of my good friends, I cannot forget you of whose love I desire to be ever assured, and whom I would desire to satisfie in all things that I shall do. If you be troubled with the suddenness of my unlooked for journey, let my resolute purpose to perform it, which could not be without secrecie, excuse me: if you call it rashness, I will better allow it to be heresie then error; for many moneths ago it was resolved: if you doubt of the success or event thereof, I say, that the same God who hath given me a mind to undertake, may according to his good pleasure make me in it, or it with me, to prosper or die, as it shall seem best unto him. And so purposing that you shall see me return happy, or never, I take my leave. Let me be commended to your good self, and such other of my good friends, as in my absence you find I am beholden to, especially to Sir *Drew Drury,* and Sir *Edward Waterhouse.*

Your assured friend,
R. ESSEX.

Again, to Secretary Davison.

SIR,

I Had speech with her Majesty yester-night after my departure from you; and I find that the success of my speech (although I hoped for good) yet did much over-run my expectation. To repeat many speeches and by-matters, as of my acquaintance with you, and such like, it will be fitter for such a time when I shall have conference with you. But in effect, our end was thus: I made her Majesty see, what in your health, in your fortune, and in your reputation with the world you had suffered since the time that it was her pleasure to commit you; I told her how many friends and well-wishers the world did afford you, and how, for the most part, throughout the whole Realm her best subjects did wish that she would do her self the honour to repair for you, and restore to you, that state which she had overthrown; your humble suffering of these harms, and reverend regard to her Majesty, must needs move a Princess so noble and so just, to do you right; and more I had said, if my gift of
speech

speech had been any way comparable to my love. Her Majesty seeing her judgment opened by the glory of her own actions, shewed a very feeling compassion of you; she gave you in many praises, and among the rest, that which she seemed to please her self in, was, that you were a man of her own choice. In truth, she was so well pleased with those things that she spake and heard of you, as I dare (if of things future there be any assurance) promise to my self that your peace will be in due to your own content, and the desires of your friends, I mean, in her favour, and your own fortune, to a better estate then, or at least the same, you had, which with all my power I will imploy my self to effect. And so in haste, I commit you to God.

Your friend most assured,
R. ESSEX.

The Earl of Essex, to Mr. Secretary Davison, upon the death of Mr. Secretary Walsingham.

SIR,

Upon this unhappy accident, I have tryed to the bottom what the Queen will do for you, and what the credit of your Sollicitor is worth. I urged not the comparison between you and any other: But in my duty to her, and zeal to her service, I did assure her that she had not any other in *England* that would for these three or four years know how to settle himself to support so great a burthen. She gave me leave to speak; heard me with patience, confessed, with me, that none was so sufficient; and could not deny but that which she layes to your charge was done without hope, fear, malice, envy, or any respect of your own, but meerly for her safety both of state and person. In the end she absolutely denied to let you enjoy that place, and willed me to rest satisfied, for she was resolved. Thus much I write to let you know I am more honest to my friends, then happy in their cases. What you will have me do for your suit, I will, as far as my credit is any thing worth. I have told most of the Councel of my manner of dealing with the Queen; my Lord Chamberlain tells me he hath dealt for you also, and they all say they wish as I do; but in this world that is enough. I will commit you to God for this time, and rest,

Your constant and true friend,
R. ESSEX.

The Earl of Essex, to the Queen.

MY dutifull affections to your Majesty alwaies overweighed all other worldly respects; that seeking in all particulars to manifest my truth, I have maimed my estate in generall, as I dare, in the heat of my thoughts, compare with the greatest that ever vowed for faithful service; so is there not the meanest that hath overslipped me; I will not say in recompence, but in some gracious estate of service. Thus whilest my state wrestleth with my fortune, the one winns breath to beat the other down. Though I have no hope to repair the ruines of my oversight, yet I cannot but presume your Majesty will suffer me to preserve them from blowing up; and what youth and forward belief hath undermined in mine estate, providence by a retired life may underlay. In which discontinuance from Court there shall be added (if any thing he added) increase of loyalty: Nor so solitary shall be my course, as it shall seem to proceed of discontment, but of necessity; and all actions both with living and my life so forward, as though some may have overrun me in fortunes, none shall in duty.

Next my allegiance to your Majesty, which shall be held most sacred and inviolable, the report of mine Honor challengeth chief interest; which that I may preserve in my wonted state, Reason draws me to stay my self slipping from falling. That of late (by what secret and venomous blow I know not) my faith hath received some wounds, your Majesties wonted grace withdrawn assures me: But truth and my patience, in this case, were one with me; and time, in your Princely thoughts, did wear it out from me. Let time be Judge; I will leave you with as great loathness, as i were to lose that I love best. But your favour failing, in which I have placed all my hopes, and my self less graced, after seven years, then when I had served but seven daies, may be a reason to excuse, if there were no other reason. These things pressed out of a distressed minde, and offered in all humility, I hope it shall not be offensive if I choose this wearisom course, rather to be retired then tired. If any of envy take advantage

Sir Thomas Egerton, *to the Earl of* Essex.

of absence, seeking by cunning to draw me into suspicion of discontentment, my conscience is setled in your never-erring Judgment, that if he come with *Esau*'s hands and *Jacob*'s voice, your Highness will censure it a wrought malice under such simplicity. It is true, that grief cannot speak; but this grief hath made me write, lest, when I leave you, I should so far forsake my self as to leave this unsaid. To your gracious acceptance I commit it, and with all humble and reverent thoughts that may be, rest ever to be commanded to die at your Majesties feet,

RO. ESSEX.

The Earl of Essex, *to the Queen.*

FRom a mind delighting in sorrow, from spirits wasted with passion, from a heart torn in pieces with care, grief, and travel; from a man that hateth himself, and all things that keep him alive, what service can your Majesty expect, since your service past deserves no more then banishment or proscription in the cursed'st of all other Countreys? Nay, nay, it is your Rebels pride and success that must give me leave to ransom my life out of this hatefull prison of my loathed body: which if it happen so, your Majesty shall have no cause to mis-like the fashion of my death, since the course of my life could never please you.

Your Majesties exiled Servant,
RO. ESSEX.

Sir Thomas Egerton, *Lord Chancellor, to the Earl of* Essex.

My very good Lord,

IT is often seen, that he that stands by seeth more then he that playeth the game; and, for the most part, every one, in his own cause, standeth in his own light, and seeth not so clearly as he should. Your Lordship hath dealt in other mens causes, and in great and weighty affairs, with great wisdom and judgment; now your own is in hand, you are not to contemn or refuse the advice of any that love you, how simple soever. In this order I rank my self, among others that love you; none more simple, and none that love you with more true and honest affection; which shall plead my excuse, if you shall either mistake, or mistrust my words or meaning: but, in your Lordships honourable wisdom, I neither doubt nor suspect the one nor the other. I will not presume to advise you; but shoot my bolt, and tell you what I think. The beginning, and long continuance, of this so unseasonable discontentment, you have seen and proved, by which you aim at the end: If you still hold this course, which hitherto you find to be worse and worse, (and the longer you go, the further you go out of the way) there is little hope or likelihood the end will be better. You are not yet gone so far, but that you may well return: the return is safe, but the progress is dangerous and desperate, in this course you hold. If you have any enemies, you do that for them, which they could never do for themselves: Your friends you leave to scorn and contempt; you forsake your self, and overthrow your fortunes, and ruinate your honour and reputation. You give that comfort and courage to the forreign enemies, as greater they cannot have; for what can be more welcome and pleasing news, then to hear that her Majesty and the Realm are maimed of so worthy a member, who hath so often, and so valiantly, quailed and daunted them? You forsake your Countrey, when it hath most need of your counsel and aid: And, lastly, you fail in your indissoluble duty which you ow unto your most gracious Sovereign; a duty imposed upon you, not by nature and policy onely, but by the religious and sacred bond wherein the Divine Majesty of Almighty God hath by the rule of Christianity obliged you.

For the four first, your constant resolution may, perhaps, move you to esteem them as light; but, being well weighed, they are not light, nor lightly to be regarded: And for the four last, it may be, that the cleerness of your own conscience may seem to content your self, but that is not enough; for these duties stand not onely in contemplation, or inward meditation, and cannot be performed, but by external actions; and where that faileth, the substance also faileth. This being your present state and condition, what is to be done? what is the remedy, my good Lord? I lack judgment and wisdom to advise you, but I will never want an honest true heart to wish you well; nor, being warranted by a good conscience, will fear to speak that I think. I have begun plainly, be not offended if I proceed so. *Bene cedit qui*

cedit

cedit tempori: and Seneca saith, *Cedendum est fortunæ.* The medicine and remedy, is, not to contend and strive, but humbly to yield and submit. Have you given cause, and yet t ke a second turn unto you? then all you can be, is too little to make satisfaction. Is t e use of scandal given unto you? yet policy, duty, and Religion, enforce you to sue, yield and submit to our Soveraign; between whom and you there can be no equal proportion of duty, where God requires it as a principal duty and care to himself; and when it is evident, that great good may ensue of it to your friends, your self, your Countrey, and your Sovereign, and extreme harm by the contrary. There can be no dishonour, to yield; but in denying, dishonour and impiety. The difficulty (my good Lord) is, to conquer your self, which is the height of true valour and fortitude, whereunto all your honourable actions have tended. Do it in this, and God will be pleased, her Majesty (no doubt) well satisfied, your Countrey will take good, and your Friends comfort by it; and your self (I mention you last, for that of all these you esteem your self least) shall receive honour; and your Enemies (if you have any) shall be disappointed of their bitter sweet hope.

I have delivered what I think, simply and plainly; I leave you to determine, according to your own wisdom: if I have erred, it is *error amoris*, and not *amor erroris*, Construe and accept it, I beseech you, as I meant it; not as an advice, but as an opinion, to be allowed or cancelled at your pleasure. If I might conveniently have conferred with your self in person, I would not have troubled you with so many idle blots. Whatsoever you judge of this my opinion, yet be assured, my desire is to further all good means that may tend to your Lordships good, And so wishing you all happiness and honour, I cease.

Your Lordships most ready and faithfull,
though unable poor Friend,
Tho. Egerton, *Cust. Sigil.*

The Earl of Essex his Answer.

My very good Lord,

THough there is not that man this day living, whom I would sooner make Judge of any question that might concern me, then your self; yet you must give me leave to tell you, that in some cases I must appeal from all earthly Judges: And if in any, then surely in this, when the highest Judge on earth hath imposed upon me the heaviest punishment, without trial, or hearing. Since then I must either answer your Lordships arguments, or else forsake mine own just defence, I will force mine aking head to do me service for an hour. I must first deny my discontent (which was forced) to be an humorous discontent; and in that it was unseasonable, or is so long continuing, your Lordship should rather condole with me, then expostulate: natural seasons are expected here below, but violent and unreasonable storms come from above: There is no tempest to the passionate indignation of a Prince, nor yet at any time so unseasonable as when it lighteth on those that might expect an harvest of their carefull and painfull labours. He that is once wounded must needs feel smart till his hurt be cured, or the part hurt become senseless: But cure I expect none, her Majesties heart being obdurate; and be without sense I cannot, being of flesh and blood. But you may say, I may aim at the end: I do more then aim, for I see an end of all my fortunes, I have set an end to all my desires. In this course do I any thing for mine enemies? when I was present, I found them absolute; and, therefore, I had rather they should triumph alone, then have me attendant upon their Chariots: Or do I leave my friends? when I was a Courtier, I could sell them no fruit of my love; and now, that I am an Hermit, they shall bear no envie for their love to me. Or do I forsake my self, because I do not enjoy my self? Or do I overthrow my fortunes, because I build not a fortune of paper-walls, which every puff of wind bloweth down? Or do I ruinate mine honour, because I leave following the pursuit, or wearing the false mark, or the shadow of honour? Do I give courage or comfort to the enemies, because I neglect my self to encounter them? or because I keep my heart from business, though I cannot keep my fortune from declining? No, no, I give every one of those considerations his due right; and the more I weigh them, the more I find my self justified from offending in any of them. As for the two last objections, that I forsake my Countrey when it hath most need of me, and fail in that indissoluble duty which I ow to my Sovereign, I answer, That if my Countrey had at this time any need of my publick service, her Majesty, that governeth it, would not have driven me to a private life. I am tied to

my

Sir Thomas Egerton, *to the Earl of* Essex.

my Countrey by two bonds; one publick, to discharge carefully and industriously that trust which is committed to me; the other private, to sacrifice for it my life and carcase, which hath been nourished in it. Of the first, I am free, being dismissed by her Majesty: Of the other nothing can free me but death, and therefore no occasion of performance shall sooner offer it self, but I will meet it half way. The indissoluble duty I ow unto her Majesty, the service of an Earl and Marshal of *England*, and I have been content to do her the service of a Clerk; but I can never serve her as a villain or a slave. But you say, I must give way to time. So I do; for now that I see the storm come, I have put my self into harbour. *Seneca* saith, we must give way to Fortune: I know that Fortune is both blind and strong, and therefore I go as far as I can out of the way. You say, the remedy is not to strive: I neither strive, nor seek for remedy. But you say, I must yield and submit: I can neither yield my self to be guilty, nor this my imprisonment lately laid upon me to be just; I ow so much to the Author of Truth, as I can never yield Truth to be Falshood, nor Falshood to be Truth: Have I given cause, you ask, and yet take a scandal? No, I gave no cause to take up so much as *Fimbria* his complaint: for I did *totum telum corpore accipere*, I patiently bear and sensibly feel all that I then received when this scandal was given me. Nay, when the vilest of all indignities are done unto me, doth Religion enforce me to sue? Doth God require it? Is is impiety not to do it? Why? cannot Princes err? Cannot Subjects receive wrong? Is an earthly power infinite? Pardon me, pardon me, my Lord, I can never subscribe to these principles. Let *Solomons* fool laugh when he is stricken; let those that mean to make their profit of Princes, shew to have no sense of Princes injuries; let them acknowledge an infinite absoluteness on earth, that do not believe an absolute infiniteness in heaven. As for me, I have received wrong, I feel it; my cause is good, I know it; and whatsoever comes, all the powers on earth can never shew more strength or constancy in oppressing, then I can shew in suffering whatsoever can or shall be imposed upon me. Your Lordship, in the beginning of your Letter, makes me a player, and your self a looker on; and me a player of my own game, so you may see more then I: but give me leave to tell you, that since you do but see, and I do suffer, I must of necessity feel more then you. I must crave your Lordships patience, 'to give him that hath a crabbed fortune, leave to use a crooked stile: But whatsoever my stile is, there is no heart more humble, nor more affected towards your Lordship, then that of

Your Lordships poor friend,
ESSEX.

Sir Thomas Egerton, *Chancellor, after Lord* Ellesmere, *to the Earl of* Essex.

SIR,

HOw things proceed here, touching your self, you shall partly understand by these inclosed. Her Majesty is gracious towards you, and you want not friends to remember and commend your former services: Of these particulars you shall know more when we meet. In the mean time, by way of caution, take this from me; There are sharp eyes upon you; your actions, publick and private, are observed: It behooveth you, therefore, to carry your self with all integrity and sincerity, both of hands and heart, lest you overthrow your own fortunes, and discredit your friends that are tender and carefull of your reputation and welldoing. So, in haste, I commit you to God, with my very hearty commendations, and rest,

At the Court at Richmond,
*Octob.*21. 1599.

Your assured loving friend,
THO. EGERTON, C.S.

Lord Chancellor Ellesmere, *to King* James.

Most gracious Sovereign,

I Find, through my great age, accompanied with griefs and infirmities, my sense and conceipt is become dull and heavy, my memory decayed, my judgment weak, my hearing imperfect, my voice and speech failing and faltering, and in all the powers and faculties of my mind and body great debility. Wherefore, *conscientia imbecilitatis*, my humbly suit to your most saered Majesty is, to be discharged of this great Place, wherein I have long served; and to have some comfortable Testimony under your Royal hand, that I leave it at this humble suit, with your gracious favour: So shall I, with comfort, number and spend the few days I have to live, in meditation, and prayers to Almighty God, to preserve your Majesty, and all yours, in all heavenly and earthly felicity and happiness.

This suit I intended some years past. *ex dictamine rationis & conscientiæ*; Love and Fear stayed it: Now Necessity constrains me to it; I am utterly unable to sustain the burthen of this great service; for I am come to St. *Paul*'s desire, *Cupio dissolvi, & esse cum Christo*. Wherefore I most humbly beseech your Majesty most favourably to grant it.

Your Majesties most humble and loyal poor Subject and Servant,
THO. ELLESMERE, *Canc.*

Lord Chancellor Ellesmere, to King James.

A most gracious Soveraign,

YOur Royal favour hath placed and continued me many years in the highest place of ordinary Justice in this your Kingdom, and hath most graciously borne with my many, but unwilling, errours and defects, accepting, in stead of sufficiency, my zeal and fidelity, which never failed. This doth encourage and stir in me an earnest desire to serve still: But when I remember, St. *Paul*'s rule, *Let him that hath an office wait on his office*; and do consider, withall, my great age, and many infirmities, I am dejected, and do utterly faint: For I see and feel sensibly, that I am not able to perform those duties as I ought, and the place requires; and thereupon I do seriously examine my self, what excuse or answer I shall make to the King of Kings, and Judge of all Judges, when he shall call me to accompt; and then my conscience shall accuse me, that I have presumed so long to undergo and wield so mighty and great a charge and burthen; and I behold a great cloud of Witnesses ready to give evidence against me.

1. Reason telleth me, and by experience I find, *Senectus est tarda & obliviosa, & insanabilis morbus.*

2. I heard the precepts and counsel of many reverend, sage, and learned men, *Senectuti debetur otium, solve senectutem mature, &c.*

3. I reade in former Laws, that old men were made *emeriti & rude donati*: And one severe Law that saith, *Sexagenarius de ponte*, whereupon they are called *Depontani*. And *Plato*, *lib. 6. de legibus*, speaking of a great Magistrate which was *Præfectus legibus servandis*, determineth thus, *Minor annis 50 non admittatur; nec major annis 70 permittatur in eo perseverare*: And to this Law, respecting both mine office, and my years, I cannot but yield. But leaving forreign Laws, the Stat. *anno 13 E. 1.* speaketh plainly, *Homines excedentes ætatem 70 annorum non ponantur in Assisis & Juratis*. So as it appeareth, that men of that age are, by that Law, discharged of greater, painfull, and carefull, especially Judicial, Offices.

4. Besides, I find many examples, of men of great wisdom, knowledge and judgment, meet and worthy to be followed; of which (leaving all other) I will remember that of *William Warham*, Archbishop of *Canterbury*, and Chancellor of *England*, who after long service, was, upon his humble suit, discharged of the Office of Chancellor of *England*, in respect of his great age. Seeing then such a cloud of witnesses against me, which, in my private Soliloquies and Meditations, are daily and continually represented to my view, and mine own conscience (more then a thousand witnesses) concurring with me; Pardon me, my most gracious Soveraign, to conclude with good *Barzillai*, *Quot sunt dies annorum vitæ meæ? quare servus tuus sit oneri domino nostro Regi? obsecro ut revertar servus tuus & moriar, &c.* So I most humbly beseech your sacred Majesty, graciously to regard the great age, infirmity, and impotency of your most devoted, obedient, loyal, and faithfull servant: Let me not be as *Domitius* after was, *Maluit desiccere quam desinere*; but, with your Princely favour, give me leave to retire my self from the carefull service of this great Office, and from the troubles of this world, and to spend the small remant of my life in meditation and prayer; and I will never cease to make my humble supplications to Almighty God, to bless and prosper your Majesty, the Queen, the Prince, all your Royal Issue, with all heavenly and earthly felicity; which is the last and best service your poor, aged, weak, and decayed servant, can do for you.

THO. ELLESMERE, *Canc.*

The Emperor Ferdinand, to Don Balthazar.

Ferdinand *the Emperour, to* Don Balthazar de Zuniga.

To the Honourable and sincerely beloved, Don Balthazar de Zuniga, *Cousin and Counsellor, of State to the most excellent and Catholique King of* Spain.

Honourable, and sincerely beloved,

WHat my mind and purpose is touching the translation of the Electorship to the Duke of *Bavaria*, according to the promise I made him, and wherefore I think that business so necessary and profitable, as for *Germany* in general, so particularly, for securing our House from all attempts of Heretiques, as his Holiness exhorts me not to be further delayed: You shall understand, as well by conference with Father *Jacinthus*, whom his Holiness hath for that purpose addressed unto me, his Majesty of *Spain* my Nephew, and other Catholique Princes of *Germany*, as by these ensuing reasons, whereof the principal are; That when I repeat from the beginning the whole course of my Reign, and the difficulties through which I have attained my Kingdoms and Provinces, I behold with reverence the admirable providence of God over me, which makes me the more bound to repose my trust in him, and not to omit any occasion which may tend to the advancement of his glory, and the honour of so admirable tried providence: and therefore that I should use that most notable victory to the honour of God, and extirpation of all seditious factions, which are nourished chiefly among the *Calvinists*; and that I should withdraw my self from that judgment that the Prophet threatens to the King of *Israel*, *Because thou hast dismissed a man worthy of death, thy soul shall be for his soul.* The Palatine keeps now in *Holland*, exiled not onely from the Kingdom which he rashly attempted, but despoiled almost of all his own Territories, expecting as it were the last cast of Fortune; whom, if by any impious kind of commiseration and subtile Petitions, I be perswaded to restore to his Electoral dignity, and nourish in my bosome a troden half-living Snake, what can I expect less then a deadly stinging? For it is in vain for me to think that he should be able to discern the greatness of such a benefit: For the Politicians saying is true, *Ultionem quaesivi, gratiam oneri habere*; especially since the injuries he did me are so heynous, his projects so subtile, that although I should overcome him with Christian charity, yet I should never be able to take him from the guilt of his offences, and make him soundly faithfull unto me; but he will alwaies gape at all occasions whereby he may free himself from fear of his ill deservings, and cover his own prostituted honour with new attempts. Add hereunto the *Calvinists* institution, of whose Sect the proper genius is to hold nothing unlawful, either fraud or wickedness, which is undertaken for the Religion; no sanctity of oath, nor fear of dishonour, hinders them. From such an one, what caution can either the house of *Austria*, or other Catholique Princes, with whom he is no less in enmity, because for Religion, as because they are interessed in the war; receive? The King of *England* will be engaged, but of the same Religion; nor is there any thing more easie, then when there is occasion of perpetrating any wickedness, to palliate it with a pretext of a breach of the League. Histories are fraughted with examples; in some there are no cautions sufficient in such a business: then to drive him where he cannot hurt, all other means are frail, and he which once believed is despised. It is likewise a consideration of no less moment, that the *Palatinate* being restored will draw all his power and policy, as hitherto, so hereafter, where he thinks he can do most hurt, and that most easily, to wit, to *Bethlem-Gabor* and the *Turks*, whom he hath already incited to hostility against me, and will never cease hereafter to instigate the *Calvinists* entire hopes in them. These, until they recover breath, and recollect their fortes, they endeavour to disarm and exexhaust me of moneys, ranging in my territories as they have done hitherto, by fire and sword. But if with them also, whom notwithstanding I cannot trust alike, I should make peace, what conditions will *Gabor*, who remains yet unconquered, require, if I should restore the *Palatine* (already conquered) to his Electoral dignity.

Therefore since long before God granted me that famous victory, I firmly forecast with my self, that the *Palatine* could not be restored to his Electoral dignity without the extream danger of the Catholiques and my house, I offered freely, on my own motion; but being directed questionless by God, the Electorship to the Duke of *Bavaria*, a most eager Defender of the Catholique cause, whose Territories on the other side lye as a Rampire between me and other Princes of *Germany*; and since I made so good use of his help, and so profitable, in the recovery of my Kingdoms and Provinces, and continue yet to this day, time it self, more then the said Duke doth, cry out that I should accomplish my promise without further delay

delay, and by a translation of the Electorship take away quite all hopes from the Palatine and them that sollicite us so importunately for a restitution, that we may be freed from all molestation; which thing, since it needs the help of his Majesty of *Spain*, although I know his Majesty be propense enough of himself to all things which appertain to the honour of God, and the security of our house, yet I thought good to admonish you of this occasion, lest this opportunity of establishing of our Religion and Family escape, which I conceive might conveniently be done by you. Neither do I suppose his Majesty to be ignorant, that it was alwaies judged of our Ancestors, that the House of *Austria*, which by Gods permission doth now seigniorize far and neer upon the earth, to have its chief foundation here in *Germany*, which is the more to be defended, the nearer its ruine depends thereupon. In times past this House hath had proof of many adversaries to its greatness, as the Histories under *Maximilian* the first, *Charles* the fifth, *Ferdinand* the second, and *Rodulf* the second, do shew: the perfidiousness of *Holland* against his Majesties Grandfather, *Philip* the second, fetched her food from the Palatinate; neither can his Majesty ever reduce the rebellious *Hollanders* to obedience, unless his root be pluckt up; which only motive, besides these which I alledged before, might justly induce him not to suffer, a fallen enemy, to rise, and resume (as his stomack will never fail him) strength again.

But albeit it is not to be dissembled, that the *Lutheran* Princes, especially the Elector of *Saxony*, will not approve haply of this translation, because they fear it conduceth too much to the corroborating of the Catholique Cause: Nevertheless, since he cannot accuse that act of *Charles* the fifth, who for a far lighter cause deprived *John Frederick* of the Electorship, and conferred it on *Maurice*, this Dukes great Uncle; and perceiving that all the Councels of the *Calvinists* do aim to bring in the Turk, he will not condemn this translation: For no less is the *Lutherans* hatred against the *Calvinists*, as the Catholiques and they think less danger do proceed from the later. It is to be hoped, therefore, that the Elector of *Saxony*, and other *Lutheran* Princes, when they see the business brought to this point, will not so far disapprove thereof, as to put themselves in Arms; which I shall shortly understand of the most excellent Archduke *Charles*, my brother, who is for this cause to treat with the Elector of *Saxony*. And these motives, as they are of great consequence, so I imagine you, which are daily of his Majesties Councel, have pondered them as diligently as my self; and therefore that you will omit nothing that is pertinent to establish this business, whereby we may obtain the long and wished fruit thereof, which is the propagation of the honour of Almighty God through the Empire, and the augmentation of the common safety, Family, and Dignity.

Beloved, *Don Balthazar*, I understand that there was a motive of great consideration omitted in my Letter; to wit, that if we had more countenance of his Catholique Majesty then we have at this present, the Empire should alwaies remain in the hands of Catholiques; and so, according to reason, in our House; to whose advancement the Duke of *Bavaria* will willingly concur in recognition of such a benefit, being promoted by an Emperour of that House, to so eminent and high a dignity, as in our letters.

Vienna, Octob. 15. 1621.

The *Lord* Faulklands *Petition to the King*.

MOst humbly shewing, that I had a Sonne, until I lost him, in your Highness displeasure, where I cannot seek him, because I have not will to find him there. Men say, there is a wild young man now prisoner in the Fleet, for measuring his actions by his own private sence. But now that for the time your Majesties hand hath appeared in his punishment, he bows and humbles himself before, and to it: Whether he be mine, or not, I can discern by no light, but that of your Royal Clemency; for only in your forgiveness can I own him for mine. Forgiveness is the glory of the supremest powers, and this the operation, that when it is extended in the greatest measure, it converts the greatest offenders into the greatest lovers, and so makes purchase of the heart, an especial priviledge peculiar and due to Sovereign Princes.

If now your Majesty will vouchsafe, out of your own benignity, to become a second nature, and restore that unto me which the first gave me, and vanity deprived me of, I shall keep my reckoning of the full number of my sons with comfort, and render the tribute of my most humble thankfulness; else my weak old memory must forget one.

A

A Declaration of Ferdinand, Infanta of Spain.

Unto all those to whom this present writing shall come, greeting.

FRance having, contrary to reason and justice, moved and maintained War in the States of the Emperour, and of my Lord the King, given extraordinary Succours both of men and money to their rebellious subjects; procured the Swedes to invade the Empire, received and bought of them the Towns of *Alsatia*, and other hereditary Countreys of our most Royal House, not sparing the Catholick League it self, which had taken Arms for no other end but for the good of Religion: And it being notorious, that the same *France*, (after all these publick and manifest contraventions to the Treaties of Peace) hath finally proceeded to a breach thereof; whereas we had cause to denounce the War, in that she hath sent her Armies to over-run the Low Countreys, the Dutchie of *Millain*, and other Feoffees of the Empire in *Italy*, and now lately the Countrey of *Burgundy*; contrary to the Lawes of Neutrality, contrary to the Publick Faith, and contrary to the express promises of the Prince of *Condé*, Disguising, in the mean time, these attempts and breaches of Faith before all Christendom, with certain weak pretexts and false surmises, contained in divers Declarations, approved in the Parliament of *France*; and accompanying all these unjust proceeding with sundry Insolencies, Calumnies, and Contempts of sacred persons. And having also observed, that this so long continence of ours at so manifold injuries hath served to no other purpose, but to make our enemies more audacious and insolent, and that the compassion we have had of *France* hath drawn on the ruine of those whom God had put under the obedience of their Majesties: For these considerations, according to the power which we have received from his Imperial Majesty, we have commanded our Armies to enter into *France*, with no other purpose then to oblige the King of *France* to come to a good and secure Peace, for removing those impediments which may hinder this so great a good. And for as much as it principally concerneth *France* to give end to these disorders, we are willing to believe that all the Estates of that Kingdom will contribute not onely their Remonstrances, but also, if need be, their Forces, to dispose their King, to chastise those who have been the Authors of all these Warrs, which these seven or eight years past have been in Christendome; and who after they have provoked and assayled all their neighbours, have brought upon France all those evils which she doth now suffer, and draw on her those other which do now threaten her. And although we are well informed of the weakness and divisions into which these great disorders and evil counsels have cast her; yet we declare, that the intentions of their Majesties are not to serve themselves of this occasion, to ruine her, or to draw from thence any other profit, then by that means to work a Peace in Christendom, which may be stable and permanent.

For these reasons, and withall to shew what estimation their Majesties do make of the prayers of the Queen Mother of the most Christian King, we do give to understand, that we will protect and treat as friends all those of the *French* Nation, who either joyntly or severally shall second these our good designes; and have given Order that Neutrality shall be held with those of the Nobility, and with the Towns, which shall desire it, and which shall refuse to assist those who shall oppose the good of Christendome, and their own safety; against whom shall be used all manner of hostility, without giving quarter to their persons, or sparing either their houses or goods. And our further will is, that all men take notice that it is the resolutions of their Majesties not to lay down Arms, till the Queen Mother of the most Christian King be satisfied and contented, till the Princes, unjustly driven out of their estates, be restored; and till they see the assurances of Peace more certain then to be disturbed by him who hath violated the treaties of *Ratisbon*, and others made before, and sithence he hath had the managing of the affairs of *France*. Neither do we pretend to draw any other advantage from the good success which it shall please God to give unto our just prosecutions, then to preserve and augment the Catholick Religion, to pacifie *Europe*, to relieve the oppressed, and to restore to every one that which of right belongeth unto him.

Given at Ments, July 5. 1636.

Master

An unknown person, to the Conde Gondomar.

Mr. Gargrave, to the Lord Davers.

My very good Lord,

I Have heretofore many times both sent and written to you, touching the insupportable burthen of wrong which hath many years lain upon my shoulders, but you were not pleased to return me any answer for my satisfaction therein: my opinion, at the first, was, that it was meerly the respect of some, whom you would not, or might might not offend, that you suffered your name to be used by others, to wound and afflict me in my estate: to which so fair an opinion I was induced, partly by ancient Judgment of your honourable disposition, partly, and much rather, by the privity of my heart, which ever constantly affected a good correspondency with you every way. But since now this oppression which I suffer hath had its continuance so many years without relaxation, in which I smart beyond all example, and the admiration of the world hath concurred with my sense of so great a bitterness from so neer Allies; I cannot but, to my grief and wonder, observe your too much either consent or connivency to these my harms, which before I have not easily suffered my thoughts to admit; wherein, if I have not mistaken your Lordships interest, I have yet conceived hope, that although you had in the beginning a just ground to make me feel the weight of your displeasure and alienation from me, yet that the sufferance of so many years, and such a sufferance under pretence, of Justice, as can hardly be parallell'd, might yet, at the last, have satiated a very deeply intended revenge, much more, satisfied a moderate mind possessed with Honour or Religion, as I conceive your Lordships to be. Herein, after a various agitation in my self, I am enforced to honour the wonderful providence of God, who hath pleased to convert the affinity which I affected with your Noble house, for my comfort and assistance, to my ruine; and that in the bosome of our neerest and dearest friendship should breed so intestine a hatred, as should tend to the overthrow of my credit, wealth, lands, liberty, house, wife and children, and all those comforts which should either support or sweeten the life of man.

Wherefore I have adventured, after so long silence, to mind your Lordship of this my unfortunate estate, wherein I rather dye then live, whereunto I have been so long since precipitated by your Lordships countenance, as I hope, pretended only by the instruments of my mischief to proceed from you; that if now your Lordship shall think it enough that I have so many years, so many waies, endured the crosses of so high a nature, and can be induced to affect a reparation, or at least a determination of those injuries which undeservedly have been heaped upon me, I may yet at length conclude this Tragedy, of my life past with some comfortable fruit of that love and kindness which at the first I aimed at in seeking your Lordships Alliance, and which I endeavoured to deserve for the continuance, and which after so long intermission, I shall think my self happy to enjoy, if so be your Lordship shall out of your charitable consideration think my motion to concur with my desire, that I may not be enforced to advance my complaint further; which I wish may be prevented by this my Expostulation, springing from the sence of so great and intolerable a misery wherein I languish every day.

Ab ignoto, to the Conde Gondomar, concerning the death of Philip the third.

Upon the last day of *February*, being Sunday, 1620. his Catholick Majesty, after he had heard Mass and the Sermon in the Chappel, was taken with a Fever, which continued with him eight daies, with a ruddiness, and pimples which appeared plainly in his face, which afterwards began to diminish: but he was suddenly taken with a vomiting and a great Fever, which continued with him till the 21 day; and the Physitians were of opinion to have him rise out of his bed, which was accordingly done both that day and the next: but about dinner time there happen'd unto him a great swouning, which much astonish'd him; and the 23. day, in the night, his fever did redouble upon him, with a vomiting and a flux in the belly, and a great melancholly, and an opinion that he should die: which feaver continued with divers reduplications, the Physitians having an ill opinion of him, till on Saturday night the 27. when his reduplications were more violent, his water bad; and the King persevered in saying how he saw well that he should die, he commanded that the Image of our Lady of *Atochia* should be carried about, which was performed on Sunday the 28. in a solemn Procession, wherein the Councellors of *Spain* assisted.

In the evening, commandment was given to the Churches, that the Blessed Sacrament should be set upon the Altar, and the Body of S. *Isidore* should be placed in the Court. On Munday the 29. about four of the clock in the evening, his disease then grew violent, and some ulcers appeared on his belly, on his reins, and on his thighes, and the King still assuring himself that he should die; the Physicians then feeling his pulse, affirmed, that undoubtedly they assented unto the King in the opinion he conceived of his infirmity. At the same time, the President of *Castile* was sent for, and the Confessor; who having had some speech with the King, and the Duke of *Ossuna*, they went and fetch'd the Councellors, before whom, and the Grandees of *Spain* who were present, the King sealed his Testament, which *John de Scrita*, Secretary of State, had set down in writing in his presence. Afterwards they caused him to eat somewhat; and being advised how it would be good for him to sleep, he made this answer in Spanish, *En jornada tan longa y tiempe tan brvene convièue reposar*; Upon so long a journey, and so short a time to perform it, I must not rest. Then he sent for the Prince, and the young Child *Don Carlo*; to whom having spoken for a good while, at length in particular to the Prince he said aloud, how he recommended unto him the Child, and that he grieved that he should have been unprovided, but he hoped he left him in the hands of a good and loving Brother. Then said he to the Prince, that he requested him, that he would not do as he did at his coming to the Crown, in removing his Fathers old Officers and servants; but that he would employ those who were experienced in affairs of the Common-wealth: He then commended unto him, particularly, *John de Luenza*, Secretary of the Memorials, and his Confessor, and afterwards the Duke of *Ossuna*. Then was presently brought in the Infanta *Maria*, and the Infant-Cardinal. He cried out when he saw the Infanta, and said, *Maria*, I am full sorry that I must die before I have married thee; but this thy Brother shall have care of. He then turned towards her Brother, and said unto him, Prince, do not forsake her; till you have made her an Empress. Then he spake unto the Cardinal Infant, whom he appointed to be a Priest, so soon as he should come to be of fit age; and said, that he should be much grieved, if he thought he would not undertake this profession. He had sent for Madam the Princess, but she swooned upon her entry at the Chamber-door, which was the cause that she was conducted back again unto her own Chamber, fearing lest it might be prejudicial unto her, being great with child. Which being reported to the King, he shewed great compassion thereat, and said, that he ever constantly believed, that Madam the Princess loved him as well as any of his own children. After that he began to speak of the Queen, saying, how she should lose a good Husband, and that he had always loved her dearly. Afterwards he distributed, between the Prince and the Infanta, the Reliques and other memorials he had, except one Crucifix, which hung at the testern of the bed, and said unto the Prince, that he could not give it him then, because it was the same with which his Grandfather and Father had died; but he commended it to him, to be held with great reverence after his death, and that the Popes had given unto it special Indulgences. Afterwards, giving them all his blessing, he caused them to go forth; and so calling for the Blessed Sacrament, which was administred unto him about midnight, he received the Extreme Unction at two of the clock in the morning, and so commended himself unto God. Yet did he not, for all this, forbear to seal to a great number of Papers which were brought him: And complaining very much, he refused such meat as they would have had him take. About noon, the Body of St. *Isidore* was placed neer unto his bed, his Confessor and Father *Florence* perswading him to make a vow for his health, and that he would build a Chappel to the same Saint; which he did, but withal said, *Però ya es tarde*, But now it is very late. He continued all the rest of the day, speaking continually to the Father Confessor, Father *Florence*, and *Rochas*. Many processions of penance were solemnized in the Town, and the Councel assembled twice. About the evening, his infirmity renewed with violence; and having languished the whole night, in the morning his departure was published, though indeed it was not till about nine of the clock in the morning, the last of *March*, the self-same day of our return; which will inform you of all things passed, at least, of such as came any ways to our knowledge. The Queen stirr'd not out of her bed all that day, for fear lest either trouble or grief of mind (whereof she give plentifull testimony by her tears) might prejudice her health, or the fruit of her body, which she hath passed over (thanks be to God ;) whereof we send you word, that the good news may shut up the discourse of an acident so lamentable and unlooked for,

To Count Gondomar.

My Lord,

I Thought my hands bound, that I could no sooner have occasion to write unto you, being forced, against my will, to delay my writing from day to day in expectation of the news of your arrival at that Court, assuring my self, that I should then receive from you some ground whereupon to write. But after a long expence of time before that I could hear of your arrival, and, in the Paequet that his Majesties Embassadour sent thereafter, receiving no Letters nor word from you, as I expected, I do now by these break my long silence unto you.

As for news from hence, I can in a word assure you, that they are, in all points, as your heart could wish: for here is a King, a Prince, and a faithfull friend and servant unto you, besides a number of your other good friends, that long so much for the happy accomplishment of this Match, as every day seems a year unto us ; and I can assure you, in the word of your honest friend, that we have a Prince here, that is so sharp set upon the business, as it would much comfort you to see it, and her there to hear it. Here are all things prepared upon our parts ; Priests and Recusants all at liberty, all the *Roman* Catholicks well satisfied ; and, which will seem a wonder unto you, our Prisons are emptied of Priests and Recusants, and filled with zealous Ministers, for preaching against the Match ; for no man can sooner, now, mutter a word in the Pulpit, though indirectly, against it, but he is presently catched, and set in streight prison. We have also published Orders, both for the Universities, and the Pulpits, that no man hereafter shall meddle, but to preach Christ crucified ; nay, it shall not be lawfull hereafter for them to rail against the Pope, or the Doctrine of the Church of *Rome*, further then for edification of ours: and for proof hereof, you shall, herewith, receive the Orders set down and published. But if we could hear as good news from you, we should think our selves happy men: But, alas ! now that we have put the ball at your feet, although we have received a comfortable Dispatch from his Majesties Embassadour there ; yet from all other parts in the world the effects appear directly contrary. For Mr. *Gage* brings us news from *Rome*, that the Dispensation there is at a stand, except a number of new Conditions be granted, which we never dreamed of, and can tend to no other end, but to bring our Master in jealousie with the greatest part of his Subjects; nay, which is strangest of all, we find some points, yielded unto by us, (which would have given the Pope good satisfaction) to be concealed from him by the King your Masters Ministers there. We were never more troubled to put a good face upon an ill game, then we were upon *Gage*'s arrival here, which, in your phrase, is to put a good sauce to an unsavoury dish.

For the whole world being in expectation of bringing the Dispensation with him, we are now forced to make him give it out here to all his friends, that 'tis past in *Rome*, and sent from thence to *Spain*. And from *Bruxels* we find, that notwithstanding both of the King your Masters promises, and undertaking of the *Infanta* there, who hath long ago acknowledged to have had power from the Emperour for granting of this long-talked of Cessation ; yet now after innumerable delays on her part, *Heidelbergh* is besieged by Count *Tilley*, and that at such a time, as his Majesty cannot imagine what ground or shadow of excuse can be found for his Commission. For the Treaty hath been twice reformed at her desire, and all the Auxiliaries, such as *Brunswick* and *Mausfelt*, have taken another course ; his Majesties Son in Law staying privately in *Sedan*, ready to obey all his Majesties directions ; and the places in the *Palatinate*, which are not already in his enemies hands, being onely possessed by his Majesties Souldiers. So as now, if the War shall continue, it must be directly between the Emperor and our Master ; his Majesty having sent a Commandment to his Embassadour at *Bruxels*, that if *Tilley* will needs go on with that siege, that he return hither with all speed: For, his Majesty in honour cannot endure, that whilest he is treating for a Cessation of Arms, at *Bruxels*, the War should go on in the *Palatinate*, especially, when they have no body to invade, but his Majesties own Subjects and Servants. And indeed, his Majesty thinks he is very ill dealt withal, for all that great sincerity and candour, wherewith he hath constantly carried himself, from the very beginning of this business, that no less can satisfie the Emperours revenge, then the utter extermination of his Children, both of Honour, and Inheritance, and not without a direct breach of his former promise, avowedly set down in his last Letter to his Majesty.

And now, let me, I pray you, in the name of your faithfull friend and servant, beseech you to set apart all partiality in this case ; and that you would be pleased indifferently to consider of the streights we are driven into, if the Emperour shall in this fashion conquer the

Palatinate,

Palatinate, the ancient inheritance of his Majesties children, what can be expected, but a bloody and unreconcileable war between the Emperour and my Master, wherein the King of *Spain* can be an Auxiliary to the Emperour against any other party but his Majesty. And therefore, as my Master lately offered to the *Infanta*, for satisfaction of her desire, that in case the Auxiliaries would not be contented with reason, but still perturb the Treaty, he offered, in that case, to assist the Emperour and her against them; so can he, in justice, expect no less of the King your Master, that if the Emperour will, contrary to all promises, both by his Letters, and Embassadours, proceed in his conquest, and refuse the cessation, that the King your Master will, in that case, and in so just a quarrel, assist him against the Emperour, in imitation of the King my Masters just and real proceedings in the business from the beginning, who never looked (as you can well be witness) to the rising or falling hopes of his Son in Law's fortunes; but constantly kept on that course that was most agreeable to honour and justice, to the peace of Christendom, and for the fastening of a firm and indissoluble knot of amity and alliance betwixt the King your Master and him, which was begun in the time of the Treaty with *France*, and then broken, at your desire, that we might embrace this alliance with you. You are the person that many times, before your departure hence, besought his Majesty once to suffer himself to be deceived by *Spain*: We, therefore, do now expect to find that great respect to honour in your Master, that he will not take any advantage by the changing of fortune, and success of time, so to alter his actions, as may put his Honour in the terms of interpretation. You see how all the rest of Christendom envy and malign this match and wished conjunction; how much greater need then hath it of a hasty and happy dispatch? And what comfort can the Prince have in her, when her friends shall have utterly ruined his Sister, and all her babes? You remember how your self praised his Majesties wisdom, in the election of so fit a Minister as Sir *Richard Weston*, in this business, but you saw what desperate Letters he writes, from time to time, of their cold and unjust treating with him in this business: you could not but wonder that any spark of Patience could be left us here: And to conclude this point in a word, we ever received comfortable words from *Spain*, but find such contrary effects from *Bruxels*, together with our intelligences from all other parts of the world, as all our hopes are not onely cold, but quite extinguished, here. Thus far for the By; and yet such a By, as may put by the main, if it be not well and speedily prevented. As to the Main, which is the Match, his Majesty, and we all here, thought we had done our part, and put the ball at your foot, when we agreed upon the twenty and five Articles more: whereupon, as your self often answered, and assured us, the best Divines in *Spain* concluded, That the Pope not onely might, but ought to grant a Dispensation to this Marriage; but now we are surcharged with a number of new Articles from *Rome*, and, in the mean time, the Dispensation is as far off as ever it was.

His Majesty hopes, that you are not ignorant, that the Treaty is between him, and your Master; He hath no Treaty with *Rome*, neither lies it in his way to dispute with them upon this question: Yet that his readiness to embrace your Masters friendship may the better appear, he is contented to yield to so many of their demands as either his Conscience, Honour, or Safety can permit, if so the King your Master shall think it necessary. But, on the other part, we three remember, that whenas you first moved this match unto him, and perswaded him to break off with *France*, you then promised, That he should be pressed to nothing, in this business, that should not be agreeable to his Conscience, and Honour, and stand with the Love of his People. As to the particular Articles new added at *Rome*, I will not clog this Paper with them, which, I fear, without them, will be too troublesome unto you: For what his Majesties opinion is of them, his Majesties Embassadour there will particularly acquaint him.

But whereas the Pope desires, in the end of his Articles, that he may see what *bonum publicum* the King our Master will grant unto, that may perswade to grant this Dispensation; I will remit it to your conscience and knowledge, Whether the favours his Majesty daily grants to those of his Religion, and is resolved still to continue, if not to increase them, if they shall by their good behaviour deserve it, be not a real *bonum publicum*? considering, that if the match should break off, (which God forbid) his Majesty would be importunately urged by his people (to whose assistance he must have his recourse) to give life and execution to all the penal Laws now hanging upon their heads.

It onely rests now, that as we have put the ball to your foot, you take a good, and speedy resolution there, to hasten a happy conclusion of this Match. The Prince is now two and twenty years of age, and so a year more then full ripe for such a business; the King our Master longeth to see an issue proceed from his Loins; and, I am sure, you have reason to expect more friendship from the posterity that shall proceed from him, and that little Angel, your

Infanta, then from his Majesties Daughters Children. Your friends here are all discomforted with this long delay; your enemies are exasperated and irritated thereby; and your neighbours, that envy the felicity of both Kings, have the more leisure to invent new Plots for the cross and hinderance of this happy business: And for the part of your true friend and servant, *Buckingham*, I am become odious already, and counted a betrayer both of King and Countrey.

To conclude all, I will use a similitude of hawking, (which you will easily understand, being a great Faulconer;) I told you already, that the Prince is (God be thanked) extremely sharp set upon this Match; and you know, that a Hawk, when she is first dressed, and made ready to flie, having a great will upon her, if the Faulconer do not follow it at that time, she is in danger to be dulled for ever after.

Take heed, therefore, lest in the fault of your delays there, our Prince, and Faulcon-gentle, (that you know was thought slow enough, to begin to be eager after the Feminine prey) become not so dull, upon these delays, as in short time hereafter he will not stoop to the Lure, though it were thrown out to him.

And here I will end to you, my sweet friend, as I do in my prayers to God, (*Onely in thee is my trust*,) and say, as it is written on the out-side of the Pacquets, *Haste, Haste, Post-haste.*

The Conde de Gondomar, *to the Duke.*

Most Excellent Sir,

AT last, Sir, the Earl of *Gondomar* goes for *England*: There will be many good discourses made in *Holland* about this voyage; but the truth is, that the intention of his journey is not to offend any one, but onely to desire and procure peace, and the publick good: And onely with this intent the King my Master commands me to go thither, and I go with a great deal of joy, as well for this, as for to kiss his Majesties and his Highness his hands, and your Excellencies, in particular.

And therefore I do appoint for the field of our Battel, your Excellencies Gallery over the *Thames*, where, I hope, your Excellency shall see, that the Earl of *Gondomar* is an honest man, and that he hath been, is, and ever will be, a faithfull and true servant and friend to Sir *George Villiers*, Duke of *Buckingham*, whom God preserve many happy years.

The Countess my Wife, and my self, kiss my Lady the Countess, and my Lady Dutchess their hands.

Febr. 13. 1625.

Your Excellencies constant and faithfull servant,
Gondomar.

King Henry *the Eighth, to the Clergy of the Province of* York, *Anno* 1533. *touching his Title of* Supreme Head of the Church of *England.*

Right Reverend Father in God, Right Trusty and Well-beloved, We greet you well; and have received your Letters dated at *York* the 6th of *May*, containing a long discourse of your mind and opinion concerning such words as have passed the Clergy of the Province of *Canterbury*, in the Proeme of their Grant made unto us, the like whereof should now pass in that Province. Albeit ye interlace such words of submission of your Judgment, and discharge of your duty towards us, with humble fashion and behaviour, as we cannot conceive displeasure, nor be mis-content with you, considering what you have said to us in times past, in other matters, and what ye confess, in your Letters, your selves to have heard and known, noting also the effect of the same; We cannot but marvel at sundry Points and Articles, which we shall open unto you, as hereafter followeth.

First, ye have heard (as ye say ye have) the said words to have passed in the Convocation of *Canterbury*, where were present so many learned in Divinity and Law, as the Bishops of *Rochester, London,* S. *Asaph,* Abbots of *Hyde,* S. *Bennets*, and many other; and in the Law, the Archbishop of *Canterbury*, and the Bishop of *Bath*; and in the Lower House of the Clergy, so many notable and great Clerks, whose Persons and Learning you know well enough. Why do ye not, in this case, with your self, as you willed us, in our great matter, conform your conscience to the conscience and opinion of a great number? Such was your advice to us in the same (our great matter) which now, we perceive, ye take for no sure counsel; for ye search the grounds, not regarding their sayings. Nevertheless, forasmuch as ye examine their grounds, causes, and reasons; in doing whereof, ye seem rather to seek and examine that thing which might disprove their doings, then that which might maintain the same; We shall answer you briefly, without long discourse, to the chief Points of your said Letters. Wherein taking for a ground, that words were ordained to signifie things, and cannot, therefore, by sinister interpretation, alter the truth of them, but onely in the wits of perverse persons that would blinde or colour the same: by reason whereof, to good men, they signifie, that they mean onely doing their office; and, to men of worse sort, they serve for maintenance of such meaning as they would imagine: So in using words, we ought onely to regard and consider the expression of the truth in convenient speech and sentences, without over-much scruple of super-perverse interpretations, as the malice of men may excogitate: wherein both overmuch negligence is not to be commended, and too much diligence is not onely, by daily experience in mens Writings and Laws, shewed frustrate and void; insomuch as nothing can be so cleerly and plainly written, spoken, and ordered, but that subtile wit hath been able to subvert the same; but also the Spirit of God, which in his Scripture taught us the contrary, as in the places which ye bring in and rehearse: —— if the Holy Ghost had had regard to that which might have been perversly construed of these words, *Pater major me est*, and the other, *Ego & Pater unum sumus*, there should have been added to the first, *humanitas*, to the second, *substantia*. And wherefore doth the Scripture call Christ, *primogenitum?* whereupon, and the Adverb *donec*, was maintained the errour, *contra perpetuam virginitatem Mariæ*. Why have we in the Church S. *Paul's* Epistle, which S. *Peter* writeth to have been the occasion of errours? Why did Christ speak many words, which the Jews drew *ad calumniam*, and yet reformed them not? as when he said, *Destruite Templum hoc, &c.* meaning of his body, where *Templum* with them had another signification; and such other like? There is none other cause but this, *Omnia quæ scripta sunt, ad nostram doctrinam scripta sunt*. And by that Learning, we ought to apply and draw words to the truth, and so to understand them as they may signifie truth, and not so to wrest them as they should maintain a lie. For otherwise, as Hereticks have done with the Holy Scripture, so shall all men do with familiar speech: and if all things shall be brought into familiar disputation, he that shall call us *Supremum & unicum Dominum*, by that means, and as goeth your argument, might be reproved: for Christ is indeed *unicus Dominus & Supremus*, as we confess him in the Church daily; and now it is in opinion, that *Sancti* be not Mediators: the contrary whereof ye affirm in your Letters, because of the Text of S. *Paul, Unus est Mediator inter Deum & hominem.* And after that manner of reason which ye use in the entry, if any man should say, This Land is mine own, and none hath right in it but I; he might be reproved by the Psalm, *Domini est terra:* For why should a man call *terram aliquam* onely his, whereof God is the chief Lord and Owner? Why is it admitted in familiar speech to call a man dead, of whom the soul, which is the chief and best part, yet liveth? How is it that we say, this man or that man to be founder of this Church, seeing that in one respect God is onely founder? We say likewise, that he is a good man to the Church, a special benefactor of the Church: and that the Church is fallen down, when the stones be fallen down, the people preserved and living; And in all this manner of speech, when we hear them, it is not accustomed nor used to do as ye do, that is to say, to draw the word *Church* to that sence wherein the speech may be a lie, but to take it in that wherein it signifieth truth. Which accustomed manner if ye had followed, you should not have needed to have laboured so much in the declaration of the word *Ecclesia*, in that signification wherein it is most rarely taken, and cannot, without maintenance of too manifest a lie, be applied to any man. For, taking *Ecclesia* in that sence ye take it, S. *Paul* wrote amiss, writing to the *Corinthians*, saying, *Ecclesia Dei quæ est Corinthi:* for, by your definition, *non circumscribitur loco Ecclesia*. In the Gospel, where Christ said, *Dic Ecclesiæ*, must needs have another interpretation and definition then ye make *de Ecclesia* in your said Letters, or else it were hard to make complaint to all Christendom, as the case in the Gospel requireth. *Sed est candidi pectoris verba veritati accommodare, ut ipsam referre quod eorum officium est non corrumpere videantur*. Furthermore, the Lawyers that write how *Ecclesia fallit & fallitur*, what blasphemy do they affirm, if that definition should be given to *Ecclesia* which you write in your Letters; wherein albeit ye write the truth for so far, yet forasmuch as ye draw that to the words spoken of us to the reprobation of them, yet ye shew your selves contrary to the teaching of Scripture, rather inclined, by applying a divers definition, to make that a lie which is truly spoken, then *genuino sensu addita & candida interpretatione* to verifie the same. It were *nimis absurdum*, for Us to be called *Caput Ecclesiæ repræsentans corpus Christi mysticum, & Ecclesia quæ sine ruga est & macula*

quam

quam Christus sibi Sponsam elegit, illius partem vel oblatam accipere vel arrogare. And therefore albeit *Ecclesia* is spoken of in these words, touched in the Proeme, yet there is added, *Et Cleri Anglicani*: which words conjoyned restrain, by way of interpretation, the word *Ecclesiam*, and is as much to say, as the Church, that is to say, the Clergy of *England*. Which manner of speaking in the Law ye have professed, ye many times find; and likewise in many other places.

But proceeding in your said Letter, ye have shewed Christ to be *Caput Ecclesia*, ye goe about to shew how he divided his power in earth after the distinction *temporalium & spiritualium*, whereof the one, ye say, he committed to Princes, the other *Sacerdotibus*; for Princes, ye alledge Texts which shew and prove obedience due to Princes of all men without distinction, be he Priest, Clerk, Bishop, or Lay-man, who make together the Church: and albeit your own words make mention of temporal things, wherein ye say they should be obeyed; yet the Texts of Scripture which ye alledge having the general words *obedite & subditi estote*, contain no such words, whereby spiritual things should be excluded; but whatsoever appertaineth to the tranquillity of mans life is of nececessity included, as the words plainly import, as ye also confess; wherefore *Gladium portat Princeps*, not only against them that break his Commandment and Laws, but against him also that in any wise breaketh Gods Laws; For we may not more regard our Law then God, nor punish the breach of our Laws, and leave the transgressour of Gods Laws unreformed: so as all spiritual things by reason whereof may arise bodily trouble and inquietatation, be necessarily included in Princes power, and so proveth the Text of Scripture by you alledged: and also the Doctors by you brought in confirm the same. After that ye intend to prove, which no man will deny, the ministration of spiritual things to have been by Christ committed to Priests, to Preach and minister the Sacraments, them to be as Physicians to mens souls; but in these Scriptures neither by spiritual things so far extended, as under colour of that vocabule be now adaies, nor it proveth not that their office being never so excellent, yet their persons, acts and deeds, should not be under the power of their Prince by God assigned: whom they should acknowledge as their Head; the excellency of the matter of the office doth not alwaies in all points extoll the dignity of the Minister. Christ who did most perfectly use the office of a Priest, *& nihil aliud quam vere curavit animas*, gainsaid not the authority of *Pilate* upon that ground; and St. *Paul* executing the office of a Priest, said, *ad tribunal Cæsaris sto, ubi me judicari oportet:* And commanded likewise, indistinctly, all others to obey Princes; and yet unto those Priests, being as members executing that Office, Princes do honour, for so is Gods pleasure and commandment; wherefore, howsoever ye take the words in the proeme, we indeed do shew, and declare, that Priests and Bishops preaching the word of God, ministring the Sacraments according to Christs Law, and refreshing our people with ghostly and spiritual food, we not only succour and defend them for tranquillity of their life, but also with our presence, and otherwise, do honour them as the case requireth, for so is Gods pleasure: Like as the husband, although he be head of the wife, yet, saith St. *Paul, Non habet vir potestatem sui corporis, sed mulier*, and so is, in that respect, under her: And having our Mother in our Realm, by the commandment of God we shall honour her, and yet she, for respect of our dignity, shall honour us by Gods commandment likewise: And the minister is not alwaies the better man, *sed cui ministratur*, the Physician is not better then the Prince, because he can do that the Prince cannot, viz. *curare morbum*. In consecration of Archbishops, do not Bishops give more dignity by their ministration then they have themselves? The Doctors ye bring in, taking for their Theme to extol Priesthood, prefer it to the dignity of a Prince; after which manner of reasoning it may be called *dignius imperare affectibus quam populis*, and so every good man in consideration of every dignity to excell a King not living so perfectly as he doth. And why is a Bishop better then a Priest, seeing and considering, in the matter of their office, *Episcopus etiam si administret plura, non tamen administrat majora*. Emperours and Princes obey Bishops and Priests as doers of the message of Christ, and his Ambassadours for that purpose: which done *statim fiunt privati*, and in order and quietness of living, acknowledge Princes as head. For what meant *Justinian* the Emperour to make Laws *de Episcopis & Clericis*, and such other spiritual matters, if he had not been perswaded *Illi esse curam Ecclesiæ a Deo mandatam*? This is true, that Princes be *filii Ecclesia*, that is to say, *illius Ecclesia* which ye define: wherewith it may agree, that they be nevertheless *Suprema Capita* of the Congregations of Christian men in their Countries; like as in smaller number of Christian men, *Non est absurdum vocare Superiores capita*, as they be called indeed, and may be called *Primi & Supremi*, in respect of those Countries. And why else doth the Pope suffer any other besides himself to be called Archbishop,

bishop, seeing that he himself indeed challengeth to be *Princeps Apostolorum, & Episcoporum* in *Peters* stead, which the name of an Archbishop utterly denieth. But by addition of the Countrey they save the sence: whereunto in us to be called *Ecclesiæ Anglicanæ* yet at the last agree, so that there were added *in temporalibus*; which addition were superfluous, considering that men being here themselves earthly and temporal, cannot be head and Governour to things eternal, nor yet spiritual, taking that word *spiritual* not as the common speech abuseth it, but as he signifieth indeed: For, *quæ spiritu aguntur, nulla lege astringuntur*, as the Scripture saith, *Quæ Spiritu Dei aguntur libera sunt.* And if you take Spiritualibus for Spiritual men, that is to say, Priests, Clerks, their good acts and deeds worldly, in all this both we and all other Princes be at this day chief and heads, after whose ordinance, either in general, or in particular, they be ordered and governed. For, leaving old stories, and considering the state of the world in our time, is there any Convocation where Laws be made for the order of our Clergy, but such as by our authority is assembled? And why should not we say as *Justinian* said, *Omnia nostra facimus quibus a nobis impartitur auchoritas?* Is any Bishop made but he submitteth himself to us, and acknowledgeth himself as Bishop to be our Subject? Do not we give our Licence and assent to the election of Abbotts? And this is concerning the Persons and Laws spiritual. As touching their goods, it is in all mens opinions learned in our Laws, *Extra controversiam*, that debate and controversie of them appertaineth to our occasion and Order. And as for the living of the Clergy, some notable offences we reserve to our correction, some we remit by our sufferance to the Judges of the Clergy; as murther, felony, and treason, and such like enormities we reserve to our examination; other crimes we leave to be ordered by the Clergy; not because we may not intermeddle with them, for there is no doubt but as well might we punish adultery and insolence in Priests, as Emperours have done, and other Princes at this day do; which ye know well enough; so as in all those Articles concerning the persons of Priests, their Laws, their Acts and order of living, forasmuch as they be indeed all temporal, and concerning this present life only, in those we (as we be called) be indeed in this Realm *Caput*; and because there is no man above us here, be indeed *supremum Caput*. As to spiritual things, meaning by them the sacraments, being by God ordained as instruments of efficacy and strength, whereby grace is of his infinite goodness conferred upon his people; forasmuch as they be no worldly nor temporal things, they have no worldly nor temporal head, but only Christ that did institute them, by whose ordinance they be ministred here by mortal men, elect, chosen and ordered as God hath willed for that purpose, who be the Clergy; who for the time they do that, and in that respect *tanquam ministri versantur in his quæ hominum potestati neu subjiciuntur inquibus si male versantur sine scandalo Deum ulterem habent, si eum scandalo hominum cognitio & videtta est.* Wherein, as is before said, either the Prince is chief doer, this authority proceedeth to the execution of the same; as when by sufferance or priviledge the Prelats intromit themselves therein; wherefore in that which is derived from the Prince at the beginning, why should any obstacle or scruple be to call him Head from whom that is derived? Such things as although they be amongst men, yet they be indeed *Divina, quoniam supra nos sunt nihil ad nos.*——And being called Head of all, we be not in deed, nor in name, to him that would sincerely understand it head of such things being not spiritual as they be not temporal, and yet to those words spoken of us *ad evitandam illam calumniam*, there is added *quantum per legem Christi licet*; for interpretation of which Parenthesis your similitude added of *homo immortalis est quantum per naturæ legem licet*, is nothing like; for *naturæ lex* is not immortality, as *lex Christi* to superiority: for *lex naturæ* nor speaketh, nor can mean of any immortality at all, considering that the law of Nature ordaineth mortality in all things, but Christs law speaketh of superiority admitteth superiority, sheweth also and declareth *obediendum esse Principibus*, as ye do alledge. Wherefore if the law God permitteth superiority, and commandeth obedience: to examine and measure *modum obedientiæ & superioritatis*, there can to no other thing so good a relation be made. For as ye understand the Scripture, though it say nay to part, it saith not nay to the whole, whereas nature denieth utterly all immortality; and so though in speaking of immortality of man it were superfluous to say *quantum per naturæ legem licet*; yet is not so speaking *de superioritate & modo Principatus*, referring the certain limits to the law of Christ, *ad cujus normam quicquid quadrat planum & rectum est, quicquid non quadrat pravum & iniquum.* And as touching the doubt and difficulty you make to give a single answer, yea or no, for that the question propounded containeth two things, whereof the one is true, the other false, as ye say, meaning, as ye write, that in *temporalibus*, we be *Caput*, and in *Spiritualibus* we be not. It seemeth that neither your example agreeth in similitude with that ye bring it in for, nor is there in learning or common speech used the scrupulosity in answers ye write of. Truth it is, that the question in

plain

plain words containeth two parts expresly, whereof the one is true, the other false; our yea or nay cannot be answered: for there should appear a manifest lye, which Gods law detesteth; and naturally is abhorred, as if it should be asked us, if we were King of *England* and of *Denmark*, our nay or yea should not suffice. But it is far otherwise both in matters of Learning and common speech, where the words in the question may by divers interpretations or relations contain two things, and yet in expression contain but one: As if a man should ask us *An filius & Pater unum sunt?* We would not doubt to answer and say, Yea, as the scripture saith, for it is truly answered, and to make a lye is but sophistication, drawing the word *unum* to person, wherein it is a ly. If one were asked the question, whether the man and wife were one, he might boldly and truly say, Yea, and yet it is *distinctione corporum naturalium* a lie; and to the question, *Utrum Ecclesia constet ex bonis & malis*, Yea, and yet, as ye define *Ecclesiam*, it is a lye. The reason of diversity is this, for that it is not supposed men would abuse words, but apply them to signifie truth, and not to signifie a lye, wherein the *Arrians* offending, took occasion of heresies.

For that which is in Scripture written is a most certain truth; and as it is there written, so and no otherwise would Christ have answered, if the question had been asked *An Pater esset major illo?* he would have said yea, as it is written, And if the *Arrians* would have taken for a truth that of him that is truth, and speaketh truth, and from whom proceedeth but truth, they would have brought a distinction with them to set forth truly, and not disprove that it was truly written, by sophistication of the word. When St. *James* wrote, *Fides sine operibus mortua est*, he wrote truth, and so did St. *Paul*, *Quod fides justificat absque operibus legis*: which it could not do, if it were *mortua*. Either of these made a single asseveration of a sentence, by interpretation containing two; trusting that the Reader would *pio animo* so understand them, as their sayings might, as they do indeed, agree with truth. It is never to be thought men will willingly and without shame lye; And therefore the sence, if any may be gathered true, or like to be true, is to be taken, and not that which is a lye. And when we write to the Pope *Sanctissimo*, we mean not holier then St. *Peter*, though it sound so; and he that in our Letters should object that, should be thought ridiculous. He that should say he rode beyond the Sea, were not conveniently interrupted in his tale by him that would object sayling upon the Sea, where he could not ride at all, And rather then men would note a lye when they know what is meant, they will sooner by allegory or methaphor draw the word to the truth, then by cavillation of the word note a lye. Hath not the Pope been called *Caput Ecclesiæ*? and who hath put any addition to it? Have not men said that the Pope may dispence *cum Jure divino*, and yet in a part *Juris divini*, viz. *moralis & naturalis*, the same men would say he might not dispence: wherefore if in all other matters it was never thought inconvenient to speak absolutely the truth without distinction, why should there be more scruple in our case? The truth cannot be changed by words: that we be, as Gods law suffereth us to be, whereunto we do and must conform our selves. And if ye understand, as ye ought to understand, *Temporalibus* for the passing over this life in quietness, ye at last descend to agree to that which in the former part of your Letters you intend to impugne; and sticking to that, it were most improperly spoken, to say, We be *illius Ecclesiæ Caput in temporalibus*, which hath not *temporalia*.

Sir John Hipsley, to the Duke.

My Noble Lord,

I Find that all my Lord of *Bristols* actions are so much extolled, that what you command me to say is hardly believed. I will say no more in it, but leave the rest to Mr. *Greihams*; only this, that you have written much to the King in some mans behalf, and Mr *Grisley* hath a 100 (a year) given him during his life; all which, I think, is without your knowledge; and Mr. *Killegrew* hath the like, that came for your sake after the other was granted. Mr. *Greihams* can tell you how that came. My Lord of *Southampton* hath offered his son to marry with my Lord Treasurers Daughter, and tells him this reason, that now is the time he may have need of friends, but it is refused as yet; the event I know not what that will be.

I have spoken to the King of all that you gave me in command, and he doth protest, that what he hath done was meerly for your sake, and indeed he is very carefull of all your business, as if you were here your self; but yet for Gods sake make what haste you may home, for fear of the worst. For the carriage of Captain *Hall*, I will not trouble you, till you come home, only this by the way, that my Lord treasurer hath it; but upon what terms I know

The Lord Herbert, to the King.

not, nor indeed defire you fhould be troubled with it. Sir *George Goring* came home but this laft night, and is gone to the Court, and defires to be excufed for writing to you. My Lady *Hatton*, and my Lady *Purbeck*, came home with him from the *Hague*.

My Lord of *Arundel* hath not been at Court fince the death of his Son. I fear the newes, that *Charles Gleman* did fhew you was true. For I can affure you, Marqueſs *Hamilton* was much troubled till I had fpoken with him. There be fome have done no good offices betwixt you. Pray have a care of the Letter, I mean the man Mr. *Gleman* did fhew you, and keep as many friends as you may. I have fpoken with no man, but my Lord Keeper, who is yours, or not his own, as he fweares. And Mr. Secretary *Conway* is yours, body and foul; I never heard of the like of him, for he flies at all men that be not yours. Here is much admiration, that they hear not from you; but I thank God, the King is not troubled at it; for I do affure him, that it is the better, that he heares not from you; for now he may be confident, that you keep your day in coming away, which doth much pleafe him. I will write nothing of my own bufineſs, though there be nothing done in it, but do hope, that you will not fee your Servant perifh.

If I be too tedious, I pray pardon me, it is my love that makes me fo, and yet I have an humble fuite unto you, which is to beg at your hands for patience; for now is the time to fhew it, or never; for all the eyes of the world are upon you, and this is the time to win Honour, and fame; and for Gods fake carry the bufineſs with patience betwixt my Lord of *Briſtol*, and you; for here be thoſe that do laugh in their fleeves at you both. I befeech you, let me hear from you, what you will command me, for I will do nothing (as near as I can) but what will give content: For you have that power in me, that you need but fay, and it is done (if it lie in my power) fo ſhall you ever command

London 1. Septemb.
1623.

Your faithful, and obedient fervant,
till death,
Jo. Hipfley.

The Lord Herbert, to his Majeſty.

My moſt Gracious Sovereign,

NOw, that, I thank God for it, his Highneſs according to my continual prayers, hath made a fafe, and happy return, unto your Sacred Majefties prefence, I think my felf bound by way of Compleat obedience to thefe Commandments I received from your Majefty, both by Mr. Secretary *Calvert*, and my Brother *Henry*, to give your Majefty an account of that fence which the generall fort of people doth entertain here concerning the whole frame and Context of his Highneſs voyage. It is agreed on all parts, that his Highneſs muſt have received much contentment, in feeing two great Kingdoms, and confequently, in enjoying that fatisfaction, which Princes, but rarely, and not without great peril, obtain. His Highneſs difcretion, diligence, and Princely behaviour every where likewife is much praifed. Laftly, fince his Highneſs journey hath fallen out fo well, that his Highneſs is come back, without any prejudice to his perfon, or dignity; they fay, the fucceſs hath fufficiently commended the Counfel. This is the moſt common cenfure (even of the biggeſt party, as I am informed) which I approve in all, but in the laſt point, in the delivery whereof I find fomething to diſlike, and therefore tell them, that things are not to be judged alone, by the fucceſs, and that, when they would not look fo high as Gods providence, without which no place is fecure, they might find even in reaſon of State, fo much, as might fufficiently warrant his Highneſs perfon, and liberty to return.

I will come from the ordinary voice to the felecter judgement, of the Miniſters of State, and more intelligent people in this Kingdom, who, though they nothing vary from the above recited opinion, yet as more profoundly looking into the ſtate of this long treated of Alliance betwixt your Sacred Majefty, and *Spain*, in the perſons of his Highneſs, and the Infanta, they comprehended their fentence thereof (as I am informed) in three Propofitions.

Firſt, that the proteſtation which the King of *Spain* made to his Highneſs upon his departure, whereby he promifed to chafe away, and dif-favour all thoſe who ſhould oppofe this marriage, doth extend no further, then to the faid Kings Servants, or at furtheſt, not beyond the temporal Princes, his Neighbours; fo that the Pope being not included herein, it is though this confent muſt be yet obtained, and confequently, that the bufineſs is in little more forwardneſs then when it firſt began.

Secondly,

The Earl of Holland, to his Majesty.

Secondly, that the Pope will never yield his consent, unless your Sacred Majesty grant some notable priviledges and advantage to the Roman Catholick Religion in your Sacred Majesties Kingdoms.

Thirdly, that the said King of *Spain* would never insist upon obtaining those priviledges, but that he more desires to form a party in your Sacred Majesties Kingdoms, which he may keep alwayes obsequious to his will, then to maintain a friendly correspondence between your Sacred Majesty, and himself. I must not, in the last place, omit to acquaint your Sacred Majesty, very particularly, with the sense which was expressed by the *bons Francois*, and body of those of the Religion, who heartily wish, that the same Greatness which the King of *Spain* doth so affect over all the world, and still maintains even in this Country, which is to be Protector of the Jesuited, and Bigot party, your Sacred Majesty would embrace, in being defender of our faith. The direct answer to which, though I evade, and therefore reply little more, then that this Counsel was much fitter, when the union in *Germany* did subsist, then at this time; Yet do I think my self obliged to represent the affection they bear unto your Sacred Majesty. This is as much as is come to my notice, concerning that point your Sacred Majesty gave me in charge, which therefore I have plainly laid open before your Sacred Majesties eyes, as understanding well, that Princes never receive greater wrong, then when the Ministers they put in trust do palliate and disguise those things which it concerns them to know. For the avoiding whereof let me take the boldness to assure your Sacred Majestie, that those of this Kings Councel here will use all means they can, both to the King of *Spain*, and to the Pope (In whom they pretend to have very particular interest) not only to interrupt; but if it be possible to break off your Sacred Majesties Alliance with *Spain*. For which purpose the Count *de Tilliers* hath strict command, to give all punctuall advice, that accordingly they may proceed. It rests, that I most humbly beseech your Sacred Majesty to take my free relation of these particulars in good part, since I am of no faction, nor have any passion, or interest, but faithfully to perform that service, and dutie which I owe to your Sacred Majesty, for whose perfect health, and happiness, I pray with the devotion, of

From *Morton* Castle,
the 31. of *October*,
1623. Stil No.

*Your Sacred Majesties most obedient, most
Loyal, and most affectionate Subject
and Servant,*

Herbert.

The Earl of Holland, to his Majesty.

May it please your most excellent Majesty,

WE are in all the pain that may be, to know what to answer to the malicious and continual complaints made by *Blanvile*, of wrongs and violences done him, even to the assaulting of him in his own lodging, the which he hath represented with so much bitterness as it took great impression here in the hearts of all, especially of the Queen Mother, whom yesterday I saw in the accustomed priviledge hath ever been given me, to have at all times my entrance free into the *Louvre*. And I the rather went, because I would not shrink at all their furies and clamours; and it came to such a height, as Petitions were given by Madam *de Blanvile*, that she might, for the injuries done to her husband your Embassadour, have satisfaction upon our persons. But she was (as she deserved) despised for so passionate a folly; yet was it in consideration (as I suspect) by a word that the Queen Mother uttered in her passion to me, who with tears before all the World, being accompanied by all the Princes and Ladies, told me, (but softly) That if your Majesty continued to affront, and suffer such indignities to be done to the Embassadour of the King her Son, your Majesty must look that your Embassadours shall be used *a la pareylie*. I confess this stirred me so much, as I told her, That if the intentions of your Majesty were no better considered by the King here, your Majesty commanding us for the good and happiness of his Kingdom, to endeavour to bring, and give him (the which we have done) the greatest blessing in this World, Peace in his Country, then to be balanced with a person, that in requital hath stirred up, and daily desires to do it, disputes, and jarres, even between your Majesty and the Queen, we had reason to believe your Majesty most unjustly, and most unworthily, requited. And it might take away, upon any such occasion, the care that otherwise you would have had to do the like. And for my part, it took from me all desire ever to be imployed

upon

The Earl of Holland, to the Duke.

upon any occasion hither, where our Actions, that their acknowledgements have been acceptable but a few dayes past, are now of so little consideration, as we are of no more weight then the unworthiest Minister that ever was imployed. Upon that I found, she was sorry for having expressed so much. But this day we had from her a more favourable audience, and from the King the effects and circumstances of that which we have in our Dispatch presented unto my Lord Conway.

Sir, the malice of this *Blainvile* is so great unto your worthy servant, my Lord Duke, as he hath written a private Letter unto the King, the which I saw, by the favour of a friend, that he is in a condition of danger to be ruined by the fury and power of the Parliament. And to confirm him in that opinion, hath sent all the passages amongst them that concern my Lord Duke; adding to that, of great factions against him at the Councel Table, and naming some Lords, the which makes me see, he hath intelligence with all those that he believes may contribute any thing towards the mischieving of him. But those that know the magnanimity and noblenes of your Majesties heart, know that so noble a vessel of honour and service as he is, shall never be in danger for all the storms that can threaten him: when it is in your Majesties hands not only to calm all these tempests, but to make the Sun, and beams of your favour to shine more clearly upon his deservings then ever, the which upon this occasion your courage and vertue will not doubt to do, to the encouragement of all deserving and excellent servants, & to his honour and comfort that is the most worthy that ever Prince had: And so affectionate, that the world hath no greater admirations, then the fortunes that the Master and servant have run together. And certainly, our good God will ever preserve that affection, that in so many accidents, and (one may say) afflictions, hath preserved your Persons.

Sir, this boldness that I take proceeds not from the least doubt these foolish rumours give me of changes, but out of a passionate meditation of those accidents that your courage and fortune hath carried you through, blessing God for your prosperity, the which will be by his grace most glorious, and lasting, according to the prayers of

Your Majesties

Most humble, and most obedient

Paris $\frac{3}{13}$ March.   *Subject, and servant,*

1625.   Holland.

The Earl of Holland, to the Duke.

My dearest Lord,

WE have made a final conclusion of this great Treatie. Upon what terms the Dispatch at large will shew your Grace: We have concluded honourably, that which we could not do safely; for to recieve words, that obliged not, would have appeared an unwise and unperfect Treaty, of our part, and no way worthy of the greatnes of our Master, nor the passion of his Highnes, the which now hath a brave expression, since his Mistress is only considered, and desired, and the only object of our Treaty. But I must tell you, that since we have proceeded thus, they say, they will out-go us in the like bravery, doing ten times more then we expect, or they durst promise, fearing the World would conceive all their doings conditionally; the which would be dishonourable for Madam. But that being safe, they now say their interest is greater then ours for the recovering of the *Palatinate*, and they will never abandon us in that action. I hope we shall shortly have the honour and happines to see your Grace here; where you will be (as justly you deserve) adored. You must make haste, for we are promised our sweet Princess within six weeks. I beseech you let me know your resolution, that I may contrive which way I may best serve you against your coming. I have carefully laboured according unto your Commands in that with the Marquess *de Fiat*. You may assure him of a speedy and good success in it, the which he will more fully understand, when Mounsieur *de la Ville-aux-Cleres* shall be in *England*. He begins his journey from hence within three dayes, He is worthy of the best reception that can be given him, having throughout all this Treaty carried himself discreetly and affectionately. I beseech you put the Prince in mind to send his Mistris a Letter: And though I might, as the first Instrument imployed in his amours, expect the honour to deliver it; yet will I not give my Colleague that cause of envie. But if his Highness will write a private Letter unto Madam, and in it express some particular trust of me, And that my

relations

relations of her, have increased his passion, and affection unto her service, I shall receive much honour, and some right, since I onely have expressed what concerned his passion and affection towards her. If you think me worthy of this honour, procure a Letter to this purpose, and send it me to deliver unto her, and likewise your Commands, the which I will receive for my greatest comforts: living in unhappiness until I may by my services express how infinitely, and eternally I am

Your Graces
Most humble, and most obliged, and devoted Servant,
Holland.

Post-script.
The Presents that the Prince will send unto Madam, I beseech you hasten.

The Earl of Holland, to the Duke.

My dear Lord,

THis Messenger is so rigid, and such an enemy to all *Jantileise*, as by him I will not send any news in that kind; but when the little *Mercury* comes, you shall know that which shall make you joy, and grieve that you cannot enjoy what your fate and merit hath so justly destined unto you. We have such daily Alarms here out of *England* from *Blanvile*, of the beating of his servant, and at the last, the danger that of late he himself hath been in, of being assassinated in his own house; for the first word that his servant said unto the King, and the whole Court was; The Embassadour had run such a hazard of his life, as no man that heard him believed he had escaped with less then 5 or 6 wounds. Insomuch as your friend *Bonteve* asked, *Fait un belle sine*: And this hath so animated this Court, being (as your Lordship knows) apt upon all occasions to be fired and stirred up, as the King hath been moved to forbid us our entries, and liberties here. And yesterday Madam *de Blanvile* did openly petition the King, to imprison us for the wrongs and injuries done unto her husband and his Embassadour, that she feared was by this time dead. But that had no other effect but to be laugh'd at. I never (I confess) saw the Queen Mother in so much distraction and passion, for she never speaks of her Daughter but with tears, and yesterday with some heat and bitterness, to me, about it: the Circumstances I have taken the boldness to present unto his Majesty. That which distracts me infinitely, is to hear, that they do traduce you as the cause of all these misfortunes, and that you stirre up the King to these displeasures. And so much impression it hath made into the Queen Mother, as this day at the Audience she told me, That you had made the marriage, and were now, as she imagined, and was informed, resolved to destroy your work. I asked her what particularity could make her say, and believe so, against the general, and continual actions and endeavours, that the whole world ought to be satisfied of your infinite care and affection, to fasten and tye together a good and constant intelligence and friendship between these Crowns. She told me, that you intreated Madam *de St. George* to do some service for you to the Queen, the which she did, and instead of giving her thanks, you threatned the sending of her away. I told her, Though I had as yet heard nothing of this particularity, yet I knew your nature to be so generous, as you would never do any action unjust. I told her, that she must distinguish between what you say, as Commanded by the King, and what you say of your self: for if it be his pleasure to make the instrument to convey his will upon any occasion of his displeasure, you are not to dispute, but to obey his Command in that, and in all other things. I told her further, that I saw the continual malice of the Embassadour, that invents daily injuries and falshoods of your Lordship, to unload himself from his insolencies and faults; but I hoped that nothing should light upon your Lordship but what you deserved, the which, to my knowledge, was more value and esteem then any man in the world could, or can ever merit from this Kingdom. And I desired her, not to entertain the belief of these things too hastily, until we had news out of *England*, that we knew would contradict all these malicious discourses. And I must tell your Grace, that by a friend (whom I am tied not to name) I was shewed the private Letter that *Blanvile* wrote to the King, in the which he sent him the whole proceedings of the Parliament, and concludes they will ruine you, naming great Factions against you, and as it were a necessity to destroy you. But I hope he, and the whole world here, will fall, before any misfortune tunes should fall upon so generous, and so noble a deserver of his Master, and so excellent a friend and Patron unto

Your Graces
Most humble, and most obedient servant,
Holland.

Post-script.

Though the Embassadour deserves nothing but contempt and disgrace, as *Blanvile*, yet I hope, as Embassadour, he shall receive (for publick honours and accustomed respect to Embassadours) all possible satisfaction, and it will be conceived a generous action.

The Earl of Holland, to the Duke.

My dearest Lord,

ALL the joy I have hath such a flatness set upon it by your absence from hence, as, I protest to God, I cannot relish it as I ought; for though beauty and love I find in all perfection and fulness, yet I vex, and languish to find impediments in our designs and services for you: first in the business, for I find our mediation must have no place with this King, concerning a Peace. We must only use our power with those of the Religion, to humble them to reasonable conditions, and that done, they would, as far as I can guess have us gone, not being willing that we should be so much as in the Kingdom, when the Peace is made, for fear the Protestants may imagine we have had a hand in it. For our Confederation, made by you at the *Hague*, they speak so of it, as they will do something in it, but not so really or friendly as we could wish. But for these things, you allow me, (I trust) to refer you to the general Dispatch: I come now to other particulars; I have been a careful Spie, how to observe intentions, and affections towards you. I find many things to be feared, and none to be assured of a safe and real welcome. For the ♄ continues in his suspects, making (as they say) very often discourses of it, and is willing to hear *Villanes* say, That ♥ hath infinite affections, you imagine which way. They say there is whispered amongst the foolish young Bravado's of the Court, That he is not a good Frenchman that suffers ♂ to return out of *France*, considering the reports that are raised, many such bruits she up and down. I have since my coming given the Queen Mother, by way of discourse, occasion to say somewhat concerning your coming, as the other might when she complained to me, That things were carried harshly in *England* towards *France*; I then said, That the greatest unkindness and harshness came from hence, even to forbid your coming hither, a thing so strange, and so unjust, as our Master had cause, and was infinitely sensible of it. She fell into discourse of you, desiring you would respect and love her daughter; and likewise that she had, and would ever command her to respect you above all men, and follow all your Counsels (the matter of her Religion excepted) with many professions of value and respect unto your Person; but would never either excuse what I complained of, or invite you to come upon that occasion. But though neither the business gives me cause to perswade your coming, nor my reason for the matter of your safety; yet know, you are the most happy, unhappy man alive, for ♥ is beyond imagination right, and would do things to destroy her fortune, rather then want satisfaction in her mind. I dare not speak as I would, I have ventured, I fear, too much, considering what practices accompany the malice of the people here. I tremble to think whether this will find a safe conveyance unto you. Do what you will, I dare not advise you; to come is dangerous; not to come is unfortunate. As I have lived with you, and only in that enjoy my happiness, so I will die with you, and, I protest to God, for you, to do you the least service, &c.

Post-script.

Have no doubt of the party that accompanied me, for he is yours with his soul, and dares not now (as things go) advise your coming.

The Earl of Holland, to the University.

Mr. Vice-chancellor and Gentlemen, the Senate of the University of Cambridge,

THE condition of man is so frail, and his time so short here, that in the sum of his account there are few accidents can deliver him worthy to posterity: yet to prevent my destiny in this defect, you have made my name to live, by your general and free election of me to be your Chancellor; the which will give me so to the world, not as my merit. I take but my beginning by this Creation, and will endeavour to proceed with such strength, in my serious affection to serve you all, as you shall see this honour is not conferred upon an unthankful person. It is my hap to succeed the most excellent example of the best Chancellor, who had both will and power to oblige you: for the first, none can exceed me, that I am tyed by my education to serve you: for my power, although it be but short in all other things; yet in what concerns you:, my Master, whose word you have, and whose thanks you will receive in my behalf, will for his own sake, if not for mine, accept of all humble requests for you, which may conduce to the support of every particular good, that can any way advantage your whole Body, or advance the several members of your University. For whose increase of fame and honour I do wish, from an affectionate heart, as I profess my self obliged, being

Your most thankful friend,
and humble servant,
Henry Holland.

The Lady Elizabeth Howard, to the King.

WHen I waited upon you at *Theobalds*, to beseech your Majesty that my Lord of *Suffolk* might not come into the Star-chamber, you protested that you loved the man, but that you must shew cause to the world why you took the Staff from him, but for his fortune, that your Majesty would not meddle with it; the same my Lord of *Buckingham* told me, with this assurance of your promise, I went away secure in that point. Sithence his cause was heard, he moved all that heard it with much compassion to him, and the people did think, that when you sent him to the Tower, you would have sent for him to have kissed your hand. But your Majesty is abused, for they do not let you know, what is thought of the proceeding against this good man, knowing how truly he loveth you, with the truth of his cause, that you would not follow him and his children with cruelty. My Lord hath spent in running a Tylt, in Masques, and following the Court, above 20000 *l*. And Sir, shall his reward now be to be turned out of this place without any offence committed. Sir, I am the child of your old Servant, and am now great with child, I know it will kill me; and I shall willingly die, rather then desire life to see my unfortunate self, and mine, thus miserably undone. Sir, I beseech your Majesty, remember my Father that is dead, and me his distressed child; for if he could know any worldly thing, he would wonder to see me, and those that shall come of me, thus strangly used. But my hope is still in your Majesties goodness, and that you will not be carried away with the malice of other men. In this confidence I rest, with my daily prayers for your health and happiness, as

Which might have been better spent.

Yours, &c.
E. H.

The History of the Reign of King Henry the Eighth, King Edward the Sixth, Queen Mary, and part of the Reign of Queen Elizabeth.

✻ THE Books which are written do, in their kinds, represent the faculties of the mind of man: Poesie, his Imaginations; Philosophy, his Reason; and History, his Memory; of which three faculties, least exception is commonly taken to memory, because Imagination is often times idle, and Reason litigious. So likewise, History of all writings deserveth least taxation, as that which holdeth least of the Author, and most of the things themselves. Again, the use which it holdeth to mans life, if it be not the greatest, yet assuredly it is the freest from ill accident or quality. For those that are conversant much in Poets, as they

attain

attain to greater variety, so withal they become conceited; and those that are brought up in Philosophy and Sciences do wax (according as their nature is) some of them too stiff and opinionative, and some others too perplexed and confused; whereas History possesseth the mind with conceits which are nearest allied unto action, and imprinteth them, so as it doth not alter the Complexion of the mind, neither to irresolution, nor pertinacity? But this is true, that in no sort of writings there is a greater distance between the good and the bad, no not between the most excellent Poet, and the vainest Rimer; nor between the deepest Philosopher, and the most frivolous School-men; then there is between good Histories, and those that unworthily bear the same, or the like title. In which regard, having purposed to write the History of *England*, from the beginning of the Reign of King *H. 8.* of that name, neer unto the present time wherein Queen *Elizabeth* Reigneth in good felicity; I am delivered of the excuse wherewith the best writers of Histories are troubled in their Poems, when they go about (without breaking the bounds of modesty) to give a reason why they should write that again, which others have written well, or at least tolerably, before. For those which I am to follow are such, as I may fear, rather, the reproach of coming unto their number, than the opinion of presumption, if I hope to do better than they: But in the mean time, it must be considered; That the best of the ancient Histories were contrived out of divers particular Commentaries, Relations and Narrations, which it was not hard to digest with ornament, and thereof to compound one entire Story. And as, at first, such Writers had the ease of others labours; so since they have the whole Commendation, in regard their former writings are for the most part lost, whereby their borrowings do not appear. But unto me the disadvantage is great, finding no publick memories of any consideration or worth, that the supply must be out of the freshness of memory and tradition; and out of the Acts, Instruments, and Negotiations of State themselves, together with the glances of Forreign Histories; which, though I do acknowledge to be the best Originals and Instructions out of which to write an History, yet the travel must be much greater, than if there had been already digested any tolerable Chronicle, as a single Narration of the Actions themselves, which should onely have needed, out of the former helps, to be enriched with Counsels and Speeches, and notable particularities. And this was the reason, while I might not attempt to go higher to more ancient times, because those helps and grounds did more and more fail; although, if I be not deceived, I may truly affirm, that there have no things passed ever in this Nation, which have produced greater Actions, nor more worthy to be delivered to the Ages hereafter; For they be not the great Wars and Conquests (which many times are works of Fortune, and fall out in barbarous times) the rehearsal whereof maketh the profitable and instructing History; but rather times refined in policies and industries, new and rare variety of accidents and alterations, equal and just encounters of State and State in forces, and of Prince and Prince in sufficiency, that bring upon the stage the best parts for observation. Now if you look into the general natures of the times (which I have undertaken throughout *Europe*, whereof the times of this Nation must needs participate; you shall find more knowledge in the World, than was in the Ages before; whereby the wits of men (which are the shops wherein all actions are forged) are more furnished and improved: Then if you shall restrain your Consideration to the state of this Monarchy; first, there will occur unto you Changes rare, and altogether unknown unto Antiquity, in matters of Religion, and the State Ecclesiastical. Then to behold the several Reigns of a King, that first, or next the first, became absolute in the Sovereignty; of a King, in minority; of a Queen, married to a Forreigner; and lastly, of a Queen that hath governed without the help, either of a marriage, or of any mighty man of her blood, is no small variety in the affairs of a Monarchy; but such, as (perhaps) in four Successions in any State, at any time, is hardly to be found. Besides, there have not wanted Examples, within the compass of the same times, neither of an Usurpation, nor of Rebellions under heads of greatness, nor of Commotions meerly popular, nor of sundry desperate Conspirators (an unwonted thing in hereditary Monarchies) nor of Forreign Wars of all sorts, invasive, repulsive, of Invasion open and declared; covert and under hand, by Sea, by Land, Scottish, French, Spanish Succors, Protections, new and extraordinary kinds of Confederations with Subjects: Generally, without question, the State of this Nation had never a longer reach to import the unusual Affairs of *Europe*, as that which was in the former part of the time the Counterpoise between *France* and *Spain:* and in the Latter, the only encounter and opposition against *Spain*. Adde hereunto, the new Discoveries and Navigations abroad, the new Provisions of Laws and Presidents of State at home; and the Accidents memorable, both of State and of Court, and there will be no doubt, but the times which I have chosen are of all

former

former times in this Nation, the fittest to be registred, if it be not in this respect, that they be of too fresh a memory; which point, I know very well, will be a prejudice, as if this story were written in favour of the time present. But it shall suffice unto me, without betraying mine own name and memory, or the liberty of a History, to procure this commendation to the time with the Posterity; namely, That a private man living in the same time, should not doubt to publish an History of the time, which should not carry any shew or taste at all of flattery; a point noted for an infallible Demonstration of a good time.

King Henry the Seventh of that name, after he had lived about 52 years, and thereof Reigned 23 and some months, deceased of a Consumption the 22 day of *April*, in the Palace which he had built at *Richmond*, in the year of our Redemption, 1509. This King attained unto the Crown, not only from a private fortune, which might endow him with moderation; but also from the fortune of an exiled man, which had quickned in him all seeds of observation and Industry. His times were rather prosperous, than calme; for he was assailed with many troubles, which he overcame happily; a matter that did not less set forth his wisdom, than his fortune; and yet such a wisdom, as seemed rather a dexterity to deliver himself from dangers when they pressed him, than any deep foresight to prevent them afar off; Jealous he was over the greatness of his Nobility, as remembring how himself was set up. And much more did this humour increase in him, after he had conflicted with some such Idols and Counterfeits, as were *Lambert Symnell*, and *Perkin Warbeck*. The strangeness of which dangers made him think nothing safe; whereby he was forced to descend to the employment of secret Espials, and suborned Conspirators, a necessary remedy against so dark and subtile practices, and not to be reprehended, except it were true which some report; That he had intelligence with Confessors, for the revealing matters disclosed in Confession; and yet if a man compare him with the King his Concurrents in *France* and *Spain*, he shall find him more politick than *Lewis* the Twelfth of *France*, and more entire and sincere than *Ferdinando* of *Spain*; upon whom, nevertheless, he did handsomly bestow the envy of the death of *Edward Plantagenet* Earl of *Warwick*. Great and devout reverence he bare to Religion, as he that employed Ecclesiastical men in most of his affairs and negotiations, and as he that was brought hardly, and very late, to the abolishing of the priviledges of Sanctuaries in case of Treason, and that, not before he had obtained it by way of suite from Pope *Alexander*; which Sanctuaries, nevertheless, had been the forges of most of his troubles. In his Government he was led by none, scarcely by his Laws; and yet he was a great observer of formality in all his proceedings, which notwithstanding, was no impediment to the working of his will, and in the suppressing and punishment of the Treasons which during the whole time of his Reign were committed against him; he had a very strange kind of interchanging of very large and unexpected pardons, with severe executions; which, his wisdom considered, could not be imputed to any Inconstancy or Inequality, but to a discretion, or at least to a principle that he had apprehended, that it was good, not obstinately to pursue one course, but to try both ways. In his Wars, he seemed rather confident than enterprizing; by which also he was commonly not the poorer, but generally he did seem inclinable to live in peace, and made but offers of War to mend the conditions of peace; and in the quenching of the commotions of his Subjects, he was ever ready to atchieve those Wars in person, sometimes reserving himself, but never retiring himself, but as ready to second. Of nature, he coveted to accumulate treasure, which the people (into whom there is infused, for the preservation of Monarchies, a natural desire to discharge their Princes, though it be with the unjust Charge of their Counsellors and Ministers) did impute unto Cardinal *Morton* and Sir *Reynold Bray*, who, as it after appeared, as Counsellors of ancient Authority with him, did so second his humour, as nevertheless they tempted it, and refrained it; whereas *Empson* and *Dudley*, that followed, being persons that had no reputation with him, otherwise than following of his own humour, gave him way, and shaped him way to these extremities, wherewith himself was touched with remorse at his death, and with his Successor disavowed. In expending of Treasure, he never spared Charge that his Affairs required; and in his Foundations, was Magnificent enough, but his Rewards were very limited; so that his Liberality was rather upon his own state and memory, than towards the deserts of others. He chose commonly to employ cunning persons, as he that knew himself sofficient to make use of their uttermost reaches without danger of being abused with himself.

The rest is wanting.

A

King James, to the Major and Aldermen of London, after he was proclaimed.

To our trusty and well-beloved, Robert Lee, Lord Major of our City of London, and to our well-beloved, the Aldermen and Commons of the same.

TRusty and well-beloved, we greet you heartily well. Being informed of your great forwardness in that just and honourable action of proclaiming us your Sovereign Lord and King, immediately after the decease of our late deceased Sister the Queen; wherein you have given a singular good proof of your ancient fidelity, a reputation hereditary to that our City of *London*, being the Chamber of our Imperial Crown, and ever free from all shades of tumultuous and unlawfull courses: We could not omit, with all possible speed we might, to give you hereby a Test of our thankfull mind for the same; and withal, assurance, that you cannot crave any thing of us, fit for the maintenance of you all in general, and every one of you in particular, but it shall be most willingly performed by us, whose special care shall ever be, to provide for the continuance and increase of your present happiness: Desiring you, in the mean time, to go constantly forward in doing all and whatsoever things you shall find necessary or expedient for the good Government of our said City, in execution of justice, as you have been used to do in our said dearest Sisters time, till our pleasure be known to you in the contrary. Thus not doubting but you will do, as you may be fully assured of our gracious favour towards you in the highest degree; we bid you heartily farewell.

Holy-rood House, March 28. 1603.   *JAMES R.*

King James, to the University of Cambridge.

JACOBUS Dei gratia Magnæ Britanniæ, Franciæ, & Hiberniæ Rex, Fidei defensor, &c. Academiæ Cantabrigiæ communi, salutem.

SI jus civitatis impetret à nobis Cantabrigia, veremur ne æmula urbis potentia crescente minuatur Academiæ securitas, sat erit apud nos metus vestri judicium fecisse; nec enim tam vobis convenit Academiæ periculum deprecari quam nobis, sponte nostra quicquid in speciem illi noxium sit avertere. Glorietur urbs illa se a Majoribus nostris electam doctrinarum sedem, ingeniorum officium, sapientia palæstram. Quicquid his titulis addi potest, & non honestatur plebeia Civitatis appellatione, Musarum domicilium vel sanè literatorum dicatur Civitas, vel quod in villa villæ & in inclarum tegitur celebritate. Hæc ejus fuerint privilegia Academiæ dignitatem comiter observare (cujus frequentia facta & seipsa major affluentia bonarum artium studiosos amicè excipere quorum congressu dilatata est) Literatorum deinque honori ancillari unde hæc illa nata est fœlicitas, ke artes quibus crevit tenendo, non aucupanda titulorum novitas incerti eventus facessat popularis vocabuli fastus, unde certa oriatur æmulationis necessitas quæ eo turpior urbi est futura quo majori erga Academiam obstricta est reverentia, nolumus sacrum illum musarum asylum minuti Prætoris ense temerari nec strepere tetrica edicta, ubi septem geminus vestri Chori auditur concentus satis & in veteri purpura invidia nova pompa tam illi futura, & supervacua quam vobis suspecta. In nostra tutela salva est, & post Deum opt. max. Alma scientiarum Mater nostro sevebitur sceptro, indefessa illius fœcunditas non abortiet, ad prætorii gladii terriculum nullum honoris titulum Cantabrigiæ indulgemus, qui cum Academiæ sollicitudine conjunctus sit. Valete. Datum è Palatio nostro Westmonast. 4 Calend. Mar. 1616.

JACOBUS REX.

The University of Cambridge, to King Charles.

Serenissimo invictissimoq; Principi ac Domino nostro, CAROLO Dei gratia, Magnæ Britanniæ, Franciæ, & Hiberniæ, Regi, Fidei Defens. &c.

SErenissime Domine noster, invictissime Carole, multum nos fortuna nostra, sed tua clementia infinitum quantum debemus; satis nempe erat judicio nostro satisfecisse, cum illum nobis præficeremus, quem unum certissime præfici posse constabat. At tua admirabilis bonitas *non patitur nos gra.ts u.l.sinatissis benefacere, sed tibi imputari vis quod nobis sicimm beneficium. Primum arduam aliquam sibi materiam obsequium nostrum poscebat, & cujus tenuitas sublimitatem vestram ajsequi min posset difficultatem——se, & molestia commendaret. Tu autem a te gratiam—— quod toti Patroni beneficio usi sumus, qui ita nos amat, ut plurimum velit, ita à te amatur, ut plurimum nostra causa posset per quem vestra in nos transeat benignitas, & difficultates nostras dissentia: si qua tamen in hac divina bonitate tua existere possit difficultas superasti, nempe majrum tuorum Clementiam, qua & easdem nobis immunitates indulges, & idetiam prospicis, ut iis r tissime utamur. Et quod unum tantæ fœlicitati reliquum erat ut esset perpetua, id ipsum precibus nostris superesse non sinis; præcurris enim vota nostra, & spem ipsam, qua nihil est imp rimius, exuperas: nam & ipsa fines suos habet, quos tuæ bonitati nullos esse experti sumus. Exhausisti votorum nostrorum materiam, Serenissime Regum, nec quicquam nobis deinceps optandum est, quam ut tu regnes ut vincas, ut nos in perpetuum simus quod sumus,*

Datæ frequentissimo Senatu
nostro, sexto Idus Junii;
1626.

Excellentissimæ Majestatis vestræ
humillimi servi & subditi,
*Procancellarius, & reliquus Senatus
Academiæ Cantabrigiensis.*

A Copy of a Letter from his Majesty, to the Lords, read at the Board, Novemb. 21. 1617. *touching the abatement of his Majesties Houshold Charge.*

My Lords,

NO worldly thing is so precious as Time: Ye know what task I gave you to work upon, during my absence; and what time was limited unto you, for the performance thereof. This same Chancellor of *Scotland* was wont to tell me, twenty four years ago, that my house could not be kept upon *Epigrams*; long discourses and fair tales will never repair my estate. *Omnis virtus in actione consistit.* Remember, that I told you, the shooe must be made for the foot; and let that be the Square of all your proceeding in this business. Abate superfluities in all things, and multitudes of unnecessary Officers, where ever they be placed. But for the Houshold Wardrobe, and Pensions, cut and carve as many as may agree with the possibility of my means. Exceed not your own rule of 50000*l.* for the Houshold. If you can make it less, I will account it for good service. And that you may see I will not spare mine own person, I have sent, with this Bearer, a note of the superfluous charges concerning my mouth, having had the happy opportunities of this Messenger, in an errand so nearly concerning his place. In this, I expect no answer in word, or writing, but onely the real performance, for a beginning to relieve me out of my miseries. For now the Ball is at your feet, and the world shall bear me witness, that I have put you fairly to it; and so praying God to bless your labours, I bid you heartily farewell.

Your own,
JAMES R.

A Copy of his Majesties second Letter.

My Lords,

I Received from you, yesternight, the bluntest Letter that, I think, ever King received from his Councel. Ye write, that the Green-Cloth will do nothing, and ye offer me no advice. Why are ye Councellors, if ye offer no Counsel? An ordinary Messenger might have brought me such an answer. It is my pleasure, that my charges be equalled with my Revenue; and it is just and necessary so to be. For this a project must be made, and one of the main branches thereof, is, my house.

This Project is but to be offered unto you, and how it may be better laid, then, to agree with my honour and contentment, ye are to advise upon, and then have my consent.

If this cannot be performed without diminishing the number of Tables, diminished they must be; and, if that cannot serve, two or three must be thrust into one. If the Green-Cloth will not make a Project for this, some other must do it: If ye cannot find them out, I must. Onely remember two things; That time must no more be lost; and that there are twenty ways of abatement, besides the house, if they be well looked into. And so farewell.

JAMES R.
King

King James, *to the Earl of* Bristol, *Embassador in* Spain.

Right Trusty, and right Well-beloved Cousin and Counceller, We greet you well.

THere is none knows better then your self, how we have laboured, ever since the beginning of these infortunate troubles of the Empire, notwithstanding all opposition to the contrary, to merit well of our dear Brother, the King of *Spain*, and the whole House of *Austria*, by a long and lingring patience, grounded still upon his friendship, and promises, That care should be had of our Honour, and of our Childrens Patrimony and Inheritance. We have acquainted you also, from time to time, since the beginning of the Treaty at *Bruxels*, how craftly things have there proceeded, notwithstanding the fair professions made unto us, both by the King of *Spain*, the Infanta, and all his Ministers, and the Letters written by him unto the Emperour, and them effectually, (at the least, as they endeavoured to make us believe:) but what fruits have we of all these, other then dishonour and scorn? Whilest we are treating, the Town and Castle of *Heidelbergh* taken by force, our Garrison put to the sword, *Manheim* besieged, and all the hostility used that is within the power of an Enemy, as you will see by the relation which we have commanded our Secretary to send you.

Our pleasure therefore is, That you shall immediately, as soon as you can get audience, let the King understand, how sensible we are of those proceedings of the Emperour towards us; and withal, are not a little troubled, to see that the *Infanta*, having an absolute Commission to conclude a suspension and cessation of Arms, should now at last, when all objections were answered, and the former (solely pretended) obstacles removed, not onely delay the conclusion of the Treaty, but refuse to lay her command upon the Emperours Generals, for abstaining from the siege of our Garrisons, during the Treaty, upon pretext of want of authority: So as, for avoiding of further dishonour, we have been enforced to recall both our Embassadors, as well the Chancellor of the Exchequer, (who is already returned to our presence) as also the Lord *Chichester*, whom we intended to have sent unto the Emperour to the Diet at *Ratisbone*. Seeing, therefore, that out of our extraordinary respect meerly to the King of *Spain*, and the firm confidence we ever put in the hopes and promises which he did give us; desiring nothing more then, for his cause principally, to avoid all occasions that might put us into ill understanding with any of the House of *Austria*; We have hitherto proceeded with a stedfast patience, trusting to the Treaties, and neglecting all other means which might probably have secured the remainder of our Childrens inheritance; those Garrisons which we maintained in the *Palatinate*, being rather, for Honours sake, to keep a footing until the general accommodation, then that we did rely so much upon their strength as upon his friendship; and by that confidence and security of ours, are thus exposed to dishonour and reproach. You shall tell that King, That seeing all those endeavours and good offices which he hath used towards the Emperour in this business, on the behalf of our Son in Law, upon confidence whereof that our security depended, which he continually, by his Letters, and Ministers here, laboured to beget and confirm in us, have not sorted to any other issue, then to a plain abuse both of his trust and ours; whereby we are both of us highly injured in our Honour, though in a different degree; we hope, and desire, that out of a true sence of this wrong offered unto us, he will, as our dear and loving Brother, faithfully promise and undertake, upon his Honour, confirming the same also under his Hand and Seal, either that the Castle and Town of *Heidelbergh* shall, within threescore and ten days after this your audience and demand made, be rendred into our hands, with all things therein belonging to our Son in Law, or our Daughter, as near as may be, in the state wherein they were taken; and the like for *Manheim* and *Frankendale*, if both or either of them shall be taken by the enemy whilest these things are in treating; as also, that there shall be, within the said term of threescore and ten days, a cessation or suspension of Arms in the *Palatinate* for the future, upon the seven Articles and Conditions last propounded by our Embassadour, Sir *Richard Weston*; and that the general Treaty shall be set on foot again, upon such honourable terms and conditions as were propounded unto the Emperor, in a Letter written unto him in *November* last, and with which the King of *Spain* then (as we understand) seemed satisfied: or else, in case all these particulars be not yielded unto, and performed by the Emperour, as is here propounded, but be refused, or delayed beyond the time afore-mentioned; that then the King of *Spain* do joyn his Forces with ours, for the recovery of our Childrens Honours and Patrimony, which upon this trust hath been thus lost: Or if so be his Forces, at this present, be otherwise so employed, as that they cannot give us that assistance which we here desire, and, as we think, we have deserved; yet, t the least he will permit us a free and friendly passage through his Territories and Dominions, for such Forces as we shall send and employ into *Germany* for this service: Of all which disjunctively, if you receive not of the King of *Spain*, within ten days, at the furthest, after your Audience and Proposition made, a direct assurance under his Hand and Seal, without delay, or putting us off to further Treaties and Conference; that is to say, of such Restitution, Cession of Arms, and proceeding to a general Treaty, as is before mentioned; or else, of assistance, and joyning his Forces with ours against the Emperour, or, at least, permission of passage for our Forces through his said Dominions; that then you take your leave, and return unto our Presence, without further stay; otherwise, to proceed in the negotiation of the Marriage of our Son, according to the instruction we have given you. Given, &c. at *Hampton-Court*, Octob. 3. 1622.

King James, to Ferdinand the Emperour, concerning the Palatinate.

James, by the Grace of God, King of *Great Britain*, *France*, and *Ireland*, Defender of the Faith, &c. wisheth health and constant peace unto the most mighty and invincible Prince *Ferdinando*, by the same Grace elected *Roman* Emperour, King of *Germany*, *Hungary*, and *Bohemia*, Archduke of *Austria*, &c. our loving Friend, and Cousin.

Most mighty and invincible Prince, Brother, Cousin, and special loving Friend; It is not unknown unto the whole world, much less to your Imperial Majesty, how earnestly we have hitherto sought and endeavoured, as well by the diligence of our Embassadours whom we have sent, as by the intercession of the chief *German* Princes, the appeasing of those *Bohemian* wars, ever since they first began; and with what ardent zeal and affection we have so much hunted after the desire of peace: Let it not, therefore, seem strange to any man, that we take it ill, that all the very time when we were (to the uttermost of our power) treating of peace, and giving out best furtherance for the overture of wholsom means to effect it; even then, notwithstanding, we found clean contrary effects to ensue thereupon: Whereat we much marvelled, seeing the Treaty was in hand, and already begun on all sides: As namely, among the rest, that our Son in Law was wholly despoiled and robbed of his hereditary Patrimony that remained unto him, excepting the lower *Palatinate*, which was all, by commandment of your Imperial Majesty, taken and possessed by the Duke of *Bavaria*, according as himself confessed, with strong hand and force of Arms, and that for such reasons as are meerly new, and such, as the like were never hitherto once heard of. That notwithstanding it plainly appeareth, by the answer given unto our Embassadour; that your Imperial Majesty had caused the suspension of that Bann or Proscription in those Countreys; yet did your Imperial Majesty permit the taking of Arms again in hand: which, also after the same your Imperial Majesties answer, was yet again likewise commanded to be done in the Lower *Palatinate*, whereby there hath therein been since raised a grievous and cruel War, and most part of the Countrey taken in by the *Spaniards* powerfull strength. But as we diligently observed those things, we cleerly see, what great trouble and misery hath been occasioned by this our great patience, and long delaying, forbearing and doubtfulness, which, without all doubt, may be hereafter further occasioned, and which may, perhaps, prove heavier then the chief reasons of this misery it self. And therefore we hold it best, and most expedient, that your Imperial Majesty do at length put a period to this most unhappy business: And for that end and purpose, have thought good, at this time, to propound what we prescribe our Son in Law, on the one part, to perform towards your Imperial Majesty, which we have always counselled and exhorted our Son in Law to do; nor will we so much as, in the least, once doubt of the contrary, and adverse success therein; but are perswaded, that your Imperial Majesty will be most graciously moved to receive our Son in Law into grace and favour, to re-deliver unto him his hereditary Lands and Titles, which he had enjoyed before those *Bohemian* Wars, and fully to restore him to his former Honours and Dignities. In regard whereof the Count *Palatine* shall perform unto your Imperial Majesty as followeth.

1. He shall, for himself and his Son, wholly renounce and acquit all pretence of right and claim unto the Crown of *Bohemia*, and the incorporated Countreys thereof.

2. He shall from henceforward yield all constant due devotion unto the Imperial Majesty, as do other obedient Princes Electors of the Empire.

3. He shall, upon his knee, crave pardon of the Imperial Majesty.

4. He shall not hereafter, any manner of way, either unfittingly carry or demean himself towards the Imperial Majesty, or disturb your Kingdoms or Countreys.

5. He

His Imperial Majesty, to King James.

5. He shall upon reasonable conditions reconcile himself with other his neighbour Princes and States of the Empire, and hold good friendship with them.

6. And shall really do all other like things as is above contained, and that shall be reasonable and necessary.

Which proposed Conditions if your Imperial Majesty shall please to receive and accept of, the same will be a notable testimony of your Imperial Majesties goodness and grace: which how well and acceptable it will be unto us, shall be acknowledged and shewed by our very willing service and unfeigned friendship as well towards your Imperial Majesty as towards the most renowned house of *Austria*. But if it shall fall out, contrary to our expectation, that these our just demands and well-willed presentation shall not find acceptance, or after this our diligent endeavour you shall seek to delay us by the using some new tergiversation, and pretend to use that long counsel and deliberate advice of the Princes of the Empire upon these our propounded conditions, whereas notwithstanding your Imperial Majesty expresly promised in your last answer freely to declare what should be your purpose and resolution therein: So that there being no ground to the contrary (as we call God and the world to witness there is not) and being forced and constrained by the duty and natural affection which we owe and bear to our children for the preservation of their honour and welfare, we are resolved to try the uttermost of our power for their relief, especially seeing we sue for, desire, and would obtain and retain no new title of honour for our Son-in-Law, but only to have again those of his own now lost, which he then had and enjoyed when [we matched him with our dear and only daughter: For if, in this distress, we should leave our children and their Partisans without counsel, help, and protection, it would be a foul stain to our honour.

Let not therefore your Imperial Majesty in regard hereof blame us at all, if we with a mighty and puissant Army, by force and strong hand, seek to recover that which by propounded and reasonable conditions we could not obtain for the continuance of our friendship. But for as much as it is most certain this cannot be without the great hurt and prejudice of all Christendom, the breach of publique peace, and the wounding of our contracted aimity and friendship with the house of *Austria*, which we have ever hitherto by manifold testimonies uprightly, faithfully and inviolably observed: It is therefore requisite and necessary, that your Majesty of your innate gracious mildness and goodness, and of that most reverent discretion wherewith you are endowed, to seek in time to meet with and prevent these so great evils likely to ensue, and use brotherly love and good will. God almighty long preserve your Imperial Majesties life, and at last so direct your heart, that sweet Peace and the concord of all Christendom, now rent asunder, may be recovered and again maintained.

At our Royal Residence-Town of Royston,   JACOBUS REX.
Novemb. 12. 1631.

His Imperial Majesty, to King James.

COnstans atque eadem nobis semper fuit mens, idem desiderium, non tam verbis quam re ipsa demenstrandi quanti tranquillitatem in Imperio publicam & mutuæ amicitiæ cum vicinis Principibus, potissimum Serenitatis vestræ sincere colendæ studium æstimaremus. Inde si præteriti temporis successus de rebus in utroque Palatinatu, tam superiore quam inferiore, innovat, de quo literis ad nos datis Serenitas vestra conqueritur deflexisse videre possint, illi culpa venit omnis imputanda; quem ab improba cupiditate aliena regna capiendi, nec divini nec humani juris respectus, nec supremi Domini sui reverentia, nec sacri ?us-jurandi religio, nec prudentissimi Socers concilium cohibere potuerint; imo qui justo Dei judicio ea acie in fugam profligatus usque adeo obstinatione sua pertinaciter etiam nunc inhæret, ut continuis machinationibus per Jagerndorfium, Mansfeildum, aliosque crudeles pacis publicæ perturbatores, Acherouta potius movere quam sanioribus acquiescere consiliis ab usurpateque regni nostri titulo desistere (non officiis per Serenitatem vestram per quam sane diligenter interpositis, sua ex parte quid deferens) videatur, nec ullum in hanc usque horam animi pœnitentis signum dederit. Itaque in tractatu de pace instituenda uti condescendamus videt Serenitas vestra ab eis quos principaliter id concernit quam nulla nobis causa vel occasio præbeatur. Id quidem ingenue profitemur, in exulceratissimo eo negotio, cujus calamitas universum pene orbem involvit, eum Serenitatis vestræ candorem, eam animi moderationem, & equitatis justitiæque respectum emituisse, ut nihil sit vicissim quod non ejusdem desidriis salva suprema authoritate nostra Cæsarea, salvisque Imperii legibus, libenter tribuamus, qui non innata nobis benignitate———aquisque conditionibus Arma poni & optatam afflictissimæ Germaniæ pacem restitui

quem

quam legitimæ executi: res insisti per cædes & sanguinem Christianum gloriosa nomini nostro trophæa figi nunquam non maluimus. In gratiam itaque Serenitatis vestræ, ut res ipsa deprehendat quanti nobis sit perpetuum eum eadem amicitia cultum novo semite subinde revocari, licet hactenus prosperos militiæ nostræ successus divina benignitas tribuit, acquiescimus, ut bonavolo tractatu almæ pacis redintegrandæ rati nes opportuna in. antur, eumque in sinum advitandum viarum temporumque dispendia, nunc in co sum. ut ut serenissimæ Principi Dominæ Elizabethæ Claræ Eugeniæ natæ, Infanti Hispaniarum, Archiducissæ Austriæ, Ducissæ Burgundiæ, Stiriæ, Carinthiæ, Carniolæ, & Wirtingburgiæ, & Provinciarum Belgiæ, Burgundiarumque Dominæ, Consobrinæ ac sorori nostræ charissimæ, ut istic in aula sua, quersum vestra quæque Serenitas si ita libuerit suos cum plena facultate ablegare poterit primum eumque proximum assequenda pacis gradum cessationem ab armis æquis conditionibus nomine nostro Cæsarii stabiliendum permittemus, prope diem expedituri Legatum nostrum, virum nobilem, qui diligentissime in gravissimo hoc negotio mentem nostram plenius aperiet, atque inde ad Serenitatem vestram animum nostrum ad redintegranda pacis studia proclivem, qui nom aliter quam quibuscunque benevolentie officiis cum Serenitate vestra certa se studes magis magisque testificetur, cujus interim consilia generosa præpotens Deus publico orbis commodo in fælicissimos eventus dispensat.

Dat *Vienna*, 14 *Jan.* 1621.

The Earl of Worcester, Arundel *and* Surrey, Montgomery, *to the King.*

May it please your excellent Majesty,

ACcording to the orders and Constitutions made and established by your Majesty, and all the Companions of the Order, at the last general Chapter held at *Whitehall*, the 21 of *May* last past, we are bold to inform your Majesty, that we having diligently viewed divers of the Records of the said Order, do in the black book find, that the keeping of the little Park at *Windsor*, next adjoyning unto the Castle, is, in direct words, annexed for ever to the office of the Usher for the said Order. So humbly kissing your Royal hands, We rest,

Your Majesties humble and faithful Subjects and servants,

Whitehall, 1. July, 1622. E. Worcester, Arundel *and* Surrey, Montgomery.

King James, *to the Earl of* Bristol.

WE have received yours brought us by *Griesley*, and the Copy of yours to our dear Son: and we cannot forbear to let you know how well we esteem your dutifull, discreet and judicious relation, and humble advice to our self and our Son: whereupon having ripely deliberated with our self, and communicated with our dear Son, we have resolved, with the great liking of our Son, to rest upon that security (in point of doubt of the *Infanta's* taking a Religious house) which you in your judgment shall think meet. We have farther thought meet to give you knowledge, that it is our special desire that the betrothing of the *Infanta* with words *de præsenti*, should be upon one of the daies in Christmas *new stile*, that holy and joyfull time best fitting so notable and blessed an action.

But first, we will that you repair presently to that King, and give him knowledg of the safe arrival of our dear Son to our Court, so satisfied and taken with the great entertainments, personal kindness, favour and respect he hath received from that King and Court, as he seems not able to magnifie it sufficiently, which makes us not know how sufficiently to give thanks; but we will that by all means you endeavour to express our thankfulness to that King, and the rest to whom it belongs, in the best and most ample manner you can. And hereupon you may take occasion to let that King know, that according to our constant affection to make a firm and indissoluble amity between our Families, Nations and Crowns, and not seem to abandon our honour, nor at the same time we give joy to our onely son, to give our only Daughter her portion in tears: By the advice of that Kings Ambassadours, we have entred a Treaty concerning the restitution of the *Palatinate*, as will more particularly appear to you by the Copies herewith sent. Now we must remember you, that we ever understood and expected, that upon the marriage of our Son with the *Infanta*, we should have a clear restitution of the *Palatinate*, & Electoral dignity to our son-in-law, to be really procured by that King, according to the obligation of our honour, as you have well expressed in your reasons why the person of our Son-in-law should not be left out of the Treaty, but that the Emperor should find out a great title, or by increasing the number of Electorate titles wherewith to satisfie the Duke of *Bavaria.* We now therefore require you, that presently in your first audience you procure from that King a punctual answer what course that King will take for the restitution of the *Palatinate* and Electorate to our son-in law; and in case that either the Emperour or the Duke of *Bavaria* oppose any part of the expected restitution, what course that King will take to give us assurance for our content in that point, whereof we require your present answer; and that you so press expedition herein, that we may all together receive the full joy of both in Christmass, resting our self upon that faithfull diligence of yours we have approved in all your service. Though almost wish we must remember to you, as a good ground for you to work on, that our Son did write us out of *Spain,* that that King would give us a Blank in which we might form our own Conditions concerning the *Palatinate*, and the same our Son confirms to us now. What observation and performance that King will make, we require you to express, and give us a speedy account, &c. *Given, &c.*

Earl of Bristol, *in answer to King* James.

May it please your most excellent Majesty,

I have received your Majesties Letters of the 8. of *October* on the 21 of the same moneth, some hours within night; and have thought fit to dispatch back unto your Majesty with all possible speed, referring the answer to what your Majesty hath by these Letters commanded me, to a Post that I shall purposely dispatch when I shall have negotiated the particulars with this King, and his Ministers; wherein God willing all possible diligence shall be used.

But forasmuch as I find both by your Majesties Letter, as likewise by Letters which I have received from the Prince his Highness, that you continue your desires of having the Match proceeded in, I held it my duty that your Majesty should be informed, that although I am set free in as much as concerneth the doubt of the *Infanta's* entring into Religion, for the delivering of the powers left with me by his Highness, yet by this new direction I now received from your Majesty, that the Deposories should be deferr'd till Christmass, the said powers are made altogether uselefs and invalid, it being a clause in the bodies of the said powers, that they shall only remain in force till Christmass and no longer, as your Majesty may see by the copie I send herewith inclosed.

Your Majesty, I conceive, will be of opinion, that the suspending of the execution of the powers untill the force and validity of them be expired, is a direct and effectual revoking of them; which not to do, how far his Highness is in his Honour engaged, your Majesty will be best able to judge by viewing the powers themselves. Further, if the date of these powers do expire, besides the breach of the Capitulations, although the match it self, jealousies, and mistrusts be hazarded, yet the Princesses coming at the Spring, will be almost impossible: For by that time new Commissions and powers shall be after Christmass granted by the Prince, which must be to the satisfaction of both parties, I conceive so much of the year will be spent, that it will be impossible for the fleets and other preparations to be in a readiness against the Spring; for it is not to be imagined that they will here proceed effectually with their preparations, untill they be sure of the Desposorio's, especially when they shall have seen them several times deferred on the Prince his part, and that upon pretexts that are not new, or grown since the granting of the Powers, but were before in being, and often under debate, and yet were never insisted upon, to make stay of the business; so that it will seem that they might have better hindred the granting of them, then the execution of them. Now, if there were not staggering in former resolutions, the which although really there is not, yet can it not but be suspected; and the clearing of it between *Spain* and *England* will cost much time. I most humbly crave your Majesties pardon, if I write unto you with the plainess of a true-hearted and faithfull servant, who ever hath co-operated honestly unto your Majesties ends. I knew them, I know your Majesty hath been long time of opinion, that the greatest assurance you could get, that the King of *Spain* would effectually labour the entire restitution of the Palatinate, was, that he really proceeded to the effecting of the match; and my instructions under your Majesties hands, were, to insist upon restoring the Prince Palatine; but not to annex it to the treaty of the match, as that thereby the match should be hazarded; for that your Majesty seemed confident that here it would never grow to a perfect conclusion without a setled resolution to give your Majesty satisfaction in the business of the *Palatinate.*

The

The same course I observed in the carriage of the business by his Highness and my Lord Duke at their being here, who though they insisted on the business of the Palatinate, yet they held it fit to treat of them distinctly, and that the marriage should proceed as a good pawn for the other.

Since their departure my Lord Ambassadour, Sir *Walter Aston*, and my self, have been pressed to have this Kings resolution, in writing, concerning the *Palatinate*; and the dispatches which your Majesty will receive herewith, concerning that business, were writ before the receit of your Majesties Letters; and doubtless it is now a great part of their care, that that business may be well entred before the *Infanta's* coming into *England*: And his Highness will well often remember, that the Conde *de Olivarez* often protested a necessity of having this busi fs compounded and setled before the marriage, saying, otherwise they might give a Daughter, and a War within three moneths after, if this ground and subject of quarrel should still be left on foot. The same language he hath ever held with *Sir Walter Aston* and my self, and that it was a firm peace and amity, as much as an alliance, which they sought with his Majesty. So that it is not to be doubted, but that this King, concluding the match, resolveth to employ his uttermost power, for your satisfaction, in the restitution of the Prince Palatine.

The question now will be, whether the business of the Prince Palatine having relation to many great Princes that are interessed therein, living at distance, and being (indeed) for the condition and nature of the business it self, impossible to be ended but by a formal treaty, which of necessity will require great length, whether the conclusion of the match shall any way depend upon the issue of this business, which I conceive to be far from your majesties intention; for so the Prince might be long kept unbestowed by any aversness of those which might have particular interest in the Princes remaining unmarried, or dislike with his matching with *Spain*. But that which I understand to be your Majesties aim, is onely to have the conclusion of this match accompanied with as strong an engagement as can be procured from this King, for the joyning with your Majesty not onely in all good Offices for the entire restitution of the *Palatinate*, but otherwise, if need require, of his Majesties assistance herein.

These days past I have laboured, with all earnestness, and procured this Kings publique answer, which I am told is resolved of, and I shall within these few dayes have it to send to your Majesty, as also a private Proposition which will be put into your hands; and shall not fail further to pursue your Majesties present directions, of procuring this Kings Declaration, in what sort your Majesty may rely upon this Kings assistance, in case the Emperour or the Duke of *Bavaria* hinder the entire restitution of the Prince Palatine. But I conceive (if it be your intention) that I should first here procure this Kings peremptory answer in the whole business, and how he will be assistant unto your Majesty in case of the Emperours or the Duke of *Bavaria's* aversness. And that if I should send it to your Majesty, and receive again your answer, before I deliver the powers for the Desposorios, the match would thereby if not be hazarded, yet I conceive the *Infanta's* going at Spring would be rendred altogether impossible. For if upon the arrival of the Approbation I cannot refuse them, but upon some grounds; If I alledge your Majesties desire of having the Desposorios deferred until Christmass, they know, as well as my self, that his Highness Proxy is then out of date, besides the infringing of the Capitulations; and they will judge it is a great scorn put upon this King, who ever since the Princes granting of the powers hath called himself the *Infanta's* Desposado, and to that effect the Prince hath writ unto him in some of his Letters. Besides, it will be held here a point of great dishonour unto the *Infanta*, if the powers called for by her friends should be detained by the Prince his part: and whosoever else may have deserved it, she certainly hath not deserved disrespect nor discomfort. Further, upon my refusal to deliver the powers, all preparations which now go on cheerfully and apace will be stayed, there will enter in so much distrust, and so many troubles and jealousies, that if the main business run not hazard by them, at least much time will be spent to cleer them.

I must therefore, in discharge of my duty, tell your Majesty, that all your Majesties businesses here are in a fair way; the Match, and all that is capitulated therein, they profess punctually to perform.

In the business of the *Palatinate*, I continue my earnest and faithfull endeavours, and they protest they infinitely desire, and will, to the utmost of their powers, endeavour to procure your Majesties satisfaction.

The Prince is like to have a most worthy and vertuous Lady, and who much loveth him, and all things else depending upon this match are in a good and hopefull way.

This is now the present state of your Majesties affairs, as it appeareth unto me and to Sir *Walter Aston*, with whom I have communicated this Dispatch, as I do all things else concerning your Majesties service. And I must cleerly let your Majesty understand, I conceive by
the

the retaining of the powers when this King shall call for them, and offering to defend the Deposorios until *Christmas*, that your Majesties business will run a hazard, what by the distaste and disgust that will be raised here, and what by the art and industry of those which are enemies to the Match, whereof every Court hath plenty in Christendom.

That therefore which I presume with all humility, is, That you would be pleased to give me order, with all possible speed, that when the business shall come cleered from *Rome*, and that the powers of the marriage shall be demanded of me, in the behalf of this King, that I may deliver them, and no ways seek to interrupt or suspend the *Deposories*, but assist and help to a perfect conclusion of the Match.

And for the business of the Palatinate, I continue my earnest and faithful endeavours to engage this King as far as shall be possible, both for the doing of all good offices, and for the Palatinates entire restitution; herein I will not fail (as likewise for this Kings declaration of assistance, in case the Emperor or Duke of *Bavaria* shall oppose the said restitution) to use all possible means; and I conceive the dispatch of the Match will be a good pawn in the business, and the help and assistance which the Princes being once betrothed, would be able to give in this Court to all your Majesties business, would be of good consideration.

So fearing I have already presumed too far upon your Majesties patience, I humbly crave your Majesties pardon, and recommend you to the holy protection of God, resting

Madrid, Octob. 29.
1 6 2 3.

Your Majesties most humble and faithful subject and servant,

BRISTOL.

King James *his Instructions to the Archbishop of* Canterbury, *concerning Orders to be observed by Bishops in their Dioceses.* 1622.

1. THat the Lords, the Bishops, be commanded to their several Sees, excepting those that are in necessary attendance at Court.

2. That none of them reside upon his land or lease that he hath purchased, nor on his Commendam if he hold any; but in one of his Episcopal Houses if he have any, and that he waste not the woods where any are left.

3. That they give their charge in their Triennial Visitations, and at other convenient times, both by themselves and the Archdeacons, and that the Declaration for setling all questions in difference be strictly observed by all parties.

4. That there be a special care taken by them all, that the Ordinations be solemn, and not of unworthy persons.

5. That they take great care concerning the Lecturers in their several Diocess, for whom we give these special Directions following.

First, That in all Parishes the after-noon Sermons may be turned into Catechising by Question and Answer, when and wheresoever there is no great cause apparent to break this ancient and profitable order.

Secondly, that every Bishop ordain in his Diocess, that every Lecturer do read Divine Service according to the Liturgy printed by authority, in his Surplice and Hood, before the Lecture.

Thirdly, That where a Lecture is set up in a Market Town, it may be read by a company of grave and Orthodox Divines neer adjoyning, and in the same Diocess, and that they preach in Gowns, not in Cloaks, as too many use to do.

Fourthly, that if a Corporation do maintain a single Lecturer, he be not suffered to Preach till he profess his willingness to take upon him a living with cure of Souls within that Incorporation, and that he actually take such Benefice or Cure so soon as it shall be fairly procured for him.

Fifthly, That the Bishops do countenance and encourage the grave and Orthodox Divines of their Clergy, and that they use means by some of the Clergy, or others, that they may have knowledge how both Lecturers and Preachers within their Diocess do behave themselves in their Sermons, that so they may take order for any abuse accordingly.

Sixthly, That the Bishops suffer none under Noblemen, or men qualified by Law, to have any private Chaplain in his house.

Seventhly, That they take special care that Divine Service be diligently frequented, as well for Prayers and Catechismes as for Sermons, and take particular note of all such as absent themselves, as Recusants, or others.

Eighthly, That every Bishop that by our grace and favour, and good opinion of his service shall be nominated by us to another Bishoprick, shall from that day of nomination not presume to make any Lease for three lives or one and twenty years, or concurrent Lease, or any way renew any estate, or cut any Wood or Timber, but meerly receive his Rents due, and to quit the place. For we think it an hateful thing, that any man leaving the Bishoprick should almost undo his Successor. And if any man shall presume to break this Order, We will refuse him Our Royal assent, and keep him at the place he hath so abused.

Ninthly and lastly, We command you to give us an account, every year, the second of *January*, of the performance of these our commands. Subscribed at *Dorchester*.

J. R.

King James, to the Palsgrave.

My most dear Son,

WE have been careful, and are at this present, to perform the promise which we made unto you, to imploy all our power to re-establish you into your estate and dignities; and having, by the patience and industry which we have used, reduced matters within a more neer circle, and of a less extent then the generality in which they were heretofore: We have thought good to give you knowledge of such things, whereof hope is given to us that we shall in all appearance obtain them, to the end you may have recourse to your wisdom, and after a mature deliberation make choice agreeable to the providence, honour, and safety of your estates, duly weighing and examining all circumstances: and therefore we present unto you these Propositions, to wit, In the first place a due submission to the Emperour, under convenient limitations, which first shall be granted and agreed in conformity to that which is Noble, with a safe conduct and assurance requisite and sufficient for the free and safe going and return of your Person and Train. This being done, we make you offer of a present and full restitution of all the Palatinate unto the person of your son, and that you shall be his Administrator during your life; and that after the death of the Duke of *Bavaria*, your son be re-established in the Electoral dignity; And for the better confirming the sound Amity, and assuring your Possessions, and enjoying of all according to the contract, which is presently to be made, and also to serve for a preparation for the bettering of the said conditions to your person, which will be, in all likelyhood, when the marriage will be resolved and concluded to be made betwixt your eldest Son our Grand-child, and one of the Emperours daughters. In contemplation whereof they have approached a degree neerer, to wit, that the Electoral dignity shall come again to your person after the Duke of *Bavaria's* death. In which Treaty of marriage, to clear the principal difficulty, which consisted with the education of your Son with the Emperour, we have taken from them all hope therein (wherein we assure our selves you will be content) and are purposed that he shall have his education with our Son, and with and in the presence of the Infanta, when she shall be in our Court, We have exactly shewed you the state of this Negotiation, which chiefly concerns you and yours, to the end you may fix your eyes upon your necessity and bare condition and manner of living, which dependeth on the courtesie and assistance of others, and that you may judge advisedly, whether your ready entrance into the possession of your own, and with a kind of present liberty of living (with insurance in time to recover the possession of it) shall not be more convenient for you then a hazardous long expectation, upon other uncertain means: The former whereof I prefer before the later. We pray you to consider, what probable and feasible means we may undertake to reduce your condition to that state as you promise your self; wherein we doubt not, but you will weigh our forces, and those of our Allies, and such other whereof we may hope to be assured, to the end, that if it should happen that we cannot obtain to the entire of that we desire, by way of Treaty, or that we should take another course, you may be partaker of Counsels, as well as the issues and uncertain events. And forasmuch as we are desirous to consider with you for your personal estate, and as we are obliged to have regard to the right of our only daughter, and to the inheritance of your children, with the hope of their posterity, by what way it may be most easily established, and by what fit means provision may be made best to that effect. And herein I remain your most affectionate Father,

From *White-Hall*, Novemb. 20.   *Jacobus Rex.*

The Palsgraves Answer to King James.

Sir,

I Take as a great honour and favour your Majesties Letter of the 20th of *November*, delivered unto me by the hands of your Embassadour, Sir *Dudley Carleton*, who hath further explained your Majesties intention, touching that which concerneth my restitution unto my honours and patrimonial estate, that you continue firm and constant (in conformity to your promises) to labour and effect by one way or other, so that the said restitution may be entire and total, as well in that which concerneth the Electoral dignity as the Palatinates; and that the Propositions which your Majesty makes by your Letter (to content my self to be Administrator to my Son, and he to be invested with the said dignity, and put into present possession of the Palatinate) is but, in all events, if so be your Majesty could not attain to the total restitution (the desired effect of your intentions) leaving me nevertheless to be at liberty to chuse the lesser of the two evils (if I may be permitted to term them so) the one by the total restitution of my Estates, but with diminution, or rather annihilation (for so in effect it will be) in respect of my person of the Electoral dignity, th'other, of the recovery of both by war, the events whereof are uncertain. First, I most humbly thank your Majesty, for the paternal care which you continue and shew, in this occasion; and which doth more comfort me, and my dear wife, in our afflictions, then the fear of humane events can grieve or incline us to be willing to recover the loss of goods with the loss of honours. I will therefore use the liberty which your Majesty is pleased to give me, in answering every particular point of your Letter. In the first whereof I observe the proceeding of my enemies, who require a personal submission (intended to precede all other things) under the safe conduct of the Emperour; whereas by natural order used in these occasions, the restitution which is material and substantial, ought by reason to precede the other, being but a point of ceremony; at the least it is necessary, that all things be resolved, and concluded under such assurances as shall be held convenient; and then if the intentions on the Emperours part be real and sincere, and without any aim to take advantage upon my person (as the Emperour *Charles* 5. did upon the Lant-grave of *Hessen*, under the subtilty of a distinction of a syllable in safe conduct *Ewig* for *Einig*) the said submission may as well be made by a Deputy as otherwise, whereby I shall be freed from the apprehension which the execution at *Prague* and other crueltie exercised by the Imperialists, may easily impress in the mind of him who is unwilling to lose himself by a *quiete de Cœur*. Besides, a simple consent to such a submission under the specified condition, to yield the Electorate to the Duke of *Bavaria*, will be sufficient to prejudice my cause for ever. For the Electors of *Saxony* and *Brandenburgh*, who have always protested against the translation of the Electorate; and the other Princes of *Germany* who have like feeling, will disavow their protestations in regard of him who shall abandon his own pretentions, and in stead of favouring me upon some breach of the Treaty, or otherwise, may be my opposites. Moreover, the experience of things past teacheth us what issue we may hereafter expect of the like conditions, consented to on our part; The Emperour having manifestly abused us in two already. First, in the instrument which I signed for the conditional resignation of the Crown of *Bohemia*, in the year 1621. Then in my ratification of the suspension of Arms this last Summer. The first having served the Emperour to accelerate his Treaty then on foot with *Bethlem Gabor*: The second, to intimidate the Electors of *Saxony* and *Brandenburgh*, that they might not undertake any thing against the Emperour, both the one and the other being divulged to the same effect, according to the knowledge which the Emperour had of these designs before any thing was therein resolved and concluded: And so will the Emperour in all appearance make his profit of this present proposition, and strike with one stone two blows, by hindering the progress of *Gabor* on the one side, and by continuing on the other, the intimidation of the Princes of *Germany*, who may with reason excuse themselves if they move not for him, who hath bound himself hand and foot, and consented to a submission, which being yielded to, it will be always in the Emperours power to break or go on, as he shall hold it expedient for himself. I do also promise my self that your Majesty will have regard that by such submission and intreaty, by undue proscription and banishment (which being done in prejudice of the constitutions of the Empire, are therefore held by the Electors of *Saxony* and *Brandenburgh* of no validity) be not approved, and thereby a mark of infamy set upon me and my posterity. Touching the second point, your Majesty may be pleased to remember, that on the part of *Spain* hope hath always been given me from the beginning, of a total and intire restitution to my own person; yea the Earl of *Bristol* hath assured me by his Letters from *Madrid*, in *November* 1622. when the marriage was not so much advanced as at this time, That the King of *Spain* (in case of refusal of the total restitution) would joyn his forces with those of your Majesty against the Emperor to constrain him thereunto: And yet in ste d of the said restitution, the transition of my Electorate to the Duke of *Bavaria* was since at *Ratisbone* agreed, and congratulated unto him from *Bruxels*; the inferior Palatinate dismembred by the grant of the *Bergstreat*, one of the best pieces thereof, to the Elector of *Mentz*, the superior (with the Bailywicks) granted to the Duke of *Newburgh*, thereby to engage them further in the quarrel by the particular defence of that which generally the Imperialists have usurped upon me; they confiscate and seise the goods of my subjects, and those that follow my party, sparing neither widow nor orphans.

It seems therefore necessary, above all things, to have sufficient assurance, for the total restitution of my Electorate and Palatinates, before any new Treaty of marriage be proposed: Of the which Treaties, as they are ordinarily handled and managed by the house of *Austria*, and drawn to length and delays, with the onely aim to the augmentation of their greatness, without respect to civil honesty, word or promise, I have a doleful experience in my own house, in the person of one of my predecessors, *Frederick* the Second, who contributed more to the first foundation which was laid, for the greatness of the house of *Austria*, then any other German Prince; and for recompence, was allured and drawn by the space of many years with Treaties and promises of marriage, without any real intention (as was seen by the effect) ever to bring them to execution. Seeing therefore, that he who had so well deserved of the house of *Austria*, (which, in all external appearance, held him in greater estimation then any other German Prince) was (nevertheless) so unworthily used by them in a Treaty of marriage; I who have been unduly put into the Ban of the Empire, and spoiled of all my honours and goods, by the eagerness, hatred and usurpation of the Emperor himself (whose daughter is propounded for the marriage in question) know not what to hope but the same effect of fraud and deceit which my forenamed predecessor found, with a sorrowful repentance of the evil when it was past remedy. And the Emperor wanteth but two or three years of leisure, which he shall easily gain by a Treaty of a marriage, to establish in *Germany* the translation of my Electoral dignity and Patrimonial estate, without any hope ever hereafter to recover the like opportunity as at this time, that my pretensions are not prejudiced by a long interposition of time, and that the memory of undue proceeding in the publication of the Ban against my person, and the said translation of my Electoral dignity, and seisure of my patrimonial inheritance, are yet fresh in the affections and minds of the Princes of *Germany*, who are by the consideration of their own interests moved with the greater compassion to see the wounds of my miseries yet fresh and bleeding, and with passion and earnest desire to see them remedied. And in this place, I will say something in answer to the last point of your Majesties Letter, wherein you commanded me to consider the means probable and feasible, whereby my condition may be reduced to the former state, and to weigh your Majesties forces with those of your Allies, and others whereof your Majesty may hope and be assured.

If your Majesty hopeth for my restitution in *Germany*, as an effect of the marriage with *Spain*, nothing else is to be done but to attend the event with patience: And if you continue to distinguish between the Spaniards and the Imperialists, there is no more to be said on this subject, but as they have with joynt consent conspired my ruine with the same forces, the same counsels, and the same designs, your Majesty will find (if you please to unmask the fair seeming, and hidden malice of the Spaniard, the same effect, as in the end you found the open and declared violence and hostility of the Imperialists, who besieged your Majesties Garrisons in my Towns taken into your protection. I will use the liberty you have given me to discourse of: your Majesties forces, and those of your Allies, and what may further with good probability be hoped from other friends and well-willers.

In the last rank I place what may be hoped from the Princes of *Germany*, who, to wit, the two Electors of *Saxony* and *Brandenburgh*, and in effect all the rest, except those of the Catholick league, have sufficiently declared the disavowing of the Emperors proceeding against me, and their opinions that the peace of *Germany* dependeth upon my restitution; besides the Levies which they made in the beginning of the last summer, though by the unlucky accident of the Duke *Christian* of *Brunswick*, they were soon after dismissed. And certainly no want of any other thing to be converted to my aid, but the countenance of a great Prince, to support them against the power of the house of *Austria*, the same affections remaining

still

still in them, and the same resolution to embrace the first good occasion that shall be presented for the liberty of *Germany*. Will there want hands for the accomplishing of such a work, when it shall be undertaken openly and earnestly? seeing that the number of those that have their interest conjoyned with mine, is great and mighty: For the greater part of the people, both horse and foot, which marched under the Catholick banner, were of a contrary Religion to the Catholick, and of affection (as it is notorious to all the world) more inclined to the ruine of those Leagues, then to their preservation. But the conduct of some powerfull Prince is necessary, as well to the men of war, as we have seen by experience the last year. The King of *Denmark* is he upon whom all have set their eyes; but he being a Prince full of circumspection, and unwilling to enter into play alone, answereth unto all instances which are made unto him to that end, That as the other Princes have their eyes upon him, so hath he his upon your Majesty.

It is not for me to judge; but since you have commanded me, I will weigh them by the balance of common judgement. That the felicity wherewith God hath blessed the person of your Majesty, having conjoyned the three Crowns of *England*, *Scotland* and *Ireland* upon one head; the power of the one of the three alone having done great matters in the affairs of *Europe* on this side the Sea, yea when it was counterbalanced by the other, gives demonstration what your Majesty may do with the joynt forces of the three together, when you shall be pleased to take a resolution therein, chiefly the question being for the interest of your own Children; and by the voluntary contribution which we have already had in our support from your Majesty, we may easily comprehend what may be promised of them when the publick authority of your Majesty shall be conjoyned with their particular affections; there being no Prince in the world more loved and reverenced of his subjects, nor more sovereign over their affections and means for the service of your person and Royal house. Touching the Allies, it is to my great grief that the unhappiness of this time hath separated a great part of them, the united Provinces of *Germany*, who make profession of the same Religion whereof they acknowledge your Majesty for Defender and Protector. But the same affection remaineth still in them entire and firm, though they have been constrained to yield to the present necessity of their affairs; and the occasion presenting it self, your Majesty may account of them.

The rest, the Estates of the united Provinces, to whom we have recourse in our afflictions, who support themselves by the help of God, and the situation of their Country, and Forces of their people alone, untill this time, against the puissance of *Spain*, seconded by the Imperialists. And in stead of fainting under such a burthen, or of giving ear unto the overtures and submissions which from day to day are presented unto them, they now put themselves to the offensive, by a good Fleet prepared and ready to set sail to the *West-Indies*, to the end they may at least interrupt the peaceable and annual return of the gold and silver of those parts, by which the house of *Austria* doth continually advance their greatness. This is commended by all good men and lovers of the publick liberty, as the sole and only means to cast to the ground the fearfull power of *Spain*, even as a great tree of large extent cut up by the root; but is held too great for such a little extent of Country as this is, and yet practically, and to be done by forces answerable to the importance of such an enterprize: And if your Majesty would be pleased to use the Forces of this estate by sea and land, to the opposition of their enemies, and by consequence of mine, their profession of a loyall and sincere affection, with the hazard of their lives and goods for the service of your Majesty, grounded upon the experience of things past, their present interest, and the judgement which may be made of the future, makes me assured that your Majesty may absolutely dispose of them; and by their means being firmly conjoyned with your Majesty, give the Law to *Europe*.

It is in obedience to your Majesties commandment that I have enlarged my self so far into this discourse, which I will send with my most humble thanks for the continuance of your most gracious and paternall bounty, particularly shewed in the care you have of the education of my eldest son in your Court, who with all the rest are at your Majesties disposing; and we hope to live, notwithstanding our hard and dolefull condition, to yield unto your Majesty the fruits of a devout and filial gratitude; and I will remain, untill the last day of my life,

From the Hague, Decemb. 30.   *Your Majesties most,* &c.
1623. *new stile.*

                                            FREDERICK.

                                                          Post-script.

Post-script.

I am advertised from a good party, that the Elector of *Mentz*, and the other Princes of the Popish league, are very instant with the Elector of *Savony* and *Brandenburgh*, to perswade them to acknowledge the Duke of *Bavaria* as an Elector of the Empire: which if they obtain, it were easie to judge how much it would prejudice my affairs, and the common cause of the Empire. I therefore most humbly beseech your Majesty, that you will be pleased to prevent and hinder such an evil, by the interposition of good offices, and exhortations to the said secular Electors, be it by some Embassadour, by serious Letters, or such other way as you shall hold meet and suitable to the importance of the matter, which above all requireth singular celerity. Your Majesty shall increase more and more my obligations, and that of the publick of *Germany*, &c.

King James, *to my Lord* Bacon, *by occasion of a Book; it was the* Organon.

MY Lord, I have received your Letter, and your Book, then which ye could not have sent a more acceptable Present unto Me; how thankful I am for it, cannot better be expressed by Me, then by a firm resolution I have taken, first, to read it through, with care and attention, though I should steal some hours from My sleep, having otherwise as little spare time to read it as ye had to write it; and then to use the liberty of a true friend, in not sparing to ask you the question in any point whereof I shall stand in doubt, *Nam ejus est explicare cujus est condere*: As for the other part, I will willingly give a due Commendation to such places as, in My Opinion, shall deserve it. In the mean time, I can with Comfort assure you, that ye could not make choice of a Subject more befitting your place, and your universal and Methodick knowledge; and in the general, I have already observed, that ye jump with me in keeping the middle way, between the two extreams; as also in some particulars, I have found that ye agree fully with my opinion; and so praying God to give your work as good success as your heart can wish, and your labours deserve, I bid you heartily farewell.

James R.

King James *his Letter to his Trusty and Well-beloved,* Thomas Coventry, *Our Attorney General.*

TRusty and Well-beloved, We greet you well; whereas our Right Trusty, and Right Well-beloved Cosen, the Viscount of St. *Alban*, upon a sentence given in the Upperhouse of Parliament full three years since, and more, hath endured loss of his place, Imprisonment and Confinement also for a great time, which may suffice for the satisfaction of Justice, and example to others; We being alwayes graciously inclined to temper Mercy with Justice, and calling to minde his former good services, and how well and profitably he hath spent his time since his Troubles, Are pleased to remove from him that blot of Ignominy which yet remaineth upon him, of incapacity, and disablement; and to remit to him all penalties whatsoever inflicted by that sentence; having therefore formerly pardoned his Fine, and released his Confinement; These are to will and require you to prepare for Our Signature a Bill containing a Pardon in due Form of Law, of the whole sentence: For which this shall be your sufficient Warrant.

Ab ignoto, *from Madrid.*

THe *Spaniard* begins now to be sensible of the great dis-obligation and gross oversight he committed in suffering the Prince to go away without his *Infanta*: For it hath given an occasion of advantage to the *English* (who now seem indifferent whether they match with him or no) to proceed more stoutly, and to add to the former Articles which the Prince had sworn at his being here certain new Propositions about the *Palatinate*, which was thought to be unfit to motion at his being here, by reason of the engagement of his person.

Of the affairs of Spain, France, and Italy.

And there is a Commission sent to the Earl of *Bristol* to treat of these two businesses joyntly; and if the King of *Spain* give not a satisfactory answer therein, then he is to return home. *Buckingham* hath little obligation to *Spain*, therefore for his own particular he hath good reason, if he cannot prop himself this way, to find other means for his support: unkindnesses passed between him and *Olivarez*, and a hot heart-burning between him and *Bristol*, who told him here before the Prince, that being so far his superior in honour and might he might haply contemn him, but he could never hate him. Ever since his departure he hath attempted to crush *Bristol* to pieces, who is out of purse two thousand pound of his own since his coming hither, and he is so crossed that he cannot get a peny from *England*. If he cannot get a surrender of the *Palatinate* to the Kings mind, he is in a poor case; for he must hence presently: he is much favoured of the King here and *Olivarez*, therefore they will do much for him before *Buckingham* work his revenge upon him: he hath received lately more comfortable dispatches from *England*; and in the last the King sent him, he requires his advice in certain things. The Proxie the King of *Spain* had to marry the *Infanta* in the Princes name, is prorogued till *March*. There is great resentment of the delays in the Court here; and the *Infanta* hath given over studying of *English*. The two Embassadours here, ever since the Princes departure, have visited the *Infanta* as vassals; but now they carry themselves like Embassadours again. We are all here in suspence, and a kind of maze, to see the event of things; and how matters will be pieced together again, we know not.

Ab Ignoto, *Of the Affairs of* Spain, France, *and* Italy.

SIR,

Though it be now full three moneths since I received any line from you, yet I dare not, nor will I for that respect discontinue my writing to you; and because no private business occurreth, I will be bold to advise a line or two concerning the publick affairs of *Italy*: *Cassalle* is still made good against the *Spaniard*, not by the Duke of *Mantua*, for he poor Prince was long since bankrupt, but by the succours of *France* and this Seigniory, the former contributing monethly 40000 Dollars, the latter 20000, not only to maintain the *Cassalleschi*, but also to enable the Duke to stand fast against all other the *Spaniards* attempts; mean while we hear say boldly, that a league offensive and defensive against the *Spaniards* in *Italy* is concluded between the *French* and the *Venetians*; and that the *French* King hath already sent out two Armies, one under the Duke of *Guise* by Sea, who they say is landed at *Nizza*; the other under the Marquess *de Cœure*, who is marching hitherward through the *Valtoline*; and though I doubt something these proceedings of the *French*, yet I am sure the Seignior doth daily give out new Commissions for the levying of Souldiers in that number, that now every one demands what strange enterprize this State hath in hand, and all jump in this, that it is against the *Spaniard*. The Pope is still adverse to the *Spaniard*, and inclines strongly to the good of *Italy*, animating this State to meet the *French* with a declaration, and the *French* to conclude a peace on any honorable terms with us, that they may the more safely follow their present designs, which is to suppress the *Spaniards* in *Italy*. His Catholick Majesty hath lost a great deal of credit in these parts, by the loss of his Silver Fleete; and that he is in extreme want of money, is collected here from the present state of some of his publick Ministers. *Ognate* his ordinary Embassadour at *Rome*, being lately recalled, in stead of going home into *Spain*, hath retired himself privately to *Monte Pincio*, being in such premunire that he is not able to accommodate himself with necessaries for his journey. And *Mounterei*, who is to succeed him, is arrived as far as *Sienna*; but being foundred in his purse, is able to get no farther; mean while, living there in an Inne. Moreover, the Merchants in *Rome* are advised by their correspondents in *Spain*, to be wary in letting either of them have moneys; this is from a good hand in *Rome*. Sir *Kenhelm Digby* hath lately been at *Delos*, where he hath laden great store of Marble; he is said to be in very good plight and Condition. I trouble you no more.

Venice 5. January *Your faithful servant,* C. H.
1629. *Stilo novo.*

Ab ignoto, *concerning the Estate of* Rochel *after the surrender.*

SIR,

I Presume you have long since heard the particulars of *Rochel*; and that by far better relations then mine; notwithstanding you may be pleased to know what I have observed and learned there my self eight dayes after the Kings entrance, whither curiosity and some other causes drew me. For the siege and Dike, they *præ cæteris excellent*, were in all parts most royall, and far more perfect and uniform then relation could make me conceive: The misery of the Siege almost incredible, but to such only as have seen it, or some part thereof: Corn was worth after the rate of 800 Franks the bushel; an Oxe or Cow sold after the rate of 2000 Franks. The host(where I lay) sold a Jade horse, worth it may be four or five pounds, for 800 Franks, and for five and twenty weeks tasted no bread: of twelve persons in his family, only he and his wife are living; who also within two dayes had dyed, if the Town had not been rendred. He and his wife made a Collation the day before the Town was rendred, which cost him about six or seven pound sterling; their chear was a pound of bread, made of Straw, Sugar, and other Spices; half a pound of horse flesh, three or foure ounces of Comfits, and a pint of Wine, which they imagin'd was the last good chear they should make together; and in like case were all the rest of the Town, only two or three families of the better sort excepted; by which you may conjecture what rates such kind of provision were at. There were eaten between 3000 & 4000 Cow-hides, all the dogs, cats, mice and rats they could get; not a horse left alive, which was food for the better sort; only Madam *Rohan*, after having eaten her Coach-horse, and her servants the Leather of her Coach, removed, though full sore against her will, her lodging from *Rochel* to the Castle of *Niœul*, where she is under guard, and since (it is said) to the Bastile in *Paris*: God send her and hers to Heaven. There died, for want of food, in *Rochel* 15000. and rested living, when the King entred, between three and four thousand, of which there are since very many dead; they dayly discover new miseries, which when I was there were not spoken of; the mother and the child at the brest both dead, the child having eaten most part of the mothers brest; a souldier was found dead with a piece of his fellows flesh in his mouth; a Burger having a servant killed, powdred her, which fed him and his wife a long time, and dainty meat too: many languishing and finding themselves draw neer their ends, caused their coffins to be carried into the Churches, laid them down in them and so dyed; these were of the better sort. The common sort laid themselves down in Coffins in the Church-yards, and there dyed; others in the streets, others not able to go out of their houses, dyed and remained there, their friends being not able to remove them thence. So that when the first Forces of the King entered, there were in the Town of Corps unburied, some in the Church-yards, others in the streets, some in their houses, some on the floore, others in their beds, besides them that died without the Gates under hedges, and in ditches round about the Town, which I saw my self when I was there; half devoured with Ravens, and other beasts, and fowls of the aire; In fine, the like misery hath not been seen nor heard of.

The King, on All-Saints day, which was the day of his entry, with a wax Candle in his hand, together with the Cardinall and all the Nobility, in like manner, went all over the Town in procession with the B. Sacrament. The chief Temple of the *Hugenots* shall be converted into a Church Cathedral, and *Rochel* to be a Bishoprick. All the fortifications and walls to Landwards to be razed, and the Fosses filled, so that a plough may pass, as in arable Land. The Major, with some of the chiefest, are banish'd for ever, others for a certain time limited, though quietly to possesse their goods, moveable and immoveable, and a general remission of all crimes past: and all others that were in the Town before the descent of the English into *Rhee*, and when the Town was rendred, shall likewise enjoy the same priviledge, though no child or heir absent, is, or shall be, capable to inherit the goods or lands of his parents deceased, but all is at the Kings disposing. The King hath granted them free liberty of their Religion in the Town of *Rochel*, which in short time will all be rooted out; for no Forreiner (though naturalized) shall be admitted to repair and inhabit in *Rochel*, nor *French*, but *Roman* Catholicks The King hath added to the revenues of his Crown 20000 Franks *per annum*, which was a rent belonging to the Town-house, for the maintenance of the fortifications and State of *Rochel*. The Town-house is to be razed, and a pillar or pyramide with an ample inscription of the particulars of the siege and rebellion, there to be erected. The forts of the Isle of *Rhee* and *Oleron*, to be razed, and (as it is said) most of all the chief forces of *France*, except on the frontiers. Four Regiments are yet in *Rochel*, the rest of the Army (at least the most part) are gone to winter in those parts of *France* towards the Coasts of *Italy*, to be ready on all occasions to succour the Duke of *Mantua*, as it is thought. The Fathers of the society have very fair buildings given them for their establishing there, and 1000 Franks to begin to build; to which is added a revenue which I know not; the place is said to be where the Hereticks kept their schools of Divinity, and Councel of War, or rebellion. And where the *English* had their Church, the *Oratorians* are likewise established with large augmentations; the Capuchins are where was the chiefest Fort, called *Le Bastion de Levangile*; The Minors are where the Dike was, and divers other elsewhere. There are at least 8000 houses in *Rochel*, which are fain to fall to the King to dispose of for want of heirs. The *Parisians* are preparing a most sumptuous and magnificent reception for the King, which is the cause he hath not been at *Paris*, since his return from *Rochel*, but is at St. *Germains*, and thereabouts, till all things are ready for his entry, which is thought will exceed in bravery and magnificence all the presidents of many years. The *Jesuites* are by the body of *Paris* imployed to make the speeches and inscriptions for that purpose, which the body of the *Sorbon* take ill; The Prince of *Conde* doth daily get ground of *Rohan*, and hath lately taken prisoners (as it is said) thirty Captains and eight hundred soldiers. Those of *Montauban* boast (as it is said) that they have provision for three or four years, and will stand out till the last: though some of the best esteem think it is only to draw the King to the best composition they can.

To King James, ab ignoto.

Your Majesty,

BOth in the eminency of your regal dignity, and in the excellencie of your judgment, doth truly represent the common sense, whose part it is to judge and discern of all things; whereas the other senses do but report their particular objects. And in that manner do I humbly offer to your Majesties consideration in this importune *Crisis* of the affairs of Christendom, so much as I have observed in *France*, that may now concern your service, in which place I have been heretofore employed in your affairs.

And first considering the present estate of things in *France*, and weighing against it the seizure made of the *Valteline* by the King of *Spain*, the late invasion of the *Palatinate*, and now this new defeat arrived in *Bohemia*, I do put this for an infallible ground, that either the King of *France* will resolve out of jealousie of the progressions of the house of *Austria* effectually to succour the *Palatinate*, or else abandoning the affairs of *Germany* to their own success, and neglecting the increase of the house of *Austria* on that side, he will think more then to recompence himself, by taking this opportunity to extinguish the body of those of the Religion in *France*. And as undoubtedly he will resolve on one of those two points, so on both of them, for sundry reasons, he cannot. To move him to the succour of the *Palatinate*, the main motive will be, the jealousie between those two Monarchies, which can never die, so long as they do both subsist in no greater a disproportion of strength and power; As also that *France* shall by their usurpation of the *Palatinate* be on all sides circled by the house of *Austria*, and particularly on that part where *France* hath before usurped on the Empire; in which regard his interest of state is greater then your Majesties in the Conservation of the *Palatinate*, though your personal interest be incomparable with his. Then he cannot but think of the loss of his Correspondencies, and breach of his Confederacies in *Germany*, which have been very ancient, and very particular with the house of the *Palatine*, And if the reason of mutual gratitude, and vindication of injuries, may move *French*-men, there are plentifull arguments on both kinds to move them to defend the house of the *Palatine* against that of *Austria*. But now, on the other side to move him against those of the Religion at home, first doth present it self, his successfull beginning against them in the business of *Bearn*, then which nothing could be more unjust, both in regard of the matter it self, and of his own faith and promise, and of the desert of those of the Religion towards him, in these late troubles; nor could any thing be more suddenly, or violently (I do not say, cruelly) executed, then that was. And again the present terms, wherein that King, and those of the Religion do stand, will push him on. Then there will not want, to this purpose, the powerfull perswasions of the Pope, and his adherents, both by propounding overtures to lay asleep the jealousies of the house of *Austria*, and offering huge sums towards the charge of the War; which if he should attempt, and prevail therein, it would prove of far greater prejudice, for many reasons that may be given, in the interest of Estate, to your Majesty, though not in the interest of your affection, then the loss of the *Palatinate*.

What may in *France* be resolved upon these motives, is uncertain.

But I do conceive hereupon, that it may be usefull for your Majesties service, effectually to propound in *France* a Confederacy for the Conservation of the *Palatinate*, to which if they do hearken, your Majesty shall proceed in that design with greater strength and reputation, and occasion the King of *Spain* to proceed with greater remisness, or else absolutely to relinquish the *Palatinate* by a Treaty: But if in *France* it be not hearkened to, your Majesty may take it for an assured argument, that they mean to proceed against those of the Religion; in which case, your Majesty may make use of the same Embassage, to revive again some of their factions in the Court, whereby those of the Religion may be strengthened in their defence; and it will not be hard to effect, if it be well proceeded in. And herein doth properly offer it self the person of the Duke of *Bovillon*, who for his great experience and wit, and intelligence in that Court, is best able to guide and further your Majesties intentions; and for his interest in the person of the *Palatine*, and in the conversation of those of the Religion, doth precisely square with your Majesties ends; whose advice you may first suddenly and secretly inquire. &c.

To King James, ab ignoto.

My most gracious King,

THese things which your Majesty did lately command to be spoken unto you, and now to be repeated in writing, are not such as they can be made to appear by Legal and Judicial Proofs; both because they by whose testimony they may be confirmed do, for fear of a most potent adversary, withdraw themselves; and also, because they think it a crime to come into the Embassadours house; yea, even they are afraid to do it who have commandment from your Majesty: But neither was it lawfull for the Embassadours themselves to speak these things, especially, not to such as they directed, when the order of the affairs required it, because they had never the freedom to speak unto your Majesty, and no audience was given or granted them in the absence of the Duke of *Buckingham*: An example, certainly, unusual with other Kings, and never to be taken in good part, unless it be, perhaps, when the King himself wanting experience, and being of weak judgment, and no wisdom, some one that is familiar and inward with the King, a man wise and circumspect, of great judgment, and no less experience, supplies the Kings place. But here, when all things go preposterously, and the King himself being a most prudent and experienced Prince, he that is familiar, or Favourite, doth in all things shew himself a rash, heady young man, a Novice in managing of business, and to the Crown of *Spain* most offensive: Certainly, by all just right, this man was to be kept away from the audience of the Embassadour of the State. We may also be bold to say, that his presence, so earnestly desired of him, doth argue a great fear in him, and a great distrust in him, as well of his own upright conscience, as also the Kings wisdom. Hence, therefore, it is come to pass, that your Majesties most faithfull Vassals dare not so much as indirectly disclose their minds to the King, though they take it in very ill part, that a very good King should be driven into such streights, and that a man pleasing himself in his own designs should use the favours of Princes so sinisterly, as he doth, of set purpose, to stir up breach of friendship, and enmity, between most Mighty Kings.

Besides, who can, without a discontented mind, endure, that the greatest affairs, and of greatest moment (if any in the Christian world can be so termed) shall be ordered, or concluded, at the pleasure of your Parliament, and from thence all things carried on with a headlong violence, at his will and pleasure, and a most deadly War to be preferred before a most happy Peace; when as, nevertheless, I am not ignorant, that not so much the restitution of the *Palatinate*, as the very claim to it, will very difficultly be obtained, or recovered, by force of Arms. Let your Majesty exactly consider, as it is used to do, whether this be not an evident argument of that I have said, that the Conference or Treaty about the *Palatinate* was taken from the Councel of State, a society of most prudent men, onely for this cause, that almost every one of them had, with one consent, approved the Proposition of the most Catholick King, and did not find in it any cause of dissolving that Treaty. Hereupon, the Parliament of this Kingdom was procured by the Duke, because he thought his plots would be most acceptable to the Puritans, not without great injury to your Councel of State, from which he fled, and disclaimed by way of an appeal; and with such success, that we may be bold to say, that the Parliament is now above the King; nay, which is more, that this daring Duke propounded many

things

things to the Parliament in the Kings name, your Majesty being neither acquainted with them, nor willing to them: Yea, and that he propounded many things contrary to your Majesties service. Who is there that doth not see and commend the royal disposition of the Prince, adorned with so great endowments of his mind, that he doth not, in them all, shew and approve himself to be a very good Son of a very good King? And yet, nevertheless, that the Duke doth so much presume upon his favour, that he contemneth all men, as knowing, that those who are obedient to his Highness will also subject themselves to his will. I would to God, he did direct those his actions to the good of the Prince: But that is a thing so far from the opinion of good men, that they rather believe, that he who hath overthrown the Marriage with *Spain*, will be of no less power to the breaking of any other Marriage, and that is it which many do prophesie.

They knew in *Spain*, that very same day that he had received Letters from the most Illustrious Prince *Palatine*, that he caused the Procuration to be revoked, and in a few days after, when the coming of the foresaid Princes Secretary, and the confirmation of his hope of having his Daughter married to her Highness's Son, all things were utterly dashed in pieces. Let your Majesty have a care of your self, and the Prince, and foresee the hurts and damages which a man of such a turbulent humour may stir up; whose heady spirit, your Majesty saith, you have noted, and have desired to mitigate.

A man (I say) that is ambitious of popular air, as plainly appeared in Parliament; when, casting of all odious matter upon your Majesty, he did arrogate the thanks of all things that were acceptable to himself, being stiled, The Redeemer of his Countrey. I say again, a man that hath envied so great a good to the Christian world, and, principally, to the Kingdoms of *England* and *Spain*, having used some certain means, which do argue, that he aimed at such an end, as many already do fear, and to prophesie in it the worst event that can be. If the Puritans desire a Kingdom (which they do against their wills) they wish it not to the most Illustrious Prince, the best and true Heir of your Majesty, but to the Prince *Palatine*, whose Spie and Scout *Mansfelt* is, what shew soever he makes. He that makes these things known to your Majesty, dischargeth the part of a good man, as well towards God, as your Majesty, and the Illustrious Prince; whom it now standeth in hand to foresee the vengeance of God provided by the Dukes plots, and the fury of the Parliament; there having been so many and so great Testimonies published against *Spain*, contrary to truth; so many, and so frequent, infamous Libels begotten and brought forth; and many such other things, so full of bitterness and ignominy, that they cannot be read, even of our enemies, without some taint upon the *English* Nation.

It is most apparent, and stories will testifie, that here Leagues have been broken by the will and pleasure of them whom it especially concerneth to provide for your peace and quiet; and to wish, from the bottom of their hearts, that after many, and these most happy, years, that Motto of yours (*Blessed are the peace-makers*) might be verified, in Letter, of the person of your Majesty; and to propound the same Counsel to the most Illustrious Prince, to be imitated, which your Majesty hath done to the whole world, to be commended, and admired. A happy Prince will he be, if he comes and succeeds peaceably into the Hereditary possession of his Kingdom, and which will be of no less advantage to him, having his peace established with those Princes whose friendship and amity your Majesty hath procured, and deserved. He would certainly love and commend those that had given him those Counsels of peace. Peace and tranquillity are by Hereditary Right devolved to the most Illustrious Prince, in as much as he is born of the Father, who hath with so much industry procured them, not onely to this Island, but to the Continent also, esteeming them at a higher value then his Kingdoms themselves.

Which since it is thus, and that the blood of his Father which is in him, and the love wherewith he is carried towards your Majesty, and the experience of this your most happy Government, and that great example wherewith your Majesty hath drawn and won the Christian world to an admiration and love of you, did all direct the most Illustrious Prince, with a kind of connatural motion, to the same counsel and purpose of peace as might have heretofore been likewise hoped: Certainly, this machination is very strong, violent, and mighty, which doth suddenly labour to turn him into a clean contrary course.

And, questionless, if the very entrance into a War, the War it self, if it want justice, it will want also happy success. It cannot be unknown to your Majesty, that the Duke of *Buckingham* carrieth himself so lofty, that he would have all men perswaded that he hath and doth exercise a kind of dominion over the will of your Majesty, and of his Highness. All things shall be made manifest to your Majesty, if you will have them so; for there are not means wanting, whereby you may free your vassal from fear and diffidence, who will otherwise

otherwise dare nothing, nor say nothing; which certainly appears so far to be true, that, all things standing as they do, it is an easie matter to find who will speak against your Majesty, yet there is none that dare speak against the Duke.

Let your Majesty call some certain men unto you, and sift out of them the opinion of the more moderate Parliament; and enquire of those that come out of *Spain*, who did first give the first cause of falling out? whether the complaints against the King of *Spain* be true, or no? Whether that foresaid King were not desirous to satisfie the desire of the Prince his Highness? whether he did not faithfully endeavour to effect the Marriage? Whether the Duke of *Buckingham* did not many things against the authority and reverence due to the most illustrious Prince? Whether he was not wont to be sitting, whilest the Prince stood, and was in presence; and also having his feet resting upon another seat, after an undecent manner? Whether, when the Prince was uncovered, whilest the Queen and Infanta looked out at the windows, he uncovered his head, or no? Whether, sitting at the Table with the Prince, he did not behave himself unreverently? Whether he were not wont to come into the Prince's Chamber with his clothes half on, so that the doors could not be opened to them that came to visit the Prince from the King of *Spain*, the Door-keepers refusing to go in for modesties sake? Whether he did not call the Prince by ridiculous names? Whether he did not dishonour and profane the Kings Palace with base and contemptible women? Whether he did not divers obscene things, and used not immodest gesticulations and wanton tricks with Players, in the presence of the Prince? Whether he did not violate his faith given to the *Conde Olivarez*? Whether he did not presently communicate his discontents, offences, and complaints, to the Embassadours of other Princes? Whether, in doing of his business, he did not use frequent threatnings unto the Catholick Kings Ministers, and to Apostolical Nuntio's? Whether he did not affect to sit at Plays, presented in the Kings Palace, after the manner and example of the King and Prince, being not contented with the honour that is ordinarily given to the High Steward, or *Major Domo* of the Kings house? Besides all these things, which have heretofore been told your Majesty, there is yet this more, that is new.

That the Duke of *Buckingham* (with what intention let others judge) hath divulged in Parliament some secret Treaty negotiated betwixt your Majesty and the King of *Spain*, touching the affairs of *Holland*; the secrecie whereof, nevertheless, your Majesty had so recommended, that, besides the King, and the *Conde Olivarez*, no man in *Spain* knew of it.

If the Duke do not appear guilty of all these things, let him be still your Majesties most faithfull servant, and let your Majesty yet conferr upon him greater Honours, if you can. For I would have these things conceived to be spoken for the security of your Majesty; not for the hurt of him, to whom I wish prosperity, if by him the Christian world might be in prosperity.

It onely remaineth, that your Majesty will be pleased to take in good part this my service and obedience shewed to your Commandments.

To the King, ab ignoto.

Best, and most Excellent King,

YOu will wonder, that he who, at first, protesteth to be neither Papist nor Puritan, Spaniard nor *Hollander*, or yet in any *delirium* fit, should presume, in this Libel-like way, to lay down to your Majesty the strong zeal he beareth to the safety of your Majesty, and his Countrey, by shewing, in this dark Tablet, (drawn by the worst Painter) the common opinion of all those which are not possessed as above.

They say, the business of greatest consequence that ever your Majesty handled, is now at point to go well, or ill; the Marriage, or none; and (as it is carried) a present War, or a continued Peace. The Match of your Son, they wish, you may perfect in your own time; and think, that, for the quiet of your Self and Kingdoms, the shortest time's the best; and that this, already traced, will far sooner piece, then any new one have beginning, and accomplishment.

They fear this suspension, carried by *Killegrew*, was wrought by *Buckingham*, not for what he pretends; and plainly say, It was not onely to prevent his Highness Marriage there, but any where.

Whereby, 1. His particular Greatness may still stand absolute.

2. His Wife, and Tribe, still present the Princess person.

3. And your Majesty be, and remain, their Pupil.

The Parliament, so much urged, they say, is to be a marrying his Mightiness unto the Com-

An unknown person, to the King.

Common-Weal; that as your Majesty is his good Father, It may be his Mother, and so he stand, not only by the King, but by the People, and popular humour, that he hath lately so earnestly courted, and especially from those who are noted to be of the most troubled humour.

How your Majesty should gain upon a Parliament, they cannot imagine, seeing all are resolved to sell your Courtesies at the dearest rate, both by ill words, and for double as much again; the humour of it being so unconstant, that, twenty to one, but those very tongues which in the last did cry, *War, war, war*, will now curse him that urgeth for one poor Subsidie to raise a War; and miserable is he that is to make a War, or to defend against it, with money that is to be given, or gathered, from them.

They say, our Great Duke hath, certainly, a brave desire to War; but, in that also, he hath some great end of enriching himself: which he too well loveth, being carried away with that sweet sound, how *Nottingham* gained yearly, during that sickness, 40000 *l*. by his Admirals place; but what his Majesty gained, they find not, either in the Exchequer, or Kingdom.

Somewhat also they fear this his Grace's precipitate humour, and change of humour; both of pride, to shew his power as great here, as is *Olivarez's* there; as also, of revenge against him in particular. For were it love to his now much beloved Countrey, they say, there was as much reason for breach, both of the Match, and Peace, when the Parliament urged it, as there is now.

They say, there is a rumour of his Grace's, a match for his *Mary* with the young *Palatine*. It is no *Gorgon*; and will concern his Highness, if they that are now our best friends, the *Hollanders*, should change their Copy.

In this his Highness coming off from *Spain*, they say, He hath advised him to no worse then he did himself; for how many did he deflour, abuse, and couzen with marriage, by his grace in Court, and power with your Majesty?

In short, your Subjects, that have sense of your estate, do most earnestly beseech your Majesty, to have more especial care of your own preservation then ordinarily you have, both in respect of the desperate staggering which their Priests now stand in, and of your own *Phaeton* himself; who, in truth, wanteth nothing of man enough, but a good nature; and being in custome to carry all with a high hand, must be desperate, if he fail in any *Punto* of his violent will.

We know, your Majesty, according to the sweetness and virtue of your nature, agreeing with Gods blessed will, hath long preserved your people in all peace and plenty: And all good and sensible people pray you, even for Gods sake, not to be couzened of your own life and liberty. Oh be not mis-led, to trouble your own Kingdoms quiet; but that, after many and many a happy year, you may die happily in peace.

To his Sacred Majesty, ab ignoto.

May it please his most Excellent Majesty to consider,

THat this great opposition against the Duke of *Buckingham* is stirred up and maintained by such, who, either maliciously, or ignorantly and concurrently, seek the debating of this free Monarchy; which because they find not yet ripe to attempt against the King himself, they endeavour it through the Dukes side. These men, though agreeing in one mischief, yet are of divers sorts and humours, *viz.*

1. Medling and busie persons, who took their first hint at the beginning of King *James*, when the Union was treated of in Parliament. That learned King gave too much way to those popular speeches, by the frequent proof he had of his great abilities in that kind.

Since the time of *H.* 6. these Parliamentary discoursings were never suffered, as being the certain symptomes of subsequent Rebellions, civil Wars, and the dethroning of our Kings: But these last twenty years, most of the Parliament-men seek to improve the reparation of their Wisdoms by these Declamations; and no honest Patriot dare oppose them, lest he incur the reputation of a Fool, or a Coward in his Countreys Cause.

2. Covetous Landlords, Inclosers, Depopulators, and Justices of the Peace, who have got a habit of Omni-regency, and in hope to extend the same against the King in Parliament, as they do on his Subjects in the Countrey. Hereby the King loseth 24000 *l*. in every whole Subsidy; for *Anno* 1600. it was 80000. *l*. and now it is but 56000. *l*. which cometh by the decay of the Yeomandry, who were three and four pound men. And these Gentlemen (most of them of the Parliament) do ease themselves, to afflict those who are the true Commons, and yet perswade them, that the grievances are caused by the Duke, and the ill government of the King.

3. Retu-

3. Recusants and Church-Papists, whose hatred is irreconcileable against the Duke, for the breach of the *Spanish* Match. The *French* Lady, though as zealous a Catholique, doth not please them, for they were tyed to *Spain* by their hopes of a change of Religion that way. All the Priests are sent from the *Spanish* Dominions, and the sons and daughters of the Papists remain as hostages of their fidelities in the Colledges and Nunneries of the King of *Spain*. And though the Papists have no place in the house of Commons, yet privately they aggravate all scandals against the Duke, to kindle a separation between the King and his people, and avert them from enabling the King to resist, or be avenged of our great enemy. Remember the course held by these men in the Parliament of undertakers; also Dr. *Eglesham*, and all the Priest duly practice libelling against all great men about the King.

4. Needy and indebted persons in both Houses who endeavour by these Parliamentary stirrs not so much the Dukes overthrow, as a rebellion, which they hope will follow if it be not done. This is much to be suspected, as well by their Calumniations against his Majesty, as for their own wants; many of them being out-lawed, and not able to shew their heads, but in Parliament time, by priviledge thereof; and they know, that there are enough to follow them in the same mischief.

5. Puritans, and all other Sectaries, who, though scarce two of them agree in what they would have, yet they all, in general, are haters of Government. They begun in Parliament, about *Anno* 23. *Eliz.* and spit their venom not only against the Bishops, but also against the Lord Chancellor *Hatton*, and others, the Queens favourites and Councellours, as they do now against the Clergy and the Duke. But their main discontentment is against the Kings Government, which they would have extinguished in matters Ecclesiastical, and limited in Temporal. This is a fearsull and important Consideration, because it pretends Conscience and religion; and they now more deadly hate the Duke, because he sheweth himself to be no Puritan, as they hoped he would at his return from *Spain*.

6. Male-contents censured, or decourted, for their deserts, as the kindred and dependants of the Earl of *Suffolk*, and of Sir *Henry Yelverton*, *Coke*, *Lake*, *Middlesex*, though all of them (the last excepted) were dejected by King *James*, without any Concurrency of the Duke. Others because they are not preferred, as they do imagine that they deserve, as the Lord *Say*, Earl of *Clare*, Sir *John Eliot*, *Selden*, and *Glanvile*, Sir *Dudley Diggs*, and the Bishops of *Norwich* and *Lincoln*. These, and many others, according to the nature of envy, look upon every one with an evil eye, especially upon the Duke, who either hath, or doth not prefer them to those places, or retain them in them, which their ambition expecteth.

7. Lawyers in general, for that (as Sir *Edward Coke* could not but often express) our Kings have upholden the power of their Prerogatives, and the rights of the Clergy, whereby their comings in have been abated. And therefore the Lawyers are fit ever, in Parliaments, to second any complaint against both Church and King, and all his servants, with their Cases, Antiquities, Records, Statutes, Presidents, and Stories. But they cannot, or will not, call to mind, that never any Nobleman, in favour with his Sovereign, was questioned in Parliament, except by the King himself, in case of Treason, or unless it were in the nonage, and tumultuous times of *Rich.* 2. *Hen.* 6. or *Edw.* 6. which happened to the destruction both of the King and Kingdom. And that, not to exceed our own, and Fathers memories, in King *Hen.* 8. time, *Wolsies* exorbitant power and pride, and *Cromwels* contempt of the Nobility and the Laws, were not yet permitted to be discussed in Parliament, though they were most odious and grievous to all the Kingdom. And that *Leicester's* undeserved favour, and faults, *Hatton's* insufficiency, and *Rawleigh's* insolence, far exceeded what yet hath been (though most falsly) objected against the Duke: yet no Lawyer durst abet, nor any man else begin any Invectives against them in Parliament.

8. The Merchants and Citizens of *London*, convinced (not by the Duke, but) by *Cranfield* and *Ingram*, to have deceived the King of Imposts and Customs, and deservedly fearing to be called to account for undoing all the other Cities and good Towns, and the poor Colonie of *Virginia*, as also for transporting of our Silver into the *East-Indies*; these vent their malice upon the Duke in the *Exchange*, *Pauls*, *Westminster-Hall*, with their suggestions, and therein they wound, both to Subjects and strangers, the honour of his Majesty, and his proceedings.

9. Innovators, *Plebicola*, and King-haters. At the later end of Queen *Elizabeth* it was a phrase to speak, yea to pray for the Queen and State. This word (*State*) was learned by our neighbourhood and Commerce with the Low-Countries, as if we were, or affected to be governed by States. This the Queen saw, and hated. And the old Earl of *Oxford* his Propositions at her death, they awakened King *James* to prevent this humour, and to oppose the conditions and limitations, and presented unto him by the Parliaments. The

The Lawyers, Citizens, and Western men (who are most hot infected with Puritanisme) stood strong against him under a colour of Parliaments, and Parliamentary priviledges. His Majesty therefore strengthened himself ever with some Favourite, as whom he might better trust then many of the Nobility tainted with this desire of Oligarchie. It behoveth, without doubt, his Majesty to uphold the Duke against them; who if he be but decourted, it will be the Corner-stone on which the demolishing of his Monarchie will be builded. For, if they prevail with this, they have hatched a thousand other demands to pull the feathers of the Royalty, they will appoint him Counsellours, Servants, Alliances, Limits of his expences, Accompts of his Revenue, chiefly, if they can (as they mainly desire) they will now dazle him in the beginning of his reign.

10 King *James*, and King *Charles*, lastly, are the Dukes Accusers; (my meaning is, with all humble reverence to their Honours, and Memories, and to speak in the sence of the House of Commons) both their Majesties are *Conjuncta Persona* in all the aspersions that are laid upon the Duke, For instance, The Parliaments money destined for the Wars, spent in the Treaties, Messages, Ambassadours, and Entertainments of the Kings marriage, and the burial of his Father, and the War in the name of the Count *Palatine*, the breach of both the Treaties, which then Canonized the Duke, but now is made evidence against him; the Honours and Offices conferred upon him by King *James*, That his Majestie might with his own Councels direct their managing, the setting forth of the Navy, though to the Duke's great charge, by both their Commandments; the Match with *France*, and generally whatsoever hath not been successful to mens expectations. All these, though the Acts of the Kings, are imputed to the Duke; who if he suffer for obeying his Sovereigns, the next attempt will be to call the King to account for any thing he undertakes, which doth not prosperously succeed as all men would desire.

If it please his Majesty to remove, and set aside all these disadvantages, He shall find the Charge laid against the Duke will prove very empty, and of small moment. And for them, if his Majesty and the Duk's Grace think it no impeachment to their Honours, all that the Parliament hath objected against the Duke is pardoned at the Kings Coronation, which benefit every poor Subject enjoyeth; Three things onely excepted, which may most easily be answered.

The Copy of a Letter written by his Majesty to the Lord-Keeper, the Bishops of London, Winton, Rochester, St. Davids, *and* Exceter, *Sir* Henry Hubbert, *Mr. Justice* Dodderidge, *Sir* Henry Martin, *and Dr.* Steward, *or any six of them, whereof the Lor Keeper, the Bishops of* London, Winton, *and* St. Davids, *to be four.*

IT is not unknown unto you; what happened the last Summer to our trusty and welbeloved Councellour, the Lord Archbishop of *Canterbury*, who shooting at a Deer with a Crossbow in *Bramzil* Park, did with that shot casually give the Keeper a wound, whereof he dyed. Which accident (though it might have happened to any other man, yet) because his eminent rank and function in the Church hath (as we are informed) ministred occasion of some doubt, as making the cause different in his person, in respect of the scandal (as is supposed,) we being desirous (as it is fit we should) to be satisfied therein, and reposing especial trust in your learnings, and judgments, have made choice of you to inform us concerning the nature of this Cause, and do therefore require you to take presently into your Considerations the Scandal that may arise thereupon, and to certifie us what in your Judgments the same may amount unto, either to an irregularity, or otherwise. And lastly, what means may be found for the redress thereof (if need be,) of all which points we shall expect to have your Reports, with what diligence and expedition you may. Dated at *Thiebalds*, Octob. 3. 1621.

The Justices of Peace in the County of Devon, *to the Lords of the Councel.*

THe Letters from his sacred Majesty unto the Justices of Peace in this County, together with your Lordships, have been opened and read, according to the directions in your Lordships Letter to our high Sheriff expressed, and the weighty business therein contained,
hath

hath been maturely and speedily debated, according to our most bounden duties to his excellent Majesty, and the many concurring necessities which press the expedition of such a service: and in those respects we can do no less then give your Lordships a timely knowledg of the vote and opinion of us all, which was this day almost in the s. me words delivered by every of us.

That the sum enjoyned to be levied by the first of March, is not to be so suddenly raised out of this County by any means, much less by way of perswasion; and hereof we had lately a certain experience in the business of the loans, which notwithstanding the fear apprehended by the presence of the Pursivant, hath come at least 6000. l. short of the expected sum, and without him we suppose would have been much less, and we are confident that nothing but extremities, which had need also be back'd by Law, will raise his Majesty a sufficient quantity of Treasure for his occasions. For our selves, at the time of the proposition of the forementioned Loans, we did, according to his Majesties Proclamation and instruction then sent us, engage our faithfull promise to our Countreymen, that if they willingly yielded to his Majesties necessities at this time, we would never more be instruments in the levy of aids of that kind, his Majesties intentions so clearly manifested not to make that a president, was the cause of that engagement, and we conceive it cannot be for his honour or service for us to be the means of such a breach. That his Majesties affairs, and of his Allies, do all want an instant supply of Royal provisions his provident and Princely Letter hath fully taught us; but we have much more cause to wish then hope, that these parts so lately, and so many ways, impoverished can yield it.

Your Lordships may vouchsafe to remember how much this County hath been charged since the beginning of the war (though sometimes refreshed with payment, which we acknowledge with humble thanks) By our own late Loan of 35000. l. and 6000. l. more sent by Sir *Thomas Wise* and Mr. *Stroad*, and yet there remains due to it, for the Coat and Conduct of their own imprest Soldiers, for divers voyages for the Recruits intended for the Isle of *Ree*, for the Conduct of the whole Army hence, besides three Companies stand yet here for *Silly*, and no small number of scattered sick, whose mortal infection hath more discouraged the people then the charge.

That many and almost unaccountable are our ways of expence; few or none have we of in-come for want of Trade, how then can there be any quantity of money to disburse? their bodies and goods are left, which (we are assured) will be ever ready for his Majesties defence, and to be imployed in his Majesties service, as far forth as ever our forefathers have yielded them to his Majesties Royal Progenitors.

Particular proofs we would have made of the peoples disability to have satisfied his Majesties demands; but we had rather adventure our selves, and this humble advertisement upon your Lordships private and favourable instructions, then to expose his Majesties honour to publique denial, and misspend his precious time, which applied to more certain courses may attain his Princely and religious ends; wherein to be his Majesties Instruments will be our earthly happiness, and singular comfort to be your Lordships obedient servants.

Instructions for the Ministers, and Church-Wardens, of London.

1. THat his Majesties declaration, published *Anno Dom.* 1628. before the Articles of Religion, for setling all questions in difference, be strictly observed.

2. That special care be had concerning Lectures in every Parish.

3. That the Minister and Church-wardens in every parish, or one of them, do by writing under his or their own hands, certifie unto the *Arch-Deacon of London*, or his official, at, or before the 28 of this present *January*: and afterwards at, or before every visitation, the Christian and Sir-names of every Lecturer in their parishes, and the place where he preacheth, whether exempt, or not exempt; together with his quality or degree.

4. That they do, in like manner, certifie the names of such men, as being not qualified by Law, do keep Chaplains in their houses.

5. That they do further certifie the names of all such as absent themselves from, or are negligent in coming to divine service, as well Prayers, as Catechising and Sermons.

6. That the Minister and Church-Wardens of every Parish, successively, do keep a several copie of those Instructions by them, whereby they may be the better informed of their duty; and that the said Copies be shewed at every visitation, when they shall present all such persons as have disobeyed these instructions; that according to his Majesties pleasure, such as do conforme may be encouraged, and such as are refractory may be punished. Subscribed, *Tho Paske*, Archdeacon of *London*.

Jan. 28. 1628.

Lord

Lord Keeper Williams

HIS

LETTERS,

&c.

Lord Keeper WILLIAMS
HIS
Letters, &c.

The Lord Keeper, to the Duke, about the Liberties of Westminster.

My most Noble Lord,

I Humbly beseech your Lordship, to be a little sensible of those injurious affronts offered, without any shew of equity, unto this poor Liberty of *Westminster.* And for Gods sake let me not want that protection, which not your Lordship only, but the two *Cecils,* and the Earl of *Somerset,* who neither regarded the Church, Learning, nor Honour, in any measure as you do, have ever afforded every Dean of this Church. When I had (to my thinking) given the Knight Marshal full, and too much satisfaction, this day a Letter was offered to the Table (in my presence) violently pursued by the Lord Steward, and the Earl Marshal, to command this liberty, (which had stood unquestioned these 700 years) to shew reason to Mr. Attorney, and Mr. Sollicitor, why they prescribe against the Knight Marshal. A Course (as my Lord President said openly) not to be offered to any Subject of *England.* It is our Charter, and freehold of inheritance, to be shewed only in a Court of Justice, and at the Kings Bench, which we are very ready to do. And we may as well be questioned by a Letter from the Councel, for all the Land we have, as for this. My Lord, the jurisdiction of this place brings not a penny to my purse, but it hath brought much sorrow to my heart, and now tears to my eyes, that I should be that unfortunate and contemptible man, who, for all the King, and your Lordships favour, and the true pains I take in answer thereunto, must be trampled down above all the Deans that lived in this place. Nor would it ever grieve me, if I had deserved it from these Lords, by the least disrespect in all the world. I beseech you for the Churches sake, and your Honours sake, to be sensible hereof, and to know of the Bishop of *Winchester, London, Duresme,* Mr. *Packer,* or Sir *Robert Pye,* whether ever any question hath been made to this Liberty in this kind. If a Letter had been recorded to question the same, when the Lord Admiral was Steward, and the Lord Keeper Dean thereof, judge you, in your wisdom, what would become thereof in future posterity, &c.

May 6. 1621.

The Lord Keeper to the Duke.

My Noble Lord,

WIth my truest affections, and thankfulness, premised; I do not doubt but his Majesty and your Lordship do now enjoy the general applause of your goodness to the Earl of *Southampton. Saturday* last he came; and dined with me and I find him more cordially affected to the service of the King, and your Lordships love and friendship, then ever he was, when he lay a prisoner in my house. Yet the Sun-shine of his Majesties favour, though most bright upon others (more open offenders) is noted to be somewhat eclipsed towards him. What directions soever his majesty gave, the order is somewhat tart upon the Earl. The word of Confinement, spread about the City (though I observed not one syllable so quick to fall from his Majesty) his Keeper much wondred at. The act of the Councel published in our names, who were neither present thereat, or heard one word of the same: yet upon my credit the Earl takes all things patiently, and thankfully, though others wonder at the same.

Mr. Secretary signed a Petition of one *Rookwood* a Papist, and prisoner in the Fleet upon five several executions, that I should grant him his liberty. The Kings name is used, and the mediation of the Spanish Embassadour. If I break rules so fouly, in favour of a Papist, (which I am resolved to keep straight against all men whatsoever) I shall infame my self in the very beginning. If his Majesty will have any special indulgence in this kind, I expect intimation immediately from the King, or your Lordship, and no third Person. Your Lordship will not expect from me any account of Councel business, nor the setting at liberty of the late prisoner. Mr. Secretary is secret enough for imparting any thing unto me, so as I must remain in a necessary ignorance.

There is a Country man of mine, one *Griffith*, a suiter unto the Court for the reversion of an Auditors place, recommended thereunto by his Master the Lord Treasurer. The place is of great Consequence for the disposing of his Majesties Revenues. The man is unfit for this, as presumptuous and daring for any place. Sir *Robert Pye* saith, he hath already written to your Lordship, and I doubt not of your care thereof. Doctor *Lamb* (the bearer) is a very sufficient, and (and for ought I ever heard of him) an honest man. The King hath employed him in discovery of counterfeit Witchcrafts, in reforming of no counterfeit, but hearty Puritanes, and he hath done good service therein. If his Majesty (now in our pure air of *Northamptonshire*) do not shew him some favour, or grace, either by Knighting, or by using him courteously, The Brethren (having gotten out their *Yelverton* again) will neglect and molest him too unsufferably. God from Heaven bless you. Remember your Deanry, and Dean of *Westminster*, &c.

July 22. 1621.

The Lord Keeper, to the Duke.

My most Noble Lord,

AN unfortunate occasion of my Lords Grace, his killing of a man casually (as it is here constantly reported) is the cause of my seconding of my yesterdays Letter unto your Lordship. His Grace (upon this accident) is by the Common Law of *England* to forfeit all his estate unto his Majesty, and by the Canon Law (which is in force with us) irregular, *ipso facto*, and so suspended from all Ecclesiastical function, until he be again restored by his Superiour, which (I take it) is the Kings Majesty, in this rank and order of Ecclesiastical jurisdictions. If you send for Dr. *Lamb*, he will acquaint your Lordship with the distinct penalties in this kind. I wish, with all my heart, his Majesty would be as merciful, as ever he was in all his life; but yet I held it my duty to let his Majesty know, by your Lordship, that his Majesty is fallen upon a matter of great advice, and deliberation. To adde affliction to the afflicted (as no doubt he is in mind) is against the Kings nature; to leave *virum Sanguinum*, or a man of blood, Primate and Patriarch of all his Churches, is a thing that sounds very harsh in the old Councels, and Canons of the Church. The Papists will not spare to descant upon the one and the other. I leave the knot to his Majesties deep wisdom to advise and resolve upon. A rheume faln into mine eye (together with the humour I last wrote unto your Lordship about) hath fastened me unto my bed: which makes this Letter the more unhandsome. But I will take nothing to heart that proceeds from his Majesty, or from that King who hath raised me from the dust, to all that I am. If the truth were set down. 1. That my self was the first mover for a temporary Keeper. 2. That his Majesty hath promised me, upon the relinquishing of the Seal (or before) one of the best places in this Church, as most graciously he did. 3. The year and a halfs probation left out, which is to no purpose, but to scare away my men, and to put a disgrace upon me. 4. That my assisting Judges were desired, and named by my self, which your Lordship knows to be most true: Such a declaration would neither shame me, nor blemish his Majesties service in my person. And it were fitter, a great deal, the penning thereof were referred to my self, then to Mr. Secretary, or the Lord Treasurer, who (if he had his demerit) deserves not to hold his staff half a year. I do verily believe, they will hasten to finish this Act, before I shall hear from your Lordship, which if they do, God send me patience, and as much care to serve him, as I have, and ever had, to serve my Master; And then all must needs be well. I send your Lordship a Copy of that Speech I have thought upon, to deliver at *London* upon *Munday* next, at the Commission of the Subsidies: If his Majesty have leisure to cast his eye thereupon, and to give direction to have any thing else delivered, or any point of this suppressed, I would be directed by your Lordship, whom I recommend, in my prayers to Gods good guiding and protection. And do rest, &c.

July 27. 1621.

The Lord Keeper, to the Duke, concerning the Earl of Southampton.

My most Noble Lord,

I Humble crave your pardon, for often troubling your Honour with my idle Lines, and beseech you to remember, that amongst many miseries my sudden greatness comes accompanied with, this is not the least, that I can no otherwaies enjoy the happiness of your presence. God is my witness, the Lord Keeper hath often (not without grief of heart) envied the fortunes of a poor Scholar, one Dr. *Williams*, late Dean of *Westminster*, who was so much blessed in the free accesses in that kind, as his Lordship (without a great quantity of goodness in your self) may scarce hope for. This enclosed will let your Lordship understand, that somewhat is to be finished in that excellent piece of mercy, which his Majesty (your hand guiding the Pencil) is about to express in the Earl of *Southampton*. It is full time his Attendant were revoked, in my poor opinion, and himself left to the Custody of his own good Angel. There is no readier way to stop the mouthes of idle men, nor to draw their eyes, from this remainder of an object of Justice, to behold nothing but goodness and mercy. And the more breathing time you shall carve out between this total enlargement, and the next access of the Parliament, the better it will be for his Majesties service. Onely remember this, that now you are left to be your own Remembrancer. Of all actions, forget not those of mercy and goodness, wherein men draw nighest to God himself: Nor of all Persons, prisoners and afflicted *Josephs*. Celerity doth redouble an act of mercy. But why do I turn a Preacher of goodness unto him, who (in my own particular) hath shewed himself to be composed of nothing else? Remember your Noble Self, and forget the aggravations of malice and envy, and then forget if you can, the Earl of *Southampton*. God bless you, and your royal Guest, and bring you both, after may years yet most happily run over here upon earth, to be his blessed Guests in the Kingdom of Heaven.

August 1. 1621.

The Lord Keeper, to the Duke, concerning the Earl Marshals Place.

My most Noble Lord,

I Beseech your Lordship to interpret this Letter well and fairly, which no malice (though never so provoked) but my duty to his Majesty, and love to your Lordship, hath drawn from me: both which respects as long as I keep inviolably, I will not omit, for the fear of any man, or the loss of any thing in this world, to do any act which my Conscience shall inform me to belong unto that place, wherein the King, by your favour, hath intrusted me. I received this morning two Commands from his Majesty, the one about a Pension of 2000 *l*. yearly, and the other concerning the office of the Earl *Marshal*, both conferred on the Right Honourable the Earl of *Arundel*. For the former, although this is a very unseasonable time to receive such large Pensions from so bountiful a King, and that the Parliament so soon approaching is very like to take notice thereof, and that this Pension might (under the correction of your better judgment) hath been conveniently deferred till that Assembly had been over. Yet who am I that I should question the wisdom and bounty of my Master? I have heretofore sealed the same, praying secretly unto God, to make his Majesty as abounding in wealth, as he is in Goodness. But the latter I dare not seal (my good Lord) until I hear your Lordships resolution to these few Questions.

1. Whether

The Lord Keeper, to the Duke.

1. Whether his Majesty by expressing himself in the delivery of the staff to my Lord of *Arundel*, that he was moved thereunto for the easing of the rest of the Commissioners, who had, before the execution of that office, did not imply, that his Majesty intended to impart unto my Lord no greater power then was formerly granted to the Lords Commissioners. If it be so, this Patent should not have exceeded their Patent; whereas it doth inlarge it self beyond that by many dimensions.

2. Whether it is his Majesties meaning, that the Patent leaping over the powers of the three last Earls, *Essex*, *Shrewsbery*, and *Somerset*, should refer only to my Lords own Ancestors, *Howards*, and *Mowbrayes*, Dukes of *Norfolk*, who claimed this place by a way of inheritance. The usual reference of Patents being unto the last, and immediate predecessour, and not unto the remote, whose powers (in those unsetled and troublesome times are vage, uncertain, and unpossible to be limited.

3. Whether it is his Majesties meaning, that this great Lord should bestow those offices setled of a long time in the Crown, Sir *Edward Zouch* his in the Court, Sir *George Reinel's* in the Kings Bench, and divers others. All which this new Patent doth sweep away, being places of great worth and dignity.

4. Whether that his Majesties meaning, and your Lordships, that my Lord *Stewards* place shall be (for all his power of Judicature in the *Verge*,) either altogether extinguished, or at leastwise subordinated unto this new Office? A point considerable, because of the greatness of that person, and his neerness in blood to his Majesty, and the Prince his Highness.

5. Lastly, Whether it be intended, that the offices of the Earl Marshal of *England*, and the Marshal of the Kings house, which seem in former times to have been distinct offices, shall be now united in this great Lord? A power limited by no Law, or Record, but to be searcht out from Chronicles, Antiquaries, Heralds, and such obsolete Monuments, and thereupon held these 60 years, (for my Lord of *Essex* his power was clearly bounded, and limited) unfit to be revived by the policy of this State.

These Questions, if his Majesty intended only the renewing of this Commission of the Earl Marshals, in my Lord of *Arundel*, are material and to the purpose. But if his Majesty aimed withal, at the reviving of this old office, *A la ventura*, whose face is unknown to the people of this age; upon the least intimation from your Lordship, I will seal the Patent. And I beseech your Lordship to pardon my discretion in this doubt, and irresolution. It is my place to be wary what innovation passeth the Seal. I may offend that great Lord in this small stay, but your Lordship cannot but know, how little I lose, when I lose but him, whom (without the least cause in the world) I have irreconcileably lost already. All that I desire is, that you may know what is done, and I will ever do what your Lordship (being once informed) shall direct as becometh, &c.

That there is a difference betwixt the Earl Marshal and the Marshal of the Kings house; See *Lamberts Archiron*: or of the High Courts of Justice in *England*.

Circa Medium.

The Marshal of *England*, and the Constable, are united in a Court, which handleth only Duels out of the Realm, matters within the Realm, as Combats, Blazon, Armorie, &c. but it may meddle with nothing triable by the Lawes of the Land.

The Marshal of the Kings Houshold is united in a Court with the Seneschal or Steward, which holds plea of Trespasses, Contracts, and Covenants made within the Verge, and that according to the Lawes of the Land, *Vid. Artic. Super Cart.* C. 3, 4, 5.

We do all of us conceive the King intended the first place only for this great Lord, and the second to remain in the Lord Stewards managing. But this new Patent hath comprehended them both. This was fit to be presented to your Lordship.

Septemb. 1. 1621.

The Lord Keeper, to the Duke.

My most Noble Lord,

I Humbly thank your Lordship for your most sweet and loving Letter, which (as Sir *George Goring* could not but observe) hath much revived me drooping under the unusual weight of so many businesses. Let God suffer me no longer to be, then I shall be true, plain, faithful, and affectionately respectful of your Lordship, as being most bound unto your Lordship for these so many fruits, but far more for the tree that bore them, your love and affection.

If your Lordſhip ſhall not think it inconvenient, I do beſeech your Lordſhip to preſent this Petition encloſed, either by word or writing, unto his Majeſty, and to procure a ſpeedy diſpatch thereof, becauſe we are to meet on Thurſday next. Alſo to acquaint his Majeſty, that I ſtumble at the Proclamation (now coming to the Seal) againſt any that ſhall draw, or preſent any Bill for his Majeſties ſignature, beſides thoſe Clerks which uſually draw them up, by vertue of their places. It is moſt prejudicial to my place, the Lord Treaſurer, and the Judges itinerant who are often occaſioned to draw up, and preſent to his Majeſty divers matters, and eſpecially pardons of Courſe. It is alſo too ſtrong a tie upon your Lordſhips hands; being intended by his Majeſty againſt Projectors and Scriveners only; if it ſhall pleaſe his Majeſty, therefore, to make an exception of the Lords of his Councel, and Judges of Aſſize, it may paſs to the contentment of all men. Mr. Attorney ſaith he meant this exception, but I find it not ſufficiently expreſſed in the Proclamation.

Alſo, I humbly beſeech your Lordſhip to meddle with no pardon for the Lord of St. Albans, until I ſhall have the happineſs to confer with your Lordſhip; the pardoning of his fine is much ſpoken againſt, not for the matter, (for no man objects to that) but for the manner, which is full of knavery, and a wicked preſident. For by this aſſignation of his fine, he is protected from all his Creditors, which (I dare ſay) was neither his Majeſties, nor your Lordſhips meaning.

I have preſumed to ſend your Lordſhip a true Copy of that ſpeech, which I made at *Weſtminſter* Hall at my entrance upon this office; becauſe ſomewhat was to be ſpoken at ſo great a change and alteration in ſo high a Court; And I was never ſo much troubled in my life, not how, but what to ſpeak. I humbly crave pardon, if I have failed in point of diſcretion, which a wiſer man (in ſuch a caſe) might eaſily do.

With my heartieſt prayers unto God, to continue all his bleſſings upon your Lordſhip, I reſt deſervedly, &c.

Poſt-ſcript.

MY Lord, I find my Lord Treaſurer affectionately touched with removing from the Court of Wards; and do wiſh, with all my heart, he may have contentment in that, or any thing elſe, but orderly, and in a right method. Let him hold it, but by your Lordſhips favour, not his own power, or wilfulneſs. And this muſt be apparent, and viſible: Let all our greatneſs depend (as it ought) upon yours, the true originall. Let the King be *Pharaoh*, your ſelf *Joſeph*, and let us come after as your half-brethren. God bleſs you, &c.

The Lord Keeper to the Duke, concerning the Lord of St. Albans.

My moſt Noble Lord,

I Have received your Lordſhips expreſſion concerning the Pauſe I made upon the two Patents. The Proclamation of writing to the Kings hand, and my Lord of St. *Albans* pardon. The former I have ſealed this morning, in duty, and obedience to your Lordſhips intimation. The latter I have not yet ſealed, but do repreſent (in all lowlineſs and humility) theſe few Conſiderations by your Lordſhip to his Sacred Majeſty, wherein let your Lordſhip make no queſtion, but I have adviſed with the beſt Lawyers in the Kingdom. And after this repreſentation, I will perform whatſoever your Lordſhip ſhall direct.

1. His Majeſty and your Lorſhip do conceive, that my Lord of S. *Albans* pardon and grant of his fine came both together to my hands, and ſo your Lordſhip directs me to paſs the one and the other. But his Lordſhip was too cunning for me. He paſſed his fine (whereby he hath deceived his Creditors) ten dayes before he preſented his pardon to the Seal. So as now, in his pardon, I find his Parliament fine excepted, which he hath before the ſealing of the ſame obtained and procured. And whether the houſe of Parliament will not hold themſelves mocked and derided with ſuch an exception, I leave to your Lordſhips wiſdom. Theſe two Grants are oppoſite and contradictory (in this point) the one to the other.

2. The King pardons in particular words, All ſums of money, and rewards taken for falſe judgements or decrees. And therefore the exception of the Parliamentary Cenſure (being inflicted but for the ſame taking of moneys and rewards) coming a good way after falleth too late in Law, and is of no force to ſatisfie the Lords (as I am informed) and I believe this clauſe was never ſeen in any other pardon.

3. The King pardoneth in my Lord of St. *Alban* the ſtealing away, altering, raſing, and
interlining

interlining of his Majesties Rowls, Records, Briefs, &c. which are more in a Lord Chancellors pardon, then the imbezeling of his Majesties Jewels in a Lord Chamberlains. And yet the Lord Chancellour *Elsmere* could not endure that clause in my Lord of *Somersets* Pardon, unless he would name the Jewels in particular.

4. I will not meddle or touch upon those mistakings which may fall between the Parliament and his Majesty, for the mis-interpretation that enemies may make hereof to your Lordships prejudice, because I see (in his Majesties great wisdom) these are not regarded. Onely I could have wished, the Pardon had been referred to the Councel-board, and so passed. I have now discharged my self of those poor scruples, which (in respect only to his Majesties service, and your Lordships honour) have wrought this short stay of my Lord of St. *Albans* Pardon. Whatsoever your Lordship shall now direct, I will most readily (craving pardon for this not undutiful boldness) put in execution. Because some speech may fall of this dayes speech, which I had occasion to make in the Common Pleas, where a Bishop was never seen sitting there these 70. years, I have presumed to enclose a Copy thereof, because it was a very short one.

Your Lordship shall not need to take that great pains (which your Lordship to my unexpressible comfort, hath so often done) in writing. What Command soever your Lordship shall impose upon me as touching this pardon, your Lordships expression to Mr. *Packer*, or the bearer shall deliver it sufficiently. God from heaven continue the showring and heaping of his blessings upon your Lordship, &c.

Octob. 27. 1621.

The Lord Keeper, to the Duke.

Most Noble Lord,

I Have seen many expressions of your love in other mens Letters (where it doth most naturally and purely declare it self) since I received any of mine own. It is much your Lordship should spare me those thoughts, which pour out themselves in my occasions: But to have me and my affaires in a kind of affectionate remembrance, when your Lordship is saluting of other Noble men, is more then ever I shall be able otherwayes to requite then with true prayers and best wishes. I received this afternoone (by Sir *John Brook*.) a most loving Letter from your Lordship, but dated the 26th. of *Novemb.* imparting your care over me for the committing of one *Beeston* for breach of a Decree. My Noble Lord, Decrees once made must be put in execution, or else, I will confess this Court to be the greatest imposture and Grievance in this Kingdom. The damned in Hell do never cease repining at the Justice of God, nor the prisoners in the Fleet, at the Decrees in Chancery; of the which hell of prisoners this one, for antiquity and obstinacy, may pass for a Lucifer. I neither know him, nor his cause, but as long as he stands in Contempt, he is not like to have any more liberty.

His Majesties last Letter, though never so full of honey (as I find by passages reported out of the same, being, as yet, not so happy as to have a sight thereof) hath notwithstanding afforded those Spiders which infest that noble House of Commons, some poyson, and ill constructions to feed upon, and to induce a new diversion, or plain Cessation of weightier businesses. His Majesty infers, (and that most truly, for where were the Commons before *Henry* the first give them authority to meet in Parliament?) that their priviledges are but Graces and favours of former Kings, which they claim to be their inheritance, and natural birth-rights. Both these assertions (if men were peaceably disposed, and affected the dispatch of the common businesses) might be easily reconciled.

These priviledges were originally the favours of Princes, and are now inherent in their persons: Nor doth his Majesty go about to impair or diminish them. If his Majesty will be pleased to qualifie that passage with some milld and noble exposition, and require them strictly to prepare things for a Session, and to leave this needless dispute, his Majesty shall thereby make it appear to all wise and just men, that these persons are opposite to those common ends: whereof they vaunt themselves the only Patrons. But do his Majesty what he please, I am afraid (although herein the Lord Treasurer and others do differ from me) they do not affect a Session, nor intend to give at this time any Subsidie at all.

Will the King be pleased therefore to add in this Letter (which must be here necessarily upon Munday morning) that if they will not prepare bills for a Session, his Majesty will break up this Parliament without any longer Prorogation, and acquainting the Kingdom with their undutifulness and obstinacy, supply the present wants by some other means. Or will his

his Majesty (upon their refusal) presently rejourn the Assembly until the appointed 8th of *February*. This course is fittest for further advice, but the other to express a just indignation. I dare advise nothing in so high a point; but humbly beseech Almighty God to illuminate his Majesties understanding, to insist upon that course which shall be most behoovefull for the advancement of his service. In our House, his Majesties servants are very strong, and increase every day; nor is there the least fear of any Malignant opposition. God reward all your Lordships goodness and affection towards, &c.

Decemb. 16. 1621.

The Lord Keeper, to the Duke, about Mr. Thomas Murray's *Dispensation,&c.*

My most Noble Lord,

I Should fail very much of my duty to his Majesty, if, before the sealing of Mr. *Thomas Murray's* Dispensation, I should not acquaint his Majesty explicitely, and freely, with the nature of this act, far differing from any Dispensation in this kind, ever granted by his Majesty, since his happy coming to the Crown of *England*. For (to say nothing of the right of the election of this Provost, which being originally, not in the King, but in the Fellows, and now by their neglect devolved unto me, shall be fully and absolutely at his Majesties command) the place is a Living, with cure of Souls, and I am to institute and admit him to the Cure of Souls of the Parish of *Eaton*, by the express Letter of the Statute: Without admission, it is impossible he should receive any real or rightfull possession of the same. Now that his Majesty, or any of his Predecessors, did ever dispence with a Lay-man to hold cure of souls, I think, will be hard for any man to shew, by any warrantable president, or record whatsoever: And I know his Majesty to be as much averse from giving any such president, as any Prince in Christendom living this day. This is altogether differing from a Deanery, or an Hospital; which being Livings without cure, have been, and may be, justly conferred by his Majesty upon Lay-men, with Dispensations *de non promovendo*. If Sir *Henry Savil's* example be objected, I answer, (besides that the Queen made claim to the gift of the place by *lapse*, occasioned through the promotion of the Provost to the Bishoprick of *Chichester*, whereas his Majesty hath no such claim thereunto at this time) That *Savil* never durst take true possession of the place, but was onely slipt in by the Bishop, (who for fear of the Earl of *Essex* made bold with the conscience) *Ad Curam & regimen Collegii*, that is, to the care and government of the Colledge: Whereas, by the express words of the Foundation, he is to be admitted, *Ad Curam animarum Parochianorum Ecclesiæ Ætonianæ*, to the Cure of the souls of all the people of the Parish of *Eaton*. Secondly, I hold it no disparagement to Mr. *Murray* (nor do I find him altogether averse from the same) to enter into Orders, in the Reign of a King so favourable to our Coat, as (Gods name be praised for it) reigns now over us. This will give satisfaction to all the Church, bring him into this place according to the Statute, and the Foundation of that dead King, prevent such a dangerous president for a Layman to possess cure of souls in the Eye and Centre of all the Realm, and be an everlasting testimony of his Majesties Piety to the Church of *England*. Thirdly, what opinion this Gentleman hath of our Church-Government, is better known to his Majesty, then to me. If he should be averse thereunto, it were such a blow unto the Church (the number of the Fellows and Students there considered) as the like was never given by publick Authority these fifty years. Fourthly, howsoever his Majesty, and the Prince his Highness, shall resolve thereof, (at whose feet I lie to be wholly disposed) I hope, it is neither of their Royal intendments, to transferr the Bishoprick of *Lincoln* upon the Fellows of that House, who have rashly usurped a Power of admitting their Provost contrary to any example seen before. Whereas all Provosts, as well the Church-men, who come in by election, as the Lay-men, recommended by the late Queen, were (as the Foundation exactly requires it) admitted by the Bishop of *Lincoln*, their Diocesan and Visitor. I hope, it was Mr. *Murray's* inexperience, rather then neglect (never deserved by me) that directed them to this strange course: Subscription, and other conformities, to be acted in the presence of the Visitor, are essentially to be required, before he can be admitted Provost of *Eaton*. Lastly, Mr. *Murray* hath hitherto mistaken all his course: He must be first dispensed withal (if his Majesty in his wisdom shall hold it fit) and then Elected, first Fellow, and then Provost, of the Colledge (if he will come in regularly, and safely) whereas now, contrary to *Savil's* president, he is first Elected, and then goes on with his Dispensation.

All this I most humbly intreat your Lordship to make known to the Prince his Highness, and, as much as your Lordship thinks fit thereof, to his Majesty. I will onely add one note, and so end: It will be no more disparagement for Mr. *Murray*, his Highness School-master, to enter into Order, then it was for *Coxe*, King *Edward's* School-master, a Master of Requests, and Privy Councellor, to do the like, who afterwards became a worthy Prelate of this Church. I have discharged my duty to the King, Prince, and the Church of *England*. It remains now, that I should (as I will) religiously obey whatsoever I shall be directed in the sequel of this business. And so I rest, &c.

Post-script.

My Lord, Mr. *Murray*, since, came unto me; to whom I shewed this Letter, and told him, I would send it unto you, to be shewed to the King, and the Prince. I find him willing to run all courses, Priesthood onely excepted. If the King will dispence with him, my Letter notwithstanding, I humbly beseech his Majesty, to write a Letter unto me, as a Warrant to admit him onely *Ad Curam & Regimen Collegii*, instead of the other word, *Ad Curam animarum*. I schooled him soundly against Puritanism; which he disavows, though somewhat faintly: I hope his Highness and the King will second it.

Febr. 23. 1621.

Passages between the Lord Keeper, and Don Francisco.

1. HE was very inquisitive, if I had already, or intended to impart, what he had told me, the night before, in secret; to which he did add a desire of secrecie.

Because
{
1. The King had charged him and the Friar to be very secret.
2. The Embassadours did not know that he had imparted these things unto me.
3. The Pope's were secret instructions, which they gave to the Friar, to urge and press the same points which himself had done to the King.
}

2. He confessed, that the greatest part of the Friars instructions were, to do all the worst offices he could against the Duke; and to lay the breach of the Marriage, and disturbance of the Peace, upon him.

3. He excused the bringing the Copy of that Paper unto me, because the Marquess had it yet in his custody; but said, he would procure it with all speed. I desired him to do it, the rather, because, besides my approbation of the form and manner of the writing, I might be by it instructed how to apply my self to do his Majesty service therein, as I found, by that Conference, his Majesties bent and inclination.

4. He having understood, that there was, though a close, yet an indissoluble friendship betwixt the Duke and my self, desired me to shew some way, how the Duke might be won unto them, and to continue the peace. I answered, I would pursue any fair course that should be proposed that way; but for my self, that I never medled with matters of State, or of this nature; but was onely employed (before this journey of the Prince's) in matters of mine own Court, and in the Pulpit.

5. He desired to know, if they might rely upon the King, whom onely they found peaceably addicted; otherwise, they would cease all mediation, and prepare for War. I answered, That he was a King that never broke his word, and he knew what he had said unto them.

6. He commended much the courage and resolution of the Lord Treasurer, which, I told him, we all did, as a probable sign of his innocency.

7. He said, that the Marquess had dispatched three *Curreos*, and expected large Propositions, from *Spain*, to be made unto his Majesty, concerning the present restitution of the *Palatinate*: And that if this failed, they were at an end of Treaty, and the Embassadours would forthwith return home.

April 11. 1622.

The Lord Keeper to the Duke, concerning Sir John Michel.

My most noble Lord,

IN the cause of Sir *John Michel*, which hath so often wearied this Court, vexed my Lady your Mother, and now, flyeth (as it seemeth) unto your Lordship, I have made an order the last day of the Term, assisted by the Master of the Rolls, and Mr. Baron *Bromley*, in the presence, and with the full consent of Sir *John Michel*, who then objected nothing against the same; but now in a dead vacation, when both the adverse party, and his Councel, are out of Town, and that I cannot possible hear otherwise then with one ear, he clamours against me, (most uncivilly,) and would have me, contrary to all conscience and honesty, reverse the same. The same substance of the order is not so difficult and intricate, but your Lordship will easily find out the equity or harshness thereof.

Sir *Lawrence Hide* makes a motion in behalf of one *Strelley* (a party whose face I never saw,) that whereas Sir *John Michel* had put a bill into this Court against him, and one *Sayers*, five years agoe, for certain Lands and Woods, (determinable properly at the Common Law) and having upon a certificate betwixt himself and *Sayers*, without the knowledge of the said *Strelley*, procured an injunction from the last Lord Chancellour, for the possession of the same; locks up the said *Strelley* with the said injunction, and never proceeds to bring his cause to hearing within five years.

It was moved therefore, that either Sir *Johns* bill might be dismissed to a Tryal at the Common Law, or else that he might be ordered to bring it to hearing in this Court, with a direction to save all wastes of Timber trees (in favour of either party, that should prove the true owner) untill the cause should receive hearing.

Sir *John*, being present in Court, made choice of his last offer, and so it was ordered accordingly. And this is that order that this strange man hath so often, of late, complained of to your Mother, and now, as it seemeth, to your Lordship. God is my witness, I have never denied either justice, or favour (which was to be justified,) to this man, or any other, that had the least relation to your good and most noble Mother. And I hope your Lordship is perswaded thereof. If your Lordship will give me leave (without your Lordships trouble) to wait upon you, at any time this day your Lordship shall appoint, I would impart two or three words unto your Lordship, concerning your Lordships own business; Remaining ever, &c.

8. *Aug.* 1622.

The Lord Keeper, to the Duke.

My most noble Lord,

YEsterday, upon the receipt of your Lordships Letters of the 19th. of this instant concerning the hastning of the business of the original Writs, I sent presently for Mr. Attourney, and Mr. Sollicitor, who were altogether unprovided for their parts of the dispatch, and are casually forced so to be, because three several Officers, in whose records they are to search, are now out of Town, and do not return yet these 7 dayes. But your Lordship shall not fail to have all things concluded three weeks before the Term; and I will (of purpose) put off all general sealing until it be effected.

In the mean time (your Lordships Letter notwithstanding) it will be nothing for your Lordships ease to have Sir *George Chaworth* any way interested in this office of the originals; but I hold it fitter to leave it (as it is in Law and Equity) forfeited for non-payment of rent, in his Majesties hand; for upon that issue I do not doubt but my Lord of St. *Albans*, and Sir. *George*, will be content to hear reason.

I have received extraordinary respects and expressions from my Noble Lord, the Lord Marquess *Hamilton*, which doth exceedingly comfort and encourage me to goe on, with some more alacrity, through the difficulties of this restless place. I beseech your Lordship (who are *Causa Causarum*, the first Cause, that sets all these other Causes of my Comforts in going) to take notice of the same, and to undertake this favour to be placed upon a poor honest hearted man, who would (if he were any way able) requite it. Gods blessings, and the prayers of a poor Bishop ever attend your Lordship, &c.

Post script.

The *Spanish* Ambassadour took the alarum very speedily of the titulary Romish Bishop,

Sir Tobie Mathews. and before my departure from his house at *Islington*, (whither I went privately to him) did write both to *Rome* and *Spain* to prevent it. But I am afraid that *Tobie* will prove but an Apocryphal, and no Canonical, Intelligencer; acquainting the State with this project, for the Jesuites, rather then for Jesus, sake.

Aug. 23. 1622.

The Lord Keeper, to the Duke, about the Lord Treasurer.

My most Noble Lord,

THat I neither wrote unto your Lordship, nor waited upon your Lordship, sithence my intolerable scandalizing by the Lord Treasurer, this is the true and onely cause: I was so moved to have all my diligent service, pains, and unspotted justice, thus rewarded by a Lord, who is reputed wise, that I have neither slept, read, written, nor eaten any thing, since that time; until the last night, that the Ladies sent for me (I believe of purpose) to *Wallingford* house, and put me out of my humour. I have lost the love and affection of my men, by seizing upon their Papers, perusing all their answers to Petitions, casting up their moneys, received by way of fees, (even to half Crowns, and two shillings) and finding them all to be poor honest Gentlemen, that have maintained themselves in my service by the greatness of my pains, and not the greatness of their fees. They are, most of them, landed men, that do not serve me for gain, but for experience, and reputation; and desire to be brought to the Test, to shew their several Books, and to be confronted by any one man, with whom they contracted, or from whom they demanded any Fee at all; the greatest sum in their Books is five pounds, and those very few, and sent unto them from Earls and Barons: All the rest are, some 20*s*. 10*s*. 5*s*. 2*s*. 6*d*. and 2*s*. And this is the oppression in my house, that the Kingdom (of the common Lawyers, peradventure, who have lost, I confess, hereby 20000*l*. at the least, saved in the purses of the Subjects) doth now groan under.

Now I humbly beseech your Lordship, to peruse this paper here enclosed, and the issue I do joyn with the Lord Treasurer; and to acquaint (at the least) the King, and the Prince, how unworthily I am used by this Lord; who (in my soul and conscience I believe it) either invents these things out of his own head, and ignorance of this Court, or hath taken them up from base, unworthy, and most unexperienced people. Lastly, because no act of mine (who am so much indebted for all my frugality) could, in the thoughts of a Devil incarnate, breed any suspicion that I gained by this Office, excepting the purchase of my Grandfathers Lands, whereunto my Lord Chamberlains nobleness, and your Lordships encouragement, gave the invitation, I do make your Lordship (as your Lordship hath been often pleased to honour me) my faithfull Confessor in that business, and do send your Lordship a note inclosed, what money I paid, what I borrowed, and what is still owing for the purchase.

I beseech your Lordship to cast your eye upon the paper, and lay it aside, that it be not lost. And having now poured out my soul, and sorrow, into your Lordships breast, I find my heart much eased, and humbly beseech your Lordship to compassionate the wrongs of

Sept. 9. 1622.

Your most humble and honest servant,
J. L. C. S.

The fair and familiar Conference which the Lord Treasurer had with the Lord Keeper, after some Expostulations of his own, and the issue joyned thereupon, at White-Hall, Septemb. 7. 1661.

Object. 1, 2. THere is taken 40000*l*. for Petitions, in your house, this year.

Sol. Not much above the fortieth part of the money, for all the dispatches of the Chancery, Star-Chamber, Councel-Table, Parliament, the great Diocess of *Lincoln*, the Jurisdiction of *Westminster* and S*t*. *Martins le Grand*; all which have resort to my house by Petitions.

Obj. 2. You have your self a share in the money.

Sol. Then let me have no share in Gods Kingdom; it is such a baseness, as never came within the compass of my thoughts.

The Lord Keeper, to the Duke.

It is commonly reported, you pay to my Lord Admiral 1000. l. *per mensem*.   *Object. 3.*
As true as the other. The means of my place will reach to no more then two moneths.   *S.l.*
You never receive any Petition with your own hands, but turn them to your Secretaries, *ob. 4.* who take double Fees, one for receiving, and the other for delivering.
Let the Cloysters at *Westminster* answer for me. I never to this day received any Petition *Sol.* from my Secretaries, but which I had formerly delivered unto them with my own hands. This is a new fashion, which my Lord hath found in some other Courts.
You sell dayes of hearing at higher rates then ever they were at.   *ob. 5.*
I never disposed of any since I came to this place, but leave them wholly to the Six Clerks, *Sol.* and Registers, to be set down in their Antiquity. Unless his Lordship means hearing of motions in the paper of Peremptories, which I seldom deny upon any Petition, and which are worth no money at all.
You usually reverse Decrees upon Petitions.   *ob. 6.*
I have never reversed, altered, explained, or endured a motion, or Petition, that touch- *S.l.* ed upon a decree once pronounced: but have sometimes made orders in pursuance of the same.
You have three Door-keepers, and are so locked up, that no man can have access un- *ob. 7.* to you.
I have no such officer in all my house, unless his Lordship means the Colledge Porters; nor *Sol.* no locks at all, but his Majesties business, which I must respect above Ceremonies and Complements.   *ob. 8.*
You are cryed out against over all the Kingdom for an unsufferable oppression and grievance.   *Sol.*
His Lordship (if he have any friends) may hear of such a Cry, and yet be pleased to *ob. 9.* mistake the person cryed out against.
All the Lords of the Councel cry out upon you, and you are a wretched and a friendless man, if no man acquaints you with it.   *Sol.*
I am a wretched man indeed if it be so, And your Lordship (at the least) a very bold man if it be otherwise.   *ob. 10.*
I will produce particular witnesses, and make all these Charges good.   *S.l.*
I know your Lordship cannot. And I do call upon you to do it, as suspecting all to be but your Lordships envie and malice to that service of the Kings, and ease of his Subjects, which God hath enabled me to accomplish and perform, in this troublesome Office.

J. L. C. S.

The Lord Keeper, to the Lord Viscount Anan.

Right Honourable,

I Ow more service to that true love, and former acquaintance, which your Lordship hath been pleased to afford me, now, these full ten years, then to be sparing, or reserved, in satisfying your Lordship about any doubt whatsoever, the resolution whereof shall lie in my power. Concerning that offence, taken by many people, both on this side the Borders, and in *Scotland*, from that clemency which his Majesty was pleased to extend to the imprisoned Lay-Recusants of this Kingdom, and my Letter written unto the Justices for the regulating of the same; which your Lordship did intimate unto me, yesterday, at Mr. *Henry Gibbs* his house, out of some news received from a Peer of *Scotland*. This is the plainest return I can make unto your Lordship. In the general, as the Sun in the firmament appears unto us no bigger then a Platter, and the Stars but as so many nails in the pummel of a saddle, because of the elongement and disproportion between our eyes and the object; so is there such an unmeasurable distance betwixt the deep resolution of a Prince, and the shallow apprehension of common and ordinary people, that as they will be ever judging and censuring, so must they be obnoxious to errour and mistaking.

Particularly, for as much as concerns my self, I must leave my former life, my profession, my continual preaching, my writing, (which is at the instant in the hands of many) my private endeavours about some great persons, and the whole bent of my actions, (which in the place I live in cannot be concealed, to testifie unto the world, what favour I am likely to importune for the Papists in their Religion. For the King my Master, I will tell you a story out of *Velleius Paterculus*. A Surveyor bragging to *M. Livius Drusus*, that he would so contrive his house, *Ut libera a conspectu immunis, & ab omnibus arbitris esset*, that it shou'd stand removed

moved out of fight, and be put all danger of peeping, or eaves-dropping; was answered again by *Drusus*, *Tu vero, si quid in te artis est, ita cum pone dimicare, ut quicquid agam ab omnibus conspici possit*; Nay, my good friend, if you have any devices in your head, contrive my house after such a manner, that all the world may see what I do therein. So, if I should endeavour to flourish up some artificial Vault, to hide and conceal the intentions of his Majesty, I know, I should receive the same thanks that the Surveyor did from *Drusus*. I was not called to Councel by his Royal Majesty, when the resolution of this Clemency to the Lay-Recusants was first concluded: But if I had been asked my opinion, I should have advised it without the least hæsitation. His Majesty was so Popishly addicted at this time, that (to the incredible exhaustments of his Treasury) he was a most zealous interceder for some ease and refreshment to all the Protestants in *Europe*, his own Dominions, and *Denmark*, onely excepted.

Those of *Sweden* (having lately provoked the *Pole*) had no other hope of Peace; those of *France*, of the exercise of their Religion; those of the *Palatinate*, and adjoyning Countreys, of the least connivency to say their Prayers, then by the earnest mediation of our gracious Master. And advised by the late Assembly of Parliament to insist a while longer in this milkie way of intercession, and Treaty. What a preposterous argument would this have been, to desire those mighty Princes (armed, and victorious) to grant some liberty and clemency to the Protestants, because himself did now imprison, and execute the rigour of his Laws against the *Roman* Catholicks. I must deal plainly with your Lordship. Our viperous Countrey-men, the *English* Jesuites in *France*, to frustrate these pious endeavours of his Majesties, had, many moneths before that favour granted, retorted that argument upon us, by writing a most malicious Book (which I have seen, and read over) to the *French* King, inciting him, and the three Estates, to put all those Statutes in execution against the Protestants in those parts, which are here enacted, and (as they falsely informed) severally executed upon the Papists. I would, therefore, see the most subtile State-monger in the world chalk out a way for his Majesty to mediate for grace and favour for the Protestants, by executing, at this time, the severity of the Laws upon the Papists. And that this favour should amount to a Toleration, is a most dull (and yet a most devillish) misconstruction.

A Toleration looks forward, to the time to come: This favour, backward onely, to the offences past. If any Papist, now set at liberty, shall offend the Laws again, the Justices may (nay must) re-commit him, and leave favour and mercy to the King, to whom onely it properly belongeth. Nay, let those two Writs directed to the Judges be as diligently perused by those rash Censurers, as they were by those grave and learned, to whom his Majesty referred the penning of the same, and they shall find, that these Papists are no otherwise out of prison, then with their shackles about their heels, sufficient sureties, and good recognizances to present themselves again at the next Assises. As therefore that Lacedemonian posed the Oracle of *Apollo*, by asking his opinion of the Bird which he grasped in his hand, whether he were alive or dead; so it is a matter yet controverted, and undecided, whether those Papists (closed up, and grasped in the hands of the Law) be still in prison, or at liberty. Their own demeanours, and the success of his Majesties negotiations, are Oracles that must decide the same. If the Lay-papists do wax insolent with this mercy, insulting upon the Protestants, and translating this favour from the person to the cause, I am verily of opinion his Majesty will remand them to their former state and condicition, and renew his writ no more. But if they shall use these graces modestly, by admitting Conference with learned Preachers, demeaning themselves neighbourly and peaceably, praying for his Majesty, and the prosperous success of his pious endeavours, and relieving him bountifully (which they are as well able to do as any of his Subjects,) if he shall be forced and constrained to take his sword in hand, then it cannot be denied, but our Master is a Prince that hath (as one said) *plus humanitatis pene quam hominis*, and will at that time leave to be mercifull, when he leaves to be himself. In the mean while, this argument fetcht from the Devils topicks, which concludes a *Concreto ad abstractum*, from a favour done to the English Papists, that the King favoureth the Romish Religion, is such a composition of follie, and malice, as is little deserved by that gracious Prince, who by word, writing, exercise of Religion, acts of Parliament, late directions for catechizing, and preaching, and all professions and endeavours in the world, hath demonstrated himself so resolved a Protestant. God by his holy Spirit open the eyes of the people, that, these aierie representations of ungrounded fancies set aside, they may clearly discern, and see how by the goodness of God, and the wisdom of their King, this Island, of all the Countreys in *Europe*, is the sole nest of peace and true Religion, and the inhabitants thereof unhappy

happy only in this one thing, that they never look up to heaven, to give God thanks for so great a happiness.

Lastly, for mine own Letter to the Judges, (which did onely declare, not operate the favour,) it was either much mis-penned, or much misconstrued. It recited four kinds of recusancies only capable of his Majesties clemency, not so much to include these, as to exclude many other crimes bearing amongst the Papists the name of Recusancies, as using the function of a Romish Priest, seducing the Kings liege people from the Religion established, scandalizing and aspersing our King, Church, State, or present Government. All which offences (being outward practices, and no secret motions of the conscience,) are adjudged by the Laws of *England* to be meerly civil, and political, and excluded by my Letter from the benefit of those Writs which the bearer was imployed to deliver unto the Judges.

And thus I have given your Lordship a plain account of the carriage of this business, and that the more suddenly, that your Lordship might perceive it is not *Aurea Fabula*, or prepared tale, but a bare Narration, which I have sent your Lordship. I beseech your Lordship to let his Majesty know, that the Letters to the Justices of Peace concerning those four heads recommended by his Majestie, shall be sent away as fast as they can be exscribed. I will trouble your Lordship no more at this time; but shall rest ever,

September, 17. 1622.   *Your Lordships servant, and true friend,*
                                        Jo. Lincoln. C. S.

The Lord Keeper, to the Duke.

My most noble Lord,

MY Lord *Brook* dis-warning me (from his Majesty) from coming to *Theobalds* this day I was enforced to trouble your Lordship with these few lines. My most humble thanks to your Lordships most free and loving Letter, I do willingly confess my errour, yet still of the mind, that your Lordship only, who justly taxed it, hath made it to be an errour. If your love to me had not exceeded all reason, and desert of mine, my complaints were not effects of melancholly, but of a real suffering, and misery. I do confess (and rest satisfied withall) that his Majesties Justice, and your Lordships love, are anchors strong enough; for a mind more tossed then mine is, to ride at. Yet pardon me, my Noble Lord, upon this consideration, if I exceeded a little in passion, the natural effect of honesty, and innocency. A Church-man, and a woman, have no greater Idol under heaven, then their good name. And yet they cannot fight at all. Nor, with credit, scold, and least of all recriminate, to protect and defend the same. Their only revenge left them, is, to grieve, and complain.

My misery I took to be this. I am one of those that labour in his Majesties Coal-mines under the earth, and out of sight. My pains from five a clock in the morning to 10. or 12. at night are restless, and endless, but under earth, and out of his Majesties sight. What other men do (or but seem to do,) it is ever before the Kings face; and if his Majesty will not look on it, if he hath ears about him, he shall be told of it so often by the parties themselves, that he must hear of it whether he will or no.

And as my service (by this remoteness) is hidden from the King, so is it liable to be traduced to the King, and my relief (as in dispatching the motions of poore men by Petitions allowable to my orders,) made to be a grievance to the Common-Wealth. But in all these fourteen daies (wherein, by the voice of the City, I have remained a prisoner in my house,) where is that one party grieved, that hath troubled his Majesty with complaints against me? Onely my Lord Marshal hath dealt with my noble Lord Marquess *Hamilton*, my Lord of *Carlisle*, my Lord Treasurer (as your Lordship may soon know by asking the question) to make a faction to disgrace the poor Lord Keeper, who never dream'd thereof.

Sir *Gilbert Haughton* hath complained to my Lord Treasurer of my men for taking, (*Hugh Holland* was by and heard him,) If your Lordship do but ask him his reason, I think it will appear how well grounded their complaints be. Upon those two former Anchors I will therefore rest, and that so far from Cowardliness, that I will either challenge them before his Majesty to make good their suggestions, or else (which I hold the greater valour of all, and which I confess I wanted before this check of your Lordships) go on in my Course, and scorn all these base and unworthy scandals, as your Lordship shall direct me.

I have sent a Copy of a Letter of mine to my Lord *Anan*, which his Majesty hath seen, and given his assent it should not be kept private; yet I would humbly crave your Lordships opinion thereof (by Mr. *Packer*) before any Copy goeth from me.

I am ever &c.

The Lord Keeper, to the Duke.

My most Noble Lord,

I Will speak with the Jesuite to morrow, and deliver him his admonition from the King, but do send your Lordship here enclosed a Copie of the Conference which I procured from him without his privity, onely to make his Majesty, and your Lordship, merry. I have also received a Letter concerning the French Ambassadour, which I will be ready to put in execution as your Lordships servant, and Deputy, but not otherwise. Yet your Lordship will give me leave, out of that freedom (which was wont to be well interpreted by your Lordship) to let your Lordship understand, that I find all businesses of restitution of ships, and goods thus taken, to have been handled before the Councel in Star-chamber all the reigns of *Henry* 7th and H. 8h without any contradiction of the Lord Admiral for the time being. But this to your Lordship in secret. I will be very carefull of the Earl of *Desmond*, that neither his cause, nor your Lordships reputation, shall suffer thereby; and this is all the account I can yet give of your Lordships Letter, save that I humbly expect that answer which your Lordships own luckie hand hath promised in the Postscript of one of them, I would ease your Lordship in this place, but to prevent complaint, that (peradventure) may be first invented, and then presented. Your Lordship shall hear of a long narrative of our Councel-Table dispatches. That passage of our Letter, which (as it now goeth) doth hope that his Majesty will spare to confer any suits of moment in *Ireland* until the return of the *Irish* Committee, was a blunt request to the King, to grant no suits there without our advice. Against this (concluded in my absence the first day of the Term) I spake first to the Prince privately (who allowed of my reasons) then (when the President would not mend it) at the Table openly, that I did utterly dislike we should tutor his Majesty, how to grant suits, especially in Letters, that are to remain upon Record. My Lord of *Cantuar*. and the Earl Marshal said, they had many Presidents in that kind. I answered, I knew they had none, but in the Kings time and that I wished them (as I do) all torn out of the book, and cast into the fire. I concealed my reasons, which now I will reveal unto your Lordship; because this is the third time I have expressed unto your Lordship, under my hand my dislike of this kind of limiting his Majesty, otherwise then by word of mouth.

First, if his Majesty (which we see so often done) shall dispose of these suits otherwise, here are so many Records remaining to malicious men, to observe his Majesties aversness from following the advice of the Councel board.

Secondly, if your Lordship shall procure any suits in this kind, here are Records also in time to come, that you cross and thwart the Government of the Kingdom. And I pray God, this be but mine own jealousie. The passage in the Letter, with my prating, and his Highness help, was altered, and for fear of mis-reporting, I make bold to relate the truth hereof to you Lordship.

My Lords proceeded very resolutely in those reformations which concerned other men. The Commission of fees enables the Committees to call before them all the Judges as well as their under-Officers (which was more then the King express'd at *Hampton* Court) amongst whom the Lord Keeper is one, who, from the conquest to this day, was never subjected to the call of any power in the Kingdom, but the King and the Parliament. And although I have not one Penny of Fee which hath not continued above one hundred years, yet for the honour of the prime place in the state (though now disgraced by the contemptibleness of the Officer) I am an humble suiter unto your Lordship, that my Person may be exempted from the command of Sir *Edwin Sandys*, or (indeed) any man else, besides the King my Master. Otherwise I shall very patiently endure it, but the King hereafter may dislike it. The Justices of the Peace are also appointed, but (if the Judges and my self be not utterly deceived) to no purpose in the world, nor service to his Majesty. But when their Lordships came to surrender the under-Lieutenantships to his Majesties hands, whom the Lord President, and I, held fit to be created, henceforward, by several Commissions under the Great Seal, it was stiffly opposed, and stood upon, that the King should name them in

their

The Lord Keeper, to the Duke.

their Lordships Commissions only (according to a President in the late Queens time) that is, the King shall have the naming, but they still the appointing of them. And now it was pressed, that his Majesty intended not to disgrace his Lords, &c. and your Lordship is to have a Letter from Mr Secretary to know his Majesties mind herein. If his Majesty shall not ordain them to be created by several Patents, it were better a great deal they should continue as they do. I am very tedious in the manner and (peradventure) in the matter of this Letter. I humbly crave pardon, &c.

Octob. 12. 1622.

The Lord Keeper, to the Duke.

May it please your Grace,

I Have no business of the least Consideration to trouble your Grace withal at this time, but that I would not suffer Mr. *Greyham* to return without an expression of my respect and obligation. I would advertise your Grace, at large, of the course held with our Recusants, but that I know Mr. Secretary is enjoyned to do so, who best can. His Majesty at *Salisbury* having referred the suit of these Embassadours to the Earl of *Carlile*, and Mr. Secretary *Conway*, sent (by their resolutions) some Articles unto us (the Lord Treasurer, Secretary *Calvert*, Sir *Richard Weston*, and my self) to this effect.

1. To grant a pardon of all offences past, with a dispensation for those to come, to all the Roman Catholicks, obnoxious to any laws made against the Recusants.

2. And then to issue forth to general Commands under the Great Seal, the first, to all the Judges, and Justices of the Peace ; and the other to all Bishops, Chancellors, and Commissaries, not to execute any Statute made against them.

Their general pardon we have passed, and sent unto his Majesty (from whence it is not returned) in as full and ample manner as they could desire, and pen it. The other general and vast prohibition I prevailed with the rest of the Lords to stop as yet, and gave (in three days conference) such reasons to the two Embassadours, that (although it is no easie matter to satisfie the Caprichiousness of the Latter of them) yet they were both content it should rest, until the Infanta had been six Months in *England*. My reason, if it may please your Grace, was this. Although this general favour and connivence, whereof there are twenty of the Prime Counsel know nothing as yet, must at last be known to all the Land; yet is there a great difference between the publishing thereof *A Golpe*, at one push as it were, and that instilling of it into their knowledge by little and little, by reason of favours done to particular Catholicks. The former course might breed a general impression, if not a mutiny. This Latter will but loosen the tongues but of some few particulars, who understand of their neighbours pardon, and having vented their dislikes, when they have not many to Sympathize with them , they grow coole again ; so as his majesty afterwards may enlarge these favours without any danger at all.

Secondly, to forbid Judges (against their oaths) and Justices of the Peace (sworn likewise) to execute the Law of the Land, is a thing unpresidented in this Kingdom, *& Durus Sermo*, a very harsh and bitter pill to be digested upon a suddain, and without some preparation. But to grant a pardon, even for a thing that is *Malum in se*, and a dispensation with Penal Laws (in the profit whereof the King onely is interested) is usual and full of presidents, and examples. And yet is this Latter onely tending to the safety, the former but to the glory and insolency of the Papists, and the magnifying the service of the Embassadours ends too dearly purchased, with the endangering of a tumult in three Kingdoms.

Thirdly and Lastly, his Majesty useth to speak to his Bishops , Judges and Justices of the peace , by his Chancellour, or Keeper (as your Grace well knoweth) and by his Great Seal ; and I can signifie his Majesties pleasure unto them, with less noise and danger, which I mean to do hereafter, (if the Embassadours shall press it,) to this effect, unless your Grace shall from his Highness, or your own judgement) direct otherwise.

That whereas his Majesty being at this time to mediate for favour to many Protestants in forreign parts, with Princes of another Religion, and to sweeten the entertainment of the Princess into this Kingdom, who is as yet a Roman Catholick, doth hold a mitigation of the rigour of those Laws made against Recusants to be a necessary inducement to both those purposes, and hath therefore issued forth some pardons of Grace and favour to such Roman Catholicks, of whose faithfulness and fidelity to the State he rests assured. That therefore you the Lords, Bishops, Judges, and Justices, (each of those to be written unto by by themselves) do take notice of this his Majesties pardon and dispensation, with all such penal Laws, and demean your selves accordingly, &c.

Thus have I been too tedious and troublesome unto your Grace, and crave your pardon therefore, and some directions (which you may cause Sir *Francis Cottington*, or some other, to write, without your Graces trouble) if there shall appear any cause of alteration. Doctor *Bishop*, the new Bishop of *Calcedon*, is come to *London* privately, and I am much troubled thereabouts, not knowing what to advise his Majesty in this posture, as things stand at this present. If you were shipped (with the Infanta) the onely Counsel were, to let the Judges proceed with them presently, hang him out of the way, and the King to blame my Lord of *Cantuar.* or my self for it. But before you be shipped in such form and manner, I dare not assent, or connive at such a course. It is (my gracious Lord) a most insolent part, and an offence (as I take it) against our Common Law (and not the Statutes onely, which are dispenced withal) for an English man to take such a consecration without the Kings consent, and especially to use any Episcopal Jurisdiction in this Kingdom, without the royal assent; and Bishops have been, in this State, put to their fine and ransom, for doing so, three hundred years ago.

I will cease to be further troublesome, and pray to Almighty God to bless your Grace, and in all humbleness take my leave, and rest, &c.

Aug. 30. 1623.

The Lord Keeper, to the Duke.

May it please your Grace,

DOn *Francisco* being with me this night, about a pardon for a poor *Irish* man, whom I reprieved from execution, at the suit of those Gentlemen of *Navarra*, which are here with the Marquess, let fall by a kind of supposition (affirming the matter to be as yet in the womb, and not fully shaped, and digested) words to this effect.

That if the King of *Spain* should make a double marriage with the second Brother of *France*, and his Sister, and bestow the Palatinate as a Dower upon his Sister, in what case were we then?

I answered, That we should be, then, in no worse case (for ought I knew) then we are now: but that *Germany* might be in a far better case. Peradventure it was but a word let fall, to terrifie me withal.

But your Grace may make that use of it, as to understand the language, if your Grace shall hear any mention thereof hereafter. I am very glad, and do give God thanks *par le mejora de su hijuela hermosissima*. And do rest, &c.

Surely the French Embassadour is secret, and more suspected then formerly by the People.

January 6. 1623.

The Lord Keeper, to the Duke.

May it please your Grace,

NOT presuming to write unto your Grace, being so offended at me, but resolved with sorrow and Patience to try what I was able to suffer, without the least thought of opposition against your absolute pleasure, his Highness hath encouraged, and commanded the contrary, assuring me (which I cannot repeat again without tears) that, upon his credit, your Grace neither did, nor doth conceive any such real distast againste me, but did onely suspect I had conceived his Highnesses mind in that full manner, which his Highness himself is now fully satisfied I did not. In the which errour, and mistake of the Princes resolution, for want of conference with your Grace, or some other, I did (as I freely confessed) offend his Highness, but not your Grace at all. Being ever resolved to stand, or fall (though diversified in opinion) Your Graces most faithful and constant servant. I humbly therefore beseech your Grace; first, to receive back this enclosed Letter of Mr. *Packers*, and to burn the same, then to receive my soul, in gage and pawn.

1. That I never harboured in this breast one thought of opposition to hurt your Grace, from the first hour I saw your face.

2. I never consulted (much less practised) with any Lord of that Committee to vote on the one or the other side.

The Lord Keeper, to the Duke.

3. I do not know that Lord in *England* that hath any design against your Grace, and when I shall know any such, whosoever it be, I shall be his enemy as long as he continueth so unto your Grace.

4. I do not know (nor do I believe,) but that your Grace stands as firm in his Majesties favour, and in his Highness, as ever you did in all your life.

5. I never made the least shew of siding with any opposite Lord unto your Grace, and I defie any man that shall avow it.

6. I never divulged your Graces, or the secrets of any man.

In the next place, I do most humbly and heartily crave your Graces pardon, for suspecting (that is the utmost of my offence) so true, real, and noble a friend. Yet that I may not appear a very beast, give me leave once to remember, and ever after to forget, the motives which drew me so to do. And I will do it in the same order they came into my head.

1. Your Graces charge upon me at *York* house, that I was a man odious to all the world.

2. *Michels* Voluntary Confession, that my Lord *Mandevil* shewed him a Letter from *Spain*, avowing, that the first action your Grace would imbarque your self in should be to remove me out of this place, which the least word of your mouth unto me is able to do.

3. A report of the *Venetian* Embassadour, that amongst others, your Grace intended to sacrifice me this Parliament, to appease the dislike of immunities exercised towards the Catholicks.

4. Your Graces motion unto my self concerning my place (which now I absolutely know proceeded out of love) at *White-hall*.

5. A most wicked lie, that one told, he heard your Grace move his Highness, to speak unto me to quit my place, after your Graces professions of friendship to me.

6. Mr. Secretary *Conwaies* and my Lord *Carlile's* estrangedness from me, which I suspected could not be (for I ever loved them both) but true copies of your Graces displeasure.

I have opened to my truest friend all my former thoughts; and being fully satisfied by his Highness how false they are in every particular, do humbly crave your Graces pardon, that I gave a nights lodging to any of them all.

Although they never transported me a jot further, then to look about how to defend my self, being resolved (as God shall be my protector) to suffer all the obloquie of the world, before I would be drawn to the least ingratitude against your Grace. All that I beg is an assurance of your Graces former Love, and I will plainly profess what I do not in the least beg or desire from your Grace.

1. No Patronage of any corrupt or unjust act which shall be objected against me this Parliament.

2. No defence of me, if it shall appear I betrayed my King, or my Religion, in favour of the Papist, or did them any real respect at all, besides ordinary complements.

3. No refuge in any of my causes, or clamours against me (which upon a false supposal of your Graces displeasure may be many) otherwise then according to justice, and fair proceeding.

And let this paper bear record against me at the great Parliament of all, if I be not, in my heart and soul, your Graces most faithful and constant poor friend and Servant.

His Highness desires your Grace to move his Majesty to accept of my Lord *Sayes* Commission, and procure me leave to send for him. Also to move his Majesty that my Lord of *Hartfort* may be in the house, accepting his Fathers place, and making his protestation to sue for his Grandfathers, according to his Majesties Laws, when the King shall give him leave. His Highness, and my Lords, do hold this a modest and submissive Petition.

His Highness, upon very deep reasons, doubts whether it be safe to put all upon the Parliament, for fear they should fail to examine particular Dispatches, wherein they cannot but find many Contradictions. And would have the proposition onely to aid for the recovery of the Palatinate. To draw on an engagement I propound it might be, to advise his Majesty how this recovery shall be effected, by reconquering the same, or by a War of diversion. This will draw on a breach with *Spain*, with ripping up of private dispatches. His Highness seemed to like well hereof, and commanded me to acquaint your Grace therewith, and to receive your opinion. I humbly crave again two lines of assurance, that I am in your Grace's opinion, as I will ever be indeed, &c.

February 2. 1623

The Heads of that Discourse which fell from Don Francisco, *7. Die Aprilis,* 1624. 11. *of the Clock at night.*

This Relation was sent by the Lord Keeper to the Duke.

1. How he came to procure his accesses to the King. The Marquess putting *Don Carlos* upon the Prince and Duke in a discourse, thrust a Letter into the Kings hand, which he desired the King to read in private; The King said he would; thrust it into his pocket, and went on with his discourse, as if he had received none. The effect was, to procure private access for *Don Francisco* to come and speak with the King, which his Majesty appointed by my Lord of *Kelley*; and he by his secrecie, who designed for *Don Francisco* time and place.

2. At his first access, he told the King That his Majesty was a prisoner, or at leastwise besieged, so as no man could be admitted to come at him. And then made a complaint against the Duke, that he aggravated, and pretended accusations against *Spain*; whereas its onely offence was, that they refused to give unto him equal honour, and observance, as they did unto his Highness. And that this was the onely cause of his hatred against them.

3. At the last access, which was some 4 days ago, he made a long invective, and remonstrance unto the King, which he had put into writing in Spanish, which he read unto me, corrected with the hand of *Don Carlos*, which I do know. It was somewhat general, and very rhetorical, if not tragical, for the stile. The heads of what I read, were these, *viz.*

   1. That the King was no more a Freeman, at this time, then King *John* of *France*, when he was prisoner in *England*, or King *Francis*, when he was at *Madrid*, being besieged and closed up with the servants and vassals of *Buckingham*.

   2. That the Embassadours knew very well, and were informed 4 moneths ago, that his Majesty was to be restrained, and confined to his Country house, and pastimes, and the Government of the State to be assumed and disposed of by others, and that this was not concealed by *Buckinghams* followers.

   3. That the Duke had reconciled himself to all the popular men of the State, and drawn them forth out of prisons, restraints, and confinements, to alter the Government of the State at this Parliament, as *Oxford, Southampton, Say*, and others, whom he met at Suppers and Ordinaries, to strengthen his popularity.

   4. That the Duke, to breed an opinion of his own greatness, and to make the King grow less, hath oftentimes brag'd openly in Parliament, that he had made the King yield to this and that, which was pleasure unto them. And that he mentioned openly before the Houses his Majesties private oath, which the Embassadours have never spoken of to any creature to this hour.

   5. That these Kingdoms are not now governed by a Monarch, but by a *Triumviri*, whereof *Buckingham* was the first and the chiefest, the Prince the second, and the King the last; and that all look towards *Solem Orientem*.

   6. That his Majesty should shew himself to be, as he was reputed, the oldest and wisest King in *Europe*, by freeing himself from this Captivity, and eminent danger wherein he was, by cutting off so dangerous and ungrateful an affecter of greatness and popularity, as the Duke was.

   7. That he desired his Majesty to conceal this his free dealing with him, because it might breed him much peril and danger. And yet if it were any way available for his service, to reveal it to whom he pleased, because he was ready to sacrifice his life, to do him acceptable service.

And this was the effect of so much of the penned Speech, as I remember was read unto me out of the Spanish Copy.

His Majesty was much troubled in the time of this Speech.

His Offer to the King, for the restitution of the Palatinate.

To have a Treaty for three moneths for the restitution, and that money was now given in *Spain*, to satisfie *Bavaria*. That in the mean time, because the people were so distrustful of the Spaniard, the King might fortifie himself at home, and assist the Hollanders with men or money at his pleasure. And the King of *Spain* should not be offended therewith.

The Lord Keeper, to the Duke.

His opinion of our preparing of this Navy.

It was a defign of the Duke, to go to the Ports of *Sevil*, and there to burn all the Ships in the Harbour; which he laugh'd at.

Speeches which (he faid) fell from his Majefty, concerning the Prince.

1. That when he told the King, that his greatnefs with the Duke was fuch as might hinder his Majefty from taking a courfe to reprefs him; His Majefty replyed; He doubted nothing of the Prince, or his own power, to fever them two, when he pleafed.

2. His Majefty faid, That when his Highnefs went to *Spain*, he was as well affected to that Nation as heart could defire, and as well difpofed as any Son in *Europe*; but now he was ftrangely carried away with rafh and youthful Councels, and followed the humour of *Buckingham*, who had (he knew not how many) Devils within him fince that journey.

Concerning the Duke.

1. That he could not believe yet, that he affected popularity, to his difadvantage. Becaufe he had tried him, of purpofe, and commanded him to make difaffecting motions to the Houfes, which he performed, whereby his Majefty concluded, he was not popular.

2. That he defired *Don Francifco*, and the Embaffadours, (and renewed this requeft unto them by *Padre Maeftro* two days ago,) to get him any ground to charge him with any popular courfes, or to increafe a fufpicion of it, and he would quickly take a courfe with him.

3. That he had good caufe to fufpect the Duke of late, but he had no fervant of his own, that would charge him with any particular; nor knew he any himfelf.

The end (as was conceived) of Don Francifco's *defiring this Conference.*

He had heard that the Duke had pufh'd at me in Parliament, and intended to do fo again, when he had done with the Treafurer; and therefore fhewed, that if I would joyn to fet upon him with the King, there was a fit occafion.

I anfwered, that the Prince and the Duke had preferred me into my place, and kept me in it, and if I found them purfuing, I would not keep it an hour. That what favour foever I fhewed the Embaffadour, or Catholicks, I did it for their fakes, and had thanks of them for it. And that I would deal by way of Counfel with the Duke to be temperate, and moderate; but to be in oppofition to my friend, and Patron, I knew he (being one that profeffed fo much love unto me) would never expect from an honeft man. Upon the which anfwer he feemed fatisfied, and never replyed word in that kind.

I made an end of writing thefe notes about two of the clock in the morning.

The Lord Keeper, to the Duke, concerning Sir Richard Wefton.

May it pleafe your Grace,

I Hold it my duty to give your Grace a prefent account of this Patent made for Sir *Richard Wefton*. Having put off the Sealing of the fame as fairly as I could (though not without the clamour of one *Lake*, a fervant of Mr. *Chancellours*, who very faucily preft for a difpatch,) this morning, Mr. *Chancellour* fpake with me himfelf; to whom I made anfwer, That I would Seal his Patent, according to his Majefties Warrant, but would retain it in my hands (as I was directed,) until I either fpake with the King or received his farther Command in that behalf. He told me he would write unto your Grace concerning the ftay thereof, and the ftand of the Kings bufinefs, until it were delivered; which courfe (I told him) was very fair. After I acquainted his Highnefs with my Sealing and retaining of the Patent, and asked him, if he knew thereof. His Highnefs anfwered, he did know thereof, but gave no approbation of the courfe, and (although he durft not fpeak to crofs it) he hoped I fhould have directions from the King to pull off the Seals again. Three hours after I went to his Highnefs the fecond time, and asked him, if he meant really as he fpake, or intended onely to make me believe fo. I defired to know his mind, left I might fteer my courfe contrary to his intendment. His Highnefs anfwered, He meant really, and would endeavour to effectuate all that he fpake. Which I thought very fitting for your Grace to know with all fpeed.

But

The Lord Keeper, to the Duke.

But for the man himself, I must deliver unto your Grace my conscience. For ought I ever saw in him he is a very honest, and a very sufficient man, and such a one, as I never in all my life could observe to be any way false, or unfaithful unto your Grace. He was brought in by your Grace sore against my will, (as your Grace may call to mind what I said to your Grace at *Woodstock* to that effect) not that I disliked the Gentleman, but because I was afraid he would be wholly the Treasurers, who began then to out-top me, and appeared, to my thoughts, likely enough, by his daring and boldness, (two vertues very powerful and active upon our Royal Master,) in time to do as much to your Grace. From that time to this, I never observed in *Weston* any unworthiness, or ingratitude to your Grace. Nay, craving pardon, I will proceed one step farther, I know no fitter man in *England* for the office, if he come in as a creature of the Prince, and your Grace's; nor unfitter, if he should offer to take it, without your likings. I think your Grace will remember, that this fortnight, this hath been my constant opinion.

Upon the death of one Mr. *Read*, the Secretaries place for the Latine tongue is void. The Dean of *Winchester*, and I, moved the King for *Patrick Young*, the fittest man in *England* for that place. And the Prince did, and will second the motion. I beseech your Grace to assist us, or else the immodesty of his Competitor (that *Lake* I spake of in the beginning of this Letter) will bear down this most honest, and bashful creature.

God be thanked for your Graces recovery, and still preserve it. And so, &c.

May 24. 1624.

The Lord Keeper, to the Duke.

May it please your Grace,

I Could not suffer Sir *George Goring* to depart without these few lines, although the greatest matter of their contents must be this, to express unto your Grace my sorrow and affliction, that I have no matter or occasion at all, wherein to shew actually my affections and earnest desires to comply with my bounden duty in serving your Grace, and humbly to desire your Grace to believe, that there is no soul living shall do it more sincerely, and faithfully, to the utmost of my understanding, then my self will do. I add this Caution the rather, because if ever I have offended your Grace, I take Almighty God to witness, it was only for want of a perfect understanding of those high matters, and the persons bent, whom they concerned, not out of any corruption of affections towards your Grace, or the least staggering in a continued resolution to live, and die, your Graces most constant, and most faithful servant.

This, God in heaven (who seeth what I now write,) and the King, and Prince upon earth, do perfectly know, and I (nothing doubt it) will acknowledge unto your Grace. And thus with my most humble thanks unto your Grace for that assurance I received, that I remain (though unimployed and unprofitably) yet in your Graces good affection, I beseech Almighty God to preserve your health, and to increase your favour day by day with God, with the King, with the Prince, and with all good men. The daily vowes of, &c.

July 21. 1624.

The Lord Keeper, to the Duke.

May it please your Grace,

I Humbly thank your Grace for your favourable and Gracious remembrance, sent by my Neighbour, Sir *George Goring*. Though I despair to be able to make any other requital, yet will I never fail to serve your Grace most faithfully, and when I grow unuseful in that kind, to pray for you.

I beseech your Grace, that I may receive from the Prince's Highness, and your Grace, some directions how to demean my self to the *French* Embassadour, in matters concerning Recusants, and that Mr. Secretary may either address himself to Mr. Attorney General in these causes, or else write unto me plainly what I am to do.

His last letter required of me, and the Judges (who neither are, nor will be in Town these six weeks yet,) an account of this their supposed persecution, neither so much as intimating unto me what, or when I should return an answer, and supposeth some directions his Majesty should give me therein, the which (particularly, or dividedly from the Judges) I never received.

I ad-

The Lord Keeper, to the Duke.

I adventured, out of mine own head, to write that answer I imagine your Grace hath seen; whether I did well, or ill therein, I know not; but conceived his Majesty expected some answer. Yesterday the Embassadour sent unto me, to know if I had received any order from his Majesty to stay this (as he termed it) persecution. I assured him, there was no such matter in this State, and that, as yet, I had received no order from his Majesty of late, but was in expectation to hear from the Court very shortly. I humbly crave your Graces directions, what I am to say, or do, in the premises, being otherwise a meer stranger in all these proceedings. I write to no body herein besides your Grace; so as if I receive no direction, (which upon my head, and livelihood, I shall bury in all secrecie) I shall be in a pitiful perplexity, if his Majesty shall turn the Embassadour upon me, altogether unprovided how to answer. And so with my heartiest prayers for your Graceshealth, I rest,

August 22. 1624.   *Yours*, &c.

The Lord Keeper, to the Duke.

May it please your Grace,

WIth my most humble and hearty thanks for all your favours extended, and multiplied daily towards me, in sicknesse and health, which are such, and so many, that (although, I trust in God, I shall never prove so inhumane as to fail in any service, or faithfulness to your Grace,) I must for all that ever live, and die ungrateful. I thought fit to return unto your Grace this account of the message received by your Grace's Steward.

I spake with that Lord, and although he seemed to be quite off from the businesse, and had (to my knowledge) disposed of his money for a great and a fair purchase here in *London*, and was resolved never to touch any more upon *Wat Steward*, (who had touched somewhat of his,) and with whom he had agreed for 4000 l. yet hearing the proposition to come so intirely from me, as proceeding immediately from your Grace, whose good favours this Lord (I protest unto your Grace) hath earnestly desired; and if at any time he hath straggled aside from the Princes desires, and yours, it was meerly, and solely, because he thought he was not so much relied upon as others of his rank. He promiseth me sometime to morrow a reasonable answer.

His material Objections were these.

1: Quantity of the money; so as first and last he is out 16000 l. whereas *Cavendish*, his Countryman and neighbour, got up, from a Gentleman, for 14000 l. I answered; That I observed your Grace never got by any of these bargains, but that in this compass of a year or two, your favours exceed any gratuity presented.

2. Precedency before *Wallingford*, and especially *Vane*. I did promise (for your service) to dispute the latter, but could say nothing to the former, because he was a Viscount, and his far ancienter Baron.

3. Your Grace's favour, and reflection upon himself, (bred up in the experience of war and peace,) and upon his sons, all of them well bred, but most towards the War. I did answer generally, that upon his application of himself towards your Grace, I made little doubt, but he should receive good satisfaction in those expectances.

4. Times of payment. I told him, I knew he would demand but a convenient time therein; and that I knew your Grace would never stand upon.

If I have erred in any of these addresses, I pray let your Steward come; and reform me therein; as also to tell me, whether if I find him coming forward, I may not say unto him; That your Lordship, upon a former motion of mine, was willing upon the next change of the Commission for the Councel of the War, to add him unto the number.
        I propose this,

1. Because 'tis a new thing.
2. Because he desires some excuse unto the World, by reason of some future services, why his Majesty should receive him unto this honour. I have wearied my self, and by this time (which doth less become me) your Grace too. I beseech your Grace to pardon the blottings and extravagancies, my head being yet but meanly setled. I beseech God to blesse your Grace: And so, &c.

Post-script.

MAy it please your Grace, this Lord hath returned his answer, which, in good, faith seemeth to be with due respect unto your Grace.

1. That although the place was offered him for 4000 l. yet because the Offer proceeds
                                from

from your Grace, (which he voweth to esteem as an especial favour as long as he liveth) he will pay, to whom you shall assign 5000 l. and account it a real obligation of service to your Grace for ever, if you shall remit him the other thousand pound.

2. That for the time, with humble thanks for your noble favour (which becometh not him to take in appointing the time) he returns it to your Grace to nominate two dayes of payment, as your Steward, or the person assigned, shall think meet and fit for your Graces occasions, desiring some small respite for the former, but as little as the party please afterwards for the second payment: for his Lordship will send in for his moneys forthwith. And he will give his bonds, or (which I hold superfluous from so sure a Card) his Morgage in present for both payments.

3. If your Grace shall make him your servant with this favour so nobly condition'd, he hopes your Grace may proceed on with his Patent thus forward, without any stay for any other Corrival, which notwithstanding he humbly refers.

4. But desires, if his presentment be accepted, he may have leave by me to render his thanks unto your Grace personally sometime to morrow.

And so I leave your Grace, for this time, in Gods protection. And rest,

Octob. 11. 1624.   Yours, &c.

The Lord Keeper to the Duke, concerning the Countess of South-hampton.

May it please your Grace,

I Know how few arguments I need to use to perswade your Grace to works of Nobleness, and charity. Your fashion hath been, ever since my happiness of dependance upon you, to out-run, and prevent all Petitions in this kind. Yet pardon my boldness to be an humble suitor unto your Grace to go on, as I know you have already begun, in extending your Grace and goodness towards the most distressed widow, and children of my Lord of *South-hampton*. Your Grace cannot do any work of charity more approved of by God, more acceptable unto men, and that shall more recommend the memory of your Nobleness to future posterity. Sir *William Spencer* (the onely Sollicitor this sorrowful Lady hath now to imploy,) will present some particulars unto your Grace, whom God ever preserve in all health, and happiness. And so, &c.

Novemb. 17. 1624.

The Lord Keeper, to the Duke.

My most Gracious Lord,

I Most humbly beseech your Grace, for Gods sake, and his Churches, to consider of this motion, which I do make unto your Grace, concerning the Deanery of *York* now vacant, the Dean being struck dead suddenly, by a Letter, which one Dr. *Scot* procured from his Majesty, to he his Coadjutour.

It is not for any man in particular; but against Doctor *Scot*, that he may not by the importunity of any one upon your Grace be promoted to this place, being the sixth, or seventh place of preferment Ecclesiastical within this Kingdom; but that your Grace would be pleased to remove Doctor *White*, or Doctor *Hall*, or whom your Grace shall please, unto this great Deanry, and bestow the lesser Deanery (far above his merit) upon him.

For these Reasons.

1. I know that he hath sold away all his Livings which he hath had in this Church, and hath at this day never an one.

2. I am credibly informed, he oweth 5000l. at the least. A vast summe for a poor Scholar, and too much to be got up in a poor Church. And most of this money in *York*.

3. I know he is a great Gamester, and of no fitting conversation for a Church-man; but of very mean parts, either of Learning, or government.

4. I am certified at this time, that he is a man often overseen in drink; but this I do not know.

If therefore your Grace shall be pleased, upon my Lord *Mordant's* importunity, to procure him any Deanery, I do not doubt but his Lordship will be satisfied, and that Church eternally obliged unto you for that Commutation. And I beseech your Grace to believe him that is no way interested herein, that it concerns your Grace very much, in credit and reputation, that so mean a man (amongst such a choice as the Church of *England* doth afford,) be not by your

favour

The Lord Keeper, to the Duke.

favour preferred to so high a dignity. God be merciful to my sins, as I have no end herein but your honour, and the good of that Church; and therefore I recommend no particular man unto your Grace, but do rest

Decemb. 24. 1624.   *Yours,* &c.

The Lord Keeper, to the Duke, concerning Dr. Scott.

May it please your Grace,

I Humbly beseech you, interpret favourably what I said unto his Majesty or his Highness, as intending to put off Dr. *Scott* from this place: and no way (God be my witness) to cross your Grace, nor to hurt *Scott*, who might have been otherwise sufficiently provided for.

But I should have written or spoken unto your Grace? so I did in this Letter enclosed, upon *Christmass-eve*: But, I confess, I durst not send it, for fear of offending your Grace, which I do take all possible diligence to avoid.

But, I spake unto the King and Prince; I did so; but with this caution, (which I know they do remember) that if your Grace would not, upon the motion, exchange *Scott* to some other preferment, I did not hold it fit to press these charges against him, but would do my endeavour to still and quiet those of the Church of *York*, who (I confess unto your Grace) are the men that have written against him.

But I recommended Dr. *White*, and another to the Prince, and Dr. *Warner* to your Grace; I confess it; but must distinguish the times, and the manner. I commended Dr. *Warner*, when I was informed Dr. *White* had his answer, and denial, and that your Grace was off from Dr. *Scott*, and did desire to hear from me what Doctor *Warner* was, whom I recommended onely in general terms, upon the suit of another. What I said of him, I believe, and know to be true; but he is so far from being any creature of mine, that, I protest before the Almighty God, I never spake one word with the man, to this very hour, in all my life. I did conceive so meanly of Doctor *Scott*, that no worthy man in the Kingdom should have failed of my recommendations in this particular.

Now I know your Grace's resolution, I do alter my opinion, and humbly crave your Grace's pardon for my medling therein, although I know his Highness will bear me witness, it was with all dutifull respect unto your Grace. I shall be very carefull of giving your Grace the least cause of jealousie in this kind again. And whereas I had put a poor suit in your Grace's hands, about the helping of my poor fortunes, I will let that, and all others, fall, and desire onely to be accounted

January 5. 1624.   *Yours,* &c.

The Lord Keeper, to the Duke.

May it please your Grace,

THis heavy and unexpected accident of my Lord Stewards death makes me to be troublesom unto your Grace at this time. In safety and discretion, I might very easily spare this labour: But my obligation to your Grace is such, as if that I conceal any thing, which but my self apprehends fit to be represented to your Grace, whilest I affect the title of a reserved, close, and wise, I may lose the other of an honest, man, which I more esteem.

Thus much by way of preface.

I represent this Office of a Lord Steward, as a place to be either accepted of by your self, or else to be discontinued, (as for many years, towards the latter end of Queen *Elizabeth*, and the beginning of our Masters Reign it was,) and in any case, not to be placed upon another, without the deliberation of some few years at the least: Being an Office, that none but the King's Kinsmen, or Favourites, or Counter-favourites (raised up of purpose to balance the great one) have anciently possessed: I could desire your Grace had it in your own person, for these Reasons.

1. It is an Office of fair and very competent gettings: but that is scarce considerable.
2. It keeps you, in all changes and alterations of years, neer the King; and gives unto you all the opportunities of accesses, without the envy of a Favourite. I beseech your Grace, pause well upon this, and call to mind, if the Duke of *Richmond* was not in this case.
3. It gives you opportunities to gratifie all the Court, great and small, *Virtute Officii,*

in right of your place: which is a thing better accepted of, and interpreted, then a court:sie from a Favorite; because in this you are a dispenser of your own, but in the other (say many envious men) of the Kings goodness, which would flow fast enough of it self, but that it is restrained to this pipe and channel onely.

4. There must be, one day, an end of this attendance as a Bed-chamber man; but, I hope; never of being next unto the King, as a great Councellor, and Officer, and above all others: which you cannot be, but by this Office. The Master of the Horse is but a Knights place, at the most; and the Admiral's (in time of action) either to be employed abroad personally, or to live at home in that ignominy and shame, as your Grace will never endure to do so.

I will trouble your Grace with a tale of *Dante*, the first *Italian* Poet of note: Who, being a great and wealthy man in *Florence*, and his opinion demanded, Who should be sent Embassador to the Pope? made this answer, that he knew not who; *Si jo vo, chi sta, Si jo sto, chi va*; if I go, I know not who shall stay at home; if I stay, I know not who can perform this employment. Yet your Grace, staying at home in favour and greatness with his Majesty, may, by your designs and directions, so dispose of the Admiral, as to enjoy the glory, without running the hazard of his personal employment. My gracious Lord, if any man shall put you in hope, that the Admiralty will fill your coffers, and make you rich; call upon them to name one Admiral that ever was so. As in time of hostility there is some getting, so are there hungry and insatiable people presently to devour the same. God made man to live upon the land, and necessity onely drives him to sea. Yet is not my advice absolutely for your relinquishing of this; but, in any case, for the retaining of the other place, though with the loss of the Admiralty.

5. I beseech your Grace, observe the Earl of *Leicester*, who (being the onely Favourite, in Queen *Elizabeth's* time that was of any continuance) made choice of this place onely, and refused the Admiralty two several times, as being an occasion, either to withdraw him from the Court, or to leave him there laden with ignominy: And yet, being Lord Steward, wise, and in favour, he wholly commanded the Admiralty, and made it ministerial, and subordinary to his directions.

6. Remember, that this Office is fit for a young, a middle, and an old man to enjoy; and so is not any other, that I know, about his Majesty: Now God Almighty having given you favour at the first, and since a great quantity (I never flattered your Grace nor do now) of wit, and wise experience; I would humbly recommend unto your Grace, this opportunity to be neerest unto the King in your young, your middle, and your decreasing age; that is, to be on earth, as your Piety will one day make you in heaven, an everlasting Favourite. There are many objections which your Grace may make; but if I find any inclination in your Grace to lay hold upon this Proposition, I dare undertake to answer them all. Your Grace may leave any Office you please (if your Grace be more in love with the Admiralty then I think you have cause) to avoid envy. But my final conclusion is this, to desire your Grace most humbly, to put no other Lord into this Office, without just and mature deliberation; and to pardon this boldness, and haste, which makes me to write so weakly in a Theme that, I perswade my self, I could maintain very valiantly. I have no other copy of this Letter, and I pray God your Grace be able to read this. I send your Grace a Letter, delivered unto me from *Conde Gondomar*, and dated either at *Madrid*, or (as I observe it was written first) at *London*: There is no great matter at whether of the places it was invented. I humbly beseech your Grace, to send, by this Bearer, the resolution for the Parliament: And do rest

March 2. 1624.   *Yours*, &c.

The Lord Keeper, to the Duke, about Sir Robert Howard.

May it please your Grace,

SIr *Robert Howard* appeared yesterday, and continues obstinate in his refusal to swear When we came to examine the Commission for our power to fine him for this obstinacie, we found, that Sir *Edward Coke* (fore-seeing, out of a prophetical spirit, how neer it might concern a Grand-child of his one day) hath expunged this clause (by the help of the Earl of *Salisbury*) out of the Commission, and left us nothing but the rustic sword of the Church, Excommunication, to vindicate the Authority of this Court. We have given him day until Saturday next, either to conform, or to be excommunicated. She hath answered wittily, and cunningly, but yet sufficient for the Cognisance of the Court: Confesseth a fame of incontinencie against her and *Howard*; but saith, it was raised by her Husbands kindred. I do not doubt,

doubt, but the businefs will go on well; but (peradventure) more flowly, if Howard continue refractory, for want of this power to fine and amerce him. I befeech your Grace, either to procure me the favour to come, or to excufe my not feeing his Majefty in this time of his indifpofition, which, I hear, ftill continueth. I befeech Almighty God (as in eternal duty I am bound) prefently to eafe him, and reftore him to his perfect health. Mr. *Packer's* being away makes me unmannerly. I am humbly tod efire your Grace, to be pleafed to move his Majefty (at your firft opportunity) to fign this Commiffion, for the proroguing of the Parliament; and to read unto his Majefty this Paper of names here enclofed, (which his Majefty is not to fign) knowing his pleafure, whether he alloweth of them for Commiffioners for the laft fubfidy of the Lords. I have added to the former the Earl of *Montgomery*, according to your Grace's direction, whom God Almighty ever preferve. It is the prayer of, *&c.*

March 11. 1624.

The Lord Keeper, to the Duke.

May it pleafe your Grace,

FOr your Brothers bufinefs, this is all I have to acquaint your Grace with: Sir *Robert Howard* appeared, yefterday, at *Lambeth*, pretended want of Councel, (the Doctors being out of Town) defired refpite until to morrow, and had it granted by my Lords Grace. Moft men think, he will not take his Oath at all; I do incline to the contrary opinion, becaufe (to my knowledge) he hath fent far and near, for the moft able Doctors in the Kingdom, to be feed for him, which were great folly, if he intended not to anfwer. He is extremely commended for his clofenefs and fecrecie by the major part of our auditors, (the He and She good-fellows of the Town;) and though he refufeth to be a Confeffor, yet is fure to die a Martyr, and moft of the Ladies in Town will offer at his Shrine. The Lady *Hatton*, fome nine dayes fince, was at *Stoke*, with the good Knight, her Husband, for fome counfel in this particular: but he refufed to meddle therewithall, and difmift her Ladyship, when fhe had ftaid with him very lovingly half a quarter of an hour.

The caufe of my troubling your Grace is this: The French Embaffadour is fired with fome complaints of our Recufants, who (I verily believe) work upon him purpofely, finding him to be of a combuftible difpofition. To morrow he is refolved to come upon you and our Mafter, with complaints, for lack of performances to the Papifts. And becaufe I would furnifh your Grace with as much anfwer as I am acquainted with, (nothing doubting but your Grace is otherwife better provided) I make bold to prefent your Grace with thefe particulars.

1. With a Letter from my Lord Archbifhop of *York*, in anfwer to another of mine; which fhews how really his Majefties promife hath been in that kind performed. I befeech your Grace to keep it fafe in your pocket, until I fhall have the honour to wait upon your Grace, when you have made ufe of the fame.

2. If your Grace fhall hear him complain of the Judges in their charges, and of their receiving of Indictments; your Grace may anfwer, That thofe Charges are but Orations of courfe, opening all the penal Laws; and the Indictments, being prefented by the Countrey, cannot be refufed by the Judges: But the Judges are ordered to execute nothing actually againft the Recufants; nor will they do it, during the negotiation.

3. Your Grace may put him in mind, that my Lord Keeper doth every day, when his (the Lord Embaffadour's) Secretary calls upon him, grant forth Writs to remove all the perfons indicted in the Countrey, into the Kings Bench, out of the power and reaches of the Juftices of the Peace: And that, being there, the King may, and doth, releafe them at his pleafure.

4. That the *Spanifh* Embaffadour never had, nor defired, more then thefe favours.

5. That you are informed, that copies of Letters, written from the King to both the Archbifhops, are fpread abroad in *Stafford-fhire*, to his Majefties difadvantage, (for fo it is;) and that thereby my Lord Embaffadour may perceive the bent of the *Englifh* Catholicks, which is, not to procure eafe and quietnefs to themfelves; but fcandals to their neighbouring Proteftants, and difcontentments againft the King and State.

I humbly crave your Grace's pardon for this boldnefs and tedioufnefs; and, with my hearty prayers for your health, do reft

March 13. 1624.

Yours, &c.

The Lord Keeper, to the Duke.

May it please your Majesty,

I Send your Grace here inclosed, the Kings Commission, and the Prince's Proxie, not fairly written, (which the Ambassadours upon the place may procure in a french hand,) but yet legibly, and possibly. The Prince's Proxie refers the manner unto the articles, and particularly to the second, third, and fourth Section of those Articles; which gives me occasion to begg of your Grace pardon, to desire your Grace to think seriously upon the third Section, to advise with the Prince, and to give Mr. *Packer* charge to inform your Grace punctually what he knoweth, and may inform himself concerning those particulars. That is, How the Queen *Margaret* of *France* was married to *Henry* the fourth, and how Madam his sister was married to the Prince of *Lorrein*. For although they are both made alike in in the article, yet surely they were not married after the same fashion. For the Dutchess of *Barr* was married in a closet, without a Mass, by words only of the present tense, as I believe, I have read in the History of *Thuanus*. A favour, which will hardly be granted to your Grace. And how Queen *Margaret* was married, my Lords the Ambassadours will soon learn, if your Grace will be pleased to write unto them.

I hold it (in a manner) necessary, that your Grace do carry over with you, in your company, one Civilian, to put your Grace in mind of the formalities required; and if your Grace be of that mind, your own Doctor, Doctor *Reeves*, is as fit as any man else, who is a good Scholar, and speaks that language. Your Grace hath revived my Lord of *Clare*, sithence I spake with your Grace. And I beseech your Grace to follow that resolution, and to let Mr. *Packer* draw up a warrant of three or four lines signed by the King to me, to place him with the rest of the Councel of War. It will be an occasion to take up more of that time which he now spends with the Lady *Hatten*. For now I am resolved, that I was of the right in my conjecture to your Grace, that his Lordship had utterly refused my Lady *Purbecks* cause (of the which the very common people begin to be ashamed) but is deeply engaged against my Lady *Dutchess of* of *Richmond*, in the business of that famous (or rather notorious) fœminine Contract and *Richmond* bargain, of sixteen hundred pounds by the year, for a house to sleep in.

When your Grace shall draw up your Instructions, you will be pleased to use the words, to contract, Espouse, and marry Our Welbeloved Son, &c. because they do in those parts contract alwaies before marriage. And your Grace will be pleased to express his Majesties pleasure, that this is to be done by your self, and no other: Because although the two Earls, upon the place, have some such general words in their Commission, yet your Grace only is named in the Prince's Proxie, and now solely imployed by the King to that purpose. Although I conceived this restrait to be fitter a great deal for the instructions, then the Commission.

I am extream sorry to hear what a grievous fit his Majesty had this last night. But I hope it is a farewell of the Agues, and I pray God it be the last fit. And now am an humble suitor again, that I may come and look upon his Majesty, resolved to say nothing, but that which I will never cease to say, God bless him. If your Grace Holds it inconvenient, I beseech your Grace to excuse me, and to account me as I will ever be found,

March, 22. 1624. *Yours &c.*

The Lord Keeper, to the Duke.

May it please your Grace.

I Received your Graces Letter by Mr. *Killegrew*, so full of that sweetness, as could never issue from any other Fountain then that one breast so fraught with all goodness and virtue; *Dick Winne* may write freely (as he talks) but alas! what can my wretched self perform, that should deserve the least acknowledgment from him to whom I owe so infinitely much more then the sacrificing of my life amounts to? only my love makes me sometimes write, and many times fear, fondly and foolishly, for the which I hope your Grace will pardon me. I have been frighted more about three weeks since (about quarrels and jarrs, which now *Dick Greyhams* hath related in part unto the King) then at this present, I am. For Gods sake be not offended with me, if I exhort you to do that which I know you do, to observe

The Lord Keeper, to the Duke. 309

serve his Highness with all lowliness, humility, and dutifull obedience, and to piece up any the least seam-rent; that heat and earnestness might, peradventure, seem to produce. I know (by looking into my self) these are the symptomes of good natures. And for Gods sake I beg it, as you regard the prayers of a poor friend, if the great Negotiation be well concluded, let all private disagreements be wrapped up in the same, and never accompany your Lordships into *England*, to the joy and exultation of your enemies, if any such ingratefull Devils are here to be found: I am in good earnest, and your Lordship would believe it, if your Grace saw but the tears that accompany these lines.

I beseech you, in your Letter to the Marquess *Hamilton*, intimate unto him your confidence, and reliance upon his watchfulness and fidelity in all turns which may concern your Grace. I have often lied unto his Lordship, that your Grace hath, in many of my Letters, expressed as much, and so have pacified him for the time. If we did know, but upon whom to keep a watchfull eye, for disaffected reports concerning your service; it is all the intelligence he and I do expect. His Majesty (as we conceive) is resolved to take certain oaths, which you have sent hither; and I pray God, afterward, no further difficulties be objected. I have had an hours discourse with his Majesty, yesterday morning, and do find him so disposed towards your Lordship as my heart desireth; yet he hath been informed of the discontentments, both with the *Conde de Olivarez*, and the Earl of *Bristol*. Here is a strange Creation passed of late, of a Vice-Countessship of *Maidenhead*, passed to the Heirs Males, who must be called hereafter Vice-Countess *Fynch*: But my Lady Dutchess hath the Land, and (as they say) hath already sold it to my Lord Treasurer, or shared it with him. I stayed the Patent, until I was assured your Lordship gave way thereunto.

My good Lord, because I have heard that they have, in those parts, a conceipt of our Church, as that they will not believe that we have any Liturgy, or Book of Common-prayer, at all, I have (at mine own cost) caused the Liturgy to be translated into *Spanish*, and fairly Printed; and do send you, by this Bearer, a couple of the Books, one for his Highness, the other for your Grace; not sending any more, unless your Grace will give directions. His Majesty was acquainted therewith, and alloweth of the business exceedingly. The Translatar is a *Dominican*, a zealous Protestant, and a good Scholar; and I have secured him to our Church, with a Benefice, and a good Prebend. Because we expect, every day, the dispatching of Sir *Francis Cottington* thitherward, I will not trouble your Grace further, at this time; but do earnestly pray unto God to bless your Grace, both now, and ever hereafter, with all his favours and blessings, spiritual and temporal; and rest, &c.

The Lord Keeper, to the Duke.

May it please your Grace,

NOw that I understand, by Sir *John Hipsley*, how things stand between your Grace and the Earl of *Bristol*, I have done with that Lord, and will never think of him otherwise then as your Grace shall direct: nor did I ever write one syllable to that effect, but in contemplation of performing true service to your Grace.

I was much abused in the Lady *Hennage* her Vice-Countess-ship, being made to believe, it was your Grace's act, or else I had stayed it finally, (until the Princes return) as I did for a time. If your Grace will give any directions in matters of that nature, I can pursue them. My Lord Treasurers sons Wardship is a thing of no moment at all, and not worthy your Grace's thinking of: And, in good faith, as far as getting and covetousness will give him leave, I do not see, but that Lord is (since your absence) very respective of your Grace, especially in your own person and affairs. I never received any answer from your Grace, concerning the Provostship of *Eaton*; nor was it good manners for me to press for the same, because in my Letters I did presume to name my self. The place is mine to bestow, for this time, and not his Majesties, nor the Colledges: But I do very willingly reserve the Collation of the same, to be disposed as your Grace shall please: Yet this will be a sufficient answer to any former promise, or any reasonable competitor.

His Majesty (as your Grace best knoweth) promised me, at the delivery of the Seal, a better Bishoprick, and intended it, certainly, if any such had fallen. My Charge is exceeding great, my Bribes are very little, my Bishoprick, Deanry, and other *Commendams*, do not clear unto me above one thousand pounds a year, at the uppermost: It hath pleased God, that the casualties of my Office (which is all the benefit of the same, and enriched my Lord

Ellesmere)

The Lord Keeper, to the Duke.

Ellesmere) hath not been worth to me, these two years past, one shilling: It may mend, when it pleaseth God.

I leave all these, and my self, who am your Vassal, at your Lordships feet, and do rest, &c.

Your Grace's, &c.

J. L. C. S.

Post-script.

May it please your Grace, I troubled his Highness with a long relation of the *Consulto* we had about his Majesties taking of the Oath: Which I had written to your Grace, and not to his Highness, but that I was frighted by great men, that I had done his Highness a displeasure, in pressing his Majesties assent unto the same: And, I protest, I was so poorly accompanied in my opinion, that I was truly afraid I had not done well: And therefore I took occasion to write my Reasons, at large, unto the Prince; which, I heard by Sir *John Hipsley*, from your Grace, was well taken. I humbly thank your Grace, who, I know, forwarded the same. And so I perceive by a Letter from his Highness, so full of sweetness, as I am over-whelmed.

J. L. C. S.

The Bishop of Lincoln, (sometime Lord Keeper) to the Duke.

Most gracious Lord,

BEing come hither, according unto the duty of my place, to do my best service for the preparation to the Coronation, and to wait upon his Majesty for his Royal pleasure and direction therein; I do most humbly beseech your Grace, to crown so many of your Grace's former favours, and to revive a creature of your own, struck dead onely with your displeasure, (but no other discontentment in the universal world) by bringing of me to kiss his Majesties hand, with whom I took leave in no dis-favour at all. I was never hitherto brought into the presence of a King by any Saint besides your self: turn me not over (most noble Lord) to offer my prayers at new Altars. If I were guilty of any unworthy unfaithfulness for the time past, or not guilty of a resolution to do your Grace all service for the time to come, all considerations under Heaven could not force me to beg it so earnestly, or to profess my self, as I do before God and you,

Your Grace's most humble, affectionate, and devoted servant,

Jan. 7. 1625.

Jo. Lincoln.

The

The Lord of KENSINGTON'S
Letters, &c.

The Lord of Kensington, *to the Duke.*

My Noblest Lord,

I Find the Queen-Mother hath the only power of governing in this State; and I am glad to find it so, since she promiseth, and professeth, to use it to do carefull, and good offices in the way of increasing the friendship that is between us and this State, and likewise to relieve and assist the united provinces, the which they are preparing to do fully, and bravely: for she hath now a clear sight of the pretentions of the King of *Spain* unto the Monarchie of Christendom; during the absence of the King, who went out of this Town early the next day after I arrived here (before I was prepared to attend him) I have been often at the *Louvre*, where I had the honour to entertain the Queen Mother. She was willing to know upon what terms stood our Spanish alliance; I told her that their delays had been so tedious, that they had somewhat discouraged the King, and had so wearied the Prince and State, with the dilatorie proceedings in it, as that Treaty (I thought) would soon have an end; She strait said of marriage, taking it that way; I to'd her I believed the contrary, and I did so the rather, because the *Spanish* Ambassadour hath given it out, since my coming, that the Alliance is fully concluded, and that my journey had no other end, then to hasten his Master unto it, only to give them jealousies of me, because he at this time fears their dispositions stand too well prepared to desire, and affect a conjunction with us. And truly his report, and instruments, have given some jealousies to the persons of power in this State, especially since they find I can say nothing directly unto them; yet thus much I have directly from them. *Monsieur de Vieuville*, and others, (but he is the chief guider of all affairs here) That never was the affection of any State so prepared to accept all offers of amity and alliance, so we will clearly, and as disengaged persons, seek it, as is this; but as a wise minister, he saies, that until we have wholly and truly abandoned the Treaty with *Spain*, they may lose the friendship of a Brother-in-Law, that is already so, in hope of gaining another that they may fail of. But when we shall see it really, by a publique Commission, that may declare all dissolved that touches upon the way of *Spain*, we shall then understand their hearts not to be capable of more joy, then that will bring them. And the Queen-Mother told me she had not lost those inclinations that she hath heretofore expressed, to desire her Daughter may be given to the Prince, with many words of value unto the King, and person of the Prince, and more then this she could not (she thought) well say, it being most natural for the woman to be demanded and sought. It is most certain, that under-hand *Spain* hath done all that is possible to procure this State to listen to a cross marriage; but here they are now so well understood, as this bait will not be swallowed by them. This I have from a grave, and honest man, that would not be brought to justifie it; therefore he must not hear of it. It is the *Savoy* Ambassadour, that is resident here, a wise, and gallant Gentleman, who vows this to be most true. So general a desire was never expressed, as is here, for alliance with us: And if the King and Prince have as many reasons of State at this time, besides their infinite affection here, to have it so continued, let it be roundly, and clearly

pursued;

The Lord Kensington, to the Duke.

pursued, and then I dare promise as respective and satisfactory a reception as can be imagined, or desired. And if it were not too much sawciness for me to advise, I could wish that the propositions of a league and marrige may not come together, but may be treated a part. For I doubt whether it may not be thought a little dishonourable for this King to give his Sister condition lly, that if he will make war upon the King of *Spain* his brother, we will make the alliance with him; on the other part, if the league should be propounded here, with all those reasons of State that are now pressing for them to make it, they have causes to doubt. and so have we too, that we may both be interrupted in that; for certainly the King of *Spain* will (if he can possibly) please one side, the which they think here may be us, with the restitution of the *Palatinate*, and we may likewise fear may be them, with the rendring of the *Valtoline*, these being the only open quarrels we must ground upon. Now as long as these doubts may possess us both, this will prove a tedious and jealous work on both sides; But if we fall speedily upon a treaty, and conclusion of a marrige, the which will find (I am perswaded) no long delays here: neither will they strain us to any unreasonableness in conditions for our Catholiques (as far as I can find) then will it be a fit time for to conclude a league, the which they will then for certain do, when all doubts, and fears of failing off, are by this conjunction taken away, and the necessity of their own affairs, and safety, will then make them more desire it then we; and so would they now, if they could think it so sure, and so honorable for them. For the King of *Spain* hath so imbraced them of all sides, as they fear, and justly, that he will one day crush them to their destruction. My Lord, I do not presume to say any thing immediatly to the King, through your hands, this I know will pass unto him; and if he should find any weakness in this that I have presumed to say, let the strength of your favour exercise those accustomed Noblenesses that you have alwaies expressed unto

Your Graces most humble and obliged servant,
Kensington.

Postscript.
Within these few daies your Grace shall hear again from me; for as yet I have not seen the King, no otherwise then the first night I arrived here. This night he is come unto the Town again.

The Lord Kensington, to the Prince.

May It please your Highness,

I Find here so infinite a value of your person, and virtue, as what Instrument soever (my self the very weakest) having some commands (as they imagine) from you, shall receive excess of honours from them. They will not conceive me, scarce receive me, but as a publique instrument for the service of an Alliance, that above all the things in this world, they do so earnestly desire. The Queen Mother hath expressed, as far as she thinks is fit for the honour of her Daughter, great favour and good will in it. I took the boldness to tell her (the which she took extreamly well) that if such a Proposition should be made, your Highness could not believe, that she had lost her former inclinations, and desires in it; She said, your trust of her should find great respect; there is no preparation I find towards this business but by her, and all perswasions of amity made light, that look not towards this end. And Sir, if your intentions proceed this way, as by many reasons of State, and wisdom (there is cause now rather to press it, then slacken it) you will find a Lady of as much loveliness and sweetness to deserve your affection, as any creature under Heaven can do. And Sir, by all her fashions since my being here, and by what I hear from the Ladies, it is most visible to me, her infinite value, and respect unto you. Sir, I say not this to betray your belief, but from a true observation, and knowledg of this to be so; I tell you this, and must somewhat more, in way of admiration of the person of Madam, for the impressions I had of her were but ordinary, but the amazement extraordinary to find her, as I protest to God I did, the sweetest Creature in *France*. Her growth is very little, short of her age; and her wisdome infinitely beyond it. I heard her discourse with her Mother, and the Ladies about her, with extraordinary discretion and quickness. She dances (the which I am a witness of) as well as ever I saw any Creature; They say she sings most sweetly, I am sure she looks so. Sir, you have thousinds of servants here, that desire to be commanded by you, but most particularly the D. of *Chevereux*, and Monsieur *Le Grand*, who seek all opportunities to do you service, and have Credit and power to do so. Sir, if these that are strangers are thus ambitious of your Commands, with what infinite passion have I cause to beg them, that am your Vassal, and have no other glory but to serve you, as your Highness, &c.

Feb. 26 1624. Kensington.
Postscript.

The Lord Kensington, to the Prince.

Post-script.

Sir, The obligations you have unto this young Queen are strange, for with that same affection that the Queen your sister would do, she asks of you with all the expressions that are possible of joy, for your safe return out of *Spain*, and told me, that she durst say, you were weary with being there, and so should she, though she be a *Spaniard*: yet I find she gives over all thought of your Alliance with her sister. Sir, you have the fortune to have respects put upon you unlookd for; for as in *Spain* the Queen there did you good offices: so I find will this sweet Queen do. Who said, She was sorry, when you saw them practise their Masques, that Madam her sister (whom she dearly loves) was seen at so much disadvantage by you, to be seen afar off, and in a dark room, whose person and face hath most loveliness to be considered neerly. She made me shew her your Picture, the which she let the Ladies see, with infinite Commendations of your Person, saying, She hoped some good occasion might bring you hither, that they might see you like your self.

The Lord Kensington, to the Prince.

May it please your Highnesse,

I Cannot but make you continual repetitions of the value you have here, to be (as justly we know you) the most Compleat young Prince and person in the world. This reputation hath begotten in the sweet Princesse Madam so infinite an affection to your fame, as she could not contain her self from a passionate desiring to see your Picture, the shadow of that person so honoured; and knowing not by what means to compasse it, it being worn about my neck; for though others, as the Queen and Princesses, would open it, and consider it, the which ever brought forth admiration from them, yet durst not this poor young Lady look any otherwise on it then afar off, whose heart was nearer it then any of the others that did most gaze upon it. But at the last (rather then want that sight the which she was so impatient of) she desired the Gentlewoman of the house where I am lodged, that had been her servant, to borrow of me the picture, in all the secrecy that may be, and to bring it unto her, saying, She could not want that Curiositie, as well as others, towards a person of his infinite reputation. As soon as she saw the party that brought it, she retired into her Cabinet, calling only her in; where she opened the picture in such haste as shewed a true picture of her passion, blushing in the instant at her own guiltiness. She kept it an hour in her hands, and when she returned it, she gave it many praises of your person. Sir, this is a business so fit for your secrecy, as I know it shall never go farther then unto the King your Father, my Lord Duke of *Buckingaam*, and my Lord of *Carliles* knowledge. A tenderness in this is honourable; for I would rather die a thousand times, then it should be published, since I am by this young Lady trusted, that is for beauty and goodness an Angel.

I have received from my Lord of *Buckingham* an advertisment, that your Highness opinion is to treat of the General league first, that will prepare the other.

Sir, whatsoever shall be propounded will have a noble acceptation; though this give me leave to tell you, when you are free, as by the next news we shall know you to be; they will expect, that upon those declarations they have here already made towards that particularitie of the Alliance, that your Highness will go that readier and nearer way to unite and fasten by that knot the affection of these Kingdoms.

Sir, for the general, they all here speak that language that I should, and do, unto them, of the power and usurpation of the *Spaniards*, of the approaches they make to this Kingdom, the danger of the *Low-Countries*, the direct Conquest of *Germany* and the *Veltoline*. By which means we have cause to joyn in opposition of the Ambitions and mightiness of this King. The which, they all here say, cannot be so certainly done as by an Alliance with us. This they speak perpetually, and urge it unto my consideration.

Sir, unless we proceed very roundly, though they be never so well affected, we may have interruptions by the arts of *Spain*, that make offers infinite to the advantage of this State, at this time. But they hearken to none of them, untill they see our intentions towards them. The which if they find to be real indeed, they will give us brave satisfaction.

But Sir, your Fathers and your will, not my opinion, must be followed; and what Commandments your Highness shall give me shall be most strictly obeyed by the most devoted,

Your Highness most dutiful and humblest servant,
Kensington.

The Lord Kensington, to the Duke.

My Lord,

I Have already acquainted your Grace how generally our desires are met with here; much more cannot be said, then I have already, for that purpose. There was never known, in this Kingdome so entire an agreement for any thing, as for an Alliance with *England*, the Count of *Soissons* only excepted, who hath had some pretentions unto Madam; but those are now much discouraged, upon a free discourse the Cardinal of *Rochfalcont* made unto the Countess his Mother, telling her, That if she or her son believed, or could expect, the King would give him his sister in marriage, they would (as he conceived) deceive themselves; for he imagined, upon good grounds, that the King would bestow his Sister that way that might be most for her honour and advancement, and likewise for the advantage of his Crown and Kingdom; and he professed, for his part, although he much honoured the Count, as a great Prince of the blood, yet was he so faithful unto his Master, as he would advise him to that purpose.

The Queen-Mother and Monsieur *Le Grand* have advised me to say something unto the King concerning my business. I told them, I could say nothing very directly unto him, and yet would I not so much as deliver my opinion of the King my Masters inclinations to wish an alliance with him, unless I were assured, his answers might make me see his value and respect unto him. They then spake unto him, and assured me, I should in that be satisfied. Having that promise from them, I told the King, that I had made this journey of purpose to declare unto him my humble service and thankfulness for all his Honours and favours, the which I thought I could not better expresse, then by informing his Majesty, that our Prince whom he had ever so much valued, would be, as I conceived, free, and dis-engaged from our Spanish Treatie, by reason that the King could not find them answer his expectation in those things that made him principally desire their Conjunction; the which your Lordship, seeing you have exercised your interest and credit with the King your Master, and the Prince, to convert those thoughts towards his Majesty, from whom you were perswaded nothing but truth and honour would be returned, the which at this time, more then ever, would be an infinite advantage to both these Kingdoms, and that, I believe, if his Majesty would shew a disposition, as affectionate to receive Propositions to this purpose, as the King my Master had to make them, a long time would not passe before the effects of this might appear; the which would shew the report raised here of the ends of my coming to be false, and me to be free of all other designs then those which I had expressed unto him. He told me, that he had not heard that the Spanish Match was yet broken, the which justly might give him cause to be reserved; yet thus far he would assure me, in the general, That whatsoever should be propounded unto him from the King of Great *Britain*, he would most heartily and affectionately receive it: but this was with such a fashion of Courtesie, as shewed that he desired cause to have said more; and I am fully satisfied not only from him, but the Queen, and (most of all) of Madam her self, who shews all the sweetness and contentment that may be; and likewise from all the Officers of the Crown, and State, that they can desire nothing equal with this alliance. A better and more large preparation then this my instructions cannot make; and I wonder to see it thus fair, considering the hinderances and defacings the *Spanish* Embassadour desires to cast upon it, who, besides the *Redomontads's* and threatnings of the preparations of his Master, doth here take a contrary, but cunning way, letting them know, that the Prince cannot have two Wives, for their *Infanta* is surely his, only to create a jealousie and shiness in them towards me, that (he suspects) labours to do offices that are not to his liking.

You will therefore, I hope, speedily put this State out of these doubts, and clearly and freely proceed with them. Upon my credit and reputation, they are all of that disposition that we can wish them to be; and it appears, by their tender care of the States, and their resolution to ayd them: And likewise in sending Captain *Coborn*, that came from the Duke of *Brunswick* to demand a supply of men, who is returned with answer unto him, that he shall have double what he required, and great satisfaction to the Count *Mansfelt*, that sent a Gentleman hither, to let the King know, he was not yet in such disorder, but that he could assemble his Troops to such a number as might do his Majesty good service, if he would be pleased to take him into his protection and favour.

And the King hath sent a Gentleman of the Religion, a *Sedanois*, to *Leige*, to give information to this State of the proceedings of the *Spaniards* there, and to be ready to receive (if the

the Town shall seek it) the protection of them. But these passages I am sure you continually understand from our Embassadour; the which makes me omit many particularities in this kind, that I could inform you of. I have sent this Bearer of purpose, the which I beseech your Grace return with some speed, and with him the resolutions of our dear and Sacred Master, whom God ever bless and keep to our glory and comfort.

My Lord, I am the humblest and most
obliged of all your Graces servants,

Kensington.

The Lord Kensington, to the Duke.

My Lord,

YEsternight, being Sunday, I arrived safe here at *Paris*. I was informed as soon as I came, that the King was resolved, after sight of the Queens Masque (that was to be performed that same night,) that he would go a private journey, for five or six dayes, to *Shautelie*, a house of Mounsieur *de Memerancies*.

Being desirous therefore to kisse his hands before his going, and to see the Court in that glory and lustre, as must for certain be found upon such an extraordinary occasion, I went to the *Leuvre* to the D. of *Chevereux* Chamber, where I found him and his Lady, apparelling themselves for the Masque, and in such infinite riches of Jewels, as I shall never be a beholder of the like worn by Subjects. I had not been there above an hour, but the Queen and Madam came thither, where they staid a great while. And it was observed, that Madam hath seldom put on a more cheerful countenance then that night. There were some that told me, I might guesse at the cause of it. My Lord, I protest to God, she is a lovely, sweet young Creature. Her growth is not great yet, but her shape is perfect; and they all swear, that her sister the Princesse of *Piedmount* (who is now grown a tall and a goodly Lady) was not taller then she is, at her age. I thought the Queen would have put a fashion of reservation upon me, as not pleased with the breach, and disorder of the Spanish Treatie; but I found it far otherwise. She is so truly *French*, as (it is imagined) she rather wishes this alliance, then with her own sister. The King (that was so early to go out of the Town) took his rest, while the Ladies were making themselves ready; but as soon as he waked, he sent for me, and purposed to have received me as an Embassadour. But I intreated the D. of *Chevereux* before I went, to let him understand, that I came as an humble and thankful servant only to kisse his Majesties hands, and had no other end then to do him service. He then received me with much freedom and cheerfulness, with many questions how the King is satisfied with his Present by Mounsieur *de Bonevan*, who, when I related the Kings liking, and value of it, he was infinitely pleased. He commanded me to attend him to the Masque, which was danced by sixteen of the greatest Princes of *France*, St. *Luke* only being by the Queen received amongst them, to put a singular honour and value upon her. The King with his Brother had danced a Masque the last Tuesday, with the same number of persons of the best quality; who this night were to cast Lots, who should dance with the sixteen Ladies, they only being allowed to dance with them. And all those were so infinitely rich in Jewels, (embroidery of gold and silver being here forbidden) as they had almost all imbroidered their clothes as thick with Diamonds, as usually with purle.

I cannot give your Lordship any particular account of my service in any thing, yesternight being an unproper time for any such thing: But I am advised by the Prince *Jenvile* to stay here till the Kings return, and I shall understand how all things stand; and that no mans affection is so straight and true for the service of the King and Prince as his is, who of himself falls into passionate wishes for an Alliance, but tells me, in much libertie, they have been informed the cause and plot of my journey was to set an edge upon *Spain*, rather to cut off their delays, then to cut the throat of the businesse. But I gave him great satisfaction in that point.

My Lord, these are passages of my first nights being here, matters of ceremony; and yet I omit much of that. I thought these too sleight to trouble his Majesty, or the Prince with, yet I thought it fit, since this Messenger goes, to let you see this outward shew and face of this Court, to have as much sweetness, smoothness, and clearness towards our design, as is possible. My next Letters shall inform you of a further search made by me, the which I am confident will be of the same nature. And I conceive it the rather, because I find them in a great alarum at the newes that they have received from *Leige*, that the King of *Spain* makes

The Lord Kensington, to the Lord Conway.

makes a Fort upon the ruine there, to command both that, and the Town. This, they say, hath made them more clearly see his vast ambition to enlarge his Monarchy, and do all speak the carefull and honest language of our Lower house men, how it may be prevented.

I have said enough, the Messenger, I dare say, thinks too much; yet this I will add, That I will study to make it appear to the world, and your self, by a thankful heart, and to God himself in my prayers for your Lordship, that I am

Your Lordships most devoted, and most humble servant,

Kensington.

Post-script.

IF the *French* Embassadour, or my Lord of *Carlile*, wonder I have not written unto them, I beseech your Lordship, let them know this Messenger is not of my sending, and in such haste as he cannot be stayed.

The Lord Kensington, to the Lord Conway.

Right Honourable,

ACcording to his Majesties order, which your last of *April* the 14. derived unto me, I have represented such reasons to the King, and his Ministers of State here, against the sending of any person, in what quality soever, to the Duke of *Bavaria*, as they acquiesce in them, specially for that they come commanded under his Majesties desire, which they professe to be very willing to comply with, not only in this, but in any other occasion wherein his Majesty may directly, or indirectly, be any way interessed.

I took the same opportunity of preparing the way a little farther to a formal treaty of alliance, by feeling once again their pulse in matters of Religion, and find, that it beats so temperately, as promises a very good Crisis of any thing that may concern that particular.

I dealt plainly with the Marquess *de la Vieville*, touching the course that his Majesty may be driven to hold against Jesuites and Priests, of banishing them the Kingdom; and of quickning the Lawes against other Catholicks, as well out of necessity of reducing them within the bounds of sobriety and obedience, as of keeping good intelligence with his Parliament, without which he could not possibly go thorow with such a weighty work as he is now to undertake. He approved of the course for the ends sake; under hope, notwithstanding, that his Majesty would not tie his own hands from some moderate favour hereafter, which is all they pretend unto, and desire it may flow from the mediation of this State, upon an alliance here, for the saving of their honour, who otherwise will be hardly reputed Catholicks.

In representing a facility in these things, I leave no other difficulties to be imagined.

Their good inclination to the Match, in general, they are willing to demonstrate, (as by many other evidences, so) by the care they are now under, of lodging, and defraying my Lord of *Carlile*, and my self, in a more splendid and Magnifick manner then ever yet they did any Embassadour whatsoever; for such is the language that *Ville-aux Cleres* holds to me upon that subject.

The Count of *Soissons* sees it, and stormes, and manifests his discontent towards me (who am the instrument) more sellie then discreetly. I encountred him the other day, and gave him the due that belonged to his rank; but instead of returning me my salute, he disdainfully turned back his head. I was somewhat sensible thereof, and I told *Monsieur de Grandmont* of it; and as he and I were discoursing of it the day following, *Soissons* offered himself full butt upon us a second time. I again repeated my courtesie, and he his childish incivility. *Grandmont* found it strange, and intimated to the Marquesse *de la Valette*, a familiar, and confident of the Counts, both my observation, and his own distaste of such an uncivil kind of proceeding. *Valette* conveys the same to *Soissons* himself, who answered, that he could not afford me a better countenance, not for any ill will he bore unto my person, but to my errand and negotiation; which (were it not in the behalf of so great a Prince) went so near his heart, as he professed, he would cut my throat if he could. Nay, were any

Prince

The Lord Kensington, to the Lord Conway.

Prince of *Savoy*, *Mantua*, or *Germany*, here in person to sollicite for themselves, in the like nature, he would hazard his life in the cause. Such is the language that despair brings forth, which put me into an expectation of no less then a challenge, to decide the quarrel. And I once verily believed it sent; for the Count *de Lude* came very soberly to me, and told me, he had a message to deliver me from a great Personage, which he intreated he might do without offence.

I desired him to speak freely what it was, and from whom. He told me he was sent by the Count of *Soissons*; and I presently replyed, that nothing should come amiss from him. In conclusion, the errand was to signifie an extream liking that the Count took to one of my Horses, which he was desirous to buy of me at any rate. I answered, that if the Count would express to me his desire himself, and receive him of gift, he should be at his service, otherwise he should remain still as he was. Since that I have met him, and been prevented with a very courteous salute from him. I have been thus ample in these particular passages betwixt the Count and my self, that by the trouble you find in his disconsolate breast, you may judge of the constancy of Madams heart towards our prince, upon whom, assuredly, it is most strongly set, (as she continually expresses upon all occasions.) Yesterday I had the honour to entertain her two hours together, and received so many testimonies of respect, as witnessed very warm affections towards the Personage I did represent. Amongst other discourse, She fell to speak of Ladies riding on horseback, which, she said, was rare here, but frequent in *England*, and then expressed her delight in that exercise.

There is lately arrived here a French Gentleman (*Dupert* by name) with commission from the King of *Bohemia* to sollicit this Kings favour (in consequence of his Majesties generous and gracious declaration in his behalf) for the recovering of his rightful inheritance, to intreat that *Bavaria* may no wayes be countenanced in his unjust pretentions, and to crave (in this his extremity) a reimbursement of the remainder of that sum which his father lent to *Henry* the fourth in the times of his necessities, which may arise to the sum of 30000 Crowns; the facilitating of this negotiation is recommended unto me, who contribute what I can to the good success thereof. There hath happened here, this last *Munday*, a dispute between the Marquess *de Courtenvant*, one of the first Gentlemen of the Kings Chamber, and the Colonel *de Ornano* (*Monsieur's* Governour) about a lodging, which this pretended unto as most convenient for him, in regard that it adjoyned to that of *Monsieur's*; but the other claimed a right unto it by a former assignation, and possession. *Ornano* at the first prevailed, till the other complained to the King, who commanded the Colonel to quit the lodging to him; which his people refusing (out of a presumption, perhaps, that the commandment was rather formal then real) the King sent 3 or 4 of his guard to reiterate the commandment, and, in case of refusal to obey, to cast out all the stuff, and to kill all such as should oppose. Thus *Courtenvant* got the day; perhaps by *Vievilles* recommendation, in opposition of *Toirax*, between whom there hath been lately a little contestation, upon this occasion. *Vieville* being desirous to strengthen himself, and to stand upon the surest bottom he could, endeavoured to joyn a confident of his in equal commission with the *Garde des Seaux*, that so he might in time work it out, and prevail himself of that office at his devotion. The *Garde des Seaux* finding feeble resistance in himself, addressed his course to *Toirax*, to seek under his Covert shelter from that disgrace and injury. *Toirax* undertakes his defence; *Vieville* expostulates the matter with him, and alleadges many reasons to justifie his intentions; which the other gainsaying, with some little warmness, hath occasioned, by that heat, a coldness of affection between them ever since, and that so far forth, as it hath grown to be notorious.

To the same original I reduce the Cardin I *de Richlieu's* introduction into the Council of the Cabinet by the favour of *Vieville* (being made also an Instrument thereunto by the Queen) that by making his own party strong in Council, he may the more easily crush any adversary that shall grapple with him. Yesterday he was admitted; so that now that Council is composed of the Queen Mother, the Cardinal *de la Rouch-foulcant*, *Richlieu*, the Constable *Vieville*, and the *Garde des Seaux*.

Before I had finished this Letter, I had occasion to visit the Constable, to whom I used the same language that formerly I had done to *la Vieville*, and with the like approbation. And when I touched upon the point of dispensation, how it might be passed over, he assured me, in general, that such was the disposition of this King and State to give the Prince content, as he might be (in a manner) his own Carver how he pleased.

This is the account I can give you of the publick: but how shall I express the deep sense I have of my obligations to your favour in particular? shall I multiply in thanks? It is too

ordinary

ordinary a payment for so many Noble expressions of your love, I will rather endeavour by my deeds constantly and continually to witness unto you, that I entirely rest

Your most Faithful and most
Humble Servant,
Kensington.

The Lord Kensington, *to the Duke.*

My most dear, and Noble Lord,

BEsides that joynt Letter to your Lordship, from my Colleague and my self, I think fit to adde this particular account of what passed yesterday at *Ruel*, betwixt Queen Mother and me; whither going to give her double thanks; as for the liberty she had given me of access at all times to Madam, to entertain her, henceforth, with a more free and amorous kind of language from the Prince; so for having so readily condescended to an humble suit of mine, in the behalf of my Lord of *Carlile*, for a favourable Letter for him to your Lordship; she was pleased to oblige me further, in telling me she did it meerly for my sake. I redoubled my thanks, and added, that I knew your Lordship would esteem it one of the greatest happinesses that could befall you, to have an occasion offered, whereby you might witness, how much you adored her Majesties royal virtues, and how infinitely you were her Servant, ready to receive law from her, whensoever, by the least syllable of her blessed Lips or Pen, she should please to impose it. And this I did (as on the one side to gratifie my Colleague, who would be infinitely sensible of the disgrace he apprehends in the miss of the *Ribbon*, being thus brought upon the Stage for it) as also to help to mesnage that your Gracious favour which *Monsieur de Fiatts* to my Lord represents unto him, by giving you means withal to oblige this sweet and blessed Queen, who hath your Lordship in a very high account, and would be glad to find occasions how she may witness it. The mention of my Lord of *Carlile* upon this occasion refreshed her remembrance of the late falling out betwixt the Cardinal and him; and though she were sufficiently informed of the particulars by the Cardinal himself, yet she would needs have a relation from me, who in a merry kind of fashion obeyed her command, and salved every thing the best I could. She would needs know my opinion of the Cardinal, who so magnified to her his wisdom, his courage, his courtesie, his fidelity to her service, his affection to our business, as pleased her not a little. Neither did my heart and my tongue differ, for I esteem him such. This discourse she left to fall upon a better subject, the Prince, concerning whose voyage into *Spain*, the censure of *Italy* (she said) was, that two Kings had therein committed two great errours. The one in adventuring so precious a pledge to so hazardous an enterprise, the other in badly using so brave a guest. The first, Madam, (answered I) may be excused from the end, the common good of all Christendom, which then standing upon desperate terms, had need of a desperate remedy. The second had need of a better advocate then I, to put any colour of defence upon it.

But his Highness had observed as great a weakness and folly as that, in that after they had used him so ill, they would suffer him to depart, which was one of the first speeches he uttered after he was entred into the Ship. But did he say so? said the Queen. Yes Madam, I will assure you (quoth I) from the witness of my own ears. She smiled, and replyed, Indeed I heard he was used ill. So he was (answered I) but not in his entertainment, for that was as splendid as that Country could afford it, but in their frivolous delaies, and in the unreasonable conditions which they propounded, and pressed (upon the advantage they had of his Princely Person.) And yet (smiling added I) you here (Madam) use him far worse. And how so? presently demanded she? In that you press (quoth I) upon that most worthy, and Noble Prince, (who hath with so much affection to your Majesties service, so much passion to Madam, sought this Alliance.) The same, nay more unreasonable conditions then the other; and what they traced out for the breaking of the match, you follow, pretending to conclude it very unseasonably in this Conjuncture of time, especially when the jealousies that such great changes in State are apt to beget are cunningly fomented by the Spanish Embassadour in *England*, who vaunts it forth, that there is not so great a change in *La Vievilles* particular person, as there is in the general affections, which did but follow before the stream of his greatness and credit.

Thus casting in the Kings mind the seed of doubts, whereunto the *Conde de Olivares* in
Spain

The Lord Kensington, to the Duke.

Spain hath been willing to contribute by this braving speech, to our Royal Masters Embassadour there; That if the Pope ever granted a dispensation for the match with *France*, the King of *Spain* would march with an Army towards *Rome* and sack it. *Vrayement nous l' en empescherous bien* (promptly answered She) *Car nous lui taglierons assez de besongne ailleurs. Mais qu' est-ce qui vous presse le plus.* I represented unto her the unfitness of the seventh Article (even qualified by that interpretation that it is) and the impossibility of the last, which requires, and prescribes an oath. And desired that the honour of the Prince (with whom she pretended a will to match her Daughter) might be dearer to her, then to be balanced with that which could adde nothing to their assurance. I also, humbly, besought her to imploy her Credit with the King her Son, and her authority with the Ministers, for a reformation of those two Articles especially, and a friendly and speedy dispatch of all.

And if we must come to that extreamity, that more could not be altered then already was, yet, at least, she would procure the allowance of this protestation, by the King our Master, when he should swear them, that he intended no further to oblige himself by that oath, then might well stand with the safety, peace, tranquillity, and conveniency of his State. This she thought reasonable, and promised to speak with the King and Cardinal about it. And if you speak as you can (replied I) I know it will be done, Though when all is done, I know not whether the King my Master will condescend so far, yea, or no. Here I intreated I might weary her Majesty no further, but take the liberty she had pleased to give me, in entertaining Madam with such Commandments as the Prince had charged me withal to her. She would needs know what I would say. Nay then (smiling, quoth I) your Majesty will impose upon me the like Law that they in *Spain* did upon his Highness. But the case is now different (said she) for there the Prince was in person, here is but his Deputy. But a Deputy (answered I) that represents his person. *Mais pour tout cela (dit elle) qu' est ce que vous direz?* Rien (dis-re) qui ne Soit digne des oreilles d'vne si vertueuse Princesse. Mais qu' est ce?* redoubled she. Why then, Madam, (quoth I) if you will needs know, it shall be much to this effect; That your Majesty having given me the liberty of some freer Language then heretofore, I obey the Prince his Command, in presenting to her his service, not by way of Complement any longer, but out of passion and affection, which both her outward and her inward beauties (the vertues of her mind) so kindled in him, as he was resolved to contribute the uttermost he could to the Alliance in question, and would think it the greatest happiness in the world, if the success thereof might minister occasion of expressing, in a better and more effectual manner, his devotion to her service; with some little other such like amorous Language. *Allez, Allez, Il n'y a point de danger en tout cela* (smilingly answered she) *je me fie en vous, je me fie en vous.* Neither did I abuse her trust, for I varied not much from it, in delivering it to Madam, save that I amplified it to her a little more, who drank it down with joy, and with a low Courtesie acknowledged it to the Prince; adding, that she was extremely obliged to his Highness, and would think her self happy in the occasion that should be presented of meriting the place she had in his good Graces affection.

After that, I turned my speech to the old Ladies that attended, and told them, That sith the Queen was pleased to give me this liberty, it would be henceforth fit for them to speak a suitable Language. I let them know, that his Highness had her Picture, which he kept in his Cabinet, and fed his eyes many times with the sight and contemplation of it; sith he could not have the happiness to behold her person. All which, and other such like speeches, she (standing by) took up, without letting any one fall to the ground.

But I fear your Lordship will think I gether together too much to enlarge my Letter thus far: but it is, that by these Circumstances your Lordship may make a perfect judgment of the issue of our negotiation, which I doubt not but will succeed to his Majesties, his Highness, and your Lordships contentment: And so yield matter of triumph to you, and infinite joy to me

Your Lordships
Most humble, and most obliged, and
most obedient servant,

Kensington.

The Lord Kensington, to the Duke.

My most dear Lord,

THis Bearer your Cousen's going is in such haste, as what you receive from me must be in very few words. I was yesterday with the Marquess *de l'ieville*, whom I find cordial to do good offices between ours and this Kingdom; and he assures me by all the promises and protestations that may be, he wil ever use his credit and power to do so, knowing these Kingdoms can (as the King of *Spain's* power and ambition increases) have no true safety and good, unless we joyn in friendship and alliance. He is very free to me, telling me, That to prevent this, the King of *Spain* offers now the largest conditions of satisfaction and friendship that can be imagined, but their thoughts here are wholly bent towards us; And although, as yet, the King cannot with honour or wisdom say more then he hath done, yet we may be assured, whenwe are free, to be satisfied in all we can desire.

This day I understand the Earl of *Argile* is like lightning passed by from *Spain*, and by a special Command from the King, it is to put us in more terrour; That he will use his service in *Scotland*, where I believe he hath little credit and power to offend us. But how soever they omit nothing they may to dishearten us; but we are of too noble and constant a temper, either to fear their cunning or power.

My Lord, give me leave to beseech you, not to defer our business, for never can this State be found so rightly and truly inclined in love and affection towards us. And the rather hasten it, because, all the art that may be is daily used from *Spain* to prevent us; and if we go not roundly and clearly with them here, they may have jealousies and discouragements, that may change them: Take them therefore now, when I dare promise they are free, very free from those thoughts. My Lord, pardon the haste of this Letter, that hath no more time given me but to tell you, that you never can have any servant more devotedly yours, then is

Your Graces most Obliged, and most
Humble Servant,

Kensington.

Mr. Lorkin, to the Duke.

May it please your Grace,

FRom an honest and truly devoted heart to receive the sacrifice of most humble thanks, which come here offered for that excess of favour which I behold in those gracious lines, that you are so nobly pleased to honour me withal; and which derive unto me, farther, the height of all contentment, his Majesties gracious acceptance of my poor endeavours; which howsoever they cannot shoot up to any high matter from so low an earth, yet (in their greatest force) are eternally vowed (with the price of my dearest blood) as to his Masters faithful service, in the first place, so to your Graces in the next; who have received, I doubt not, ere this, what my former promised in the *Savoyard* Embassadours behalf, and that as well from his own pen, as mine. But this State is a very *Euripus*, that flows, and reflows, 7 times a day, and in whose waies is neither constancy, nor truth. The changes your Grace will find in my Letters to my Lord *Conway*, whereunto I therefore make reference, because, I suppose, there will be but one Lecture thereof to his Majesty, and your self.

Therein, likewise, your Grace will see a suddain Commandment laid upon *Monsieur de Blanville premire Gentilhome de la chambre du Roy*, speedily to provide himself to go extraordinary Embassadour into *England*. The cause thereof I rove at in my dispatch, taking my aim from two dark speeches of the Queen Mother, and the Cardinal. I have since learned the interpretation of the riddle, not from the Cardinals lips (who yet being sounded by me, pretended a further end then *Ville-aux-cleres* had done, viz; to entertain good intelligence betwixt the Queen of *England* and your Grace, and to do you all the best offices and services that are possible; but from the Duke *de Chevereux*, who (whatsoever pretexts may be taken) makes the true end of that Voyage to be, first, to try whether this man can mend what (they conceive here) the Duke hath marred, in shewing himself more a servant to the King of *England*, then to his own King and Master. Secondly, to spie and discover what he can; and (according as he shall find cause) to frame Cabals and factions, whereunto he is esteemed very proper, being characterized with the marks of a most subtile, prying, penetrating, and dangerous

And

Mr. Lorkin, to the Duke.

And therefore, as an Antidote against the poison, he brings, the Duke gives this Caveat afore-hand, That every one keep close and covert towards him, and avoid familiarity with him, though (otherwise) he wishes him a kind and honourable entertainment.

Thus much I received from the Dukes own lips yesternight, (*Bonocil* being witness, perhaps counsellour of all that passed;) he promised a Memorial in writing this day; which I have attended till this evening, and even now received it.

I have not touched the least syllable hereof to my Lord *Conway*, because I think both your Grace's, and the Duke *de Chevereux*'s, will, may concur in this, that these things be not subject to many eyes.

Even now the *Savoy* Embassadour sends an express Messenger unto me, to hasten to *Fountain-Bleau*.: Perhaps, it may be, to facilitate the Treaty with *Rochel*, either by some Letter, or journey of mine thither.

But, upon the conference I have had with the Duke *de Chevereux*, I shall temporize, till I hear his Majesties pleasure, or see good evidences of generous effects like to ensue: being desirous to shape my course so as may be most acceptable to his Majesty, and pleasing to your Grace, whose virtues I adore, in quality of

Aug. 30. 1625.

Your Grace's most humble, most faithfull, and most obedient servant,
Tho. Lorkin.

Post-script.
The Duke *de Chevereux* expects the Cipher from your Grace, if I be not deceived.

Mr. Lorkin, to the Duke.

May it please your Grace,

TO read and consider two contrary advertisements; the one given me on Munday evening by *des Porcheres*, who repeating what he had told me before, (*D'avoir destrompé la Royne mere en mil et mil choses*) assured me, that her thoughts were now so far changed from what they were, as she remitted every thing to his Majesties pleasure, to do what he list, (provided, that he attempted not upon the conscience of the Queen her Daughter, which was the onely point she was tender in, and scrupulous;) that she had written a very sharp Letter, full of good Lessons and Instructions, to her : That she had as cleer a heart to your Grace, as was possible; had sent for *Blainville*, expressly to alter his Instructions; and that, howsoever he (like a hollow-hearted man) had uttered, in confidence, to a friend of his, That he would perswade the Queen of *England* to put on a reconciled countenance for a time, till the way should be better prepared to give your Grace a dead lift, yet the Queen Mothers intentions were assuredly sincere and good. The *Savoy* Embassadours voyage was not then resolved, but his Secretary prepared to make it in his room : Of whom *Porcheres* (by the way) gave this touch, That there was a great correspondence between *Madamoiselle de Truges* and him, (contracted upon occasions of frequent visits that had passed betwixt her Mother and the Embassadour) and that therefore a carefull eye was to be had of him.

Another (who must be namelesse) sent for me, yesterday in the fore-noon, to tell me, That *Pere Berule's* errand hither, was onely to make out-cries against the Decree, or Proclamation against the Catholicks; and to accuse your Grace as the principal, if not the onely, author, who was now, of a seeming friend, become a deadly foe. That the Earl of *Arundel* had (out of his respect unto this State) purposely absented himself, that he might not be guilty of so pernicious a Counsel. That your Grace, and my Lord of *Holland*, had both but very slippery hold in his Majesties affections; that if this King would employ his credit as he might, it would be no hard matter to root you both out thence; that there were good preparatives for it already, and that my Lords, *Arundel* and *Pembroke*, would joyn hands and heads together to accomplish the effect. Whereupon *Blainville* was sent for back, to be more particularly instructed in the ways how to compass it, and would speedily post away in diligence. The same party added, That the Propositions which the Marquess *de Fiatt* had made about the League and Fleet, were, before *Berule's* arrival, somewhat well tasted, but since sleighted, as those that became cheap, (by their offer to divers others, as well as them;) that the Marquess should have visited *Blainville* at *Paris*, and sounded him about his errand, after this manner.

First, whether he had order to dis-nestle Madam *de St. George*? Whereto the answer was, No; and that it was against all reason of State so to do. And when the other replied, that the world was come to a bad pass, if reason of State descended as low as her, *Blainville* remained silent.

Secondly, whether he had commission to introduce the Duchess of *Buckingham* and the Countess of *Denbigh* into the Queens Bed-chamber? Answer was made, that it was a nice and tender point; and if that were once condescended to, they would be continually whispering in the Queens ear, how dear she would be to the King her Husband, how plausible and powerfull among the people, how beloved of all, if she would change her Religion, against which they were in conscience here bound to provide, and therefore conclude with a refusal of that likewise.

Thirdly, whether he carried any good instructions about an offensive or defensive League? whereunto the negative was still repeated, but that he carried brave offers for the entertainment of *Mansfelt*. And when the Marquess replied, that if that were all the contentment he carried, he feared, she would find but a very cold welcome; the other added, that perhaps he might be an Instrument to make the Queen and Duke friends. This were good (quoth the Marquess) if the Queen had not as much need of the Dukes friendship, as the Duke of hers: and upon these terms they parted. The same lips that uttered all this gave caution likewise against the *Savoyard* Embassadour, as a cunning, deep, hollow-hearted, man: And, being felt by me, how his pulse beat towards *Porcheres*, told me, he was a mercenary man, and no way to be trusted. In the issue of all this, his Counsel was, That your Grace would consider well your own strength, and what ground you have in his Majesties favour: If it be solid and good, then a Bravado will not do amiss, but may be powerfull here, to make them to see their own errour, and to walk upright, so it end with a good close: but if your station be not sure, then he counsels to prevent the storm; for to break with all, *Spain*, *France*, Puritans, Papists, were not wisdom: And desires, that, by any means, you instantly dispatch a Courrier to me, to represent the true state of things at home, and how you desire matters should be ordered for your service here abroad, so that there may be fabricked a more solid contentment to your Grace, whose hands I most humbly kiss in quality of

Septemb. 17. 1625.

Your Grace's most humble, most faithfull, most obedient, and most obliged servant,
Tho. Lorkin.

Post-script.

If my stay be intended long, it will be necessary that I use a Cipher, which I humbly beseech your Grace to send me, or to give me leave to frame one as I can.

As I was closing up my Letter, Mr. *Gerbier* arrived, who hath been somewhat indisposed in his health by the way, but now is reasonably well, God be thanked: His coming is very seasonable, and, I assure my self, will be usefull.

By the discourse I have had with Mr. *Gerbier*, I see a little clearer into the state of things here, and think *Porcheres* his advertisement may be truer, as being, perhaps, grounded upon knowledge, the other springing onely upon conjecture, built upon *Berule's* clamours, and overtures, and the sudden sending for Monsieur *Blainville* back. Your Grace will see day in all shortly. But, assuredly, the latter advice comes from a heart that is affectionately devoted to your Grace's service. This Bearer will kiss your Grace's hands from the Author, and thereby you will know his name, which he stipulated might not come in writing.

The Lords of the Council of England, *to the Lords of the Council in* Ireland, *January* 31. 1629.

BY your Letter, dated the ninth of *January*, we understand, how the seditious riot, moved by the Friars and their adherents at *Dublin*, hath by your good order and resolution been happily suppresst; and, we doubt not, but by this occasion you will consider how much it concerneth the good Government of that Kingdom, to prevent, in time, the first growing of such evils: for where such people be permitted to swarm, they will soon grow licentious, and endure no Government but their own, which cannot otherwise be restored then by a due and seasonable execution of the Law, and of such directions as from time to time have been sent from his Majesty and this Board. Now it redoundeth much to the honour of his Majesty, that the world shall take notice of the ability and good service of his Ministers there, which in person he hath been pleased openly in Councel, and in most gracious manner, to approve and commend; whereby you may be sufficiently encouraged to go on with like resolution

solution and moderation, till the work be fully done, as well in the City, as in other places of your Kingdom, the carriage whereof we must leave to your good discretions, whose particular knowledge of the present state of things can guide you better, when and where to carry a soft or harder hand; onely this we hold necessary to put you in mind, that you continue in that good agreement amongst your selves, for this, and other services, which your Letters do express, and for which we commend you much, that the good servants of the King and State may find encouragement equally from you all; and the ill-affected may find no support or countenance from any; nor any other connivances used, but by general advice, for avoiding of further evils, shall be allowed; and such Magistrates and Officers, if any shall be discovered, that openly, or under-hand, favour such disorders, or do not their duties in suppressing them, and committing the offenders, you shall do well to take all fit and safe advantages, by the punishment, or displacing of a few, to make the rest more cautious. This we write, not as mis-liking the fair course you have taken, but to express the concurrency of our Judgments with yours, and to assure you of our assistance in all such occasions wherein, for your further proceedings, we have advised. And his Majesty requireth you accordingly to take order, first, that the house wherein Seminary Friars appeared in their habits, and wherein the Reverend Archbishop, and the Mayor of *Dublin*, received the first affront, be speedily demolished, and be the mark of terror to the resisters of Authority; and that the rest of the houses erected or employed there, or elsewhere, to the use of suspicious societies, be converted to houses of Correction, and to set the people on work, or to other publick uses, for the advancement of Justice, good Arts, or Trades; and further, that you use all fit means to discover the Founders, Benefactors, and Maintainers, of such Societies and Colledges, and certifie their names; and that you find out the Lands, Leases, or Revenues, applied to their uses, and dispose thereof according to the Law; and that you certifie also the places and institutions of all such *Monasteries, Priories, Nunneries,* and other Religious houses, and the names of all such persons as have put themselves to be Brothers and Sisters therein, especially such as are of note, to the end such evil plants be not permitted to take root any where in that Kingdom, which we require you take care of. For the supply of Munition, which you have reason to desire, we have taken effectual order that you shall receive it with all convenient speed. And so, &c.

Lord Keeper.
Lord Treasurer.
Lord President.
Lord Privy Seal.
Lord High Chamberlain.
Earl of Suffolk.
Earl of Dorset.

Earl of Salisbury.
Earl of Kelly.
Lord Viscount Dorchester.
Lord Newbergh.
Mr. Vice-Chamberlain.
Mr. Secretary Cook.
Sir William Alexander.

Sir Robert Mansel, *to the Duke.*

Right Honourable, and my singular good Lord,

HAving used all the possible speed I could to repair to *Algier*, where I should have been by the 15th of *March* last, I held it my duty, humbly to present unto your Lordship the particular account of my proceedings.

Before my arrival, I furnished the two Prizes, three Brigandines, and a fourth Boat, with Fire-locks, and combustible materials, for the burning of the Pyrates ships within the Mole, and had trained my men in the execution of their several duties, and likewise appointed a squadron of Boats, with small shot, to rescue the vessels of execution, in their advancement and retreat.

The first night of my arrival, being the 21. of *May* last, the Vessels of execution were all advanced; but, by reason of contrary winds, they were commanded to retire.

The second and third nights they were also in a readiness, but were with-held with calms.

The fourth night it pleased God to bless us with a fair gale, and they being advanced again, and the two ships with the Fire-works having almost recovered the mouth of the *Mole*, the wind (to our great grief) turned to the opposite point of the Compass.

The Boats performed their directions in towing of the ships; but considering, that by the continuance of the course, they should expose their principallest men to hazard, by reason

son of the great store of Ordnance and small shot, which played upon them, they debated amongst themselves what to do; Captain *Hughs* (who commanded one of the Brigandines) replied, Go on, and give the attempt with the Boats; which they cheerfully pursued, crying out without cessation, King *James*, King *James*, God bless King *James*; and fearless of danger (even in the mouth of the Cannon, and small-shot, which showred like hail upon them) they fired the ships in many places, and maintained the same, to the great comfort of us that were spectators, so long as they had any powder left in their Bandileers, striving in the end, who should have the honour to come off last; the which at length, as a due to his former resolution and courage, they left to Captain *Hughes*, and so retired, all the ships continuing still their cheerfull cry, King *James*, with the loss of 20 that were slain, and hurt; and leaving the fire flaming up in seven several places, which continued in some of them long after their retreat, and being aboard his Majesties ships.

The cowardly Turks, who before durst not shew themselves to so weak a force, but from the walls, or the tops of their houses, so soon as they perceived all the Boats retired, opened their Ports, and sallied out in thousands; and, by the help of so great multitudes, and a sudden shower of rain, seconded with a calm, which then happened, the fire was after extinguished, without doing any more hurt then making two of their ships unserviceable.

During that stay there, there came out of the Mole onely one Frigot, which we forced to run on shore.

Other service by us there performed, was the sinking of one of their best Men of War by Sir *Thomas Wilford*, and Captain *Chidleigh*; she was mann'd with 130 Turks, and 12 Christians, whereof 12 onely escaped, the rest were either slain, or drowned; which appeared, both by the relation of divers Christians which nightly escaped aboard us, and by divers of the dead bodies that floted upon the water by our ships. We took likewise, before their faces, in the Bay, a Fly-Boat, which the Pyrates had formerly taken from the Christians, and sold to *Legorn*; in her Merchandize, to be exchanged for Pyrates goods, and some money, amounting to 2000. and odd pounds; the exact account whereof I shall not fail to addresse to your Lordship, as soon as the same is perfected by the Councel of War.

The Turks hereupon presently mann'd out three Galleys to rescue her; but Captain *Giles*, and Captain *Herbert*, with the help of three Brigandines, which I sent out to second them, soon fetch'd her up, and brought her unto me, and the Galleys were put to flight by Sir *Thomas Wilford*, Captain *Pennington*, and Captain *Chidleigh*.

During the time of my abode there, after the attempt made by the Boats, I attended ten days for an opportunity to send in the ships with the fire-works, to finish the service begun by the Boats; but in all that time there hapned not one breath of wind fit for their attempt, notwithstanding the ships were always ready at the instant that they should receive my directions to advance. But at last, understanding by the Christian (that escaped by swimming) aboard me, how the Pyrates had boomed up the Moles with Masts, and Rafts, set a double guard upon their Ships, planted more Ordnance upon the Mole, and the Walls, and mann'd out twenty Boats to guard the Boom; and perceiving, likewise, that they had sent out their Galleys and Boats, both to the Eastward, and Westward, to give advice to all the Ships upon the coast, that they should not come in during my abode there; and so finding no hope remaining, either by stratagem to do service upon them in the Mole, or to meet with any more of them; in the regard of the daily complaints brought unto me, both from some of the Kings Ships, and most of the Merchants, of their want of victuals; I resolved, by the advice of the Councel of War, to set sail; whence I made my repair to this place, where I met my Brother *Roper*, with your Lordships directions, which I have received, and at the instant obeyed, by signifying his Majesties pleasure, declared by your Lordships Letter, unto the worthy Commanders of those four Ships, whom his Majesty hath pleased to call home.

But, my Lord, in the duty I ow your Lordship, and my zeal to his Majesties honour and service, I humbly beg your Lordships pardon to advertise your Lordship, that seeing we have now made this attempt upon the Pyrates, and that they perceive, that our intent is to work their utter ruine and confusion, the recalling of these his Majesties Forces, before the arrival of others in their stead, and the bereaving us of so many worthy and experienced Commanders, I fear, may prove more prejudicial to the service, then upon one days consideration I dare presume to set down in writing, by encouraging the Pyrates to put in execution such stratagems upon us, as, to my knowledge, they have already taken into their consideration. My reasons for the same, I shall be bold, upon more mature deliberation, to offer, in all humbleness, unto your Lordships judicious view, either by the Commanders that are to return unto your Lordship, or by a messenger which divers of the Councel of War advise to be addressed over land on purpose with the same. And

Sir Robert Mansell, to the Duke.

And so being ready (so soon as we have received in our water, and dispatched divers other businesses, which of necessity must be ordered in this place) to set sail for *Malaga*, there to receive in our remainder of Victuals, and to take my leave of these four Ships, and such other of the Merchants as cannot be made serviceable in these parts. With my endless prayers for your Lordships increase of all honour, I cease your Lordships farther trouble for the present; And rest,

From aboard the Lyon, *in* Alegant
Rode. June 9. 1621.

*Your Lordships most humble, most faithfull,
and sad servant,*
Robert Mansel.

Sir Robert Mansel, to the Duke.

Right Honourable, and my singular good Lord,

IT is not unknown unto your Lordship, that Sir *Thomas Button*, before his coming out, thought himself much wronged in that he did not hold the place of Vice-Admiral in this Fleet, whereof I must acknowledge him very worthy, and that for my part I had engaged Sir *Richard Hawkins*, a very Grave, Religious, and experienc'd Gentleman, before I was assured whether Sir *Thomas Button* would leave his employment in *Ireland*, or no; and that afterwards Sir *Thomas Button*, by your Lordships mediation, was contented to undertake the charge he now holdeth, which, God knows, I laboured for no other end, then for the security and advancement of his Majesties service, by reason of the experience I have had of his sufficiency and ability.

Since that time, I have doubled that injury. A wrong was done unto him which cannot be denied; he patiently appealed to me for Justice, which I must confess I denied him. But the name of the person that offered the wrong, and the reasons why I denied him Justice, I must leave unto Sir *Richard Hawkins* and Sir *Henry Palmer* to relate unto your Lordship, and if that will not give your Lordship satisfaction, I must humbly submit my self to your Lordships Censure.

Notwithstanding the impression that these injuries took with him; yet thus much I must truly confess in his behalf, that there was no man more zealous to advance his Majesties service, nor more forward to undergo any danger or hazard, then himself; whereof he hath given assured testimony to the World in these three particulars.

First, in the service performed by him on a Christmass-day at night, whereof I have formerly advertised your Lordship at large.

Secondly, Then in going over to *Algier* cheerfully, without complaining, when his Ship was so grievously infected, that he had not able men in her to manage her Sails.

Also in imploying the most choice men in his Ship, under the command of his Nephew, for the firing of the Pyrates ships within the Mole of *Algier*.

And lastly, in his joyning with Sir *Richard Hawkins* in the towing off one of the Prizes, when she was becalmed within Musquet shot of the *Mole*.

My Lord, I must protest unto your Lordship, that I had no ends of mine own for the injuries done to Sir *Thomas Button*; and therefore your Lordship cannot cast a greater honour upon your poore servant, then in repairing him, which I humbly begg of your Lordship.

If Sir *Richard Hawkins* do return unto me, then I shall be an humble suitor unto your Lordship in the behalf of Sir *Thomas Button*, that he may return to his employment in *Ireland*; from whence, at my earnest desires to enjoy his company and assistance, I was the only means to withdraw him; and that he may receive such allowance and entertainment as was formerly usually paid unto him; by which means your Lordship will take away the Curses of his Children, whose bloods are neer unto me, and oblige me with my continual prayers for your Lordships increase of honour, ever to remain,

From aboard the Vantguard,
July 10, 1621.

*Your Lordships most humble, and
faithful servant,*
Robert Mansell.

Padre Maestre *at* Rome, *to the* Spanish *Ambassadour in* England.

My Lord,

I Have received two Letters from your Lordship, the one of the 15th of *March*, brought me by Mr. *George Gage*, and the other of the 30th of *April* which came by the Ordinary. In both which Letters I have received a special favour from you, and much comfort. The coming of Mr. *Gage* hath given me infinite contentment, then which there could nothing have happened more fitly and to the purpose, for the matter which is in negotiation; nor any man have come hither that could better advance the business, then he, as well in respect of his good affection, as for his wisdome and dexterity in all things. And if the King of Great *Britain* will withall help now a little, the business will be quickly done, and in a good manner. I beseech your Lordship, preach to him a Christian Sermon as is most needfull: for there comes from thence, divers waies, such reports hither, that I am ashamed, and out of countenance, in the Streets as I go; and they do me a favour, that they do not stone me, knowing that I am treating, and labouring this business at the same time, when the poor Catholiques are so cruelly used in *England*, *Scotland*, and *Ireland*. And when I excuse it, that it is not by the Kings order, but by the abuse and malice of some ill affected Ministers, it will not be received, neither do they want Replies. Besides, there is a rumour all over *Rome*, that the King, in a Speech which he made at the beginning of the Parliament, affirmed publiquely, *That for all this marriage with* Spain, *The Catholique party in* England *should not be in one jot better condition then they are*.

But I cannot be yet discouraged; My confidence is in the King, and in the desire which I know he hath to procure a good Wife for his Son. And now that the time is come, let him play the part of a Couragious Wooer, and frustrate the intentions and desires of all those that are adverse to it. It is a comfort unto me, that I do not find here an Impossibility; but that though there be difficulties, yet I find many here that desire to overcome them. And above all, I hope that God will assist this business as his own Cause. I am going to prepare my self for the Congregation of the Cardinals, and a Consultation of Divines, to whom I understand we shall be remitted this next week. I shall give your Lordship an account punctually of all things that happen in those Conferences. Our Lord, &c.

Your Lordships &c.
Padre Maestre.

Magdibeg, *to his Majesty*.

May it please your most Excellent Majesty,

I Make bold, after a long silence, to prostrate my self before your Majesty; and being the Ambassadour of a great King, that counteth it an honour to stile himself your friend, I do beseech you to afford me that justice which I am sure you will not refuse to the meanest of your Subjects.

At my first arrival into this your happy Kingdom, I was informed by the general relation of all that had recourse unto me, that one here (who had the title of Ambassadour from my Master) did vainly brag that he had married the King of *Persia's* Niece, which kindled in me such a vehement desire to vindicate my Masters honour, from so unworthy and false a report, that at my first enterview with him, my hand being guided by my duty, I endeavoured to fasten upon him a Condign disgrace to such an imposture. But the caution that I ought to have of my own justification, when I return home, biddeth me the more strictly to examine the truth of that which was told me (whereon my action with Sir *Robert Shirley* was grounded) and to have it averred in the particulars, as well as by a general voice. Therefore I humbly beseech your Majesty, that out of your Princely goodness you will be pleased to give such order, that this point may be fully cleared. Wherein, for the manner of proceeding, I wholly and humbly remit my self to your Majesty: And this being done, I shall return home with some measure of joy, to balance the grief which I have, for having done ought that may have clouded your Majesties favour to me. And so committing your Majesty to the protection of the greatest God, whose shadows and elect instruments Kings are, on earth, I humbly take my leave, and rest, &c.

The Earl of Middlesex, to his Majesty.

Sacred Majesty, and my most gracious Master,

YOur goodness is such to me your oppressed servant in this my time of persecution, as I know not how to express my thankfulness otherwise then by pouring forth my humble and hearty prayers to the great God of Heaven and Earth, to grant your Majesty all happiness here, and everlasting happiness hereafter.

Between 5. and 6. of the clock, upon Saturday in the evening, I received my Charge from the Lords assembled in Parliament, with an Order by which I am commanded to make my appearance at the Barr, upon Thursday next, by 9. of the clock in the morning, with my answer: And in the mean time to examine my witnesses.

This Charge of mine hath been in preparing, by examining of witnesses upon oath, and otherwise, 23. daies. And hath been weighed by the wisdom of both Houses, and doth concern me so neerly in point of honour, and faith to your Majesty, to answer well, as I value my life at nothing in comparison of it.

I may grieve, though I will not complain of any thing my Lords shall be pleased to Command; but do hope, that upon a second consideration they will not think three daies a fitting time for me to make my answer, and to examine witnesses in a cause of such importance, and so neerly concerning me, when twenty three daies have been spent almost from morning until night in preparing my charge.

I know the House (whose Judgment I shall never desire to wave) is the proper place for me to move to be resolved herein, and therefore shall, upon Wednesday morning, make my humble motion there to have 7 daies longer time; as well to make my answer, and appearance, as to examine my witnesses, which are many, and upon several heads.

But because the Prince his Highness, and many of the principal Lords, are now with your Majesty at *Windsor*, my most humble suit to your Majesty is, that you would be pleased to move them, on my behalf, to yield me so much further time, that my Cause may not suffer prejudice for want of time to make my just defence, that which I have propounded being as moderate as is possible.

With my most humble and hearty prayer to Almighty God for continuance of your health, with all happiness, I humbly kiss your Royal hands, and will ever rest,

April. 26. 1624.   *Your Majesties most humble &c.*
                                                          Middlesex.

The Earl of Middlesex, to the Duke.

Right Noble, and my most honoured Lord,

I Have received divers Letters from your Lordship since your going from *Theobalds*, which though they concern several men, and in sundry kinds, yet they all conclude upon diminution of his Majesties estate, contrary to your general ground; when his Majesty delivered me the Staff, and contrary to your Lordships private directions given me at *Theobalds*; with which I did your Lordship the right to acquaint the King.

I have of late had cause to take into consideration the miserable condition of my present estate, who since I received the staff, have led such a life as my very enemies pity me, which I foresaw, the distraction of the Kings estate; and burthen of that place, would of necessity throw upon me. Yet my duty, love and thankfulness to his Majesty, and my love and thankfulness to you, contrary to my own judgment, and advice of my friends, made me undertake it, little expecting these cross accidents, which have lien heavy upon me, and more troubled me then the continual cares and vexations of my place.

I do most freely and willingly acknowledg, one man cannot be more bound unto another, then I am to your Lordship; and if I do not make a thankful return, let me be held an ungrateful Monster, which is the worst of Villains.

I have been so ambitious as to desire to extend my gratitude so far, as that the King may have cause to thank you for preferring me, and that your Lordship may bless the time you did it. To effect that, I shall delight to live a miserable life for a time. The course which must of necessity be held, to do it, I will acquaint your Lordship with very shortly, which I hope you will be pleased to approve, and assist me in. And then I will express my thankfulness to you
                                                                                                    that

Sir Toby Mathew, *to the Duchess of* Buckingham.

that way: If that course shall not like you, I will not only deliver you up my places, but whatsoever I hold from the King, and live privately upon mine own estate. For I will never sell so good and gracious a Master, nor see so noble and constant a friend ruined, and undone. God bless you, and send you your hearts desire. As for my self, I never desired to quit the world, and all the fooleries in it, till now.

Your Lordships faithfullest servant, and Kinsman,
Middlesex.

Sir Tobie Mathew, *to the Duchess of* Buckingham.

Madam;

THere was no cause, till now, why I should trouble your Ladyship with presenting my unprofitable service to you: but now I shall venture to do it, by reason of the good news I shall send with it.

For our Queen arrived here yesterday, and I was glad at the heart to see her such as she hath seemed; she is more grown then I had thought, being higher by half the head then my Lady Marquess. And whatsoever they say, believe me, she sits already upon the very skirts of womanhood. Madam, upon my faith, she is a most sweet lovely Creature, and hath a countenance which opens a window into her heart, where a man may see all Nobleness and Goodness; and I dare venture my head (upon the little skill I have in Physiognomie) that she will be extraordinarily beloved by our Nation, and deserve to be so; and that the actions of her self, which are to be her own, will be excellent. Me thought I discerned in her countenance a little remnant of sadness, which the fresh wound of parting from the Queen Mother might have made, yet perhaps I was deceived. Her Attire was very plain, for so great a Queen can be thought to have nothing mean about her. But I hope that amongst many other blessings, which God will have provided for us by her means, her example will be able to teach our Countrey wit in this kind.

I had the happiness to see, and hear her, at a short distance, by the Commandement which my Lady of *Buckingham* laid upon me to interpret for her; and believe me, she is full of wit, and hath a lovely manner in expressing it. But I confess I was sorry, with all my heart, to hear that her courage was so great, as to carry her instantly (after my Lady of *Buckingham* had taken her leave for that time) to Sea in a poor little Boat, in the company of her brother, whom I have not yet had the honour to see. I dare give my word for her, that she is not afraid of her own shadow, who could find in her heart to put her self, at the first sight, upon an element of that danger, and disease, for meer pastime: Unless it were, perhaps, that she might carry some Steel about her, and that there is some Adamant at *Dover*, which already might begin to draw her that way.

I am extreamly sorry, that we have lost the hope of seeing the two other Queens; for if they had come, we might have had beauty here as well in the preterperfect, and in the present tense, as now we have in the future.

But the Queen Mothers indisposition hath arrested her at *Amiens*, in punishment of that malice, wherewith she dissembled it too long at the first, through the extream desire she had of coming hither.

Our Queen received my Lady of *Buckingham* with strange courtesie and favour; and now there is no remedy, but that the King will needs defray and treat her after a high manner, And I have been told, that *Monsieur* will needs descend so much as to visit her in her lodging; and the Duchess of *Chevereux* (being that great Princess, as she is, both by match, and blood) will perforce give precedence not only to my Lady of *Buckingham*, but to my Ladies her daughters also: And I assure my self, that a less puissant example then this will serve to convert our great Ladies, even to exceed, in *England*, towards the Ladies which are strangers, and do but come, and go.

But the while this Court doth so apply it self to do my Lady of *Buckingham* all imaginable honour, I look on it so, as that I am no way discouraged thereby for bearing devotion to the blessed Virgin, when I see that men, who are sick of love towards the Son, are put, even by a kind of Law of nature, into pain, till they revenge themselves upon the Mother. I beseech Jesus, &c.

From Bulloign. *June* 9. 1625.

Sir Toby Mathew, *to the King of* Spain.

Don Tobia Mathei Cavallero Ynglesy Catholico Romano beseecheth your Catholick Majesty, with all humility and reverence, to give him leave to speak these few words unto you.

He understandeth that the *Theologi* have persisted precisely upon the *Voto*, which they gave before, and he findeth clearly that the Prince conceiveth, that he can by no means submit himself thereunto with his Honour. And besides, my Lord the King hath expresly required him to return with all possible speed, in case that *Voto* would not be qualified. And it is certain that he will depart for *England* within very few daies. And whosoever shall inform your Majesty, that the Treaty of this marriage may be truly kept on foot, after the departure of the Prince, upon these terms, doth deceive your Majesty through the ignorance wherein he is of the State of *England*. So that the Prince departing thus, the Catholick Subjects of all my Lord the Kings Dominions are to be in lamentable case. For although the Prince did yesterday vouchsafe to have Compassion of me, in respect of the grief wherein he saw I had upon these occasions, and to say, That although the marriage were broken, yet he would procure that his Catholick Subjects should not fare the worse for that, yet I know that it is morally impossible, for that honourable design of his to take place, in respect of the people, and the importunity and malice of the Puritans; and especially, because it will now be a case of meer necessity for my Lord the King, to run in a course of very streight Conjunction with them of his Parliament, that he may be able the better to serve himself of them in other occasions: from which Parliament, as now the case will stand, what Catholick can expect any other, then the extremity of rigour?

In consideration whereof, I cast my self with a sad heart at the feet of your Majesty, beseeching you, that you will take into your royal remembrance the love which you owe, and procure to pay to our holy Mother, the Church, and that some course may be taken, and with speed (for otherwise it will be too late) to give the Prince some foot of ground, upon which he may be able to stand in such sort, as that without loss of honour, and breach of that word which he hath given to the world, and without prejudice to that obedience which he oweth to the least commandment of the King his Father; his Highness may be enabled to comply with the incomparable affection which he beareth the Infanta, your Majesties Sister. And that by means hereof, the two Crowns may be kindly, in perfect union, and the Catholick Religion may be, highly, advantaged, not onely in the Dominions of my Lord the King, but in many other parts of Christendom, into which the Authority of these Dominions doth flow.

For my part, I take the eternal God to witness, whom I procure to serve, and who hath given me a heart which disclaimeth from all other interesses then to serve God and my King, that I conceive my self not to comply with a good conscience, without laying this protestation under the Eye of your Majesty, that if the Catholick Subjects of the King my Lord shall grow liable to persecution, or affliction, by occasion of breaking this Match, through the disgust of the King my Lord, and his Councel, or through the power which infallibly the Puritans assembled in Parliament will have with him, upon this occasion, that blood, or misery whatsoever, it may partly be required at their hands who have advised your Majesty not to accept of those large conditions for Catholicks, which my Lord the King, and the Prince hath condescended to, and of that more then moral Security, which they have offered for the performance thereof.

And on the other side, I undertake to your Majesty, under the pain of infamy, in case that be not made good which here I affirm, that if your Majesty will be pleased to give some such ground to the Prince, as whereupon he may with Honour stay, and perfect the Treaty of the Marriage by any such way, or means, as may occur to your Majesties royal wisdom, the whole bodies of the Catholicks in *England*, both religious and secular, shall acknowledge it as a great blessing of God, and shall oblige themselves to pay incessantly for happy Estate, &c.

The Lord Mountjoy, to the Earl of Essex.

Most Noble Lord,

THE Queen is now removing towards a Progress; wherein, after I have somewhat waited upon her, I shall have a desire to write to your Lordship of some things more at large, which I will do as safely as I can; your Lordships vertue, and your clear conscience, must be your own brazen wall: for we that are not of the Councel do see no hope to keep long together this State from assured ruine. I pray God, the Queen may with all prosperity out-live their negligence, and your care; to be a just Judge, if not a rewarder thereof. In the mean time, you owe unto her and your own vertue, extraordinary patience. Your Lordships mind (I do protest) cannot labour more in the storm wherein you are, then mine doth in this dangerous and miserable calm. For it is some comfort to perish doing somewhat; and yet, my Lord, why should we despair, since there is a Providence that looks beyond, and concludes contrary to the practices of the world; which Providence hath shewed us ways, how rugged soever they be, which will bring unto true happiness; and though we lose these mortal Barkes we sail in, yet he will assuredly save the passengers. Noble Lord, in respect of that great Haven, contemn these tempests and shipwracks at sea. Your Lordships servant Mr. *Bushel,* doth fear to have you impute his slow dispatch unto any want of his diligence, and hath shewed his fear in exceeding sorrow that it could not be sooner, and with as much care with all his best means to effect it. I much thank your Lordship for your favour to Sir *Charles Blunt,* of whom (if he be not thankful) I shall not onely be deceived, but also revenged. I will pray continually for your Lordships prosperity,——— and that it shall be impossible to make me otherwise then

Your Lordships most honest and faithful Servant,

MOUNTJOY.

The Duke of Modena, to the Duke of Savoy.

WHen I was deprived of my Mistriss the *Infanta Izabella,* so intimately beloved of me, I was suddenly possessed with a most ardent desire of finding the means how to follow her into Paradise; and distrusting, in regard of my weakness and life past, that I was not able to stand in those dangers wherein that holy soul knew how to find security and tranquillity, I resolved to retire my self out of the tempestuous Sea of Government, and to shelter my self in the harbour of Religion, rejoycing to sacrifice that unto God which useth to be so highly esteemed in the world; and knowing, that truly to reign, is to serve his Divine Majesty, hitherto I deferred the execution of my purpose, because, being bound in this, to depend upon the Counsel of him that governed my soul, it seemed not expedient to him, that I should retire my self while there was need of assistance, both in respect of the age of the Duke my Father (which was *Cæsar d' Este,* who dyed 1628.) and of the nonage of the Prince my Son (which is *Don Francisco,* who now governeth.) Now that these impediments are removed, I go most contentedly whither the Lord doth call me, namely, to take upon me the Capuchin Religion, out of *Italy*; and I do promise to find for my self, in one little Cell, that repose which all the greatness of the world cannot give me. True it is, if I should look back upon my life past, I should find motives rather of terrour, then of comfort: But the mercy of God doth make me confident, and my having (for his love, and to perform his will) renounced all that I could or had, I departed also most comforted, because I leave the Prince my Son so well qualified, that I may confidently expect an excellent issue of his Government, especially if your Highness shall vouchsafe to direct him with your most prudent Counsels, and to shrowd him under your benign protection, whereunto, with reverent affection, I do recommend him, together with the rest of my Sons, especially *Carlo Alexandro* (who is now living in your Highness his Court) since that (as a man may say) they have no other Father then your Highness, and are branches of your Princely house.

Unto your Highness was, in all respects, due from me the accompt which I have given you of my vocation; I beseech you to accept it, and to believe that I will always be answerable to my duty, and will pray for the spiritual and temporal encrease of your Highnes, whose hands I reverently kiss.

From *Salsuolo* the 30th
of *July*, 1629.

*Your Highness most humble and most
Obliged Servant,*
Alfonso d' Este.

Thomas *Duke of* Norfolk, *to Queen* Elizabeth.

O Most dear and dread Sovereign and Lady Queen, and most gracious Mistress, when I consider with my self, how far I have transgressed my duty to your most gracious Majesty, I dare not now presume to look up, or hope for your gracious favours, I confess my self so far unworthy thereof: but again, when I look into your Highness manifold merciful and most pitiful nature, of which so many have so abundantly tasted of, since your Majesties most prosperous reign, I am emboldened with penitent and sorrowful heart, to make my trembling hand to offer unto your Highness my most rueful and lowly submission, having none other means to ease my oppressed mind, I am for my sins and disobedience to ask pardon, that is, of Almighty God, and of your most excellent Majesty: the first, I have done to Almighty God, and so I by the grace of him will continue with a new heart and full mind of amendment, not doubting, but asking mercy, to receive it, according to the Scripture, he that knocketh at the door shall have it opened unto him. Now do I prostrate my self at your Highness most gracious feet, my poor children, and all that I have, hoping more in your Majesties most gracious clemency, then in any of mine unadvised deserts; I seek to excuse my self no way, but wholly submit my self to what what shall please your most merciful heart, like a most gracious Queen, to a man that hath been astray, who finding mercy hath afterwards with bad service oftentimes redoubled his former folly. O most noble Queen, it is in your most gracious power to make of my wretched mould what it pleaseth you, my faith and religion reserved to my Saviour, my body being already to your Highness subject, and imprisoned for my most just desert, I dedicate my mind and heart, to be hereafter as it shall please your Majesty to direct it; I do not seek favour at your Majesties hands, in respect of my former good service, I confess undutifulness hath now blotted the same out; neither dare I remember, which heretofore was my greatest comfort, because, I deserve not that honour, which was, that it hath pleased your Highness to account me indeed your unworthy kinsman. Wo, wretch, that day when I entred into that matter which hath made such alteration of your Majesties most gracious favour unto me, and hath heaped upon my self these intolerable troubles. O unworthy that I am, that in all the days of my life, counting upon nothing but a quiet life, I take God to witness, whatsoever some have judged the contrary of me, I was so unhappy: to give ear to that which hath done, and ever was like to bring me to the contrary.

Sir Francis Norris, *to King* James.

Most gracious Sovereign,

THE advantage which mine adversary hath taken, in, first presenting his complaint freely and uncontrolled, would have afflicted me greatly, had I not known that your Majesty hath given to your Judges injunction, *Audire alteram partem*. That I entered into discourse with the Lord *Willoughby*, in Church or Church-yard, may make it manifest, that I had no disposition at all to quarrel. The rest of the world is wide enough for men so affected. They that prophane such places trust more to the place then their own worth. That I was improvidently in such a place by him surprized, muffled in my own Cloak, and treacherously buffeted, shewed, that I suspected no such assault as was there made upon me, and where I was so disgracefully and ignobly assaulted by the Lord *Willoughby*, and he in no sort by me, yet well I hope to satisfie every indifferent judgement, much more the supream Judge, that I had nothing in my intention either towards the Master or the Man. It is true, most gracious Sovereign, that after the Lord *Willoughby's* dishonorable Indignity by me expelled, I seeing an unknown face coming fiercely, with his sword, upon me, for my life, (in defence whereof God himself, the law of Nature and Nations, doth warrant us to contend) I was forced to have forgone it at a Ruffians command, or by resisting, to yield it up to your Majesty, to whom I have vowed it (whensoever you shall command it) to your service. This I presume to write to a King, in whom rests the spirit of honour; and by that spirit I hope your Majesty will judge, that he which will run from his own defence, being injuriously assaulted,

The Lord Nithisdail, to the Duke.

will also run from the defence of his Sovereign Master. I also presume, in all humility, to address my self to a Prince endued with the spirit of Justice, joyned to the divine vertue of compassion; by both which I nothing doubt your Majesty will judge, when you shall be truly informed, of the preceding and succeeding wrongs offered me, that I am and will be

Your Majesties most humble and Loyal Subject,
FR. NORRIS.

The Countess of Nottingham, to the Danish Embassadour.

SIR,

I Am very sorry this occasion should have been offered me by the King your Master, which makes me troublesom to you for the present. It is reported to me by men of honour, the great wrong the King of the *Danes* hath done me, when I was not by to answer for my self: For if I had been present, I would have letten him know, how much I scorn to receive that wrong at his hands. I need not urge the particular of it, for the King himself knows it best. I protest to you Sir, I did think as honourably of the King your Master, as I did of my own Prince; but now I perswade my self there is as much baseness in him, as can be in any man: For although he be a Prince by birth, it seems not to me that there harbours any Princely thought in his breast; for, either in Prince or Subject, it is the basest thing that can be to wrong any woman of honour: I deserve as little that name he gave me, as either the mother of himself or of his children; and if ever I come to know what man hath informed your Master so wrongfully of me, I should do my best for putting him from doing the like to any other: but if it hath come by the tongue of any woman, I dare say, she would be glad to have companions. So leaving to trouble you any further, I rest, Your friend
M. NOTTINGHAM.

The Lord Nithisdail, to the Duke.

My most Noble Lord,

FInding matters at great uncertainty when I came hither, I resolved to make farther tryal before I should part from hence. What thanks is due to the Embassadours, for their painful and discreet Carriage, can hardly be expressed.

Matters now being drawn to such a conformity (which I confess I thought impossibilities, though withal I found much respect alwaies to the Prince, with a sensible desire of the Match expressed, both by the King, and those I spake withal) our Embassadours seem still to be discontent, that all things are not remitted to our Masters verbal promise, which though it may be assurance sufficient to all Catholicks, who have the sence to consider, that it must be our Masters, and the Princes, gracious disposition must be our safety, more then either word or writ: yet the writ being desired privately (as they pretend) merely to draw the Popes consent (without the which nothing is to be finished) the difference is not so great, their Princely promise being given already.

What cause of jealousie the refusing hereof should procure, you may consider: besides, my judgment failes me, if a more easie way shall be assented unto upon this side. If the Embassadours have bestirred themselves to get this out of the publick Articles, I can bear witness. Thus much I dare avow, that neither time nor place have been omitted by them to do good; though I must confess, what intelligence I had in the proceeding hath rather been from the *French* then from them. Their Reasons (as I conceive) was their doubts, that did bring me hither, having neither Letters from the King, the Prince, nor your Grace.

Whereupon, to remove these conceits, I shewed them, that I did onely take this in my way, intending to go see the Jubilees, wherewith though his Majesty, nor the Prince, neither yet your Grace, were acquainted with at my parting, you will be pleased to make my excuse. I am infinitely beholden to the Embassadours noble Courtesie, which I know hath proceeded from that relation which they know I have to you.

My Lord, let the happiness which shall come to the Prince by matching with such a Lady as, I protest before God, hath those perfections, to my thinking, can hardly be equalled, be a means to hasten a happy conclusion; And let not matter of Ceremony draw delaies where the substance is agreed upon. So shall all that belong to our Master be made happy, in general, and you in particular, for that love which they express here to your self.

Once

The Lady Elizabeth Norris, to the Duke.

Once more I humbly beg, you will confider particularly upon each one of the Articles; and I hope, you fhall not find fuch unreconcileable difference as an affected Puritan may pretend. Whereupon if I have looked more with eyes of a Papift then was fitting, it is my lick of judgement, and not of zeal to my Mafters Honour, which of all earthly things fhall be preferred. Befeeching God to give a happy fuccefs hereunto, with a found recovery of your own health, I humbly take my leave,

Dated at *Compion.*

Your Graces faitifful fervant,

Nithisdail.

The Lady Elizabeth Norris, to the Duke.

My Lord,

EVer fince your Lordfhips firft recommendation of my husband to me, I have thought my felf much engaged to your Lordfhip; for I muft confeffe after he had taken his leave of me, I did love him never the lefs: for immediately after my fathers death (when in my Confcience he leaft expected to hear from me) I did both fend and write to him, which he might enterpret an encouragement, or rather an invitation. I did it the rather, becaufe I did not believe thofe which did him ill offices; for thofe which were moft for him, on a fudden were moft againft him. I muft confefs, that pitie did confirm my affection, and I truft your Lordfhip will commiferate his eftate, as you do the fall of all mankind; for I was the *Eve,* and he was the *Adam:* and I pray God, the King and your Lordfhip may forgive us, as I am confident God will pardon us. Your Lordfhip may imagine my Mother was of the plot, but I take God to witnefs, that fhe was not only againft it, but contrarily. I did believe fhe was wholly for your Brother: And for your Brother, my Mother recommended him to me, whom I ufed like a Gentleman of high worth and qualitie. But I did by no means abufe him by promife, or taking gifts, which I falfely fuffer for, in the opinion of the world. I only took a Ring, by my Mothers appointment, which came as a token from my Lady your Mother, which was of very fmall value. My husband and I am refolved rather to fuffer in the opinion of the world, then contradict any thing which fhall be aggravated againft us. We muft both honour you, and think our felves much ingaged to your Lordfhip. After God, I proteft you are the only authour of it: for by your means, I firft fetled my affection. I know there are thofe which do my husband and me ill offices. I have reafon to be jealous of the Lord *Montgomery*, for he would have put tricks upon me in making me deny the Contract; and when he failed in that, he went about to make me believe Mr. *Wray* had denied his. And to tell your Lordfhip true, his violence and overearneftnefs made me the more averfe. If my husband had not fetched me, I would have come to him, and fo I fent him word.

Thus humbly befeeching your Lordfhip, as you are happie in your wife, that you would be pleafed to make our peace with the King; and feeing it is Gods act, that you would honour us with your favour. We fhall be both bound to joyn in prayer, that you may be ever happy in your Wife, and in your Childrens Children. And fo with my humble refpect to your Lordfhip, I reft,

Your Lordfhips humble fervant,

Elizabeth Norris.

Sir John Ogle, to the Duke.

Right Excellent, and moft Gracious Lord,

ANd becaufe you are fo, why fhould not I put my foul in your hand? that I have not done it fooner, was not through want of will in me; but it hath been the will of God, that mine acknowledgement fhould be the fuller, your goodnefs the greater. Your Grace cannot be ignorant of the many motions I have had thereto; but my judgement hath been made irrefolute by feveral diftractions. I lay now my felf, and the fortunes of me and mine, at your Graces feet. Take me up then (nobleft Lord) as becometh the fame which

you

The Earl of Oxford, to the Duke.

you have, and the confidence which I have of you with a hand of goodnesse. If I had wilfully sinned against you (when I was wickedly ensnared and beguiled by that wretch at *Utrecht*, to whom I gave some Extract out of your Letters; as also out of the Lord Embassadours,) or did yet with obstinacy maintain such indiscreet proceeding, your Grace might in justice reject me as unworthy.

But since you have long discerned in me a propension to crave your pardon, though still unhappily diverted till this time; I trust your true Noblenesse, generousnesse and goodnesse to be such, as you will not only not turn this heartie submission to any disadvantage on my part; but looking upon mine ingenuitie, with a right eye of gracious inclination, both pardon my fault, and folly towards your self, and also (to bind my prayers to be offered in the greater zeal for you, for I shall not be able to do you better service then in prayer) be a strong mediator to his gracious Majesty, that my errours of weaknesse, and want of discretion, committed then towards his late Majesty of ever blessed memory, and his Embassadour, with what other over-sights may have been gathered up since, may be freely and fully forgiven and remitted, that so my soul being discharged of all fear of displeasure against me, I may with a chearful heart and quiet conscience go on in such a vocation as the Lord shall have appointed for me. My Lord, this wound hath long festered neer my heart; and though false skins have been drawn over it sometimes by unskilful hands, yet have I ever judged it the surest cure to rip it up by Confession, and heal it by Contrition. And sure I judge that it favours more of a right generous spirit to confesse a fault, then to conceal it, especially when the party offending is free from malice, and the party offended of a nature so noble and full of goodnesse, as nothing can be wished to be added unto it, and which is yet more; and this have you graciously done to me, (my Lord) signed himself with his own hand a true and faithful friend unto him, the more to invite him to trust him. And trust you I do, my Lord, and in you (next my Gracious Sovereign) as much as may be in any arm of flesh. The God of Heaven (I hope) will speak peace to my soul, if the King, and your Grace, will send peace to my heart. I trust you will, and will pray to God you may, that I may in all chearfulnesse and thankfulnesse ever remain,

Exceter 3. *June*,
1625.

*Your Grace's most humble, and faithful,
and obliged servant,*

Jo. Ogle.

Post-script.

I Beseech your Grace to send some other man to take this Charge which I too weakly, for fear of offending by denial, have thus far undergone, but upon hope of being withdrawn. Yet still I submit my self to your Graces good pleasure.

The Earl of Oxford, to the Duke.

My Lord,

I Cannot but believe that I have had some undeserved ill offices done me unto your Lordship, otherwise I should not find this difficultie in being preferred, if not afore, at least equally, in balance with my Accusers. It is common unto all mens understanding, that it is not the guilt of the accused, but the legal and just proceeding, which cleares the Kings honour; and this I do, and ever will acknowledge to have been held towards me. Neither was it ever known, that the Kings Grace, the more it came sweetned with his favour, did lessen or diminish his honour, but rather seemed as a lustre to make his goodnesse shine brighter, and oblige the Receiver in a more strict Tie of gratitude. My Lord, it cannot wrong you to oblige me to your service, nor add reputation to you to throw me upon Rocks. I appeal to the King, and your own Conscience, whether ever I have harboured any treasonable thoughts, either against his Majesty, or his issue, that should make me uncapable of receiving his grace, without imputation to those faithful and dutiful respects, with which I have ever served his Majesty; If it shall please him to line me out my path to death (the period whither we must all travel to) by imprisonment, I shall be far from repining at the sentence, but with all humblenesse will undergo it, and employ my heartiest prayers for the long continuance of his honour and happinesse.

I be-

An Order made at Whitehal, *&c.*

I beseech your Lordship receive my Character of what I am, and have ever been towards you, not from Conjectures and reports of others, but from my own mouth, and actions. For yet I have reason to suspect your opinion of me, else sure I should have found better fruits of your power. I was alwayes (as much as lay in me) desirous to outstrip, rather then come short of, any in doing you service; and the same affections still remain with me; of the truth of which I pray you be confident.

To this only I will add one request more, which is, That since your Lordship is pleased to mediate with his Majesty for my freedom, you will procure it so free from rubs, as that my obligation may be the greater, which I will ever willingly and faithfully pay unto your Lordship in all respects, like him who truly is

Your Lordships, &c.

H. O.

An Order made at Whitehall *betwixt the University and Town of* Cambridge. *Decemb.* 4. 1629.

Lord Keeper.	*Lord Chamberlain.*	*Earl of* Kelly.
Lo. Arch. of York,	*Earl of* Suffolk.	*Lord Visc.* Dorchester.
Lord Treasurer.	*Earl of* Dorset.	*Lord Visc.* Grandison.
Lord President.	*Earl of* Salisbury.	*Lord L. Bp.* of Winton.
Lord Privie Seal.	*Earl of* Bridgewater.	*Master of the Wards.*
Lord high Chamberlain.	*Earl of* Holland.	*Master Chamberlain.*
Earl Marshal.	*Earl of* Danby.	*M. Secretary* Cook.
Lord Steward.		

THis day his Majesty sitting in Councel did hear at large the controversie between the University of *Cambridge*, and certain Burgers of the Town, concerning the rating and setting the price of *Victualia*, and particularly of Candles, and other necessaries comprized under the terms of *Focalia*; and of the consequences lately fallen out upon the controversie: which having been long debated by Counsel learned on both sides, his Majesty finally ordered, by advice of the Board, That as well the late Major and Bayliff, and *William Bridges*, as *Edward Almond, John Ball, Jonas Scot,* and *Thomas Oliver*, shall acknowledge and submit themselves (by setting their hands to this Order in the Councel-book) to the Jurisdiction and Priviledges of the University, as well for the rating and setting the price of all manner of *Victualia*, and of Candles, and all other necessaries under the term of *Focalia*, as for the correcting and punishing of all such inhabitants of the Town as shall break and exceed the said rates and prices so set by the Vice-Chancellor, or such Officers of the University as are in that behalf authorized. And it is further ordered, That all the parties fined by the Vice-Chancellor, shall pay the Fines, and such charges of the Court as were set upon them by the Vice-Chancellor; and shall make publick confession, in the Vice-Chancellors Court, of their fault, in breaking the said rates and prizes so set, and refusing to pay the Fines so assessed upon them, and questioning the Priviledges of the University. And as touching the discommuning of any of the said persons in this Order mentioned; It is ordered, That peace and agreement shall be setled between the parties, according to the performance of that respect and submission which is due from the inhabitants of the said Town of *Cambridge* to the said University.

Ex. Will. Becher.

Sir John Perrots *Commission for Lord Deputy of* Ireland.

ELizabetha *Dei gratia &c. omnibus ad quos præsentes literæ pervenerint, salut. Sciatis quod nos certis urgentibus causis & considerationibus nos specialiter moventibus, de provida circumspectione & industria prædilecti & fidelis nobis* Johannis Perrot *milit. plenius confidentes de advisamento Concilii nostri assignavimus, facimus, ordinavimus, constituimus & deputavimus, & per præsentes assignamus, &c. eundem* Johannem Perrot *milit. Deputat.*

tit. nostrum Generalem Regni nostri Hiberniæ, habend. tenend. gaudend. exercend. & occupand. officium prædict. eidem Johanni Perrot *milit. durante beneplacito nostro, dantes & concedentes eidem Deputat. nostro Generali plenam tenore præsentium potestatem ad p cem nostram ac ad leges & consuetudines regni nostri prædict. custodiend. & custodiri faciend. & ad omnes & singulas leges n-stras, &c.*

The whole Contents of the Commission, for Lord Deputy.

TO conserve the peace, to punish offenders; to make Orders and Proclamations, to receive offenders to grace, to give pardons and impose fines, to levy forces, to fight and make peace, to dispose Rebels lands, to pardon all treasons saving touching the Queens person, and counterfeiting of coyn; to give offices, saving the Chancellor, Treasurer, two chief Justices, chief Baron, and Master of the Rolls; to dispose of Ecclesiasticall livings, except Arch-bishops and Bishops; to receive homage and the oath; to make provision for his houshold according to the ancient custome; to assemble the Parliament with her Majesties privity, to receive the account of Officers, saving the Treasurers, to exercise martiall Law.

The Queens Warrant to the Lords, &c. of Ireland, for ministring the Oath, and delivery of the Sword to him, Jan. 31. 1583.

Right Reverend Father in God, right trusty and welbeloved, and trusty and right welbeloved, we greet you well: Whereas upon the departure from thence of our right trusty and welbeloved the Lord *Gray* of *Wilton*, late our Deputy there, we thought it meet for our government there, to appoint you joyntly to have the place of our Justices, untill such time as we should resolve to send another thither to be our Deputy there; We let you to wit, that meaning now no longer to burthen you with such a charge, wherein you have, according to the trust imposed in you, very wisely behaved your selves, greatly to our contentation, we have chosen and appointed our right trusty and welbeloved Sir *Je. Perrot* Knight, this bearer, to be our Deputy of that our said Realm, and that for that purpose to send him presently thither: Wherefore our will and pleasure is, and by vertue of these our Letters we authorize you, upon the view of our Letters Patents made and delivered unto him in that behalf, both to minister unto him the oath accustomed to be given unto the Deputy there; and also to deliver unto him the Sword, as heretofore hath been used. And further, that you communicate unto him amply the present estate of that our Realm, and of all our affairs there, for his better instruction, at his entrance into that Government, and the advancement of our service. And these our Letters shall be your sufficient warrant and discharge in this behalf. Given under our Signet, &c. the last of *January*, 1583. the 26 year of our Reign.

Another, for his Entertainment there.

Trusty and welbeloved, we greet you well. Whereas we have now appointed our right trusty and welbeloved Sir *John Perrot* Knight to be our Deputy in that our Realm of *Ireland*, for which Office allowance as well of diets as of entertainments for certain Horsemen is to be given him: These be therefore to let you to wit, that we allow unto him for his ordinary dyet one hundred pounds sterling, according to the last Establishment in *March* 1580. and for his Retinue fifty Horsmen and fifty Footmen, with such wages for every Horsman, and Footman, and for their Officers, as was allowed to Sir *William Fitzwilliams*, and Sir *Henry Sydney*, Knights, in the late times of their Governments in that Realm, After which rates as well for his own dyet, as for the said fifty Horsmen, and fifty Footmen, and for their Officers, We will and command you to make payment to him during his employment and service in that place, from the date of our Letters Patents, authorizing him to that Government; And these our Letters shall be sufficient Warrant as well to you as to any Treasurer or Vice treasurer

there

there, for the time being, and to your and their Substitutes, as also to the Auditor, or his Deputies, and to all other Commissioners to be appointed over your Accompts, to pass and allow the same payments to you accordingly. Given, &c. the fourth of *April*, 1583. in the 26. year of our Reign of *England*, &c.

The Queens Instructions to Sir John Perrot,

YOu shall see, immediately upon your arrival into that Realm, assembled our Council there, and confer with them, what course of Government, upon due consideration had of the present estate of the said Realm, may be held, so as Justice may take place, our Charges be lessened, our Revenues encreased, and our Subjects there not oppressed.

You shall also consider what Forces are meet to be continued in pay, and how the rest, chargeable unto us, and burthensom unto the Countrey, may be discharged; and also, how the Horse-men and Foot-men serving there may be reduced to their old pay, which by reason of the general Rebellion in that Realm (the Countrey being wasted) we were driven to encrease: And therefore, we see no reason but the Band residing in those Countreys that are not wasted may live well enough of the old pay, especially, being victualled by us: And for the ease and diminishing of our charges in that behalf, We do think it meet, that you should treat with those Countreys that are not wasted, as well in *Munster*, or elsewhere in that Realm, to see if you can draw them, with good contentment, to contribute something towards the finding of that Garrison, as *Carberrie* heretofore hath done.

And for that our Subjects in that Realm, &c.

To advise of the inhabiting of *Munster*, the attainted Lands to be lett out at easie rents. Survey, certifie what States. 5. Port-Corn. 6. Th'attainted Lands to be bestowed in reward upon Servitors. 7. Younger Brothers of Noble-men, Diminish Pensioners. 9. Review former Instructions. 10.——11. Renewing of forfeited Leases for three years: Beef, Remittal of Arrearages. 12. Reversion of Lands to the Governours. 13. Lands of the attainted to be appointed to house-keeping. 14. Reservation of Timber-woods. 15. Residence of Officers. 16. Report to the State, outrages of disloyal Subjects. 17. Profits of Customs, Escheats, &c. 19. Establishment for *Connaught*. 20. President for *Munster*, allowance begin at *May*, Transportation. 21. Councellors, B. of *Meath*, *John Norris*, *Richard Bingham*, *Tho. Strange*. 22. Refer the choice of a person to the Chancellor, and others. 23. Certificate of the last Treasurers Receipts and Expences.

Every one of these Articles doth contain half a side of Paper; and therefore, it is rather thought fit to abbreviate them, then to transcribe them at large, the whole Contents being contained in this abbreviation.

Sir John Perrot, to the Lords of the Council.

May it please your good Lordships,

ALthough I and this Councel have, by our joynt-Letters, truly declared unto you the dutifull state of things here, and the causes, both forreign, and domestical, whereupon we gather it; and withall have shewed our extreme wants, and what supplies are desired: Yet understanding thence, but not from your Lordships, (for I have had no kind of advertisements, answer, or resolution, for the same, these twelve moneths) that there is a great preparation made by the *Spanish* King against the Realm, and that your Lordships have intelligence thereof; I cannot but, as one whose chief charge and care it is, importune your Lordships to cast your eye more carefully this way; humbly praying you to consider, in what case we are in, to try with a most mighty Prince, whether this Realm shall be still her Majesties, or his; if there be any such matters (as your Lordships know best) then I beseech your Lordships to think, whether it be more safety to say, that we have sent provision to encounter the danger, or else, you will send, when, perhaps, it will be too late. And withal, for mine own discharge, if I shall tarry, and have nothing wherewith: I have but a life to yield for her Majesty, and my Countrey; for the loss thereof I grieve not, but rather for the harm that through defects, I fear, may come to her Majesty and the State, and the shame I shall leave behind me. This forreign preparation, if there be any such thing, is likely to be spent against *Munster*, to seize upon, and to spoil the Cities and Towns of the same, which in truth are very weak. If I shall go thither; what for the late wars, and this last bad season, there is not so much to be had

there,

there, as will maintain that one Band of 200. that is under Mr. *Thomas Norris*, the Vice-President there, but that I am enforced to shift them from Town to Town, who, by reason of their extreme penury do receive them with great grief and grudge. And though I had men sufficient to encounter the Enemy that should come, yet, for want of victuals, I should be driven to abandon the place with danger and shame; where they that are to come over are like to bring their provision with them, and to settle it in some Town that they will soon seize upon for that purpose: whereof what may ensue, amongst this unconstant people, naturally delighting in change, your Lordships may soon gather. Besides this that I have said of the bare estate of *Munster*, where there is not so much to be had as will serve for my own Family, or yet to feed my horses till grass grow, I refer you to understand, not onely the same more fully; but also the great wants of the rest of the Realm, by the Declaration here enclosed; which, as *Beverly* the Victualler maketh it, so I know it to be true. And therefore, I most humbly beseech your Lordships, to send speedy order, that such a Staple of Victuals may be provided, and be sent over, as your Lordships shall think requisite to serve, as well for the numbers here already, as also for those that are to be sent over, to encounter such an accident as may fall out. And herein I would wish your Lordships to consider the winds and weather, how untowardly they have framed this year: For as some have lain at *Chester* nine weeks to come over hither, so hath there been no passage hence this six weeks. Moreover, if there be such purposes in hand, it were good some shipping were dispatch'd, for the guard of the Coasts. And to all these and other difficulties, may I, with your Lordships favour, add one more, to be considered of, How weakly I am seconded, if need fall out, by those forreign attempts, whereof I would say little for any other cause: The Marshall is old, and not able either to ride or go; the Master of the Ordnance is both absent and old, and I wish there were a more sufficient man in his place: the Lord President, and Sir *William Stanley*, who are men of good conduct, are drawn away: Sir *H. Harrington*, Mr. *Edward Barkley*, and the Seneschal *Dantry*, are suffered to remain still there; but I humbly pray, they may be sped away, together with all other that are Servitors, by any manner of pay, there. And so having herein discharged my duty, I humbly end.

From the Castle of Dublin,   *Your Lordships, most humble at commandment,*
January 31. 1585.   JOHN PERROT.

The Petition of Francis Philips, to King James, for the release of Sir Robert Philips, Prisoner in the Tower.

Most dread Sovereign,

IF the Thrones of Heaven and Earth were to be sollicited one and the same way, I should have learned, by my often praying to God for your Majesty, how to pray to your Majesty for others: But the Liturgies of the Church and Court are different, as in many other points, so especially in this, That in the one, there is not so poor a friend, but may offer his vows immediately to the Almighty; whereas in the other, a right loyal subject may pour out his soul in vain, without an *Ora pro nobis*. Now such is the obscure condition of your humble suppliant, as I know no Saint about your sacred Majesty, to whom I can address my orisons, or in whose mediation I dare repose the least assurance: Let it be, therefore, lawfull for me, in this extraordinary occasion, to pass the ordinary forms; and raising my spirits above uncertainties, to fix my entire faith upon your Majesties supreme goodness, which is, and ever ought to be, esteemed, both the best Tribunal, and the best Sanctuary, for a good cause. But how good soever my cause be, it would be high presumption in me to stand upon it: I have, therefore, chosen rather to cast my self at your Majesties feet, from whence I would not willingly rise, but remain a monument of sorrow and humility, till I have obtained some gracious answer to my Petition: For though your Majesties thoughts cannot discern so low, as to conceive how much it importeth a poor distressed suppliant to be reviled, & neglected; yet you may be pleased to believe, that we are as highly affected, and as much anguished with the extremities that press our little fortunes, as Princes are with theirs. Which I speak, not out of any pride I take in comparing small things with great, but onely to dispose your Majesty to a favourable construction of my words, if they seem to be overcharged with zeal and affection, or to express more earnestness then, perhaps, your Majesty may think the business merits, as my self values it. The suit I am to make to your Majesty, is no sleight one, yet it may be easily granted without references: For, I dare assure your Majesty, upon my life, it is neither against the

Laws

The Petition of Francis Philips, to King James.

Laws of the Kingdom, nor will diminish any of your treasure, either that of your coffers, or that of your peoples hearts; it being an act of clemency, or rather a word, for even that will satisfie to create in your poor dejected Suppliant a new heart, and send him away as full of content as he is now of grief and despair. Nor is it for my self I thus implore your Majesties grace, but for one that is far more worthy, and in whom all that I am consists, my dear Brother, who, I know not by what misfortune, hath fallen, or rather been pushed, into your Majesties displeasure; not in dark and crooked ways, as corrupt and ill-affected subjects use to walk, and neer to break their necks in; but even in the great road, which both himself, and all good *English-men*, that know not the paths of the Court, would have sworn, would have led most safely and most directly to your Majesties service from your Majesties displeasure; there needs no other invention to crucifie a generous and honest-minded suppliant, upon whom hath issued, and been derived, a whole torrent of exemplary punishment, wherein his reputation, his person, and his estate, grievously suffered.

For having (upon the last process of Parliament) retired himself to his poor house in the Countrey, with hope a while to breathe after these troublesome affairs, and still breathing nothing but your Majesties service; he was sent for, ere he had finished his Christmas, by a Sergeant at Arms, who arrested him in his own house, with as much terror as belongs to the apprehending of Treason it self: But (thanks be to God) his conscience never started; and for his obedience herein shewed, it was not in the power of any authority to surprize it: For at the instant, without asking one minutes time of resolution, he rendred himself to the Officers discretion, who (according to his directions) brought him up captive, and presented him at the Council-Table as a Delinquent, from whence he was as soon committed to the Tower; where he ever since hath been kept close prisoner, and that with so strict a hand, as his own beloved wife, and my self, having sometime since urgent and unfeigned occasion to speak with him, about some private business of his Family, and hereupon making humble Petition to the Lords of your Majesties most Honourable Privy Council, for the favour of access, we were, to our great discomforts, denied it, by reason, as their Lordships were pleased to declare unto us, that he had not satisfied your Majesty fully in some points; which is so far from being his fault, as, I dare say, it is the greatest part of his affliction, that he sees himself debarred from the means of doing it. The Lords Commissioners that were appointed by your Majesty to examine his offence, since the first week of his imprisonment, have not done him the honour to be with him; by which means, not onely his body, but (the most part of his mind) his humble intentions to your Majesty, are kept in restraint. May it please, therefore, your most excellent Majesty, now at length, after five moneths imprisonment, and extreme durance, to ordain such expedition in this cause, as may stand with your justice, and yet not avert your mercy: either of them will serve our turns; but that which is most agreeable to your Royal and gracious inclination, will best accomplish our desire. To live still in close prison, is all one as to be buried alive; and for a man that hath any hope of salvation, it were better to pray for the day of Judgment, then to lie languishing in such waking misery; yet not ours, but your Majesties will be done: For if in your Princely wisdom you shall not think it a fit season to restore him to his former condition, or to accept the fruit of his correction, an humble and penitent submission for his unhappiness in offending your Majesty, which, I assure my self, is long since ripe, and grown to full perfection, in so forward affection, and so proper for all duties, as his hath ever been: If (I say) it be not yet time to have mercy, but that he must still remain within the walls of bondage, to expiate that which he did in these priviledged ones, my hope is, that he will die at any time for your Majesties service; and will find patience to live any where for your Majesties pleasure; onely thus much let me beseech your Majesties grace, again and again, not to deny your humble and most obedient suppliant, that you will, at least, be pleased to mitigate the rigour of his sufferings so far, as to grant him the liberty of the Tower, that he may no longer groan under the burthen of those incommodities which daily prejudice his health and fortune, in a higher degree (I believe) then either your Majesty knows, or intends. I am the more bold to importune your Majesty in the point of favour, because it concerns my own good and preservation: For your Majesty shall deign to understand, that I, your supplicant, have no means to live, but what proceeds from his brotherly love and bounty; so as if I may not be suffered to go to him, and receive order for my maintenance, I know none but *Our Father which art in heaven* to beg my daily bread on; he that was my father on earth is long since departed (if I have not been mis-informed) who was then beyond sea; your Majesties anger was, to him, little better then the messenger of death, though, I perswade my self, it was rather sent in your Majesties Name, then in you: Warrant.

For what use could your Majesty have of his not being, who neither was, nor could be

Sir Robert Philips, to the Duke of Buckingham.

ever but your faithfull and affectionate servant, who in his soul adored your Royal Majesty, as much as ever mortal man did any mortal God; lastly, whose heart was so bent to please your Majesty, as the very sound of your displeasure was enough to break it. And more perfect obedience then this can no subject shew, to make his Sovereigns favour equal to life and death.

Pardon me, dread Sovereign, if, on this occasion, I cannot hinder my Father's ghost from appearing: For how can it possibly be at rest, as long as your fatal displeasure reigns still in his family, and makes it the house of continual mourning? Remove then (if it be your blessed will) the clouds that have been so long hanging over our heads; and let not the present storm, that wants matter to produce, extort a thunder-bolt: For what is *Philips*, or the son of *Philips*, that your Majesty should so destroy them? We are unworthy of *Cæsar's* anger, as well in regard of our means, as of our innocency.

To conclude my prayers, I most humbly beseech your Majesty, to forgive them; and let not the ignorance of the stile, or ceremonies used in the Court, be imputed to your humble and well-meaning Suppliant, as a willing want of reverence; in whose breast these two legal qualities, Love, and Fear, do more vigorously meet, or who could more willingly part with his essence, to add the least acquisition to the Greatness and Majesty of his Sovereign. True it is, that the subject that employed the faculties of my soul, at this present, is of such a nature, as I could not deny it the uttermost of my affection; and he that thinks he can never speak enough, may easily speak too much. That neither my self, nor my brother, have failed in any thing but words, that your Majesty will pardon; without that, all crimes are equal, and as much danger lies in an humble Petition, as in a plot of high Treason.

Be pleased then (most gracious Sovereign) to give us back one gracious word, and keep our undoubted hearts; at least, shew us so much mercy, as to judge us according to your own goodness: For, if we had not liberty to appeal thither, we should be in danger of losing the best part of our birthright, and, instead of your Majesties subjects, become other mens slaves. From your Majesty, therefore, and from no other, your faithfull suppliant craves and expects the joyfull word of grace; which if I may be so happy as to carry my poor brother, before he grows any elder in misery, I shall find an honest heart with prayers and thanksgiving: And for my particular, your Majesties greatest favour and liberality shall not more oblige, or better affect, others, then your Royal clemency shall me. In memory whereof, I shall daily pray, that your Majesty may obtain all your desires of Heaven, and so be obeyed in all your commandments on earth, that we may live to see your holy intentions to take effect for the good of Christendom, and so you may honour the age you live in with the miracles of your wisdom. Finally, that your felicity in this world may overtake that in the highest, to make you wear a perpetual Crown, to Gods glory, and your own.

Your Majesties most humble, loyal, and true-hearted English subject,
Francis Philips.

Sir Robert Philips, to the Duke of Buckingham.

May it please your Grace,

BEfore the receipt of that Dispatch, with which you were pleased to honour me, from *Apthorp*, dated the last of *July*, I was fully determined, at your return to *Woodstock*, to have presented your Grace my most humble and faithfull service, and by that means to have obtained the knowledge, in what state and condition of health you had passed this part of the Progress. Your former weakness, together with the dangerous temper of the season, giving me cause both to doubt, and pray against the worst: But I found my self then to be more strictly obliged to the performance of this duty, when I received from your Grace so clear and abundant a testimony, as well of your good opinion, as of the trust you reposed in me. Obligations, certainly, of that nature, and of so large an extent as do with reason deprive me of all degree of liberty, and justly subject me to a perpetual of servitude, and obedience to all your Grace's commandments.

I have diligently perused my Lord of *Bristol's* answer, which it pleased your Grace to communicate unto me. And although it become me not, neither will I presume, to give my opinion of the strength, or weakness, thereof; yet will I take the liberty to say thus much, That I find, in his case, that to be verified which I have observed at other times, (to wit) That
when

when able and prudent men come to act their own parts, they are then for the most part not of the clearest sight, and do commonly commit such errors, as are both discernable and avoidable, even by men of mean abilities.

Being now fallen to speak of this Lord, I humbly beseech your Lordship to give me leave plainly and briefly to set before you some Cogitations of mine own, touching his present occasion.

First, that it may be maturely considered, whether the tendring him any further charge, unto which he may be able to frame a probable satisfactory answer, will not rather serve to declare his innocency, then to prepare his Condemnation, and so instead of pressing him, reflect back with disadvantage upon the proceeding against him.

Secondly, That your grace would be pleased to consult with your self, whether you may not desist from having him further questioned, without either blemish to your Honour or manifest prejudice to the service: Considering that you have (to your perpetual glory) already dissolved and broken the Spanish party, and rendred them without either the means, or the hope, of ever conjoyning in such sort together again, as may probably give the least disturbance or impediment to your Graces waies and designs.

And lastly, Although his Lordship, in sundry places of his answer, especially in the later part, doth seem directly to violate the rule of the * prudent Mariner, who in foul weather, and in a storm, is accustomed (to prevent shipwrack) rather to pull down, then to set up his sails. Nevertheless, as this case stands, it deserves to be throughly pondered, which of the two waies will most conduce to your Graces purpose, and is likely to receive the better interpretation and success, either to have him dealt with after a quick and round manner, or otherwise to proceed slowly and moderately with him, permitting him for a time to remain where he is, as a man laid aside, and in the way to be forgotten. A state of being (if I mistake not his complexion) which will be by him apprehended equivalent to the severest and sharpest censure that possibly can be inflicted on him.

* Providdent.

Thus have I over-boldly adventured to present unto your Grace these few Queries and Proposals, which might be both enlarged, and more forcibly urged; yet to avoid the being too tedious, I have chosen to omit the further insisting upon them, till such time as I may have the honour and felicity of being neer your person. At this present it shall suffice, humbly to beseech your Grace, to be assuredly perswaded, that what I have now delivered in this subject doth not proceed from any over-indulgent respect I bear either to the person, or fortune of my Lord of Bristol; though I should not be sorry, that like a prudent man he might, by his discreet application to your Grace, render himself capable to be again readmitted to your love and favour. But the motive which hath induced me principally to use this plainess and liberty, is, the Consideration how importantly (as I conceive) the well ordering and disposing this particular, doth concern your Graces service. Unto the advancement and furtherance whereof, if I may be able, now, or at any time, to contribute the least proportion, I shall esteem my self most happy, and more then abundantly rewarded, in case that my right humble endeavours in that kind may receive from your Grace a favourable and acceptable construction.

I will conclude this Letter with a two-fold prayer; first to you for my self, that your Grace will be pleased to pardon this boldness. Next to God for you, that he will give you health, and length of days, for his Majesties service, and the good and honour of this Common-wealth. I humbly crave leave to remain,

Aug. 21. 1624.

Your Graces most obedient, and most devoted servant;
Robert Philips.

King Philip, the third, of Spain, to the Conde Olivarez.

THe King my Father declared at his death, that his intention never was to marry my sister the *Infanta Donna Maria* with the Prince of *Wales*; which your Uncle *Don Baltezer* well understood, and so treated this match with an intention to delay it; notwithstanding it is now so far advanced, that, considering withall the averseness unto it of the *Infanta*, as it is high time to seek some means to divert the treaty, which I would have you find out, and I will make it good whatsoever it be; but in all other things procure the satisfaction of the King of *Great Britain*, who hath deserved very much, and it shall content me, so that it be not the match.

Conde

Conde Olivarez, *his Answer to the King.*

Sir,

Considering in what estate we find the Treaty of marriage between *Spain* and *England*, and knowing certainly how the Ministers did understand this business, that treated it in the time of *Philip* the third, Who is now in heaven, that their meaning was never to effect it; but by enlarging the treaties and points of the said marriage, to make use of the friendship of the King of *Great Britain*, as well in the matter of *Germany* as those of *Flanders*; and suspecting likewise that your Majesty is of the same opinion (although the demonstrations do not shew so) joyning to those suspitions, that it is certain that the *Infanta Donna Maria* is resolved to put her self into the Monastery the same day that your Majesty shall press her to make the marriage, I have thought fit to present to your Majesty that which my good zeal hath afforded me in this occasion, thinking it a good time to acquaint your Majesty withall, to the end you may resolve of that which you shall find most convenient, with the advice of those Ministers that you shall think fit.

The King of *Great Britain* doth find himself at this time equally in the two businesses, the one is the marriage to which he is mov'd by the conveniencies which he finds in your Majesties friendship with making an agreement with those Catholiques that he thinks are secretly in his Kingdom, and by this to assure himself of them; as likewise to marry his son to one of the house of *Austria*, knowing that the *Infanta Donna Maria* is the best born Lady in the world. The other business is, the restitution of the Palatinate, in which he is yet more engaged. For (besides that his reputation is at stake there is added) the love and interest of his Grandchildren, sons of his only daughter. So that, both by the law of Nature, and reason of State, he ought to put them before whatsoever conveniencies might follow by dissembling what they suffer. I do not dispute whether the King of *Great Britain* be governed, in this business of the Palatinate, by Art of friendship, I think a man may say he hath used both; but as a thing not precisely necessary to this discourse, I omit it. I hold it for a maxime, that these two engagements in which he finds himself, are unseparable: for although the marriage be made, we must fail in that which in any way of understanding is most necessary, which is the restitution of the Palatinate. This being supposed, having made the marriage in the form as it is treated, your Majesty may find your self, together with the King of *Great Britain*, engaged in a war against the Emperour, and the Catholique league; so that your Majesty shall be forced to clear your self with your Arms against the Emperour and the Catholique league, a thing which, to hear, will offend your Majesties Godly ears: or declaring your self for the Emperour and the Catholique League, as certainly you will, your Majesty will find your self engaged in a war against the King of *England*, and your sister married with his son, with the which, all whatsoever conveniencies that was thought upon with this marriage, do cease, if your Majesty shall shew your self Neutral, as it may be some will expound ———

The first will cause every great scandal, and with just reason, since in matters of less opposition then of Catholiques against Heretiques, the Armes of this Crown hath taken the godly against the contrary part; and at this time the *French* men have taken part with the *Hollanders* against your Majesty, your Piety hath been such, that you have sent your Arms against the Rebels of that Crown, leaving all the great considerations of State, only because those men are enemies of the faith and the Church. It will oblige your Majesty, and give good occasion to those of the league, to make use of the King of *France*, and other Catholique Princes ill affected to this Crown, for it will be a thing necessary for them to do so; and those, even against their own Religion, will foment and assist the Heretiques, for hatred to us; without doubt they will follow the conttary part, onely to leave your Majesty with that blemish that never hath befaln any King of these Dominions.

By the second the King of *England* will remain offended and disobliged, seeing that neither interesses nor hopes do follow the Alliance with this Crown, as likewise the pretext of particular resentment for having suffered his daughter and Grand-children to be ruined for respect of the said Alliance. The Emperour, though he be well affected, and obliged to us, in making the transition at this time, as businesses now stand (the Duke of *Bavaria* being now possessed of all the Dominions) although he would dispose of all according to our conveniencies, yet it will not be in his power to do it, as you and every body may see: And the memorial that the Emperours Ambassadour gave your Majesty yesterday makes it certain, since in the List of the Soldiers, that every one of the league is to pay, he shews your

The Protestants of France, to King Charles.

Majesty, that *Bavaria* for himself alone will pay more then all the rest joyned together; the which doth shew his power and his intention, which is not to accommodate matters, but to keep to himself the superiority of all in this broken time. The Emperour is now in the Dyet, and the translation is to be made in it. The opposition in this estate is, by conserving the means for conference, which your Majesties Ministers will do with their capacities, zeal and wisdom; and it is certain they will all have enough to do, for the difficulty consists to find a way to make the present state of affairs straight again, which with lingring, as it is said, both the power and time will be lost. I suppose that the Emperour, as your Majesty knows by his Ambassadour, desires to marry his Daughter with the King of *Englands* son, I doubt not but he will be likewise glad to marry his second Daughter with the Palatines son.

Then I propound, that these two marriages be made, and that they be set on foot presently, giving the King of *England* full satisfaction in all his propositions for the strict union and correspondency that he may agree to it: I hold for certain, that all the conveniencies that would have followed the Alliance with us, will be as full in this; it doth accommodate the matter of the Palatinate, and the succession of his Grand-children, with his honour, and without drawing a sword, or wasting treasure.

After I would reduce the Prince Elector, that was an enemy, to the obedience of the Church, by breeding his sons in the Emperours Court, with Catholique Doctrine.

This business is great, the difficulty greater then perchance hath been in any other case, I have found my self obliged to represent to your Majesty, and to shew (if you please to command me) what I think fit for the disposing of the things, and of the great Ministers that your Majesty hath; I hope with the particular notice of these things, (and all being helped with the good zeal of the *Conde de Gondomar*) it may be that God will open a way to it; a thing so much for his and your Majesties service.

The Protestants of France, to Charles King of Great Britain.

SIR,

The knowledg and resentment which it hath pleased your Majesty to take of the misery of the afflicted Churches of *France* hath given us the boldness to awaken your Compassion in such measure, as our calamities are aggravated by the unmercifull rigour of our persecutors, and as the present storm doth threaten neer at hand the total ruine, and lamentable destruction of that which the mercy of God had yet kept entire unto us since the desolation of *Rochel*: and as we have adored with humility the judgment of God in this bad success (which we impute only to his wrath justly kindled against us for our sins) so our silence could be thought no less then ingratitude, if we had not at the beginning of our Assembly resolved the most humble and most affectionate acknowledgment which we now render to your Majesty, for the great succour which you have sent us, interesting your self so far in the grief of our oppression, and in the means of our deliverance. The most humble supplication which we do offer to your Majesty next after this our thanksgiving, is, that your Majesty (according to the sweet inclination of your goodness) would permit us still to present our complaints, and discover our wounds before the eyes of your Royal charity, protesting unto your Majesty, that we see none other hand under of heaven by which we may be healed, but your Majesties, in case your Majesty will still vouchsafe to lift it up on the behalf of oppressed innocents, and of the Church of our Lord outragiously persecuted by the most invenom'd passion that our age, or any age precedent, hath seen: we most humbly beseech your Majesty, to read this letter which is written with our tears and with our blood; and (according to your exquisite judgment, your incomparable wisdome, and the devotion of your zeal, to the glory of God) to consider our estate, which is such, that our persecutors, upon the loss of *Rockell*, supposing we had been put to utter discomfiture, and into a weakness without recovery or resistance, and boasting themselves, that now there remained no more any eyes unto us, but to bewaile our selves, nor any sense, but to feel the smart thereof, without further employing our hands or our arms for our defence, have made use of this advantage, with so much fierceness, insultation, and cruelty, that they have not only sacked the houses, and with an unheard of rudeness and barbarisme rifled the goods of our poor brethren of this Province of *Languedock*, relying themselves upon publick faith, and the benefits of the edicts of pacification (especially of the last which your Majesty had favourably procured and confirmed unto us) dissipating whole families, and exiling them with perfidious inhumanity, but also they have laid waste and destroyed almost
all

all the Churches of the same, which are at their command and discretion under the liberty of edicts; employing Monks (the Popes Emissaries) assisted with force of soldiers, and of the tyrannical authority of Governours, to ravish mens souls, and to draw the most constant with violence to Mass, and to the feet of the Idol, interdicting assemblies, and all exercise of true Religion in the same places, beating, imprisoning, ransoming, assassinating the faithful and their pastors with an enraged fury, which hath exceeded all the inhumanities of the Inquisition, profaning and demolishing of Temples; their violence having proceeded so farre, as publickly to burn, in pomp and triumph, the sacred books of Gods Covenant in presence of the Governour of the Province, with damnable sacriledge, which cryeth for vengeance before God, and doth elevate its voice to the ears, (Sir) of a most puissant Monarch, professing the purity of the Gospel, zealous of his Glory, and capable to revenge so outragious an injury. But your Majesty shall understand, that all this hath produced an effect much contrary to the intention of our persecutors; for so farre it is from us, that their objects of pity and grief, whereof the very thought doth make us repine, should render us faint-hearted, and cause us to yield our selves in prey to their rage, that, on the contrary, seeing the Mask taken off, and the pretext which they had alledged of the Army of rebellion whereof they accused us, quite removed; and that without any more dissimulation, their design goes on to the ruinating of our Religion, and the extirpation of our Church, and that there remained no more hope of safety and liberty, but general resolution to die in the Arms of our just and vigorous defence, and that our persecutors possessing the spirit of our King, and hindring the effects of his bounty, have obtained a declaration of the fifteenth of December last, which alluring us to implore his grace and mercy, yet leaveth us not any hope of enjoying the benefits of any edict, nor by consequence of any tolerable peace, and soliciting us to disarm our selves, and to put our selves into the condition of sacrifices destined, by one, and by one, to the slaughter, to be all at one stroak offered up to the fury of Antichrist, by one general Massacre throughout the whole Kingdome, whereof we do not only hear the vaunts, but do almost see great armies upon our backs for execution. This makes us (Sir) have recourse to your Royal and undoubtable puissance, as to a place of refuge, which God hath yet left open to us, in your Ardent charity, to find within your assistance assured and effectual means to avoid ruine, which is ready inevitably to fall upon our heads, And to attain thereunto; (Sir) we have religiously renewed, in this Assembly, the Oath of Union, which bindes us with a sacred bond unto the Arms of your Majesty; of the violating whereof your Majesty may be assured that we will never make our selves guilty, being encouraged to this resolution by the reiterate confirmations which my Lord the Duke of *Roban* hath lately given us, that your Majesty continues to take to heart the assistance and deliverance of our Churches according to your Royal promises, being debtors to his sage and valorous conduct, and to his pious magnanimity, for all that strength and liberty which we yet enjoy: and we will leave unto posterity memorable examples of our Constancy which prefers death before reproachfull cowardize and shamefull servitude, hoping that out of our ashes God will draw matter for his glory, and the propagation of his Church; being perswaded (Sir) that you are the instrument of his election to give us comfort and deliverance from our evils in time convenient. Be you assured also that he will uphold us in that extraordinary valour wherewith he hath inspired us to endure all extremities with a patience invincible, expecting the succour of his hands through yours. Of all (Sir) which a great Monarch could ever do in the world, nothing can be more just then this enterprize, nor more glorious then this deliverance: the Lord having exalted you to the most eminent degree of dignity and power to be the nursing father of his Church, she hath right, being thus mangled and bloody, to stretch forth her arms unto you, even she that Spouse of Jesus Christ, the common mother of Christians, and your mother also, by the respect of her bruised members, and of the searing of her innocent brest, covered with wounds, she will move your pity; She assures her self (Sir) that the glorious title which you bear of the Defender of the faith, shall intercede for your accepting of her humble request: if you do extend unto us your cares, your affections, and your formidable Arms, you shall nourish in our hearts affections of our honour and obedience which shall never die; you shall daunt all powers that would raise themselves against your Crown; you shall raise your glory to such a height, that all the earth shall admire it, all Christendome shall celebrate it, and your name shall be of sweet odour unto Angels and men; and in perpetual benediction unto all posterity of Saints, and your reward shall be great and eternal in heaven. May it please your Majesty to pardon us, if our necessities pressing us, we all do press your Majesty by our instant supplications accompanied

companied with a most humble respect to strengthen our selves so soon as may be with the honour of your commandments, and the declaration of your favour, the wholesome effects of your assistance, according to the sweetness of your compassion, and charity, and we will redouble our prayers to the divine clemency for the length and safety of your life, and the prosperity of your estate, being ready with a most holy and ardent affection to expose our goods and lives to render us worthy of the quality which we dare take of your most humble, most obedient, and most faithful servants, the Deputies of the reformed Churches of *France*, in their general Assembly held at *Nismes*, and for all *Jaques de Maresey adjunct la Reque.*

The Pope, to the Duke of Buckingham. Gregorie P. P. XV.

Nobleman, health, and the light of Divine Grace,

THe authority wherein we have understood your Nobleness to flourish in the *British* Court is accounted not only the reward of your merits, but also the patronage of vertue; certainly an excellent renown, and every way so worthy, that the people desire a diuturnity to be annexed unto it. But it is almost ineffable, what an increase of glory thorowout the world would be annexed unto it, if by Gods favour it should become the defence of the Catholick Religion.

Certainly you have gained an opportunity by which you may insert your self into the Councels of those Princes, who obtaining an immortal name have attained the Celestial Kingdom.

Suffer not then (O Nobleman) this occasion presented to you from God, and commended by the Bishop of *Rome*, to slip out of your hands.

You that are privie to their royal Councels cannot choose but know in what estate the affaires of *Britain* at this time stand, and with what voyces of the Holy Ghost (speaking in them) they daily sound in the ears of your Princes. What Glory would redound unto your Name, if by your exhortation and perswasion, the English Kings should again recover their Celestial inheritance of that Glory left unto them by their Ancestours in those Kingdomes in abundant manner, by providing for the increase of Gods Worship, and by not only defending, but propagating the jurisdicton of the Pontifical authority. There have been many, and shall be hereafter, whom the bountie of Kings hath enriched with fading riches, and advanced to envied titles, and yet mindful posterity will not celebrate your name with eternal Praises for having attained these: but if your Councels should reduce those most powerful Kings and people unto the bosom of the *Romane* Church, the name of your Nobleness would be written in the book of the living, whom the torment of Death toucheth not; and the Monument of Histories shall place you amongst those wise men in whose splendor Kings walked; but with what comforts in this life, and what rewards in the life to come, God who is rich in mercy would reward you, they easily see who know the art and force by which the Kingdom of heaven is conquered. It is not only our Pontifical charity (to whose care the salvation of mankind pertaineth) but also the piety of your Mother, who as she brought you into the world, so she desireth to bear you again to the *Romane* Church, which she acknowledgeth for her mother, that moved us to desire, that you were made Partaker of so great felicity. Therefore when our beloved Son, the religious man *Didactus de la Fuente*, who hath wisely administred the affaires of your Princes in this City) prepared his journey for *Spain*, we commanded him to come unto your Nobleness, and present these our Apostolical Letters, by which the Greatness of our Pontifical charity, and the desire of your salvation may be declared. Your Nobleness may therefore hear him as the interpreter of our mind, and as one endued with these vertues which have won him the love of forreign nations, being a Catholick, and religious Priest: He certainly hath reported those things of you in these parts of the world, that he is worthy to be embraced of you with singular affection, and defended by your authority, being a servant to the Glory, and salvation of the *British* Kings, and people. This thing, truly, will we pray for to the father of mercies, that he will open to your Nobleness the gates of his Celestial Kingdom, and afford you frequent Documents of his Clemency. Given at *Rome*, at St. *Mary* the Greater, under the Ring of the *Fisherman*, the 19. of *May*, 1623. and of our *Popedom* the thrd,

John Champolus.

The Lady Purbeck, to the Duke.

My Lord;

Though you may judge what pleasure there is in the conversation of a man in the distemper you see your Brother in; yet the duty I owe to a husband, and the affection I bear him, (which sickness shall not diminish,) makes me much desire to be with him, to adde what comfort I can to his afflicted mind, since his onely desire is my Company: Which if it please you to satisfie him in, I shall with a very good will suffer with him, and think all but my duty, though I think every wife would not do so. But if you can so far dispence with the Laws of God; as to keep me from my Husband, yet aggravate it not by restraining from me his means, and all other contentments; but, which I think is rather the part of a Christian, you especially ought much rather to study comforts for me, then to adde ills to ills, since it is the marriage of your Brother makes me thus miserable. For if you please but to consider, not onely the lamentable estate I am in, deprived of all Comforts of a Husband, and having no means to live of: besides, falling from the hopes my fortune then did promise me; for you know very well, I came no beggar to you, though I am like so to be turned off.

For your own Honour and Conscience sake, take some course to give me satisfaction, to tye my tongue from crying to God and the world for vengeance, for the unworthy dealing I have received. And think not to send me again to my Mothers, where I have stayed this quarter of a year, hoping (for that my Mother said you promised) order should be taken for me, but I never received penny from you. Her confidence of your Nobleness made me so long silent; but now believe me, I will sooner beg my bread in the streets, to all your dishonours, then any more trouble my friends, and especially my Mother, who was not onely content to afford us part of the little means she hath left her; but whilest I was with her, was continually distempered with devised Tales, which came from your Family, and withal lost your good opinion, which before she either had, or you made shew of it; but had it been real, I cannot think her words would have been so translated, nor in the power of discontented servants Tales to have ended it.

My Lord, if the great honour you are in can suffer you to have so mean a thought as of so miserable a creature as I am, so made by too much Credulity of your fair promises, which I have waited for performance of almost these five years: And now it were time to despair, but that I hope you will one day be your self, and be governed by your own noble thoughts; and then I am assured to obtain what I desire, since my desires be so reasonable, and but for mine own. Which whether you grant or no, the affliction my poor husband is in (if it continue) will keep my mind in a continual purgatory for him, and will suffer me to sign my self no other, but

Your unfortunate Sister,

F. Purbeck.

Mr. John Packer, to the Lord Keeper.

May it please your Lordship,

Since my coming hither, finding my Lord at good opportunity, I have acquainted him in what perplexity I found your Lordship at my coming from *Westminster*, and upon what reason. And though I am sorry I can make no comfortable relation of his answer, yet because it so much importeth your Lordship to know in what terms you stand, I could not conceal it from you, being agreeable to those reports your Lordship hath already heard; saving that his Grace told me, he doth not seek your ruine (as some others had related) but onely will hereafter cease to study your fortune, as formerly he hath done; and withal added the reason, that your Lordship hath run a course opposite to him, which though he had cause to take ill at your hands, yet he could have passed it over, if it had been out of conscience, or affection to his Majesties service, or the publick good; but being both dangerous to your country, and prejudicial to the cause of religion (which your Lordship above all other men should have laboured to uphold) he thought, he could not with reason continue that strictness of friendship, where your Lordship had made such a separation, especially

having

having divers times, out of his love to you, assayd to bring you into the right way, which once you promised to follow; but the two last times you met in Councel, he found, that you took your kue just as other men did, and joyned with them in their opinions, whose aim was to tax his proceedings in the managing of the Princes business. But instead of laying it upon him, they did no less, then throw dirt in the Princes teeth. For either they would make him a *minor*, or put the refusal of the Lady upon his Highness, and to lay an aspersion upon his carriage there. His Lordships Conclusion with me was, that for any carriage of his, he desireth no other favour, but that the greatest Councel in *England* may be Judge of it, and the like he wisheth for other mens actions. Yet I did what I could to perswade his Grace to expostulate the matter with your Lordship, which he told me, he would no more do having done it already, but found no other satisfaction, but that by your practice you rejected what he had said, and besides, divulged what had passed between you, as he evidently perceived, meeting with it among others. Whereby you gained only thus much, that they esteemed of you, as of a man fit, by reason of your passion, to set all on fire, but held you not worthy of trust, because you, that would not be true to him, would never be so to them.

My Lord, this is a part I would never have chosen; but being imposed by your Lordship, I could do you no better service then faithfully, and plainly, to discharge it, leaving the use to your Lordships wisdome, and ever resting,

Your Lordships most humbly at command,

J. P.

22. of May, 1624.

Having made visits at sundry times to the Spanish *Embassadours, I do here under my hand declare, what passed betwixt them and me, so neer as my memory serveth; lest in my absence any such matter should fall in question; I now intending to travel for a space.*

WHen his Highness was in *Spain*, being upon my journey in *Scotland*, I went to *Elie*-House to take leave of *Don Carlos*, where *Vanvail* was present, I expressing much joy of the Match (which in my mind would without all question be perfected) did find no such humour, nor inclination on their part, which did much astonish me; for they grumblingly did alledge, that the King my Master did perform nothing that he promised; or how could any thing be expected the *Infanta* being here, whereas nothing was performed, the Prince being in *Spain*? I besought them to do better offices, then without reason to put jealousies betwixt my Master and theirs, who would never have sent his son to *Spain* without a real intention. Which only act was reason sufficient to remove all doubts.

Yet did they still continue their challenge of divers Bracks, specially, against the sending of Ships to *Scotland* to bring away the two *Dunkirkers*, and not perfecting such conditions as were promised to Catholicks. I did intreat them again, that such conceits of my Master might be removed, for they might be confident of full performance of what he had promised, by reason he had never broke his promise to any. I desired them likewise to consider with what love our Prince was gone, and what a stain it should be to the State of *Spain*, if uncourteously he should return with distaste; Besides, it might fall out to be the worst act that ever they committed; where, on the contrary, if they had love to their Master they would prove good Instruments. What was spoke by me in *English* was related in *Spanish* to *Don Carlo*; so was it to me what they spoke in *Spanish*. Sometimes *Don Carlo* spoke in *French*, so that not a word passed which each man did not know.

I went again after the Treaties were given up, and did remember *Don Carlo* of what I had forespoken; when the Marquess was present, and took the speech; they did demand of me, whether I was come of my self, or by Commission, for they professed to account me their friend.

I answered, that I came meerly of my self, and was sorry that by their own deserving they had procured such alterations, and I thought strange of such demands as they had made at

Hampton

Hampton Court, which did both express much spleen, and lack of good intelligence. They did avow their demands were reasonable; but, from that time they would make visits to the Duke, and love him better then before, because they were in doubt before, but now they know him to be an Enemy. I did answer, that I was sorry for their proceeding, and was their friend so long as they were friends to my Master.

After a few haughty words, such as, it was a wrong way to deal with their Master by threatnings, who gave pay daily to 300000 Souldiers, that they had followed the wars a long time, and had seen men killed by the Cannon, Musket, Pike, and Sword, but never saw men killed with words, they desired me to speak to his Majesty, that they might either be dismissed, or have freedome to go about their businesse with securitie. They did desire me likewise to speak to his Majesty, that the treatise for the *Palatinate* might continue.

I did demand of them how these two things did agree, both to threaten and intreat? whereupon they passed upon me with odd complaints. I went once more of late to give them a farwel. I said, they proved themselves good Servants to their Master in pressing to raise jealousies in this State, but they were now too well known to do harm. The Marquess swore, that by this time the *Infanta* had been here, and the *Palatinate* restored, if the blame had not been on our part. I did intreat I might be excused not to believe that. I did ask whether they did not condemn their own judgements in accusing the Duke of *Buckingham* of that whereof he was cleared, both by the King, and State. Their answer was, He was cleared by those who were his confederates, all as guiltie as himself.

I demanded, why they should still express their malice against the Duke of *Buckingham*. Did they not think but our Prince was a man sensible of what injuries he had received? their answer was, if the Duke were out of the way, the Prince would be well disposed. They said farther, his Highness was an obedient son before the Duke guided him, but since, he was not. So that when we speak of his Majesty, they speak with much respect; but for that the Prince did not use them kindly, they did make the less account of him. So after I took my leave and parted,

Nithisdail.

Post-script.

Much I have omitted, for brevitie, wherein they did express much respect to his Majesty, and much of their threatning to the Duke of *Buckingham*.

Captain John Pennington, to the Duke.

May it please your Grace,

MY last to your Lordship was of the 18. of this present, from *Stokes Bay*, since which time I have received two from your Grace, at *Diep*, one by your Secretary Mr. *Nicholas*, whereby your Grace commands me to deliver up his Majesties Ship, and the rest under my Command, to the hands of such *Frenchmen* as his Christian Majesty shall appoint, according to his Majesties pleasure signified by my Lord *Conway*. And that I and the rest of the Masters take securitie of them for our Ships severally, according to the true valuation. And to see this put in execution, you sent your Secretary Mr. *Nicholas*. And the other by Mr. *Ingham*, in answer of mine written from *Stokes Bay*. The former part whereof being only a command to put your former in practice, and the latter a denial of my humble suit for my being called home from this Service. Which said part confirms absolutely, that it was not your Graces pleasure that I should yield up the Ships into their hands, and dispossesse my self and company of them: for I trust your Grace had no such unjust thought as to continue me here alone, after the *French* had possession of her to be their slave, as I am sure they would have made me, if they had had their wills.

To give your Grace an account of what I have done since I came to *Diep* (which was the 21th. at this instant, about nine of the clock at night) would be too tedious for this time. The 22th. in the morning early I sent my boat ashore with my Lieutenant, to find out your Graces Secretary, to receive my Letters, whereby I might know your Graces pleasure, and to kiss my Lord Embassadours hands from me, and to let him know, I was come with his Majesties Ship to do him service, but could not command the rest to come along with me, their Masters not being there, and all their companies in a mutiny. But his jealousie was such, that he would not suffer your Graces Secretary to come aboard, or to send me your Letters, or that my Lieutenant should speak to him, but in his presence, but presently sent a Gentleman aboard to me, commanding me

to

to come ashoar to him, which I confess, I was very loath to do, in regard my people were much discontented, and ready daily to mutiny, being all wonderous unwilling to go against *Rochel*, or those of their religion. And besides, I never having been ashoar, since I came into my command, neither on our own Coast, or elsewhere: (It being not my use) yet notwithstanding these particulars, knowing his Greatness, and your Graces pleasure, for the giving him all due respect, I presently went to him, where he taking me into a room apart with your Graces Secretary, he first delivered me my Lord *Conways* Letter, or rather a warrant, (for so he tearms it himself) for the delivery of the Ship into their hands (as they interpreted it) and then your Graces Letter, commanding me to see his Majesties pleasure (signifyed by my Lord *Conway*) put in execution. And lastly, a Letter from the King of *France*, thereby willing me to receive his Souldiers aboard that he had provided, and his Cousin the *D. de Mommorencie*, and to go presently, and to joyn with his Great Fleet against his rebellious Subjects. This is the effect of that Letter. Having read all these Letters, he would presently have possession of the Ship that night, for that he could not stay longer. I told him, that I did not understand it so, but that I was to render all service to his most Christian Majesty; but nothing would serve him, save the present possession, which because I would not yield unto, he grew into a strange fury, telling me, that your Grace had sent your Secretary to see her delivered, and security to be taken for her. My answer was, that I was ready to obey, according as I understood the warrant, which was to do his Christian Majesty service, and to receive a convenient number of Souldiers aboard me. But to dispossesse my self of my command, I had no such order: but still nothing would satisfie him but the Ship, telling me, he would not entertain at the most (if they were willing) above 60 or 80 of our people. My answer was, I had no order to discharge a man of them, neither could I; but if they were discharged, what they should do, or how they should get home, having neither meat, money, nor clothes, I knew not. To the first of these, he told me, that Mr. *Nicholas* had order, by word of mouth, from your Grace to discharge us, which Mr. *Nicholas* confirmed, as also to see the Ship delivered, which he commanded me to do. But, with your Graces pardon, I durst not do it upon words, it being a business of too high consequence; neither if I had been willing, would my Company ever have condescended to it. To the second, for our passage, he promised to have provided Barques for us; but to conclude this, and not to insist upon the rest of the particulars (they being too tedious) his rage and fury was such, that I must of necessity give a little way thereto, or else I think he would have kept me ashoar, so as I told him I was content if my Company would yield thereunto, and therefore desired to go aboard to speak with them, and to give order for the drawing up of the Inventory. And upon this he suffered me to depart, but not without promises of a large sum of money, which should be given me at the surrender, besides a royal pension during my life, he sending his Secretary, and many others, aboard with me to see all things put in execution, and your Graces Secretary to perswade me to do it. But when I had them aboard, I told them, it was a thing not presently done, neither was my Company willing to deliver over the Ship, without a more ample warrant, yet I would do my best to bring both to pass so soon as I could. So using them with the best respect I could, and fair promises, that I would use all diligence for the accomplishing of their desires; though I must confess I never meant it, till I should hear further from your Grace, and have an especial Warrant from his Majesty, or your Grace, for it, it being a business of so high a nature. Upon these hopes they departed, and went ashoar, where they had not been long, till some of them returned back with a strange Allarum from his Lordship, that he would presently have possession of her, or my resolution to the contrary. And although I alleadged, that the Inventory and other business would not be dispatched in two days, it would not suffice, except I would receive 400 Souldiers aboard in the mean time, till things were perfected.

Thus seeing I could not delay him till I heard farther from your Grace, I was forced to give him this resolute answer, That upon this Warrant I would not deliver over the Ship unto him; neither if I would, would the Company give way unto the same, we not holding it a sufficient discharge for us: But that we were ready to receive a competent number of Souldiers aboard, with a chief Commander, and to go upon such service, as his Christian Majesty should direct us, according to the agreement with the King my Master; but nothing would satisfie him, but to have her delivered over to him, which if I did not presently, my head should pay for it. I desired his patience for two or three days, till I had written, and sent to your Grace, and that he would let me have a Shallop for that purpose; but he denied both the one and the other; notwithstanding sent away a Barque himself, with one to your Grace, but

but would not suffer me to send thereby, which made me the more jealous of the real intent of the businesse. The 23 he sent your Lordships Secretary aboard to work and perswade me; but I could not give other answer, then I had done formerly, onely that I would attend until I heard farther from your Grace; though I must confesse, I had much ado to perswade my Company, who were very unwilling to it. But I had hope still to have a more ample Order how to proceed in this great and weighty businesse. And upon the 24. at two of the clock in the morning, Mr. *Ingham* (whom I sent from *Stokes Bay* to your Grace) returned unto me with two Letters, one from your Grace, and another from my Lord *Conway*, the former Commands in execution: but the latter part prohibiting me to depart with my charge, gave me the more courage to stand upon my former tearms.

This day your Graces Secretary came aboard me again, after I had sent your Graces Letter to him, being sent by the Embassadour to prosecute the businesse, for the delivery of the Ship unto them. But after I had shewed him, that part of your Graces Letter, he knew not what to say to it. I willed him to tell the Embassadour, that this Letter was nothing but an answer of mine written from *Stokes Bay*, concerning the not coming of the rest of the Ships. I further offered his Lordship this day, for the more expedition of the businesse, to take 150. of his men aboard, and to run over for the Coast of *England*, and to send presently to your Grace, that we were ready to surrender over there, upon an Authentick Warrant from his Majesty, or your Grace. His answer to this was, That he would not put his men into be prisoners, nor that we should be the major part. I then offered him to take in as many French as I had English, man for man, but without arms; yet nothing would satisfie him, but the possession of the Ship, either by delivering of her over into their hands, or by receiving 400 armed men aboard, wherewith they would quickly have taken her from us, as you may plainly see their intent by their proceeding. Which I refusing to do, this night about ten of the clock he sent his Secretary aboard with three or four others, to make a protestation against me, as a Rebel to my King and Countrey, as you may perceive by the Copy of it, which I send your Grace herewith; and this, he said, was the last he would have to do with me, for that on the morrow he would away for *Paris*. Whereupon, the next morning I sent this Gentleman Mr. *Ingham* unto him to know, what farther service he would command me, and whether he would have me attend his pleasure longer here, for that I was ready to go upon any service they would command, according to the former agreement, and to receive as many men aboard as possibly I could; but he said, he had nothing to do except I would either deliver up the Ship, or take in the 400 Souldiers. In the interim came his Secretary, with the same company he had before, and made another protestation against me, in regard I would not take in his 400 men, and therewithal brought me a Letter from your Graces Secretary, (for he is so jealous that he will not suffer him to come aboard but when he listeth) which Letter was, That the Embassadour would stay till *Thursday* next, if I would give it him under my hand, to deliver up the Ship then, if I had not order to the contrary before, which I had as good have done at the present; for I expect no Letters from your Grace, in regard they would not suffer me to write to you, as I desired. And if your Grace should write to me by his messenger, they would be sure not to deliver them, till the day were past, except such as were for their turn.

In all which your Grace may see their intents, that there hath been no sleights or waies left unassayed, to bring their purpose to passe: first by fair words, then by seeking to get me become the Kings servant, with promises of a great Pension, and brave employment, with offers of good sums to be laid down upon the surrender of the Ship, as aforesaid. And when none of these courses could preval with me, then followed their threatnings of having my head, and such like. All which (I thank God) I have withstood; for I had rather live all my life with bread and water, then betray my King and Country of so precious a Jewel as this; and had rather the King should take my life, then to have a hand in the surrender, or undervaluing such a Bulwark of the Kingdom.

Upon the making of the last Protest, and with the threats they gave us, my Company grew into such a fury and tumult, that they got up their Anchors, and set sail for *England*, without acquainting me with it, or order from me, saying, They would rather be hanged at home, then surrender the Kings Ships, or be slaves to the French, or fight against those of the Religion. But I must confesse, I heard what they were a doing, but let them alone, because I saw they had reason; otherwise, I should rather have died amongst them, then to have suffered it.

And thus I have related the paincipal passages unto your Grace, wherein, if I have offended his Majesty, or your Grace, it hath been for want of discretion, and not of true zeal to

do

do his Majesty, your Grace, and my Country service; which if it be found to be an offence, I humbly crave pardon.

I am now come to an anchor in the Downs, where I shall attend your Grace's farther pleasure, to be disposed of as his Majesty, and your Grace shall please. But to return again to *France*, I can assure your Grace, that all the people in the Ship will rather be hanged then do it, they have been so well used there. Thus praying for your Graces many happy and prosperous daies, I humbly rest

From aboard the *Vanguard* in
the *Downs*, 27 *July* 1625.

*Your Graces most humble, and
faithful servant*,
Jo. Pennington.

Captain Pennington, to the Duke.

May it please your Grace,

TO take into your consideration these Particulars following:

First, That there is no clause in the contract for our quiet enjoying, and celebrating our Divine service to God morning and evening, according to the ancient order of the Seas.

Secondly, That they may bring as many of their own Nation aboard as they will, and they speak of putting in as many French as English, which will amount to 500 in all, which the Ship is neither able to carry, neither will it be for the health of those that go in her, or safety of the Ship to his Majesty. All which I desire may be considered of, and a course setled with the Embassadour of the just number I shall receive aboard.

Thirdly, That we are bound to fight against any Nation that they command us, except our own; which you may likewise please to consider of.

Fourthly, That there is no clause for the supply of the Victuals, and other provisions, before the six moneths be expired; so that they may keep us till that time, and then turn us off naked and destitute of all provisions, to be a prey to our enemies.

Fifthly, That we may know where we shall receive our supplies of powder, and other munition from them, for that the three last; which we have in here, with the appurtenance, is not sufficient to maintain a fight of three hours.

The former five Articles I humbly desire your Grace judiciously to consider of; and what your Grace will have me therein perform may be inserted in my instructions.

Now further I humbly desire your Grace;

First, That all we English may be of a squadron, and not separated upon any occasion, the accidents of the Sea excepted, and that we may be ready at all times to aid and assist one another.

Secondly, That I may have power in my instructions, or otherwise, for the command of the rest of the English that go along with me, if not, every man may take his course, and do what liketh him best, which may prove prejudicial to the service, dishonourable to the State, and dangerous for the safety of his Majesties Ship.

Lastly, I humbly desire, that your Grace will be pleased to give order, that there may be some provision of Cloaths laid in for naked men, (whereof there are many in the Ship) as hose, shooes, and shirts, (at least.) As also some provision of store for sick men, of Oatmeal, Rice, Sugar, and Fruit, and some little stock of money to relieve them, if necessity require it. It may afterwards be deducted out of their wages, if your Grace will have it so.

*Your Graces Loyal, and Faithful Servant,
ever to be commanded*,
Jo. Pennington.

A Patent for the Admiralty of Ireland.

RIght trusty and welbeloved Cousin, and Councellor, We greet you well. Whereas we are graciously pleased, as well for the increase of our Navy and Navigators, as also, for the better enabling & enriching of our Subjects in our Realm of *Scotland*, to give way and licence unto our loving Subjects of *Scotland*; and so many of them as may make a full, able, and
compleat

Sir Thomas Roe, to the Marquess of Buckingham.

compleat company for Traffick and Merchandizing into the *East Indies*, to erect and set up among themselves a Company, to be called *The East Indian Company of Scotland*, making their first Magazine Storehouse for the said Company, in some parts of our Realm of *Ireland*. But for that our Ports and Seas, upon the Coasts of our said Realm of *Ireland*, have of late, and still are likely, without our special aid and assistance, to be much troubled and annoyed with Pirats, and other Sea-Robbers, to the great discouragement of our loving Subjects and Merchants, passing that way: We, for the Avoyding of those inconveniences, and for the better heartning of the said Company in their intended voyage and traffick, have, for reasons to us best known, resolved (notwithstanding any other employments of our Ships there) by our Letters Patents under our great Seal of *England*, and at the humble request and Petition of our loving Subjects of the said Company, do nominate and appoint *A. B.* our trusty servant, to be employed in those Seas and Coasts of *Ireland*, as fully and amply as our servant Sir *F. H.* is now for our narrow Seas. And to the end he may with more courage and less prejudice to our said servant Sir *F. H.* by his diligence and industry in the said employment, free those Seas from the said annoyances, our pleasure is, That you by your Deed Poll do give unto our said servant such and the like power and authority for the *Irish* Seas and Chanel of St. *George*, as the said Sir *F. H.* hath for the Narrow Seas: So always as the power and authority of the said *A. B.* may begin where the power and authority of the said Sir *F. H.* doth end, that is to say, from our Island of *Scillie* in our Realm of *England*, unto and alongst the Coast of *Ireland*, and the Chanel of St. *George*. So not doubting of your speedy effecting of what is here required, for the furtherance of so good a work, We bid you heartily farewel.

From our Court at, &c.

Sir Thomas Roe, *to the Marquess of* Buckingham, *Lord Admiral.*

My Lord,

I Can give your Lordship no great account of any thing that hath occurred since my departure. I was bold to write to Mr. Secretary *Calvert* from *Malaga*, of the great increase of the Pyrates in those Seas, and of the danger of the Merchants, with my own thoughts, if his Majesty have any farther purpose to attempt their destruction, which is both honourable and necessary: if these Trades, or the other of *Spain*, to the south of the *North-Cape*, be of any consequence to his Majesties Kingdoms; if they be suffered to increase, they will brave the Armies of Kings at Sea in a few years, and attempt even the Coasts and Shoars with peril. And because they carry the name only of Thieves, they are yet contemned, or neglected; but they will become a dangerous enemy, when they shall rob with Fleets, and therefore would be in time considered. The Spaniards now make great offers to continue the Contract, though their performance be slow, and their own Estates chiefly interessed; yet besides the danger and ruine of the Merchant, it is considerable, that this Army increasing is at the obedience of the Grand Seignior, the common Enemy, who hath no strength but Gallies. I know your Lordship will collect enough out of this, without further pressure. The Armado's of *Spain*, *Naples* and *Sicily*, have been in the *Archipelago*, the Turks Forces absent in the black Sea. Yet they have done nothing of consequence, taken a few Carmisales and slaves, and are returned to the Port, where *Don Philibert* of *Savoy*, *Generalissimo*, is present, who is made Vice-Roy of *Sicily*, with absolute power to dispose of all offices, without attendance from *Spain*, which is more then Vice-Roy. He hath used me, for his Majesties honour, with very great respect, as I have in particular advertised Mr. Secretary. Among many courtesies, finding 13 English Captives in the Gallies, I thought it my duty to succour them. His Highness at the first instance, to express his good affection to my Master, gave them to me all free, which I think is a good work, and not ordinary. I beseech your Lordship, that his Majesty may be pleased to take knowledge of it in *Spain*, for the Princes honour, that he may on the like occasion not think himself neglected.

The advice from *Constantinople* is seconded, of the overthrow of the Turk. God grant it be true; and yet the pride of the Grand Seignior is not assuaged, but he threatens a new attempt in the spring. I hope I have hitherto done his Majesty no dishonour, nor can I boast of services; but being under your Lordships protection, I will hope for a good interpretation, beseeching you to present my name to his Majesty, that I be not forgotten in these great distances, wherein my humble fortune hath kept me; and as I have observed your Lordship to be the *Amparo* of those that pretend to virtue and honour, and not to

desert

desert them till they have forsaken themselves: So I beseech you, take me upon those conditions, which cannot shame you, and leave me, when I am other then

Messina, $\frac{7}{17}$ *Decemb*. 1621.   *Your Lordships faithfull and honest servant*,
Tho. Roe.

Cardinal *Richlieu*, to the Roman Catholicks of *Great Britain*.

VIri præclari, longius differo ad vos scribere, quia res vestra facta non verba desiderant, vota vestra nostra sunt studia, & utraque propitio Deo, aliqua ex parte, saltem optatos speramus exitus inventura; spondet hoc nobis Rex Christianissimus, qui aut nullas, aut certè honorificas Religioni, pro Regia sua indole, conditiones fœderis unquam admissurus est; Ita à nobis formatus, ita animo præparatus est, ut se rei divinæ augendæ non minus quam finibus propagandis natum vocatumque esse meminerit : serenissima Regina ejus Mater, sedula opera, intenta cura cavebit, non modo ne quid detrimenti Religio capiat, sed etiam ut quà possit promoveri, promoveatur, & adjuvetur. Equidem ita me rerum vestrarum miseret, ut si non dico consilio, non fide, non authoritate (quæ sentio quam sint exigua:) sed si vita ipsa & sanguine vos eripere vel levare etiam malis possem, libentissime facerem. Ex animo dico, testis est conscientia, qua me vestrum omnium, libertatisque vestræ semper & omni loco fore studiosissimum pollicitor, Vobis ex animo addictissimus,

Amandus, Cardinalis Richlieu.

Apud Sanctum German.
25 August. 1624.

The *Duke of* Rohan, *to his Majesty of* Great Britain.

SIR,

THe deplorable accident of the loss of *Rochel*, which God hath suffered, to humble us under his hand, hath redoubled in the hearts of our enemies their passionate fierceness to our utter ruine, with an assured hope to attain thereunto. But it hath not taken away from the Churches of those Provinces either the heart, or the affection, to oppose their unjust plots by a just and lively defence. This is it hath made them take resolution to assemble themselves to conjoyn, in the midst of these commotions, to assist me with their good counsels, and, with me, to provide the means of their deliverance. And forasmuch as the greatest support which God hath raised unto them upon earth, is, the succour our Churches have, and do look to receive from your Majesty; the general Assembly hath desired, that my Letters, which alone hitherto have represented unto your Majesty the interest of the publick cause, might be joyned to their most humble supplications put up to your Majesty. I do it, Sir, with so much the more affection, because I am a witness, that these poor people, who with sighs and groans implore your assistance, having once laid down their weapons, which the oppression of their enemies made so necessary, because they knew such was your desire to take them up again, so soon as they heard that your Majesty did oblige them thereunto by your Counsel and Promises; they have, upon this onely assurance, continued all dangers, surmounted all oppositions, accounted their estates as nothing, and are still ready to spend their blood till the very last drop: They esteem your love and favour more precious then their own lives; and whatsoever promises or threatnings have been used to shake their constant resolution, they could never be brought to make any breach in that they had tied themselves to, nor ever to hear of any Treaty without your consent. This great zeal for the preservation of all the Churches of this Kingdom, which is naturally knit to the preservation of these few we have left, and that fidelity, without example, are worthy and glorious subjects to exercise your Charity and Power. You are (Sir) Defender of that Faith whereof they make Profession, suffer it not therefore to be so unjustly oppressed; you have stirred up their affection in this defence by your Royal Promises, and those Sacred words, that your Majesty would employ all the power in your Dominions, to warrant and protect all our Churches from the ruine that threatned them, have been (after Gods favour) the onely foundation of all their hope; so the Churches should think no greater a Crime could be committed by them, then doubt of your Royal performance thereof, if their miseries and calamities have at the beginning moved your Compassion. This wofull subject hath encreased with such violence, that nothing but your succour can prevent their utter undoing: for, at this day, the greatest offence our Enemies lay to our charge, (and proclaim, nothing can expiate but our blood) is, to have implored your aid, and hope for it: For this cause, our Lands and Possessions are taken away, and destroyed; our houses made desolate, and reduced to ashes; our heads exposed to file to murtherers; our families banished; and wheresoever the cruelty of them that hate us can extend, men and women are dragg'd and beaten to Mass with Bastinadoes. To be short, the horrour of the persecution we suffer is so great, that our words are too weak to express it. Moreover, we see great and mighty Armies at our Gates, that wait their onely fit time to fall with impetuosity upon the places of retreat that remain; and after that, to expel and banish the exercise of Religion, and massacre all the faithfull ones throughout the whole Kingdom. These things considered (Sir) I do beseech your Majesty, not to forsake us. I should fear by such words to offend so great, so potent, and so faithfull a King: But because of urgent necessity that presseth us, I have presumed importunately to entreat the hastening of your assistance, to keep us from failing under the heavy burthen of our Enemies endeavours. Your Majesty need not to draw, but out of the source of your own profound wisdom, for the fit means how to make your succour dreadfull and powerfull to those that contemn it, and salutiferous to so many people that wait and long for it. Your Majesty shall, by this means, acquire the greatest glory that can be desired, pluck out from the fire and sword Three hundred thousand families, that continually pray to God for your prosperity; preserve a people whom God hath purchased with his most precious blood, and which hath (even in the middest of most eminent dangers, and cruellest torments) kept entire a sound and upright faith, both towards God and man: You shall settle the fidelity of your word, the reputation of your Kingdoms and Arms, to a pitch worthy of your grandeur; and, in repressing of the audaciousness of those that go about every day to blemish the same through their vile and unworthy reproaches, you shall add to your Titles that of the Restorer of a people, the most innocent, and most barbarously persecuted, that ever was. In that which concerns me, Sir, I will not make mention to your Majesty of my own Interest, though I might do it, having, as it seems, the honour to be unto you what I am: But I have so long since consecrated all things with my self to the publick good, that I shall esteem my self happy enough, so that the Church were not miserably distressed; and that I may have this advantage, that through my actions (which your Majesty will not disavow) I may make it known, that I am

March 12. 1628.

Your Majesties most humble, and most obedient servant,
Henry de Rohan.

Sir Walter Raleigh, *to the Duke.*

IF I presume too much, I humbly beseech your Lordship to pardon me, especially, in presuming to write to so great and worthy a person, who hath been told, that I have done him wrong: I heard it but of late; but most happy had I been, if I might have disproved that villany against me, when there had been no suspicion, that the desire to save my life had prevented my excuse.

But, my worthy Lord, it is not to excuse my self that I now write: I cannot; for I have now offended my Sovereign Lord: For all past, even all the world, and my very enemies have lamented my loss, whom now, if his Majesties mercy alone do not lament, I am lost. Howsoever, that which doth comfort my soul in this offence, is, that, even in the offence it self, I had no other intent then his Majesties service, and to make his Majesty know, That my late enterprize was grounded upon a truth, and which with one Ship speedily set out, I meant to have ssured, or to have died; being resolved (as it is well known) to have done it from *Plymouth*, had I not been restrained: Hereby I hoped, not onely to recover his Majesties gracious opinion, but to have destroyed all those malignant reports which had been spread of me. That this is true, that Gentleman in whom I so much trusted, (my Keeper) and to whom I opened my heart, cannot but testifie, and wherein, if I cannot be believed living, my death shall witness: Yea, that Gentleman cannot but avow it, that when we came back towards *London*, I desired to save no other Treasure, then the exact description of those places in the *Indies*. That I meant to go hence as a discontented man, God, I trust, and mine own Actions, will disswade his Majesty; whom neither the loss of my estate, thirteen years imprisonment,

and

and the denial of my Pardon, could beat from his service; nor the opinion of being accounted a fool, or rather distract, by returning as I did, balanced with my love to his Majesties Person and Estate, had no place at all in my heart.

It was that last severe Letter fom my Lords, for the speedy bringing of me up, and the impatience of dishonour, that first put me in fear of my life, or enjoying it in a perpetual imprisonment, never to recover my reputation lost, which strengthened me in my late, and too late lamented resolution, if his Majesties mercy do not abound; if his Majesty do not pity my age, and scorn to take the extremest and utmost advantage of my errours; if his Majesty, in his great charity, do not make a difference between offences proceeding from a life-saving-natural impulsion, without all ill intent, and those of an ill heart; and that your Lordship, remarkable in the world for the Nobleness of your disposition; do not vouchsafe to become my Intercessor; whereby your Lordship shall bind an hundred Gentlemen of my kindred to honour your memory, and bind me, for all the time of that life which your Lordship shall beg for me, to pray to God that you may ever prosper, and over-bind me to remain

Your most humble servant,
W. Raleigh.

Sir Walter Raleigh, *to King* James, *before his Tryal.*

IT is one part of the Office of a just and worthy Prince, to hear the complaints of his vassals, especially, such as are in great misery. I know not, amongst many other presumptions gathered against me, how your Majesty hath been perswaded, that I was one of them who were greatly discontented, and therefore the more likely to prove disloyal: But the great God so relieve me, in both worlds, as I was the contrary; and I took as great comfort to behold your Majesty, and always learning some good, and bettering my knowledge, by bearing your Majesties discourse. I do most humbly beseech your Sovereign Majesty, not to believe any of those, in my particular, who, under pretence of offences to Kings, do easily work their particular revenge. I trust, no man, under the colour of making examples, shall perswade your Majesty to leave the word *Mercifull* out of your Stile; for it will be no less profit to your Majesty, and become your greatness no less then the word *Invincible*. It is true, that the Laws of *England* are no less jealous of the Kings, then *Cæsar* was of *Pompey's* wife: For, notwithstanding she was cleared for having company with *Claudius*, yet, for being suspected, he condemned her. For my self, I protest before Almighty God, and I speak it to my Master and Sovereign, that I never invented treason against him; and yet I know I shall fall *in manus eorum a quibus non possum evadere*, unless by your Majesties gracious compassion I be sustained. Our Law, therefore, (most mercifull Prince) knowing her own cruelty, and knowing that she is wont to compound treason out of presumptions and circumstances, doth give this charitable advice to the King her Supreme, *Non solum sapiens esse, sed & misericors, &c. cum tutius sit reddere rationem misericordiæ quam judicii*. I do, therefore, on the knees of my heart, beseech your Majesty, from your own sweet and comfortable disposition; to remember that I have served your Majesty twenty years, for which your Majesty hath yet given me no reward; and it is fitter I should be endebted unto my Sovereign Lord, then the King to his poor Vassal: Save me therefore, most mercifull Prince, that I may ow your Majesty my life it self, then which there cannot be a greater debt: Limit me, at least, my Sovereign Lord, that I may pay it for your service when your Majesty shall please. If the Law destroy me, your Majesty shall put me out of your power, and I shall have none to fear but the King of Kings.

WALTER RALEIGH.

Sir Walter Raleigh, *to Sir* Robert Car, *after, Earl of* Somerset.

SIR,

After many losses, and many years sorrows, of both which, I have cause to fear, I was mistaken in their ends: It is come to my knowledge, that your self (whom I know not but by an honourable favour) hath been perswaded to give me and mine my last fatal blow; by obtaining from his Majesty the Inheritance of my Children and Nephews, lost in Law for want of a word. This done, there remaineth nothing with me, but the name of life:

His Majesty, whom I never offended, (for I hold it unnatural, and unmanlike, to hate goodness) staid me at the graves brink; not that I thought his Majesty thought me worthy of many deaths, and to behold mine cast out of the world with my self; but, as a King that knoweth the poor in truth, hath received a promise from God, that his Throne shall be established.

And for you, Sir, seeing your fair day is but in the dawn, mine drawn to the setting, your own vertues, and the Kings grace, assuring of many fortunes, and much honour; I beseech you, begin not your first building upon the ruines of the innocent, and let not mine and their sorrows attend your first plantation. I have ever been bound to your Nation, as well for many other graces, as for the true report of my trial to the Kings Majesty; against whom had I been malignant, the hearing of my cause would not have changed enemies into friends, malice into compassion, and the minds of the greatest number then present into the commiseration of mine estate: It is not the nature of foul Treason to beget such fair passions; neither could it agree with the duty and love of faithfull Subjects, (especially of your Nation) to bewail his overthrow that had conspired against their most natural and liberal Lord. I therefore trust, that you will not be the first that shall kill us out-right, cut down the tree with the fruit, and undergo the curse of them that enter the fields of the fatherless; which, if it please you to know the truth, is far less in value then in fame: But that so worthy a Gentleman as your self will rather bind us to you (being six Gentlemen, not base in birth and alliance) which have interest therein; and my self, with my uttermost thankfulness, will remain ready to obey your commandments.

WALTER RALEIGH.

Monsieur *Richer*, forced, recants his Opinions against the Papal Supremacy over Kings.

Ego Librum quem composui Ecclesiasticæ potestatis, & meipsum measque omnes Propositiones subjicio Ecclef. Cathol. Apost. & Roman. & sanctæ sedi Apostolicæ, quam matrem omnium Ecclesiarum esse agnosco; & in qua semper viguit infallibile Judicium veritatis in rebus fidei decernendis. Vehementerque doleo in prædicto meo Libro quasdam esse Propositiones quæ scandalum genuerint, & quæ sint veritati Catholicæ, ut sonant, contraria.

The Lord Viscount Rochfort, *to the* Duke *of* Buckingham.

My Lord,

I Have received great wrongs, about my Lord of *Oxford*, by reports which can find no author; yet have they wrought such impressions in the hearts of some, that it is hard to remove those calumniations: For divers are possessed, that I am to be his accuser; which is so strange, and so maliciously bruited, that it is somewhat suspected. Yet know I not any one particular for which he is in the Tower; neither, if I knew any such slip (in so noble a person as might deserve the Kings displeasure) would my nature give me leave to play the Informer, except it neerly concerned the safety, or the honour, of my King; and then should my discovery be publick, to the face, and not private, behind the back; for that I account too base to be found faulty in.

Sorry I am to be so much as suspected; but since ill-disposed persons will raise ill rumours, without any ground, the cleerness of my heart is sufficient content unto me: And as my heart hath been always most faithfull and watchfull to do you service; so, good my Lord, let me intreat you, that, for my sake, my Lord of *Oxford* may receive some testimonies of your great favour for his speedy enlargement, and that it may appear you are the more willing to do it for my earnest intreaty. My Lord, you shall not onely hereby oblige all my Lord of *Oxford's* friends, but likewise the Lady *Diana's*, who doth lose a great deal of precious time by my Lords imprisonment; and therefore, let all be arguments to excite your noble heart to procure his freedom. And so I kiss your hands, and rest

More yours then his own,
H. R.

Post-script.

Pray, make all haste from *Spain*; for neither are your pleasures and contents so great there as you may find them here, neither have you so faithfull friends there as you deserve: but

but sure I am you have many false ones, for I have work enough both in Court and City to falsifie their reports of you; yea some of them (about women) very base ones, and much tending to your great dishonour. And it is current among very great ones, that the Prince hath been somewhat displeased with you of late. I have sent you another Letter of larger contents, and I should be glad to hear from you.

Mr. Ruthen, to the Earl of Northumberland.

My Lord,

IT may be interpreted discretion sometimes to wink at private wrongs, especially for such a one as my self, that have a long time wrastled with a hard fortune, and whose actions, words and behaviour are continually subject to the censure of a whole State; yet not to be sensible of publique and national disgrace, were stupidity and baseness of mind: For no place, nor time, nor State, can excuse any man from performing that duty and obligation wherein Nature hath tied him to his Countrey and to himself. This I speak in regard of certain infamous verses lately by your Lordships means dispersed abroad to disgrace my Countrey and my self, and to wrong and stain by me the honour of a worthy and vertuous Gentlewoman, whose unspotted and immaculate vertue your self is so much more bound to admire and uphold, in that having dishonourably assaulted it, you could not prevail. But belike, my Lord, you dare do any thing but that which is good and just. Think not to bear down these things either by greatness or denyal; for the circumstances that prove them are too evident, and the vail wherewith you would shadow them is too transparant. Neither would I have you flatter your self, as though, like another *Giges*, you could pass in your courses invisible. If you owe a spight to any of my countrey-men, it is a poore revenge to rail upon me in verse: or it the repulse of your lewd desire at the Gentlewomans hands hath inflamed and exasperated your choler against her, it was never known that to refuse *Northumberlands* unlawfull lust was a crime for a Gentlewoman deserving to have her honour called in question. For her part, I doubt not but her own unspotted vertue will easily wipe out any blot which your malice would cast upon it; and for me and my Countreymen know, (my good Lord) that such blows as come in rime are too weak to reach or harm us. I am asham'd in your Lordships behalf for these proceedings, and sorry that the world must now see how long it hath been mistaken in *Northumberlands* spirit: and yet who will not commend your wisdome in chusing such a safe course to wrong a woman and a prisoner? The one of which cannot and the other, by nature and quality of the place, may not right his own wrongs. Wherefore (setting aside the most honourable order of the Garter, and protesting that whatsoever is here said is no way intended to the Nobility and Gentry of *England*, in general, which I doubt not but will condemn this your dishonourable dealing, and for which both my self, and, I dare truly say, all my Countreymen shall be even as ready to sacrifice our bloods as for our own mother *Scotland*) I do not only in regard of our own persons affirm, that whatsoever in those infamous verses is contained, is utterly false and untrue, and that your self hath dealt most dishonourably, unworthily, and basely; but this I'll ever maintain. If these words sound harshly in your Lordships ear, blame your self; since your self forgetting your self hath taught others how to dishonour you: And remember that though Nobility makes a difference of persons, yet injury acknowledgeth none.

Patrick Ruthen.

The Copy of a Letter sent from Spain, *concerning the Princes arrival there.* &c.

I Presume his Highness being now returned, you may by Conference have such choice and free relations of his proceedings in *Spain*, that I may well hold my Pen, (it being not priviledged with that freedom that the tongue is;) yet to comply with that constant obligation I purpose still to owe you, I will write something, and point at some passages, where others perhaps may not so punctually inform you.

The Princes coming hither seemed not so strange, as acceptable, and pleasing unto all. The Common sort expressed it by extraordinary shouts, and acclamations of joy, offering, and marrying the *Infanta* (as it were) presently, by publique voice, as having wonne, and truly deserved her, by so brave an adventure. The King and State studied how to do him all the honour that might be: The first decree that the Councel of State made, was, that at all occasions

sions of meetings, he should have the precedency of the King. That he should make entry into the Palace in the form of State, as the Kings of *Spain* do in the first day of their Coronation. That he should have one of the chief Quarters of the Kings House for his lodgings, one hundred of the Guard to attend him, all the Councel to obey him, as the Kings own person. All prisoners were released, the new Proclamation against excess in apparel revoked, and sundry other arguments of joy. But a wonder lasteth not but for nine days.

a you so?

For which God be thanked.

This universal joy was grounded upon hopes, that the Prince came not only to fetch a wife, but also to make himself a Catholique. The Pope incited him hereunto by Letters, which his Nuncio delivered. He sent a charge to the Inquisitor general, to use all possible diligence herein. Many Processions, and shews were made to stirr him. But they soon saw how improbable it was to win him, how amongst all his servants there was not one Catholique about him: what sleight esteem they made of the Churches, and Religion here: some committing irreverent and scandalous actions in the Kings own Chappel, so that they began to behold the English with an ill aspect, to inveigh against the *Conde de Gondomar*, that he should inform the King and State, that the Prince had a disposition easie to be wrought upon to be made a Catholique. Add hereunto the ill offices that the *Irish* do, who to preserve themselves in the *Spanish* pension did prejudice the business, by casting aspersions upon the *English*, the misinformation of the persecution in their Countrey, and in *England*, notwithstanding being here, and the abuse of the Ambassadours servants in *London*.

When the Prince came, there wanted nothing for the final consummation of all things but the dispensation, which came two moneths after. And whereas it was expected to come absolute, and full; it came infringed with Cautions and limitations, *viz.* That the Infanta should not be married till matters in *England* were in perfect execution; that in case the King of *England* could not give sufficient security, The King of *Spain* himself should swear, and under take the oath for him. Hereupon a *Junto* of Divines was appointed to determine hereof, whether the King might do this with a safe Conscience or no. These Divines went gravely and tediously to work; which put the Prince upon that impatiency, that he was upon point of departure. When at last the business came to a resolution, and so the Match was publiquely declared. The Prince had then often (though publiquely) access to the Infanta, the King being still himself present, and in hearing. After this a Ratification was sent for from *Rome*, but the Pope dying in the interim, and the new Pope falling suddenly sick, it could not be speedily procured. For want of this Ratification there was no Contract made, and the Prince himself seemed not to desire it. A little before his departure, the King and the Councel of State, with the Patriarch of the *Indies*, and the Prince-Prelate, after the Bishop of *Toledo*, (who is under age) swore to all the Capitulations, so that the Prince seemed to depart well satisfied. The King brought him to the *Escurial*; and a little before his departure, the King and he went into a close Coach, and had a large discourse together, (my Lord of *Bristel* being in another Coach hard by, to interpret some hard words, when he was called.) And so they parted with many tender demonstrations of love. A Trophey of Marble is erected in the place where they parted. Many rich Presents were given on both sides. The Prince bestowed upon the Queen the biggest Crown Pearl in the world between two Diamonds. He gave the Infanta a Rope of Pearl, and an Anchor of great Diamonds, with many other Jewels. He hath been very bountiful to every one of the Kings house, and all the Guard. Never Prinae parted with such an universal love of all. He left every mouth filled with his Commendations; every one reporting him to be a truly Noble, discreet, and well deserving Prince, I write what I hear, and know, and that without passion, for all he is the Prince of my Countrey.

My Lord of of *Buckingham*, at first, was much esteemed, but it lasted little; his *French* garb, with his stout hastiness in negotiating, and over-familiarity with the Prince, was not liked. Moreover; the Councel of *Spain* took it ill, that a green head should come with such a superintendent power to treat of an affair of such Consequence, among so many grave Ministers of State, to the prejudice of so able and well deserving a Minister as my Lord of *Bristel*, who laid the first stone of this building. Hereupon his power was called in question and found imperfect, in regard it was not confirmed by the Councel. Thus the business began to gather ill blood between *Olivarez* and him, and grew so far out of square, that unless there had been good heads to peece them together again, all might have fallen quite off the hinges. He did not take his leave of the Countess of *Olivarez*, and the farewell he took of the *Conde* himself was harsh; for he told him, he would be an everlasting servant to the King of *Spain*, the Queen, and the Infanta, and would endeavour to do the best offices he could, for the concluding of this business, and strengthening the amity between the two

Kingdoms;

A Privy Seal, for Transporting of Horse.

Kingdoms; but for himself, he had so far disobliged him, that he could make no profession of friendship to him at all. The *Conde* turned about, and said he accepted of what he had spoken, and so parted.

Since his Highness departure, my Lord of *Bristol* negotiates closely, he is daily at the Palace to attend the Infanta, and he treats by means of the Countess of *Olivarez*.

There is a new *Junto* appointed for the disposing of the Infanta's affairs, and we hope here, that all things will be ripe against the next Spring to bring her over, And so I rest, &c.

From Madrid, Septemb. 30. 1623.

A Privy Seal, for transporting of Horse.

CHARLES by the Grace of God, King of *England*, *Scotland*, *France*, and *Ireland*, Defender of the Faith, &c. To the Treasurer and under-Treasurer of our Exchequer for the time being, greeting. We do hereby will and command you, that out of our Treasure remaining in the receipt of our said Treasury, forthwith to pay, or cause to be paid unto *Philip Burlamack* of *London* Merchant, the sum of 30000 l. to be by him paid over to the Low-Countreys by bill of Exchange, and *Germany*, unto our Trusty and Welbeloved Sir *William Belfour* Knight, and *John Dabler* Esq; or either of them, for levying and providing a certain number of Horse, with Arms for Foot and Horse to be brought over into this Kingdom for our Service; viz. for the levying and transporting of 1000 Horse, 15000 l. for 5000 Muskets, 5000 Corslets, 5000 Pikes, 10500 l. for 1000 Curasiers compleat, 200 Corslets and 200 Carbines, 4500 l. amounting to the whole to the said said sum of 30000 l. And this your Letter shall be our sufficient warrant and discharge in this behalf. *Given under Our Privy Seal, at our Palace of Westminster, January 30 in the third year of Our Reign,* Anno Domini, 1627.

The Earl of Suffolk, to his Majesty.

Gracious Sovereign,

IN this grievous time of my being barred from your presence, which to me is the greatest affliction that can lye upon me; and knowing by my former service to you, the sweet and Princely disposition that is in you naturally, together with that unmatchable judgment which the world knoweth you have, is the occasion, that I presume at this time to lay before your Majesty my most humble suit; which is, that you would be pleased to look upon the case of your poor servant, who after so many faithfull desires of mine to do you service, I do not say that success hath fallen out as I wished, should now not only have suffered for my weakness, and errours, but must be further questioned to my disgrace. I would to God your Majesty did truly understand the thoughts of my heart, and if there you could find out the least of ill affections to you, I wish it pulled out of my body.

Now to add to my miseries, give me leave to let your Majesty know the hard estate I am in; for I do owe at this present (I dare avow upon my fidelity to you) little less then 40000 l. which I well know will make me and mine poor and miserable for ever.

All this I do not lay down to your Majesties best judging eyes, that I mean this by way of complaint; For I do acknowledge the reason that your Majesty had to do what you did: neither do I go about to excuse errours to have escaped me, but will now and ever acknowledge your Gracious favourable dealing with me, if you will be pleased now to receive me again to your favour after this just correction; without which I desire not to enjoy fortune of Goods, or life in this world, which in the humblest manner that I can I begg at your Princely feet, as &c.
Yours, &c.
T. Suffolk.

The Earl of Southampton's Letter to the Bishop of Lincoln.

My Lord,

I Have found your Lordship already so favourable, and affectionate unto me, that I shall be still hereafter desirous to acquaint you with what concerns me, and bold to ask your
advise

The Lord Keeper, to the Earl of Southampton.

advice, and Councel; of which makes me to send this bearer to give your Lordship an account of my answer from Court, which I cannot better do, then by sending unto you the answer it self, which you shall receive here enclosed. Wherein you may see what is expected from me, that I may not only magnifie his Majesties Gracious dealing with me, but cause all my friends to do the like, and restrain them from making any extenuation of my errours; which if they be disposed to do, or not to do, is impossible for me to alter, that am not likely for a good time to see any other then mine own family. For my self, I shall ever be ready (as is fit) to acknowledg his Majesties favour to me, but can hardly perswade my self, that any errour by me committed deserved more punishment then I have had, and hope that his Majesty will not expect, that I should not confess my self to have been subject to a Star-chamber sentence, which God forbid I should ever do. I have, and shall do, according to that part of my Lord of *Buckinghams* advice, to speak of it as little as I can; and so shall I do in other things, to meddle as little as I can. I purpose (God willing) to go to morrow to *Tichfield* (the place of mine own confinement) there to stay as long as the King shall please.

Sir *William Parkhurst* must go with me, who hoped to have been discharged at the return of my Messenger from Court, and seems much troubled, that he is not, pretending that it is extream inconvenient for him, in regard of his own occasions. He is fearfull he should be forgotten. If therefore when your Lordship writes to the Court, you would but put my Lord of *Buckingham* in remembrance of it, you shall (I think) do him a favour. For my part, it is so little to trouble me, and of so small moment, as I mean to move no more for it. When this bearer returns, I beseech you return by him this inclosed Letter, and believe that whatsoever I am, I will ever be,

Your Lordships most assured friend, to do you service,
H. Southampton.

The Lord Keepers Answer, to the Earl of Southampton's Letter.

My Lord,

I Have perused your Lordships Letter, and that enclosed I return back again, and doubt nothing of my Lord Admirals remembring of you upon the first opportunity. Great works (as I hope this will be a perfect reconciling of his Majesties affections to you, of your best studies, and endeavours to the service of his Majesty) do require some time: They are but poor actions, and of no continuance, that are slubbered up in an instant. I know (my Lord) mens tongues are their own, nor lieth it in your power to prescribe what shall be spoken for you, or against you. But to avoid that *Complacentia* (as the Divines call it) that itching and inviting of any interpretation, which shall so add to your innocency as it shall derogate from the Kings mercy, which (I speak as I would do before God) had a great cloud of jealousies and suspicions to break through, before it came to shine upon you. This (I take it) is the effect of my Lords exhortation, and I know it ever hath been your Lordships resolution. How far you could be questioned in the Star-chamber, is an unreasonable time to resolve. The King hath waved off all judgment, and left nothing for your meditation, but love and favour, and the increasing of both these. Yet I know (upon my late occasions to peruse Presidents in that Court) that small offences have been in that Court (in former times) deeply censured, In the sixteenth of *Edward* the second (for the Court is of great antiquity) *Henry* Lord *Beaumont*, running a way of his own about the invading of *Scotland*, and dissenting from the rest of the Kings Councel, because of his absenting himself from the Councel Table, was fined and imprisoned, though otherwise, a most worthy and deserving Nobleman. But God be thanked, your Lordship hath no cause to trouble your head about these meditations. For (if I have any judgment) you are in a way to demean your self so, as you may expect rather more new additions, then suspect the least diminution from his Gracious Majesty. For mine own part, assure your self, I am your true and faithful servant, and shall never cease so to continue, as long as you make good your professions to this Noble Lord. Of whose extraordinary goodness your Lordship, and my self, are remarkable reflexions. The one of his sweetness, in forgetting of wrongs, the other of his forwardness in conferring of courtesies.

With my best respect to your Lordship, and my Noble Lady, and my Commendations to Sir *William Parkhurst*, I recommend your Lordship, &c.

Aug. 2. 1621.

Oliver

Oliver St. John, *to the Major of* Marlborough, *against the Benevolence.*

AS I think, this kind of Benevolence is against Law, Reason, and Religion.
First, the Law is in the Statute called *Magna Charta*, 9 H. 3. *cap.* 29. That no Freeman be any way destroyed, but by the Laws of the Land.

Secondly, besides that the said Statute of *Magna Charta* is by all Princes since established and confirmed, it is, in the special case of voluntary or free Grants, enacted and decreed, 25 E. 1. *cap.* 5. That no such be drawn into custom: and *cap.* 6. That henceforth be taken no such Aids, Tasks, free Grants, or Prizes, but by assent of all the Realm, and for the good of the same. And in *primo* R. 3. *cap.* 2. That the Subjects and Commons in this Realm from henceforth shall in no wise be charged by any charge or imposition called a Benevolence, or any such like charge; and that such exactions, called a Benevolence, shall be damned and annulled for ever.

First, it is not onely without, but against reason, that the Commons, in their several and particulars, should be made relievers or suppliers of his Majesties wants, who neither know his wants, nor the sums that may be this way raised to supply the same.

Secondly, it is against reason, that the particular and several Commons, distracted, should oppose their judgment and discretion to the judgment and discretion of the wisdom of their Land assembled in Parliament, who have there denied any such aid.

It argueth in us want of love and due respect of our Sovereign Lord and King, which ought to be in every of us towards each other, which is, to stay every one which we see falling, and reduce the current. What prosperity can be expected to befall either our King or Nation, when the King shall, haply out of ignorance, or ('tis I hope) out of forgetfulness or headiness, commit so great a sin against his God, as is the violating of his great and solemn Oath taken at his Coronation, for the maintaining of his Laws, Liberties, and Customs of this Noble Realm; and his Subjects, some for fear, some in pride, some to please others, shall joyn hands to forward so unhappy an atchievement? Can he any way more highly offend the Divine Majesty (whom he then invocated?) as also, can he then give unto another *Hen.* 4. (if such an one should rise up, which God forbid) a greater advantage? Let those Articles put up against *R.* 2. be looked on, it will appear, that the breach of the Laws, infringing the Liberties, and failing in this his Oath, were the main blemishes wherewith he could distain and spot the Honour of that good and gentle Prince; who, indeed, was rather by others abused, then of himself mischievously any way disposed.

Secondly, As very irreligiously, and uncharitably, we help forward the Kings Majesty in that grievous sin of perjury; so into what an hellish danger we plunge our selves, even so many of us as contribute, is to be learned out of the several Curses and Sentences of Excommunication given out against all such givers, and, namely, the two following, *viz.* the great Curse given out, the 36 H. 3. against all breakers of the Liberties and Customs of the Realm of *England,* with their Abettors, Counsellors, and Executioners; wherein, by the sentence of *Boniface,* Archbishop of *Canterbury,* and the chief part of all the Bishops of this Land, are *Ipso facto* excommunicated. And that of 24 *Ed.* 1. denounced immediately upon the Acts made against such Benevolence, free Grants and Impositions, had and taken without common assent; which, because it is not so large as that former, I will set down as our Books deliver the same.

IN the Name of the Father, Son, and Holy Ghost, *Amen.* Whereas our Sovereign Lord the King, to the Honour of God, and of the Holy Church, and for the common Profit of the Realm, hath granted, for Him and his Heirs for ever, these Articles above-written: *Robert* Archbishop of *Canterbury,* Primate of all *England,* admonished all his Province, once, twice, and thrice, because that shortness will not suffer so much delay, as to give knowledge to all the people of *England* of these presents in writing. We, therefore, enjoyn all persons, of what estate soever they be, that they, and every of them, as much as in them is, shall uphold and maintain those Articles granted by our Sovereign Lord the King in all points; and all those that, in any point, do resist or break those Ordinances, or in any manner hereafter procure, counsel, or in any ways assent to, resist, or break those Ordinances, or go about it by word or deed, openly or privately, by any manner of pretence or colour: We therefore, the said Archbishop, by our Authority in this Writing expressed, do excommunicate and accurse. and from the Body of our Lord Jesus Christ, and from all the Company of Heaven, and from all the Sacraments of the holy Church, do sequester and exclude.

Sir,

Sir, hearing that to morrow the Justices will be here about this busie work of Benevolence, wherein you have both sent unto, and talked with me, and thinking that, it may be, you would deliver up the names of the not-givers: Forasmuch as, I think, I shall scarcely be at home to make my further answer, if I should be called for, I pray you, both hereby to understand my mind your self, and, if cause so require, to let the Justices perceive as much. So leaving others to their own consciences, whereby in that last and dreadfull day they shall stand or fall before him who will reward every man according to his deeds, I commend you to the grace of the Almighty, and rest

Your loving Neighbour and Friend,
OLIVER S^t. JOHN.

The Earl of Suffolk, to the Duke.

My Honourable good Lord,

AT the first minute of mine and my Wives delivery out of the Tower, I had returned such acknowledgment due for so great a favour, but that Sir *George Goring* onely desired to be the Messenger, as well as he was of the other. Let not (my Lord) my late misfortunes make me or mine more unable to serve and thank you, then any he that thus takes advantage thereby to wrong me in your belief: For, what I have received, both in abatement of my fine, and speedy liberty, I must confess to come from your Noble mediation to his Majesty; whose displeasure hath been more grievous to my soul, then all the rest this world can inflict upon me.

As your Lordships kindness hath begun to ease me, so now let the same hand cure and preserve me from a worse relapse wherein I am like to fall, if your power prevent it not. The motion of his Majesty for my perswading my Sons out of their places, was the grievousest sound that ever entred me; for thereby I still breathed under the heavy weight of all my afflictions, not despairing but their care (charged upon them with my blessing) might somewhat redeem my errours, and assure his Majesty, that my will was never tainted with offending him.

I know, my Lord, there is little benefit in serving against Masters minds; but they are unworthy servants, that will leave such Masters upon any conditions: Such as make suit to chop or change for their own advantage are better lost then kept; but as for mine, my curse should follow them, if ever I could think, they followed his Majesty with such indifferency. My obedience to his Majesty was ever of more force with me, then mine own ends any way laid; nor ever joyed I more, then in running to his Commands. But this (my Lord) rends my heart, to think, that unfortunate I should bury my Sons alive, and pronounce that Sentence which would make me and them Scorns to posterity. Whilest I have knee to bend, eye to lift up, or tongue to beg, I must implore his Majesties pardon and mercy in this kind. As for that more drossie part of my estate, it still lies at his Majesties feet; and if he now please to recal what he remitted, without further condition I must obey, and let his Majesty see, no change of time or place can change me, my love, my duty, or my zeal to him,

My Lord, here you may read me, in my greatest griefs that ever did fall to me: Weigh them well, and think that one day you may be a father, and be as neerly touched as now I am. The favour you shall do me herein shall prove no hidden talent; for the increase shall not onely be the happiness of a good work well done, but the hearty acknowledgment of a whole family, and all theirs, that shall as faithfully serve and honour you, as the best of those that would succeed them, which I hope your Lordship will believe from me, who will ever be

Your, &c.
T. SUFFOLK.

The Earl of Suffolk, to his Majesty.

Most gracious Soveraign,

YOur Princely favour, in delivering me and my Wife out of the Tower, must, and shall ever be acknowledged of us with all humble thanks. And now be pleased to give me leave to be an humble suitor to your Majesty, that out of the tender compassion of your Princely heart, you will be pleased to cast your eye upon the miserable estate of your distressed, afflicted,

Sir Philip Sidney, to Queen Elizabeth.

afflicted, and old Servant, now brought into fear of never recovering of your Majesties favour; and so wretched my case is, as the little hope that remained in me to live in your memory, was by my two Sons service to your gracious self, and the Prince. It is now required of me, to impose upon them the resignation of their places; which, with all humility, I beseech you to give me leave to say, I would sooner use my power over them, to will them to bury themselves quick, then by any other way then enforcement to give up their places of service, which onely remains to me, to be either my dying comfort, or my living torment.

Besides, they are now past my government, being both married, and have children; onely I have a Paternal care of them; which I humbly beseech your best judging Majesty to weigh respectively, how unhappy I must of necessity think my self, if I should be the perswader of that misfortune to my children, that their children, within a few years, would curse me for, either living, or dead. Upon all these just considerations (most gracious Master) give me leave to turn my cruel and unnatural part, of perswading them to yield to that for which I should detest my self, to my humblest desire, upon the knees of my heart, to beg humbly of your Majesty, that whatsoever favour you have ever had to me for any service done, that your Majesty will be pleased to spare the ruine of these two young men; whom I find so honestly disposed in their desire of spending their fortunes and lives in your Majesties and your Princely Son's service, as if your displeasure be not fully satisfied with what I have suffered already, that you lay more upon me, and spare them. I have written to my Lord of *Buckingham*, to be my mediator to your Majesty in this behalf, which I assure my self he will nobly perform, as well as he hath formerly done, in being my means to your Majesty in obtaining this great begun favour. To conclude, with my prayer to God, that your Majesty may ever find the same zeal and love to your person in whomsoever you shall employ, that my hearts sole-affection did, and ever shall carry unto you, which, God knows, was and is more to your Majesty, then to my wife and children, and all other worldly things, which God measure unto me according to the truth, as

Yours, &c.
T. Suffolk.

Sir Philip Sidney, unto Queen Elizabeth, touching her Marriage with Monsieur.

Most feared and beloved, most sweet and gracious Sovereign,

* TO seek out excuses of this my boldness, and to arm the acknowledging of a fault with reasons for it, might better shew, I knew I did amiss, then any way diminish the attempt, especially, in your Judgment; who being able to discern lively into the nature of the thing done, it were folly, to hope, by laying on better Colours, to make it more acceptable. Therefore carrying no other Olive-branch of Intercession, then the laying of my self at your feet; nor no other Insinuation, either for attention, or pardon, but the true vowed sacrifice of unfeigned Love; I will, in simple and direct terms (as hoping they shall onely come to your mercifull eyes) set down the over-flowing of my mind, in this most important matter; importing, as I think, the continuance of your safety, and (as I know) the joys of my life. And, because my words (I confess, shallow, but coming from the deep Well-spring of most loyal Affection) have delivered unto your most gracious ear, what is the general sum of my travelling thoughts therein; I will now but onely declare, what be the Reasons that make me think, That the Marriage with Monsieur will be unprofitable unto you; then will I answer the Objections of those Fears which might procure so violent a Refuge.

The Good or Evils that will come to you by it, must be considered, either according to your Estate, or Person. To your Estate: What can be added to the being an absolute born, and accordingly respected, Princess? But as they say, The *Irish-men* are wont to call over them that die, They are rich, they are fair, what needed they to die so cruelly? Not unfitly of you, endowed with Felicity above all others, a man might well ask, What makes you, in such a calm, to change course? to so healthfull a Body, to apply so unsavoury a Medicine? What can recompence so hazardous an adventure? Indeed, were it but the altering of a well-maintained, and well-approved, Trade: For, as in Bodies Natural, every sudden change is full of peril; so, this Body Politick, whereof you are the onely Head, it is so much the more dangerous, as there are more humours to receive a hurtfull impression: But hazards are then most to be regarded, when the nature of the Patient is fitly composed to occasion them.

The Patient I account your Realm, the Agent *Monsieur*, and his Design; for neither outward

outward accidents do much prevail against a true inward strength; nor doth inward weakness lightly subvert it self, without being thrust at by some outward force.

Your inward force (for as for your Treasures, indeed, the Sinews of your Crown, your Majesty doth best, and onely, know) consisteth in your Subjects, generally unexpert in warlike defence; and as they are divided now into mighty Factions (and Factions bound upon the never dying knot of Religion) the one of them to whom your happy Government hath granted the free exercise of the Eternal Truth; with this, by the continuance of time, by the multitude of them, by the principal Offices and strength they hold; and, lastly, by your dealings both at home and abroad against the adverse party, your State is so entrapped, as it were impossible for you, without excessive trouble, to pull your self out of the party so long maintained. For such a course once taken in hand is not much unlike a Ship in a tempest, which how dangerously soever it be beaten with waves, yet is there no safety or succour without it: These, therefore, as their souls live by your happy Government, so are they your chief, if not your sole strength. These, howsoever the necessity of humane life makes them lack, yet can they not look for better conditions then presently they enjoy: these, how their hearts will be galled, if not aliened, when they shall see you take a Husband, a *French-man*, and a Papist, in whom (howsoever fine wits may find further dealings, or painted excuses) the very common people well know this, that he is the Son of a *Jezabel* of our Age; that his Brother made oblation of his own Sisters Marriage, the easier to make Massacres of our Brethren in Belief. That he himself, contrary to his promise, and all gratefulness, having had his liberty and principal estate by the *Hugonots* means, did sack *Lacharists*, and utterly spoil them with fire and sword: This, I say, even at the first sight, gives occasion to all, truly Religious, to abhor such a Master, and consequently, to diminish much of the hopefull love they have long held to you.

The other Faction (most rightly indeed to be called a Faction) is the Papists; men, whose spirits are full of anguish, some being infested by others, whom they accounted damnable, some having their Ambition stopped, because they are not in the way of Advancement; some in prison, and disgraced; some, whose best friends are banished Practisers; many thinking you are an Usurper; many thinking, also, you had disannulled your Right, because of the Popes Excommunication: All burthened with the weight of their Conscience; men of great numbers, of great riches (because the Affairs of State have not lain on them) of united minds, (as all men that deem themselves oppressed naturally are;) with these I would willingly joyn all discontented persons, such as want and disgrace keeps lower then they have set their hearts; such as have resolved what to look for at your hands; such, as *Cæsar* said, *Quibus opus est Bello civili*; and are of his mind, *Malo in acie quàm in foro cadere*: These be men so much the more to be doubted, because, as they do embrace all Estates, so are they, commonly, of the bravest and wakefullest sort, and that know the advantage of the world most. This double rank of people, how their minds have stood, the Northern Rebellion, and infinite other practices, have well taught you: Which, if it be said, it did not prevail, that is true indeed; for, if they had prevailed, it were too late now to deliberate. But, at this present, they want nothing so much as a Head, who, in effect, needs not but to receive their Instructions, since they may do mischief enough onely with his Countenance. Let the *Sigingniam*, in *Hen.* 4. time; *Perkin Warbeck*, in your Grand-fathers; but, of all, the most lively and proper is that of *Lewis*, the *French* Kings Son, in *Hen*, 3. time, who having at all no shew of Title, yet did he cause the Nobility, and more, to swear direct Fealty and Vassalage, and they delivered the strongest Holds unto him: I say, let these be sufficient to prove, That occasion gives minds and scope to stranger things then ever would have been imagined. If then the affectionate side have their affections weakned, and the discontented have a gap to utter their discontent; I think, it will seem an ill preparative for the Patient, I mean, your Estate, to a great sickness.

Now the agent party, which is *Monsieur*, whether he be not apt to work upon the disadvantage of your Estate, he is to be judged by his will and power: His will to be as full of light Ambition as is possible, besides the *French* disposition, and his own education; his inconstant attempt against his Brother, his thrusting himself into the Low-Countrey matters, his sometime seeking the King of *Spain's* Daughter, sometimes your Majesty, are evident testimonies of his being carried away with every wind of hope; taught to love Greatness any way gotten: and having for the motioners and ministers of the mind, onely such young men as have shewed, they think evil contentment a ground of any *Rebellion*; who have seen no Common-wealth but in faction, and divers of which have defiled their hands in odious murthers; with such fancies, and favourites, what is to be hoped for? or that he will contain himself

Sir Philip Sidney, *to* Queen Elizabeth. 365

self within the limits of your conditions, since, in truth, it were strange, that he that cannot be contented to be the second Person in *France*, and Heir apparent, should be content to come to be second person, where he should pretend no way to Sovereignty? His power, I imagine, is not to be despised, since he is come into a Countrey where the way of evil-doing will be presented unto him; where there needs nothing but a Head, to draw together all the ill-affected Members: Himself, a Prince of great Revenues, of the most popular Nation of the world, full of Souldiery, and such as are used to serve without pay, so as they may have shew of spoil; and, without question, shall have his Brother ready to help him, as well for old revenge, as to divert him from troubling *France*, and to deliver his own Countrey from evil humours. Neither is King *Philip's* Marriage herein any example, since then it was between two of one Religion; so that he, in *England*, stood onely upon her strength, and had abroad King *Henry* of *France*, ready to impeach any enterprize he should make for his greatness that way: And yet what events time would have brought forth of that Marriage, your most blessed Reign hath made vain all such considerations. But things holding in present state, I think I may easily conclude, that your Countrey, as well by long peace, and fruits of peace, as by the poyson of division, (wherewith the faithfull shall by this means be wounded, and the contrary enabled) made fit to receive hurt; and *Monsieur* being every way likely to use the occasions to hurt, there can, almost, happen no worldly thing of more eminent danger to your Estate Royal. And as to your person, in the scale of your happiness, what good there may come by it, to balance with the loss of so honourable a constancy, truly, yet I perceive not. I will not shew so much malice, as to object the universal doubt, the Races unhealthfulness; neither will I lay to his charge the Ague-like manner of proceedings, sometimes hot, and sometimes cold, in the time of pursuit, which always rightly is most fervent: And I will temper my speeches from any other unreverend disgracings of him in particular; (though they might be never so true;) this onely will I say, that if he do come hither, he must live here in far less reputation then his mind will well brook, having no other Royalty to countenance himself with; or else you must deliver him the Keys of your Kingdom, and live at his discretion; or, lastly, he must be separate himself, with more dishonour, and further dis-uniting of heart, then ever before. Often have I heard you, with protestation, say, No private pleasure, nor self-affection, could lead you unto it; but if it be both unprofitable for your Kingdom, and unpleasant to you, certainly, it were a dear purchase of Repentance: Nothing can it add unto you, but the bliss of Children, which, I confess, were a most unspeakable comfort; but yet no more appertaining unto him, then to any other, to whom the height of all good haps were allotted, to be your Husband; and therefore I may assuredly affirm, that what good soever can follow Marriage, is no more his, then any bodies; but the evils, and dangers, are peculiarly annexed to his Person and Condition. For, as for the enriching of your Countrey with treasure, which either he hath not, or hath otherwise bestowed it; or the staying of your servants minds with new expectation and liberality, which is more dangerous then fruitfull; or the easing of your Majesty of cares, which is as much to say, as the easing of you to be Queen and Sovereign; I think, every body perceives this way either to be full of hurt, or void of help. Now resteth to consider, what be the motives of this sudden change, as I have heard you, in most sweet words, deliver: Fear of standing alone, in respect of forreign dealings; and in them from whom you should have respect, doubt of contempt. Truly, standing alone, with good fore-sight of Government, both in peace, and war-like defence, is the honourablest thing that can be to a well-established Monarchy; those buildings being ever most strongly durable which lean to none other, but remain from their own foundation.

So yet, in the particulars of your estate at present, I will not altogether deny, that a true *Massinissa* were very fit to countermine the enterprize of mighty *Carthage*: But how this general truth can be applied to Monsieur, in truth, I perceive not. The wisest, that have given best Rules where surest Leagues are to be made, have said, That it must be between such as either vehement desire of a third thing, or as vehement fear, doth knit their minds together. Desire is counted the weaker Bond; but yet that bound so many Princes to the Expedition of the *Holy Land*. It united that invincible *Hen. 5.* and that good Duke of *Burgundy*: the one desiring to win the Crown of *France* from the *Dauphin*; the other desiring to revenge his Fathers murther upon the *Dauphin*; which both tended to one. That coupled *Lewis* the Twelfth, and *Ferdinando* of Spain, to the Conquest of *Naples*. Of Fear, there are innumerable examples. *Monsieur's* desires, and yours, how they should meet in Publick matters, I think, no Oracle can tell: For as the Geometricians say, That Parallels, because they maintain divers lines, can never joyn; so truly, two, having in the beginning contrary Principles,

Sir Philip Sidney, to Queen Elizabeth.

to bring forth one Doctrine, must be some Miracle. He of the *Romish* Religion; and, if he be a man, must needs have that manlike property, to desire that all men be of his mind: You the Erecter and Defender of the contrary; and the only Sun that dazleth their eyes. He *French*, and desiring to make *France* great; Your Majesty *English*, and desiring nothing less then that *France* should grow great. He, both by his own fancy, and his youthful Governorus, embracing all ambitious hopes, having *Alexanders* Image in his head, but, perhaps, evil painted: Your Majesty, with excellent vertue, taught what you should hope; and by no less wisdom, what you may hope; with a Council renowned over all *Christendom*, for their well tempered minds, having set the utmost of their Ambition in your Favour; and the study of their Souls in your Safety.

Fear hath as little shew of outward appearance, as Reason, to match you together; for in this estate he is in, whom should he fear? his Brother? Alas! his Brother is afraid, since the King of *Navar* is to step into his place, Neither can his brother be the safer by his fall; but he may be the greater by his Brothers; whereto whether you will be an accessary, you are to determine. The King of *Spain*, certainly cannot make war upon him, but it must be upon all the Crown of *France*; which is no likelihood he will do. Well may *Monsieur* (as he hath done) seek to enlarge the bounds of *France* upon his State; which likewise, whether it be safe for you to be a Countenance to, any other way, may be seen; So that if neither desire, nor fear, be such in him as are to bind any publick fastness; it may be said, That the only Fortress of this your Marriage is, of his private Affection; a thing too incident to the person laying it up in such knots.

The other Objection of contempt in the Subjects, I assure your Majesty, if I had heard it proceed out of your mouth, which of all other I do most dearly reverence, it would as soon (considering the perfections both of body and mind have set all mens eyes by the height your estate) have come to the possibility of my imagination, if one should have told me on the contrary side, That the greatest Princess of the world should envy the State of some poor deformed Pilgrim. What is there either within you or without you, that can possibly fall into the danger of contempt, to whom fortunes are tyed by so long descent of your Royal Ancestors? But our minds rejoyce with the experience of your inward Vertues, and our eyes are delighted with the sight of you. But because your own eyes cannot see your self, neither can there be in the world any example fit to blaze you by, I beseech you vouchsafe to weigh the grounds thereof. The Natural causes are lengths of Government, and uncertainty of succession: The effects, as you term them, appear by cherishing some abominable speeches which some hellish minds have uttered, The longer a good Prince Reigneth, it is certain the more he is esteemed; there is no man ever was weary of well being. And good encreased to good maketh the same good both greater and stronger; for it useth men to know no other cares, when either men are born in the time, and so never saw other; or have spent much part of their flourishing time, and so have no joy to seek other: in evil Princes, abuse growing upon abuse, according to the nature of evil, with the increase of time ruines it self. But in so rare a Government, where neighbours fires give us light to see our quietness, where nothing wants that true Administration of Justice brings forth, certainly the length of time rather breeds a mind to think there is no other life but in it, then that there is any tediousness in so fruitfull a Government. Examples of good Princes do ever confirm this, who the longer they lived, the deeper still they sunk into their Subjects hearts. Neither will I trouble you with examples, being so many and manifest. Look into your own estate, how willingly they grant, and how dutifully they pay such subsidies as you demand of them? How they are no less troublesome to your Majesty in certain requests, than they were in the beginning of your Reign: and your Majesty shall find you have a people more then ever devoted to you.

As for the uncertainty of succession, although for mine own part I have cast the utmost Anchor of my hope, yet for *Englands* sake I would not say any thing against such determination; but that contention in good should bring contempt to a certain good, I think it is beyond all reach of Reason: nay, because if there were no other cause (as there are infinite) common reason and profit would teach us to hold that Jewel dear, the loss of which would bring us to we know not what: which likewise is to be said of your Majesties Speech of the rising Sun, a Speech first used by *Scilla* to *Pompey* in *Rome*, as then a popular City, where indeed men were to rise or fall, according to the Flourish and breath of a many headed confusion. But in so Lineal a Monarchy; where-ever the Infants suck the love of their rightfull Prince who would leave the Beams of so fair a Sun, for the dreadful expectation of a divided Company of Stars? Vertue and Justice are the only bonds of peoples love: and as for that

point,

point, Many Princes have loft their Crowns whose own children were manifest succeffors, and some, that had their own children used as inftruments of their ruine; not that I deny the bliss of children, but only to shew Religion and equity to be of themselves sufficient ftaies: Neither is the love was born in the Queen, your Sifters dates, any contradiction hereunto; for she was the Oppreffor of that Religion which lived in many mens hearts, and whereof you were known to be the favourer; by her loss, was the moft excellent Prince in the World to fucceed; by your loss, all blindneffs light upon him that fees not our misery. Laftly, and moft properly for this purpose, she had made an odious marriage with a ftranger (which is now in queftion, whether your Majefty fhould do or no,) fo that if your Subjects do at this time look for any after-chance, it is but as the Pilot doth to the Ship-boat, if his Ship should perifh; driven by extremity to the one; but, as long as he can with his life, tendring the other. And this I fay, not only for the lively parts that be in you; but even for their own fakes, fince they muft needs fee what tempefts threaten them.

The laft proof in this contempt fhould be the venomous matter certain men impoftumed with wickedneffs fhould utter againft you. Certainly not to be evil fpoken of, neither Chrifts holineffs, nor *Cafars* might, could ever prevent or warrant: There being for that no other rule, then fo to do, as that they may not juftly fay evil of you; which whether your Majefty have not done, I leave it in you, to the finecereneffs of your own Confcience, and wifdom of your judgment; in the world, to your moft manifeft fruits and fame through *Europe*; *Auguftus* was told, that men fpake of him much hurt; it is no matter, faid he, fo long as they cannot do much hurt; and laftly, *Charles* the 5th. to one that told him, *Le Hollandeur parlent mal, mais Ilz. patient bien*, anfwered *Le*. I might make a Scholar-like reckoning of many fuch examples. It fufficeth that thefe great Princes knew well enough upon what waies they flew, and cared little for the barking of a few Currs: And truly, in the behalf of your fubjects, I durft with my blood anfwer it, That there was never Monarch held in more precious reckoning of her people; and before God how can it be otherwife? For mine own part, when I hear fome loft wretch hath defiled fuch a name with his mouth, I confider the right name of Blafphemy, whofe unbridled foul doth delight to deprave that which is accounted generally moft high and holy. No, no, moft excellent Lady, do not raze out the impreffion you have made in fuch a multitude of hearts, and let not the fcum of fuch vile minds bear any witneffs againft your fubjects devotions: Which, to proceed one point further, if it were otherwife, could little be helped, but rather nourifhed, and in effect begun by this. The only means of avoiding contempt, are Love and Fear: Love as you have by divers means fent into the depth of their fouls; fo if any thing can ftain fo true a form, it muft be the trimming your felf, not in your own likeneffs, but in new colours unto them: Their fear by him cannot be encreafed without appearance of French Forces, the manifeft death of your eftate; but well may it againft him bear that face, which (as the Tragick *Seneca* faith.) *Metus in Authorem redit*, as becaufe both in will and power he is like enough to do harm. Since then it is dangerous for your State, as well becaufe by inward weakneffs (principally caufed by divifion) it is fit to receive harm; fince to your perfon it can no way be comfortable, you not defiring marriage, and neither to perfon nor ftate he is to bring any more good then any body, but more evil he may, fince the caufes that fhould drive you to this are either fears of that which cannot happen, or by this means cannot be prevented; I do with moft humble heart fay unto your Majefty (having affayed this dangerous help) for your ftanding alone, you muft take it for a fingular Honour God hath done you, to be indeed the only Protector of his Church; and yet in worldly Refpects your Kingdom very fufficient fo to do, if you make that Religion upon which you ftand, to carry the only ftrength, and have abroad thofe that ftill maintain the fame courfe, who as long as they may be kept from utter falling, your Majefty is fure enough from your mightieft Enemies.

As for this man, as long as he is but *Monfieur* in Might, and a Papift in profeffion, he neither can, nor will greatly fhield you: And if he grow to be King, his defence will be like *Ajax* fhield, which rather weighed them down, then defended thofe that bare it. Againft contempt, if there be any, which I will never believe, let your excellent vertues of Piety, Juftice and Liberality, daily, if it be poffible, more and more fhine; let fuch particular actions be found out (which be eafie, as I think, to be done) by which you may gratifie all the hearts of your people: Let thofe in whom you find truft, and to whom you have committed truft in your weighty Affairs, be held up in the eyes of your Subjects. Laftly, doing as you do, you fhall be as you be, the Example of Princes, the Ornament of this Age, the Comfort of the afflicted, the delight of your people, and the moft excellent fruit of your Progenitors, and the perfect mirrour of your Pofterity.

The Lord Sanquir's Case.

IN this cause of the life and death, the Juries part is in effect discharged, for after a frank and formal confession, their labour is at an end; so that what hath been said by Mr. Attorney, or shall be said by my self, is rather convenient than necessary.

My Lord Sanquire, your fault is great, it cannot be extenuated, and it cannot be aggravated; and if it needed, you have made so full an Anatomy of it out of your own feeling, as it cannot be matched by my self, or any man else, out of Conceit: so as that part of aggravation I leave.

Nay more, this Christian and penitent course of yours draws me thus far, that I will agree in some sort to extenuate it; for certainly, as even in extreami evils there are degrees; so this particular of your offence is such, as though it be foul spilling of blood, yet there are more foul; for if you had sought to take away a mans life for his Vineyard, as *Achab* did; or for envy, as *Cain* did; or to possess his bed, as *David* did; surely the murder had been more odious.

Your temptation was revenge, which the more natural it was to man, the more have Laws both divine and humane sought to repress it; *Mihi vindicta*. But in one thing you and I shall never agree. That generous spirits (you say) are hard to forgive; no, contrariwise, generous and magnanimous minds are readiest to forgive; and it is a weakness and impotency of mind to be unable to forgive; *Corpora magnanima satis est prostrasse Leoni.*

But howsoever Murther may arise from several motives, less or more odious, yet the Law both of God and man involve them in one degree, and therefore you may read that in *Joabs* case, which was a Murther upon revenge, and matcheth with our case; he for a dear brother, and you for a dear part of your own body, yet there was never a severe charge given, that it should not be unpunished.

And certainly the circumstance of time is heavy upon you; it is now five years since this unfortunate man *Turner*, be it upon accident, or be it upon despight, gave the provocation, which was the seed of your malice: all passions are assuaged with time, love, hatred, grief, all, fire it self burns out with time, if no new fuel be put to it. Therefore for you to have been in the gall of bitterness so long, and to have been in restless chase of this blood for so many years, is a strange example; and I must tell you plainly, that I conceive you have suck'd those affections of dwelling in malice rather out of *Italy*, and Outlandish manners where you have conversed, than out of any part of this Island, *England* or *Scotland*.

But that which is fittest for me to spend time in, (the matter being confessed) is, to set forth and magnifie to the hearers the Justice of this day; first of God, and then of the King.

My Lord, you have friends and entertainments in Forreign parts; It had been an easie thing for you to set *Carlile*, or some other blood-hound on work, when your person had been beyond the Seas, and so this news might have come to you in a packet, and you might have looked on how the storm would pass; but God bereaved you of this fore-sight, and bound you here under that hand of a King, that though abundant in Clemency, yet is no less zealous of justice.

Again, when you came in at *Lambeth*, you might have persisted in the denial of the procurement of the fact. *Carlile*, a resolute man, might perhaps have cleared you (for they that are resolute in mischief are commonly obstinate in concealing their procurers) and so nothing should have been against you but presumption. But then also God, to take away obstructions of Justice, gave you the grace, (which ought indeed to be more true comfort to you, than any device, whereby you might have escaped) to make a clear and plain Confession.

Other impediments there were (not a few) which might have been an interruption to this daies Justice, had not God in his Providence removed them.

But now that I have given God the Honour, let me give it likewise where it is next due, which is, to the King our Sovereign.

This Murther was no sooner committed, and brought to his Majesties ears; but his just indignation wherewith he first was moved, cast it self into a great deal of care and Prudence to have Justice done: First came forth his Proclamation somewhat of a rare Form, and devised and in effect dictated by his Majesty himself, and by that he did prosecute the Offendors, as it were, with the breath and blast of his mouth: Then did his Majesty stretch forth his long Arms (for Kings have long Arms, when they will extend them) one of them to the Sea, where he took hold of *Grey* shipped for *Luedia*, who gave the first light of Testimony; the other Arm to *Scotland*, and took hold of *Carlile*, ere he was warm in his house, and brought him the length of his Kingdom under such safe watch and custody, as he could have no means to to escape, no nor to mischief himself, no nor learn no lessons to stand mute; in which case, perhaps, this dayes Justice might have received a stop; so that I may conclude, his Majesty hath shewed himself Gods true Lieutenant, and that he is no Respecter of persons; but *English*, *Scotish*, Noblemen, Fencer, are to him alike in respect of Justice.

Nay, I must say further, That his Majesty hath had, in this, a kind of Propheticall Spirit; for what time *Carlile* and *Grey*, and you my Lord your self, were fled, no man knew whither, to the four winds; the King ever spake in a confident and undertaking manner, That wheresoever the Offenders were in *Europe*, he would produce them forth to Justice; of which noble word God hath made him Master.

Lastly, I will conclude, towards you my Lord, That though your Offence hath been great, yet your Confession hath been free, and your behaviour and speech full of discretion; and this shews, That though you could not resist the Tempter, yet you bear a Christian and generous spirit, answerable to the noble Family of which you are descended. This I commend in you, and take it to be an assured Token of Gods mercy and favour, in respect whereof all worldly things are but Trash; and so it is fit for you, as your state now is, to account them; and this is all I will say for the present.

My Lady Shrewsburies Cause.

Your Lordships do observe the Nature of this Charge.

MY Lady of *Shrewsbury*, a Lady wise, and that ought to know what duty requireth is charged to have refused, and to have persisted in refusal to answer, and to be examined in a High cause of State, being examined by the Councel-table, which is a Representative body of the King.

The nature of the cause upon which she was examined is an essential point which doth aggravate and increase this contempt and presumption, and therefore of necessity with that we must begin.

How graciously and Parent-like his Majesty used the Lady *Arabella*, before she gave him cause of Indignation, the world knoweth.

My Lady, notwithstanding, extreamly ill-advised, transacted the most weighty and binding part and action of her life, which is her Marriage, without acquainting His Majesty, which had been a neglect even to a mean Parent. But being to Our Sovereign, and she standing so near to His Majesty as she doth, and then choosing such a Condition as it pleased her to choose, all parties laid together, how dangerous it was, my Lady might have read it in the fortune of that house wherewith she is matched; for it was not unlike the case of Mr. *Seymers* Grand-mother.

The King, nevertheless, so remembred He was a King, as He forgot not He was a Kinsman, and placed her only *sub libera custodia*.

But now did my Lady accumulate and heap up this offence with a far greater than the former, by seeking to withdraw her self out of the Kings Power into Forreign Parts.

That this flight or escape into Forreign Parts might have been seed of trouble to this State, is a matter whereof the conceit of a Vulgar person is not capable.

For although my Lady should have put on a mind to continue her Loyalty, as nature and duty did bind her; yet when she was in another sphere, she must have moved in the motion of that Orb, and not of the Planet it self. And God forbid the Kings felicity should be so little, as he should not have envy and enviers enough in Forreign Parts.

It is true, if any forreigner had wrought upon this occasion, I do not doubt but the intent would have been, as the Prophet saith *They have conceived mischief, and brought forth a vain thing*. But yet your Lordships know that is Wisdom in Princes, and it is a watch they owe to themselves, and to their people, to stop the beginnings of evils, and not to despise them. *Seneca* saith well, *Non jam amplius levia sunt pericula si levia videantur*; dangers cease to be light, because by despising they grow and gather strength.

And accordingly hath been the practice both of the Wisest and stoutest Princes to hold; for matter pregnant of peril, to have any near them in blood to flie into Forreign Parts. Wherein I will not wander, but take the example of King *Hen.* 7. a Prince not unfit to be parallel'd with his Majesty; I mean not the particular of *Perkin Warbeck*; for he was but an idol, or a disguise; but the example I mean, is that of the Earl of *Suffolk*, whom the King extorted from *Philip* of *Austria*. The story is memorable, That *Philip* after the death of *Isabella* coming to take Possession of His Kingdom of *Castile* (which was but Matrimonial to His

Father in Law *Ferdinand*, of *Arragon*,) was cast by weather upon the Coast of *Tamouth*, where the *Italian* story saith, King *Henry* used him in all things else as a Prince, but in one thing as a Prisoner; for he forced upon him a Promise to restore the Earl of *Suffolk* that was fled into *Flanders*; and yet this I note was in the 21 year of his Reign, when the King had a goodly Prince at mans estate, besides his daughters, nay, and the whole line of *Clarence* nearer in title; for that Earl of *Suffolk* was Descended of a Sister of *Edward* 4. so far off did that King take his aim.

To this action of so deep consequence, it appeareth you (my Lady of *Shrewsbury*) were privy) not upon forreign suspicions or strained inferences, but upon vehement presumptions, now clear and particular testimony, as hath been opened to you; so as the King had not only Reason to examine you upon it, but to have proceeded with you upon it as for a great contempt; which if it be reserved for the present, your Ladiship is to understand it aright, that it is not defect of proof, but abundance of grace that is the cause of this proceeding. And your Ladyship shall do well to see into what danger you have brought your self: All offences consist of the fact which is open, and the intent which is secret; this fact of Conspiring in the flight of this Lady, may bear a hard, and gentler construction; if upon over-much affection to your Kinswoman, gentler; if upon practice or other end, harder; you must take heed how you enter into such actions, whereof if the hidden part be drawn unto that which is open, it may be your overthrow; which I speak not by way of charge, but by way of caution.

For that which you are properly charged with, you must know that all Subjects, without distinction of degrees, owe to the King tribute and service, not only of their deed and hand, but of their knowledge and discovery.

If there be any thing that imports the Kings service, they ought themselves, undemanded, to impart it; much more if they be called and examined, whether it be of their own fact, or of anothers, they ought to make direct answer; Neither was there ever any subject brought into causes of estate to trial judicial, but first he passed examination; for examination is the entrance of Justice in criminal causes; it is one of the eyes of the Kings politick body; there are but two, Information, and Examination; it may not be endured that one of the lights be put out by your example.

Your excuses are not worthy your own judgement; rash vowes of lawful things are to be kept, but unlawful vowes not; your own Divines will tell you so. For your examples, they are some erroneous traditions. My Lord of *Pembroke* spake somewhat that he was unlettered, and it was but when he was examined by one private Councellor, to whom he took exception. That of my Lord *Lumley* is a fiction; the preheminencies of Nobility I would hold with to the last graine; but every dayes experience is to the contrary. Nay, you may learn dutie of my Lady *Arabella* her self, a Lady of the Blood, of an higher Rank than your self, who declining (and yet that but by request neither to declare your fact) yieldeth ingenuously to be examined of her own; I do not doubt but by this time you see both your own error, and the Kings grace in proceeding with you in this manner.

Dr. Sharp, to King James.

The Complaint of Europe our Mother, aged, and oppressed.

TO whom? To the Kings and Princes of *Europe*. Of whom? Of the Pope of *Rome*. For what matter? For causing by his Catholick League so much blood to be spilt within these few years in *Europe*. To this effect, as that excellent Poet speaks, with a little change of his words,

> *Quis non Europæo sanguine pinguior.*
> *Campus sepulchris impia prælia*
> *Testatur? auditumq; Turcis*
>   *Europæ sonitum ruinæ?*
> *Qui gurges aut quæ flumina lugubris*
> *Ignara belli? quo Mare Civicæ*
>   *Non decoloravæ cades?*
>   *Quæ Caret ora cruore nostro?*

And what further danger is it like to breed? Even to bring the *Turk* into *Austria*, *Italy*, *Germany*, into *Vienna*, and into *Rome* it self, as it hath brought him into *Pannonia*, and of late into late into *Polonia*, to the great danger of all Christendom. Which danger she doth foresee, and lament, and telleth, That no *European* King hath sought to compound these bloody home-quarrels, but the King of Great *Britain*. She most humbly desires the rest of the Princes, that they would commiserate her most afflicted estate; her Cities taken, her houses spoiled, her children murthered, her Matrons and Virgins defloured, her waies full of Thieves, her Seas of Pyrates, all the helps of life taken from her in many parts, her flocks and herds scattered, her Tillage ceased, her Trade decayed, the Laws silent, Learning fallen, good manners ruined, neither fear of God left, nor care of men, that all things seem to tend to the first Chaos, &c. And therefore she doth beseech the Princes, to whose trust God hath committed, not to whose power he hath permitted his two Wards, two Twins, the Common-Wealth, and the Church, as to Guardians, that they will look better to their charge.

And first, not suffer the Common-Wealth of Christendom by their Arms (at the Popes secret instigation) to be destroyed; and to this end, she first useth the example of good Heathen Emperours, to perswade them, as *Augustus, Vespasian, Titus, Nerva, Trajan, Antoninus, Marcus Aurelius, Alexander Severus, Probus*; that they will settle peace at home, and by joynt Forces make war abroad upon the Common enemy of their Kingdomes, and so make the Common-Wealth to Honour them, being made by them rich in wealth, strong in power, famous in glory, honest in manners, the felicity of every earthly Common-Wealth.

Now for the other Ward, or Twin, the Church, the Heavenly Common-Wealth, because she hath before professed, that as she had been long a Pagan, so now, by the grace of God, hath long been a Christian, and did take this to be her greatest honour, to be the harbour of the Christian Church, she stirres them up to be more careful by the example of the best Christian Emperours, *Constantine, Jovinian, Gratian, Theodosius, Arcadius, Honorius, Charlemaign*, and his Sons, *Lotharius*, and *Ledovicus*, to defend her from heresies within, and from violence without.

And now she begins to tell them, That as one walking with others in the Sun, not thinking on it, must needs be Sun-burned; so she walking with her reformed children in this new-risen Sun of the Gospel of Christ, did feel her self coloured (as it were) with the Spirit of Christ, by observing the differences between the two Churches with great indifferency.

Here, because she hath before challenged the Pope and the Jesuites of cruelty, and perswading first, that as men they should spare humane blood.

Secondly, as *Europeans*, they should spare *European* blood.

Thirdly, as Christians they should spare Christian blood.

She is first thus answered by the Pope, speaking for himself and his Jesuites, That they are not the authors of shedding Christian blood, but Heretical blood: and that her reformed Sons (as she terms them) are not Christians, because they be no Catholicks; And therefore Hereticks to be taken away by death, according to the sentence of St. *Paul, Hæreticum hominem post unam aut alteram admonitionem devita*; *Hoc est, de vita tolle*, as Cardinal *Allen* doth expound it, and according to the Decree of the Councel of *Lateran*.

And where, I pray you, was this your Reformed Church before *Luther?* And as for my Jesuites, you call them bloody, even as you call your Physitians bloody, who, for driving away a Pestilential Feaver, do take more corrupt and putrified blood from the party then they would.

And thereupon, he doth twit *Europe* as an old doubting *Sybilla*, in her youth, being the Concubine of one *Taurus*, whom she feigned to be *Jupiter*, to cover her fault with the greatness of her lover, who did also give her the name of this divided World, that by the honour of her title she might excuse the shame of her fact; And bites the fond Oratour, that put this person upon her, a whelp of *Luthers*, that makes this Minion to accuse him before the Princes of Homicide, or an insensible piece of Earth to plead his Cause.

To which *Europe* answereth,

First, for her self;

Then, for the Church

This Summe I thought good to present to your Majesty; if it please your judgment, I shall bring the whole work to your Majesty when I am recovered.

And thus, craving pardon of your Majesty for troubling your greater thoughts, though this tend to the good of Christendom which you intend, I rest

Your Majesties most humble Chaplain,

Leonel Sharp.

Dr. Sharp, to the Duke of Buckingham.

May it please your Grace,

'Tis not my purpose to advise, but to attend what others shall determine of the Match of the *Palatinate*; but if that be broken off, and this not restored according to promise, every one may conceive that Peace must give place to War abroad; but with whom, and where, and how it is to be made, it is for an higher Council, then for any private man to resolve.

Peace were best, if it had *Nihil insidiarum*, as *Tully* saith; but it is to be feared, that the malice of the Catholick League doth and will hinder the work of the Kings most Noble and Christian heart, and then it will be a War wrapt in the name of Peace.

A just War is the exercise of Faith, as *Peter Martyr* well collects out of those Wars which those Worthy Kings and Princes *Heb.* 11. fought for their God and his *Israel*: so War is just which is made for the maintenance of Gods true Religion, and for the safety of the Common Wealth, either for the keeping of that we have, or recovering of that we have lost.

Every one therefore doth rejoyce to see the King and his Subjects so joyned in love together, and in the purpose of this defence; every one, I mean that is a true Christian, and good subject; and do wish that two things presently were added, care at home to Coupe up all false-hearted Subjects, that are known; and provision to meet with the secret and open practices of such forreign Enemies as are like to abet them.

The good policies of the former reign in such times is the best president for this, at this time. The heads were then committed *liberali Custodia*, divided from their inferiour parts, the Papists disarmed, their clawes pared, that they might not hurt us, the lawes executed upon the Jesuites and Priests, fire-brands of sedition and rebellion withal: Or if not blood drawn of them, yet close imprisonment, or banishment enjoyned them.

Large subsidies granted to prepare the Navy, and pay the Armies. And a great while no war proclaimed, but brave Adventurers sent forth, as to *Portugal*, the *Groine*, to the *West-Indies*, &c. And before Letters of surprisal granted to the Merchants to make up their losses, a *Rowland*, for an *Oliver*, because they had granted Letters of Mart against us. By this means Carricks were brought in, the treasure of their *West-Indian* mines laid for at their return, so to make war upon them with their own money, till they had made the *Ausburg.* enemy bankrupt, and to break with their Banquers of *Ausburg*, and *Genua*, that he was not able to pay his Souldiers and Garrisons; and still the Low-countries strongly assisted, and war made upon the enemy there, or at home at his own doors, which was more Noble, gainful, and safe for us; for we still had peace and plenty at home, though war abroad.

I know not how the case stands now between us and the Spaniards, but me thinks it should not be very well, when nothing will satisfie him, but the head of him that spake the truth for the good of the King and Kingdom. Certainly if we break with him, as they which sit at the Helm know what is best to do, he is ready to strike, and will peradventure strike quickly, before we be fully prepared; therefore our preparations had need to be more speedy thorough, lest we fall into the snare. While they were treating of Peace in 88, they did even then invade us. I pray God they have not used this Treaty of marriage to as bad a purpose; for it seems they never did intend it, but for delaies, and to make it serve their turn, they have plainly abused us in the *Palatinate* thereby. But I can say nothing for the present; yet what is to be done, it is proper to an higher judgment; onely I tell what was then, when we were enemies.

I remember in 88 waiting upon the Earl of *Leicester* at *Tilbury* Camp, and in 89 going into *Portugal* with my Noble Master the Earl of *Essex*, I learned somewhat fit to be imparted to your Grace.

The Queen lying in the Camp one night, guarded with her Army, the old Treasurer *Burleigh* came thither, and delivered to the Earl the examination of *Don Pedro*, who was taken, and brought in by Sir *Francis Drake*, which examination the Earl of *Leicester* delivered unto me, to publish to the Army in my next Sermon. The sum of it was this,

Don Pedro's Confession. *Don Pedro* being asked what was the intent of their coming, stoutly answered the Lords, What? But to subdue your Nation, and root it out.

Good, said the Lords, and what meant you then to do with the Catholicks? He answered, We meant to send them (good men) directly unto Heaven, as all you that are Hereticks to Hell. Yea but, said the Lords, what meant you to do with your whips of Cord,

and

Dr. Sharp, to the Duke of Buckingham.

and wyer? (whereof they had great store in their Ships) What? said he, We meant to whip you Hereticks to death, that have assisted my Masters Rebels, and done such dishonours to our Catholick King, and people? Yea, but what would you have done (said they) with their young Children? They (said he) which were above seven years old should have gone the way their fathers went, the rest should have lived, branded in the forehead with the Letter *L.* for *Lutheran*, to perpetual bondage.

This, I take God to witness, I received of those great Lords upon examination taken by the Councel, and by commandment delivered it to the Armie.

The Queen the next morning rode through all the Squadrons of her Army, as Armed *Pallas*, attended by Noble Footmen, *Leicester*, *Essex*, and *Norris*, then Lord Marshal, and divers other great Lords. Where she made an excellent Oration to her Army, which, the next day after her departure, I was commanded to re-deliver to all the Army together, to keep a Publick Fast.

Her words were these.

MY loving people, we have been perswaded by some that are careful of our safety, to take heed how we commit our self to armed multitudes, for fear of treachery: but I assure you, I do not desire to live to distrust my faithful and loving people. Let Tyrants fear, I have alwayes so behaved my self, that under God I have placed my chiefest strength and safeguard in the loyal hearts and good will of my subjects. And therefore I am come amongst you, as you see, at this time, not for my recreation, and disport, but being resolved, in the midst and heat of the battle, to live or die amongst you all, to lay down for my God, and for my Kingdom, and for my people, my Honour, and my blood, even in the dust. I know I have the body but of a weak and feeble woman, but I have the heart and Stomach of a King, and of a King of *England* too, and think foul scorn that *Parma* or *Spain*, or any Prince of *Europe*, should dare to invade the borders of my Realm; to; which rather then any dishonour shall grow by me, I my self will take up arms, I my self will be your General, Judge, and Rewarder of every one of your vertues in the field. I know, already for your forwardness, you have deserved rewards, and crowns; and we do assure you, in the word of a Prince, they shall be duly paid you. In the mean time, my Lieutenant General shall be in my stead, then whom never Prince commanded a more Noble or worthy subject, not doubting but by your obedience to my General, by your Concord in the Camp, and your valour in the field, we shall shortly have a famous victory over those enemies of my God, of my Kingdoms, and of my People.

This I thought would delight your Grace, and no man hath it but my self, and such as I have given it to; and therefore I made bold to send it unto you, if you have it not already.

I would I could perswade your Grace, either to read your self, or to command your Secretary to gather out of the History of *Spain*, translated into *English*, towards the end, five or six leaves, which hath matter of great importance fit for the Parliament, especially for two points; the one concerning the setled intention of the State of *Spain* against *England*, whensoever they can get an opportunity; the other concerning the main reasons of State, which moved the Queen, and Councel, then to take upon her the protection of the *Low-Countries*.

They were of two sorts, the first inherent in the Person of the Prince then being, which died with her, (as some think) the Quarrel being then between the Queen and King of *Spain*, *Philip* the second, which are said to be buried in their graves; the other inherent in their Estates, which live with them, and remain in the heart of the State of *Spain* against us, whosoever is their King.

And this appeareth by a large Disputation of State had before the King of *Spain*, and blab'd out by their Chronicler in many words, wherein, *pro & contra*, two do argue. The one, who proves that the *Netherlands* their Rebels are first to be conquered, that it may serve them as a rise to the Conquest of *England*, and the reasons for that project. The other, who proves, that the *English* are first to be conquered, the supporters of those their Rebels, and for a rise to the Empire of Christendome, and the reasons for the project; and specially for that it is more easie now for the disuse of armes in *England*, for that *England* is not now that *England* which it hath been, &c,

And the mean, how they may win themselves into us by a Treatie of Marriage, as *Mariana* blabs it out in general, that which the Prince hath tryed, and your Grace hath uttered in Parliament in special, that *Colloquia de Contractibus* are with them *Mera ludibria parata tantum*

tantum Regum animis, Ne noceant distinendis, dum ea qua ipsi intendunt perficiantur. Which *Guicciardine* also doth, in general, affirm, That the *Spaniards* bring more things to passe by Treaties, and subtilties, then by force of Armes.

And that you may truly understand the full intention of the *Spaniard* to the state of this Kingdom, and Church, I would your Grace would read a notable Discourse of the late most Noble Earl of *Essex*, made by the Commandment of Queen *Elizabeth*, and debated before her Majesty and her Councel, concerning this point, Whether Peace or War was to be treated with *Spain*? The Lord *Buckhurst* speaking for a Treatie of Peace, to the which the Noble Queen, and her old Lord Treasurer, inclined: The Earl speaking for War, because no safe Peace could be made with that State, for three special Reasons, which are in that Treatise set down at large, which is not fit for me yet to deliver by writing, but there you shall find them. Your Grace may have the book of divers Noblemen your friends. If you have it not (if I may understand your pleasure) I will get it for you. It was of that affect, that it brought the Queen, and Treasurer, contrary to their purpose, to his side, for the very necessity of the common safety.

Your Lordship having angred them, and endeared your self to us, you had need to look to your self; you are as odious to them as ever the Earl of *Essex* was.

The Jesuite *Walpool* set on one of the stable (*Squire*) one well affected to my Lord, to poyson the rest of his Chair. And seeing they strike at the Ministers, which deal effectually for his Church, (witness worthy Doctor *White*) what will they do to such Pillars of State as you are? The Lord preserve your Grace, and watch over you, And thus I rest,

Your Grace his most humble at Commandment,

Leonel Sharp.

Sir Nicholas Throckmorton, *then Ambassadour in* France, *to Queen* Elizabeth, *touching a free Passage for the Queen of* Scots, *through* England *into* Scotland.

IT may please your Majesty to understand that the 17 of *July* I received your Letters at *Poisey* of the 14 of the same, by *Francisco* this bearer; and for that I could not, according to your Majesties instructions in the same Letters, accomplish the contents of them, until *Mounsieur d' Oysell* had delivered your Letters to the *French* King, the Queen of *Scotland*, and the Queen Mother (who did not arrive at this Court till the 20th of this present) I did defer to treat with any of the Princes, of your Majesties answer to the said *Mounsieur d' Oysell*. Nevertheless, the 18th of this moneth I required Audience of the *French* King, which was granted me; the same day in the after-noon I repaired to his Court being at Saint *Germanes*, and there the Queen-Mother, accompanied with the King of *Navarre* and sundry other great personages, was in the place of State to hear what I had to say to the King her Son who was absent, unto her I declared your Majesties pleasure according to my instructions, concerning your acceptation of the Hostages already received, and hereafter to be received, signified to me by your Majesties Letters of the 17 of *June*; and, as I wrote to your Majesty lately, brought to me by *Mounsieur de Noailles* the 16 of *July*; for answer whereunto the Queen-Mother said, *Mounsieur l' Ambassadour*, we marvail greatly how it cometh to pass that the Queen your Mistress doth not make more stay to receive the King my sons Hostages, than she hath done heretofore; for from the beginning since the Hostages were sent into *England*, neither the King my late Lord and Husband, nor the late King my Son, did either recommend the sufficiency of their Hostages by their Letters, or cause their names to be recommended unto you the Ambassadour; but the presentation of them by our Ambassadour in *England* did suffice: thereunto I said, Madam, you know they be Hostages for a matter of some moment; and if they should neither have the Kings assurance for their Validity, nor the Queen my Mistris Ambassadours allowance of their sufficiency, some personages might be sent which were neither meet for the King to send, nor for the Queen my Mistris to receive; and yet, Madam, the Queen my Mistris doth not require the manner of recommending the sufficiency of the Hostages, for any doubt she hath that unmeet persons should be sent; but rather, because a friendly and sincere fashion of dealing should be betwixt her good Brother and her, with whom her Majesty is so desirous to have a perfect and assured A-

mity

Sir Nicholas Throckmorton, to Q. Elizabeth, &c.

mity: I said also, That the King her Son hath notified both to my Lord of *Bedford* at his being here, and unto me, the names of some of the Hostages; as the Count of *Benox* before his going into *England*, as *Mounsieur de Suult*, who had the charge so to do, could well inform her; so as this motion need not seem strange for the newness. The Queen answered, *Mounsieur l' Ambassadour*, we be well pleased, seeing your Mistriss doth require it, that from henceforth either the Hostages shall have the King my Sons Letters of Recommendation, or else their names should be notified unto you, or any other her Ambassadour here; and I pray you *Mounsieur l' Ambassadour*, quoth she, give the Queen your Mistris, my good Sister, to understand from me, That if there be any thing in this Countrey that may please her, she shall have it, if I may know her liking; I told the said Queen, That I was sure your Majesty was of the same mind towards her, for any pleasures to content her in your Realm; and so I took my leave of her for that time.

It may farther please your Majesty, Having Intelligence that *Mounsieur d' Oysell* had advertised the Queen of *Scotland*, by *Rollet* her Secretary, the 17th. of this present, what answer your Majesty had made him; and hearing also of the sundry Praises and discourses made here, of that your Majesty answered, I sent to *Dampier* (a house of the Cardinal of *Lorrains*) the 19th. of this Moneth, to the Queen of *Scotland*, to require Audience of her, which she appointed me to have the next day in the afternoon at St. *Germaines*; She was (accompanied) at *Dampier* with her Unkles the Cardinals of *Lorrain* and *Guise*, and the Duke of *Guise*; there was also the Duke of *Nemours*, who the same day arrived there in Post out of *Savoy*, and visited the said Queen before he came to this Town.

The 20th of this present, in the afternoon, I had access to the said Queen of *Scotland*, with whom I found *Mounsieur d' Oysel* talking when I entred into her Chamber; she dismissed *Mounsieur d' Oysel*, and rose from her Chair when she saw me; unto whom I said, Madam, whereas you sent lately *Mounsieur d' Oysel* to the Queen my Mistris to demand her Majesties safe conduct for your free passage by Sea into your own Realm, and to be accommodated with such favours as upon events you might have need of upon the Coast of *England*, and also did farther require the free passage of the said *Mounsieur d' Oysel* into *Scotland* through *England*; The Queen my Mistris hath not thought good to suffer the said *Mounsieur d Oysel* to pass into *Scotland*, nor to satisfie your desire for your passage home, neither for such other favours as you required to be accommodated withall at her Majesties hand, in as much as you have not accomplished the ratification of the treaty accorded by your Deputies in *July*, now twelve Moneths ago, at *Edenburgh*, which in honour you are bound many wayes to perform; for besides, that you stand bound by your hand and seal, whereby your Commissioners were authorized, it may please you, Madam, to remember, that many promises have been made for the performance thereof, as well in the King your Husbands time, as by your self since his death, and yet notwithstanding the Treaty remaineth unratified, as before, a whole year being expired since the Accord thereof, which by your Commissioners was agreed to have been ratified within sixty dayes: So as upon this unamicable and indirect dealings, the Queen my Mistris hath refused you these favours and pleasures by you required, and hath grounded this her Majesties strangeness unto you upon your own behaviour, which her Majesty doth uncomfortably, both for that your Majesty is, as she is, a Queen, her next Neighbour and next Kinswoman; nevertheless, her Majesty hath commanded me to say unto you, Madam, (quoth I) that if you can like to be better advised, and to ratifie the treaty, as you in Honour are bound to do, her Majesty will not only give you and yours free passage, but also will be most glad to see you pass through her Realm, that you may be accommodated with the pleasure thereof, and such friendly conference may be had betwixt you, as all unkindness may be quenched, and an assured perfect amity betwixt you both for ever Establisht. Having said thus much unto her, the said Queen sat down, and made me sit also by her; she then commanded all the audience to retire them further off, and said, *Mounsieur l' Ambassadour*, I know not well my own infirmity, nor how far I may with my passion be transported: but I like not to have so many witnesses of my passions, as the Queen your Mistris was content to have, when she talked with *Mounsieur d' Oysel*; there is nothing that doth more grieve me, then that I did so forget my self, as to require of the Queen your Mistriss that favour which I had no need to ask; I needed no more to have made her privy to my Journey, than she doth me of hers; I may pass well enough home into my own Realm, I think, without her Pass-port or License; for though the late King your Master (said she) used all the impeachment he could both to stay me, and catch me when I came hither, yet you know, *Mounsier le Ambassadour*, I came hither safely, and I may have as good means to help me home again, as I had to come hither, if I would imploy

ploy my Friends: Truly (said she) I was so far from evil meaning to the Queen your Mistriss, that at this time I was more willing to employ her Amity to stand me instead, than all the Friends I have; and yet you know, both in this Realm, and elsewhere, I have both Friends and Allies, and such as would be glad and willing to employ both their Forces and Aid to stand me instead; you have, *Mounsieur l' Ambassadour* (quoth she) oftentimes told me, That the Amity between the Queen your Mistriss and me were very necessary and profitable for us both; I have some Reason (quoth she) now to think that the Queen your Mistriss is not of that mind, for I am sure, if she were, she would not have refused me thus unkindly; it seemeth she maketh more account of the Amity of my disobedient Subjects, than she doth of me their Sovereign, who am her equal in degree, though inferiour in Wisdome and experience, her nighest Kinswoman, and her next neighbour; and trow you (quoth she) that there can be so good meaning between my Subjects and her, which have forgotten their principal duty to me their Sovereign, as there should be betwixt her and me? I perceive that the Queen your Mistriss doth think, that because my Subjects have done me wrong, my Friends and Allies will forsake me also: indeed your Mistriss doth give me cause to seek friendship where I did not mind to ask it; but *Mounsieur l' Ambassadour*, let the Queen your Mistriss think that it will be thought very strange amongst all Princes and Countries, that she should first animate my Subjects against me, and now being widow, to impeach my going into my own Countrey: I ask her nothing but friendship; I do not trouble her State, nor practise with her Subjects: And yet I know there be in her Realm that be inclined enough to hear offers; I know also they be not of the mind she is of, neither in Religion, nor other things. The Queen your Mistriss doth say that I am young, and do lack experience, indeed (quoth she) I confess, I am younger then she is, and do want experience: But I have age enough and experience to use my self towards my friends and Kinsfolks friendly and uprightly; And I trust my discretion shall not so fail me, that my Passion shall move me to use other language of her then it becometh of a Queen, and my next Kinswoman. Well, *Mounsieur l' Ambassadour*, I could tell you that I am as she is, a Queen allied and friended, as is known; and I tell you also, that my heart is not inferiour to hers, so as an equal respect would be had betwixt us on both parts; but I will not contend in comparisons: first, you know (quoth she) that the accord was made in the late King my Lord and Husbands time; by whom, as reason was, I was commanded and governed; and for such delays as were then in his time used in the said ratification, I am not to be charged; since his Death, my Interest failing in the Realm of *France*, I left to be advised by the Councel of *France*, and they left me also to mine own Councel; indeed (quoth she) my Unkles being, as you know, of the affaires of this Realm, do not think meet to advise me in my Affairs; neither do my Subjects, nor the Queen your Mistriss, think meet that I should be advised by them, but rather by the Councel of my own Realm; here are none of them, nor none such as is thought meet that I should be Counselled by; the matter is great, it toucheth both them and me; and in so great a matter it were meet to use the advice of the wisest of them; I do not think it meet in so great a matter to take the Counsel of private and unexpert persons, and such as the Queen your Mistriss knoweth be not most acceptable to such of my Subjects as she would have me be advised by; I have (quoth she) oftentimes told you, that as soon as I had their advices, I would send the Queen your Mistriss such an answer as should be reasonable; I am about to haste me home as fast as I may, to the intent the matter might be answered; and now the Queen your Mistriss will in no wise suffer neither me to pass home, nor him that I sent into my Realm; so as *Mounsieur l' Ambassadour* (quoth she) it seemeth the Queen your Mistriss will be the cause why in this manner she is not satisfied, or else she will not be satisfied; but liketh to make this matter a quarrel still betwixt us, whereof she is the Author: The Queen your Mistriss saith, that I am young; she might as well say, that I were as foolish as young, if I would in the State and Countrey that I am in proceed to such a matter of my self, without any Counsel; for that which was done by the King my late Lord and Husband must not be taken to be my act; so as neither in Honour, nor in conscience, I am bound, as you say I am, to perform all that I was by my Lord and Husband commanded to do; and yet (quoth she) I will say truly unto you, and as God favours me, I did never mean otherwise unto her than becometh me to my good Sister and Cousin, nor meant her no more harm than to my self; God forgive them which have otherwise perswaded her, if there be any such; what is the matter, pray you, *Mounsieur l' Ambassadour* (quoth she) that doth so offend the Queen your Mistriss, to make her thus evil-affected to me? I never did her wrong, neither in Deed, nor Speech; it should the less grieve me, if I had deserved otherwise than well; and though the World may be of divers judgements of us and our doings one to another, I do well know,

God

Sir Nicholas Throckmorton, *to* Queen Elizabeth.

God that is in Heaven can and will be a true Judg, both of our doings & meanings. I answered, Madam, I have declared unto you my Charge commanded by the Queen my Mistris, & have no more to say to you on her behalf, but to know your answer for the Ratification of the Treaty.

The Queen answered, I have aforetime shewed you, and do now tell you again, that it is not meet for to proceed in this matter, without the advice of the Nobles and States of mine own Realm, which I can by no means have until I come amongst them. You know (quoth she) as well as I, there is none come hither since the death of the King my late Husband and Lord, but such as are either come for their private business, or such as dare not tarry in *Scotland*. But, I pray you, *Monsieur l'Ambassadour* (quoth she) tell me, how riseth this strange affection in the Queen your Mistris towards me? I desire to know it, to the intent I may reform my self, if I have failed. I answered, Madam, I have, by the Commandment of the Queen my Mistress, declared unto you the cause of her mis-contentation already: But seeing you so desirous to hear how you may be charged with any deserving, as one that speaketh of mine own mind, without instruction, I will be so bold, Madam, by way of discourse, to tell you; As soon as the Queen my Mistris, after the death of her Sister, came to the Crown of *England*, you bore the Arms of *England* diversly quartered with your own, and used in your Countrey, notoriously, the stile and title of the Queen my Mistris, which was never by you put in ure in Queen *Maries* time: And if any thing can be more prejudicial to a Prince, then to usurp the Title and Interest belonging to them, Madam, I do refer it to your own judgment. You see, such as be noted usurpers of other folks States cannot patiently be born withall for such doings; much more the Queen my Mistris hath cause to be grieved (considering her undoubted and lawfull Interest) with the offer of such injury. *Monsieur l'Ambassadour*, said she, I was then under the commandment of King *Henry* my Father, and of the King my Lord and Husband; and whatsoever was done then by their Order and Commandments, the same was in like manner continued until both their deaths, since which time, you know, I neither bore the Arms, nor used the Title, of *England*: Methinks (quoth she) these my doings might ascertain the Queen your Mistris, that that which was done before was done by commandment of them that had the power over me; and also in reason she ought to be satisfied, seeing I order my doings as I tell you. It were no great dishonour to the Queen, my Cousin, your Mistris, though I, a Queen also, did bear the Arms of *England*; for, I am sure, some, inferiour to me, and that be not on every side so well apparented as I am, do bear the Arms of *England*. You cannot deny (quoth she) but that my Grand-mother was the King her Fathers Sister, and (I trow) the eldest Sister he had. I do assure you, *Monsieur l'Ambassadour*, and do speak unto you truly as I think, I never meant nor thought matter against the Queen my Cousin. Indeed (quoth she) I know what I am, and would be loth either to do others wrong, or suffer too much wrong to my self: And now that I have told you my mind plainly, I pray behave your self betwixt us like a good Minister, whose part is, to make things betwixt Princes rather better then worse. And so I took my leave of the said Queen for that time.

The same day, after this my Audience, I required Audience in like manner of the *French* King, which was assigned me, on the 21 of this present, at Afternoon: At which time, I did set forth, as well as I could, to the Queen-Mother, the good reasons, and just occasions, according to your Majesties Instructions, why your Majesty did refuse the Queen of *Scotland* your safe Conduct, for her free passage into her Countrey; and declared, at good length, the Causes why your Majesty did not accommodate the said Queen of *Scotland* with such favours as she required in her passage, not forgetting the reasons that moved your Majesty to return *Monsieur d'Oysell* back hither again.

The Queen-Mother answered, *Monsieur l'Ambassadour*, the King my Son, and I, are very sorry to hear, that the Queen my good Sister, your Mistris, hath refused the Queen my Daughter free passage home into her own Realm; this may be an occasion of further unkindness betwixt them, and so prove to be a cause and entry into War: They are Neighbours, and neer Cousins, and either of them hath great Friends and Allies; so, as it may chance, that more unquietness shall ensue of this matter then is to be wished for, or then is meet to come to pass. Thanks be to God (quoth she) all the Princes of Christendom are now in peace, and it were great pity that they should not so continue: and where (said she) I perceive the matter of this unkindness is grounded upon the delay of Ratification of the Treaty, the Queen my Daughter hath declared unto you, That she doth stay the same, until she may have the advice of her own Subjects; wherein methinks (said she) my Daughter doth discreetly, for many respects: And though she have her Uncles here, by whom it is thought (as reason is) she should be advised; yet considering they be Subjects and Counsellors to the King my

Ccc   Son,

Son, they be not the meetest to give her Council in this matter; the Nobles and States of her own Realm would neither like it, nor allow it, that their Sovereign should resolve, without their advice, in matter of consequence: Therefore, *Monsieur l'Ambassadour*, (quoth she) methinks the Queen your Mistris might be satisfied with this Answer, and accommodate the Queen my Daughter, her Cousin and Neighbour, with such favour as she demandeth. I answered, Madam, the Queen, my Mistris, trusteth you will, upon the reasons before by me declared, as her good Sister and Friend, interpret the matter as favourably on her part, as on the Queen of *Scotland's*; and that you will also indifferently consider, how much it importeth my Mistris, not to suffer a matter so dangerous to her and her State as this is to pass unprovided for; it seemeth, by the many delays which in this matter have been used, after so many fair and sundry promises, that the Queen of *Scotland* hath not meant so sincerely and plainly as the Queen my Mistris hath done; for by this time the said Queen might have known the minds of her Subjects in *Scotland*, if she liked to propound the matter unto them. There have been, since the death of the King, your Son, and her Husband, two or three Assemblies of the Nobles and States in *Scotland*, and this matter was never put forth amongst them: Hither have come, out of *Scotland*, many of sundry Estates, and some that the Queen did send with Commission thither, as the Lord of *Finliter*, to treat on her behalf with the Estates of that Realm, and of other matters; so as, if she had minded an end in this matter of the Treaty, before this time she might have heard her Subjects advices. Thereto the Queen-Mother said, The King my Son, and I, would be glad to do good betwixt the Queen my Sister, your Mistris, and the Queen my Daughter, and shall be glad to hear that there were good amity betwixt them; for neither the King my Son, nor I, nor none of his Council, will do harm in the matter, nor shew our selves other then friends to them both.

After this, I took my leave of the said Queen-Mother, and addressed my speech to the King of *Navarre*; unto whom I declared as I had done to the Queen-Mother, adding, That your Majesty esteemed his amity and friendship entire; that you did not doubt of his good acceptation of your doings and proceedings with the Queen of *Scotland*: and said further, That for your Majesties purpose to have reason, at all times, and in all things, of the Queen of *Scotland*, it were better she were in her own Countrey then here. The said King conceived, that your Majesty needed not doubt, that the King his Sovereign would shew himself, in this matter, more affectionate to the Queen of *Scotland*, then to you, his good Sister; and thereof he bade me assure your Majesty. Then taking my leave of the said King of *Navarre*, I went to the Constable, and declared unto him, as I had done unto the King of *Navarre*, on your Majesties behalf. The Constable humbly thanked your Majesty, that you would communicate your affairs with him, which argued your good opinion of him: He said, he trusted that your expectation should not be deceived of him; but would rather so behave himself towards your Majesty, as your good opinion of him should be increased. As to the matter of the Queen of *Scotland*, he was sorry that the occasions were such, as your Majesty could not bestow such kindness on her, as was meet betwixt Princes, so neer Neighbours and Kinsfolks; but he trusted that time would repair these unkindnesses betwixt you. As for his part, he prayeth your Majesty to think, that he would never give other advice to the King his Sovereign, but such as should rather increase the good amity betwixt both your Majesties, then diminish it; and so prayed me to present his most humble commendation and service to your Majesty, wherewith I took my leave of him. And to the intent I might the better decipher whether the Queen of *Scotland* did mind to continue her voyage, I did, the same 21 of *July*, (after my former Negotions finished) repair to the said Queen of *Scotland*, to take my leave of her; unto whom I then declared, That in as much as I was your Majesties Ambassadour, as well to her, for the matters of *Scotland*, as to the *French* King, your good Brother, and hearing, by common bruit, that she minded to take her voyage very shortly, I thought it my Duty to take my leave of her, and was sorry she had not given your Majesty so good occasion of Amity, as that I, your Minister, could not conveniently wait upon her to her embarquing. The said Queen made Answer, *Monsieur l'Ambassadour*, if my preparations were not so much advanced as they are, peradventure the Queen your Mistrisses unkindness might stay my voyage; but now I am determined to adventure the matter, whatsoever come of it: I trust (quoth she) the wind will be so favourable, as I shall not need to come on the Coast of *England*; and if I do, then, *Monsieur l'Ambassadour*, the Queen your Mistris shall have me in her hands to do her will of me; and if she be so hard-hearted as to desire my end, she may then do her pleasure, and make sacrifice of me; peradventure, that casualty might be better for me, then to live: in this matter (quoth she) Gods will be fulfilled. I answered, she might amend all this matter, if she would, and find more Amity of your Majesty and your Realm,

Sir Nicholas Throckmorton, to Queen Elizabeth.

Realm, then of any other Prince or Countrey. The Queen answered, I have (me thinketh) offered and spoken that that might suffice the Queen my Sister, if she will take any thing well at my hand: I trust (said she) for all this, we shall agree better then some would have us; and, for my part, I will not take all things to the worst: I hope also (said she) the Queen, my Sister and Cousin, will do the like; whereof (quoth she) I doubt not, if Ministers do no harm betwixt us. And so the said Queen embraced me.

This is the sum of my Negotiations, at these my last Audiences with the *French* King, the Queen-mother, the King of *Navarre*, the Queen of *Scotland*, and the Constable; whereof I have thought meet to enlarge to your Majesty, in such sort as the same passed, and was uttered betwixt us. As far as I can perceive, the said Queen of *Scotland* continueth her voyage still; and I hear that *Villageignon* and *Octavian* have the principal order of her said voyage, and mean to sail along the coast of *Flanders*, and so to strike over to the North-part of *Scotland*, as the wind shall serve: She did once mean to use the West-passage, but now she dares not trust the Duke of *Chastilheraults*, nor the Earl of *Argyle*, and therefore dareth not to pass by the West-seas.

The said Queen, as I hear, desireth to borrow of the *French* King an hundred thousand Crowns, the same to be received again of her Dowry, which is twenty eight thousand Crowns by the year: The Queen-mother is willing to help her; the King of *Navarre* doth not further the matter, but seeketh to abridge the sum. After I had done my Negotiations at the Court, I was constrained to dis-lodge from *Poissey*, for the Assembly of the Clergy, who meet there to the end of this moneth, and the Embassadours are now appointed to lodge at *Paris*.

The Queen of *Scotland* departed from St. *Germains* yesterday, the 25 of *July*, towards her voyage, as she bruiteth it; she sendeth most of her Train straight to *New-haven* to embarque, and she her self goeth such a way between both as she will be at her choice, to go to *New-haven*, or to *Calice*: Upon the sudden, what she will do, or where she will embarque, she will be acknown to never a *Scotch-man*, and but to few *French*: And, for all these shews and boasts, some think she will not go at all; and yet all her stuff is sent down to the Sea, and none other bruit in her house but of her hasty going. If it would please your Majesty, to cause some to be sent privily to all the Ports on this side, the certainty shall be better known to your Majesty that way, by the laying of her Vessels, then I can advertise it hence. She hath said, that at her coming into *Scotland* she will forthwith rid the Realm of all the *English-men* there; namely, of your Majesties Agent there; and forbid mutual traffick with your Majesties Subjects. If she make the haste to embarque that she seemeth to do, she will be almost ready to embarque by that time this shall come to your Majesties hands. Two or three days ago the *French* King was troubled with a pain in his head, and the same beginneth to break from him by bleeding at the nose, and running at his ear: It is taken to be the same disease in his head, whereof his Brother died; but by voiding it (which the other could not do, that organ being stopped) this King is well amended.

At the dispatch hereof, the King of *Navarre* was disquieted by a Flux and a Vomit, and the Queen-mother with a Fever. I hear, that in *Gascoigny* the people stir apace for Religion (as they do in many other places) and being there assembled, to the number of four thousand, have entred a Town, thrown down the Images, and put out the Priests, and will suffer no Mass to be said there.

My Lord of *Leviston*, being ready to go homewards into *Scotland*, through *England*, went to the Queen of *Scotland* for her leave so to do; but she hath commanded him to tarry and wait on her, and to meet her at *Abbeville*, without letting him know any thing else: He, in doubt what she will do, is content to expect her coming thither, and to do then as she shall command him; and, seeing no likelihood of her short passing, (which, he saith, is uncertain) but that she will go to *Calice*, there to hover, and hearken what your Majesty doth to stop her, and according thereunto to go or stay. He mindeth to get him home: he hath required my Letters of recommendations to your Majesties Officers, at his landing in *England*; which, for his good devotion towards your Majesty, and for that he is one that wisheth the same well, I have not refused him; and so I humbly beseech your Majesties good favour towards him, at his coming to your Majesty for his Pass-port. Here is a bruit, that the *Turk* is greatly impeached, both by a sort of *Jews* within his own Countrey, and also by the *Sophy*. And thus I pray God long to preserve your Majesty in health, honour, and all felicity.

Paris, July 26.
1561,

Your Majesties most humble, and most
obedient Subject and Servant,
N. Throckmorton.

Monsieur Toyrax, to the Duke of Buckingham.

My Lord,

YOur courtesies are sufficiently known to all the world ; and you place them with so much judgment, that those onely may hope after them that make themselves worthy by their actions. Now I know no action so worthy of that merit, as for a man to employ himself,——if in the defence of this place he vanquish not all difficulties——so that no despair of succour, nor fear of rigour, in case of extremity, can make me quit a design so generous ; as also, I shall esteem my self unworthy of any of your favours, if in this action I omit the least point of my duty, the issue whereof cannot be but honourable : And by how much you add to this glory by your valour and courage, by so much I am more bound to remain during my life,

Your Lordships humble and most obedient servant,

Toyrax.

Mr. Trumbal, to the Secretary.

Right Honourable,

WIth my former, dated the 11th of this moneth, I sent your Honour two Letters for his Majesty, and promised, by my next, to write unto your Honour at large, about the matter they did contain.

In performance whereof, and for the discharge of my duty, I will now desire permission hereby freely to deliver my mind, for so much as is yet come to my knowledge, and I judge meet to be committed to paper, concerning the same. And seeing this Packet is to be sent by an express Messenger, and a * person of trust, I will, for your Honours greater ease, abstain from the use of a Cipher.

*Mr. Carie.

After I had been at *Lovain*, and *Antwerp*, to take some Depositions, for the discovering of the Authors and Correctors of that most pernicious Libel, *Corona Regia*, (as by a dispatch to the late Mr. Secretary *Lake*, I did advertise his Majesty) there came unto me a certain person, living about this Town, going by the name of *Nicholas de Laken*, and brought me the Packet which a good while since I sent to your Honour. Amongst other things, he told me, that heretofore, by accident, he fell into the company of a Canon of *Lovain*, with whom he had some speech about that devilish Book ; and that, if I would send thither, he was very confident, he should penetrate further by his private industry, in the space of a few days, into the mystery, then I had been able to do, in the compass of divers years, with my publick information.

Hereupon, to make a trial, and desiring to employ *Le fee et Le verd*, for the manifesting of a truth which I knew his Majesty so much longed to understand ; I furnished him with money, and some instructions, and sent him to *Lovain*. At the end of six or seven days he returned from thence, and, as his own Letters do testifie, and (he hath protested with many Oaths) he avouched to me, that he had discovered that secret to the very bottom. I inquired of him, by what means ? He made answer, by the help of the said Canon, and some young Scholars, his Countrey-men, Students in that University, who had brought him to the acquaintance of a certain *Italian* living there, that had served the Author of the Book, both while he did compose it, and while it was in Printing. He averreth also, that *Puteanus*, and some others, had their fingers in that unsavoury Pye. And he saith, that when I began to make search for those persons which had done his Majesty that intollerable wrong, that the principal Author, and *Flavius* the Printer, were secretly warned to get them out of this Countrey, and had some means given them to maintain them abroad. He affirmeth likewise, that both of them, ever since that time, have remained, and are at this present remaining out of the Territories of the Archduke : That he hath often seen the said Author in this City, and knoweth his name, and sirname, and his person, so well, as no change of his apparel, nor disguising of his body, can cause him to mistake or be deceived. By his report, that party is no Clergy man, though he be a good Scholar, and reputed to have an excellent *Latin* Pen : But those commendable qualities are drowned by his greater vices, he being much addicted to lewd women, and unsatiable drinking. He is now (by this mans information) resident in a Town upon the Frontiers of *Germany*. And as for

Flavius,

Mr. Trumbal, *to the Secretary.*

Flavius, he can (if he will) truly declare where he lurketh, and assureth me, that his wife is at a place within ten leagues of this Town. The Canon that did oversee the press, and withdrew the leaves of this book, as they were Printed, is called (as he heard) Mr. *Claud*, and dwelleth at *Nostre Dame de Hales*, whither I purpose to send him this Easter Holydaies, to make farther inquiry. More then these, and some other particulars (which are so transcendent as I dare neither believe, nor set them down in writing) he will not impart unto me, until he be assured of his Majesties protection, by a Letter under his hand, and a competent reward for his labours. And the reason he alledgeth therefore is, that if once it be known he did meddle in this matter, there can be no more safety for him to continue in these Provinces. He doth further undertake, that in case his Majesty will be further pleased to grant him his demands, allow money for the expences of the Journey, and to give him two persons of courage and fidelity to accompany him, he will either lose his life, or put the said Authour into their hands who may carry him (as he thinketh) with little danger, either into the Pallatinate, or the united Provinces. Hereupon I guess, that if this report be well grounded) that wicked fellow must be in, or near about the Town of *Cullen*. I cannot, amongst all those of my acquaintance, and his Majesties subjects here, call to mind any one so fit for this enterprize, as the Gentleman whose name is written in Cipher in my Letter to his Majesty. For he is universally well spoken of for his honesty, and other good parts, and in sundry occasions hath given good testimony of his ardent desire to do his Majesty some remarkable and meritorious service. And his sufficiency being better known to his Majesty then to my self, I will not commend it any further. The want of imployment and some disgusts he received in *Holland*, while he served there, compelled him by necessity to look for preferment under the King of *Spain*. But hitherto his religion, the respect he beareth to his Majesty, and my perswasions, have detained him from those Courses. By him I am told, that he hath heard out of the mouths of one Captain *Carpentine*, and his son in law, Captain *Hamilton*, pensioners to the King of *Spain*, but Subjects to his Majesty, that they being one day walking in a street at *Antwerp* called the Major Brugg (where they reside) with 4. or 5. others in their company, and there happening some speech amongst them, about a book his Majesty had then published against the Pope, it fell out that one of them apprehending that opportunity said, that he had subject enough to furnish a book which should more vex the King of *Great Britain*, then his Majesties book could offend his Holiness; and if he could meet with a Scholar that were able to put it into a method, and good latine, he would be ready to perform his word. Another of the Troop made answer, that he would undertake the work upon that condition, and they both (for a great while after) were absent at *Lovain*, even about the same time that the Libel was forged. Perhaps some part of this may draw neer to the verity. But they both depending upon the King of *Spain* (as is before mentioned) and being averse in religion, I am much afraid, I shall do little good upon them by examining them before the Arch-Dukes Commissioners, seeing they may delude me, and the truth, with equivocation, and mental reservation. Although he conceiveth, that if they were called before a Judge, and summoned upon their oaths to speak the truth, they would not refuse to discharge their consciences. I have seriously intreated him to bestow his best endeavour in attempting what he can further learn about this relation, and he hath accepted to perform my request. The said Gentleman from whom I had it is not willing to be brought publiquely upon the Stage, for this business, lest thereby he should incurre the note of an informer, then which nothing is, or can be, more odious in these parts. Nevertheless he hath promised (if his Majesty like to have is so, and will be pleased to give commandement for it) to justifie what is before rehearsed to their faces.

Whether both these parties encounter upon one and the same Authour, or understand them to be divers men, I can neither judge, nor foretell: yet it seemeth that one of them may hit on the right; And as I will not spare any pains, charges, nor peril whatsoever, to bring the parent of this child of darkness into the light, so I hope his Majesty (whose cause it is) will not refuse to hazard a little money to give himself satisfaction.

These things having passed in this manner, I humbly beseech your honour at a fit opportunity when the King is alone, to acquaint him with these particulars, and intreat his Majesty to keep them secret; for I am of opinion (being spoken under humble correction, and without offence) that had not his Majesty by communicating this business at the first to *Monsieur Borscot*, given him means to advertize it to his wife (who by tatling divulged it, and foyled the way) we had never been put to half this trouble, but had taken *Flavius*, in the form, and by him discovered the Authour. My intention is not, that his Majesty should be induced

Mr. Trumbal, to the Secretary.

to put 2000. Pistols (or the summe that shall be allotted *Laken*) into his hands, before the service be done; but that his Majesty would vouchsafe (if he approve the project) to cause so much money, as in his profound wisdom he shall think meet for this ocation to be forthwith remitted to me by Mr. *John Afere*, by the means of Mr. *Ducket* a Merchant dwelling in Milk-street in *London*, to be repayed at *Antwerp* by Mr. *Lionel Wake* trading there, or by the company of our English Merchants at *Midelberough* in *Zealand*, in the name of reward for service done, or to buy Tapestries, or Linnen for his Majesty. And I will either return it back again by exchange, if this design cannot be effected, or default the remains thereof upon my entertainment. All that I would venture in this case should only be for those mens necessary expences that are to be employed therein; and that also I would have not to exceed, but to be limited within the compass of 200. pounds sterling.

By apprehending these men, the Arch-Dukes cannot take any just occasion of offence against his Majesty or his Ministers, seeing one of them is not their Vassal, and both are out of their Dominions.

It may (for these considerations) please your Honour to advise with his Majesty, whether it be fitter to proceed herein *Via facti*, or *Via Juris*: to send *Laken* to seek out the Authour and others to apprehend him, or the Printer; or upon promise of a reasonable recompence for his pains, to deal with him effectually to declare their names, and habitations, and afterwards leave it to his Majesties gracious and Princely pleasure to prosecute or let fall his action. In either of which kind, I will yield humble obedience to his Majesties Commands, and your Honours directions, as things to my self indifferent. But I am doubtful, that by continuing of the course formerly holden in the carriage of this business, we shall never attain our desired ends. I am not so sleight as to give credit to all reports, nor so prodigal as to part with money for nothing.

My most humble and earnest suit is, that his Majesty, and your Honour, after mature deliberation upon the several points of this Letter, will vouchsafe to send me by my servant *Marsham* (who is now at *London*) particular and distinct answers for my better direction. I have been the more prolix upon this subject, in hope that this I have written shall serve once for all.

In that matter concerning the Countess of *Argyle*, which it pleased your Honour to recommend unto my Care, I have done as much already as I can for the present. We must of necessity with a little patience expect the success, whereof your Honour shall in due time be punctually advertised. In the mean while, I do with all reverence, desire your Honour to excuse the tediousness of this Letter; And so take my leave,

Bruxels, $\frac{21}{31}$ of *March*, $\frac{1618}{1619}$

Your Honours very humble, and ready to be commanded,

W. Trumball.

Mr. Trumbal, to the Secretary.

Right Honourable,

THose that are employed in such place as I am must admit all manner of men into their company. And the Oath I have taken to his Majesty will not permit me to conceal any thing from his knowledg that cometh to mine, and may in any sort have relation to his Royal service. For these considerations I assume the boldness so soon to renew your Honours trouble, after the dispatch of those Volumnes of Letters which I sent you yesterday by one of my servants.

This Bearer *de la Forrest* is better known to your Honours then to my self, although I remember many years agoe to have seen him in *England*. During his stay in this Town, he brought unto me a certain *French* Gentleman, calling himself the Viscount of *L'orme*, and Sir *De la Pommeraye*, who hath (by his own relation) been a great Navigator, and been authorized by 18. of the chief Pyrates in the *Levant*, to search for their pardon, and retreat into some Christian Countrey, being sorry for the ill they have done, and desirous to spend the rest of their daies in peace. With this Commission he came into *France*, and there travelled so far with the King and his Ministers, as he obtained a general abolition for the said Pyrates, a safe Conduct to bring them into his Dominions, and a procuration (which I have seen under the great Seal of *France*) to treat, and conclude with them, upon certain conditions. But he being envied by some Grandees of
that

that Kingdom, and by misfortune happening to kill a man he was forced (as he pretendeth) for the safety of his life to flye into these Countreys, before he could bring that work to perfection.

And being now disinabled to return thither again, he desireth to make tryal, whether his Majesty will vouchsafe to lend his ear to that Treaty, and grant unto the said Pyrates a generall Pardon. To which effect, he sendeth over *La Ferrest*, and hath intreated me to accompany him with his Letters to my Lord Admiral, your Honour, and Mr. Secretary *Calvert*. For retribution of this grace, the said Pyrates offer to give 45000 l. sterling to be shared amongst you three, or to be disposed of as his Majesty shall appoint. But your Honour may see the Conditions proposed to the French King were more advantagious. For they were to give him their Ships, Artillery, and Munition, and to furnish means to set out some men of War for his service.

And I see no reason (in case his Majesty should incline to such capital offenders, and common enemies) why he should not have as much, or more benefit then another Prince, the greatest part of them being his Vassals.

Your Honour, if you please, may peruse these adjoyned Papers, and impart the contents of them to my Lord Admiral. They agree with their Originals; and if his Majesty do not taste this overture, there is no more harm done (for any thing I can perceive) then the loss of my labour to peruse and subscribe them.

There remaineth only two points, wherein I should speak to your Honour, the one is, that this matter may be concealed from the French Ambassadour *Monsieur le Count de Tilliers*, for fear of ruining *de L' Orme*. The other with gratifying *La Forrest* with the pay of a Pacquet (if your Honour shall think it meet) for the carrying of these Letters, who saith your Honour is his great Patron, and hath promised him a good turn.

Monsieur de L' Orme hath given him power to sollicite this businefs, and procure him an answer; wherein I joyn my humble prayer, that the poor man may not here languish in hopes, and spend his money to no purpose.

When I shall know whether his Majesty will rellish this overture, or not, I will write thereof more largely (if there be cause) otherwise let it remain as it was before. In the mean while I humbly take my leave; And rest,

Bruxels, 23. *Octob.* 1618.   *Your Honours, in all humblenefs, to be commanded,*
W. Trumball.

Mr. Ch. Th. to the Duke of Buckingham.

My Lord,

IT is intimated to your Lordship, first, that you would procure his Majesty to desire the Lords to choose six (or so many as you shall think fit) of whom they have most confidence to attend him to morrow morning, to whom his Majesty may be pleased to declare, That he hath endeavoured to divert the charges against your Lordship, because his Majesty hath had found knowledge and experience of the service and fidelity (though in outward shew the contrary might justly appear) and because also he saw it was urged with a great deal of private spleen, and perhaps not without some Papistical device of troubling his Majesties businefs; in Parliament but seeing no suit, or persuasion, could prevail to appease the distempered course, his Majesty is now forced, and so pleased to reveal some secrets, and *Arcana* of State, which otherwise in the wisdom of Kings were unfit to be opened. Here his Majesty may let them know, that the King his Father finding the Palatinate more then in danger to be lost, and after his Majesty being in *Spain*, and there deluded, and his abode, and return, both unsafe. It was a necessity of State to sweeten, and content the *Spaniards* with a hope of any thing that might satisfie and redeem those engagements, and therefore willed your Lordship to yield discreetly to what you should find they most desired, and this was chiefly the point of religion; so as in this and all of the like kind, your Lordship (upon his Majesties knowledge) was commanded, and but the instrument trusted by your Master in this exigent, or (if you will) extremity. And this with other more potent overtures (such as your Lordship best understands) may Cancel all those objections of that nature. Upon this same ground, though not in so high a degree, the sending of the ships to *Rochel* may be excused (and this is not the least fault objected, in the opinion of the wisest.) Touching the vast creation of Nobility his Majesty may ask those Lords (whereof perchance
some

some of them may be concerned in this article,) whether they conceive any reason of King *James* his doing herein; to which, I suppose, they will stand mute. Then his Majesty may say, I will tell you, and therein discover a truth, and a secret of State. My Father who was born a King, and had long experience of that Regiment, especially more traversed in this point then perhaps ever any King, found that this State inclined much to Popularity, a thing apparent universally in all the Courts, viz. in that of Star-chamber, which was at first erected to restrain the insolence of great men, in great outrages, but now for every petty offence, the meanest Tenant may be bold to call thither his Lord. A thing also appearing in the fawcie approaches of the Puritans upon the Bishops, &c; and plainly in the boldness of the house of Commons against the Kings Patents and edicts, which in all good times (out of their necessity) have been powerfull. And especially this humour hath been comforted by the sturdy example of their Neighbour States of the Low-Countries, as in their insolencies in the *East-Indies* &c. From this place an enticing voice hath sounded in our ears of liberty and freedom, though indeed a feigned voice, and (but in sound) unsound I say, when the King my Father had well beheld these things, he could not foresee a remedy more proper, or easier, as being serviceable, and in his own gripe, then to enlarge the number of his Nobles, that these being dispersed into several Counties might as Limbs of Sovereignty, in their own degree, and at their own charge, inure the people with respect and obedience to greatness; and yet, not to amate and discourage them, he thought good to raise some neer, or of their own rank, whereby they might see themselves in possibility of the like honour, if either by vertue, wealth, or honesty they make themselves worthie. This, I protest, was a child of my Fathers best judgment, in this point, and the Duke but the instrument thereof. And if you say, that there was money many times given for these Honours; nay if you say, that money hath been given for places of Clergie, and Judicature, I pray take this of me, that this is so in all other Countreys, as in *France*, and *Spain*. And those Councels seem a little to smile at our dulness, that we have so lately apprehended their soundness herein; for (so they) when men pay well for such places, it is the best kind of security for their honesties, especially when faylig in their duty they shall be sure to be as much punished as they were advanced. Howbeit I am not satisfied in this opinion. And if it be said, that the King should have had the money which the Duke took to his own use; I believe this last is more then any can prove; neither will I deliver what I know therein. Howsoever, it matters not much, being no popular disbursment. Only this I will say, that I know the Dukes particular service, and affection to me, and that he and his will lay down themselves, and all they have, at my feet. Neither is this bare opinion, since the Duke alone hath disbursed, and stands engaged more for my affairs, and the States, then any Number of any Noble men of *England* whatsoever, and therefore there is reason, that from a King he should receive his own, and more.

And now (my Lords) since I have thus far opened a Kings Cabinet unto you, at least by the measure of this foot of answer, you may discover, what may be said concerning that great body and bulk of accusations of the Highest kind made against the Duke. I desire you would take it to heart, remembring, that it is your King that speaketh this, who therefore expects your service, and love herein, and who will requite the same assuredly; hoping you will believe me indeed, and do accordingly and that you will also rest assured, that my spirit is not so young (though a young King) as that I would bring this testimony in mine own wrong, were not that I say true in my own knowledg. And being so, you also will grant, that it is not for a King to use his Servant, and Instrument, as he doth his Horses, which being by hard riding in his service foundred, and lamed, to turn them off to grass, or to the Cart. I must therefore, in right of the King my Fathers Honour, and my own, protect a man (though I have said, justly, seeming guilty, yet) in mine own knowledg innocent, and free, as I have delivered it; will you then deny the King to favour whom he please, which the King hath never denyed you that are his subjects? will now controll me your Head and Governour, in things wherein your selves have taken liberty uncontrolled? Would you that I should require accompt of your liberality? nay of all your failings, which are lyable to my authority? well, commend me to my Lords, and tell them, that if any thing had been formerly done amiss by others, I have power and will to redress it, and to prevent the like. I speak it in the word of a King, neither Lords, nor Commons can desire of me any thing that is honest, which I am not ready to give them. Let not therefore the world, by these mistakings, make Table-talk any longer of your King and his negotiations? nay of his secrets and necessities, for, alas, what greater wrong, or indignity, can the glory of the

State

Mr. Ch. Th. to the Duke.

State receive, then that the private grudges of Subjects (accusing to the ignorant, when in their consciences they could excuse) should be the business of our Parliament, and that the King himself should be forced to appear as a party? No doubt, this is a Cocatrice egg, that the crafty heads of our enemies seek to hatch, whilest the weighty Affairs that, at present concern the Honour and welfare of the King and State, and the peace of all Christendom, are by us utterly neglected.

I end, hoping your Lordship (now privy to these things) will be tender of your Sovereigns Honour, and will so satisfie, and treat with the rest, that those particular janglings may be, by some other course, and in some other place and time, discussed and determined; that so our minds and time may be employed in the care of better things, which earnestly invoke our aid at this instant.

Thus much spoken, or written, or the like, (for I seek but to awaken your Lordships higher spirit and invention) I conceive it may get this effect: That these six Lords, won by these Reasons, and by other the Kings invitations, may deliver to the House, That, for their parts, they have received unexpected satisfaction in those greatest points of the accusation against your Lordship, and of such secret nature as are not fit to be published without further deliberation: Wherefore since it pleased their Lordships to have made choice of them to be trusted in this employment, they have faithfully served accordingly; and do, upon their Honours, freely, and without any engagement or respect, protest the same: and therefore humbly desire their Lordships, that they would intreat his Majesty to be President in advice with their Lordships, What further were to be done in this private Contention betwixt your Lordship and the Lord *Digby*. Which obtained, something may then follow for your Lordships good, by yielding up that Cause into the Kings hands. And his Majesty hath great Reason to bend it that way, because it is conceived, that the Lords will be loth to admit the King to be supreme Judge and Accuser; which point will much touch his Majesty: And his Majesty were better give some ease to the Lord *Digby*, then permit that dispute.

And now for my self, I beseech your Lordship to pardon my strange boldness; I know, I am a meer stranger to you; and if ever you have heard of me, it must be as of a friend of such you then did not love. I know it shews me a medler in business, or an insinuator, which are suspicions that may distaste you, and make you suspect my pretences, though they were not altogether witless. I know this disadvantage, and am, in my own nature, offended for putting my self thus into your notions: But yet I resolved to undergo all this; First, because you made my Brother a Captain in *Ireland*, who had otherwise perished; Next, for the favour you did to my Lord of *Northumberland*, and the retiring of disfavour from my Lord of *Somerset*; and Lastly, for your firm hand, that advanced the now Lord Treasurer; to all which Lords I am familiarly known, and bound; but (neerest to you) your Lordship may hear of me from the Lord Treasurer.

I am confident of your Lordships noble interpretation, since I seek no ends, no acquaintance, no other thanks, being one that have no Court-suits to your Lordship; but being one that loves not ruines, (which my friends have tasted) nor that the publick should wrestle with a private In-turn of Spleen: And I offer it but as a simplicity, yet with good will enough; for, what can a man, that is not privy to the Elements of State, demonstrate any conclusion thereof; yet I hear sometimes how the world goes, as other men do.

I conceive, I have said something to your Lordship; and though, perhaps, short, yet enough to occasion and stir up your deeper thoughts: I also may have deeper; but also I know, that little pins of wood do sustain the whole building. More I could have said touching the other points; but these greatest elided, the fall of the others may be easily directed. What I have said against those objections I touche ddoth arise from grounds of truth, and they must win, and prevail; and my conceit is fitted to the Kings part, and to the occasions now on foot.

I humbly cease your Lordship further trouble, and wish you all good; desiring your Lordship also to pardon my tedious and hasty scribled hand.

Your Lordships unknown servant,
Ch. Th.

Post-script.
Your Lordship shall be pleased to take off some part of my boldness, and impute it to the obligation and service I ow this worthy Lady, the Bearer.

Pope Urban, to Lewis the Thirteenth.

To our dearest Son in Christ Jesus, Lewis, the most Christian King of France, Pope Urban sendeth greeting.

MOst dear Son in Christ, Health, and Apostolical Benediction: The high exploits of your Royal valour, which have drawn upon them all the eyes of Christendom, bring a great deal of comfort to our Fatherly care, as well in regard of the glory of your Arms, as the hope of your triumphs. For, considering, as we do, with much grief, the impiety of Hereticks, living in some places without fear or danger, we now thank the Lord of Hosts, that hath, in so fit an opportunity, made your Majesty to maintain with Arms the Dignity of the Catholick Religion. Oh fair Apprenticeship of Royal Warfare, and worthy of a most Christian King! What an admirable thing it is, that the age which other Princes, out of a kind of softness and idleness, use to pass away in sports and delights, your Majesty should employ so generously, so fortunately, in appeasing differences, conducting Armies, and besieging the strongest places of Hereticks, and all not without the special counsel of God, by which Kings reign! Is it almost credible, that the very first steps of your thoughts should carry you on in so high and troublesome an enterprize; and that the dangers and difficulties which have stopped others in their course, should onely serve for a spur to the greatness of your courage? Enjoy (dear Son) the Renown your Name hath got, and follow the God that fights for you; to the end, that as you are now held the Thunder-bolt and Buckler of War, so you may hereafter be esteemed the Praise of *Israel*, and the Glory of the World. From the heighth of our Apostolick Dignity, whereto it hath pleased God of his goodness to raise us, unworthy of so great grace, we assist your Arms with heart and affection, and by our frequent Prayers prepare the Divine remedies. And though we doubt not but your own Vertue will make you constant in the work you have begun; nevertheless, we have thought good to add Exortations, that the World may see the care we have of the advancement of true Religion, and how willing we are to give way to your Glory. You have been hitherto infinitely bound to God for his bounty towards you; and, as we hope and wish, you shall hereafter a great deal more. For you having your mind endued with Celestial Doctrine, and not with the bare Precepts of humane Wisdom, do well know, that Kingdoms have their foundation upon the Truth of Orthodox Faith: And unless God keep the City, what Principality can subsist with any assurance? It may easily be judged with what fidelity they are likely to defend your Royal Throne that have cast the very Saints themselves out of their Temples, and done as much as in them lay, to put them out of the number of the Blessed, yea, out of Paradise it self; that with impious temerity condemn the Institutions of our Fathers, the Custom of Kings, the Decrees of Popes, and the Ceremonies of the Church: These are the disturbers of the Christian Common-wealth, and the reproaches of *France*, whom the great God hath reserved to be exterminated, as it were, in the beginning of your Reign. Know then, that all *Europe* (which the event of your Arms holds all this time in suspence) hopes shortly it will hoise sail upon the Ocean, under the conduct of your Greatness and Power, and go to the place which serves now for Sanctuary and protection to the Hereticks and Rebels. and it will shortly serve for a Trophie of your Victories. We are confidently perswaded, that neither fear, nor inconstancy, shall ever be able to divert you from the pursuit of your so glorious enterprize, nor hinder you to subvert that unsanctified people. Onely, by the way, we would have you remember, that the Saints in Heaven assist that Prince who takes upon him the defence of Religion, and fight on his side like Fellow-souldiers. The same God that hardned the waters like dry land, and turned the waters of the Sea into walls, to give safe passage to his Childrens Army, will certainly, in this most pious action be as favourable to you: and then we shall have good cause to hope, that having established your own Kingdom, and crushed the impiety that was and yet is there, you may one day, by the progress of your victorious Arms, joyn the Orient to the Occident; imitating the Glories of your Ancestors, who have ever born as much respect to the Exhortations of Popes, as to the Commandment of God. Saint *Lewis*, whose name you bear, and whose steps you follow, invites you to it; so did the first of your Race, who, in defending the Apostolick Authority, and propagating Christian Religion, laid the best and surest foundation to your Royal House. Follow (dear Son) them which are the Ornaments of the World, and the Commandments of Heaven: Pour out your wrath and indignation

The University of Cambridge, to the Duke. 387

tion upon those people that have not, nor will not know God, and our Apostolick benignity; to the end the Divine treasure of Heaven may belong unto you by a just acquisition. In the mean time, we send you, most affectionately, our Apostolick benediction.

Given at Rome, at great St. Maries, under the Seal of the Fisher, the 4. day of August, 1629. being the seventh year of our Pontificate.

The University of Cambridge, to the Duke.

Illustrissime Princeps,

QUam paterno cum affectu, quam divina cum charitate vestra hujus Academiæ salutem utilitatemque vestra Celsitudo semper procuraverit, nec nos effari possumus, nec ætas ulla conticere.

Ingentia beneficia sæculum præsens admiratione obruunt; nec alio queunt quam perennis famæ & immortalitatis præmio compensari. Vestræ Celsitudinis singulari patrocinio, de Typographis Londinensibus triumphavimus. Hostium undequaque ferociam persensimus imminutam, auctamque Academiæ dignitatem: Nihil nos votis expetiscere, nihil vestra Celsitudo conferre potuit, quod a vestra benignitate non accepimus. Et quid nos præter hanc sterilem cultus nostri messem rependimus? At beneficia vestra, quam sancte posteritas alet, quibus præconiis, quam æternis laudibus vestræ Celsitudinis memoriam nepotes nostri celebrabunt, facile conjiciet is qui norit quantum Academia tranquille administrata, vindicata privilegia, immunitates conservatæ, otium, libertas, ipsa vita Musis donata, promereantur! Quot hostes Reipublicæ Litterariæ infensos vestra Celsitudo profligavit, quot in nos munera contulerit, nec illi sine gemitu agnoscere, nec nos sine stupore recitare valeamus. Dum te licet conspici, dum tua genua prehendere, flocci faciamus mortalium iras, & in recessibus nostris abditi tuto literis indulgeamus.

Jam vestra Celsitudo novam parat Militiam (quam vestro nomini gloriosam, Religioni Christianæ faustam, nobis omnibus fœlicem, omnipotens Deus faxit) quibus nos periculis exponimur? Alii flumen nostrum siccare, eumque ablatum a quo forsan ipsi aquas olim ingrati hauserunt: alii nobis Imprimendi facultatem rursus adimere conabuntur. Illustrissime Princeps, pauca sunt nostra bona, suppellex curta, angusta Athenarum pomœria: nullæ tamen opes Crœsi vel Midæ perditorum hominum insidiis petuntur atrocius, quam inermis & nuda paupertas nostra. Videt vestra Celsitudo quam in ipsa fiduciam collocamus, qui, tempestas priusquam ingruit, ad vestras aras confugimus. Et quamvis haud ignari sumus quanta moles vestræ Celsitudinis humeros jam premat, audacter tamen tot curarum montibus nostrum Parnassum superaddimus. Perficiat vestra Celsitudo hanc suam Academiam, ut incipit: florentem ornet, trepidantem excitet, depressam sustentet, periclitantem expediat; ac Deum perpetuo imploret, ut omnia tua gloriosa molimina vestra Celsitudo consequatur, & illa vestræ Celsitudinis patrocinio fruatur in æternum.

Dat' e frequenti Senatu nostro,
Nonas Julii, 1628.

Celsitudinis vestræ devinctissimi,
Procancellarius, reliquusque
Senatus Academiæ vestræ
Cantabrigiensis.

The Dukes Answer.

Gentlemen,

SUch and so cordial have your respects been unto me, that no other Pen then your own can express them, nor no other heart then mine can apprehend them: and therefore, I labour not any verbal satisfaction, but shall desire you to believe, that what service soever you please to think I have hitherto done for you, I cannot so much as call an expression of that I would willingly do for you. And whereas, in your Letters, you seem to fear, that my absence may be an advantage of time, to make your adversaries active and stirring against you, and your Affairs consequently meet with partiality and opposition; I have therefore most humbly recommended them to the Justice of my Royal Master, and to the bosomes of some friends, where they shall likewise meet with mediation and protection, to what part of the world soever my Master or the States service shall call me. I can carry but one Chancellor of your University along with me, but, I hope,

The University of Cambridge, to the King.

hope I shall leave you many behind me, And I shall presage likely of the success of our actions, since they are all so followed by your wishes and devotions; which I shall endeavour you may always continue unto

Chelsey, July 30. 1628. *Your most affectionate friend, and humble servant,*
BUCKINGHAM.

Directed,
To my very worthy and much respected friends, The Vice-Chancellor and Senate of the University of Cambridge.

The Vice-Chancellor of Cambridge, *to the King, upon the Dukes death.*

Dread Soveraign,

THe fatal blow given your most loyal servant, whom your Majesty made our Patron and Chancellor, hath so stounded our University, as (like a Body without a Soul) she stirs not, till your Majesties Directions breathe life again, in the choice of another. And although I am but one of many, and therefore (having to do with a multitude) cannot absolutely assure the effecting of your pleasure; yet I dare undertake for my self, with the rest of the Heads, and many others, truly and faithfully to labour in your Majesties desires, and now presume to send fair and strong hopes to give them full satisfaction: Humbly intreating the continuance of your Majesties love and care of your University, the onely stay and comfort of this her sad and mournfull estate, occasioned by such an unexpressible disaster; cherishing her self with that blessed word your Majesty used upon her last Election, That howsoever your Majesties appointment shadowed out another, yet your Self in substance would be her Chancellor. This, as an indelible Character in her memory, shall ever return, as all thankfull observance, so to God prayers full of cordial zeal, for your Majesties long and happy Reign.

The University of Cambridge, *to the King.*

Serenissimo, & Magnificentissimo Principi, *CAROLO*, Dei gratia, Britanniæ Regi, &c.

**Serenissime & Potentissime Monarcha,
Carole, Defensor Fidei, Pater Patriæ:**

DUm ad Majestatis tuæ pedes discumbimus, veniam humillime deprecamur temeritatis nostræ, Quod Majestati tuæ in illud gloriæ fastidium evecta, ad quod nulli Principes a multis retro seculis pervenere, Chartas has ineptas ausi sumus, & querimonias obtrudere; sed nullum jam in terris effulget Majestate tua aut illustrius, aut magis beneficum sidus, cujus cœlesti aspectu mortales afflicti ab adversis ad salutis momentum perduci possint. Sensimus nos persæpe, læti sensimus vivificam charitatis tuæ auram, divinam clementiam amplectimur, & benignitatem incredibilem sempiterna veneratione adoramus. Quæ enim per te nobis pax data sit, quæ privilegia indulta & confirmata, quæ gratia, candor, misericordia, beneficentia nobis impertita, nec nos effari possumus, nec ulla secula conticere. O nos fœlicissimos sub tuo Sceptro, Carole! qui certe miserrimi essemus, si Regio Majestatis tuæ Patrocinio ac favore destitueremur: irruunt in nos omne genus illiteratorum hominum, longum hærent in nostris malis, & sine magno numine non amoventur. Centum olim annos cum oppidanis nostris de summa privilegiorum decertavimus, quinquaginta cum Typographis Londinensibus, adeo crudelis est ac pertinax malitia, quæ literis bellum indicit; Typographis per tuam in nos pietatem nuper compositis, oppidani veterem odii Camarinam incipiunt commovere. Ita ab Oppidanis ad Typographos, a Typographis ad Oppidanos, nostra in gyrum calamitas circumacta volvitur, & infinitis controversiarum nodis astringimur, & jugulamur. Deflexis genibus Excellentissimam Majestatem tuam imploramus, ut qua serenitate tuam Academiam semper aspexeris, eadem digneris huic causæ ad dictum a te diem interesse. Et Deum Optim. Max. precabimur, ut te nobis quam diutissime conservet clementissimum Principem, & Patrem indulgentissimum: In cujus salute totius Regni incolumitas, tranquillitas Literarum, publica seculi fœlicitas, & bonorum omnium vota abunde continentur.

Servi Majestati tuæ devoti & fideles subditi,
Procanc' & Senat'.

The University of Cambridge, to the Archbishop of York.

Reverendissimo in Christo Patri, & summo Archi-præsuli, Samueli, Dei gratia, Archiepiscopo *Eboracensi*, Patrono nostro æternum colendo.

Reverendissime in Christo Pater, Archi-præsul amplissime,

NIsi perspecta esset Paternitatis tuæ in Academiam gratia & favor supra quam meremur immensius, vereremur, sine multis ambagibus, ad tam illustre in Ecclesia caput accedere; verum ea semper fuit indulgentia tua, & stabile nobis patrocinium, ut in difficultatibus nostris ultro fueris magis ad accurrendum alacer, quam nos esse potuimus ad implorandum; temerarii incidimus in veterem controversiæ lacunam cum nostris Oppidanis. Novit sat Paternitas tua ab exp. rientia multiplici, quas illi erga nos mentes gerant, quam atra lolligine & invidia succo a teneris unguiculis pasti fuerint; neque jam incipiunt ferocire, nec unquam, credimus, desinent homines insulsi, tam dignitatis nostræ immemores, quam rationis suæ, nonnullis eorum commercium cum nostris interdiximus dum procacius, quam par erat fasces nostros videbantur contemnere; sed grave est, & permolestum quicquid cadit in præcipites animos, & ira impotentes. Illi tanquam fulmine perculsi ad publica judicum subsellia Lymphatice festinant, cum possent consultius forsan in domibus suis ——— Nos autem veriti ne Majestas Reipub. Literariæ minueretur, in foro publico prostituta Academia de privilegiis, & summa rerum trepidaret, Senatus Regis tribunali appellavimus. In quo cum jam auspicatissime consedisse tuam Paternitatem intelligeret Alma Mater, & de honore tuo, & sua fœlicitate eximie triumphabat, nunquam oblita virtutis tuæ, & magnanimitatis invictæ, qua solebas hic toties Vice-cancellarius ad immortalem neminis tui laudem istiusmodi perduelles contundere, humillime rogamus Paternitatem tuam, pro suo summo in nos affectu & pietate, ut quemadmodum semper Academiam ornare studuit, ita nunc dignetur eidem periclitanti succurrere.

Pat' tuæ devotiss.
Procanc' & Senat.

The University of Cambridge, to the Earl of Manchester.

Illustrissimo, nobilissimo, nostroque amantissimo Domino, Comiti *Manchestriæ*, Privati Sigilli Custodi, Regiæ Majestati a Sanctioribus Consiliis, Patrono nostro plurimum colendo.

HOnoratissime nosterque amantissime Domine Montacute, Nescimus an ipsi nobis vana credulitate blandiamur, sed cum singula tua pro nobis gesta perpendimus, fruimur hac opinione, vix quenquam vivere, qui nostram salutem, literarum incrementum, tranquillitatem Academiæ magis ex animo velit quam nobilissimus Montacutus; tot indies apparent indubitata testimonia amoris tui erga nos integerrimi & profusissimæ benevolentiæ. Quid dicemus de Typographis, quos tandem aliquando post varios casus & tot discrimina subegimus, quamvis nodum controversiæ Gordianum confuerant non nisi Alexandri gladio explicabilem, & tanquam sepia piscis longa perplexæ litis caligine capita involverant ne caperentur. Ac hæc ultima sententia vestra momento beneficii, favoris magnitudine, celeritate conficiendi trajecit, quicquid ulla spes nobis dictare potuit, aut suggerere, sententia celebris, sancta memorabilis ad opprimendam in perpetuum morosam oppidanorum insolentiam; sententia quam quo penitius contemplamur, eo magis sub stupore bonitatis vestræ, & admirationis onere laboramus.

Noli (nec enim fas est) metiri observantiæ nostræ rationem, ex nostro scribendi modulo. Majora de te sentimus quam verba nostra expedire valeant, multo minus rependere, Illud nostrum erga te tantum est & tam firmum, ut nulla novæ opportunitatis accessione augere queat, aut temporum injuria diminui.

Honori tuo æternum obligati, Procanc'
& Senatus reliquus Academiæ.

The University of Cambridge, to Sir Humphrey May.

Clarissimo & spectatissimo Domino, *Humphredo May*, Equiti Aurato, & Regiæ Majestatis Procamerario, amico & fautori nostro æternum observando.

ÆTernas agimus tibi gratias, Clarissime Domine Procamerarie, quod favore tam subito, tam propensa & inclinata benevolentia ad nostram causam ultro accesseris: subiit forsan & pupugit (clarissime Domine) conditionis nostræ pia commiseratio cum videre Musas litibus implicatas circa Tribunalia tremere, quas æquius erat inter lauros & virgulata pacifica in veritatis disquisitione occupari. Verum est, & in hac ætate improba sic vivimus, ut frequenter deposita toga & calamo, pallia & Clientum soccos induere cogamur: Maxime vero nos ad incommoda pellunt opidani nostri, qui hoc a natura principium mordicus tenent, & nullo dimittunt sato, turbare semper pacem literarum, et bonis Academiæ quovis modo insidiari. O quam magna merces est prudentia, et sobria mens, æqua in utriusque sortis importunitate! sunt quos ipsum sœlicitatis tædium satigat ad mortem, & dira contentionis ambitio fanatico quodam œstro impellit ad suam perniciem. Post triginta annos simulatæ pacis & induciarum, oppidani nostri quietis impatientia, & invidiæ aculeis alti, nuper tentare voluerunt quantum possunt calcibus contra spinas, aut contra Solem jaculis; at præter pænitentiam ac suspiria nihil domum reportarunt; Ita Musas in æternum sibi devinxit Senatus ille tremendus & gloriosus, in quo Majores dii gentis nostræ sedent. Tu in illa scena splendida Regiæ Majestati adstare maluisti, quam tuam inter divos reliquos classem retinere, ut nostro momento inservires, & illud pectus sacrum proprius attingeres, in quo omnes gratiæ nidificant, & nostra beatitudo reconditur. Magna sunt hæc amoris tui testimonia, nolis vero messem sementi parem a nobis expectare; Musæ non sunt pares solvendo. Et tamen, si preces, vota, laudes, encomia, pro nobis sufficere possint, Nihil nos tuis meritis debituros confidenter promittimus.

Dignitati tuæ devinctiss. Procanc' & Senat'
vel Academ. Cantabrigiens.

The University of Cambridge, to the Lord Chief Justice Richardson.

Honoratissimo Domino, *Thomæ Richardson*, Communium Placitorum Proto-Justiciario, & Proedro amico Academiæ, & Patrono singulari.

AMplissime et honoratissime Domine, superiori et Termino et Anno te nostris literis & negotiis graviter defatigavimus, & nunc novas afferre molestias nentiquam dubitamus; sed tu pro candore quo polles maxime hanc nostram morositatem benigne interpretare, & da veniam impatienti nostræ occasioni ad Sacerdotium Hallingburii, quod de cujusdam papicole, lapsu in manus nostras ex diplomate serenissimi Regis Jacobi nobis indulto, et per Senatum Regni solennem confirmato venit. Hunc Magistrum Love Collegii divi Petri promovimus, virum fide, doctrina, integritate, sanctimonia præclarum, qui Procuratoris Officium, magistratum apud nos amplissimum, insigniter administravit, & non sine magna laude fasces ante biennium deposuit, unde liquido constet dominationi tuæ, quibus opulentiis abundat Alma mater, cum virum consularem, et de republica nostra tam bene meritum, tali sacerdotiolo auctum & remuneratum dimittimus. Utinam tamen vel tantillum hoc quod est beneficii homini nostro placide concederent mortales Dii, et se precibus ad æquanimitatem flecti paterentur. Enim vero nescimus quo malo sato nostro id comparatum sit, ut inter sacrum & saxum semper hæreamus, quemadmodum in proverbio est, Inter sacrum quod ambimus, & hominum præcordia saxo duriora, nihil nos sine controversia impetrare possumus; sed cogimur virtute nostra nos involvere, & probam pauperiem sine dote quærere, cum Poeta Horatio; nam in tanta dominorum & captatorum turba, difficile est ad omnes articulos sic excubare, ut qui modeste prensat in lutum non detrudatur; & certe usque adeo præclusus est industriæ nostræ ad eadem honoris & emolumenti aditus, ut multi repudia literis in æternum renunciare mallent, quam post tot laboribus consumptam juventutem & senectam studiis immature acceleratam, vanæ spei cassa nuceiludificari; cum non solum sua nobis negare beneficia, sed et nostra abripere terrarum Domini flagitiose contendant. Quid ad te hæc verba spectant, facile conjicias: Nos te Patronum appellamus, quem adversarii nostri Judicem; & per omnia patrocinia tua nobis ante hac graviter concessa, per omnia sacra clementiæ tuæ & amoris in Academiam te obtestamur, ut huic Alumno nostro

Sir Isaac Wake, to the Secretary.

jus suum et Academiæ dignitatem, sartam tectam, authoritate tua conservare velis: et cum tua merita non alia re consequi valeamus, quam debiti agnitione etsi sumus impares, memorisque animi grata testificatione, utrumque tibi sempiternum religiose pollicemur.

Honoris tui Clientes assidui, Procancel. et Senatus integer Academ.
Dat. e *frequenti Senatu nostro, pridie Calend. Maij, 1630.*   *Cantabrig.*

Sir Henry Wallop, to the Queen.

IT may please your Majesty, a rumour hath been raised not long since at *Dublin* (I know not how, nor by what particular person, but strongly confirmed since the last passage out of *England*) (neither doth your service now in hand upon this Northern border suffer me to examine it) that your Majesty conceived some hard opinion of me, from which your Highness is not yet removed; but what the offence is, or how conceived, is neither by the reporters published, nor secretly revealed unto me: And like as it is easie to judge what effects this may work in the service of your Majesty, or to a man in publick office, as I am, in such a government as this is, where the obedience, for the most, is constrained, and all reputation, the people either growing or diminishing as your Majesty either graceth or disgraceth your Officers; so how much this quiet burthen over-presseth my most devoted and dutifull mind towards your Majesty, I feel to my exceeding grief and discomfort. In examining my self in what root this your judgment should spring, I confess, Madam, I have viewed in my self many imperfections, some in nature, others, perhaps, for lack of ability and sufficiency to be a co-operator or an assistant in so great and so ticklish a government and charge; into which not ambition in me, but your Majesties will and commandement, hath intruded me. But in all that my memory can hitherto present unto me I find my loyalty in your service, and my sincerity in imploying your Majesties treasure according to your intent, so unspotted and direct, as I cannot but comfort my self in opposing my innocency to the envy of the informer, or to any other his hard construction whatsoever: yet since, in general consideration, I cannot feel such a particular error as might settle in your Majesties grave judgment an offence meriting your disfavour, I am most humbly to beseech your Majesty, that by knowing my fault I may either purge my self by a just denial, or by confessing it crave pardon of your Highness, and reform my self. If therefore it shall stand with your Majesties good pleasure to declare it to my honourable good friend Mr. Secretary *Walsingham*, commanding him to charge me with it, I will thereupon simply answer, even as before the Lord God, without concealing any matter of truth in any wise, for mine own defence. This grace the sooner I shall obtain, the apter I shall be found for your other services, from which I find my self distracted, because the end of my travels is none other but to purchase that grace and favour which I may now fear to be alienated from me till my cause be better explained. And so I humbly end, praying the Lord to bless you with a long and prosperous reign.

Your Majesties most humble servant and subject,
At your town of Dundalk, August 11. 1583.   Henry Wallop.

Sir Isaac Wake, to the Secretary.

Right Honourable,

I Have safely received the Letter wherewith your Honour hath been pleased to favour me, dated at *Theobalds* the 19 h. of July Stil. Vet. and have, to my singular comfort, understood, that you have been pleased not only to give favourable acceptance unto such weak dispatches as I have made bold to address unto you, but done me the honour likewise to acquaint his Majesty with the contents of them, and to direct my proceedings in this intricate business, with instructions dictated by his Majesties wisdome; this light will be sufficient to direct my steps in the middest of an *Egyptian* darkness, which doth not only obscure the *Horizon* of this Province where I reside, but almost the whole face of *Europe*, by reason of the great mists which are cast artificially in all mens eyes, to cover the designs of those who do presume, that they have in all places *arbitrium Belli et Pacis*.

I most humbly crave pardon of your Honour, if you do not receive my answer so soon as, perhaps, you might expect. For yours having stayed upon the way a moneth and a day, did

Sir Isaac Wake, to the Secretary.

did not come to my hands until the 20th of August, Stil. Vet. At which time it was brought unto me by Mr. *Rowlandson*, whom I had dispatched into *Germany*, to advertise those Princes of the motion made to the Duke of *Savoy* for the passage of Spanish forces through his State. My Lord of *Doncaster* under whose cover I received that Letter, did not think fit to send it to me by an express messenger for fear of increasing the suspition of some in those parts, who are jealous that his Majesty doth favour the Duke of *Savoy* more then they could wish. And I must confess, that the same reason induced me likewise to send that Gentleman of the Duke of *Savoy's* into *Germany* rather then any servant of mine own, for fear least allees, and vennes of messengers betwixt my Lord of *Doncaster* and me in these doubtfull times might so far injealous the contrary party, as might prejudice the service of his Majesty in that Negotiation.

The instructions that your honour hath been pleased to give me from his Majesty, concer-
52. c. the ning my treating with 52. c. in favour of 93. a. Having reference unto the inclination of
Duke of 95. a. to peace, or the probability of defence to be made by 93. a. I held it more safe for me
Savoy. to govern my self by such informations of the state of those affairs as I have received from
93. a. the the favour of the 1. 32. 7. 5. 47. 48. 2. 10. 40. 45. of 51. a. in 97. a. And for the better justi-
Bohemians. fication of my proceedings I send your Honour here enclosed the copy of his Letter unto me,
Emperour wherein you will see, that I have no reason as yet to spend the name of 51. a. in favour of
Ferdinand. 93. a. nor to imbargue 52. c. in a business which may draw a great charge and envie upon
51. a. the himself, and not much advantage the 93. a. I must confess that the 50. b. in general, and
King of particularly the 54. b. and the 41. 45. 23. 34. 9. 12. of 5. 22. 4. 30. 50. have represented
England. the state of those affairs at this present unto 52. b. in a manner not only different from
97. a. Ger- the advertisements sent me, but almost contrary; and they do seem not only to be confident
many. of the prevailing of 93. a. but likewise they continue to give hope that the 10. 51. 29. 15. of
99. the 48. 3. 59. 15. will concur with 51. b. and 52. b. in the 12. 30. 13. 9. 50. 27. 40. 35. of 99.
King of the a. But because I have reason to suspect that they make relation of those affairs,
Romans. rather as they wish they were, then as they be indeed, and that their intention to
51. c. the draw somewhat from 52. c. towards the succours of 93. a. I will forbear to joyn with
Agent of them therein, until I can have some better ground then their advertisements, which may be
England. thought to favour of Partiality; and I have reason to be backward therein, because I know
51. b. the that 52. c. would presently take me *eu mot*, and put to the account of 51. a. that which he
son a Fa- is most willing to do of himself. I do not affirm this out of conjecture, but upon good ground;
vorite. for besides that he did signifie so much unto me at my return out of *England*,
51. b. the I do know that within this fortnight he hath sent unto 56. b. 3000. 41. 24. 48. 49. 40. 30. 47.
Marquess in part of 42. 2. 60. 32. 15. 35. 50. and in the conveyance of this 33. 39. 34. 35. 61. there
Branden- was extraordinary diligence used to conceal it from the knowledge of the 71. c. whereof
bergh. no other construction can be made, but that 52. c. would fain be intreated by 71. c. to do that,
54. b. the which he hath already a mind to do.
Marquess
Huspa b. If upon more fresh Letters, which I expect from my Lord of *Doncaster*, I shall find that
50. b. the the affairs there have changed face since the writing of his last unto me, I will govern my
Princes of self accordingly as I shall receive warrant from him.
the Union.
51. b. Count We are here at a stand, expecting with devotion the issue of the affairs of *Germany*. The
Ern-st Army in the Kingdom of *Naples* is still retained, and no order given, either for the dis-
Mansfelt. missing of those Troops, or the employing them in any service. Prince *Philibert* is at *Messi-
na* with the Gallies, and hath with him 10 or 12000 men. The ships and Galleons remain at *Naples*, and the *Walloons*, *Lombardes* and *Neapolitans* which should have come to *Vado*, are since their disimbarquing again quartered round the City of *Naples*. It is impossible to guess what they mean to do; but the most probable conjecture is, that under the colour of suspecting the Duke of *Ossuna*, the *Spaniards* will keep their Potent Army on foot, and by that means keep all *Italy* in awe, and as it were *sub Ferula*, and delude the reiterated promises and oaths that have passed by them, to assure the Duke of *Savoy* and the *Venetians*, that they would dismiss those Forces. The season is now past for any enterprise by Sea, so that Prince *Philibert* must be forced to return without doing any thing. And many are of opinion, that the Duke of *Ossuna* had secret order to counterfeit madness, and to cross the Kings Commandemen expresly to deprive Prince *Philibert* of the honour which would have redounded unto him if he had been possessed of the absolute command of so potent an Army. The Duke of *Savoy* on the other side, would fain make you believe, that undoubtedly *Ossuna* hath entertained rebellious thoughts; and that if *Don Octavio D'Arragona* do not bring a good answer out of *Spain*, he will break out into open contumacy. His demands of the King of *Spain* are these.

First,

Sir Isaac Wake, to Mr. Secretary.

First, That he may be continued in the Government four years longer.

Secondly, That he may be permitted to enter with his Fleet into the Gulph of *Venice*, and to dispute his Majesties Title to that Sea by the force of Arms.

Lastly, That in case the King of *Spain* will not let him Contest so far with the *Venetians*, that there may then be sent him so much money out of *Spain* as may license his Army, considering that the Kingdom of *Naples* is so far exhausted, as that they cannot contribute any longer, either to the maintaining, or to the dismissing of those Forces.

The *Venetians* did lately chase a small Gally of the *Vicocchi*, which was entred into the Gulph to rob and spoil, and followed her unto the shoars of *Apuglia*, where *Ferlitick* the Captain of those Thieves saved himself and the most part of his fellows, by flight into the mountains; but *Seignior Philippo Belegno* recovered the Gally, and carried her away as a prize; having found two Banners displayed, the one with the Arms of *Spain*, the other with the Arms of *Ossuna*; And not onely a formal Patent and Commission, to take any thing that he could from the *Venetians*, but some Letters likewise from some principal Ministers of *Ferdinand*, wherein this *Capo di Banditi* is encouraged, and requested to do the *Venetians* as much hurt and dammage as he might be able. Now the Duke of *Ossuna* is fallen into a great rage with the *Venetians*, *quod non totum telum corpore acceperunt*; and he doth threaten to be revenged upon them, for not suffering these *Vicocchie* to rob and spoyl their subjects.

The Duke of *Savoy* hath done me the honour to intreat my company with him into *Savoy*, whither he doth purpose very shortly to go, that he may receive at the confines of his Estate the Prince of *Piedmont*, and Madam his wife. And because his request hath the power of a command over me in *Licitis, & honestis*; I must be enforced to pass the Mountains again at an unseasonable time, before I have sufficiently refreshed my self after my last voyage; and I know not whether I shall have the opportunity of writing unto your Honour again before my going, which is uncertain, as depending upon the going of the Duke. So with my hearty prayers unto Almighty God for the preservation of his Majesty in health, and the prosperity of his Estate, in all humility I take leave; And rest

Turin 27. Septemb.
     22. August. } 1619.

Your Honours most faithfully to command,
Isaac Wake.

Sir Isaac Wake, to Mr. Secretary.

Right Honourable,

I Have received the Letter wherewith your Honour hath been pleased to favour me, dated at *White-Hall* the 27. of *February*, as having to my singular comfort understood, that his Majesty hath declared his gracious approbation of my proceedings here, with the Duke of *Savoy*, and the *Venetians*. And I do, with all thankfulness, acknowledge to receive that favour from the hand of your Honour, as my only *Gratum faciens*——

I will not fail to govern my self precisely, by the rule of those Instructions which you have been pleased to give me. And as you have favoured me with passing your word for me, that I will not spend his Majesties name without particular Warrant and direction; so will I promise faithfully to perform as much as you have undertaken for me, and both in this, as in all things else, you may assure your self, that his Majesties revealed will, and that onely, shall be a Law unto me.

Your Honour will have understood, by my former Dispatches, that the Duke of *Ossuna* is re-confirmed in his Government of *Naples*: He hath not (as far as I can learn) any certain time prefixed, but is to remain there *durante Regis beneplacito*: And when his Patent was presented unto him, he had likewise order (which was delivered by word of mouth) that the King his Master did require him immediately to dismiss all his Army, and to send the *Wallocns*, and *Neopolitanes* into *Germany*, to the succours of the Emperour. The same party did likewise signifie unto him, that as the King of *Spain* had shewed to have a care of the honour of the Duke of *Ossuna*, in establishing him anew in that Regency, at this time when the world had made some doubt, that his late actions had not been conformable to the will and pleasure of his Master, so he did expect that he should voluntarily; and of himself, ask leave to go into *Spain*, and offer to give an account of all his proceedings. Which course the King did recommend unto him as most honourable, for the justification of his own innocency, and the confusion of his enemies. This Message the said Duke hath wisely suppressed, and hath published the Patent of his Confirmation, without taking notice of the private Articles which were annexed thereunto, and delivered verbally. He doth profess to understand very well, that in *Spain* they wish him ill, and that their design is under the fair bait of this establishing him in that Government, to make him swallow the hook of dismissing his army, that so they may afterwards dispose of him at their pleasure, when he shall remain utterly disarmed. But his heart did not serve him to throw away the scabbard when he had drawn his sword: and I am perswaded, that as in *Spain* they will judge of his proceedings by the rule of *Tacitus, Qui deliberant desciverant*: so he will repent of not having observed that other *Maxime, Aut nunquam tentes, aut perfice*. His best hope is, that *Chi ha tempo ha vita*, and if he can make his peace at home upon any conditions, he will not much care to turn honest, and change his dangerous designs into faithful service of his Master. To play *Le bon valett*, he hath now obeyed his Masters Commandment in sending the *Walloons* and *Neapolitans* into *Lombardie*, and they are all so safely arrived at *Vado* upon 19 Galleons, being in number 6, or 7000.

The landing of these Troops, and their passing along the skirt of this State, doth not only give a little jealousie to the Duke of *Savoy*, but put him likewise to some Cost and trouble. For as he doth well know how dangerous it is to stand to the discretion of a reconciled enemy, so doth he evidently see, that their ill talent towards him doth not onely continue; but increase; and therefore to assure himself, and his State, he hath caused at this present a general muster to be made of all his Cavalry, and trained Infantery, which he doth send to the confines of his State that way, which these newly landed Troops are to pass. And although their order be to march towards *Switzerland*, and to pass that way into *Germany*, yet will this Prince stand upon his Guard untill they are quite gone out of *Lombardie*; and hath given order to the Count *Guido* St. *George* in his absence, not to let him lodge in *Monferrat* upon any terms whatsoever, nor to linger too long neer the Confine of this Province. He hath this reason to conclude, that the Spaniards wish him ill, because he doth see that they do mistrust him. For whereas they had a fair promise of the passage for their army through this State, by vertue of antient capitulations betwixt the King of *Spain* and the Duke of *Savoy*, they have chosen rather to buy the passage at the hands of the *Swissers* at a very dear rate, then adventure to take it here Gratis. Whereby it may appear unto all the world how little confidence they have in this Prince, and how much they mistrust him for being partially affected to the Prince *Palatine*, and all that party. Howsoever your Honour doth conceive, that the season of the year is too far passed for the transportation of this Army of the *Spaniards* into *Germany*, yet you will see that necessity doth make men strive with many inconveniencies, for they must pass whatsoever weather happen; and indeed, the Alpes are passable enough until the months of *January* and *February*, if the Souldiers be well cloathed; for there is no danger but of cold, until the deluges of Snow which fall late do shut up the passages.

Perhaps they will not find the passages of *Switzerland* so favourable as they do conceive, and as is figured unto them, for they have bought it onely of the little Popish *Cantons*, without asking leave of the *Seigniory* of *Zurich* and *Berne*; and it is to be supposed, that the State of *Berne* will take a hot Alarum, considering that their controversie with *Friburg* is not accommodated, and that the Governour of *Millain* hath made offer unto those of *Friburg*, and the little *Cantons*, of all this army for the defence of the Catholick Religion in the *Bailiage* of *Eschalens*, whereof I have given notice to our *Seigniory* of *Berne* by an express Currier, that they may have time to save themselves from a surprise.

The voice doth run current over all *Italy*, that the Duke of *Parma* is to undertake a voyage shortly for the service of the King of *Spain*, but whither he is to go they cannot tell; for some send him into *Germany*, others into *Flanders*, and the most men into *Spain*. For all which discourse I know no other ground, but that his brother, the Cardinal *Farnese*, hath asked leave of the Pope to retire himself for a time to *Parma*; and I do imagine that the *Speculativi* have concluded thereupon, that he is to govern the State in the absence of his brother.

Prince *Philibert* having failed of the enterprise of *Susa* did intend, in his second setting out from *Sicily*, to meet with the Turkish Fleet and fight with them. The first part of his design succeeded happily, for he had the good fortune to encounter the whole Fleet between *Zant* and *Cephalonia*; but finding them more strong then he was aware, and well resolved to give him battail, he was counselled to retire to *Messina*, where he is at this present, without having effected any thing. The two Armies of *Venice*, and the Turk, did likewise meet on those Seas, not far from *Corfu*; but as soon as they did know each the other, the two Generals, and all the principal Officers, did interchangeably present one the other with wine, and *Rinfrea Camenti*; and so much kindness passed betwixt them, that the *Visier Bassa* did offer to joyn his Fleet with the *Venetian*, and to set upon the Spanish *Armado*; which charitable offer the *Venetian* General had so much Christianity as to refuse with modest thanks.

Seigniour

Sir Isaac Wake, to the Duke.

Seigniour *Antonio Donato* hath sent a servant of his hither, who had the fortune to arrive in an ill Conjuncture. For the Duke of *Savoy* having lately called upon the *Venetians* for that money which is wanting in Seigniour *Donato's* account, they did excuse themselves upon his pleading not guilty, and did send unto the Duke a Copy of his Letter written to the Senate, when he was yet Embassadour, and not convicted. This Letter arrived here from *Venice* the very day before Seigniour *Donato's* servant; and if your honour will be pleased to cast an eye upon the Copy which I send here inclosed, you will not blame the Duke of *Savoy* for refusing to give him audience, or to receive his Masters Letters; for he doth give the Duke the Lie three several times in that Letter, which is strange language to be used of a Prince; and I do much wonder, that the *Venetians* would upon any occasion whatsoever publish such a Petulancy, committed by one that was their Embassadour at that time.

He brought me a Letter from his Master, of nicer Ceremony, and Complement, and had his principal address unto the Popes Nuntio in this Court, whereat I did wonder somewhat formally at the first, as conceiving that in Congruity he ought to have interrupted his Correspondence with the Popes Ministers, as long as he doth live under the protection of his Majesty; but when I understood, that the Duke had lodged him in a prison, with an intent to send him to *Venice*; I was glad that I had so little to do with him, and the Nuntio so much.

The Duke of *Savoy* doth assure himself, that when his Majesty shall have perused this Letter of Seigniour *Donato's*, he will withdraw his countenance, and protection from him, and account him unworthy of any favour, for having wronged, in so high a degree, a Prince that is so much a servant of his Majesty.

I may not likewise conceal from his Majesties knowledge, that Seigniour *Donato* hath not been wanting to ruine (as far as he could) *Padre Paolo*, and *Fulgentio* in *Venice*; two persons that have done his Majesty very long and faithful service, as by an inclosed Paper, your Honour may see, which is an abstract of a Letter written from *Fulgentio*.

The Prince of *Piedmont* having made a posting voyage hither to receive his Fathers blessing, before he bring his Lady into the Country, I did present unto him his Majesties Letters of Congratulation, whereunto he hath returned answer, which I send here inclosed. So with my hearty prayers unto Almighty God for the preservation of his Maiesties Person in all happiness and prosperity, in all humility I take leave, And rest

Turin $\frac{5}{15}$ of *Octob*. 1619.

Your Honours
Most faithfully to command,
Isaac Wake.

Sir Isaac Wake, to the Duke.

Right Honourable, and my very singular good Lord,

IN these parts we have nothing of moment worthy the relating, the storms which do vex our neighbours round about us, keeping us here in calm and quiet, as it were *per anteperistasin*. Howsoever I am of opinion, that we shall enter into the Dance either actively or passively, before the next summer pass over. All over *Italy* there doth reign a great dearth, which did lately cause in *Naples* a dangerous Cullevation of the people against the Cardinal *Zappata* Vice-Roy, who had somewhat to do to save himself from the fury of the *Popolarzo*.

In the State of *Millain* likewise some insurrections were beginning to be made in *Novarra*, *Allessandria* and *Cremona*, both for want of bread, and for the insolency of the Garrison Souldiers, who having had no pay for many moneths did commit many violent excesses upon the people, which did drive them into despair; but those commotions were appeased betimes, and no great matter of Consideration hath ensued, although there are some neighbour Princes who did stand *aux Escoutes*, and would be ready to have acted a troublesome part, if the scene had been ready.

The Duke of *Parma* hath imprisoned his natural son *Don Octavio*, the mystery whereof is not well known, but it must needs be for some great matter, because he did make shew to love him passionately. The Infanta *Isabella* of *Modena* hath been in danger of her life, by being surprized with a violent Feaver, neer the time of her child-birth: from hence the Duke of *Savoy* sent his Physitians to help her, and we hear now that she hath escaped that danger, and is safely delivered of a daughter.

Count *Mansfelt* is grown formidable, and doth daily increase in strength and reputation. Although he hath hitherto intitled his armes unto the service of the King of *Bohemia*, yet

I beleeve he will neither difarm, nor fuspend his arms, when he shall be commanded so to do by that King. For being now entertained by the State of *Venice*, with an honourable provision of 12000 Crowns *per annum*, in peace, during his life, and the pay of 10000 Foot, and 2000 Horse in the time of War, he will try what he can do for the franchifing of the *Grifons*, when the affairs of the *Palatinate* shall be accommodated. And if the *Austriaci* do not bend all their forces against him very speedily, and break his Army before it grow more strong, he is like to give them a greater blow then they have had these many years. That which he hath gotten already in *Alsatia* is much more worth then the lower *Palatinate*; and although he hath hitherto made those people to swear Allegiance unto the King of *Bohemia*, yet when the said King shall make his peace with the Emperour, it may be doubted whether Count *Mansfelt* will resign up what he hath conquered; and it is thought, that he will either keep it for himself, or intitle some other Prince thereunto. The *Austriaci* were never so matched as with Count *Mansfelt*, for he is a perpetual motion, and doth not stand upon the defensive (as others have done hitherto, and lost by the bargain) but he is alwaies setting upon them, and doth make War at their cost; let them take heed how they proceed with him; for he, who hath nothing to lose, is ready to hazard the Paquet upon all occasions; And if he do chance to overthrow them once in battel, they will run danger to lose all that they have in *Germany*. Let me in all humility beseech your Lordship, to continue me in the honour of your good opinion, and to favour me with your honourable protection, especially with a good word to my Lord Treasurer, for the sending me some relief, without which I cannot possibly subsist, having for want of my pay consumed all that I had in the world. God Almighty increase upon your Lordship all happiness and prosperity, as is unfeinedly wished unto you by him that is

Turin $\frac{13}{23}$ of *Febr.* 1621.

Your Lordships most humbly obliged Creature and Servant,
Isaac Wake.

Sir Isaac Wakes *Proposition for the King of* Denmark.

IT seemeth that the Glory of this State, which at all times was great, doth shine brighter now adays; since that besides so many Neighbouring Kings and Princes, whereof some are in a made league with us, and some do keep a good correspondence, & all a good intelligence with us. Now the friendship of your Highness is sought by the mighty King of *Denmark*, a Monarch of those nations that in time past have left the remembrance of their *prowesse* in *Italy*, *France*, *Spain*, and in whole Europe behind them. This Great King of the North, who like a Second *Atlas* holds up the *Artick-pole*, rich in treasure, numerous in men, dreadful for his invincible generosity and courage doth here offer himself unto your Highness. And acquainting you of his actions, doth confidently promise you to stand firm, and stout in the defence of the common cause, if so be that he receive that assistance as he hath reason to expect from those that are interested in the same cause. His Majesty of *Denmark* hath had from the King my Master as much as can be given; and it is no small matter, that his Majesty of great *Britain* doth still continue the same assistance, having withal still those great expences that are required for the surety of his Realms, and for the offence of the common enemy.

His Majesty of *France* hath also contributed to this good work somewhat, and there is great hope that he will bring forth in a short time some fit remedy against this evil. The Lords States do as much as they are able. And the Princes of *Low Saxony* do not want in their duties. There remaineth now, that your Highness put also your powerful hand to this work, and with a vigorous succour, worthy of your great heart, do encourage all the rest to continue their Empress. The two Kings are not ignorant of the great sincerity wherewith this most Excellent State doth observe the capitulations made with Allies of the league, and that rather then to be wanting in things agreed upon, you have surpassed in necessary provisions for the advancement of the designs, and that you have not been partakers, nor agreers of the Treaty made at *Moncon*. But that you do continue to keep some forces in your Dominions, and likewise some Troops in the *Valtoline*, for the effecting (as much as is in you) of what was first thought fit, and of the agreement of the League.

And as that generous resolution and constancy of this State is never enough praised, so there is great hope that you will not bring this same in the reckoning of the two Kings, who never will miss to praise the wisdom and generosity of this State, though not obliged

Sir Henry Wootton, to the Duke.

for their particular for any thing whatsoever done till now, either by the league in general, or by whomsoever of the united in particular, because that the league was made two years and more before his Majesty of great *Britain* broke with *Spain*, or that the King of *Denmark* had declared himself. Since the time that these two Kings are come to the dance, your Highness hath not levied one man; and the Forces which you do yet keep, as they were not levied, so are they not maintained in Contemplation of the two Kings, but only for the first reasons of the League.

The only thing here sought for is to go with a common pace, that those that are now too heavily laden may be supported by their friends, either by way of diversion, or by way of assistance. And therefore your Highness and other Princes are now requested to help, seeing there is small appearance of diversion. And set the case, that the Peace between *Spain* and *France* should be firm, would it not turn against the Common Cause, *Italiæ incendium ruina Germaniæ extinguere*? To quench a little fire in *Italy* by the ruine of whole *Germany*? In Chronical diseases Physitians do not so much respect the symptoms and accidents, as they do the causes of the evil.

The *Valtoline, Palatinate, Hussia, Marchisat* of *Baden*, Dukedome of *Brunswick*, and so many other Countries attempted, and oppressed by the *Spanish* and *Austrian* usurpation, are grievous and dangerous symptoms and accidents: but the Cause, and fewel of the evil remains yet in the ambitious bowels of the *Spaniard*, who now with spread sailes goeth on towards the universal Monarchie; unless there be applied betimes some fit remedies, all to-pick remedies will do but little good.

The King of *Denmark* doth offer himself ready to apply such an issue whereby he may be brought back to terms of modestie; and with the assistance he doth expect from your Highness and other interessed Princes he hopeth to bring his good intent to pass. And being prodigal of his great Soul, there is no doubt he will never go back, unless he be forsaken.

Thus there remains the Common liberty almost in your hands; and if this most excellent Senate resolves to give ayd unto that King, that libertie will be preserved. If you do forsake him, that will also be indangered, yea lost. I therefore beseech your Highness to ponder well this matter, and to grant such an assistance as is requested by the King of *Denmarks* Embassadour.

Sir Henry Wootton, to the Duke.

My most Noble Lord,

I Will be bold by this opportunity to give his Majesty, through your Lordships hands, an account of a Command which I had from him at *Theobalds*, about sounding how the *Venetian* Embassadour stood satisfied with the late determination touching his predecessour *Donato*.

I did visit the said Embassadour immediately at my return from the King, and saluted him as by express Commandment; interjecting some words of mine own gladness, that he had received contentment in this tender point, which would signalize his beginnings. This I said, because in truth I had found him alwayes before the more passionate in it by some reflection upon himself. His answer (after due thanks for his Majesties gracious remembrance of him from abroad) was, That for his own part, he was *Contentissimo*, and had represented things home in the best manner. He hoped likewise it would be well tasted there also, though with some doubt, because the State out of their own devotion towards his Majesty might form a confidence of expecting more. I replyed, that the King, upon the matter, (if we consider disgrace) had done more then themselves: for he was but once banished at *Venice*, and twice here; *viz.* once from the Verge of the Court; and secondly, from *London*, which was as much as could be done with preservation of National immunities, and more then would have been done at the suit of any other Embassadour here resident, or perhaps of any of their own hereafter, if the like case shall occur. For (as I told him) it was the Kings express will, that his particular respect to the Republick, & to him in this business, should not be drawn into examples. With this point he was not a little pleased for his own glory, and said, that indeed Mr. Secretary *Nanton* had told him so. This was the summe of what passed between us, omitting impertinencies. Let me end (my dear Lord) as I am bound in all the use, either of my pen, or of my voice, with an humble and hearty acknowledgement of my great obligations towards your Lordship, which will make me resolve, and in good faith unhappy, till I can some way shew my self,

January 25th.
1619.

Your Lordships most thankful and faithful servant,

Henry Wootton.

Sir Henry Wootton, *to the Duke.*

My most honoured Lord, and Patron,

THese poor lines will be presented unto your Lordship by my Nephew (one of your obliged servants) and withal some description (as I have prayed him) of my long infirmities, which have cast me behind in many private, and often interrupted even my publick Duties; with which yet I do rather seek to excuse some other defects of service then my silence towards your Lordship.

For to importune your Lordship seldom with my pen, is a choice in me, and not a disease, having resolved to live at what distance soever from your sight, like one who had well studied before I came hither, how secure they are to whom you once vouchsafe any part of your love. And indeed I am well confirmed therein by your own gracious lines: for thereby I see that your Lordship had me in your meditation, when I scant remembred my self.

In answer of which Letter, after some respite from mine own evils, I have deputed my said Nephew to re-deliver my fortune into your Noble hands, and to assure your Lordship, that as it should be cheerfully spent at your Command, if it were present and actual (from whose mediation I have derived it) so much more am I bound to yield up unto your Lordship an absolute disposition of my hopes: But if it should please you therein to grant me any part of mine own humour, then I would rather wish some other satisfaction, then exchange of Office; yet even in this point likewise I shall depend on your wil, which your Lordship may indeed challenge from me, not only by an humble gratitude, and reverence due to your most worthy person, but even by that natural charity and discretion which I owe my self: For what do I more therein, then only remit to your own arbitrement the valuation of your own goodness? I have likewise committed to my foresaid Nephew some Memorials touching your Lordships familiar service (as I may term it) in matter of art and delight.

But though I have laid these Offices upon another, yet I joy with mine own pen to give your Lordship an account of a Gentleman, worthier of your love, then I was of the honour to receive him from you.

We are now after his well-spent travailes in the Towns of purer language, married again till a second Divorce, for which I shall be sorry, whensoever it shall happen. For in truth (my good Lord) his conversation is both delightful, and fruitful; and I dare pronounce, that he will return to his friends as well fraught with the best observations as any that hath ever sifted this Country, which indeed doth need sifting; for there is both flower and bran in it.

He hath divided his abode between *Sienna* and *Rome:* The rest of his time was for the most part spent in motion. I think his purpose is to take the *French* tongue in his way homewards; but I am perswading with him to make *Bruxels* his Seat, both because the *French* and *Spanish* Languages are familiar there, whereof the one will be after *Italian* a sport unto him, so as he may make the other a labour: And for that the said Town is now the scene of an important Treatie, which I fear will last till he come thither: but far be from me all ominous conceit.

I will end with cheerful thoughts and wishes; beseeching the Almighty God to preserve your Lordship in health, and to cure the publick diseases. And so I ever remain,

Venice 29. of
July, 1622.

Your Lordships

Most devoted, obliged servant,

Henry Wootton.

Sir Henry Wootton, to the Duke.

My most honoured, and dear Lord,

TO give your Lordship occasion to exercise your Noble nature, is withal one of the best exercises of mine own duty; and therefore I am confident to pass a very charitable motion through your Lordships hands, and mediation to his Majesty. There hath long lain in the prison of Inquisition a constant worthy Gentleman, *viz.* Mr. *Mole*; In whom his Majesty hath not only a right as his Subject, but likewise a particular interest in the cause of his first imprisonment. For having communicated his Majesties immortal work touching the alleageance unto Sovereign Princes with a *Florentine* of his familiar acquaintance, this man took such impression at some passages, as troubling his conscience he took occasion at next shrift to confer certain doubts with his Confessor, who out of malicious curiosity, inquiring into all circumstances, gave afterwards notice thereof to *Rome*, whither the said *Mole* was gone with my Lord *Rosse*, who in this story is not without blame; but I will not disquiet his Grave.

Now having lately heard, that his Majesty, at the suit of I know not what Embassadours, (but the *Florentine* amongst them is voiced for one) was pleased to yield some releasement to certain restrained persons of the Roman faith: I have taken a conceit upon it, that in exchange of his clemency therein, the Great Duke would be easily moved by the Kings Gracious request, to intercede with the Pope for Mr. *Moles* delivery. To which purpose if it shall please his Majesty to grant his Royal Letters, I will see the business duly pursued. And so needing no arguments to commend this proposition to his Majesties goodness, but his goodness it self, I leave it (as I began) in your Noble hand.

Now touching your Lordships familiar service (as I may term it) I have sent the complement of your bargain upon the best provided and best manned Ship that hath been here in a long time, called the *Phœnix*; and indeed the cause of their long stay hath been for some such sure vessel as I might trust. About which, since I wrote last to your Lordship, I resolved to fall back to my first choice. So as now the one piece is the work of *Titian*, wherein the least figure (*viz.* the child in the Virgins lap playing with a bird) is alone worth the price of your expence for all four, being so round, that I know not whether I shall call it a piece of sculpture, or picture; and so lively, that a man would be tempted to doubt, whether nature or art had made it. The other is of *Palma*, and this I call the speaking piece, as your Lordship will say it may well be termed: for except the Damosel brought to *David*, whom a silent modesty did best become, all the other figures are in discourse, and action. They come both distended in their frames; for I durst not hazard them in rowles, the youngest being 25 years old, and therefore no longer supple, and pliant. With them I have been bold to send a dish of Grapes to your Noble Sister, the Countess of *Denbigh*, presenting them first to your Lordships view, that you may be pleased to pass your censure, whether *Italians* can make fruits as well as *Flemings*, which is the common Glory of their Pencils. By this Gentleman, I have sent the choicest Melon-seeds of all kinds, which his Majesty doth expect, as I had order both from my Lord of *Holdernesse*, and from Mr. Secretary *Calvert*. And although in my Letter to his Majesty (which I hope, by your Lordships favour, himself shall have the honour to deliver, together with the said seeds) I have done him right in his due attributes; yet let me say of him farther as *Architects* use to speak of a well chosen foundation, that your Lordship may boldly build what fortune you please upon him, for surely he will bear it vertuously. I have committed to him, for the last place, a private memorial touching my self, wherein I shall humbly beg your Lordships intercession upon a necessary motive. And so with my heartiest prayers to heaven for your continual health and happiness, I most humbly rest,

Venice $\frac{2}{12}$ Decemb.
1622.

Your Lordships ever obliged devoted Servant,
Henry Wootton.

Post-script.

MY Noble Lord, it is one of my duties to tell your Lordship, that I have sent a servant of mine (by profession a Painter) to make a search in the best Towns through *Italy* for some principal pieces, which I hope may produce somewhat for your Lordships contentment and service.

Sir Henry Wotton, to the Duke.

May it please your Grace,

HAving some dayes by sickness been deprived of the comfort of your sight, who did me so much honour at my last Access, I am bold to make these poor lines happier then my self. And withal to represent unto your Grace (whose noble Patronage is my refuge, when I find any occasion to bewail mine own fortune) a thing which seemeth strange unto me. I am told (I know not how truly) that his Majesty hath already disposed the *Venetian* Embassage to Sir *Isaac Wake*; from whose sufficiency if I should detract, it would be but an argument of my own weakness.

But that which herein doth touch me,(I am loath to say in point of reputation,surely much in my livelihood, as Lawyers speak) is, that thereby after 17 years of forreign continual imployment either ordinary or extraordinary, I am left utterly destitute of all possibility to subsist at home, much like those Seale Fishes which sometimes (as they say) over-sleeping themselves in an ebbing water, feel nothing about them but a dry shoare when they awake. Which comparison I am fain to seek among those Creatures, not knowing, among men that have so long served so gracious a Master, any one to whom I may resemble my unfortunate bareness. Good my Lord, as your Grace hath vouchsafed me some part of your Love, so make me worthy in this of some part of your Compassion. So I humbly rest,

Your Graces, &c.

Henry Wotton.

Sir Henry Wotton, to the Duke.

My most Noble Lord,

WHen, like that impotent man in the Gospel, I had lyen long by the Pools side, while many were healed, and none would throw me in, it pleased your Lordship, first of all, to pity my infirmities, and to put me into some hope of subsisting hereafter. Therefore I most humbly and justly acknowledge all my ability and reputation from your favour. You have given me encouragement, you have valued my poor endeavours with the King, you have redeemed me from ridiculousness, who had served so long without any mark of favour. By which arguments being already,and ever bound, to be yours, till either life or honesty shall leave me, I am the bolder to beseech your Lordship to perfect your own work; and to draw his Majesty to some setling of those things that depend between Sir *Julius Cæsar* and me, in that reasonable form, which I humbly present unto your Lordship by this my Nephew likewise your obliged servant, being my self by a late indisposition confined to my Chamber, but in all estates such as I am,

Your Lordships

Henry Wotton.

Sir Henry Wotton, to the Earl of Portland, Lord Treasurer.

My most honoured Lord,

I Most humbly present (though by some infirmities a little too late) a straying new years gift unto your Lordship, which I will presume to term the cheapest of all that you have received, and yet of the richest Materials.

In short, it is only an image of your self drawn by memory from such discourse as I have taken up here and there of your Lordship among the most intelligent, and unmalignant men. Which to portraict before you I thought no servile office, but ingenuous and real. And I could wish, that it had come at that day, that so your Lordship might have begun the new year somewhat like *Plato's* definition of felicity, with the contemplation of your own *Idea*. They say, that in your forreign imployments under King *James* your Lordship wan the opinion of a very able and searching judgement, having been the first discoverer of the intentions against the *Palatinate*, which were then in brewing, and masqued with much

much Art; and that Sir *Edward Conway* got the ſtart of you, both in title, and employment, becauſe the late Duke of *Buckingham* wanted then, for his own ends, a Martial Secretary.

They ſay, That, under our preſent Sovereign, you were choſen to the higheſt charge, at the loweſt of the State, when ſome inſtrument was requiſite of indubitable integrity, and provident moderation; which attributes I have heard none deny you.

They diſcourſe thus of your actions ſince, That though great exhauſtations cannot be cured without ſudden remedies, no more in a Kingdom then in a natural body: yet your Lordſhip hath well allayed thoſe bluſtring clamours wherewith, at your beginning, your houſe was, in a manner, daily beſieged.

They note, That there hath been made changes, but that none hath brought to the place a Judgment ſo cultivated and illuminated with various erudition, as your Lordſhip, ſince the Lord *Burleigh*, under Queen *Elizabeth*, whom they make your parallel in the Ornament of Knowledge.

They obſerve in your Lordſhip divers remarkable combinations of Virtues and Abilities rarely ſociable.

In the character of your Aſpect, a mixture of Authority and Modeſty; in the faculties of your Mind, quick Apprehenſion and Solidity together; in the ſtile of your Port and Train, as much Dignity, and as great Dependency as was ever in any of your place, and with little noiſe, and outward form.

That your Table is very abundant, free, and noble, without Luxury; that you are by nature no Flatterer, and yet of greateſt power in Court: That you love Magnificence and Frugality both together; that you entertain your Gueſts and Viſitours with noble Courteſie, and void of complement: Laſtly, That you maintain a due regard to your Perſon and Place, and yet an Enemy to frothy-formalities.

Now in the diſcharge of your Function, they ſpeak of two things that have done you much Honour, *viz.* That you had always a ſpecial care to the ſupply of the Navy; and likewiſe, a more worthy and tender reſpect towards the Kings onely Siſter, for the continual ſupport from hence, then ſhe hath found before.

They obſerve your Greatneſs as firmly eſtabliſhed as ever was any, of the love, and (which is more) in the eſtimation of a King who hath ſo ſignalized his conſtancy, beſides your additions of ſtrength (or at leaſt of luſtre) by the nobleſt Alliances of the Land.

Amongſt theſe notes, it is no wonder, if ſome obſerve, that between a good willingneſs in your affections to ſatiſfie all, and impoſſibility in the matter, and yet an importunity in the perſons, there doth, now and then, I know not how, ariſe a little impatience, which muſt needs fall on your Lordſhip, unleſs you had been cut out of a Rock of Diamonds, eſpecially having been long before ſo converſant with liberal ſtudies, and with the freedom of your own mind.

Now after this ſhort Collection touching your moſt honoured Perſon, I beſeech you, give me leave to add likewiſe a little what men ſay of the Writer.

They ſay, I want not your gracious good will towards me, according to the degrees of my poor talent and travels; but they ſay, I am wanting to my ſelf. And, in good faith (my Lord) in ſaying ſo, they ſay the truth: For I am condemned, I know not how, by nature, to a kind of unfortunate baſhfulneſs in mine own buſineſs; and it is now too late to put me in a new Furnace.

Therefore, it muſt be your Lordſhips proper work, and not onely your noble, but even your charitable goodneſs, that muſt, in ſome bleſſed hour, remember me. God give your Lordſhip many healthfull and joyfull years, and the bleſſing of the Text, *Beatus qui attendit ad attenuatum.* And ſo I remain, with all humble and willing heart,

At your Lordſhips command,
Henry Wotton.

Sir Richard Weſton, *to the Duke.*

May it pleaſe your Lordſhip,

I Fear I have taken too much of that liberty of not writing you were pleaſed to allow me by Sir *George Goring*; but I hope, your Lordſhip will meaſure my devotion to ſerve you, by no other rule then your own intereſt and deſert: For, as I underſtand by Sir *George Goring* how often I come into your thoughts, and how great a part I have in your cares; ſo is there no man to whom I would more willingly give daily account of my ſelf, then to your Lordſhip, to whoſe grace and favour I ow ſo much.

Sir Richard Weston, to the Duke.

I forbear to trouble your Lordship with any relation of business, because, I presume, your Lordship is acquainted with all my dispatch; and it is not long since I intreated my Lord Treasurer to tell your Lordship what I thought of things then: I have yet little reason to change my opinion.

And if your Lordship please to know the State of things now, I have sent this Gentleman, the Bearer hereof, especially, to do your Lordship reverence in my name, and to give you full information. For my return, or stay, I humbly submit it to his Majesties pleasure.

Though this Negotiation be like to spin it self out into much length, I weigh not my own interest: I shall willingly be there where I shall be thought most able to do his Majesty service. And so intreating that I may be continued in that good opinion and grace, wherein your Lordships own affection, not any merit of mine, hath placed me, I humbly kiss your hands, and remain

Bruxels, June 26. 1622.

Your Lordships faithfull and devoted servant,
Richard Weston.

Sir Richard Weston, to the Duke.

My very good Lord,

I Have understood, by my Lord Treasurer, the way you have made with his Majesty for my calling home; for which this present doth give your Lordship most humble thanks, though I have forborn to press or sollicite it, because I would approve my obedience to his Majesty, and take away from them all occasion, who otherwise might have accused my departure, and imputed the want of success here to my want of patience to expect an answer.

I have, almost in all my Dispatches, since we entred into this Treaty, signified what opinion I had of their proceedings here; and my chief comfort was, that whatsoever the success were, that the clearness of his Majesties intentions would appear to the whole world, and that the failing is not of his side, which, I think, is manifest enough: for, notwithstanding that his Majesty hath followed them in all their desires, and the Prince Elector hath conformed himself to what was demanded; that the Count *Mansfelt*, and Duke of *Brunswick*, the pretended obstacles of the Treaty, are now, with all their Forces, removed; no face of an Enemy in the *Palatinate*, but his Majesties power in the Garrisons; all other places repossessed which *Mansfelt* had taken; no cause of continuing any War now, nor any cause of jealousie or fear, for the future, considering his Majesties fair and honourable offers: yet are they so far from a Cessation, that they are fallen upon *Heidlebergh*, and either want the will, or power, to remove the siege. And all I can get, is, two Letters of intreaty from her Highness to the Chiefs of the Emperour, to proceed no further: and after some eighteen days since I made my Proposition for the Cessation, I have yet no answer; so that being able to raise no more doubts, they make use of delays. I have said, and done, and used all diligences within my power to bring forth better effects, and can go no further; and therefore, I humbly beseech your Lordship, that I may have leave to return, when I shall hear that they will not remove the siege at *Heidleberg*. For their pretending to restore all, when all is taken, is a poor comfort to me, and as little honour to his Majesty: And how far they are to be believed in that, is to be examined, more exactly then by writing, by weighing how the weak hopes given me here agree with the strong assurances given by my Lord *Digby* out of *Spain*.

I hope, therefore, his Majesty will be pleased to think it reasonable to speak with me; and as your Lordship hath ever been a happy and gentle Star to me, so have I now more need of your favourable aspect then ever, that his Majesty may receive my obedience as a sacrifice, and interpret well of my endeavours, what success soever I bring home with me. Wherein humbly intreating your Lordships wonted grace and favour, I humbly kiss your hands, and vow unto you the faithfull observance of

Bruxels, Septemb. 3. 1622.

Your Lordships most humble and devoted servant,
Richard Weston.

Sir Richard Weston, *to the Duke.*

May it please your Grace,

YOur Grace shall add much to the infinite favours I have received from you, to read a few lines from me, much more to vouchsafe them an answer; which I am the more bold to beg, and the more hopefull to obtain, because I understand by Sir *George Goring*, that howsoever I have had many ill-offices done me, your Grace will not easily depart from that opinion you have hitherto conceived of me; for which I humbly thank your Grace, and intreat the continuance of it no longer then I shall be able to make good the integrity of my heart unto you. But that which with all humility and importunity I sue for at your Grace's hands, is, to let me know my Accuser; and if your Grace think it unseasonable now, that I may have a promise to know him at your return. Whatsoever, or how great soever he be, (though respect and reverence of those eyes which shall read these lines make me forbear ill language now) I shall dare to tell him whatsoever becomes a wronged innocence to say. In the mean time, I despise him, if there be any such that hath accused me, since your Grace's departure, to have done, or said, or given way to the hearing of any thing that may be wrested to the impeachment of my faith and sincere professions towards your Grace: And yet, till it come to the tryal, I rely (as I wrote to Sir *George Goring*) no less upon your Grace's wisdom and goodness, then my own innocency, that such Calumnies shall not lessen the estimation I had with you; wherein being most confident, praying for the continuance and increase of your Graces honour and happiness, I remain

July 17. 1623.   *Your Grace's most humble and devoted servant,*
Richard Weston.

Sir Richard Weston, *to the Duke.*

May it please your Grace.

I Humbly thank your Grace for the Message I received from you yesterday by Mr. *Packer:* And withal, I humbly beseech your Grace to believe, that no man should condemn me more then I would my self, if I had omitted any possible diligence, either to interest, or acquaint your Grace with the Commission of the Treasury. Wherein I appeal to Mr. Secretary *Conway*, who first declared his Majesties pleasure unto me; which I could not ascribe more to any cause, then your Grace's favour, and good opinion of me: And at my last being with your Grace I began to speak with you of it; but finding your Grace to grow into some indisposition, I forbore, thinking it not onely incivility, but a violence, to have spoken any thing of my self to your Grace at that time. This I intreated Sir *George Goring* to relate unto your Grace, and withal, to renew the professions of my love and reverence to your Grace's person; which I had rather make good by real performances, then by words, and therefore I will trouble your Grace no longer upon this subject.

I am now extremely importuned by the Earl of *Middlesex*, to sollicite his Majesty for the first testimony of his gracious disposition towards him: And your Grace remembers, that in the beginning of his Lordships troubles, his Majesty commanded me to deliver unto his Majesty whatsoever his Lordship should petition of him.

Now I humbly beseech your Grace, to direct me what to do: His Lordship sues for his enlargement, and, I know, desires to derive that favour from his Majesty by your Grace's mediation. And I am carefull to perform all duties, my obedience to his Majesty, my respect to your Grace, and my care of him (that relieth upon me) being in affliction. And therefore, I humbly beseech your Grace, to vouchsafe me an answer to this particular, because his Majesty goeth from hence to morrow, and the Earl of *Middlesex* will languish with expectation, till he receive some comfort from him. And so continually praying for the increase of your Grace's health, I remain

May 29. 1624.   *Your Grace's most humble servant,*
Richard Weston.

Sir Richard Weston, to the Duke.

May it please your Grace;

I Have, according to his Majesties Command signified to me by Mr. Secretary *Conway*, delivered to the Earl of *Middlesex* his Majesties pleasure concerning his Fine: The news of it did extremely dismay him, as being far contrary to his expectation. He used not many words; but thereof I having given Mr. Secretary a particular account, in answer of the charge I received from his Majesty, I will not trouble your Grace with the repetition of them.

The chief cause of this unto your Grace, is, to acquaint your Grace with a short Dialogue that passed between Mr. *Brett* and me, touching his Pension.

He sent his man to me this week, to demand it; to whom I made this answer, That the charge of the Progress being settled, I would consider of the payment of his Masters pension, amongst others; before which time I could not, in that case, give satisfaction to any. He went away with this answer; and immediately after (within less then a quarter of an hour) Mr. *Brett* himself came to me, and asked me at the first word, Whether I had any Command to stay his Pension? I replied, No other command then the want of money. He told me, That the rest of his fellows were paid. I said, It was true, I was to have care of them that immediately followed his Majesty, when I was forced to intreat others to have patience till more moneys came in. He asked me again, Whether I had any Command to stay his? I answered as before; wherewith he parted from me, as it seemed, not pleased.

This, peradventure, is not worth troubling your Grace withal; but that, because his Majesty was pleased to acquaint me with his just indignation against him at *Wansteed*, I would be glad to receive some direction, what answer I shall make, upon his next importunity. And so humbly intreating your Grace ever to number me amongst those that do most honour and pray for you, I remain

Chelsey, July 23. 1624.

Your Grace's most humble and faithfull servant,
Richard Weston.

Sir Richard Weston, to the Duke.

May it please your Grace,

I Did scarce esteem my Letter worthy your Grace's reading, much less worthy your pains to answer it:. It is my duty, upon all occasions, great and small, to pay unto your Grace those observances I ow you; and when your Grace vouchsafes to take knowledge of them, it is your favour; and therefore I humbly thank your Grace for vouchsafing an answer.

I have, according to his Majesties commandment, signified by your Grace unto me, taken the best order I can about the Wardship of the Lady *Craven's* Son. The most of the Officers of the Court of Wards being out of the Town, I have spoken with Sir *Benjamin Ruddiard*, who assured me, that there is nothing yet done, nor can be, till there be a Master, or that the Officers meet together; and that he will take care that nothing shall be done to the prejudice of his Majesty.

And for the more caution, I have commanded the Clerk of the Court, if any man Petition, or sue about the Wardship, that there be no proceeding till he acquaint me with it. This is all can be done for the present; and thereof I think fit to give your Grace account, in answer of the charge I have received from his Majesty. And so humbly craving leave to kiss your Grace's hands, I wish your Grace continual increase of honour and happines, and remain

Chelsey, Aug. 12. 1624:

Your Grace's most humble and faithfull servant,
Richard Weston.

The Lord Wimbledon, to the Duke.

My gracious Lord,

IT hath not a little troubled your faithfull servant, at my last being with your Excellency in *White-Hall* Garden, to understand (after I had attended so long) that I had ill offices done me to his Majesty, and yet the world is of opinion, that I have your Excellencies favour.

The Lord Wimbledon, to the Duke.

your, I presently went home, and ever since I have mused and considered, and can find no reason or policy for my being kept from his Majesties presence, which maketh me and my neer friends astonished. For hitherto I have received no favour, but rather the most strictest proceeding that ever was used (and without example) to any man that had such a charge.

And whereas there is no Commission of any force, or validity, without the assistance of the State, and Prince he serveth; for he that commandeth is but one man, and the rest are many thousands, which are great odds, yet I have been publikely heard before the whole body of the Councel (my adversaries standing by) so curiously, as no inquisition could have done more.

For first, I was examined upon mine instructions, then upon my acts of Councel, then upon my journal, then upon a journal compounded of ten sundry persons, which were under my Command both Landmen and Seamen, which was never heard of before; and I did not only answer in particular to all points that were demanded, but by writing, which is extant: yet cannot I get any judgment or report made to his Majesty, but rather time is given to my enemies (as I hear) to make an ill report of me and my actions to the King. But when I was to be accused, there was no time delayed nor deferred, and such men as I have proved guilty, and failed in the Principal point of the service, to have fired and destroyed the Shipping, are neither examined, or any thing said against them, which is strange, especially Sir *Michael Geere.* So that I know not how my Lord of *Essex* can take any thing ill from your Excellency, unless it be to have you do injustice, or against all reason. He may rather give your Excellency many thanks, that his Lordship is not called into question for letting pass the King of Spains ships, that offered him fight, which would have been the chief service, having instructions not to let any flie, or break out, without fighting with them.

Now (my Lord) I humbly beseech your Excellency to consider my Case, that hath been so severely examined, and no body else, and that after my examination I have lingred so long in my wrongs and disgraces, and by the ill offices your Grace doth see are done me to his Majesty, which will rather encrease then diminish, so long as I shall be kept from the presence of his Majesty, that is, I know, of himself the justest Prince in the world, and yet to be in your Excellencies favour.

And I hold my self clear of all imputations in despight of all malice and practice that hath been against me, to obscure all my endeavours which my adversaries in their consciences can best witness, that when they slept, I waked; when they made good chear, I fasted; and when they rested, I toyled. And besides, when they went about to hinder the journey at *Plimouth*, by railing on the beggarliness of it, and discrediting of it, I was content to take it upon me, though against my judgment, as I did secretly deliver both to his Majesty and your Grace, before I departed from the Coast: Nominating in my Letter to his Majesty all the inconveniencies that did after happen unto the fleet: for had it not been in my obedience to his Majesty, and my good affection to your Excellency, (that I did see so much affect it, and was so far engaged) I would rather have been torne in pieces, then to have gone with so many ignorant and malicious people, that did shew so little affection or courage to his Majesties service, or any affection at all to your Excellency. Yet for all this, all hath been laid upon me, having had rather hard courses taken against me, then any way maintained in my Commission which was given me, which no State, that I ever heard of did before. I pray God his Majesties future service do not suffer for it; for where his Majesties Officers are not obeyed, he can never be served.

Wherefore my suit is, that if I have any ill offices done me to his Majesty, that I may clear my self before him by your favour, which I have so long attended after; or by way of Petition, which the meanest subject is not to be hindred in; for as I continue now, I have not only wrong done to me, but I suffer as much punishment (without any fault) as if I had been condemned.

And that your Excellency will do me the favour to deal plainly with me, to let me know, why I am deferred from his Majesties presence, which is not denied to any, having received much wrong.

If my suffering be to adde any service to your affairs in these troublesome times, let but this honest friend of mine know so much, and I will suffer any inconvenience, as I have, misery, danger, and decay of my fortunes, for your Excellencies sake. And so I rest,

28. April, 1622.

Your Excellencies most devoted, and faithful,
and thankful servant and Creature,
Wimbledon.

The

The Lord Wimbledon, to the Duke.

My gracious Lord,

I Understand, that it pleased the Lords to grant the Colonels leave to accuse me anew; and they have taken to them the most discontented Sea-men they could get, to help their malice forward. I had thought, that before my coming they should have had time and advantage sufficiently to have shewn all their envy: And I was perswaded, that they could not have defired more then to have been present when I should be examined, and my journal read. At the reading whereof they took all the exceptions that might be, and I did answer them all in your Excellencies presence, as I thought, fully; whereupon they seemed to be so content, as they had no more to say; neither did they, at that time, desire to make a journal, or to say any more.

Then the Lords resolutions were onely to hear the Sea-men speak, upon whom all the business did lie. If they may be suffered, upon new combinations, to bring new slanders upon me, I cannot tell what to think of it. But this I can say, that if this course be taken, his Majesty will never be without a mutinous Army, (which all States, in policy, do shun.) For when the Common Souldiers shall see their Chiefs give them such examples, they will soon follow; being that all Armies are subject to it, especially, a new Army. I had thought that one tryal had been sufficient, being it was before such an Assembly. But if I should be accused, I should desire to have new accusers, and not the same that have already accused me, (for so there would be no end;) and that, upon their Petition, I might have been heard what I could justly say, why they should not have leave to make a journal, and not to give them leave before I were heard. I am afraid, there was never any such president before; and what inconveniences may come of it, time will shew.

I have sought to none of the Lords, as I fear my enemies have done, (I know not whether I shall suffer for it, or no) but my trust hath onely been in your Excellency, and the justness of my Cause. I have been your Excellencies Officer in as difficult and as miserable an action as ever any one hath undertaken, and with as little assistance as ever any one had. For many of those that should have assisted me were more carefull in betraying me, then in forwarding his Majesties service: and if this course be held to encourage them, there is no man shall suffer more then his Majesties service will. For, it will be folly for any man to look to his Majesties service, or to take any pains to prevent or hinder that which may be committed against it, but to let every man do what he will; so all will be pleased; and he that commands shall have no man to slander him, which is the way to live in quiet.

Thus much, I thought, was fit for me to let your Excellency understand; and withal, that I held it a great unhappiness for me (that have taken such toil and pains, and suffered so many slanders) to be kept back by my enemies from that honour that never any one of my rank and place was hindered in, which is, from kissing the hand of my Sovereign Lord the King. All Power is in your Lordships hands, whether you will uphold me in my just cause, or no, or let me be ruinated for want of it: So that I can say no more, but that if I suffer, I shall be your Excellencies Martyr; if not, I shall all my life rest

Your Excellencies most humble, and most thankfull Servant and Creature,
Wimbledon.

Sir Francis Walsingham, *Secretary*, to *Monsieur* Critoy, *Secretary of* France.

SIR,

WHereas you desire to be advertised touching the proceedings here in Ecclesiastical Causes, because you seem to note in them some inconstancy and variation, as if we sometimes inclined to one side, sometimes to another; and as if that clemency and lenity were not used of late that was used in the beginning: all which you impute to your own superficial understanding of the affairs of this State; having, notwithstanding, her Majesties doing in singular reverence, as the real pledges which she hath given unto the world of her sincerity in Religion, and of her wisdom in Government, well meriteth. I am glad of this occasion to impart that little I know in that matter to you, both for your own satisfaction, and to the end you may make use thereof towards any that shall not be so modestly and so reasonably minded as you are. I find, therefore, her Majesties proceedings to have been grounded upon two principles.

1. The one, That Consciences are not to be forced, but to be won, and reduced, by the force of truth, with the aid of time, and the use of all good means of instruction and perswasion.

2. The

Sir Francis Walsingham Secr. to the Secr. of France.

2. The other, That the Causes of Conscience wherein they exceed their bounds, and grow to be matter of faction, lose their nature; and that Sovereign Princes ought distinctly to punish the practice in contempt, though coloured with the pretence of Conscience and Religion.

According to these principles, her Majesty at her coming to the Crown, utterly disliking the tyranny of *Rome* which had used by terrour and rigour to settle commandments of mens faiths and consciences, though as a Prince of great wisdome and magnanimity she suffered but the exercise of one Religion, yet her proceedings towards the Papists was with great lenity, expecting the good effects which time might work in them. And therefore her Majesty revived not the Laws made in the 28. and 35 year of her Fathers reign, whereby the Oath of Supremacy might have been offered at the Kings pleasure to any Subject though he kept his conscience never so modestly to himself; and the refusal to take the same oath without further circumstance was made Treason. But contrariwise, her Majesty not liking to make windows into mens hearts and secret thoughts, except the abundance of them did overflow into overt and express acts or affirmations, tempered her Laws so as it restraineth every manifest disobedience in impugning and impeaching advisedly and maliciously her Majesties supream power, maintaining and extolling a forreign jurisdiction. And as for the Oath, it was altered by her Majesty into a more grateful form, the hardness of the name and appellation of Supream Head was removed, and the penalty of the refusal thereof turned only into disablement to take any promotion, or to exercise any charge, and yet with liberty of being re-invested therein if any man should accept thereof during his life. But after, when *Pius Quintus* had excommunicated her Majesty, and the Bulls of Excommunication were published in *London*, whereby her Majesty was in a sort proscribed; and that thereupon, as upon a Principal motive or preparative, followed the Rebellion in the North: yet because the ill humors of the Realm were by that Rebellion partly purged, and that she feared at that time no forreign invasion, and much less the attempt of any within the Realm not backed by some potent succour from without, she contented her self to make a Law against that special case of bringing and publishing of any Bulls or the like Instruments, whereunto was added a prohibition upon pain not of treason, but of an inferior degree of punishment, against the bringing in of *Agnus Dei*, hallowed bread, and such other merchandise of *Rome*, as are well known not to be any essential part of the Romish Religion, but only to be used in practice as Love-tokens, to enchant the peoples affections from their allegiance to their natural Sovereign. In all other points her Majesty continued her former lenity: but when, about the 20. year of her reign, she had discovered in the King of *Spain* an intention to invade her Dominions, and that a principal point of the plot was to prepare a party within the Realm that might adhere to the Forreigner; and that the Seminaries began to blossome and to send forth daily Priests and professed men, who should by vow taken at Shrift reconcile her Subjects from their obedience, yea and bind many of them to attempt against her Majesties sacred person; and that by the poyson which they spread the humours of most Papists were altered, and that they were no more Papists in conscience and of softness, but Papists in faction, then were there new Laws made for the punishment of such as should submit themselves to such reconcilements or renunciations of obedience. And because it was treason carried in the clouds, and in wonderful secrecie, and came seldome to light, and that there was no pre-suspition thereof so great as the Recusants to come to Divine Service, because it was set down by their Decrees, that to come to Church before reconcilement was absolutely heretical and damnable: Therefore there were added Laws containing punishment pecuniary against such Recusants, not to enforce Conscience, but to enfeeble and impoverish the means of those of whom it resteth indifferent and ambiguous whether they were reconciled or no. And when notwithstanding all this provision this poyson was dispersed so secretly, as that there was no means to stay it, but by restrayning the Merchants that brought it in; then lastly there was added another Law, whereby such seditious Priests of new erection were exiled, and those that were at that time within the Land shipped over, and so commanded to keep hence upon pain of Treason.

This hath been the proceeding, though intermingled not only with sundry examples of her Majesties grace towards such as in her wisdom she knew to be Papists in conscience, and not in faction and singularity, but also with an ordinary mitigation towards the offenders in the highest degree committed by Law, if they would but protest that in case this Realm should be invaded with a forreign Army by the Popes authority for the Catholique cause, as they term it, they would take party with her Majesty, and not adhere to her Enemies. For the other part which have been offensive to this State, though in other degree, which named themselves Reformers, and we commonly call Puritans, this hath been the proceeding toward them a

great

great while: When they inveighed against such abuses in the Church, as Pluralities, Non-residence, and the like; their zeal was not condemned, only their violence was sometimes censured: When they refused the use of some Ceremonies and Rites as superstitious, they were tolerated with much conniuencie and gentlenesse, yea when they called in question the Superiority of Bishops, and pretended to bring a Democracy into the Church, yet their Propositions were heard, considered, and by contrary writings debated and discussed. Yet all this while it was perceived that their course was dangerous and very popular: As because Papistry was odious, therefore it was ever in their mouths, that they sought to purge the Church from the reliques of Popery, a thing acceptable to the people, who love ever to run from one extream to another. Because multitudes of Rogues, and poverty, were an eye-sore and dislike to every man; therefore they put it into the Peoples head, that if Discipline were plantive, there should be no Beggars nor Vagabonds; a thing very plausible. And in like manner they promise the people many other impossible wonders of their Discipline, Besides they opened the people a way to Government by their Consistory and Presbytery, a thing though in consequence no less prejudicial to the liberties of private men then to the Sovereignty of Princes, yet in the first shew very popular. Neverthelesse this (except it were in some few that entred into extream contempt) was borne with, because they pretended but in dutifull manner to make Propositions, and to leave it to the Providence of God, and the authority of the Magistrate. But now of late years, when there issued from them a Colony of those that affirmed the consent of the Magistrate was not to be attended; when under pretence of a Confession to avoid slanders and imputations, they combined themselves by Classes and Subscriptions; when they descended into that vile and base means of defacing the Government of the Church by ridiculous Pasquils; when they began to make any Subjects in doubt to take an Oath, which is one of the fundamental points of justice in this Land and in all places; when they began both to vaunt of their strength and number of their partizans and followers, and to use the communications that their Cause would prevail, though with uprore and violence; then it appeared to be no more zeal, no more conscience, but meer faction and division: And therefore though the State were compelled to hold somwhat a harder hand to restrain them then before, yet it was with as great moderation as the peace of the Church and State could permit. And therefore, to conclude, consider uprightly of these matters, and you shall see her Majesty is no Temporizer in Religion. It is not the successe abroad, nor the change of servants here at home, can alter her; only as the things themselves alter, so she applyed her religious wisdom to correspond unto them, still retaining the two rules before mentioned, in dealing tenderly with consciences, and yet in discovering Faction from Conscience. Farewell.

Your loving friend,

Francis Walsingham.

Dr. Williams, to the Duke.

My most noble Lord,

IT hath pleased God to call for the Bishop of *London*. I am so conscious of mine own weaknesse and undeservings, that, as I never was, so now I dare not be a suiter for so great a charge. But if his Majesty, by your Honors mediation, shall resolve to call me to perform him the best service I can in that place, I humbly beseech your Honour to admit me a suiter in these three circumstances.

First, that whereas my Lord of *London* hath survived our Lady day, and received all the profits, that should maintain a Bishop until *Michaelmass*, I may by his Majesties favour retain all my own means until the next day after Michaelmas day; this is a Petition which I shall be necessitated to make unto his Majesty (if his Majesty by your favour shall advance me to this place) and injureth no man else in the world.

Secondly, that whereas the Commissioners challenge from the Bishops revenues a matter of 200 l. *per annum*, (this Bishoprick being already very meanly endowed in regard of the continual charge, and exhaustments of the place) it would please his Majesty to leave in my hands (by way of *Commendam*) one Benefice of mine, which falls into his Majesties dispose upon my remove, until it be determined by the said Commissioners, whether any part of the Bishops means be due unto the Fabrique. My humble suit is for *Walgrave*, a Benefice with Cure in *Northhamptonshire*, where I have laid out all my estate in temporal Lands.

Lastly,

The Marquess Ynoiosa, to the Lord Conway.

Lastly, that if it be found, that the Bishop is to joyn with the Residentiaries of *Pauls* in the repair of the Church, his Majesty would qualifie me by a certain *salvo* to hold one of my own Prebends, when it shall fall to be a Residentiary also; that if I be charged with the burthen of Residentiary, I might enjoy the profits of a Residentiary.

These three requests do (I confess) adde unto me, but do not prejudice any one else whatsoever. I submit them and my self to your Honours wisdom, &c.

The names of such Ecclesiastical promotions as I now retain, and will fall to be disposed of by the King, if I should be removed.

1. Deanry of *Westminster*.
2. Rectory of *Dinam*.
3. Rectory of *Walgrave*.
4. Rectory of *Grafton*.
5. Rectory of *Peterborough*.
6. Chaunter of *Lincoln*.
7. Prebendary of *Asgarbie*.
8. Prebendary of *Nonnington*.
9. Residentiaries place of *Lincoln*.

The Marquess Ynoiosa, to the Lord Conway.

I Answered not long since to both your Letters, and now I will add this, that only the sport, and pleasure that *Don Carlos*, and I, consider his Majesty hath in his progress, may make tolerable the deferring (by reason of that) and not hearing the newes we expect to hear of his Majesties good health. For by that means we might not only satisfie more often our desire in this point (having his Majesty nearer) but also our desire to bring these businesses to an end, which are ordinarily more delayed, and less well executed, when they are to pass through the hands of Ministers (though they be very zealous, and well affected to it) as these Lords are with whom we treat here; who are desirous that the King should be known for just, though unnecessarily, when nothing is pretended contrary to that which is agreed upon. This knowledge whereupon I ground my reasons may perhaps make me (*Sin Embargo*) incurre the Censure of an impatient man; But I am perswaded, that if that which hath been done here had been setled there by your Honour, and the Lord Count of *Carleil* (whose good disposition and proceeding is as much to be esteemed as it is praised by *Don Carlos* and my self) we would have made an end, and those things, which I have seen and observed here, had not happened unto us. For in the conference, in which my Lord Keeper did assist, it was agreed (as we thought) that his Majesty should give order to the Judges and Justices of Peace, Arch-bishops and Bishops signed with his royal hand under the little Seale within three moneths, or at the Princess her arrival. He hath persisted afterwards, as also Sir *George Calvert*, in that (though it was plain) that his Majesty would give the said warrant, afterwards, there being no term nor day appointed. Neverthelesse, at last we have condescended, that it should be within six moneths, or at her Highness arrival, if she comes afore that time, that we may shew how happy we think our selves in being Servants to his Majesty, whom God save.

The dispatches that we are to have are contained in the relation here enclosed. I pray you to take order, that those that are to be sent back to that effect may be subscribed, and Sealed; for I have differred the dispatching of a Currier (with an evident danger that he will now arrive too late, and put in hazard a business of mine of consideration, which obligeth me to dispatch him) that he may not go without them; And that it may not be an occasion to doubt of the assurance we have given of his Majesties good will and intention; whose Royal hands, I, and *Don Carlos*, do intreat your Honour to kiss, in our name, and to continue us in his Majesties good Favour, and your Honour likewise in yours; for we deserve it with a particular affection, and equal desire to serve you. God save your Honour, as I desire.

Septemb. 5.
1623.

Your Honours ser vant,
The Marquess Ynoiosa.

Sir Henry Yelverton, to the Duke.

May it please your Grace,

MY humble heart and affection hath wrote many lines, and presented many Petitions to your Grace before this time, though none legible but one sent by my Lord *Rochford*, within five dayes after your most welcomed arrival from *Spain*.

I have learned the plain phrase of honest speech. My Lord, I have honoured your name long, and your own vertue much. I never found mis-fortune greater then this, that still failing after you in all humble desires of dutie, I was still cast behind you. I excuse nothing, wherein your Grace may judge me faultie, but will be glad to expiate my errours at any price.

Your noble heart (I hope) harbours no memory of what did then distaste you. Your own merits which have so much ennobled you will be the more compleat, if I may but merit your forgetfulness of wrongs past. If I seek your Grace before I deserve it, enable me, I beseech you, to Deserve, that I may seek. If any, on whom you have cast your eye most, endear himself more to your service then I shall, let me not follow the vintage at all. Till this day I feared the rellish of sowr Grapes, though I have sought you with many broken sleeps. But this Noble Earl, whose honour for this work shall ever with me be second to yours, hath revived me, with the assurance of your gracious pardon, and libertie to hope, I may be deemed your servant.

I protest to God, it is not the affluence of your honour makes me joy in it, nor the power of your Grace, that trains me on to seek it; but let the trial of your fortunes speak thus much for me, that I will follow you, not as *Cyrus* his Captains and Souldiers followed him, the one for spoil, the other for place: but if with safetie to your Grace, though with peril to my self, I may serve you, let me die if I do it not, rather then want any longer what my humble love ever led me to, and I still affect the honour

March 15.   *To be yours,*
1623.
                                        Henry Yelverton.

Sir Henry Yelvertons *submission in the* Star-chamber.

My Lords;

I Humbly beseech you to think that I stand not here either to out-face the Court, or to defend this cause otherwise then justly I may; only I desire in mine own person to second the submission which hath been opened by my Councel: for hitherunto hath nothing been opened unto you but that which hath passed under the advised pen of others, and hitherto hath appeared from my self neither open nor inward acknowledgement.

My Lords, it may seem strange to the hearers, that against a Bill so sharpned I should abruptly fall upon a submission or confession, whereby I may seem to bow down my neck to the stroke. But, my Lords, in this I weighed not my self, but I did it to amplifie the honour and mercy of his Majesty, from whom I may say Clemency springs as the blood that runs in his own veins. For, my Lords, when this Charter was sometime questioned, and divers of my Lords here present had out of their great wisdoms discovered that shame in it (which I must here confess I did not then see) and had related the same to his Majesty, it pleased his Majesty out of his great favour to me, his unworthy servant, to send me this message by two great honorable persons here present; and therefore, under your Lordships favour, I think not fit to hide so great a favour of his Majesty from the eyes of the people, who offered to my choice either to submit to himself in private, or defend here openly; and when I saw I fell into such faithful hands, I remember my answer then was, that the offer was gracious, and the choice was easie, and his mercy free. After came this Information against me: I took it but as trial whether I would make his Majesty King of my confidecce, or not: And though there was offered unto me and my Councel such a way of defence as I might have escaped, yet I protest I did reject it, because I would not distrust his Majesties mercy to let go the anchorhold I had thereof; and whatsoever becomes of me, I protest I shall still honour the King, though I go lame to my grave. I humbly confess the manifold errors of this Charter to your Lordships, wherein I have miscarried; and I beseech his Majesty and your Lordships to think they are rather crept in unawares, then usher'd in by consent. The errors are of divers natures, some of negligence, some of ignorance, some of misprision; I mistook many things, I was improvident in some things, too credulous in all things. But I who was chosen, when I had so much provoked his Majesty by mine unperienced years, and having since found so many favours from his Majesties hands, and this day having served him full seven years, who this day hath translated me from a low estate unto a place whereof I enjoy now only the name, and now since hath so much quickned and enlightned me by his gracious countenance,

nance, and assured me by his daily favours to make me to depend upon him; and that I should deliberately and determinately take any flowers from his Crown, to place them on the heads of others, or to betray his Majesties interest into the hands of others, I hope his Majesty will vouchsafe me so much favour not to value me at so low a rate, as to think these things came in *de industria*: For if I had felt any such Eccho arise in my breast, I protest I would have laid hands on my self, and judged my self unworthy of any society.

My Lords, the corruption of my hands is far inferior to the corruption of the heart; and the hand that runs wilfully into error works meerly from the corruption of the heart, and that makes it the more inexcusable; as the bleeding of a wound inwardly ever becomes mortal; and were I conscious to my self, I would not have any colour of excuse. I thank his Majesties Councel, that howsoever these hands were at first mistrusted, yet since they are not at all misdoubted, nor the least corruption laid to my charge. But this doth most grieve me, that my faithfulness to his Majesty should be suspected: And I humbly desire upon my knees, that his Clemency, in this case, may stop the issue of his Justice; that though a long time his face hath been hid, yet now at length his mercy will break through the clouds, to support me that am now fallen. I lay my self at his Majesties feet to do with me as it pleaseth him, and humbly desire his Majesty would take me to his own sentence. I never thought of my self otherwise then clay in his Majesties hands, to mould me to honour or dishonour. When I look and behold this solemnity and spectacle about me, I make no other account of it then *Pompa mortis*; and such a Prince as he is, knows that Life and Reputation are equal, if the last be not the greatest. I know your Lordships have such power, and his Majesty takes such pleasure in you, you are so dear in his eyes, that he can deny you nothing, and therefore I would desire you that you would be suiters in my behalf, that his favour might once again shine upon me. I know his grace and clemency sleepeth, if I be not unworthy to partake, and the rather because the River that did run another way is now turned into the Sea again, and the Charter given up, surrendred and cancelled. I know much life might be added to the sinewes of my happiness by your Lordships intercessions for me; in vouchsafing whereof I shall pledge a perpetuall assurance of better service for the time to come, and shall be bound and engaged to every one of your Lordships: so that my desire is, that his Majesty might first be acquainted with this submission, before you proceed into the merits of the cause, remaining still a prisoner to his Justice, knowing his Majesty may, if he please, turn me to vanity.

An Appendix

Of such Letters as by accident were omitted, and not placed in their due Order; Yet are referred to in the Table.

King James, to Pope Gregory the 15th.

James by the Grace of God, King of Great Britain, France and Ireland, Defender of the Faith, &c. To the most Holy Father Pope Gregory the 15th. Greeting, and all manner of Felicity.

Most Holy Father,

YOur Holiness will perhaps marvel, that we differing from you in point of Religion should now first salute you with our Letters. Howbeit, such is the trouble of our mind for these calamitous discords and bloodsheds, which for these late years by-past have so miserably rent the Christian World, and so great is our care, and daily sollicitude to stop the course of these growing evils betimes, so much as in us lies, as we could no longer abstain, considering that we all worship the same most blessed Trinity, nor hope for salvation by any other means, then by the blood and merits of our Lord and Saviour Christ Jesus; but breaking this silence to move your Holiness by these our Letters, friendly and seriously, that you would be pleased, together with us, to put your hand to so pious a work, and so worthy of a Christian Prince.

It is, truly, to be wished, and by all means to be endeavoured, that this mischief creep on no farther, but that these storms at the last ceasing, and the rancor being removed, by which they were at the first raised, the hearts of those Princes, whom it any way concerns, may be re-united in a firm and unchangeable friendship, and, as much as may be, knit together in stricter obligations then before, one unto another.

This we have alwaies had in our desires, and, to bring it to pass, have not hitherto spared any labour or pains, not doubting but your Holiness, out of your singular piety, and for the credit and authority that you have with the parties, both may and will further this work in an extraordinary manner. No way can any man better merit of the state of Christendom, which if it shall take the desired effect in your daies, and by your assistance, your Holiness shall worthily reap the glory and the reward due to so excellent a work.

That which remains for us further to say concerning this matter, this Gentleman, our Subject, *George Gage* will deliver unto you more at large. Praying your Holiness, that you will give him in all things full credence and belief, beseeching Almighty God from our heart to preserve you in safety, and to grant you all other happiness.

From our Palace at Hampton Court, the last of Septemb. 1622.

Sir John Eliot, to the Duke.

Right Honourable,

WIth what affection I have served your Grace, I desire rather it should be read in my actions, then my words, which made me sparing in my last relation to touch those difficulties wherewith my Letters have been checkt, that they might the more fully speak themselves. I shall not seek to gloss them now, but, as they have been, leave them to your Graces acceptance, which I presume so noble, that scandal or detraction cannot decline it. It were an injury of your worth, which I dare not attempt, to insinuate the opinion of any merit by false colours or pretences, or with hard circumstances to endear my labours, and might beget suspition, sooner then assurance in your credit, which I may not hazard. My innocence, I hope, needs not these; nor would I shadow the least errour under your protection. But where my services have been faithful, and not altogether

vain,

The Lord Cromwell, to the Duke.

vain, directed truly to the honour and benefit of your place, onely suffering upon the disadvantage of your absence, I must importune your Grace to support my weakness, that it may cause no prejudice of your rights and liberties, which I have studied to preserve, though with the loss of mine own. My insistance therein hath exposed me to a long imprisonment, and great charge, which still increaseth, and threatens the ruine of my poor fortunes, if they be not speedily prevented. For which, as my endeavours have been wholly yours, I most humbly crave your Graces favour both to my self, and them; In which I am devoted.

Novemb. 8. 1623.

Your Graces thrice-humble Servant,
J. Eliot.

The Lord Cromwell, to the Duke.

May it please your Grace.

I Am now returned from mine own home, and am here at *Fulham* neer Mr. *Burlemachi*, making my self ready to attend your Command in the best manner my poor fortunes will give me leave, and with what speed I may. Some things I have sent to *Plymouth*, and some Gentlemen, so as when I come there, I hope to find that your Lordship hath appointed me a good sailing Ship, and one that shall be able to play her part with the best and proudest enemy, that dare look danger in the face.

Though your Grace hath placed a Noble Gentleman in the Regiment was intended to my Lord of *Essex*, yet I will not despair of your favour, or that you will not give me some taste of it, as well as to any other. I will study to be a deserving Creature; and whether you will please to look on me with an affectionate eye, or no, I will love, honour, and serve you, with no less truth and faith then those you have most obliged. What concerns me I will not here speak of, for fear I offend. My prayers shall ever attend you, and my curses those that wish you worse then their own souls. Divers I do meet, that say your Grace hath parted with your place of the Mastership of the Horse, which makes the world suspect; that some disfavour your Lordship is growing into: And that this prime feather of yours being lost, or parted with (be it as it will) it will not be long ere the rest follow.

They offer to lay wagers, the Fleet goes not this year, and that of necessity shortly a Parliament must be; which when it comes, sure it will much discontent you. It is wondered at, that since the King did give such great gifts to the Duchess of *Chevereux*, and those that then went, how now a small sum in the Parliament should be called for at such an unseasonable time: And let the parliament sit when it will, begin they will where they ended. They say, the best Lords of the Councel knew nothing of Count *Mansfelts* journey, or this Fleet; which discontents even the best sort, if not all; They say, it is a very great burthen your Grace takes upon you, since none knows any thing but you. It is conceived, that not letting others bear part of the burthen you now bear, it may ruine you (which heaven forbid) Much discourse there is of your Lordship here and there, as I passed home and back, and nothing is more wondered at, then that one Grave man is not known to have your Ear, except, my good and Noble Lord *Conway*. All men say, if you go not with the Fleet, you will suffer in it, because, if it prosper, it will be thought no act of yours; and if it succeed ill, they say, it might have been better, had not you guided the King. They say, your undertakings in the Kingdom, and your Engagements for the Kingdom, will much prejudice your Grace.

And if God bless you not with goodness, as to accept kindly what in duty and love I here offer; questionless my freedom in letting you know the discourse of the world may much prejudice me. But if I must lose your favour, I had rather lose it for striving to do you good in letting you know the talk of the wicked world, then for any thing else, so much I heartily desire your prosperity, and to see you trample the ignorant multitude under foot.

All I have said is the discourse of the world, and when I am able to judge of your actions, I will freely tell your Lordship my mind. Which when it shall not be alwaies really inclined to serve you, may all noble thoughts forsake me. Because I seldom am honoured with your Ear, I thus make bold with your all-discerning eye, which I pray God may be inabled with power and strength, daily to see into them that desire your ruine. Which if it once be, I will never believe, but so good a King will constantly inable you daily with power to confound them.

Many

The Lord Conway, to the Earl of Bristol.

Many men would not be thus bold and saucy. If I find you distaste me for my respect to you, I will respect my poor self (who ever hath honoured you) so much, as hereafter to be silent. So I kiss the noble hands of your Grace.

Septemb. 8. 1625.

Your Lordships servant during life,
Tho. Cromwell.

The Lord Conway, to the Earl of Bristol.

My Lord,

I Received a Letter from your Lordship dated the 4th of this month, written in answer to a former which I directed to your Lordship by his Majesties Commandment. This last Letter (according to my duty) I have shewed unto his Majesty; who hath perused it, and hath commanded me to write back this unto you again. That he finds himself nothing satisfied therewith; the question propounded to your Lordship from his Majesty was plain and clear; Whether you did rather choose to sit still without being question'd for any errours past in your negotiation in *Spain*, and enjoy the benefit of the late gratious pardon granted in Parliament, whereof you may have the benefit; or whether, for the clearing of your innocency (whereof your self, your friends, and your followers are so confident) you will be contented to wave the advantage of that pardon, and put your self into a legal way of examination, for the tryal thereof? His Majesties purpose hereby is not to prevent you of any favours the Law hath given you: but if your assurance be such as your words and letter import, he conceiveth it stands not with that publick and resolute profession of your integrity, to decline your tryal. His Majesty leaves the choice to your self, and requires from you a direct answer, without Circumlocution, or bargaining with him for future favours before hand.

But if you have a desire to make use of that pardon which cannot be denyed to you, nor is it any way desired to be taken from you; His Majesty expects, that you should at least forbear to magnifie your service, and out of the opinion of your own innocency cast an aspersion upon his Majesties Justice, in not affording you that present fulness of liberty and favour which cannot be drawn from him but in his own good time, and according to his own good pleasure. Thus much I have in command to write unto your Lordship, and to require your answer cleerly and plainly by this Messenger sent on purpose for it. And so, &c.

March 21. 1625.

To King James, ab ignoto.

Most wise, and Glorious Prince,

BEcause the departure of your Majesty doth not permit me to hope for the honour of seeing you, and that the advertisements and orders which I have to communicate unto you, do merit your speedy review and magnanimous resolution, I have presumed to trust them unto this paper, which I do humbly desire may rest in the hands of your Majesty alone.

The Treaty of restoring all that had been taken by Sea (which by a motion from *Spain* was put into the hands of some Ministers in *Rome*) is accompanied with so little hope of obtaining the end that was pretended, that by reason of their continuing at *Naples* to dissipate and waste such goods as they had taken in our Ships, and the Cardinal *Borgias* reservedness to promise any thing, that negotiation may be held as vain, and as an insidious invention to gain time. Nevertheless, my Masters marching still with a constant desire of purchasing the publick tranquillity have been content to render all such vessels as they had taken within their Gulph, in hope that having gotten the advantage of the cause by this honest proceeding, they might prevail in the Address which they had made at *Naples*, for the restitution of their Galleasses, and of the Ship called *Rosse*.

But the actions and operations of the Spaniards do not answer unto what is desired and hoped. For in the Kingdom of *Sicilie*, *Naples*, and *Calabria*, they do muster new Souldiers, and they make great preparations for a war by the Sea. The subjects of those Kingdoms

doms are taxed with extraordinary Contributions of money, and in daily Counsels held by the Duke of *Ossuna*, the Marquess *Santa Croce*, and other ministers, they do consult of the means of making war, and doing hurt. But that which is most important is, that in the conjuncture, there is likewise in divers parts of *Spain* a terrible concourse of great provisions. For they have put in a readiness armour for 30000 men, they have ingrossed all the ammunition that could be purchased, and have put in good equipage 60 tall ships which being added unto those they have already in the Streights make 80, at *Naples* they have 20 ships more, besides all their own Gallies, and an order they have obtained for the Gallies of *Malta*, *Florence*, and the Pope, to joyn with them.

All the *Italian* Souldiers are quartered along the Coast of *Apulia*, which is opposite to our Gulph, and they have 14000 Foot, of *Walloons*, *French*, and *Spaniards*, lodged within the Kingdom of *Naples*. In *Flanders*, at this present, they make a new Leavy of 6000 Foot and a 1000 Horse. And in the state of *Millan*, they do retain still 3000 Horse supernumeraries. All which forces and provisions, as they do deserve for their greatness to be regarded, and looked upon with a jealous eye of every one; so those, who do suffer at the present many injuries and acts of hostility at the hands of the *Spaniard*, and in particular the State of *Venice*, which is betrayed by their fraudulent Treaties, cannot chuse but fear and doubt, more then any other. Neither can any pretences of enterprises or designs against the Turk secure those who see the sword bended against their breasts, and the fire kindled in their own houses.

Whereupon your Majesty is humbly desired, that you will be pleased to consider seriously of what hath been remonstrated, and to take such a resolution as may best befit your wisdom and greatness, and the safety and indemnity of a State so observant of your Majesty, as ours is, and of a member so important of the liberty of *Italy*, and of *Europe*. There is not at this day (Invincible Sir) any Prince in the whole world upon whom the Conservation of the publick tranquillity doth more rely then upon your Majesty. For there being none that doth equal your Majesty in wisdom and experience, possessing your Kingdoms in perfect peace, quietness, and plenty, to the infinite praise of your name, and being free from the mollestation of all storms and tempests, it seemeth that the eyes of all men are turned towards your Majesty as towards a Sun that ought to clear the Skie, and that they expect deliverance onely from your hand. These resolutions (oh most wise King) will be the strongest walls upon which your eternity can be reared. These will be the Jewels and the Crown, which will adorn you on earth, and in Heaven. These will be the immortal Glory of your powerful name.

The resolutions in cases of such weight and danger, ought to be magnanimous, quick, and powerful. The very noise of your putting in order your Royal Navy, the sending a person of quality to the place from whence the danger is feared, and the declaring your self in favour of those whom you shall find to have the right on their side, may perhaps prove sufficient to procure a peace. If words will not prevail deeds must follow, and such a resolution will prove the true Antidote to all their poysons. For the better effecting whereof, the world doth attend with great devotion to see a good correspondency renewed betwixt your Majesty and the French King; and for the disposing your Majesties heart thereunto, the State of *Venice* doth joyn her humble prayers unto the earnest intreaty of many others.

In the mean time, I am to request your Majesty, that you will be pleased to forbid the exportation of Artillery, Ships and Mariners, out of your Kingdoms for the service of the Spaniards, it being neither just nor agreeable to your Majesties Piety, that your Arms should be stayned with the blood of a State, and Prince, that hath no equal in love to your Royal Crown, and that will ever testifie to all the world, by effects of their observance, the pure and sincere devotion that they have to your Glorious Name. For my own particular, I humbly crave leave to kiss your Royal hands.

The King of Spain, to Pope Urban.

MOst Holy Father, I condescended that my forces should be imployed in the execution of *Mountferrat*, to divert the introduction of strangers into *Italy*, with so evident danger of Religion: I suffered the Siege of *Cassalle* to run on so slowly, to give time that by way of negotiation those differences might be composed with the reciprocal satisfaction of the parties interessed; and to shew in effect, what little reason all *Italy* had to be

jealous

The King of Spain, to Pope Urban.

jealous of the Arms of my Crown, for having possessed many places of importance; some I have freely given away, and others, after I had defended them in a time the owners had need, I presently restored with much liberality. Upon this moderation the Duke of Nevers, being hardned against the Emperour my Uncle, and he perhaps and other Princes calling thither the most Christian King, who not contenting himself to have attained that which he publickly professed to desire, and having left a Garrison in *Monjovet*, and in *Suse*, and as (I am told) having fortified some places, hath thereby given occasion to the Emperour my Uncle, to give order his Army should pass into *Italy*, to maintain the Authority, Jurisdiction and preheminency of the Empire, with whom I can do no less then concurre, and give him assistance, in respect of the great and strict obligation by blood, of Honour, and of Conveniency which I hold with his Imperial Majesty, and for the ——— which I do acknowledge from the sacred Empire; declaring now, as I have done heretofore, and as my Embassadours have told your Holiness, that in this business, I do neither directly nor indirectly aim at any other end of my own particular interest. But, beholding the numerous Armies of the Emperour in *Italy*, and with extreme grief foreseeing the harmes, inconveniences, and dangers that *Italy* must thereby suffer in matter of Religion, being that which most importeth; I do not onely resent it, in respect of that portion which God hath given me in Christendom, but especially as a King and Prince of *Italy*, the peace of those Provinces being disturbed, which my Progenitors with so much Judgement and Providence, and with so much Authority and benefit of the Natives had so many years preserved. Wherefore, I thought it my duty to present unto your Beatitude that experience hath demonstrated that to oppose and streighten the Jurisdiction of the Emperour, and to resist his commandments, hath brought matters to these difficult terms, and this way being still persisted in, there must needs follow those mischiefs which we desire to shun. Now the most convenient manner how to compose these businesses, is that your Holiness do effectually perswade the Duke of *Nevers* to accommodate himself to the Justice and obedience of the Emperour, and the King of *France* to recal his Armies out of *Italy*, and the Princes that do aid *Nevers*, no more to interest themselves in the business, even as from the beginning my Ministers have propounded to your Beatitude; because, this difference being ended juridically, all the persons interessed shall come off with honour and reputation, and so all of them shall have a ground to beseech the Emperour, that out of his wonted clemency, he will take off that impression which he justly might have conceived against the Duke of *Nevers*; whereupon things inclining to this issue, I shall with a very good will imploy my best offices, to the end that speedy and exact justice may be administred, and also that his *Cæsarean* Majesty may give experimental effects of his magnanimity and stability, desiring with a most sincere affection, that so much Christian blood may be spared as would be spilt in this war, and that those forces might be imployed to the service, and not to the prejudice of Christendom. Thus have I cleerly and sincerely delivered my meaning unto your Holiness, to the end that knowing my intention, you may do those offices which your manifold wisdom shall find proper for the place whereto God hath advanced you; and if God for our sins have decreed to chastise Christendom, by continuing the war, let this dispatch be a testimony of my good will, and real intention towards peace; for the prosecuting whereof, I on my part, will alwaies embrace any reasonable and proportionable means. Our Lord God preserve your Beatitude a thousand years.

Septemb. 21. 1629.

FINIS.

A TABLE

OF THE

Principal Matters Contained in this CABALA.

A.

ANNE *Bullen* Queen of *England*, sues to king *Henry* for an open *Trial*, alleadging many cogent reasons, and that her Enemies may not be her Accusers and Judges, protests her innocency, declares the cause of the Kings change, beggs the lives of her brother, and the other Gentlemen with passionate expressions. *pag.*1,2

Ashley Sir *Anthony* secretly gives Intelligence to the Duke of *Buckingham* of designs against him, and upon what grounds. 2

Aston Sir *Walter*, adviseth the Duke of *Buckingham* of the arrival of the Dispensation. 3.

Delivers a Memorial to the King of *Spain*, pressing a Restitution of the *Palatinate*, by command from the King his master 3, 4

Congratulates the Duke of *Buckingham* for his favours in Court, and acquaints him with important passages touching the intended marriage. 4

Informes Secretary *Conway* of the Report there of a Treaty of marriage with *France*, and *Olivarez* of the revocation of my Lord of *Bristol*, who offers him a blank signed by the King of *Spain*, bids him choose what was in his power, but he stoutly refuseth it: Preparations in *Spain* for war: Jewels left with the King of *Spain*, by the Prince, for the Infanta. 5,6

My Lord of *Bristols* return, *Don Carlos* made Vice-roy of *Portugal*. 7

Differences touching Merchants and Trades. 8

Violence offered to the Assistant of *Sevil*; and three Scotish Masters of Ships condemned to the Gallies, but an Appeal admitted. 9

Great discontents and preparations in *Spain*, a French man burnt for contempt to the Sacrament: A Procession solemnly performed for Expiation. 10

Sir *Walter Aston* prosecutes the Marquess of *Inoiosa*, in defence of the honour of *England*; but he is delivered from exemplary punishment by the power of *Olivarez*: He sues to return home. 10,11

To the Duke, how he was provoked to be an enemy to the match, but withal tels him, that he hath been a principal means for the compassing of it. (11,) (12)

The Dukes favour raised him many enemies, but he relies upon his own sincerity, and the Dukes goodness. *ibid.*

A memorial delivered by him to the King of *Spain*, touching a discovery made by his Embassadours, of a Conspiracy against the King, and the matter of it, but they refuse to discover their Conspirators; some of the Council of State examined about it, and found innocent; but the punishment and the reparation thereof left to the King of *Spain*. (13, (14)

Don Carlos Entry into *Madrid*, and the State and manner of it: Sir *Walter* refuses to see him, and the reason: The Duke of *Brandenbergh* assents to transfer the Electoral dignity upon the Duke of *Bavaria*. 11

Two matches propounded with the Infanta *Donna Maria*. 12

Jealousie touching the Invasion of *Ireland*, by reason of the Troops delivered to Count *Mansfelt*: The match with the Prince of *Spain*, and Madam *Christiene* the King of *France* his Sister: *Conde de Gondomar* commanded to return for *England*. 3

Anderson Edmond, craves the Duke *Buckingham* his favour for his assistance in some discontents. 14

B.

BAcon Sir *Francis*, after Lord *Verulam*, and Viscount Saint *Alban*, To the Lord Treasurer, touching the Sollicitors Place, Apologizeth with him about his speech in Parliament, concerning the Subsidy: That Variety is allowed in Council, as a discord in Musick to better it: Excuses his want of experience by some examples, and courts him to assistance. 17

Not as a man born under *Sol*, that loves honour, nor under *Jupiter*, that loveth business: place of any reasonable countenance commands more wits then a mans own. 18

Assures him that his endeavour shall not be in fault, if diligence can entitle him unto it, wishes to share his service with as good proof, as he can say it in good faith. 19

Bacon Anthony, with many excellent reasons, disswades the Earl of *Essex* (then in disfavour) from despair: The Earles quaint answer. 19, 20,21

H h h   *Bacon*

A Table of the Principal Matters.

Bacon Sir Francis, sues to the Earl of Salisbury to obtain the Sollicitors Place. 21
Perswades the Earl of Essex to take upon him the management of Irish affairs. 22
To him touching a Treaty with Tyrone. 23
Gives him excellent advice before his going into Ireland, touching the Deputyship. 23, 24, 25.
Assures his Lordship of all true effects and offices of his affection. 25
Caresses the Earl of Northumberland. ibid.
The Entrance of King James, a fair morning before the Sun rising: This State performed the part of good Attorneys, in delivering the King quiet Possession. 26
To Sir Robert Cecil, touching a way of reducing Ireland to civility, and the reasons for it. 26, 27
Excuses himself for his speech in Parliament, touching a Subsidy. 27
No reason the world should reject truth in Philosophy, although the Author dissents in Religion. 28
Advice to the King, touching his Revenue. ibid.
The Kings Attorneys place, and the value of it honestly: The Chancellors place usually conferred upon the Kings Council, and not upon a Judge: Reasons against the Lords Coke and Hubbart, and the Archbishop. 29
The body of Parliament men is Cardo rerum: Part of the Chancellors place is Regnum Judiciale, and since his Fathers time too much inlarged. ibid.
A Narration in several Letters of the differences between the Chancery and Kings Bench, and the grounds thereof Stated to the King. 33, 34, 35
The proceedings against Somerset, and divers private transactions touching that business. 33, 34, 35, 36, 37, 38, 53, &c.
His Advice to Sir George Villiers concerning Ireland, wherein three Propositions are acutely scanned. The first is touching the Recusant Magistrates of Towns there. 2. About reducing the number of the Council, from 50 to 20. 3. That a means may be found to re-enforce the Army by 500 or 1000 men, without increase of charge. 39, 40
From him to the Duke, when he first became a Favourite, with some directions for his demeanour in that Eminent Place, ranked into eight material heads, with an ample and quaint Gloss upon each of them, most elegantly penned. 40, 41, 42, &c.
Sir Francis Bacons considerations touching the Queens service in Ireland, divided into 4 points. 1. The extinguishing of the Reliques of War. 2. The recovery of the hearts of the people. 3. The removing of the root and occasions of new troubles. 4. Plantations and buildings, with an excellent amplification of all those particulars. (49.) (50.) &c.
To the Earl of Northumberland, upon the coming in of King James, together with some Character of him. (51)
A Discourse touching helps for the intellectual powers, in the mind and Spirit, and there again, not onely in his appetite and affection, but in his powers of wit and reason; an exquisite Philosophical Discourse. (52.) (53.) (54)
To the King, when he was in a lapsed condition, something in excuse of his faults, and imploring the Kings mercy. (55.) (55)
Again to him upon sending his Patent for Viscount Villiers, with several Advisors, and in cidently a censure of the Cecils, the Father and the Son. 55, 56
Sends the King a Certificate from the Lord Coke. 56
He is sorry for Mr. Mathews being seduced, advises him to continue within the bounds of Loyalty, and Piety to his Country, and tels him, that Superstition is far worse then Atheism. 56, 57
The Sollicitors Place not the thing it hath been, time having wrought an alteration therein, and in the profession. 57
Explains his meaning to the King touching the Duke of Buckingham. ibid.
Perswades the King to rectifie, and settle his Estate and means. 58
Being under a Cloud of troubles, Characterizeth himself to the King plainly and humbly, and denies the taking of Bribes, to pervert Justice. ibid.
Sends to the King an Essay of History of his Majesties time. 59
Desires the History of Britain may be written for three observations. 59, 60
Sixty four years of in age, and three years and five moneths in misery, desires neither Means, Place, nor employment; but a total remission of the Sentence of the Upper House, by the Example of Sir John Bennet. 60
To the King, touching the Plantation of Ireland, as formerly of the Union, as being brother thereunto. 61
To the Earl of Salisbury, touching his Book of Advancement of Learning, saying, he is but like a Bell-ringer, to awake better Spirits. ibid.
To the Lords, ingeniously confessing, and declining all Justification of himself, he faith there are vitia temporis, as well as vitia hominis. 61, 62
My Lord of Suffolk and his Lady Fined at 30000 li. with imprisonment, and Bingley at 2000 li. 63
Several Letters to Great Personages, in sending unto them his Book of Advancement of Learning, and the presenting of it to the King. ibid.
To Doctor Plaser touching the Translation of it into Latine, with many excellent reasons to that inducement. 64
To Sir Thomas Bodley, in sending the same Book, and a long and elaborate Answer from Sir Thomas upon that new Philosophy. 64, 65
To divers friends upon sending unto them some other of his Books. 68, 69
To Mr. Savil touching the Education of youth, and the improving the Intellectual powers. 69
A Factious Book, stiling the Queen Misera famina, the addition of the Popes Bull. 71
The business of the Commendams, and the carriage of the Judges therein related to the King. 72
Three examples of great Calamity, Demosthenes, Cicero, and Seneca: A Discourse concerning his own Books. 73, 74.
A Learned and ample Discourse, touching a Digest to be made of the Laws of England. 74, 75, 76
To the Earl of Devonshire, a Letter Apologetical touching a common fame, as if he had been false or ingratefull to the Earl of Essex, something long, but exquisitely penn'd. 77, 78, 79, 8., &c.

The

A Table of the Principal Matters.

The majesty of the Kings person is not inclosed for a few, nor appropriate to the great. 86

To the Earl of *Northumberland*, concerning the Expediency of a Proclamation before the Kings Entry. 87

To Sir *Edward Coke*, Expostulatory. 88

To him in disgrace, bitter, but wholsome. 88, 89, 90, &c.

To Sir *Vincent Skinner*, Expostulatory. 91

Importunate for Preferment. 92, 93

Bristol Earl to King *James*, touching the business of the Match, and the restitution of the *Palatinate*. The Popes demands about Religion, impossible to be agreed unto. The Spaniard ignorant thereof, Disclaimes the siege of *Heidelbergh*, if the Palatine will not conform, King *James* will declare against him, and for the Emperour. The King of *Spain* promises assistance to regain *Heidelbergh*; They premise the King satisfaction in the Match; which if not intended, they are falser then all the Devils in Hell. 95, 96

Protests his zeal for the Match, but the Treaty being ended, desires one of the Kings Ships may be sent to waft him over, having a great charge of the Princes with him. 97

Sues for reconciliation to the Duke, ill used by him, and therefore pitied by the *Spaniards*; a scandalous thing for Ministers of a Prince to differ in a strange Court. The Princes return Variance between the King of *Spain* his Ministers, and the Duke; They will rather put the *Infanta* headlong into a Well, then into his hands. 97, 98

Two millions the portion, and how paiable. 98, 99

The Prince greatly beloved in *Spain*; the Duke but little. 99

The Capitulations of the Marriage. 100, 101

Denied the Kings presence, desires to be heard, and to justifie himself. 101

Removed from his Offices, and denied to sit in Parliament as a Peer, accepts the Pardon of 21 *Jacobi*. 102

A Match propounded with the second Daughter of *Spain*, to stay the Treaty with *France*; and for other reasons; difference in Religion the maine obstacle. 102, 103, &c.

Where a Woman betrothed, *& post matrimonium ratum*, may before consummation become Religious; held by the King and the Prince the fittest match in the world, for her birth, portion, vertue, and her affection is to make the match out of zeale onely to the Princes service. 107, 108

Arch-bishop *Abbot* encourages a war in *Germany*. 108

The Arch-bishop to the Bishops, with King *James* his Letter touching directions for Preachers, and the directions themselves, with their limitations, and cautions at large. 109

The Bishops of *Rochester*, *Oxford*, and *St. Davids*, to the Duke, touching Mr. *Montague*, and in vindication of his Book. The King and the Bishops only Judges in a National Synod, for five reasons; and a sharp glance at the Synod of *Dort*. Mr. *Montagues* great learning. 111

The Bishop of *Winton* to his Arch deacon, in pursuance of the Kings Directions for Preachers above-mentioned. 112

The Bishop of *Lincoln*, Lord Keeper, to the Bishop of *London*, touching the abuse of Preaching then used, preferring Catechizing, with the reasons which induced the King to prescribe those Directions: The Doctrine is contained in the Articles of Religion, the two Books of Homilies, and the Catechismes. 112, 113

The Bishop of *Exceter*, to the House of Commons, a Letter of moderate Advice. 113

The Arch-bishop of *York* to King *James*, touching a Toleration of Religion, with free and strong reasons against it, something passionate. 114

The Bishop of *Lincoln* (then in displeasure) to the King. 114, 115

The Bishop of *St. Davids* to the Duke, desiring his name may be inserted in the High Commission, and the reasons. 115

The Bishop of *Landaff*, to the Duke, complaining of Injuries, and suing to be Removed to *Hereford*. 115, 116

The Bishop of *St. Davids*, to the Duke, upon his Return, congratulating him with joy for the birth of a son. 116

Doctor *Mountague*, Bishop of *Chichester*, to the Duke, touching his questioning in the House of Commons, undertakes to Answer what can be objected out of his Books; His three Challenges to the papists, with much confidence, 116, 117

A jolly and merry conceited Letter from the Bishop of *Landaff*, to the Duke, for a Remove, either to *Eli*, or *Bath* and *Wells*. 117, 118

From Monsieur *Bevoyr*, Chancellor of *France* discharged, to the French King, most elegantly penn'd, but with much tartness and plainness. 118

Balsac to the Cardinal *de la Valette*, Satyrical, deriding most Princes, and States. 119, 120

The same to King *Lewis*, in praise of his father, and of himself. 121

The Lord *Brooks* to the Duke, touching the marriage of the *Palgraves* eldest son with the Emperours youngest Daughter; a solid and political discourse. 121, 122

To his wife expostulatory. 123

Doctor *Balcanquel* to Secretary *Nanton*, giving an account of passages at the Synod of *Dort*. 123, 124

Monsieur *de Luines* advance by the death of Marshall *d' Anchre*, applyes himself wholly to the Kings person. 125

Complements between the Duke of *Buckingham*, Chancellor of *Cambridge*, and the Universitie. 125, 127

The Duke chides Sir *Walter Aston* for concurring with the Earl of *Bristoll*, for prefixing a day for the Deposorios, with restitution of the *Palatinate*, the portion, and temporal Articles. 127, 128

The Duke by the Protestants divulged a Papist; by the Papists avowed to be their greatest enemy: since his being at *Madrid*; better beloved of all: the King very reserved in the business of *Spain*, advises the Prince, and the Duke to return,' advises him, that the Lord of *Bristoll* had a great party in Court. 129

C.

Sir *Robert Cecil* to his father, meets with the President of *Rohan*, commends him much: The marriage of *Tremoville* with Count *Maurice* his Sister: Sir *Thomas Wilks* sick of a Lethargy. 133

Sir *William Cecil* to Sir *Henry Norris*, Ambassadour in *France*, about his entertainment there, being extraordinary, & what the reason should be:

A Table of the principal Matters.

be. *Shan Oneal* sues to be received into the Queens favour. 134
Taxes Monsieur *de Foix* for breach of promise, in not delivering *Lestrille*. The news of the death of the King of *Scots*, and the manner of it: Earl *Bothwell* suspected. 135, 136
Calice demanded to be restored to the Queen, according to the treaty of *Cambray*. More of the murther of the King of *Scots*; words which touched that Queen, but fit to be suppressed. 136
If *Calice* be not delivered, 500:0 *l.* is to be forfeited. Matters in *Flanders* go hard against the Protestants. 137
Those of the Order of *France* (if Life or Honour be touched) to be tried by the King, and others of the same Order. 137, 138
Marriage of the Queen of *Scots* to *Bothwell*; the prime Nobility against it. 138
The *French* Kings Letter touching *Calice* ill resented by the Queen. The Queen of *Scots* married the 15th of *May*. 138, 139
Bothwell prosecuted for the murther, defended by the Queen and the *Hamiltons*: the Queen under restraint. *Shan Oneal* slain in *Ireland*, by certain *Scots*. 139
Sir *Nicholas Throckmorton* sent into *Scotland*, to negotiate a pacification: the two Factions of the *Hamiltons*, and *Lenox*'s. 139
The Prince of *Scotland* crowned at *Sterling*, the 29. of *July*. 140
Queen *Elizabeth* offended at the *Scotch* Lords: *Murray* like to be made Regent. Advice to Sir *Henry Norris*, touching his expences. 140, 141
Murray made Regent. My Lord of *Sussex* with the Emperor. All Judges, Officers, &c. at *Antwerp*, compelled to attest the Catholick Faith. 141
Bothwell reported to be taken at sea. 142
Dunbar rendred to the Regent, the Keeper adjudged to a new punishment. 142
Expectation of Marriage between the Queen and the Archduke *Charles*. 143
Troubles in *France*, between the Prince of *Conde* and the King. 143, 144
The Queen of *Scots* noted by the Parliament there to be privy to the murther of her Husband. 144
The Earl of *Desmond*, and his Brother, in the Tower. 145
Fishermen of *Diepe* taken at *Rye* with unlawfull Nets. 145
The Popes Ministers prefer the State of their corrupt Church before the weal of any Kingdom. 146
The Earl of *Sussex* his return: the Prince of *Orange* his Son to be sent into *Spain*, and doubted *Edmond* and *Horn* must follow. ibid.
Emanuel Tremelius sent into *England* by the Elector Palatine: the Prince of *Orange* refuseth to be judged by the Duke of *Alva*: the *Hamiltons* continue their Faction: the death of Sir *Ambrose Cave*. 147
Beaton sent from *Scotland* into *France* for 1000 Harquebusiers, Money, and Ordnance. 148
Devilish practice against the Queen: the Queen of *Scots* removed to *Bolton* Castle; her demands of the Queen denied. 149
The Queen of *Scots* submits her Cause to be heard and determined in *England*. 149, 150
Honourably used by the Queen. 150
The Duke of *Norfolk*, the Earl of *Sussex*, and Sir *Walter Mildmay*, Commissioners touching the treaty betwixt the Queen of *Scots* and her Subjects. 151
The Queen of *Scots* makes *Argyle* and *Huntley*

Lieutenants, and the Duke of *Chastilherault* over all; they raise Forces against the Regent, but are routed. 152
A couragious Answer from Queen *Elizabeth* to the *French* Embassador, and the Audience put off. 152
She sends a Ring to Marshal *Montmorancies* Wife. 153
The Bishop of *Rhemes*, Embassador from *France*, is offended, that the Doctrine of *Rome* is said to be contrary to Christs, deducing, consequently, that his Master should be reputed no Christian; and how that speech was salved. 153
The Cardinal *Chastillons* Wife comes over. 154
The reason of the Cardinals coming into *England*: Ships sent by the Queen to preserve the *Burdeaux* Fleet; the Queen of *Scots* case not defensible, and the consequence thereof. 154
Matters about the Queen of *Scots*. *Chastillon* highly commended. 155
The Cause of the Queen of *Scots* to be heard here. 155
Passages touching the differences between the King and the Prince of *Conde*. 156
Matters against the Queen of *Scots* very bad. ibid.
Sir *Henry Norris* claims the Lord *Dacres* lands. 157
Three manner of ways proposed for ending the *Scotish* differences. 157
Spanish treasure stayed. ibid.
The Parliament of *Scotland* declared the Queen of *Scots* privy to the murther of her Husband. 158
D'Assonleville comes over without commission, and desired conference with the *Spanish* Embassador, but denied. 158, 159
Hawkins his return to *Mounts bay*, from the *Indies*, with treasure: the Queen of *Scots* at *Tetbury*, under the charge of the Earl of *Shrewsbury*. 159
The *French* Embassadors Courrier searched, and the reason of it. ibid.
The *English* Embassador complains of two discourtesies offered unto him: the Queen refuseth to give Monsieur *D'Assonleville* audience, but permits him conference with the Councel, and denies him restitution of the *Spanish* money. 160
The *French* Embassador disperseth news of *Montgomery's* overthrow, and the rest of that party. 161
The Prince of *Conde* slain; the *English* Embassador evilly entreated; the 13th. of *March* had two great effects. 161
The differences in *Scotland* accorded, but not observed. 162
Sir *William Cecil* laments the misfortune of *France*: means made to accord with the *Low Countreys*: *Scotish* Nobility reconciled. 163
Original Letters intercepted by persons of credit in the *French* Court, of advertisement, concerning the Queen of *Scots*, and Duke of *Anjou*. 163
That the said Queen should transfer her title on the said Duke; to learn more truth hereof, and advertise with speed: the Queens Ships far excel others. ibid.
The Queen of *Scots* excuseth her transaction with the Duke of *Anjou*. 164
A Rebellion in the west part of *Ireland*, and the *Spaniards* aid feared. 164
My Lord of *Shrewsbury* stricken with a Palsie, and Phrensie. 165
The *Parisians* execute two Merchants whom the King had pardoned: the *English* Embassador taxed for dealing with the Kings Rebels. 165
The Earl of *Desmond's* great Rebellion in *Ireland*, but dispersed. 166
An *Italian* sent hither upon a devilish attempt:

A Table of the Principal Matters.

an infurrection in *Suffolk*, Queen *Elizabeth* defires to be rid of the Queen of *Scots*. 157
The Queen offended with the Duke of *Norfolk* about his marriage, Sir *William Cecil* his good fcient therein, my Lords of *Arundel* and *Pembroke* confined to their lodgings about it, and fo is my Lord *Lumley*; my Lord of *Huntington* joyned with the Earl of *Shrewsbury* in the cuftody of the *Scots* Queen. 68
The Duke of *Norfolk*, *Arundel*, and *Lumley*, in cuftody, the Duke takes all in good part. 169
The grand Rebellion in the North, and the pretences thereof, and their numbers, and names. 169, 170
A report of the death of the Count *Naffau*, the Northern Rebellion fcattered, and their Ringleaders fled. 170
The two Rebellious Earls in *Liddefdale*, but flye from thence: The Countefs of *Northumberland* and her attendants robbed in *Scotland*, the Earls flye with about fifty horfe; *Weftmerland* changes his Coat of Plate and Sword, and travails like a Scotifh Borderer: Many others taken: The Regent of *Scotland* takes the Earl of *Northumberland* and others; the Lords *Fernhurft* and *Bucklugh*, aiders of them. 171
The murder of the Regent of *Scotland* at *Lithgo*, by *Hambleton* of *Bothwell-Hall*: The Earl of *Suffex* his wife and noble carriage: The *Hambletons* ftrongly fufpected for the murder, and why. 172
The French Embaffadour makes three demands to the Queen, in behalf of the Queen of *Scots*: Sir *William Cecil* names to the Queen Mr. *Francis Walfingham*, and Mr. *Henry Killigrew*, to fucceed Sir *Henry Norris* in *France*. 173
The Earl of *Suffex* goes again into *Scotland*: The Bifhop of *Roffe* writes a Book in defence of the Queen of *Scots*, and dangerous againft Queen *Elizabeth*: The Earls of *Worcefter* and *Huntington* made Knights of the Order: The Earl of *Suffex* and the Lord *Hunfdon* enter *Scotland* with fire and fword, 50 Caftles, and 300 Villages burnt. 174, 175
My Lord of *Suffex* commands the Frontiers; the Bifhop of *Roffe* deals treacheroufly with the Queen; Sir *Henry Norris* to be revoked, and Mr. *Walfingham* to go into his place. 177
The Marfhal of *Berwick* betrayed by the Bifhop of St. *Andrews* and other Lords, who under colour of Treaty with him intended to have flain him; he deftroyes the *Hambletons* Caftles, and Houfes. 177, 178
The Earl of *Southampton* for compliance with the Bifhop of *Rofs* is committed clofe prifoner to the Sheriff of *London*; the fond Lord *Morley* withdraws to *Loain*. 178
The French King mediates for the Queen of *Scots*, the Queen keeps fome Caftles in *Scotland*, until her fubjects of *England* fhould have fatisfaction. ibid.
Sir *William Cecil* and Sir *Walter Mildmay* are fent Commiffioners to the Scotch Queen. 179
Sir *Edward Cecil* complains to Secretary *Conway* of the States, and the fupplying of them with forces, conftrained to buy ten pieces of Ordnance. ibid.
Many called Souldiers, but few that are fo, the knowledge of war being the higheft of humane things. 180
Sir *Edward Cecil* congratulates the Duke for his favours; is offended that Sir *Horatio Vere* is to be made a Baron; fues to the Duke to be made General. 181, 182

Wittily but fcoffingly defcribes the fituation of the *Low Countries*, and the inconveniencies of his long fervice there. 182
Propofitions made by Sir *Dudley Carleton* to the States, touching the reftitution of the Towns in *Cleave* and *Juliers*, much conference between him and *Barnevelt*: The French King incens'd againft the Duke of *Bouillon*: A rumour of marrying the Prince with *Spain*, the Remora of his chief affairs with the States, the contra Remonftrants have leave to Preach in the Englifh Churches and others: The Kings Letter or Meffage defired againft the Novelifts, and their opinions. 183, 184, 185
Moves the Duke of *Buckingham* for the return of Sir *John Ogle* into *England*; a rancor between Sir *Horatio Vere* and Sir *Edward Cecil*, and the extent of their Commands: The Princes of *Orange* and *Conde* at variance, paffages about the renewing the Truce between the Spaniards and the States, whether the old one be confirmed, or a new one be eftablifhed. 185, 187
The Siege of *Oftend*, and feveral old Englifh Commanders flain, Count *Mansfield* his advance towards *Breda*, and recommendation of the Queen of *Bohemia*. 187, 188
The Lord of *Buckleugh* his pretentions to the States, Colonel *Brague* his Regiment given unto him for his pretentions: The Emperours violent proceedings againft the Elector Palatine; The Army of *Mansfelt* and *Brunfwick*, and their condition and hopes: The Jugling of the Spaniard with the Emperour, to abufe King *James*. 189, 190
A long conference between Sir *Dudley Carleton* and the Prince of *Orange* concerning the States, and their demeanour towards the King. 190, 191
Propofitions made to the King and Queen of *Bohemia*: The upper Palatinate and Electorate given to the Duke of *Bavaria*, and the lower to the Elector of *Mentz*: *Gabor* in Arms againft the Emperour: the King of *France* and *Sweden* Godfathers to the *Palfegraves* Son. 192, 193
The Hollanders Maxime, that *Spain* will never Match with our King for love, but either for hope or fear; and the reafons of it. 194
Captain *Giffords* Plot to take a Galeon of Treafure coming from *Nova Spagna* to *Havana*, and the manner of it: Letters of Mart againft the Spaniard in the name of the King and Queen of *Bohemia*. 195
Fair overtures of a Reftitution of the Palatinate; but a well armed Treaty neceffary. 196
Sir *Dudley Carleton* gives the Duke two grand Advertifements in matter of Action. 197
That friendfhip is ftrongeft, when Intereft is moft conjoined. 198
Agreed by Articles, that in no cafe but that of Scandal, Englifh Subjects ought to be troubled in *Spain* for their Confciences. 199
A High and violent complaint by Sir *Charles Cornwallis* to the Spanifh King, touching the Viceroy of *Sardinia* for fome outrages. 199, 200
A bitter Invective againft Englifh and Irifh fugitives into *Spain*. 199, 200, 201
A large Enumeration of oppreffions of Englifh Subjects in *Spain*, a redrefs fharply importuned by Sir *Charles Cornwallis* Embaffadour there in that behalf. 201, 202, 203
Briftol, Earl, reprehended by King *Charles* for giving the Spaniards hopes of his inclination to a change in Religion, for his demeanor in the bufinefs of the match, and undervaluing the Kingdom of *England*; Approves the Education

Hhh 3

A Table of the principal Matters.

of the Prince Palsgrave in the Emperors Court, which King *Charles* takes ill. 203
King *Charles* his Letter to the University of *Cambridge*, in approbation of their election of the Duke Chancellor. 203
The Universities Answer of Thanks to King *Charles*. 257
Instructions by the King, to the Vice-Chancellor, &c. for Government, &c. 204
To the Lords Spiritual and Temporal, in vindication of his prerogative, touching the committing of offenders against the State and Government ibid
To the University of *Cambridge*, for electing the Earl of *Holland* their Chancellor. 205
Commissioners, and their names, for delivering up *Flushing*, *Brill*, &c. 206,207
The Council of *Ireland* to the King, in defence of the Lord Deputy *Faulkland*; with an ample relation of his prudent demeanor in that great employment. 208,209
An Order at the Councel-Table, 10 *Mart*.1629. against hearing Mass at Embassadors houses, prisons, or other places. 210,211
Discourses of State between the *Spanish* Embassadors, and Sir *Arthur Chichester*, enclosed in a Letter to the Duke of *Buckingham*. 211,212
Earl of *Carlisle* advises the King of three things which trouble the people: three ways of redress propounded by him. 212,214
Popish Lords disarmed, by occasion whereof the Lord *Vaux* was committed to the Fleet, Sir *Thomas Gerrard* accused of treachery against the Kings person. 214
The *Infanta* sues to the King on her knees for the restitution of the *Palatinate*. 216
The Lord *Coke* to King *James*, touching the trial of Duels out of *England*, upon the Act of 1 H. 4. *cap*. 14. upon Sir *Francis Drake*'s putting to death *Dowrie* beyond the seas. 216
The terrour and mischiefs done by *Turkish* Pyrates in the Ocean, and Mediterranean: they lie in wait for the East *Indian* Fleet. 217
Sir *James Mackonel* escapes out of *Edenburgh*, and flies into *Spain* for his Religion, and refuge. 218
The sum of 130000 *l*. raised by Fines in the Star-Chamber. 219
Don *Carlos* to the Lord *Conway*, in excuse of the King of *Spain*, and the *Infanta*, their visiting the Duke of *Bavaria*; perswades the Palsgraves submission, and to renounce amity with the Rebels of the King of *Spain*, and House of *Austria*. 220
Papists orthodox in point of Allegiance, and the Puritans onely Recusants. ibid.
Carr Earl of *Somerset* sues to King *James* for Pardon and Estate, 221

D.

The Earl of *Desmond* to the Earl of *Ormond*, in acknowledgment of his folly, with promise of future loyalty to the Queen. 223
Sir *Kenhelm Digby* to Sir *Edward Stradling*, a Philosophical Analysis upon the 22*th*. Staff of the 9*th*. Canto in the second Book of *Spencer's Fairy-Queen*, replenished with variety of profound learning. 223,224,&c.
Doctor *Donne* congratulates the Duke, for having the love of King, Prince, Kingdom, and Church; Gods Privy Seal is the testimony of a good Conscience, and his Broad Seal the outward Blessings of this life. 228
A blasphemous Defiance sent by *Solyman* the *Turk* to *Maximilian* the second. 229

E.

Queen *Elizabeth* comforts the Lady *Norris* after the death of her Son. 229
Essex intercedes to *James* King of *Scotland*, for secretary *Davison*, then in disgrace. 230
Comforts him with excellent counsel, and hopeth to obtain restitution to the Queens favour. 232
Apologizeth for him to the Queen elegantly and pathetically. 232,233
The Lord Chancellor *Egerton's* Letter to the Earl of *Essex*, in eight grave and plain Avisoes. 234
And the Earls particular Answer. 234,235
The Lord Chancellor to King *James*, suing to be discharged of his place, for several Reasons Divine and Humane, and his great age and infirmities. 235,236

F.

The Emperor *Ferdinand* to Don *Balthazar de Zuniga*, touching the translation of the Electorship to the Duke of *Bavaria*, and divers grand Reasons of State for it. 237
The Lord *Faulklands* Petition to the King, in behalf of his rebellious Son. 238
A Declaration of *Ferdinand*, Infanta of *Spain*, principally against *France*, for the preservation of the Catholick Religion, pacification of Europe, relief of the oppressed, and restitution of right to others. 239

G.

Mr. *Gargrave* to the Lord *Davers* expostulatory, and bitter. 240
To *Gondemar*, concerning the death of *Philip* third; the manner of it, and ceremonies then used. 240,241
To him, concerning the Match with *Spain*; ample, but rarely penn'd. 242,243

H.

King *Henry* the Eighth to the Clergy of the Province of *York*, touching his Title of *Supreme Head of the Church*; with many cogent, but mystical Reasons for it. 244,245,&c.
Sir *John Hipsley* to the Duke, of cautionary advice touching the differences between him and the Earl of *Bristol*. 248,249
The Lord *Herbert* advertises the King of the judgment of the most intelligent people touching the Match with *Spain*, in three Propositions. 249
The Earl of *Holland* to the King, touching the complaints of the affronts offered unto *Blanville*, the *French* Embassadour, and his malice and plots against the Duke. 250,251
Informs the Duke, that the Match with *France* is concluded. 251
The Queen Mother of *France* offended at the Duke. 252
Advises the Duke secretly, but doubtfully, touching his coming into *France*. 253
Congratulates the University of *Cambridge*, for his election of Chancellor. 254
The Lady *Howard*, to the King, in the behalf of my Lord

A Table of the principal Matters.

Lord of Suffolk, prisoner in the Tower. 254
The History of the Reign of King Henry 8. King Edward 6. Queen Mary, and part of the Reign of Queen Elizabeth; a well polished Discourse, but left imperfect, 254,255

I.

A Letter of King James, congratulatory, to the City of London, after he was proclaimed. 257
The Kings Letter to the University of Cambridge, upon their desire to be made a City. 257
From the King to the Lords, touching the abatement of his Majesties Houshold charge. 258
King James advertiseth the Earl of Bristol, touching the dishonour and abuses offered in the Palatinate; commands him to acquaint the King of Spain, that he expects restitution, and cessation of Arms, and assistance from him against the Emperor, or passage for his Forces through his Dominions. 259
King James to the Emperor, desiring the restitution of the Palatinate and Electorship, for which six Propositions are offered; and the Emperors Answer thereunto. 260,261
The custody of the little Park at Windsor is annexed to the office of the Usher of the Knights of the Garter. 262
The King to the Earl of Bristol, to return thanks to the King of Spain, for the King, for the Prince's entertainment; and to declare himself fully, touching the restitution of the Palatinate. And the Earl of Bristol returns his Answer to the King. 264
Instructions from the King to the Archbishop of Canterbury, to be observed by Bishops respectively, 1622. 265
The King to the Palsgrave, touching his restitution, and upon what terms, denies the Palsgrave's Son to be bred in the Emperors Court. 266
The Palsgrave's Answer to every particular at large; very elaborate. 267,268
The Elector of Mentz, and other Popish Princes, are earnest with the Electors of Saxony and Brandenburgh, to acknowledge the Duke of Bavaria as an Elector of the Empire. 270
The King to my Lord Bacon, in commendation of his Organon. ibid.
The King totally pardons my Lord Bacon. ibid.
The Spaniard sensible of his oversight, in suffering the Prince to go away without his Infanta, and the reasons. Unkindness between the Duke and Olivarez, and also between the Duke and Bristol, who is much favoured of that King and Olivarez. 270,271.
A League offensive and defensive, by the French, and other Nations, against the Spaniard: the Pope against the Spaniard in Italy; the loss of the Spaniards Silver-Fleet. 271
The calamitous condition of Rochel, after the surrender, fully and particularly expressed. 272,273
To the King, secret advice, either to assist the Palatine, or to extinguish those of the Religion in France. 273
To the King, touching the insolency of the Duke: the Puritans work for the Palatine, whose Spy Mansfelt is. 274,275
More aggravations against the Duke. 275
The Duke and his demeanor defended; an elaborate discourse. 277,278
A Letter from the King to the Lord Keeper, and divers others, touching my Lord of Canterbury's killing the Keeper of Bramzil Park, and their opinions therein. 279
The Justices of Devon, to the Lords of the Councel, touching an advance of Moneys. Instructions for the Ministers and Church-wardens of London, particularly therein mentioned. 280

K.

THe Lord Keeper to the Duke, in maintenance of the Liberties of Westminster. 283
Touching the Earl of Southampton, and his confinement. Doctor Lamb commended, and employed to reform the Puritans. 284
His opinion touching my Lord of Canterbury, and of my Lord of Canterburies accident. 284
More concerning the Earl of Southampton, and of mercy to be shewed to him. Touching the Earl Marshals place, in five particular questions; and about the sealing of the Patent, and the extent thereof. 285,286
Opposeth my Lord Bacon's Pardon, as it is drawn. 287
The reasons thereof. 287,288
Touching the priviledges of the House of Commons, and their obstinacy. 288,289
Denies to seal Mr. Murray's Dispensation for the Provostship of Eaton, in regard he was a Layman, and that Cure of Souls belongs thereunto: and that Savile was admitted onely Ad curam & regimen Collegii; and for several other weighty Reasons there urged. 289, 290
Passages of State between the Lord Keeper and Don Francisco, where, amongst other things, the Duke is censured. 290
Touching Sir John Michel, and his clamour. 291
To the Duke, touching the business of Original Writs. 291
Much scandalized by the Lord Treasurer, but vindicates himself. 292
Expostulations between them, by way of Objection and Answer. 292,293
Touching favour and liberty shewed to some Papists, and the Reasons. 294,295,297
In some disgrace, upon frivolous surmizes. 295
Thinketh it not fit to limit the King in dispensing his favours, without the advice of the Councel-Table. 295
Doctor Bishop, the new Bishop of Chalcedon, his coming to London, and his Keepers design how to proceed against him. Excuseth himself to the Duke, in several high matters. 299
The Heads of that Discourse which fell from Don Francisco, the 7th. of Decemb. 1624. wherein the Duke is much concern'd, as aiming at too much Popularity. 300,301
The Lord Keeper to the Duke, concerning Sir Richard Weston, and his Patent. 301
To the Duke, in behalf of the Countess Dowager of Southampton. 304
To the Duke, in opposition of advancing Doctor Scot to the Deanry of York. 304,305
The death of the Lord Steward, advising it may be discontinued, or that his Grace will accept thereof, for divers Reasons. 305,306
To the Duke, concerning Sir Robert Howard, and his obstinacy in the matter of incontinency with the Lady Purbeck. 306,307
More matter touching Recusants. 307
More touching the Princess Marriage 308
The English Liturgy translated into Spanish by a Dominican,

A Table of the Principal Matters.

Dominican, who is secured to our Church with a benefice and a good Prebend, and the book sent into Spain. 309

Promised a better Bishoprick, when he was made Lord Keeper, all his places amounting not to above 1000 l. per annum. 309

Prepares for his service at the Coronation, and begs of the Duke to kiss the Kings hand. 310

The Lord Kensington, to the Duke, of overtures of a marriage with France, if that of Spain abandoned; Jealousie touching the King of Spain to be Monarch of Christendome, a league thought fit to be first concluded with France. 311, 312

The Queen-mother earnest in the match, high commendations of Madame. ibid.

Madame obtains wittily from my Lord of Kensington a sight of the Princes Picture; the power of Spain feared. 313

That Match opposed by the Spanish Embassadour. 314

My Lords of Carlile, and Kensington, entertained more magnificently then any Embassadors formerly: The Count of Soissons storms at my Lord Kersington's negotiation. 314

But is after reconciled. A Commission from the King of Bohemia, to sollicite the French King, for the recovering of his inheritance, and a reimbursement of moneys lent by his Father Henthe 4.th. Cardinal Richlieu made of the Cabinet Councel. 317

More Conference about the Match. 318

The necessity of joyning Alliance with France, considering the growing power of Spain. 320

Presseth in the Match. ibid.

Monsieur de Blanville sent Embassadour extraordinary into England, as a subtile spye, whereof the Duke de Chevereux gives a Caveat. 320, 321

The business of the Match remitted to the Kings pleasure, only not to attempt the Queens conscience: Blanville plots against the Duke, who is accused for the Proclamation against the Catholicks. Arundel and Pembroke combine against the Duke. 321

L.

Lorkin advises the Duke to be circumspect. 321, 322

Sedition at Dublin by Friars, and their adherents, Directions from the Councel here, to the Councel there, for the future: suspicious houses there to be made houses of Correction; the Founders Lands, and persons professed, to be discovered, and punished. 322, 323

M.

Sir Robert Mansell signifies to the Duke divers passages of service at Algier. 324

Sir Thomas Button sues to be Vice-Admiral in the Algier Fleet, but Sir Richard Hawkins preferred Sir Thomas much commended. 325

Padre Maestre earnest at Rome, for the Match with Spain. 325

Magdibeg complains to the King against Sir Robert Shirley, for reporting that he had married the King of Persia's Niece. 326

The Earl of Middlesex questioned, and sues for longer time to examine Witnesses. 327

Thanks the Duke, for the Seff. ibid.

The Queen her coming over, extreamly commended by Sir Toby Mathew. 318

Sir Toby perswades the King of Spain, with strong reasons, to comply with the Prince in the March. 329

Mountjoy counsels the Earl of Essex to patience. 330

The Duke of Medena acquaints the Duke of Savoy of his becoming a Capuchin. ibid.

N.

The Duke of Norfolk Prisoner, beggs pardon of the Queen, with a total submission. 331

Sir Francis Norris, to the King in defence, or rather excuse of his quarrel with the Lord Willoughby. ibid.

The Countess of Nottingham inveighs against the King of Denmark for words. 332

Jubilees. ibid.

The Lady Elizabeth Norris to the Duke, in excuse of her Marriage with Mr. Wray. 333

O.

Sir John Ogle to the Duke, mediating for pardon, for faults against the King. 333, 334

The Earl of Oxford to the Duke, something expostulatory, and yet submissive. 334, 335

An Order at White hall, for the University of Cambridge, against the Burgers. 335

P.

Sir John Perrots Commission, (and the Contents thereof) for Deputy of Ireland, a warrant to the Lords there to swear him, and deliver the sword, and for his entertainment; Instructions from the Queen unto him. 335, 336, 337

Writes to the Lords of the Councel of an Invasion from Spain, and of the want of strength in Munster, and other places, and divers Military Officers there weak and old. 337, 338

A most ingenious, and effectual Petition of Francis Philips to the King, for the release of his Brother Sir Robert Philips Prisoner in the Tower. 338, 339

When prudent men act their own parts, they are seldom of the cleerest sight, but subject to many and plain errors. Sir Robert Philips his Proposals to the Duke touching the Earl of Bristol, and the differences between them. 341

The King of Spain reveals to Olivarez, that the Match of the Infanta with the Prince was never intended by her Father, nor her self, and commands him to seek means how to divert it with expedition 341

Olivarez propounds, in answer to the King, that the Emperours daughter should marry our Prince, and another daughter the Palatines son, whom he would have bred a Catholick in the Emperors Court. 343

A deplorable Letter from the Protestants of France to the King, after the loss of Rochel. 343, 344

Their great cruelty over them, and a Massacre threatned. ibid.

Pope Gregory the 15th to the Duke, perswading him with many zealous reasons, not only to become a Catholick himself, but the King and Kingdom, by the example of his Mother. 345

From the Lady Purbeck to the Duke, expostulating with

A Table of the principal Matters.

with him, for the separation from her husband, and depriving her of her means for divers years. 345
Mr. Packer, to the Lord Keeper, sharply admonishing him of his unfaithful and opposite carriage towards the Duke. ibid.
Nithisdales conference with the Spanish Embassadours about the Match, vindicating the Prince and the Duke in the management of that business, 347, 348
Captain Pennington refuseth to deliver up the Kings ships, for the service of the French King, notwithstanding the Embassadours large promises, and fierce menaces, or to fight against them of the Religion. 349, 350
Again to the Duke, desiring satisfaction in several Articles touching that business. 351
An Admiral constituted for the Irish Seas. 352

R.

Sir Thomas Ree, to the Lord Admiral, touching the great encrease of Pyrates about Malaga, and the dangerous consequence thereof to Merchants. 352
A consolatory Letter from Cardinal Richlieu, to the Catholicks of Great Britain. 353
The Duke of Rohan complains to the King of the grievous persecution against the Protestants in France, and sues for assistance and protection. 353, 354
Sir Walter Raleigh to the Duke, desiring him to intercede to the King for his life, with an extenuation of his fault. ibid.
To King James, before his Tryal, suing unto him not to give heed to his private enemies, and that the word merciful, in his Stile, is as honourable, as the word invincible, that he serv'd the King 20 years without any reward, and thereupon beggs his life. 355
To Sir Robert Carr, questioning with him about begging his inheritance from the King, lost in Law for want of a word, desires him that he will not cut down the tree with the fruit, and incurre the curse of the Fatherless, 325, 326
Monsieur Richer's Recantation of his opinion, against the Papal Supremacy over Kings, Viscount Rochfort sollicites the Duke for the enlargement of my Lord of Oxford out of the Tower. 356
An angry expostulatory Letter, from Mr. Ruthen, to the Earl of Northumberland. 357

S.

The manner of the Princes Reception in Spain, and the manner of his departure from thence exactly related. 357, 358
A Privy Seal for 30000 l. to be paid to Philip Burlamack, and by him to Sir William Belfour, and John Dabler, for transporting of Horse and Arms into England. 359
The Earl of Suffolk sues to the King to be restored to his favour, the acknowledgment of his errours, that he is 40000 l. in debt, the Earl of Southampton confined to his house at Tichfield whom Sir William Parkhurst was to accompany: small offences in former time deeply censur'd in the Star-Chamber, an instance thereof in the 16th. of Ed. the second, of Henry Lord Beaumont. 360
Oliver St. John to the Major of Marlberough, against the Benevolence, and his reasons and arguments against it. 361
The Earl of Suffolk Congratulates the Duke for his delivery out of the Tower, in the behalf of him and his family with hearty acknowledgment. 362
To the King in behalf of his Sons, and their places in Court. 363
Sir Philip Sidney to the Queen, disswading her from her Marriage with Monsieur most elegantly and judicially penned. 363, 364, 365, 366, 367
A most quaint Speech made by the Lord Bacon, (then Sollicitor General) at the Arraignment of the Lord Sanquir, as well in extenuation as aggravation of the Murther of Turner. 368, 369
The Countess of Shrewsburies Case, touching the marriage of the Lady Arabella, and her refusal to be examined therein. 359
Dr. Sharp, King James Chaplain, his complaint of Europe our mother, against the Pope and Jesuites, to Christian Princes, to whose Trust God hath committed his two Twins, the State and Church. 370, 371
Urging the example of heathen Emperours, and Christian, Invective against the Pope, and magnifying King James. 371
To the Duke, a just War is the exercise of faith; when war is just: the invasion in 88. Don Pedro's examination and Confession Frank and plain. The Queens Oration to her Army. A Discourse made by the Earl of Essex by the Queens command, whether Peace or War was to be made with Spain, Squire abetted to poison the Earl of Essex. 372, 373, 374

T.

Sir Nicholas Throckmorton Ambassadour in France to Queen Elizabeth, touching a free passage for the Queen of Scots, therow England into Scotland, several publick reasons urg'd on both sides between him and the Queen of Scots, and the Queen-mother of France. 374, 375, 376, &c.
Mr. Trumbal to the Secretary, about a pernicious Libel called Corona Regia, for discovery of the Authour; great designs laid. 380, 381
Maketh an overture to King James for pardoning 18 grand Pyrates, most of them being the Kings Vassals, and upon what terms, they offer 450000 l. 382, 383
A Letter of much secrecy from Mr. Ch. Th to the Duke, concerning his Accusation in Parliament, and the reasons of the Kings vindicating of him: Upon what grounds King James created so many Noblemen, wherefore money was given for such Honour or places of Clergy and Judicature; it is so in all other Countreys, as France and Spain, The Duke more engaged for the King then any number of Noblemen. 383, 384, &c.

U.

Pope Urban to Lewis the 13th. encouraging him, and perswading to proceed in the subversion of Hereticks and enemies of the Church, and in applause of his victories. 386
The University of Cambridge to the Duke, congratulatory, and his Answer. 387
The University of Cambridge to the King, another to the Archbishop of York, to the Earl of Manchester, to Sir Humphry May, to the Lord Chief Justice Richardson: All in Latine. 388, 389, 390

Sir

A Table of the Principal Matters.

W.

Sir *Henry Wallop*, to the Queen, in vindication of himself from a false and malicious rumor raised at *Dublin* against him. 391

Advertisements from Sir *Isaac Wake*, touching affaires in *Germany, Savoy, Spain, Naples*, and severall other places: The Duke of *Ossuna* his demand of the King of *Spain*. 392, 393

Under a Cloud; Seignior *Donato* an Enemy to *Padre Paolo*, and *Fulgentio*, friends to the King. 394, 395

A great dearth in *Italy*: The Duke of *Parma* imprisons his natural son *Ottavio*: Count *Mansfelt* groweth formidable: Is entertained by the State of *Venice*: gaineth in *Alsatia*: and affrighteth the *Austrian*. 396

Propositions by Sir *Isaac Wake* to severall Princes, and States, to oppose the ambition of *Spain*. 395, 397

Severall quaint Letters from Sir *Henry Wotton*, to the Duke: Some rare Pieces of *Titian*, and others sent unto him: Mr. *Mole* a prisoner in the Inquisition, and wherefore; means propounded for his enlargement: Thinks it strange, that after seventeen years forreigne employment, Sir *Isaac Wake* should be sent Ambassadour to *Venice*. 399, 400

Sues to him for some part of his Compassion. ibid.

To the Earl of *Portland* his Character, making him parallel with the Lord *Burleigh*: a short representation of himself. 400, 401

Sir *Richard Weston* to the Duke, touching affaires in the *Palatinate*, and the siege of *Heidleberg*, desires to return home. 402

Ill offices done between him and the Duke, but justifies himself. ibid.

Touching the Earl of *Middlesex* enlargement, earnest therein. 403

He is fined: Mr. *Brett* angry because his Pension is not paid: order taken about the Wardship of the Lady *Cravens* Son. 404

The Lord *Wimbledon* to the Duke, complaining of ill offices done him to the King: strictly examined by the Councel, desires to be admitted to the Kings presence, there to clear himself. 405

Relyes wholly upon the Duke. 406

Secretary *Walsingham*, to the Secretary of *France*, touching the Queens proceedings in Ecclesiasticall Causes, grounded upon two Principles;
her lenity towards the Papists, her difference between Papists in conscience, and in faction: The Proceedings against the Puritans, and their dangerous designes: A solid Discourse. 406, 407, 408

Dr. *Williams* to the Duke, after the death of the Bishop of *London*, obliquely suing to succeed therein, and desiring three requests, by way of augmentation: The Names of such Ecclesiasticall promotions, as then he held. 408, 409

The Marquess *Inoiosa* to the Lord *Conway*, touching some passages, for the speedier expediting of the Match with *Spain*. 409

Y.

Sir *Henry Yelverton* to the Duke, submissively apologeticall desiring pardon, and restitution to his favour. 4, 9 410

His submission to the Lords in the *Star-Chamber*, touching a Charter, wherein were divers Errors, some of negligence, some of ignorance, and some of misprision; and humbly desiring their intercessions in his behalf to the King. 410, 411,

From King *James* to Pope *Gregory* the 15 th, perswading, and desiring him, to give his best assistance to stop the course of discords then in agitation in the Christian world. 412

Sir *John Eliot*, prisoner, for preserving the Dukes rights, and liberties. 512, 413

A report of the Dukes loss of the Mastership of the Horse; severall plain avisoes given him by the Lord *Cromwell*. 413, 414

The Lord *Conway* to the Earl of *Bristoll*, by command from the King, whether he will take the benefit of the Parliaments pardon, or clear himself by a legall course, for errors committed in *Spain*. ibid.

Severall Remonstrances to King *James*, concerning great preparations of Forces by the *Spaniards*, and desiring him to forbid the exportation of ammunition for the *Spaniards* service. 415

The King of *Spain* to Pope *Urban*, desiring him to perswade the Duke of *Nevers* to an accommodation with the Emperour, and the *French* King to recall his Armies out of *Italy*, and such Princes as aid *Nevers* to dis-interest themselves in that business for preventing of Warr in Christendom, and hazarding of Religion, and therein promises his best assistance. 415, 416

The End of the Table.

ERRATA.

Page 4: lin. 26. r. ordinary Post. p. 7. l. 6. r. Procutadores. p. 23. l. 10. r. that most, p. 43. l. 3. r. superstition. p. (52.) l. 1. r. fortunæ suæ. p. 58. l. b. r. Stats. p. 87. l. 30. r. shall not deceive. p. 143. l. ult. r. shortly. p. 146. l. 6. dele for. p. 149. l. 19. r. preparation. p. 151. l. 17. r. to be sent. p. 193. l. antipenult. r. answered. p. 198. l. 2. r. because p. 195. l. 48. r. so much. p. 205. l. antipenult. for our affections, r. your affections. p. 218. l. 21. r. at least he says. p. 219. l. 18. r. withal. p. 237. l. 44. r. surces. p. 249. l. penult, r. thought his. p. 256. l. 24. r. Kings. p. 265. l. 7. for defend, r. deser. p. 292. l. 40. for 1661. r. 1612. p. 329. l. 31. r. profess. ibid. in fine. r. to pray incessantly for your. p. 340. l. 51. dele of. p. 358. l. 44. r. Prince. p. 359. l. 16. r. John Dalbert. p. 360. l. 40. r. his own accord. p. 361. l. 40. r. ipso. p. 367. l. 12 for t. r. He. p. 367. l. 23 for waies r. wings. p. 368. l. antipenu. r. Suedia p. 290. l. 1. r. Falmouth. l. 18. r. un accord. p. 391. l. 16. r. great burthen. p. 392. l. 9. for Vennes, r. venues. p. 400 l. 21. r. whilst. 408. l. 12. r. planted. p. 412. circa finem, r. to your worth.

Some few other literal faults have escaped, which the candid Reader is requested courteously to correct, and excuse.

www.ingramcontent.com/pod-product-compliance
Lightning Source LLC
Chambersburg PA
CBHW022134300426
44115CB00006B/177